THE PSYCHOLOGY AND LAW OF CRIMINAL JUSTICE PROCESSES

THE PSYCHOLOGY AND LAW OF CRIMINAL JUSTICE PROCESSES

ROGER J. R. LEVESQUE

Nova Science Publishers, Inc.
New York

For permission to use material from this book please contact us:
Telephone 631-231-7269; Fax 631-231-8175
Web Site: http://www.novapublishers.com

LIBRARY OF CONGRESS CATALOGING-IN-PUBLICATION DATA
Available upon request

ISBN 1-59454-312-7

Published by Nova Science Publishers, Inc. ✢ New York

CONTENTS

PREFACE

This text fills an empty niche. Individuals interested in understanding connections between psychological sciences and the legal system's response to crime often demonstrate interest in real-life cases and situations to help them distill, understand and apply massive amounts of psychological theory and research. Yet, no text examines cases and situations in ways that also present evidence from psychological science to evaluate how society, researchers, and the law conceptualize and respond to crime. Likewise, no text provides students with a firm understanding of psychological sciences relevant to legal mandates that could allow us to foster more effective efforts to address crime and, at the very least, understand the appropriateness of current responses.

This book seeks to fill the above gaps. To do so, the text begins with a comprehensive introduction. The introduction analyzes the major legal themes and values that guide criminal justice processes and points to the many psychological issues they raise. Although it often is tempting to skip introductions, this one appears quite important for introducing readers to the interdisciplinary nature of the field as well as to the types of issues criminal justice processes raise and ask us to address. The introduction is followed by chapters grouped into three substantive parts. Part I examines how the legal system investigates and apprehends criminal suspects. Topics range from the identification, searching and seizing to the questioning of suspects. Part II focuses on how the legal system establishes guilt. To do so, it centers on the process of bargaining and pleading cases, assembling juries, providing expert witnesses, and considering defendants' mental states. Part III focuses on the disposition of cases. Namely, it highlights the process of sentencing defendants, predicting criminal tendencies, treating and controlling offenders, and determining eligibility for such extreme punishments as the death penalty. As this brief overview suggests, the format seeks to give students a feeling for the entire criminal justice process and for the role psychological science has and can play in it.

Readers will be impressed by how much we know and, equally importantly, how much we still do not know about how our legal system responds to crime. Despite dramatic growth in research related to criminal justice processes, we will find that many points remain largely uninvestigated, which will require that we extrapolate from other areas of research to get a sense of what we know and what we should know. As we will see, the limits of psychological science are often paralleled by the limits of legal responses to crime. It is hoped that the materials will provide readers with a firm understanding of key themes and trends and will allow them to understand why our science may offer much but the legal system remains hesitant, and often unable, to benefit from it. By taking both psychological science and the law on its own terms, it is hoped that readers will be able to divine better what type of research and legal response would be most useful, needed, and beneficial. This is an optimistic note, one that I have found necessary to keep in mind if we are to guard against getting too depressed when we take seriously the materials that follow. The significance of the effort, including the need to remain optimistic, hardly can be underestimated. The manner the state takes a person's liberty or life and justifies its protections against error reveals the state's most consequential power. Criminal justice processes, then, pose an awesome challenge to everyone's civic responsibility to evaluate, understand, and improve our society's actions done in our name. At its core, this text seeks to help us recognize that challenge.

Chapter 1

CRIMINAL JUSTICE PROCESSES: COMPETING IDEOLOGIES, RECURRING PRINCIPLES AND CONSIDERING THE ROLE OF PSYCHOLOGICAL SCIENCE

INTRODUCTION

Explorations of relationships between criminal law enforcement and psychological sciences necessarily make two initial choices. The first choice involves a commitment to mastering many fields of scientific psychology as well as fundamental legal principles and even highly technical legal rules. That task certainly is enormous. The task means becoming familiar, for example, with the nature of psychological experiments, survey methodologies, psychiatric syndromes, epidemiological findings, crime reports, and other forms of inquiry fundamental to the understanding of crime. The task also requires the ability to interpret scientific results in ways that recognize their promise; it means drawing conclusions from limited and flawed data. Once reasonable conclusions are drawn, it means placing them in relevant legal contexts. That task, in turn, requires understanding the nature of law, its driving principles, and the ability to make broad policy decisions to ensure that the use of scientific facts moves law enforcement in appropriate directions.

The second choice that must be made by those exploring relationships between psychological sciences and criminal law enforcement involves deciding whether the sciences or legal processes will serve as the primary guide. It may be feasible and legitimate to consider both simultaneously when considering discrete aspects of law enforcement, but examining how the law and psychology interact requires selecting one as the essential guide. Choosing which area as the primary guide is more than a matter of taste. The choice dictates how and what certain phenomena gain significance and which ones will be important to consider, investigate, and take seriously in addressing responses to crime. The choice also means that analyses will focus on different assumptions; for the law and sciences make different assumptions and present their own benefits and limitations in their responses to crime. The difficulties posed by these two choices help explain why no text attempts to do what this one seeks to accomplish.

The two choices necessarily impact the development and presentation of materials included in this casebook. The following pages necessarily provide enormous amounts of materials not readily made available to either those interested in understanding the legal rules of criminal law enforcement or those interested in psychological sciences examining responses to crime. Given the desire to understand the place of psychological sciences throughout criminal justice processes, this text takes the legal system on its own terms. The text does so by examining how law enforcement could benefit from taking psychological findings and theories seriously as well as why, in many instances, law enforcement remains unable to take scientific findings seriously. The goal, then, is simple: to provide an overview of relevant psychological findings and the legal context for understanding law enforcement's use (or non-use) of those findings.

To understand the legal system guiding responses to crime, it is important to begin with understanding basic principles and ideologies (general ways of conceiving and viewing particular issues) that guide criminal justice processes. Fortunately, many who have studied criminal justice processes have offered models to help examine and explain tensions in the manner the state processes individuals suspected, accused, and found guilty of crimes. By far, the most successful conceptual attempt takes the form of two competing models. One focuses on due process concerns, which includes ensuring that the state treats individuals fairly when they are suspected or have been found guilty of committing crimes. The other model, known as the crime control model, focuses on public safety and expands the power of law enforcement as it trusts that the system will treat individuals appropriately. Given the dominance of this way to conceptualize tensions that dominate criminal justice processes, the approach has been the subject of much elaboration and criticism. Yet, the two core ideologies can help us understand the complexity of the manner the legal system responds to criminal activity. They still continue to dominate and actually become increasingly relevant in light of recent developments in constitutional law regulating criminal justice processes.

As we will soon see, it is not enough to know the nature of the ideologies guiding responses to crime. Often ignored in efforts to understand the balancing of crime control and due process concerns has been the principles within those ideologies that give them their substance. These principles range widely, from who should have discretion to enforce laws, the manner we respect individual dignity, and the extent to which we rely on the state to address crime, to the types of rights provided those accused and found guilty of crime. Those principles actually are as important as the overarching ideologies themselves. As we will see, the focus of any principle often varies according to the stage in legal processes and the extent to which either the ideology of due process or of crime control has gained dominance in particular stages. Equally importantly, we also shall see how these models and principles play a large role in determining the use of psychological sciences. The importance of the models to understanding the role of psychological sciences in criminal justice processes explains why we must focus so much on criminal justice principles at the beginning of a text dealing with the psychological understanding of responses to crime.

Competing Ideologies of Criminal Justice Processes

Ideologies that dominate criminal justice processes are best understood through two metaphors that capture the essence of competing interests in criminal justice processes. One metaphor concerns the ideology of crime control as it describes the criminal process as a high speed assembly-line conveyor belt operated by police and prosecutors seeking guilty pleas. The other involves core principles of due process as it presents criminal justice processes as obstacle courses in which defense counsels ensure that the police and prosecution respect the accused's rights. The differences between the two ideologies generally are understood as the former's preoccupation with speed, efficiency and finality in criminal justice processes and outcomes and the latter's concern for ensuring proper respect for the rights of offenders so that the system exhibits fairness to the accused and maintains society's faith in the system.

Those familiar with the study of criminal justice immediately will recognize the striking resemblance of the competing metaphors to Herbert Packer's approach to understanding criminal justice systems.[1] The resemblance is intentional. Packer first effectively conceptualized the above ideologies and those who have followed him have tried to embellish, criticize, and even debunk his guiding ideological models. Those criticisms and concerns will recur throughout the pages that follow. The limitations and criticisms may well be accurate, but, for now, it is important to note that they do not diminish the significance of the ideologies for understanding the broad contours and dilemmas guiding law enforcement.[2] We will investigate the

---

[1] Herbert L. Packer, Two models of the criminal process, 113 U. Pa. L. Rev. 1 (1964).

[2] It does seem fair to note that prevailing and emerging doctrine does not fold neatly into two ideological categories. Matters of due process may be (and often are) important concerns for the crime control model, and vice versa. Likewise, when

ideologies not only as they operate but also in terms of the directions suggested by their ultimate goals. We will seek to understand the type of criminal justice processes that would be in place if we favored one approach to the other. It is only by understanding competing forces that we can understand the proper role of psychological science's claims.

Although the ideologies may appear extreme at first glance, we will see in the following chapters that the ascending approach to criminal justice processes in many ways responds to what is known as the due process revolution. Legal commentators generally understand that revolution as having been launched most forcefully in the 1960s and as having dissipated quickly in the 1970s through current times, with the contemporary response to criminal justice forces placeable squarely within a crime control model. Yet, due process concerns still are taken seriously and vary in different contexts as much as they sometimes vary among members of the judiciary who interpret laws and among policy makers who enact laws. The different ideologies, then, present general contours to help frame many of the legal issues that follow as well as sharpen our understanding of the potential place of social science in criminal justice processes. The ideologies help remind us that criminal processes involve a balance between liberty and order; and the fundamental question for society and its legal system is to determine how that balance should be struck in order to preserve individuals' basic rights against state encroachment while, at the same time, accommodating to the need for legitimate state encroachment to protect individuals and fetter crime. Not surprisingly, it is in that balancing that psychological sciences may offer considerable assistance. But, before getting to some of the issues psychological sciences may raise and help address, we need to preview the relevant legal context.

Ideologies of Crime Control

The efficient suppression of crime serves as the primary value underlying the ideologies of crime control. Concern with efficiency derives from the real limits of law enforcement resources. As a result, the approach places a premium on speed and finality. The legal system achieves efficiency through expert front-line administrators, the police and prosecutors, who screen out the innocent and expeditiously secure the conviction of the guilty. Given that it would be inefficient for administrators to select and press cases forward involving innocent individuals, the model assumes that law enforcement legitimately applies the law. Given that law enforcement are presumed to act efficiently, the approach systematically presumes guilt and seeks to minimize challenges and opportunities for reviewing decisions made by law enforcement personnel. The approach seeks to avoid reliance on the formal court system. The approach further views the criminal sanction as a positive guarantor of social freedom and as necessary for the effective maintenance of public order. To better understand the ideals and nature of this model, we take a quick look at how this model would guide the development of laws across the various stages of criminal justice processes.

The prominence of crime prevention, investigation, and punishment under this model leads to a preference for providing police with broad, discretionary powers. Concern centers on factual guilt. An accusation by law enforcement means that the accused probably committed the charged criminal act. The model makes secondary the need to establish legal guilt, which occurs only after a defendant is found or accepts guilt in a court of law. The approach focuses on ensuring more of a quick plea bargain that avoids efforts to establish guilt beyond a reasonable doubt through admissible evidence and after careful consideration of all the accused's rights and defenses. The orientation encourages bestowing police with broad powers to conduct searches since it assumes that only the factually guilty have something to hide and that society has an obligation to arrest and punish offenders. Taken to its logical conclusion, the approach would provide police with broad investigative powers to arrest people for questioning and establishing

considering the utility of broad ideologies, it is important to recall that neither corresponds perfectly to reality or represents the ideal to the exclusion of the other.

factual guilt. Individualized suspicion would be unnecessary. For example, law enforcement would be allowed to round up "the usual suspects," would be able to detain or arrest without following objective criteria, and would have the general power to search and question suspects. The presumption that the innocent have nothing to hide and no reason to fear injustice counters considerations of inconvenience and harms that could occur as a result of such police power. Police power also would include the state's ability to use even illegally seized evidence against defendants simply because seized evidence reveals the obvious truth of guilt. And that guilt would still be important to prosecute and punish even if law enforcement obtained its evidence illegally, such as without the conditions needed to justify a proper search of an individual's home. Importantly, the model does not assume that police are immune from making errors or violating laws. Rather, it assumes that disciplinary, civil and even criminal proceedings against individual officers best respond to blundering law enforcement personnel. It would use those mechanisms to ensure proper police behavior instead of not prosecuting a case and punishing offenders. The approach would limit the use of the exclusionary rule[3] simply because the rule is seen as unfair to law enforcement, victims and broader society. In general, then, the crime control model espouses the view that police in the streets and station-houses conduct most of the fact-finding and that the collected facts should be used against offenders.

The power of police to investigate could reach quite broadly. The approach views custodial interrogation by law enforcement as absolutely good. The reality that interrogation may provide critical clues supports the argument that law enforcement should not be required to follow strict rules regarding the length or condition of inquiry, including limitations on the nature of questions. The approach would discourage detained suspects' contact with attorneys, simply because defense counsel may impede the efficient accumulation of information and unfairly benefit the guilty who remain silent on their attorney's advice. Not surprisingly, the model rejects the notion of appointed counsel given that defense counsel undermine law enforcement's efficient objective of corralling the factually guilty. If a right to counsel must be recognized, the model would curtail its use to critical trial proceedings and not extend it to investigations. Importantly, even though the model seeks to provide police with immense discretion, it still recognizes the need to reject coerced confessions. Coerced confessions raise the possibility that they are unreliable and that the suspect was probably not factually guilty.

The presumption of guilt permits detaining suspects; individuals need not be proven guilty in order to be detained. The assumption that the system uses accurate screening procedures yields the presumption that those charged with crimes are in fact criminals, which legitimizes their detainment. Since they are presumed guilty, the system fears that their release before trial or before pleading guilty could unfairly give them the opportunity to abscond from the jurisdiction or commit more crimes. Detainment secures immediate societal protection and has the added benefit of encouraging defendants to acknowledge their wrongdoings and accept their punishments. Importantly, the longer individuals remain in the system, the more they are presumed guilty; staying in the system makes it more likely that they are culpable simply because those best situated to determine guilt – policemen and prosecutors – have deemed suspects guilty.

The crime control ideology considers a guilty plea the most efficient outcome, for it allows the state to expend the least resources in its disposal of the largest number of cases. To achieve this effectiveness, law enforcement may use all reasonable means to encourage a defendant's plea. Short of using physical torture, the government may use essentially any tool to encourage a plea. To the extent courts are to have a role in overseeing the plea processes, they should help encourage defendants to plead guilty. A court only would examine facts relevant to the issue of sentencing, rather than, for example, probing the factual basis for a guilty plea. The approach also would not provide counsel to defendants as long as defendants understood the nature and consequences of an admission and the plea agreement resulted from free will. As a result, even if the court were to uncover prosecutorial misconduct in the plea bargaining process, the appropriate remedy would not be to dismiss the case but rather to appraise the defendant of his rights and accept a guilty plea as long as the defendant understood his legal rights. Importantly, this view of courts as sources

[3] As we will see, the rule generally forbids the use of evidence against suspects when the evidence was illegally obtained.

of administrative fact-finding means that prosecutors acquire somewhat more importance than judges. Just as it views police, the approach views prosecutors as administrators of justice who can be trusted to not waste limited time and resources on innocent suspects.

Under the crime control model, trials should center on factual innocence and play down legal technicalities. The assumption again is that police and prosecutors appropriately have screened out the factually innocent and that remedies allow for convicting the factually guilty even when law enforcement inappropriately may have encroached on individuals' rights. To maximize efficiency, the approach would narrowly construe the right to trial by jury. Jury panels would be economically small in size because their functions would not depend on the particular number of the body that makes up the jury. A defendant need not necessarily be tried by a jury of his "peers"given that the law only would require juries to understand the nature of the crime charged and determine factual guilt. Similarly, jury members would not need to agree on their verdict since unanimity does not contribute much to the exercise of commonsense judgment. Again, the belief is that early protections and trustworthy administrators of justice already have screened out the innocent. That focus also means that the prosecution would not always need to hold the burden of proving guilt, nor should the burden be high. A jury determination of probable guilt would suffice to uphold a conviction and the accused could hold the burden to establish his innocence affirmatively, rather than having the state prove guilt beyond a reasonable doubt. Defendants still may retain a privilege against self-incrimination, but they still could be required to invoke that right before the jury and prosecutors could comment on their failure to testify. The crime control model encourages the highest possible conviction rate, even if it means that a person may need to prove their innocence.

Given the emphasis on what happens early in criminal justice processes, the crime control ideology's concern with efficiency and finality conflicts with judicial review after conviction. Judicial appeals are deemed fruitless given that individuals are presumed guilty and already had protections throughout their trials. The argument is that post-conviction appeals unnecessarily expend scarce resources and undermine the efficient findings of guilt. This view emerges from the assumption that police investigating crime act in good faith and that magistrates, prosecutors, and clerical personnel adequately protect defendants' rights. If required by law, the model would allow appeals if the accused were able to establish that no reasonable trier of fact could have convicted on the proffered evidence. If the legal system required review, the scope of review would include only clear fact-finding errors; but even if eventually determined truly erroneous, such errors would not suffice to overturn a conviction if a reasonable jury could still have found the defendant guilty. Government misconduct and claims unrelated to factual guilt are deemed irrelevant to the defendant's actual culpability and thus beyond the purview of appeals.[4]

The crime control model generally would reject external limitations on the form and length of punishment. The model focuses on forceful criminal sanctions, as it rejects the principle of proportionality. The punishment need not fit the crime. The minimum content of constitutional rights might forbid clear acts of torture, but even torturous acts could be justified given exigent circumstances. Exigencies may call for extreme measures that would otherwise shock the conscience. Importantly, constitutional rights would not impact the length of incarceration. If some minor disturbances could pose a major societal threat, the model recognizes that such urgencies may justify life imprisonment and even the death penalty. The model even would place few restraints on the ultimate penalty – capital punishment. The model, in fact, would welcome execution of the factually guilty of appropriate crimes; for execution would efficiently further the double goals of deterrence and finality.

Ideologies of Due Process

---

[4] Again, the model does not want to have criminals benefit from bundling administrators. The argument is that the civil justice system should deal with those who make grievous errors and violate people's rights.

The model that focuses on ideologies of due process seeks to shield individuals from the harmful consequences that the criminal process may have for individuals. It is not that the model would forego punishment. Rather, the model concerns itself with ensuring that the system should not punish on its way to determining warranted punishment. To protect individuals, the model seeks to offer the accused basic safeguards to ensure their fair treatment, such as the right to attorneys throughout criminal processes. The model focuses on ensuring that legal processes do not function in a way that systematically and unfairly treats certain groups and vulnerable individuals, an approach that takes seriously the extent to which certain groups, such as minorities and the poor, may bear the brunt of police abuse and prosecutions. The argument is that only by protecting the rights of the most disadvantaged can we protect the rights of everyone else.

To achieve its goals, the approach imposes significant restraints on law enforcement. Unlike the crime control model, this model does not favor expanding police powers and presuming the just administration of justice. As a result, the model protects the rights of suspects by minimizing informal fact-finding in the streets and police stations. The effort seeks to enact clear, objective, and stringent standards to guide decisions to intervene in people's everyday lives rather than entrust discretion to police who may engage in prejudicial enforcement and find ways to skirt even clear standards. Rather than granting police broad discretion to determine who suspects are and what to do with them, the approach focuses on individualized suspicion, which clearly delineates why particular individuals became suspects. Only a warrant supported by probable cause and issued by an impartial magistrate properly would justify state interference in people's affairs. Although these requirements limit the efficiency of law enforcement's arrests and guilty pleas, the model finds them necessary to protect individuals' dignity. Indeed, the model does not even deem these inefficiencies as costs; the protections simply are signs of fair law enforcement.

The due process model would seek to curb the powers of law enforcement during the time between arrest and arraignment (when formal charges are made). The approach discourages the use of charges and detention for interrogating and gathering information. Formal arrests constitute the only legitimate purpose for charging suspects. The approach seeks to grant defendants a prompt arraignment and a right to counsel at least by the time of arrest. Respecting these rights necessarily requires explicitly informing a suspect of his right to counsel and his right against self-incrimination. Law enforcement's failure to warn suspects of their constitutional rights would result in exclusion of the subsequent statement at trial. Also inadmissible would be confessions made without free will or during prolonged periods between arrest and arraignment. In addition, court proceedings would exclude any evidence derived from such statements. Although such confessions and derivative evidence could be quite reliable and indicate guilt, their reliability would not justify their use. A fair criminal justice system forces the government to make its case without coercion and without the defendants' help.

The due process model views the moment of arrest as fraught with disparity in resources between the state and the accused. To protect the accused from unfair self-incrimination, criminal trials would exclude any statements taken absent an accused's clear and voluntary waiver of their rights. The rationale for excluding confessions does not relate to the confession's trustworthiness, unreliability or veracity. Exclusion prevents the state from capitalizing on a defendant's ignorance of his legal rights; the state should not make its case against a defendant by forcing him to co-operate in the process. Actions could be taken against police who ignore suspect's rights, but the model concerns itself with ensuring that the violations do not allow the state to hold suspects responsible. Because the system encourages police and prosecutors to take short cuts (such as plea bargaining or encouraging consensual searches), the model seeks to penalize within trials any violations of the accused's rights. Given the dominance of plea bargaining and the reduced chance that police abuse will not be uncovered, the model seeks to ensure the use of strong exclusionary rules. The argument is that letting the factually guilty go free forces the system to act fairly.

Unlike the crime control approach's presumption that individuals suspected by law enforcement are guilty, the due process model firmly adheres to the presumption of innocence. Although clear factual evidence may point to guilt, an accused does not become criminal until proven legally guilty. Only a conviction pursuant to the highest standard of proof brings legal guilt and legitimately brands suspects as criminals. Individuals who are only factually guilty are innocent. Pretrial confinement contradicts this fundamental presumption. The model fears that pretrial incarceration based on a presumption of guilt can become a self-fulfilling prophesy. Incarceration presumably limits the effectiveness of a defendant's ability to assist in their defense by, for example, hampering consultation with their counsel and their ability to uncover exculpatory evidence or witnesses. Moreover, pretrial incarceration results in de facto punishment even in the absence of a final verdict, such as the loss of employment and reputation. To minimize inadvertent punishments, limits on an individual's liberties would require individualized responses to each defendants' particular circumstances. To prevent miscarriages of justice and to exonerate the presumption of innocence, the prevailing legal norm would champion pretrial freedom and provide basic legal tools for suspects to defend themselves against the state's power. The government shoulders the full burden to establish guilt beyond a reasonable doubt.

The due process model advocates the need to abolish (or at least significantly reform) plea bargaining. Bargaining is inherently suspect given how the overwhelming power of the state fosters systematic injustice in the manner it encourages even innocent defendants to plead guilty in an effort to avoid oppressive sentences. Vulnerable defendants, such as those who are indigent, are particularly open to the evil of plea bargaining. In addition, plea bargaining is presumptively invalid because it essentially forecloses review and thus problematically allows governmental misconduct to escape any disinterested scrutiny. The model would only accept a plea bargain system if courts had an affirmative duty to ensure that strong factual bases supported the pleas. Even bargains with strong factual indicators would be accepted only if they were untainted by other governmental abuses. Plea agreements would only receive the imprimatur of the court when the court would be convinced of the defendants' guilt and the propriety of law enforcement practices. If society deemed plea bargaining necessary, the model would require rigorous efforts to guard against having defendants accept undeserved convictions solely because of the lack of means and will to challenge the charges.

The due process model embraces defense attorneys as necessary participants in the criminal justice system. The model does not assume that the government's own self-discipline can vindicate a defendant's constitutional rights. Criminal trials of any accused must address violations of their rights because those subject to police abuse – the poor, the ignorant, the illiterate, the unpopular – are not necessarily able to bring separate civil, disciplinary, or criminal actions. As a result, the model seeks to provide everyone with defense attorneys. Only effective defense attorneys can help innocent suspects avoid the danger of conviction by responding to legal technicalities and procedures backed by prosecuting attorneys with vast state resources. Even the clearly guilty should be provided the presence and effective assistance of counsel. The overriding theme is that a system that seeks to deprive individuals of their liberties also must not deprive the accused of their only hope of avoiding that fate.

The model does not trust prosecutors to screen valid from invalid charges any more than it trusts the police to be able to do so. As a result, the model necessarily relies on impartial judges and juries to vindicate a suspect's rights. Thus, trials would be encouraged to establish legal guilt. Regardless of factual guilt, culpability rests on whether the prosecutor can establish legal guilt beyond a reasonable doubt on the basis of legally obtained evidence. Juries would be sufficiently large to foster effective group deliberation and participation of minority views while enhancing accurate factfinding. Likewise, convictions only would be had after juries unanimously agreed on a defendant's guilt; unanimity would help ensure the strongest presumption of innocence and highest burden of proof. The right to be tried by a jury of one's peers is deemed a necessary safeguard against possibly corrupt or overzealous prosecutors and against compliant, biased, or eccentric judges. The ultimate burden of proof would never shift to the defendant. The prosecution would be barred from calling defendants as witnesses so that they would be forced to invoke their privilege against self-incrimination before the jury; prosecutors would not be allowed to force defendants to imply that they have something to hide. A jury verdict would foreclose any further prosecution, even in another jurisdiction, whether for civil or criminal sanctions. The approach would grant broad rights of appeal given the even minor risks of convicting innocent individuals. Appellate courts would reverse convictions whenever trial judges failed to protect the accused's rights, regardless of the defendant's obvious guilt. The belief is that reversals of criminal convictions are small prices to pay for affirming proper societal values and effectively deterring crime.

The sentencing stage of criminal justice processes shifts the focus away from determining culpability toward controlling punishment in light of the defendant's guilt. The due process ideology focuses on the proportionate nature of the punishment and the defendant's moral culpability. To do so, sentencing would consider both the nature of the offense and the unique characteristics of the offender. No punishment would use the defendant as a means to a societal goal; retribution would not factor into criminal sanctions. The model leaves open options for review. All errors could be raised on appeal, regardless of whether they were aired before the trial court. And errors would be taken seriously. Unlike the crime control approach, the due process model allows even harmless, technical mistakes to justify reversal if they violated the defendant's fundamental rights. Moreover, the danger of condemning the innocent requires full and unrestricted access to the appellate process, a series of benefits ranging from providing transcripts and appointing counsel, to eliminating filing fees. It is believed that the threat of appeals that can result in reversals provides a systematic check on legal processes. The argument is that overturning individual cases, rather than imposing sanctions against those who fail to follow legal rules, effectively curbs misconduct and properly educates law enforcement on the boundaries of governmental power.

Dominant Ideologies of Criminal Law Enforcement

Crime control values	**Due process values**
Assembly line justice	Obstacle, adversarial course
Quick speed to reach finality	Deliberate speed to guard against error
Administrative expertise	Adjudicative expertise
Presumption of guilt	Presumption of innocence
Need to control crime	Need to control the state
Faith in pre-trial/extra judicial procedures	Faith in courts and adversarial processes
Focus on informal fact finding	Focus on formal fact finding
Factual guilt	Legal guilt
Deterrence and retribution	Proportionality
Treat all similarly	Treat all individually

Notes and Queries

In seeking to understand the two dominant tensions in criminal justice processes, it may be useful to attempt to understand where one stands on these issues. For example, should someone be presumed guilty or innocent? We know that our system theoretically assumes innocence, but consider how it sometimes actually assumes guilt. Where do you stand on this matter? Likewise, what are your thoughts on factual guilt and legal guilt? If we know, for example, that someone is guilty but cannot prove it because of legal technicalities, should we treat that person as guilty anyway? What would be needed to find him guilty even if we technically cannot prove it – would it be a severe mental illness that makes us afraid of him, a slew of outrageous crimes, expert testimony that he is extremely dangerous? Consider going through the chart delineating the components of each model and determine which values you tend to support. To do so, attempt to envision examples so that you can better determine where you stand.

In considering where you stand, ponder the Dirty Harry dilemma, which we can adapt from the film *Dirty Harry* (Warner Bros 1971). Inspector Harry Callaghan – "Dirty Harry" – of the San Francisco Police Department, played by Clint Eastwood, battles with Scorpio, an evil child-kidnapper and serial killer. Harry agrees to carry a ransom to Scorpio even though he believes that Scorpio will kill his child kidnap victim anyway, if he has not done so already. When Harry and Scorpio meet, Scorpio attempts to kill Harry. Before barely escaping, Harry manages to wound Scorpio severely with a swift switchblade to the leg. Knowing that time is running out (the ransom stated that the girl was buried alive, with a limited amount of oxygen), Harry hunts down Scorpio, first to a hospital then to Scorpio's home in the basement of a football stadium. Harry breaks into Scorpio's home, seizes the gun that was used in Scorpio's murders, and chases Scorpio into the stadium. As Scorpio attempts to escape, the stadium lights flash on and Harry shoots Scorpio, who is unarmed, in his good leg. Harry approaches, points his .44 at Scorpio's head and demands to know where he buried the kidnap victim. Scorpio cries for a lawyer as he refuses to reveal where he hid the girl. Harry then viciously stomps on Scorpio's wounded leg and again demands that Scorpio disclose his victim's location. Screaming in pain and still crying out for a lawyer, the kidnapper finally reveals where he buried the girl. She is found dead. Consider how the scenario could be approached from both the Due Process Model and Crime Control Model. Consider, for example, what you should make of Harry's seizure of evidence and entrance into Scorpio's home without a warrant? What do you make of the manner Harry seized (stopped) Scorpio from escaping? Did Harry act reasonably? What do you make of his interrogation? Is the information Harry retrieved reliable? What do you make of Scorpio's right to an attorney? Did Harry act criminally? When the body is found, could it be used as evidence against Scorpio? Once in the stadium, Harry knows Scorpio is the kidnapper. But, as Harry steps on his leg, should he still assume Scorpio guilty or assume him innocent? Which model do you find most appealing in your efforts to balance the many considerations that go into fighting crime?

Prevailing Legal Principles and Dilemmas

We have seen how the law enforcement system seems to balance two competing orientations. In order to understand fully those orientations, it is important to consider what factors tend to be balanced. Several factors repeatedly emerge. At this point, it makes sense simply to highlight the nature of those factors and give examples that we will return to in much more depth in the chapters that follow.. Several questions, which go to the issue of basic policy orientations to guide law enforcement, will recur in balancing efforts: To what lengths should society go to prevent crime? Who within the law enforcement system should have the most control? What is the disjuncture between law on the books and law in action? How should the law change to address the needs of a changing society? How much emphasis should law enforcement place on truth-seeking? As we will see, the need to address these questions and balance numerous factors provides psychology with opportunities to assist law enforcement's efforts to address tensions identified by the dominant ideologies guiding future developments in criminal justice processes. As we also shall see, the legal system plays the dominant role and psychological sciences often only can serve as guide for envisioning options.

Discretion

Criminal procedure doctrine seeks to regulate the conduct of various actors in the criminal justice system. Yet, the criminal justice system heavily relies on selectivity in enforcement as it grants to an array of government officials the discretionary authority to administer the selection process. In particular, the system vests police with enormous discretion to arrest individuals.[5] The creation of a rule granting officers such wide discretion to arrest protects police officers from suits premised on the abuse of their discretion; it provides them with even more protection than they already have under the doctrine of qualified immunity.[6]

---

[5] Most recently in *Atwater v. City of Lago Vista*, 532 U.S. 318 (2001), for example, the Supreme Court bestowed on police virtually unbridled power to arrest an ordinary citizen for merely violating any number of misdemeanors, regardless of the actual need to arrest.

[6] Qualified immunity protects public officials from being sued for damages unless they violated clearly established law of which a reasonable official in their position would have known. Courts apply the test articulated by the Supreme Court in *Anderson v. Creighton*, 483 U.S. 635 (1987), to determine whether the right is "sufficiently clear that a reasonable official would understand that what he is doing violates that right." Id. at 639-40. It is not necessary that the specific

As the Due Process Model would suggest, this authority is extremely significant not only because it broadens the inherent power of law enforcement to intrude upon citizens' liberty and privacy but also because it affords police even more discretion to enforce the law selectively and to give effect to possible discriminatory motives.

The criminal justice system also vests prosecutors with considerable discretion in determining which cases and which defendants to prosecute. Courts rarely review a prosecutor's affirmative charging decision, and will almost never second-guess the prosecutor's decision not to prosecute. The power is rather immense in that it directly affects constitutional rights. Most notably, the Fifth Amendment provides that an individual cannot be held to answer a felony offense unless the grand jury has rendered an indictment or presentment[7] on the charges. The Amendment presupposes an investigative body acting independently of either the prosecuting attorney or judge whose mission is to clear the innocent. In this regard, the grand jury is intended as a protection against an overly aggressive government. However, prosecutorial discretion means that these fundamental principles are not as secure as they may seem. Since prosecutors control the information they present to grand juries, prosecutors virtually can guarantee that grand juries will find the probable cause needed to bring a formal indictment and ensure a trial or guilty plea against the defendant.[8]

Judicial discretion also figures prominently throughout other criminal justice processes. Much of the focus of commentaries on judicial discretion has focused on sentencing and, more recently, with efforts to control judicial discretion by implementing sentencing guidelines. Yet, the discretion runs much deeper than that. In the admission of evidence, for example, the trial judge retains the discretion to determine what scientific evidence could be admitted.[9] The standard reviewing courts would take to evaluate a trial court's judgment is that of "abuse of discretion." Such abuse occurs only when the trial judge acts with disregard to logic and with disregard to settled law in its application of the law to the offered testimony. This rule highlights the discretionary nature of judicial decision making which helps determine the outcomes of criminal justice processes.

The legal system also bestows upon correction officials immense discretion. The Supreme Court has found that the Eighth Amendment allows holding prison guards and prison officials responsible when they fail to protect prisoners or do not adequately respond to their needs.[10] However, the Eighth Amendment

---

action in question previously have been declared unconstitutional, so long as the unlawfulness was apparent in light of preexisting law. Id. at 640.

[7] An indictment is the formal written accusation of a crime, as framed by the prosecuting authority of the state, which is affirmed by a grand jury and presented to a court to begin criminal proceedings against that accused. The formal charge states that there is enough evidence that the defendant committed the crime to justify having a trial; it is used primarily for felonies. Presentments are accusations of crime made by a grand jury on its own initiative, rather than on behalf of a prosecutor's office.

[8] The Supreme Court, in *United States v. Williams*, 504 U.S. 36 (1992), held that prosecutors have no duty to present substantial exculpatory evidence that opposes a finding of probable cause in grand jury proceedings. This is arguably the most important prosecutorial power and the strongest example of the influence and reach of prosecutorial discretion. The prosecutor retains the sole discretion in charging a particular defendant with a crime, from the decision whether to prosecute at all to the selection of the nature and the number of charges to bring before the grand jury. As a result of *Williams*, the prosecutor can single-handedly cause the grand jury to indict for additional or more severe offenses based on the evidence he chooses to present. Strategically, it is within the prosecutor's interest to charge more and greater offenses than can be proved beyond a reasonable doubt. By overcharging, prosecutors have more influence during plea negotiations where the defendant faces numerous or very serious charges because the defendant will be willing to plead to reduced charges to avoid conviction for all of them. Instead of charging the defendant with a lesser crime fully supported by probable cause in light of all the evidence, *Williams* allows the prosecutor to convince the grand jury that probable cause exists for a greater crime without showing substantial exculpatory evidence.

[9] This was the Supreme Court's ruling in *General Electric v. Joiner*, 522 U.S. 136 (1997). *Joiner* affirmed the judge's role as the gatekeeper who applies the law in determining what constitutes admissible scientific evidence. The Court did so by affirming that the standard reviewing courts would take of such judgments is that of "abuse of discretion."

[10] For example, *Hudson v. McMillian*, 503 U.S. 1 (1992), tells us that a cause of action under the Eighth Amendment (which, in part, prohibits cruel and unusual punishment) can arise when a prison guard uses excessive force against an inmate. Likewise, *Hudson v. Palmer*, 468 U.S. 517, 526-27 (1984), held that a similar action could be filed when a guard does not provide adequate food, clothing, and medical care. It further held that prison officers must "take reasonable measures to guarantee the safety of the inmates." Id. at 526-527.

does not protect inmates from every injury received in prison. The standard used to determine liability is very high for inmates to reach, which results in granting correctional officers immense discretion.[11]

Importantly, the extent to which criminal procedure satisfactorily regulates those involved in the criminal justice system impacts discretion outside the system. Most notably, it impacts victims' behaviors as well as those of offenders (and potential offenders). The extent that the system is perceived as fair, for example, impacts the extent to which individuals will follow society's laws. A number of studies have demonstrated that many individuals act as though they hold a generalized norm of fairness. An important association exists between perceptions of fair procedures and increased criminal law compliance: people who perceive that they are treated fairly feel respected and more readily adhere to other group norms.[12] The extent to which the system effectively administers justice, then, impacts the extent to which victims will use their discretion, for example, not to report victimization, as has been the case in the legal system's efforts to address sexual violence and violence against women.[13]

Privacy

The extent to which we should protect individuals' private lives by not intruding on them runs rampant throughout all stages of law enforcement. Privacy presents itself as a key concern in the investigation of crime, in the intrusiveness of police interrogation, in evidence presented at trials, in sentencing reports, in prison environments, and in what communities learn about victims and offenders. The major legal example of the need to protect privacy, however, comes in Fourth Amendment analyses that examine searches and seizures. The touchstone of Fourth Amendment analysis is whether a person has a constitutionally protected reasonable expectation of privacy. This involves inquiring whether the individual manifested a subjective expectation of privacy in the object of the challenged search and whether society is willing to recognize that expectation as reasonable. Consider, for example, the constitutional definition of "searches." If an action constitutes a "search" or "seizure," then it might, or might not, be "reasonable" within the meaning of the Fourth Amendment. In contrast, if it is neither a "search" nor a "seizure," then the action does not even involve the Fourth Amendment, no matter how unreasonable.

Much concern revolves around the extent to which the Fourth Amendment requires privacy to be a broad concept. For example, the Amendment clearly deals with informational privacy – what the state can have you say or reveal about yourself. We also know that the Amendment deals with more than informational privacy, but what it would protect remains contentious. It most likely speaks to humiliation, inconvenience, embarrassment, and violence which go to the core of what many consider privacy concerns. Even if one confines one's attention to searches, many invasions that the Fourth Amendment regulates impose little risk to informational privacy. For example, frisks on the street usually reveal little information about the individual. The Fourth Amendment nonetheless constrains these searches because they impose on dignitary and autonomy interests, which may be viewed as privacy concerns. For example, a typical frisk delays a suspect from going about his business, forces him to assume a vulnerable and uncomfortable position, embarrasses him before others, and humiliates him through physical contact with all parts of his

[11] In order for a prison guard to be held liable for an Eighth Amendment violation, *Farmer v. Brennan*, 511 U.S. 825, 834-837 (1994), teaches us that two requirements must be fulfilled. First, the alleged injury, based on an objective standard, must be "sufficiently serious." Specifically, the guard's act must have deprived the prisoner of the minimal civilized measure of life's necessities. Second, the prison official must have had a sufficiently culpable state of mind at the time of the act. This subjective standard is based on "deliberate indifference" to the inmate's health and safety. The Court stated that correctional officers fulfill the deliberate indifference standard if they know of "an excessive risk to inmate health or safety" and disregard that risk. "The official must both be aware of facts from which the inference could be drawn that a substantial risk of serious harms exists, and he must also draw the inference."

[12] See generally E. Allan Lind and Tom R. Tyler, The Social Psychology of Procedural Justice (1988); Tom R. Tyler, Why People Obey the Law (1990); and Tom R. Tyler and Steven L. Blader, Cooperation in Groups: Procedural Justice, Social Identity and Behavioral Engagement (2000).

[13] Stacy Futter and Walter R. Mebane, Jr., The effects of rape law reform on rape case processing, 16 Berkeley Women's L.J. 72 (2001).

body. Even less intrusive searches, like opening a paper bag or requiring a suspect to get out of his car, may be experiences fraught with fear, anxiety, and feelings of invasive intrusions. These invasions require a close look at the interests being affected by law enforcement and at efforts to determine the extent to which those interests should weigh in equations balancing law enforcement needs with individuals' basic rights to be let alone.

Waiver of Rights

The Court has long permitted criminal defendants to waive constitutional rights. Some of the most obvious examples involve the Fourth Amendment right to be free from searches and seizures absent probable cause,[14] the Fifth Amendment right against compulsory self-incrimination, the Sixth Amendment right to a jury trial, the Sixth Amendment right to confrontation, and the Sixth Amendment right to counsel.[15] The Supreme Court has established specific requirements for a waiver of rights, such as in the context of the right to counsel and of the prohibition against compulsory self-incrimination. We also know that waivers of trial rights must be voluntary as well as "intelligent and knowing."[16] Current controversy centers on the extent to which this view of waiver extends to other types of waivers in criminal justice processes. Controversy also centers on the appropriateness of current conceptualizations of waiver.

Throughout criminal justice processes, the term "waiver" actually refers to a broad range of circumstances in which a party loses a right. Many types of waivers exist and this variety raises the fundamental issue of which form best fits particular rights. First, there can be intentional waivers, which are the waivers that most likely come to mind when we think of waiving rights. Intentional relinquishment involves the explicit, premeditated and theoretically unilateral decision to forego the benefits of a personal right. As the Court has noted, waivers of this kind "not only must be voluntary but must be knowing, intelligent acts done with sufficient awareness of the relevant circumstances and likely consequences."[17] However, some rights may not be relinquished, such as the right to be free from slavery and right to be tried by a court with appropriate jurisdiction.[18] Second, a waiver can be a simple forfeiture. Forfeiture involves the failure to make the timely assertion of a right. Unlike the intentional relinquishment type of waiver, forfeiture need not be intentional or conscious, competent or intelligent, counseled or on the record.[19] For example, a defendant who fails to raise an Eighth Amendment issue at the appropriate time will waive that claim, and failure to follow certain state procedural rules will result in the waiver of all

---

[14] *Schneckloth v. Bustamonte*, 412 U.S. 218 (1973).

[15] *Boykin v. Alabama*, 395 U.S. 238 (1969).

[16] *Godinez v. Moran*, 509 U.S. 389 (1993).

[17] *Brady v. United States*, 397 U.S. 742, 248 (1970).

[18] Similarly, the Supreme Court suggests that even if a defendant stipulated to trial by twelve orangutans, the conviction would be invalid notwithstanding consent. Other unwaivable rights identified by the Supreme Court include the right to conflict-free representation where there is an actual conflict of interest, and the right to a unanimous jury verdict in a criminal case. In the plea bargaining context, courts consistently have held that a defendant may not waive the requirement that a guilty plea be voluntary and intelligent, and that it be entered upon the effective assistance of counsel. Daniel P. Blank, Plea bargain waivers reconsidered: A legal pragmatist's guide to loss, abandonment, and alienation, 68 Fordham L. Rev. 2011 (2000).

[19] For example, in *Schneckloth v. Bustamonte*, 412 U.S. 218 (1973), the Supreme Court rejected the requirements for intentional relinquishment of a known right in determining whether a defendant effectively waived his Fourth Amendment rights by consenting to a warrantless search of his automobile. Although purporting to analyze the "voluntariness" of Bustamonte's consent, the Court stated that voluntariness in that context cannot be taken literally to mean a "knowing choice." Instead, the Court analogized to principles governing coerced confessions in explaining that the determination of consent "reflects an accommodation of the complex of values implicated in police questioning of a suspect," including "the need for police questioning." Id. at 224-25. For a valid Fourth Amendment "waiver," the *Bustamonte* Court held, the prosecution need not necessarily prove "that the defendant knew he had a right to refuse to answer the questions that were put." Id. at 226. Rather, as applied to consent searches, the trial court should look to "the totality of all the surrounding circumstances" to determine "whether a consent to a search was in fact "'voluntary' or was the product of duress or coercion, express or implied...." Id. at 227. The courts must perform this inquiry by balancing "two competing concerns... the legitimate need for such searches and the equally important requirement of assuring the absence of coercion." Id.

claims.[20] Third, one can elect to choose one right over another.[21] In the context of criminal procedure, the Fifth Amendment privilege against self-incrimination illustrates this type of waiver. The Supreme Court has repeatedly held that, pursuant to the Fifth Amendment, every criminal defendant is privileged to testify in his own defense, or to refuse to do so. However, in any given prosecution, the same defendant cannot exercise both of those alternative aspects of the Fifth Amendment simultaneously.[22] If one testifies, he loses the right to plead the Fifth. Other forms of waiver certainly exist. But these basic forms illustrate the many options we may consider when we seek to determine when individuals can (ideally or realistically) control criminal justice processes.

Exclusionary Rule and Harmless Errors

The exclusionary rule requires that evidence obtained directly or indirectly through government violations of constitutional mandates may not be introduced by the prosecution at trial, at least for the purpose of providing direct proof of the defendant's guilt. In fact, suppression of illegally seized evidence has been the principal method of sanctioning Fourth Amendment violations.[23] The rule was created on the theory that denying the state the fruits of unconstitutional conduct would constrain future constitutional violations. Importantly, the rule is not designed as a specific remedy for individual defendants whose constitutional rights have been violated. Rather, the rule is meant to discourage police officers from violating the constitutional right to be free from unreasonable and arbitrary searches. By denying the state the ability to present to a jury evidence uncovered via an unconstitutional search, the rule intends to discourage officers from unconstitutionally searching anyone, law-abiding or criminal, by making the value of such searches zero.

The general rule has been the subject of important developments. Thus, the Fourth Amendment normally requires that police obtain a warrant, issued by a neutral and detached magistrate, before making a non-exigent search of a home. In the past three decades, however, the Supreme Court has created numerous exceptions to the exclusionary rule's application. Virtually all of these exceptions are grounded on one of two theories of deterrence, the good faith theory or the secondary process theory. The good faith theory justifies foregoing exclusion when officers conduct an illegal search or seizure relying on what would have appeared to be a valid warrant, statute or arrest report.[24] In all of these situations, one can plausibly claim that the threat of exclusion does not act as a deterrent. Police officers who believe they are operating with a valid warrant or under a duly enacted statute, the theory goes, are unlikely to believe that their actions violate the Fourth Amendment. The secondary process theory rejects the use of the exclusionary remedy when it would be applied in proceedings[25] or procedures[26] deemed ancillary to making the prosecution's *prima facie* case.[27] Exclusion is not necessary in such situations because sufficient

---

[20] Even the timing of other court decisions may allow a defendant to be executed despite a constitutional violation in the case. *Coleman v. Thompson*, 501 U.S. 722, 752-54 (1991).

[21] Election occurs when a party having two coexistent but inconsistent remedies chooses to exercise one, in which event he forfeits the right thereafter to exercise the other.

[22] Like any witness, a defendant who testifies relinquishes the privilege against self-incrimination. *Mitchell v. United States*, 526 U.S. 314 (1999). By the same token, a defendant who exercises the privilege against self-incrimination as a factual matter relinquishes the opportunity to testify on his or her own behalf. Yet no formal "waiver" of the right to testify is required in order for the defendant to elect to remain silent.

[23] This has been the case since *Mapp v. Ohio*, 367 U.S. 643 (1961).

[24] See *United States v. Leon*, 468 U.S. 897, 922 (1984) (facially valid warrant), *Illinois v. Krull*, 480 U.S. 340, 349-50 (1987) (statute) and *Arizona v. Evans*, 514 U.S. 1, 15-16 (1995) (computerized arrest report).

[25] Examples include grand jury proceedings, *United States v. Calandra*, 414 U.S. 338, 354-55 (1974), and sentencing hearings, *United States v. McCrory*, 930 F.2d 63 (D.C. Cir. 1991).

[26] Examples include the impeachment of the defendant. *United States v. Havens*, 446 U.S. 620, 627-28 (1980).

[27] *Prima facie* literally means "at first view." It refers to the minimal amount of evidence a plaintiff/prosecutor must have to avoid having a case dismissed.

deterrence is achieved through preventing use of illegal evidence in the government's case-in-chief,[28] the supposed focus of all law enforcement efforts.[29] The secondary process theory also justifies the introduction of illegally obtained evidence in noncriminal adjudications, such as tax deficiency proceedings, at least when the evidence is obtained by police who are looking for evidence of crime,[30] because again the possibility of exclusion at the criminal trial is seen as sufficient deterrence. The second example demonstrates well how the state can use illegally obtained evidence in many ways, and the extent to which we do use illegally obtained evidence reveals how we either follow the crime control model (which allows it) or due process model (which prohibits it).

In addition to emerging exceptions to exclusions, the exclusionary rule itself limits its impact. Most notably, a trial court improperly admits evidence in violation of the exclusionary rule, reversal is required unless the error was harmless beyond a reasonable doubt. The harmless error rule's purpose is to avoid setting aside convictions for small errors or defects that have little, if any, likelihood of having changed the result of the trial. In the case of constitutional error, the Supreme Court has stated that a court may label the error harmless only upon determination beyond a reasonable doubt that the error did not contribute to the verdict. For nonconstitutional error, the Court has rejected an examination of the correctness of the result; an appellate court need only determine with fair assurance that the judgment was not substantially swayed by the error. Curative measures taken at trial increase the likelihood of an appellate court finding the error harmless.

Typically, a court analyzes an error by distinguishing classic trial errors, which are subject to harmless error analysis, from structural defects in the trial mechanism, which are not.[31] Other types of error, however, are immune from harmless error analysis because the right involved is so basic to a fair trial that an infraction can never be considered harmless, such as right to an impartial judge.[32] That these violations are probably understandable to those who have not formally studied criminal justice processes testifies to the fact that these would seem to be very basic protections. Yet, controversy still remains as to which context to apply the harmless error analysis.

Right to Effective Counsel and Experts

---

[28] A case-in-chief is one side's evidence presented at trial. In a criminal trial, the prosecution presents its evidence (case-in-chief) first. The defense then can rebut it. After the prosecution rests its case, the defense presents its evidence (case-in-chief).

[29] *United States v. Calandra*, 414 U.S. 338, 351 (1974).

[30] *United States v. Janis*, 428 U.S. 433, 454 (1976).

[31] A list of errors subject to harmless error analysis may not mean much to those who have not been formally initiated to the study of criminal justice processes. Regardless, consider the following list and realize that you most likely will understand what they all mean once you have studied the chapters of this book. Errors subject to harmless error analyses include certain grand jury procedural violations, variance between the indictment and the proof, misjoinders of offenders or offenses, errors in the plea colloquy, the admission of evidence in violation of a defendant's Fourth, Fifth, or Sixth Amendment rights including admission of coerced confessions, errors in voir dire examination of prospective jurors, juror misconduct, prosecutorial misconduct, Confrontation Clause violations, the absence of the defendant from trial proceedings, improper exclusion of evidence, errors in jury instructions, failure to inquire whether a guilty plea is voluntary, absence of the defendant from the return of a death verdict, and errors in sentencing.

[32] In *Arizona v. Fulminante*, 499 U.S. 279 (1991), the Court noted that such violations include denial of the right to counsel, the right to an impartial judge, the right to a public trial, and the right to self-representation at trial. The Court also has held that harmless error analysis may not be applied to cases involving erroneous jury instructions regarding reasonable doubt, racial discrimination in grand jury selection, the improper removal of potential jurors for cause in capital trials, and certain discovery violations. Furthermore, circuit courts have declined to apply harmless error analysis in the following circumstances: (1) egregious violation of the right to a fair trial, (2) violation of the right to choice of counsel, (3) improper amendment to the indictment, (4) failure to determine if the defendant understands the nature of charges, (5) failure to inform the defendant of the right to appeal his or her conviction, (6) impairment of the defendant's right to peremptory challenges, and (7) denial of right to jury trial. In cases that follow, determine the exclusionary rule's effectiveness.

Given the nature of adversarial proceedings, few procedural rights have the status of fundamental than the Sixth Amendment right to counsel. A criminal defendant needs counsel not only to scrutinize the government's case and to present the defendant's side of the story, but also to ensure that the state honors all of the defendant's other rights. Included in those rights are those that apply before a criminal defendant even becomes a defendant, such as the Fourth Amendment protection against unreasonable search and seizure. Moreover, because suppression motions brought by criminal defendants remain the principal enforcement mechanisms for all criminal procedure rights, even people who are never charged with crimes depend, albeit indirectly, on criminal defense attorneys to keep law enforcement and the powers of the state in check. The belief is that the less criminal defense we have, the less enforcement we have of constitutional criminal procedure. The Supreme Court reveals the remarkable extent to which the right is taken seriously through the requirement that the government provide an attorney for every felony defendant who cannot afford one.[33] The potential breadth of this right appears quite impressive.

Numerous issues arise from the Court's approach, four of which are important to consider at this juncture. First, the Court never has determined how much the government must support defense counsels. The legal system has imposed only the weakest of demands on the kind of representation the government purchases.[34] Second, the Court rarely has sought to clarify the type of support defense counsel may have, such as the ability to acquire needed expertise by retaining experts.[35] Third, the Court has assessed the constitutional adequacy of appointed counsel, and it has set the standard on which to sustain challenges quite high.[36] Lastly, difficulties arise in efforts to determine when the right to counsel attaches.[37] All of

---

[33] This has been the case since *Gideon v. Wainwright*, 372 U.S. 335 (1963).

[34] As a result, few people familiar with criminal litigation in the United States – attorneys, judges, or scholars – believe that poor defendants routinely receive adequate legal assistance. And most defendants are poor, or poor enough to need appointed counsel. Many researchers have examined indigent defense systems in the United States. Results reveal that public defender offices suffer from chronically under staffing and cannot pay enough to retain experienced attorneys. Lawyers appointed from private practice are paid far below market rates and often face unrealistically low fee caps. Consequently, poor defendants represented under either system often receive substandard representation: Attorneys lack the time and resources to mount the kind of defense any informed, paying client would expect. Commentators report that the situation is worst for poor defendants with the most at stake, those charged with capital murder, and it has been getting progressively worse for all poor defendants. Stephen B. Bright, Counsel for the poor: The death sentence not for the worst crime but for the worst lawyer, 103 Yale L.J. 1835 (1994).

[35] Most notably, the Supreme Court has found effective assistance of experts to be constitutionally required under narrow conditions, such as psychiatric expertise in capital defense cases. See *Ake v. Oklahoma*, 470 U.S. 68 (1985). But the Court has yet to clarify the needed effectiveness and qualifications of such expertise. As *Ake* entitled an indigent defendant to his own independent expert advocate, it simultaneously left to the state the power to determine how to implement that right. As a result, lower federal courts have struggled to decide whether: an indigent defendant is entitled to an independent expert, separate from the state's expert; due process entitles an indigent to a "competent" expert (one "qualified" to conduct "appropriate" tests and provide "helpful" opinions consistent with Federal Rules of Evidence); the right applies narrowly to psychiatric examination or non-psychiatric assistance; and the harmless error analysis applies to an *Ake* violation. Although state court opinions generally comply with *Ake's* call for a preliminary showing and an expert different from that of the prosecutor, they differ on whether *Ake* requires an indigent to receive an expert of his own choice and on whether *Ake* should extend to non-psychiatric assistance. Carlton Bailey, *Ake v. Okldahoma* and indigent defendant's "right" to an expert witness: A promise denied or imagined?, 10 Wm. and Mary Bill of Rts. J. 401 (2002).

[36] The Court's two-part test announced in *Strickland v. Washington*, 466 U.S. 668 (1984), governs post-conviction challenges to the adequacy of any criminal law related assistance of counsel, whether appointed or privately retained. Under *Strickland*, a conviction will be set aside on grounds of ineffective assistance of counsel only if the attorney's performance fell below "prevailing professional norms" and the defendant establishes "a reasonable probability that, but for counsel's unprofessional errors, the result of the proceeding would have been different." Id. at 688, 694. Although the standard is not impossible to meet, the reality is that mistakes and omissions by defense counsel often are excused as "strategic decisions" or "isolated" errors – or not even addressed, because the reviewing court finds the evidence of guilt so strong that there is no "reasonable probability" that any deficiencies in the defendant's representation affected the verdict. See Richard Klein, The constitutionalization of ineffective assistance of counsel, 58 Md. L. Rev. 1433, 1435-45 (1999). To complicate matters, the high evidentiary standard is problematic to the extent that the very lawyer whose competence is challenged made the record under attack: evidence of injury to the defendant may be missing from the record precisely because of the incompetence of defense counsel.

[37] The case controlling this area is *United States v. Wade*, 388 U.S. 218 (1967). In that case, the Supreme Court held that the Sixth Amendment right to counsel attaches to "critical stages" of pretrial proceedings. Concerned that a suggestive pretrial lineup might lead to the conviction of innocent persons, the Wade Court held that a postindictment, pretrial lineup is a critical stage of a criminal proceeding where the defendant has a right to the assistance of counsel. The Court

these issues figure prominently in our efforts to understand how to structure criminal justice procedures and systems. As we will see, the legal system places considerable emphasis on representation to protect people's rights. If that representation does not met expectations, ti becomes difficult to uphold the rationales relying on it.[38]

Need for Governmental Action

By now, we know that criminal procedure embodies the rights that must be afforded to suspects and defendants in the criminal justice system. Some protections restrict the activities and discretion of law enforcement, while others affect the amount and type of process required in pre-trial and trial litigation. All criminal procedure rights, however, share a common purpose. All limit the means by which the government can investigate, prosecute, and punish crime. The concern is with what the state's representatives (e.g., police and prosecutors) do or fail to do.

Understanding what the government can do often leads to discussions of negative and affirmative governmental obligations. An affirmative right against the government is a right to have the government do something; it is a legal power to impose on the government an affirmative obligation. A negative right against the government is a right to have the government not do something; it is a legal power to impose on the government a negative obligation. The distinction between affirmative and negative obligations of the government, and between affirmative and negative rights against the government, is tightly connected to the distinction between benefits and burdens. An affirmative right is the right to a benefit; a negative right is the right to avoid a burden. The most common and influential view of the Constitution suggests that it creates, almost exclusively, negative obligations of government and negative rights. At least two different kinds of considerations underlie this view. The first is ideological; it draws on the deep and longstanding commitments in Anglo-American political culture to individualism and limited government. The second is institutional; it builds on the notion that doing something generally costs money, whereas refraining from action typically does not. Affirmative rights therefore generally have budgetary implications. Many find courts ill-suited to make decisions with such implications. Yet, it is debatable which approach actually guides.[39] When it comes to law enforcement and the constitutional provisions guiding it, the rights are almost entirely negative; defendants have the right to be free from certain kinds of government conduct. More particularly, they have the right to be free from criminal conviction except when the government follows a given set of procedures. Thus, defendants' rights really are the system's rules, rules that regulate the conduct of the various actors who take part in the process of convicting and punishing criminal defendants.

Although constitutional rights do tend to be viewed as negative rights, we will see that governmental obligations also may involve both negative and positive obligations. For example, the right to counsel is paradigmatically quasi-affirmative: It requires the government to do something affirmative, but only for people it chooses to charge with crimes. Outside the field of criminal procedure, perhaps the most familiar examples of quasi-affirmative rights directly impacting law enforcement are the obligations of protection

---

reasoned that the presence of counsel may guard against suggestive procedures and enable counsel to reconstruct and challenge those procedures at trial. It is important to highlight what the right to counsel established in *Wade* does not encompass. It does not reach identification procedures that occur before the start of adversarial judicial proceedings or procedures that do not require the defendant's presence. Nor does *Wade* encompass "other preparatory steps, such as systematized or scientific analyzing of the accused's fingerprints, blood sample, clothing, hair, and the like." The Court reasoned that counsel is not required for these preparatory steps because knowledge of the techniques of science and technology is sufficiently available, and the variables in techniques few enough, that the accused has the opportunity for a meaningful confrontation of the Government's case at trial through the ordinary processes of cross-examination.

[38] For example, we will see that many cases turn on the fact that a defendant had counsel and that he had been adequately represented. The case in the previous footnote is illustrative.

[39] David P. Currie, Positive and negative constitutional rights, 53 U. Chi. L. Rev. 864 (1986). For a more recent and more elaborate defense, see Frank B. Cross, The error of positive rights, 48 U.C.L.A. L. Rev. 857, 864-74 (2001).

and support the government owes to those placed in its custody,[40] such as prisoners and those held for treatment.[41] Calling these "affirmative obligations," however, runs the risk of missing or over-simplifying a fundamental point. The cases actually do not require anything from the government, so long as the government leaves people alone. In this regard, then, the rights are also somewhat negative in that they simply bar the government from acting in particularly abusive or egregious manners. The significance of these rights will emerge as we move from investigative to correctional law enforcement.

Federalism

Federalism presents one of the most enduring and now resurgent themes in the development of standards regulating law enforcement. Federalists believe that decisions can often be best made at the local governmental level as opposed to the national level. Given the constitutionalization of criminal procedure cases, a tension that continues involves federalist concerns – the extent to which the federal government should control or otherwise monitor state responses to crime. Federalist concerns reach both the extent to which state legislatures and constitutions should preempt federal laws as well the extent to which constitutional principles should be expanded to reach what may be viewed as within state jurisdictions.[42] For our purposes, these concerns contribute two important themes.

One theme involves examining how courts, particularly federal courts, police the boundaries of power between the federal and state governments. This includes, for example, how the Supreme Court requires states to follow the Bill of Rights, incorporated through the Due Process Clause of the Fourteenth Amendment and how federal courts interpret congressional power under the Commerce Clause or Section 5 of the Fourteenth Amendment. The interaction is significant. As we will see, many aspects of trial functioning, for example, vary systematically by jurisdiction or are left to the discretion of the particular judge hearing the case. These aspects include instructions given to the jury, the degree of agreement required for a verdict, the number of jurors serving on the jury, acceptable behavior by the jury, the inclusion of lesser charges, the set of verdict options, and the manner and sequence in which courtroom events take place. Yet, the immense discretion left to state courts and legislatures has not stopped the federal courts to examine, for example, the extent to which these matters offend constitutional mandates.

The second federalist theme relates to the interaction of federal and state courts. Examples include the impact of jurisdictional and other procedural requirements in federal court by past, concurrent, or future litigation in state court; how state courts adjudicate issues of federal law; how the Supreme Court reviews such adjudication; and how state courts have interpreted their own constitutions to protect rights to an extent not found in federal constitutional law. In the cases that follow, issues of federalism will arise repeatedly when discussing the extent to which state courts should have the power to determine their own criminal laws and procedures, such as the extent to which a defendant must sustain a certain burden of proof regarding their mental state (e.g. sanity or competence) and the extent to which judges should retain discretion to determine whether a defendant should be provided an expert to help support their defenses (e.g., offering a battered woman defense).

Importantly, the impact and role of federalism is often difficult to detect. A notable example, which recurs in the cases that we will examine, involves the use of the "totality of circumstances" analysis. The Supreme Court, with some important exceptions, opts for this standard which utilizes a case-by-case approach to determine constitutional violations. For an officer to stop a vehicle, for example, he must have reasonable suspicion that the driver is engaged in criminal activity and the stop must meet the "totality of circumstances" test, looking at the whole picture.[43] This approach varies from a preference for specific

[40] *DeShaney v. Winnebago County Dep't of Soc. Servs.*, 489 U.S. 189 (1989).
[41] *Estelle v. Gamble*, 429 U.S. 97 (1976); and *Youngberg v. Romeo*, 457 U.S. 307 (1982).
[42] See Richard H. Fallon, Jr., Daniel J. Meltzer, and David L. Shapiro, Hart and Wechsler's The Federal Courts and the Federal System 492-509 (4th ed. 1996).
[43] *United States v. Arvizu*, 534 U.S. 266 (2002).

rules to guide law enforcement officers as well as the courts that evaluate their behaviors. The result is that the case-by-case approach diminishes the precedential value of cases. That is, legal rules are difficult to determine from legal opinions when the court's decisions seem to rest on the specific facts of the presented cases rather than on broad legal principles. Reliance on facts tends to leave discretion to lower courts. When this is coupled by the view that state court determinations of factual issues relating to even federal constitutional claims be accorded a presumption of correctness, the legal system essentially reduces constitutional (federal) restrictions on law enforcement. It is debatable whether this constitutes a sound approach to resolving disputes. For our purposes, it means that we need to look at the standards adopted by the Supreme Court if we are to understand the extent to which the legal system protects rights in a universal or contextual manner.

NOTES AND QUERIES

After having considered the Dirty Harry scenario for where you stand in terms of the Due Process and Crime Control ideologies, reconsider the scenario for where you stand in terms of the principles we have highlighted above. For example, should there be uniform, federal standards to guide law enforcement's responses to exigent circumstances requiring the use of force to obtain information from suspects? Should Scorpio be deemed as having waived his rights? Should the legal system respect Scorpio's right to privacy in terms of Harry's invasion of his home and admittedly rough interrogation? Should the legal system allow prosecutors to retain the discretion not to prosecute people like Scorpio (or, for that matter, renegade officers like Harry)? Assume that Harry violated too many of Scorpio's rights to allow for a successful prosecution. Should the evidence be used in the civil system to, for example, institutionalize Scorpio because he is dangerous? Would the legal system act fairly if it allowed the use of the evidence if the same information and roughing were done by vigilantes not acting under the authority of the sate?

PREVIEWING PSYCHOLOGICAL SCIENCE'S PLACE IN RESOLVING LEGAL DILEMMAS

Each of the identified legal principles may seem foreign to readers more accustomed to examining psychological research than exploring legal complexities. Yet, the principles raise numerous psychological issues. Importantly, it is not that psychology provides easy answers to dealing with most legal issues. Rather, psychological sciences help raise concerns and point to possible remedies. In the end, whether the legal system can and should respond to psychological findings and theories is an entirely different matter. That matter generally depends on the extent to which society seeks to move toward either the due process or crime control models at particular stages of criminal justice processes. A few examples may help clarify this point and prepare us for thinking through the use, non-use or misuse of psychological sciences in the chapters that follow.

We have identified the enormous discretionary power given to police, attorneys, judges, juries, correctional officers, and virtually anyone involved in criminal justice processes. Psychological sciences can help us determine whether and how to allow, limit, or even foster that discretion. We know, for example, that people are inherently biased and that bias manifests itself differently in different contexts. The central concern arising from that reality involves how we are to control such bias. For example, if a potential juror states that she is biased by pretrial publicity but that she can control that bias, should we believe her? How should the law deal with such jurors and the problems of pretrial publicity? Likewise, should we leave it to the discretion of individual psychologists and psychiatrists to determine the form of psychological treatment an offender should receive, or should we rely on standards established by relevant professional organizations or by courts? Should we grant prosecutors discretion to plea bargain, either aggressively or leniently, when we know that suspects do not necessarily make decisions based on objectively sound reasoning? Should we leave sentencing to judicial discretion or devise guidelines? Should we still require the use of such guidelines when we know that judges simply cannot apply them properly because we know that two judges may apply the guidelines differently due to their psychological abilities and inabilities?

The legal conception of privacy, which we may view as dealing with the psychological integrity of individuals, also points to the possible use of psychological science. Issues involving privacy may concern, for example, the extent to which society can justify intrusion and how it offers protections from unwarranted intrusions. We know that issues of privacy certainly arise when police seek to search one's home, car or draw blood samples for testing. And these issues can quickly become complex and highly politically charged. For example, should racial profiling be abolished because it may disproportionately target a group of individuals, diminish their dignity and inflict them with emotional harm? Should we still abolish profiling if it leads to the same effect when used to target white males for domestic terrorism or serial murder? Numerous other important psychological issues also arise when we attempt to determine the extent to which we will protect someone else's privacy. Do we, for example, underestimate the extent to which others feel intrusions because we are not the ones suspected of the crime? Could those who rarely suffer invasions of privacy by police adequately judge how intrusive police practices can be to those who are more often likely to be stopped and frisked as suspects? Can we really place ourselves in another's position? What are we to do with the finding indicating that, in some circumstances, asking us to place ourselves in another's position (such as a rape victim) does not raise the anticipated response (such as sympathy and understanding) but its opposite (such as anger and fear)? Other concerns about psychological integrity are more obvious but equally difficult to address. Should defendants be allowed to reject medications even if it means that they have lost contact with reality and cannot be prosecuted until they regain contact with reality? Should we medicate individuals so that they are able to know what is happening to them? This could include medication to allow them to understand why they are being executed before they are to be executed. In the alternative, are we simply to execute them without their knowing what is happening to them or are we not to execute them at all? How are we to determine what medications they need? Should a mental health professional be involved in such matters when their code of ethics requires them to do no harm?

Requesting individuals to waive their rights remains one of the fundamental ways that the legal system retains efficiency. If people agree to waive certain rights, the state need not provide them with what otherwise would be required protections. Although waivers are necessary for maintaining a smoothly functioning system, the psychology of how people respond to requests from authority figures raises many concerns. Many psychological findings challenge the presumption that people are in fact capable of waiving their rights. This raises the concern of whether individuals should be allowed to waive their rights at all. In addition, issues arise as to what law enforcement can do to have suspects waive their rights. Should police be allowed to use psychological pressure? Should a persons' particular psychological vulnerabilities matter when law enforcement personnel have no way of knowing those vulnerabilities without having a suspect undergo intensive psychological evaluations? Relatedly, do we have reliable methods to determine the nature, extent and significance of individuals' vulnerabilities?

The exclusionary rules also raise many psychological concerns in that they deal with the extent to which people can be treated fairly by the legal system when the system acted inappropriately toward them. For example, could a judge ignore improperly obtained evidence when deciding guilt? Could a jury ignore such evidence when they are told to do so? How can we go about remedying trial situations involving inappropriately admitted evidence? Should we allow police to illegally obtain evidence in order to generate a list of suspects? If so, what does that do to police officers? What does that do to society and to people's socialization into our legal system? How does it affect the trust we have in the legal system? Does trust matter and, if so, how? Do harmless error rules reflect reality to the extent that they assume that judges can properly determine the extent to which tainted evidence influenced juries?

Our adversarial system relies heavily on the ability to empower defendants to defend themselves against claims of wrong-doing. This is seen most obviously through the provision of legal counsel and even experts to help attorneys provide testimony regarding psychological conditions. This reliance on attorneys and experts also raises numerous psychological issues. For example, should an expert be allowed to testify for prosecutors in an insanity case when every defendant that he has examined turns out to be sane? How about an expert who always finds defendants dangerous to the community, which makes those defendants likely to receive the death penalty? How much should counsel be expected to understand his client's inability to interact with him to prepare his defense? Should a psychologist report all that she knows about a defendant she examined or only report what she has been told to report by those who hired her? Should an expert offer an opinion in court about a matter, such as offering a diagnosis, when the law allows it but his professional association finds it unethical to offer such a diagnosis (e.g., when an evaluator provides a diagnosis without personally interviewing the client)? Could attorneys actually put their biases aside when defending people they do not like? What about the natural biases of prosecutors; should they, for example, be allowed to be vindictive or racially motivated in their decisions to prosecute? How are we to determine if they were?

The manner our criminal justice system uses procedural rules that seek to protect individuals from state officials also raises important psychological issues. One notable concern involves what we should consider as people's free will when they interact with law enforcement. For example, what if someone confesses to a crime because their delusions (they believe they are Jesus Christ) urge them to confess that they committed a crime (because of yet another delusion, thinking they were the devil)? Should police require them to seek the advice of an attorney first and then talk to them or should police simply take their statement? Is the person confessing under inappropriate duress? What would be a fair way to deal with their mental illness and respect their rights (as well as those of victims and broader society)? What are we to do of a law that requires a child sex offender to inform future neighbors about his past crimes? Should it matter that the offender may be harmed by the future neighbors acting as concerned citizens? Should the state be held responsible when requiring such notification leading to vigilantism? How would you respond if your new neighbor told you that he had just been released from prison for sexually abusing five 4-year-old girls? Should your gut instincts play into your consideration of what the law should be? Issues of state action also figure into people's responses to crime. For example, should a person be held responsible when they fail to notify police to stop a crime that is occurring a few feet from them, especially when reporting would not place the reporter in danger? What if it can be shown that many psychological reasons explain why even reasonable and otherwise responsible people tend not to call for help?

Issues regarding federalism also will recur frequently and raise important concerns relating to psychological matters. For example, assuming that psychologists identify a principle that leads to unjust outcomes in responses to crime. Should the federal government require states to remedy their procedures accordingly in their responses to crime? For example, what should happen if it is shown that certain types of line-ups increase the risk of erroneous identification of suspects? Should states be banned from using those line-up procedures? What if allowing people with certain beliefs to serve on juries leads to a biasing effect in favor of prosecutors and even to the biased imposition of the death penalty? Should people with those beliefs be automatically excused from serving on juries in every state and federal death penalty case? What if it is shown that *Miranda* warnings[44] are not effective in helping individuals exercise their right not to consent to interrogations. Further suppose that research shows how *Miranda* may actually play into the hands of law enforcement because police can use subtle psychological pressures to have subjects waive their rights and because we know that individuals tend to submit to legitimate authority even when it is against their best interests. Should *Miranda* warnings still be required in every jurisdiction? What if the Constitution mandates the warnings?

---

[44] *Miranda* warnings derive from *Miranda v. Arizona*, 384 U.S. 436 (1966), which was based on the Fifth Amendment right against compelled self-incrimination. In that case, the Supreme Court held that when police have a suspect in custody and prior to conducting any interrogation, they must warn the suspect that she has the right to remain silent; that if she gives up that right, anything she says may be used against her in court; that she has a right to an attorney's presence during questioning; and that if she is indigent, an attorney may be appointed for her. After hearing these warnings, a suspect may waive her rights and submit to interrogation. If she chooses to exercise her rights, however, the police must

NOTES AND QUERIES

Return again to Dirty Harry. Physically assaulting Scorpio to obtain information may seem justified but also a bit barbaric. Should we instead permit the use of a mind-altering drug that would achieve the same effect? Should we leave it to the discretion of an expert to determine whether Scorpio manifests the appropriate level of insanity so as to not be held legally responsible for his actions? Should an expert be involved in testifying about Scorpio's dangerousness, which is a determination needed to keep Scorpio incarcerated but which is the type of testimony that an expert is likely to be worse than chance in predicting correctly? Should a court uphold a jury's guilty verdict based, in part, on illegally obtained evidence (perhaps Scorpio's gun and his statements made under duress) when it is clear that the evidence played an important part in the jury's verdict and we know that Scorpio is guilty anyway? Should some states be allowed to not provide *Miranda* rights to suspects like Scorpio because the vast majority of voters in that state believe that such suspects do not deserve those rights? Should Scorpio be tried by a jury that has characteristics that would be biased against him both in terms of finding him guilty and imposing the death penalty? Should Scorpio have a right to an expert to help determine if some members of the jury are in fact biased against people like him?

CONSIDERING THE LIMITS OF USING PSYCHOLOGICAL SCIENCES

It is important to recognize the limits of our own abilities to use psychological sciences, in addition to understanding the limits of psychological sciences themselves. As we will soon see, the variety of empirical research we will investigate in the pages that follow inevitably have some drawbacks as well as some advantages. The general argument made in this text is that we should take the findings seriously to the extent that they allow us to examine the current approaches to criminal justice processes. It is not to say that we should change processes; rather, it is to say that we should consider what the empirical evidence reveals in terms of limitations and remedies to identified concerns. This may seem like an all too obvious point. But, the reality is that many consumers of empirical research have a tendency to disregard methodological nuances and fail to tie research, theory and practice together. As a result, they run the risk of accepting empirical results at face value and then using their interpretation as a source of answers to complex legal or policy issues. Or, in the alternative, they run the risk of rejecting findings because relevant studies failed to address thoroughly the legal concerns or conditions. How people respond to scientific findings, then, creates an important obstacle to their proper use.

Obvious ways exist to counter the above tendency to reject evidence out of hand or embrace it at face value, but none may be adequate. For example, one obvious solution is to provide in depth reports of psychological studies and to let readers judge materials for themselves. That, however, quickly becomes impractical: studies often are very complex and some areas of research produce hundreds of detailed studies. Relatedly, readers may be unable to decipher the significance or relevance of findings. That inability leads to the other obvious solution often offered by those who explore the use of psychological findings in legal settings: encourage training in both disciplines. But, that too may be impractical, especially in terms of time, cost, and whether there is in fact a need to study both disciplines in much depth. These two obvious solutions, and any other that may arise, are further limited by basic psychological obstacles. Most notably, people tend not to act randomly when they dismiss or accept an empirical study. The process involves cognitive and motivational biases which actually constitute what psychologists view as the phenomenon of "biased assimilation."[45] The tendency provides an important obstacle which, as we will see in the pages that follow, can best be addressed by understanding and recognizing its existence.

---

respect that choice and refrain from questioning her. If she nonetheless initiates interrogation, her answers are inadmissible to prove her guilt at trial.

45 See Robert J. MacCoun, Biases in the interpretation and use of research results, 49 Ann. Rev. Psych. 259 (1998).

Biased assimilation is the tendency for evaluations of the methodology and persuasiveness of empirical research to be influenced by the extent to which research results are consistent with the attitudes or expectations of the person conducting the evaluation.[46] Our expectations and theories bias our judgements about the validity,[47] reliability,[48] relevance, and sometimes even the meaning of proffered evidence. The classic study of biased assimilation, for example, found that people who evaluate empirical research related to capital punishment actually evaluate identical methodologies differently depending on whether they produced findings that were consistent with the evaluators' existing attitudes and beliefs.[49] The basic phenomenon of biased assimilation has been widely replicated using different populations of evaluators. Judges and law students, for example, have been found to judge research as more relevant to the legal issues, more likely to be admissible, and to have greater dispositive weight (affect the eventual court decision) when the results were consistent with their personal attitudes than when the results contradicted those attitudes.[50]

Research exploring the mechanisms that underlie the biased assimilation effect identify important motivational and cognitive influences that help us understand the extent to which biased assimilation poses a serious obstacle to evaluations of research. Research supports, for example, the general conclusion that people's emotional convictions impact their judgements. Biased assimilation effects seem mediated by the different emotional responses evaluators have to research results that are either congruent or incongruent with their attitudes. This area of research tends to come from examinations of prejudices. People evaluating studies reporting results consistent with their prejudices find those studies to be of better methodological quality and people feel more positive emotions after reading stereotypical results consistent with their

---

[46] Charles G. Lord, Lee Ross, and Mark R. Lepper, Biased assimilation and attitude polarization: The effects of prior theories on subsequently considered evidence, 37 J. Personality and Soc. Psych. 2098 (1979).

[47] Validity refers to the degree to which a study accurately reflects or assesses the specific concept that the researcher is attempting to measure. Generally, we concern ourselves with both external and internal validity. External validity refers to the extent to which the results of a study are generalizable or transferable. Internal validity refers to the rigor with which the study was conducted (e.g., the study's design, the care taken to conduct measurements, and decisions concerning what was and was not measured) and the extent to which the designers of a study have taken into account alternative explanations for any causal relationships they explore.

[48] Reliability is the extent to which an experiment, test, or any measuring procedure yields the same result on repeated trials. Without the agreement of independent observers able to replicate research procedures, or the ability to use research tools and procedures that yield consistent measurements, researchers would be unable to satisfactorily draw conclusions, formulate theories, or make claims about the generalizability of their research.

[49] The study recruited participants who either favored capital punishment and believed it to have a deterrent effect or who opposed capital punishment and questioned its deterrent effect. Participants were asked to evaluate two empirical studies of the deterrent effect of capital punishment, with one study described as finding an effect and the other described as failing to find such evidence. This meant that each participant read about one study that corroborated their initial beliefs about capital punishment and deterrence and one that refuted these beliefs. For each study, participants were provided a description of the procedures used in the study, the results, a set of criticisms, and a rebuttal. For half of the participants, the study finding a deterrent effect was described as using a longitudinal methodology involving a comparison of homicide rates in a number of states before and after each state adopted a system of capital punishment. The study finding no deterrent effect was described as using a cross-sectional methodology comparing homicide rates across states with and without capital punishment. For the other participants, the methodologies of the studies were described in the opposite manner. Participants were asked to rate the methodology of each study as well as its persuasiveness. Studies described as having results that were consistent with the participants' prior beliefs were rated as having higher methodological quality and as being more convincing than were studies described as having results that contradicted these prior beliefs, regardless of which methodology was described. Thus, participants who favored capital punishment and believed it to have a deterrent effect found the prodeterrence study to be of higher quality and persuasiveness than the antideterrence study and vice versa. Charles G. Lord, Lee Ross, and Mark R. Lepper, Biased assimilation and attitude polarization: The effects of prior theories on subsequently considered evidence, 37 J. Personality and Soc. Psych. 2098 (1979).

[50] The study found a pattern of biased assimilation for state court judges and law students who were asked to make judgments about social science research on capital punishment and deterrence. The study had varied the results of the empirical studies that were presented in a leading death penalty case to the U.S. Supreme Court so that the studies either supported or failed to support the death penalty. Richard E. Redding and N. Dickon Reppucci, Effects of lawyers' socio-political attitudes on their judgments of social science in legal decision making, 23 L. and Hum. Beh. 31 (1999). The case was *Furman v. Georgia*, 408 U.S. 238 (1972), in which a majority of Justices agreed that capital punishment, as then administered, was plagued by arbitrariness, unpredictability, and capriciousness.

prejudices (while feeling more negative emotion after reading the non-stereotypical results).[51] Research also generally supports the finding that evaluators tend to rapidly reduce the complexity of information and remember only a few well-chosen supportive impressions when results are consistent with their attitudes, expectations, or theories. When evaluating information that disconfirms their attitudes, theories and expectations, evaluators tend to become more sensitive to the quality of information as they consider alternative hypotheses, request more information to make decisions, and generate more arguments.[52] People, then, tend to accept empirical results that confirm previously held attitudes at face value and to seek to reject results that disconfirm or conflict with those attitudes. As expected, researchers have a term for this tendency, "disconfirmation bias," which holds that evidence inconsistent with an evaluator's prior beliefs are scrutinized more extensively.[53]

NOTES AND QUERIES

The phenomenon of biased assimilation provides an important concept for us to consider as we read empirical research. As you consider the vast amount of empirical research in the pages that follow, consider not only questioning the findings themselves but also why you seem to accept or reject those findings. In that determination, consider evaluating your thoughts in terms of the Due Process and Crime Control models presented above.

We have noted that the legal system exerts considerable dominance over the extent to which certain empirical findings will be taken seriously. When you examine the nature of that dominance in the cases that follow, consider that dominance in terms of biased assimilation. Consider it not only in terms of how the law works but also in terms of how justices may be operating under similar biases, often described as political orientations.

It should be noted that there are no "silver bullet" techniques to counter assimilation bias. Researchers, however, have identified some debiasing techniques. These are readily obvious to those trained in law: encouraging consideration of alternative hypotheses, engaging in devil's advocacy, and using adversarial discussions. As we will see, however, these techniques also bring their own limitations.

As the more empirically-minded likely report, there actually may be nothing inherently wrong with accepting differing opinions about imperfect and limited research on complex, multifaceted phenomena. Indeed, and as those more law-minded likely report, there is nothing wrong with adopting an advocate's

---

[51] Kari Edwards and Edward E. Smith, A disconfirmation bias in the evaluation of arguments, 71 J. Personality and Soc. Psych. 5 (1996); and Geoffrey D. Munro and Peter H. Ditto, Biased assimilation, attitude polarization, and affect in reactions to stereotype-relevant scientific information, 23 Personality and Soc. Psych. Bull. 636 (1997).

[52] Kari Edwards and Edward E. Smith, A disconfirmation bias in the evaluation of Arguments, 71 J. Personality and Soc. Psych. 5 (1996); Geoffrey D. Munro and Peter H. Ditto, Biased assimilation, attitude polarization, and affect in reactions to stereotype-relevant scientific information, 23 Personality and Soc. Psych. Bull. 636 (1997); and Petter H. Ditto, James A. Scepansky, Geoffrey D. Munro, Anne Marie Apanovitch, and Lisa K. Lockhart, Motivated sensitivity to preference-inconsistent information, 75 J. Personality and Soc. Psych. 53 (1998).

[53] Kari Edwards and Edward E. Smith, A disconfirmation bias in the evaluation of arguments, 71 J. Personality and Soc. Psych. 5 (1996).

role, provided that we are self-conscious about our views, stances, standards and make those explicit to the extent that we can.

Part I. Investigating and Apprehending Criminal Suspects

Chapter 2

IDENTIFYING SUSPECTS

INTRODUCTION

The criminal justice system relies heavily on eyewitness accounts,[1] and the lesson we will learn is that such reliance does not mean that law enforcement responds effectively to them. Our everyday notions of how the legal system responds to crime brings into sharp focus the manner law enforcement devotes itself to collecting and using eyewitness accounts. Much of criminal justice processing, however, also involves devoting an enormous amount of resources and creating numerous mechanisms to avoid or correct errors. The system does so, for example, through the provision of appointed counsel when suspects are identified through lineups as well as through the use of prosecutorial discretion to drop charges based on unreliable eyewitness accounts, cross-examination by counsel to fetter out unreliable witnesses, evidentiary rulings by judges to ensure proper use of eyewitness evidence, juries to assure the credibility of accounts, and appellate review processes to guard against the failure to follow correct legal mandates in the use of testimony. Taken together, these constitute rather impressive protections.

Yet, studies of wrongful convictions provide clear examples of the extent to which the error-avoidance and error-correction mechanisms seem inadequate to remedy misidentifications. For example, one highly-cited study of wrongful convictions reported that misidentification was the most frequent kind of error, occurring in over 50% of the surveyed cases.[2] Importantly, over 40% of wrongful convictions were for murder, suggesting that wrongful incarceration was likely to be lengthy and even life-threatening. Relatedly, the National Institute of Justice recently conducted a study of felony convictions that had later been identified as wrongful through DNA evidence.[3] The study identified twenty-eight such cases, all involving sexual assault, in which DNA evidence later exonerated the convicted person. All of the cases involved eyewitness identifications, and in the vast majority of them, 86%, the primary evidence that had produced the conviction was an erroneous eyewitness identification. Accumulating research points to the conclusion that the task for the eyewitness may seem simple at first glance, but the task may lead to mistaken identifications that become responsible for more actual cases of wrongful convictions by juries

---

[1] Each year, identifications through lineups make over 75,000 suspects criminal defendants. Alvin G. Goldstein, June E. Chance, and Gregory R. Schneller, Frequency of eyewitness identification in criminal cases: A survey of prosecutors, 27 Bull. of the Psychonomic Soc. 71 (1989). The completeness and perceived accuracy of eyewitness accounts often determine whether or not law enforcement brings appropriate charges against defendants and solves cases. As we will see, eyewitness accounts greatly impact those who administer criminal justice process – from police, prosecutors, judges, and defense attorneys, to juries.

[2] Arye Rattner, Convicted but innocent: Wrongful conviction and the criminal justice system, 12 L. and Hum. Beh. 283, 287 (1988).

[3] Edward Connors,Thomas Lundregan, Neal Miller, and Tom McEwen, Convicted By Juries, Exonerated by Science: Case Studies in the Use of DNA Evidence to Establish Innocence after Trial (1996).

than all other causes combined.[4] Importantly, these research findings do not necessarily reflect the wide impact of eyewitness accounts. We will learn that most cases end with plea bargains, and such bargains generally mean that no one challenges unreliable evidence that appeared irrefutable at first glance. These studies support the claim that incorrect eyewitness identifications serve as the leading cause of wrongful criminal convictions. The criminal justice system does not necessarily respond effectively to mistakes and, as we will see, actually may exacerbate the unreliability of eyewitness accounts.

Psychological research has long shown that juries place great weight on eyewitness testimony and that eyewitnesses can play critical key roles in miscarriages of justice. For example, a ground-breaking study revealed that the addition of an eyewitness' identification to circumstantial evidence pointing to a suspect increased the percentage of subjects voting to convict from 18% to 72%.[5] Importantly, even with additional information showing that the eyewitness was unreliable (e.g., that he was legally blind and not wearing his glasses at the time of the events; that it was dark and that he was 1/4 mile away from the defendant), 68% of subjects still voted to convict.[6] In addition to being taken perhaps a bit too seriously by juries, we know that eyewitnesses can make mistakes. Another ground-breaking study reported how subjects were pervasively unreliable when they had watched a staged purse-snatching on television and had a clear view of the suspect's face: Only 14% of the subjects correctly chose the purse-snatcher out of a six person lineup. Despite having been provided with a clear view of the suspect, the witnesses performed worse than if they had guessed at random.[7] Put differently, with recognition beaning close to chance for nearly 2,000 television-viewer witnesses, it seems rather remarkable that over 1,800 witnesses made mistaken identifications. Research since then has continued to confirm the remarkable unreliability of eyewitness accounts.

Obviously, realization that eyewitness accounts may be inaccurate are not new. The legal system always has struggled with the reliability of witnesses and it continues to contend with the extent to which inaccuracies impact criminal justice processes and outcomes. What seems different now is that researchers know that the risks seem much higher than ever imagined,[8] even though those who administer criminal justice processes overwhelmingly tend to believe witnesses anyway. What also seems different now is the enormous amount of scientific research findings indicating reasons for high error risks and charting ways for reform. Our task is to examine some of these findings and suggestions and to explore how the legal system does or could respond to them.

THE PSYCHOLOGICAL MAKE-UP OF MEMORIES

How to address issues of inaccuracies requires understanding the processes that lead to the formation of inaccuracies. Several studies have focused on the conditions which contribute to the misidentifications of suspects. These conditions typically involve three phases: the initial perception of the suspect (the encoding phase), the period in which memory stores the memory trace (the retention interval phase), and the subsequent recall or identification of the suspect (the retrieval phase). Each of these phases poses different problems as different factors can influence the reliability of memory formation, retention and retrieval. The bulk of research most relevant to criminal justice processes, however, focuses on encoding

---

[4] See Barry Scheck, Peter Neufeld, and Jim Dwyer, Actual Innocence: When Justice Goes Wrong and How to Make it Right (2000); and Gary L. Wells, Mark Small, Steven Penrod, Roy S. Malpass, Solomon M. Fulero, and C.A.E. Brimacombe, Eyewitness identification procedures: Recommendations for lineups and photospreads, 22 L. and Hum. Beh. 603 (1998).

[5] Elizabeth F. Loftus, Eyewitness Testimony 9-10 (1979).

[6] Elizabeth F. Loftus, Eyewitness Testimony 9-10 (1979).

[7] Also note that those witnesses tended to believe that they were correct, otherwise they would not have taken part in the experiment. Robert Buckhout, Nearly 2000 witnesses can be wrong, 16 Bull. of Psychonomic Soc. 307 (1980).

[8] Although we know that inaccuracy may be high, not everyone believes it. For example, 84% of prosecutors believe that eyewitness identifications are "probably correct" at least 90% of the time. Jennifer L. Devenport, Steven D. Penrod, and Brian L. Cutler, Eyewitness identification evidence: Evaluating commonsense evaluations, 3 Psych. Pub. Pol'y. and L. 338 (1997).

and on retrieval. Exactly how all of those stages could be examined, though, remains a challenge, for researching and discussing one aspect of memory tends to involve another.[9] For our purposes, we will focus largely on the first and last stages.

Encoding and Retaining Memories

During the initial perception of the event or suspect, several factors may influence an eyewitness' ability to encode accurately the stimulus (in this case, the criminal event and the criminal's appearance) in memory. Without doubt, an individual's expectations of the event can influence the manner by which details about the event are recalled. Eyewitnesses generally report scenarios that are consistent with their expectations, a psychological mechanism known as the confirmation bias.[10] We know that once impressions are made, we seek confirming information rather than disconfirming information.[11] The way the confirmation bias works in terms of perception has been noted in police shootings of unarmed black suspects mistakenly believed to possess a weapon. The argument is that stereotypes associating blacks with violence lead police to "see" a weapon rather than the actual object or empty hand. Although it is possible that officers were lying, it also is possible that they were telling the truth in terms of what they saw. A recent study compellingly demonstrates the power of expectations associating blacks with violence. The study demonstrated that merely seeing a black face led subjects to be more likely to mistake objects for weapons, even when the objects were presented independently of the face. Thus, the associations to weapons and violence elicited by the black face were so strong as to create perceptions of objects not physically associated with the black face.[12] The phenomenon is of course complicated but it nevertheless has been replicated and found to shape people's perceptions quite powerfully.[13]

The above example certainly is complex, as it relates to unconscious and unintended prejudices as much as it does to confirmation biases. We know, for example, that people who do not see themselves as prejudice may act prejudicially in unconscious ways.[14] That research suggests that there may well be something much more psychologically rooted than simple efforts to confirm what we have seen. It may well be that seeing certain factors and making attributions to them (such as attaching positive attributes to physically attractive individuals and then confirming positive attributes to confirmation bias) is moderated by stable individual differences in the tendency to rely on external stimulus qualities in forming social

---

[9] For example, it is difficult to talk about encoding without somehow having subjects report their accounts, which means that research also necessarily must focus on the retrieval of information.

[10] John M. Darley and Paget H. Gross, A hypothesis-confirming bias in labeling effects, 44 J. Personality and Soc. Psych. 20 (1983).

[11] Joshua Klayman and Young-Won Ha, Confirmation, disconfirmation, and information in hypothesis testing, 94 Psych. Rev. 211, 211 (1987). Note that this becomes especially important in the manner people are questioned. Research on selective exposure to information consistently shows that, after having made a decision, people prefer supporting over conflicting information. Eva Jonas, Stefan Schultz-Hardt, Dieter Frey and Norman Thelen, Confirmation bias in sequential information search after preliminary decisions: An expansion of dissonance theoretical research on selective exposure to information, 80 J. of Personality and Soc. Psych. 557 (2001).

[12] B. Keith Payne, The role of automatic and controlled processes in misperceiving a weapon, 81 J. Pers. and Soc. Psych. 181 (2001).

[13] See, e.g., Anthony G. Greenwald, Mark A. Oaks, and Hunter G. Hoffman, Targets of discrimination: Effects of race on responses to weapons holders, 39 J. of Exper. Soc. Psych. 399 (2003). In this study, rapid actions to persons holding weapons were simulated using desktop virtual reality. Subjects responded to simulated (a) criminals, by pointing the computer's mouse at them and left-clicking (simulated shooting), (b) fellow police officers, by pressing the spacebar (safety signal), and (c) citizens, by inaction. In one of two tasks, Black males holding guns were police officers while White males holding guns were criminals. In the other, Whites with guns were police and Blacks with guns were criminals. In both tasks Blacks or Whites holding harmless objects were citizens. Signal detection analyses revealed two race effects that led to Blacks being incorrectly shot at more than Whites: a perceptual sensitivity effect (guns held by Blacks were less distinguishable from harmless objects) and a response bias effect (objects held by Blacks were more likely to be treated as guns).

[14] Anthony G. Greenwald and Mahzarin R. Banaji, Implicit social cognition: Attitudes, self-esteem, and stereotypes, 102 Psych'l Rev. 4 (1995).

impressions.[15] Accordingly, there may be purely perceptual-based forms of bias. If this is the case, how to deal with such hard-wired biases raises enormous challenges.

Factors beyond somewhat pure perception biases also may be at work. We know, for example, that an individual's state of mind or the nature of the event observed largely determines what is perceived and stored in memory. Psychologists who explore these two factors frequently report that they largely account for the possible distortion and incompleteness of memories. For example, research on the weapon focus effect indicates that when a witness is threatened with a weapon (e.g., a knife or gun), the witness' attention focuses on the weapon, lessening the possibility of accurately encoding the appearance of the person wielding the weapon.[16] Social psychologists refer to the outcome of the narrowed attention and heightened psychological focus on the source of the emotional arousal as "tunnel memory."[17] Events witnessed under this narrow processing mode will tend to promote better memory for central information, the details of the emotion provoking part of the event. In contrast, this narrow processing mode will tend to inhibit processing of and memory for peripheral details, the types of details that are either irrelevant or spatially peripheral to the core source of arousal. Numerous studies have supported this conclusion, and it is seen as one of the most reliable findings in this area of study.[18]

The weapon focus effect helps us understand why people may be paying attention and not seeing anything. We know, for example, that a victim or eyewitness may be paying a great deal of attention to the event, but that attention may be countered by levels of arousal that likely interfere with their ability to encode accurately details of the event. This works, for example, when people simply focus on objects rather than on the perpetrator's face.[19] As we already have seen, research on stress and memory does not support the conclusion that arousal inevitably leads to memory impairment.[20] Rather, arousal and stress impact certain aspects of encoding, such as not remembering peripheral information as well in an arousing event as compared to memory of neutral and unusual events.[21] Likewise, the complexity of events leads to predictable results. People tend to overestimate the duration of complex events; and underestimations apparently are rare. People even have a tendency to overestimate the duration of less complex events: on average, overestimations tend to be more in the range of two or three to one. More extreme overestimations are not uncommon, such as the mistaken belief that a thirty-second bank robbery lasted over fifteen minutes.[22]

The above findings point to the need to consider the quality of attention paid to events and the depth and specificity of processing with which we process those events. These two factors are important to understand and can be illustrated nicely through the creative manner researchers investigate the phenomenon of "change blindness."[23] "Change blindness" refers to failure to detect changes in scenes or

---

[15] A series of three studies illustrated the effect. The first introduced the Perceptual Reliance Index (PRI) and provided psychometric data on the measure. The second study showed that high PRI participants make significantly different social evaluations for targets of high versus low physical attractiveness, whereas low PRI participants do not. The last study further extended these findings by demonstrating that within-race variations in phenotypic appearance (e.g., skin color and facial features) produce differential priming effects for high but not low PRI participants. The researchers concluded that systematic bias in social judgment on the basis of physical cues alone suggests the existence of a purely perceptual-based form of prejudice. Robert W. Livingston, What you see is what you get: Systematic variability in perceptual-based social judgment, 27 Personality and Soc. Psych. Bull. 1086 (2001).

[16] Nancy M. Steblay, A meta-analytic review of the weapon focus effect, 16 L. and Hum. Beh. 413 (1992).

[17] Martin A. Safer, Sven-Ake Christianson, Marguerite W. Autry, and Karin Oesterlund, Tunnel memory for traumatic events, 12 Appl. Cogn. Psych. 99, 99 (1998).

[18] Jeffrey M. Brown, Eyewitness memory for arousing events: Putting things into context, 17 Appl. Cog. Psych. 93 (2003).

[19] Claudia Stanny and Thomas C. Johnson, Effects of stress induced by a simulated shooting on recall by police and citizen witnesses, 113 Am. J. of Psych. 359 (2000).

[20] Sven-Ake Christianson, Emotional stress and eyewitness memory: A critical review, 112 Psych. Bull. 84 (1992).

[21] Jeffrey M. Brown, Eyewitness memory for arousing events: Putting things into context, 17 Appl. Cog. Psych. 93 (2003).

[22] Elizabeth F. Loftus, Jonathan W. Schooler, Stanley M. Boone, and Donald Kline, Time went by so slowly: Overestimation of event duration by males and females, 1 Appl. Cog. Psych. 3 (1987). Further, arousal and stress tend to lead to even greater overestimation. Sven-Ake Christianson and Elizabeth F. Loftus, Memory for traumatic events, 1 Appl. Cog. Psych. 225 (1987).

[23] Daniel T. Levin and Daniel J. Simons, Failure to detect changes to attended objects in motion pictures, 4 Psych. Bull. Rev. 501 (1997).

objects under continuous observation. Nearly half to two-thirds of subjects in a series of situations tend not to notice, for example, that a person in a film was replaced by another,[24] that the person to whom they are giving directions has been replaced by another after their conversation was obstructed momentarily by a door,[25] or that a person to whom they were asking questions was replaced by another when they apparently had just bent behind a counter to get forms.[26] Interestingly, knowing about the effect may not influence its impact. Almost half of the participants in the counter study had heard of the change blindness research, and some recently had seen videos of the door study. Nevertheless, two thirds of these "savvy" participants failed to detect the change. The explanation for this failure to realize change is that subjects only encode the gist of the scene without specific details, that subjects use "shallow encoding."[27] When individuals fail to encode the features of details that distinguish one stimulus from another, they are unable to detect change. The "gist" of similar objects or the same object in a slightly different position or configuration is the same. As this research suggests, change blindness with respect to people may be an unrecognized source of errors in eyewitness identifications.

Importantly, the research does not stand alone; the literature on "inattentional blindness" has shown that attention to some facets of a scene can prevent the encoding of others.[28] The "inattention" research illustrates two widely observed phenomena. In particular, processing goals selectively direct attention, and attention then determines which features of a scene individuals will encode and remember. Unattended features of the environment are often not encoded at all. As one researcher found, even experienced pilots who pay close attention to display consoles can proceed with their landing in flight simulators even though clearly visible airplanes block the runway.[29] Similarly, witnesses to crimes are often present at the scene with their own goals in mind, which selectively direct their attention to some aspects of the environment, and often result in shallow processing of other people and events irrelevant to these goals. The extent to which attention to others is limited due to personal processing goals or other distractions reduces encoding specificity regarding the other people and their actions. In turn, this shallow processing would be expected to enhance the probability of source monitoring errors – in both detecting differences between innocents

---

[24] This study had observers watch a movie in which an actor performed a simple action. Unknown to the observers, one actor was replaced by another during the course of the scene. Two thirds of the observers failed to notice the change. Daniel T. Levin and Daniel J. Simons, Failure to detect changes to attended objects in motion pictures, 4 Psych. Bull. Rev. 501 (1997).

[25] In a more real-life study, researchers had a confederate on a college campus request directions from subjects. While the confederate and subjects were talking, two men walked between them to hold a door, which momentarily obscured the subject's view of the confederate. By the time the door past, the confederate changed places with another. The subject was then confronted with a different person who continued the conversation as if he was the original. Less than half of the subjects noticed the change. Daniel J. Simons and Daniel T. Levin, Failure to detect changes to people during a real-world interaction, 4 Psych. Bull. Rev. 644 (1998).

[26] This study was even closer to common robbery crime scenarios where robber and clerk interact across a counter – but in reverse. That is, participants approached a counter to participate in an experiment. After a brief interaction with the experimenter, the participant signed a consent form and handed it to the experimenter. The experimenter then ducked down behind the counter to put the form away, and a second experimenter arose to conclude the interaction. Again, seventy five percent of participants failed to detect the change in experimenters. Daniel T. Levin, Daniel J. Simons, Bonnie L. Angelone, and Christopher F. Chabris, Memory for centrally attended changing objects in an incidental real-world change detection paradigm, 93 Brit. J. of Psych. 289 (2002).

[27] Daniel J. Simons and Daniel T. Levin, Change blindness, 1 Trends in Cog. Sci. 261 (1997).

[28] In a dramatic illustration of this effect, a study asked participants to watch two teams dressed in black and white passing a ball back and forth. While watching, they were to count the number of passes between either the black or white team. As the game unfolded, a large person dressed in either white clothing carrying an umbrella or a black gorilla costume walked right through the middle of the group. Those who were counting the white team passes, presumably because their attention was directed away from black objects, largely failed to notice the gorilla, whereas those counting the black team passes largely failed to notice the umbrella woman in white. Further, those given a more difficult counting task, presumably involving stronger demands for attention, were less likely to notice the targets than those given an easier counting task. Across all conditions, 46% of participants failed to notice the target. Daniel J. Simons and Christopher F. Chabris, Gorillas in our midst: Sustained inattentional blindness for dynamic events, 28 Perception 1059 (1999). See also Arien Mack and Irvin Rock, Inattentional Blindness (1998).

[29] Arien Mack, Inattentional blindness: Looking without seeing, 12 Cur. Dir. in Psych. Sci. 180 (2003).

and perpetrators at the time they are observed, as well as incorrectly distinguishing between them when later asked to identify perpetrators.

The failure to detect change relates to what the eyewitness accuracy literature has identified as "unconscious transference."[30] Unconscious transference essentially refers to the misidentification of an innocent person who is familiar from a different context. That is, unconscious transference is considered a form of source monitoring error, where the person fails to remember accurately the source of exposure to the misidentified person.[31] The eyewitness literature has illustrated the phenomenon two ways. The first way involved the misidentification of persons who are familiar because they were previously seen in mug shots, rather than at the scene of the crime,[32] and the second example involved the misidentification of persons who were at the scene of the crime, but were not the perpetrator.[33] Importantly, only one study has attempted to identify conditions under which this confusion leading to unconscious transference is most likely to occur.[34] Subjects in that study who observed the perpetrator and bystander simultaneously were less likely to later misidentify the bystander, presumably because they were forced to notice the distinction between the two. Absence of a trigger to compare representations of two persons observed in a scene means that the observer will be less likely to detect the difference between them. People need to be paying attention. Thus, changes are more likely to go unnoticed unless the change itself is noticeable and surprising, and unless something suggests a change in persons or objects. If the meaning of a scene remains unchanged, and the change itself does not draw attention, the observer may not directly compare their representations of the two actors, and thereby fail to notice the difference. This leads us to the conclusion that we know what can help prevent the problem from happening, but the problem sill remains to the extent that it derives from the failure of individuals to pay attention in the first place.

In addition to research focusing on blindness and attention, a long history of research indicates that who is with you when you witness an event impacts what you see. A well-known series of studies on conformity conducted by Solomon Asch in the 1950's reveals the powerful influence people may have on one another's judgments under various conditions of potential for group influence. An illustrative example of his studies is one that asked subjects to judge the length of lines. The task required subjects to examine two cards, one with a target line and another with three comparison lines. The subjects were to choose which comparison line matched the target line. The task was quite easy, with nearly a zero error rate when subjects completed the comparison task alone. The task, however, resulted in strikingly different results when the subjects conducted the comparison in groups. When in groups, Asch had varying numbers of confederates announce incorrect judgments on eighteen of twenty-four trials before the subjects' turn. Among subjects who heard the incorrect responses from others, only 10% remained free of error. A full 90% of the subjects incorrectly responded on at least one of eighteen possible trials, and 25% responded incorrectly on all trials. Importantly, when just one other person made an accurate match, errors were reduced by three-quarters, even if a strong majority had conspired to respond incorrectly. His research revealed that even a modest variation in the experimental conditions makes other people's judgments influence our own.

These are impressive results for at least two reasons. First, virtually no subjects completely resisted the influence of what they could clearly see were false judgments of others. Second, many subjects completely succumbed to that influence. Importantly, Asch's subjects did not merely bow to the group's pressure to

---

[30] Elizabeth F. Loftus, Unconscious transference, 2 L. and Psychiatry Rev. 93 (1976).

[31] Stephen D. Lindsay, Memory source monitoring and eyewitness testimony, in Adult Eyewitness Testimony: Current Trends and Development 27 (David F. Ross, J. Don Read, and Michael P. Toglia, eds. 1994).

[32] Jennifer E. Dysart, R.C.L. Lindsay, Robin Hammond and Paul Dupuis, Mug shot exposure prior to lineup identification: Interference, transference, and commitment effects, 86 J. of Appl. Psych. 1280 (2001).

[33] R. Edward Geiselman, David Haghighi, and Ronna Stown , Unconscious transference and characteristics of accurate and inaccurate eyewitnesses, 2 Psych. Crim. and L. 197 (1996); R. Edward Geiselman, Amber MacArthur, and Shelly Meerovitch, Transference of perpetrator roles in eyewitness identifications from photo arrays, 11 Amer. J. of Foren. Psych. 5 (1993); Arien Mack, Inattentional blindness: Looking without seeing, 12 Cur. Direct. in Psych. Sci. 180 (2003).

[34] Mark R. Phillips, R. Edward Geiselman, David Haghighi, and Cynthia Lin, Some boundary conditions for bystander misidentification, 24 Crim. Jus. and Beh. 370 (1997).

make a public claim that differed from a personal observation. Later research showed that even when subjects in Asch's paradigm responded anonymously, the group norm still influenced their responses.[35] Asch's results have been replicated in many studies that followed, although more recent studies indicate that conformity has moderately decreased since Asch's findings.[36] But the general findings remain. Subjects are more influenced by the judgments of those they perceive as more expert than they are and those viewed as particularly credible, well-liked, or part of their own in-group. Subjects also are more influenced on judgments of stimuli where they are uncertain of their own judgment.[37]

The social conformity literature does more than demonstrate the power of social influence to alter reports of judgments and perceptions. Evidence from the eyewitness literature demonstrates that having others present, such as co-witnesses, can influence both the accuracy of one another's testimony as well as their confidence in those accounts. For example, some leading researchers found that participant-witnesses incorporated misleading details from other witnesses' written descriptions into their own descriptions of target faces.[38] Other researchers also reveal that other witnesses can influence memory for cars and that bogus responses of others can influence people's later memory reports for details from a written story.[39] In addition, we know that misleading interview questions create more errors in witness reports. Witnesses also commit more errors, however, when they receive incorrect information both directly from other witnesses and indirectly via the misleading questions of the interviewers. Discussions between co-witnesses have great potential to influence the testimony of all of the witnesses.[40] Importantly, the "social contagion effect"[41] persists even when individuals are explicitly warned about the possibility that a confederates' responses might induce false memories.[42]

Characteristics of the eyewitness and the suspect also interact to influence identification accuracy. The most commonly cited example of such an interaction involves the own-race bias in facial recognition.[43] This robust phenomenon reflects the finding that recognition memory tends to be better for faces of one's own race than for faces of other races. In addition, many report a cross-race effect phenomenon whereby people are better able to recognize persons of their own race as compared with those of other races.[44] For example, a review of research on differential recognition of own-race versus other-race faces revealed that approximately 80% of the participants in those studies demonstrated the cross-race effect.[45] Related to the difficulty of cross race identifications is the likelihood that witnesses are more likely to believe that they

---

[35] Morton Deutsch and Harold B. Gerard, A study of normative and informational social influences upon individual judgment, 51 J. Abnormal and Soc. Psych. 629, 632 (1955).

[36] Rod Bond and Peter B. Smith, Culture and conformity: A meta-analysis of studies using Asch's (1952b, 1956) Line Judgment Task, 119 Psych. Bull. 111 (1996).

[37] Researchers advance several reasons people may be influenced by others to alter their reported judgments. People are sometimes unsure of the correct answer and use other judgments as a source of information about what is true. Likewise, people sometimes conform just to please others or avoid social rejection. Whether or not people actually believe what they are reporting may be a concern, but this area of research makes the important point that people are influenced by others when they report perceptions and judgments.

[38] Elizabeth F. Loftus and Edith Greene, Warning: Even memory for faces may be contagious, 4 L. and Hum. Beh. 323 (1980).

[39] Daniel B. Wright, Gail Self and Chris Justice, Memory conformity: Exploring misinformation effects when presented by another person, 91 Brit. J. Psych. 189 (2000); Andrew L. Betz, John J. Skowronski, and Thomas M. Ostrom, Shared realities: Social influence and stimulus memory, 14 Soc. Cog. 113 (1996).

[40] John S. Shaw III, Sena Garven, James M. Wood, Co-witness information can have immediate effects on eyewitness memory reports, 21 L. and Hum. Beh. 503 (1997).

[41] In social psychological experiments, this effect occurs when a confederate recounts a false memory of an event, and that false memory then becomes incorporated in the memory of another subject. See Henry L. Roediger, III, Michelle L. Meade, and Erik T. Bergman, Social contagion of memory, 8 Psychonomic Bull. and Rev. 365 (2001).

[42] Michelle L. Meade and Henry L. Roediger III, Explorations in the social contagion of memory, 30 Mem. and Cog. 995 (2002).

[43] June E. Chance and Alvin G. Goldstein, The other-race effect and eyewitness identification, in Psychological Issues in Eyewitness Identification 153 (Siegfried Ludwig Sporer, Roy S. Malpass, and Guenter Koehnken, eds., 1996).

[44] Christian A. Meissner and John C. Brigham, Eyewitness identification: Thirty years of investigating the own-race bias in memory for faces: A meta-analytic review, 7 Psych. Pub. Pol'y and L. 3 (2001).

[45] Robert K. Brothwell, JackC. Brigham, and Roy S. Malpass, Cross-racial identification, 5 Personality and Soc. Psych. Bull. 19 (1989).

have previously seen an other-race face when they have not.[46] These findings raise important concerns; the potential for false identifications increases if people in general are poor at recognizing others of a different race and many eyewitness identifications occur across racial lines.

Important sex differences in eyewitness abilities also exist. Some research reports that the differences are more notable when comparing memory of faces and names. Women, on average, outperform men in facial processing tasks.[47] However, other notable sex differences also reveal how the particularities of the event and law enforcement responses contribute to different outcomes.[48] Females, for example, are more accurate than males when providing structured testimony. Females are also more accurate when the questioner is supportive rather than antagonistic. Likewise, females are superior to males when identifying a female bystander but not when identifying a male assailant in a crime scene. Females also are both more accurate eyewitnesses and more resistant to misleading suggestions about female-oriented details than are males, whereas males are more accurate eyewitnesses and less susceptible to distorted information about male-oriented details. It seems difficult to dispute that an eye-witness' sex does not influence eyewitness accounts.

The growing body of research on sex differences suggests that sex differences in eyewitness reliability could be explained by the existence of an own-sex bias. That bias suggests that eyewitnesses are better at identifying members of their own sex than they are at identifying members of the opposite sex, a bias similar to the well-established own-race bias.[49] Relatedly, sometimes expertise or familiarity links to gender. One study of eyewitness performance examined male and female ability to accurately recall features of an event considered more male or female oriented (i.e., of greater interest and familiarity to males versus females). As expected, each sex was more accurate and less easily influenced by misleading questions on the issues "oriented" toward their gender. Thus, to the extent that gender-related features of an event are the subject of witness testimony, it is important to note that each gender (or indeed, each individual) will tend to be more accurate in areas of particular interest or expertise.[50]

Recalling Memories

A number of factors also can influence a witness' later recall of an event or suspect from memory. This period, the retention phase, includes the many things that can happen from the time the individual perceives and encodes the information to the time they retrieve the information from memory (e.g., view a lineup). The findings from the Asch study clearly are relevant here. The major finding emerging from efforts to understand this phase has been that witnesses are highly susceptible to suggestions regarding their memory for the previously viewed event. The biasing may come from numerous sources. Suggestions leading to inaccurate identifications come from overhearing the recall of other witnesses or from questioning by field officers investigating a crime, and may involve aspects of the situation or facial characteristics of the suspect.[51] For example, if witnesses are given another eyewitness' description of the suspect, they will be biased toward selecting a member of the photo lineup who most closely matches the other witness' description.[52] This misinformation effect has been shown to be quite powerful across a vast

---

[46] Ashlyn E. Slone, John C. Brigham, Christian A. Meissner, Social and cognitive factors affecting the own-race bias in whites, 22 Basic and Appl. Soc. Psych.71 (2000).

[47] David C. Geary, Male, Female: The Evolution of Human Sex Differences (1998).

[48] Jerry I. Shaw and Paul Skolnick, Sex differences, weapon focus, and eyewitness reliability, 134 J. of Soc. Psych. 413 (1994).

[49] Jerry I. Shaw and Paul Skolnick, Sex differences, weapon focus, and eyewitness reliability, 134 J. of Soc. Psych. 413 (1994).

[50] Peter A. Powers, Joyce L. Andriks, and Elizabeth F. Loftus,, Eyewitness accounts of males and females, 64 J. Appl. Psych. 339 (1979).

[51] John S. Shaw, III, Sena Garven, and James M. Wood, Co-witness information can have immediate effects on eyewitness memory reports, 21 L. and Hum. Beh. 503 (1997).

[52] Felicity Jenkins and Graham Davies, Contamination of facial memory through exposure to misleading composite pictures, 70 J. Appl. Psych. 164 (1985).

number of studies, stimuli, and situations. Overall, it appears that individuals tend to "commit" to the post-event misinformation by accepting it as if it were an accurate account, which renders the witness' original memory inaccessible.[53]

The potential for immediate influence between witnesses has far reaching consequences. They not only shape one another's initial reports. A witness's first statements shapes that witness's later reports during subsequent interviews or court appearances. In other words, once a witness reveals a version of what happened, that witness most likely clings to that account in future reports.[54] This "freezing effect" phenomenon means that the passing of time makes it increasingly difficult for a witness to change from an initial statement or identification. Given what we have learned so far, this should not be surprising. The effect works similarly to the confirmation bias. We have seen how that bias works in perceptual judgments, but it also works to maintain memories. Research on selective exposure to information consistently shows that, after having made a decision, people prefer supporting over conflicting information. Note that even stronger preference for supporting information arises if information is presented and processed sequentially instead of simultaneously;[55] and this is precisely what trials do. The increase in confirmation bias under sequential presentation is caused by heightened commitment due to the participants' increased focusing on their decision.

Numerous examples of this type of confirmation bias exist in the literature,[56] but for our purposes, research on physical attractiveness bias serves us well. People make evaluations based on someone's relative attractiveness, which biases the information they use to judge them. The most intriguing criminal justice research comes from research on judges' bias toward good looking people. Defendant attractiveness associates with judges levying smaller fines and lower bail levels in actual misdemeanor cases.[57] This was the result of a study that had police escorts rate the physical attractiveness of defendants in over 1500 misdemeanor cases in Texas and then correlated the physical attractiveness with the monetary fines given by the judge. A strong negative correlation was found between the physical attractiveness and the amount of money the person was fined. Again, there obviously are many factors at work, but it does seem that bias builds into people's decisions and that it impacts their eventual judgments.

Numerous factors also influence the process of retrieving the memory of the event or suspect's characteristics. For example, the manner in which eyewitnesses are requested to provide a description of suspects influences their ability to subsequently identify them. It often is assumed that asking witnesses an open question about the suspect or event increases accuracy. ("Tell me what you saw.") Yet, the opposite may be true. For example, when people are strongly urged to provide a full and "complete" description of the suspect, they tend to guess (often inaccurately) about uncertain features. These inaccurate guesses interfere with their later ability to recognize the person's face in a lineup, producing a higher level of misidentifications than for those who were not urged to give a "complete" description. At the time of retrieval, factors surrounding identification of the suspect from a lineup are critically important. The unconscious transference phenomenon (or the bystander effect), wherein different memory images may become combined or confused with one another, plays an important role. In identification processes, for example, this phenomenon occurs when a witness misidentifies an individual from a photo lineup as the actual suspect when, in reality, the witness previously saw the individual either as a bystander at the event

---

[53] John C. Brigham, Anida W. Wasserman and Christian A. Meissner, Disputed eyewitness identification evidence: Important legal and scientific issues, 36 Ct. Rev. 12 (1999).

[54] Elizabeth F. Loftus, Eyewitness Testimony (1979).

[55] Eva Jonas, Stefan Schultz-Hardt, Dieter Frey, and Norman Thelen, Confirmation bias in sequential information search after preliminary decisions: An expansion of dissonance theoretical research on selective exposure to information, 80 J. of Personality and Soc. Psych. 557 (2001).

[56] For example, we have seen the powerful weapon focus effect. That effect, however, may very depending on expectations. One study, for example, had the target shown dressed either as a police officer or as a Catholic priest, and he carried either a handgun or a cellular phone. The witnesses' descriptions were poorer if the target carried an object that was inconsistent with his occupation (as indicated by his clothing style) and better if the object and occupation were not inconsistent. Kerri L. Pickel, The influence of context on the "weapon focus" effect, 23 L. and Hum. Beh. 299 (1999).

[57] Chris A. Downs and Phillip M. Lyons, Natural observations of the links between attractiveness and initial legal judgments, 17 Personality and Soc. Psych. Bull. 541 (1991). Note that this relationship was weaker or absent in felony cases.

or in a completely different context.[58] Additionally, selecting an incorrect person from a showup or lineup strongly increases the likelihood that the same individual will be selected in future lineups or in-court identifications, despite the inaccuracy of the original identification.[59] As would be expected and predicted from our understanding of the confirmation bias, witnesses actually do tend to commit to a response and provide the same response in subsequent attempts at retrieval.

Other eyewitness characteristics are important to note. Age influences the accuracy of memory and the subsequent identification of suspects. Although children tend to recall less information when compared with adults, the standard proportion of correct information recalled by adults and children does not typically differ.[60] Elderly adults, however, tend to perform more poorly than other age groups. Of most importance, children and the elderly also appear to be more susceptible to the effects of suggestive questioning or post-event misinformation.[61] Relatedly, older elderly (those above age 75) tend to be less accurate in testifying, more likely to accent their testimonies with subjective impressions, and more likely to stray off topic. Surprisingly, jurors tend not to recognize the poor quality of the elderly's accounts. Indeed, they actually place a high value on it apparently because the elderly provide more interesting stories, are more informative, and are better storytellers than are young adults.[62] Jurors, perhaps like most of us, like to hear stories and tend to listen carefully when an older person recounts them.

In addition to age, occupation would presumably be an important variable, especially since it could be assumed that people with different talents and training seek different occupations. Available evidence suggests that occupations pervasively have little effect on encoding, although occupations may have an effect on communicating the memory. For example, we tend to assume that law enforcement officials are better at identifying faces than are other citizens. Yet, officers perform no better in identifying the faces of perpetrators than do laypersons. However and when compared to laypersons, officers may be able to provide more detailed accounts of events and be less susceptible to the effects of post-event misinformation.[63] This finding follows the more general finding about attempts to train individuals to remember events and faces. Individuals' accuracy can be improved for recalling details of an event, but that improvement does not transfer to facial identification.[64] It also may be thought that characteristics of the suspect have an influence. However, available evidence reveals that even facial typicality may not be a powerful influence on eyewitness accounts. For example, the presence of unusual attributes that make a face distinctive from other faces also makse it easier to remember. But such distinctive characteristics also appear to make it more difficult to construct an appropriate lineup, due to the difficulty of finding other individuals with similar distinctive features. Alternatively, faces that are more typical in appearance are significantly more difficult to recall later or to identify from a photo lineup, and often result in a higher likelihood of false identification.[65]

---

[58] J. Don Read, Patricia Tollestrup, Richard Hammersley, Eileen McFadzen, and A. Christensen, The unconscious transference effect: Are innocent bystanders ever misidentified?, 4 Appl. Cog. Psych. 3 (1990).

[59] Gabriel W. Gorenstein and Phoebe C. Ellsworth, Effect of choosing an incorrect photograph on a later identification by an eyewitness, 65 J. Appl. Psych. 616 (1981).

[60] Joanna D. Pozzulo and R.C.L. Lindsay, Identification accuracy of children versus adults: A meta-analysis, 22 L. and Hum. Beh. 549 (1998).

[61] Jonathan W. Schooler and Elizabeth F. Loftus, Multiple mechanisms mediate individual differences in eyewitness accuracy and suggestibility, in Mechanisms of Everyday Cognition 177 (James M. Puckett and Hayne W. Reese, eds., 1993)

[62] See C.A. Elizabeth Brimacombe, Sandy Jung, Lynn Garrioch, and Meredith Allison, Perceptions of older adult eyewitnesses: Will you believe me when I'm 64?, 27 L. and Hum. Beh. 507 (2003).

[63] John C. Yuille, Research and teaching with police: A Canadian example, 33 Int. Rev. Appl. Psych. 5 (1984).

[64] M. M. Woodhead, A. D. Baddeley, and D. C. V. Simmonds, On training people to recognize faces, 22 Ergonomics 333 (1979).

[65] Judith A. Hosie and Alan B. Milne, The effect of experimental design on memory for typical and distinctive faces, 4 Memory 175 (1996). Note, however, that the matter remains highly complex. See Peter E. Morris and Lee H. V. Whickham, Typicality and face recognition: A critical re-evaluation of the two factor theory, 54A Q. J. of Exper'l Psych.: Hum. Exper'l Psych. 863 (2001); and Lee H. V. Wickham, Petter E. Morris, and Catherine O. Fritz, Facial distinctiveness: Its measurement, distribution and influence on immediate and delayed recognition, 91 Brit. J. of Psych. 99 (2000).

Also important to note is the failure to find clear answers to whether traumatic memories will be superior or inferior to memories for more mundane events. What is clear is that the memories may be either very clear and accurate or very inaccurate. Victims of rape, for example, reveal the familiar tendency toward better memory for central than peripheral details, along with reasonable accuracy and good retention over time. However, when memories for rape are compared to memories for other intensely unpleasant experiences, memories for rape appear less accurate, less clear and vivid, less meaningfully organized, less thought and talked about, but more emotionally intense.[66] The victim's ability to describe race, sex, age, height, weight, build, complexion, hair color, and eye color of their assailants inversely relates to the severity of the crime. For example, rape victims and injured victims are less accurate and complete than robbery and uninjured victims.[67] Importantly, care must be made to not overgeneralize; the reality seems to be that the vast majority of rape victims actually know their assailants. The research does confirm, however, the need to proceed cautiously when intuition could tell us that certain observations would be more accurate when reality reveals the opposite.

Issues regarding the veracity of memories also have led to investigating the extent to which even adults may not be immune to monitoring difficulties, and may also be led to falsely report autobiographical memories. A now classic study examined efforts to implant into college students a memory of being lost in a shopping mall as a child. In this study, the "misinformation" came from the researchers, who gave subjects a description of an incident in which they supposedly were lost in a mall for an extended period, became upset and cried, and were comforted by an elderly woman. Subjects were told that the descriptions had come from the subjects' parents. The parents, however, had verified that the incident had never occurred. Subjects were asked to write as much as they could recall about the incident that never was. Later, in follow-up interviews, subjects were asked to report as much detail about the incident as they could remember. Fully 25% of their subjects falsely "remembered" having been lost in the mall, and many provided very detailed descriptions of the event, including much detail not included in the original suggested event. Similar results were obtained for other implanted childhood events.[68]

Facilitating Recollections

One of the more promising developments in social science research in this area is the refinement of techniques, supported by both laboratory and field research, known as the Cognitive Interview ("CI").[69] CI capitalizes on the research findings concerning the accuracy of uninfluenced recovery and likely sources of contamination and inhibition to identify techniques that support the natural processes of memory retrieval by cooperating witnesses. The CI operates from two principles of memory. The first principle is that the effectiveness of a retrieval cue is related to the amount of feature overlap with the encoded event. The second principle is that there may be several retrieval paths to the encoded event, so that information not accessible with one retrieval cue may be accessible with a different cue. The CI's four general instructions derive from those principles: (1) mentally reinstating the environmental and personal context that existed at the time of the original event, (2) reporting everything, even partial information, regardless of its perceived importance, (3) recounting the events in a variety of orders, and (4) reporting the events from a variety of perspectives.

---

[66] Mary P. Koss, Shannon Tromp, and Melinda Tharan, Traumatic memories: Empirical foundation, forensic, and clinical Implications, 2 Clin. Psych. Sci. Prac. 111 (1995); and Shannon Tromp, Mary P. Koss, Aurelio Jose Figueredo, and Melinda Tharan, Are rape memories different? A comparison of rape, other unpleasant, and pleasant memories among employed women, 8 J. Trauma. Stress 607 (1995).

[67] Lowell L. Keuhn, Looking down a gun barrel: Perception and violent crime, 39 Percept. Mot. Skills 1159 (1974).

[68] Elizabeth F. Loftus and Jacqueline E. Pickrell, The formation of false memories, 25 Psychiatric Annals 720 (1995).

[69] Ronald P. Fisher, Michelle R. McCauley, and G. Edward Geiselman, Improving eyewitness testimony with the cognitive interview, in Adult Eyewitness Testimony, 245-69 (David F. Ross, J. Don Read, and Michael P. Toglia, eds., 1994).

The CI, like a structured clinical interview, proceeds in a planned sequence to maximize recovery of useful information. The sequence includes the rapport-establishing stage, the open-ended narration stage, the probing stage, the review stage, and the closing stage. The CI also provides guidance about what the interviewer should not do. For example, although the use of open-ended questions to prompt the witness to provide a narrative account of the event is a well-recognized technique, law enforcement investigators may nevertheless frequently interrupt the witness. The belief is that such interruptions can derail the witness's natural memory processes, encourage cognitive passivity on the witness's part, and discourage volunteering or elaboration of information. These problems are compounded when interruptions take the form of rapid-fire, closed-ended questions (sometimes from a standard list of questions), or questions that prematurely seek to take the witness back to a previous point in the narrative flow. Overall, the CI calls for a more patient, reflective, and supportive interpersonal style than some law enforcement investigators may either possess dispositionally or have developed during their patrol days and through contact with non-cooperative subjects. The CI also takes more time than the standard law enforcement interview, because it does not seek quickly to get to the point, but instead tolerates and even encourages the witness to recall every aspect of the event, no matter how ultimately tangential to the investigation's focus. It is up to the investigator later to cull through the interview material, which preferably will have been recorded both to preserve it and to reduce the cognitive load of memory and note-taking on the investigator during the interview.

Beyond helping interviewers increase their ability to obtain accurate information, the CI raises important systemic issues that may contribute to the risk of error – from both contamination and insufficient trace recovery – in eyewitness interviews.[70] Researchers who have worked with the CI point to inadequate training, over-emphasis on an aggressive interpersonal style, and a work-assignment system in which rookies are assigned to routine patrol duties where they acquire interviewing techniques poorly suited to maximizing accurate recall from cooperative witnesses. They also point to possible motivational biases as a potential source of error. In an adversarial, politically influenced system that provides strong external incentives to obtain convictions, investigators who (on whatever basis) believe they already have identified the guilty party may be under pressure to search more diligently for evidence that inculpates rather than exonerates. In such situations, the most efficient approach would be to ask direct, closed-ended, and often leading questions to obtain witness responses that confirm the investigator's suspicions.

The CI approach has become so popular that enough research studies have emerged to allow for a meta-analysis on the effects of the cognitive interview on correct and incorrect recall.[71] The database for the meta-analysis was comprised of 42 studies with 55 individual comparisons involving nearly 2,500 interviewees. A strong overall effect size was found for the increase of correctly recalled details with the cognitive interview compared to a control interview. The overall effect size for the increase in incorrect details, although considerably smaller, was also significant toward the cognitive interview. However, the accuracy rates (proportion of correct details relative to the total amount of details reported) were almost identical in both types of interview (85% for the cognitive interview and 82% for standard interviews, respectively). Furthermore, the enhanced version of the cognitive interview produced more errors than the original version. These findings have been interpreted as positive developments in creating more effective interviews and highlighting the fundamental point that the interviewer's technique does in fact matter.

Overestimating Abilities

The large amount of research may appear somewhat obvious, but the reality is that most people tend to overestimate people's abilities to witness events; and they also overestimate their own abilities. For

---

[70] Ronald P. Fisher, Interviewing victims and witnesses of crime, 1 Psych., Pub. Pol'y and L. 732, 41-42 (1995).

[71] Guenter Koehnken, Rebecca Milne, Amina Memon, and Ray Bull, The cognitive interview: A meta-analysis, 5 Psych. Crime and L. 3 (1999).

example, most people feel that they are well aware of what they can and cannot remember about the events they observe and in which they participate and that they know about the factors that make their memories accurate. For example, most agree or strongly agree with the following statements:

Memory is like a video recording of your observations that can be played back at will to remind you of what you saw.

When you are very confident about your memory for an event you observed, you are much more likely to be correct.

Your memory is stable over time.

Your memory for what you originally saw can be kept separate from things you learned after observing the event.

People's faces stand out when you observe them and it is easy to remember faces, so recognition of faces is rarely in error.

An eyewitness report is accurate evidence as to who was present and what happened.

Having to tell the same story of what happened over and over reinforces it and makes it more resistant to change.

*When a weapon is visible during a crime, witnesses are more accurate in remembering the details of the crime.

Personally experienced traumatic events are remembered more accurately than everyday ones.

Observed violent events are remembered more accurately than everyday events. F

Yet, when these statements are judged by experts who examine these issues, the majority disagrees with each statement. That disagreement is supported by a considerable amount of scientific evidence contradicting each of these statements.[72]

The above study relates to the important point that people pervasively consider themselves immune from bias. For example, people doubt that they would succumb to social influence if they themselves were placed in the Asch experiment. When asked to predict what they themselves would do, people predict that they would give a response contrary to everyone else in the group a much higher percentage of the time than is actually observed.[73] People are, of course, mistaken. Similar findings have been noted in the change blindness research. Researchers have coined the term "change blindness blindness" to refer to the metacognitive error of overestimating change detection ability both in oneself and others.[74] Participants in their experiments observed videos of changes in scenes previously shown to go largely undetected by subjects in change blindness experiments. The participants were asked to indicate whether they or others would have detected the changes in question. For the original "door" experiment we discussed earlier, 97.6% of participants predicted that they would have noticed the change in persons, whereas only 46% of pedestrians confronted with the real change noticed. Further, participants were quite confident that they would have detected the change (4.43 on a 5 pt scale). Similar results were obtained for predictions of whether other persons would detect the changes, and for detection of other types of changes in people and other features of the scenes, both focal and peripheral.[75] People confidently predicted that they would notice the change, even when faced with the findings that most people involved in the experiment did not notice changes. Clearly, like other features of memory and witness performance, "change blindness" is diametrically inconsistent with lay understanding of how memory or perception works.

---

[72] Ralph Norman Haber and Lyn Haber, Experiencing, remembering and reporting events, 6 Psych. Pub. Pol'y and L. 1057 (2000).

[73] Robert J. Wolosin, Steven J. Sherman, and Arnie Cann, Predictions of own and other's conformity, 43 J. Personality 357, 372-76 (1975).

[74] Daniel T. Levin, Nausheen Momen, Sarah B. Drivdahl, and Daniel J. Simons, Change blindness blindness: The metacognitive error of overestimating change-detection ability, 7 Visual Cognition 397 (2000).

[75] Daniel T. Levin, Change blindness blindness as visual metacognition, 9 J. of Consciousness Studies 111 (2002).

The Psychology of Law Enforcement Responses to Eyewitnesses

The enormous potential for erroneous identification contributes to a surge of interest in understanding how law enforcement responds to eyewitnesses. A staple of the investigatory process involving eyewitnesses is the formal identification procedure through which witnesses select suspects. As our discussion thus far suggests, investigators' efforts to maximize recovery of useful material while minimizing contamination face severe challenges. Witnesses face not only a cognitive problem-solving setting created by the recollection task but also a social problem-solving task presented by the encounter with law enforcement investigators. Given that the susceptibility of memory evidence to post-event contamination – the so-called "misinformation" or "post-event information contamination" effect – has been so well documented, the central concern becomes how law enforcement can best deal with what can be viewed as "memory traces." The trace residing in the witness' memory raises the essential concern about the manner investigators can or should treat eyewitness evidence like physical trace evidence, such as blood alcohol concentration as measured by a breath test such as the Breathalyzer, a fingerprint impression lifted from a crime scene, or a DNA sample linked to suspects.

Yet, intuition and tradition rather than scientific findings guide the processes involved in handling eyewitness evidence. Law enforcement has used three procedures to address inadequacies in eyewitness accounts during pre-trial identifications. The standard or simultaneous lineup presents a number of "suspects" at the same time and a witness or victim chooses from those persons presented. Alternatively, a sequential lineup presents the "suspects" one at a time and asks the witness to decide at the time of presentation whether the subject matches his or her memory of the criminal. Both lineup forms can be performed with live persons or with photographs. Lastly, identifications may be obtained through showups. Showups involve bringing suspects to eyewitnesses to determine if they will identify that person as the perpetrator. Unlike a lineup, there are no fillers (distractors, foils) in showup procedures.

The above identification options have achieved different reliability results. Innocent suspects are far more likely to be identified in otherwise fair target-absent lineups, when they are only more similar to the real perpetrator than the foils. In fact, misidentification rates for blank lineups (containing only subjects known to be innocent) are extremely high, ranging from 81-93%. The basis for this type of misidentification may lie in the fact that witnesses view lineups as problems to be solved and believe that they must choose at least one from the lineup.[76] These are critical findings given that lineups are a standard control measure in eyewitness identifications: the more photographs a witness examines, for example, the more likely it is that he or she will pick out the wrong person.[77] Yet, people's intuition suggests that the more photographs are sifted through, the more reliable the eventual identification.

In terms of showups, experimental data clearly show that they are inferior to lineups in terms of the chances of a mistaken identification.[78] Many reasons may account for this. One of the most obvious is that innocent suspects have protections in lineups to the extent that there are lineup foils. Likewise, selecting a foil renders an eyewitness unreliable. In addition, showups are understood as being a one-time opportunity to identify the suspect, while sequential lineups provide the option of choosing more. Relatedly, showups

---

[76] J. Don Read, Understanding bystander misidentifications: The role of familiarity and contextual knowledge, in Adult Eyewitness Testimony 56, 77 (David F. Ross, J. Don Read, and Michael P. Toglia, eds., 1994).

[77] Graham Davies, John Shepherd, and Hayden D. Ellis, Effects of interpolated mugshot exposure on accuracy of eyewitness identification, 64 J. Appl. Psych. 232 (1979); and Hunter A. McAllister, Heather A Stewart, and James Loveland, Effects of mug book size and computerized pruning on the usefulness of dynamic mug book procedures, 9 Psych. Crime and L. 265 (2003).

[78] R. C. L. Lindsay, Joanna D Pozzulo, Wendy Craig, Kang Lee, and Samantha Corber, Simultaneous lineups, sequential lineups, and showups: Eyewitness identification decisions of adults and children, 21 L. and Hum. Beh. 391 (1997); and A. Daniel Yarmey, Meagan J. Yarmey, and A. Linda Yarmey, Accuracy of eyewitness identifications in showups and lineups, 20 L. and Hum. Beh. 459 (1996).

reveal police suspicion. Less obvious, though, is the problem of clothes bias. Showups tend to be done in the field and shortly after the crime; this tendency creates the risk that police and witnesses will focus on the witnesses' description of clothes and inadvertently provide a match because of clothing.[79]

Regardless of the identification option, equally important to consider is what occurs after the eyewitness makes an identification. Recent research has shown that if the eyewitness is told, immediately following the lineup administration, that he or she correctly identified the suspect, two results can occur, one obvious and one more subtle. First, not surprisingly, the eyewitness becomes more confident in the accuracy of the identification. Second, though, the feedback also is likely to change his or her memory for the crime itself. The witness is likely to remember that he or she saw the suspect longer, and under better viewing conditions, than previously reported.[80] Both of these factors are likely to impact the eyewitness' future recollections as they go through criminal justice processes; it also likely impacts how officials respond to the suspect.

Solid empirical evidence indicates that the confidence with which eyewitnesses present identification testimony is the most important single quality of testimony in terms of whether jurors (and study participants acting as jurors) will believe that the witness correctly identified the actual perpetrator or relevant evidence. In fact, a confident witness tends to make jurors ignore the witnessing conditions themselves and believe the eyewitness at a rate that exceeds the actual rate of accuracy. According to one comprehensive review of the literature in this area, including specifically the relationship between witness confidence and accuracy in the context of lineup identifications, jurors misplace their faith in witness confidence as a reliable guide to witness accuracy.[81] Yet, little correlation exists between the accuracy of eyewitness identification and the confidence of eyewitnesses in there selection.[82] Regardless of this repeated finding, most people – including police, prosecutors, jurors, trial judges, and appellate judges – rely heavily on witness confidence as a guide to witness accuracy.[83] Taken together, these studies demonstrate the fallibility of the human mind in the context of eyewitness identification, and cast considerable doubt over trials that rely on eyewitness testimony.

To address some of the above concerns, the first "Scientific Review Paper," created by a special committee of the American Psychology-Law Society, reported research studies indicating a number of "system variables" influential during the construction and administration of lineups.[84] The report highlighted several factors that could be considered in efforts to increase the reliability of identification: (1) having the lineup administered by someone who is unaware of which lineup member is the suspect (also known as "double-blind testing"); (2) using unbiased instructions that explicitly state that the perpetrator "may or may not be present" in the lineup, and that the witness may elect to select no one from the lineup; (3) using sequential lineups, in which the eyewitness views one photo at a time and makes an identification decision before viewing the next photo, since research indicates that there are fewer "false alarms" (erroneous identifications) with this method than with the typical simultaneous lineup, in which the

---

[79] See Nancy Steblay, Jennifer Dysart, Solomon Fulero, and R.C.I. Lindsay, Eyewitness accuracy rates in police showup and lineup presentations: A meta-analytic comparison, 27 L. and Hum. Beh. 523 (2003). Note too that the same clothing bias increases choices of innocent people but not of guilty people when investigators use mugshots. R.C.L. Lindsay, Gleen J. Nosworthy, Ronald Martin, and Craig Marynuck, Using mug shots to find suspects, 79 J. of Appl. Psych. 121 (1994).

[80] Gary L. Wells and Amy L. Bradfield, "Good, you identified the suspect": Feedback to witnesses distorts their reports of the witnessing experience, 83 J. Appl. Psych. 360 (1998).

[81] Steven Penrod and Brian Cutler, Witness confidence and witness accuracy: Assessing their forensic relation, 1 Psych. Pub. Pol'y and L. 817, 817-22 (1995); and Siegfried Ludwig Sporer, Steven Penrod, Don Read, Brian Cutler, Choosing, confidence, and accuracy: A meta-analysis of the confidence-accuracy relation in eyewitness identification studies, 118 Psych. Bull. 315 (1995).

[82] Elizabeth Loftus and Gary L. Wells, Eyewitness identification confidence, in Adult Eyewitness Testimony 201 (David F. Ross, J. Don Read, and Michael P. Toglia, eds., 1994).

[83] Steven Penrod and Brian Cutler, Witness confidence and witness accuracy: Assessing their forensic relation, 1 Psych. Pub. Pol'y and L. 817, 817-22 (1995).

[84] Saul M. Kassin, Eyewitness identification procedures: The fifth rule, 22 L. and Hum. Beh. 649 (1998); and Gary L. Wells, Mark Small, Steven Penrod, Roy S. Malpass, Solomon M. Fulero, and C.A.E. Brimacombe, Eyewitness identification procedures: Recommendations for lineups and photospreads, 22 L. and Hum. Beh. 603 (1998).

eyewitness views all photos at the same time; and (4) videotaping the entire identification process so that independent evaluations of the procedures can be made later, such as through expert testimony.

Importantly, the above findings reach significance to the extent that they reflect the realities of criminal law enforcement. As we will see, the manner the legal system operates has important implications.[85] Photo lineups may be unreliable in studies, but they seem to be used more often, perhaps simply because suspects have a right to counsel for lineups, and not for photo spreads. Likewise, showups may be more reliable in practice simply because people may guess more when they have different options, police may be more certain when they use showups (which increases the chances that identifications also will be correct), and people may be more cautious when they accuse someone right in front of them (a real possibility which actually serves to justify the Constitution's Confrontation Clause). Lastly, defense attorneys actually may not want the best procedures, since such procedures may well diminish the number of possible arguments available to challenge the government's prosecution.

NOTES AND QUERIES

A great upsurge in eyewitness memory research began in the early 1970s, and much of this research has revealed a disturbingly high error rate and ever more ways in which eyewitness identifications and recollections are susceptible to error. Mistakes in eyewitness accounts may be common. But, as we have seen, their significance depends on the manner the criminal justice system responds to these inadequacies. The above research may indicate a need for courts to take heed of current developments in social psychological research and proceed cautiously in accepting eyewitness testimony. However, studies demonstrating general inaccuracies in procedures may not necessarily impact criminal justice processes. The research may amount to nothing more than interesting information for the court to acknowledge and promptly dismiss. As you examine the following cases, consider what role psychological science does and can play in the identification of suspects.

Explain the nature and potential significance of the confirmation bias, tunnel memory, change blindness, change blindness blindness, shallow encoding, social contagion effect, and unconscious transference. What significance do you attach to the numerous race and gender effects identified by eyewitness research? What do you make of research on traumatic memories and the impact of violence on memory?

As you read the cases that follow, consider these questions: Does the legal system recognize the limitations of eyewitness accounts? How does the legal system respond to the recognized limitations of eyewitness fallibility? How could the legal system respond more effectively? How, for example, can the legal system deal effectively with the finding that witness confidence does not relate to accuracy but does relate to the believability of witnesses?

---

[85] The first U. S. Supreme Court decisions that specifically addressed eyewitness evidence issues were a trio of 1967 cases: *United States v. Wade*, 388 U.S. 218 (1967), *Gilbert v. California*, 388 U.S. 263 (1967), and *Stovall v. Denno*, 388 U.S. 293 (1967). The legal rulings that emerged from these cases sought to determine rights to counsel during identification proceedings, standards regarding suggestibility within identification procedures, and laws regarding in-court identifications if the original identification procedure was determined to be highly suggestive. The *Wade* decision granted a suspect the right to an attorney during a live lineup. However, five years later the Supreme Court reversed (or at least clarified) in part the *Wade* ruling in *Kirby v. Illinois*, 406 U.S. 682 (1972), limiting the right to counsel only after the initiation of criminal proceedings. In *United States v. Ash*, 413 U.S. 300 (1973), the Supreme Court ruled that there is no right to counsel at any photographic identification procedures. It was believed that since a photo lineup could be reconstructed and subsequently analyzed for suggestivity, counsel was not necessary at the time of the identification. Lastly, the Court examined the admissibility of eyewitness identification obtained under suggestive circumstances in *Neil v. Biggers*, 409 U.S. 188 (1972), and *Manson v. Brathwaite*, 432 U.S. 98 (1977). In evaluating the admissibility of the identification, the Court considered whether, under the totality of circumstances, the identification was reliable, even though the confrontation procedure may have been suggestive. Importantly, if suspects allege errors prior to the point at which their right to an attorney would attach, the Court still recognizes the possibility of redress under the Constitution's Due Process Clause.

Does the scientific knowledge base concerning eyewitness memory have valid insights to offer that fact finders do not already know? Do jurors need help in evaluating eyewitness reports? If so, what qualities of jurors and trials form the bases of this need? Can expert testimony, theoretically, deliver this help? Will expert testimony, in practice, deliver the help and improve jurors' ability to evaluate eyewitness testimony validly? If so, how and when can it best be used in the court system? What is so wrong with relying on common sense intuition rather than science which challenges that intuition?

As you consider the potential role of psychological sciences, consider these important concerns: Which rights are implicated in challenges to eyewitness accounts? What are the standards the legal system sets in approaching those rights? What are the remedies for violation of those rights? What does psychological science tell us about the legal standards and remedies? What alternatives does psychological science suggest? Note, for example, that framing the affected rights in a certain manner may result in ignoring psychological sciences while framing the rights involved in another manner may make psychological sciences more relevant.

CONSIDERING THE SIXTH AMENDMENT

U.S. v. WADE
388 U.S. 218 (1967)

MR. JUSTICE BRENNAN delivered the opinion of the Court.

The federally insured bank in Eustace, Texas, was robbed on September 21, 1964. A man with a small strip of tape on each side of his face entered the bank, pointed a pistol at the female cashier and the vice president, the only persons in the bank at the time, and forced them to fill a pillowcase with the bank's money. The man then drove away with an accomplice who had been waiting in a stolen car outside the bank. On March 23, 1965, an indictment was returned against respondent, Wade, and two others for conspiring to rob the bank, and against Wade and the accomplice for the robbery itself. Wade was arrested on April 2, and counsel was appointed to represent him on April 26. Fifteen days later an FBI agent, without notice to Wade's lawyer, arranged to have the two bank employees observe a lineup made up of Wade and five or six other prisoners and conducted in a courtroom of the local county courthouse. Each person in the line wore strips of tape such as allegedly worn by the robber and upon direction each said something like "put the money in the bag," the words allegedly uttered by the robber. Both bank employees identified Wade in the lineup as the bank robber.

At trial, the two employees, when asked on direct examination if the robber was in the courtroom, pointed to Wade. The prior lineup identification was then elicited from both employees on cross-examination. At the close of testimony, Wade's counsel moved for a judgment of acquittal or, alternatively, to strike the bank officials' courtroom identifications on the ground that conduct of the lineup, without notice to and in the absence of his appointed counsel, violated his Fifth Amendment privilege against self-incrimination and his Sixth Amendment right to the assistance of counsel. The motion was denied, and Wade was convicted. The Court of Appeals for the Fifth Circuit reversed the conviction and ordered a new trial at which the in-court identification evidence was to be excluded, holding that, though the lineup did not violate Wade's Fifth Amendment rights, "the lineup, held as it was, in the absence of counsel, already chosen to represent appellant, was a violation of his Sixth Amendment rights . . ." We reverse the judgment of the Court of Appeals and remand to that court ...

I.

Neither the lineup itself nor anything shown by this record that Wade was required to do in the lineup violated his privilege against self-incrimination. We have only recently reaffirmed that the privilege "protects an accused only from being compelled to testify against himself, or otherwise provide the State with evidence of a testimonial or communicative nature . . . ."

We have no doubt that compelling the accused merely to exhibit his person for observation by a prosecution witness prior to trial involves no compulsion of the accused to give evidence having testimonial significance. It is compulsion of the accused to exhibit his physical characteristics, not compulsion to disclose any knowledge he might have. ... ... compelling Wade to speak within hearing distance of the witnesses, even to utter words purportedly uttered by the robber, was not compulsion to utter statements of a "testimonial" nature; he was required to use his voice as an identifying physical characteristic, not to speak his guilt. ... the distinction to be drawn under the Fifth Amendment privilege against self-incrimination is one between an accused's "communications" in whatever form, vocal or physical, and "compulsion which makes a suspect or accused the source of 'real or physical evidence.'" We [have] recognized that "both federal and state courts have usually held that . . . [the privilege] offers no protection against compulsion to submit to fingerprinting, photography, or measurements, to write or speak for identification, to appear in court, to stand, to assume a stance, to walk, or to make a particular gesture." None of these activities becomes testimonial within the scope of the privilege because required of the accused in a pretrial lineup.

II.

The fact that the lineup involved no violation of Wade's privilege against self-incrimination does not, however, dispose of his contention that the courtroom identifications should have been excluded because the lineup was conducted without notice to and in the absence of his counsel. ... it is urged that the assistance of counsel at the lineup was indispensable to protect Wade's most basic right as a criminal defendant – his right to a fair trial at which the witnesses against him might be meaningfully cross-examined.

The Framers of the Bill of Rights envisaged a broader role for counsel than under the practice then prevailing in England of merely advising his client in "matters of law," and eschewing any responsibility for "matters of fact." ... When the Bill of Rights was adopted, there were no organized police forces as we know them today. The accused confronted the prosecutor and the witnesses against him, and the evidence was marshalled, largely at the trial itself. In contrast, today's law enforcement machinery involves critical confrontations of the accused by the prosecution at pretrial proceedings where the results might well settle the accused's fate and reduce the trial itself to a mere formality. In recognition of these realities of modern criminal prosecution, our cases have construed the Sixth Amendment guarantee to apply to "critical" stages of the proceedings. The guarantee reads: "In all criminal prosecutions, the accused shall enjoy the right . . . to have the Assistance of Counsel for his defence." The plain wording of this guarantee thus encompasses counsel's assistance whenever necessary to assure a meaningful "defence."

...we recognized that the period from arraignment to trial was "perhaps the most critical period of the proceedings . . . ,"during which the accused "requires the guiding hand of counsel . . . ," if the guarantee is not to prove an empty right. That principle has since been applied to require the assistance of counsel at the type of arraignment ... where certain rights might be sacrificed or lost: "What happens there may affect the whole trial. Available defenses may be irretrievably lost, if not then and there asserted . . . ."

In sum, ... [the principle from] succeeding cases requires that we scrutinize any pretrial confrontation of the accused to determine whether the presence of his counsel is necessary to preserve the defendant's basic right to a fair trial as affected by his right meaningfully to cross-examine the witnesses against him and to have effective assistance of counsel at the trial itself. It calls upon us to analyze whether potential substantial prejudice to defendant's rights inheres in the particular confrontation and the ability of counsel to help avoid that prejudice.

III.

The Government characterizes the lineup as a mere preparatory step in the gathering of the prosecution's evidence, not different – for Sixth Amendment purposes – from various other preparatory steps, such as systematized or scientific analyzing of the accused's fingerprints, blood sample, clothing, hair, and the like. We think there are differences which preclude such stages being characterized as critical stages at which the accused has the right to the presence of his counsel...

IV.

...the confrontation compelled by the State between the accused and the victim or witnesses to a crime to elicit identification evidence is peculiarly riddled with innumerable dangers and variable factors which might seriously, even crucially, derogate from a fair trial. The vagaries of eyewitness identification are well-known; the annals of criminal law are rife with instances of mistaken identification. ... A major factor contributing to the high incidence of miscarriage of justice from mistaken identification has been the degree of suggestion inherent in the manner in which the prosecution presents the suspect to witnesses for pretrial identification. ... Suggestion can be created intentionally or unintentionally in many subtle ways. And the dangers for the suspect are particularly grave when the witness' opportunity for observation was insubstantial, and thus his susceptibility to suggestion the greatest.

Moreover, "it is a matter of common experience that, once a witness has picked out the accused at the line-up, he is not likely to go back on his word later on, so that in practice the issue of identity may (in the absence of other relevant evidence) for all practical purposes be determined there and then, before the trial."

The pretrial confrontation for purpose of identification may take the form of a lineup, also known as an "identification parade" or "showup," as in the present case, or presentation of the suspect alone to the witness .... It is obvious that risks of suggestion attend either form of confrontation and increase the dangers inhering in eyewitness identification. ... For the same reasons, the defense can seldom reconstruct the manner and mode of lineup identification for judge or jury at trial. Those participating in a lineup with the accused may often be police officers; in any event, the participants' names are rarely recorded or divulged at trial. The impediments to an objective observation are increased when the victim is the witness. Lineups are prevalent in rape and robbery prosecutions and present a particular hazard that a victim's understandable outrage may excite vengeful or spiteful motives. In any event, neither witnesses nor lineup participants are apt to be alert for conditions prejudicial to the suspect. And if they were, it would likely be of scant benefit to the suspect since neither witnesses nor lineup participants are likely to be schooled in the detection of suggestive influences. Improper influences may go undetected by a suspect, guilty or not, who experiences the emotional tension which we might expect in one being confronted with potential accusers. Even when he does observe abuse, if he has a criminal record he may be reluctant to take the stand and open up the admission of prior convictions. Moreover, any protestations by the suspect of the fairness of the lineup made at trial are likely to be in vain; the jury's choice is between the accused's unsupported version and that of the police officers present. In short, the accused's inability effectively to reconstruct at trial any unfairness that occurred at the lineup may deprive him of his only opportunity meaningfully to attack the credibility of the witness' courtroom identification.

What facts have been disclosed in specific cases about the conduct of pretrial confrontations for identification illustrate both the potential for substantial prejudice to the accused at that stage and the need for its revelation at trial. ...

Similarly state reports, in the course of describing prior identifications admitted as evidence of guilt, reveal numerous instances of suggestive procedures, for example, that all in the lineup but the suspect were known to the identifying witness, that the other participants in a lineup were grossly dissimilar in appearance to the suspect, that only the suspect was required to wear distinctive clothing which the culprit allegedly wore, that the witness is told by the police that they have caught the culprit after which the defendant is brought before the witness alone or is viewed in jail, that the suspect is pointed out before or during a lineup, and that the participants in the lineup are asked to try on an article of clothing which fits only the suspect.

The few cases that have surfaced therefore reveal the existence of a process attended with hazards of serious unfairness to the criminal accused and strongly suggest the plight of the more numerous defendants who are unable to ferret out suggestive influences in the secrecy of the confrontation. We do not assume that these risks are the result of police procedures intentionally designed to prejudice an accused. Rather we assume they derive from the dangers inherent in eyewitness identification and the suggestibility inherent in the context of the pretrial identification. ... "The fact that the police themselves have, in a given case, little or no doubt that the man put up for identification has committed the offense, and that their chief pre-occupation is with the problem of getting sufficient proof, because he has not 'come clean,' involves a danger that this persuasion may communicate itself even in a doubtful case to the witness in some way . . ."

Insofar as the accused's conviction may rest on a courtroom identification in fact the fruit of a suspect pretrial identification which the accused is helpless to subject to effective scrutiny at trial, the accused is deprived of that right of cross-examination which is an essential safeguard to his right to confront the witnesses against him. And even though cross-examination is a precious safeguard to a fair trial, it cannot be viewed as an absolute assurance of accuracy and reliability. Thus in the present context, where so many variables and pitfalls exist, the first line of defense must be the prevention of unfairness and the lessening of the hazards of eyewitness identification at the lineup itself. The trial which might determine the accused's fate may well not be that in the courtroom but that at the pretrial confrontation, with the State aligned against the accused, the witness the sole jury, and the accused unprotected against the overreaching, intentional or unintentional, and with little or no effective appeal from the judgment there rendered by the witness – "that's the man."

Since it appears that there is grave potential for prejudice, intentional or not, in the pretrial lineup, which may not be capable of reconstruction at trial, and since presence of counsel itself can often avert prejudice and assure a meaningful confrontation at trial, there can be little doubt that for Wade the post-indictment lineup was a critical stage of the prosecution at which he was "as much entitled to such aid [of counsel] . . . as at the trial itself." Thus both Wade and his counsel should have been notified of the impending lineup, and counsel's presence should have been a requisite to conduct of the lineup, absent an "intelligent waiver." No substantial countervailing policy considerations have been advanced against the requirement of the presence of counsel. Concern is expressed that the requirement will forestall prompt identifications and result in obstruction of the confrontations. ... And to refuse to recognize the right to counsel for fear that counsel will obstruct the course of justice is contrary to the basic assumptions upon which this Court has operated in Sixth Amendment cases...

In our view counsel can hardly impede legitimate law enforcement; on the contrary, for the reasons expressed, law enforcement may be assisted by preventing the infiltration of taint in the prosecution's identification evidence. That result cannot help the guilty avoid conviction but can only help assure that the right man has been brought to justice.

V.

We come now to the question whether the denial of Wade's motion to strike the courtroom identification by the bank witnesses at trial because of the absence of his counsel at the lineup required, ... the grant of a new trial at which such evidence is to be excluded. We do not think this disposition can be justified without first giving the Government the opportunity to establish by clear and convincing evidence that the in-court identifications were based upon observations of the suspect other than the lineup identification. Where, as here, the admissibility of evidence of the lineup identification itself is not involved, a per se rule of exclusion of courtroom identification would be unjustified. A rule limited solely to the exclusion of testimony concerning identification at the lineup itself, without regard to admissibility of the courtroom identification, would render the right to counsel an empty one. The lineup is most often used, as in the present case, to crystallize the witnesses' identification of the defendant for future reference. We have already noted that the lineup identification will have that effect. The State may then rest upon the witnesses' unequivocal courtroom identification, and not mention the pretrial identification as part of the State's case at trial. Counsel is then in the predicament in which Wade's counsel found himself – realizing that possible unfairness at the lineup may be the sole means of attack upon the unequivocal courtroom identification, and having to probe in the dark in an attempt to discover and reveal unfairness, while bolstering the government witness' courtroom identification by bringing out and dwelling upon his prior identification. Since counsel's presence at the lineup would equip him to attack not only the lineup identification but the courtroom identification as well, limiting the impact of violation of the right to counsel to exclusion of evidence only of identification at the lineup itself disregards a critical element of that right.

We think it follows that the proper test to be applied in these situations is ... "'Whether, granting establishment of the primary illegality, the evidence to which instant objection is made has been come at by exploitation of that illegality or instead by means sufficiently distinguishable to be purged of the primary taint.'"Application of this test in the present context requires consideration of various factors; for example, the prior opportunity to observe the alleged criminal act, the existence of any discrepancy between any pre-lineup description and the defendant's actual description, any identification prior to lineup of another person, the identification by picture of the defendant prior to the lineup, failure to identify the defendant on a prior occasion, and the lapse of time between the alleged act and the lineup identification. It is also relevant to consider those facts which, despite the absence of counsel, are disclosed concerning the conduct of the lineup.

We doubt that the Court of Appeals applied the proper test for exclusion of the in-court identification of the two witnesses. The court stated that "it cannot be said with any certainty that they would have recognized appellant at the time of trial if this intervening lineup had not occurred," and that the testimony of the two witnesses "may well have been colored by the illegal procedure [and] was prejudicial." Moreover, the court was persuaded, in part, by the "compulsory verbal responses made by Wade at the instance of the Special Agent." This implies the erroneous holding that Wade's privilege against self-incrimination was violated so that the denial of counsel required exclusion.

On the record now before us we cannot make the determination whether the in-court identifications had an independent origin. This was not an issue at trial, although there is some evidence relevant to a determination. That inquiry is most properly made in the District Court...

The judgment of the Court of Appeals is vacated and the case is remanded to that court with direction to enter a new judgment vacating the conviction and remanding the case to the District Court for further proceedings consistent with this opinion.

It is so ordered.

THE CHIEF JUSTICE joins the opinion of the Court except for Part I, from which he dissents for the reasons expressed in the opinion of MR. JUSTICE FORTAS.

MR. JUSTICE DOUGLAS joins the opinion of the Court except for Part I. [omitted]

MR. JUSTICE CLARK, concurring. [opinion omitted]

MR. JUSTICE BLACK, dissenting in part and concurring in part.

The Court in Part I of its opinion rejects Wade's Fifth Amendment contention. From that I dissent. In Parts II-IV of its opinion, the Court sustains Wade's claim of denial of right to counsel in the out-of-court lineup, and in that I concur. In Part V, the Court remands the case to the District Court to consider whether the courtroom identification of Wade was the fruit of the illegal lineup, and, if it was, to grant him a new trial unless the court concludes that the courtroom identification was harmless error. I would reverse the Court of Appeals' reversal of Wade's conviction, but I would not remand for further proceedings. Since the prosecution did not use the out-of-court lineup identification against Wade at his trial, I believe the conviction should be affirmed.

I.

In rejecting Wade's claim that his privilege against self-incrimination was violated by compelling him to appear in the lineup wearing the tape and uttering the words given him by the police, the Court relies on the recent holding in Schmerber v. California. In that case the Court held that taking blood from a man's body against his will in order to convict him of a crime did not compel him to be a witness against himself. I dissented from that holding and still dissent. The Court's reason for its holding was that the sample of Schmerber's blood taken in order to convict him of crime was neither "testimonial" nor "communicative" evidence. I think it was both. It seems quite plain to me that the Fifth Amendment's Self-incrimination Clause was designed to bar the Government from forcing any person to supply proof of his own crime, precisely what Schmerber was forced to do when he was forced to supply his blood. The Government simply took his blood against his will and over his counsel's protest for the purpose of convicting him of crime. So here, having Wade in its custody awaiting trial to see if he could or would be convicted of crime, the Government forced him to stand in a lineup, wear strips on his face, and speak certain words, in order to make it possible for government witnesses to identify him as a criminal. Had Wade been compelled to utter these or any other words in open court, it is plain that he would have been entitled to a new trial because of having been compelled to be a witness against himself. Being forced by the Government to help convict himself and to supply evidence against himself by talking outside the courtroom is equally violative of his constitutional right not to be compelled to be a witness against himself. Consequently, because of this violation of the Fifth Amendment, and not because of my own personal view that the Government's conduct was "unfair," "prejudicial," or "improper," I would prohibit the prosecution's use of lineup identification at trial.

III.

I would reverse Wade's conviction without further ado had the prosecution at trial made use of his lineup identification either in place of courtroom identification or to bolster in a harmful manner crucial courtroom identification. But the prosecution here did neither of these things. After prosecution witnesses under oath identified Wade in the courtroom, it was the defense, and not the prosecution, which brought out the prior lineup identification. While stating that "a per se rule of exclusion of courtroom identification would be unjustified," the Court, nevertheless, remands this case for "a hearing to determine whether the in-court identifications had an independent source," or were the tainted fruits of the invalidly conducted lineup. From this holding I dissent.

In the first place, even if this Court has power to establish such a rule of evidence, I think the rule fashioned by the Court is unsound. The "tainted fruit" determination required by the Court involves more than considerable difficulty. I think it is practically impossible. How is a witness capable of probing the recesses of his mind to draw a sharp line between a courtroom identification due exclusively to an earlier lineup and a courtroom identification due to memory not based on the lineup? What kind of "clear and convincing evidence" can the prosecution offer to prove upon what particular events memories resulting in an in-court identification rest? How long will trials be delayed while judges turn psychologists to probe the subconscious minds of witnesses? All these questions are posed but not answered by the Court's opinion. In my view, the Fifth and Sixth Amendments are satisfied if the prosecution is precluded from using lineup identification as either an alternative to or corroboration of courtroom identification. If the prosecution does neither and its witnesses under oath identify the defendant in the courtroom, then I can find no justification for stopping the trial in midstream to hold a lengthy "tainted fruit" hearing. The fact of and circumstances surrounding a prior lineup identification might be used by the defense to impeach the credibility of the in-court identifications, but not to exclude them completely.

I would affirm Wade's conviction.

MR. JUSTICE WHITE, whom MR. JUSTICE HARLAN and MR. JUSTICE STEWART join, dissenting in part and concurring in part.

The premise for the Court's rule is not the general unreliability of eyewitness identifications nor the difficulties inherent in observation, recall, and recognition. The Court assumes a narrower evil as the basis for its rule – improper police suggestion which contributes to erroneous identifications. The Court apparently believes that improper police procedures are so widespread that a broad prophylactic rule must be laid down, requiring the presence of counsel at all pretrial identifications, in order to detect recurring instances of police misconduct. I do not share this pervasive distrust of all official investigations. None of the materials the Court relies upon supports it. Certainly, I would bow to solid fact, but the Court quite obviously does not have before it any reliable, comprehensive survey of current police practices on which to base its new rule. Until it does, the Court should avoid excluding relevant evidence from state criminal trials.

The Court goes beyond assuming that a great majority of the country's police departments are following improper practices at pretrial identifications. To find the lineup a "critical" stage of the proceeding and to exclude identifications made in the absence of counsel, the Court must also assume that police "suggestion," if it occurs at all, leads to erroneous rather than accurate identifications and that reprehensible police conduct will have an unavoidable and largely undiscoverable impact on the trial. This in turn assumes that there is now no adequate source from which defense counsel can learn about the circumstances of the pretrial identification in order to place before the jury all of the considerations which should enter into an appraisal of courtroom identification evidence. But these are treacherous and unsupported assumptions, resting as they do on the notion that the defendant will not be aware, that the police and the witnesses will forget or prevaricate, that defense counsel will be unable to bring out the truth and that neither jury, judge, nor appellate court is a sufficient safeguard against unacceptable police conduct occurring at a pretrial identification procedure. I am unable to share the Court's view of the willingness of the police and the ordinary citizen-witness to dissemble, either with respect to the identification of the defendant or with respect to the circumstances surrounding a pretrial identification.

I share the Court's view that the criminal trial, at the very least, should aim at truthful factfinding, including accurate eyewitness identifications. I doubt, however, on the basis of our present information, that the tragic mistakes which have occurred in criminal trials are as much the product of improper police conduct as they are the consequence of the difficulties inherent in eyewitness testimony and in resolving evidentiary conflicts by court or jury. I doubt that the Court's new rule will obviate these difficulties, or that the situation will be measurably improved by inserting defense counsel into the investigative processes of police departments everywhere.

But, it may be asked, what possible state interest militates against requiring the presence of defense counsel at lineups? After all, the argument goes, he may do some good, he may upgrade the quality of identification evidence in state courts and he can scarcely do any harm. Even if true, this is a feeble foundation for fastening an ironclad constitutional rule upon state criminal procedures. Absent some reliably established constitutional violation, the processes by which the States enforce their criminal laws are their own prerogative. The States do have an interest in conducting their own affairs, an interest which cannot be displaced simply by saying that there are no valid arguments with respect to the merits of a federal rule emanating from this Court.

Beyond this, however, requiring counsel at pretrial identifications as an invariable rule trenches on other valid state interests. One of them is its concern with the prompt and efficient enforcement of its criminal laws. Identifications frequently take place after arrest but before an indictment is returned or an information is filed. The police may have arrested a suspect on probable cause but may still have the wrong man. Both the suspect and the State have every interest in a prompt identification at that stage, the suspect in order to secure his immediate release and the State because prompt and early identification enhances accurate identification and because it must know whether it is on the right investigative track. Unavoidably, however, the absolute rule requiring the presence of counsel will cause significant delay and it may very well result in no pretrial identification at all. Counsel must be appointed and a time arranged convenient for him and the witnesses. Meanwhile, it may be necessary to file charges against the suspect who may then be released on bail, in the federal system very often on his own recognizance, with neither the State nor the defendant having the benefit of a properly conducted identification procedure.

Finally, I think the Court's new rule is vulnerable in terms of its own unimpeachable purpose of increasing the reliability of identification testimony.

Law enforcement officers have the obligation to convict the guilty and to make sure they do not convict the innocent. They must be dedicated to making the criminal trial a procedure for the ascertainment of the true facts surrounding the commission of the crime. To this extent, our so-called adversary system is not adversary at all; nor should it be. But defense counsel has no comparable obligation to ascertain or present the truth. Our system assigns him a different mission. He must be and is interested in preventing the conviction of the innocent, but, absent a voluntary plea of guilty, we also insist that he defend his client whether he is innocent or guilty. The State has the obligation to present the evidence. Defense counsel need present nothing, even if he knows what the truth is. He need not furnish any witnesses to the police, or reveal any confidences of his client, or furnish any other information to help the prosecution's case. If he can confuse a witness, even a truthful one, or make him appear at a disadvantage, unsure or indecisive, that will be his normal course. Our interest in not convicting the innocent permits counsel to put the State to its proof, to put the State's case in the worst possible light, regardless of what he thinks or knows to be the truth. Undoubtedly there are some limits which defense counsel must observe but more often than not, defense counsel will cross-examine a prosecution witness, and impeach him if he can, even if he thinks the witness is telling the truth, just as he will attempt to destroy a witness who he thinks is lying. In this respect, as part of our modified adversary system and as part of the duty imposed on the most honorable defense counsel, we countenance or require conduct which in many instances has little, if any, relation to the search for truth.

I would not extend this system, at least as it presently operates, to police investigations and would not require counsel's presence at pretrial identification procedures. Counsel's interest is in not having his client placed at the scene of the crime, regardless of his whereabouts. Some counsel may advise their clients to refuse to make any movements or to speak any words in a lineup or even to appear in one. To that extent the impact on truthful factfinding is quite obvious. Others will not only observe what occurs and develop possibilities for later cross-examination but will hover over witnesses and begin their cross-examination then, menacing truthful factfinding as thoroughly as the Court fears the police now do. Certainly there is an implicit invitation to counsel to suggest rules for the lineup and to manage and produce it as best he can. I therefore doubt that the Court's new rule, at least absent some clearly defined limits on counsel's role, will measurably contribute to more reliable pretrial identifications. My fears are that it will have precisely the opposite result. It may well produce fewer convictions, but that is hardly a proper measure of its long-run acceptability. In my view, the State is entitled to investigate and develop its case outside the presence of defense counsel. This includes the right to have private conversations with identification witnesses, just as defense counsel may have his own consultations with these and other witnesses without having the prosecutor present.

MR. JUSTICE FORTAS, with whom THE CHIEF JUSTICE and MR. JUSTICE DOUGLAS join, concurring in part and dissenting in part.

...I agree with the Court that the exhibition of the person of the accused at a lineup is not itself a violation of the privilege against self-incrimination. ...

...In my view, however, the accused may not be compelled in a lineup to speak the words uttered by the person who committed the crime. I am confident that it could not be compelled in court. It cannot be compelled in a lineup. It is more than passive, mute assistance to the eyes of the victim or of witnesses. It is the kind of volitional act – the kind of forced cooperation by the accused – which is within the historical perimeter of the privilege against compelled self-incrimination.

I completely agree that the accused must be advised of and given the right to counsel before a lineup – and I join in that part of the Court's opinion; but this is an empty right unless we mean to insist upon the accused's fundamental constitutional immunities. One of these is that the accused may not be compelled to speak. To compel him to speak would violate the privilege against self-incrimination, which is incorporated in the Fifth Amendment.

This great privilege is not merely a shield for the accused. It is also a prescription of technique designed to guide the State's investigation. History teaches us that self-accusation is an unreliable instrument of detection, apt to inculpate the innocent-but-weak and to enable the guilty to escape. But this is not the end of the story. The privilege historically goes to the roots of democratic and religious principle. It prevents the debasement of the citizen which would result from compelling him to "accuse" himself before the power of the state. The roots of the privilege are deeper than the rack and the screw used to extort confessions. They go to the nature of a free man and to his relationship to the state.

Accordingly, while I join the Court in requiring vacating of the judgment below for a determination as to whether the identification of respondent was based upon factors independent of the lineup, I would do so not only because of the failure to offer counsel before the lineup but also because of the violation of respondent's Fifth Amendment rights.

NOTES AND QUERIES

What do you make of the simple statement that lineups do not implicate the 5th Amendment privilege against self-incrimination? The Court reasons that lineups do not because they are neither testimonial nor communicative. Persuasive?

According to the majority, the 6th Amendment applies to critical stages of a criminal prosecution. What implications arise from formulating the Amendment in this fashion? What do you make of the focus on post-indictment? Consider Justice White's dissenting opinion to evaluate concerns about providing counsel at that stage in proceedings. Do you find that opinion persuasive in light of the majority's view?

Given the psychological science we have examined, do you find the majority opinion psychologically insightful? If you do, keep that idea in mind when we examine the cases that follow. As you examine those cases, consider the extent to which they remain faithful to the Court's views announced in *Wade*.

The majority conducts a standard taint analysis. That analysis considers whether or not the evidence that was used can be purged from the tainted evidence, with the tainted evidence being the evidence that was obtained illegally. The goal is to determine whether the evidence remaining after exclusion of the tainted evidence was obtained by exploiting the illegally obtained evidence or whether the evidence is sufficiently distinguishable from the tainted evidence and thus can be purged from the primary taint.

Do you find that the in-court identification had an independent origin? Can we be sure, at least sure enough to be convinced, that the suspect was properly identified in court? Justice Black's opinion finds that such taint analysis simply is not possible. Note, however, that he still would uphold the conviction. Why?

Justice Black would concern himself with whether the identification was "harmless error." We will examine that concept more closely in another chapter. For now, it makes sense to understand the concept as simply stating that a conviction should hold if the result would have been the same without the problem evidence, hence the error is deemed harmless.

NOTES ON GILBERT V. CALIFORNIA

What do you make of the following identification, presented in *Gilbert v. California*, 388 U.S. 263 (1967) and argued with *Wade* to the Supreme Court?

The lineup occurred on March 26, 1964, after Gilbert had been indicted and had obtained counsel. It was held in an auditorium used for that purpose by the Los Angeles police. Some ten to thirteen prisoners were placed on a lighted stage. The witnesses were assembled in a darkened portion of the room, facing the stage and separated from it by a screen. They could see the prisoners but could not be seen by them. State and federal officers were also present and one of them acted as 'moderator' of the proceedings. Each man in the lineup was identified by number, but not by name. Each man was required to step forward into a marked circle, to turn, presenting both profiles as well as a face and back view, to walk, to put on or take off certain articles of clothing. When a man's number was called and he was directed to step into the circle, he was asked certain questions: where he was picked up, whether he owned a car, whether, when arrested, he was armed, where he lived. Each was also asked to repeat certain phrases, both in a loud and in a soft voice, phrases that witnesses to the crimes had heard the robbers use: "Freeze, this is a stickup; this is a holdup; empty your cash drawer; this is a heist; don't anybody move." Either while the men were on the stage, or after they were taken from it, it is not clear which, the assembled witnesses were asked if there were any that they would like to see again, and told that if they had doubts, now was the time to resolve them. Several gave the numbers of men they wanted to see, including Gilbert's. While the other prisoners were no longer present, Gilbert and 2 or 3 others were again put through a similar procedure. Some of the witnesses asked that a particular prisoner say a particular phrase, or walk a particular way. After the lineup, the witnesses talked to each other; it is not clear that they did so during the lineup. They did, however, in each other's presence, call out the numbers of men they could identify.

At the guilt stage, after the first witness, a cashier of the savings and loan association, identified Gilbert in the courtroom, defense counsel moved, out of the presence of the jury, to strike her testimony on the ground that she identified Gilbert at the pretrial lineup conducted in the absence of counsel in violation of the Sixth Amendment made applicable to the States by the Fourteenth Amendment. He requested a hearing outside the presence of the jury to present evidence supporting his claim that her in-court identification was, and others to be elicited by the State from other eyewitnesses would be, "predicated at least in large part upon their identification or purported identification of Mr. Gilbert at the showup . . . ." The trial judge denied the motion as premature. Defense counsel then elicited the fact of the cashier's lineup identification on cross-examination and again moved to strike her identification testimony. Without passing on the merits of the Sixth Amendment claim, the trial judge denied the motion on the ground that, assuming a violation, it would not in any event entitle Gilbert to suppression of the in-court identification. Defense counsel thereafter elicited the fact of lineup identifications from two other eyewitnesses who on direct examination identified Gilbert in the courtroom. Defense counsel unsuccessfully objected at the penalty stage, to the testimony of the eight witnesses to the other robberies that they identified Gilbert at the lineup.

The Court ruled that admission of the in-court identifications without first determining that they were not tainted by the illegal lineup but were of independent origin was constitutional error. The Court had held that a post-indictment pretrial lineup at which the accused is exhibited to identifying witnesses is a critical stage of the criminal prosecution; that police conduct of such a lineup without notice to and in the absence of his counsel denies the accused his Sixth Amendment right to counsel and calls in question the admissibility at trial of the in-court identifications of the accused by witnesses who attended the lineup. However, as in *Wade*, the Court did not view the record as permitting an informed judgment whether the in-court identifications at the two stages of the trial had an independent source. The Court ruled that Gilbert was entitled only to a vacation of his conviction pending the holding of such proceedings as the California Supreme Court would deem appropriate to afford the state the opportunity to establish that the in-court identifications had an independent source, or that their introduction in evidence was in any event harmless error.

KIRBY v. ILLINOIS
406 U.S. 682 (1972)

MR. JUSTICE STEWART announced the judgment of the Court and an opinion in which THE CHIEF JUSTICE, MR. JUSTICE BLACKMUN, and MR. JUSTICE REHNQUIST join.

On February 21, 1968, a man named Willie Shard reported to the Chicago police that the previous day two men had robbed him on a Chicago street of a wallet containing, among other things, traveler's checks and a Social Security card. On February 22, two police officers stopped the petitioner and a companion, Ralph Bean, on West Madison Street in Chicago. When asked for identification, the petitioner produced a wallet that contained three traveler's checks and a Social Security card, all bearing the name of Willie Shard. Papers with Shard's name on them were also found in Bean's possession. When asked to explain his possession of Shard's property, the petitioner first said that the traveler's checks were "play money," and then told the officers that he had won them in a crap game. The officers then arrested the petitioner and Bean and took them to a police station.

Only after arriving at the police station, and checking the records there, did the arresting officers learn of the Shard robbery. A police car was then dispatched to Shard's place of employment, where it picked up Shard and brought him to the police station. Immediately upon entering the room in the police station where the petitioner and Bean were seated at a table, Shard positively identified them as the men who had robbed him two days earlier. No lawyer was present in the room, and neither the petitioner nor Bean had asked for legal assistance, or been advised of any right to the presence of counsel.

More than six weeks later, the petitioner and Bean were indicted for the robbery of Willie Shard. Upon arraignment, counsel was appointed to represent them, and they pleaded not guilty. A pretrial motion to suppress Shard's identification testimony was denied, and at the trial Shard testified as a witness for the prosecution. In his testimony he described his identification of the two men at the police station on February 22, and identified them again in the courtroom as the men who had robbed him on February 20. He was cross-examined at length regarding the circumstances of his identification of the two defendants. The jury found both defendants guilty, and the petitioner's conviction was affirmed on appeal. The Illinois appellate court held that the admission of Shard's testimony was not error ... holding that the Wade-Gilbert per se exclusionary rule is not applicable to pre-indictment confrontations.

We granted certiorari, limited to this question.

I.

In a line of constitutional cases in this Court ... it has been firmly established that a person's Sixth and Fourteenth Amendment right to counsel attaches only at or after the time that adversary judicial proceedings have been initiated against him.

This is not to say that a defendant in a criminal case has a constitutional right to counsel only at the trial itself. ... But the point is that, ... all of those cases have involved points of time at or after the initiation of adversary judicial criminal proceedings – whether by way of formal charge, preliminary hearing, indictment, information, or arraignment.

The initiation of judicial criminal proceedings is far from a mere formalism. It is the starting point of our whole system of adversary criminal justice. For it is only then that the government has committed itself to prosecute, and only then that the adverse positions of government and defendant have solidified. It is then that a defendant finds himself faced with the prosecutorial forces of organized society, and immersed in the intricacies of substantive and procedural criminal law. It is this point, therefore, that marks the commencement of the "criminal prosecutions" to which alone the explicit guarantees of the Sixth Amendment are applicable.

In this case we are asked to import into a routine police investigation an absolute constitutional guarantee historically and rationally applicable only after the onset of formal prosecutorial proceedings. We decline to do so. Less than a year after Wade and Gilbert were decided, the Court explained the rule of those decisions as follows: "The rationale of those cases was that an accused is entitled to counsel at any 'critical stage of the prosecution,' and that a post-indictment lineup is such a 'critical stage.'" We decline to depart from that rationale today by imposing a per se exclusionary rule upon testimony concerning an identification that took place long before the commencement of any prosecution whatever.

II.

What has been said is not to suggest that there may not be occasions during the course of a criminal investigation when the police do abuse identification procedures. Such abuses are not beyond the reach of the Constitution. As the Court pointed out in Wade itself, it is always necessary to "scrutinize any pretrial confrontation . . . ." The Due Process Clause of the Fifth and Fourteenth Amendments forbids a lineup that is unnecessarily suggestive and conducive to irreparable mistaken identification. When a person has not been formally charged with a criminal offense, Stovall strikes the appropriate constitutional balance between the right of a suspect to be protected from prejudicial procedures and the interest of society in the prompt and purposeful investigation of an unsolved crime.

The judgment is affirmed.

MR. CHIEF JUSTICE BURGER, concurring. [opinion omitted]
MR. JUSTICE POWELL, concurring in the result. [opinion omitted]

MR. JUSTICE BRENNAN, with whom MR. JUSTICE DOUGLAS and MR. JUSTICE MARSHALL join, dissenting.

After petitioner and Ralph Bean were arrested, police officers brought Willie Shard, the robbery victim, to a room in a police station where petitioner and Bean were seated at a table with two other police officers. Shard testified at trial that the officers who brought him to the room asked him if petitioner and Bean were the robbers and that he indicated they were. The prosecutor asked him, "And you positively identified them at the police station, is that correct?" Shard answered, "Yes." Consequently, the question in this case is whether it was constitutional error to admit Shard's testimony that he identified petitioner at the pretrial station-house showup when that showup was conducted by the police without advising petitioner that he might have counsel present. Gilbert held, in the context of a post-indictment lineup, that "only a per se exclusionary rule as to such testimony can be an effective sanction to assure that law enforcement authorities will respect the accused's constitutional right to the presence of his counsel at the critical lineup." I would apply Gilbert and the principles of its companion case, United States v. Wade, and reverse.

In Wade, after concluding that the lineup conducted in that case did not violate the accused's right against self-incrimination, the Court addressed the argument "that the assistance of counsel at the lineup was indispensable to protect Wade's most basic right as a criminal defendant – his right to a fair trial at which the witnesses against him might be meaningfully cross-examined." The Court began by emphasizing that the Sixth Amendment guarantee "encompasses counsel's assistance whenever necessary to assure a meaningful 'defense.'" ...

The Court then pointed out that "nothing decided or said in the opinions in ... links the right to counsel only to protection of Fifth Amendment rights." To the contrary, the Court said, those decisions simply reflected the constitutional

> principle that in addition to counsel's presence at trial, the accused is guaranteed that he need not stand alone against the State at any stage of the prosecution, formal or informal, in court or out, where counsel's absence might derogate from the accused's right to a fair trial. The security of that right is as much the aim of the right to counsel as it is of the other guarantees of the Sixth Amendment . . . .

This analysis led to the Court's formulation of the controlling principle for pretrial confrontations:

> In sum, the principle requires that we scrutinize any pretrial confrontation of the accused to determine whether the presence of his counsel is necessary to preserve the defendant's basic right to a fair trial as affected by his right meaningfully to cross-examine the witnesses against him and to have effective assistance of counsel at the trial itself. It calls upon us to analyze whether potential substantial prejudice to defendant's rights inheres in the particular confrontation and the ability of counsel to help avoid that prejudice.

While it should go without saying, it appears necessary, in view of the plurality opinion today, to re-emphasize that Wade did not require the presence of counsel at pretrial confrontations for identification purposes simply on the basis of an abstract consideration of the words "criminal prosecutions" in the Sixth Amendment. Counsel is required at those confrontations because "the dangers inherent in eyewitness identification and the suggestibility inherent in the context of the pretrial identification," mean that protection must be afforded to the "most basic right [of] a criminal defendant – his right to a fair trial at which the witnesses against him might be meaningfully cross-examined." Indeed, the Court expressly stated that "legislative or other regulations, such as those of local police departments, which eliminate the risks of abuse and unintentional suggestion at lineup proceedings and the impediments to meaningful confrontation at trial may also remove the basis for regarding the stage as 'critical.'" Hence, "the initiation of adversary judicial criminal proceedings" is completely irrelevant to whether counsel is necessary at a pretrial confrontation for identification in order to safeguard the accused's constitutional rights to confrontation and the effective assistance of counsel at his trial.

In view of Wade, it is plain, and the plurality today does not attempt to dispute it, that there inhere in a confrontation for identification conducted after arrest the identical hazards to a fair trial that inhere in such a confrontation conducted "after the onset of formal prosecutorial proceedings." The plurality apparently considers an arrest, which for present purposes we must assume to be based upon probable cause, to be nothing more than part of "a routine police investigation" and thus not "the starting point of our whole system of adversary criminal justice." An arrest, according to the plurality, does not face the accused "with the prosecutorial forces of organized society," nor immerse him "in the intricacies of substantive and procedural criminal law." Those consequences ensue, says the plurality, only with "the initiation of judicial criminal proceedings," "for it is only then that the government has committed itself to prosecute, and only then that the adverse positions of government and defendant have solidified." If these propositions do not amount to "mere formalism," it is difficult to know how to characterize them. An arrest evidences the belief of the police that the perpetrator of a crime has been caught. A post-arrest confrontation for identification is not "a mere preparatory step in the gathering of the prosecution's evidence." A primary, and frequently sole, purpose of the confrontation for identification at that stage is to accumulate proof to buttress the conclusion of the police that they have the offender in hand. The plurality offers no reason, and I can think of none, for concluding that a post-arrest confrontation for identification, unlike a post-charge confrontation, is not among those "critical confrontations of the accused by the prosecution at pretrial proceedings where the results might well settle the accused's fate and reduce the trial itself to a mere formality."

The highly suggestive form of confrontation employed in this case underscores the point. This showup was particularly fraught with the peril of mistaken identification. In the setting of a police station squad room where all present except petitioner and Bean were police officers, the danger was quite real that Shard's understandable resentment might lead him too readily to agree with the police that the pair under arrest, and the only persons exhibited to him, were indeed the robbers. "It is hard to imagine a situation more clearly conveying the suggestion to the witness that the one presented is believed guilty by the police." The State had no case without Shard's identification testimony, and safeguards against that consequence were therefore of critical importance. Shard's testimony itself demonstrates the necessity for such safeguards. On direct examination, Shard identified petitioner and Bean not as the alleged robbers on trial in the courtroom, but as the pair he saw at the police station. His testimony thus lends strong support to the observation, quoted by the Court in Wade, that "it is a matter of common experience that, once a witness has picked out the accused at the line-up, he is not likely to go back on his word later on, so that in practice the issue of identity may (in the absence of other relevant evidence) for all practical purposes be determined there and then, before the trial."

MR. JUSTICE WHITE, dissenting.

United States v. Wade and Gilbert v. California govern this case and compel reversal of the judgment below.

Notes and Queries

Kirby deals with a station-house showup. What do you make of these forms of identification? Consider the difference between the majority and dissent's characterization of the showp. Which one sways your opinion about the legitimacy of the majority's legal approach to showups?

The Court finds that there were no formal proceedings against the defendants, thus their rights were not violated. Persuasive? Why not extend the rights identified in *Wade* to this form of pre-trial identifications of suspects/defendants?

Considering the Fifth Amendment

STOVALL v. DENNO
388 U.S. 293 (1967)

MR. JUSTICE BRENNAN delivered the opinion of the Court.

Dr. Paul Behrendt was stabbed to death in the kitchen of his home in Garden City, Long Island, about midnight August 23, 1961. Dr. Behrendt's wife, also a physician, had followed her husband to the kitchen and jumped at the assailant. He knocked her to the floor and stabbed her 11 times. The police found a shirt on the kitchen floor and keys in a pocket which they traced to petitioner. They arrested him on the afternoon of August 24. An arraignment was promptly held but was postponed until petitioner could retain counsel.

Mrs. Behrendt was hospitalized for major surgery to save her life. The police, without affording petitioner time to retain counsel, arranged with her surgeon to permit them to bring petitioner to her hospital room about noon of August 25, the day after the surgery. Petitioner was handcuffed to one of five police officers who, with two members of the staff of the District Attorney, brought him to the hospital room. Petitioner was the only Negro in the room. Mrs. Behrendt identified him from her hospital bed after being asked by an officer whether he "was the man" and after petitioner repeated at the direction of an officer a "few words for voice identification." None of the witnesses could recall the words that were used. Mrs. Behrendt and the officers testified at the trial to her identification of the petitioner in the hospital room, and she also made an in-court identification of petitioner in the courtroom.

Petitioner was convicted and sentenced to death. The New York Court of Appeals affirmed without opinion. Petitioner pro se sought federal habeas corpus in the District Court for the Southern District of New York. He claimed that among other constitutional rights allegedly denied him at his trial, the admission of Mrs. Behrendt's identification testimony violated his rights under the Fifth, Sixth, and Fourteenth Amendments because he had been compelled to submit to the hospital room confrontation without the help of counsel and under circumstances which unfairly focused the witness' attention on him as the man believed by the police to be the guilty person. The District Court dismissed the petition after hearing argument on an unrelated claim of an alleged invalid search and seizure. On appeal to the Court of Appeals for the Second Circuit a panel of that court initially reversed the dismissal after reaching the issue of the admissibility of Mrs. Behrendt's identification evidence and holding it inadmissible on the ground that the hospital room identification violated petitioner's constitutional right to the assistance of counsel. The Court of Appeals thereafter heard the case en banc, vacated the panel decision, and affirmed the District Court. We granted certiorari...

II.

We turn now to the question whether petitioner ... is entitled to relief on his claim that in any event the confrontation conducted in this case was so unnecessarily suggestive and conducive to irreparable mistaken identification that he was denied due process of law. This is a recognized ground of attack upon a conviction independent of any right to counsel claim. The practice of showing suspects singly to persons for the purpose of identification, and not as part of a lineup, has been widely condemned. However, a claimed violation of due process of law in the conduct of a confrontation depends on the totality of the circumstances surrounding it, and the record in the present case reveals that the showing of Stovall to Mrs. Behrendt in an immediate hospital confrontation was imperative. The Court of Appeals, en banc, stated,

> Here was the only person in the world who could possibly exonerate Stovall. Her words, and only her words, 'He is not the man' could have resulted in freedom for Stovall. The hospital was not far distant from the courthouse and jail. No one knew how long Mrs. Behrendt might live. Faced with the responsibility of identifying the attacker, with the need for immediate action and with the knowledge that Mrs. Behrendt could not visit the jail, the police followed the only feasible procedure and took Stovall to the hospital room. Under these circumstances, the usual police station line-up, which Stovall now argues he should have had, was out of the question.

The judgment of the Court of Appeals is affirmed.

It is so ordered.

MR. JUSTICE DOUGLAS is of the view that the deprivation of the right to counsel in the setting of this case should be given retroactive effect ...

MR. JUSTICE FORTAS would reverse and remand for a new trial on the ground that the State's reference at trial to the improper hospital identification violated petitioner's Fourteenth Amendment rights and was prejudicial. ...

MR. JUSTICE WHITE, whom MR. JUSTICE HARLAN and MR. JUSTICE STEWART join. [opinion omitted]

MR. JUSTICE BLACK, dissenting.

In United States v. Wade and Gilbert v. California, the Court holds that lineup identification testimony should be excluded if it was obtained by exhibiting an accused to identifying witnesses before trial in the absence of his counsel. I concurred in part in those holdings as to out-of-court lineup identification on the ground that the right to counsel is guaranteed in federal courts by the Sixth Amendment and in state courts by the Sixth and Fourteenth Amendments. The first question in this case is whether other defendants, already in prison on such unconstitutional evidence, shall be accorded the benefit of the rule. In this case the Court holds that the petitioner here, convicted on such unconstitutional evidence, must remain in prison, and that besides Wade and Gilbert, who are "chance beneficiaries," no one can invoke the rule except defendants exhibited in lineups in the future. I dissent from that holding. It keeps people serving sentences who were convicted through the use of unconstitutional evidence. This is sought to be justified on the ground that retroactive application of the holding in Gilbert and Wade would somehow work a "burden on the administration of justice" and would not serve the Court's purpose "to deter law enforcement authorities." It seems to me that to deny this petitioner and others like him the benefit of the new rule deprives them of a constitutional trial and perpetrates a rank discrimination against them. Once the Court determines what the Constitution says, I do not believe it has the power, by weighing "countervailing interests," to legislate a timetable by which the Constitution's provisions shall become effective. ...

The Court goes on, however, to hold that even though its new constitutional rule about the Sixth Amendment's right to counsel cannot help this petitioner, he is nevertheless entitled to a consideration of his claim, "independent of any right to counsel claim," that his identification by one of the victims of the robbery was made under circumstances so "unfair" that he was denied "due process of law" guaranteed by the Fourteenth Amendment. Although the Court finds petitioner's claim without merit, I dissent from its holding that a general claim of "unfairness" at the lineup is "open to all persons to allege and prove." The term "due process of law" is a direct descendant of Magna Charta's promise of a trial according to the "law of the land" as it has been established by the lawmaking agency, constitutional or legislative. No one has ever been able to point to a word in our constitutional history that shows the Framers ever intended that the Due Process Clause of the Fifth or Fourteenth Amendment was designed to mean any more than that defendants charged with crimes should be entitled to a trial governed by the laws, constitutional and statutory, that are in existence at the time of the commission of the crime and the time of the trial. The concept of due process under which the Court purports to decide this question, however, is that this Court looks at "the totality of the circumstances" of a particular case to determine in its own judgment whether they comport with the Court's notions of decency, fairness, and fundamental justice, and, if so, declares they comport with the Constitution, and, if not, declares they are forbidden by the Constitution. Such a constitutional formula substitutes this Court's judgment of what is right for what the Constitution declares shall be the supreme law of the land. This due process notion proceeds as though our written Constitution, designed to grant limited powers to government, had neutralized its limitations by using the Due Process Clause to authorize this Court to override its written limiting language by substituting the Court's view of what powers the Framers should have granted government. Once again I dissent from any such view of the Constitution. Where accepted, its result is to make this Court not a Constitution-interpreter, but a day-to-day Constitution-maker.

But even if the Due Process Clause could possibly be construed as giving such latitudinarian powers to the Court, I would still think the Court goes too far in holding that the courts can look at the particular circumstances of each identification lineup to determine at large whether they are too "suggestive and conducive to irreparable mistaken identification" to be constitutional. That result is to freeze as constitutional or as unconstitutional the circumstances of each case, giving the States and the Federal Government no permanent constitutional standards. It also transfers to this Court power to determine what the Constitution should say, instead of performance of its undoubted constitutional power to determine what the Constitution does say. And the result in this particular case is to put into a constitutional mold a rule of evidence which I think is plainly within the constitutional powers of the States in creating and enforcing their own criminal laws. I must say with all deference that for this Court to hold that the Due Process Clause gives it power to bar state introduction of lineup testimony on its notion of fairness, not because it violates some specific constitutional prohibition, is an arbitrary, wholly capricious action.

I would not affirm this case but would reverse and remand for consideration of whether the out-of-court lineup identification of petitioner was harmless error. If it was not, petitioner is entitled to a new trial because of a denial of the right to counsel guaranteed by the Sixth Amendment which the Fourteenth Amendment makes obligatory on the States.

NOTES AND QUERIES

This case provides yet another means to challenge the identification of suspects: the Fifth Amendment's Due Process Clause. The Court enumerates the standard quite clearly. The confrontation must be unnecessarily suggestive and conducive to irreparable mistaken identification. Note two key phrases. The first is "unnecessarily suggestive," which means that in some instances the identification may be suggestive but still be appropriate if it were necessary. The second is "irreparable mistaken identification," meaning that the identification cannot be cured. Also note that the Court evaluates the due process claim by using a totality of circumstances test, a test that we will repeatedly use in many of the legal rules in the cases that follow.

Do you agree with the Court's application of the facts to the legal rule in this case?

The dissent makes the powerful argument that there are no due process claims in this case. He argues that the right is not explicit in the Constitution and that the Court should simply leave these matters to the states. What do you think of this approach?

APPLYING STANDARDS: UNNECESSARILY SUGGESTIVE IDENTIFICATIONS

FOSTER v. CALIFORNIA
394 U.S. 440 (1969)

MR. JUSTICE FORTAS delivered the opinion of the Court.

Petitioner was charged by information with the armed robbery of a Western Union office... The day after the robbery one of the robbers, Clay, surrendered to the police and implicated Foster and Grice. Allegedly, Foster and Clay had entered the office while Grice waited in a car. Foster and Grice were tried together. Grice was acquitted. Foster was convicted. The California District Court of Appeal affirmed the conviction; the State Supreme Court denied review. We granted certiorari, limited to the question whether the conduct of the police lineup resulted in a violation of petitioner's constitutional rights.

Except for the robbers themselves, the only witness to the crime was Joseph David, the late-night manager of the Western Union office. After Foster had been arrested, David was called to the police station to view a lineup. There were three men in the lineup. One was petitioner. He is a tall man – close to six feet in height. The other two men were short – five feet, five or six inches. Petitioner wore a leather jacket which David said was similar to the one he had seen underneath the coveralls worn by the robber. After seeing this lineup, David could not positively identify petitioner as the robber. He "thought" he was the man, but he was not sure. David then asked to speak to petitioner, and petitioner was brought into an office and sat across from David at a table. Except for prosecuting officials there was no one else in the room. Even after this one-to-one confrontation David still was uncertain whether petitioner was one of the robbers: "truthfully – I was not sure," he testified at trial. A week or 10 days later, the police arranged for David to view a second lineup. There were five men in that lineup. Petitioner was the only person in the second lineup who had appeared in the first lineup. This time David was "convinced" petitioner was the man.

At trial, David testified to his identification of petitioner in the lineups, as summarized above. He also repeated his identification of petitioner in the courtroom. The only other evidence against petitioner which concerned the particular robbery with which he was charged was the testimony of the alleged accomplice Clay.

In United States v. Wade and Gilbert v. California, this Court held that because of the possibility of unfairness to the accused in the way a lineup is conducted, a lineup is a "critical stage" in the prosecution, at which the accused must be given the opportunity to be represented by counsel. That holding does not, however, apply to petitioner's case, for the lineups in which he appeared occurred before June 12, 1967. But in declaring the rule of Wade and Gilbert to be applicable only to lineups conducted after those cases were decided, we recognized that, judged by the "totality of the circumstances," the conduct of identification procedures may be "so unnecessarily suggestive and conducive to irreparable mistaken identification" as to be a denial of due process of law.

Judged by that standard, this case presents a compelling example of unfair lineup procedures. In the first lineup arranged by the police, petitioner stood out from the other two men by the contrast of his height and by the fact that he was wearing a leather jacket similar to that worn by the robber. When this did not lead to positive identification, the police permitted a one-to-one confrontation between petitioner and the witness. This Court pointed out in Stovall that "the practice of showing suspects singly to persons for the purpose of identification, and not as part of a lineup, has been widely condemned." Even after this the witness' identification of petitioner was tentative. So some days later another lineup was arranged. Petitioner was the only person in this lineup who had also participated in the first lineup. This finally produced a definite identification.

The suggestive elements in this identification procedure made it all but inevitable that David would identify petitioner whether or not he was in fact "the man." In effect, the police repeatedly said to the witness, "This is the man." This procedure so undermined the reliability of the eyewitness identification as to violate due process.

...the judgment is reversed and the case remanded for further proceedings not inconsistent with this opinion.

Reversed and remanded.

MR. JUSTICE WHITE, with whom MR. JUSTICE HARLAN and MR. JUSTICE STEWART concur, being unwilling in this case to disagree with the jury on the weight of the evidence, would affirm the judgment.

MR. JUSTICE BLACK, dissenting.

...Court in this case looks behind the evidence given by witnesses on the stand and decides that because of the circumstances under which one witness first identified the defendant as the criminal, the United States Constitution requires that the conviction be reversed. The Court, however, fails to spell out exactly what should happen to this defendant if there must be a retrial, and thus avoids the apparently distasteful task of specifying whether (1) at the new trial the jury would again be permitted to hear the eyewitness' testimony and the in-court identification, so long as he does not refer to the previous lineups, or (2) the eyewitness' "tainted" identification testimony must be entirely excluded, thus compelling Foster's acquittal. Objection to this ambiguity is the first of my reasons for dissent.

I.

The Court declares the judgment of conviction is reversed and the case remanded for further proceedings not inconsistent with this opinion. I am compelled to say that if I were the trial judge in this case I would not know how to proceed or how to decide whether the "error" in this case was harmless. Of course, when a confession is held to have been compelled, that confession must not be admitted to convict the defendant at all. But the situation in this case is not that simple. For the Court has in effect decided here that the officers of the law have so "arranged" lineups that the eyewitness to the robbery has been led to make an "irreparable mistaken identification." In other words, no one now or hereafter can believe his identification of Foster as the robber. Since he and the accomplice are the only eyewitnesses, and since, in order to convict, California law requires evidence of an accomplice to be corroborated, the Court's direction means, I suppose, that the trial judge here should dismiss the case. The Court's dilemma, which leads to its ambiguous judgment as to the further disposition of this case, points, I think, to the irreparable harm done to the cause of justice by the Court's holding in this case.

II.

Far more fundamental, however, is my objection to the Court's basic holding that evidence can be ruled constitutionally inadmissible whenever it results from identification procedures that the Court considers to be "'unnecessarily suggestive and conducive to irreparable mistaken identification.'" One of the proudest achievements of this country's Founders was that they had eternally guaranteed a trial by jury in criminal cases ... Of course it is an incontestable fact in our judicial history that the jury is the sole tribunal to weigh and determine facts. That means that the jury must, if we keep faith with the Constitution, be allowed to hear eyewitnesses and decide for itself whether it can recognize the truth and whether they are telling the truth. It means that the jury must be allowed to decide for itself whether the darkness of the night, the weakness of a witness' eyesight, or any other factor impaired the witness' ability to make an accurate identification. To take that power away from the jury is to rob it of the responsibility to perform the precise functions the Founders most wanted it to perform. And certainly a Constitution written to preserve this indispensable, unerodible core of our system for trying criminal cases would not have included, hidden among its provisions, a slumbering sleeper granting the judges license to destroy trial by jury in whole or in part.

This brings me to the constitutional theory relied upon by the Court to justify its invading the constitutional right of jury trial. The Court here holds that:

> Judged by the 'totality of the circumstances,' the conduct of identification procedures may be 'so unnecessarily suggestive and conducive to irreparable mistaken identification' as to be a denial of due process of law. . . .
>
> Judged by that standard, this case presents a compelling example of unfair lineup procedures.

I do not deny that the "totality of circumstances" can be considered to determine whether some specific constitutional prohibitions have been violated, such, for example, as the Fifth Amendment's command against compelling a witness to incriminate himself. Whether evidence has been compelled is, of course, a triable issue of fact. And the constitutional command not to compel a person to be a witness against himself, like other issues of fact, must be determined by a resolution of all facts and the "totality" of them offered in evidence. Consequently were the Court's legal formula posed for application in a coerced testimony case, I could agree to it. But it is not. Instead the Court looks to the "totality of circumstances" to show "unfair lineup procedures." This means "unfair" according to the Court's view of what is unfair. The Constitution, however, does not anywhere prohibit conduct deemed unfair by the courts...

For the above reasons I dissent from the reversal and remand of this case.

NOTES AND QUERIES

Note that the challenged lineup came after *Wade*. To address the claim, then, the Court conducts a due process analysis. The majority finds a due process violation. Do you agree?

The majority's analysis may appear straightforward, but what do yo make of the dissent's claim? What do you make of the claim that a jury, not a judge, should decide whether the procedures were fair? What about the claim that the jury should be allowed to hear the eyewitness?

There may be a belief that those who take their time to scrutinize and identify a suspect out of a lineup are more accurate than those who quickly identify suspects. Evidence actually supports the opposite conclusion. Eyewitness researchers have shown that witnesses accurately choosing the culprit out of a lineup reach their decisions more quickly than those erroneously choosing an innocent individual. Researchers also have examined how quickly or slowly witnesses must be, in absolute terms, to indicate that they are accurate or inaccurate. Across 4 studies, a group of researchers discovered that a time boundary of roughly 10 to 12 seconds best differentiated accurate from inaccurate positive identifications. Witnesses making their identification faster than 10 to 12 seconds were nearly 90% accurate; those taking longer were roughly 50% accurate. This finding is consistent with previous research showing that accurate witnesses are more likely than inaccurate witnesses to reach their decisions automatically, that is, quickly, without conscious thought or effort. David Dunning and Scott Perretta, Automaticity and eyewitness accuracy: A 10- to 12-second rule for distinguishing accurate from inaccurate positive identifications, 87 J. Appl. Soc. Psych. 951 (2002).

APPLYING STANDARDS: SUGGESTIVE YET RELIABLE IDENTIFICATIONS

NEIL v. BIGGERS
409 U.S. 188 (1972)

MR. JUSTICE POWELL delivered the opinion of the Court.

In 1965, after a jury trial in a Tennessee court, respondent [Biggers] was convicted of rape and was sentenced to 20 years' imprisonment. The State's evidence consisted in part of testimony concerning a station-house identification of respondent by the victim. ...

...We granted certiorari to decide ... whether the identification procedure violated due process.

II.

...The victim testified at trial that on the evening of January 22, 1965, a youth with a butcher knife grabbed her in the doorway to her kitchen:

> A. He grabbed me from behind, and grappled – twisted me on the floor. Threw me down on the floor.
>
> Q. And there was no light in that kitchen?
>
> A. Not in the kitchen.
>
> Q. So you couldn't have seen him then?
>
> A. Yes, I could see him, when I looked up in his face.
>
> Q. In the dark?
>
> A. He was right in the doorway – it was enough light from the bedroom shining through. Yes, I could see who he was.
>
> Q. You could see? No light? And you could see him and know him then?
>
> A. Yes.

When the victim screamed, her 12-year-old daughter came out of her bedroom and also began to scream. The assailant directed the victim to "tell her [the daughter] to shut up, or I'll kill you both." She did so, and was then walked at knifepoint about two blocks along a railroad track, taken into a woods, and raped there. She testified that "the moon was shining brightly, full moon." After the rape, the assailant ran off, and she returned home, the whole incident having taken between 15 minutes and half an hour.

She then gave the police what the Federal District Court characterized as "only a very general description," describing him as "being fat and flabby with smooth skin, bushy hair and a youthful voice." Additionally, though not mentioned by the District Court, she testified at the habeas corpus hearing that she had described her assailant as being between 16 and 18 years old and between five feet ten inches and six feet tall, as weighing between 180 and 200 pounds, and as having a dark brown complexion. This testimony was substantially corroborated by that of a police officer who was testifying from his notes.

On several occasions over the course of the next seven months, she viewed suspects in her home or at the police station, some in lineups and others in showups, and was shown between 30 and 40 photographs. She told the police that a man pictured in one of the photographs had features similar to those of her assailant, but identified none of the suspects. On August 17, the police called her to the station to view respondent, who was being detained on another charge. In an effort to construct a suitable lineup, the police checked the city jail and the city juvenile home. Finding no one at either place fitting respondent's unusual physical description, they conducted a showup instead.

The showup itself consisted of two detectives walking respondent past the victim. At the victim's request, the police directed respondent to say "shut up or I'll kill you." The testimony at trial was not altogether clear as to whether the victim first identified him and then asked that he repeat the words or made her identification after he had spoken. In any event, the victim testified that she had "no doubt" about her identification. At the habeas corpus hearing, she elaborated in response to questioning.

> A. That I have no doubt, I mean that I am sure that when I – see, when I first laid eyes on him, I knew that it was the individual, because his face – well, there was just something that I don't think I could ever forget. I believe –
>
> Q. You say when you first laid eyes on him, which time are you referring to?
>
> A. When I identified him – when I seen him in the courthouse when I was took up to view the suspect."

We must decide whether this identification and the circumstances surrounding it failed to comport with due process requirements.

III.

Some general guidelines emerge from these cases as to the relationship between suggestiveness and misidentification. It is, first of all, apparent that the primary evil to be avoided is "a very substantial likelihood of irreparable misidentification." While the phrase was coined as a standard for determining whether an in-court identification would be admissible in the wake of a suggestive out-of-court identification, with the deletion of "irreparable" it serves equally well as a standard for the admissibility of testimony concerning the out-of-court identification itself. It is the likelihood of misidentification which violates a defendant's right to due process .... Suggestive confrontations are disapproved because they increase the likelihood of misidentification, and unnecessarily suggestive ones are condemned for the further reason that the increased chance of misidentification is gratuitous. ...

What is less clear from our cases is whether ... unnecessary suggestiveness alone requires the exclusion of evidence. While we are inclined to agree with the courts below that the police did not exhaust all possibilities in seeking persons physically comparable to respondent, we do not think that the evidence must therefore be excluded. The purpose of a strict rule barring evidence of unnecessarily suggestive confrontations would be to deter the police from using a less reliable procedure where a more reliable one may be available, and would not be based on the assumption that in every instance the admission of evidence of such a confrontation offends due process. ...

We turn, then, to the central question, whether under the "totality of the circumstances" the identification was reliable even though the confrontation procedure was suggestive. As indicated by our cases, the factors to be considered in evaluating the likelihood of misidentification include the opportunity of the witness to view the criminal at the time of the crime, the witness' degree of attention, the accuracy of the witness' prior description of the criminal, the level of certainty demonstrated by the witness at the confrontation, and the length of time between the crime and the confrontation. Applying these factors, we disagree with the District Court's conclusion.

We find that the District Court's conclusions on the critical facts are unsupported by the record and clearly erroneous. The victim spent a considerable period of time with her assailant, up to half an hour. She was with him under adequate artificial light in her house and under a full moon outdoors, and at least twice, once in the house and later in the woods, faced him directly and intimately. She was no casual observer, but rather the victim of one of the most personally humiliating of all crimes. Her description to the police, which included the assailant's approximate age, height, weight, complexion, skin texture, build, and voice, might not have satisfied Proust but was more than ordinarily thorough. She had "no doubt" that respondent was the person who raped her. In the nature of the crime, there are rarely witnesses to a rape other than the victim, who often has a limited opportunity of observation. The victim here, a practical nurse by profession, had an unusual opportunity to observe and identify her assailant. She testified at the habeas corpus hearing that there was something about his face "I don't think I could ever forget."

There was, to be sure, a lapse of seven months between the rape and the confrontation. This would be a seriously negative factor in most cases. Here, however, the testimony is undisputed that the victim made no previous identification at any of the showups, lineups, or photographic showings. Her record for reliability was thus a good one, as she had previously resisted whatever suggestiveness inheres in a showup. Weighing all the factors, we find no substantial likelihood of misidentification. The evidence was properly allowed to go to the jury.

Affirmed in part, reversed in part, and remanded.

MR. JUSTICE BRENNAN, with whom MR. JUSTICE DOUGLAS and MR. JUSTICE STEWART concur, concurring in part and dissenting in part. [opinion omitted]

NOTES AND QUERIES

Note the shift from suggestibility, which was the major concern in prior cases, to reliability. What do you make of that shift?

What are the "court factors" the Court identifies as important to consider in evaluating eyewitness testimony? Do you find that those are good indicators of reliability? How about when applied to this case? What does that tell you about the possible utility of psychological science?

CONSIDERING NON-CORPOREAL IDENTIFICATIONS

MANSON v. BRATHWAITE
432 U.S. 98 (1977)

MR. JUSTICE BLACKMUN delivered the opinion of the Court.

I.

Jimmy D. Glover, a full-time trooper of the Connecticut State Police, in 1970 was assigned to the Narcotics Division in an undercover capacity. On May 5 of that year, about 7:45 p.m., and while there was still daylight, Glover and Henry Alton Brown, an informant, went to an apartment building at 201 Westland, in Hartford, for the purpose of purchasing narcotics from "Dickie Boy" Cicero, a known narcotics dealer. Cicero, it was thought, lived on the third floor of that apartment building. Glover and Brown entered the building, observed by backup Officers D'Onofrio and Gaffey, and proceeded by stairs to the third floor. Glover knocked at the door of one of the two apartments served by the stairway. The area was illuminated by natural light from a window in the third floor hallway. The door was opened 12 to 18 inches in response to the knock. Glover observed a man standing at the door and, behind him, a woman. Brown identified himself. Glover then asked for "two things" of narcotics. The man at the door held out his hand, and Glover gave him two $ 10 bills. The door closed. Soon the man returned and handed Glover two glassine bags. While the door was open, Glover stood within two feet of the person from whom he made the purchase and observed his face. Five to seven minutes elapsed from the time the door first opened until it closed the second time.

Glover and Brown then left the building. This was about eight minutes after their arrival. Glover drove to headquarters where he described the seller to D'Onofrio and Gaffey. Glover at that time did not know the identity of the seller. He described him as being "a colored man, approximately five feet eleven inches tall, dark complexion, black hair, short Afro style, and having high cheekbones, and of heavy build. He was wearing at the time blue pants and a plaid shirt." D'Onofrio, suspecting from this description that respondent might be the seller, obtained a photograph of respondent from the Records Division of the Hartford Police Department. He left it at Glover's office. D'Onofrio was not acquainted with respondent personally, but did know him by sight and had seen him "[s]everal times" prior to May 5. Glover, when alone, viewed the photograph for the first time upon his return to headquarters on May 7; he identified the person shown as the one from whom he had purchased the narcotics.

Respondent was arrested on July 27 while visiting at the apartment of a Mrs. Ramsey on the third floor of 201 Westland. This was the apartment at which the narcotics sale had taken place on May 5.

Respondent was charged, in a two-count information, with possession and sale of heroin.... At his trial in January 1971, the photograph from which Glover had identified respondent was received in evidence without objection on the part of the defense. Glover also testified that, although he had not seen respondent in the eight months that had elapsed since the sale, "there [was] no doubt whatsoever" in his mind that the person shown on the photograph was respondent. Glover also made a positive in-court identification without objection.

No explanation was offered by the prosecution for the failure to utilize a photographic array or to conduct a lineup.

Respondent, who took the stand in his own defense, testified that on May 5, the day in question, he had been ill at his Albany Avenue apartment ... and that at no time on that particular day had he been at 201 Westland. His wife testified that she recalled, after her husband had refreshed her memory, that he was home all day on May 5. ..

The jury found respondent guilty on both counts of the information. He received a sentence of not less than six nor more than nine years. ...

... On appeal, the United States Court of Appeals for the Second Circuit reversed, with instructions to issue the writ unless the State gave notice of a desire to retry respondent and the new trial occurred within a reasonable time to be fixed by the District Judge.

In brief summary, the court felt that evidence as to the photograph should have been excluded, regardless of reliability, because the examination of the single photograph was unnecessary and suggestive. And, in the court's view, the evidence was unreliable in any event. We granted certiorari.

Petitioner at the outset acknowledges that "the procedure in the instant case was suggestive [because only one photograph was used] and unnecessary" [because there was no emergency or exigent circumstance]. The respondent, in agreement with the Court of Appeals, proposes a per se rule of exclusion that he claims is dictated by the demands of the Fourteenth Amendment's guarantee of due process. He rightly observes that this is the first case in which this Court has had occasion to rule upon strictly post-Stovall out-of-court identification evidence of the challenged kind.

Since the decision in Biggers, the Courts of Appeals appear to have developed at least two approaches to such evidence. The first, or per se approach, employed by the Second Circuit in the present case, focuses on the procedures employed and requires exclusion of the out-of-court identification evidence, without regard to reliability, whenever it has been obtained through unnecessarily suggested confrontation procedures. The justifications advanced are the elimination of evidence of uncertain reliability, deterrence of the police and prosecutors, and the stated "fair assurance against the awful risks of misidentification."

The second, or more lenient, approach is one that continues to rely on the totality of the circumstances. It permits the admission of the confrontation evidence if, despite the suggestive aspect, the out-of-court identification possesses certain features of reliability. Its adherents feel that the per se approach is not mandated by the Due Process Clause of the Fourteenth Amendment. This second approach, in contrast to the other... serves to limit the societal costs imposed by a sanction that excludes relevant evidence from consideration and evaluation by the trier of fact.

The respondent here stresses the same ... for deterrence of improper identification practice, a factor he regards as pre-eminent. Photographic identification, it is said, continues to be needlessly employed.... He argues that a totality rule cannot be expected to have a significant deterrent impact; only a strict rule of exclusion will have direct and immediate impact on law enforcement agents. Identification evidence is so convincing to the jury that sweeping exclusionary rules are required. Fairness of the trial is threatened by suggestive confrontation evidence, and thus, it is said, an exclusionary rule has an established constitutional predicate.

There are, of course, several interests to be considered and taken into account. The driving force behind United States v. Wade, Gilbert v. California, and Stovall, all decided on the same day, was the Court's concern with the problems of eyewitness identification. Usually the witness must testify about an encounter with a total stranger under circumstances of emergency or emotional stress. The witness' recollection of the stranger can be distorted easily by the circumstances or by later actions of the police. Thus, Wade and its companion cases reflect the concern that the jury not hear eyewitness testimony unless that evidence has aspects of reliability. It must be observed that both approaches before us are responsive to this concern. The per se rule, however, goes too far since its application automatically and peremptorily, and without consideration of alleviating factors, keeps evidence from the jury that is reliable and relevant.

The second factor is deterrence. Although the per se approach has the more significant deterrent effect, the totality approach also has an influence on police behavior. The police will guard against unnecessarily suggestive procedures under the totality rule, as well as the per se one, for fear that their actions will lead to the exclusion of identifications as unreliable.

The third factor is the effect on the administration of justice. Here the per se approach suffers serious drawbacks. Since it denies the trier reliable evidence, it may result, on occasion, in the guilty going free. Also, because of its rigidity, the per se approach may make error by the trial judge more likely than the totality approach. And in those cases in which the admission of identification evidence is error under the per se approach but not under the totality approach – cases in which the identification is reliable despite an unnecessarily suggestive identification procedure – reversal is a Draconian sanction. Certainly, inflexible rules of exclusion that may frustrate rather than promote justice have not been viewed recently by this Court with unlimited enthusiasm.

The standard, after all, is that of fairness as required by the Due Process Clause of the Fourteenth Amendment. Stovall, with its reference to "the totality of the circumstances" and Biggers, with its continuing stress on the same totality, did not, singly or together, establish a strict exclusionary rule or new standard of due process. ...

We therefore conclude that reliability is the linchpin in determining the admissibility of identification testimony for both pre- and post-Stovall confrontations. The factors to be considered are set out in Biggers. These include the opportunity of the witness to view the criminal at the time of the crime, the witness' degree of attention, the accuracy of his prior description of the criminal, the level of certainty demonstrated at the confrontation, and the time between the crime and the confrontation. Against these factors is to be weighed the corrupting effect of the suggestive identification itself.

V.

We turn, then, to the facts of this case and apply the analysis:

The opportunity to view. Glover testified that for two to three minutes he stood at the apartment door, within two feet of the respondent. The door opened twice, and each time the man stood at the door. The moments passed, the conversation took place, and payment was made. Glover looked directly at his vendor. It was near sunset, to be sure, but the sun had not yet set, so it was not dark or even dusk or twilight. Natural light from outside entered the hallway through a window. There was natural light, as well, from inside the apartment.

The degree of attention. Glover was not a casual or passing observer, as is so often the case with eyewitness identification. Trooper Glover was a trained police officer on duty - and specialized and dangerous duty - when he called at the third floor of 201 Westland in Hartford on May 5, 1970. Glover himself was a Negro and unlikely to perceive only general features of "hundreds of Hartford black males," as the Court of Appeals stated. It is true that Glover's duty was that of ferreting out narcotics offenders and that he would be expected in his work to produce results. But it is also true that, as a specially trained, assigned, and experienced officer, he could be expected to pay scrupulous attention to detail, for he knew that subsequently he would have to find and arrest his vendor. In addition, he knew that his claimed observations would be subject later to close scrutiny and examination at any trial.

The accuracy of the description. Glover's description was given to D'Onofrio within minutes after the transaction. It included the vendor's race, his height, his build, the color and style of his hair, and the high cheekbone facial feature. It also included clothing the vendor wore. No claim has been made that respondent did not possess the physical characteristics so described. D'Onofrio reacted positively at once. Two days later, when Glover was alone, he viewed the photograph D'Onofrio produced and identified its subject as the narcotics seller.

The witness' level of certainty. There is no dispute that the photograph in question was that of respondent. Glover, in response to a question whether the photograph was that of the person from whom he made the purchase, testified: "There is no question whatsoever." This positive assurance was repeated.

The time between the crime and the confrontation. Glover's description of his vendor was given to D'Onofrio within minutes of the crime. The photographic identification took place only two days later. We do not have here the passage of weeks or months between the crime and the viewing of the photograph.

These indicators of Glover's ability to make an accurate identification are hardly outweighed by the corrupting effect of the challenged identification itself. Although identifications arising from single-photograph displays may be viewed in general with suspicion, we find in the instant case little pressure on the witness to acquiesce in the suggestion that such a display entails. D'Onofrio had left the photograph at Glover's office and was not present when Glover first viewed it two days after the event. There thus was little urgency and Glover could view the photograph at his leisure. And since Glover examined the photograph alone, there was no coercive pressure to make an identification arising from the presence of another. The identification was made in circumstances allowing care and reflection.

Surely, we cannot say that under all the circumstances of this case there is "a very substantial likelihood of irreparable misidentification." Short of that point, such evidence is for the jury to weigh. We are content to rely upon the good sense and judgment of American juries, for evidence with some element of untrustworthiness is customary grist for the jury mill. Juries are not so susceptible that they cannot measure intelligently the weight of identification testimony that has some questionable feature.

The judgment of the Court of Appeals is reversed.

It is so ordered.

MR. JUSTICE STEVENS, concurring. [opinion omitted].

DISSENT: MR. JUSTICE MARSHALL, with whom MR. JUSTICE BRENNAN joins, dissenting.

...the Court considers two alternatives, a per se exclusionary rule and a totality-of-the-circumstances approach. The Court weighs three factors in deciding that the totality approach, which is essentially the test used in Biggers, should be applied. In my view, the Court wrongly evaluates the impact of these factors.

First, the Court acknowledges that one of the factors, deterrence of police use of unnecessarily suggestive identification procedures, favors the per se rule. Indeed, it does so heavily, for such a rule would make it unquestionably clear to the police they must never use a suggestive procedure when a fairer alternative is available. I have no doubt that conduct would quickly conform to the rule.

Second, the Court gives passing consideration to the dangers of eyewitness identification recognized in the Wade trilogy. It concludes, however, that the grave risk of error does not justify adoption of the per se approach because that would too often result in exclusion of relevant evidence. In my view, this conclusion totally ignores the lessons of Wade. The dangers of mistaken identification are, as Stovall held, simply too great to permit unnecessarily suggestive identifications. ... While the Court is "content to rely on the good sense and judgment of American juries," the impetus for Stovall and Wade was repeated miscarriages of justice resulting from juries' willingness to credit inaccurate eyewitness testimony.

Finally, the Court errs in its assessment of the relative impact of the two approaches on the administration of justice. The Court relies most heavily on this factor, finding that "reversal is a Draconian sanction" in cases where the identification is reliable despite an unnecessarily suggestive procedure used to obtain it. Relying on little more than a strong distaste for "inflexible rules of exclusion," the Court rejects the per se test. In so doing, the Court disregards two significant distinctions between the per se rule advocated in this case and the exclusionary remedies for certain other constitutional violations.

First, the per se rule here is not "inflexible." Where evidence is suppressed, for example, as the fruit of an unlawful search, it may well be forever lost to the prosecution. Identification evidence, however, can by its very nature be readily and effectively reproduced. The in-court identification, permitted under Wade and Simmons if it has a source independent of an uncounseled or suggestive procedure, is one example...

Second, other exclusionary rules have been criticized for preventing jury consideration of relevant and usually reliable evidence in order to serve interests unrelated to guilt or innocence, such as discouraging illegal searches or denial of counsel. Suggestively obtained eyewitness testimony is excluded, in contrast, precisely because of its unreliability and concomitant irrelevance. Its exclusion both protects the integrity of the truth-seeking function of the trial and discourages police use of needlessly inaccurate and ineffective investigatory methods.

Indeed, impermissibly suggestive identifications are not merely worthless law enforcement tools. They pose a grave threat to society at large in a more direct way than most governmental disobedience of the law. For if the police and the public erroneously conclude, on the basis of an unnecessarily suggestive confrontation, that the right man has been caught and convicted, the real outlaw must still remain at large. Law enforcement has failed in its primary function and has left society unprotected from the depredations of an active criminal.

For these reasons, I conclude that adoption of the per se rule would enhance, rather than detract from, the effective administration of justice. In my view, the Court's totality test will allow seriously unreliable and misleading evidence to be put before juries. Equally important, it will allow dangerous criminals to remain on the streets while citizens assume that police action has given them protection. According to my calculus, all three of the factors upon which the Court relies point to acceptance of the per se approach.

...The Court holds, as Neil v. Biggers failed to, that a due process identification inquiry must take account of the suggestiveness of a confrontation and the likelihood that it led to misidentification, as recognized in Stovall and Wade. Thus, even if a witness did have an otherwise adequate opportunity to view a criminal, the later use of a highly suggestive identification procedure can render his testimony inadmissible. Indeed, it is my view that, assuming applicability of the totality test enunciated by the Court, the facts of the present case require that result.

I consider first the opportunity that Officer Glover had to view the suspect. Careful review of the record shows that he could see the heroin seller only for the time it took to speak three sentences of four or five short words, to hand over some money and later after the door reopened, to receive the drugs in return. The entire face-to-face transaction could have taken as little as 15 or 20 seconds. But during this time, Glover's attention was not focused exclusively on the seller's face. He observed that the door was opened 12 to 18 inches, that there was a window in the room behind the door and, most importantly, that there was a woman standing behind the man. Glover was, of course, also concentrating on the details of the transaction – he must have looked away from the seller's face to hand him the money and receive the drugs. The observation during the conversation thus may have been as brief as 5 or 10 seconds.

As the Court notes, Glover was a police officer trained in and attentive to the need for making accurate identifications. Nevertheless, both common sense and scholarly study indicate that while a trained observer such as a police officer "is somewhat less likely to make an erroneous identification than the average untrained observer, the mere fact that he has been so trained is no guarantee that he is correct in a specific case. His identification testimony should be scrutinized just as carefully as that of the normal witness." Moreover, "identifications made by policemen in highly competitive activities, such as undercover narcotic agents..., should be scrutinized with special care." Yet it is just such a searching inquiry that the Court fails to make here.

Another factor on which the Court relies – the witness' degree of certainty in making the identification – is worthless as an indicator that he is correct. Even if Glover had been unsure initially about his identification of respondent's picture, by the time he was called at trial to present a key piece of evidence for the State that paid his salary, it is impossible to imagine his responding negatively to such questions as "is there any doubt in your mind whatsoever" that the identification was correct. As the Court noted in Wade: "'It is a matter of common experience that, once a witness has picked out the accused at the [pretrial confrontation], he is not likely to go back on his word later on.'"

Next, the Court finds that because the identification procedure took place two days after the crime, its reliability is enhanced. While such temporal proximity makes the identification more reliable than one occurring months later, the fact is that the greatest memory loss occurs within hours after an event. After that, the dropoff continues much more slowly. Thus, the reliability of an identification is increased only if it was made within several hours of the crime. If the time gap is any greater, reliability necessarily decreases.

Finally, the Court makes much of the fact that Glover gave a description of the seller to D'Onofrio shortly after the incident. Despite the Court's assertion that because "Glover himself was a Negro and unlikely to perceive only general features of 'hundreds of Hartford black males,' as the Court of Appeals stated," the description given by Glover was actually no more than a general summary of the seller's appearance. We may discount entirely the seller's clothing, for that was of no significance later in the proceeding. Indeed, to the extent that Glover noticed clothes, his attention was diverted from the seller's face. Otherwise, Glover merely described vaguely the seller's height, skin color, hairstyle, and build. He did say that the seller had "high cheekbones," but there is no other mention of facial features, nor even an estimate of age. Conspicuously absent is any indication that the seller was a native of the West Indies, certainly something which a member of the black community could immediately recognize from both appearance and accept.

From all of this, I must conclude that the evidence of Glover's ability to make an accurate identification is far weaker than the Court finds it. In contrast, the procedure used to identify respondent was both extraordinarily suggestive and strongly conducive to error. In dismissing "the corrupting effect of the suggestive identification" procedure here, the Court virtually grants the police license to convict the innocent. By displaying a single photograph of respondent to the witness Glover under the circumstances in this record almost everything that could have been done wrong was done wrong.

In the first place, there was no need to use a photograph at all. Because photos are static, two-dimensional, and often outdated, they are "clearly inferior in reliability" to corporeal procedures. While the use of photographs is justifiable and often essential where the police have no knowledge of an offender's identity, the poor reliability of photos makes their use inexcusable where any other means of identification is available. Here, since Detective DOnofrio believed that he knew the seller's identity, further investigation without resort to a photographic showup was easily possible. With little inconvenience, a corporeal lineup including Brathwaite might have been arranged. Properly conducted, such a procedure would have gone far to remove any doubt about the fairness and accuracy of the identification.

Worse still than the failure to use an easily available corporeal identification was the display to Glover of only a single picture, rather than a photo array. With good reason, such single-suspect procedures have "been widely condemned." ...

The Court discounts this overwhelming evidence of suggestiveness, however. It reasons that because D'Onofrio was not present when Glover viewed the photograph, there was "little pressure on the witness to acquiesce in the suggestion." That conclusion blinks psychological reality. There is no doubt in my mind that even in D'Onofrio's absence, a clear and powerful message was telegraphed to Glover as he looked at respondent's photograph. He was emphatically told that "this is the man," and he responded by identifying respondent then and at trial "whether or not he was in fact 'the man.'"

I must conclude that this record presents compelling evidence that there was "a very substantial likelihood of misidentification" of respondent Brathwaite.

The suggestive display of respondent's photograph to the witness Glover likely erased any independent memory that Glover had retained of the seller from his barely adequate opportunity to observe the criminal.

NOTES AND QUERIES

This case applies the Court factors identified in *Neil v. Biggers*. How would you have applied those factors in this case?

The major concern is this case centers on which rule should be used once there is evidence that the identification was unfair and unnecessarily suggestive. The Court addresses two possible standards: a *per se* approach and a totality of the circumstances approach. Which one would you find appropriate? Note that a *per se* approach would require exclusion if it is determined that the evidence fits into a particular category (like unnecessarily suggestive) while the totality of circumstances allows for a more nuanced look at the evidence. Importantly, the *per se* approach demands the exclusion of testimony concerning unnecessarily suggestive identifications, but it does permit the admission of testimony concerning a subsequent identification, including an in-court identification, if the subsequent identification is determined reliable. The totality approach, in contrast, is simpler: if the challenged identification is reliable, then testimony as to it and any identification in its wake is admissible.

RESEARCH NOTE ON THE "COURT FACTORS"

The U. S. Supreme Court established in *Neil* – and reaffirmed in *Manson* – five factors that should be taken into account in evaluating the reliability of an identification: (1) the witness's opportunity to view the criminal during the crime; (2) the length of time between the crime and the subsequent identification (retention interval); (3) the level of certainty demonstrated by the witness at the identification; (4) the (apparent) accuracy of the witness' prior description of the criminal; and (5) the witness' degree of attention during the crime. In the *Neil* and *Manson* cases, the Court's emphasis appeared to shift from a concern with suggestibility, as demonstrated in the *Wade*, *Gilbert*, and *Stovall* decisions, to an overriding concern with the reliability of an identification, even if it was obtained under suggestive circumstances. At the time of the *Neil* decision, there existed little published scientific research on eyewitness memory. The Supreme Court could, therefore, make only "educated guesses" about the factors that might affect eyewitness accuracy. However, scientific research conducted in the ensuing years permits a systematic evaluation of the validity of the five criteria enumerated by the Court.

Research findings indicate that only two of the five *Neil* factors are clearly related to accuracy in the way that the Court assumed. First, the Court suggested that witnesses with a better opportunity to observe the criminal (e.g., better lighting, closer view, longer viewing time) are more likely to make accurate identifications. Second, the length of the retention interval (i.e., the time between the crime and the identification) generally relates to accuracy, with longer retention intervals yielding poorer accuracy. But research shows that this relationship is not always simple. Other factors such as race or stress may interact with the length of the retention level and affect eyewitness accuracy. The importance of the other three factors for estimating accuracy – witness certainty, description accuracy, and degree of attention – have received mixed support by researchers.

With respect to witness certainty, results of thirty-five staged-event studies showed only a very weak relationship between witnesses' degree of certainty and identification accuracy. Robert K. Bothwell, Kenneth A. Deffenbacher, and John C. Brigham, Correlation of eyewitness accuracy and confidence: Optimality hypothesis revisited, 72 J. Appl. Psych. 691 (1987). However, several recent studies have demonstrated that varying witnessing conditions to make later identification easier or more difficult (e.g., by shortening or extending the time of encoding) can create a rather substantial relationship between identification accuracy and confidence of the eyewitness. D. Stephen Lindsay, J. Don Read, and Kusum Sharma, Accuracy and confidence in person identification: The relationship is strong when witnessing conditions vary widely, 9 Psych. Sci. 215 (1998). To further complicate things, research has demonstrated that witnesses may become more certain of the identification as time passes. Such "confidence hardening" is likely to occur whenever people have publicly committed themselves to their identification, or when they are told that their identification was correct. Gary L. Wells, Tamara J. Ferguson, and R.C. Lindsay, The tractability of eyewitness confidence and its implications for triers of fact, 66 J. Appl. Soc. Psych. 688 (1981). Overall, then, self-reported confidence in the accuracy of identification, especially if it is given a considerable time after the identification was made, is not a good indicator of accuracy.

With respect to the apparent quality of a witness' initial description of the suspect, the Court opined that the accuracy of that description would be related to the probable accuracy of the identification. But contrary to the Court's assumption, research consistently has demonstrated that accuracy of description generally is not related to accuracy of identification. Further, the apparent "completeness" of a description, the number of attributes that are recalled, also is not related to identification accuracy. See Melissa A. Pigott, John C. Brigham, and Robert K. Bothwell, A field study of the relationship between description accuracy and identification accuracy, 17 J. Police Sci. and Admin. 84 (1990).

The final factor – degree of attention – many not be as predictive as we may have hoped. Eyewitnesses who pay a moderate degree of attention to a situation are likely to be more accurate when compared to those who do not pay attention or to those who are distracted because they were in a stressful crime situation. Kenneth A. Deffenbacher, The influence of arousal on reliability of testimony, in Evaluating Witness Evidence 235 (Sally M.A. Lloyd-Bostock and Brian R. Clifford, eds., 1983). Even if someone is trying to be attentive, high fear or stress (if present) likely interferes with memory and impairs the accuracy of subsequent identifications. The perceptual situation is made even more difficult if a weapon is involved, because the perceiver is likely to focus attention on the weapon rather than on the individual holding the weapon. As a consequence, the witness fails to acquire a strong representation of the suspect in memory.

REVIEW PROBLEM

At trial Reynolds testified that at about 11:30 p. m. on July 24, 1966, he was engaged in changing a tire when three men approached from across the highway. One of them shot him from a short distance away. The three then ran up to within three or four feet. Reynolds arose from his stooped position and held on to his wife, who had left the car to watch him as he worked. One of the men put his hand on Mrs. Reynolds' shoulder. Reynolds testified that this was Coleman. Within a few seconds a car with its lights on approached, and the three men turned and "ran across the road. . . ." As they turned to go, Reynolds was shot a second time. He identified Stephens as the gunman, stating that he saw him "in the car lights" while "looking straight at him." Reynolds repeated on cross-examination his testimony on direct examination; he said he saw Coleman "face to face"; "I looked into his face," "got a real good look at him." Coleman and Stephens sought to suppress the identification evidence at a pretrial hearing. At that hearing, Detective Fordham testified that he had spoken briefly to Reynolds at the hospital two days after the assault and about two weeks later, and that on neither occasion was Reynolds able to provide much information about his assailants. At the hospital he gave a vague description – that the attackers were "young, black males, close to the same age and height." Although Stephens and Coleman were both black, Stephens was 18 and 6'2', and Coleman, 28 and 5'4 ½'. Detective Fordham also testified that at the time Reynolds gave this description he was in considerable pain, and that consequently the questioning was very brief. The detective further stated that Reynolds did not identify any of his assailants from mug shots, but it does not appear whether pictures of petitioners were among those shown him. Detective Hart testified that a lineup was held on October 1 at the request of the police. He stated that Reynolds identified Stephens spontaneously before the formal lineup even began. "The six men were brought in by the warden, up on the stage, and as Otis Stephens – he didn't get to his position on the stage, which was number one, when Mr. Reynolds identified him as being one of his assailants." Reynolds gave similar testimony: "As soon as he stepped inside the door – I hadn't seen him previous to then until he stepped inside the door, and I recognized him. . . . Just as soon as he stepped up on the stage, I said, 'That man, there, is the one; he is the one that shot me.'" Reynolds also testified that he identified Coleman at the lineup before Coleman could act on a request Reynolds had made that the lineup participants speak certain words used by the attackers. Reynolds admitted that he did not tell Detective Hart of his identification until later during the lineup, and the detective stated he could not recall whether Reynolds told him of the identification before or after Coleman spoke the words.

Would you find that Reynolds' in-court identification of Coleman and Stephens stemmed from an identification procedure at the lineup so impermissibly suggestive as to give rise to a very substantial likelihood of irreparable misidentification? The Court, in *Coleman v. Alabama*, 399 U.S. 1 (1970), did not think so.

Would you find that failure to provide Coleman and Stephens with counsel at the lineup stage violative of their rights? Recall that, in *U.S. v. Wade*, the Supreme Court held that a person accused of crime requires the guiding hand of counsel at every step in the proceedings against him and that that constitutional principle is not limited to the presence of counsel at trial: "It is central to that principle that in addition to counsel's presence at trial, the accused is guaranteed that he need not stand alone against the State at any stage of the prosecution, formal or informal, in court or out, where counsel's absence might derogate from the accused's right to a fair trial." The "critical stage" may apply to preliminary hearings. But, what if the preliminary hearing is not a required step in the particular state's (here Alabama's) prosecution? Here, the prosecutors may seek an indictment directly from the grand jury without a preliminary hearing. Does that mean that the preliminary hearing is not a critical stage requiring provision of counsel? The Court ruled that the preliminary hearing was a "critical stage". The Court reasoned as follows:

> ... the determination whether the hearing is a "critical stage" requiring the provision of counsel depends upon an analysis "whether potential substantial prejudice to defendant's rights inheres in the . . . confrontation and the ability of counsel to help avoid that prejudice." Plainly the guiding hand of counsel at the preliminary hearing is essential to protect the indigent accused against an erroneous or improper prosecution. First, the lawyer's skilled examination and cross-examination of witnesses may expose fatal weaknesses in the State's case that may lead the magistrate to refuse to bind the accused over. Second, in any event, the skilled interrogation of witnesses by an experienced lawyer can fashion a vital impeachment tool for use in cross-examination of the State's witnesses at the trial, or preserve testimony favorable to the accused of a witness who does not appear at the trial. Third, trained counsel can more effectively discover the case the State has against his client and make possible the preparation of a proper defense to meet that case at the trial. Fourth, counsel can also be influential at the preliminary hearing in making effective arguments for the accused on such matters as the necessity for an early psychiatric examination or bail.

What remedy? The Court noted that the test to be applied is whether the denial of counsel at the preliminary hearing was harmless error under *Chapman v. California*, [.... *United States v. Wade*]. The Court found that it could not be said on the record whether or not Coleman and Stephens were otherwise prejudiced by the absence of counsel at the preliminary hearing. Given the lack of record, the Supreme Court remanded since that inquiry in the first instance should be made by the Alabama courts.

UNITED STATES v. ASH
413 U.S. 300 (1973)

MR. JUSTICE BLACKMUN delivered the opinion of the Court.

I.

On the morning of August 26, 1965, a man with a stocking mask entered a bank in Washington, D. C., and began waving a pistol. He ordered an employee to hang up the telephone and instructed all others present not to move. Seconds later a second man, also wearing a stocking mask, entered the bank, scooped up money from tellers' drawers into a bag, and left. The gunman followed, and both men escaped through an alley. The robbery lasted three or four minutes.

A Government informer, Clarence McFarland, told authorities that he had discussed the robbery with Charles J. Ash, Jr., the respondent here. Acting on this information, an FBI agent, in February 1966, showed five black-and-white mug shots of Negro males of generally the same age, height, and weight, one of which was of Ash, to four witnesses. All four made uncertain identifications of Ash's picture. At this time Ash was not in custody and had not been charged. On April 1, 1966, an indictment was returned charging Ash ... in five counts related to this bank robbery ...

Trial was finally set for May 1968, almost three years after the crime. In preparing for trial, the prosecutor decided to use a photographic display to determine whether the witnesses he planned to call would be able to make in-court identifications. Shortly before the trial, an FBI agent and the prosecutor showed five color photographs to the four witnesses who previously had tentatively identified the black-and-white photograph of Ash. Three of the witnesses selected the picture of Ash, but one was unable to make any selection. ... This post-indictment identification provides the basis for respondent Ash's claim that he was denied the right to counsel at a "critical stage" of the prosecution.

... The trial judge held a hearing on the suggestive nature of the pretrial photographic displays. The judge did not make a clear ruling on suggestive nature, but held that the Government had demonstrated by "clear and convincing" evidence that in-court identifications would be "based on observation of the suspect other than the intervening observation."

At trial, the three witnesses who had been inside the bank identified Ash as the gunman, but they were unwilling to state that they were certain of their identifications. ... The fourth witness, who had been in a car outside the bank and who had seen the fleeing robbers after they had removed their masks, made positive in-court identifications... After a conference at the bench, the trial judge ruled that all five color photographs would be admitted into evidence. [Note that it was admitted because Ash's co-defendant's attorney brought out the fact that this witness had selected another man as one of the robbers. At this point the prosecutor became concerned that the jury might believe that the witness had selected a third person when, in fact, the witness had selected a photograph of Ash.] The Court of Appeals held that this constituted the introduction of a post-indictment identification at the prosecutor's request and over the objection of defense counsel.

The jury convicted Ash on all counts. ...

The five-member majority of the Court of Appeals held that Ash's right to counsel, guaranteed by the Sixth Amendment, was violated when his attorney was not given the opportunity to be present at the photographic displays conducted in May 1968 before the trial. ...

II.

The Court of Appeals relied exclusively on that portion of the Sixth Amendment providing, "In all criminal prosecutions, the accused shall enjoy the right . . . to have the Assistance of Counsel for his defence." The right to counsel in Anglo-American law has a rich historical heritage, and this Court has regularly drawn on that history in construing the counsel guarantee of the Sixth Amendment. ...

III.

Although the Court of Appeals' majority recognized the argument that "a major purpose behind the right to counsel is to protect the defendant from errors that he himself might make if he appeared in court alone," the court concluded that "other forms of prejudice," mentioned and recognized in Wade, could also give rise to a right to counsel. These forms of prejudice were felt by the court to flow from the possibilities for mistaken identification inherent in the photographic display.

We conclude that the dangers of mistaken identification, mentioned in Wade, were removed from context by the Court of Appeals and were incorrectly utilized as a sufficient basis for requiring counsel. Although Wade did discuss possibilities for suggestion and the difficulty for reconstructing suggestivity, this discussion occurred only after the Court had concluded that the lineup constituted a trial-like confrontation, requiring the "Assistance of Counsel" to preserve the adversary process by compensating for advantages of the prosecuting authorities.

...Wade has shown that the traditional Sixth Amendment test easily allowed extension of counsel to a lineup. The similarity to trial was apparent, and counsel was needed to render "Assistance" in counterbalancing any "overreaching" by the prosecution.

After the Court in Wade held that a lineup constituted a trial-like confrontation requiring counsel, a more difficult issue remained in the case for consideration. The same changes in law enforcement that led to lineups and pretrial hearings also generated other events at which the accused was confronted by the prosecution. The Government had argued in Wade that if counsel was required at a lineup, the same forceful considerations would mandate counsel at other preparatory steps in the "gathering of the prosecution's evidence," such as, for particular example, the taking of fingerprints or blood samples.

The Court concluded that there were differences. Rather than distinguishing these situations from the lineup in terms of the need for counsel to assure an equal confrontation at the time, the Court recognized that there were times when the subsequent trial would cure a one-sided confrontation between prosecuting authorities and the uncounseled defendant. In other words, such stages were not "critical." Referring to fingerprints, hair, clothing, and other blood samples, the Court explained:

> Knowledge of the techniques of science and technology is sufficiently available, and the variables in techniques few enough, that the accused has the opportunity for a meaningful confrontation of the Government's case at trial through the ordinary processes of cross-examination of the Government's expert witnesses and the presentation of the evidence of his own experts.

The structure of Wade, viewed in light of the careful limitation of the Court's language to "confrontations," makes it clear that lack of scientific precision and inability to reconstruct an event are not the tests for requiring counsel in the first instance. These are, instead, the tests to determine whether confrontation with counsel at trial can serve as a substitute for counsel at the pretrial confrontation. If accurate reconstruction is possible, the risks inherent in any confrontation still remain, but the opportunity to cure defects at trial causes the confrontation to cease to be "critical."...

The Court of Appeals considered its analysis complete after it decided that a photographic display lacks scientific precision and ease of accurate reconstruction at trial. That analysis, under Wade, however, merely carries one to the point where one must establish that the trial itself can provide no substitute for counsel if a pretrial confrontation is conducted in the absence of counsel. ...

We now undertake the threshold analysis that must be addressed.

IV.

A substantial departure from the historical test would be necessary if the Sixth Amendment were interpreted to give Ash a right to counsel at the photographic identification in this case. Since the accused himself is not present at the time of the photographic display, and asserts no right to be present, no possibility arises that the accused might be misled by his lack of familiarity with the law or overpowered by his professional adversary. Similarly, the counsel guarantee would not be used to produce equality in a trial-like adversary confrontation. Rather, the guarantee was used by the Court of Appeals to produce confrontation at an event that previously was not analogous to an adversary trial.

Even if we were willing to view the counsel guarantee in broad terms as a generalized protection of the adversary process, we would be unwilling to go so far as to extend the right to a portion of the prosecutor's trial-preparation interviews with witnesses. ... The traditional counterbalance in the American adversary system for these interviews arises from the equal ability of defense counsel to seek and interview witnesses himself.

That adversary mechanism remains as effective for a photographic display as for other parts of pretrial interviews. No greater limitations are placed on defense counsel in constructing displays, seeking witnesses, and conducting photographic identifications than those applicable to the prosecution. Selection of the picture of a person other than the accused, or the inability of a witness to make any selection, will be useful to the defense in precisely the same manner that the selection of a picture of the defendant would be useful to the prosecution. ... Although we do not suggest that equality of access to photographs removes all potential for abuse, it does remove any inequality in the adversary process itself and thereby fully satisfies the historical spirit of the Sixth Amendment's counsel guarantee.

The argument has been advanced that requiring counsel might compel the police to observe more scientific procedures or might encourage them to utilize corporeal rather than photographic displays. This Court has recognized that improved procedures can minimize the dangers of suggestion. ...

Pretrial photographic identifications, however, are hardly unique in offering possibilities for the actions of the prosecutor unfairly to prejudice the accused. Evidence favorable to the accused may be withheld; testimony of witnesses may be manipulated; the results of laboratory tests may be contrived. In many ways the prosecutor, by accident or by design, may improperly subvert the trial. The primary safeguard against abuses of this kind is the ethical responsibility of the prosecutor, who, as so often has been said, may "strike hard blows" but not "foul ones." If that safeguard fails, review remains available under due process standards. These same safeguards apply to misuse of photographs.

We are not persuaded that the risks inherent in the use of photographic displays are so pernicious that an extraordinary system of safeguards is required.

We hold, then, that the Sixth Amendment does not grant the right to counsel at photographic displays conducted by the Government for the purpose of allowing a witness to attempt an identification of the offender. This holding requires reversal of the judgment of the Court of Appeals...

Reversed and remanded.

MR. JUSTICE STEWART, concurring in the judgment.

A photographic identification is quite different from a lineup, for there are substantially fewer possibilities of impermissible suggestion when photographs are used, and those unfair influences can be readily reconstructed at trial. It is true that the defendant's photograph may be markedly different from the others displayed, but this unfairness can be demonstrated at trial from an actual comparison of the photographs used or from the witness' description of the display. Similarly, it is possible that the photographs could be arranged in a suggestive manner, or that by comment or gesture the prosecuting authorities might single out the defendant's picture. But these are the kinds of overt influence that a witness can easily recount and that would serve to impeach the identification testimony. In short, there are few possibilities for unfair suggestiveness – and those rather blatant and easily reconstructed. Accordingly, an accused would not be foreclosed from an effective cross-examination of an identification witness simply because his counsel was not present at the photographic display. For this reason, a photographic display cannot fairly be considered a "critical stage" of the prosecution...

Preparing witnesses for trial by checking their identification testimony against a photographic display is little different, in my view, from the prosecutor's other interviews with the victim or other witnesses before trial. While these procedures can be improperly conducted, the possibility of irretrievable prejudice is remote, since any unfairness that does occur can usually be flushed out at trial through cross-examination of the prosecution witnesses. The presence of defense counsel at such pretrial preparatory sessions is neither appropriate nor necessary under our adversary system of justice "to preserve the defendant's basic right to a fair trial as affected by his right meaningfully to cross-examine the witnesses against him and to have effective assistance of counsel at the trial itself."

MR. JUSTICE BRENNAN, with whom MR. JUSTICE DOUGLAS and MR. JUSTICE MARSHALL join, dissenting.

The Court holds today that a pretrial display of photographs to the witnesses of a crime for the purpose of identifying the accused, unlike a lineup, does not constitute a "critical stage" of the prosecution at which the accused is constitutionally entitled to the presence of counsel. In my view, today's decision is wholly unsupportable in terms of such considerations as logic, consistency, and, indeed, fairness. As a result, I must reluctantly conclude that today's decision marks simply another step towards the complete evisceration of the fundamental constitutional principles established by this Court, only six years ago, in United States v. Wade, Gilbert v. California, and Stovall v. Denno. I dissent.

III.

As the Court of Appeals recognized, "the dangers of mistaken identification . . . set forth in Wade are applicable in large measure to photographic as well as corporeal identifications." To the extent that misidentification may be attributable to a witness' faulty memory or perception, or inadequate opportunity for detailed observation during the crime, the risks are obviously as great at a photographic display as at a lineup. But "because of the inherent limitations of photography, which presents its subject in two dimensions rather than the three dimensions of reality … a photographic identification, even when properly obtained, is clearly inferior to a properly obtained corporeal identification." Indeed, noting "the hazards of initial identification by photograph," we have expressly recognized that "a corporeal identification . . . is normally more accurate" than a photographic identification. Thus, in this sense at least, the dangers of misidentification are even greater at a photographic display than at a lineup.

Moreover, as in the lineup situation, the possibilities for impermissible suggestion in the context of a photographic display are manifold. Such suggestion, intentional or unintentional, may derive from three possible sources. First, the photographs themselves might tend to suggest which of the pictures is that of the suspect. For example, differences in age, pose, or other physical characteristics of the persons represented, and variations in the mounting, background, lighting, or markings of the photographs all might have the effect of singling out the accused.

Second, impermissible suggestion may inhere in the manner in which the photographs are displayed to the witness. The danger of misidentification is, of course, "increased if the police display to the witness … the pictures of several persons among which the photograph of a single such individual recurs or is in some way emphasized."...

Third, gestures or comments of the prosecutor at the time of the display may lead an otherwise uncertain witness to select the "correct" photograph. ... Thus, as is the case with lineups, "improper photographic identification procedures, . . . by exerting a suggestive influence upon the witnesses, can often lead to an erroneous identification . . . ." And "regardless of how the initial misidentification comes about, the witness thereafter is apt to retain in his memory the image of the photograph rather than of the person actually seen . . . ." As a result, "'the issue of identity may (in the absence of other relevant evidence) for all practical purposes be determined there and then, before the trial.'"

Moreover, as with lineups, the defense can "seldom reconstruct" at trial the mode and manner of photographic identification. It is true, of course, that the photographs used at the pretrial display might be preserved for examination at trial. But "it may also be said that a photograph can preserve the record of a lineup; yet this does not justify a lineup without counsel." Indeed, in reality, preservation of the photographs affords little protection to the unrepresented accused. For, although retention of the photographs may mitigate the dangers of misidentification due to the suggestiveness of the photographs themselves, it cannot in any sense reveal to defense counsel the more subtle, and therefore more dangerous, suggestiveness that might derive from the manner in which the photographs were displayed or any accompanying comments or gestures. Moreover, the accused cannot rely upon the witnesses themselves to expose these latter sources of suggestion, for the witnesses are not "apt to be alert for conditions prejudicial to the suspect. And if they were, it would likely be of scant benefit to the suspect" since the witnesses are hardly "likely to be schooled in the detection of suggestive influences."

Finally, and unlike the lineup situation, the accused himself is not even present at the photographic identification, thereby reducing the likelihood that irregularities in the procedures will ever come to light.

Thus, the difficulties of reconstructing at trial an uncounseled photographic display are at least equal to, and possibly greater than, those involved in reconstructing an uncounseled lineup.

IV.

...Although apparently conceding that the right to counsel attaches, not only at the trial itself, but at all "critical stages" of the prosecution, the Court holds today that, in order to be deemed "critical," the particular "stage of the prosecution" under consideration must, at the very least, involve the physical "presence of the accused," at a "trial-like confrontation" with the Government, at which the accused requires the "guiding hand of counsel." According to the Court a pretrial photographic identification does not, of course, meet these criteria.

The fundamental premise underlying all of this Court's decisions holding the right to counsel applicable at "critical" pretrial proceedings, is that a "stage" of the prosecution must be deemed "critical" for the purposes of the Sixth Amendment if it is one at which the presence of counsel is necessary "to protect the fairness of the trial itself." ...

There is something ironic about the Court's conclusion today that a pretrial lineup identification is a "critical stage" of the prosecution because counsel's presence can help to compensate for the accused's deficiencies as an observer, but that a pretrial photographic identification is not a "critical stage" of the prosecution because the accused is not able to observe at all. In my view, there simply is no meaningful difference, in terms of the need for attendance of counsel, between corporeal and photographic identifications. And applying established and well-reasoned Sixth Amendment principles, I can only conclude that a pretrial photographic display, like a pretrial lineup, is a "critical stage" of the prosecution at which the accused is constitutionally entitled to the presence of counsel.

NOTES AND QUERIES

Note 3 of Justice Blackmun's opinion reveals that Ash did not assert a right to counsel at the black-and-white photographic display in February 1966 because Ash recognized that *Kirby v. Illinois*, 406 U.S. 682 (1972), foreclosed application of the Sixth Amendment to events before the initiation of adversary criminal proceedings.

The Court finds that protections against identifications do not go to prosecutors' trial preparation interviews of witnesses. Given what you now know about memory, does this seem fair? Although it may seem unfair, it is difficult to imagine that constitutional protections would apply given the obvious impact it could have on preparation for trials and prosecutors' interactions with witnesses. Or is the impact not that obvious?

What do you make of the Court's argument that "the ethical responsibility of the prosecutor" is in itself a sufficient "safeguard" against impermissible suggestion at a photographic display? The same argument might, of course, be made with respect to lineups. Moreover, the prosecutor is not always present at such pretrial displays. Indeed, in this very case, one of the four eyewitnesses was shown the color photographs on the morning of trial by an FBI agent in the absence of the prosecutor. And even though "the ethical responsibility of the prosecutor" might be an adequate "safeguard" against intentional suggestion, prosecutors are not unaffected by human biases. His behavior may be fraught with unintentional and unconscious nuances that might effectively suggest the "proper" response. And, as *Wade* makes clear, unlike other forms of unintentional prosecutorial "manipulation," even unintentional suggestiveness at an identification procedure involves serious risks of "freezing" the witness' mistaken identification and creates almost insurmountable obstacles to reconstruction at trial.

Review Problem Two

Evidence at trial showed that two men entered a Chicago savings and loan association. One of them pointed a gun at a teller and ordered her to put money into a sack which the gunman supplied. The men remained in the bank about five minutes. After they left, a bank employee rushed to the street and saw one of the men sitting on the passenger side of a departing white 1960 Thunderbird automobile with a large scrape on the right door. Within an hour police located in the vicinity a car matching this description. They discovered that it belonged to the sister-in-law of petitioner Simmons. She told the police that she had loaned the car for the afternoon to her brother, Andrews. At about 5:15 p. m. the same day, two FBI agents came to Andrews' mother's house, about half a block from the place where the car was then parked. The agents searched the house and found two suitcases. One suitcase contained, among other items, a gun holster, a sack similar to the one used in the robbery, and several coin cards and bill wrappers from the bank which had been robbed. The following morning the FBI obtained from another of Andrews' sisters some snapshots of Andrews and of petitioner Simmons, who was said by the sister to have been with Andrews the previous afternoon. These snapshots were shown to the five bank employees who had witnessed the robbery. Each witness identified pictures of Simmons as representing one of the robbers. Simmons and others subsequently were indicted and tried for the robbery. During the trial, all five bank employee witnesses identified Simmons as one of the robbers. On appeal, Simmons asserted that his pretrial identification by means of photographs was in the circumstances so unnecessarily suggestive and conducive to misidentification as to deny him due process of law.

The Supreme Court held that each case must be considered on its own facts, and that convictions based on eyewitness identification at trial following a pretrial identification by photograph will be set aside on that ground only if the photographic identification procedure was so impermissibly suggestive as to give rise to a very substantial likelihood of irreparable misidentification. The Court found that the resort to photographic identification was not unnecessary given that a serious felony had been committed; the perpetrators were still at large; inconclusive clues led to Simmons; and it was essential for the FBI agents swiftly to determine whether they were on the right track, so that they could properly deploy their forces in Chicago and, if necessary, alert officials in other cities. The Court also found that there was little chance that the procedure utilized led to misidentification of Simmons. Five bank employees had been able to see the robber later identified as Simmons for periods ranging up to five minutes. Those witnesses were shown the photographs only a day later, while their memories were still fresh. At least six photographs were displayed to each witness. Apparently, these consisted primarily of group photographs, with Simmons appearing several times in the series. Each witness was alone when he or she saw the photographs. There was no evidence to indicate that the witnesses were told anything about the progress of the investigation, or that the FBI agents in any other way suggested which persons in the pictures were under suspicion. *Simmons v. U.S.*, 390 U.S. 377 (1968).

Note the Court's reasoning for the use of this standard in non-corporeal identifications. The Court had reasoned that, despite the hazards of initial identification by photograph, this procedure had been used widely and effectively in criminal law enforcement, from the standpoint both of apprehending offenders and of sparing innocent suspects the ignominy of arrest by allowing eyewitnesses to exonerate them through scrutiny of photographs. It further reasoned that the danger that use of the technique may result in convictions based on misidentification may be substantially lessened by a course of cross-examination at trial which exposes to the jury the method's potential for error. Importantly, however, in this case, the prosecutor had been unable to state which pictures had been used and had not returned the pictures. The Court held that the trial Court had not abused its discretion in not requiring the prosecutors to present the pictures. Fair?

NOTE ON THE EFFECTIVENESS OF ERROR DETECTION AND CORRECTION ABILITIES

Commentators suggest several factors that question the extent to which criminal litigation processes can be viewed as a reliable source of error-detection and -correction. Most generally, the usual measures relied on in that process all rely on the adversarial system. Litigation safeguards may be inadequate to the task of catching and correcting eyewitness error. For example, the presence-of-counsel safeguard is of questionable effectiveness because attorneys are rarely present at identification tests, and, when they are, they may not fully understand the factors that influence suggestiveness. In addition, the process of uncovering bias during jury selection – voir dire – is unlikely to be effective because characteristics identifiable before trial, such as attitudes toward eyewitnesses, do not predict juror bias. Likewise, cross-examination appears to be ineffective because jurors tend to rely on factors that do not predict identification accuracy and ignore factors that do affect accuracy. Furthermore, as we will see below, expert testimony has shown some success at sensitizing jurors to factors affecting eyewitness memory, but such testimony usually is ruled inadmissible. Lastly, traditional judicial instructions about eyewitness memory do not sensitize jurors effectively, but some evidence suggests that careful instructions can assist jurors. If attorneys either do not make or do not prevail on a motion to suppress possibly biased eyewitness evidence, then it will be left for the jury – aided perhaps by cross-examination, expert testimony, or closing argument – to evaluate the credibility of the eyewitness evidence. Regrettably, studies taking a variety of approaches to assessing jurors' beliefs and assumptions, including surveys, "postdiction" studies (which ask jurors to postdict the outcome of a previously conducted identification procedure), and mock trials reveal that jurors do not protect reliably against erroneous convictions based on false eyewitness evidence. Veronica Stinson, Jennifer L. Devenport, Brian L. Cutler, and David A. Kravitz, Judges' perceptions of the suggestiveness and fairness of biased lineup procedures, 82 J. Appl. Psych. 211 (1997).

RESEARCH NOTE ON EYEWITNESS EXPERT TESTIMONY

The adversarial system of justice traditionally has relied on cross-examination to alert the jury to any inaccuracies or inconsistencies in the testimony of an eyewitness. When coupled with proper cautionary instructions regarding eyewitness testimony, the legal system presumes the jury's ability to assess the credibility and reliability of each witness. However, cross-examination may not be as effective as intended. Problematic facts are easily elicited on cross-examination, but juries may well discount the damage. To complicate matters, cross-examination tends to target, shape, and make salient exactly what can most mislead jurors: eyewitness confidence. Although witness confidence can be undermined by cross-examination, it does not necessarily enhance the fact-finders' ability to detect eyewitness error. In addition, the pretrial briefing of witnesses often bolsters their confidence against attacks. Likewise, it may well be that attorneys do not know the correct accuracy-relevant factors to highlight during cross-examination or summation. Evidence also reveals that judges' instructions do not effectively teach jurors about how to evaluate eyewitness testimony. Despite these possibilities, the judiciary has not warmly received expert testimony. A leading commentator has challenged that failure and offered evidence to debunk the five major reasons not to offer expert testimony: 1. The scientific basis of research and theory is insufficient; 2. juror knowledge is sufficient already; 3. experts would usurp the jury's role; 4. prejudicial effects exceed probative value; and 5. traditional devices for challenging eyewitnesses are effective. What the evidence does reveal in terms of the predictable impact of expert testimony on juries is that it heightens juror skepticism – reduces belief in the eyewitness, reflected in ratings of his or her credibility, verdict preferences, or both. The skepticism effect transcends the eyewitness-presentation context and occurs with real eyewitnesses and with reasonably realistic trial simulations. Michael R. Lieppe, The case for expert testimony about eyewitness memory, 1 Psych. Pub. Pol'y and L. 909 (1995).

Chapter 3

SEARCHING SUSPECTS

INTRODUCTION

The Fourth Amendment's twin probable cause and warrant requirements prohibit law enforcement from conducting arbitrary searches of someone's home, papers, belongings or their physical person. To protect citizens from such searches, the Amendment imposes four fundamental requirements on the issuance and execution of search warrants.[1] First, the search warrant must be issued by a "neutral and detached magistrate" to ensure that the assessment of probable cause remains unbiased. Second, the Fourth Amendment requires law enforcement agents to support their request for a search warrant with a showing of probable cause. Third, the Fourth Amendment commands that officers attest to the legitimacy of all search warrants by oath or affirmation.[2] Fourth, the Fourth Amendment requires law enforcement agents to draft search warrants "particularly describing" the items to be seized.

The Amendment's language obviously presents difficulties for law enforcement; and the legal system attempts to adjust.[3] For example, the inherent difficulties of describing something not yet seen pose obvious problems. To address that challenge, the legal system looks to the purpose of this requirement and focuses on the need to describe "particularly." As a result, the focus centers on the need to discourage exploratory searches. The search warrant only need be sufficiently definite so as to allow the executing officer to identify the property sought with reasonable certainty. Requirements regarding the need to describe places follow a similar approach; the search warrant will be valid if the officer executing the warrant can with reasonable effort identify the described place. Relatedly, requirements that warrants be supported by oaths typically lead courts to inquire whether the procedures followed were such that a charge of perjury could be claimed against the officer.

In addition to adjusting the Amendment's literal language regarding the nature of warrants, the Supreme Court now recognizes various exceptions to these procedural safeguards.[4] These exceptions legitimize searches conducted without following the Constitution's explicit warrant requirement. First, Fourth Amendment jurisprudence permits searches without warrants if the searches fall within a traditional exception, such as those incident to arrest, justified by exigent circumstances, and part of routine inventories. Second, several types of searches do not even qualify as "searches" for 4th Amendment

---

[1] The Fourth Amendment provides "The right of the people to be secure in their persons, houses, papers, and effects, against unreasonable searches and seizures, shall not be violated, and no Warrants shall issue, but upon probable cause, supported by Oath or affirmation, and particularly describing the place to be searched, and the persons or things to be seized."

[2] Note that an oath simply means that the officer attests to the veracity of his claims made to the neutral magistrate. An affirmation is a solemn declaration that serves the same purpose as an oath (if an oath is objectionable to the person on religious or ethical grounds).

[3] See Wayne R. LaFave and Jerold H. Israel, Criminal Procedure (2d ed. 1992).

[4] Joshua Dressler, Understanding Criminal Procedure 183-240 (3rd ed. 2002); and Charles H. Whitebread and Christopher Slobogin, Criminal Procedure: An Analysis of Cases and Concepts (4th ed. 2000).

purposes. Law enforcement may rummage through garbage, fly airplanes and helicopters over backyards, deploy undercover agents, subpoena bank records, and use a host of other investigative activities. The Supreme Court interprets these activities as not infringing on reasonable expectations of privacy and therefore as not constituting searches for purposes of Constitutional regulation. As a result, these "searches" are not regulated by the Fourth Amendment, which means that they need not be authorized by a warrant, nor be based on probable cause, nor be in any other way "reasonable." Third, even if particular law enforcement conduct infringes on reasonable expectations of privacy to the extent necessary to constitute a "search," only a person whose own "reasonable" expectations of privacy have been violated may invoke Fourth Amendment protections. The most clear example of this exception is the exclusionary rule the Court developed to deter Fourth Amendment violations; the rule makes it difficult to use the tainted evidence against a suspect. Fourth, a suspect may have standing to contest to a search; that is, the legal system may recognize the search as one that could be intrusive enough to implicate Fourth Amendment protections. Even in those cases, however, the search may not be subject to the "usual" warrant and probable cause requirements if it is thought to invade relatively less significant privacy interests. The Court holds, for instance, that people may have reduced expectations of privacy when in certain roles or contexts. This allows, for example, searches of mobile vehicles without a warrant and permits warrantless, suspicionless, drug and alcohol testing of certain employees. This approach coincides with the many exceptions highlighted above in that it deems certain situations unreasonable for any citizen to expect Fourth Amendment protection, such as a prison inmate's cell and anyone's property readily observable by the public. Lastly, searches without warrants, including those based on no suspicion of criminal activity and those that would invade one's reasonable expectations of privacy, are permissible based on a voluntary consent by an individual with the authority to consent to the search.

The basic rules regulating 4th Amendment law may seem simple enough. In fact, that is how they are meant to be. If doubt exists that a search can be done without a warrant and the search does not readily fall within an exception to the need for warrants, officers should get a warrant. This would seem to be consistent with the obvious language of the 4th Amendment. The rules are, however, rather complex when applied in real life situations. More importantly for our purposes, psychological sciences reveal realities that do not support well the fundamental assumptions on which the rules rest. Although we will continue to explore psychological issues relating to the 4th Amendment in the next chapter, two important areas of research – the current psychological understanding of privacy and the complexities of consent – go to the heart of this aspect of criminal justice processes and provide a good starting point to understand the psychological contours of 4th Amendment law.

Complexities of Consent

It is now well accepted that law enforcement considerably relies on consent searches. Estimates reveal that about ninety-eight percent of searches police conduct are executed without a warrant and pursuant to consent.[5] As we have just seen, the consent exception is valid only if the consent is voluntary and given by one with the authority to give such consent. This rule, especially in light of its rampant use, raises several issues worthy of close scrutiny: Why do individuals voluntarily consent to searches? Exactly what is meant by "voluntariness?" Do we simply mean the absence of coercion? Are we concerned with the behavior of the police, such as whether they have acted reasonably? Should the background, experience, race, or beliefs of the suspect matter? All of these issues actually raise important psychological issues, many aspects of which we will address in other chapters. For now, we look at the assumptions supporting the law's approach to consent and explore what basic psychological findings reveal about their validity.

[5] Richard Van Duizend, L. Paul Sutton, and Charlotte A. Carter, The Search Warrant Process: Preconceptions, Perceptions, and Practices 21 (1984).

Properly addressing the above concerns begins with understanding two realities surrounding issues of consent in the context of 4th Amendment law. One reality, of course, is that not all consensual searches uncover inculpating evidence. The other reality concerns the apparently irrational behavior of guilty suspects who, in the face of police authority, consent to searches. These points raise two preliminary policy issues. First, by not requiring procedural safeguards for consent searches, the approach plays down the impact that suspicionless consent searches have on innocent suspects. Because these searches are bound by the laws of probability to plague the innocent as well as the guilty, a substantial number of suspicionless consent searches inevitably target innocent suspects. In order to safeguard legitimate privacy interests, the rules require innocent suspects to assert their rights in defiance of police authority and to expect law enforcement to respect that assertion in the absence of a warrant or exceptions to the warrant rule. Second, for guilty suspects, the approach places considerable significance on their ability to refuse police requests. If the guilty voluntarily consent to searches, then law enforcement may use the fruits of those searches simply because it is good law enforcement: we want law enforcement to respond to crime, and consent to the privacy invasion is permissible without other due process procedures because the individual did not object to the search. Both of these concerns go to the heart of the nature of consent and both are subjects of debates regarding whether consent rules are consistent with the abilities of human nature.

A psychological perspective raises important concerns about the abilities of ordinary people to perform in a manner consistent with legal ideals. Common sense suggests that very few people, if any, feel comfortable refusing a police request, even when the encounter is otherwise perceived as amicable. In fact, even in the "best" of circumstances – a polite officer, without gun drawn, and familiar circumstances for the consenter – often results in a suspect's consent where they only have something to lose. This common sense proposition about the manner we respond to authority has received a fair amount of empirical attention and resulted in some of the most popular and widely accepted social science research. In this section, we explore some of those classic studies and apply them to encounters with police. In addition, we compliment those studies with more recent research dealing with the psychology of requests. To reflect on whether the research has practical significance, we complete our discussion with one more step. We examine available research on citizens' encounters with police to determine the extent to which psychological research actually reveals what our understanding of law enforcement suggests.

The Psychological Significance of Authority

Psychological theory and experiments on obedience to authority support the notion that many mechanically obey legitimate authority. The works of Stanley Milgram[6] and Leonard Bickman[7] together support the general premise that people have a deeply ingrained need to obey authority even when it is against their own best interest to do so, and that obedience increases when authority figures exhibit recognizable trappings of authority. Milgram and Bickman's work further reveals that obedience depends primarily on the perceived legitimacy of the authority figure, not on possibilities of punishment and compliance. Obedience does not depend on the presence or absence of physical coercion; physical coercion does not determine the voluntariness of an actor's decision. Most of us probably do not feel free to deny a request by a police officer simply because the request comes from an officer.

Milgram's experiments are widely understood as revealing the remarkable extent to which adults display obedience to authority figures. That respect for authority was exemplified by the manner subjects appeared to inflict severe pain on mock victims. Specifically, experimenters directed subjects to give progressively stronger electrical shocks to experimental learners if the learners gave incorrect replies to simple word-pair learning tasks. An actor – a confederate of the experimenter – was strapped in a chair with his arms restrained, and a subject was "selected" to be a teacher. Each actor pretended to fail the

[6] Stanley Milgram, Obedience to Authority (1974).
[7] Leonard Bickman, The social power of a uniform, 4 J. Appl. Soc. Psych. 47 (1974).

learning task so that the teacher would be able to follow the directive to administer a shock as negative feedback for failure to perform. The degree of obedience in continuing to administer shocks was measured in four situations of differing proximity, from a separate room to direct hand-to-hand contact between the subject and the "learner." In each setup, the "learner" gave stronger and stronger verbal protests as increasing voltage was applied, including a scream of great distress and a statement of withdrawal from the experiment at 300 volts, and a final scream of pain at 315 volts. A convincing fake shock generator provided the "energy" for the electric shocks. Its control panel consisted of a series of switches arranged in fifteen-volt increments, ranging in intensity from 15 to 450 volts. Additionally, a clearly labeled sign marked each group of four switches. Thus, the control panel displayed the following messages from left to right: "Slight Shock," "Moderate Shock," "Strong Shock," "Very Strong Shock," "Intense Shock," "Extremely Intense Shock," and "Danger: Severe Shock." Set apart at the far right of the panel were two lone switches marked "XXX" to ominously note extreme danger.

Before conducting the experiment, Milgram had surveyed a variety of sources, essentially all of which had predicted that subjects would refuse to obey the experimenter when the shocks obviously hurt another person. The predictions proved surprisingly inaccurate. With no visual cues about the distress of the learner, 65% of the subjects continued to deliver shocks to the maximum level, 450 volts. With vocal cues alone, 62.5% of the subjects delivered shocks to the maximum value. When confronted with victims in the same room, the percentage that shocked to the maximum dropped to 40%, and when required to have tactile contact, just 30% of the subjects reached the maximal shock. Some subjects obeyed experimenters even when they heard that the "learner" had a heart condition.

Milgram concluded that the unexpectedly high levels of obedience to authority derived from three basic factors. First, a variety of social forces prepare individuals to obey authority figures most of their lives (from parents in the family, ushers in movie theaters, to teachers in the classroom) in ways that define the individual's perception of legitimate authority. He argued that the power of the authority stems not from personal characteristics but from the authority figure's perceived position in a social structure. Second, subjects tended to see themselves as agents of the experimenters, not as the principle directors of the administration of shocks. The subjects assumed a submissive role that undermined their resolve to break with the experimenter's legitimate authority. Third, each subject brought traits that encouraged obedience, including politeness, a desire to adhere to the agreement with the researcher, anxiety, awkwardness at the prospect of stopping the experiment, and a tendency to continue in an experiment involving a series of small sequential steps. These factors help to explain how obedience depends on a number of interrelated factors. In this situation, all those factors operated independently of physical compulsion or the threat of physical compulsion to undermine the voluntariness of the subjects' behavior. Importantly, when the subjects were debriefed after the experiment, nearly all of them freely admitted that shocking the learner contradicted their sense of morality and reasoned judgment. Yet, nearly two-thirds performed acts inconsistent with their professed beliefs, even though no coercion or threat of coercion was brought to bear upon them.

Bickman conducted another group of classic studies. He investigated how the type of dress of individuals directing pedestrians to carry out simple tasks affects the degree of compliance to simple commands. To do so, he created three situations to examine the relationship between uniforms and social power. In the first situation, the wearer approached the randomly selected subject, pointed to a paper bag lying on the ground, and said, "Pick up this bag for me!" In the second situation, the wearer stopped the chosen subject, pointed to a confederate standing beside a car parked at a parking meter, and said, "This fellow is over-parked at the meter but doesn't have any change. Give him a dime!" In the third and final situation, the wearer approached a subject standing alone at a bus stop and exclaimed, "Don't you know you have to stand on the other side of the pole? The sign says 'No Standing'." The sign, of course, referred only to the fact that it was illegal for a car to park at a bus stop.

Bickman discovered that adult pedestrians obeyed young men wearing either a higher authority uniform or a lower authority uniform at a statistically significant increased rate than actors who wore a sports jacket and tie when commanding the experimental subjects. Those wearing a guard's uniform (even without a weapon) achieved significantly greater compliance than actors who wore either a milkman's uniform or a jacket and tie. For example, 82% of the subjects picked up trash when the "guard" directed them, versus 64% when a "milkman" told them to, and 36% when a civilian so directed. Similarly, 89% attempted to comply with a guard's request to find pocket change for someone else's parking meter, versus 57% and 33% compliance with a milkman and civilian request, respectively. Even with an unreasonable demand to leave an appropriate bus stop waiting area, 56% of the subjects complied with "guard" given instructions, versus 20-21% compliance with lower authority uniforms or no uniforms. Importantly, Bickman also conducted an experiment with college students as subjects to determine how well they could predict compliance with commands given by figures in the three types of garb. The students predicted no statistically significant effect from the presence of uniforms. These predictions proved woefully inaccurate, just as Milgram's study had first found that people would not inflict pain on others while the study found the complete opposite.

These experiments obviously remain limited. Critics of Milgram's study, for example, may charge that the study may not offer conclusive proof of the "power of the situation." Subjects may have obeyed the experimenter because he may have conveyed that nothing serious has or could happen. Likewise, the subjects could have taken for granted that the experimenter was responsible for the entire situation. In addition, the lessons of Milgram and Bickman's experiments may not prove very helpful to understanding actual police-citizen encounters. The magnitude of the harm/consequences to the individual, such as a minor inconvenience or minor emotional discomfort, may pale in comparison to the consequences of arrest and conviction. That possibility makes problematic analogizing between the reactions of persons to authority in the Milgram and Bickman experiments and police-citizen encounters. The experiments also may not translate to real-life encounters simply because they involved clear demands to do something by authority figures, not simple requests by those figures. The studies do not seem analogous to the consent situation because there may be obedience to a direct order by an authority figure but there still may be greater ability to resist a "request" issued by that same person. The experiments document that people readily comply with authority figures' demands, not the critical question of whether there is a "demand" in the first place (an issue we address below).

Despite their limitations, the studies may still provide useful insight. They may provide viable explanations as to why people follow or obey a police officer's "request" simply because officers occupy authority positions in situations where there is likely harm. Both the obedience and social power of the uniform theories reveal that the average citizen will find it difficult to avoid responding to a police officer. Regarding the limit to analogizing the experiments to the consent scenario, the parallels certainly are clear (such as the sequential questioning and uniform). The central issue becomes, however, whether individuals perceive requests by individuals in authority as demands. We already know that immense diversity exits, and even that some individuals from minority groups do view requests as demands to the extent that they are more likely to consent to searches.[8] Likewise, we know that individuals on the street are considerably more likely to comply with requests from persons perceived as having authority than with requests from those without such status: the role of those who make requests impacts our response.[9] This diversity and tendencies may reflect much broader psychological tendencies that emerge in the context of encounters with police.

---

[8] David Rudovsky, Law enforcement by stereotypes and serendipity racial profiling and stops and searches without cause, 3 U. Pa. J Const. L. 296 (2001).

[9] Like the Bickman investigation, another dressed individuals as a "bum," a business executive, or a fireman, and requested minor help from a pedestrian. Compliance ranged from 44% for requests from the "bum" to 82% for those from the fireman. Brad J. Bushman, Perceived symbols of authority and their influence on compliance, 14 J. Appl. Soc. Psych. 501, 506 (1984). Similar studies were conducted with women as the person making requests when wearing either a uniform, professional attire, or sloppy clothing. The results also suggested that a uniform is a certificate of legitimacy for females as well as males and that both sexes are influenced by a female dressed in a uniform. Brad J. Bushman, The effects of apparel on compliance: A field experiment with a female authority figure, 14 Personality and Soc. Psych. Bull. 459 (1988).

The Psychological Significance of Polite Requests

We have seen that a potential limitation of the research on people's obedience to authority is that its findings may not transfer to police demands that typically are framed as requests. The research suggested that, even if requests for searches are phrased as polite questions, they still may be perceived less as options than imperatives. This is within the realm of possibility. Most students who have not been exposed to the intricacies of criminal procedure, for example, are surprised to hear that they have a right to turn down a police "request" to search. Framing the demand as a request also raises many practical concerns. Most notably, unlike strict demands, requests may create situations in which people honestly misremember the circumstances surrounding consent, which makes it difficult to ever know whether the person consented, let alone felt pressure to consent. As it turns out, considerable psychological science theory and research offer support for these possibilities. This section examines that psychological research as well as research that addresses the issue that arises from it: what should the legal system do about these findings?

The research we have reviewed reveals that, because she is perceived as an authority, an officer need not rely on coercive statements to achieve a goal. Authorities need not demand compliance in order to communicate coercive potential; it is assumed. As a result, their speech is perceived to be powerful regardless of the type of directive they communicate. Despite the fact that neither imperatives nor suggestions explicitly mention a negative sanction, they most likely are interpreted by others as warnings of punishment for noncompliance. Research on verbal communication and social influence supports this point. When authorities make suggestions, they appear more sensitive than when they express imperatives, and that apparent sensitivity to those questioned increases the chances of compliance.[10]

The above understanding of requests actually has been the subject of research related to consent and searches. Researchers argue that any police suggestion, request, command, or threat is fraught with implications of legal control.[11] This creates a general willingness to comply with apparent public servants. These two factors mean, and studies have shown, that a police officer's friendly, nonthreatening initial approach actually is significantly *more* likely to produce compliance than is a forceful initial stance.[12] In the area of consent searches, search requests phrased interrogatively are more likely to produce the requested consent compared to those phrased declaratively.[13] Ironically, then, a consensual encounter may be effective precisely because it is deemed not confrontational, and consensual encounters may lead to more willingness to comply with officer commands than, for example, stops.

The creation of consensual encounters has important implications. As we already have seen, when encounters with police are deemed consensual, the Court interprets these interactions as outside of 4th Amendment protections. Given the possibility of acquiescence, the research seems to support some legal commentators who champion the need to require police to warn citizens of their right to refuse a request to search.[14] These commentators often argue that citizens partly feel coercion from lack of knowledge of their right to refuse the request. This appears quite reasonable: One cannot refuse if one is not aware that refusal is an option. By requiring police to advise suspects that they can refuse to cooperate with the request to search, the argument and assumption goes, we remove the coercive aspect of the request and allow citizens to make a free and informed choice. A further assumption is that if police are required to issue

---

[10] Sik Hung Ng and James J Bradac, Power in Language: Verbal Communication and Social Influence (1993); Jennifer L. Vollbrecht, Michael E. Roloff, and Gaylen D. Paulson, Coercive potential and face threatening sensitivity: The effects of authority and directives in social confrontation, 8 Int'l J. Conflict Mgmt. 235, 236 (1997); and Peter Tiersma, The judge as linguist, 27 Loyola LA L. Rev. 269 (1993); Herbert H. Clark and Michael F. Schober, Asking questions and influencing answers, in Questions About Questions 15, 15 (Judith M. Tanur, ed., 1992).

[11] Stephen D. Mastrofski, Jeffery B. Snipes, and Anne E. Supina, Compliance on demand: The public's response to specific police requests, 33 J. Res. Crime and Delinq. 269, 271 (1996).

[12] Stephen D. Mastrofski, Jeffery B. Snipes, and Anne E. Supina, Compliance on demand: The public's response to specific police requests, 33 J. Res. Crime and Delinq. 269, 271 (1996).

[13] Dorothy K. Kagehiro, Psycholegal research on the Fourth Amendment, 1 Psych.. Sci. 187, 188 (1990).

[14] Devon W. Carbado, Erasing the Fourth Amendment, 100 Mich. L Rev. 946, 1030 (2002); and Carol S. Steiker, How much justice can you afford? A response to Stuntz, 67 Geo. Wash. L. Rev. 1290, 1294 (1999).

Miranda-type warnings in consent search cases, the compliance rate will necessarily decrease because, armed with the knowledge that refusal is an option, some people will choose to refuse. That assumption turns out to be mistaken, at least in instances where it has been directly examined empirically. One ground-breaking study examined Ohio State Police consent search data both before and after the Ohio Supreme Court ruled that motorists who are stopped for traffic violations must be warned that they are free to leave prior to being asked by police for consent to search their vehicle.[15] The study examined all Ohio highway stops conducted between 1995 and 1997 and found no decrease in consent rates after police were required to advise motorists of their right to refuse to cooperate with a request for consent to search.[16] In fact, the same number of citizens consent with the warnings as without the warnings. Apparently, people are unaffected by the warnings because they do not believe them. People feel that they will be searched regardless of whether or not they consent. The study's comparison revealed that the rate at which motorists consented to searches actually *increased* nominally after the institution of warnings. An examination of data from a control group (Maryland, in which warnings were never instituted) revealed that a similar nominal increase occurred there during the same time period, suggesting that the Ohio warnings actually had no effect whatsoever on rates of consent to searches. It seems that people tend to know that polite requests are actually demands.

The Psychology and Significance of Decision Making under Time Pressure

Police encounters undoubtedly are complex. It does seem that they produce not only pressures in terms of roles people adopt but also pressures in terms of what the encounters require. Pressures to provide immediate answers challenge effective decision making. Numerous studies reveal that decisions made under time pressure use different processes from decisions made without time stress. Those studies also reveal that the use of those processes reduces the effectiveness of decision making.[17] People making decisions under time pressure engage in what has been termed "premature closure": they end their decision process prior to considering all the relevant information and alternatives.[18] For example, people under time pressure may seize onto the first information that attracts their attention and will ignore other more diagnostic information.[19] Likewise, people solving problems under time pressure fail to consider relevant information that people not under time pressure successfully do consider.[20] They also engage in defensive reactions, such as denying the importance of pieces of information.[21] People making decisions under time

---

[15] Note that the Supreme Court subsequently reversed and held that no such warning was necessary. *Ohio v. Robinette*, 519 U.S. 33 (1996).

[16] Illya D. Lichtenberg, Miranda in Ohio: The effects of *Robinette* on the "voluntary" waiver of Fourth Amendment rights, 44 Howard L. J. 349 (2001).

[17] Irving L. Janis, Stress, Attitude, and Decisions (1982); Dan Ariely and Dan Zakay, A timely account of the role of duration in decision making, 108 Acta Psychologica 187, 197 (2001); John W. Payne, James R. Bettman, and Mary Frances Luce, When time is money: Decision behavior under opportunity-cost time pressure, 66 Organ'l Beh. and Hum. Decision Processes 131 (1996); Jose H. Kerstholt, The effect of time pressure on decision-making behavior in a dynamic task environment, 86 Acta Psychologica 89 (1994); and Edward M. Bowden, Accessing relevant information during problem solving: Time constraints on search in the problem space, 13 Mem. and Cognition 280 (1985).

[18] Jay J. Christiansen-Szalanski, A Further examination of the selection of problem-solving strategies: The effects of deadlines and analytic aptitudes, 25 Organ'l Beh. and Hum. Decision Processes 107 (1980).

[19] Arie W. Kruglanski and Ofra Mayseless, Contextual effects in hypothesis testing: The rule of competing alternatives and epistemic motivations, 6 Soc. Cog. 1, 12-17 (1988).

[20] Edward M. Bowden, Accessing relevant information during problem solving: Time constraints on search in the problem space, 13 Mem. and Cog. 280, 284 (1985).

[21] Dan Ariely and Dan Zakay, A timely account of the role of duration in decision making, 108 Acta Psychologica 187, 197 (2001).

pressure also tend to rely on "accessible constructs" like stereotypes.[22] It is difficult to find research that finds positive effects of time pressure on decision making.

Social and cognitive psychologists understand the failures arising from time pressures as predictable results of our reliance on scripts to understand our social world. Recall that a script is a mental representation of a social situation as it unfolds over time.[23] Once activated, a script allows us more easily to interpret our perceptions and observations in a given situation. Events that always follow the same order become chronically associated, so that when we experience the first event we expect the next one to follow. In fact, our mental readiness to perceive events in a standard situation means that we often carry out what would be the next event in the script even when the prior event did not occur, simply because the superficial features of the situation follow the same form as the script.[24] The significance of these scripts derives from the remarkable extent to which people ordinarily have numerous event scripts at their disposal. In fact, scripts are so commonplace and so often used that we rely on them without realizing it – scripts are both automatic and pervasive.[25] This "automaticity" (automatic use of scripts) means that the social interaction, evaluation and judgment, and the operation of internal responses to the situation can all proceed without the intervention of conscious acts of will and guidance.[26] Once we become accustomed to relying on a particular script, the situation no longer requires the same level of conscious deliberation. Indeed, most of moment-to-moment psychological life must occur through nonconscious means if it is to occur at all.[27]

Script and automaticity theory and research suggest that, even though we do not necessarily interact often with police, our popular culture creates scripts for interacting with police officers that undoubtedly involve ready cooperation and compliance with requests. Automatic processing of scripts intensifies when the script involves interacting with an authority. The argument is that on-the-spot decisions about whether to comply with the request of an authority lead people to react, not think, in that people often react and respond to legitimate authority in a mindless, automatic, thoughtless, fast, and shallow manner with little processing.[28] Automatic activation and use of scripts play to our advantage as they allow us to avoid cognitive overload in our everyday affairs, but that advantage raises the specter that similar processing may well end up to our disadvantage.

The pressures of police-citizen encounters central to the complexities of consent are complicated further by the manner our memories work. The way our memories work challenges our best efforts to remember stressful encounters and raises issues regarding how best to fashion rules regulating those encounters. Police-citizen encounters are ripe with conditions that would cause individuals to misremember interactions. For example, requests to search may be responded to by uncertain and tentative communications with the officer, rather than clear rejections. This is exacerbated by the extent to which

---

[22] See Chi-yue Chiu, Michael W. Morris, Ying-yi Hong, and Tanya Menon, Motivated cultural cognition: The impact of implicit cultural theories on dispositional attribution varies as a function of need for closure, 78 J Personality and Soc. Psych. 247, 255-56 (2000).

[23] See Robert P. Abelson, Psychological status of the script concept, 36 Am. Psych. 715 (1981). For a more detailed review of how we make routine decisions, see Tilmann Betsch, Susanne Haberstroh, and Cornelia Hoehle, Explaining routinized decision making: A review of theories and model,12 Theory and Psych. 453 (2002).

[24] Ellen J. Langer, Arthur Blank, and Benzion Chanowitz, The mindlessness of ostensibly thoughtful action: The role of "placebic" information in interpersonal interaction, 36 J Personality and Soc. Psych. 635, 641 (1978); and John A. Bargh, Automaticity in social psychology, in Social Psychology: Handbook of Basic Principles 169, 179 (Tory Higgins and Arie W. Kruglanski, eds., 1996).

[25] Ellen J. Langer and Allison I. Piper, The psevention of mindlessness, 53 J Personality and Soc. Psych. 280, 280 (1987).

[26] John A. Bargh and Melissa J. Ferguson, Beyond behaviorism: On the automaticity of higher mental processes, 126 Psych. Bull. 925 (2000).

[27] Researchers have identified three major forms of automatic self-regulation: an automatic effect of perception on action, automatic goal pursuit, and a continual automatic evaluation of one's experience. From the accumulating evidence, researchers conclude that these various nonconscious mental systems perform the lion's share of the self-regulatory burden, beneficently keeping the individual grounded in his or her current environment. John A. Bargh and Tanya L. Chartrand, The unbearabale automaticity of being, 54 Am. Psych 462 (1999).

[28] John A. Bargh, Automaticity in social psychology, in Social Psychology: Handbook of Basic Principles 169, 170 (Tory Higgins and Arie W. Kruglanski, eds., 1996).

law enforcement need not take a "no" as an answer and may continue to request in order to obtain consent, unlike confessions which preclude the police from trying to encourage suspects to consent. These situations provide officers with the reasonable claim that, while they did not remember the exact words, the individual had no clear objection to the search. The suspect also will likely share the same fate and suffer from memory problems over time. The memory "problems" stem from the nature of the interaction.

The interaction may lead individuals to recall selectively what occurred in their encounter. The reason both officers and suspects have difficulty recalling many specifics partly stems from the manner our minds operate to restore cognitive dissonance. It is well known that individuals try to reduce internal inconsistencies between their beliefs and observations in order to establish internal harmony, consistency or congruity among opinions, attitudes, knowledge and values. As a result, when cognitive elements are in conflict, individuals tend to view their experiences in a modified manner, by using, among other psychological mechanisms, selective recall.[29] The power of selective recall is well understood; in fact, the gatekeeper to our memory is a process known as selective attention. We have seen how the process works to create distortions in what eyewitnesses perceive and later recall. This was, for example, a key component of "change blindness" discussed more fully in Chapter Two.[30] Many motivations also can create distortions, causing us to remember ourselves in a more favorable manner than we deserve, so that our memories become self serving. Importantly, our self-serving memories are rarely (or at least need not be) attempts to deceive others. Rather, they are unconscious reconstructions that bolster our self esteem, so that we can continue to think of ourselves in a positive light. As we have seen in Chapter One, individual differences in values and attitudes factor heavily in human perception, and we interpret massive amounts of information in ways that are most useful to us; we are biased in our assimilation.[31] That different actors in a police encounter may have different motivations supports the claim that even simple police requests may turn out considerably difficult to evaluate.

The Significance of Consent

The challenge to consent raises the practical issue of what we are to do to ensure appropriate respect for 4th Amendment principles. Accepting that requests for consent may be problematic means that we must return to consider the need for warrants or reconsider what the 4th Amendment actually requires. Whether warrants themselves are that protective actually is difficult to tell. The most authoritative information about the warrant process comes from a seven-jurisdiction study conducted by the National Center for State Courts (NCSC).[32] We already have reported a key finding of the study, that the "vast majority" of searches are conducted without a warrant, a finding that directly undercuts the ideal that warrants play a significant role in regulating police behavior. The study also reported, however, that warrants do figure prominently in searches of premises, universally considered the most private space. But findings about the warrant process make it difficult to determine whether warrants actually do provide any real privacy protection.

Many findings question the utility of warrants at least in terms of how they are supposed to offer a level of protection beyond the investigating officer. The NCSC study revealed that when police did seek a warrant, magistrates spent less than three minutes reviewing their application in 65% of the cases, devoted more than five minutes to the application in only 11% of the cases, and rejected only 8% of the applications. A separate study found that judges are even less likely to reject law enforcement requests for electronic surveillance warrants; of the 20,107 applications submitted for such warrants at the federal level

---

[29] Leon Festinger, A Theory of Cognitive Dissonance 260 (1957).

[30] Daniel T. Levin and Daniel J. Simons, Failure to detect changes to attended objects in motion pictures, 4 Psych. Bull. Rev. 501 (1997).

[31] See Robert J. MacCoun, Biases in the interpretation and use of research results, 49 Ann. Rev. Psych. 259 (1998).

[32] Richard Van Duizend, L. Paul Sutton, and Charlotte A. Carter, The Search Warrant Process: Preconceptions, Perceptions, and Practices 21 (1984).

between 1968 and 1995, only 27 were denied, and none were denied between 1988 and 1995.[33] The findings from that study have been reinforced by another study that examined 1748 warrant requests and found that a warrant was rejected in only one case.[34] These findings suggest that magistrates usually "rubberstamp" police applications, which has led some to conclude that the law's theoretical mandate for a neutral, independent judgment rarely takes place in practice. That conclusion is reinforced by the NCSC's finding that police often sought out particular magistrates believed to be friendly to police views on investigation.

Despite the above findings, at least three reasons support the belief that the warrant process discourages illegal searches.[35] First, the process may reduce judicial bias favoring the police (and therefore police reliance on such bias) because a magistrate grants or denies a warrant application before he knows whether the police will find the evidence. In contrast, judicial review of a warrantless search occurs after the search, typically during a hearing to suppress evidence. Because the magistrate in this hearing inevitably knows the police have found incriminating evidence, a real possibility exists that he may use hindsight reasoning,[36] which is known to infect other assessments of police behavior and may taint a judge's probable cause determination. Second, the warrant process may reduce illegality by making police fabrication difficult, again because the probable cause determination occurs before the search takes place. Yet, fabrication is relatively simple during ex post review of a warrantless search, when the officer can more easily concoct "justifications" for his actions based on known prior events.[37] Lastly, it may be that the warrant process works to curb inappropriate behavior because officers routinely request that their supervisors or the prosecutor check their application before submitting it to the magistrate. This leads some to the conclusion that the applications are so rarely rejected because they are meritorious. Conceivably, a three-minute review is all that is necessary in many cases, because police knowledge that a judicial officer will check their investigative efforts and reasoning, even if only in a cursory fashion, encourages genuine requests. However, the fact that prosecutors and police are involved does not necessary ensure that a neutral party has reviewed the warrant request. The factors identified as potentially creating a bias for police may still be at work, a possibility highlighted by the finding that only 5% of the warrants that are issued are subsequently found invalid.[38] This may mean several things, but it does at least indicate that the need for exclusion virtually disappears when the police do avail themselves of the warrant process.

Whether illegal searches would increase if the warrant requirement were abolished or relaxed remains unknown. Although studies have found that only approximately ten percent of those warrant-based searches that were challenged were found invalid, that failure rate is only slightly lower than the suppression rate of 14.6% for all searches.[39] Furthermore, even if police are found to violate the Fourth Amendment at a higher rate when they conduct warrantless searches, that differential could be due to a number of third factors, including a reviewing court's reluctance to second-guess a fellow judicial officer's warrant decision. A warrant requirement may even detract from effective law enforcement. According to the NCSC study, drafting and submitting a warrant application may take as long as half a day (although the advent of telephonic warrants in some jurisdictions has significantly reduced that period). If the only searches discouraged by this process are those for which the police lack probable cause, then the warrant requirement is functioning properly. But the requirement creates perverse incentives if the hassle of

---

[33] Christopher Slobogin, Criminal Procedure-Regulation of Police Investigation: Legal, Historical, Empirical and Comparative Materials 192 (2d ed. 1998).

[34] Craig D. Uchida and Timothy S. Bynum, Search warrants, motions to suppress and "lost cases": The effects of the exclusionary rule in seven jurisdictions, 81 J. Crim. L. and Criminology 1034, 1058 (1991).

[35] William J. Stuntz, Warrants and Fourth Amendment remedies, 77 Va. L. Rev. 881, 910-18 (1991).

[36] Psychologists identify the phenomenon as hindsight bias. Ralph Hertwig, Carola Fanselow, and Ulrich Hoffrage, Hindsight bias: How knowledge and heuristics affect our reconstruction of the past, 11 Memory 357 (2003).

[37] William J. Stuntz, Warrants and Fourth Amendment remedies, 77 Va. L. Rev. 881, 910-18 (1991).

[38] Richard Van Duizend, L. Paul Sutton, and Charlotte A. Carter, The search warrant process: Preconceptions, perceptions, and practices (1984).

[39] Peter Nardulli, The societal cost of the exclusionary rule: An empirical assessment, 1983 Am. Bar Found. Res. J. 585, 597 tbl.7 (1983). Note that the 10% is higher than the 5% noted above. The reason for the disparity apparently derives from the differences between challenging warrants and challenging searches resulting from such warrants.

obtaining a warrant discourages police from conducting searches in cases where probable cause exists. The cumbersome nature of the process may even encourage illegal searches if police try to evade it through dubious consent searches or arrests staged in areas where warrants are not required (e.g., the car). As one officer quoted in the NCSC study stated, 98% of his searches were conducted after securing the target's "consent," sometimes obtained through (often unfounded) threats to secure a warrant unless the target granted entry.

COMPLEXITIES OF PRIVACY

Supreme Court cases suggest a reliance on what the average citizen would feel about the impact of police investigative techniques on their privacy and autonomy. The Fourth Amendment does not protect expectations of privacy that only a criminal would have, intrusiveness under the Fourth Amendment must be considered from the viewpoint of an innocent person. These fundamentals of 4th Amendment law reveal the importance of understanding how citizens feel about police practices and the factors individuals consider in evaluating the intrusiveness of a search or seizure. Yet, surprisingly few studies have examined empirically the nature of privacy affected by 4th Amendment searches. In fact, only one groundbreaking study has sought to examine directly these complexities. Fortunately, that study has revealed important findings that help orient our understanding of the cases that follow.[40]

The study requested subjects to rank brief scenarios obtained from Supreme Court holdings to determine concurrences between legal views and community views of invasions of privacy. The study broadly confirmed Supreme Court holdings, which viewed, for example, forced hospital surgery on a shoulder to locate evidence and searches of a bedroom and bugging a phone as very intrusive searches. Likewise, they also viewed as much less intrusive searches of jail cells and flying over backyards, again in conformity with the Court's decisions. Yet, despite overall agreement, numerous instances of apparent disagreement with other Court holdings emerged in terms of the extent to which particular types of investigative actions implicate privacy interests. Key among those differences were the use of undercover agents to obtain information, which the Court does not view as a justifiable intrusion because one assumes the risk that one's acquaintances will reveal confidences. Relatedly, subjects viewed the government's use of bank deposits to be highly invasive, yet the Court has not viewed the use of bank deposit slips by officials as an inappropriate invasion of privacy. Likewise, police entry onto fenced-in private property outside the curtilage of the home was seen as highly intrusive, while the Court has not even seen it as a search; and "dog sniffs" were also seen as highly intrusive by layperson but not even a search according to the Court. Lastly, the many factors of general agreement listed at the beginning of this paragraph – inspections of jail cells and helicopter overflights, also were somewhat different in that subjects did view them as intrusive yet the Supreme Court does not even view them as searches.

The researchers posited many possible factors to explain the apparent incongruences. Most notably, individuals perceive searches of their own property or person as more intrusive than those of others. That is, individuals find privacy invasions less intrusive if they involve someone else. Likewise, the objective of the investigation matters. A search with a specified objective (such as a stop on the street to frisk for a gun or drugs) is viewed as less intrusive than an investigative action with no particular aim (such as a stop on the street), because the former action seems more justified. Relatedly, a search that is beneficial (to stop weapons from being carried on airplanes) may not even be viewed as searches at all. People may even be grateful for the intrusion.

---

[40] Christopher Slobogin and Joseph E. Schumacher, Reasonable expectations of privacy and autonomy in Fourth Amendment cases: An empirical look at "understandings recognized and permitted by society," 42 Duke L.J. 727 (1993); and Christopher Slobogin and Joseph E. Schumacher, Rating the intrusiveness of law enforcement searches and seizures, 17 L. and Hum. Beh. 183 (1993).

The above findings have important implications. These findings call into question judicial evaluations of the privacy and autonomy interests implicated by searches. Regarding the proposition that we undervalue the privacy of others compared to our own, judges whose cases invariably involve police actions that happen to other people might undervalue the intrusiveness of searches and seizures, at least as perceived by those members of society who have experienced them or something similar to them. Courts may suffer from a "distancing effect" in evaluating intrusiveness; they are evaluating the intrusion of others.[41] Regarding the view that the objective of the investigation matters heavily in determinations of appropriate intrusiveness, if we are to gauge the intrusiveness of a search from the perspective of an "innocent" person, then the courts may systematically underestimate the intrusiveness of various police actions given that they usually evaluate a search only if it has met its objective. Knowledge of the police objective lowers the perceived intrusiveness of police action. Even in those cases in which a target knows the police objective, the courts' evaluation is likely to be tainted by their further knowledge that the objective was achieved (for example, the gun was found) since such knowledge does not facilitate understanding of the innocent person's perspective. This finding reflects to some extent a "hindsight bias" effect, an effect caused by knowing or assuming the outcome of the action. In terms of reviewing courts, the finding suggests that the courts, which know not only the objective of the police but also that it was met, may find it difficult to evaluate intrusiveness from the perspective of the innocent individual the Supreme Court asks them to assume.

The implications of the inference of guilt and dangerousness theories challenge judicial assumptions of 4th Amendment jurisprudence. As earlier noted, the Court has held that intrusiveness under the Fourth Amendment should be considered from the viewpoint of an innocent person. And, it logically would seem that to the extent an intrusiveness rating rests on assumed guilt of the particular target or repugnance toward the criminal activity investigated, it should be invalid for Fourth Amendment purposes. Thus, for instance, the mere fact that the police have decided a person is subject to arrest, or are investigating organized crime rather than some lesser crime, should not normally affect measurement of the action's insult to privacy or autonomy. Similarly, the mere fact that the police do not appear to be after wrongdoing (but are merely asking, for example, about destination) should not elevate the level of intrusiveness above what it would be if the police's objective were unknown. Moreover, if the Fourth Amendment is at least partly about protecting individuals' privacy expectations, the state's needs should be irrelevant to what the individual is presumptively entitled to expect. The harm to the individual remains the same regardless of the nature and size of the governmental need. Strong state needs justify some intrusions on individual expectations but do not logically defeat the existence of those expectations or their reasonableness. Rather, whether to recognize the existence of a reasonable privacy expectation is best understood as a normative question turning on fundamental notions of individual and group identity.

NOTES AND QUERIES

Do you find persuasive the psychological findings relating to people's responses to authority? Do you find them useful to understanding encounters with police? Why do you supposed that most students tend to accept, for example, Milgram's findings yet also tend to ignore those analyses when determining whether someone consented to searches? In addition, if we took this area of research seriously in thinking about the law's approach to consent in Fourth Amendment contexts, it would seem that it would undermine the legal

---

[41] Social psychologists long have revealed that we distance ourselves from others when the others have characteristics that we fear in ourselves. Jeff Schimel, Tom Pyszczynski, Jeff Greenberg, Heather O'Mahen and Jamie Arndt, Running from the shadow: Psychological distancing from others to deny characteristics people fear in themselves, 78 J. of Personality and Soc. Psych. 446 (2000). As we will see in later chapters on punishment, we also may try to distance ourselves from others who have experienced events we fear. To make matters worse, we actually may have a tendency to project fear of what we are like, or what may happen to us, onto others. Jeff Schimel, Jeff Greenberg, and Andy Martens, Evidence that projection of a feared trait can serve a defensive function, 29 Personality and Soc. Psych. Bull. 969 (2003).

system's approach. When you read the cases that follow, attempt to envision how the legal system reflects an awareness of the phenomena identified by psychological research and the extent to which they could be taken more seriously.

What do you make of the argument that time pressure and polite requests contribute to automaticity in our interactions with officers? Reasonable argument? Should it be taken seriously or ignored? What about the studies challenging the utility of warrants? Believable? What implications arise from those findings? What other information would you need before you take the findings seriously? Does that suggest that even better data may not impact appreciably Fourth Amendment jurisprudence?

In its analysis of search law, the Supreme Court places great emphasis on whether the police investigative action infringes on "reasonable expectations of privacy" or produces certain feelings that would be deemed "reasonable" intrusions effecting certain "reasonable" responses. To determine those factors, the Court has stated that community values about intrusiveness should heavily influence, if not dictate, those determinations. The results and explanations set forth above provide some initial evidence about those values; they also suggest that the Supreme Court's conclusions about the scope of the Fourth Amendment are often not consistent with commonly held attitudes about police investigative techniques. In considering the validity of searches, then, much of our concern will focus on determining their appropriateness, the standard to determine appropriateness, as well as the extent to which relevant considerations relate to popular conceptions and important policy objectives. As a result, we necessarily will return to the need to balance the Due Process Model and Crime Control Model we identified in Chapter One.

The results reveal that searches of people who appear to be "guilty" will be ranked less intrusively than searches and seizures of "innocent" people. They also show that the investigative method used to search will be rated as relatively unintrusive if it is believed that the crime being investigated is particularly dangerous. Does that seem appropriate? Note that the above findings do not necessarily mean that the legal system should alter its approaches. It may well be, for example, that judges are able to take the view of innocent individuals. It also may be that the findings, even if accurate and reflective of judicial abilities, are inconsequential to the extent that law enforcement must be given freedom to investigate and prevent criminal activity. It may also be that laymen do not quite understand the need for privacy intrusions which, properly understood, would lead to more concordance between laymen and the Court's decisions. As it currently is, however, which view do you think the legal system should respect: the Court's view or that of laymen who provide commonsense judgments that reflect current societal realities?

FRAMING THE LAW'S APPROACHES

KATZ v. U.S.
389 U.S. 347 (1967)

MR. JUSTICE STEWART delivered the opinion of the Court.

The petitioner [Katz] was convicted in the District Court for the Southern District of California under an eight-count indictment charging him with transmitting wagering information by telephone from Los Angeles to Miami and Boston, in violation of a federal statute. At trial the Government was permitted, over the petitioner's objection, to introduce evidence of the petitioner's end of telephone conversations, overheard by FBI agents who had attached an electronic listening and recording device to the outside of the public telephone booth from which he had placed his calls. In affirming his conviction, the Court of Appeals rejected the contention that the recordings had been obtained in violation of the Fourth Amendment, because "there was no physical entrance into the area occupied by [the petitioner]." We granted certiorari in order to consider the constitutional questions thus presented.

Because of the misleading way the issues have been formulated, the parties have attached great significance to the characterization of the telephone booth from which the petitioner placed his calls. The petitioner has strenuously argued that the booth was a "constitutionally protected area." The Government has maintained with equal vigor that it was not. But this effort to decide whether or not a given "area," viewed in the abstract, is "constitutionally protected" deflects attention from the problem presented by this case. For the Fourth Amendment protects people, not places. What a person knowingly exposes to the public, even in his own home or office, is not a subject of Fourth Amendment protection. But what he seeks to preserve as private, even in an area accessible to the public, may be constitutionally protected.

The Government stresses the fact that the telephone booth from which the petitioner made his calls was constructed partly of glass, so that he was as visible after he entered it as he would have been if he had remained outside. But what he sought to exclude when he entered the booth was not the intruding eye – it was the uninvited ear. He did not shed his right to do so simply because he made his calls from a place where he might be seen. No less than an individual in a business office, in a friend's apartment, or in a taxicab, a person in a telephone booth may rely upon the protection of the Fourth Amendment. One who occupies it, shuts the door behind him, and pays the toll that permits him to place a call is surely entitled to assume that the words he utters into the mouthpiece will not be broadcast to the world. To read the Constitution more narrowly is to ignore the vital role that the public telephone has come to play in private communication.

The Government contends, however, that the activities of its agents in this case should not be tested by Fourth Amendment requirements, for the surveillance technique they employed involved no physical penetration of the telephone booth from which the petitioner placed his calls. It is true that the absence of such penetration was at one time thought to foreclose further Fourth Amendment inquiry, for that Amendment was thought to limit only searches and seizures of tangible property. But "the premise that property interests control the right of the Government to search and seize has been discredited." ... Once this much is acknowledged, and once it is recognized that the Fourth Amendment protects people – and not simply "areas" – against unreasonable searches and seizures, it becomes clear that the reach of that Amendment cannot turn upon the presence or absence of a physical intrusion into any given enclosure.

We conclude that the underpinnings of ... [prior opinions grounding search and seizure law in property interests] have been so eroded by our subsequent decisions that the "trespass" doctrine there enunciated can no longer be regarded as controlling. The Government's activities in electronically listening to and recording the petitioner's words violated the privacy upon which he justifiably relied while using the telephone booth and thus constituted a "search and seizure" within the meaning of the Fourth Amendment. The fact that the electronic device employed to achieve that end did not happen to penetrate the wall of the booth can have no constitutional significance.

The question remaining for decision, then, is whether the search and seizure conducted in this case complied with constitutional standards. In that regard, the Government's position is that its agents acted in an entirely defensible manner: They did not begin their electronic surveillance until investigation of the petitioner's activities had established a strong probability that he was using the telephone in question to transmit gambling information to persons in other States, in violation of federal law. Moreover, the surveillance was limited, both in scope and in duration, to the specific purpose of establishing the contents of the petitioner's unlawful telephonic communications. The agents confined their surveillance to the brief periods during which he used the telephone booth, and they took great care to overhear only the conversations of the petitioner himself.

Accepting this account of the Government's actions as accurate, it is clear that this surveillance was so narrowly circumscribed that a duly authorized magistrate ... could constitutionally have authorized, with appropriate safeguards, the very limited search and seizure that the Government asserts in fact took place...

The Government urges that, because its agents ... did no more here than they might properly have done with prior judicial sanction, we should retroactively validate their conduct. That we cannot do. It is apparent that the agents in this case acted with restraint. Yet the inescapable fact is that this restraint was imposed by the agents themselves, not by a judicial officer. They were not required, before commencing the search, to present their estimate of probable cause for detached scrutiny by a neutral magistrate. They were not compelled, during the conduct of the search itself, to observe precise limits established in advance by a specific court order. Nor were they directed, after the search had been completed, to notify the authorizing magistrate in detail of all that had been seized. In the absence of such safeguards, this Court has never sustained a search upon the sole ground that officers reasonably expected to find evidence of a particular crime and voluntarily confined their activities to the least intrusive means consistent with that end. Searches conducted without warrants have been held unlawful "notwithstanding facts unquestionably showing probable cause," for the Constitution requires "that the deliberate, impartial judgment of a judicial officer . . . be interposed between the citizen and the police . . . ." "Over and again this Court has emphasized that the mandate of the [Fourth] Amendment requires adherence to judicial processes," and that searches conducted outside the judicial process, without prior approval by judge or magistrate, are per se unreasonable under the Fourth Amendment – subject only to a few specifically established and well-delineated exceptions.

The Government does not question these basic principles. Rather, it urges the creation of a new exception to cover this case. It argues that surveillance of a telephone booth should be exempted from the usual requirement of advance authorization by a magistrate upon a showing of probable cause. We cannot agree. Omission of such authorization bypasses the safeguards provided by an objective predetermination of probable cause, and substitutes instead the far less reliable procedure of an after-the-event justification for the . . . search, too likely to be subtly influenced by the familiar shortcomings of hindsight judgment.

And bypassing a neutral predetermination of the scope of a search leaves individuals secure from Fourth Amendment violations "only in the discretion of the police."

...Wherever a man may be, he is entitled to know that he will remain free from unreasonable searches and seizures. The government agents here ignored "the procedure of antecedent justification....that is central to the Fourth Amendment," a procedure that we hold to be a constitutional precondition of the kind of electronic surveillance involved in this case. Because the surveillance here failed to meet that condition, and because it led to the petitioner's conviction, the judgment must be reversed.

It is so ordered.

MR. JUSTICE MARSHALL took no part in the consideration or decision of this case.

MR. JUSTICE DOUGLAS, with whom MR. JUSTICE BRENNAN joins, concurring. [opinion omitted]

MR. JUSTICE HARLAN, concurring.

As the Court's opinion states, "the Fourth Amendment protects people, not places." The question, however, is what protection it affords to those people. Generally, as here, the answer to that question requires reference to a "place." My understanding of the rule that has emerged from prior decisions is that there is a twofold requirement, first that a person have exhibited an actual (subjective) expectation of privacy and, second, that the expectation be one that society is prepared to recognize as "reasonable." Thus a man's home is, for most purposes, a place where he expects privacy, but objects, activities, or statements that he exposes to the "plain view" of outsiders are not "protected" because no intention to keep them to himself has been exhibited. On the other hand, conversations in the open would not be protected against being overheard, for the expectation of privacy under the circumstances would be unreasonable.

MR. JUSTICE WHITE, concurring. [opinion omitted]

MR. JUSTICE BLACK, dissenting.

My basic objection is twofold: (1) I do not believe that the words of the Amendment will bear the meaning given them by today's decision, and (2) I do not believe that it is the proper role of this Court to rewrite the Amendment in order "to bring it into harmony with the times" and thus reach a result that many people believe to be desirable.

While I realize that an argument based on the meaning of words lacks the scope, and no doubt the appeal, of broad policy discussions and philosophical discourses on such nebulous subjects as privacy, for me the language of the Amendment is the crucial place to look in construing a written document such as our Constitution. The Fourth Amendment says that

> The right of the people to be secure in their persons, houses, papers, and effects, against unreasonable searches and seizures, shall not be violated, and no Warrants shall issue, but upon probable cause, supported by Oath or affirmation, and particularly describing the place to be searched, and the persons or things to be seized.

The first clause protects "persons, houses, papers, and effects, against unreasonable searches and seizures . . ." These words connote the idea of tangible things with size, form, and weight, things capable of being searched, seized, or both. The second clause of the Amendment still further establishes its Framers' purpose to limit its protection to tangible things by providing that no warrants shall issue but those "particularly describing the place to be searched, and the persons or things to be seized." A conversation overheard by eavesdropping, whether by plain snooping or wiretapping, is not tangible and, under the normally accepted meanings of the words, can neither be searched nor seized. In addition the language of the second clause indicates that the Amendment refers not only to something tangible so it can be seized but to something already in existence so it can be described. Yet the Court's interpretation would have the Amendment apply to overhearing future conversations which by their very nature are nonexistent until they take place. How can one "describe" a future conversation, and, if one cannot, how can a magistrate issue a warrant to eavesdrop one in the future? It is argued that information showing what is expected to be said is sufficient to limit the boundaries of what later can be admitted into evidence; but does such general information really meet the specific language of the Amendment which says "particularly describing"? Rather than using language in a completely artificial way, I must conclude that the Fourth Amendment simply does not apply to eavesdropping.

Tapping telephone wires, of course, was an unknown possibility at the time the Fourth Amendment was adopted. But eavesdropping (and wiretapping is nothing more than eavesdropping by telephone) was ... recognized, [as] "an ancient practice which at common law was condemned as a nuisance. In those days the eavesdropper listened by naked ear under the eaves of houses or their windows, or beyond their walls seeking out private discourse." There can be no doubt that the Framers were aware of this practice, and if they had desired to outlaw or restrict the use of evidence obtained by eavesdropping, I believe that they would have used the appropriate language to do so in the Fourth Amendment. They certainly would not have left such a task to the ingenuity of language-stretching judges. No one, it seems to me, can read the debates on the Bill of Rights without reaching the conclusion that its Framers and critics well knew the meaning of the words they used, what they would be understood to mean by others, their scope and their limitations. Under these circumstances it strikes me as a charge against their scholarship, their common sense and their candor to give to the Fourth Amendment's language the eavesdropping meaning the Court imputes to it today.

...I simply cannot in good conscience give a meaning to words which they have never before been thought to have and which they certainly do not have in common ordinary usage. I will not distort the words of the Amendment in order to "keep the Constitution up to date" or "to bring it into harmony with the times." It was never meant that this Court have such power, which in effect would make us a continuously functioning constitutional convention.

The Fourth Amendment protects privacy only to the extent that it prohibits unreasonable searches and seizures of "persons, houses, papers, and effects." No general right is created by the Amendment so as to give this Court the unlimited power to hold unconstitutional everything which affects privacy. Certainly the Framers, well acquainted as they were with the excesses of governmental power, did not intend to grant this Court such omnipotent lawmaking authority as that. The history of governments proves that it is dangerous to freedom to repose such powers in courts.

For these reasons I respectfully dissent.

NOTES AND QUERIES

Katz breaks new ground as it frames Fourth Amendment principles in terms of privacy protections. What do you make of Justice Black's dissent of that approach? Do you think Justice Black has the better argument?

Katz teaches us that officers must show probable cause before searching and they must limit their search to what is approved in advance. The simple reason for that protection is that people must know that they are free from unreasonable searches and seizures. What do you make of the complications in this case due to being unable to apply this rule to conversations? The issue is addressed by the Court in its discussion of *Osborn.* The Court notes that, although the protections afforded the petitioner in *Osborn* were "similar . . . to those . . . of conventional warrants," they were not identical. A conventional warrant ordinarily serves to notify the suspect of an intended search. But if *Osborn* had been told in advance that federal officers intended to record his conversations, the point of making such recordings would obviously have been lost; the evidence in question could not have been obtained. In omitting any requirement of advance notice, the federal court that authorized electronic surveillance in *Osborn* simply recognized that officers need not announce their purpose before conducting an otherwise authorized search if such an announcement would provoke the escape of the suspect or the destruction of critical evidence.

Justice White, in his concurring opinion, makes the important note that the case leaves undisturbed prior cases that the Court upheld as reasonable under the Fourth Amendment and therefore admissible at trial of evidence obtained (1) by an undercover police agent to whom a defendant speaks without knowledge that he is in the employ of the police, (2) by a recording device hidden on the person of such an informant, and (3) by a policeman listening to the secret micro-wave transmissions of an agent conversing with the defendant in another location. He points out that, when one man speaks to another he takes all the risks ordinarily inherent in so doing, including the risk that the man to whom he speaks will make public what he has heard. The Fourth Amendment does not protect against unreliable (or law-abiding) associates. It is but a logical and reasonable extension of this principle that a man takes the risk that his hearer, free to memorize what he hears for later verbatim repetitions, is instead recording it or transmitting it to another. The present case deals with an entirely different situation, for as the Court emphasizes the petitioner "sought to exclude ... the uninvited ear" and spoke under circumstances in which a reasonable person would assume that uninvited ears were not listening.

Is it your view that *Katz* offers very broad Fourth Amendment protections? How do later cases deal with this approach to Fourth Amendment law?

TECHNOLOGICALLY ENHANCED SEARCHES

KYLLO v. U.S.
533 U.S. 27 (2001)

JUSTICE SCALIA delivered the opinion of the Court.

I.

In 1991 Agent William Elliott of the United States Department of the Interior came to suspect that marijuana was being grown in the home belonging to petitioner Danny Kyllo, part of a triplex on Rhododendron Drive in Florence, Oregon. Indoor marijuana growth typically requires high-intensity lamps. In order to determine whether an amount of heat was emanating from petitioner's home consistent with the use of such lamps, at 3:20 a.m. on January 16, 1992, Agent Elliott and Dan Haas used an Agema Thermovision 210 thermal imager to scan the triplex. Thermal imagers detect infrared radiation, which virtually all objects emit but which is not visible to the naked eye. The imager converts radiation into images based on relative warmth – black is cool, white is hot, shades of gray connote relative differences; in that respect, it operates somewhat like a video camera showing heat images. The scan of Kyllo's home took only a few minutes and was performed from the passenger seat of Agent Elliott's vehicle across the street from the front of the house and also from the street in back of the house. The scan showed that the roof over the garage and a side wall of petitioner's home were relatively hot compared to the rest of the home and substantially warmer than neighboring homes in the triplex. Agent Elliott concluded that petitioner was using halide lights to grow marijuana in his house, which indeed he was. Based on tips from informants, utility bills, and the thermal imaging, a Federal Magistrate Judge issued a warrant authorizing a search of petitioner's home, and the agents found an indoor growing operation involving more than 100 plants. Petitioner was indicted on one count of manufacturing marijuana. He unsuccessfully moved to suppress the evidence seized from his home and then entered a conditional guilty plea.

The Court of Appeals for the Ninth Circuit remanded the case for an evidentiary hearing regarding the intrusiveness of thermal imaging. On remand the District Court found that the Agema 210 "is a non-intrusive device which emits no rays or beams and shows a crude visual image of the heat being radiated from the outside of the house"; it "did not show any people or activity within the walls of the structure"; "the device used cannot penetrate walls or windows to reveal conversations or human activities"; and "no intimate details of the home were observed." Based on these findings, the District Court upheld the validity of the warrant that relied in part upon the thermal imaging, and reaffirmed its denial of the motion to suppress. A divided Court of Appeals ... held that petitioner had shown no subjective expectation of privacy because he had made no attempt to conceal the heat escaping from his home, and even if he had, there was no objectively reasonable expectation of privacy because the imager "did not expose any intimate details of Kyllo's life," only "amorphous 'hot spots' on the roof and exterior wall." We granted certiorari.

II.

One might think ... that examining the portion of a house that is in plain public view, while it is a "search" despite the absence of trespass, is not an "unreasonable" one under the Fourth Amendment. But in fact we have held that visual observation is no "search" at all .... In assessing when a search is not a search, we have applied somewhat in reverse the principle first enunciated in Katz v. United States. ... As Justice Harlan's oft-quoted concurrence described it, a Fourth Amendment search occurs when the government violates a subjective expectation of privacy that society recognizes as reasonable. We have subsequently applied this principle to hold that a Fourth Amendment search does not occur – even when the explicitly protected location of a house is concerned – unless "the individual manifested a subjective expectation of privacy in the object of the challenged search," and "society [is] willing to recognize that expectation as reasonable."..

The present case involves officers on a public street engaged in more than naked-eye surveillance of a home. We have previously reserved judgment as to how much technological enhancement of ordinary perception from such a vantage point, if any, is too much. ...

III.

...While it may be difficult to refine Katz when the search of areas such as telephone booths, automobiles, or even the curtilage and uncovered portions of residences are at issue, in the case of the search of the interior of homes – the prototypical and hence most commonly litigated area of protected privacy – there is a ready criterion, with roots deep in the common law, of the minimal expectation of privacy that exists, and that is acknowledged to be reasonable. To withdraw protection of this minimum expectation would be to permit police technology to erode the privacy guaranteed by the Fourth Amendment. We think that obtaining by sense-enhancing technology any information regarding the interior of the home that could not otherwise have been obtained without physical "intrusion into a constitutionally protected area" constitutes a search – at least where (as here) the technology in question is not in general public use. This assures preservation of that degree of privacy against government that existed when the Fourth Amendment was adopted. On the basis of this criterion, the information obtained by the thermal imager in this case was the product of a search.

The Government maintains, however, that the thermal imaging must be upheld because it detected "only heat radiating from the external surface of the house." The dissent makes this its leading point, contending that there is a fundamental difference between what it calls "off-the-wall" observations and "through-the-wall surveillance." ... While the technology used in the present case was relatively crude, the rule we adopt must take account of more sophisticated systems that are already in use or in development. ... As for the dissent's extraordinary assertion that anything learned through "an inference" cannot be a search, that would validate even the "through-the-wall" technologies that the dissent purports to disapprove. Surely the dissent does not believe that the through-the-wall radar or ultrasound technology produces an 8-by-10 Kodak glossy that needs no analysis (i.e., the making of inferences). ...

The Government also contends that the thermal imaging was constitutional because it did not "detect private activities occurring in private areas." It points out that in Dow Chemical we observed that the enhanced aerial photography did not reveal any "intimate details." Dow Chemical, however, involved enhanced aerial photography of an industrial complex, which does not share the Fourth Amendment sanctity of the home. The Fourth Amendment's protection of the home has never been tied to measurement of the quality or quantity of information obtained. ... In the home, our cases show, all details are intimate details, because the entire area is held safe from prying government eyes...

Limiting the prohibition of thermal imaging to "intimate details" would not only be wrong in principle; it would be impractical in application, failing to provide "a workable accommodation between the needs of law enforcement and the interests protected by the Fourth Amendment." To begin with, there is no necessary connection between the sophistication of the surveillance equipment and the "intimacy" of the details that it observes – which means that one cannot say (and the police cannot be assured) that use of the relatively crude equipment at issue here will always be lawful. The Agema Thermovision 210 might disclose, for example, at what hour each night the lady of the house takes her daily sauna and bath – a detail that many would consider "intimate"; and a much more sophisticated system might detect nothing more intimate than the fact that someone left a closet light on. We could not, in other words, develop a rule approving only that through-the-wall surveillance which identifies objects no smaller than 36 by 36 inches, but would have to develop a jurisprudence specifying which home activities are "intimate" and which are not. And even when (if ever) that jurisprudence were fully developed, no police officer would be able to know in advance whether his through-the-wall surveillance picks up "intimate" details – and thus would be unable to know in advance whether it is constitutional.

We have said that the Fourth Amendment draws "a firm line at the entrance to the house." That line, we think, must be not only firm but also bright – which requires clear specification of those methods of surveillance that require a warrant. While it is certainly possible to conclude from the videotape of the thermal imaging that occurred in this case that no "significant" compromise of the homeowner's privacy has occurred, we must take the long view, from the original meaning of the Fourth Amendment forward.

Where, as here, the Government uses a device that is not in general public use, to explore details of the home that would previously have been unknowable without physical intrusion, the surveillance is a "search" and is presumptively unreasonable without a warrant.

Since we hold the Thermovision imaging to have been an unlawful search, it will remain for the District Court to determine whether, without the evidence it provided, the search warrant issued in this case was supported by probable cause – and if not, whether there is any other basis for supporting admission of the evidence that the search pursuant to the warrant produced.

The judgment of the Court of Appeals is reversed; the case is remanded for further proceedings consistent with this opinion.

It is so ordered.

JUSTICE STEVENS, with whom THE CHIEF JUSTICE, JUSTICE O'CONNOR, and JUSTICE KENNEDY join, dissenting.

There is, in my judgment, a distinction of constitutional magnitude between "through-the-wall surveillance" that gives the observer or listener direct access to information in a private area, on the one hand, and the thought processes used to draw inferences from information in the public domain, on the other hand. The Court has crafted a rule that purports to deal with direct observations of the inside of the home, but the case before us merely involves indirect deductions from "off-the-wall" surveillance, that is, observations of the exterior of the home. Those observations were made with a fairly primitive thermal imager that gathered data exposed on the outside of petitioner's home but did not invade any constitutionally protected interest in privacy. Moreover, I believe that the supposedly "bright-line" rule the Court has created in response to its concerns about future technological developments is unnecessary, unwise, and inconsistent with the Fourth Amendment.

I.

There is no need for the Court to craft a new rule to decide this case, as it is controlled by established principles from our Fourth Amendment jurisprudence. One of those core principles, of course, is that "searches and seizures inside a home without a warrant are presumptively unreasonable." But it is equally well settled that searches and seizures of property in plain view are presumptively reasonable. Whether that property is residential or commercial, the basic principle is the same: "'What a person knowingly exposes to the public, even in his own home or office, is not a subject of Fourth Amendment protection.'" That is the principle implicated here.

Indeed, the ordinary use of the senses might enable a neighbor or passerby to notice the heat emanating from a building, particularly if it is vented, as was the case here. Additionally, any member of the public might notice that one part of a house is warmer than another part or a nearby building if, for example, rainwater evaporates or snow melts at different rates across its surfaces. Such use of the senses would not convert into an unreasonable search if, instead, an adjoining neighbor allowed an officer onto her property to verify her perceptions with a sensitive thermometer. Nor, in my view, does such observation become an unreasonable search if made from a distance with the aid of a device that merely discloses that the exterior of one house, or one area of the house, is much warmer than another. Nothing more occurred in this case.

...Heat waves, like aromas that are generated in a kitchen, or in a laboratory or opium den, enter the public domain if and when they leave a building. A subjective expectation that they would remain private is not only implausible but also surely not "one that society is prepared to recognize as 'reasonable.'"

To be sure, the homeowner has a reasonable expectation of privacy concerning what takes place within the home, and the Fourth Amendment's protection against physical invasions of the home should apply to their functional equivalent. But the equipment in this case did not penetrate the walls of petitioner's home, and while it did pick up "details of the home" that were exposed to the public, it did not obtain "any information regarding the interior of the home." In the Court's own words, based on what the thermal imager "showed" regarding the outside of petitioner's home, the officers "concluded" that petitioner was engaging in illegal activity inside the home. It would be quite absurd to characterize their thought processes as "searches," regardless of whether they inferred (rightly) that petitioner was growing marijuana in his house, or (wrongly) that "the lady of the house [was taking] her daily sauna and bath." In either case, the only conclusions the officers reached concerning the interior of the home were at least as indirect as those that might have been inferred from the contents of discarded garbage, or pen register data, or, as in this case, subpoenaed utility records. For the first time in its history, the Court assumes that an inference can amount to a Fourth Amendment violation.

Notwithstanding the implications of today's decision, there is a strong public interest in avoiding constitutional litigation over the monitoring of emissions from homes, and over the inferences drawn from such monitoring. Just as "the police cannot reasonably be expected to avert their eyes from evidence of criminal activity that could have been observed by any member of the public," so too public officials should not have to avert their senses or their equipment from detecting emissions in the public domain such as excessive heat, traces of smoke, suspicious odors, odorless gases, airborne particulates, or radioactive emissions, any of which could identify hazards to the community. In my judgment, monitoring such emissions with "sense-enhancing technology," and drawing useful conclusions from such monitoring, is an entirely reasonable public service.

On the other hand, the countervailing privacy interest is at best trivial. After all, homes generally are insulated to keep heat in, rather than to prevent the detection of heat going out, and it does not seem to me that society will suffer from a rule requiring the rare homeowner who both intends to engage in uncommon activities that produce extraordinary amounts of heat, and wishes to conceal that production from outsiders, to make sure that the surrounding area is well insulated. The interest in concealing the heat escaping from one's house pales in significance to the "the chief evil against which the wording of the Fourth Amendment is directed," the "physical entry of the home," and it is hard to believe that it is an interest the Framers sought to protect in our Constitution.

Since what was involved in this case was nothing more than drawing inferences from off-the-wall surveillance, rather than any "through-the-wall" surveillance, the officers' conduct did not amount to a search and was perfectly reasonable.

II.

...I would not erect a constitutional impediment to the use of sense-enhancing technology unless it provides its user with the functional equivalent of actual presence in the area being searched.

It is clear, however, that the category of "sense-enhancing technology" covered by the new rule is far too broad. It would, for example, embrace potential mechanical substitutes for dogs trained to react when they sniff narcotics. But in United States v. Place, we held that a dog sniff that "discloses only the presence or absence of narcotics" does "not constitute a 'search' within the meaning of the Fourth Amendment," and it must follow that sense-enhancing equipment that identifies nothing but illegal activity is not a search either. Nevertheless, the use of such a device would be unconstitutional under the Court's rule, as would the use of other new devices that might detect the odor of deadly bacteria or chemicals for making a new type of high explosive, even if the devices (like the dog sniffs) are "so limited in both the manner in which" they obtain information and "in the content of the information" they reveal. ...

The application of the Court's new rule to "any information regarding the interior of the home," is also unnecessarily broad. If it takes sensitive equipment to detect an odor that identifies criminal conduct and nothing else, the fact that the odor emanates from the interior of a home should not provide it with constitutional protection. The criterion, moreover, is too sweeping in that information "regarding" the interior of a home apparently is not just information obtained through its walls, but also information concerning the outside of the building that could lead to (however many) inferences "regarding" what might be inside. ...

I respectfully dissent.

Notes and Queries

Do you take Justice Scalia's opinion as one that limits the use of technologically sophisticated intrusions or one that increases the probability of their use by law enforcement? What do you make of his focus on whether or not the device is in general public use?

What do you make of the dissent's view that, essentially, the information received by the device was the same that could be had by a plain view? What about the claim that the privacy interest was trivial to the state interest in allowing such searches?

In deciding whether a particular type of physical surveillance is a search and, if so, how to regulate it, the courts have adopted a multi-factor approach. Although factors considered by courts inevitably overlap, it does seem that courts tend to apply seven major factors when examining the appropriateness of physical surveillance, whether or not it is technologically-aided: 1. The nature of the place subjected to physical surveillance (e.g., someone's home, cars, public areas); 2. The steps taken to enhance privacy (ten feet high fence, thick curtains); 3. The degree to which surveillance must physically intrude onto private property (dog sniffs, opening luggage); 4. The nature of the object of activity observed (growing illicit drugs, discarded trash); 5. The availability of the technology to the general public (binoculars, heat sensors, cameras); 6. The extent to which technology enhances the natural senses (satellites, flashlights, night-vision equipment); and 7. The steps taken to minimize intrusion (invasive, pervasiveness, etc.).

Why are dog sniffs not searches for the purposes of Fourth Amendment protections?

On July 3, 2001, the Tampa, Florida, Police Department began using FaceIt, a video surveillance system based on face-recognition software, in Ybor City, a downtown nightlife district. Three dozen security cameras scanned crowds while the software, using complex mathematical formulas to represent facial features, searched for database matches to the faces of wanted criminals. When no match was found, the scanned image was deleted, a precaution voluntarily undertaken by the system's owner, Visionics Corporation of Jersey City, New Jersey, but not required by law. If a match was found, however, a systems operator would then determine whether there was enough of a match to notify a uniformed officer to investigate and possibly make an arrest. Signs in the area warned passersby, "Smart CCTV in use," though most interviewed for a news story on the system did not know what the message meant. The technology is growing; the Pentagon funds a fifty-million dollar initiative to use face-recognition technology as a means for combating terrorism. Importantly, the technology has been used at the Super Bowl, casinos, Sat Lake Winter Olympics, and at Tampa airport. The FaceIt system represents the tip of the iceberg in the growing potential use of surveillance technologies, including "ray-gun distance frisks," mandatory, nationwide DNA databases covering all United States residents, long-distance, hard-to-detect cyber-searches, retinal scanning, and radioactive "tag" alerts. Susan McCoy, O'big brother where art thou?: The constitutional use of facial-recognition technology, 20 J. Marshall J. Computer and Info. L. 471 (2002). For an analysis of other technologies, see Christopher Slobogin, Technologically-assisted physical surveillance: The American Bar Association's tentative draft standards, 10 Harv. J.L. and Tech. 383 (1997).

INVASIVE SEARCHES

SCHMERBER v. CALIFORNIA
384 U.S. 757 (1966)

MR. JUSTICE BRENNAN delivered the opinion of the Court.

Petitioner was convicted in Los Angeles Municipal Court of the criminal offense of driving an automobile while under the influence of intoxicating liquor. He had been arrested at a hospital while receiving treatment for injuries suffered in an accident involving the automobile that he had apparently been driving. At the direction of a police officer, a blood sample was then withdrawn from petitioner's body by a physician at the hospital. The chemical analysis of this sample revealed a percent by weight of alcohol in his blood at the time of the offense which indicated intoxication, and the report of this analysis was admitted in evidence at the trial. Petitioner objected to receipt of this evidence of the analysis on the ground that the blood had been withdrawn despite his refusal, on the advice of his counsel, to consent to the test. He contended that in that circumstance the withdrawal of the blood and the admission of the analysis in evidence denied him due process of law under the Fourteenth Amendment, as well as specific guarantees of the Bill of Rights secured against the States by that Amendment: his privilege against self-incrimination under the Fifth Amendment; his right to counsel under the Sixth Amendment; and his right not to be subjected to unreasonable searches and seizures in violation of the Fourth Amendment. The Appellate Department of the California Superior Court rejected these contentions and affirmed the conviction. ... we granted certiorari. We affirm.

I.

THE DUE PROCESS CLAUSE CLAIM

Breithaupt was also a case in which police officers caused blood to be withdrawn from the driver of an automobile involved in an accident, and in which there was ample justification for the officer's conclusion that the driver was under the influence of alcohol. There, as here, the extraction was made by a physician in a simple, medically acceptable manner in a hospital environment. There, however, the driver was unconscious at the time the blood was withdrawn and hence had no opportunity to object to the procedure.

We affirmed the conviction there resulting from the use of the test in evidence, holding that under such circumstances the withdrawal did not offend "that 'sense of justice' of which we spoke in Rochin v. California. Breithaupt thus requires the rejection of petitioner's due process argument, and nothing in the circumstances of this case or in supervening events persuades us that this aspect of Breithaupt should be overruled.

II.

THE PRIVILEGE AGAINST SELF-INCRIMINATION CLAIM

It could not be denied that in requiring petitioner to submit to the withdrawal and chemical analysis of his blood the State compelled him to submit to an attempt to discover evidence that might be used to prosecute him for a criminal offense. He submitted only after the police officer rejected his objection and directed the physician to proceed. The officer's direction to the physician to administer the test over petitioner's objection constituted compulsion for the purposes of the privilege. The critical question, then, is whether petitioner was thus compelled "to be a witness against himself."

If the scope of the privilege coincided with the complex of values it helps to protect, we might be obliged to conclude that the privilege was violated. ... The withdrawal of blood necessarily involves puncturing the skin for extraction, and the percent by weight of alcohol in that blood, as established by chemical analysis, is evidence of criminal guilt. Compelled submission fails on one view to respect the "inviolability of the human personality." Moreover, since it enables the State to rely on evidence forced from the accused, the compulsion violates at least one meaning of the requirement that the State procure the evidence against an accused "by its own independent labors."

...however, the privilege has never been given the full scope which the values it helps to protect suggest. History and a long line of authorities in lower courts have consistently limited its protection to situations in which the State seeks to submerge those values by obtaining the evidence against an accused through "the cruel, simple expedient of compelling it from his own mouth. . . . In sum, the privilege is fulfilled only when the person is guaranteed the right 'to remain silent unless he chooses to speak in the unfettered exercise of his own will.'" ...

It is clear that the protection of the privilege reaches an accused's communications, whatever form they might take, and the compulsion of responses which are also communications, for example, compliance with a subpoena to produce one's papers. On the other hand, both federal and state courts have usually held that it offers no protection against compulsion to submit to fingerprinting, photographing, or measurements, to write or speak for identification, to appear in court, to stand, to assume a stance, to walk, or to make a particular gesture. The distinction which has emerged, often expressed in different ways, is that the privilege is a bar against compelling "communications" or "testimony," but that compulsion which makes a suspect or accused the source of "real or physical evidence" does not violate it.

Although we agree that this distinction is a helpful framework for analysis, we are not to be understood to agree with past applications in all instances. There will be many cases in which such a distinction is not readily drawn. Some tests seemingly directed to obtain "physical evidence," for example, lie detector tests measuring changes in body function during interrogation, may actually be directed to eliciting responses which are essentially testimonial. To compel a person to submit to testing in which an effort will be made to determine his guilt or innocence on the basis of physiological responses, whether willed or not, is to evoke the spirit and history of the Fifth Amendment. Such situations call to mind the principle that the protection of the privilege "is as broad as the mischief against which it seeks to guard."

In the present case, however, no such problem of application is presented. Not even a shadow of testimonial compulsion upon or enforced communication by the accused was involved either in the extraction or in the chemical analysis. ...

III.

THE RIGHT TO COUNSEL CLAIM

This conclusion also answers petitioner's claim that, in compelling him to submit to the test in face of the fact that his objection was made on the advice of counsel, he was denied his Sixth Amendment right to the assistance of counsel. Since petitioner was not entitled to assert the privilege, he has no greater right because counsel erroneously advised him that he could assert it. ...

IV.

THE SEARCH AND SEIZURE CLAIM

...But if compulsory administration of a blood test does not implicate the Fifth Amendment, it plainly involves the broadly conceived reach of a search and seizure under the Fourth Amendment. That Amendment expressly provides that "the right of the people to be secure in their persons, houses, papers, and effects, against unreasonable searches and seizures, shall not be violated . . . ." It could not reasonably be argued, and indeed respondent does not argue, that the administration of the blood test in this case was free of the constraints of the Fourth Amendment. Such testing procedures plainly constitute searches of "persons," and depend antecedently upon seizures of "persons," within the meaning of that Amendment.

...In other words, the questions we must decide in this case are whether the police were justified in requiring petitioner to submit to the blood test, and whether the means and procedures employed in taking his blood respected relevant Fourth Amendment standards of reasonableness.

In this case, as will often be true when charges of driving under the influence of alcohol are pressed, these questions arise in the context of an arrest made by an officer without a warrant. Here, there was plainly probable cause for the officer to arrest petitioner and charge him with driving an automobile while under the influence of intoxicating liquor. The police officer who arrived at the scene shortly after the accident smelled liquor on petitioner's breath, and testified that petitioner's eyes were "bloodshot, watery, sort of a glassy appearance." The officer saw petitioner again at the hospital, within two hours of the accident. There he noticed similar symptoms of drunkenness. ...

While early cases suggest that there is an unrestricted "right on the part of the Government, always recognized under English and American law, to search the person of the accused when legally arrested to discover and seize the fruits or evidences of crime," the mere fact of a lawful arrest does not end our inquiry. The suggestion of these cases apparently rests on two factors – first, there may be more immediate danger of concealed weapons or of destruction of evidence under the direct control of the accused; second, once a search of the arrested person for weapons is permitted, it would be both impractical and unnecessary to enforcement of the Fourth Amendment's purpose to attempt to confine the search to those objects alone. Whatever the validity of these considerations in general, they have little applicability with respect to searches involving intrusions beyond the body's surface. The interests in human dignity and privacy which the Fourth Amendment protects forbid any such intrusions on the mere chance that desired evidence might be obtained. In the absence of a clear indication that in fact such evidence will be found, these fundamental human interests require law officers to suffer the risk that such evidence may disappear unless there is an immediate search.

Although the facts which established probable cause to arrest in this case also suggested the required relevance and likely success of a test of petitioner's blood for alcohol, the question remains whether the arresting officer was permitted to draw these inferences himself, or was required instead to procure a warrant before proceeding with the test. Search warrants are ordinarily required for searches of dwellings, and, absent an emergency, no less could be required where intrusions into the human body are concerned. The requirement that a warrant be obtained is a requirement that the inferences to support the search "be drawn by a neutral and detached magistrate instead of being judged by the officer engaged in the often competitive enterprise of ferreting out crime." The importance of informed, detached and deliberate determinations of the issue whether or not to invade another's body in search of evidence of guilt is indisputable and great.

The officer in the present case, however, might reasonably have believed that he was confronted with an emergency, in which the delay necessary to obtain a warrant, under the circumstances, threatened "the destruction of evidence." We are told that the percentage of alcohol in the blood begins to diminish shortly after drinking stops, as the body functions to eliminate it from the system. Particularly in a case such as this, where time had to be taken to bring the accused to a hospital and to investigate the scene of the accident, there was no time to seek out a magistrate and secure a warrant. Given these special facts, we conclude that the attempt to secure evidence of blood-alcohol content in this case was an appropriate incident to petitioner's arrest.

Similarly, we are satisfied that the test chosen to measure petitioner's blood-alcohol level was a reasonable one. Extraction of blood samples for testing is a highly effective means of determining the degree to which a person is under the influence of alcohol. Such tests are a commonplace in these days of periodic physical examinations and experience with them teaches that the quantity of blood extracted is minimal, and that for most people the procedure involves virtually no risk, trauma, or pain. ...

Finally, the record shows that the test was performed in a reasonable manner. Petitioner's blood was taken by a physician in a hospital environment according to accepted medical practices. ...

We thus conclude that the present record shows no violation of petitioner's right under the Fourth and Fourteenth Amendments to be free of unreasonable searches and seizures. ... That we today hold that the Constitution does not forbid the States minor intrusions into an individual's body under stringently limited conditions in no way indicates that it permits more substantial intrusions, or intrusions under other conditions.

Affirmed.

MR. JUSTICE HARLAN, whom MR. JUSTICE STEWART joins, concurring. [omitted]

MR. CHIEF JUSTICE WARREN, dissenting. [omitted]

MR. JUSTICE BLACK with whom MR. JUSTICE DOUGLAS joins, dissenting.

...I disagree with the Court's holding that California did not violate petitioner's constitutional right against self-incrimination when it compelled him, against his will, to allow a doctor to puncture his blood vessels in order to extract a sample of blood and analyze it for alcoholic content, and then used that analysis as evidence to convict petitioner of a crime.

The Court admits that "the State compelled [petitioner] to submit to an attempt to discover evidence [in his blood] that might be [and was] used to prosecute him for a criminal offense." To reach the conclusion that compelling a person to give his blood to help the State convict him is not equivalent to compelling him to be a witness against himself strikes me as quite an extraordinary feat...

In the first place it seems to me that the compulsory extraction of petitioner's blood for analysis so that the person who analyzed it could give evidence to convict him had both a "testimonial" and a "communicative nature." The sole purpose of this project which proved to be successful was to obtain "testimony" from some person to prove that petitioner had alcohol in his blood at the time he was arrested. And the purpose of the project was certainly "communicative" in that the analysis of the blood was to supply information to enable a witness to communicate to the court and jury that petitioner was more or less drunk.

I think it unfortunate that the Court rests so heavily for its very restrictive reading of the Fifth Amendment's privilege against self-incrimination on the words "testimonial" and "communicative." These words are not models of clarity and precision as the Court's rather labored explication shows. ...

How can it reasonably be doubted that the blood test evidence was not in all respects the actual equivalent of "testimony" taken from petitioner when the result of the test was offered as testimony, was considered by the jury as testimony, and the jury's verdict of guilt rests in part on that testimony? ...

MR. JUSTICE DOUGLAS, dissenting.

We are dealing with the right of privacy which, ... we have held to be within the penumbra of some specific guarantees of the Bill of Rights. Thus, the Fifth Amendment marks "a zone of privacy" which the Government may not force a person to surrender. Likewise the Fourth Amendment recognizes that right when it guarantees the right of the people to be secure "in their persons." No clearer invasion of this right of privacy can be imagined than forcible bloodletting of the kind involved here.

MR. JUSTICE FORTAS, dissenting.

I would reverse. In my view, petitioner's privilege against self-incrimination applies. I would add that, under the Due Process Clause, the State, in its role as prosecutor, has no right to extract blood from an accused or anyone else, over his protest. As prosecutor, the State has no right to commit any kind of violence upon the person, or to utilize the results of such a tort, and the extraction of blood, over protest, is an act of violence.

NOTES AND QUERIES

Schmerber makes numerous constitutional claims. Why does extracting someone's blood not shock the conscience and thereby violate the Fourth Amendment? Why is the evidence neither testimonial nor communicative when the evidence will be incriminating? Note that the search and seizure did fall under the protection of the Fourth Amendment. Once that was established, there was a need to examine its reasonableness. The Court finds the intrusion both minor and reasonable. What arguments can you make against that claim?

Schmerber cites to *Rochin v. California*, 342 U.S. 165 (1952), another leading case which had held that certain types of investigative intrusions into the body are impermissible even under the authority of search warrants. In that case, three sheriffs had "some information" that the suspect, Rochin, was selling narcotics. On arriving at the two-story dwelling house in which Rochin lived with his mother, common-law wife, brothers and sisters, the found the outside door open. They then entered and forced open the door to Rochin's room on the second floor. Inside they found him sitting partly dressed on the side of the bed, upon which his wife was lying. On a "night stand" beside the bed the deputies spied two capsules. When asked "Whose stuff is this?" Rochin seized the capsules and put them in his mouth. A struggle ensued, in the course of which the three officers "jumped upon him" and attempted to extract the capsules. The force they applied proved unavailing against Rochin's resistance. He was handcuffed and taken to a hospital. At the direction of one of the officers, a doctor forced an emetic solution through a tube into Rochin's stomach against his will. This "stomach pumping" produced vomiting. In the vomited matter were found two capsules which proved to contain morphine. Rochin was charged and convicted of possessing "a preparation of morphine." He appealed the admission of the two capsules into evidence on grounds that they were obtained in violation of his due process rights. On appeal, the District Court of Appeals affirmed the conviction, despite the finding that the officers "were guilty of unlawfully breaking into and entering defendant's room and were guilty of unlawfully assaulting and battering defendant while in the room," and "were guilty of unlawfully assaulting, battering, torturing and falsely imprisoning the defendant at the alleged hospital. The Supreme Court found a due process violation. It summarized the due process of law constitutional guarantees as those personal immunities which are "so rooted in the traditions and conscience of our people as to be ranked as fundamental," or are "implicit in the concept of ordered liberty." Applying those standards, the Court found that the sheriffs' conduct shocked the conscience.

Scmerber involved a sense of urgency. What if there is no such urgency and the search constitutes a highly invasive bodily intrusion? Should an officer get a warrant authorizing the specific procedure? The Supreme Court has suggested that an adversarial proceeding is required prior to invasive intrusions, at which the government will need to sustain a higher than usual burden. The leading case in this area, *Winston v. Lee*, 470 U.S. 753 (1985), involved surgery to remove a bullet from a defendant's collarbone. The Court found such intrusions impermissible, even with a warrant, as it listed three factors such cases should consider: (1) the extent to which the procedure threatens the safety or health of the individual, (2) the extent to which the intrusion impinges on the individual's "dignitary interests in personal privacy and bodily integrity," and (3) the extent to which prohibiting the intrusion would affect the community's interest in fairly and accurately determining guilt or innocence.

BOND v. U.S.
529 U.S. 334 (2000)

CHIEF JUSTICE REHNQUIST delivered the opinion of the Court.

Petitioner Steven Dewayne Bond was a passenger on a Greyhound bus that left California bound for Little Rock, Arkansas. The bus stopped, as it was required to do, at the permanent Border Patrol checkpoint in Sierra Blanca, Texas. Border Patrol Agent Cesar Cantu boarded the bus to check the immigration status of its passengers. After reaching the back of the bus, having satisfied himself that the passengers were lawfully in the United States, Agent Cantu began walking toward the front. Along the way, he squeezed the soft luggage which passengers had placed in the overhead storage space above the seats.

Petitioner was seated four or five rows from the back of the bus. As Agent Cantu inspected the luggage in the compartment above petitioner's seat, he squeezed a green canvas bag and noticed that it contained a "brick-like" object. Petitioner admitted that the bag was his and agreed to allow Agent Cantu to open it. Upon opening the bag, Agent Cantu discovered a "brick" of methamphetamine. The brick had been wrapped in duct tape until it was oval-shaped and then rolled in a pair of pants.

Petitioner was indicted for conspiracy to possess, and possession with intent to distribute, methamphetamine.... He moved to suppress the drugs, arguing that Agent Cantu conducted an illegal search of his bag. Petitioner's motion was denied, and the District Court found him guilty ... On appeal, he conceded that other passengers had access to his bag, but contended that Agent Cantu manipulated the bag in a way that other passengers would not. The Court of Appeals rejected this argument, stating that the fact that Agent Cantu's manipulation of petitioner's bag was calculated to detect contraband is irrelevant for Fourth Amendment purposes. [Note that the Government did not argue that petitioner's consent to Agent Cantu's opening the bag was a basis for admitting the evidence.] Thus, the Court of Appeals affirmed the denial of the motion to suppress, holding that Agent Cantu's manipulation of the bag was not a search within the meaning of the Fourth Amendment. We granted certiorari and now reverse.

The Fourth Amendment provides that "the right of the people to be secure in their persons, houses, papers, and effects, against unreasonable searches and seizures, shall not be violated . . . ." A traveler's personal luggage is clearly an "effect" protected by the Amendment. Indeed, it is undisputed here that petitioner possessed a privacy interest in his bag.

But the Government asserts that by exposing his bag to the public, petitioner lost a reasonable expectation that his bag would not be physically manipulated. The Government relies on our decisions ... for the proposition that matters open to public observation are not protected by the Fourth Amendment. In Ciraolo, we held that police observation of a backyard from a plane flying at an altitude of 1,000 feet did not violate a reasonable expectation of privacy. Similarly, in Riley, we relied on Ciraolo to hold that police observation of a greenhouse in a home's curtilage from a helicopter passing at an altitude of 400 feet did not violate the Fourth Amendment. We reasoned that the property was "not necessarily protected from inspection that involves no physical invasion," and determined that because any member of the public could have lawfully observed the defendants' property by flying overhead, the defendants' expectation of privacy was "not reasonable and not one 'that society is prepared to honor.'"

But Ciraolo and Riley are different from this case because they involved only visual, as opposed to tactile, observation. Physically invasive inspection is simply more intrusive than purely visual inspection. ...Although Agent Cantu did not "frisk" petitioner's person, he did conduct a probing tactile examination of petitioner's carry-on luggage. Obviously, petitioner's bag was not part of his person. But travelers are particularly concerned about their carry-on luggage; they generally use it to transport personal items that, for whatever reason, they prefer to keep close at hand.

Here, petitioner concedes that, by placing his bag in the overhead compartment, he could expect that it would be exposed to certain kinds of touching and handling. But petitioner argues that Agent Cantu's physical manipulation of his luggage "far exceeded the casual contact [petitioner] could have expected from other passengers." The Government counters that it did not.

Our Fourth Amendment analysis embraces two questions. First, we ask whether the individual, by his conduct, has exhibited an actual expectation of privacy; that is, whether he has shown that "he [sought] to preserve [something] as private." Here, petitioner sought to preserve privacy by using an opaque bag and placing that bag directly above his seat. Second, we inquire whether the individual's expectation of privacy is "one that society is prepared to recognize as reasonable." When a bus passenger places a bag in an overhead bin, he expects that other passengers or bus employees may move it for one reason or another. Thus, a bus passenger clearly expects that his bag may be handled. He does not expect that other passengers or bus employees will, as a matter of course, feel the bag in an exploratory manner. But this is exactly what the agent did here. We therefore hold that the agent's physical manipulation of petitioner's bag violated the Fourth Amendment.

The judgment of the Court of Appeals is

Reversed.

JUSTICE BREYER, with whom JUSTICE SCALIA joins, dissenting.

Does a traveler who places a soft-sided bag in the shared overhead storage compartment of a bus have a "reasonable expectation" that strangers will not push, pull, prod, squeeze, or otherwise manipulate his luggage? Unlike the majority, I believe that he does not.

Petitioner argues – and the majority points out – that, even if bags in overhead bins are subject to general "touching" and "handling," this case is special because "Agent Cantu's physical manipulation of [petitioner's] luggage 'far exceeded the casual contact [he] could have expected from other passengers.'" ... Although the agent acknowledged that his practice was to "squeeze [bags] very hard," he testified that his touch ordinarily was not "hard enough to break something inside that might be fragile." Petitioner also testified that Agent Cantu "reached for my bag, and he shook it a little, and squeezed it."

How does the "squeezing" just described differ from the treatment that overhead luggage is likely to receive from strangers in a world of travel that is somewhat less gentle than it used to be? I think not at all. The trial court, which heard the evidence, saw nothing unusual, unforeseeable, or special about this agent's squeeze. It found that Agent Cantu simply "felt the outside of Bond's softside green cloth bag," and it viewed the agent's activity as "minimally intrusive touching." The Court of Appeals also noted that, because "passengers often handle and manipulate other passengers' luggage," the substantially similar tactile inspection here was entirely "foreseeable."

The record and these factual findings are sufficient to resolve this case. The law is clear that the Fourth Amendment protects against government intrusion that upsets an "actual (subjective) expectation of privacy" that is objectively "'reasonable.'" Privacy itself implies the exclusion of uninvited strangers, not just strangers who work for the Government. Hence, an individual cannot reasonably expect privacy in respect to objects or activities that he "knowingly exposes to the public."

Of course, the agent's purpose here – searching for drugs – differs dramatically from the intention of a driver or fellow passenger who squeezes a bag in the process of making more room for another parcel. But in determining whether an expectation of privacy is reasonable, it is the effect, not the purpose, that matters. Few individuals with something to hide wish to expose that something to the police, however careless or indifferent they may be in respect to discovery by other members of the public. Hence, a Fourth Amendment rule that turns on purpose could prevent police alone from intruding where other strangers freely tread. And the added privacy protection achieved by such an approach would not justify the harm worked to law enforcement – at least that is what this Court's previous cases suggest.

Nor can I accept the majority's effort to distinguish "tactile" from "visual" interventions, even assuming that distinction matters here. Whether tactile manipulation (say, of the exterior of luggage) is more intrusive or less intrusive than visual observation (say, through a lighted window) necessarily depends on the particular circumstances.

If we are to depart from established legal principles, we should not begin here. At best, this decision will lead to a constitutional jurisprudence of "squeezes," thereby complicating further already complex Fourth Amendment law, increasing the difficulty of deciding ordinary criminal matters, and hindering the administrative guidance (with its potential for control of unreasonable police practices) that a less complicated jurisprudence might provide. At worst, this case will deter law enforcement officers searching for drugs near borders from using even the most non-intrusive touch to help investigate publicly exposed bags. ...

For these reasons, I dissent.

Notes and Queries

Like *Schmerber*, this case involves an intrusion that is recognized as a search. Unlike that case, however, the majority finds the search unreasonable. Do you find it odd that we would not allow a search of someone's bags but would allow the extraction of blood? Should it not be the reverse if we are concerned with protecting the dignity, either psychological or physical, of individuals? What rationales support the argument that the Supreme Court has things backward? Why do those rationales lose? Which do you find to constitute the most reasonable expectation of privacy? Which police response is really the more reasonable?

What do you make of the dissent's view that we should not focus on the purpose of searches, that such a focus would unacceptably hamper law enforcement? In this case, for example, the officers' purpose was clear – they were searching for drugs. Why would we want to focus on the purpose if we are to compare officers with passengers who move and feel luggage? Does the dissent have it right?

Search Incident to Arrest

CHIMEL v. CALIFORNIA
395 U.S. 752 (1969)

MR. JUSTICE STEWART delivered the opinion of the Court

The relevant facts are essentially undisputed. Late in the afternoon of September 13, 1965, three police officers arrived at the Santa Ana, California, home of the petitioner with a warrant authorizing his arrest for the burglary of a coin shop. The officers knocked on the door, identified themselves to the petitioner's wife, and asked if they might come inside. She ushered them into the house, where they waited 10 or 15 minutes until the petitioner returned home from work. When the petitioner entered the house, one of the officers handed him the arrest warrant and asked for permission to "look around." The petitioner objected, but was advised that "on the basis of the lawful arrest," the officers would nonetheless conduct a search. No search warrant had been issued.

Accompanied by the petitioner's wife, the officers then looked through the entire three-bedroom house, including the attic, the garage, and a small workshop. In some rooms the search was relatively cursory. In the master bedroom and sewing room, however, the officers directed the petitioner's wife to open drawers and "to physically move contents of the drawers from side to side so that [they] might view any items that would have come from [the] burglary." After completing the search, they seized numerous items – primarily coins, but also several medals, tokens, and a few other objects. The entire search took between 45 minutes and an hour.

At the petitioner's subsequent state trial on two charges of burglary, the items taken from his house were admitted into evidence against him, over his objection that they had been unconstitutionally seized. He was convicted, and the judgments of conviction were affirmed by both the California Court of Appeal and the California Supreme Court. Both courts accepted the petitioner's contention that the arrest warrant was invalid because the supporting affidavit was set out in conclusory terms, but held that since the arresting officers had procured the warrant "in good faith," and since in any event they had had sufficient information to constitute probable cause for the petitioner's arrest, that arrest had been lawful. From this conclusion the appellate courts went on to hold that the search of the petitioner's home had been justified, despite the absence of a search warrant, on the ground that it had been incident to a valid arrest. We granted certiorari in order to consider the petitioner's substantial constitutional claims.

Without deciding the question, we proceed on the hypothesis that the California courts were correct in holding that the arrest of the petitioner was valid under the Constitution. This brings us directly to the question whether the warrantless search of the petitioner's entire house can be constitutionally justified as incident to that arrest. ...

...Clearly, the general requirement that a search warrant be obtained is not lightly to be dispensed with, and "the burden is on those seeking [an] exemption [from the requirement] to show the need for it. ..."

Only last Term in Terry v. Ohio, we emphasized that "the police must, whenever practicable, obtain advance judicial approval of searches and seizures through the warrant procedure," and that "the scope of [a] search must be 'strictly tied to and justified by' the circumstances which rendered its initiation permissible." The search undertaken by the officer in that "stop and frisk" case was sustained under that test, because it was no more than a "protective . . . search for weapons." But in a companion case, Sibron v. New York, we applied the same standard to another set of facts and reached a contrary result, holding that a policeman's action in thrusting his hand into a suspect's pocket had been neither motivated by nor limited to the objective of protection. Rather, the search had been made in order to find narcotics, which were in fact found.

A similar analysis underlies the "search incident to arrest" principle, and marks its proper extent. When an arrest is made, it is reasonable for the arresting officer to search the person arrested in order to remove any weapons that the latter might seek to use in order to resist arrest or effect his escape. Otherwise, the officer's safety might well be endangered, and the arrest itself frustrated. In addition, it is entirely reasonable for the arresting officer to search for and seize any evidence on the arrestee's person in order to prevent its concealment or destruction. And the area into which an arrestee might reach in order to grab a weapon or evidentiary items must, of course, be governed by a like rule. A gun on a table or in a drawer in front of one who is arrested can be as dangerous to the arresting officer as one concealed in the clothing of the person arrested. There is ample justification, therefore, for a search of the arrestee's person and the area "within his immediate control" – construing that phrase to mean the area from within which he might gain possession of a weapon or destructible evidence.

There is no comparable justification, however, for routinely searching any room other than that in which an arrest occurs – or, for that matter, for searching through all the desk drawers or other closed or concealed areas in that room itself. Such searches, in the absence of well-recognized exceptions, may be made only under the authority of a search warrant. The "adherence to judicial processes" mandated by the Fourth Amendment requires no less.

It is argued in the present case that it is "reasonable" to search a man's house when he is arrested in it. But that argument is founded on little more than a subjective view regarding the acceptability of certain sorts of police conduct, and not on considerations relevant to Fourth Amendment interests. Under such an unconfined analysis, Fourth Amendment protection in this area would approach the evaporation point. ...

Thus, although "the recurring questions of the reasonableness of searches" depend upon "the facts and circumstances – the total atmosphere of the case," those facts and circumstances must be viewed in the light of established Fourth Amendment principles.

Application of sound Fourth Amendment principles to the facts of this case produces a clear result. The search here went far beyond the petitioner's person and the area from within which he might have obtained either a weapon or something that could have been used as evidence against him. There was no constitutional justification, in the absence of a search warrant, for extending the search beyond that area.

The scope of the search was, therefore, "unreasonable" under the Fourth and Fourteenth Amendments, and the petitioner's conviction cannot stand.

Reversed.

MR. JUSTICE HARLAN, concurring

I join the Court's opinion with these remarks concerning a factor to which the Court has not alluded.

The only thing that has given me pause in voting .. is that as a result of Mapp v. Ohio ...every change in Fourth Amendment law must now be obeyed by state officials facing widely different problems of local law enforcement. We simply do not know the extent to which cities and towns across the Nation are prepared to administer the greatly expanded warrant system which will be required by today's decision; nor can we say with assurance that in each and every local situation, the warrant requirement plays an essential role in the protection of those fundamental liberties protected against state infringement by the Fourteenth Amendment.

This federal-state factor has not been an easy one for me to resolve, but in the last analysis I cannot in good conscience vote to perpetuate bad Fourth Amendment law.

MR. JUSTICE WHITE, with whom MR. JUSTICE BLACK joins, dissenting.

The rule which has prevailed, but for very brief or doubtful periods of aberration, is that a search incident to an arrest may extend to those areas under the control of the defendant and where items subject to constitutional seizure may be found. The justification for this rule must, under the language of the Fourth Amendment, lie in the reasonableness of the rule. ...

In terms, then, the Court must decide whether a given search is reasonable. The Amendment does not proscribe "warrantless searches" but instead it proscribes "unreasonable searches" and this Court has never held nor does the majority today assert that warrantless searches are necessarily unreasonable.

Applying this reasonableness test to the area of searches incident to arrests, one thing is clear at the outset. Search of an arrested man and of the items within his immediate reach must in almost every case be reasonable. There is always a danger that the suspect will try to escape, seizing concealed weapons with which to overpower and injure the arresting officers, and there is a danger that he may destroy evidence vital to the prosecution. Circumstances in which these justifications would not apply are sufficiently rare that inquiry is not made into searches of this scope, which have been considered reasonable throughout.

The justifications which make such a search reasonable obviously do not apply to the search of areas to which the accused does not have ready physical access. This is not enough, however, to prove such searches unconstitutional. ...

This is not to say that a search can be reasonable without regard to the probable cause to believe that seizable items are on the premises. But when there are exigent circumstances, and probable cause, then the search may be made without a warrant, reasonably. An arrest itself may often create an emergency situation making it impracticable to obtain a warrant before embarking on a related search. Again assuming that there is probable cause to search premises at the spot where a suspect is arrested, it seems to me unreasonable to require the police to leave the scene in order to obtain a search warrant when they are already legally there to make a valid arrest, and when there must almost always be a strong possibility that confederates of the arrested man will in the meanwhile remove the items for which the police have probable cause to search. This must so often be the case that it seems to me as unreasonable to require a warrant for a search of the premises as to require a warrant for search of the person and his very immediate surroundings.

IV.

If circumstances so often require the warrantless arrest that the law generally permits it, the typical situation will find the arresting officers lawfully on the premises without arrest or search warrant. Like the majority, I would permit the police to search the person of a suspect and the area under his immediate control either to assure the safety of the officers or to prevent the destruction of evidence. And like the majority, I see nothing in the arrest alone furnishing probable cause for a search of any broader scope. However, where as here the existence of probable cause is independently established and would justify a warrant for a broader search for evidence, I would follow past cases and permit such a search to be carried out without a warrant, since the fact of arrest supplies an exigent circumstance justifying police action before the evidence can be removed, and also alerts the suspect to the fact of the search so that he can immediately seek judicial determination of probable cause in an adversary proceeding, and appropriate redress.

...The only issue is whether a search warrant was required as a precondition to that search. It is agreed that such a warrant would be required absent exigent circumstances. I would hold that the fact of arrest supplies such an exigent circumstance, since the police had lawfully gained entry to the premises to effect the arrest and since delaying the search to secure a warrant would have involved the risk of not recovering the fruits of the crime.

...The only possible justification for the majority's rule is that in some instances arresting officers may search when they have no probable cause to do so and that such unlawful searches might be prevented if the officers first sought a warrant from a magistrate. Against the possible protection of privacy in that class of cases, in which the privacy of the house has already been invaded by entry to make the arrest – an entry for which the majority does not assert that any warrant is necessary – must be weighed the risk of destruction of evidence for which there is probable cause to search, as a result of delays in obtaining a search warrant. Without more basis for radical change than the Court's opinion reveals, I would not upset the balance of these interests which has been struck by the former decisions of this Court.

In considering searches incident to arrest, it must be remembered that there will be immediate opportunity to challenge the probable cause for the search in an adversary proceeding. The suspect has been apprised of the search by his very presence at the scene, and having been arrested, he will soon be brought into contact with people who can explain his rights. ...

An arrested man, by definition conscious of the police interest in him, and provided almost immediately with a lawyer and a judge, is in an excellent position to dispute the reasonableness of his arrest and contemporaneous search in a full adversary proceeding. I would uphold the constitutionality of this search contemporaneous with an arrest since there were probable cause both for the search and for the arrest, exigent circumstances involving the removal or destruction of evidence, and satisfactory opportunity to dispute the issues of probable cause shortly thereafter. In this case, the search was reasonable.

Notes and Queries

The case stands for confirming the point that officers may conduct a search incident to arrest. However, in this case, the Court finds the scope of the search invalid because it was not reasonable.

What do you make of the hesitation that local law enforcement simply may be unable to administer the expanded warrant rule this case rules? Should that really matter when we are discussing constitutional dimensions of the Fourth Amendment?

Do you find the dissent's view that warrantless searches should be allowed so long as the officer had probable cause for searching while arresting individuals? Do you view the Fourth Amendment as focusing on unreasonable searches rather than warrantless searches? What are the implications of taking either approach? What do you make of the argument that the arrest provides the exigent circumstances which makes searches permissible without consent? Does it just seem futile to seek a warrant when officers are already at the scene? Do you suppose empirical research would reveal that citizens find broad searches incident to arrest reasonable? If the majority of citizens do find such searches reasonable, what persuasive argument can be made against using those findings to shape Fourth Amendment jurisprudence? What do you make of the argument that the search should be allowed because the defendant will have the opportunity to challenge it in adversarial proceedings? What is problematic with that view?

We now know that a valid arrest renders automatic the right to search incident to that arrest. But can the search include a full search of the person? We may discern two rationales supporting an exception to the warrant rule for searches of individuals placed under arrest: protection of police and the prevention of evidence destruction. Should it matter that the officer conducting the search of the arrested person is not concerned about the destruction of evidence or self-protection? The Supreme Court, in *United States v. Robinson*, 414 U.S. 218, 235 (1973), held that the exception still operates even if the rationales do not necessarily apply to the arrest. In *Robinson*, an officer, upon effecting a lawful, full custody arrest of the defendant for operating a motor vehicle after revocation of his operator's permit, pursuant to established police department practice, had conducted a full field search of the defendant's person. The search led to the seizure of heroin capsules found in a crumpled cigarette package in the defendant's coat pocket. The officer did not indicate any subjective fear of the defendant, did not suspect that the defendant was armed, and was not specifically looking for weapons or anything else in the search. The Supreme Court held that after a police officer lawfully places a suspect under arrest for the purpose of taking him into custody, even where the arrest was for a traffic violation, the officer could proceed to fully search the prisoner. The Court offered two rationales: a mere patdown for weapons provides insufficient protection and a clear rule best serves the realities that officers face when they need to make quick decisions in the field. The use of a bright, easy to follow rule is significant. The general result is that the officer's intent relating to the search essentially becomes a non-issue; a lawful arrest that leads to custodial detention justifies the search. Should it matter whether an officer needs a particularized reason to believe that a search incident to an arrest would be fruitful? One worried about zealous law enforcement may suggest that this allows, for example, unscrupulous officers who lack probable cause for a search warrant to use a traffic arrest as a pretext to conduct a full search. What do you make of such concerns?

CONSENSUAL SEARCHES

SCHNECKLOTH v. BUSTAMONTE
412 U.S. 218 (1972)

MR. JUSTICE STEWART delivered the opinion of the Court

I.

While on routine patrol in Sunnyvale, California, at approximately 2:40 in the morning, Police Officer James Rand stopped an automobile when he observed that one headlight and its license plate light were burned out. Six men were in the vehicle. Joe Alcala and the respondent, Robert Bustamonte, were in the front seat with Joe Gonzales, the driver. Three older men were seated in the rear. When, in response to the policeman's question, Gonzales could not produce a driver's license, Officer Rand asked if any of the other five had any evidence of identification. Only Alcala produced a license, and he explained that the car was his brother's. After the six occupants had stepped out of the car at the officer's request and after two additional policemen had arrived, Officer Rand asked Alcala if he could search the car. Alcala replied, "Sure, go ahead." Prior to the search no one was threatened with arrest and, according to Officer Rand's uncontradicted testimony, it "was all very congenial at this time." Gonzales testified that Alcala actually helped in the search of the car, by opening the trunk and glove compartment. In Gonzales' words: "The police officer asked Joe [Alcala], he goes, 'Does the trunk open?' And Joe said, 'Yes.' He went to the car and got the keys and opened up the trunk." Wadded up under the left rear seat, the police officers found three checks that had previously been stolen from a car wash.

The trial judge denied the motion to suppress, and the checks in question were admitted in evidence at Bustamonte's trial. On the basis of this and other evidence he was convicted, and the California Court of Appeal for the First Appellate District affirmed the conviction. In agreeing that the search and seizure were constitutionally valid, the appellate court applied the standard earlier formulated by the Supreme Court of California in an opinion by then Justice Traynor: "Whether in a particular case an apparent consent was in fact voluntarily given or was in submission to an express or implied assertion of authority, is a question of fact to be determined in the light of all the circumstances." The appellate court found that "in the instant case the prosecution met the necessary burden of showing consent. ..." The California Supreme Court denied review.

Thereafter, the respondent sought a writ of habeas corpus ... The appellate court reasoned that a consent was a waiver of a person's Fourth and Fourteenth Amendment rights, and that the State was under an obligation to demonstrate, not only that the consent had been uncoerced, but that it had been given with an understanding that it could be freely and effectively withheld. Consent could not be found, the court held, solely from the absence of coercion and a verbal expression of assent. Since the District Court had not determined that Alcala had known that his consent could have been withheld and that he could have refused to have his vehicle searched, the Court of Appeals vacated the order denying the writ and remanded the case for further proceedings. We granted certiorari ....

II.

A.

The most extensive judicial exposition of the meaning of "voluntariness" has been developed in those cases in which the Court has had to determine the "voluntariness" of a defendant's confession for purposes of the Fourteenth Amendment. ... It is to that body of case law to which we turn for initial guidance on the meaning of "voluntariness" in the present context.

Those cases yield no talismanic definition of "voluntariness," mechanically applicable to the host of situations where the question has arisen. "The notion of 'voluntariness,'" Mr. Justice Frankfurter once wrote, "is itself an amphibian." It cannot be taken literally to mean a "knowing" choice. "Except where a person is unconscious or drugged or otherwise lacks capacity for conscious choice, all incriminating statements – even those made under brutal treatment – are 'voluntary' in the sense of representing a choice of alternatives. ...

Rather, "voluntariness" has reflected an accommodation of the complex of values implicated in police questioning of a suspect. At one end of the spectrum is the acknowledged need for police questioning as a tool for the effective enforcement of criminal laws. Without such investigation, those who were innocent might be falsely accused, those who were guilty might wholly escape prosecution, and many crimes would go unsolved. In short, the security of all would be diminished. At the other end of the spectrum is the set of values reflecting society's deeply felt belief that the criminal law cannot be used as an instrument of unfairness, and that the possibility of unfair and even brutal police tactics poses a real and serious threat to civilized notions of justice. "In cases involving involuntary confessions, this Court enforces the strongly felt attitude of our society that important human values are sacrificed where an agency of the government, in the course of securing a conviction, wrings a confession out of an accused against his will."

This Court's decisions reflect a frank recognition that the Constitution requires the sacrifice of neither security nor liberty. The Due Process Clause does not mandate that the police forgo all questioning, or that they be given carte blanche to extract what they can from a suspect. "The ultimate test remains that which has been the only clearly established test in Anglo-American courts for two hundred years: the test of voluntariness. Is the confession the product of an essentially free and unconstrained choice by its maker? If it is, if he has willed to confess, it may be used against him. If it is not, if his will has been overborne and his capacity for self-determination critically impaired, the use of his confession offends due process."

In determining whether a defendant's will was over-borne in a particular case, the Court has assessed the totality of all the surrounding circumstances – both the characteristics of the accused and the details of the interrogation. Some of the factors taken into account have included the youth of the accused, his lack of education, or his low intelligence; the lack of any advice to the accused of his constitutional rights; the length of detention; the repeated and prolonged nature of the questioning; and the use of physical punishment such as the deprivation of food or sleep. In all of these cases, the Court determined the factual circumstances surrounding the confession, assessed the psychological impact on the accused, and evaluated the legal significance of how the accused reacted.

The significant fact about all of these decisions is that none of them turned on the presence or absence of a single controlling criterion; each reflected a careful scrutiny of all the surrounding circumstances...

B.

Similar considerations lead us to agree with the courts of California that the question whether a consent to a search was in fact "voluntary" or was the product of duress or coercion, express or implied, is a question of fact to be determined from the totality of all the circumstances. While knowledge of the right to refuse consent is one factor to be taken into account, the government need not establish such knowledge as the sine qua non of an effective consent. As with police questioning, two competing concerns must be accommodated in determining the meaning of a "voluntary" consent – the legitimate need for such searches and the equally important requirement of assuring the absence of coercion.

In situations where the police have some evidence of illicit activity, but lack probable cause to arrest or search, a search authorized by a valid consent may be the only means of obtaining important and reliable evidence. In the present case for example, while the police had reason to stop the car for traffic violations, the State does not contend that there was probable cause to search the vehicle or that the search was incident to a valid arrest of any of the occupants. Yet, the search yielded tangible evidence that served as a basis for a prosecution, and provided some assurance that others, wholly innocent of the crime, were not mistakenly brought to trial. And in those cases where there is probable cause to arrest or search, but where the police lack a warrant, a consent search may still be valuable. If the search is conducted and proves fruitless, that in itself may convince the police that an arrest with its possible stigma and embarrassment is unnecessary, or that a far more extensive search pursuant to a warrant is not justified. In short, a search pursuant to consent may result in considerably less inconvenience for the subject of the search, and, properly conducted, is a constitutionally permissible and wholly legitimate aspect of effective police activity.

But the Fourth and Fourteenth Amendments require that a consent not be coerced, by explicit or implicit means, by implied threat or covert force. For, no matter how subtly the coercion was applied, the resulting "consent" would be no more than a pretext for the unjustified police intrusion against which the Fourth Amendment is directed. ...

The problem of reconciling the recognized legitimacy of consent searches with the requirement that they be free from any aspect of official coercion cannot be resolved by any infallible touchstone. To approve such searches without the most careful scrutiny would sanction the possibility of official coercion; to place artificial restrictions upon such searches would jeopardize their basic validity. Just as was true with confessions, the requirement of a "voluntary" consent reflects a fair accommodation of the constitutional requirements involved. In examining all the surrounding circumstances to determine if in fact the consent to search was coerced, account must be taken of subtly coercive police questions, as well as the possibly vulnerable subjective state of the person who consents. Those searches that are the product of police coercion can thus be filtered out without undermining the continuing validity of consent searches. In sum, there is no reason for us to depart in the area of consent searches, from the traditional definition of "voluntariness."

The approach of the Court of Appeals for the Ninth Circuit finds no support in any of our decisions that have attempted to define the meaning of "voluntariness." Its ruling, that the State must affirmatively prove that the subject of the search knew that he had a right to refuse consent, would, in practice, create serious doubt whether consent searches could continue to be conducted. There might be rare cases where it could be proved from the record that a person in fact affirmatively knew of his right to refuse – such as a case where he announced to the police that if he didn't sign the consent form, "you [police] are going to get a search warrant;" or a case where by prior experience and training a person had clearly and convincingly demonstrated such knowledge. But more commonly where there was no evidence of any coercion, explicit or implicit, the prosecution would nevertheless be unable to demonstrate that the subject of the search in fact had known of his right to refuse consent.

The very object of the inquiry – the nature of a person's subjective understanding – underlines the difficulty of the prosecution's burden under the rule applied by the Court of Appeals in this case. Any defendant who was the subject of a search authorized solely by his consent could effectively frustrate the introduction into evidence of the fruits of that search by simply failing to testify that he in fact knew he could refuse to consent. And the near impossibility of meeting this prosecutorial burden suggests why this Court has never accepted any such litmus-paper test of voluntariness. ...

One alternative that would go far toward proving that the subject of a search did know he had a right to refuse consent would be to advise him of that right before eliciting his consent. That, however, is a suggestion that has been almost universally repudiated by both federal and state courts, and, we think, rightly so. For it would be thoroughly impractical to impose on the normal consent search the detailed requirements of an effective warning. Consent searches are part of the standard investigatory techniques of law enforcement agencies. They normally occur on the highway, or in a person's home or office, and under informal and unstructured conditions. The circumstances that prompt the initial request to search may develop quickly or be a logical extension of investigative police questioning. The police may seek to investigate further suspicious circumstances or to follow up leads developed in questioning persons at the scene of a crime. ...

... if under all the circumstances it has appeared that the consent was not given voluntarily – that it was coerced by threats or force, or granted only in submission to a claim of lawful authority – then we have found the consent invalid and the search unreasonable. ...

...knowledge of a right to refuse is not a prerequisite of a voluntary consent. ...

C.

It is said, however, that a "consent" is a "waiver" of a person's rights under the Fourth and Fourteenth Amendments. The argument is that by allowing the police to conduct a search, a person "waives" whatever right he had to prevent the police from searching. It is argued that ... to establish such a "waiver" the State must demonstrate "an intentional relinquishment or abandonment of a known right or privilege."

But these standards were enunciated in ... the context of the safeguards of a fair criminal trial. Our cases do not reflect an uncritical demand for a knowing and intelligent waiver in every situation where a person has failed to invoke a constitutional protection. ...

The guarantees afforded a criminal defendant at trial also protect him at certain stages before the actual trial, and any alleged waiver must meet the strict standard of an intentional relinquishment of a "known" right. But the "trial" guarantees that have been applied to the "pretrial" stage of the criminal process are similarly designed to protect the fairness of the trial itself.

There is a vast difference between those rights that protect a fair criminal trial and the rights guaranteed under the Fourth Amendment. Nothing, either in the purposes behind requiring a "knowing" and "intelligent" waiver of trial rights, or in the practical application of such a requirement suggests that it ought to be extended to the constitutional guarantee against unreasonable searches and seizures.

Our decision today is a narrow one. We hold only that when the subject of a search is not in custody and the State attempts to justify a search on the basis of his consent, the Fourth and Fourteenth Amendments require that it demonstrate that the consent was in fact voluntarily given, and not the result of duress or coercion, express or implied. Voluntariness is a question of fact to be determined from all the circumstances, and while the subject's knowledge of a right to refuse is a factor to be taken into account, the prosecution is not required to demonstrate such knowledge as a prerequisite to establishing a voluntary consent. Because the California court followed these principles in affirming the respondent's conviction, and because the Court of Appeals for the Ninth Circuit in remanding for an evidentiary hearing required more, its judgment must be reversed.

It is so ordered.

MR. JUSTICE BLACKMUN, concurring. [opinion omitted]

MR. JUSTICE POWELL, with whom THE CHIEF JUSTICE and MR. JUSTICE REHNQUIST join, concurring. [opinion omitted]

MR. JUSTICE DOUGLAS, with whom MR JUSTICE BRENNAN and MR. JUSTICE MARSHALL join, dissenting. [omitted]

MR. JUSTICE BRENNAN, dissenting.

...The Court holds today that an individual can effectively waive this right even though he is totally ignorant of the fact that, in the absence of his consent, such invasions of his privacy would be constitutionally prohibited. It wholly escapes me how our citizens can meaningfully be said to have waived something as precious as a constitutional guarantee without ever being aware of its existence. In my view, the Court's conclusion is supported neither by "linguistics," nor by "epistemology," nor, indeed, by "common sense." I respectfully dissent.

MR. JUSTICE MARSHALL, dissenting.

Several years ago, MR. JUSTICE STEWART reminded us that "the Constitution guarantees . . . a society of free choice. Such a society presupposes the capacity of its members to choose." I would have thought that the capacity to choose necessarily depends upon knowledge that there is a choice to be made.

But today the Court reaches the curious result that one can choose to relinquish a constitutional right – the right to be free of unreasonable searches – without knowing that he has the alternative of refusing to accede to a police request to search. I cannot agree, and therefore dissent.

I.

I believe that the Court misstates the true issue in this case. That issue is not, as the Court suggests, whether the police overbore Alcala's will in eliciting his consent, but rather, whether a simple statement of assent to search, without more, should be sufficient to permit the police to search and thus act as a relinquishment of Alcala's constitutional right to exclude the police. ...

The Court assumes that the issue in this case is: what are the standards by which courts are to determine that consent is voluntarily given? It then imports into the law of search and seizure standards developed to decide entirely different questions about coerced confessions.

The Fifth Amendment, in terms, provides that no person "shall be compelled in any criminal case to be a witness against himself." Nor is the interest protected by the Due Process Clause of the Fourteenth Amendment any different. The inquiry in a case where a confession is challenged as having been elicited in an unconstitutional manner is, therefore, whether the behavior of the police amounted to compulsion of the defendant. Because of the nature of the right to be free of compulsion, it would be pointless to ask whether a defendant knew of it before he made a statement; no sane person would knowingly relinquish a right to be free of compulsion. Thus, the questions of compulsion and of violation of the right itself are inextricably intertwined. The cases involving coerced confessions, therefore, pass over the question of knowledge of that right as irrelevant, and turn directly to the question of compulsion.

In contrast, this case deals not with "coercion," but with "consent," a subtly different concept to which different standards have been applied in the past. Freedom from coercion is a substantive right, guaranteed by the Fifth and Fourteenth Amendments. Consent, however, is a mechanism by which substantive requirements, otherwise applicable, are avoided. In the context of the Fourth Amendment, the relevant substantive requirements are that searches be conducted only after evidence justifying them has been submitted to an impartial magistrate for a determination of probable cause. There are, of course, exceptions to these requirements based on a variety of exigent circumstances that make it impractical to invalidate a search simply because the police failed to get a warrant. But none of the exceptions relating to the overriding needs of law enforcement are applicable when a search is justified solely by consent. On the contrary, the needs of law enforcement are significantly more attenuated, for probable cause to search may be lacking but a search permitted if the subject's consent has been obtained. Thus, consent searches are permitted, not because such an exception to the requirements of probable cause and warrant is essential to proper law enforcement, but because we permit our citizens to choose whether or not they wish to exercise their constitutional rights. Our prior decisions simply do not support the view that a meaningful choice has been made solely because no coercion was brought to bear on the subject.

...I am at a loss to understand why consent "cannot be taken literally to mean a 'knowing' choice." In fact, I have difficulty in comprehending how a decision made without knowledge of available alternatives can be treated as a choice at all.

If consent to search means that a person has chosen to forgo his right to exclude the police from the place they seek to search, it follows that his consent cannot be considered a meaningful choice unless he knew that he could in fact exclude the police. ...

If the burden is placed on the defendant, all the subject can do is to testify that he did not know of his rights. And I doubt that many trial judges will find for the defendant simply on the basis of that testimony.

Precisely because the evidence is very hard to come by, courts have traditionally been reluctant to require a party to prove negatives such as the lack of knowledge.

In contrast, there are several ways by which the subject's knowledge of his rights may be shown. .... Denials of knowledge may be disproved by establishing that the subject had, in the recent past, demonstrated his knowledge of his rights, for example, by refusing entry when it was requested by the police. The prior experience or training of the subject might in some cases support an inference that he knew of his right to exclude the police.

The burden on the prosecutor would disappear, of course, if the police, at the time they requested consent to search, also told the subject that he had a right to refuse consent and that his decision to refuse would be respected. The Court's assertions to the contrary notwithstanding, there is nothing impractical about this method of satisfying the prosecution's burden of proof. It must be emphasized that the decision about informing the subject of his rights would lie with the officers seeking consent. If they believed that providing such information would impede their investigation, they might simply ask for consent, taking the risk that at some later date the prosecutor would be unable to prove that the subject knew of his rights or that some other basis for the search existed.

The Court contends that if an officer paused to inform the subject of his rights, the informality of the exchange would be destroyed. I doubt that a simple statement by an officer of an individual's right to refuse consent would do much to alter the informality of the exchange, except to alert the subject to a fact that he surely is entitled to know. ... What evidence there is, then, rather strongly suggests that nothing disastrous would happen if the police, before requesting consent, informed the subject that he had a right to refuse consent and that his refusal would be respected.

I must conclude, with some reluctance, that when the Court speaks of practicality, what it really is talking of is the continued ability of the police to capitalize on the ignorance of citizens so as to accomplish by subterfuge what they could not achieve by relying only on the knowing relinquishment of constitutional rights. Of course it would be "practical" for the police to ignore the commands of the Fourth Amendment, if by practicality we mean that more criminals will be apprehended, even though the constitutional rights of innocent people also go by the board. But such a practical advantage is achieved only at the cost of permitting the police to disregard the limitations that the Constitution places on their behavior, a cost that a constitutional democracy cannot long absorb.

... Permitting searches in such circumstances, without any assurance at all that the subject of the search knew that, by his consent, he was relinquishing his constitutional rights, is something that I cannot believe is sanctioned by the Constitution.

III.

The proper resolution of this case turns, I believe, on a realistic assessment of the nature of the interchange between citizens and the police, and of the practical import of allocating the burden of proof in one way rather than another. ...

NOTES AND QUERIES

While the *Schneckloth* Court helped determine what is not necessary for voluntary consent, it did not explore fully when coercion exists. The Court held that lower courts should look to the totality of the circumstances surrounding the consent in determining voluntariness. Importantly, the Court noted that determinations of coercion must take account of the subtly coercive police questions as well as the possibly vulnerable subjective state of the person who consents. Voluntary consent means that the consenter had a choice to refuse and the police obtained the consent without practicing any coercive tactics. Some of the courts routinely consider the number of uniformed officers present, officer display of weapons, the existence of prior illegal police action, the defendant's psychological characteristics (maturity, sophistication, mental or emotional state), the defendant's previous or subsequent refusal of consent, whether the defendant is in custody, the defendant's belief that the officers would not find any incriminating evidence, physical mistreatment of the defendant by police, and the defendant's awareness of his right to refuse consent. Some circuits apply the same specific factors to each case, and others view each case individually. Rebecca Strauss, We can do this the easy way or the hard way: The use of deceit to induce consent searches, 100 Mich. L. Rev. 868 (2002).

Although the Court may allow for a focus on subtle coercion, it is explicit in noting that voluntary does not necessarily mean a knowing choice. As the Court appropriately notes, its approach to voluntariness seeks to accommodate individuals' rights with the need for police questioning as a tool for effective enforcement of criminal laws. Should police officers be required to inform suspects of their right to withhold consent upon requesting their permission to search? How protective of individuals' rights would that be? Note that the knowing, intelligent, and voluntary waiver standards are meant for trial rights, not for the waiver of investigatory rights. Is that an appropriate justification for requiring a less stringent standard for the waiver of Fourth Amendment rights? Is that justification legitimate in the first instance? As one dissenter notes, how can one waive a right if one does not know that the rights exists? What does the Court's approach reveal about criminal justice processes?

Does case law consider the reality that most people will feel compelled to allow the police to search, no matter how politely the request is phrased? Some have argued that feelings of compulsion are particularly experienced by members of certain racial and cultural groups who fear confrontation with the police. Assuming that is true, how should the legal system respond?

LAW NOTE ON CONSENT SEARCHES

Courts have yet to agree whether a refusal to allow consent can be used against the suspect by using it to develop suspicion justifying a non-consensual search. Some courts have suggested that a person's refusal to consent should be considered a factor in determining whether the officer has reasonable suspicion to detain a person or to undertake other investigatory techniques; see *United States v. Withars*, 972 F.2d 837, 843 (7th Cir. 1992); cf. *United States v. Holloman*, 113 F.3d 192, 193 (11th Cir. 1997) (driver refused consent, police used narcotics dog to sniff); *United States v. Taxacher*, 902 F.2d 867 (11th Cir. 1990) (warrant to search based on suspect's nervousness and withdrawal of consent); cf. *Illinois v. Wardlow*, 528 U.S. 119, 124 (2000) (flight from police can be factor in determining reasonable suspicion to stop). Other courts have suggested that the refusal to consent cannot be used against the suspect. *United States v. Carter*, 985 F.2d 1095, 1097 (D.C. Cir. 1993); *United States v. White*, 890 F.2d 1413, 1417 n.4 (8th Cir. 1989) (refusal to consent cannot be support for reasonable suspicion); cf. *United States v. Hyppolite*, 65 F.3d 1151 (4th Cir. 1995) (refusal to search cannot establish probable cause to search). These cases note that a rule to the contrary would vitiate the protections of the Fourth Amendment to the extent that the Amendment would mean little if officers could manufacture probable cause by asking questions until a suspect either consents or exercises constitutional rights. The answer to this question has obvious import. If law enforcement can use a citizen's negative answer against them, then they are not truly free to refuse; and the unclarity of law on this issue means that citizens cannot know whether their choice to refuse can and will be held against them. See David Cole, No Equal Justice: Race and Class in the American Criminal Justice System 33 (1999).

The reality is that ninety-eight percent of warrantless searches are conducted via consent; and the vast majority of searches are conducted without warrants. See Joshua Dressler, Understanding Criminal

Procedure 241 (2d ed. 1997). This evidence reveals that warrants may protect individuals' privacy more than consent searches, but many forces encourage law enforcement to seek consent rather than rely on warrants. We have seen that the Fourth Amendment requires search warrants to prevent general searches. The requirement serves to protect the subject of the search while the consent search offers no such protection. If police seek consent, and an owner grants it, the police have received consent to search any area in his home where they reasonably may find evidence of the crime they claimed to be investigating. The scope of their consent search is limited to the stated purpose and the scope of the consent to the search. The warrant search is more limited and protects individuals in two ways. It requires probable cause before the police can search a home, and it limits the scope of the actual search. If the police chose to search a home with a search warrant instead of the owner's consent, the police would have gone to a magistrate and demonstrated the requisite level of probable cause to obtain a search warrant. The police also would have presented an affidavit explaining their basis for suspicion, and that affidavit serves as the basis for any later legal challenge to the sufficiency of probable cause. If, after considering the affidavit, the magistrate determined that the issuance of a warrant was proper, the warrant would detail the specific items the police had cause to believe were in the home, and where police could look for the items. If the police exceeded the scope of the warrant, they would not be able to use any evidence obtained outside the permitted scope. Moreover, a court could suppress any "fruit" of the illegal search. The potential exclusion of any evidence seized outside of the warrant's scope motivates the police to stay within the specified scope. As even this brief description suggests, a warrant search clearly better protects an individual's privacy. Yet, the Supreme Court encourages consent searches, despite the impact on privacy and the contradiction with the purpose of the Fourth Amendment. The Court encourages consent searches in at least two ways: it allows consent searches after coercive police tactics that are not allowed in other contexts, and it praises the use of consent searches. *Scheckloth v. Bustamonte,* 412 U.S. 218 (1973), has played a key role in this development. *Scheckloth* actually remains the last Court decision to address consent searches comprehensively, and it was in that case that the Court highlighted the virtues of consent searches. According to the Court, consent searches offer the following benefits: the subjects of consent searches are less inconvenienced, law enforcement gathers valuable incriminating evidence that may be unavailable in the absence of a consent search, and a fruitless consent search may exculpate the innocent. Importantly, *Schneckloth* probably represents the Court's desire to maintain consistency with its Fifth Amendment jurisprudence rather than ignore evidence of coercion. The Court had previously held in *Miranda v. Arizona,* 384 U.S. 439 (1966), that psychological coercion can be presumed only when a suspect is in custody; if the Court were to presume coercion for noncustodial consent searches it would have to carve out a way to deal with the extension of *Miranda* to all forms of noncustodial questioning. The *Schneckloth* Court maintained that "consent searches will normally occur on a person's own familiar territory, the specter of incommunicado police interrogation in some remote station house is simply inapposite. *Schneckloth v. Bustamonte*, 412 U.S. 218, 247 (1973). As commentators note, the Court appears to have overstated the distinction. Warrants are most likely to be used when searches are for places and except where consent is requested in a person's home, search requests necessarily arise in areas unfamiliar and intimidating, such as by the side of the road by a police cars, or in airports or on a buses by armed officers. See Rebecca Strauss, We can do this the easy way or the hard way: The use of deceit to induce consent searches, 100 Mich. L. Rev. 868 (2000).

PRETEXTUAL SEARCHES

WHREN v. U.S.
517 U.S. 806 (1996)

JUSTICE SCALIA delivered the opinion of the Court.

On the evening of June 10, 1993, plainclothes vice-squad officers of the District of Columbia Metropolitan Police Department were patrolling a "high drug area" of the city in an unmarked car. Their suspicions were aroused when they passed a dark Pathfinder truck with temporary license plates and youthful occupants waiting at a stop sign, the driver looking down into the lap of the passenger at his right. The truck remained stopped at the intersection for what seemed an unusually long time – more than 20 seconds. When the police car executed a U-turn in order to head back toward the truck, the Pathfinder turned suddenly to its right, without signaling, and sped off at an "unreasonable" speed. The policemen followed, and in a short while overtook the Pathfinder when it stopped behind other traffic at a red light. They pulled up alongside, and Officer Ephraim Soto stepped out and approached the driver's door, identifying himself as a police officer and directing the driver, petitioner Brown, to put the vehicle in park. When Soto drew up to the driver's window, he immediately observed two large plastic bags of what appeared to be crack cocaine in petitioner Whren's hands. Petitioners were arrested, and quantities of several types of illegal drugs were retrieved from the vehicle.

Petitioners were charged in a four-count indictment with violating various federal drug laws. At a pretrial suppression hearing, they challenged the legality of the stop and the resulting seizure of the drugs. They argued that the stop had not been justified by probable cause to believe, or even reasonable suspicion, that petitioners were engaged in illegal drug-dealing activity; and that Officer Soto's asserted ground for approaching the vehicle – to give the driver a warning concerning traffic violations – was pretextual. The District Court denied the suppression motion, concluding that "the facts of the stop were not controverted," and "there was nothing to really demonstrate that the actions of the officers were contrary to a normal traffic stop."

Petitioners were convicted of the counts at issue here. The Court of Appeals affirmed the convictions, holding with respect to the suppression issue that, "regardless of whether a police officer subjectively believes that the occupants of an automobile may be engaging in some other illegal behavior, a traffic stop is permissible as long as a reasonable officer in the same circumstances could have stopped the car for the suspected traffic violation." We granted certiorari.

II.

The Fourth Amendment guarantees "the right of the people to be secure in their persons, houses, papers, and effects, against unreasonable searches and seizures." Temporary detention of individuals during the stop of an automobile by the police, even if only for a brief period and for a limited purpose, constitutes a "seizure" of "persons" within the meaning of this provision. An automobile stop is thus subject to the constitutional imperative that it not be "unreasonable" under the circumstances. As a general matter, the decision to stop an automobile is reasonable where the police have probable cause to believe that a traffic violation has occurred.

Petitioners accept that Officer Soto had probable cause to believe that various provisions of the District of Columbia traffic code had been violated. [("An operator shall . . . give full time and attention to the operation of the vehicle"); ("No person shall turn any vehicle . . . without giving an appropriate signal"); ("No person shall drive a vehicle . . . at a speed greater than is reasonable and prudent under the conditions").] They argue, however, that "in the unique context of civil traffic regulations" probable cause is not enough. Since, they contend, the use of automobiles is so heavily and minutely regulated that total compliance with traffic and safety rules is nearly impossible, a police officer will almost invariably be able to catch any given motorist in a technical violation. This creates the temptation to use traffic stops as a means of investigating other law violations, as to which no probable cause or even articulable suspicion exists. Petitioners, who are both black, further contend that police officers might decide which motorists to stop based on decidedly impermissible factors, such as the race of the car's occupants. To avoid this danger, they say, the Fourth Amendment test for traffic stops should be, not the normal one (applied by the

Court of Appeals) of whether probable cause existed to justify the stop; but rather, whether a police officer, acting reasonably, would have made the stop for the reason given.

...Petitioners' difficulty is not simply a lack of affirmative support for their position. Not only have we never held, outside the context of inventory search or administrative inspection, that an officer's motive invalidates objectively justifiable behavior under the Fourth Amendment; but we have repeatedly held and asserted the contrary. ... We flatly dismissed the idea that an ulterior motive might serve to strip the agents of their legal justification. In United States v. Robinson, we held that a traffic-violation arrest (of the sort here) would not be rendered invalid by the fact that it was "a mere pretext for a narcotics search," and that a lawful postarrest search of the person would not be rendered invalid by the fact that it was not motivated by the officer-safety concern that justifies such searches. ... We described Robinson as having established that "the fact that the officer does not have the state of mind which is hypothecated by the reasons which provide the legal justification for the officer's action does not invalidate the action taken as long as the circumstances, viewed objectively, justify that action."

We think these cases foreclose any argument that the constitutional reasonableness of traffic stops depends on the actual motivations of the individual officers involved. We of course agree with petitioners that the Constitution prohibits selective enforcement of the law based on considerations such as race. But the constitutional basis for objecting to intentionally discriminatory application of laws is the Equal Protection Clause, not the Fourth Amendment. Subjective intentions play no role in ordinary, probable-cause Fourth Amendment analysis.

B.

Recognizing that we have been unwilling to entertain Fourth Amendment challenges based on the actual motivations of individual officers, petitioners disavow any intention to make the individual officer's subjective good faith the touchstone of "reasonableness." They insist that the standard they have put forward – whether the officer's conduct deviated materially from usual police practices, so that a reasonable officer in the same circumstances would not have made the stop for the reasons given – is an "objective" one.

But although framed in empirical terms, this approach is plainly and indisputably driven by subjective considerations. Its whole purpose is to prevent the police from doing under the guise of enforcing the traffic code what they would like to do for different reasons. Petitioners' proposed standard may not use the word "pretext," but it is designed to combat nothing other than the perceived "danger" of the pretextual stop, albeit only indirectly and over the run of cases. Instead of asking whether the individual officer had the proper state of mind, the petitioners would have us ask, in effect, whether (based on general police practices) it is plausible to believe that the officer had the proper state of mind.

Why one would frame a test designed to combat pretext in such fashion that the court cannot take into account actual and admitted pretext is a curiosity that can only be explained by the fact that our cases have foreclosed the more sensible option. If those cases were based only upon the evidentiary difficulty of establishing subjective intent, petitioners' attempt to root out subjective vices through objective means might make sense. But they were not based only upon that, or indeed even principally upon that. Their principal basis – which applies equally to attempts to reach subjective intent through ostensibly objective means – is simply that the Fourth Amendment's concern with "reasonableness" allows certain actions to be taken in certain circumstances, whatever the subjective intent. But even if our concern had been only an evidentiary one, petitioners' proposal would by no means assuage it. Indeed, it seems to us somewhat easier to figure out the intent of an individual officer than to plumb the collective consciousness of law enforcement in order to determine whether a "reasonable officer" would have been moved to act upon the traffic violation. While police manuals and standard procedures may sometimes provide objective assistance, ordinarily one would be reduced to speculating about the hypothetical reaction of a hypothetical constable – an exercise that might be called virtual subjectivity.

Moreover, police enforcement practices, even if they could be practicably assessed by a judge, vary from place to place and from time to time. We cannot accept that the search and seizure protections of the Fourth Amendment are so variable and can be made to turn upon such trivialities. The difficulty is illustrated by petitioners' arguments in this case. Their claim that a reasonable officer would not have made this stop is based largely on District of Columbia police regulations which permit plainclothes officers in unmarked vehicles to enforce traffic laws "only in the case of a violation that is so grave as to pose an immediate threat to the safety of others." This basis of invalidation would not apply in jurisdictions that had a different practice. And it would not have applied even in the District of Columbia, if Officer Soto had been wearing a uniform or patrolling in a marked police cruiser.

In what would appear to be an elaboration on the "reasonable officer" test, petitioners argue that the balancing inherent in any Fourth Amendment inquiry requires us to weigh the governmental and individual interests implicated in a traffic stop such as we have here. That balancing, petitioners claim, does not support investigation of minor traffic infractions by plainclothes police in unmarked vehicles; such investigation only minimally advances the government's interest in traffic safety, and may indeed retard it by producing motorist confusion and alarm – a view said to be supported by the Metropolitan Police Department's own regulations generally prohibiting this practice. And as for the Fourth Amendment interests of the individuals concerned, petitioners point out that our cases acknowledge that even ordinary traffic stops entail "a possibly unsettling show of authority"; that they at best "interfere with freedom of movement, are inconvenient, and consume time" and at worst "may create substantial anxiety." That anxiety is likely to be even more pronounced when the stop is conducted by plainclothes officers in unmarked cars.

It is of course true that in principle every Fourth Amendment case, since it turns upon a "reasonableness" determination, involves a balancing of all relevant factors. With rare exceptions not applicable here, however, the result of that balancing is not in doubt where the search or seizure is based upon probable cause...

Where probable cause has existed, the only cases in which we have found it necessary actually to perform the "balancing" analysis involved searches or seizures conducted in an extraordinary manner, unusually harmful to an individual's privacy or even physical interests – such as, for example, seizure by means of deadly force, unannounced entry into a home, entry into a home without a warrant, or physical penetration of the body. The making of a traffic stop out of uniform does not remotely qualify as such an extreme practice, and so is governed by the usual rule that probable cause to believe the law has been broken "outbalances" private interest in avoiding police contact.

Petitioners urge as an extraordinary factor in this case that the "multitude of applicable traffic and equipment regulations" is so large and so difficult to obey perfectly that virtually everyone is guilty of violation, permitting the police to single out almost whomever they wish for a stop. But we are aware of no principle that would allow us to decide at what point a code of law becomes so expansive and so commonly violated that infraction itself can no longer be the ordinary measure of the lawfulness of enforcement. And even if we could identify such exorbitant codes, we do not know by what standard (or what right) we would decide, as petitioners would have us do, which particular provisions are sufficiently important to merit enforcement.

For the run-of-the-mine case, which this surely is, we think there is no realistic alternative to the traditional common-law rule that probable cause justifies a search and seizure.

Here the District Court found that the officers had probable cause to believe that petitioners had violated the traffic code. That rendered the stop reasonable under the Fourth Amendment, the evidence thereby discovered admissible, and the upholding of the convictions by the Court of Appeals for the District of Columbia Circuit correct. The judgment is

Affirmed.

NOTES AND QUERIES

What do you make of the majority's argument that motives do not invalidate a search? Is the Court right in making the point that the issue is not whether a reasonable officer would stop and search but rather whether an officer could do so?

Many scholars have criticized these decisions on a number of grounds, including the concern that the police will use the power granted them under these decisions to target minority members. A brief filed in the *Bostick* case by the ACLU claimed that reported bus sweep prosecutions all involved defendants who were African-American or Hispanic. Joshua Dressler and George C. Thomas III, Criminal Procedure; Principles, Policies and Perspectives 380 (1999); see also David Cole, No Equal Justice: Race and Class in the American Criminal Justice System 21 (1999) (bus stops and traffic stops affect minority community disproportionately). Statistics reveal that traffic stops also disproportionately affect minorities. See Kenneth Gavsie, Making the best of *Whren*: The problems with pretextual traffic stops and the need for restraint, 50 Fla. L. Rev. 385, 391-92 (1998) (in one study, seventy percent of all traffic stops involved African-Americans, even though African-Americans made up less than ten percent of the drivers on the highway; African-Americans were two times more likely to have cars searched subsequent to the stop). In *Whren*, the occupants of the car pulled over were black; in the "facts" section of the opinion, the Court's only description of the occupants was that they were "youthful." See Anthony C. Thompson, Stopping the usual suspects: Race and the Fourth Amendment, 74 N.Y.U. L. Rev. 956, 979 (1999). See also David A. Sklansky, Traffic stops, minority motorists and the future of the Fourth Amendment, 1997 Sup. Ct. Rev. 271 (1997).

Whren gains significance in that it increases the likelihood that the police will try to utilize the doctrine of consent to search a person or their property. By unanimously upholding "pretextual searches," where police officers may stop a car for the purpose of asking consent, even on a hunch, so long as the driver commits some type of traffic violation, the Supreme Court increased the chances that police would conduct such stops. Lower courts have noted the effect that, "[b]y all indications, pretextual traffic stops have increased markedly all over the country since the Whren decision." *Whitehead v. State*, 698 A.2d 1115, 1117 (Md. Ct. Spec. App. 1997). Such stops are important in that they inevitably involve a police officer requesting consent to search, even though the officer has no articulable suspicion that the search will reveal anything. Wesley MacNeil Oliver, With an evil eye and an unequal hand: Pretextual stops and doctrinal remedies to racial profiling, 74 Tul. L. Rev. 1409, 1411 (2000). *Whren* gains even more significance in light of *Florida v. Bostick*, 501 U.S. 429, 431-436 (1991), the Supreme Court approved suspicionless drug interdiction practices, which also significantly increase the likelihood of police searches based on consent. In *Bostick*, two police officers boarded a bus en route to Atlanta from Miami when it stopped in Fort Lauderdale. Without any articulable suspicion, the police officer picked out Bostick and asked him for his identification and ticket. Although nothing about these items was remarkable, the police officer asked for his consent to search his luggage. Bostick said yes; the police found illegal narcotics in his luggage. Bostick argued that he had been illegally seized, and therefore, that his consent was invalid. The Court disagreed, finding that while a reasonable person would have not felt free to leave (the traditional test for a seizure under the Fourth Amendment), that is not an appropriate question in this instance. Bostick would not have felt free to leave even if the police were not present by virtue of being on a bus. Thus, the real issue, according to the Court, was whether a reasonable (innocent) person would feel free to ignore the police officer and go about his or her business. In Bostick's situation, a reasonable person would have felt free to decline the officer's requests or otherwise terminate the encounter. *Bostick v. State*, 593 So. 2d 494 (Fla. 1992) (on remand, Florida Supreme Court found the encounter consensual). Taken together, these two cases point toward important developments encouraging searches.

LAW NOTE ON WARNING SUSPECTS PRIOR TO SEARCHES

In *Shneckloth*, the Court reasoned that it would be impractical to impose the detailed warnings required in a custodial interrogation for a normal consensual search, as such searches are a standard investigatory technique. The Court further reasoned that the community has a real interest in encouraging consent, for the resulting search may yield necessary evidence for the solution and prosecution of crime. Thus, under what they reasoned to be a lesser standard, the *Schneckloth* Court held that an individual's consent to a search need not be knowing or intelligent, only voluntary. Should a suspect have the right to be informed that he has the right not to consent to a search? The Court reinforced the notion that individuals need not be informed of their rights in *Ohio v. Robinette*, 519 U.S. 33 (1996). There, a police officer stopped a car for speeding. The driver was ordered out of the car. After checking the driver's license and finding no outstanding violations, the officer issued the driver a verbal warning and returned his license. The officer then said: "One question before you get gone: Are you carrying any illegal contraband in your car? Any weapons of any kind, drugs, anything like that?" The driver said no. The officer then asked if he could search the car and the driver consented. The search revealed a small amount of marijuana and a pill later found to be a controlled substance. Possession of the pill formed the basis for the arrest. The defendant argued that the consent should be deemed involuntary because he was not told that he was free to go before he consented to a search of his car. The Ohio Supreme Court agreed, holding that the allegedly consensual search of the car was invalid, since it was the product of an unlawful seizure. Fearing that the shift from a lawful traffic stop to a consensual encounter is so nebulous that a motorist being questioned would not realize it, the state supreme court established a bright line rule, requiring that once a valid traffic stop is concluded, the police officer must tell the motorist that he or she is free to go before engaging in consensual questioning or requesting consent to search. The Supreme Court, 8-1, disagreed. Rejecting the constitutional necessity for such a warning, the Court found that, like in *Schneckloth*, it would be unrealistic to require police officers to always inform detainees that they are free to go before a consent to search may be deemed voluntary. Incidently, *Robinette* is white. David A. Sklansky, Traffic stops, minority motorists and the future of the Fourth Amendment, 1997 Sup. Ct. Rev. 271, 320-23, n.241 (1997).

Whether even warnings would suffice, however, may be disputable. Arguably, criminal defendants confess or consent in the face of police authority less because of an absence of knowledge and more because of the inherent psychological vulnerability of facing the state as a criminal suspect. Both the obedience and social power of the uniform theories reveal that absent preliminary warning, average citizens find it difficult to tell an approaching officer that they rather not talk to them. The irrational behavior of guilty suspects in the face of police authority provides strong evidence not only that people attribute legitimacy to the police officer's uniform but also that they obey police authority reflexively. The research confirms that police authority confronting the individual may be much more instrumental in shaping the decision to consent than the recognition that consent relinquishes protected rights in place and thing. Because warnings merely supply information, warnings only superficially improve the voluntariness of consent. If the real problems undermining the capacity of criminal defendants to voluntarily relinquish constitutional rights are the inherent psychological vulnerability of facing the state alone as well as lack of legal expertise, then an effective solution would be to require the presence of counsel in such settings. Arguably, defense counsel would seldom, if ever, advise a client to consent to a search. What could be the outcome of that requirement? Should consent be removed as a basis to search and seize in traffic stops? That is, if no probable cause or other basis to search the car exists at the conclusion of the routine traffic stop, should the car still be searched?

PROBABLE CAUSE AND STANDARDS FOR REVIEW

ORNELAS v. U.S.
517 U.S. 690 (1996)

CHIEF JUSTICE REHNQUIST delivered the opinion of the Court

Petitioners each pleaded guilty to possession of cocaine with intent to distribute. They reserved their right to appeal the District Court's denial of their motion to suppress the cocaine found in their car. The District Court had found reasonable suspicion to stop and question petitioners as they entered their car, and probable cause to remove one of the interior panels where a package containing two kilograms of cocaine was found. The Court of Appeals opined that the findings of reasonable suspicion to stop, and probable cause to search, should be reviewed "deferentially," and "for clear error." We hold that the ultimate questions of reasonable suspicion and probable cause to make a warrantless search should be reviewed de novo.

The facts are not disputed. In the early morning of a December day in 1992, Detective Michael Pautz, a 20-year veteran of the Milwaukee County Sheriff's Department with 2 years specializing in drug enforcement, was conducting drug-interdiction surveillance in downtown Milwaukee. Pautz noticed a 1981 two-door Oldsmobile with California license plates in a motel parking lot. The car attracted Pautz's attention for two reasons: because older model, two-door General Motors cars are a favorite with drug couriers because it is easy to hide things in them; and because California is a "source State" for drugs. Detective Pautz radioed his dispatcher to inquire about the car's registration. The dispatcher informed Pautz that the owner was either Miguel Ledesma Ornelas or Miguel Ornelas Ledesma from San Jose, California; Pautz was unsure which name the dispatcher gave. Detective Pautz checked the motel registry and learned that an Ismael Ornelas accompanied by a second man had registered at 4 a.m., without reservations.

Pautz called for his partner, Donald Hurrle, a detective with approximately 25 years of law enforcement experience, assigned for the past 6 years to the drug enforcement unit. When Hurrle arrived at the scene, the officers contacted the local office of the Drug Enforcement Administration (DEA) and asked DEA personnel to run the names Miguel Ledesma Ornelas and Ismael Ornelas through the Narcotics and Dangerous Drugs Information System (NADDIS), a federal database of known and suspected drug traffickers. Both names appeared in NADDIS. The NADDIS report identified Miguel Ledesma Ornelas as a heroin dealer from El Centro, California, and Ismael Ornelas, Jr., as a cocaine dealer from Tucson, Arizona. The officers then summoned Deputy Luedke and the department's drug-sniffing dog, Merlin. Upon their arrival, Detective Pautz left for another assignment. Detective Hurrle informed Luedke of what they knew and together they waited.

Sometime later, petitioners emerged from the motel and got into the Oldsmobile. Detective Hurrle approached the car, identified himself as a police officer, and inquired whether they had any illegal drugs or contraband. Petitioners answered "No." Hurrle then asked for identification and was given two California driver's licenses bearing the names Saul Ornelas and Ismael Ornelas. Hurrle asked them if he could search the car and petitioners consented. The men appeared calm, but Ismael was shaking somewhat. Deputy Luedke, who over the past nine years had searched approximately 2,000 cars for narcotics, searched the Oldsmobile's interior. He noticed that a panel above the right rear passenger armrest felt somewhat loose and suspected that the panel might have been removed and contraband hidden inside. Luedke would testify later that a screw in the doorjam adjacent to the loose panel was rusty, which to him meant that the screw had been removed at some time. Luedke dismantled the panel and discovered two kilograms of cocaine. Petitioners were arrested.

Petitioners filed pretrial motions to suppress, alleging that the police officers violated their Fourth Amendment rights when the officers detained them in the parking lot and when Deputy Luedke searched inside the panel without a warrant. The Government conceded in the court below that when the officers approached petitioners in the parking lot, a reasonable person would not have felt free to leave, so the encounter was an investigatory stop. An investigatory stop is permissible under the Fourth Amendment if supported by reasonable suspicion and a warrantless search of a car is valid if based on probable cause.

After conducting an evidentiary hearing, the Magistrate Judge concluded that the circumstances gave the officers reasonable suspicion, but not probable cause. The Magistrate found, as a finding of fact, that there was no rust on the screw and hence concluded that Deputy Luedke had an insufficient basis to conclude that drugs would be found within the panel. The Magistrate nonetheless recommended that the District Court deny the suppression motions because he thought, given the presence of the drug-sniffing dog, that the officers would have found the cocaine by lawful means eventually and therefore the drugs were admissible under the inevitable discovery doctrine.

The District Court adopted the Magistrate's recommendation with respect to reasonable suspicion, but not its reasoning as to probable cause. The District Court thought that the model, age, and source-State origin of the car, and the fact that two men traveling together checked into a motel at 4 o'clock in the morning without reservations, formed a drug-courier profile and that this profile together with the NADDIS reports gave rise to reasonable suspicion of drugtrafficking activity; in the court's view, reasonable suspicion became probable cause when Deputy Luedke found the loose panel. Accordingly, the court ruled that the cocaine need not be excluded.

The Court of Appeals reviewed deferentially the District Court's determinations of reasonable suspicion and probable cause; it would reverse only upon a finding of "clear error." [The Court notes that, while the Seventh Circuit uses the term "clear error" to denote the deferential standard applied when reviewing determinations of reasonable suspicion or probable cause, we think the preferable term is "abuse of discretion."] The court found no clear error in the reasonable-suspicion analysis and affirmed that determination. With respect to the probable-cause finding, however, the court remanded the case for a determination on whether Luedke was credible when testifying about the loose panel.

On remand, the Magistrate Judge expressly found the testimony credible. The District Court accepted the finding, and once again ruled that probable cause supported the search. The Seventh Circuit held that determination not clearly erroneous.

We granted certiorari to resolve the conflict among the Circuits over the applicable standard of appellate review.

Articulating precisely what "reasonable suspicion" and "probable cause" mean is not possible. They are commonsense, nontechnical conceptions that deal with "'the factual and practical considerations of everyday life on which reasonable and prudent men, not legal technicians, act.'" As such, the standards are "not readily, or even usefully, reduced to a neat set of legal rules." ...

The principal components of a determination of reasonable suspicion or probable cause will be the events which occurred leading up to the stop or search, and then the decision whether these historical facts, viewed from the standpoint of an objectively reasonable police officer, amount to reasonable suspicion or to probable cause. ...

... We have never, when reviewing a probable-cause or reasonable-suspicion determination ourselves, expressly deferred to the trial court's determination. A policy of sweeping deference would permit, "in the absence of any significant difference in the facts," "the Fourth Amendment's incidence [to] tur[n] on whether different trial judges draw general conclusions that the facts are sufficient or insufficient to constitute probable cause." Such varied results would be inconsistent with the idea of a unitary system of law. This, if a matter-of-course, would be unacceptable.

In addition, the legal rules for probable cause and reasonable suspicion acquire content only through application. Independent review is therefore necessary if appellate courts are to maintain control of, and to clarify, the legal principles.

Finally, de novo review tends to unify precedent and will come closer to providing law enforcement officers with a defined "'set of rules which, in most instances, makes it possible to reach a correct determination beforehand as to whether an invasion of privacy is justified in the interest of law enforcement.'"

It is true that because the mosaic which is analyzed for a reasonable-suspicion or probable-cause inquiry is multifaceted, "one determination will seldom be a useful 'precedent' for another." ... And even where one case may not squarely control another one, the two decisions when viewed together may usefully add to the body of law on the subject.

The Court of Appeals, in adopting its deferential standard of review here, reasoned that de novo review for warrantless searches would be inconsistent with the "'great deference'" paid when reviewing a decision to issue a warrant. We cannot agree. The Fourth Amendment demonstrates a "strong preference for searches conducted pursuant to a warrant," and the police are more likely to use the warrant process if the scrutiny applied to a magistrate's probable-cause determination to issue a warrant is less than that for warrantless searches. Were we to eliminate this distinction, we would eliminate the incentive.

We therefore hold that as a general matter determinations of reasonable suspicion and probable cause should be reviewed de novo on appeal. ...

A trial judge views the facts of a particular case in light of the distinctive features and events of the community; likewise, a police officer views the facts through the lens of his police experience and expertise. The background facts provide a context for the historical facts, and when seen together yield inferences that deserve deference. ...

In a similar vein, our cases have recognized that a police officer may draw inferences based on his own experience in deciding whether probable cause exists. To a layman the sort of loose panel below the back seat armrest in the automobile involved in this case may suggest only wear and tear, but to Officer Luedke, who had searched roughly 2,000 cars for narcotics, it suggested that drugs may be secreted inside the panel. An appeals court should give due weight to a trial court's finding that the officer was credible and the inference was reasonable.

We vacate the judgments and remand the case to the Court of Appeals to review de novo the District Court's determinations that the officer had reasonable suspicion and probable cause in this case.

It is so ordered.

JUSTICE SCALIA, dissenting.

The Court today decides that a district court's determinations whether there was probable cause to justify a warrantless search and reasonable suspicion to make an investigatory stop should be reviewed de novo. We have in the past reviewed some mixed questions of law and fact on a de novo basis, and others on a deferential basis, depending upon essentially practical considerations. Because, with respect to the questions at issue here, the purpose of the determination and its extremely fact-bound nature will cause de novo review to have relatively little benefit, it is in my view unwise to require courts of appeals to undertake the searching inquiry that standard requires. I would affirm the judgment of the Court of Appeals.

The facts of this very case illustrate the futility of attempting to craft useful precedent from the fact-intensive review demanded by determinations of probable cause and reasonable suspicion. On remand, in conducting de novo review, the Seventh Circuit might consider, inter alia, the following factors relevant to its determination whether there was probable cause to conduct a warrantless search and reasonable suspicion justifying the investigatory stop: (i) the two NADDIS tips; (ii) that the car was a 1981 two-door General Motors product; (iii) that the car was from California, a source State; (iv) that the car was in Milwaukee; (v) that it was December; (vi) that one suspect checked into the hotel at 4 a.m.; (vii) that he did not have reservations; (viii) that he had one traveling companion; (ix) that one suspect appeared calm but shaking; and (x) that there was a loose panel in the car door. If the Seventh Circuit were to find that this unique confluence of factors supported probable cause and reasonable suspicion, the absence of any one of these factors in the next case would render the precedent inapplicable.

In the present case, an additional factor counseling against de novo review must be mentioned: The prime benefit of de novo appellate review in criminal cases is, of course, to prevent a miscarriage of justice that might result from permitting the verdict of guilty to rest upon the legal determinations of a single judge. But the issue in these probable-cause and reasonable-suspicion cases is not innocence but deterrence of unlawful police conduct. That deterrence will not be at all lessened if the trial judge's determination, right or wrong, is subjected to only deferential review.

The Court is wrong in its assertion, that unless there is a dual standard of review – deferential review of a magistrate's decision to issue a warrant, and de novo review of a district court's ex post facto approval of a warrantless search – the incentive to obtain a warrant would be eliminated. ... we [have] held that "reliable physical evidence seized by officers reasonably relying on a warrant issued by a detached and neutral magistrate . . . should be admissible in the prosecutor's case in chief." Only a warrant can provide this assurance that the fruits of even a technically improper search will be admissible. Law enforcement officers would still have ample incentive to proceed by warrant.

Finally, I must observe that the Court does not appear to have the courage of its conclusions. In an apparent effort to reduce the unproductive burden today's decision imposes upon appellate courts, or perhaps to salvage some of the trial court's superior familiarity with the facts that it has cast aside, the Court suggests that an appellate court should give "due weight" to a trial court's finding that an officer's inference of wrongdoing (i. e., his assessment of probable cause to search) was reasonable. The Court cannot have it both ways. This finding of "reasonableness" is precisely what it has told us the appellate court must review de novo; and in de novo review, the "weight due" to a trial court's finding is zero. In the last analysis, therefore, the Court's opinion seems to me not only wrong but contradictory.

* * *

I would affirm the judgment of the Seventh Circuit on the ground that it correctly applied a deferential standard of review to the District Court's findings of probable cause and reasonable suspicion.

NOTES AND QUERIES

Petitioners also alleged that they had not given their consent to search the interior of the car. The Magistrate Judge rejected this claim, finding that the record "clearly established consent to search the Oldsmobile" and that "neither [petitioner] placed any restrictions on the areas the officers could search." The Magistrate ruled that this consent did not give the officers authority to search inside the panel, however, because under Seventh Circuit precedent the police may not dismantle the car body during an otherwise valid search unless the police have probable cause to believe the car's panels contain narcotics.

Ornelas holds that appellate courts must review reasonable suspicion and probable cause cases *de novo*, while giving due weight to the factual inferences of the trial judge and law enforcement. The Court employed a *de novo* review rather than deferring to the trial judge's determination for three reasons. First, deference would create inconsistent results because each trial judge may draw different inferences from the same set of facts. Second, *de novo* review allows "appellate courts ... to maintain control of, and to clarify, the legal principles," because "the legal rules for ... reasonable suspicion acquire content only through application." Third, *de novo* review allows appellate courts to create uniform rules, giving law enforcement clearer rules to follow when deciding whether to conduct an investigatory stop. The majority also notes that using the *de novo* standard is appropriate because we want police to use magistrates who will scrutinize the process as they issue warrants. Justice Scalia vigorously dissents, arguing that appellate courts should review reasonable suspicion cases with deference to the trial court rather than *de novo* because reasonable suspicion cases are fact-intensive, making a *de novo* review practically useless. Should reviewing courts be deferential as Justice Scalia suggests?

Ornelas established that, to determine whether an officer had probable cause to make an arrest, a court must examine the events leading up to the arrest, and then decide whether these historical facts, viewed from the standpoint of an objectively reasonable police officer, amount to probable cause. What would you make of the following case from Maryland? A police officer stopped a car for speeding at 3:16 a.m.; he searched the car, and seized $763 from the glove compartment and cocaine from behind the back-seat armrest. The officer then arrested the car's three occupants after all denied ownership of the drugs and money. The front-seat passenger, Pringle, was convicted of possession with intent to distribute cocaine and possession of cocaine. He was sentenced to 10 years' incarceration without the possibility of parole. Maryland law authorizes police officers to execute warrantless arrests where the officer has probable cause to believe that a felony has been committed or is being committed in the officer's presence. Here, it is uncontested that the officer, upon recovering the suspected cocaine, had probable cause to believe a felony had been committed; the question is whether he had probable cause to believe Pringle committed that crime. Would an officer have probable cause if the definitions of probable cause is a reasonable ground for belief of guilt, and that belief must be particularized with respect to the person to be searched or seized? The Maryland Court of Special Appeals affirmed, but the State Court of Appeals reversed, holding that, absent specific facts tending to show Pringle's knowledge and dominion or control over the drugs, the mere finding of cocaine in the back armrest when Pringle was a front-seat passenger in a car being driven by its owner was insufficient to establish probable cause for an arrest for possession. The U.S. Supreme Court unanimously held that, as it is an entirely reasonable inference from the facts here that any or all of the car's occupants had knowledge of, and exercised dominion and control over, the cocaine, a reasonable officer could conclude that there was probable cause to believe Pringle committed the crime of possession of cocaine, either solely or jointly. The Court found Pringle's attempt to characterize this as a guilt-by-association case unavailing. *Maryland v. Pringle*, 540 U.S. 366 (2003).

Legal Note: The Supreme Court Revisits Reasonable Suspicion

How must a court apply the "totality of circumstances" test to determine what constitutes reasonable suspicion? Consider this scenario. On January 19, 1998, Agent Clinton Stoddard ("Stoddard") was on duty at the Douglas Arizona checkpoint. In the afternoon, a magnetic sensor located on Leslie Canyon Road detected a vehicle. Stoddard decided to investigate the activation of the sensor for three reasons. First, smugglers often use Leslie Canyon Road to avoid the checkpoint. Second, the sensor was triggered during a shift change, which meant that no roving patrols were in the area and that, in turn, meant that smuggling activity generally increased. Third, Stoddard knew that another agent stopped a minivan containing marijuana in the area a few weeks earlier. As he traveled down the road, Stoddard noticed a vehicle approaching in the distance. He pulled off the road to watch the vehicle pass, believing it to be the vehicle that activated the sensors. Stoddard noted that the approaching vehicle was a minivan, because smugglers often use them. The minivan was traveling at about fifty miles per hour until it came close to Stoddard, when it rapidly slowed to about twenty-five to thirty miles per hour. In the minivan, Stoddard could see a man driving, a woman in the passenger seat, and three children in the back. The man sat very stiff and straight, keeping his eyes on the road. Normally, drivers usually either look at Stoddard out of curiosity or wave. In addition, the children's knees were raised, suggesting their feet rested on something on the floor.

Based on these initial observations, Stoddard decided to follow the minivan. As he began to follow the minivan, the children started moving their hands as if they were waving at him. This action was suspicious to Stoddard for three reasons. First, the children waved facing forward even though Stoddard was behind the minivan. Second, the children waved in an abnormal way, as if they were instructed to wave. Third, the children waved for about four or five minutes. At that point and just before reaching an intersection, the driver turned his right turn signal and quickly turned right, onto a road used mostly by four-wheel-drive vehicles. Stoddard noted that if the vehicle had continued without turning, it would have headed to the checkpoint and, had it turned left, it would have headed toward picnic and camping areas. Still following the minivan, Stoddard performed a registration check over the radio; the check revealed that the minivan was registered in an area notorious for alien and narcotics smuggling. Based on his observations and the registration check, Stoddard stopped the minivan to briefly investigate. The driver revealed that his name was Ralph Arvizu. Stoddard asked Arvizu if he could search the minivan and Arvizu consented. During his search, Stoddard found over 128 pounds of marijuana with a street value of almost $100,000. Stoddard arrested Arvizu who was charged with possession with intent to distribute marijuana. During trial, Arvizu moved to suppress the evidence, because "Stoddard did not have reasonable suspicion to stop the vehicle as required by the Fourth Amendment." Was Stoddard's suspicion reasonable? The trial court thought so.

The appellate court did not. Among other findings, the court found that the minivan slowing rapidly was an inappropriate factor, because slowing down when seeing law enforcement was a perfectly natural response. Second, not waving to an officer may demonstrate that a person is unfriendly, but not a criminal. Third, the children's waving was not relevant to the analysis. If every bizarre act of a child was relevant, law enforcement could stop almost any parent. Fourth, the fact that an officer stopped a minivan containing marijuana on the same road a month earlier was an inappropriate factor because an officer hardly can infer that all minivans on the road contain drugs based on one isolated incident. Fifth, Stoddard's inability to recognize Arvizu's minivan was irrelevant given that both locals and tourists use the road on which Arvizu was stopped. Sixth, the minivan's registration to an address in an area known for alien and drug smuggling was an inappropriate factor since not all individuals have control over where they live due to financial difficulties. Seventh, the children's raised knees were irrelevant to the analysis. Although it suggests their feet were propped on cargo, the cargo just as easily could have been picnic and camping supplies as it was marijuana. Eighth, the fact that Arvizu was driving on a road smugglers frequently use was not particularly significant, because both locals and tourists use the road either as a shortcut or to visit the national monument. Ninth, the fact that Arvizu drove a minivan, a vehicle smugglers use often, is also insignificant, because minivans are a popular family vehicle in the United States. Finally, the fact that Arvizu was on the road during a shift change is not significant, because the time actually was forty-five minutes before the shift change. The court found these factors not enough to constitute reasonable suspicion either singly or collectively. It then suppressed the marijuana evidence, because Stoddard did not have reasonable suspicion to conduct an investigatory stop.

Chief Justice Rehnquist wrote the opinion for a unanimous Court, holding that Stoddard had the requisite level of reasonable suspicion needed under the Fourth Amendment to stop Arvizu based on all facts and circumstances of the case. The Court noted that the law requires a look at the totally of circumstances, not at each factor individually, because each may appear innocent but taken together may amount to reasonable suspicion. *United States v. Arvizu*, 534 U.S. 266 (2002).

Chapter 4

SEIZING SUSPECTS

INTRODUCTION

The Fourth Amendment protects individuals from unreasonable seizures and requires that law enforcement use warrants supported by probable cause.[1] On its face, the Amendment requires a probable cause that a crime has been committed before the state can seize an individual. The reality of police-citizen encounters, however, challenges that requirement. It would be impossible to operate a system where police did not interact with citizens except to arrest them. As a result, the legal system seeks to achieve a reasonable balance between the needs of law enforcement and the protection of individuals' liberties to move freely and not be humiliated, harassed, or otherwise bothered by police encounters.

The legal system has developed three levels of police-citizen encounters in order to balance the need to be left alone with the need for law enforcement to interact with the public. The first involves consensual encounters. These types of encounters resemble those that strangers would have on a street; they involve non-intrusive questions and no show of force or authority. The next, intermediary level involves a more formal interaction which is conceived as a "stop" for questioning. This level typically requires reasonable suspicion that the individual is implicated in some form of criminal activity. The third level is a custodial arrest. This level constitutes a seizure based on probable cause that the individual has committed a crime. Note that such seizures are known as arrests, which the law deems lawful without warrants as long as they are based on probable cause supporting the belief that the suspect committed a crime for which he can be arrested.[2] Importantly, the Fourth Amendment concerns itself only with the second and third levels of police-citizen encounters.

Given that only the second and third levels implicate constitutional protections, analyses tend to examine the implications of what constitutes reasonable suspicion and probable cause. These are rather complex standards. For example, the test for determining whether probable cause exists can be stated as whether at the time of the action the facts and circumstances within the officers' knowledge and of which they had reasonably trustworthy information were sufficient to warrant a prudent person in believing that the suspect had committed or was committing an offense. The legal system generally refers to this evidentiary standard as less than that which would justify conviction, but more than a bare suspicion.[3] This

---

[1] Recall that the Fourth Amendment reads as follows: "The right of the people to be secure in their persons, houses, papers, and effects, against unreasonable searches and seizures, shall not be violated, and no Warrants shall issue, but upon probable cause, supported by Oath or Affirmation, and particularly describing the place to be searched, and the persons or things to be seized."

[2] At common law, an arrest could be made without a warrant for a misdemeanor or felony committed in a peace officer's presence, or for a felony committed outside the officer's presence if there was reasonable ground for making the arrest. The Supreme Court's interpretation of the Fourth Amendment reflects the common-law view. See *Atwater v. City of Lago Vista*, 532 U.S. 318 (2001).

[3] Probable cause concerns not technical probabilities, but factual and practical considerations of everyday life on which prudent persons, not legal technicians, act. As stated by the Court in *United States v. Cortez*, 449 U.S. 411, 418 (1981): "The process does not deal with hard certainties, but with probabilities. Long before the law of probabilities was articulated as such, practical

vague approach finds support from the Supreme Court. The Court envisions probable cause as a fluid concept – turning on the assessment of probabilities in particular factual contexts – not readily, or even usefully, reduced to a neat set of rules. As we will see, similarly vague standards guide determinations of whether officers had reasonable suspicions to stop individuals. Importantly, even though consensual encounters fall outside of constitutional concerns, consensual interactions still leave us with the challenge of determining whether particular encounters were, in fact, consensual. For, if they were not consensual, they may fall under constitutional mandates that protect individuals from state intrusions.[4]

The above rules raise important psychological issues. The following materials examine psychological research relevant to issues about the seizure of individuals. The discussion necessarily explores two analyses. The first deals with suspects' responses to police and how individuals evaluate those responses. The second focuses on available evidence relating to how police officers make decisions to stop or seize individuals and how to control police officers so that they will not unfairly use their powers. As with our previous discussions, we will find that much still remains unknown or simply ignored. As a result, we necessarily extrapolate from psychological findings as well as from other fields of study to evaluate behaviors and legal assumptions. Again, our task will be to consider the utility of existing research for examining legal responses.

THE PSYCHOLOGY OF FEELING SEIZED

A key concern involving law enforcement's seizure of suspects deals with determining when the seizure actually occurs. The law frames this issue in terms of arrest and clearly defines an arrest as occurring when individuals are taken into custody against their will for the purposes of criminal prosecution. But precisely when this occurs remains legally contentious. And that contentiousness is quite significant given that determinations of whether or not someone is under arrest determines the extent to which they gain protection for basic rights.[5]

The legal system provides a deceptively simple test to determine when a seizure occurs. As with searches, seizures are defined in a manner that evaluates the reasonableness of an officers' actions to determine the extent to which the police's authority was within the limits of the Fourth Amendment's mandates. The law focuses on the nature and extent of officers' interference with people's liberty and freedom of movement. Thus, a seizure depends on whether a reasonable person would conclude that they are not free to leave. If a reasonable person would feel free to leave (and thus feel free to disregard the police), the law considers the encounter consensual. As we will see,[6] an officer's mere show of authority does not constitute a seizure. The seizure occurs when the officer uses physical force or the suspect submits to the officer's show of authority. If the encounter is consensual, the Constitution does not protect evidence obtained during that encounter; the Court deems such evidence as freely and legally provided to the state.

The legal system makes many important assumptions regarding police-suspect encounters. Most importantly, the Supreme Court assumes that individuals know that they are free to terminate their contact with officers who have no grounds for questioning. To a large extent, the Court takes a very narrow view of consent, one that does not require that individuals actually be aware of their rights or that they actually do not feel free to walk away. The assumption is that most people know that they can refuse some officer's requests or can challenge unreasonable or warrantless searches. Psychologically, this is quite striking, as

people formulated certain common-sense conclusions about human behavior; jurors as factfinders are permitted to do the same – and so are law enforcement officers. Finally, the evidence thus collected must be seen and weighed not in terms of library analysis by scholars, but as understood by those versed in the field of law enforcement."

[4] This typically means that the evidence is illegally obtained and thus, generally cannot be used against the individual. Note, however, that this area of law remains exceedingly complex, as we soon will see in the cases that follow.

[5] As we have seen in Chapter 2, for example, when the legal system formally begins to view the suspect as a defendant, he gains the right to counsel.

[6] Most notably in *California v. Hodari*, 499 U.S. 621 (1991).

striking as the Court's belief that individuals feel free to reject an officer's request to search their belongings. If we take a psychological view of voluntariness and coercion, little if no psychological evidence supports the Supreme Court's claim, and much anecdotal evidence seems to refute it. As we already have seen in the previous chapter, research reveals a tendency to comply with authorities, even when individuals have something to lose. The empirical literature we reviewed that dealt with people's pressures to consent or obey authority obviously applies to this context. Two other areas of established psychological research also clearly are relevant to evaluating how the legal system approaches consent to interact with officers.

Proxemics Research

One of the clearest factors at work when officers interact with civilians is the invasion of people's spaces. The concern involves the extent to which officers use that space to interact in a manner that may well be deemed coercive from the civilian's perspective. This area of research, known as the study of proxemics,[7] seeks to understand the amount of territory or space individuals need around themselves to feel comfortable. Generally, people like their personal space, and discomfort arises when individuals invade that space. The degree of discomfort experienced is proportional to the degree of intrusion into one's personal space.[8] For example, subjects approached by another person report feeling "slightly uncomfortable" at about 27 inches, "moderately uncomfortable" at about 20 inches, and "very uncomfortable" at about 12 inches. People who feel invasion of their personal space may become aroused or stressed and even tense, anxious, or angry.[9] And once aroused, people tend to prefer greater distance, which in turn runs the risk of creating even more anxiety.[10]

The relevance of this research to our discussion stems from the finding that individuals do not similarly experience invasions of personal space. Social roles affect comfort zones. For example, people naturally provide high-status individuals with more personal space than low-status individuals. Although we may be unaware of it, we grant special deference to high-status people by keeping a distance from them. We do so not necessarily because it is the polite thing to do, but mainly because it makes us feel comfortable. The prerogative to invade others' space resides with people who have higher status and power.[11] The use of personal space, then, reveals control, comfort, and social power.[12]

Given the social dynamics of encounters with police, proxemics research would suggest that individuals could be compelled to interact with officers even when they would otherwise prefer not to do so

---

[7] Proxemics is commonly defined as personal space or social distance. More recently, this area of study has been called nonverbal communication research.

[8] Leslie A. Hayduk, Personal space: Where we now stand, 94 Psych. Bull. 293 (1983).

[9] Nancy J. Felipe and Robert Sommer, Invasions of personal space, 14 Soc. Problems 206 (1966); Michael A. Dosey and Murray Miesels, Personal space and self protection, 11 J. Personality and Soc. Psych. 93 (1969).

[10] Edgar C. O'Neal, Mark A. Brunault, James F. Marquis, Michael Carifio, Anger and the body-buffer zone, 108 J. of Soc. Psych.135 (1979); and Adele T. Brady and Michael B. Walker, Interpersonal distance as a function of situationally induced anxiety, 17 Brit. J. of Soc. and Clin. Psych. 127 (1978).

[11] The Nonverbal Communication Reader: Classic and Contemporary Readings (Laura K. Guerrero, Joseph A. DeVito, and Michael L. Hecht, eds, 2nd ed., 1999); and Handbook of Communication and Emotion: Research, Theory, Applications, and Contexts (Peter Andersen and Laura K. Guerrero, eds., 1998).

[12] Many draw connections between social inequality and several patterns of nonverbal communication. Some of the most frequently presented conclusions include the general rule that: (1) social power is expressed through the command of personal space and control over the physical distance between self and others; (2) lower-status people more often wait for the time of higher status people, while higher-status people may command immediate access to the time of lower-status people when they choose to do so; (3) people with more power and status are accorded the conversational privileges of interrupting, contradicting, manipulating silence, and demanding speech; (4) subordinates are expected to display a bodily formality in interactions with superiors, while superiors demonstrate their superiority with bodily relaxation; (5) higher-status people may legitimately initiate touch of subordinates, while the symmetrical privilege is denied to subordinates; and (6) higher-status people exhibit greater visual dominance behavior than people with lower status. Nancy M. Henley, Body politics, in Self and Society 288 (Ann Branaman, ed., 2001).

and when officers do not have reason to suspect criminal conduct. As we have seen, if these two facts can be true, then the Constitution should perhaps protect the interaction. And, again, the important implication of this line of reasoning is that evidence gained in that interaction would be subject to the exclusionary rule – the evidence could not be used in a case-in-chief against the defendant simply because the evidence would not be voluntarily given to law enforcement.[13]

The above possibility actually receives support from proxemic studies on compliance and police behavior. Research investigating the relationship between interpersonal distance and compliance demonstrates that people feel more pressure to comply with a request when the requester speaks to them from a close physical distance. Rather strikingly, research reports that compliance increases when the person who requests moves from 36-48 inches to 12-18 inches.[14] This research reveals, then, that people approached at a close distance by an authority in a tightly enclosed space without opportunities to adjust to that intrusion experience discomfort and tension; and people who find their space invaded in that manner more "willingly" comply with the request of the person making them feel uncomfortable. This information becomes important in light of typical police behavior. Research examining police officers' use of personal space reveals that they observe a narrower interpersonal distance than non-officers. This is not surprising. Interestingly, though, the research also reveals that, because police do invade space, police actually create suspects. This occurs because officers create defensive behaviors and officers who view defensive behaviors (i.e., certain trunk and arm movements aimed at reducing the tension evoked by a violation of personal space and restoring a psychologically comfortable distance) wrongly interpret such defensive behavior as suspicious.[15] In a real sense, officers create suspects. Whether this type of policing is acceptable or problematic may be debatable; but the reality seems to be that police behavior does impact individuals.

A long line of research and commentaries urging attorneys to make use of a witness, jury and judge's personal space supplements research on the proxemics of law enforcement. For example, some propose that trial attorneys use the tactic of entering into and withdrawing from an adverse witness' close personal zones. The belief is that such intrusion and exit from zones usefully increases the anxiety level of witnesses. The argument is that distraught or guilty people have a greater than average need to maintain extended space between themselves and others. Responding to questions from close personal zones makes confident testimony increasingly difficult. When counsel invades a witness's personal zones, the witness often becomes anxious and testimony may appear more hesitant and uncertain. To cap matters off, attorneys are asked to not look at the adverse witness's eyes but to his forehead, which increases witness anxiety but makes the attorney appear considerate and respectful from the perspective of jurors. Experts also encourage invasion of personal space in order to establish dominance, which increases the attorney's credibility and decreases the witness's credibility by challenging the witness's status and importance. They also suggest moving slowly toward witnesses to draw their attention away from questions.[16]

The extent to which this area of research reveals important tendencies supports the need to consider how officers can use space to achieve obedience by ensuring that individuals feel the need to respond to law enforcement's requests.

---

[13] The argument, which we have seen in Chapter 1, is that law enforcement should collect its own evidence without the assistance of defendants. Whether this holds true in real life is an entirely different matter. Note too that the rule only protects individuals from prosecutions based on tainted evidence, it does not protect individuals from police invasions of privacy or from police harassment when the police do not wish to use the evidence.

[14] Robert A. Baron and Paul A. Bell, Physical distance and helping: Some unexpected benefits of "crowding in" on others, 6 J. Appl. Soc. Psych. 95 (1976). See also Robert C. Ernest and Ralph E. Cooper, "Hey Mister, do you have any change?" Two real world studies of proxemic effects on compliance with a mundane request, 1 Personality and Soc. Psych. Bull. 158 (1974); and David B. Buller, Communication apprehension and reactions to proxemic violations, 11 J. Nonverbal Beh. 13 (1987).

[15] See Frans W. Winkel, Leendert Koppelaar, and Aldert Vrij, Creating suspects in police-citizen encounters: Two studies on personal space and being suspect, 3 Soc. Beh. 307 (1988).

[16] See Stephan H. Peskin, Nonverbal communication in the courtroom, 3 Trial Diplomacy 8 (1980); Constance Bernstein, Winning trials nonverbally: Six ways to establish control in the courtroom, 30 Trial 61 (1994); Roberto Aron, Julius Fast, and Richard B. Klein, Trial Comunicaiton Skills, c.9, §§ 1-14 (1986); and Stanley L. Brodsky, Nicole E. Hooper, Donald G. Tipper, and S. Brian Yates, Attorney invasions of witness space, 23 L. and Psych. Rev. 49 (1999).

The Pervasive Inability to Recognize Constraints on Others

Perhaps more important than a person's feeling seized is an officer or a judge's evaluation of the encounter to determine its level of voluntariness. We already have seen in Chapter 3 that a large gap seems to exist between what people predict they would do in a situation and what they actually do. For example, we saw this phenomenon at work in research dealing with people's responses to authority and social pressure. People predict that they will not fall prey to these biases and pressures, even when confronted with evidence that most people actually do not resist them in practice. That finding corresponds well to social psychological experiments supporting the view that our imaginations are not as good as we think. We tend to think that we would do better than others in situations that research shows people simply do not perform well and that there is no reason to believe why anyone would do any better.[17]

The gap arises from the manner we tend to grossly overestimate the voluntariness of others' actions. A vast empirical literature reveals that situational forces systematically pull and push behavior, but our ability to recognize these forces depends on whether we are explaining our own behavior or someone else's behavior. Generally, we understand and explain another person's behavior in terms of internal causes (such as their intentions and dispositions), while ignoring aspects of the situation that could account for our own actions.[18] As a result, it may well be that behavior that looks voluntary from the outside feels constrained by the situation from the actor's perspective. In the context of police-citizen encounters, this means that observers outside of the situation systematically overestimate the extent to which citizens feel free to refuse consenting to interactions with officers. We are not good at identifying coerciveness. Importantly, this inability to discern occurs even when we are observing interactions, even in those situations we do not reliably appreciate the strength and consequences of situational constraints on another's behavior.[19]

This area of research may lead us to important conclusions. First, we recognize the influence other people can have on individuals. Second, we see the extent of the influence as relatively large and excessive even though we ourselves most likely would have been influenced similarly. Lastly, we are likely to make rather harsh moral judgments about those who are seen as easily influenced and manipulated on the rationale that we would not have given in to such pressure. These findings have been repeated as researchers frequently conclude that when the degree of influence shown by others is noted, we view the response as relatively excessive even though we also might have been influenced an equal amount; we tend to believe that we would be immune from such pressure.[20] People have difficulty accurately imagining the extent to which situational constraints shape their behavior; they overestimate their competencies and judge others a bit too harshly.

---

[17] For example, one classic laboratory study found that people listening to special beeps tend to overestimate the number of beeps they heard if other people who answer first also overestimate – in this sense, we conform with the decisions of others. This is not a surprising finding in light of what we have learned thus far. What is a bit surprising and more important to this analysis is the remarkable extent to which observers who secretly watch the laboratory sessions about others predicting actually predict that they themselves would be more accurate than the participants. Robert J. Wolosin, Steven J. Sherman, and Arnie Cann, Predictions of own and other's conformity, 43 J. Personality 357, 374 (1975).

[18] Daniel T. Gilbert and Patrick S. Malone, The correspondence bias, 117 Psych. Bull. 21 (1995).

[19] Daniel G. Lassiter, Andrew L. Geers, Patrick J. Munhall, Ian M. Handley, and Melissa J. Beers, Videotaped confessions: Is guilt in the eye of the camera?, 33 Adv. in Exper'l Soc. Psych. 189 (2001).

[20] One of the most interesting examples reveals that observers who read about a job candidate who is asked inappropriate interview questions predict that if they were in that situation themselves, they would confront the interviewer directly; yet, actual candidates who were placed in the very same situation capitulated and answered the question. Julie A. Woodzicka and Marianne LaFrance, Real versus imagined gender harassment, 57 J. Soc. Issues 15 (2001).

The Psychology of Officer Decision Making

If a seizure has occurred, the Fourth Amendment requires that the seizure be reasonable. To be a seizure, however, the legal system must consider the specific encounter as a recognizable seizure. The legal system permits stops, for example, because stops are not fully seizures and they are justifiable if the officer has a reasonable suspicion that the person is involved in criminal activity.[21] An officer has reasonable suspicion if the situation provides specific articulable facts to conclude that the suspect was reasonably stopped to investigate the occurrence of a crime. The facts justifying the stop must be objectively reasonable (another person would see them as sufficient to arouse "reasonable suspicion"). The reality, however, is that officers typically supply descriptions after the stop has occurred and after the discovery of incriminating evidence. In addition, the Court allows some stops to be done without reasonable suspicion; the stops are assumed to be reasonably suspicious and no reason exists to explain them. The requirements of the Fourth Amendment are loosened, for example, at border crossings, during exigent circumstances, sobriety checkpoints, and other circumstances in which societal interests outweigh the liberty or privacy interests of individuals.[22] Even these broad exceptions, however, raise the need to evaluate more closely the reasonableness of police officers' behaviors.

The significance of reasonableness, coupled with the failure to provide a clear definition of it, raises the psychological issue of what level of certainty a police officer must possess under the reasonableness approach. Research has not addressed this issue in terms of individual officers' own decisions but rather in terms of those who would evaluate officers' reasonableness: judges. A leading study surveyed 171 federal judges to determine their views of reasonable suspicion and probable cause. The study found that 66% indicated a belief that the reasonable suspicion standard requires 30% certainty or less that evidence of crime would be found by an officer after a stop; 74% indicated a belief that the reasonable suspicion standard requires 40% certainty or less; and 93% of the judges indicated that 50% certainty or less was necessary for reasonable suspicion.[23] Importantly, 36% would require 20% or less suspicion.[24] In terms of probable cause, 20% put it at 30% certainty or lower, 46% placed it at 40% certainty or lower, while only 6% placed it at 70 percent or certainty; 53% placed it at 50% certainty or higher.[25] Taken together, the average level of certainty needed to establish reasonable suspicion was thirty percent, while that needed for probable cause was the somewhat higher forty-five percent. This empirical evidence makes it quite clear that Fourth Amendment jurisprudence leaves open just how much liberty should be circumscribed. Police seem to enjoy considerable flexibility. There does not seem to be much difference between the standards that implicate very different levels of interaction – a mere stop versus a full arrest. Equally importantly, an officer can be deemed as acting reasonably even though they are likely to be wrong.

---

[21] *Terry v. Ohio*, 392 U.S. 1 (1968), was the seminal case establishing a new type of police-citizen encounter called the investigatory stop. Although the Fourth Amendment requires a police officer to have probable cause to arrest a suspect, the officer may detain a person for a short amount of time to investigate or question the person based on the less stringent requirement of reasonable suspicion. The original justification behind this increase in police power was a concern for police safety. In *Terry*, the Court held that the police officer was justified in detaining the defendant and in searching his person for weapons after the officer's observation of the defendant led him to suspect that the defendant was planning a robbery. The Supreme Court reasoned that this police power was necessary to promote effective law enforcement and to protect police officers from armed criminals. Since this decision, warrantless stops by police officers designed to confirm suspicions of criminal activity have been referred to as *Terry* stops.

[22] But the exceptions allowing for these stops have their limits; suspicionless roadblocks to stop cars in order to find drugs or to check drivers' licenses are impermissible on the rationale that suspicion would be needed. *Indianapolis v. Edmund*, 531 U.S. 32 (2000).

[23] C.M.A. McCauliff, Burdens of proof: Degrees of belief, quanta of evidence, or constitutional guarantees?, 35 Vand. L. Rev. 1293, 1328 (1982).

[24] C.M.A. McCauliff, Burdens of proof: Degrees of belief, quanta of evidence, or constitutional guarantees?, 35 Vand. L. Rev. 1293, 1328 (1982).

[25] C.M.A. McCauliff, Burdens of proof: Degrees of belief, quanta of evidence, or constitutional guarantees?, 35 Vand. L. Rev. 1293, 1327 (1982).

The major approach research has taken to assess the reasonableness of officers' decisions to stop has been to examine the extent to which their stops lead to arrests. Thus far, the most comprehensive study in this area was conducted by the New York Office of the Attorney General. That study used what are known as "UF-250s."[26] According to the NYPD's Patrol Guide, a police officer who stops and frisks an individual on the street must complete a UF-250 if a person is (1) stopped by force, (2) stopped and frisked, (3) arrested, and (4) stopped and refuses to identify oneself. In police-suspect encounters that fall outside these four contexts, a police officer may fill out a form if he or she desires to do so, but does not necessarily have to do so. The pool of forms analyzed in the study contained about three quarters mandated reports and the rest voluntary. The forms covered stops that occurred in 1998 and the first three months in 1999.

The Attorney General's study examined the characteristics of "good" stops, those that lead to an arrest. Citywide, that ratio was 9:1. That is, nine stops were made by the NYPD for every eventual arrest. The study also reported, however, many other important findings. The comparison between the stop-to-arrest rates were 2:1 for Blacks and Whites (the differential held across precincts with different percentages of minorities). For stops with reasonable suspicion, 7 stops were made for every one arrest. For stops without reasonable suspicion (voluntary questioning), the ratio was 29 to 1 (29 stops to 1 arrest). And stops for running from police in a high crime area had a stop-to-arrest ratio of 45:1. Although officers stop individuals for different reasons, not only to arrest but also, for example, to obtain leads for other crimes, the findings do reveal a significant amount of officer-citizen interactions. The findings also reveal an enormous amount of police discretion, apparently both in terms of stopping suspects and arresting them.

In addition to focusing on good/effective stops, research efforts have focused on variables that factor into an officer's decision to stop and decision to arrest. Researchers investigating police behavior have devoted considerable attention to the influence of extralegal variables – citizens' race, sex, age, and demeanor – on officers' use of their authority. The hypothesized effects of several extra-legal variables, such as race, have been confirmed by some studies and disconfirmed by others.[27] Nearly every study, however, reveals that a suspect's demeanor influences police behavior toward suspected offenders. Police are more likely to use their authority (by invoking the law or by using force) against suspects who are disrespectful or hostile toward police, or who more generally fail to show deference to the police.[28] Yet this clearly is not the definitive word on the relationship between suspects' demeanor and police action: the effect of demeanor might not simply be additive but interactive. Findings are complicated by the visibility of the encounter to complainants or to supervisors, the types of legal grounds for arrest or citation (e.g., drunk driving encounters versus interpersonal disputes), and the gravity of offense. Researchers have yet to conduct systematically the needed explorations of interactions between suspects' demeanor and other extralegal and legal variables in an effort to understand and explain more clearly the effects of demeanor. We do not know, then, whether the effects of demeanor are contingent on suspects' characteristics such as their race or sex, or on other features of police-citizen interactions, such as the seriousness of the offense or

---

[26] Eliot Spitzer, Office of the N.Y. State Attorney Gen., The New York City Police Department's "Stop and Frisk" Practices 92-110 (Dec. 1, 1999).

[27] For a complete review of these findings, see Eric C. Riksheim and Steven M. Chermack, Causes of police behavior revisited, 21 J. of Crim. Jus. 353 (1993).

[28] This finding remained undisputed until one researcher argued that suspects' demeanor had been conceived and measured improperly in previous research, and that previous studies had failed to control adequately for suspects' criminal behavior. David A. Klinger, Demeanor or crime? Why 'hostile' citizens are more likely to be arrested, 32 Criminology 475 (1994). His analysis of arrest in a sample of interpersonal disputes indicated that a suspect's demeanor was not statistically significant when demeanor was measured properly and controls for crime were included in the model. Since that time, researchers have reanalyzed previous findings while taking Klinger's criticisms into account. Their results confirm previous findings: although the magnitude or sometimes the significance of the effects is contingent on how demeanor is operationalized, a careful assessment of the most theoretically grounded analyses shows that police are more likely to take coercive action against antagonistic or hostile suspects. Robert E. Worden, Robin L. Shepard, and Stephen D. Mastrofski, On the meaning and measurement of suspects' demeanor toward the police: A comment on 'demeanor and arrest,' 33 J. of Res. in Crime and Delinq. 324 (1996).

the visibility of the encounter. It also is plausible that the effect of demeanor varies with the gravity of the offense, independent of the evidentiary basis for legal action.[29]

In addition to research on decisions to arrest, research increasingly examines whom police stop, or at least whom police hassle more often. The best research comes in analyses of motorist stops when police suspect them of criminal activity. That research reveals considerable racial profiling, a finding consistent with the disparity in the way the criminal justice system treats minorities.[30] That research, however, also is not without controversy. Few doubt that minority motorists are in fact stopped more often, but what that means remains open to interpretation. Some view, for example, the differential as legitimate based on findings of hit rates.[31] For example, research from a sector of I-95 in Maryland reveals 63% of the persons stopped and searched by state police were African-American and 29% were white (of a total of 1,590 observations). Given that the assumed proportion of African-American drivers on the road was approximately 18%, the officers' behaviors would seem to constitute obvious discrimination. However, 34 % of searches uncovered evidence of drug carrying when African Americans were searched and 32% of the searches revealed evidence of drugs when police searched white mororists.[32] The 33 percent average of successful searches of white and African-American drivers is much higher than success rates at nondiscretionary road blocks, noted to be around 4 percent.[33] The higher hit rate apparently results from the reality that officers do not profile on race alone. They profile on car models, vehicle attributes, motorist appearance, age, and other factors to narrow rather successfully the pool of likely suspects. Regardless of these findings of apparent effectiveness, however, some commentators focus on raw disparities in searches to argue that the disparities themselves produce large numbers of innocent motorists subjected to negative police interactions and state surveillance. They find such disparity unacceptable on its own terms.[34] Whether police are using their reasonable suspicion effectively still remains subject to interpretation, even though this currently seems to be the most researched area of police decision making.

Other areas of police decision making, however, do seem to report bias. In arrests for less-serious, non-Index crimes, ample reasons support the belief that police roles may well be more proactive than reactive, resulting in the overarrest of African-Americans compared to whites.[35] For instance and as we have seen, the Office of the Attorney General for the State of New York recently concluded that black and Hispanic males in New York City were subject to unfair practices through police "stop and frisk" operations.[36] Officials stated that racial disparities in stops exist and, furthermore, that these disparities do not go away when race-specific crime rates are taken into account. Similarly, the U.S. Customs Office recently reported that black women airline travelers were nine times as likely to be subject to invasive searches by Customs officers – despite the fact that black women's rate of offending was actually lower than that of white women. The report found that black women (U.S. citizens) were nine times more likely

---

[29] Robert E. Worden and Robin L. Shepard, Demeanor, crime, and police behavior: A reexamination of the Police Services Study Data, 34 Criminology 83 (1996).

[30] See Saundra Lee Browning, Francis T. Cullen, Liqun Cao, Renee Kopache, and Thomas J. Stevenson, Race and getting hassled by the police, 17 Police Stud. 1 (1994); and Katheryn K. Russell, The Color of Crime (1998).

[31] Hit rates simply are the percentage of the times officers' suspicions/stops uncover the targeted illegal activity, such as drug carrying.

[32] John Knowles, Nicola Persico, and Petra Todd, Racial bias in motor vehicle searches: Theory and evidence, 109 J. of Political Economy 203 (2001).

[33] The statistics of the leading case regarding the permissibility of random road blocks to search cars for drugs, *Indianapolis v. Edmund*, 531 U.S. 32 (2000), netted drug possession in 4.7 percent of the total number of stops.

[34] David Rudovsky, Law enforcement by stereotypes and serendipity: Racial profiling and stops and searches without cause, 3 U. Penn. J. of Const'l L. 298 (2001); and Albert W. Alschuler, Racial profiling and the Constitution, 2002 U. of Chic. Legal Forum 163 (2002).

[35] Anthony R. Harris and James A. W. Shaw, Looking for patterns: Race, class, and crime, in Criminology: A Contemporary Handbook 129, 135 (Joseph F. Sheley ed., 3d ed., 1999).

[36] Eliot Spitzer, Office of the N.Y. State Attorney Gen., The New York City Police Department's "Stop and Frisk" Practices 92-110 (Dec. 1, 1999).

than white women to be subjected to invasive searches, even though they "were less than half as likely to be found carrying contraband as white women who were U.S. citizens."[37]

Research asking those stopped by police also reveals important points about police decision making. A nationally representative sample collected as part of the 1999 annual National Crime Victimization Survey was used to randomly select over seven thousand reports of traffic stops in which the subjects were the driver.[38] Researchers asked these subjects their perception of the legitimacy of the stop and their perception of whether police had acted properly. The study found that, net of other important explanatory variables (e.g., driver's age and social class), the data indicated that police make more traffic stops for African-Americans (both males and females) and are more likely to stop males than females. In addition, African-American and Hispanic drivers were less likely to report that the police had a legitimate reason for the stop and also were less likely to report that the police had acted properly. These are important results that confirm other research findings suggesting that police use pretexts to stop drivers of color for minor traffic law violations that otherwise would go ignored. The study also reported that females are stopped significantly less often, presumably because police officers are more reluctant to stop female drivers for fear that they will press harassment charges. Officers treat women differently, and better than they treat men.[39] Although this area of research remains limited to basic explanations of race and gender, the research does explore important dynamics. The finding that officers consider race and gender provides important supportive evidence for our earlier discussions.

Although research investigating people's responses to police behavior remains in its infancy, it is important to not play down its significance. Surveys of individuals stopped by police relate to the overall impact of police discretion to arrest on public opinion. Researchers have studied extensively public opinion and attitudes on injustice and criminal law enforcement. Studies have sought to identify significant correlates of public opinions toward the police, the courts, various legal sanctions, and the legal system.[40] Surveys consistently have found that a nontrivial portion of the general population believes that the legal system treats minorities unfairly; and researchers also consistently have found a significantly greater level of perceived bias in the legal system among minorities.[41] In particular, African-American perception of racial discrimination in criminal law enforcement has been consistently identified in empirical research and opinion polls.[42] Note, however, that evidence does not always point in the direction of racial discrimination

---

[37] U.S. Gen. Accounting Office, Pub. No. GAO/GGD-00-38, U.S. Customs Service: Better Targeting of Airline Passengers for Personal Searches Could Produce Better Results 10 (2000). The report summarizes an investigation of U.S. Customs' policies and procedures involving searches of airline passengers at four airports [John Fitzgerald Kennedy International Airport (JFK) in New York, O'Hare International Airport in Chicago, Los Angeles International Airport (LAX), and Miami International Airport] in 1997 and 1998.

[38] Richard J. Lundman and Robert L. Kaufman, Driving while Black: Effects of race, ethnicity, and gender on citizen self-reports of traffic stops and police actions, 41 Criminology 195 (2003).

[39] This was supported by the finding that women are significantly more likely to report that officers acted properly.

[40] See, e.g., Timothy J. Flanagan and Michael S. Vaughn, Public opinion about police abuse of force, in Police Violence 113, 128 (William A. Geller and Hans Toch, eds., 1996); Timothy J. Flanagan, Edmund F. McGarrell and Edward J. Brown, Public Perceptions of the criminal courts: The role of demographic and related attitudinal variables, 22 J. Res. Crime and Delinq. 66 (1985); Phoebe C. Ellsworth and Lee Ross, Public opinion and capital punishment: A close examination of the views of abolitionists and retentionists, 29 Crime and Delinq. 116 (1983); Austin Sarat and Neil Vidmar, Public opinion, the death penalty, and the Eighth Amendment: Testing the Marshall Hypothesis, 1976 Wis. L. Rev. 171 (1976); and Tom. R. Tyler, Why People Obey the Law (1990).

[41] See David H. Bayley and Harold Mendelsohn, Minorities and the Police: Confrontation in America 42 (1969); and Ronald Weitzer, Racial discrimination in the criminal justice system: Findings and problems in the literature, 24 J. Crim. Just. 309 (1996).

[42] Several concerns and controversies arise from this finding, not the least of which is the controversy surrounding the manner police can enhance social norms. This observation led to the now broadly held conclusion that the police and communities can prevent serious crimes from overtaking a neighborhood by limiting and controlling the appearance of disorder. One particularly important – and controversial – approach is order-maintenance policing. These responses fall under the general rubric of community policing and, when properly implemented, they have been credited with controlling crime. This approach is predicated on the view that visible signs of disorder on the streetscape stimulate the commission of more serious crimes; therefore, an order-maintenance strategy seeks to minimize visible disorder through enforcement of curfew, truancy, anti-loitering, public intoxication and similar public order laws. James Q. Wilson and George L. Kelling, Broken windows: The police and neighborhood safety, Atlantic Monthly, Mar. 1982, at 29; George

but sometimes to different treatment based on sex, age, income, and degree of neighborhood disadvantage as well as police and suspect's attitudes and responses to coercive actions.[43] Like much of other research relating to police decision making, however, this line of research also still remains limited both in scope and depth. We area dealing with exceedingly complicated areas of human behavior.

Complexities of Controlling Police

The above considerations, especially in terms of the potential place of bias in policing, raise important concerns about how the legal system can control police. We know that they have considerable discretion. The probable cause requirement seeks to safeguard citizens from unfounded charges of crime, while giving fair leeway for enforcing the law to protect the community. In an effort to deter government conduct that violates the Fourth Amendment's provisions, and to impute value to the rights the Amendment embodies, the Court has developed the exclusionary rule. That rule offers a remedy that generally requires the suppression of evidence seized through an illegal search or arrest. When law enforcement violates constitutional mandates regulating searches and seizures, the courts typically exclude the evidence from the prosecution's case-in-chief, with the result that the state must often dismiss charges against the defendant.[44] Despite important exceptions to exclusion,[45] exclusion (like warrants themselves) serves to prevent police

L. Kelling and Catherine M. Coles, Fixing Broken Windows: Restoring Order and Reducing Crime in our Communities (1996). Order-maintenance advocates credit these tactics as a major force behind the precipitous reduction in the crime rate during the 1990s, especially in New York City, where their use has been particularly aggressive and widespread. Scholarly observers of urban policing are coming to agree that policing tactics did contribute to the substantial declines in urban crime rates experienced in the 1990s. But this approach to urban policing is not without its critics. Their essential argument is that this new brand of aggressive policing imposes an extremely harsh regime of surveillance and control, promotes heavy-handed police tactics based on highly ambiguous or innocuous conduct, endorses racial profiling and similar abuses, and falls disproportionately on persons of color. See, e.g., Bernard E. Harcourt, Illusion of Order: The False Promise of Broken Windows Policing 166-79 (2001); David Cole, Foreword: Discretion and discrimination reconsidered – A response to the New Criminal Justice Scholarship, 87 Geo. L.J. 1059, 1074-82 (1999); and Dorothy E. Roberts, Foreword: Race, vagueness, and the social meaning of order-maintenance policing, 89 J. Crim. L. and Criminology 775, 799-818 (1999). In many central city neighborhoods, the police and the community are often at odds over the police's order-maintenance strategies and complaints continue to charge that the police are too aggressive and are often biased against urban minorities. Accusations of racial bias have long plagued the American criminal justice system. Gary Stewart, Black codes and broken windows: The legacy of racial hegemony in anti-gang civil injunctions, 107 Yale L.J. 2249 (1998).

[43] Using those factors leads to finding, for example, that Whites may be at a disadvantage to the extent that they encounter more police disrespect. Stephen D. Mastrofski, Michael D. Reisig, and John D. McCluskey, Police disrespect toward the public: An encounter-based analysis, 40 Criminology 519 (2002).

[44] *Mapp v. Ohio*, 367 U.S. 643 (1961).

[45] Illegally seized evidence need not be excluded if it falls under any of the four traditional exceptions to exclusion. The good faith theory justifies foregoing exclusion when officers conduct an illegal search or seizure relying on a facially valid warrant, *United States v. Leon*, 468 U.S. 897, 922 (1984), a statute, *Illinois v. Krull*, 480 U.S. 340, 349-50 (1987), or a computerized arrest report, *Arizona v. Evans*, 514 U.S. 1, 15-16 (1995). The argument is that the threat of exclusion does not act as a deterrent. The presumption is that police officers who believe they are operating with a valid warrant or under a duly enacted statute are unlikely to believe their actions violate the Fourth Amendment. The secondary process theory rejects application of the exclusionary remedy in connection with proceedings, such as grand jury proceedings, *United States v. Calandra*, 414 U.S. 338, 354-55 (1974), and, although the Supreme Court has yet to so hold, lower courts routinely conclude that the rule is inapplicable at sentencing hearings, see e.g., *United States v. McCrory*, 930 F.2d 63 (D.C. Cir. 1991). The secondary process theory also rejects application of the exclusionary rule to procedures that are ancillary to making the prosecution's *prima facie* case, such as the impeachment of the defendant. *Walder v. United States*, 347 U.S. 62, 62 (1954), *United States v. Havens*, 446 U.S. 620, 627-28 (1980). The Court deems exclusion unnecessary in such situations because sufficient deterrence can be reached through preventing the use of illegal evidence in the government's case-in-chief. The secondary process theory also can be used to justify the introduction of illegally obtained evidence in noncriminal adjudications, such as tax deficiency proceedings, at least when the evidence is obtained by police who are looking for evidence of crime, *United States v. Janis*, 428 U.S. 433, 454 (1976), because the specter of exclusion at the criminal trial is seen as sufficient deterrence. The "independent source" exception applies when law enforcement has an alternative, independent source for discovering the evidence that was obtained through illegal means. *Murray v. United States*, 487 U.S. 533 (1988); *Segura v. United States*, 468 U.S. 796 (1984). Similarly, the "inevitable discovery" exception is available when law enforcement would have inevitably or ultimately discovered

abuse of their powers.[46] The reason for warrants and the exclusionary rule raises the question of whether they effectively control police. Given the practical significance of these constitutional protections, it is not surprising to find that several types of research address whether exclusion of illegally obtained evidence deters police violations of the Fourth Amendment. These efforts fall into four groups, and we examine each of them.

Police Officer Surveys

Two significant efforts have sought to determine directly from police officers whether the exclusionary rule effectively deters them from engaging in searches and seizures that violate the Fourth Amendment. The first study interviewed twenty-six narcotics police officers from the Chicago Police Department.[47] The officers were asked about officer training and experience with suppression motions and were asked to opine on how well the exclusionary rule worked, whether it should be "scrapped," whether it inhibited officers from performing searches, and whether it led officers to lie in court. With respect to whether the exclusionary rule educated police officers, 85% of the officers were informed when their evidence was suppressed and generally understood the basis for the suppression.[48] The study also revealed that at least some of the illegal searches occurred not because the police failed to understand the law of search and seizure, but because they wanted to get the weapons or drugs that were seized "off the street." Officers so motivated were, of course, not deterred by the exclusionary rule. Deterrence from the exclusionary rule was most common when police officers felt a personal sense of disappointment at the loss of a potential conviction; and several asserted that the suppression hearings themselves were a form of punishment. These findings indicate that many police officers feel a personal sense of loss when evidence is suppressed, thus giving the police an incentive to comply with the Fourth Amendment.

Importantly, the study also examined the extent to which institutional responses to suppression of evidence punish and deter police officers. The unit had a policy of demoting or transferring officers with two suppressions, a policy that was well known to the responding officers. Although that policy may have highlighted the potential deterrent effect of the exclusionary rule and led to greater protection of individuals' rights, it may have contributed to other unintended results. The study further revealed that almost all the officers admitted that police occasionally lie in suppression hearings. Seventy-six percent disclosed that police often "shade the facts" to establish that they had probable cause; nineteen percent stated that it was "reasonably common" for the officers to lie at the hearings. (Yet, five percent of the officers stated that they did not believe that officers lied in court and 56% stated that they believed that the police lied "infrequently.") All of the officers approved of the exclusionary rule, although several cited a need for a good faith exception. More than half of the police officers said that the exclusionary rule frequently kept them from making a search that they thought they should make; and 50% of the officers found that the rule harmed police work. Importantly, all of the police officers said they preferred the exclusionary rule to a system that would permit victims of improper searches to sue the offending officers. Ninety-five percent of the responding officers stated that allowing victims to sue officers would have a

---

the illegally obtained evidence, even without the illegal search. *Nix v. Williams*, 467 U.S. 431, 432 (1984). The belief is that the exclusionary rule loses its deterrent value in, and thus should not apply to, these circumstances. The final exception is for "attenuation," which occurs when an intervening act occurs that separates the Fourth Amendment violation from the discovery of the evidence. These circumstances are said to remove the "taint," which then renders the evidence admissible. *Brown v. Illinois*, 422 U.S. 590 (1975); and *Wong Sun v. United States*, 371 U.S. 471 (1963).

[46] Indeed, the exclusionary rule exists to deter police misconduct. *United States v. Calandra*, 414 U.S. 338 (1973).

[47] Myron W. Orfield, Jr., The exclusionary rule and deterrence: An empirical study of Chicago narcotics officers, 54 U. Chi. L. Rev. 1016 (1987).

[48] Note that this was an important finding because an offending officer must be informed of his mistakes if he is to leran from and correct them.

chilling effect on the officers' ability to do their jobs. Based on these and similar findings, the study concluded that the exclusionary rule deters illegal searches.

The second study focused on two fundamental questions: Do the police understand the law of search and seizure? And how frequently do police believe that they in fact violate search or seizure rules?[49] The officers responded to a series of hypotheticals involving warrantless police intrusion and numerous questions about Fourth Amendment Law. For purposes of comparison, the researchers also posed both sets of questions to groups of prosecutors, public defenders, and college students in an introductory course in criminal justice. In answering the hypotheticals, the officers reached the correct conclusion about the lawfulness of the intrusion 56.7% of the time, whereas lawyers were correct 73.3% of the time. Officers answered the multiple-choice questions correct less than 50 percent of the time. More than one-third of the officers would engage in conduct that would constitute an unwitting violation of search and seizure rules. The researchers concluded that the large number of unwitting violators (34%) shows the extent to which the rule can not operate as a deterrent. (There can be no deterrence in the absence of police understanding the law.) Importantly, fifteen percent of the more than 500 officers responding said that they would intentionally follow an illegal course of conduct; that is, one in six was willing to knowingly disregard the rights of the accused. The fact that 15% of the participants admitted such an inclination suggests a higher actual (not admitted) rate of non-compliance. Unlike the study reviewed above, this one concluded that the exclusionary rule may deter some police misconduct but that its effectiveness still leaves much to be desired.

Surveys of Other Criminal Justice Personnel

Three important studies have sought to determine opinions held by participants in the criminal justice system concerning the efficacy of the exclusionary rule. A survey of police chiefs, prosecuting attorneys, judges, defense attorneys, and A.C.L.U. officials reported important findings.[50] This study sought to exmine the impact of *Mapp v. Ohio,*[51] the Supreme Court decision that announced the exclusionary rule. The study compared results from 23 states that had an exclusionary rule prior to the 1961 *Mapp* decision (noninitiating states) to the 24 states that had been forced to initiate the exclusionary rule by the *Mapp* decision (initiating states). Noninitiating states reported a 57% increase in police adherence to search and seizure rules since *Mapp*, while initiating states reported a 75% increase; likewise, police departments increased their emphasis in educating their officers in the law of search and seizure, a 51% increase in the initiating states compared to a 27% increase in the noninitiating states. Following *Mapp*, 57% of the respondents in the initiating states reported an increase in the number of searches declared illegal, while 36% of those respondents reported no change. This is compared to 35% reporting an increase in the noninitiating states and 53% indicating no change. The study next examined the number of criminal defendants released because of the exclusion of evidence. Forty-five percent of the respondents from the initiating states reported an increase in releases and 43% reported no change. By contrast, 34% of the respondents from the noninitiating states reported an increase and 53% reported no change. The study neither repudiates nor confirms the exclusionary rule as a deterrent to illegal police conduct, but it does reflect that, after *Mapp*, both desirable and undesirable effects were felt, even in jurisdictions that previously had in place an exclusionary rule.

---

[49] William C. Heffernan and Richard W. Lovely, Evaluating the Fourth Amendment exclusionary rule: The problem of police compliance with the law, 24 U. Mich. J.L. Reform 311 (1991).

[50] Stuart S. Nagel, Testing the effects of excluding illegally seized evidence, 1965 Wis. L. Rev. 283 (1965). Those responding included 22 police chiefs, 27 prosecuting attorneys, 17 judges, 24 defense attorneys, 19 A.C.L.U. officials, and 4 with unknown occupations.

[51] *Mapp v. Ohio*, 367 U.S. 643 (1961).

Another important study examined the impact of the exclusionary rule in a jurisdiction (North Carolina) that had adopted the rule 10 years prior to *Mapp*.[52] Surprisingly, five (18%) of the trial judges, fourteen (34%) of the prosecutors and six (29%) of the defense lawyers did not know that North Carolina required exclusion of illegally seized evidence prior to *Mapp*. That is, more than 1 out of 4 participants in the adjudicative process did not know that illegally seized evidence needed to be excluded. Only 8% of the judges and 10% of the defense attorneys, compared with 59% of the prosecutors, approved of admitting reliable evidence regardless of whether it was legally obtained. Thirty-nine percent of defense attorneys felt that the "legal search" should be expanded; and 71% of the judges favored an expanded definition. Seventy-nine percent of police officers and prosecutors felt it hindered law enforcement, 80% felt that morale had decreased because of the rule, and 100% felt there was an increase in the number of guilty people going free.

The third significant effort interviewed personnel in fourteen randomly selected felony trial courtrooms in the Criminal Division of the Circuit Court of Cook County.[53] The study concluded that the exclusionary rule effectively deters illegal searches and educates police officers. However, the study showed two significant "costs" associated with the exclusionary rule: pervasive police perjury in an effort to avoid suppression and judicial abdication of the duty to suppress evidence in serious cases. A majority of judges and public defenders reported that perjury was the main factor limiting the deterrent effect of the exclusionary rule; 81% of all respondents believed that the possibility of suppression sometimes caused police officers to change their testimony rather than their behavior. Additionally, 38% of the respondents believed that police superiors encouraged police perjury, while 67% felt that police superiors "tolerated" it. The study also indicated that 93% of all respondents believed that, at least some of the time, prosecutors knew, or had reason to know, that police were lying at suppression hearings. Some respondents even felt that prosecutors encouraged perjury in the way that they prepared police officers to testify. Seventy percent of all respondents indicated that judges sometimes failed to suppress evidence when required by law to do so because it would be unjust; they also felt that judges would fail to suppress evidence because of the judge's desire to avoid adverse publicity (60% of respondents) and fear that it would hurt the judge's chances for re-election (48% of respondents). These findings, as a whole, challenge the belief that the exclusionary rule effectively controls police conduct.[54]

Observational Studies

Jerome H. Skolnick's classic observational study of policing asked police officers about the exclusionary rule and its effects on them.[55] He found that police officers faced two principal dilemmas. First, the officer had to consider what behavior constituted a legal arrest, because most searches were made incident to an arrest, and therefore were without a warrant. Second, officers had to adopt a particular strategy to make their activity appear legal, even if that was not the case. Officers reported that courts had not clearly set forth the boundaries of legal searches and seizures, which led officers to be able to reconstruct events in ways, subsequent to the arrest, that would allow a court to find probable cause. As a result, the exclusionary rule created many dangers, such as falsification of the arrest report, perjury at a suppression hearing, and other abuses of police authority, each of which defeated the purpose for having an exclusionary rule.

---

52 Michael Katz, The Supreme Court and the states: An inquiry into *Mapp v. Ohio* in North Carolina. The model, the study, and the implications, 45 N.C. L. Rev. 119, 119 (1966).

53 Myron W. Orfield, Jr., Deterrence, perjury and the heater factor: An exclusionary rule in the Chicago criminal courts, 63 U. Colo L. Rev. 75 (1992).

54 Note that these findings typically are used to support the argument that other methods, such as lawsuits against specific officers, would offer much needed remedies.

55 Jerome H. Skolnick, Justice Without Trial (1966).

Skolnick also pointed to circumstances within the police environment that hamper the deterrent effect of the exclusionary rule. First, the average police officer would feel embarrassed to report to a superior that he hesitated to search someone on the street because he had first to meditate on the suspect's legal rights, and that, because of his hesitation, the suspect had in the meantime escaped or had disposed of the incriminating evidence. Thus, the deterrent value of the exclusionary rule was slight when compared to the pressures on a particular police officer to satisfy his superiors or his department. Second, the Fourth Amendment rights competed against the officers' need to make an arrest to ensure public safety. Typically, police officers fear that if they spend too much time debating whether their actions meet constitutional standards, the suspect might make a getaway. If the officer could justify his search to his superiors, the worst that might happen was a lost conviction, and if the search failed to yield any incriminating evidence, then all the involved parties could drop the matter. On the other hand, if incriminating evidence was found, the burden shifted toward the defendant, or the suspect. The legality of the search may still be an issue, but it was likely to be offset by the fact that something actually was found. Finally, even if the individual police officer lost a conviction, Skolnick noted that sympathy from the officer's superiors helped smooth over the situation, even if the officer did not have the reasonable cause required to make the arrest, provided that the search was administratively reasonable.[56] Although derived from a very different research method, Skolnick's findings support many of the points made by other researchers.

Arrest and Legal Outcomes Research

A last group of studies attempting to gauge the effectiveness of the exclusionary rule involved the analysis of criminal justice statistics, including arrests, convictions, returns of seized property, and suppression motions.[57] For example, one study divided the states into "own rule states," which included those states that had an exclusionary rule before the advent of *Mapp*, and "imposed rule states," which included those states whose use of the exclusionary rule began with *Mapp*.[58] The study examined nineteen cities and arrest rates for three types of offenses (gambling, narcotics, and weapons violations) and focused on statistics from four or five pre-*Mapp* years (1956 or 1957-60) and for four post-*Mapp* years (1962-65). Based on the relative increases or decreases in the arrest rates after *Mapp*, the study concluded that *Mapp* had a significant impact on 34.8% of the "imposed rule states" and no significant impact on the remaining 65.2% of those states. In comparison, the study found that *Mapp* significantly impacted arrest rates in 43.5% of the "own rule" states, but not the remaining 56.5% of the "own rule" states. This surprising finding, which at first blush appears to be upside down, led the researchers to speculate that the only way *Mapp* has a strong impact is if it reinforces an already existing exclusionary rule policy; or it could also be argued, based on this finding, that the impact of *Mapp* as a deterrent was greatly exaggerated.

Unfortunately, the pre/post studies were seriously flawed. Post-*Mapp* changes in the number of search warrants issued, arrest and conviction rates, or the amount of recovered stolen property and seized contraband – in theory, possible indicators of the rule's effect – turned out to be confounded by a number of other factors as well. These other potential influences include changes in crime rates, police priorities,

---

56 Skolnick also noted that officers knew that civil suits for false arrest are difficult to prove, and if the suspect does indeed turn out to be a criminal, such as an addict, the suspect's position would prevent him from filing a complaint against the police.

57 Comment, Effect of *Mapp v. Ohio* on police search-and-seizure practices in narcotics cases, 4 Colum. J.L. and Soc. Probs. 87, 102 (1968); Dallin H. Oaks, Studying the exclusionary rule in search and seizure, 37 U. Chi. L. Rev. 665, 675 (1970); James E. Spiotto, Search and seizure: An empirical study of the exclusionary rule and its alternatives, 2 J. Legal Stud. 243 (1973); Bradley C. Canon, Is the exclusionary rule in failing health? Some new data and a plea against a precipitous conclusion, 62 Ky. L.J. 681 (1973); Bradley C. Canon, Testing the effectiveness of civil liberties policies at the state and federal levels, 5 Am. Pol. Q. 57 (1977); Comptroller General U.S., General Accounting Office, Impact of the Exclusionary Rule on Federal Criminal Prosecutions (Rep. No. GGD-79-45) (1979); National Institute of Justice, The Effects of the Exclusionary Rule: A Study in California 2 (1982); and Craig D. Uchida and Timothy S. Bynum, Search warrants, motions to suppress and "lost cases": The effects of the exclusionary rule in seven jurisdictions, 81 J. Crim. L. and Criminology 1034, 1035 (1991).

58 Bradley C. Canon, Testing the effectiveness of civil liberties policies at the state and federal levels, 5 Am. Pol. Q. 57 (1977).

and Fourth Amendment rules. Poor record-keeping prior to *Mapp* also afflicted the studies. These difficulties critically undermined pre/post research on the exclusionary rule and reveal, if anything, the difficulty of determining whether rules in fact have their desired effects.

Reaching Conclusions about Controlling Officers' Decisions

Taken together, these studies reveal many important points. Even rules that seem rather strict and theoretically straight-forward may not transfer well in practice. Efforts to assess whether rules reach effectiveness face many challenges that question the results of even the most comprehensive research efforts. Much of the research appears quite dated, and whether we could expect different findings from more recent research remains to be seen. Lastly, it actually is surprising to find that many charged with the mandate to enforce laws simply do not know key laws and do not abide by them. This last problem obviously compounds the others we have identified, such as the unwittingly biased implementation of laws.

NOTES AND QUERIES

What do you make of the psychological assumptions the legal system makes about individuals' consenting to interact with police? Note that research directly on point does not exist. It is unclear, for example, when people would feel free to leave and decline an officer's request for a brief encounter. Also not examined are officers' perceptions of when individuals would feel free to leave or feel under the authority of police. The anecdotal and theoretical work may help us understand current rules, but much more remains to be investigated. In the cases that follow, determine the extent to which (and how) social science can shed light on these very basic assumptions the law makes about citizen-police encounters and how such evidence could be best utilized, if at all.

The use of the totality of the circumstances test to determine the legality of searches makes psychological research significant. For example, the totality of the circumstances analysis may not take into account the general human inability to discern coercion in a particular set of circumstances from the perspective outside of the questioned situation. Using our imaginations may increase our bias and overestimate a suspect's abilities to resist the power of situations. Most of us probably think that the exaggerated perception of voluntariness may be easily overcome if we simply imagine the suspect's perspective and how the coerciveness of situational constraints would feel on us. By imagining oneself in the shoes of the citizen whom the police are targeting, such as in bus sweeps, we may think that we can understand the situational pressures that the target feels, and thus more accurately determine whether they are in a position to choose freely whether to consent to police officers' requests. The reality seems to be that this is problematic. Because people have difficulty imagining situational influences that constrain choice when such imagining takes place outside of the situation, people tend to grossly overestimate the voluntariness of even their own hypothetical actions.

What significance do you attach to the strikingly broad range of certainty federal judges require of reasonable suspicion and probable cause standards?

What do you make of research on the effectiveness of the exclusionary rule. Which studies do you find most persuasive? To what extent do you think these studies should matter to rethinking how to control police officers effectively? Do you think more recent research would reveal similar results challenging the effectiveness of efforts to control police through the exclusionary rule?

STOPPING SUSPECTS

TERRY v. OHIO

392 U.S. 1 (1968)

MR. CHIEF JUSTICE WARREN delivered the opinion of the Court

... Officer McFadden testified that while he was patrolling in plain clothes in downtown Cleveland at approximately 2:30 in the afternoon of October 31, 1963, his attention was attracted by two men, Chilton and Terry, standing on the corner of Huron Road and Euclid Avenue. He ... was unable to say precisely what first drew his eye to them. However, he testified that he had been a policeman for 39 years and a detective for 35 and that ... he had developed routine habits of observation over the years and that he would "stand and watch people or walk and watch people at many intervals of the day." He added: "Now, in this case when I looked over they didn't look right to me at the time."

His interest aroused, Officer McFadden took up a post of observation in the entrance to a store 300 to 400 feet away from the two men. "I get more purpose to watch them when I seen their movements," he testified. He saw one of the men leave the other one and walk southwest on Huron Road, past some stores. The man paused for a moment and looked in a store window, then walked on a short distance, turned around and walked back toward the corner, pausing once again to look in the same store window. He rejoined his companion at the corner, and the two conferred briefly. Then the second man went through the same series of motions, strolling down Huron Road, looking in the same window, walking on a short distance, turning back, peering in the store window again, and returning to confer with the first man at the corner. The two men repeated this ritual alternately between five and six times apiece – in all, roughly a dozen trips. At one point, while the two were standing together on the corner, a third man approached them and engaged them briefly in conversation. This man then left the two others and walked west on Euclid Avenue. Chilton and Terry resumed their measured pacing, peering, and conferring. After this had gone on for 10 to 12 minutes, the two men walked off together, heading west on Euclid Avenue, following the path taken earlier by the third man.

By this time Officer McFadden had become thoroughly suspicious. He testified that ... he suspected the two men of "casing a job, a stick-up," and that he considered it his duty as a police officer to investigate further. He added that he feared "they may have a gun." ... Deciding that the situation was ripe for direct action, Officer McFadden approached the three men, identified himself as a police officer and asked for their names. At this point his knowledge was confined to what he had observed. He was not acquainted with any of the three men by name or by sight, and he had received no information concerning them from any other source. When the men "mumbled something" in response to his inquiries, Officer McFadden grabbed petitioner Terry, spun him around so that they were facing the other two, with Terry between McFadden and the others, and patted down the outside of his clothing. In the left breast pocket of Terry's overcoat Officer McFadden felt a pistol. He reached inside the overcoat pocket, but was unable to remove the gun. At this point, keeping Terry between himself and the others, the officer ordered all three men to enter Zucker's store. As they went in, he removed Terry's overcoat completely, removed a .38-caliber revolver from the pocket and ordered all three men to face the wall with their hands raised. Officer McFadden proceeded to pat down the outer clothing of Chilton and the third man, Katz. He discovered another revolver in the outer pocket of Chilton's overcoat, but no weapons were found on Katz. The officer testified that he only patted the men down to see whether they had weapons, and that he did not put his hands beneath the outer garments of either Terry or Chilton until he felt their guns. So far as appears from the record, he never placed his hands beneath Katz' outer garments. Officer McFadden seized Chilton's gun, asked the proprietor of the store to call a police wagon, and took all three men to the station, where Chilton and Terry were formally charged with carrying concealed weapons.

On the motion to suppress the guns the ... court denied the defendants' motion on the ground that Officer McFadden, on the basis of his experience, "had reasonable cause to believe . . . that the defendants were conducting themselves suspiciously, and some interrogation should be made of their action." Purely for his own protection, the court held, the officer had the right to pat down the outer clothing of these men, who he had reasonable cause to believe might be armed. ...

I.

We have recently held that "the Fourth Amendment protects people, not places," and wherever an individual may harbor a reasonable "expectation of privacy," he is entitled to be free from unreasonable governmental intrusion. Of course, the specific content and incidents of this right must be shaped by the context in which it is asserted. For "what the Constitution forbids is not all searches and seizures, but unreasonable searches and seizures." Unquestionably petitioner was entitled to the protection of the Fourth Amendment as he walked down the street in Cleveland. The question is whether in all the circumstances of this on-the-street encounter, his right to personal security was violated by an unreasonable search and seizure.

We would be less than candid if we did not acknowledge that this question thrusts to the fore difficult and troublesome issues regarding a sensitive area of police activity ...

On the one hand, it is frequently argued that in dealing with the rapidly unfolding and often dangerous situations on city streets the police are in need of an escalating set of flexible responses, graduated in relation to the amount of information they possess. For this purpose it is urged that distinctions should be made between a "stop" and an "arrest" (or a "seizure" of a person), and between a "frisk" and a "search." Thus, it is argued, the police should be allowed to "stop" a person and detain him briefly for questioning upon suspicion that he may be connected with criminal activity. Upon suspicion that the person may be armed, the police should have the power to "frisk" him for weapons. If the "stop" and the "frisk" give rise to probable cause to believe that the suspect has committed a crime, then the police should be empowered to make a formal "arrest," and a full incident "search" of the person. This scheme is justified in part upon the notion that a "stop" and a "frisk" amount to a mere "minor inconvenience and petty indignity," which can properly be imposed upon the citizen in the interest of effective law enforcement on the basis of a police officer's suspicion.

On the other side the argument is made that the authority of the police must be strictly circumscribed by the law of arrest and search ... The heart of the Fourth Amendment, the argument runs, is a severe requirement of specific justification for any intrusion upon protected personal security, coupled with a highly developed system of judicial controls to enforce upon the agents of the State the commands of the Constitution. Acquiescence by the courts in the compulsion inherent in the field interrogation practices at issue here, it is urged, would constitute an abdication of judicial control over, and indeed an encouragement of, substantial interference with liberty and personal security by police officers whose judgment is necessarily colored by their primary involvement in "the often competitive enterprise of ferreting out crime." This, it is argued, can only serve to exacerbate police-community tensions in the crowded centers of our Nation's cities.

In this context we approach the issues in this case mindful of the limitations of the judicial function in controlling the myriad daily situations in which policemen and citizens confront each other on the street. The State has characterized the issue here as "the right of a police officer . . . to make an on-the-street stop, interrogate and pat down for weapons (known in street vernacular as 'stop and frisk'). "But this is only partly accurate. For the issue is not the abstract propriety of the police conduct, but the admissibility against petitioner of the evidence uncovered by the search and seizure. Ever since its inception, the rule excluding evidence seized in violation of the Fourth Amendment has been recognized as a principal mode of discouraging lawless police conduct. Thus its major thrust is a deterrent one, and experience has taught that it is the only effective deterrent to police misconduct in the criminal context, and that without it the constitutional guarantee against unreasonable searches and seizures would be a mere "form of words." The rule also serves another vital function – "the imperative of judicial integrity." Courts which sit under our Constitution cannot and will not be made party to lawless invasions of the constitutional rights of citizens by permitting unhindered governmental use of the fruits of such invasions. Thus in our system evidentiary rulings provide the context in which the judicial process of inclusion and exclusion approves some conduct as comporting with constitutional guarantees and disapproves other actions by state agents. A ruling admitting evidence in a criminal trial, we recognize, has the necessary effect of legitimizing the conduct which produced the evidence, while an application of the exclusionary rule withholds the constitutional imprimatur.

The exclusionary rule has its limitations, however, as a tool of judicial control. It cannot properly be invoked to exclude the products of legitimate police investigative techniques on the ground that much conduct which is closely similar involves unwarranted intrusions upon constitutional protections. Moreover, in some contexts the rule is ineffective as a deterrent. Street encounters between citizens and police officers are incredibly rich in diversity. They range from wholly friendly exchanges of pleasantries or mutually useful information to hostile confrontations of armed men involving arrests, or injuries, or loss of life. Moreover, hostile confrontations are not all of a piece. ... Regardless of how effective the rule may be where obtaining convictions is an important objective of the police, it is powerless to deter invasions of constitutionally guaranteed rights where the police either have no interest in prosecuting or are willing to forgo successful prosecution in the interest of serving some other goal.

Proper adjudication of cases in which the exclusionary rule is invoked demands a constant awareness of these limitations. The wholesale harassment by certain elements of the police community, of which minority groups ... frequently complain, will not be stopped by the exclusion of any evidence from any criminal trial. Yet a rigid and unthinking application of the exclusionary rule, in futile protest against practices which it can never be used effectively to control, may exact a high toll in human injury and frustration of efforts to prevent crime. No judicial opinion can comprehend the protean variety of the street encounter, and we can only judge the facts of the case before us. ...

...we turn our attention to the quite narrow question posed by the facts before us: whether it is always unreasonable for a policeman to seize a person and subject him to a limited search for weapons unless there is probable cause for an arrest. ...

II.

Our first task is to establish at what point in this encounter the Fourth Amendment becomes relevant. That is, we must decide whether and when Officer McFadden "seized" Terry and whether and when he conducted a "search." There is some suggestion in the use of such terms as "stop" and "frisk" that such police conduct is outside the purview of the Fourth Amendment because neither action rises to the level of a "search" or "seizure" within the meaning of the Constitution. We emphatically reject this notion. ... It must be recognized that whenever a police officer accosts an individual and restrains his freedom to walk away, he has "seized" that person. And it is nothing less than sheer torture of the English language to suggest that a careful exploration of the outer surfaces of a person's clothing all over his or her body in an attempt to find weapons is not a "search." Moreover, it is simply fantastic to urge that such a procedure performed in public by a policeman while the citizen stands helpless, perhaps facing a wall with his hands raised, is a "petty indignity." It is a serious intrusion upon the sanctity of the person, which may inflict great indignity and arouse strong resentment, and it is not to be undertaken lightly.

...We therefore reject the notions that the Fourth Amendment does not come into play at all as a limitation upon police conduct if the officers stop short of something called a "technical arrest" or a "full-blown search."

In this case there can be no question, then, that Officer McFadden "seized" petitioner and subjected him to a "search" when he took hold of him and patted down the outer surfaces of his clothing. We must decide whether at that point it was reasonable for Officer McFadden to have interfered with petitioner's personal security as he did. And in determining whether the seizure and search were "unreasonable" our inquiry is a dual one – whether the officer's action was justified at its inception, and whether it was reasonably related in scope to the circumstances which justified the interference in the first place.

III.

If this case involved police conduct subject to the Warrant Clause of the Fourth Amendment, we would have to ascertain whether "probable cause" existed to justify the search and seizure which took place. However, that is not the case. We do not retreat from our holdings that the police must, whenever practicable, obtain advance judicial approval of searches and seizures through the warrant procedure, or that in most instances failure to comply with the warrant requirement can only be excused by exigent circumstances. But we deal here with an entire rubric of police conduct – necessarily swift action predicated upon the on-the-spot observations of the officer on the beat – which historically has not been, and as a practical matter could not be, subjected to the warrant procedure. Instead, the conduct involved in this case must be tested by the Fourth Amendment's general proscription against unreasonable searches and seizures.

Nonetheless, the notions which underlie both the warrant procedure and the requirement of probable cause remain fully relevant in this context. In order to assess the reasonableness of Officer McFadden's conduct as a general proposition, it is necessary "first to focus upon the governmental interest which allegedly justifies official intrusion upon the constitutionally protected interests of the private citizen," for there is "no ready test for determining reasonableness other than by balancing the need to search [or seize] against the invasion which the search [or seizure] entails." And in justifying the particular intrusion the police officer must be able to point to specific and articulable facts which, taken together with rational inferences from those facts, reasonably warrant that intrusion. The scheme of the Fourth Amendment becomes meaningful only when it is assured that at some point the conduct of those charged with enforcing the laws can be subjected to the more detached, neutral scrutiny of a judge who must evaluate the reasonableness of a particular search or seizure in light of the particular circumstances. And in making that assessment it is imperative that the facts be judged against an objective standard: would the facts available to the officer at the moment of the seizure or the search "warrant a man of reasonable caution in the belief" that the action taken was appropriate? Anything less would invite intrusions upon constitutionally guaranteed rights based on nothing more substantial than inarticulate hunches, a result this Court has consistently refused to sanction. And simple "'good faith on the part of the arresting officer is not enough.' ...If subjective good faith alone were the test, the protections of the Fourth Amendment would evaporate, and the people would be 'secure in their persons, houses, papers, and effects,' only in the discretion of the police."

Applying these principles to this case, we consider first the nature and extent of the governmental interests involved. One general interest is of course that of effective crime prevention and detection; it is this interest which underlies the recognition that a police officer may in appropriate circumstances and in an appropriate manner approach a person for purposes of investigating possibly criminal behavior even though there is no probable cause to make an arrest. It was this legitimate investigative function Officer McFadden was discharging when he decided to approach petitioner and his companions. ... It would have been poor police work indeed for an officer of 30 years' experience in the detection of thievery from stores in this same neighborhood to have failed to investigate this behavior further.

The crux of this case, however, is not the propriety of Officer McFadden's taking steps to investigate petitioner's suspicious behavior, but rather, whether there was justification for McFadden's invasion of

Terry's personal security by searching him for weapons in the course of that investigation. We are now concerned with more than the governmental interest in investigating crime; in addition, there is the more immediate interest of the police officer in taking steps to assure himself that the person with whom he is dealing is not armed with a weapon that could unexpectedly and fatally be used against him. Certainly it would be unreasonable to require that police officers take unnecessary risks in the performance of their duties...

In view of these facts, we cannot blind ourselves to the need for law enforcement officers to protect themselves and other prospective victims of violence in situations where they may lack probable cause for an arrest. When an officer is justified in believing that the individual whose suspicious behavior he is investigating at close range is armed and presently dangerous to the officer or to others, it would appear to be clearly unreasonable to deny the officer the power to take necessary measures to determine whether the person is in fact carrying a weapon and to neutralize the threat of physical harm.

We must still consider, however, the nature and quality of the intrusion on individual rights which must be accepted if police officers are to be conceded the right to search for weapons in situations where probable cause to arrest for crime is lacking. Even a limited search of the outer clothing for weapons constitutes a severe, though brief, intrusion upon cherished personal security, and it must surely be an annoying, frightening, and perhaps humiliating experience. Petitioner contends that such an intrusion is permissible only incident to a lawful arrest, either for a crime involving the possession of weapons or for a crime the commission of which led the officer to investigate in the first place. However, this argument must be closely examined.

Petitioner does not ... say that an officer is always unjustified in searching a suspect to discover weapons. Rather, he says it is unreasonable for the policeman to take that step until such time as the situation evolves to a point where there is probable cause to make an arrest. When that point has been reached, petitioner would concede the officer's right to conduct a search of the suspect for weapons, fruits or instrumentalities of the crime, or "mere" evidence, incident to the arrest.

Our evaluation of the proper balance that has to be struck in this type of case leads us to conclude that there must be a narrowly drawn authority to permit a reasonable search for weapons for the protection of the police officer, where he has reason to believe that he is dealing with an armed and dangerous individual, regardless of whether he has probable cause to arrest the individual for a crime. The officer need not be absolutely certain that the individual is armed; the issue is whether a reasonably prudent man in the circumstances would be warranted in the belief that his safety or that of others was in danger. And in determining whether the officer acted reasonably in such circumstances, due weight must be given, not to his inchoate and unparticularized suspicion or "hunch," but to the specific reasonable inferences which he is entitled to draw from the facts in light of his experience.

IV.

We must now examine the conduct of Officer McFadden in this case to determine whether his search and seizure of petitioner were reasonable, both at their inception and as conducted. ... We think on the facts and circumstances Officer McFadden detailed before the trial judge a reasonably prudent man would have been warranted in believing petitioner was armed and thus presented a threat to the officer's safety while he was investigating his suspicious behavior....

The manner in which the seizure and search were conducted is, of course, as vital a part of the inquiry as whether they were warranted at all. The Fourth Amendment proceeds as much by limitations upon the scope of governmental action as by imposing preconditions upon its initiation. The entire deterrent purpose of the rule excluding evidence seized in violation of the Fourth Amendment rests on the assumption that "limitations upon the fruit to be gathered tend to limit the quest itself." Thus, evidence may not be introduced if it was discovered by means of a seizure and search which were not reasonably related in scope to the justification for their initiation.

We need not develop at length in this case, however, the limitations which the Fourth Amendment places upon a protective seizure and search for weapons. ... The sole justification of the search in the present situation is the protection of the police officer and others nearby, and it must therefore be confined in scope to an intrusion reasonably designed to discover guns, knives, clubs, or other hidden instruments for the assault of the police officer.

The scope of the search in this case presents no serious problem in light of these standards...

V.

We conclude that the revolver seized from Terry was properly admitted in evidence against him. ... We merely hold today that where a police officer observes unusual conduct which leads him reasonably to conclude in light of his experience that criminal activity may be afoot and that the persons with whom he is dealing may be armed and presently dangerous, where in the course of investigating this behavior he identifies himself as a policeman and makes reasonable inquiries, and where nothing in the initial stages of the encounter serves to dispel his reasonable fear for his own or others' safety, he is entitled for the protection of himself and others in the area to conduct a carefully limited search of the outer clothing of such persons in an attempt to discover weapons which might be used to assault him. Such a search is a reasonable search under the Fourth Amendment, and any weapons seized may properly be introduced in evidence against the person from whom they were taken.

Affirmed.

MR. JUSTICE HARLAN, concurring

... Any person, including a policeman, is at liberty to avoid a person he considers dangerous. If and when a policeman has a right instead to disarm such a person for his own protection, he must first have a right not to avoid him but to be in his presence. That right must be more than the liberty (again, possessed by every citizen) to address questions to other persons, for ordinarily the person addressed has an equal right to ignore his interrogator and walk away; he certainly need not submit to a frisk for the questioner's protection. I would make it perfectly clear that the right to frisk in this case depends upon the reasonableness of a forcible stop to investigate a suspected crime.

Where such a stop is reasonable, however, the right to frisk must be immediate and automatic if the reason for the stop is, as here, an articulable suspicion of a crime of violence. ... There is no reason why an officer, rightfully but forcibly confronting a person suspected of a serious crime, should have to ask one question and take the risk that the answer might be a bullet.

MR. JUSTICE WHITE, concurring. [opinion omitted]

MR. JUSTICE DOUGLAS, dissenting.

I agree that petitioner was "seized" within the meaning of the Fourth Amendment. I also agree that frisking petitioner and his companions for guns was a "search." But it is a mystery how that "search" and that "seizure" can be constitutional by Fourth Amendment standards, unless there was "probable cause" to believe that (1) a crime had been committed or (2) a crime was in the process of being committed or (3) a crime was about to be committed.

The opinion of the Court disclaims the existence of "probable cause." If loitering were in issue and that was the offense charged, there would be "probable cause" shown. But the crime here is carrying concealed weapons; and there is no basis for concluding that the officer had "probable cause" for believing that that crime was being committed. Had a warrant been sought, a magistrate would, therefore, have been unauthorized to issue one, for he can act only if there is a showing of "probable cause." We hold today that the police have greater authority to make a "seizure" and conduct a "search" than a judge has to authorize such action. ...

To give the police greater power than a magistrate is to take a long step down the totalitarian path. Perhaps such a step is desirable to cope with modern forms of lawlessness. But if it is taken, it should be the deliberate choice of the people through a constitutional amendment. Until the Fourth Amendment, which is closely allied with the Fifth, is rewritten, the person and the effects of the individual are beyond the reach of all government agencies until there are reasonable grounds to believe (probable cause) that a criminal venture has been launched or is about to be launched.

Yet if the individual is no longer to be sovereign, if the police can pick him up whenever they do not like the cut of his jib, if they can "seize" and "search" him in their discretion, we enter a new regime. The decision to enter it should be made only after a full debate by the people of this country.

NOTES AND QUERIES

The Court makes the important finding that a stop and frisk is a search and seizure within the meaning of the Constitution, which means that the seizure must be reasonable. The Court then adopts a two-pronged approach to determine the reasonableness of the search and seizure: it must be justified at its inception and reasonably related in scope to the circumstances which justified the interference in the first place. To justify the intrusion, an officer must be able to point to specific and articulable facts which reasonably warrant the intrusion. Thus, there is a need to have specific reasonable inferences (suspicion) for the stop; there is no need to demonstrate probable cause. What do you make of this practical movement away from the need for officers to have probable cause before they seize a suspect? What do you make of Justice Douglas' dissent?

REVIEW NOTE ON MINNESOTA V. DICKERSON

After leaving a Minneapolis, Minnesota apartment building which was considered by police officers to be a "crack house," the accused began walking toward a marked squad car in which two police officers were patrolling. Upon making eye contact with one of the officers, the accused abruptly halted, began walking in the opposite direction, and turned and entered an alley on the other side of the building. The officers pulled the squad car into the alley and ordered the accused to stop and submit to a patdown search. The search revealed no weapons, but the officer who conducted the search felt a small lump in the front pocket of the accused's nylon jacket. As the officer later testified, the officer examined the lump with his fingers, and "it slid and it felt to be a lump of crack cocaine in cellophane." The officer then reached into the pocket and retrieved a small plastic bag containing one fifth of one gram of crack cocaine. The accused was arrested and charged with possession of a controlled substance. Prior to trial in a Minnesota county court, the accused moved to suppress the cocaine. Following *Terry v. Ohio*, should the cocaine be suppressed?

The Supreme Court unanimously held that, consistent with the Fourth Amendment, a police officer may seize nonthreatening contraband detected during a protective patdown search of a person whom the officer has briefly stopped based on the officer's reasonable conclusion that criminal activity may be afoot with respect to such person, where the officer is justified in believing that the person is armed and presently dangerous to the officer or to others nearby, so long as the officer strictly limits his search to that which is necessary for the discovery of weapons which might be used to harm the officer or others. Five Justices further held that, as in the case at hand, the Fourth Amendment did not permit the seizure of the cocaine where (a) the officer determined that the lump was contraband only after squeezing, sliding, and otherwise manipulating the contents of the pocket, which the officer already knew contained no weapon, and (b) because the officer's further search of the pocket was constitutionally invalid in that it was not authorized by *Terry v. Ohio* or any other exception to the Fourth Amendment's warrant requirement, the seizure of the cocaine that followed likewise was unconstitutional. See *Minnesota v. Dickerson*, 508 U.S. 366 (1993).

The case confirms that the protective search – permitted without a warrant and on the basis of reasonable suspicion less than probable cause – is not meant to discover evidence of crime, but must be strictly limited to that which is necessary for the discovery of weapons which might be used to harm the officer or others. If the protective search goes beyond what is necessary to determine if the suspect is armed, it is no longer valid under *Terry* and its fruits will be suppressed.

What do you make of the argument that we should extend the "plain-view" doctrine which permits police to seize an object without a warrant if they are lawfully in a position to view it, if its incriminating character is immediately apparent, and if they have a lawful right of access to it? The trial court had ruled to do just that, extend the doctrine to a "plain feel," arguing that the officers' seizure of the cocaine did not violate the Fourth Amendment because the sense of touch, grounded in experience and training, may be as reliable as perceptions drawn from other senses. The Supreme Court rejected the argument, finding the extension of the plain view doctrine too intrusive. Despite the Court's hesitancy to expand exceptions, how protective do you find the rule announced in *Dickerson*?

REVIEW NOTE ON ILLINOIS V. WARDLOW

On September 9, 1995, Officers Nolan and Harvey were working as uniformed officers in the special operations section of the Chicago Police Department. The officers were driving the last car of a four car caravan converging on an area known for heavy narcotics trafficking in order to investigate drug transactions. The officers were traveling together because they expected to find a crowd of people in the area, including lookouts and customers. As the caravan passed 4035 West Van Buren, Officer Nolan observed respondent Wardlow standing next to the building holding an opaque bag. Respondent looked in the direction of the officers and fled. Nolan and Harvey turned their car southbound, watched him as he ran through the gangway and an alley, and eventually cornered him on the street. Nolan then exited his car and stopped respondent. He immediately conducted a protective pat-down search for weapons because in his experience it was common for there to be weapons in the near vicinity of narcotics transactions. During the frisk, Officer Nolan squeezed the bag respondent was carrying and felt a heavy, hard object similar to the shape of a gun. The officer then opened the bag and discovered a .38-caliber handgun with five live rounds of ammunition. The officers arrested Wardlow. Should a trial court agree with Warldow's claim that the gun had been recovered during a lawful stop and frisk and must not be used to support a conviction of unlawful use of a weapon by a felon? See *Illinois v. Wardlow*, 528 U.S. 119 (2000).

In *Wardlow*, the trial court rejected the motion to suppress; the Illinois Appellate Court expressed the view that the gun should have been suppressed and reversed the accused's conviction; and the Illinois Supreme Court affirmed, expressing the view that sudden flight in a high crime area does not create a reasonable suspicion under *Terry v. Ohio*. On certiorari, the United States Supreme Court reversed and remanded. In an opinion by Chief Justice Rehnquist, joined by Justices O'Connor, Scalia, Kennedy, and Thomas, it was held that the police officer did not violate the Fourth Amendment when he stopped the accused, because the officer was justified in suspecting that the accused was involved in criminal activity and, therefore, in investigating further, as (1) officers are not required to ignore the relevant characteristics of a location in determining whether the circumstances are sufficiently suspicious to warrant further investigation, (2) headlong flight, which is the consummate act of evasion, is suggestive of wrongdoing, and (3) the determination of reasonable suspicion must be based on commonsense judgments and inferences about human behavior. Justice Stevens, joined by Justices Souter, Ginsburg, and Breyer, concurred in part and dissented in part, (1) agreed with the court's rejection of both the rule requested by Illinois, which rule would authorize the detention of anyone who flees at the mere sight of a police car, and the rule requested by the accused – that such flight would never, by itself, justify a stop authorized by *Terry v. Ohio* – but (2) expressed the view that even in a high crime neighborhood, unprovoked flight does not invariably lead to reasonable suspicion justifying a stop and frisk.

Wardlow raises two empirical questions. First, how good an indicator of guilt does flight from police have to be? Second, how many innocents are going to be stopped in relation to the whole? The risk of innocents being stopped may be too high to be constitutionally acceptable. One fear is that allowing police to justify stops and frisks with less evidence than is required for arrests and full searches implicitly encourages police officers to prefer these lesser intrusive actions over more serious ones.

Note on the Significance of Running Away from Officers

Why would an innocent person flee from police? What do you make of the following argument? A reasonable person may conclude that an officer's sudden appearance indicates nearby criminal activity. And criminal activity creates a substantial element of danger – either from the criminal or from a confrontation between the criminal and the police. These considerations can lead to an innocent and understandable desire to quit the vicinity with all speed. Regrettably, statistical studies of bystander victimization are rare. One study attributes this to incomplete recordkeeping and a lack of officially compiled data. See Lawrence W. Sherman, Leslie Steele, Deborah Laufersweiler, Nancy Hoffer, and Sherry Julian, Stray bullets and "mushrooms": Random shootings of bystanders in four cities, 1977-1988, 5 J. of Quant. Criminology 297, 303 (1989). Nonetheless, that study, culling data from newspaper reports in four large cities over an 11-year period, found "substantial increases in reported bystander killings and woundings in all four cities." Id. at 306. From 1986 to 1988, for example, the study identified 250 people who were killed or wounded in bystander shootings in the four survey cities.

For some citizens, particularly minorities and those residing in high crime areas, the possibility exists that fleeing constitutes entirely innocent behavior; with or without justification, they may believe that contact with the police can itself be dangerous, apart from any criminal activity associated with the officer's sudden presence. See Jean Johnson, Americans' Views on Crime and Law Enforcement: Survey Findings, National Institute of Justice Journal 13 (Sept. 1997) (reporting a study by the Joint Center for Political and Economic Studies in April 1996, which found that 43% of African-Americans consider "police brutality and harassment of African-Americans a serious problem" in their own community); President's Comm'n on Law Enforcement and Administration of Justice, Task Force Report: The Police 183-184 (1967) (documenting the belief, held by many minorities, that field interrogations are conducted "indiscriminately" and "in an abusive . . . manner," and labeling this phenomenon a "principal problem" causing "friction" between minorities and the police) (cited in *Terry v. Ohio*); Steven K. Smith, Greg W. Steadman, Todd W. Minton, and Meg Townsend, Criminal Victimization and Perceptions of Community Safety in 12 Cities 25, U.S. Dept. of Justice, Bureau of Justice Statistics (June 1998) (African-American residents in 12 cities are more than twice as likely to be dissatisfied with police practices than white residents in same community).

Seizing Suspects

U.S. v. MENDENHALL
446 U.S. 544 (1980)

MR. JUSTICE STEWART announced the judgment of the Court and delivered an opinion, in which MR. JUSTICE REHNQUIST joined. THE CHIEF JUSTICE, MR. JUSTICE BLACKMUN, and MR. JUSTICE POWELL also join all but Part II-A of this opinion.

I.

At the hearing in the trial court on the respondent's motion to suppress, it was established how the heroin she was charged with possessing had been obtained from her. The respondent arrived at the Detroit Metropolitan Airport on a commercial airline flight from Los Angeles early in the morning on February 10, 1976. As she disembarked from the airplane, she was observed by two agents of the DEA, who were present at the airport for the purpose of detecting unlawful traffic in narcotics. After observing the respondent's conduct, which appeared to the agents to be characteristic of persons unlawfully carrying narcotics [See note 1], the agents approached her as she was walking through the concourse, identified themselves as federal agents, and asked to see her identification and airline ticket.

The respondent produced her driver's license, which was in the name of Sylvia Mendenhall, and, in answer to a question of one of the agents, stated that she resided at the address appearing on the license. The airline ticket was issued in the name of "Annette Ford." When asked why the ticket bore a name different from her own, the respondent stated that she "just felt like using that name." In response to a further question, the respondent indicated that she had been in California only two days. Agent Anderson then specifically identified himself as a federal narcotics agent and, according to his testimony, the respondent "became quite shaken, extremely nervous. She had a hard time speaking."

After returning the airline ticket and driver's license to her, Agent Anderson asked the respondent if she would accompany him to the airport DEA office for further questions. She did so, although the record does not indicate a verbal response to the request. The office, which was located up one flight of stairs about 50 feet from where the respondent had first been approached, consisted of a reception area adjoined by three other rooms. At the office the agent asked the respondent if she would allow a search of her person and handbag and told her that she had the right to decline the search if she desired. She responded: "Go ahead." She then handed Agent Anderson her purse, which contained a receipt for an airline ticket that had been issued to "F. Bush" three days earlier for a flight from Pittsburgh through Chicago to Los Angeles. The agent asked whether this was the ticket that she had used for her flight to California, and the respondent stated that it was.

A female police officer then arrived to conduct the search of the respondent's person. She asked the agents if the respondent had consented to be searched. The agents said that she had, and the respondent followed the policewoman into a private room. There the policewoman again asked the respondent if she consented to the search, and the respondent replied that she did. The policewoman explained that the search would require that the respondent remove her clothing. The respondent stated that she had a plane to catch and was assured by the policewoman that if she were carrying no narcotics, there would be no problem. The respondent then began to disrobe without further comment. As the respondent removed her clothing, she took from her undergarments two small packages, one of which appeared to contain heroin, and handed both to the policewoman. The agents then arrested the respondent for possessing heroin.

It was on the basis of this evidence that the District Court denied the respondent's motion to suppress. The court concluded that the agents' conduct in initially approaching the respondent and asking to see her ticket and identification was a permissible investigative stop under the standards of Terry v. Ohio, finding that this conduct was based on specific and articulable facts that justified a suspicion of criminal activity. The court also found that the respondent had not been placed under arrest or otherwise detained when she was asked to accompany the agents to the DEA office, but had accompanied the agents "'voluntarily in a spirit of apparent cooperation.'" It was the court's view that no arrest occurred until after the heroin had been found. Finally, the trial court found that the respondent "gave her consent to the search [in the DEA office] and . . . such consent was freely and voluntarily given."

The Court of Appeals reversed the respondent's subsequent conviction, ... [and] disapproved [of] the Government's reliance on the so-called "drug courier profile," and held that the agents could not reasonably have suspected criminal activity in that case, for the reason that "the activities of the [persons] observed by DEA agents, were consistent with innocent behavior." The Court of Appeals further concluded ... that, even if the initial approach had been permissible, asking the suspects to accompany the agents to a private room for further questioning constituted an arrest requiring probable cause. Finally, the court ... held that the consent to the search in that case had not been voluntarily given, principally because it was the fruit of what the court believed to have been an unconstitutional detention.

II.

...Here the Government concedes that its agents had neither a warrant nor probable cause to believe that the respondent was carrying narcotics when the agents conducted a search of the respondent's person. It is the Government's position, however, that the search was conducted pursuant to the respondent's consent, and thus was excepted from the requirements of both a warrant and probable cause. Evidently, the Court of Appeals concluded that the respondent's apparent consent to the search was in fact not voluntarily given and was in any event the product of earlier official conduct violative of the Fourth Amendment. We must first consider, therefore, whether such conduct occurred, either on the concourse or in the DEA office at the airport.

A.

The Fourth Amendment's requirement that searches and seizures be founded upon an objective justification, governs all seizures of the person, "including seizures that involve only a brief detention short of traditional arrest." Accordingly, if the respondent was "seized" when the DEA agents approached her on the concourse and asked questions of her, the agents' conduct in doing so was constitutional only if they reasonably suspected the respondent of wrongdoing. ...

We adhere to the view that a person is "seized" only when, by means of physical force or a show of authority, his freedom of movement is restrained. Only when such restraint is imposed is there any foundation whatever for invoking constitutional safeguards. The purpose of the Fourth Amendment is not to eliminate all contact between the police and the citizenry, but "to prevent arbitrary and oppressive interference by enforcement officials with the privacy and personal security of individuals." As long as the person to whom questions are put remains free to disregard the questions and walk away, there has been no intrusion upon that person's liberty or privacy as would under the Constitution require some particularized and objective justification.

Moreover, characterizing every street encounter between a citizen and the police as a "seizure," while not enhancing any interest secured by the Fourth Amendment, would impose wholly unrealistic restrictions upon a wide variety of legitimate law enforcement practices. The Court has on other occasions referred to the acknowledged need for police questioning as a tool in the effective enforcement of the criminal laws. ...

We conclude that a person has been "seized" within the meaning of the Fourth Amendment only if, in view of all of the circumstances surrounding the incident, a reasonable person would have believed that he was not free to leave. Examples of circumstances that might indicate a seizure, even where the person did not attempt to leave, would be the threatening presence of several officers, the display of a weapon by an officer, some physical touching of the person of the citizen, or the use of language or tone of voice indicating that compliance with the officer's request might be compelled. In the absence of some such evidence, otherwise inoffensive contact between a member of the public and the police cannot, as a matter of law, amount to a seizure of that person.

On the facts of this case, no "seizure" of the respondent occurred. The events took place in the public concourse. The agents wore no uniforms and displayed no weapons. ... The respondent was not seized simply by reason of the fact that the agents approached her, asked her if she would show them her ticket and identification, and posed to her a few questions. ... In short, nothing in the record suggests that the respondent had any objective reason to believe that she was not free to end the conversation in the concourse and proceed on her way, and for that reason we conclude that the agents' initial approach to her was not a seizure.

Our conclusion that no seizure occurred is not affected by the fact that the respondent was not expressly told by the agents that she was free to decline to cooperate with their inquiry, for the voluntariness of her responses does not depend upon her having been so informed. We also reject the argument that the only inference to be drawn from the fact that the respondent acted in a manner so contrary to her self-interest is that she was compelled to answer the agents' questions. It may happen that a person makes statements to law enforcement officials that he later regrets, but the issue in such cases is not whether the statement was self-protective, but rather whether it was made voluntarily.

B.

Although we have concluded that the initial encounter between the DEA agents and the respondent on the concourse at the Detroit Airport did not constitute an unlawful seizure, it is still arguable that the respondent's Fourth Amendment protections were violated when she went from the concourse to the DEA office. Such a violation might in turn infect the subsequent search of the respondent's person.

The question whether the respondent's consent to accompany the agents was in fact voluntary or was the product of duress or coercion, express or implied, is to be determined by the totality of all the circumstances, and is a matter which the Government has the burden of proving. The respondent herself did not testify at the hearing. The Government's evidence showed that the respondent was not told that she had to go to the office, but was simply asked if she would accompany the officers. There were neither threats nor any show of force. The respondent had been questioned only briefly, and her ticket and identification were returned to her before she was asked to accompany the officers.

On the other hand, it is argued that the incident would reasonably have appeared coercive to the respondent, who was 22 years old and had not been graduated from high school. It is additionally suggested that the respondent, a female and an African-American, may have felt unusually threatened by the officers, who were white males. While these factors were not irrelevant, neither were they decisive, and the totality of the evidence in this case was plainly adequate to support the District Court's finding that the respondent voluntarily consented to accompany the officers to the DEA office.

C.

Because the search of the respondent's person was not preceded by an impermissible seizure of her person, it cannot be contended that her apparent consent to the subsequent search was infected by an unlawful detention. There remains to be considered whether the respondent's consent to the search was for any other reason invalid. The District Court explicitly credited the officers' testimony and found that the "consent was freely and voluntarily given." There was more than enough evidence in this case to sustain that view. ...

Counsel for the respondent has also argued that because she was within the DEA office when she consented to the search, her consent may have resulted from the inherently coercive nature of those surroundings. But in view of the District Court's finding that the respondent's presence in the office was voluntary, the fact that she was there is little or no evidence that she was in any way coerced. And in response to the argument that the respondent would not voluntarily have consented to a search that was likely to disclose the narcotics that she carried, we repeat that the question is not whether the respondent acted in her ultimate self-interest, but whether she acted voluntarily.

III.

We conclude that the District Court's determination that the respondent consented to the search of her person "freely and voluntarily" was sustained by the evidence and that the Court of Appeals was, therefore, in error in setting it aside. Accordingly, the judgment of the Court of Appeals is reversed, and the case is remanded to that court for further proceedings.

It is so ordered.

MR. JUSTICE POWELL, with whom THE CHIEF JUSTICE and MR. JUSTICE BLACKMUN join, concurring in part and concurring in the judgment. [opinion omitted]

MR. JUSTICE WHITE, with whom MR. JUSTICE BRENNAN, MR. JUSTICE MARSHALL, and MR. JUSTICE STEVENS join, dissenting.

MR. JUSTICE STEWART believes that a "seizure" within the meaning of the Fourth Amendment occurs when an individual's freedom of movement is restrained by means of physical force or a show of authority. Although it is undisputed that Ms. Mendenhall was not free to leave after the DEA agents stopped her and inspected her identification, MR. JUSTICE STEWART concludes that she was not "seized" because he finds that, under the totality of the circumstances, a reasonable person would have believed that she was free to leave. While basing this finding on an alleged absence from the record of objective evidence indicating that Ms. Mendenhall was not free to ignore the officer's inquiries and continue on her way, MR. JUSTICE STEWART'S opinion brushes off the fact that this asserted evidentiary deficiency may be largely attributable to the fact that the "seizure" question was never raised below. In assessing what the record does reveal, the opinion discounts certain objective factors that would tend to support a "seizure" finding, while relying on contrary factors inconclusive even under its own illustrations of how a "seizure" may be established. ...

II.

Assuming, as we should, that Ms. Mendenhall was "seized" within the meaning of the Fourth Amendment when she was stopped by the DEA agents, the legality of that stop turns on whether there were reasonable grounds for suspecting her of criminal activity at the time of the stop. To establish that there was reasonable suspicion for the stop, it was necessary for the police at least to "be able to point to specific and articulable facts which, taken together with rational inferences from those facts, reasonably warrant that intrusion."

At the time they stopped Ms. Mendenhall, the DEA agents' suspicion that she was engaged in criminal activity was based solely on their brief observations of her conduct at the airport. The officers had no advance information that Ms. Mendenhall, or anyone on her flight, would be carrying drugs. What the agents observed Ms. Mendenhall do in the airport was not "unusual conduct" which would lead an experienced officer reasonably to conclude that criminal activity was afoot, but rather the kind of behavior that could reasonably be expected of anyone changing planes in an airport terminal.

None of the aspects of Ms. Mendenhall's conduct, either alone or in combination, were sufficient to provide reasonable suspicion that she was engaged in criminal activity. The fact that Ms. Mendenhall was the last person to alight from a flight originating in Los Angeles was plainly insufficient to provide a basis for stopping her. Nor was the fact that her flight originated from a "major source city," for the mere proximity of a person to areas with a high incidence of drug activity or to persons known to be drug addicts, does not provide the necessary reasonable suspicion for an investigatory stop. Under the circumstances of this case, the DEA agents' observations that Ms. Mendenhall claimed no luggage and changed airlines were also insufficient to provide reasonable suspicion. ...

III.

Whatever doubt there may be concerning whether Ms. Mendenhall's Fourth Amendment interests were implicated during the initial stages of her confrontation with the DEA agents, she undoubtedly was "seized" within the meaning of the Fourth Amendment when the agents escorted her from the public area of the terminal to the DEA office for questioning and a strip-search of her person. ... ... the nature of the intrusion to which Ms. Mendenhall was subjected when she was escorted by DEA agents to their office and detained there for questioning and a strip-search was so great that it "was in important respects indistinguishable from a traditional arrest." Although Ms. Mendenhall was not told that she was under arrest, she in fact was not free to refuse to go to the DEA office and was not told that she was. Furthermore, once inside the office, Ms. Mendenhall would not have been permitted to leave without submitting to a strip-search. ... probable cause, which concededly was absent, was required to support the intrusion.

...There was no evidence in the record to support the District Court's speculation ... that Ms. Mendenhall accompanied "Agent Anderson to the airport DEA Office 'voluntarily in a spirit of apparent cooperation with the [agent's] investigation.'" Ms. Mendenhall did not testify at the suppression hearing and the officers presented no testimony concerning what she said, if anything, when informed that the officers wanted her to come with them to the DEA office. Indeed, the only testimony concerning what occurred between Agent Anderson's "request" and Ms. Mendenhall's arrival at the DEA office is the agent's testimony that if Ms. Mendenhall had wanted to leave at that point she would have been forcibly restrained. ...

The Court recognizes that the Government has the burden of proving that Ms. Mendenhall consented to accompany the officers, but it nevertheless holds that the "totality of evidence was plainly adequate" to support a finding of consent. On the record before us, the Court's conclusion can only be based on the notion that consent can be assumed from the absence of proof that a suspect resisted police authority. This is a notion that we have squarely rejected. ... the prosecution's "burden of proving that the consent was, in fact, freely and voluntarily given . . . cannot be discharged by showing no more than acquiescence to a claim of lawful authority." While the Government need not prove that Ms. Mendenhall knew that she had a right to refuse to accompany the officers, it cannot rely solely on acquiescence to the officers' wishes to establish the requisite consent. The Court of Appeals properly understood this in rejecting the District Court's "findings" of consent.

Since the defendant was not present to testify at the suppression hearing, we can only speculate about her state of mind as her encounter with the DEA agents progressed from surveillance, to detention, to questioning, to seclusion in a private office, to the female officer's command to remove her clothing. Nevertheless, it is unbelievable that this sequence of events involved no invasion of a citizen's constitutionally protected interest in privacy. The rule of law requires a different conclusion.

Because Ms. Mendenhall was being illegally detained at the time of the search of her person, her suppression motion should have been granted in the absence of evidence to dissipate the taint.

Note and Queries

The agent testified that the respondent's behavior fit the so-called "drug courier profile" – an informally compiled abstract of characteristics thought typical of persons carrying illicit drugs. In this case the agents thought it relevant that (1) the respondent was arriving on a flight from Los Angeles, a city believed by the agents to be the place of origin for much of the heroin brought to Detroit; (2) the respondent was the last person to leave the plane, "appeared to be very nervous," and "completely scanned the whole area where [the agents] were standing"; (3) after leaving the plane the respondent proceeded past the baggage area without claiming any luggage; and (4) the respondent changed airlines for her flight out of Detroit. Do you find that that provides sufficient reasonable suspicion or probable cause to stop/seize her?

Was Ms. Mendenhall free to leave? The DEA agents for a time took her plane ticket and driver's license. Does that matter? Is it doubtful that any reasonable person about to board a plane would feel free to leave when law enforcement officers have their plane ticket? In addition, Agent Anderson testified as follows on cross-examination at the suppression hearing: "Q. All right. Now, when you asked her to accompany you to the DEA office for further questioning, if she had wanted to walk away, would you have stopped her? "A. Once I asked her to accompany me? "Q. Yes. "A. Yes, I would have stopped her. "Q. She was not free to leave, was she? "A. Not at that point." The Court finds to the contrary, that she was free to leave because it was a public concourse, the officers were not wearing uniforms and had no weapons, and she did not have to answer the questions. What do you make of the Court's reasoning that seems to contradict what the officers actually thought?

The Court uses a totality of circumstances test. Do you support the conclusion that the district court could have found voluntariness, and that she was thus not seized and has no claim to challenge the use of the evidence against her? What do you make of Justice Stewart's dissenting view that there was no reasonable suspicion for the investigatory stop, that she was seized at the office given that she was not free to leave when asked to go to the office, and that the officers needed probable cause for the strip search?

Review Exercise with Florida v. Royer

On January 3, 1978, Royer was observed at Miami International Airport by two plainclothes detectives assigned to the county's Organized Crime Bureau, Narcotics Investigation Section. Detectives Johnson and Magdalena believed that Royer's appearance, mannerisms, luggage, and actions fit the so-called "drug courier profile." The following facts were considered to be within the profile: (a) Royer was carrying American Tourister luggage, which appeared to be heavy, (b) he was young, apparently between 25-35, (c) he was casually dressed, (d) he appeared pale and nervous, looking around at other people, (e) he paid for his ticket in cash with a large number of bills, and (f) rather than completing the airline identification tag to be attached to checked baggage, which had space for a name, address, and telephone number, he wrote only a name and the destination. Royer, apparently unaware of the attention he had attracted, purchased a one-way ticket to New York City and checked his two suitcases, placing on each suitcase an identification tag bearing the name "Holt" and the destination "La Guardia." As Royer made his way to the concourse which led to the airline boarding area, the two detectives approached him, identified themselves as policemen working out of the sheriff's office, and asked if Royer had a "moment" to speak with them; Royer said "Yes." Upon request, but without oral consent, Royer produced for the detectives his airline ticket and his driver's license. The airline ticket, like the baggage identification tags, bore the name "Holt," while the driver's license carried respondent's correct name, "Royer." When the detectives asked about the discrepancy, Royer explained that a friend had made the reservation in the name of "Holt." Royer became noticeably more nervous during this conversation, whereupon the detectives informed Royer that they were in fact narcotics investigators and that they had reason to suspect him of transporting narcotics. The detectives did not return his airline ticket and identification but asked Royer to accompany them to a room, approximately 40 feet away, adjacent to the concourse. Royer said nothing in response but went with the officers as he had been asked to do. The room was later described by Detective Johnson as a "large storage closet," located in the stewardesses' lounge and containing a small desk and two chairs. Without Royer's consent or agreement, Detective Johnson, using Royer's baggage check stubs, retrieved the "Holt" luggage from the airline and brought it to the room where Royer and Detective Magdalena were waiting. Royer was asked if he would consent to a search of the suitcases. Without orally responding to this request, Royer produced a key and unlocked one of the suitcases, which one detective then opened without seeking further assent from Royer. Marihuana was found in that suitcase. According to Detective Johnson, Royer stated that he did not know the combination to the lock on the second suitcase. When asked if he objected to the detective opening the second suitcase, Royer said "[no], go ahead," and did not object when the detective explained that the suitcase might have to be broken open. The suitcase was pried open by the officers and more marihuana was found. Royer was then told that he was under arrest. Approximately 15 minutes had elapsed from the time the detectives initially approached Royer until his arrest upon the discovery of the contraband. Prior to his trial for felony possession of marihuana, Royer made a motion to suppress the evidence obtained in the search of the suitcases. Royer argued that he had been involuntarily confined within the small room without probable cause; that the involuntary detention had exceeded the limited restraint permitted by *Terry v. Ohio* at the time his consent to the search was obtained; and that the consent to search was therefore invalid because it was tainted by the unlawful confinement. How would you rule? See *Florida v. Royer*, 460 U.S. 491 (1983).

The trial court found that Royer's consent to the search was "freely and voluntarily given," and that, regardless of the consent, the warrantless search was reasonable because "the officer doesn't have the time to run out and get a search warrant because the plane is going to take off." The District Court of Appeals reversed Royer's conviction, and accepted Royer's arguments. On certiorari, the United States Supreme Court affirmed. Although unable to agree on an opinion, five members of the court agreed that the detectives' actions exceeded the permissible bounds of an investigative stop and that the suspect's consent to the search of his suitcases was tainted by the illegal detention. Justice White announced the judgment of the court. In an opinion joined by Justices Marshall, Powell, and Stevens, he expressed the view that, although the detectives had adequate grounds for temporarily detaining the suspect and his luggage, the detention to which the suspect was subjected was a more serious intrusion on his personal liberty than was allowable on a mere suspicion of criminal activity and that the suspect's consent to the search of his suitcases was tainted by the illegal detention and was ineffective to justify the search. Justice Powell concurred and expressed the view that the suspect in this case as a practical matter was under arrest and that his surrender of the luggage key to the detectives could not be viewed as consensual. Justice Brennan also concurred in the result, expressing the view that the suspect's consent to the search of his suitcases was tainted by an illegal arrest and that the initial stop of the suspect was also illegal. Justice Blackmun dissented, expressed the view that the police conduct was minimally intrusive and reasonable and that, given the strength of society's interest in overcoming the extraordinary obstacles to the detection of drug traffickers, such conduct should not be subjected to a requirement of probable cause. Rehnquist, J., joined by Burger, Ch. J., and O'Connor, J., dissented, expressing the view that the conduct of the detectives was reasonable as that term is used in the Fourth Amendment.

Review Exercise with U.S. v. Sokolow

On a Sunday in July 1984, respondent went to the United Airlines ticket counter at Honolulu Airport, where he purchased two round-trip tickets for a flight to Miami leaving later that day. The tickets were purchased in the names of "Andrew Kray" and "Janet Norian" and had open return dates. Respondent paid $2,100 for the tickets from a large roll of $20 bills, which appeared to contain a total of $4,000. He also gave the ticket agent his home telephone number. The ticket agent noticed that respondent seemed nervous;

he was about 25 years old; he was dressed in a black jumpsuit and wore gold jewelry; and he was accompanied by a woman, who turned out to be Janet Norian. Neither respondent nor his companion checked any of their four pieces of luggage.

After the couple left for their flight, the ticket agent informed Officer John McCarthy of the Honolulu Police Department of respondent's cash purchase of tickets to Miami. Officer McCarthy determined that the telephone number respondent gave to the ticket agent was subscribed to a "Karl Herman," who resided at 348-A Royal Hawaiian Avenue in Honolulu. Unbeknownst to McCarthy (and later to the DEA agents), respondent was Herman's roommate. The ticket agent identified respondent's voice on the answering machine at Herman's number. Officer McCarthy was unable to find any listing under the name "Andrew Kray" in Hawaii. McCarthy subsequently learned that return reservations from Miami to Honolulu had been made in the names of Kray and Norian, with their arrival scheduled for July 25, three days after respondent and his companion had left. He also learned that Kray and Norian were scheduled to make stopovers in Denver and Los Angeles. On July 25, during the stopover in Los Angeles, DEA agents identified respondent. He "appeared to be very nervous and was looking all around the waiting area." Later that day, at 6:30 p.m., respondent and Norian arrived in Honolulu. As before, they had not checked their luggage. Respondent was still wearing a black jumpsuit and gold jewelry. The couple proceeded directly to the street and tried to hail a cab, where Agent Richard Kempshall and three other DEA agents approached them. Kempshall displayed his credentials, grabbed respondent by the arm, and moved him back onto the sidewalk. Kempshall asked respondent for his airline ticket and identification; respondent said that he had neither. He told the agents that his name was "Sokolow," but that he was traveling under his mother's maiden name, "Kray." Respondent and Norian were escorted to the DEA office at the airport. There, the couple's luggage was examined by "Donker," a narcotics detector dog, which alerted on respondent's brown shoulder bag. The agents arrested respondent. He was advised of his constitutional rights and declined to make any statements. The agents obtained a warrant to search the shoulder bag. They found no illicit drugs, but the bag did contain several suspicious documents indicating respondent's involvement in drug trafficking. The agents had Donker reexamine the remaining luggage, and this time the dog alerted on a medium-sized Louis Vuitton bag. By now, it was 9:30 p.m., too late for the agents to obtain a second warrant. They allowed respondent to leave for the night, but kept his luggage. The next morning, after a second dog confirmed Donker's alert, the agents obtained a warrant and found 1,063 grams of cocaine inside the bag. Respondent was indicted for possession with the intent to distribute cocaine. See *United States v. Sokolow*, 490 U.S. 1 (1989).

The United States District Court for Hawaii denied his motion to suppress the cocaine and other evidence seized from his luggage, finding that March 26, 2004 the DEA agents had a reasonable suspicion that he was involved in drug trafficking when they stopped him at the airport. The United States Court of Appeals for the Ninth Circuit reversed respondent's conviction, holding that the DEA agents did not have a reasonable suspicion to justify the stop. The Court of Appeals held that the DEA agents seized respondent when they grabbed him by the arm and moved him back onto the sidewalk. The issue was whether the agents had a reasonable suspicion that respondent was engaged in wrongdoing when they encountered him on the sidewalk. Following *Terry v. Ohio*, police can stop and briefly detain a person for investigative purposes if the officer has a reasonable suspicion supported by articulable facts that criminal activity "may be afoot," even if the officer lacks probable cause. The majority believed that such characteristics, "shared by drug couriers and the public at large," were only relevant if there was evidence of ongoing criminal behavior and the Government offered "[e]mpirical documentation" that the combination of facts at issue did not describe the behavior of "significant numbers of innocent persons." The Supreme Court found that the Court of Appeals' effort to refine and elaborate the requirements of "reasonable suspicion" created unnecessary difficulty and that the proper standard to evaluate the stop was "the totality of the circumstances – the whole picture." Any one of the factors fitting the profile is not by itself proof of any illegal conduct and is quite consistent with innocent travel. But taken together they amount to reasonable suspicion. Justice Marshall and Brennan dissented, expressing the view that (1) it was highly significant that the DEA agents stopped the traveler because he matched one of the DEA's "profiles" of a paradigmatic drug courier; (2) the factors comprising the DEA profile relied upon in the case at hand were especially dubious indices of ongoing criminal activity; and (3) under the circumstances, the facts about the traveler known to the DEA agents at the time they stopped him fell short of reasonably indicating that the traveler was engaged at the time in criminal activity.

CALIFORNIA v. HODARI
499 U.S. 621 (1991)

Justice SCALIA delivered the opinion of the Court, in which Rehnquist, C. J., and White, Blackmun, O'Connor, Kennedy, and Souter, JJ., joined.

Late one evening in April 1988, Officers Brian McColgin and Jerry Pertoso were on patrol in a high-crime area of Oakland, California. They were dressed in street clothes but wearing jackets with "Police" embossed on both front and back. Their unmarked car proceeded west on Foothill Boulevard, and turned south onto 63rd Avenue. As they rounded the corner, they saw four or five youths huddled around a small red car parked at the curb. When the youths saw the officers' car approaching they apparently panicked, and took flight. The respondent here, Hodari D., and one companion ran west through an alley; the others fled south. The red car also headed south, at a high rate of speed.

The officers were suspicious and gave chase. ... Hodari, meanwhile, emerged from the alley onto 62nd and ran north. Looking behind as he ran, he did not turn and see Pertoso until the officer was almost upon him, whereupon he tossed away what appeared to be a small rock. A moment later, Pertoso tackled Hodari, handcuffed him, and radioed for assistance. Hodari was found to be carrying $130 in cash and a pager; and the rock he had discarded was found to be crack cocaine.

In the juvenile proceeding brought against him, Hodari moved to suppress the evidence relating to the cocaine. The court denied the motion without opinion. The California Court of Appeal reversed, holding that Hodari had been "seized" when he saw Officer Pertoso running towards him, that this seizure was unreasonable under the Fourth Amendment, and that the evidence of cocaine had to be suppressed as the fruit of that illegal seizure. The California Supreme Court denied the State's application for review. We granted certiorari.

As this case comes to us, the only issue presented is whether, at the time he dropped the drugs, Hodari had been "seized" within the meaning of the Fourth Amendment. If so, respondent argues, the drugs were the fruit of that seizure and the evidence concerning them was properly excluded. If not, the drugs were abandoned by Hodari and lawfully recovered by the police, and the evidence should have been admitted. (In addition, of course, Pertoso's seeing the rock of cocaine, at least if he recognized it as such, would provide reasonable suspicion for the unquestioned seizure that occurred when he tackled Hodari.)

We have long understood that the Fourth Amendment's protection against "unreasonable . . . seizures" includes seizure of the person. From the time of the founding to the present, the word "seizure" has meant a "taking possession." For most purposes at common law, the word connoted not merely grasping, or applying physical force to, the animate or inanimate object in question, but actually bringing it within physical control....

...The present case ...does not involve the application of any physical force; Hodari was untouched by Officer Pertoso at the time he discarded the cocaine. His defense relies instead upon the proposition that a seizure occurs "when the officer, by means of physical force or show of authority, has in some way restrained the liberty of a citizen." Hodari contends (and we accept as true for purposes of this decision) that Pertoso's pursuit qualified as a "show of authority" calling upon Hodari to halt. The narrow question before us is whether, with respect to a show of authority as with respect to application of physical force, a seizure occurs even though the subject does not yield. We hold that it does not.

The language of the Fourth Amendment, of course, cannot sustain respondent's contention. The word "seizure" readily bears the meaning of a laying on of hands or application of physical force to restrain movement, even when it is ultimately unsuccessful. It does not remotely apply, however, to the prospect of a policeman yelling "Stop, in the name of the law!" at a fleeing form that continues to flee. That is no seizure....

We do not think it desirable, even as a policy matter, to stretch the Fourth Amendment beyond its words and beyond the meaning of arrest, as respondent urges. Street pursuits always place the public at some risk, and compliance with police orders to stop should therefore be encouraged....

Respondent contends that his position is sustained by the so-called Mendenhall test... "[A] person has been 'seized' within the meaning of the Fourth Amendment only if, in view of all the circumstances surrounding the incident, a reasonable person would have believed that he was not free to leave." ... Mendenhall establishes that the test for existence of a "show of authority" is an objective one: not whether the citizen perceived that he was being ordered to restrict his movement, but whether the officer's words and actions would have conveyed that to a reasonable person. ...

In sum, assuming that Pertoso's pursuit in the present case constituted a "show of authority" enjoining Hodari to halt, since Hodari did not comply with that injunction he was not seized until he was tackled. The cocaine abandoned while he was running was in this case not the fruit of a seizure, and his motion to exclude evidence of it was properly denied. We reverse the decision of the California Court of Appeal, and remand for further proceedings not inconsistent with this opinion.

It is so ordered.

Justice Stevens, with whom Justice Marshall joins, dissenting.

The decisions in Katz and Terry unequivocally reject the notion that the common law of arrest defines the limits of the term "seizure" in the Fourth Amendment. In Katz, the Court abandoned the narrow view that would have limited a seizure to a material object, and, instead, held that the Fourth Amendment extended to the recording of oral statements. And in Terry, the Court abandoned its traditional view that a seizure under the Fourth Amendment required probable cause, and, instead, expanded the definition of a seizure to include an investigative stop made on less than probable cause. Thus, the major premise underpinning the majority's entire analysis today – that the common law of arrest should define the term "seizure" for Fourth Amendment purposes – is seriously flawed. The Court mistakenly hearkens back to common law, while ignoring the expansive approach that the Court has taken in Fourth Amendment analysis since Katz and Terry.

II.

In United States v. Mendenhall, the Court "adhered to the view that a person is 'seized' only when, by means of physical force or a show of authority, his freedom of movement is restrained." The Court looked to whether the citizen who is questioned "remains free to disregard the questions and walk away," and if she is able to do so, then "there has been no intrusion upon that person's liberty or privacy" that would require some "particularized and objective justification" under the Constitution. The test for a "seizure," as formulated by the Court in Mendenhall, was whether, "in view of all of the circumstances surrounding the incident, a reasonable person would have believed that he was not free to leave." Examples of seizures include "the threatening presence of several officers, the display of a weapon by an officer, some physical touching of the person of the citizen, or the use of language or tone of voice indicating that compliance with the officer's request might be compelled." The Court's unwillingness today to adhere to the "reasonable person" standard, as formulated by Justice Stewart in Mendenhall, marks an unnecessary departure from Fourth Amendment case law.

The Court today draws the novel conclusion that even though no seizure can occur unless the Mendenhall reasonable person standard is met, the fact that the standard has been met does not necessarily mean that a seizure has occurred. ...

Even though momentary, a seizure occurs whenever an objective evaluation of a police officer's show of force conveys the message that the citizen is not entirely free to leave – in other words, that his or her liberty is being restrained in a significant way. ...

III.

In this case the officer's show of force – taking the form of a head-on chase – adequately conveyed the message that respondent was not free to leave. Whereas in Mendenhall, there was "nothing in the record [to] suggest that the respondent had any objective reason to believe that she was not free to end the conversation in the concourse and proceed on her way," here, respondent attempted to end "the conversation" before it began and soon found himself literally "not free to leave" when confronted by an officer running toward him head-on who eventually tackled him to the ground. There was an interval of time between the moment that respondent saw the officer fast approaching and the moment when he was tackled, and thus brought under the control of the officer. The question is whether the Fourth Amendment was implicated at the earlier or the later moment.

It seems equally clear to me that the constitutionality of a police officer's show of force should be measured by the conditions that exist at the time of the officer's action. A search must be justified on the basis of the facts available at the time it is initiated; the subsequent discovery of evidence does not retroactively validate an unconstitutional search. The same approach should apply to seizures; the character of the citizen's response should not govern the constitutionality of the officer's conduct.

...In an airport setting, may a drug enforcement agent now approach a group of passengers with his gun drawn, announce a "baggage search," and rely on the passengers' reactions to justify his investigative stops? The holding of today's majority fails to recognize the coercive and intimidating nature of such behavior and creates a rule that may allow such behavior to go unchecked.

The deterrent purposes of the exclusionary rule focus on the conduct of law enforcement officers and on discouraging improper behavior on their part, and not on the reaction of the citizen to the show of force. In the present case, if Officer Pertoso had succeeded in tackling respondent before he dropped the rock of cocaine, the rock unquestionably would have been excluded as the fruit of the officer's unlawful seizure. Instead, under the Court's logic-chopping analysis, the exclusionary rule has no application because an attempt to make an unconstitutional seizure is beyond the coverage of the Fourth Amendment, no matter how outrageous or unreasonable the officer's conduct may be.

It is too early to know the consequences of the Court's holding. If carried to its logical conclusion, it will encourage unlawful displays of force that will frighten countless innocent citizens into surrendering whatever privacy rights they may still have...

I respectfully dissent.

NOTES AND QUERIES

California conceded below that Officer Pertoso did not have the "reasonable suspicion" required to justify stopping Hodari, see *Terry v. Ohio*, 392 U.S. 1 (1968). That it would be unreasonable to stop, for brief inquiry, young men who scatter in panic upon the mere sighting of the police is not self-evident, and arguably contradicts proverbial common sense. The Court notes, however, that they do not decide that point in this case, but rely entirely upon the State's concession. So if he did not have reasonable suspicion, how can the stop be justified? Do we want police to be able to run after "suspects" in hope that they will reveal incriminating evidence?

Note the significance of whether he was seized at the time he dropped the drugs. If he was not seized, the drugs were abandoned and thus could be used as evidence. If he was seized, then the drugs cannot be used against him.

What do you make of the distinction between show of authority and physical restraint? Why is show of authority insufficient to qualify the interaction as a seizure? Do you think that, had he not run, he would have been seized? If so, would it be possible to use the evidence against him? If he is not caught, is he still free to leave? Should the citizen's response govern the constitutionality of an officer's conduct?

The individuals in this case were juveniles. Should the legal system adjust to that fact? The Court's holdings in cases dealing with juveniles reveals that the legal system often concludes that minors generally: (1) lack critical knowledge of their rights and have less capacity to understand the meaning of informative warnings and act on them; (2) are developing the ability, at different rates, to weigh the pros and cons of different courses of action and foresee their consequences, especially in pressure-filled situations; (3) have different perceptions of risk and time, and are undergoing emotional changes, which affect their decisionmaking capacity; and (4) are less able than adults to withstand pressure from authority figures to comply with their demands, especially in coercive settings. How could the legal system approach these differences in the context of seizures? Should these differences apply in the consent context? See Lourdes M. Rosado, Minors and the Fourth Amendment: How juvenile status should invoke different standards for searches and seizures on the street, 71 N.Y.U.L.Rev. 726 (1996).

UNITED STATES V. DRAYTON
536 US 194 (2002)

JUSTICE KENNEDY delivered the opinion of the Court.

I.

On February 4, 1999, respondents Christopher Drayton and Clifton Brown, Jr., were traveling on a Greyhound bus ... The bus made a scheduled stop in Tallahassee, Florida. The passengers were required to disembark so the bus could be refueled and cleaned. As the passengers reboarded, ... the driver allowed three members of the Tallahassee Police Department to board the bus as part of a routine drug and weapons interdiction effort. The officers were dressed in plain clothes and carried concealed weapons and visible badges.

Once onboard Officer Hoover knelt on the driver's seat and faced the rear of the bus. He could observe the passengers and ensure the safety of the two other officers without blocking the aisle or otherwise obstructing the bus exit. Officers Lang and Blackburn went to the rear of the bus...

According to Lang's testimony, passengers who declined to cooperate with him or who chose to exit the bus at any time would have been allowed to do so without argument. In Lang's experience, however, most people are willing to cooperate. ... Lang could recall five to six instances in the previous year in which passengers had declined to have their luggage searched. It also was common for passengers to leave the bus for a cigarette or a snack while the officers were on board. Lang sometimes informed passengers of their right to refuse to cooperate. On the day in question, however, he did not.

Respondents were seated next to each other on the bus. Drayton was in the aisle seat, Brown in the seat next to the window. Lang approached respondents from the rear and leaned over Drayton's shoulder. He held up his badge long enough for respondents to identify him as a police officer. With his face 12-to-18 inches away from Drayton's, Lang spoke in a voice just loud enough for respondents to hear:

> I'm Investigator Lang with the Tallahassee Police Department. We're conducting bus interdiction [sic], attempting to deter drugs and illegal weapons being transported on the bus. Do you have any bags on the bus?
>
> Both respondents pointed to a single green bag in the overhead luggage rack. Lang asked, "Do you mind if I check it?," and Brown responded, "Go ahead." Lang handed the bag to Officer Blackburn to check. The bag contained no contraband.

Officer Lang noticed that both respondents were wearing heavy jackets and baggy pants despite the warm weather. In Lang's experience drug traffickers often use baggy clothing to conceal weapons or narcotics. The officer thus asked Brown if he had any weapons or drugs in his possession. And he asked Brown: "Do you mind if I check your person?" Brown answered, "Sure," and cooperated by leaning up in his seat, pulling a cell phone out of his pocket, and opening up his jacket. Lang reached across Drayton and patted down Brown's jacket and pockets, including his waist area, sides, and upper thighs. In both thigh areas, Lang detected hard objects similar to drug packages detected on other occasions. Lang arrested and handcuffed Brown. Officer Hoover escorted Brown from the bus.

Lang then asked Drayton, "Mind if I check you?" Drayton responded by lifting his hands about eight inches from his legs. Lang conducted a pat-down of Drayton's thighs and detected hard objects similar to those found on Brown. He arrested Drayton and escorted him from the bus. A further search revealed that respondents had duct-taped plastic bundles of powder cocaine between several pairs of their boxer shorts. Brown possessed three bundles containing 483 grams of cocaine. Drayton possessed two bundles containing 295 grams of cocaine.

Respondents were charged with conspiring to distribute cocaine and with possessing cocaine with intent to distribute it. They moved to suppress the cocaine, arguing that the consent to the pat-down search was invalid. Following a hearing at which only Officer Lang testified, the United States District Court for the Northern District of Florida denied their motions to suppress. The District Court determined that the police conduct was not coercive and respondents' consent to the search was voluntary. The District Court pointed to the fact that the officers were dressed in plain clothes, did not brandish their badges in an authoritative manner, did not make a general announcement to the entire bus, and did not address anyone in a menacing tone of voice. It noted that the officers did not block the aisle or the exit, and stated that it was "obvious that [respondents] can get up and leave, as can the people ahead of them." The District Court concluded: "Everything that took place between Officer Lang and Mr. Drayton and Mr. Brown suggests that it was cooperative. There was nothing coercive, there was nothing confrontational about it."

The Court of Appeals for the Eleventh Circuit reversed .... The court held that this disposition was compelled by its previous decisions. Those cases had held that bus passengers do not feel free to disregard police officers' requests to search absent "some positive indication that consent could have been refused."

We granted certiorari...

II.

Law enforcement officers do not violate the Fourth Amendment's prohibition of unreasonable seizures merely by approaching individuals on the street or in other public places and putting questions to them if they are willing to listen. Even when law enforcement officers have no basis for suspecting a particular individual, they may pose questions, ask for identification, and request consent to search luggage – provided they do not induce cooperation by coercive means. If a reasonable person would feel free to terminate the encounter, then he or she has not been seized.

The Court has addressed on a previous occasion the specific question of drug interdiction efforts on buses. In Bostick, two police officers requested a bus passenger's consent to a search of his luggage. The passenger agreed, and the resulting search revealed cocaine in his suitcase. The Florida Supreme Court suppressed the cocaine. In doing so it adopted a per se rule that due to the cramped confines onboard a bus the act of questioning would deprive a person of his or her freedom of movement and so constitute a seizure under the Fourth Amendment.

This Court reversed. Bostick first made it clear that for the most part per se rules are inappropriate in the Fourth Amendment context. The proper inquiry necessitates a consideration of "all the circumstances surrounding the encounter." The Court noted next that the traditional rule, which states that a seizure does not occur so long as a reasonable person would feel free "to disregard the police and go about his business." ... The proper inquiry "is whether a reasonable person would feel free to decline the officers' requests or otherwise terminate the encounter." Finally, the Court rejected Bostick's argument that he must have been seized because no reasonable person would consent to a search of luggage containing drugs. The reasonable person test, the Court explained, is objective and "presupposes an innocent person."

In light of the limited record, Bostick refrained from deciding whether a seizure occurred. The Court, however, identified two factors "particularly worth noting" on remand. First, although it was obvious that an officer was armed, he did not remove the gun from its pouch or use it in a threatening way. Second, the officer advised the passenger that he could refuse consent to the search.

Relying upon this latter factor, the Eleventh Circuit has adopted what is in effect a per se rule that evidence obtained during suspicionless drug interdiction efforts aboard buses must be suppressed unless the officers have advised passengers of their right not to cooperate and to refuse consent to a search. ...

Although the Court of Appeals has disavowed a per se requirement, the lack of an explicit warning to passengers is the only element common to all its cases. ... Under these cases, it appears that the Court of Appeals would suppress any evidence obtained during suspicionless drug interdiction efforts aboard buses in the absence of a warning that passengers may refuse to cooperate. The Court of Appeals erred in adopting this approach.

Applying the Bostick framework to the facts of this particular case, we conclude that the police did not seize respondents when they boarded the bus and began questioning passengers. The officers gave the passengers no reason to believe that they were required to answer the officers' questions. When Officer Lang approached respondents, he did not brandish a weapon or make any intimidating movements. He left the aisle free so that respondents could exit. He spoke to passengers one by one and in a polite, quiet voice. Nothing he said would suggest to a reasonable person that he or she was barred from leaving the bus or otherwise terminating the encounter.

There were ample grounds for the District Court to conclude that "everything that took place between Officer Lang and [respondents] suggests that it was cooperative" and that there "was nothing coercive [or] confrontational" about the encounter. There was no application of force, no intimidating movement, no overwhelming show of force, no brandishing of weapons, no blocking of exits, no threat, no command, not even an authoritative tone of voice. It is beyond question that had this encounter occurred on the street, it would be constitutional. The fact that an encounter takes place on a bus does not on its own transform standard police questioning of citizens into an illegal seizure. Indeed, because many fellow passengers are present to witness officers' conduct, a reasonable person may feel even more secure in his or her decision not to cooperate with police on a bus than in other circumstances.

Drayton contends that even if Brown's cooperation with the officers was consensual, Drayton was seized because no reasonable person would feel free to terminate the encounter with the officers after Brown had been arrested. The Court of Appeals did not address this claim; and in any event the argument fails. The arrest of one person does not mean that everyone around him has been seized by police. If anything, Brown's arrest should have put Drayton on notice of the consequences of continuing the encounter by answering the officers' questions. Even after arresting Brown, Lang addressed Drayton in a polite manner and provided him with no indication that he was required to answer Lang's questions.

We turn now from the question whether respondents were seized to whether they were subjected to an unreasonable search, i.e., whether their consent to the suspicionless search was involuntary. In circumstances such as these, where the question of voluntariness pervades both the search and seizure inquiries, the respective analyses turn on very similar facts. And, as the facts above suggest, respondents' consent to the search of their luggage and their persons was voluntary. Nothing Officer Lang said indicated a command to consent to the search. Rather, when respondents informed Lang that they had a bag on the bus, he asked for their permission to check it. And when Lang requested to search Brown and Drayton's persons, he asked first if they objected, thus indicating to a reasonable person that he or she was free to refuse. Even after arresting Brown, Lang provided Drayton with no indication that he was required to consent to a search. To the contrary, Lang asked for Drayton's permission to search him ("Mind if I check you?"), and Drayton agreed.

The Court has rejected in specific terms the suggestion that police officers must always inform citizens of their right to refuse when seeking permission to conduct a warrantless consent search. ... Although Officer Lang did not inform respondents of their right to refuse the search, he did request permission to search, and the totality of the circumstances indicates that their consent was voluntary, so the searches were reasonable.

The judgment of the Court of Appeals is reversed, and the case is remanded for further proceedings consistent with this opinion.

It is so ordered.

JUSTICE SOUTER, with whom JUSTICE STEVENS and JUSTICE GINSBURG join, dissenting.

Anyone who travels by air today submits to searches of the person and luggage as a condition of boarding the aircraft. It is universally accepted that such intrusions are necessary to hedge against risks that, nowadays, even small children understand. The commonplace precautions of air travel have not, thus far, been justified for ground transportation, however, and no such conditions have been placed on passengers getting on trains or buses. There is therefore an air of unreality about the Court's explanation that bus passengers consent to searches of their luggage to "enhance their own safety and the safety of those around them." Nor are the other factual assessments underlying the Court's conclusion in favor of the Government more convincing.

The issue we took to review is whether the police's examination of the bus passengers, including respondents, amounted to a suspicionless seizure under the Fourth Amendment. If it did, any consent to search was plainly invalid as a product of the illegal seizure.

Florida v. Bostick established the framework for determining whether the bus passengers were seized in the constitutional sense. In that case, we rejected the position that police questioning of bus passengers was a per se seizure, and held instead that the issue of seizure was to be resolved under an objective test considering all circumstances: whether a reasonable passenger would have felt "free to decline the officers' requests or otherwise terminate the encounter." We thus applied to a bus passenger the more general criterion, whether the person questioned was free "to ignore the police presence and go about his business."

Thus, for reasons unexplained, the driver with the tickets entitling the passengers to travel had yielded his custody of the bus and its seated travelers to three police officers, whose authority apparently superseded the driver's own. The officers took control of the entire passenger compartment, one stationed at the door keeping surveillance of all the occupants, the others working forward from the back. With one officer right behind him and the other one forward, a third officer accosted each passenger at quarters extremely close and so cramped that as many as half the passengers could not even have stood to face the speaker. None was asked whether he was willing to converse with the police or to take part in the enquiry. Instead the officer said the police were "conducting bus interdiction," in the course of which they "would like . . . cooperation." The reasonable inference was that the "interdiction" was not a consensual exercise, but one the police would carry out whatever the circumstances; that they would prefer "cooperation" but would not let the lack of it stand in their way. There was no contrary indication that day, since no passenger had refused the cooperation requested, and there was no reason for any passenger to believe that the driver would return and the trip resume until the police were satisfied. The scene was set and an atmosphere of obligatory participation was established by this introduction. Later requests to search prefaced with "Do you mind… " would naturally have been understood in the terms with which the encounter began.

It is very hard to imagine that either Brown or Drayton would have believed that he stood to lose nothing if he refused to cooperate with the police, or that he had any free choice to ignore the police altogether. No reasonable passenger could have believed that, only an uncomprehending one. It is neither here nor there that the interdiction was conducted by three officers, not one, as a safety precaution. The fact was that there were three, and when Brown and Drayton were called upon to respond, each one was presumably conscious of an officer in front watching, one at his side questioning him, and one behind for cover, in case he became unruly, perhaps, or "cooperation" was not forthcoming. The situation is much like the one in the alley, with civilians in close quarters, unable to move effectively, being told their cooperation is expected. While I am not prepared to say that no bus interrogation and search can pass the Bostick test without a warning that passengers are free to say no, the facts here surely required more from the officers than a quiet tone of voice. A police officer who is certain to get his way has no need to shout.

...Brown and Drayton were seemingly pinned-in by the officers and the customary course of events was stopped flat. The bus was going nowhere, and with one officer in the driver's seat, it was reasonable to suppose no passenger would tend to his own business until the officers were ready to let him.

Notes and Queries

The majority holds that Drayton and Brown had not been seized because a reasonable person in the situation would have felt free to terminate the encounter with the police. Further, it concluded that Drayton and Brown's permission to search their persons had been voluntarily given under the totality of the circumstances. It noted that the police officers did not command passengers to answer their questions; instead they spoke in polite, quiet voices, and asked permission prior to search bags or persons. It concluded that the passengers cooperated not because they were coerced but because they knew that doing so would enhance their own safety. The dissent, on the other hand, concluded that the two men had indeed been seized for purposes of the Fourth Amendment, that the seizure was unreasonable in light of the absence of individualized suspicion of wrongdoing, and that the cocaine discovered should have been suppressed as the fruit of an unlawful seizure. The dissent argued that the three police officers had established an "atmosphere of obligatory participation" so that a reasonable person would not have felt free to end the encounter with the officers. Given this view, the dissent did not reach the issue of whether Drayton and Brown consented voluntarily to the search. Note that the police conduct in *Drayton* may have been reasonable under the circumstances, but it does not follow from that reasonable conduct that there was no seizure and no unconsented search for Fourth Amendment purposes. The standard for determining whether a citizen has been seized or subjected to an involuntary search focuses on whether a reasonable person in the situation would feel free to refuse the police requests. Do you suppose there was such freedom to refuse police requests? Given your own thoughts of how you would feel on a bus, which opinion do you find most convincing? Do you think your answer would be different if you had been asked what a reasonable bus passenger would do or feel?

Can you separate your own thoughts of what you would do from your conception of what a reasonable person would do? It would seem that your thoughts of what a reasonable person would feel or do should be dispositive. Yet, we have seen that members of the Court have difficulty agreeing on whether the passengers felt free to refuse. People's intuitions differ about the question of whether a bus passenger feels free to say no to a police officer. In addition to differences, the available research suggests that intuition alone will produce answers to this question that are skewed inappropriately in the direction of inferring more voluntariness on the part of passengers. Relying on intuition to infer why someone acted the way they did in a situation where all of the details and circumstances are important and must be taken into account almost always leads to mistaken and erroneous judgments, as we see in the note presenting research on voluntariness. The Court notes that the encounter contained "no threat, no command, not even an authoritative tone of voice." The Court also notes that the officer who kneeled backward in the driver's seat to observe the passengers "did nothing to intimidate passengers, and he said nothing to suggest that people could not exit and indeed he left the aisle clear." The officer's request to search is described as not indicating a "command to consent to the search" but rather asking permission: The officer asked Drayton "Mind if I check you?" after Brown was arrested. The officers also asked whether the passengers objected to have their persons searched, which the Court interprets as indicating to a reasonable person that they were free to refuse. The Court concludes that even though "Officer Lang did not inform respondents of their right to refuse the search, he did request permission to search, and the totality of the circumstances indicates that their consent was voluntary, so the searches were reasonable." The Court's understanding may be intuitively appealing but the perspective of bus passengers may reveal a different reality. From that perspective, it may well be that the polite requests and apparently non-threatening situation may be problematic. This view may differ from those of observers. We have seen that focusing on how we would act in the context of bus sweeps runs the risk of raising incorrect attributions. How would you analyze the officer's request from the passenger's perspective? Note that understanding language means understanding the speaker's intention and focusing on the context of the speech. Understanding the passengers' experiences means focusing not on the precise language but on what the passengers understood the officers as meaning and intending. What do you suppose the passengers understood as the officers' intentions?

One view of the passengers' perspective is that the officers boarded the bus with a specific goal in mind. The officers actually did tell the passengers that they were searching for illegal drugs and weapons, with one officer occupying the driver's seat indicating that they would complete their mission before the bus could continue its scheduled route. From this perspective, it may well be that the passengers interpreted the officers' polite requests as commands to help reach their objectives. This view gains support from research that reveals very little difference between requests and demands from authority figures. Because officers are perceived as authorities, they need not rely on coercive statements to achieve a goal. Authorities need not demand compliance in order to communicate coercive potential; it is assumed regardless of the type of directive they communicate. Despite the fact that neither imperatives nor suggestions explicitly mention a negative sanction, others interpret them as warnings of punishment for noncompliance. Importantly, when authorities make suggestions, they appear more sensitive than when they express imperatives, and that apparent sensitivity to those questioned increases the chances of compliance. Persuasive?

Some may object to the conception of consent in Fourth Amendment jurisprudence that has led to suspicionless searches of innocent citizens who "consent" to searches under coercive circumstances.

Arguably, the systematic suspicionless searching of innocent citizens may be a worthwhile price to pay in exchange for effective law enforcement. However, as we have seen, the Court has not engaged in this analysis in its Fourth Amendment consent search or seizure cases. What do you make of that apparent omission?

Drayton relies on and extends *Florida v. Bostick*, 501 U.S. 429 (1991), which had continued the movement away from *Mendenhall's* definition of seizure. In *Bostick*, two officers (complete with badges and insignia and with one of them armed with a visible pistol) boarded a bus that had made a scheduled stop. The officers picked out, without articulable suspicion, the defendant passenger and asked to inspect his ticket and identification. The ticket, from Miami to Atlanta, matched the defendant's identification and both were immediately returned to him as unremarkable. However, the two police officers persisted and explained their presence as narcotics agents on the lookout for illegal drugs. In pursuit of that aim, they then requested the defendant's consent to search his luggage. They also advised him of his right to refuse consent and, at no time, never threatened him with a gun. After finding cocaine in Bostick's bag, the officers arrested and charged him with trafficking. Bostick moved to suppress the admission of the cocaine on the grounds that it had been seized in violation of his Fourth Amendment rights. The Florida Supreme Court reasoned that Bostick had been seized because a reasonable passenger in his situation would not have felt free to leave the bus to avoid questioning by the police, and that the evidence could not then be used against him because the officers had lacked the reasonable suspicion required to justify a seizure. The Supreme Court disagreed. It reasoned that, so long as a reasonable person would feel free "to disregard the police and go about his business," the encounter is consensual and no reasonable suspicion is required. On that standard, it found that the encounter was consensual because Bostick did not feel free to leave because of coercive police conduct but because of his own decision to take the bus. What do you make of the view that Bostick placed himself in the bus voluntarily and, because of that, he was not seized by the state? What are your thoughts on this approach to state action? Are bus sweeps really fair? If they are so unfair, why do they not violate the due process clause which protects individuals from unfair state actions? The Court highlighted the proper test for determining whether a seizure took place as whether a reasonable person was not at liberty to ignore the police presence and go about his business. In light of the psychological evidence we discussed in the introduction to this chapter, what do you make of this definition of voluntary consent – complying with a request that one would prefer to refuse? Compliance in the face of discomfort, anxiety, and tension suggests that bus sweep situations coerce passengers to comply with a request that they would prefer to refuse. Is this a persuasive point? The officer told Bostick that he was free to leave, yet he persisted asking questions. Is it fair to conceive of the event as voluntary? Does the fact that the officer has a weapon figure in your analysis? Importantly, the Court noted that the reasonable person test presupposes an innocent person. Given what you know about the psychology of feeling seized, is that standard interpreted appropriately? Does that protect peoples' rights enough? In your analysis, consider the note below.

NOTE ON THE SOCIAL DETERMINATION OF BEHAVIOR

Psychologists suggest the concept of social validation to help us understand how people's susceptibility to influence by others when they are uncertain of their own opinions. Several factors explain why, in new or ambiguous situations, people follow other people's actions to decide on the correct course of action for themselves. We look to others because ambiguity fails to offer a guide to behavior and thoughts about situations. Given that failure, determining what to do first requires making sense of and attaching meaning to situations. Ambiguous situations, then, first require us to attach meaning by examining what others do or seem to be thinking. Once that has been determined, we seem to operate by the rule of thumb that equates consensus with correctness. We deem what others seem to be thinking or doing as the correct thing to do or think. Stanley Milgram, Leonard Bickman, and Lawrence Berkowitz, Note on the drawing power of crowds of different size, 31 J. Personality and Soc. Psych. 79 (1969).

Several empirical demonstrations of this phenomenon were conducted in the 1970's. One leading study, for example, arranged for subjects to complete a questionnaire in a room that slowly began filling with smoke. The subjects encountered this manufactured emergency either alone, with two confederates who sat passively as the room filled with smoke, or with two other naive subjects. When alone, seventy-five percent of the subjects called for help within the time allotted for the experiment. When the subject was with two confederates who calmly continued to fill out the questionnaire as the smoke entered the room, only ten percent called for help even though the smoke would make it difficult to see across the room. Of the groups of three naive subjects, only thirty-eight percent reported a problem to anyone. The researchers concluded that the presence of others inhibited a pro-social response, a finding that also emerged in more realistic situations, such as screams for help from a female confederate who had just been introduced to subjects before she went to another room to encounter staged violence. Bibb Latane and John M. Darley, The Unresponsive Bystander: Why Doesn't He Help? (1970); and Bibb Latane and John M. Darley, Group inhibition of bystander intervention in emergencies, 10 J. Personality and Soc. Psych. 215 (1968).

The above studies of ambiguity and the search for consensus reveal well the varied impact of social validation. They show how numerous factors influence our decision to follow others when we experience ambiguous situations. The experiments also show that a key factor includes the number of other people present. Other research demonstrates the impact of the extent to which those other people are similar to oneself. See Robert B. Cialdini and Melanie R. Trost, Social influence: Social norms, conformity and compliance, in 2 The Handbook of Social Psychology 151, 172 (Daniel T. Gilbert, Susan T. Fiske, and Gardner Lindzey, eds., 1998). Equally interesting research reveals that the behavior can sometimes follow social perception rather automatically, without any conscious thought about the decision or action. See Ap Dijksterhuis and John A. Bargh, The perception-behavior expressway: Automatic effects of social perception on social behavior, in Advances in Experimental Social Psychology 1 (Mark P. Zanna, ed., 2001). The finding is that we often do what we see others doing not because we have consciously decided to do so, but because we do the behavior automatically. To put it in the language of social psychologists, we do the behavior because it is a natural consequence of the automatic activation of behavioral representations that follow perceptions. The concept is actually quite simple. For example, we often unconsciously imitate other people's posture and tone of voice because these processes are automatic and unintentional, known as the "chameleon effect." This effect refers to nonconscious mimicry of the postures, mannerisms, facial expressions, and other behaviors of one's interaction partners, such that one's behavior passively and unintentionally changes to match that of others in one's current social environment. Researchers suggest that the mechanism involved is the perception-behavior link, that the mere perception of another's behavior automatically increases the likelihood of engaging in that behavior oneself. Tanya L. Chartrand and John A. Bargh (1999). The chameleon effect: The perception-behavior link and social interaction, 76 J. of Personality and Soc. Psych. 893 (1999). Psychologists, though, show that it may even be enough for a stereotype of behavior to become activated in order to produce actual behavior associated with that stereotype; we actually may not even need to observe other people. Henk Aarts and Ap Dijksterhuis, Category activation effects in judgment and behavior: The moderating role of perceived comparability, 41 Brit. J. Soc. Psych. 123 (2002). Observing others or even thinking about others doing an act can automatically lead to doing that act ourselves, even if we do not intend to, are not aware of doing so, or would prefer to do otherwise. Much of this research supports the findings we discusses in Chapter 3 about the automaticity of social behavior.

The above findings result from a long line of research in social psychology that reveals the remarkable extent to which people profoundly influence those around them. Arguably the most famous study in this area includes Philip Zimbardo's demonstration that he could induce people to destroy an automobile by providing a model who began to smash it with a sledgehammer. The effect of groups was shown even more profoundly by achieving similar results in violent neighborhoods simply by providing a similar automobile; the argument was that passersby destroyed the automobile because they had witnessed many examples of such activities and did not need to be induced by someone smashing with sledgehammers. Again, the point is that situations may lead to certain behaviors even in the absence of models for behavior. Phillip G.

Zimbardo, The human choice: Individuation, reason, and order versus deindividuation, impulse, and chaos, in Nebraska Symposium on Motivation 237, 287-93 (William J. Arnold and David Levie, eds., 1969).

The above studies have been used to account for people's failure to offer assistance, like simply calling police, for victims in obvious need of help. The theory posits, for example, that when we are faced with a mildly ambiguous situation, such as unidentified screams from an alley outside one's window, we look to others to help us interpret the situation. Rather than seeing people aid the victim, we often see other people looking at us for help interpreting the situation. This leads bystanders to believe that the victim does not actually need assistance, or, if they do, the other bystanders must already have requested it. It is not that the bystanders subscribe to a social norm of not helping, it is that they unwittingly influence each other's interpretation of the situation in a manner that results in assuming that others help.

What is again interesting from the above research is the remarkable extent to which people believe that they would act differently in situations involving social validation. Robert J. Wolosin, Steven J. Sherman, and Arnie Cann, Predictions of own and other's conformity, 43 J. Personality 357, 372-76 (1975). They are mistaken. What implications arise from this finding? What do you make of the argument that the Court seems to make a similar mistake when it asserts that a reasonable person could easily terminate encounters with police even once a cascade of acquiescence is under way? In addition to the Court's possible mistake due to its being an observer, do you find that this research reveals that the Court inappropriately assumes that individuals will not act against their best interests while in groups? Do you think social validation plays a role in people's consenting to be searched on buses when everyone else consents? If so, how significant a role is it?

GROUNDS FOR ARREST

ATWATER v. CITY OF LAGO VISTA
532 U.S. 318 (2001)

JUSTICE SOUTER delivered the opinion of the Court

The question is whether the Fourth Amendment forbids a warrantless arrest for a minor criminal offense, such as a misdemeanor seatbelt violation punishable only by a fine. We hold that it does not.

I.

A.

In Texas, if a car is equipped with safety belts, a front-seat passenger must wear one and the driver must secure any small child riding in front. Violation of either provision is "a misdemeanor punishable by a fine not less than $25 or more than $50." Texas law expressly authorizes "any peace officer [to] arrest without warrant a person found committing a violation" of these seatbelt laws, although it permits police to issue citations in lieu of arrest.

In March 1997, Petitioner Gail Atwater was driving her pickup truck in Lago Vista, Texas, with her 3-year-old son and 5-year-old daughter in the front seat. None of them was wearing a seatbelt. Respondent Bart Turek, a Lago Vista police officer at the time, observed the seatbelt violations and pulled Atwater over. According to Atwater's complaint (the allegations of which we assume to be true for present purposes), Turek approached the truck and "yelled" something to the effect of "we've met before" and "you're going to jail." [Turek had previously stopped Atwater for what he had thought was a seatbelt violation, but had realized that Atwater's son, although seated on the vehicle's armrest, was in fact belted in. Atwater acknowledged that her son's seating position was unsafe, and Turek issued a verbal warning.] He then called for backup and asked to see Atwater's driver's license and insurance documentation, which state law required her to carry. When Atwater told Turek that she did not have the papers because her purse had been stolen the day before, Turek said that he had "heard that story two-hundred times."

Atwater asked to take her "frightened, upset, and crying" children to a friend's house nearby, but Turek told her, "you're not going anywhere." As it turned out, Atwater's friend learned what was going on and soon arrived to take charge of the children. Turek then handcuffed Atwater, placed her in his squad car, and drove her to the local police station, where booking officers had her remove her shoes, jewelry, and eyeglasses, and empty her pockets. Officers took Atwater's "mug shot" and placed her, alone, in a jail cell for about one hour, after which she was taken before a magistrate and released on $310 bond.

Atwater was charged with driving without her seatbelt fastened, failing to secure her children in seatbelts, driving without a license, and failing to provide proof of insurance. She ultimately pleaded no contest to the misdemeanor seatbelt offenses and paid a $50 fine; the other charges were dismissed.

B.

Atwater and her husband, petitioner Michael Haas, filed suit in a Texas state court under 42 U.S.C. § 1983 against Turek and respondents City of Lago Vista and Chief of Police Frank Miller. So far as concerns us, petitioners (whom we will simply call Atwater) alleged that respondents (for simplicity, the City) had violated Atwater's Fourth Amendment "right to be free from unreasonable seizure," and sought compensatory and punitive damages.

...Given Atwater's admission that she had "violated the law" and the absence of any allegation "that she was harmed or detained in any way inconsistent with the law," the District Court ruled the Fourth Amendment claim "meritless" and granted the City's summary judgment motion. A panel of the United States Court of Appeals for the Fifth Circuit reversed. It concluded that "an arrest for a first-time seat belt offense" was an unreasonable seizure within the meaning of the Fourth Amendment and held that Turek was not entitled to qualified immunity.

Sitting en banc, the Court of Appeals vacated the panel's decision and affirmed the District Court's summary judgment for the City. Relying on Whren v. United States, the en banc court observed that, although the Fourth Amendment generally requires a balancing of individual and governmental interests, where "an arrest is based on probable cause then 'with rare exceptions . . . the result of that balancing is not in doubt.'" Because "neither party disputed that Officer Turek had probable cause to arrest Atwater," and because "there [was] no evidence in the record that Officer Turek conducted the arrest in an 'extraordinary manner, unusually harmful' to Atwater's privacy interests," the en banc court held that the arrest was not unreasonable for Fourth Amendment purposes.

We granted certiorari to consider whether the Fourth Amendment, either by incorporating common-law restrictions on misdemeanor arrests or otherwise, limits police officers' authority to arrest without warrant for minor criminal offenses. We now affirm.

II.

The Fourth Amendment safeguards "the right of the people to be secure in their persons, houses, papers, and effects, against unreasonable searches and seizures." In reading the Amendment, we are guided by "the traditional protections against unreasonable searches and seizures afforded by the common law at the time of the framing," since "an examination of the common-law understanding of an officer's authority to arrest sheds light on the obviously relevant, if not entirely dispositive, consideration of what the Framers of the Amendment might have thought to be reasonable." Thus, the first step here is to assess Atwater's claim that peace officers' authority to make warrantless arrests for misdemeanors was restricted at common law (whether "common law" is understood strictly as law judicially derived or, instead, as the whole body of law extant at the time of the framing). Atwater's specific contention is that "founding-era common-law rules" forbade peace officers to make warrantless misdemeanor arrests except in cases of "breach of the peace," a category she claims was then understood narrowly as covering only those nonfelony offenses "involving or tending toward violence." Although her historical argument is by no means insubstantial, it ultimately fails.

A.

We begin with the state of pre-founding English common law and find that, even after making some allowance for variations in the common-law usage of the term "breach of the peace," the "founding-era common-law rules" were not nearly as clear as Atwater claims; on the contrary, the common-law commentators (as well as the sparsely reported cases) reached divergent conclusions with respect to officers' warrantless misdemeanor arrest power. Moreover, in the years leading up to American independence, Parliament repeatedly extended express warrantless arrest authority to cover misdemeanor-level offenses not amounting to or involving any violent breach of the peace.

B.

An examination of specifically American evidence is to the same effect. Neither the history of the framing era nor subsequent legal development indicates that the Fourth Amendment was originally understood, or has traditionally been read, to embrace Atwater's position.

2.

Nor does Atwater's argument from tradition pick up any steam from the historical record as it has unfolded since the framing, there being no indication that her claimed rule has ever become "woven . . . into the fabric" of American law.

Small wonder, then, that today statutes in all 50 States and the District of Columbia permit warrantless misdemeanor arrests by at least some (if not all) peace officers without requiring any breach of the peace, as do a host of congressional enactments. The American Law Institute has long endorsed the validity of such legislation and the consensus, as stated in the current literature, is that statutes "removing the breach of the peace limitation and thereby permitting arrest without warrant for any misdemeanor committed in the arresting officer's presence" have "'never been successfully challenged and stand as the law of the land.'"

III.

While it is true here that history, if not unequivocal, has expressed a decided, majority view that the police need not obtain an arrest warrant merely because a misdemeanor stopped short of violence or a threat of it, Atwater does not wager all on history. Instead, she asks us to mint a new rule of constitutional law on the understanding that when historical practice fails to speak conclusively to a claim grounded on the Fourth Amendment, courts are left to strike a current balance between individual and societal interests by subjecting particular contemporary circumstances to traditional standards of reasonableness. Atwater accordingly argues for a modern arrest rule, one not necessarily requiring violent breach of the peace, but nonetheless forbidding custodial arrest, even upon probable cause, when conviction could not ultimately carry any jail time and when the government shows no compelling need for immediate detention.

If we were to derive a rule exclusively to address the uncontested facts of this case, Atwater might well prevail. She was a known and established resident of Lago Vista with no place to hide and no incentive to flee, and common sense says she would almost certainly have buckled up as a condition of driving off with a citation. In her case, the physical incidents of arrest were merely gratuitous humiliations imposed by a police officer who was (at best) exercising extremely poor judgment. Atwater's claim to live free of pointless indignity and confinement clearly outweighs anything the City can raise against it specific to her case.

But we have traditionally recognized that a responsible Fourth Amendment balance is not well served by standards requiring sensitive, case-by-case determinations of government need, lest every discretionary judgment in the field be converted into an occasion for constitutional review. Often enough, the Fourth Amendment has to be applied on the spur (and in the heat) of the moment, and the object in implementing its command of reasonableness is to draw standards sufficiently clear and simple to be applied with a fair prospect of surviving judicial second-guessing months and years after an arrest or search is made. Courts attempting to strike a reasonable Fourth Amendment balance thus credit the government's side with an essential interest in readily administrable rules.

At first glance, Atwater's argument may seem to respect the values of clarity and simplicity, so far as she claims that the Fourth Amendment generally forbids warrantless arrests for minor crimes not accompanied by violence or some demonstrable threat of it (whether "minor crime" be defined as a fine-only traffic offense, a fine-only offense more generally, or a misdemeanor). But the claim is not ultimately so simple, nor could it be, for complications arise the moment we begin to think about the possible applications of the several criteria Atwater proposes for drawing a line between minor crimes with limited arrest authority and others not so restricted.

One line, she suggests, might be between "jailable" and "fine-only" offenses, between those for which conviction could result in commitment and those for which it could not. The trouble with this distinction, of course, is that an officer on the street might not be able to tell. It is not merely that we cannot expect every police officer to know the details of frequently complex penalty schemes, but that penalties for ostensibly identical conduct can vary on account of facts difficult (if not impossible) to know at the scene of an arrest. Is this the first offense or is the suspect a repeat offender? Is the weight of the marijuana a gram above or a gram below the fine-only line? Where conduct could implicate more than one criminal prohibition, which one will the district attorney ultimately decide to charge? And so on.

But Atwater's refinements would not end there. She represents that if the line were drawn at nonjailable traffic offenses, her proposed limitation should be qualified by a proviso authorizing warrantless arrests where "necessary for enforcement of the traffic laws or when [an] offense would otherwise continue and pose a danger to others on the road." The proviso only compounds the difficulties. Would, for instance, either exception apply to speeding? At oral argument, Atwater's counsel said that "it would not be reasonable to arrest a driver for speeding unless the speeding rose to the level of reckless driving." But is it not fair to expect that the chronic speeder will speed again despite a citation in his pocket, and should that not qualify as showing that the "offense would . . . continue" under Atwater's rule? And why, as a constitutional matter, should we assume that only reckless driving will "pose a danger to others on the road" while speeding will not?

There is no need for more examples to show that Atwater's general rule and limiting proviso promise very little in the way of administrability. ...It is the difference between no basis for legal action challenging the discretionary judgment, on the one hand, and the prospect of evidentiary exclusion or (as here) personal § 1983 liability for the misapplication of a constitutional standard, on the other. Atwater's rule therefore would not only place police in an almost impossible spot but would guarantee increased litigation over many of the arrests that would occur. For all these reasons, Atwater's various distinctions between permissible and impermissible arrests for minor crimes strike us as "very unsatisfactory lines" to require police officers to draw on a moment's notice.

One may ask, of course, why these difficulties may not be answered by a simple tie breaker for the police to follow in the field: if in doubt, do not arrest. The first answer is that in practice the tie breaker would boil down to something akin to a least-restrictive-alternative limitation, which is itself one of those "ifs, ands, and buts" rules generally thought inappropriate in working out Fourth Amendment protection. Beyond that, whatever help the tie breaker might give would come at the price of a systematic disincentive to arrest in situations where even Atwater concedes that arresting would serve an important societal interest. An officer not quite sure that the drugs weighed enough to warrant jail time or not quite certain about a suspect's risk of flight would not arrest, even though it could perfectly well turn out that, in fact, the offense called for incarceration and the defendant was long gone on the day of trial. Multiplied many times over, the costs to society of such underenforcement could easily outweigh the costs to defendants of being needlessly arrested and booked, as Atwater herself acknowledges.

Just how easily the costs could outweigh the benefits may be shown by asking, as one Member of this Court did at oral argument, "how bad the problem is out there." The very fact that the law has never jelled the way Atwater would have it leads one to wonder whether warrantless misdemeanor arrests need constitutional attention, and there is cause to think the answer is no. So far as such arrests might be thought to pose a threat to the probable-cause requirement, anyone arrested for a crime without formal process, whether for felony or misdemeanor, is entitled to a magistrate's review of probable cause within 48 hours, and there is no reason to think the procedure in this case atypical in giving the suspect a prompt opportunity to request release. ...

Accordingly, we confirm today what our prior cases have intimated: the standard of probable cause "applies to all arrests, without the need to 'balance' the interests and circumstances involved in particular situations." If an officer has probable cause to believe that an individual has committed even a very minor criminal offense in his presence, he may, without violating the Fourth Amendment, arrest the offender.

IV.

Atwater's arrest satisfied constitutional requirements. There is no dispute that Officer Turek had probable cause to believe that Atwater had committed a crime in his presence. She admits that neither she nor her children were wearing seat belts. Turek was accordingly authorized (not required, but authorized) to make a custodial arrest without balancing costs and benefits or determining whether or not Atwater's arrest was in some sense necessary.

Nor was the arrest made in an "extraordinary manner, unusually harmful to [her] privacy or . . . physical interests." ...the question whether a search or seizure is "extraordinary" turns, above all else, on the manner in which the search or seizure is executed. ...The arrest and booking were inconvenient and embarrassing to Atwater, but not so extraordinary as to violate the Fourth Amendment.

The Court of Appeals's en banc judgment is affirmed.

It is so ordered.

JUSTICE O'CONNOR, with whom JUSTICE STEVENS, JUSTICE GINSBURG, and JUSTICE BREYER join, dissenting.

The Fourth Amendment guarantees the right to be free from "unreasonable searches and seizures." The Court recognizes that the arrest of Gail Atwater was a "pointless indignity" that served no discernible state interest, and yet holds that her arrest was constitutionally permissible. Because the Court's position is inconsistent with the explicit guarantee of the Fourth Amendment, I dissent.

I.

A full custodial arrest, such as the one to which Ms. Atwater was subjected, is the quintessential seizure. When a full custodial arrest is effected without a warrant, the plain language of the Fourth Amendment requires that the arrest be reasonable. It is beyond cavil that "the touchstone of our analysis under the Fourth Amendment is always 'the reasonableness in all the circumstances of the particular governmental invasion of a citizen's personal security.'"

We have "often looked to the common law in evaluating the reasonableness, for Fourth Amendment purposes, of police activity." But history is just one of the tools we use in conducting the reasonableness inquiry. And when history is inconclusive, as the majority amply demonstrates it is in this case, we will "evaluate the search or seizure under traditional standards of reasonableness by assessing, on the one hand, the degree to which it intrudes upon an individual's privacy and, on the other, the degree to which it is needed for the promotion of legitimate governmental interests." In other words, in determining reasonableness, "each case is to be decided on its own facts and circumstances."

...The Court's thorough exegesis makes it abundantly clear that warrantless misdemeanor arrests were not the subject of a clear and consistently applied rule at common law. We therefore must engage in the balancing test required by the Fourth Amendment. While probable cause is surely a necessary condition for warrantless arrests for fine-only offenses, any realistic assessment of the interests implicated by such arrests demonstrates that probable cause alone is not a sufficient condition.

A custodial arrest exacts an obvious toll on an individual's liberty and privacy, even when the period of custody is relatively brief. The arrestee is subject to a full search of her person and confiscation of her possessions. If the arrestee is the occupant of a car, the entire passenger compartment of the car, including packages therein, is subject to search as well. The arrestee may be detained for up to 48 hours without having a magistrate determine whether there in fact was probable cause for the arrest. Because people arrested for all types of violent and nonviolent offenses may be housed together awaiting such review, this detention period is potentially dangerous.

Because a full custodial arrest is such a severe intrusion on an individual's liberty, its reasonableness hinges on "the degree to which it is needed for the promotion of legitimate governmental interests." In light of the availability of citations to promote a State's interests when a fine-only offense has been committed, I cannot concur in a rule which deems a full custodial arrest to be reasonable in every circumstance. Giving police officers constitutional carte blanche to effect an arrest whenever there is probable cause to believe a fine-only misdemeanor has been committed is irreconcilable with the Fourth Amendment's command that seizures be reasonable. Instead, I would require that when there is probable cause to believe that a fine-only offense has been committed, the police officer should issue a citation unless the officer is "able to point to specific and articulable facts which, taken together with rational inferences from those facts, reasonably warrant [the additional] intrusion" of a full custodial arrest.

The majority insists that a bright-line rule focused on probable cause is necessary to vindicate the State's interest in easily administrable law enforcement rules. Probable cause itself, however, is not a model of precision. "The quantum of information which constitutes probable cause – evidence which would 'warrant a man of reasonable caution in the belief' that a [crime] has been committed – must be measured by the facts of the particular case." The rule I propose – which merely requires a legitimate reason for the decision to escalate the seizure into a full custodial arrest – thus does not undermine an otherwise "clear and simple" rule.

While clarity is certainly a value worthy of consideration in our Fourth Amendment jurisprudence, it by no means trumps the values of liberty and privacy at the heart of the Amendment's protections....

At bottom, the majority offers two related reasons why a bright-line rule is necessary: the fear that officers who arrest for fine-only offenses will be subject to "personal liability for the misapplication of a constitutional standard," and the resulting "systematic disincentive to arrest...where...arresting would serve an important societal interest." These concerns are certainly valid, but they are more than adequately resolved by the doctrine of qualified immunity.

...the city contends that arresting Atwater was constitutionally reasonable because it advanced two legitimate interests: "the enforcement of child safety laws and encouraging [Atwater] to appear for trial."

It is difficult to see how arresting Atwater served either of these goals any more effectively than the issuance of a citation. With respect to the goal of law enforcement generally, Atwater did not pose a great danger to the community. She had been driving very slowly – approximately 15 miles per hour – in broad daylight on a residential street that had no other traffic. Nor was she a repeat offender; until that day, she had received one traffic citation in her life – a ticket, more than 10 years earlier, for failure to signal a lane change. Although Officer Turek had stopped Atwater approximately three months earlier because he thought that Atwater's son was not wearing a seatbelt, Turek had been mistaken. Moreover, Atwater immediately accepted responsibility and apologized for her conduct. Thus, there was every indication that Atwater would have buckled herself and her children in had she been cited and allowed to leave.

With respect to the related goal of child welfare, the decision to arrest Atwater was nothing short of counterproductive. Atwater's children witnessed Officer Turek yell at their mother and threaten to take them all into custody. Ultimately, they were forced to leave her behind with Turek, knowing that she was being taken to jail. Understandably, the 3-year-old boy was "very, very, very traumatized." After the incident, he had to see a child psychologist regularly, who reported that the boy "felt very guilty that he couldn't stop this horrible thing . . . he was powerless to help his mother or sister." Both of Atwater's children are now terrified at the sight of any police car. According to Atwater, the arrest "just never leaves us. It's a conversation we have every other day, once a week, and it's – it raises its head constantly in our lives."

Citing Atwater surely would have served the children's interests well. It would have taught Atwater to ensure that her children were buckled up in the future. It also would have taught the children an important lesson in accepting responsibility and obeying the law. Arresting Atwater, though, taught the children an entirely different lesson: that "the bad person could just as easily be the policeman as it could be the most horrible person they could imagine."

III.

The Court's error, however, does not merely affect the disposition of this case. The per se rule that the Court creates has potentially serious consequences for the everyday lives of Americans. A broad range of conduct falls into the category of fine-only misdemeanors. In Texas alone, for example, disobeying any sort of traffic warning sign is a misdemeanor punishable only by fine, as is failing to pay a highway toll, and driving with expired license plates. Nor are fine-only crimes limited to the traffic context. In several States, for example, littering is a criminal offense punishable only by fine.

To be sure, such laws are valid and wise exercises of the States' power to protect the public health and welfare. My concern lies not with the decision to enact or enforce these laws, but rather with the manner in which they may be enforced. Under today's holding, when a police officer has probable cause to believe that a fine-only misdemeanor offense has occurred, that officer may stop the suspect, issue a citation, and let the person continue on her way. Or, if a traffic violation, the officer may stop the car, arrest the driver, search the driver, search the entire passenger compartment of the car including any purse or package inside, and impound the car and inventory all of its contents....

Such unbounded discretion carries with it grave potential for abuse. The majority takes comfort in the lack of evidence of "an epidemic of unnecessary minor-offense arrests." But the relatively small number of published cases dealing with such arrests proves little and should provide little solace. Indeed, as the recent debate over racial profiling demonstrates all too clearly, a relatively minor traffic infraction may often serve as an excuse for stopping and harassing an individual. After today, the arsenal available to any officer extends to a full arrest and the searches permissible concomitant to that arrest. An officer's subjective motivations for making a traffic stop are not relevant considerations in determining the reasonableness of the stop. But it is precisely because these motivations are beyond our purview that we must vigilantly ensure that officers' poststop actions – which are properly within our reach – comport with the Fourth Amendment's guarantee of reasonableness.

* * *

The Court neglects the Fourth Amendment's express command in the name of administrative ease. In so doing, it cloaks the pointless indignity that Gail Atwater suffered with the mantle of reasonableness. I respectfully dissent.

NOTES AND QUERIES

The arrest may seem extraordinary. As the Court notes, whether a search or seizure is done in an extraordinary manner unusually harmful to privacy or physical interests turns on the manner in which the search or seizure is executed, as we have seen above in *Winston v. Lee*, 470 U.S. 753 (1985) ("physical penetration of the body"). Do you find the current seizure appropriately executed?

Do you find that the majority appropriately balances the intrusiveness of the arrest, especially in terms of suffered indignities, with the need to provide officers with discretion? The Court admits that the officer exercised poor judgment; then why does it allow the behavior to continue? Do you find the majority's rationales persuasive? What do you make of the argument that individuals do not need protection since the problem of unwarranted seizures arises infrequently? Do you find a full custodial arrest to be the type of intrusion that is minor, as the majority suggests, or is it a severe intrusion, as the dissent suggests? The majority notes that the arrest was pointless and an indignity. Why does that not indicate that the arrest was therefore unreasonable?

The dissent fears that the majority grants police too much power to arrest for a minor traffic violation, which also ends up being the power to search, for example, either their persons or their cars. Worrisome?

Chapter 5

INTERROGATING SUSPECTS

INTRODUCTION

We have seen that the legal system assumes that individuals know their rights, such as their right not to consent to a search or right to be free to ignore "consensual encounters" with law enforcement. We also have seen that Supreme Court perceptions of reasonable beliefs and standards do not necessarily square with those of many individuals, as seen in different views regarding what should constitute reasonable expectations of privacy. The current approach to the Fifth Amendment's[1] self-incrimination clause presents many of the themes we have seen as recurring when we balance individual liberties with the interests of law enforcement. Yet, the nature of Supreme Court decisions ensures that this area of legal processes remains different from all others.

This area of law differs in two critical ways from those we have reviewed. First, the vast majority of individuals reveal an understanding of the rudiments of what constitutes the broad right against self-incrimination. A national poll conducted in the early 1990s, for example, indicated that 80% of respondents knew that they have a right to remain silent if arrested.[2] In addition, the relevant empirical and social scientific research on police interrogation suggests that, in virtually all observed police custodial interrogations, police do inform suspects of their basic 5th Amendment rights.[3] This is in many ways not surprising given that the Supreme Court, with some notable exceptions, seeks to ensure that individuals do know their rights. Most notably, the Supreme Court did so in *Miranda v. Arizona*[4] when it held that officers who wish to interrogate suspects must provide warnings to them when they are taken into custody or when officers significantly limit their liberties. The Court viewed the warnings as a more effective procedure for apprizing accused persons of the right to silence than the Due Process voluntariness test characteristic of the investigative phase of criminal justice processes. It often has been argued that the new requirement contributed to a popular diffusion of 5th Amendment law through the media and popular culture, with the result that the vast majority of people today know their *Miranda* rights. Given what we have learned from other areas of law, this seems to be quite a remarkable achievement.

---

[1] The Fifth Amendment reads: "No person shall be held to answer for a capital, or otherwise infamous crime, unless on a presentment or indictment of a Grand Jury, except in cases arising in the land or naval forces, or in the Militia, when in actual service in time of War or public danger; nor shall any person be subject for the same offence to be twice put in jeopardy of life or limb, nor shall be compelled in any criminal case to be a witness against himself, nor be deprived of life, liberty, or property, without due process of law; nor shall private property be taken for public use without just compensation."

[2] Samuel Walker, Taming the System: The Control of Discretion in Criminal Justice 1950-1990, 51 (1993).

[3] See Richard A. Leo, The impact of *Miranda* revisited, 86 J. Crim. L. and Criminology 621 (1996); and Paul G. Cassel and Bret S. Hayman, Police interrogation in the 1990s: An empirical study of the effects of *Miranda*, 43 UCLA L. Rev. 839 (1996). Note that the research was conducted after *Miranda* had taken effect.

[4] 384 U.S. 439 (1966).

That immense diffusion of knowledge and impact on police behavior attests to the Supreme Court's power to infuse the public and law enforcement's legal consciousness. *Miranda* warnings do seem effective in apprizing suspects, as well as the general public, of their right to silence and in assuring an opportunity to exercise that right. Yet, this area of law still raises important concerns and reveals the challenges faced by efforts that seek to protect individuals' liberties. Most notably, it still remains debatable whether interrogatory warnings are as protective as we would expect. In addition, it still remains difficult to assess claims that challenge the truthfulness of suspects' confessions, not only to the extent to which people could make false claims but also to the extent that we have difficulty evaluating the truthfulness of people's statements. These difficulties are further complicated by the possibility that efforts to grant suspects increased protection may hamper legitimate law enforcement. We explore research examining these issues and concerns before examining the leading cases in this area.

THE PROTECTIVE NATURE OF INTERROGATORY WARNINGS

It may seem obvious that the best way to protect rights is to inform individuals of those rights at the critical moment that they should consider invoking them. Yet, that theoretical benefit may not emerge so clearly when put in practice. The extent to which the current focus on informing suspects who are in custody and who are about to be interrogated by officers raises concerns about the actual protective nature of the warnings. Although we will address that concern in many ways, an appropriate starting point is to consider research that examines the rule's effectiveness.

A primary concern involves the extent to which the warnings actually do protect suspects' 5th Amendment rights. One way to gauge this question is to investigate the extent to which individuals invoke their right to silence. That is, a reduction in rates of interrogation, if attributable to the *Miranda* warnings, would correspond to more protection of the right against compelled self-incrimination. Evidence does suggest that *Miranda* procedures have resulted in a lower frequency of police interrogation of suspects. A series of post-*Miranda* studies revealed that an average of 20% of suspects invoke their *Miranda* rights and are not questioned by police. Some argue that pre-*Miranda* interrogation rates were much higher and that the differential may be due to the requirement of *Miranda* warnings.[5] Although the meaning of this research may remain disputed in terms of *Miranda*'s impact on interrogation rates, the research does make one point clear: invoking *Miranda* means that law enforcement must rely on evidence other than confessions. Importantly, this actually was one of the major rationales for *Miranda*'s ruling: law enforcement should be encouraged to support convictions on reliable evidence preferably from sources other than defendants themselves.

Another way to determine the protective nature of interrogative rights is to examine whether *Miranda* warnings too severely limit legitimate law enforcement. We may address this in two ways. One obvious way is to ask law enforcement officers themselves. This approach reveals that *Miranda* warnings have not impeded law enforcement. This finding may not have been expected when *Miranda* was decided, but in the mid-1980s, the American Bar Association had conducted hearings in three cities as well as a randomized telephone survey. The ABA Report concluded that "[a] very strong majority of those surveyed prosecutors, judges, and police officers agree that compliance with *Miranda* does not present serious problems for law enforcement."[6] Of course, that left a minority taking the opposite view. The materials we shall soon see, however, tends to support the majority view that *Miranda* does not impede law enforcement as much as it was feared.

---

[5] Paul G. Cassel and Bret S. Hayman, Police interrogation in the 1990s: An empirical study of the effects of *Miranda*, 43 UCLA L. Rev. 839 (1996); and Richard A. Leo, Inside the interrogation room, 86 J. Crim. L. and Criminology 266, 268 (1996).

[6] A.B.A. Special Comm. On Criminal Justice in a Free Society, Criminal Justice in Crisis 12, 28 (1988).

The second way to address the protective nature of *Miranda* is to examine how police interrogators have adapted to its requirements. The general finding emerging from this research is that the police have become adept at skirting *Miranda's* requirements. Available evidence suggests that police can minimize the *Miranda* warnings and avoid invocation of the right to silence. Research examining interrogation tactics report the frequent use of psychological ploys intended to reduce *Miranda* invocations. In one leading study of actual police interrogations, it was found that police frequently appealed to the suspect's self-interest (88% of interrogations); confronted the suspect with evidence of guilt (85%); undermined the suspect's confidence in denial (43%); identified contradictions in the story (42%); appealed to the importance of cooperation (37%); offered moral justifications or excuses (34%); confronted the suspect with false evidence of guilt (30%); used praise or flattery (30%); and minimized the moral seriousness of the offense (22%). A common strategy was to tell the suspect that they are here to discuss why, not whether, the suspect committed the crime. Consistent with their training to avoid express promises of leniency, officers effectively communicated these promises implicitly by inviting the suspect to imagine how prosecutors or juries would perceive the case if no statement was made.[7] These strategies are often deployed in what has been referred to as a confidence game – a con game, where the police interrogator seeks to induce confidence and trust from the suspect in exchange for hope of a better future for the suspect.[8]

This research undermines the claim of *Miranda*'s effectiveness in assuring an accused the continuous opportunity to exercise fully their right of silence. Many of the psychological ploys are investigative strategies deemed legitimate, even despite *Miranda*. This is rather significant; studies comparing different psychological ploys find that those deemed permissible may have the same impact as those that are not. For example, a leading study of subjects' reactions to interrogation transcripts investigated "minimization" and "maximization" strategies.[9] In the "minimization" condition, the officer offered the suspect an excuse or moral justification for the crime; in the "maximization" condition, the officer used high-pressure tactics, such as "exaggerating the strength of the evidence and the seriousness of the offense." The researchers determined that, although minimization techniques may appear non-coercive (at least under legal definitions of coercion), minimization techniques create expectations of leniency just as effectively as explicit promises of leniency (which are not permitted). Even more, researchers suggest that giving *Miranda* warnings in certain cases may actually put suspects at ease and thereby elicit confessions that would not otherwise have been obtained. The theory is that by making suspects feel more comfortable in the interrogation setting, the increased level of comfort may decrease their guard and thereby result in more confessions.[10] Some researchers present evidence from excerpts of interrogation transcripts revealing, in their opinion, that the giving of *Miranda* warnings are actually used as a way to elicit confessions. These are situations where interrogators are sometimes able to present the *Miranda* warnings so that suspects are led to believe that waiving their *Miranda* rights will be to their advantage.[11] Although this may be counterintuitive, it actually finds support from the research we reviewed on compliance to polite police requests.

The above findings should not be surprising. The thirty-five years since *Miranda* have brought numerous refinements in police interrogation techniques. Leading manuals in police interrogation, which derive from the popular "Reid Technique,"[12]describe some of the more successful techniques for eliciting

---

[7] Richard A. Leo, Inside the interrogation room, 86 J. Crim. L. and Criminology 266, 268 (1996).

[8] Richard A. Leo, *Miranda's* revenge: Police interrogation as a confidence game, 30 L. and Soc'y Rev. 259 (1996).

[9] Saul M. Kassin and Karlyn McNall, Police interrogations and confessions: Communicating promises and threats by pragmatic implication, 15 L. and Hum. Beh. 233 (1991).

[10] This proposition should not be surprising given the research on compliance and requests we reviewed in Chapter 4.

[11] Richard A. Leo and Welsh S. White, Adapting to *Miranda*: Modern interrogators' strategies for dealing with the obstacles posed by *Miranda*, 84 Minn. L. Rev. 397 (1999).

[12] The Reid Technique was developed in the 1960s and has not been revised much since, even with the passing of *Miranda*. See Fred E. Inbau, John J. Reid, and Joseph P. Buckley, Criminal Interrogation and Confessions (3d ed., 1987).

waivers and incriminating statements. As we will see, these interrogation techniques were the ones most criticized by the Supreme Court in *Miranda v. Arizona.*[13] Yet, they continue to be used.

Many of the prescribed police tactics specifically aim to increase the level of compulsion in the interrogation room in order to make it more likely that suspects waive their *Miranda* rights. The Reid Technique, for example, focuses on placing psychological pressure, including police deception, on suspects to convince them to confess. For example, the *Miranda* warnings are often read while the officers are still friendly with the suspect and have yet to become confrontational, so that the suspect feels more comfortable in waiving these rights. Officers also are trained to provide suspects with two alternatives: the first alternative leads to a significant punishment, while the second alternative leads to a lesser punishment or no punishment at all.[14] Importantly, one of the main tools of deception employed by police through the Reid Technique involves an officer lying about the amount and quality of evidence already obtained against the suspect. Officers may suggest that there is extensive incriminating evidence, which leads suspects to believe that they will be convicted even if they do not confess during the interrogation. Officers also will point to "tests" that suspects failed, such as a voice analyzer test, even when the officers know that the tests are bogus. Such lies by the police are designed to erode the confidence of suspects. The Reid Technique also instructs officers to offer excuses to suspects to make the suspect feel more comfortable with confessing to the crime. Some suggested tactics include pointing out the possibility that a victim has lied or exaggerated the nature of an offense. In some cases, the technique advises sympathizing with the suspect by condemning the victim or accomplice. It also advises suggesting, for the purpose of a socially revolting offense, a less revolting and more morally acceptable motivation or reason for the offense. The technique also focuses on the deportment of the interrogator and advises, for example, police to avoid creating the impression that the interrogator is a detective, but rather is a person "merely seeking the truth." The technique also focuses on the conditions of the confession room and preliminary preparations. For instance, it recommends privacy in the interrogation room, devoid of distractions such as telephones, vents, windows, and pictures. It even suggests types of lighting to maximize observance of the suspect without providing the suspect either a high degree of comfort or excessive discomfort. It suggests knowing as much as possible about the victim and the suspect; the social, religious, and racial attitudes of the suspect; potentials for alibi evidence; and the suspect's education level. The dominance and effectiveness of the technique can be seen by the regular criticisms from researchers investigating false confessions.[15]

It seems that *Miranda* may well be protective of individuals' 5th Amendment rights. Yet, the real possibility exists that officers can avoid the burdens imposed by *Miranda* and that some officers can even use the *Miranda* requirements to their advantage. These possibilities may simply constitute effective law enforcement. If police can obtain confessions from guilty suspects, the process works smoothly. The concern arises, however, that the techniques may be so inappropriately suggestive and coercive that they lead individuals to make false confessions.

---

[13] 384 U.S. 436 (1966).

[14] For example, suspects might be told that a murder could either have been intentional or in the heat of passion, the latter carrying a lighter sentence. The suspect must then choose between two confessions and may be tempted to claim that he or she committed the lesser offense so that an unavoidable punishment will not be as harsh. Either way, the end result is a confession.

[15] Gisli H. Gudjonsson, The Psychology of Interrogations and Confessions: A Handbook (2003). Gudjonsson is perhaps best known for the creation of a suggestibility scale to assess a subject's responses to leading questions and negative feedback. The scale uses a narrative paragraph describing a fictitious mugging, which is read to the subjects. The subjects are then asked to recall all they can about the story. After a delay of about fifty minutes, a subject is asked twenty specific questions, fifteen of which are subtly misleading. After answering these, the person is informed that he or she has made a number of mistakes (even if no errors have been made), and thus it is necessary to ask each of the questions once more. The person is instructed to try to be more accurate than before. Any change in answers from the previous trial is labeled a "shift"; the extent to which people give in to the misleading questions is scored as a "yield." "Yields" and "shifts" are added together to make up a "total suggestibility" score. See Jon Fridrik Sigurdsson and Gisli H. Gudjonsson, False confessions: The relative importance of psychological, criminal, and substance abuse variables, 7 Psych. Crime and L. 275 (2001).

The Possibility and Significance of False Confessions

The extent to which interrogator tactics may elicit false confessions presents an important concern. Previous chapters presented research indicating that citizens may feel vulnerable to law enforcement and act in ways against their best interests. Whether these factors contribute to false confessions and inappropriate convictions, however, is a different matter. Determining when a confession was false is problematic. For example, a leading researcher investigated the relative importance of numerous psychological and criminological variables in differentiating between alleged false confessors and other prison inmates. His studies found that antisocial personality characteristics and the extent and severity of criminal behavior, as judged by number of imprisonments, are the best predictors of offenders claiming to have made a false confession to police.[16] This, of course, may be the case because making a false confession is part of some individual's life style; or claiming a false confession is a calculated response by those with the most to lose and thus the most to gain from such claims. It is difficult to imagine that dilemmas associated with determining the validity of false confessions will be resolved any time soon. The reality that distinguishing between false from truthful false claims suggests that it makes sense to put aside the challenge of determining when false confessions are in fact false confessions in particular cases and proceed to examine what researchers typically conceptualize as false confessions.

Researchers typically classify false confessions in three ways, as either voluntary, coerced-compliant, or coerced-internalized.[17] As the term suggests, a voluntary false confession occurs without any external pressure from law enforcement. Researchers advance a number of reasons for this phenomenon: a morbid desire for notoriety, a need to expiate guilt over prior transgressions via self-punishment, inability to distinguish facts from fantasy, a desire to aid and protect the real criminal, the hope for a recommendation of leniency, and even a need to protect oneself from others.[18] The second form of false confessions, those deemed coerced-compliant, results from the pressures of coerciveness of the interrogation process. In this context, compliance denotes a conscious decision to carry out the behavior, whether or not a suspect has agreed to do it privately. Rather than confessing voluntarily, individuals simply give in to the pressures and demands of the interrogators for immediate instrumental gain. These gains include, for example, being allowed to return home after confessing, ending the interview, avoiding immediate incarceration, and failing to understand the long-term consequences.[19] Coerced-internalized false confessions are the third form. These involve suspects who eventually believe that they have committed the alleged acts after police interrogation. These recollections may be due to subtle manipulative influences by interrogators when suspects previously had no clear recollection or they may arise when the suspects realize that they may have committed the crime and have no recollection due to amnesia or alcohol induced memory problems.

Conceptualizations of false confessions, although not immune from criticism, make two significant distinctions among a wide variety of possible false confessions. First, they focus on whether the confession is initiated by law enforcement or by individuals themselves. Second, they focus on whether the interrogation causes the confession to occur for instrumental reasons or actually changes the suspect's belief about guilt or innocence. Both of these factors may be problematic in the real life of false confessions. Given that we already have examined in previous chapters the challenges associated with

---

[16] Jon Fridrik Sigurdsson and Gisli H. Gudjonsson, False confessions: The relative importance of psychological, criminal, and substance abuse variables, 7 Psych. Crime and L. 275 (2001).

[17] See Lawrence Wrightsman and Saul Kassin, Confessions in the Courtroom (1993). Some researchers have altered and expanded this list to the following categories: voluntary false confessions, stress-compliant false confessions, compliant false confessions, coerced-persuaded false confessions, and noncoerced-persuaded false confessions. See Richard J. Ofshe and Richard A. Leo, The decision to confess falsely: Rational choice and irrational action, 74 Denv. U. L. Rev. 979 (1997).

[18] Lawrence Wrightsman and Saul Kassin, Confessions in the Courtroom (1993); and Richard J. Ofshe and Richard A. Leo, The decision to confess falsely: Rational choice and irrational action, 74 Denv. U. L. Rev. 979 (1997).

[19] Lawrence Wrightsman and Saul Kassin, Confessions in the Courtroom (1993); and Richard J. Ofshe and Richard A. Leo, The decision to confess falsely: Rational choice and irrational action, 74 Denv. U. L. Rev. 979 (1997).

consensual encounters with law enforcement, we focus on false confessions instigated and perhaps instilled by the interrogation process.

Several areas of research help us understand why individuals come to believe and make false confessions. As we have seen, a coerced-internalized confession occurs when the suspect, through fatigue, pressures, and suggestiveness, actually comes to believe that he or she committed the offense. Many of the elements involved in coerced-compliant confessions apply to coerced-internalized confessions. However, there is an additional element where the confessor reaches a point where he fully believes in his own guilt. Should this transpire, a memory alteration effectively occurs. Two explanations for why this may occur are particularly illustrative.[20] The first reason this may occur relates to the manner some individuals may be susceptible to memory inflation.[21] Individuals differ in the extent to which they can use their imagination; some individuals who are asked to imagine that they had experienced an event significantly increase the likelihood that they will believe the event true. These vulnerabilities may be due to difficulties in reality monitoring and the ability to produce very vivid imagery. The second reason deals with the vulnerability of individuals to suggestibility and compliance, such as their trust of people in authority, lack of self-confidence, and having difficulty detecting discrepancies between real memory and what is suggested to them.[22] This area of research derives from the development of the concept of interrogative suggestibility to explain individualized responses to police questioning. Interrogative suggestibility derives, in part, from the extent to which interrogations are closed social interactions, and people in such interactions may come to accept messages communicated during formal questioning as the result of their subsequent behavioral response.[23] In addition, characteristics of the interviewee also affect the process of the interrogation. For persons likely to employ avoidance coping, there may be a greater possibility of suggestibility; persons with poor memory and low intelligence also are more generally suggestible; low self-esteem, lack of assertiveness, and anxiety also contribute to compliance.[24] Although all quite recent, these findings point to the real possibility that false confessions can occur, and that they may occur with undetected frequency.

Few researchers have examined the manner by which interrogations actually can produce false confessions. One study, however, continues to be cited and is worth a close look for the actual findings themselves and for understanding the challenges facing this area of research. The study involved a laboratory experiment on false confessions.[25] The researchers offered the following hypothesis: The presentation of false evidence can lead individuals who are vulnerable (that is, in a heightened state of uncertainty) to confess to an act they did not commit, and that it could cause those individuals to internalize their confession and perhaps fabricate memory details consistent with that belief. The experiment consisted of seventy-five college students who were given a typing test on a computer. The subjects typed at two different speeds and were instructed not to touch the "ALT" key because it would crash the computer

---

[20] Other possible explanations certainly exist, but they have not been the subject of much empirical research. For example, some claim that the interrogation may be compared to a trance-like state similar to one found in hypnosis. Lawrence Wrightsman and Saul Kassin, Confessions in the Courtroom (1993).

[21] Elizabeth F. Loftus, Imagining the past, 14 The Psychologist 584 (2001).

[22] See Richard J. Ofshe, Coerced confessions: The logic of seemingly irrational action, 6 Cultic Studies J. 1 (1989).

[23] Gudjonsson, for example, suggests five interrelated components as part of the interrogative suggestibility theory: (1) a closed social interaction between the interrogator and the interviewee; (2) a questioning procedure that involves two or more participants; (3) a suggestive stimulus; (4) acceptance of the suggestive stimulus; and (5) a behavioral response to indicate whether or not the suggestion is accepted. Gisli H. Gudjonsson, The Psychology of Interrogations and Confessions: A Handbook (2003).

[24] See Gisli H. Gudjonsson, Kristin Hannesdotter, Hannes Petursson, and Thorarinn Tyrfingsson, The effects of alcohol withdrawal on memory, confabulation and suggestibility, 54 Nord. J. Psychiatry 213 (2000); Gisli H. Gudjonsson, Kristin Hannesdotter, Hannes Petursson, and Gudbjorn Bjornsson, The effects of alcohol withdrawal on mental state, interrogative suggestibility and compliance: An experimental study, 13 J. of Forensic Psychiatry 53 (2002); Gisli H. Gudjonsson, Jon Fridrik Sigurdsson, Berglind Brynjolfscottir, and Hrafnhildur Hreinsdottir, The relationship of compliance with anxiety, self-esteem, paranoid thinking and anger, 8 Psych. Crime and L. 145 (2002); and Gisli H. Gudjonsson and Jon Fridrik Sigurdsson, The relationship of compliance with coping strategies and self-esteem, 19 European J. of Psych. Assess. 117 (2003).

[25] Saul M. Kassin and Katherine L. Kiechel, The social psychology of false confessions: Compliance, internatization, and confabulation, 7 Psych. Sci. 125 (1996).

program and ruin the experiment. At approximately one minute into the typing test, the test team made the computer crash. The team then blamed the computer failure on the subject's pressing of the "ALT" key. The researchers then used several modern interrogation techniques on the subjects. Some were falsely told that the experimenter had seen them touch the "ALT" key. Other subjects were asked directly if they had hit the "ALT" key when the computer crashed. Eventually the subjects were asked to sign a statement acknowledging that they had touched the "ALT" key and caused the computer to crash. Amazingly, sixty-nine percent of the subjects signed the false confession, twenty-eight internalized their guilt just by seeing the computer crash and being asked "what happened?" by the test team, and nine percent actually fabricated specific details to fit the allegation that they had touched the "ALT" key. The experiment clearly has inherit limitations. It may not be the strongest evidence for establishing that individuals are susceptible to false confessions through interrogations. The subjects were not accused of an actual crime, but rather accused of negligence for a relatively trivial matter. Far higher stakes await a criminal suspect in a murder investigation. Yet, the subjects were not subjected to a grueling, hostile interrogation by well trained investigators – factors that could also affect a suspect's likelihood to confess. If anything, the research does at least show the danger of false confessions under generally noncoercive circumstances. What may be striking is that people actually fabricated stories to explain what they had done, a response understandable from the perspective of cognitive dissonance theory.[26]

The study was recently replicated, and that replication revealed even more impressive results than the original study.[27] The new study found that the large majority of participants (82%) were willing to sign a false confession. Importantly, 42% of the subjects exhibited internalization by, for example, expressing the belief that they were fully responsible for the computer crash. Even more striking, 58% exhibited confabulation by, for example, giving detailed information about when, why, and how they hit the key that would crash the computer. Unlike the original study, however, this one implicated financial loss (they would receive only $2 rather than the $10 for participating in the experiment). The researchers interpreted these results as demonstrating that normal participants can be manipulated to sign a false confession even when such an act has straightforward negative consequences.[28]

Taken together, experimental and other forms of research highlight important points. False confessions can exist. Characteristics of the individual, interviewer, and situation can contribute to false confessions. Lastly, given that false confessions can occur by using techniques acceptable to our legal system, concern arises as to whether we can detect coerced from voluntary interrogations.

THE PSYCHOLOGY OF DISTINGUISHING COERCIVE FROM VOLUNTARY INTERROGATIONS

Evidence suggests that we may over rate our abilities to determine whether a confession was coerced. We have seen in earlier chapters how people may grossly overestimate the voluntariness of others' actions. People generally explain another person's behavior in terms of the individual's intentions and dispositions rather than focusing on the situation that could account for the person's actions.[29] The general finding that observers do not reliably appreciate the strength and consequences of situational constraints on an actor's behavior has been demonstrated in many different settings, including interrogations.

---

[26] Recall that, according to cognitive dissonance theory, individuals tend to seek consistency among their cognitions (i.e., beliefs, opinions). In other words, people will try to re-interpret past events, for example, in light of new, apparently contradictory, knowledge about those events. Leon Festinger, A Theory of Cognitive Dissonance (1957).

[27] Robert Horselenberg, Harald Merckelbach, and Sarah Josephs, Individual differences and false confessions: A conceptual replication of Kassin and Kiechel (1996), 9 Psych. Crim. and L. 1 (2003).

[28] Again, however, many counter-arguments can be levied against these findings. Most notably, the $8.00 was never their's in the first place. Yet, the high rates still are striking and indicate at least that the experiment did lead to false confessions, even if the actual percentage of those confessions are lower than those found through the experimental method.

[29] Daniel T. Gilbert and Patrick S. Malone, The correspondence bias, 117 Psych. Bull. 21 (1995).

Observers perceive confessions as more voluntary when comparing the police's perspective from the suspects' perspective. One study dramatically illustrated how this may well be true. The study involved videotaping a single confession with two cameras. When the audience saw everything the interrogator saw (the camera angle focused on the suspect from the interrogator's perspective), the identical confession was perceived as more voluntary than when the audience saw everything the suspect saw (the camera angle showed the interrogator from the suspect's perspective). The argument is that people attribute actions to what is most salient. In this context, when the suspect is shown, the suspect is viewed as more salient, which leads viewers to infer only a small degree of coercion because they attribute the act of confessing largely to the most salient object on the screen: the suspect. This finding conforms with a large body of evidence indicating that people attribute unwarranted causality (influence) to a stimulus simply because it is more salient or noticeable than other available stimuli. This creates the phenomenon of "illusory causation." The phenomenon has been hypothesized to occur because salient information tends to be more memorable than nonsalient information, and this difference in memory is responsible for the greater causality ascribed to salient information. Or, it may occur because of the manner people initially register information from an observed interaction and then remember that information. The argument is that the point of view from which individuals observe interactions influences the registration and organization of that information from the ongoing interaction, which, in turn, directly influences causal attributions and related judgments. Research examining confessions tends to support the second hypothesis. It follows from this phenomenon that, when the camera is focused on the interrogator, observers infer a large degree of coercion because they again attribute the act of confessing largely to the most salient object on the screen: the interrogator. Importantly, then, when the audience views what the suspect saw, the pressure from the interrogator (which are the external forces on the suspect's behavior) become more apparent and are considered significant. The significance of the changing focus cannot be underestimated. Trial simulations reveal that simply focusing the camera on the suspect actually doubles conviction rates.[30]

Four experiments with 539 undergraduates were conducted to test possible limits on the previously demonstrated point-of-view bias in videotaped confessions. Study 1 showed that deliberation did not eliminate the bias. Study 2 showed that forewarning did not eliminate the bias. Study 3 showed that directing greater attention to the content of the confession did not eliminate the bias. Study 4 showed that using a lengthier, case-based confession also did not eliminate the bias. Taken together, this research clearly indicates that the legal system needs to be concerned with the potential for bias that exists in videotaped confessions.[31]

This research comports with findings we discussed in Chapter Four. For example, the findings correspond with those we noted when we examined people's inability to recognize situational constraints on others, which leads to the overestimation that others acted more voluntarily than they did. In the context of interrogations, people tend to overestimate their capacity to detect lying in others and to underestimate their own ability to tell lies. This was found to be the case with police.[32] On a practical level, the tendency of police interrogators to overestimate their ability to detect deception could change suspicion into certainty and increase the risk of a false confession. In addition, this area of research also finds support from the

---

[30] G. Daniel Lassiter, Illusory Causation in the Courtroom, 11 Cur. Dir. in Psych. Sci. 204 (2002); and Daniel G. Lassiter, Andrew L. Geers, Patrick J. Munhall, Ian M. Handley, and Melissa J. Beers, Videotaped confessions: Is guilt in the eye of the camera? 33 Advances in Experimental Social Psychology 189 (Mark Zanna, ed., 2001).

[31] Daniel J. Lassiter, Melissa J. Beers, Andrew L. Geers, Ian M. Handley, Patrick J. Mundhall, and Paul E. Weiland, Further evidence of a robust point-of-view bias in videotaped confessions, 21 Cur. Psych.: Developmental, Learning, Personality, Social 265 (2002).

[32] These biases were demonstrated in a sample of 60 Israeli police officers (mean age 32.47 yrs). In a lie-detection task, the officers evaluated their accuracy as high and were overconfident in their judgements. In fact, their performance was below chance level. Participants also received false feedback about their performance. When the feedback suggested that they had performed better than they thought, this further enhanced their perceived lie-detection capacity and also increased their belief in their ability to conceal their own lies. When the feedback suggested they had performed worse than they thought, their ratings of both lie detection and their lie-telling abilities were lowered. The researchers discussed these results in terms of anchoring, availability, and the self-assessment bias. Eitan Elaas, Effects of feedback on the overestimated capacity to detect lies and the underestimated ability to tell lies, 17 Appl. Cog. Psych. 349 (2003).

research we examined involving how police interactions can create suspects when police stop them for questioning. That research also has been extended to interrogations. For example, studies have investigated police officers' movements. A series of studies examined the theory that an increase in a police officer's movements in an interview will lead to an increase in movements made by the suspect.[33] This was deemed as important because the increase in movements may then be interpreted by the police officer as suspicious behavior. The results supported the view that being interviewed by an officer who makes movements results in having suspects make more movements, which then results in police officers finding those suspects less credible.[34]

This research contributes important points. The possibility that following *Miranda*'s mandates may lead to false confessions raises the need to be able to determine when an interrogation was coerced. This, of course, remains a contentious matter in that it directly goes to the issue of the standard used to determine what constitutes voluntary behavior and the possible need to reconsider that standard. This possibility, in turn, rests on the extent to which society can afford the rule in terms of crimes that could go unsolved, deterred, or at least not punished if we heighten the threshold for determining coercion. As we explore in the next section, it remains difficult to evaluate how to determine appropriate levels of protections based on the cost of responding appropriately to crime.

The Impact of Interrogatory Protections on Solving Crime

Although there may be some evidence that officers can skirt the rules of *Miranda* to still obtain legitimate confessions, one of the major concerns involves *Miranda*'s impact on solving crime and on punishing offenders. This has been a major area of controversy, for it is extremely challenging to determine *Miranda*'s impact on these matters given other legal and social changes that occurred with *Miranda*. A considerable amount of pre/post research indicates that confession rates dropped after *Miranda*, although debate over precisely how much continues.[35] After considering twelve studies and excluding three of them as unreliable, one researcher concluded that the reduction in confessions resulting from *Miranda* averaged 16.1%. Another researcher, examining the same studies and also after excluding some as unreliable, concluded that *Miranda* reduced the confession rate between 6.7% and 9.1%. He argued further that the reduction may have been as low as 4 to 5% if certain other adjustments were made. Even the lower figures show that *Miranda* has had some effect on the interrogation process. One might wonder, however, why *Miranda* has not had a greater impact on the confession rate. After all, a rational guilty person who is told that he may remain silent and consult an attorney would presumably decide not to confess, at least until he had met with an attorney.

It remains equally challenging to determine *Miranda*'s impact on clearance rates, the reports of the number of crimes solved (through conviction or otherwise). One author studied the trend in clearance rates for the four-year period following *Miranda*. He found that, whereas clearance rates were relatively steady around 60% from 1950 to 1965, the rate of clearance dropped consistently during the four years after *Miranda*, and then plateaued at about 45% after that. He concluded that *Miranda* accounts for that change.[36] Another researcher, however, has demonstrated that the drop closely tracks the decline in the capacity of law enforcement to clear crimes. When the data is adjusted to reflect that decline, the data

---

[33] Lucy Akehurst and Aldert Vrij, Creating suspects in police interviews, 29 J. of Appl. Soc. Psych. 192 (1999).

[34] These were the results of Akehurst and Vrij's three studies. In Study 1, interviewees were interviewed by 1 male police officer who either made some movements or no movements at all. The movements made by the suspects were investigated. In Studies 2 and 3, police officers were asked to judge the credibility of interviewees who were interviewed by a lively or a nonlively interviewer. Lucy Akehurst and Aldert Vrij, Creating suspects in police interviews, 29 J. of Appl. Soc. Psych. 192 (1999).

[35] Paul G. Cassell, All benefits, no costs: The grand illusion of *Miranda's* defenders, 90 Nw. U. L. Rev. 1084 (1996); and Stephen J. Schulhofer, *Miranda* and clearance rates, 91 Nw. U. L. Rev. 278, 283-84, 286-87 (1996).

[36] Paul G. Cassell, All benefits, no costs: The grand illusion of *Miranda's* defenders, 90 Nw. U. L. Rev. 1084 (1996).

actually show that the number of crimes cleared per officer rose steadily during the period.[37] Researchers then subsequently revisited the first clearance rate study and found that, holding other variables constant, the *Miranda* warnings – or more appropriately, the year 1966 – correlated with reduced clearance rates for property crimes, robbery and total violent crimes, but not for murder, rape or assault. That study revealed that the *Miranda* warnings caused a 6.7% drop in the clearance rate for total violent crimes, and a 2.3% drop in the clearance rate for total property crimes.[38] The data was then replicated and reexamined with slightly different statistical methods.[39] In turn, that study concluded that, although there was a statistically significant effect with regard to larceny and total violent crimes, there was none for other property crimes or for the individual crimes that make up the category of total violent crimes (murder, robbery, rape, and assault). The re-analysis also challenged the failure to control for unquantifiable variables, including, for instance, legal changes unrelated to *Miranda* and changes in police reporting of crime. These findings reveal that there may well have been a small percentage drop in clearance rate, a small percentage that may well translate to huge numbers depending on overall crime rates themselves. The original study had argued that the *Miranda* warnings resulted in lost cases on average against 3.8% of criminal suspects in the period immediately following *Miranda*. If that rate were applied to current crime figures, the author argued, it would translate into the loss of about 28,000 arrests for serious crimes of violence, 79,000 arrests for property crimes, and almost the same number of cases being disposed of on terms more favorable for defendants

Although the impact on clearance rates may be controversial, no one challenges the proposition that *Miranda* has not impacted how the legal system views confessions. Several commentators have argued that the *Miranda* warnings also have undermined judicial scrutiny of the voluntariness of statements pursuant to the Due Process clause. They suggest that, once judges are satisfied that the suspect was informed of his rights and waived them, the subsequent voluntariness analysis may become *pro forma*. The result could be that more suspects are being compelled to self-incriminate by means of police trickery and deceit that would not be condoned absent the *Miranda* warnings. This is a provocative and important proposition, but still speculative.[40]

Evidence may well reveal that *Miranda* has not lived up to its full potential. Whether or not that is the case, however, there still may remain other justifications that would cause us to retain *Miranda*. Many values underlie the Fifth Amendment. Its key values include the need to preserve autonomy, maintain our adversarial system, curtail inhumane treatment and police misconduct, avoid false confessions, and comply with our sense of fair play. Although *Miranda* may not address all of these concerns in an empirically verifiable manner, there may well be a need to retain the approach simply for the sake of the type of society we wish our legal system to uphold. In other words, it could be the type of legal rule that seems most fair. In addition to the rationales found in the cases that follow, evidence also comes in the form of police organizations (the Police Foundation, Police Executive Research Forum, International Union of Police Associations, and National Black Police Association) and former prosecutors who filed an amicus curiae brief in *Withrow v. Williams*.[41] Their brief asked the Court not to take *Miranda* claims out of the reach of federal habeas corpus appeals in part because "the law enforcement community has seen the enforcement of *Miranda* and its progeny lead to an increased professionalism within police and sheriff's departments throughout the country. *Miranda*'s bright-line rules have proved relatively easy to follow."[42]

---

[37] Stephen J. Schulhofer, *Miranda* and clearance rates, 91 Nw. U. L. Rev. 278, 283-84, 286-87 (1996).

[38] Paul G. Cassel and Richard Fowles, Handcuffing the cops? A thirty-year perspective on *Miranda's* harmful effects on law enforcement, 50 Stan. L. Rev. 1055, 1086-88 (1998).

[39] John J. Donohue, III, Did *Miranda* diminish police effectiveness?, 50 Stan. L. Rev. 1147 (1998).

[40] Richard A. Leo, Miranda and the problem of false confessions, in The Miranda Debate: Law, Justice and Policing 276-77 (Richard A. Leo and George C. Thomas, III, eds., 1998).

[41] 507 U.S. 680 (1993).

[42] Brief Amici Curiae of The Police Foundation et al. in Support of Respondent at 7, Withrow (No. 91-1030).

NOTES AND QUERIES

Consider the different types of false confessions. What do you make of the psychological evidence supporting the possibility of such confessions? Should the legal system really concern itself with these possibilities?

Consider the significance of "illusory causation."

Describe key aspects of the "Reid technique." How effective do you think it really is when used by the "average" police interrogator? On which suspects do you think it would be most effective? What makes that consideration important? How protective do you find interrogatory warnings?

What do you make of the research indicating that the focus on suspects leads to viewing their actions as more voluntary than they would seem if we were looking at what the suspect was seeing? Note that criminal interrogations typically are videotaped with the camera lens zeroed in on suspects.

We now know that it is difficult to evaluate empirically *Miranda's* effectiveness. As you read the cases that follow, consider the Court's reasoning and evidence presented in *Miranda* and the extent to which the cases that followed remained faithful to *Miranda*.

In addition to surveying issues in interrogation contexts, this area of research and law provides us with an important opportunity to explore how differently we can approach some of the issues that we already have discussed. Consider how this area of law and research reveals the differences that alternative approaches can (or cannot) make if we made parallel changes to the other areas of law we have discussed. For example, how much focus do we want to place on the extent to which people actually know their rights before they waive them? How can we best inform them of those rights? How can the system be less coercive? Do we want the system to be coercive?

FRAMING INTERROGATION LAW

MIRANDA v. ARIZONA
384 U.S. 436 (1966)

MR. CHIEF JUSTICE WARREN delivered the opinion of the Court.

The cases before us raise questions which go to the roots of our concepts of American criminal jurisprudence: the restraints society must observe consistent with the Federal Constitution in prosecuting individuals for crime. More specifically, we deal with the admissibility of statements obtained from an individual who is subjected to custodial police interrogation and the necessity for procedures which assure that the individual is accorded his privilege under the Fifth Amendment to the Constitution not to be compelled to incriminate himself.

I.

The constitutional issue we decide in each of these cases is the admissibility of statements obtained from a defendant questioned while in custody or otherwise deprived of his freedom of action in any significant way. In each, the defendant was questioned by police officers, detectives, or a prosecuting attorney in a room in which he was cut off from the outside world. In none of these cases was the defendant given a full and effective warning of his rights at the outset of the interrogation process. In all the cases, the questioning elicited oral admissions, and in three of them, signed statements as well which were admitted at their trials. They all thus share salient features – incommunicado interrogation of individuals in a police-dominated atmosphere, resulting in self-incriminating statements without full warnings of constitutional rights.

An understanding of the nature and setting of this in-custody interrogation is essential to our decisions today. The difficulty in depicting what transpires at such interrogations stems from the fact that in this country they have largely taken place incommunicado. From extensive factual studies undertaken in the early 1930's, including the famous Wickersham Report to Congress by a Presidential Commission, it is clear that police violence and the "third degree" flourished at that time. In a series of cases decided by this Court long after these studies, the police resorted to physical brutality – beating, hanging, whipping – and to sustained and protracted questioning incommunicado in order to extort confessions. The Commission on Civil Rights in 1961 found much evidence to indicate that "some policemen still resort to physical force to obtain confessions." The use of physical brutality and violence is not, unfortunately, relegated to the past or to any part of the country....

The examples given above are undoubtedly the exception now, but they are sufficiently widespread to be the object of concern. Unless a proper limitation upon custodial interrogation is achieved – such as these decisions will advance – there can be no assurance that practices of this nature will be eradicated in the foreseeable future. ...

Again we stress that the modern practice of in-custody interrogation is psychologically rather than physically oriented. As we have stated before, "... this Court has recognized that coercion can be mental as well as physical, and that the blood of the accused is not the only hallmark of an unconstitutional inquisition." Interrogation still takes place in privacy. Privacy results in secrecy and this in turn results in a gap in our knowledge as to what in fact goes on in the interrogation rooms. A valuable source of information about present police practices, however, may be found in various police manuals and texts which document procedures employed with success in the past, and which recommend various other effective tactics...

The officers are told by the manuals that the "principal psychological factor contributing to a successful interrogation is privacy – being alone with the person under interrogation." The efficacy of this tactic has been explained as follows:

> If at all practicable, the interrogation should take place in the investigator's office or at least in a room of his own choice. The subject should be deprived of every psychological advantage. In his own home he may be confident, indignant, or recalcitrant. He is more keenly aware of his rights and more reluctant to tell of his indiscretions or criminal behavior within the walls of his home. Moreover his family and other friends are nearby, their presence lending moral support. In his own office, the investigator possesses all the advantages. The atmosphere suggests the invincibility of the forces of the law.

To highlight the isolation and unfamiliar surroundings, the manuals instruct the police to display an air of confidence in the suspect's guilt and from outward appearance to maintain only an interest in confirming certain details. The guilt of the subject is to be posited as a fact. The interrogator should direct his comments toward the reasons why the subject committed the act, rather than court failure by asking the subject whether he did it. Like other men, perhaps the subject has had a bad family life, had an unhappy childhood, had too much to drink, had an unrequited desire for women. The officers are instructed to minimize the moral seriousness of the offense, to cast blame on the victim or on society. These tactics are designed to put the subject in a psychological state where his story is but an elaboration of what the police purport to know already – that he is guilty. Explanations to the contrary are dismissed and discouraged.

The texts thus stress that the major qualities an interrogator should possess are patience and perseverance. One writer describes the efficacy of these characteristics in this manner:

> In the preceding paragraphs emphasis has been placed on kindness and stratagems. The investigator will, however, encounter many situations where the sheer weight of his personality will be

> the deciding factor. Where emotional appeals and tricks are employed to no avail, he must rely on an oppressive atmosphere of dogged persistence. He must interrogate steadily and without relent, leaving the subject no prospect of surcease. He must dominate his subject and overwhelm him with his inexorable will to obtain the truth. He should interrogate for a spell of several hours pausing only for the subject's necessities in acknowledgment of the need to avoid a charge of duress that can be technically substantiated. In a serious case, the interrogation may continue for days, with the required intervals for food and sleep, but with no respite from the atmosphere of domination. It is possible in this way to induce the subject to talk without resorting to duress or coercion. The method should be used only when the guilt of the subject appears highly probable.

The manuals suggest that the suspect be offered legal excuses for his actions in order to obtain an initial admission of guilt. Where there is a suspected revenge-killing, for example, the interrogator may say:

> Joe, you probably didn't go out looking for this fellow with the purpose of shooting him. My guess is, however, that you expected something from him and that's why you carried a gun – for your own protection. You knew him for what he was, no good. Then when you met him he probably started using foul, abusive language and he gave some indication that he was about to pull a gun on you, and that's when you had to act to save your own life. That's about it, isn't it, Joe?

Having then obtained the admission of shooting, the interrogator is advised to refer to circumstantial evidence which negates the self-defense explanation. This should enable him to secure the entire story. One text notes that "Even if he fails to do so, the inconsistency between the subject's original denial of the shooting and his present admission of at least doing the shooting will serve to deprive him of a self-defense 'out' at the time of trial."

When the techniques described above prove unavailing, the texts recommend they be alternated with a show of some hostility. One ploy often used has been termed the "friendly-unfriendly" or the "Mutt and Jeff" act:

> ...In this technique, two agents are employed. Mutt, the relentless investigator, who knows the subject is guilty and is not going to waste any time. He's sent a dozen men away for this crime and he's going to send the subject away for the full term. Jeff, on the other hand, is obviously a kindhearted man. He has a family himself. He has a brother who was involved in a little scrape like this. He disapproves of Mutt and his tactics and will arrange to get him off the case if the subject will cooperate. He can't hold Mutt off for very long. The subject would be wise to make a quick decision. The technique is applied by having both investigators present while Mutt acts out his role. Jeff may stand by quietly and demur at some of Mutt's tactics. When Jeff makes his plea for cooperation, Mutt is not present in the room.

The interrogators sometimes are instructed to induce a confession out of trickery. The technique here is quite effective in crimes which require identification or which run in series. In the identification situation, the interrogator may take a break in his questioning to place the subject among a group of men in a line-up. "The witness or complainant (previously coached, if necessary) studies the line-up and confidently points out the subject as the guilty party." Then the questioning resumes "as though there were now no doubt about the guilt of the subject." A variation on this technique is called the "reverse line-up":

> The accused is placed in a line-up, but this time he is identified by several fictitious witnesses or victims who associated him with different offenses. It is expected that the subject will become desperate and confess to the offense under investigation in order to escape from the false accusations.

The manuals also contain instructions for police on how to handle the individual who refuses to discuss the matter entirely, or who asks for an attorney or relatives. The examiner is to concede him the right to remain silent. "This usually has a very undermining effect. First of all, he is disappointed in his expectation of an unfavorable reaction on the part of the interrogator. Secondly, a concession of this right to remain silent impresses the subject with the apparent fairness of his interrogator." After this psychological conditioning, however, the officer is told to point out the incriminating significance of the suspect's refusal to talk:

> Joe, you have a right to remain silent. That's your privilege and I'm the last person in the world who'll try to take it away from you. If that's the way you want to leave this, O. K. But let me ask you this. Suppose you were in my shoes and I were in yours and you called me in to ask me about this and I told you, 'I don't want to answer any of your questions.' You'd think I had something to hide, and you'd probably be right in thinking that. That's exactly what I'll have to think about you, and so will everybody else. So let's sit here and talk this whole thing over.

Few will persist in their initial refusal to talk, it is said, if this monologue is employed correctly.

In the event that the subject wishes to speak to a relative or an attorney, the following advice is tendered:

> The interrogator should respond by suggesting that the subject first tell the truth to the interrogator himself rather than get anyone else involved in the matter. If the request is for an attorney, the interrogator may suggest that the subject save himself or his family the expense of any such professional service, particularly if he is innocent of the offense under investigation. The interrogator may also add, 'Joe, I'm only looking for the truth, and if you're telling the truth, that's it. You can handle this by yourself.'

From these representative samples of interrogation techniques, the setting prescribed by the manuals and observed in practice becomes clear. In essence, it is this: To be alone with the subject is essential to prevent distraction and to deprive him of any outside support. The aura of confidence in his guilt undermines his will to resist. He merely confirms the preconceived story the police seek to have him describe. Patience and persistence, at times relentless questioning, are employed. To obtain a confession, the interrogator must "patiently maneuver himself or his quarry into a position from which the desired objective may be attained." When normal procedures fail to produce the needed result, the police may resort to deceptive stratagems such as giving false legal advice. It is important to keep the subject off balance, for example, by trading on his insecurity about himself or his surroundings. The police then persuade, trick, or cajole him out of exercising his constitutional rights.

Even without employing brutality, the "third degree" or the specific stratagems described above, the very fact of custodial interrogation exacts a heavy toll on individual liberty and trades on the weakness of individuals....

In the cases before us today, given this background, we concern ourselves primarily with this interrogation atmosphere and the evils it can bring. In No. 759, Miranda v. Arizona, the police arrested the defendant and took him to a special interrogation room where they secured a confession…

In these cases, we might not find the defendants' statements to have been involuntary in traditional terms. Our concern for adequate safeguards to protect precious Fifth Amendment rights is, of course, not lessened in the slightest. In each of the cases, the defendant was thrust into an unfamiliar atmosphere and run through menacing police interrogation procedures. The potentiality for compulsion is forcefully apparent, for example, in Miranda, where the indigent Mexican defendant was a seriously disturbed individual with pronounced sexual fantasies.... To be sure, the records do not evince overt physical coercion or patent psychological ploys. The fact remains that in none of these cases did the officers undertake to afford appropriate safeguards at the outset of the interrogation to insure that the statements were truly the product of free choice.

It is obvious that such an interrogation environment is created for no purpose other than to subjugate the individual to the will of his examiner. This atmosphere carries its own badge of intimidation. To be sure, this is not physical intimidation, but it is equally destructive of human dignity. The current practice of incommunicado interrogation is at odds with one of our Nation's most cherished principles – that the individual may not be compelled to incriminate himself. Unless adequate protective devices are employed to dispel the compulsion inherent in custodial surroundings, no statement obtained from the defendant can truly be the product of his free choice.

II.

We sometimes forget how long it has taken to establish the privilege against self-incrimination, the sources from which it came and the fervor with which it was defended...

Today, then, there can be no doubt that the Fifth Amendment privilege is available outside of criminal court proceedings and serves to protect persons in all settings in which their freedom of action is curtailed in any significant way from being compelled to incriminate themselves. We have concluded that without proper safeguards the process of in-custody interrogation of persons suspected or accused of crime contains inherently compelling pressures which work to undermine the individual's will to resist and to compel him to speak where he would not otherwise do so freely. In order to combat these pressures and to permit a full opportunity to exercise the privilege against self-incrimination, the accused must be adequately and effectively apprised of his rights and the exercise of those rights must be fully honored.

It is impossible for us to foresee the potential alternatives for protecting the privilege which might be devised by Congress or the States in the exercise of their creative rule-making capacities. Therefore we cannot say that the Constitution necessarily requires adherence to any particular solution for the inherent compulsions of the interrogation process as it is presently conducted. Our decision in no way creates a constitutional straitjacket which will handicap sound efforts at reform, nor is it intended to have this effect. We encourage Congress and the States to continue their laudable search for increasingly effective ways of protecting the rights of the individual while promoting efficient enforcement of our criminal laws. However, unless we are shown other procedures which are at least as effective in apprising accused persons of their right of silence and in assuring a continuous opportunity to exercise it, the following safeguards must be observed.

At the outset, if a person in custody is to be subjected to interrogation, he must first be informed in clear and unequivocal terms that he has the right to remain silent. For those unaware of the privilege, the warning is needed simply to make them aware of it – the threshold requirement for an intelligent decision as to its exercise. More important, such a warning is an absolute prerequisite in overcoming the inherent pressures of the interrogation atmosphere. It is not just the subnormal or woefully ignorant who succumb to an interrogator's imprecations, whether implied or expressly stated, that the interrogation will continue until a confession is obtained or that silence in the face of accusation is itself damning and will bode ill when presented to a jury. Further, the warning will show the individual that his interrogators are prepared to recognize his privilege should he choose to exercise it.

The Fifth Amendment privilege is so fundamental to our system of constitutional rule and the expedient of giving an adequate warning as to the availability of the privilege so simple, we will not pause to inquire in individual cases whether the defendant was aware of his rights without a warning being given.

Assessments of the knowledge the defendant possessed, based on information as to his age, education, intelligence, or prior contact with authorities, can never be more than speculation; a warning is a clearcut fact. More important, whatever the background of the person interrogated, a warning at the time of the interrogation is indispensable to overcome its pressures and to insure that the individual knows he is free to exercise the privilege at that point in time.

The warning of the right to remain silent must be accompanied by the explanation that anything said can and will be used against the individual in court. This warning is needed in order to make him aware not only of the privilege, but also of the consequences of forgoing it. It is only through an awareness of these consequences that there can be any assurance of real understanding and intelligent exercise of the privilege. Moreover, this warning may serve to make the individual more acutely aware that he is faced with a phase of the adversary system – that he is not in the presence of persons acting solely in his interest.

The circumstances surrounding in-custody interrogation can operate very quickly to overbear the will of one merely made aware of his privilege by his interrogators. Therefore, the right to have counsel present at the interrogation is indispensable to the protection of the Fifth Amendment privilege under the system we delineate today. Our aim is to assure that the individual's right to choose between silence and speech remains unfettered throughout the interrogation process. A once-stated warning, delivered by those who will conduct the interrogation, cannot itself suffice to that end among those who most require knowledge of their rights. A mere warning given by the interrogators is not alone sufficient to accomplish that end. Prosecutors themselves claim that the admonishment of the right to remain silent without more "will benefit only the recidivist and the professional." Even preliminary advice given to the accused by his own attorney can be swiftly overcome by the secret interrogation process. Thus, the need for counsel to protect the Fifth Amendment privilege comprehends not merely a right to consult with counsel prior to questioning, but also to have counsel present during any questioning if the defendant so desires.

The presence of counsel at the interrogation may serve several significant subsidiary functions as well. If the accused decides to talk to his interrogators, the assistance of counsel can mitigate the dangers of untrustworthiness. With a lawyer present the likelihood that the police will practice coercion is reduced, and if coercion is nevertheless exercised the lawyer can testify to it in court. The presence of a lawyer can also help to guarantee that the accused gives a fully accurate statement to the police and that the statement is rightly reported by the prosecution at trial.

An individual need not make a pre-interrogation request for a lawyer. While such request affirmatively secures his right to have one, his failure to ask for a lawyer does not constitute a waiver. No effective waiver of the right to counsel during interrogation can be recognized unless specifically made after the warnings we here delineate have been given. The accused who does not know his rights and therefore does not make a request may be the person who most needs counsel...

Accordingly we hold that an individual held for interrogation must be clearly informed that he has the right to consult with a lawyer and to have the lawyer with him during interrogation under the system for protecting the privilege we delineate today. As with the warnings of the right to remain silent and that anything stated can be used in evidence against him, this warning is an absolute prerequisite to interrogation. No amount of circumstantial evidence that the person may have been aware of this right will suffice to stand in its stead. Only through such a warning is there ascertainable assurance that the accused was aware of this right.

If an individual indicates that he wishes the assistance of counsel before any interrogation occurs, the authorities cannot rationally ignore or deny his request on the basis that the individual does not have or cannot afford a retained attorney. The financial ability of the individual has no relationship to the scope of the rights involved here. The privilege against self-incrimination secured by the Constitution applies to all individuals. The need for counsel in order to protect the privilege exists for the indigent as well as the affluent. In fact, were we to limit these constitutional rights to those who can retain an attorney, our decisions today would be of little significance. The cases before us as well as the vast majority of confession cases with which we have dealt in the past involve those unable to retain counsel. While authorities are not required to relieve the accused of his poverty, they have the obligation not to take advantage of indigence in the administration of justice....

In order fully to apprise a person interrogated of the extent of his rights under this system then, it is necessary to warn him not only that he has the right to consult with an attorney, but also that if he is indigent a lawyer will be appointed to represent him. Without this additional warning, the admonition of the right to consult with counsel would often be understood as meaning only that he can consult with a lawyer if he has one or has the funds to obtain one. The warning of a right to counsel would be hollow if not couched in terms that would convey to the indigent – the person most often subjected to interrogation – the knowledge that he too has a right to have counsel present. As with the warnings of the right to remain silent and of the general right to counsel, only by effective and express explanation to the indigent of this right can there be assurance that he was truly in a position to exercise it.

Once warnings have been given, the subsequent procedure is clear. If the individual indicates in any manner, at any time prior to or during questioning, that he wishes to remain silent, the interrogation must cease. At this point he has shown that he intends to exercise his Fifth Amendment privilege; any statement taken after the person invokes his privilege cannot be other than the product of compulsion, subtle or otherwise. Without the right to cut off questioning, the setting of in-custody interrogation operates on the individual to overcome free choice in producing a statement after the privilege has been once invoked. If the individual states that he wants an attorney, the interrogation must cease until an attorney is present. At that time, the individual must have an opportunity to confer with the attorney and to have him present during any subsequent questioning. If the individual cannot obtain an attorney and he indicates that he wants one before speaking to police, they must respect his decision to remain silent.

This does not mean, as some have suggested, that each police station must have a "station house lawyer" present at all times to advise prisoners. It does mean, however, that if police propose to interrogate a person they must make known to him that he is entitled to a lawyer and that if he cannot afford one, a lawyer will be provided for him prior to any interrogation. If authorities conclude that they will not provide counsel during a reasonable period of time in which investigation in the field is carried out, they may refrain from doing so without violating the person's Fifth Amendment privilege so long as they do not question him during that time.

If the interrogation continues without the presence of an attorney and a statement is taken, a heavy burden rests on the government to demonstrate that the defendant knowingly and intelligently waived his privilege against self-incrimination and his right to retained or appointed counsel. This Court has always set high standards of proof for the waiver of constitutional rights, and we re-assert these standards as applied to in-custody interrogation. Since the State is responsible for establishing the isolated circumstances under which the interrogation takes place and has the only means of making available corroborated evidence of warnings given during incommunicado interrogation, the burden is rightly on its shoulders.

An express statement that the individual is willing to make a statement and does not want an attorney followed closely by a statement could constitute a waiver. But a valid waiver will not be presumed simply from the silence of the accused after warnings are given or simply from the fact that a confession was in fact eventually obtained....

> Presuming waiver from a silent record is impermissible. The record must show, or there must be an allegation and evidence which show, that an accused was offered counsel but intelligently and understandingly rejected the offer. Anything less is not waiver.

Moreover, where in-custody interrogation is involved, there is no room for the contention that the privilege is waived if the individual answers some questions or gives some information on his own prior to invoking his right to remain silent when interrogated.

Whatever the testimony of the authorities as to waiver of rights by an accused, the fact of lengthy interrogation or incommunicado incarceration before a statement is made is strong evidence that the accused did not validly waive his rights. In these circumstances the fact that the individual eventually made a statement is consistent with the conclusion that the compelling influence of the interrogation finally forced him to do so. It is inconsistent with any notion of a voluntary relinquishment of the privilege. Moreover, any evidence that the accused was threatened, tricked, or cajoled into a waiver will, of course, show that the defendant did not voluntarily waive his privilege. The requirement of warnings and waiver of rights is a fundamental with respect to the Fifth Amendment privilege and not simply a preliminary ritual to existing methods of interrogation.

The warnings required and the waiver necessary in accordance with our opinion today are, in the absence of a fully effective equivalent, prerequisites to the admissibility of any statement made by a defendant. No distinction can be drawn between statements which are direct confessions and statements which amount to "admissions" of part or all of an offense. The privilege against self-incrimination protects the individual from being compelled to incriminate himself in any manner; it does not distinguish degrees of incrimination. Similarly, for precisely the same reason, no distinction may be drawn between inculpatory statements and statements alleged to be merely "exculpatory." If a statement made were in fact truly exculpatory it would, of course, never be used by the prosecution. In fact, statements merely intended to be exculpatory by the defendant are often used to impeach his testimony at trial or to demonstrate untruths in the statement given under interrogation and thus to prove guilt by implication. These statements are incriminating in any meaningful sense of the word and may not be used without the full warnings and effective waiver required for any other statement...

The principles announced today deal with the protection which must be given to the privilege against self-incrimination when the individual is first subjected to police interrogation while in custody at the station or otherwise deprived of his freedom of action in any significant way. It is at this point that our adversary system of criminal proceedings commences, distinguishing itself at the outset from the inquisitorial system recognized in some countries. Under the system of warnings we delineate today or under any other system which may be devised and found effective, the safeguards to be erected about the privilege must come into play at this point.

Our decision is not intended to hamper the traditional function of police officers in investigating crime. When an individual is in custody on probable cause, the police may, of course, seek out evidence in the field to be used at trial against him. Such investigation may include inquiry of persons not under restraint. General on-the-scene questioning as to facts surrounding a crime or other general questioning of citizens in the fact-finding process is not affected by our holding. It is an act of responsible citizenship for individuals to give whatever information they may have to aid in law enforcement. In such situations the compelling atmosphere inherent in the process of in-custody interrogation is not necessarily present.

In dealing with statements obtained through interrogation, we do not purport to find all confessions inadmissible. Confessions remain a proper element in law enforcement. Any statement given freely and voluntarily without any compelling influences is, of course, admissible in evidence. The fundamental import of the privilege while an individual is in custody is not whether he is allowed to talk to the police without the benefit of warnings and counsel, but whether he can be interrogated. There is no requirement that police stop a person who enters a police station and states that he wishes to confess to a crime, or a person who calls the police to offer a confession or any other statement he desires to make. Volunteered statements of any kind are not barred by the Fifth Amendment and their admissibility is not affected by our holding today.

IV.

In announcing these principles, we are not unmindful of the burdens which law enforcement officials must bear, often under trying circumstances. We also fully recognize the obligation of all citizens to aid in enforcing the criminal laws. This Court, while protecting individual rights, has always given ample latitude to law enforcement agencies in the legitimate exercise of their duties. The limits we have placed on the interrogation process should not constitute an undue interference with a proper system of law enforcement. . . .

It is also urged that an unfettered right to detention for interrogation should be allowed because it will often redound to the benefit of the person questioned. When police inquiry determines that there is no reason to believe that the person has committed any crime, it is said, he will be released without need for further formal procedures. The person who has committed no offense, however, will be better able to clear himself after warnings with counsel present than without. It can be assumed that in such circumstances a lawyer would advise his client to talk freely to police in order to clear himself.

Custodial interrogation, by contrast, does not necessarily afford the innocent an opportunity to clear themselves. A serious consequence of the present practice of the interrogation alleged to be beneficial for the innocent is that many arrests "for investigation" subject large numbers of innocent persons to detention and interrogation...

V.

...We turn now to these facts to consider the application to these cases of the constitutional principles discussed above. In each instance, we have concluded that statements were obtained from the defendant under circumstances that did not meet constitutional standards for protection of the privilege.

No. 759. Miranda v. Arizona.

On March 13, 1963, petitioner, Ernesto Miranda, was arrested at his home and taken in custody to a Phoenix police station. He was there identified by the complaining witness. The police then took him to "Interrogation Room No. 2" of the detective bureau. There he was questioned by two police officers. The officers admitted at trial that Miranda was not advised that he had a right to have an attorney present. Two hours later, the officers emerged from the interrogation room with a written confession signed by Miranda. At the top of the statement was a typed paragraph stating that the confession was made voluntarily, without threats or promises of immunity and "with full knowledge of my legal rights, understanding any statement I make may be used against me."

At his trial before a jury, the written confession was admitted into evidence over the objection of defense counsel, and the officers testified to the prior oral confession made by Miranda during the interrogation. Miranda was found guilty of kidnapping and rape. He was sentenced to 20 to 30 years' imprisonment on each count, the sentences to run concurrently. On appeal, the Supreme Court of Arizona held that Miranda's constitutional rights were not violated in obtaining the confession and affirmed the conviction. In reaching its decision, the court emphasized heavily the fact that Miranda did not specifically request counsel.

We reverse. From the testimony of the officers and by the admission of respondent, it is clear that Miranda was not in any way apprised of his right to consult with an attorney and to have one present during the interrogation, nor was his right not to be compelled to incriminate himself effectively protected in any other manner. Without these warnings the statements were inadmissible. The mere fact that he signed a statement which contained a typed-in clause stating that he had "full knowledge" of his "legal rights" does not approach the knowing and intelligent waiver required to relinquish constitutional rights.

It is so ordered.

MR. JUSTICE CLARK, dissenting in Nos. 759, 760, and 761, and concurring in the result in No. 584.

...I am unable to join ... in the Court's criticism of the present practices of police and investigatory agencies as to custodial interrogation. The materials it refers to as "police manuals" are, as I read them, merely writings in this field by professors and some police officers. Not one is shown by the record here to be the official manual of any police department, much less in universal use in crime detection. Moreover, the examples of police brutality mentioned by the Court are rare exceptions to the thousands of cases that appear every year in the law reports. The police agencies – all the way from municipal and state forces to the federal bureaus – are responsible for law enforcement and public safety in this country. I am proud of their efforts, which in my view are not fairly characterized by the Court's opinion.

I.

...the majority has no support in our cases. Indeed, the Court admits that "we might not find the defendants' statements [here] to have been involuntary in traditional terms." ... Such a strict constitutional specific inserted at the nerve center of crime detection may well kill the patient. Since there is at this time a paucity of information and an almost total lack of empirical knowledge on the practical operation of requirements truly comparable to those announced by the majority, I would be more restrained lest we go too far too fast.

II.

Custodial interrogation has long been recognized as "undoubtedly an essential tool in effective law enforcement." Recognition of this fact should put us on guard against the promulgation of doctrinaire rules...

The rule prior to today ... depended upon "a totality of circumstances evidencing an involuntary...admission of guilt."...

III.

I would continue to follow that rule. Under the "totality of circumstances" rule ...I would consider in each case whether the police officer prior to custodial interrogation added the warning that the suspect might have counsel present at the interrogation and, further, that a court would appoint one at his request if he was too poor to employ counsel. In the absence of warnings, the burden would be on the State to prove that counsel was knowingly and intelligently waived or that in the totality of the circumstances, including the failure to give the necessary warnings, the confession was clearly voluntary.

...In this way we would not be acting in the dark nor in one full sweep changing the traditional rules of custodial interrogation which this Court has for so long recognized as a justifiable and proper tool in balancing individual rights against the rights of society. ...

I would affirm the convictions in Miranda v. Arizona, No. 759... I find from the circumstances no warrant for reversal. ...

MR. JUSTICE HARLAN, whom MR. JUSTICE STEWART and MR. JUSTICE WHITE join, dissenting.

While the fine points of this scheme are far less clear than the Court admits, the tenor is quite apparent. The new rules are not designed to guard against police brutality or other unmistakably banned forms of coercion. Those who use third-degree tactics and deny them in court are equally able and destined to lie as skillfully about warnings and waivers. Rather, the thrust of the new rules is to negate all pressures, to reinforce the nervous or ignorant suspect, and ultimately to discourage any confession at all. The aim in short is toward "voluntariness" in a utopian sense, or to view it from a different angle, voluntariness with a vengeance.

To incorporate this notion into the Constitution requires a strained reading of history and precedent and a disregard of the very pragmatic concerns that alone may on occasion justify such strains. ...

I turn now to the Court's asserted reliance on the Fifth Amendment, an approach which I frankly regard as a trompe l'oeil. The Court's opinion in my view reveals no adequate basis for extending the Fifth Amendment's privilege against self-incrimination to the police station. Far more important, it fails to show that the Court's new rules are well supported, let alone compelled, by Fifth Amendment precedents. Instead, the new rules actually derive from quotation and analogy drawn from precedents under the Sixth Amendment, which should properly have no bearing on police interrogation.

The more important premise is that pressure on the suspect must be eliminated though it be only the subtle influence of the atmosphere and surroundings. The Fifth Amendment, however, has never been thought to forbid all pressure to incriminate one's self in the situations covered by it...

The Court appears similarly wrong in thinking that precise knowledge of one's rights is a settled prerequisite under the Fifth Amendment to the loss of its protections...

Examined as an expression of public policy, the Court's new regime proves so dubious that there can be no due compensation for its weakness in constitutional law. ...

Without at all subscribing to the generally black picture of police conduct painted by the Court, I think it must be frankly recognized at the outset that police questioning allowable under due process precedents may inherently entail some pressure on the suspect and may seek advantage in his ignorance or weaknesses. The atmosphere and questioning techniques, proper and fair though they be, can in themselves exert a tug on the suspect to confess, and in this light "to speak of any confessions of crime made after arrest as being 'voluntary' or 'uncoerced' is somewhat inaccurate, although traditional. A confession is wholly and incontestably voluntary only if a guilty person gives himself up to the law and becomes his own accuser." ...Until today, the role of the Constitution has been only to sift out undue pressure, not to assure spontaneous confessions.

What the Court largely ignores is that its rules impair, if they will not eventually serve wholly to frustrate, an instrument of law enforcement that has long and quite reasonably been thought worth the price paid for it. There can be little doubt that the Court's new code would markedly decrease the number of confessions. To warn the suspect that he may remain silent and remind him that his confession may be used in court are minor obstructions. To require also an express waiver by the suspect and an end to questioning whenever he demurs must heavily handicap questioning. And to suggest or provide counsel for the suspect simply invites the end of the interrogation.

While passing over the costs and risks of its experiment, the Court portrays the evils of normal police questioning in terms which I think are exaggerated. Albeit stringently confined by the due process standards interrogation is no doubt often inconvenient and unpleasant for the suspect. However, it is no less so for a man to be arrested and jailed, to have his house searched, or to stand trial in court, yet all this may properly happen to the most innocent given probable cause, a warrant, or an indictment. Society has always paid a stiff price for law and order, and peaceful interrogation is not one of the dark moments of the law.

This brief statement of the competing considerations seems to me ample proof that the Court's preference is highly debatable at best and therefore not to be read into the Constitution. However, it may make the analysis more graphic to consider the actual facts of one of the four cases reversed by the Court. Miranda v. Arizona serves best, being neither the hardest nor easiest of the four under the Court's standards.

On March 3, 1963, an 18-year-old girl was kidnapped and forcibly raped near Phoenix, Arizona. Ten days later, on the morning of March 13, petitioner Miranda was arrested and taken to the police station. At this time Miranda was 23 years old, indigent, and educated to the extent of completing half the ninth grade. He had "an emotional illness" of the schizophrenic type, according to the doctor who eventually examined him; the doctor's report also stated that Miranda was "alert and oriented as to time, place, and person," intelligent within normal limits, competent to stand trial, and sane within the legal definition. At the police station, the victim picked Miranda out of a lineup, and two officers then took him into a separate room to interrogate him, starting about 11:30 a.m. Though at first denying his guilt, within a short time Miranda gave a detailed oral confession and then wrote out in his own hand and signed a brief statement admitting and describing the crime. All this was accomplished in two hours or less without any force, threats or promises and – I will assume this though the record is uncertain – without any effective warnings at all.

Miranda's oral and written confessions are now held inadmissible under the Court's new rules. One is entitled to feel astonished that the Constitution can be read to produce this result. These confessions were obtained during brief, daytime questioning conducted by two officers and unmarked by any of the traditional indicia of coercion. They assured a conviction for a brutal and unsettling crime, for which the police had and quite possibly could obtain little evidence other than the victim's identifications, evidence which is frequently unreliable. There was, in sum, a legitimate purpose, no perceptible unfairness, and certainly little risk of injustice in the interrogation. Yet the resulting confessions, and the responsible course of police practice they represent, are to be sacrificed to the Court's own finespun conception of fairness which I seriously doubt is shared by many thinking citizens in this country.

It is no secret that concern has been expressed lest long-range and lasting reforms be frustrated by this Court's too rapid departure from existing constitutional standards....

All four of the cases involved here present express claims that confessions were inadmissible, not because of coercion in the traditional due process sense, but solely because of lack of counsel or lack of warnings concerning counsel and silence. For the reasons stated in this opinion, I would adhere to the due process test and reject the new requirements inaugurated by the Court....

MR. JUSTICE WHITE, with whom MR. JUSTICE HARLAN and MR. JUSTICE STEWART join, dissenting.

First, we may inquire what are the textual and factual bases of this new fundamental rule. To reach the result announced on the grounds it does, the Court must stay within the confines of the Fifth Amendment, which forbids self-incrimination only if compelled. Hence the core of the Court's opinion is that because of the "compulsion inherent in custodial surroundings, no statement obtained from [a] defendant [in custody] can truly be the product of his free choice," absent the use of adequate protective devices as described by the Court. However, the Court does not point to any sudden inrush of new knowledge requiring the rejection of 70 years' experience. Nor does it assert that its novel conclusion reflects a changing consensus among state courts, or that a succession of cases had steadily eroded the old rule and proved it unworkable. Rather than asserting new knowledge, the Court concedes that it cannot truly know what occurs during custodial questioning, because of the innate secrecy of such proceedings. ... Insofar as appears from the Court's opinion, it has not examined a single transcript of any police interrogation, let alone the interrogation that took place in any one of these cases which it decides today. Judged by any of the standards for empirical investigation utilized in the social sciences the factual basis for the Court's premise is patently inadequate.

Although in the Court's view in-custody interrogation is inherently coercive, the Court says that the spontaneous product of the coercion of arrest and detention is still to be deemed voluntary. An accused, arrested on probable cause, may blurt out a confession which will be admissible despite the fact that he is alone and in custody, without any showing that he had any notion of his right to remain silent or of the consequences of his admission. Yet, under the Court's rule, if the police ask him a single question such as "Do you have anything to say?" or "Did you kill your wife?" his response, if there is one, has somehow been compelled, even if the accused has been clearly warned of his right to remain silent. Common sense informs us to the contrary. While one may say that the response was "involuntary" in the sense the question provoked or was the occasion for the response and thus the defendant was induced to speak out when he might have remained silent if not arrested and not questioned, it is patently unsound to say the response is compelled.

Today's result would not follow even if it were agreed that to some extent custodial interrogation is inherently coercive. The test has been whether the totality of circumstances deprived the defendant of a "free choice to admit, to deny, or to refuse to answer,"and whether physical or psychological coercion was of such a degree that "the defendant's will was overborne at the time he confessed." The duration and nature of incommunicado custody, the presence or absence of advice concerning the defendant's constitutional rights, and the granting or refusal of requests to communicate with lawyers, relatives or friends have all been rightly regarded as important data bearing on the basic inquiry. But it has never been suggested, until today, that such questioning was so coercive and accused persons so lacking in hardihood that the very first response to the very first question following the commencement of custody must be conclusively presumed to be the product of an overborne will.

If the rule announced today were truly based on a conclusion that all confessions resulting from custodial interrogation are coerced, then it would simply have no rational foundation. A fortiori that would be true of the extension of the rule to exculpatory statements, which the Court effects after a brief discussion of why, in the Court's view, they must be deemed incriminatory but without any discussion of why they must be deemed coerced. Even if one were to postulate that the Court's concern is not that all confessions induced by police interrogation are coerced but rather that some such confessions are coerced and present judicial procedures are believed to be inadequate to identify the confessions that are coerced and those that are not, it would still not be essential to impose the rule that the Court has now fashioned. Transcripts or observers could be required, specific time limits, tailored to fit the cause, could be imposed, or other devices could be utilized to reduce the chances that otherwise indiscernible coercion will produce an inadmissible confession.

On the other hand, even if one assumed that there was an adequate factual basis for the conclusion that all confessions obtained during in-custody interrogation are the product of compulsion, the rule propounded by the Court would still be irrational, for, apparently, it is only if the accused is also warned of his right to counsel and waives both that right and the right against self-incrimination that the inherent compulsiveness of interrogation disappears. But if the defendant may not answer without a warning a question such as "Where were you last night?" without having his answer be a compelled one, how can the Court ever accept his negative answer to the question of whether he wants to consult his retained counsel or counsel whom the court will appoint? And why if counsel is present and the accused nevertheless confesses, or counsel tells the accused to tell the truth, and that is what the accused does, is the situation any less coercive insofar as the accused is concerned? The Court apparently realizes its dilemma of foreclosing questioning without the necessary warnings but at the same time permitting the accused, sitting in the same chair in front of the same policemen, to waive his right to consult an attorney. It expects, however, that the accused will not often waive the right; and if it is claimed that he has, the State faces a severe, if not impossible burden of proof.

All of this makes very little sense in terms of the compulsion which the Fifth Amendment proscribes. That amendment deals with compelling the accused himself. It is his free will that is involved. Confessions and incriminating admissions, as such, are not forbidden evidence; only those which are compelled are banned. I doubt that the Court observes these distinctions today. By considering any answers to any interrogation to be compelled regardless of the content and course of examination and by escalating the requirements to prove waiver, the Court not only prevents the use of compelled confessions but for all practical purposes forbids interrogation except in the presence of counsel. That is, instead of confining itself to protection of the right against compelled self-incrimination the Court has created a limited Fifth Amendment right to counsel – or, as the Court expresses it, a "need for counsel to protect the Fifth Amendment privilege . . . ." The focus then is not on the will of the accused but on the will of counsel and how much influence he can have on the accused. Obviously there is no warrant in the Fifth Amendment for thus installing counsel as the arbiter of the privilege.

In sum, for all the Court's expounding on the menacing atmosphere of police interrogation procedures, it has failed to supply any foundation for the conclusions it draws or the measures it adopts.

IV.

Criticism of the Court's opinion, however, cannot stop with a demonstration that the factual and textual bases for the rule it propounds are, at best, less than compelling. Equally relevant is an assessment of the rule's consequences measured against community values. The Court's duty to assess the consequences of its action is not satisfied by the utterance of the truth that a value of our system of criminal justice is "to respect the inviolability of the human personality" and to require government to produce the evidence against the accused by its own independent labors. More than the human dignity of the accused is involved; the human personality of others in the society must also be preserved. Thus the values reflected by the privilege are not the sole desideratum; society's interest in the general security is of equal weight.

The obvious underpinning of the Court's decision is a deep-seated distrust of all confessions. As the Court declares that the accused may not be interrogated without counsel present, absent a waiver of the right to counsel, and as the Court all but admonishes the lawyer to advise the accused to remain silent, the result adds up to a judicial judgment that evidence from the accused should not be used against him in any way, whether compelled or not. This is the not so subtle overtone of the opinion – that it is inherently wrong for the police to gather evidence from the accused himself. And this is precisely the nub of this dissent. I see nothing wrong or immoral, and certainly nothing unconstitutional, in the police's asking a suspect whom they have reasonable cause to arrest whether or not he killed his wife or in confronting him with the evidence on which the arrest was based, at least where he has been plainly advised that he may remain completely silent. Until today, "the admissions or confessions of the prisoner, when voluntarily and freely made, have always ranked high in the scale of incriminating evidence." Particularly when corroborated, as where the police have confirmed the accused's disclosure of the hiding place of implements or fruits of the crime, such confessions have the highest reliability and significantly contribute to the certitude with which we may believe the accused is guilty. Moreover, it is by no means certain that the process of confessing is injurious to the accused. To the contrary it may provide psychological relief and enhance the prospects for rehabilitation.

...But I see no sound basis, factual or otherwise, and the Court gives none, for concluding that the present rule against the receipt of coerced confessions is inadequate for the task of sorting out inadmissible evidence and must be replaced by the per se rule which is now imposed. Even if the new concept can be said to have advantages of some sort over the present law, they are far outweighed by its likely undesirable impact on other very relevant and important interests.

The most basic function of any government is to provide for the security of the individual and of his property. These ends of society are served by the criminal laws which for the most part are aimed at the prevention of crime. Without the reasonably effective performance of the task of preventing private violence and retaliation, it is idle to talk about human dignity and civilized values.

The modes by which the criminal laws serve the interest in general security are many. First the murderer who has taken the life of another is removed from the streets, deprived of his liberty and thereby prevented from repeating his offense. In view of the statistics on recidivism in this country and of the number of instances in which apprehension occurs only after repeated offenses, no one can sensibly claim that this aspect of the criminal law does not prevent crime or contribute significantly to the personal security of the ordinary citizen.

Secondly, the swift and sure apprehension of those who refuse to respect the personal security and dignity of their neighbor unquestionably has its impact on others who might be similarly tempted. That the criminal law is wholly or partly ineffective with a segment of the population or with many of those who have been apprehended and convicted is a very faulty basis for concluding that it is not effective with respect to the great bulk of our citizens or for thinking that without the criminal laws, or in the absence of their enforcement, there would be no increase in crime. Arguments of this nature are not borne out by any kind of reliable evidence that I have seen to this date.

Thirdly, the law concerns itself with those whom it has confined. The hope and aim of modern penology, fortunately, is as soon as possible to return the convict to society a better and more law-abiding man than when he left. Sometimes there is success, sometimes failure. But at least the effort is made, and it should be made to the very maximum extent of our present and future capabilities.

The rule announced today will measurably weaken the ability of the criminal law to perform these tasks. It is a deliberate calculus to prevent interrogations, to reduce the incidence of confessions and pleas of guilty and to increase the number of trials. ... There is, in my view, every reason to believe that a good many criminal defendants who otherwise would have been convicted on what this Court has previously thought to be the most satisfactory kind of evidence will now, under this new version of the Fifth Amendment, either not be tried at all or will be acquitted if the State's evidence, minus the confession, is put to the test of litigation.

I have no desire whatsoever to share the responsibility for any such impact on the present criminal process.

Nor can this decision do other than have a corrosive effect on the criminal law as an effective device to prevent crime. A major component in its effectiveness in this regard is its swift and sure enforcement. The easier it is to get away with rape and murder, the less the deterrent effect on those who are inclined to attempt it. This is still good common sense. If it were not, we should posthaste liquidate the whole law enforcement establishment as a useless, misguided effort to control human conduct.

And what about the accused who has confessed or would confess in response to simple, noncoercive questioning and whose guilt could not otherwise be proved? Is it so clear that release is the best thing for him in every case? Has it so unquestionably been resolved that in each and every case it would be better for him not to confess and to return to his environment with no attempt whatsoever to help him? I think not. It may well be that in many cases it will be no less than a callous disregard for his own welfare as well as for the interests of his next victim.

Much of the trouble with the Court's new rule is that it will operate indiscriminately in all criminal cases, regardless of the severity of the crime or the circumstances involved. It applies to every defendant, whether the professional criminal or one committing a crime of momentary passion who is not part and parcel of organized crime. It will slow down the investigation and the apprehension of confederates in those cases where time is of the essence, such as kidnapping, those involving the national security, and some of those involving organized crime. In the latter context the lawyer who arrives may also be the lawyer for the defendant's colleagues and can be relied upon to insure that no breach of the organization's security takes place even though the accused may feel that the best thing he can do is to cooperate.

At the same time, the Court's per se approach may not be justified on the ground that it provides a "bright line" permitting the authorities to judge in advance whether interrogation may safely be pursued without jeopardizing the admissibility of any information obtained as a consequence. Nor can it be claimed that judicial time and effort, assuming that is a relevant consideration, will be conserved because of the ease of application of the new rule. Today's decision leaves open such questions as whether the accused was in custody, whether his statements were spontaneous or the product of interrogation, whether the accused has effectively waived his rights, and whether nontestimonial evidence introduced at trial is the fruit of statements made during a prohibited interrogation, all of which are certain to prove productive of uncertainty during investigation and litigation during prosecution. For all these reasons, if further restrictions on police interrogation are desirable at this time, a more flexible approach makes much more sense than the Court's constitutional straitjacket which forecloses more discriminating treatment by legislative or rule-making pronouncements.

Applying the traditional standards to the cases before the Court, I would hold these confessions voluntary. ...

Notes and Queries

Compare *Miranda's* approach to that in *Escobedo.* Although the Court endorsed *Miranda's* approach, do you find it to be more effective in balancing the rights of the accused and the needs of law enforcement?

Given the cases we have studied thus far, does *Miranda*'s imposition of a *per se* rule seem justified? Does the way Miranda was treated appear so egregious? Given the fundamental significance of this case, would you have expected more striking facts about Miranda's mistreatment? Miranda knew his rights (he signed a statement to that effect) and there was no evidence of coercion. Given that, what rationales did the Court take to develop its ruling? Note that the prior rule was a totality of circumstances standard to examine voluntariness. What was so wrong with that approach? Why reject that standard to determine whether the waiver of rights was knowing and intelligent.

Defendants may use a variety of approaches to challenge the prosecution's use of their confession. Defendants are entitled to move for suppression of evidence at pretrial hearings. In many jurisdictions defendants may challenge the voluntariness of the confession before the trier of fact at the time of trial. These challenges would be based on the argument that the confession was obtained by violating the defendants' constitutional rights. Typically, the motion would involve issues of voluntariness, such as the conditions under which the police obtained the confession. Likewise, defendants may challenge the credibility of confessions by arguing that they are false and coerced. These challenges to voluntariness and credibility of confessions can make use of expert testimony that challenges the nature of the interrogation techniques used by the police and presents defendants' peculiar vulnerabilities. Experts may testify, without providing specifics into the defendant's state of mind, that the defendant's interrogation encompassed elements present in cases of known false confessions. In other cases, experts may testify that a specific mental illness renders the defendant unusually suggestible. These cases propose that particular defendants are susceptible to suggestion and adopt stories suggested by police as their own.

As *Miranda* notes, *Miranda* warnings only come into play when the subject of the interrogation is "taken into custody, or otherwise deprived of his freedom of action in a significant way." Exactly when this happens is actually not a simple manner. Custody has not been defined by any one case, and cases reveal several factors used to determine both actual and *de facto* custody. These factors include, for example, the presence of probable cause to arrest, the subjective intent of the officers, the subjective belief of the accused, the site and physical surroundings of the interrogation, the confrontation of the suspect with evidence of guilt, the focus of the investigation, the language used to summon the accused, the duration and nature of the interrogation, and whether the accused was permitted to leave either during or following the interrogation. Faulty interrogations usually contain multiple problems and reversal of a conviction rarely occurs when challenges allege only one of these factors. See Joshua E. Kastenberg, A three-dimensional model for the use of expert psychiatric and psychological evidence in false confession defenses before the trier of fact, 26 Seattle Univ. L. R. 783 (2003).

Miranda defines interrogation as "questioning initiated by a law enforcement officer." Note, as we will see in later cases, that there are forms of interrogation that do not involve direct questioning, such as when a suspect includes himself in an officer's conversation.

Once a constitutional right is invoked, all questioning of the suspect must cease. If the suspect does not invoke his right to remain silent, law enforcement agents are permitted to question a suspect with only a few limitations, such as not using coercion and duress. As *Miranda* reveals, law enforcement agents use a variety of psychological techniques, such as deceit or trickery. Do you find that *Miranda* protects against such methods?

A confession may be challenged through the defendant's own testimony or through the cross-examination of police witnesses. Challenging confession evidence is actually more tricky than it initially may seem. Most notably, a defendant who challenges the confession may well need to forego his right to remain silent. This may not be advisable given that defendants who testify become subject to cross-examination.

In its recent and controversial *United States v. Dickerson,* 530 U.S. 428 (2000), decision, the United States Supreme Court upheld *Miranda.* In 1968, two years after *Miranda* was decided, Congress had enacted 18 U.S.C. §3501, which provided that the admissibility of confessions should be determined by the fact sensitive totality of the circumstances voluntary test. In upholding the validity of *Miranda v. Arizona,* the Court held that 18 U.S.C. §3501 was unconstitutional because it was merely an attempt to overrule the Miranda decision and reinstate the "totality of the circumstances" test that *Miranda* replaced. The *Dickerson* Court held that *Miranda* announced a constitutional rule and that Congress could not overrule that decision through legislation that did not guarantee the same rights that were made available to defendants by the decision. But experience suggests that §3501's totality-of-the-circumstances test is more difficult than *Miranda* for officers to conform to, and for courts to apply consistently. The *Dickerson* Court justified its decision to uphold *Miranda* by arguing that *Miranda* has become embedded in routine police practice to the point where the warnings have become part of our national culture.

Is the right to counsel that protective? How effective is counsel?

DETERMINING COERCIVENESS

ARIZONA v. FULMINANTE

499 U.S. 279 (1991)

Justice White delivered an opinion, Parts I, II, and IV of which are the opinion of the Court, and Part III of which is a dissenting opinion. Justice Marshall, Justice Blackmun, and Justice Stevens join this opinion in its entirety; Justice Scalia joins Parts I and II; and Justice Kennedy joins Parts I and IV.

I.

Early in the morning of September 14, 1982, Fulminante called the Mesa, Arizona, Police Department to report that his 11-year-old stepdaughter, Jeneane Michelle Hunt, was missing. He had been caring for Jeneane while his wife, Jeneane's mother, was in the hospital. Two days later, Jeneane's body was found in the desert east of Mesa. She had been shot twice in the head at close range with a large caliber weapon, and a ligature was around her neck. Because of the decomposed condition of the body, it was impossible to tell whether she had been sexually assaulted.

Fulminante's statements to police concerning Jeneane's disappearance and his relationship with her contained a number of inconsistencies, and he became a suspect in her killing. When no charges were filed against him, Fulminante left Arizona for New Jersey. Fulminante was later convicted in New Jersey on federal charges of possession of a firearm by a felon.

Fulminante was incarcerated in the Ray Brook Federal Correctional Institution in New York. There he became friends with another inmate, Anthony Sarivola, then serving a 60-day sentence for extortion. The two men came to spend several hours a day together. Sarivola, a former police officer, had been involved in loansharking for organized crime but then became a paid informant for the Federal Bureau of Investigation. While at Ray Brook, he masqueraded as an organized crime figure. After becoming friends with Fulminante, Sarivola heard a rumor that Fulminante was suspected of killing a child in Arizona. Sarivola then raised the subject with Fulminante in several conversations, but Fulminante repeatedly denied any involvement in Jeneane's death. During one conversation, he told Sarivola that Jeneane had been killed by bikers looking for drugs; on another occasion, he said he did not know what had happened. Sarivola passed this information on to an agent of the Federal Bureau of Investigation, who instructed Sarivola to find out more.

Sarivola learned more one evening in October 1983, as he and Fulminante walked together around the prison track. Sarivola said that he knew Fulminante was "starting to get some tough treatment and whatnot" from other inmates because of the rumor. Sarivola offered to protect Fulminante from his fellow inmates, but told him, "'You have to tell me about it,' you know. I mean, in other words, 'For me to give you any help.'" Fulminante then admitted to Sarivola that he had driven Jeneane to the desert on his motorcycle, where he choked her, sexually assaulted her, and made her beg for her life, before shooting her twice in the head.

...On September 4, 1984, Fulminante was indicted in Arizona for the first-degree murder of Jeneane.

Prior to trial, Fulminante moved to suppress the statement he had given Sarivola in prison, as well as a second confession he had given to Donna Sarivola, then Anthony Sarivola's fiancee and later his wife, following his May 1984 release from prison. He asserted that the confession to Sarivola was coerced, and that the second confession was the "fruit" of the first. Following the hearing, the trial court denied the motion to suppress, specifically finding that, based on the stipulated facts, the confessions were voluntary. The State introduced both confessions as evidence at trial, and on December 19, 1985, Fulminante was convicted of Jeneane's murder. He was subsequently sentenced to death.

Fulminante appealed, arguing, among other things, that his confession to Sarivola was the product of coercion and that its admission at trial violated his rights to due process ... the Arizona Supreme Court held that the confession was coerced, but initially determined that the admission of the confession at trial was harmless error, because of the overwhelming nature of the evidence against Fulminante. ... Although a majority of this Court finds that such a confession is subject to a harmless-error analysis, for the reasons set forth below, we affirm the judgment of the Arizona court.

II.

We deal first with the State's contention that the court below erred in holding Fulminante's confession to have been coerced. …

In applying the totality of the circumstances test to determine that the confession to Sarivola was coerced, the Arizona Supreme Court focused on a number of relevant facts. First, the court noted that "because [Fulminante] was an alleged child murderer, he was in danger of physical harm at the hands of other inmates." In addition, Sarivola was aware that Fulminante had been receiving "'rough treatment from the guys.'" Using his knowledge of these threats, Sarivola offered to protect Fulminante in exchange for a confession to Jeneane's murder and "in response to Sarivola's offer of protection, [Fulminante] confessed." Agreeing with Fulminante that "Sarivola's promise was 'extremely coercive,'" the Arizona Court declared: "The confession was obtained as a direct result of extreme coercion and was tendered in the belief that the defendant's life was in jeopardy if he did not confess. This is a true coerced confession in every sense of the word."

Although the question is a close one, we agree with the Arizona Supreme Court's ... finding, permissible on this record, that there was a credible threat of physical violence, we agree with its conclusion that Fulminante's will was overborne in such a way as to render his confession the product of coercion.

III.

Four of us, Justices Marshall, Blackmun, Stevens, and myself, would affirm the judgment of the Arizona Supreme Court on the ground that the harmless-error rule is inapplicable to erroneously admitted coerced confessions. We thus disagree with the Justices who have a contrary view.

The majority today abandons what until now the Court has regarded as the axiomatic proposition that a defendant in a criminal case is deprived of due process of law if his conviction is founded, in whole or in part, upon an involuntary confession, without regard for the truth or falsity of the confession and even though there is ample evidence aside from the confession to support the conviction. The Court has repeatedly stressed that the view that the admission of a coerced confession can be harmless error because of the other evidence to support the verdict is "an impermissible doctrine;" for "the admission in evidence, over objection, of the coerced confession vitiates the judgment because it violates the Due Process Clause of the Fourteenth Amendment." As [prior] decisions show, the rule was the same even when another confession of the defendant had been properly admitted into evidence. Today, a majority of the Court, without any justification, overrules this vast body of precedent without a word and in so doing dislodges one of the fundamental tenets of our criminal justice system.

In extending to coerced confessions the harmless-error rule, the majority declares that because the Court has applied that analysis to numerous other "trial errors," there is no reason that it should not apply to an error of this nature as well. The four of us remain convinced, however, that we should abide by our cases that have refused to apply the harmless-error rule to coerced confessions, for a coerced confession is fundamentally different from other types of erroneously admitted evidence to which the rule has been applied. …

[Prior cases] specifically noted three constitutional errors that could not be categorized as harmless error: using a coerced confession against a defendant in a criminal trial, depriving a defendant of counsel, and trying a defendant before a biased judge. The majority attempts to distinguish the use of a coerced confession from the other two errors ... by drawing a meaningless dichotomy between "trial errors" and "structural defects" in the trial process. ... It is clear, though, that ... [this] Court recognized that regardless of the amount of other evidence, "the admission in evidence, over objection, of the coerced confession vitiates the judgment," because "where, as here, a coerced confession constitutes a part of the evidence before the jury and a general verdict is returned, no one can say what credit and weight the jury gave to the confession." The inability to assess its effect on a conviction causes the admission at trial of a coerced confession to "defy analysis by 'harmless-error' standards," just as certainly as do deprivation of counsel and trial before a biased judge.

The majority also attempts to distinguish "trial errors" which occur "during the presentation of the case to the jury," and which it deems susceptible to harmless-error analysis, from "structural defects in the constitution of the trial mechanism," which the majority concedes cannot be so analyzed. This effort fails, for our jurisprudence on harmless error has not classified so neatly the errors at issue. ...

These same concerns counsel against applying harmless-error analysis to the admission of a coerced confession. A defendant's confession is "probably the most probative and damaging evidence that can be admitted against him," so damaging that a jury should not be expected to ignore it even if told to do so, and because in any event it is impossible to know what credit and weight the jury gave to the confession. Concededly, this reason is insufficient to justify a per se bar to the use of any confession. …

Nevertheless, in declaring that it is "impossible to create a meaningful distinction between confessions elicited in violation of the Sixth Amendment and those in violation of the Fourteenth Amendment," the majority overlooks the obvious. ... cases upon which the majority relies involved a defendant's coerced confession, nor were there present in these cases the distinctive reasons underlying the exclusion of coerced incriminating statements of the defendant. First, some coerced confessions may be untrustworthy. Consequently, admission of coerced confessions may distort the truth-seeking function of the trial upon which the majority focuses. More importantly, however, the use of coerced confessions, "whether true or false," is forbidden "because the methods used to extract them offend an underlying principle in the enforcement of our criminal law: that ours is an accusatorial and not an inquisitorial system – a system in which the State must establish guilt by evidence independently and freely secured and may not by coercion prove its charge against an accused out of his own mouth." This reflects the "strongly felt attitude of our society that important human values are sacrificed where an agency of the government, in the course of securing a conviction, wrings a confession out of an accused against his will," as well as "the deep-rooted feeling that the police must obey the law while enforcing the law; that in the end life and liberty can be as much endangered from illegal methods used to convict those thought to be criminals as from the actual criminals themselves." Thus, permitting a coerced confession to be part of the evidence on which a jury is free to base its verdict of guilty is inconsistent with the thesis that ours is not an inquisitorial system of criminal justice.

The search for truth is indeed central to our system of justice, but "certain constitutional rights are not, and should not be, subject to harmless-error analysis because those rights protect important values that are unrelated to the truth-seeking function of the trial." The right of a defendant not to have his coerced confession used against him is among those rights, for using a coerced confession "aborts the basic trial process" and "renders a trial fundamentally unfair."

For the foregoing reasons the four of us would adhere to the consistent line of authority that has recognized as a basic tenet of our criminal justice system... the prohibition against using a defendant's coerced confession against him at his criminal trial. ... the majority offers no convincing reason for overturning our long line of decisions requiring the exclusion of coerced confessions.

IV.

Since five Justices have determined that harmless-error analysis applies to coerced confessions, it becomes necessary to evaluate under that ruling the admissibility of Fulminante's confession to Sarivola. ... "before a federal constitutional error can be held harmless, the court must be able to declare a belief that it was harmless beyond a reasonable doubt." The Court has the power to review the record de novo in order to determine an error's harmlessness. In so doing, it must be determined whether the State has met its burden of demonstrating that the admission of the confession to Sarivola did not contribute to Fulminante's conviction. Five of us are of the view that the State has not carried its burden and accordingly affirm the judgment of the court below reversing petitioner's conviction.

A confession is like no other evidence. Indeed, "the defendant's own confession is probably the most probative and damaging evidence that can be admitted against him. . . . The admissions of a defendant come from the actor himself, the most knowledgeable and unimpeachable source of information about his past conduct. Certainly, confessions have profound impact on the jury, so much so that we may justifiably doubt its ability to put them out of mind even if told to do so." While some statements by a defendant may concern isolated aspects of the crime or may be incriminating only when linked to other evidence, a full confession in which the defendant discloses the motive for and means of the crime may tempt the jury to rely upon that evidence alone in reaching its decision. In the case of a coerced confession such as that given by Fulminante to Sarivola, the risk that the confession is unreliable, coupled with the profound impact that the confession has upon the jury, requires a reviewing court to exercise extreme caution before determining that the admission of the confession at trial was harmless.

In the Arizona Supreme Court's initial opinion, in which it determined that harmless-error analysis could be applied to the confession, the court found that the admissible second confession to Donna Sarivola rendered the first confession to Anthony Sarivola cumulative. The court also noted that circumstantial physical evidence concerning the wounds, the ligature around Jeneane's neck, the location of the body, and the presence of motorcycle tracks at the scene corroborated the second confession. The court concluded that "due to the overwhelming evidence adduced from the second confession, if there had not been a first confession, the jury would still have had the same basic evidence to convict"

We have a quite different evaluation of the evidence. Our review of the record leads us to conclude that the State has failed to meet its burden of establishing, beyond a reasonable doubt, that the admission of Fulminante's confession to Anthony Sarivola was harmless error. Three considerations compel this result.

First, ...a successful prosecution depended on the jury believing the two confessions. Absent the confessions, it is unlikely that Fulminante would have been prosecuted at all, because the physical evidence from the scene and other circumstantial evidence would have been insufficient to convict. Indeed, no indictment was filed until nearly two years after the murder. Although the police had suspected Fulminante from the beginning, as the prosecutor acknowledged in his opening statement to the jury, "What brings us to Court, what makes this case fileable, and prosecutable and triable is that later, Mr. Fulminante confesses this crime to Anthony Sarivola and later, to Donna Sarivola, his wife."...

Second, the jury's assessment of the confession to Donna Sarivola could easily have depended in large part on the presence of the confession to Anthony Sarivola. Absent the admission at trial of the first confession, the jurors might have found Donna Sarivola's story unbelievable. ...

Although some of the details in the confession to Donna Sarivola were corroborated by circumstantial evidence, many, including details that Jeneane was choked and sexually assaulted, were not. As to other aspects of the second confession, including Fulminante's motive and state of mind, the only corroborating evidence was the first confession to Anthony Sarivola Thus, contrary to what the Arizona Supreme Court found, it is clear that the jury might have believed that the two confessions reinforced and corroborated each other. For this reason, one confession was not merely cumulative of the other. ...

Third, the admission of the first confession led to the admission of other evidence prejudicial to Fulminante. For example, the State introduced evidence that Fulminante knew of Sarivola's connections with organized crime in an attempt to explain why Fulminante would have been motivated to confess to Sarivola in seeking protection. Absent the confession, this evidence would have had no relevance and would have been inadmissible at trial. ...

Finally, although our concern here is with the effect of the erroneous admission of the confession on Fulminante's conviction, it is clear that the presence of the confession also influenced the sentencing phase of the trial. Under Arizona law, the trial judge is the sentencer. ... In reaching this conclusion, the judge relied heavily on evidence concerning the manner of the killing and Fulminante's motives and state of mind which could only be found in the two confessions. For example, in labeling the murder "cruel," the judge focused in part on Fulminante's alleged statements that he choked Jeneane and made her get on her knees and beg before killing her. Although the circumstantial evidence was not inconsistent with this determination, neither was it sufficient to make such a finding beyond a reasonable doubt. Indeed, the sentencing judge acknowledged that the confessions were only partly corroborated by other evidence.

In declaring that Fulminante "acted with an especially heinous and depraved state of mind," the sentencing judge relied solely on the two confessions. ...

Although the sentencing judge might have reached the same conclusions even without the confession to Anthony Sarivola, it is impossible to say so beyond a reasonable doubt. ...

Because a majority of the Court has determined that Fulminante's confession to Anthony Sarivola was coerced and because a majority has determined that admitting this confession was not harmless beyond a reasonable doubt, we agree ... that Fulminante is entitled to a new trial at which the confession is not admitted. Accordingly the judgment of the Arizona Supreme Court is

Affirmed.

Chief Justice Rehnquist, with whom Justice O'Connor joins, Justice Kennedy and Justice Souter join as to Parts I and II, and Justice Scalia joins as to Parts II and III, delivered the opinion of the Court with respect to Part II, and a dissenting opinion with respect to Parts I and III.

The Court today properly concludes that the admission of an "involuntary" confession at trial is subject to harmless-error analysis. Nonetheless, the independent review of the record which we are required to make shows that respondent Fulminante's confession was not in fact involuntary. And even if the confession were deemed to be involuntary, the evidence offered at trial, including a second, untainted confession by Fulminante, supports the conclusion that any error here was certainly harmless.

I.

The admissibility of a confession such as that made by respondent Fulminante depends upon whether it was voluntarily made. "The ultimate test remains that which has been the only clearly established test in Anglo-American courts for two hundred years: the test of voluntariness. Is the confession the product of an essentially free and unconstrained choice by its maker? If it is, if he has willed to confess, it may be used against him. If it is not, if his will has been overborne and his capacity for self-determination critically impaired, the use of his confession offends due process."

The Supreme Court of Arizona stated that the trial court committed no error in finding the confession voluntary based on the record before it. But it overturned the trial court's finding of voluntariness based on the more comprehensive trial record before it, which included, in addition to the facts stipulated at the suppression hearing, a statement made by Sarivola at the trial that "the defendant had been receiving 'rough treatment from the guys, and if the defendant would tell the truth, he could be protected.'" It also had before it the presentence report, which showed that Fulminante was no stranger to the criminal justice system: He had six prior felony convictions and had been imprisoned on three prior occasions.

On the basis of the record before it, the Supreme Court stated:

> Defendant contends that because he was an alleged child murderer, he was in danger of physical harm at the hands of other inmates. Sarivola was aware that defendant faced the possibility of retribution from other inmates, and that in return for the confession with respect to the victim's murder, Sarivola would protect him. Moreover, the defendant maintains that Sarivola's promise was 'extremely coercive' because the 'obvious' inference from the promise was that his life would be in jeopardy if he did not confess. We agree.

...I am at a loss to see how the Supreme Court of Arizona reached the conclusion that it did. Fulminante offered no evidence that he believed that his life was in danger or that he in fact confessed to Sarivola in order to obtain the proffered protection. Indeed, he had stipulated that "at no time did the defendant indicate he was in fear of other inmates nor did he ever seek Mr. Sarivola's 'protection.'"...

The facts of record in the present case are quite different from those present in cases where we have found confessions to be coerced and involuntary. Since Fulminante was unaware that Sarivola was an FBI informant, there existed none of "the danger of coercion resulting from the interaction of custody and official interrogation." The fact that Sarivola was a government informant does not by itself render Fulminante's confession involuntary, since we have consistently accepted the use of informants in the discovery of evidence of a crime as a legitimate investigatory procedure consistent with the Constitution. ... Sarivola at no time threatened him or demanded that he confess; he simply requested that he speak the truth about the matter. ...

II.

Since this Court's landmark decision in Chapman v. California, in which we adopted the general rule that a constitutional error does not automatically require reversal of a conviction, the Court has applied harmless-error analysis to a wide range of errors and has recognized that most constitutional errors can be harmless.

The common thread connecting these cases is that each involved "trial error" – error which occurred during the presentation of the case to the jury, and which may therefore be quantitatively assessed in the context of other evidence presented in order to determine whether its admission was harmless beyond a reasonable doubt. In applying harmless-error analysis to these many different constitutional violations, the Court has been faithful to the belief that the harmless-error doctrine is essential to preserve the "principle that the central purpose of a criminal trial is to decide the factual question of the defendant's guilt or innocence, and promotes public respect for the criminal process by focusing on the underlying fairness of the trial rather than on the virtually inevitable presence of immaterial error."

...Justice White in dissent concludes that the principle of stare decisis requires us to hold that an involuntary confession is not subject to harmless-error analysis. ...

The admission of an involuntary confession – a classic "trial error" – is markedly different from the other two constitutional violations referred to in the Chapman footnote as not being subject to harmless-error analysis. One of those violations, involved was the total deprivation of the right to counsel at trial. The other violation was a judge who was not impartial. These are structural defects in the constitution of the trial mechanism, which defy analysis by "harmless-error" standards. The entire conduct of the trial from beginning to end is obviously affected by the absence of counsel for a criminal defendant, just as it is by the presence on the bench of a judge who is not impartial. ... other cases have added to the category of constitutional errors which are not subject to harmless error the following: unlawful exclusion of members of the defendant's race from a grand jury; the right to self-representation at trial; and the right to public trial. Each of these constitutional deprivations is a similar structural defect affecting the framework within which the trial proceeds, rather than simply an error in the trial process itself. "Without these basic protections, a criminal trial cannot reliably serve its function as a vehicle for determination of guilt or innocence, and no criminal punishment may be regarded as fundamentally fair."

It is evident from a comparison of the constitutional violations which we have held subject to harmless error, and those which we have held not, that involuntary statements or confessions belong in the former category. The admission of an involuntary confession is a "trial error," similar in both degree and kind to the erroneous admission of other types of evidence. The evidentiary impact of an involuntary confession, and its effect upon the composition of the record, is indistinguishable from that of a confession obtained in violation of the Sixth Amendment – of evidence seized in violation of the Fourth Amendment – or of a prosecutor's improper comment on a defendant's silence at trial in violation of the Fifth Amendment. When reviewing the erroneous admission of an involuntary confession, the appellate court, as it does with the admission of other forms of improperly admitted evidence, simply reviews the remainder of the evidence against the defendant to determine whether the admission of the confession was harmless beyond a reasonable doubt.

Of course an involuntary confession may have a more dramatic effect on the course of a trial than do other trial errors – in particular cases it may be devastating to a defendant – but this simply means that a reviewing court will conclude in such a case that its admission was not harmless error; it is not a reason for eschewing the harmless-error test entirely. The Supreme Court of Arizona, in its first opinion in the present case, concluded that the admission of Fulminante's confession was harmless error. That court concluded that a second and more explicit confession of the crime made by Fulminante after he was released from prison was not tainted by the first confession, and that the second confession, together with physical evidence from the wounds (the victim had been shot twice in the head with a large calibre weapon at close range and a ligature was found around her neck) and other evidence introduced at trial rendered the admission of the first confession harmless beyond a reasonable doubt.

III.

I would agree with the finding of the Supreme Court of Arizona in its initial opinion – in which it believed harmless-error analysis was applicable to the admission of involuntary confessions – that the admission of Fulminante's confession was harmless. Indeed, this seems to me to be a classic case of harmless error: a second confession giving more details of the crime than the first was admitted in evidence and found to be free of any constitutional objection. ...

Justice Kennedy, concurring in the judgment. [omitted]

NOTES AND QUERIES

The Court notes that several points also support a finding of coercion: Fulminante possesses low average to average intelligence; he dropped out of school in the fourth grade. He is short in stature and slight in build. He had not always adapted well to the stress of prison life.

The majority applies the totality of circumstances test to determine if Fulminante was coerced into admitting that he had killed his step-daughter. Do you find the circumstances coercive? What do you make of the trial court's finding that it was not coerced? Why not leave the determination in the hands of the trial court since it is the one which reviewed the evidence and typically is deemed best situated to evaluate it?

Fuliminante provides an important analysis of the differences between structural defects and trial errors, with the former leading to a *per se* rule requiring reversal and the latter leading to a harmless error rule which may not lead to reversal. Note that Part III is not part of the majority opinion of the Court. Four justices would reject the harmless error rule analysis, which means that five would accept it as applicable in this case. Do you find either of the "confessions" harmless in this case? Based on your understanding of psychological research on decision making, what do you think that research would tell us about whether impermissibly admitted evidence is ever harmless?

RESEARCH NOTE ON THE HARMLESS ERROR RULE

When conducting harmless error analysis, the reviewing court examines the ostensible effect of the error on the verdict. If the court believes that the same verdict would have been reached even in the absence of the error, then the conviction will not be set aside. Prompted by this approach, two studies evaluated the proposition that an erroneously admitted coerced confession can be considered "harmless error." Mock jurors read transcripts of a murder trial containing a confession that was (1) elicited in a high- or low-pressure interrogation, and (2) ruled admissible or inadmissible by the judge (no-confession control groups were also included). As prescribed by law, jurors saw the high-pressure confession as less voluntary, correctly recalled the judge's ruling, and reported that it had less influence on their decisions. On verdicts, however, the confession increased the conviction rate – even when it was seen as coerced, even when it was stricken from the record, and even when jurors said it had no influence. These results suggest that appellate courts should exercise caution in applying the harmless error rule to the admission of coerced confessions. These are important findings; even jurors who are told not to consider testimony cannot help but consider it. Thus, researchers have demonstrated that even jurors who aver that they are capable of following a judge's instruction to ignore a wrongfully admitted confession are in fact influenced significantly by the confession when deliberating the defendant's guilt or innocence. Importantly, there is no reason to believe that these findings are not equally applicable to appellate courts as well. If they are, the very possibility of harmless error review is called into question. The reviewing court is not permitted to use the confession to sustain the conviction – to buttress its belief that the defendant would have been convicted anyway – but if, in applying harmless error analysis, it is impossible for the court not to do so, then harmless error analysis certainly poses a formidable challenge that may well be beyond our human capacity. See Saul M. Kassin and Holly Sukel, Coerced confessions and the jury: An experimental test of the "harmless error" rule, 21 L. and Hum. Beh. 27 (1997).

DETERMINING VOLUNTARINESS

COLORADO v. CONNELLY
479 U.S. 157 (1986)

CHIEF JUSTICE REHNQUIST delivered the opinion of the Court.

I.

On August 18, 1983, Officer Patrick Anderson of the Denver Police Department was in uniform, working in an off-duty capacity in downtown Denver. Respondent Francis Connelly approached Officer Anderson and, without any prompting, stated that he had murdered someone and wanted to talk about it. Anderson immediately advised respondent that he had the right to remain silent, that anything he said could be used against him in court, and that he had the right to an attorney prior to any police questioning. Respondent stated that he understood these rights but he still wanted to talk about the murder. Understandably bewildered by this confession, Officer Anderson asked respondent several questions. Connelly denied that he had been drinking, denied that he had been taking any drugs, and stated that, in the past, he had been a patient in several mental hospitals. Officer Anderson again told Connelly that he was under no obligation to say anything. Connelly replied that it was "all right," and that he would talk to Officer Anderson because his conscience had been bothering him. To Officer Anderson, respondent appeared to understand fully the nature of his acts.

Shortly thereafter, Homicide Detective Stephen Antuna arrived. Respondent was again advised of his rights, and Detective Antuna asked him "what he had on his mind." Respondent answered that he had come all the way from Boston to confess to the murder of Mary Ann Junta, a young girl whom he had killed in Denver sometime during November 1982. Respondent was taken to police headquarters, and a search of police records revealed that the body of an unidentified female had been found in April 1983. Respondent openly detailed his story to Detective Antuna and Sergeant Thomas Haney, and readily agreed to take the officers to the scene of the killing. Under Connelly's sole direction, the two officers and respondent proceeded in a police vehicle to the location of the crime. Respondent pointed out the exact location of the murder. Throughout this episode, Detective Antuna perceived no indication whatsoever that respondent was suffering from any kind of mental illness.

Respondent was held overnight. During an interview with the public defender's office the following morning, he became visibly disoriented. He began giving confused answers to questions, and for the first time, stated that "voices" had told him to come to Denver and that he had followed the directions of these voices in confessing. Respondent was sent to a state hospital for evaluation ...

At a preliminary hearing, respondent moved to suppress all of his statements. Dr. Jeffrey Metzner, a psychiatrist employed by the state hospital, testified that respondent was suffering from chronic schizophrenia and was in a psychotic state at least as of August 17, 1983, the day before he confessed. Metzner's interviews with respondent revealed that respondent was following the "voice of God." This voice instructed respondent to withdraw money from the bank, to buy an airplane ticket, and to fly from Boston to Denver. When respondent arrived from Boston, God's voice became stronger and told respondent either to confess to the killing or to commit suicide. Reluctantly following the command of the voices, respondent approached Officer Anderson and confessed.

Dr. Metzner testified that, in his expert opinion, respondent was experiencing "command hallucinations." This condition interfered with respondent's "volitional abilities; that is, his ability to make free and rational choices." Dr. Metzner further testified that Connelly's illness did not significantly impair his cognitive abilities. Thus, respondent understood the rights he had when Officer Anderson and Detective Antuna advised him that he need not speak. Dr. Metzner ... explained that in his opinion, Connelly's psychosis motivated his confession.

On the basis of this evidence the Colorado trial court decided that respondent's statements must be suppressed because they were "involuntary." ... the court ruled that a confession is admissible only if it is a product of the defendant's rational intellect and "free will." Although the court found that the police had done nothing wrong or coercive in securing respondent's confession, Connelly's illness destroyed his volition and compelled him to confess. The trial court also found that Connelly's mental state vitiated his attempted waiver of the right to counsel and the privilege against compulsory self-incrimination. Accordingly, respondent's initial statements and his custodial confession were suppressed.

The Colorado Supreme Court affirmed. In that court's view, the proper test for admissibility is whether the statements are "the product of a rational intellect and a free will." Indeed, "the absence of police coercion or duress does not foreclose a finding of involuntariness. One's capacity for rational judgment and free choice may be overborne as much by certain forms of severe mental illness as by external pressure." The court found that the very admission of the evidence in a court of law was sufficient state action to implicate the Due Process Clause of the Fourteenth Amendment to the United States Constitution. The evidence fully supported the conclusion that respondent's initial statement was not the product of a rational intellect and a free will. The court then considered respondent's attempted waiver of his constitutional rights and found that respondent's mental condition precluded his ability to make a valid waiver. ...

II.

The Due Process Clause of the Fourteenth Amendment provides that no State shall "deprive any person of life, liberty, or property, without due process of law." ...by virtue of the Due Process Clause "certain interrogation techniques, either in isolation or as applied to the unique characteristics of a particular suspect, are so offensive to a civilized system of justice that they must be condemned."

Indeed, coercive government misconduct was the catalyst for this Court's seminal confession case, Brown v. Mississippi. In that case, police officers extracted confessions from the accused through brutal torture. The Court had little difficulty concluding that even though the Fifth Amendment did not at that time apply to the States, the actions of the police were "revolting to the sense of justice." The Court has retained this due process focus ...

Thus the cases considered by this Court over the 50 years since Brown v. Mississippi have focused upon the crucial element of police overreaching. While each confession case has turned on its own set of factors justifying the conclusion that police conduct was oppressive, all have contained a substantial element of coercive police conduct. Absent police conduct causally related to the confession, there is simply no basis for concluding that any state actor has deprived a criminal defendant of due process of law. Respondent correctly notes that as interrogators have turned to more subtle forms of psychological persuasion, courts have found the mental condition of the defendant a more significant factor in the "voluntariness" calculus. But this fact does not justify a conclusion that a defendant's mental condition, by itself and apart from its relation to official coercion, should ever dispose of the inquiry into constitutional "voluntariness."

Our "involuntary confession" jurisprudence is entirely consistent with the settled law requiring some sort of "state action" to support a claim of violation of the Due Process Clause of the Fourteenth Amendment. The Colorado trial court, of course, found that the police committed no wrongful acts, and that finding has been neither challenged by respondent nor disturbed by the Supreme Court of Colorado. The latter court, however, concluded that sufficient state action was present by virtue of the admission of the confession into evidence in a court of the State.

The difficulty with the approach of the Supreme Court of Colorado is that it fails to recognize the essential link between coercive activity of the State, on the one hand, and a resulting confession by a defendant, on the other. The flaw in respondent's constitutional argument is that it would expand our previous line of "voluntariness" cases into a far-ranging requirement that courts must divine a defendant's motivation for speaking or acting as he did even though there be no claim that governmental conduct coerced his decision.

The most outrageous behavior by a private party seeking to secure evidence against a defendant does not make that evidence inadmissible under the Due Process Clause. We have also observed that "[jurists] and scholars uniformly have recognized that the exclusionary rule imposes a substantial cost on the societal interest in law enforcement by its proscription of what concededly is relevant evidence." Moreover, suppressing respondent's statements would serve absolutely no purpose in enforcing constitutional guarantees. The purpose of excluding evidence seized in violation of the Constitution is to substantially deter future violations of the Constitution. Only if we were to establish a brand new constitutional right – the right of a criminal defendant to confess to his crime only when totally rational and properly motivated – could respondent's present claim be sustained.

... Respondent would now have us require sweeping inquiries into the state of mind of a criminal defendant who has confessed, inquiries quite divorced from any coercion brought to bear on the defendant by the State. We think the Constitution rightly leaves this sort of inquiry to be resolved by state laws governing the admission of evidence and erects no standard of its own in this area. ... "The aim of the requirement of due process is not to exclude presumptively false evidence, but to prevent fundamental unfairness in the use of evidence, whether true or false."

We hold that coercive police activity is a necessary predicate to the finding that a confession is not "voluntary" within the meaning of the Due Process Clause of the Fourteenth Amendment. We also conclude that the taking of respondent's statements, and their admission into evidence, constitute no violation of that Clause.

III.

A.

The Supreme Court of Colorado went on to affirm the trial court's ruling that respondent's later statements made while in custody should be suppressed because respondent had not waived his right to consult an attorney and his right to remain silent. That court held that the State must bear its burden of proving waiver of these Miranda rights by "clear and convincing evidence." Although we have stated in passing that the State bears a "heavy" burden in proving waiver, we have never held that the "clear and convincing evidence" standard is the appropriate one.

... this Court upheld a procedure in which the State established the voluntariness of a confession by no more than a preponderance of the evidence. We upheld it for two reasons. First, the voluntariness determination has nothing to do with the reliability of jury verdicts; rather, it is designed to determine the presence of police coercion. Thus, voluntariness is irrelevant to the presence or absence of the elements of a crime, which must be proved beyond a reasonable doubt. Second, we rejected ...[the] assertion that a high burden of proof was required to serve the values protected by the exclusionary rule. ... we rejected the argument that "the importance of the values served by exclusionary rules is itself sufficient demonstration that the Constitution also requires admissibility to be proved beyond a reasonable doubt."...

We now reaffirm our holding ... Whenever the State bears the burden of proof in a motion to suppress a statement that the defendant claims was obtained in violation of our Miranda doctrine, the State need prove waiver only by a preponderance of the evidence. If ... the voluntariness of a confession need be established only by a preponderance of the evidence, then a waiver of the auxiliary protections established in Miranda should require no higher burden of proof. ...

B.

We also think that the Supreme Court of Colorado was mistaken in its analysis of the question whether respondent had waived his Miranda rights in this case. Of course, a waiver must at a minimum be "voluntary" to be effective against an accused. The Supreme Court of Colorado in addressing this question relied on the testimony of the court-appointed psychiatrist to the effect that respondent was not capable of making a "free decision with respect to his constitutional right of silence . . . and his constitutional right to confer with a lawyer before talking to the police."

We think that the Supreme Court of Colorado erred in importing into this area of constitutional law notions of "free will" that have no place there. There is obviously no reason to require more in the way of a "voluntariness" inquiry in the Miranda waiver context than in the Fourteenth Amendment confession context. The sole concern of the Fifth Amendment, on which Miranda was based, is governmental coercion. Indeed, the Fifth Amendment privilege is not concerned "with moral and psychological pressures to confess emanating from sources other than official coercion." The voluntariness of a waiver of this privilege has always depended on the absence of police overreaching, not on "free choice" in any broader sense of the word.

...Miranda protects defendants against government coercion leading them to surrender rights protected by the Fifth Amendment; it goes no further than that. Respondent's perception of coercion flowing from the "voice of God," however important or significant such a perception may be in other disciplines, is a matter to which the United States Constitution does not speak.

IV.

The judgment of the Supreme Court of Colorado is accordingly reversed, and the cause is remanded for further proceedings not inconsistent with this opinion.

It is so ordered.
JUSTICE BLACKMUN, concurring in part and concurring in the judgment. [opinion omitted]

JUSTICE STEVENS, concurring in the judgment in part and dissenting in part.

...I agree with the State of Colorado that the United States Constitution does not require suppression of those statements, but in reaching that conclusion, unlike the Court, I am perfectly willing to accept the state trial court's finding that the statements were involuntary.

The state trial court found that, in view of the "overwhelming evidence presented by the Defense," the prosecution did not meet its burden of demonstrating that respondent's initial statements to Officer Anderson were voluntary. Nevertheless, in my opinion, the use of these involuntary precustodial statements does not violate the Fifth Amendment because they were not the product of state compulsion. Although they may well be so unreliable that they could not support a conviction, at this stage of the proceeding I could not say that they have no probative force whatever. The fact that the statements were involuntary ... does not mean that their use for whatever evidentiary value they may have is fundamentally unfair or a denial of due process.

The postcustodial statements raise an entirely distinct question. When the officer whom respondent approached elected to handcuff him and to take him into custody, the police assumed a fundamentally different relationship with him. Prior to that moment, the police had no duty to give respondent Miranda warnings and had every right to continue their exploratory conversation with him. Once the custodial relationship was established, however, ...the questioning could not thereafter go forward in the absence of a valid waiver of respondent's constitutional rights unless he was provided with counsel. ...

The Court seems to believe that a waiver can be voluntary even if it is not the product of an exercise of the defendant's "'free will.'" The Court's position is not only incomprehensible to me; it is also foreclosed by the Court's recent pronouncement in Moran v. Burbine, 475 U.S. 412, 421 (1986), that "the relinquishment of the right must have been voluntary in the sense that it was the product of a free and deliberate choice. . . ." Because respondent's waiver was not voluntary in that sense, his custodial interrogation was presumptively coercive. ...

Accordingly, I concur in the judgment insofar as it applies to respondent's precustodial statements but respectfully dissent from the Court's disposition of the question that was not presented by the certiorari petition.

JUSTICE BRENNAN, with whom JUSTICE MARSHALL joins, dissenting.

I.

The respondent's seriously impaired mental condition is clear on the record of this case. At the time of his confession, Mr. Connelly suffered from a "longstanding severe mental disorder," diagnosed as chronic paranoid schizophrenia. He had been hospitalized for psychiatric reasons five times prior to his confession; his longest hospitalization lasted for seven months. Mr. Connelly heard imaginary voices and saw nonexistent objects. He believed that his father was God, and that he was a reincarnation of Jesus.

At the time of his confession, Mr. Connelly's mental problems included "grandiose and delusional thinking." He had a known history of "thought withdrawal and insertion." Although physicians had treated Mr. Connelly "with a wide variety of medications in the past including antipsychotic medications," he had not taken any antipsychotic medications for at least six months prior to his confession. Following his arrest, Mr. Connelly initially was found incompetent to stand trial because the court-appointed psychiatrist, Dr. Metzner, "wasn't very confident that he could consistently relate accurate information." Dr. Metzner testified that Mr. Connelly was unable "to make free and rational choices" due to auditory hallucinations: "[When] he was read his Miranda rights, he probably had the capacity to know that he was being read his Miranda rights [but] he wasn't able to use that information because of the command hallucinations that he had experienced." He achieved competency to stand trial only after six months of hospitalization and treatment with antipsychotic and sedative medications.

II.

The absence of police wrongdoing should not, by itself, determine the voluntariness of a confession by a mentally ill person. The requirement that a confession be voluntary reflects a recognition of the importance of free will and of reliability in determining the admissibility of a confession, and thus demands an inquiry into the totality of the circumstances surrounding the confession.

A.

Today's decision restricts the application of the term "involuntary" to those confessions obtained by police coercion. Confessions by mentally ill individuals or by persons coerced by parties other than police officers are now considered "voluntary." The Court's failure to recognize all forms of involuntariness or coercion as antithetical to due process reflects a refusal to acknowledge free will as a value of constitutional consequence. But due process derives much of its meaning from a conception of fundamental fairness that emphasizes the right to make vital choices voluntarily: ... This right requires vigilant protection if we are to safeguard the values of private conscience and human dignity.

...A true commitment to fundamental fairness requires that the inquiry be "not whether the conduct of state officers in obtaining the confession is shocking, but whether the confession was 'free and voluntary'..."

The only logical "flaw" which the Court detects in this argument is that it would require courts to "divine a defendant's motivation for speaking or acting as he did even though there be no claim that governmental conduct coerced his decision." Such a criticism, however, ignores the fact that we have traditionally examined the totality of the circumstances, including the motivation and competence of the defendant, in determining whether a confession is voluntary...

B.

Since the Court redefines voluntary confessions to include confessions by mentally ill individuals, the reliability of these confessions becomes a central concern. A concern for reliability is inherent in our criminal justice system, which relies upon accusatorial rather than inquisitorial practices. While an inquisitorial system prefers obtaining confessions from criminal defendants, an accusatorial system must place its faith in determinations of "guilt by evidence independently and freely secured."...

Our interpretation of the Due Process Clause has been shaped by this preference for accusatorial practices and by a concern for reliability.

Our distrust for reliance on confessions is due, in part, to their decisive impact upon the adversarial process. Triers of fact accord confessions such heavy weight in their determinations that "the introduction of a confession makes the other aspects of a trial in court superfluous, and the real trial, for all practical purposes, occurs when the confession is obtained." No other class of evidence is so profoundly prejudicial. "Thus the decision to confess before trial amounts in effect to a waiver of the right to require the state at trial to meet its heavy burden of proof."

Because the admission of a confession so strongly tips the balance against the defendant in the adversarial process, we must be especially careful about a confession's reliability. We have to date not required a finding of reliability for involuntary confessions only because all such confessions have been excluded upon a finding of involuntariness, regardless of reliability. The Court's adoption today of a restrictive definition of an "involuntary" confession will require heightened scrutiny of a confession's reliability.

The instant case starkly highlights the danger of admitting a confession by a person with a severe mental illness. The trial court made no findings concerning the reliability of Mr. Connelly's involuntary confession, since it believed that the confession was excludable on the basis of involuntariness. However, the overwhelming evidence in the record points to the unreliability of Mr. Connelly's delusional mind. Mr. Connelly was found incompetent to stand trial because he was unable to relate accurate information, and the court-appointed psychiatrist indicated that Mr. Connelly was actively hallucinating and exhibited delusional thinking at the time of his confession. ...

Moreover, the record is barren of any corroboration of the mentally ill defendant's confession. No physical evidence links the defendant to the alleged crime. Police did not identify the alleged victim's body as the woman named by the defendant. Mr. Connelly identified the alleged scene of the crime, but it has not been verified that the unidentified body was found there or that a crime actually occurred there. There is not a shred of competent evidence in this record linking the defendant to the charged homicide. There is only Mr. Connelly's confession.

Minimum standards of due process should require that the trial court find substantial indicia of reliability, on the basis of evidence extrinsic to the confession itself, before admitting the confession of a mentally ill person into evidence. I would require the trial court to make such a finding on remand. To hold otherwise allows the State to imprison and possibly to execute a mentally ill defendant based solely upon an inherently unreliable confession.

III.

...I emphatically dissent from the Court's holding that the government need prove waiver by only a preponderance of the evidence, and from its conclusion that a waiver is automatically voluntary in the absence of police coercion.

In recognition of the importance of the Due Process Clause and the Fifth Amendment, we always have characterized the State's burden of proof on a Miranda waiver as "great" and "heavy." Furthermore, under the Sixth Amendment, we have required the prosecution to meet a clear and convincing standard in demonstrating that evidence is not tainted by the absence of counsel at police lineups. Imposing the weakest possible burden of proof for waiver of Miranda's right to counsel plainly ignores this precedent.

The ultimate irony is that, even accepting the preponderance of the evidence as the correct standard, the prosecution still failed to meet this burden of proof. The Colorado Supreme Court found that Dr. Metzner, the court-appointed psychiatrist and the only expert to testify, "clearly established" that Mr. Connelly "was incapable" of making a "free decision" respecting his Miranda rights. Thus the prosecution failed – even by the modest standard imposed today – to prove that Mr. Connelly voluntarily waived his Miranda rights.

B.

Since the Colorado Supreme Court found that Mr. Connelly was "clearly" unable to make an "intelligent" decision, clearly its judgment should be affirmed. ...

I dissent.

NOTES AND QUERIES

How voluntary do you find Connelly's original statements to police officers? Was it voluntary? Should it matter that the "coercion" is psychological in that it derives from his own thinking rather than from psychological pressure deriving from law enforcement? Would it be fair to law enforcement and society if we recognized an individual's own psychological pressures to confess as coercive? How fair is it to the individual? Note that, in theory, a waiver must be a free and deliberate choice. How did Connelly's waiver satisfy that requirement?

The crime control model suggests that we can play down true voluntariness and other standards as long as we can be sure that the individual is guilty anyway. Given the facts of this case, do you find the confession reliable? If you do not find it reliable, how could you justify the result in this case?

What do you make of the state action rule in this case?

The case provides an important discussion of the standard for reviewing a *Miranda* waiver. The Court notes that the waiver will be deemed constitutional if it satisfies a preponderance of the evidence standard. Given that *Miranda* protects against police overreaching, do you find that standard high enough? What would be the implication of using a higher standard? Compare the majority opinion with Justice Steven's dissenting view that a higher standard of review should be used. Persuasive?

ELICITING STATEMENTS

BREWER v. WILLIAMS
430 U.S. 387 (1977)

MR. JUSTICE STEWART delivered the opinion of the Court.

I.

On the afternoon of December 24, 1968, a 10-year-old girl named Pamela Powers went with her family to the YMCA in Des Moines, Iowa, to watch a wrestling tournament in which her brother was participating. When she failed to return from a trip to the washroom, a search for her began. The search was unsuccessful.

Robert Williams, who had recently escaped from a mental hospital, was a resident of the YMCA. Soon after the girl's disappearance Williams was seen in the YMCA lobby carrying some clothing and a large bundle wrapped in a blanket. He obtained help from a 14-year-old boy in opening the street door of the YMCA and the door to his automobile parked outside. When Williams placed the bundle in the front seat of his car the boy "saw two legs in it and they were skinny and white." Before anyone could see what was in the bundle Williams drove away. His abandoned car was found the following day in Davenport, Iowa, roughly 160 miles east of Des Moines. A warrant was then issued in Des Moines for his arrest on a charge of abduction.

On the morning of December 26, a Des Moines lawyer named Henry McKnight went to the Des Moines police station and informed the officers present that he had just received a long-distance call from Williams, and that he had advised Williams to turn himself in to the Davenport police. Williams did surrender that morning to the police in Davenport, and they booked him on the charge specified in the arrest warrant and gave him the warnings required by Miranda v. Arizona. The Davenport police then telephoned their counterparts in Des Moines to inform them that Williams had surrendered. McKnight, the lawyer, was still at the Des Moines police headquarters, and Williams conversed with McKnight on the telephone. In the presence of the Des Moines chief of police and a police detective named Leaming, McKnight advised Williams that Des Moines police officers would be driving to Davenport to pick him up, that the officers would not interrogate him or mistreat him, and that Williams was not to talk to the officers about Pamela Powers until after consulting with McKnight upon his return to Des Moines. As a result of these conversations, it was agreed between McKnight and the Des Moines police officials that Detective Leaming and a fellow officer would drive to Davenport to pick up Williams, that they would bring him directly back to Des Moines, and that they would not question him during the trip.

In the meantime Williams was arraigned before a judge in Davenport on the outstanding arrest warrant. The judge advised him of his Miranda rights and committed him to jail. Before leaving the courtroom, Williams conferred with a lawyer named Kelly, who advised him not to make any statements until consulting with McKnight back in Des Moines.

Detective Leaming and his fellow officer arrived in Davenport about noon to pick up Williams and return him to Des Moines. Soon after their arrival they met with Williams and Kelly, who, they understood, was acting as Williams' lawyer. Detective Leaming repeated the Miranda warnings, and told Williams:

> [W]e both know that you're being represented here by Mr. Kelly and you're being represented by Mr. McKnight in Des Moines, and... I want you to remember this because we'll be visiting between here and Des Moines.

Williams then conferred again with Kelly alone, and after this conference Kelly reiterated to Detective Leaming that Williams was not to be questioned about the disappearance of Pamela Powers until after he had consulted with McKnight back in Des Moines. When Leaming expressed some reservations, Kelly firmly stated that the agreement with McKnight was to be carried out - that there was to be no interrogation of Williams during the automobile journey to Des Moines. Kelly was denied permission to ride in the police car back to Des Moines with Williams and the two officers.

The two detectives, with Williams in their charge, then set out on the 160-mile drive. At no time during the trip did Williams express a willingness to be interrogated in the absence of an attorney. Instead, he stated several times that "[w]hen I get to Des Moines and see Mr. McKnight, I am going to tell you the whole story." Detective Leaming knew that Williams was a former mental patient, and knew also that he was deeply religious.

The detective and his prisoner soon embarked on a wideranging conversation covering a variety of topics, including the subject of religion. Then, not long after leaving Davenport and reaching the interstate highway, Detective Leaming delivered what has been referred to in the briefs and oral arguments as the "Christian burial speech." Addressing Williams as "Reverend," the detective said:

> I want to give you something to think about while we're traveling down the road. ... Number one, I want you to observe the weather conditions, it's raining, it's sleeting, it's freezing, driving is very treacherous, visibility is poor, it's going to be dark early this evening. They are predicting several inches of snow for tonight, and I feel that you yourself are the only person that knows where this little girl's body is, that you yourself have only been there once, and if you get a snow on top of it you yourself may be unable to find it. And, since we will be going right past the area on the way into Des Moines, I feel that we could stop and locate the body, that the parents of this little girl should be entitled to a Christian burial for the little girl who was snatched away from them on Christmas [E]ve and murdered. And I feel we should stop and locate it on the way in rather than waiting until morning and trying to come back out after a snow storm and possibly not being able to find it at all.

Williams asked Detective Leaming why he thought their route to Des Moines would be taking them past the girl's body, and Leaming responded that he knew the body was in the area of Mitchellville - a town they would be passing on the way to Des Moines. [The fact of the matter, of course, was that Detective Leaming possessed no such knowledge.] Leaming then stated: "I do not want you to answer me. I don't want to discuss it any further. Just think about it as we're riding down the road."

As the car approached Grinnell, a town approximately 100 miles west of Davenport, Williams asked whether the police had found the victim's shoes. When Detective Leaming replied that he was unsure, Williams directed the officers to a service station where he said he had left the shoes; a search for them proved unsuccessful. As they continued towards Des Moines, Williams asked whether the police had found the blanket, and directed the officers to a rest area where he said he had disposed of the blanket. Nothing was found. The car continued towards Des Moines, and as it approached Mitchellville, Williams said that he would show the officers where the body was. He then directed the police to the body of Pamela Powers.

Williams was indicted for first-degree murder. Before trial, his counsel moved to suppress all evidence relating to or resulting from any statements Williams had made during the automobile ride from Davenport to Des Moines. After an evidentiary hearing the trial judge denied the motion. He found that "an agreement was made between defense counsel and the police officials to the effect that the Defendant was not to be questioned on the return trip to Des Moines," and that the evidence in question had been elicited from Williams during "a critical stage in the proceedings requiring the presence of counsel on his request." The judge ruled, however, that Williams had "waived his right to have an attorney present during the giving of such information."

The evidence in question was introduced over counsel's continuing objection at the subsequent trial. The jury found Williams guilty of murder, and the judgment of conviction was affirmed by the Iowa Supreme Court, a bare majority of whose members agreed with the trial court that Williams had "waived his right to the presence of his counsel" on the automobile ride from Davenport to Des Moines. The four dissenting justices expressed the view that "when counsel and police have agreed defendant is not to be questioned until counsel is present and defendant has been advised not to talk and repeatedly has stated he will tell the whole story after he talks with counsel, the state should be required to make a stronger showing of intentional voluntary waiver than was made here."

Williams then petitioned for a writ of habeas corpus ... The District Court made findings of fact as summarized above, and concluded as a matter of law that the evidence in question had been wrongly admitted at Williams' trial. ...

The Court of Appeals for the Eighth Circuit, with one judge dissenting, affirmed this judgment. ...We granted certiorari to consider the constitutional issues presented.

II.

B.

...For it is clear that the judgment before us must in any event be affirmed upon the ground that Williams was deprived of a different constitutional right - the right to the assistance of counsel.

This right, guaranteed by the Sixth and Fourteenth Amendments, is indispensable to the fair administration of our adversary system of criminal justice. ...

...Whatever else it may mean, the right to counsel granted by the Sixth and Fourteenth Amendments means at least that a person is entitled to the help of a lawyer at or after the time that judicial proceedings have been initiated against him - "whether by way of formal charge, preliminary hearing, indictment, information, or arraignment."

There can be no doubt in the present case that judicial proceedings had been initiated against Williams before the start of the automobile ride from Davenport to Des Moines. A warrant had been issued for his arrest, he had been arraigned on that warrant before a judge in a Davenport courtroom, and he had been committed by the court to confinement in jail. The State does not contend otherwise.

There can be no serious doubt, either, that Detective Leaming deliberately and designedly set out to elicit information from Williams just as surely as - and perhaps more effectively than - if he had formally interrogated him. Detective Leaming was fully aware before departing for Des Moines that Williams was being represented in Davenport by Kelly and in Des Moines by McKnight. Yet he purposely sought during Williams' isolation from his lawyers to obtain as much incriminating information as possible. Indeed, Detective Leaming conceded as much when he testified at Williams' trial ...

The state courts clearly proceeded upon the hypothesis that Detective Leaming's "Christian burial speech" had been tantamount to interrogation. Both courts recognized that Williams had been entitled to the assistance of counsel at the time he made the incriminating statements. Yet no such constitutional protection would have come into play if there had been no interrogation.

III.

The Iowa courts recognized that Williams had been denied the constitutional right to the assistance of counsel. They held, however, that he had waived that right during the course of the automobile trip from Davenport to Des Moines. The state trial court explained its determination of waiver as follows:

> The time element involved on the trip, the general circumstances of it, and more importantly the absence on the Defendant's part of any assertion of his right or desire not to give information absent the presence of his attorney, are the main foundations for the Court's conclusion that he voluntarily waived such right.

In its lengthy opinion affirming this determination, the Iowa Supreme Court applied "the totality-of-circumstances test for a showing of waiver of constitutionally-protected rights in the absence of an express waiver," and concluded that "evidence of the time element involved on the trip, the general circumstances of it, and the absence of any request or expressed desire for the aid of counsel before or at the time of giving information, were sufficient to sustain a conclusion that defendant did waive his constitutional rights as alleged."

In the federal habeas corpus proceeding the District Court, believing that the issue of waiver was not one of fact but of federal law, held that the Iowa courts had "applied the wrong constitutional standards" in ruling that Williams had waived the protections that were his under the Constitution. The court held "that it is the government which bears a heavy burden... but that is the burden which explicitly was placed on [Williams] by the state courts." After carefully reviewing the evidence, the District Court concluded:

> [U]nder the proper standards for determining waiver, there simply is no evidence to support a waiver. ...[T]here is no affirmative indication... that [Williams] did waive his rights. ... [T]he state courts' emphasis on the absence of a demand for counsel was not only legally inappropriate, but factually unsupportable as well, since Detective Leaming himself testified that [Williams], on several occasions during the trip, indicated that he would talk after he saw Mr. McKnight. Both these statements and Mr. Kelly's statement to Detective Leaming that [Williams] would talk only after seeing Mr. McKnight in Des Moines certainly were assertions of [Williams'] 'right or desire not to give information absent the presence of his attorney. ...' Moreover, the statements were obtained only after Detective Leaming's use of psychology on a person whom he knew to be deeply religious and an escapee from a mental hospital - with the specific intent to elicit incriminating statements. In the face of this evidence, the State has produced no affirmative evidence whatsoever to support its claim of waiver, and, a fortiori, it cannot be said that the State has met its 'heavy burden' of showing a knowing and intelligent waiver of... Sixth Amendment rights."

The Court of Appeals approved the reasoning of the District Court...

The District Court and the Court of Appeals were also correct in their understanding of the proper standard to be applied in determining the question of waiver as a matter of federal constitutional law - that it was incumbent upon the State to prove "an intentional relinquishment or abandonment of a known right or privilege." That standard has been reiterated in many cases. We have said that the right to counsel does not depend upon a request by the defendant and that courts indulge in every reasonable presumption against waiver. This strict standard applies equally to an alleged waiver of the right to counsel whether at trial or at a critical stage of pretrial proceedings.

We conclude, finally, that the Court of Appeals was correct in holding that, judged by these standards, the record in this case falls far short of sustaining petitioner's burden. It is true that Williams had been informed of and appeared to understand his right to counsel. But waiver requires not merely comprehension but relinquishment, and Williams' consistent reliance upon the advice of counsel in dealing with the authorities refutes any suggestion that he waived that right. ...

Despite Williams' express and implicit assertions of his right to counsel, Detective Leaming proceeded to elicit incriminating statements from Williams. Leaming did not preface this effort by telling Williams that he had a right to the presence of a lawyer, and made no effort at all to ascertain whether Williams wished to relinquish that right. The circumstances of record in this case thus provide no reasonable basis for finding that Williams waived his right to the assistance of counsel.

The Court of Appeals did not hold, nor do we, that under the circumstances of this case Williams could not, without notice to counsel, have waived his rights under the Sixth and Fourteenth Amendments. It only held, as do we, that he did not.

IV.

The crime of which Williams was convicted was senseless and brutal, calling for swift and energetic action by the police to apprehend the perpetrator and gather evidence with which he could be convicted. No mission of law enforcement officials is more important. Yet "[d]isinterested zeal for the public good does not assure either wisdom or right in the methods it pursues." ... so clear a violation of the Sixth and Fourteenth Amendments as here occurred cannot be condoned. The pressures on state executive and judicial officers charged with the administration of the criminal law are great, especially when the crime is murder and the victim a small child. But it is precisely the predictability of those pressures that makes imperative a resolute loyalty to the guarantees that the Constitution extends to us all.

The judgment of the Court of Appeals is affirmed.

It is so ordered.

MR. JUSTICE MARSHALL, concurring. [omitted]

MR. JUSTICE POWELL, concurring. [omitted]

MR. JUSTICE STEVENS, concurring. [omitted]

MR. CHIEF JUSTICE BURGER, dissenting.

The result in this case ought to be intolerable in any society which purports to call itself an organized society. It continues the Court - by the narrowest margin - on the much-criticized course of punishing the public for the mistakes and misdeeds of law enforcement officers, instead of punishing the officer directly, if in fact he is guilty of wrongdoing. It mechanically and blindly keeps reliable evidence from juries whether the claimed constitutional violation involves gross police misconduct or honest human error.

Williams is guilty of the savage murder of a small child; no member of the Court contends he is not. While in custody, and after no fewer than five warnings of his rights to silence and to counsel, he led police to the concealed body of his victim. The Court concedes Williams was not threatened or coerced and that he spoke and acted voluntarily and with full awareness of his constitutional rights. In the face of all this, the Court now holds that because Williams was prompted by the detective's statement - not interrogation but a statement - the jury must not be told how the police found the body.

...I categorically reject the remarkable notion that the police in this case were guilty of unconstitutional misconduct, or any conduct justifying the bizarre result reached by the Court. ...

Under well-settled precedents which the Court freely acknowledges, it is very clear that Williams had made a valid waiver of his Fifth Amendment right to silence and his Sixth Amendment right to counsel when he led police to the child's body. Indeed, even under the Court's analysis I do not understand now a contrary conclusion is possible.

The evidence is uncontradicted that Williams had abundant knowledge of his right to have counsel present and of his right to silence. Since the Court does not question his mental competence, it boggles the mind to suggest that Williams could not understand that leading police to the child's body would have other than the most serious consequences...

One plausible but unarticulated basis for the result reached is that once a suspect has asserted his right not to talk without the presence of an attorney, it becomes legally impossible for him to waive that right until he has seen an attorney. But constitutional rights are personal, and an otherwise valid waiver should not be brushed aside by judges simply because an attorney was not present. The Court's holding operates to "imprison a man in his privileges;" it conclusively presumes a suspect is legally incompetent to change his mind and tell the truth until an attorney is present. It denigrates an individual to a nonperson whose free will has become hostage to a lawyer so that until the lawyer consents, the suspect is deprived of any legal right or power to decide for himself that he wishes to make a disclosure. It denies that the rights to counsel and silence are personal, nondelegable, and subject to a waiver only by that individual. The opinions in support of the Court's judgment do not enlighten us as to why police conduct - whether good or bad - should operate to suspend Williams' right to change his mind and "tell all" at once...

(2).

The Exclusionary Rule Should Not be Applied to Non-egregious Police Conduct

Even if there was no waiver, and assuming a technical violation occurred, the Court errs gravely in mechanically applying the exclusionary rule without considering whether that Draconian judicial doctrine should be invoked in these circumstances, or indeed whether any of its conceivable goals will be furthered by its application here.

...it is striking that the Court fails even to consider whether the benefits secured by application of the exclusionary rule in this case outweigh its obvious social costs. Perhaps the failure is due to the fact that this case arises not under the Fourth Amendment, but under Miranda v. Arizona and the Sixth Amendment right to counsel. The Court apparently perceives the function of the exclusionary rule to be so different in these varying contexts that it must be mechanically and uncritically applied in all cases arising outside the Fourth Amendment.

...Involuntary and coerced admissions are suppressed because of the inherent unreliability of a confession wrung from an unwilling suspect by threats, brutality, or other coercion. ...

But use of Williams' disclosures and their fruits carries no risk whatever of unreliability, for the body was found where he said it would be found. Moreover, since the Court makes no issue of voluntariness, no dangers are posed to individual dignity or free will. Miranda's safeguards are premised on presumed unreliability long associated with confessions extorted by brutality or threats; they are not personal constitutional rights, but are simply judicially created prophylactic measures.

Thus, in cases where incriminating disclosures are voluntarily made without coercion, and hence not violative of the Fifth Amendment, but are obtained in violation of one of the Miranda prophylaxes, suppression is no longer automatic. Rather, we weigh the deterrent effect on unlawful police conduct, together with the normative Fifth Amendment justifications for suppression, against "the strong interest under any system of justice of making available to the trier of fact all concededly relevant and trustworthy evidence which either party seeks to adduce. ... We also 'must consider society's interest in the effective prosecution of criminals. ...'" This individualized consideration or balancing process with respect to the exclusionary sanction is possible in this case, as in others, because Williams' incriminating disclosures are not infected with any element of compulsion the Fifth Amendment forbids; nor, as noted earlier, does this evidence pose any danger of unreliability to the factfinding process. In short, there is no reason to exclude this evidence.

Similarly, the exclusionary rule is not uniformly implicated in the Sixth Amendment, particularly its pretrial aspects. We have held that

> the core purpose of the counsel guarantee was to assure 'Assistance' at trial, when the accused was confronted with both the intricacies of the law and the advocacy of the public prosecutor.

Thus, the right to counsel is fundamentally a "trial" right necessitated by the legal complexities of a criminal prosecution and the need to offset, to the trier of fact, the power of the State as prosecutor. It is now thought that modern law enforcement involves pretrial confrontations at which the defendant's fate might effectively be sealed before the right of counsel could attach. In order to make meaningful the defendant's opportunity to a fair trial and to assistance of counsel at that trial - the core purposes of the counsel guarantee - the Court formulated a per se rule guaranteeing counsel at what it has characterized as "critical" pretrial proceedings where substantial rights might be endangered.

In any event, the fundamental purpose of the Sixth Amendment is to safeguard the fairness of the trial and the integrity of the factfinding process. In this case, where the evidence of how the child's body was found is of unquestioned reliability, and since the Court accepts Williams' disclosures as voluntary and uncoerced, there is no issue either of fairness or evidentiary reliability to justify suppression of truth. ...

...Rather than adopting a formalistic analysis varying with the constitutional provision invoked, we should apply the exclusionary rule on the basis of its benefits and costs, at least in those cases where the police conduct at issue is far from being outrageous or egregious.

MR. JUSTICE WHITE, with whom MR. JUSTICE BLACKMUN and MR. JUSTICE REHNQUIST join, dissenting

...The majority creates no new rule preventing an accused who has retained a lawyer from waiving his right to the lawyer's presence during questioning. The majority simply finds that no waiver was proved in this case. I disagree. That respondent knew of his right not to say anything to the officers without advice and presence of counsel is established on this record to a moral certainty. He was advised of the right by three officials of the State - telling at least one that he understood the right - and by two lawyers. Finally, he further demonstrated his knowledge of the right by informing the police that he would tell them the story in the presence of McKnight when they arrived in Des Moines. The issue in this case, then, is whether respondent relinquished that right intentionally.

Respondent relinquished his right not to talk to the police about his crime when the car approached the place where he had hidden the victim's clothes. Men usually intend to do what they do, and there is nothing in the record to support the proposition that respondent's decision to talk was anything but an exercise of his own free will. Apparently, without any prodding from the officers, respondent - who had earlier said that he would tell the whole story when he arrived in Des Moines - spontaneously changed his mind about the timing of his disclosures when the car approached the places where he had hidden the evidence. However, even if his statements were influenced by Detective Leaming's above-quoted statement, respondent's decision to talk in the absence of counsel can hardly be viewed as the product of an overborne will. The statement by Leaming was not coercive; it was accompanied by a request that respondent not respond to it; and it was delivered hours before respondent decided to make any statement. Respondent's waiver was thus knowing and intentional.

...Absent coercion - no matter how the right involved is defined - an accused is amply protected by a rule requiring waiver before or simultaneously with the giving by him of an answer or the making by him of a statement.

III.

The consequence of the majority's decision is, as the majority recognizes, extremely serious. A mentally disturbed killer whose guilt is not in question may be released. Why? Apparently the answer is that the majority believes that the law enforcement officers acted in a way which involves some risk of injury to society and that such conduct should be deterred. However, the officers' conduct did not, and was not likely to, jeopardize the fairness of respondent's trial or in any way risk the conviction of an innocent man - the risk against which the Sixth Amendment guarantee of assistance of counsel is designed to protect. The police did nothing "wrong," let alone anything "unconstitutional." To anyone not lost in the intricacies of the prophylactic rules of Miranda v. Arizona, the result in this case seems utterly senseless ... I respectfully dissent.

MR. JUSTICE BLACKMUN, with whom MR. JUSTICE WHITE and MR. JUSTICE REHNQUIST join, dissenting.

...not every attempt to elicit information should be regarded as "tantamount to interrogation." I am not persuaded that Leaming's observations and comments, made as the police car traversed the snowy and slippery miles between Davenport and Des Moines that winter afternoon, were an interrogation, direct or subtle, of Williams...

...Persons in custody frequently volunteer statements in response to stimuli other than interrogation. When there is no interrogation, such statements should be admissible as long as they are truly voluntary.

NOTES AND QUERIES

Do you find the "Christian burial speech" inappropriately coercive? How different do you find this case from *Connelly*? Both the trial and Iowa Supreme Court had found that Williams had waived his rights. The Iowa court had conducted a totality of circumstances analysis. What would be your result if you used that standard? Unlike *Connelly*, this case involves police enticement. Do you find that enticement enough to distinguish these two cases? Do you find the pressure on Williams to be coercive? If so, is it coercive enough for the legal system to worry about it?

The Supreme Court finds that the state needed to prove an "intentional relinquishment or abandonment of a known right or privilege." Using that standard, the Supreme Court finds that Williams had not relinquished his right to an attorney and that he has not waived his right to counsel. Does your analysis lead you to the same conclusion? Do you think people should have an attorney present for them to consult with when they decide whether to waive their right to counsel? How about having an adult or other individual present with them who is not involved in law enforcement? Would having someone present help those who are vulnerable, like both Connelly and William? What do you think would be the implications of such a rule? Would such a rule be fair to defendants?

In considering the above questions, note that England requires the presence of an appropriate adult (AA) safeguard for vulnerable adult (e.g., one with a mental disability) and juvenile suspects undergoing police interviews. A recent study of 501 interviews, 365 (73%) of which were with adult suspects and 136 (27%) with juveniles, revealed that an AA was present during 212 (58%) adult interviews and 135 (99%) juvenile interviews. The researchers examined the contribution (or lack of contribution) made by the AA, the extent to which they fulfilled their role, and the effect of their presence on other persons and interview outcome. The study found that AAs for juveniles, who were mainly family members and friends, contributed more during interviews, both appropriately and inappropriately, than did social workers and volunteers, although overall there was little direct intervention by the AA. Sarah Medford, Gisli Gudjonsson, and John Pearse, The efficacy of the appropriate adult safeguard during police interviewing, 8 Legal and Criminological Psych. 253 (2003). What do you make of these findings?

Do you find the exclusionary rule appropriate in this case? What purpose does it serve in this case? What do you make of the fact that Williams did in fact know his rights. Why is that knowledge being treated differently in this case than in the cases we examined in prior chapters?

What do you make of the claim that the confession was in fact reliable? They did find the body. What do you make of the view that Williams is clearly guilty and that the state would have found him guilty anyway? What protections would have Williams lost if the Court would have adopted the policy that police may entice individuals to waive their rights when they are clearly guilty? Should the exclusionary rule still be applied when it is clear that there was not a risk of convicting an innocent person?

NOTE ON REVISITING THE ELICITATION OF STATEMENTS

What do you make of this interrogation? On November 28, 1997, police officers were near a vacant lot in a residential area of Oxnard, California, investigating suspected narcotics activity. While they were questioning an individual, they heard a bicycle approaching on a darkened path that crossed the lot. They ordered the rider, Martinez, to dismount, spread his legs, and place his hands behind his head. Martinez complied. Salinas then conducted a patdown frisk and discovered a knife in Martinez's waistband. An altercation ensued. It is unclear what happened after that. What is clear is that Oliverio Martinez was shot five times during an altercation with police officers. He was arrested and taken to a hospital emergency room. One bullet rendered Martinez blind, having damaged his optic nerve; another fractured a vertebra, paralyzing his legs. Three additional bullets passed through his leg around the knee joint. The injuries were life-threatening, and Martinez drifted in and out of consciousness during medical treatment.

A police supervisor arrived, Sergeant Ben Chavez, to question Martinez while he was receiving treatment in the emergency room. Without first reciting the Miranda warnings, Chavez tape-recorded the questioning, which amounted to ten minutes over a forty-five minute period. Medical staff asked Chavez to leave the room several times, but each time he returned and resumed his questioning. The court of appeals noted that Chavez "pressed Martinez with persistent, directed questions regarding the events leading up the shooting." Based on the tape recording of the questioning, the District Court concluded that "during the questioning at the hospital, [Martinez] repeatedly begged for treatment; he told [Sergeant Chavez] he believed he was dying eight times; complained that he was in extreme pain on fourteen separate occasions; and twice said he did not want to talk any more." The sergeant stopped attempting to question Martinez only when hospital staff moved him out of the emergency room for a C.A.T. scan.

While most of Martinez's responses to Chavez's questions were non-responsive and consisted of complaints of pain and expressions of belief that he was dying, the court of appeals concluded that Martinez did utter statements that the plaintiff could reasonably believe might be used in a criminal prosecution or lead to evidence that might be so used.

What follows is an English translation of portions of the tape-recorded questioning in Spanish that occurred in the emergency room of the hospital when, as is evident from the text, both parties believed that the respondent was about to die:

> Chavez: What happened? Olivero, tell me what happened.
> O[liverio] M[artinez]: I don't know.
> Chavez: I don't know what happened (sic)?
> O. M.: Ay! I am dying. Ay! What are you doing to me? No, . . .! (unintelligible scream).
> Chavez: What happened, sir?
> O. M.: My foot hurts. . .
> Chavez: Olivero. Sir, what happened?
> O. M.: I am choking.
> Chavez: Tell me what happened.
> O. M.: I don't know.
> Chavez: 'I don't know.'
> O. M.: My leg hurts.
> Chavez: I don't know what happened (sic)?
> O. M.: It hurts. . .

Chavez: Hey, hey look.

O. M.: I am choking.

Chavez: Can you hear? look listen, I am Benjamin Chavez with the police here in Oxnard, look.

O. M.: I am dying, please.

Chavez: OK, yes, tell me what happened. If you are going to die, tell me what happened. Look I need to tell (sic) what happened.

O. M.: I don't know.

Chavez: You don't know, I don't know what happened (sic)? Did you talk to the police?

O. M.: Yes.

Chavez: What happened with the police?

O. M.: We fought.

Chavez: Huh? What happened with the police?

O. M.: The police shot me.

Chavez: Why?

O. M.: Because I was fighting with him.

Chavez: Oh, why were you fighting with the police?

O. M.: I am dying. . .

Chavez: OK, yes you are dying, but tell me why you are fighting, were you fighting with the police? . . . . .

O. M.: Doctor, please I want air, I am dying.

Chavez: OK, OK. I want to know if you pointed the gun [to yourself] at the police.

O. M.: Yes.

Chavez: Yes, and you pointed it [to yourself]? (sic) at the police pointed the gun? (sic) Huh?

O. M.: I am dying, please. ...

...

Chavez: OK, listen, listen I want to know what happened, ok?

O. M.: I want them to treat me.

Chavez: OK, they are do it (sic), look when you took out the gun from the tape (sic) of the police. .

O. M.: I am dying. . .

Chavez: Ok, look, what I want to know if you took out (sic) the gun of the police?

O. M.: I am not telling you anything until they treat me.

Chavez: Look, tell me what happened, I want to know, look well don't you want the police know (sic) what happened with you?

O. M.: Uuuggghhh! my belly hurts. . .

...

Chavez: Nothing, why did you run (sic) from the police?

O. M.: I don't want to say anything anymore.

Chavez: No?

O. M.: I want them to treat me, it hurts a lot, please.

Chavez: You don't want to tell (sic) what happened with you over there?

O. M.: I don't want to die, I don't want to die.

Chavez: Well if you are going to die tell me what happened, and right now you think you are going to die?

O. M.: No.

Chavez: No, do you think you are going to die?

O. M.: Aren't you going to treat me or what?

Chavez: Look, think you are going to die, (sic) that's all I want to know, if you think you are going to die? Right now, do you think you are going to die?

O. M.: My belly hurts, please treat me.

Chavez: Sir?

O. M.: If you treat me I tell you everything, if not, no.

Chavez: Sir, I want to know if you think you are going to die right now?

O. M.: I think so.

Chavez: You think (sic) so? Ok. Look, the doctors are going to help you with all they can do, Ok?. That they can do.

O. M.: Get moving, I am dying, can't you see me? come on.

Chavez: Ah, huh, right now they are giving you medication.

The statements, however, were not, in fact, introduced against Martinez in any criminal proceeding. The question presented by the case, then, was whether a suspect's constitutional rights are violated by the conduct of police during a coercive interrogation, or are violated only in the event that an incriminating statement is taken and introduced against him in a trial or other criminal proceeding.

The court of appeals found that Martinez had alleged viable Fifth Amendment and Fourteenth Amendment involuntariness claims on the basis of police coercion of a potentially incriminating statement. The court also held that a reasonable officer would have known that his conduct under the circumstances violated these clearly established constitutional rights. For these reasons the appeals court affirmed the district court's denial of the sergeant's motion for summary judgment based on the doctrine of qualified immunity.

Chavez appealed to the Supreme Court, arguing that neither the Fifth Amendment nor the Fourteenth Amendment protects the right of a person in police custody to be free from interrogation methods that coerce an involuntary statement. Chavez claimed that the only protection these rights provide is protection from the introduction of involuntary statements in evidence at a criminal trial. He argued that the only right that protects a suspect in custody during interrogation is a limited Fourteenth Amendment right to be free from practices that violate substantive due process by shocking the conscience. Chavez contended that there is no constitutionally protected right to remain silent when questioned by police or other government officials other than during questioning that takes place at a criminal proceeding.

The Supreme Court reiterated the fundamental principle that an officer is entitled to qualified immunity if his alleged conduct did not violate a constitutional right. Following that principle, the Court ruled that allegations failed to state a valid § 1983 claim for a violation of the arrestee's privilege against self-incrimination, under the Federal Constitution's Fifth Amendment as made applicable to the states by the Constitution's Fourteenth Amendment, where (1) the arrestee had never been charged with any crime related to the altercation; and (2) thus, the arrestee's answers to the supervisor's interrogation had never been used against the arrestee in any subsequent criminal prosecution.

The majority also noted that even assuming, for the sake of the argument, that the questioning somehow deprived Martinez of some right to liberty, the interrogation was not egregious and conscience shocking. Given that, Martinez had no claim. The Court reasoned that official conduct most likely to rise to the conscience-shocking level is conduct intended to injure in a manner unjustifiable by any government interest. Here, the Court found, there was no evidence that Chavez acted with a purpose to harm Martinez by intentionally interfering with his medical treatment. Medical personnel were able to treat Martinez throughout the interview, and Chavez ceased his questioning to allow tests and other procedures to be performed. Nor was there evidence that Chavez's conduct exacerbated Martinez's injuries or prolonged his stay in the hospital. Moreover, the need to investigate whether there had been police misconduct constituted a justifiable government interest given the risk that key evidence would have been lost if Martinez had died without the authorities ever hearing his side of the story.

Dissenters found that the police interrogation shocked the conscience, that the right against self-incrimination applies at the time and place police use severe compulsion to extract a statement from a suspect, and therefore that Martinez's rights had been violated. *Chavez v. Martinez*, 538 U.S. 760 (2003).

EXCLUDING STATEMENTS

OREGON v. ELSTAD
470 U.S. 298 (1985)

JUSTICE O'CONNOR delivered the opinion of the Court.

I.

In December 1981, the home of Mr. and Mrs. Gilbert Gross ... was burglarized. Missing were art objects and furnishings valued at $150,000. A witness to the burglary contacted the Polk County Sheriff's Office, implicating respondent Michael Elstad, an 18-year-old neighbor and friend of the Grosses' teenage son. Thereupon, Officers Burke and McAllister went to the home of respondent Elstad, with a warrant for his arrest. Elstad's mother answered the door. She led the officers to her son's room where he lay on his bed, clad in shorts and listening to his stereo. The officers asked him to get dressed and to accompany them into the living room. Officer McAllister asked respondent's mother to step into the kitchen, where he explained that they had a warrant for her son's arrest for the burglary of a neighbor's residence. Officer Burke remained with Elstad in the living room. He later testified:

> I sat down with Mr. Elstad and I asked him if he was aware of why Detective McAllister and myself were there to talk with him. He stated no, he had no idea why we were there. I then asked him if he knew a person by the name of Gross, and he said yes, he did, and also added that he heard that there was a robbery at the Gross house. And at that point I told Mr. Elstad that I felt he was involved in that, and he looked at me and stated, 'Yes, I was there.'

Elstad was transported to the Sheriff's headquarters and approximately one hour later, Officers Burke and McAllister joined him in McAllister's office. McAllister then advised respondent for the first time of his Miranda rights, reading from a standard card. Respondent indicated he understood his rights, and, having these rights in mind, wished to speak with the officers. Elstad gave a full statement, explaining that he had known that the Gross family was out of town and had been paid to lead several acquaintances to the Gross residence and show them how to gain entry through a defective sliding glass door...

Respondent was charged with first-degree burglary. ... Respondent moved at once to suppress his oral statement and signed confession. He contended that the statement he made in response to questioning at his house "let the cat out of the bag," and tainted the subsequent confession as "fruit of the poisonous tree." The judge ruled that the statement, "I was there," had to be excluded because the defendant had not been advised of his Miranda rights. The written confession taken after Elstad's arrival at the Sheriff's office, however, was admitted in evidence. The court found:

> [His] written statement was given freely, voluntarily and knowingly by the defendant after he had waived his right to remain silent and have counsel present which waiver was evidenced by the card which the defendant had signed. [It] was not tainted in any way by the previous brief statement between the defendant and the Sheriff's Deputies that had arrested him.

Elstad was found guilty of burglary in the first degree...

...respondent appealed to the Oregon Court of Appeals... The State conceded that Elstad had been in custody when he made his statement, "I was there," and accordingly agreed that this statement was inadmissible as having been given without the prescribed Miranda warnings. But the State maintained that any conceivable "taint" had been dissipated prior to the respondent's written confession by McAllister's careful administration of the requisite warnings. The Court of Appeals reversed respondent's conviction, identifying the crucial constitutional inquiry as "whether there was a sufficient break in the stream of events between [the] inadmissible statement and the written confession to insulate the latter statement from the effect of what went before." The Oregon court concluded:

> Regardless of the absence of actual compulsion, the coercive impact of the unconstitutionally obtained statement remains, because in a defendant's mind it has sealed his fate. It is this impact that must be dissipated in order to make a subsequent confession admissible. In determining whether it has been dissipated, lapse of time, and change of place from the original surroundings are the most important considerations.

Because of the brief period separating the two incidents, the "cat was sufficiently out of the bag to exert a coercive impact on [respondent's] later admissions."

II.

The arguments advanced in favor of suppression of respondent's written confession rely heavily on metaphor. One metaphor, familiar from the Fourth Amendment context, would require that respondent's confession, regardless of its integrity, voluntariness, and probative value, be suppressed as the "tainted fruit of the poisonous tree" of the Miranda violation. A second metaphor questions whether a confession can be truly voluntary once the "cat is out of the bag." Taken out of context, each of these metaphors can be misleading. They should not be used to obscure fundamental differences between the role of the Fourth Amendment exclusionary rule and the function of Miranda in guarding against the prosecutorial use of compelled statements as prohibited by the Fifth Amendment. The Oregon court assumed and respondent here contends that a failure to administer Miranda warnings necessarily breeds the same consequences as police infringement of a constitutional right, so that evidence uncovered following an unwarned statement must be suppressed as "fruit of the poisonous tree." We believe this view misconstrues the nature of the protections afforded by Miranda warnings and therefore misreads the consequences of police failure to supply them.

A.

Prior to Miranda, the admissibility of an accused's in-custody statements was judged solely by whether they were "voluntary" within the meaning of the Due Process Clause. If a suspect's statements had been obtained by "techniques and methods offensive to due process," or under circumstances in which the suspect clearly had no opportunity to exercise "a free and unconstrained will," the statements would not be admitted. The Court in Miranda required suppression of many statements that would have been admissible under traditional due process analysis by presuming that statements made while in custody and without adequate warnings were protected by the Fifth Amendment. The Fifth Amendment, of course, is not concerned with nontestimonial evidence. Nor is it concerned with moral and psychological pressures to confess emanating from sources other than official coercion. Voluntary statements "remain a proper element in law enforcement."...

Respondent's contention that his confession was tainted by the earlier failure of the police to provide Miranda warnings and must be excluded as "fruit of the poisonous tree" assumes the existence of a constitutional violation. ... It is settled law that "a confession obtained through custodial interrogation after an illegal arrest should be excluded unless intervening events break the causal connection between the illegal arrest and the confession so that the confession is 'sufficiently an act of free will to purge the primary taint.'"

But ...a procedural Miranda violation differs in significant respects from violations of the Fourth Amendment, which have traditionally mandated a broad application of the "fruits" doctrine. The purpose of the Fourth Amendment exclusionary rule is to deter unreasonable searches, no matter how probative their fruits. "The exclusionary rule, . . . when utilized to effectuate the Fourth Amendment, serves interests and policies that are distinct from those it serves under the Fifth." Where a Fourth Amendment violation "taints" the confession, a finding of voluntariness for the purposes of the Fifth Amendment is merely a threshold requirement in determining whether the confession may be admitted in evidence. Beyond this, the prosecution must show a sufficient break in events to undermine the inference that the confession was caused by the Fourth Amendment violation.

The Miranda exclusionary rule, however, serves the Fifth Amendment and sweeps more broadly than the Fifth Amendment itself. It may be triggered even in the absence of a Fifth Amendment violation. The Fifth Amendment prohibits use by the prosecution in its case in chief only of compelled testimony. Failure to administer Miranda warnings creates a presumption of compulsion. Consequently, unwarned statements that are otherwise voluntary within the meaning of the Fifth Amendment must nevertheless be excluded from evidence under Miranda. Thus, in the individual case, Miranda's preventive medicine provides a remedy even to the defendant who has suffered no identifiable constitutional harm.

But the Miranda presumption, though irrebuttable for purposes of the prosecution's case in chief, does not require that the statements and their fruits be discarded as inherently tainted. Despite the fact that patently voluntary statements taken in violation of Miranda must be excluded from the prosecution's case, the presumption of coercion does not bar their use for impeachment purposes on cross-examination. The Court ... rejected as an "extravagant extension of the Constitution," the theory that a defendant who had confessed under circumstances that made the confession inadmissible, could thereby enjoy the freedom to "deny every fact disclosed or discovered as a 'fruit' of his confession, free from confrontation with his prior statements" and that the voluntariness of his confession would be totally irrelevant. Where an unwarned statement is preserved for use in situations that fall outside the sweep of the Miranda presumption, "the primary criterion of admissibility [remains] the 'old' due process voluntariness test."

We believe that this reasoning applies with equal force when the alleged "fruit" of a noncoercive Miranda violation is neither a witness nor an article of evidence but the accused's own voluntary testimony. ...the absence of any coercion or improper tactics undercuts the twin rationales – trustworthiness and deterrence – for a broader rule. Once warned, the suspect is free to exercise his own volition in deciding whether or not to make a statement to the authorities. The Court has often noted: "'[A] living witness is not to be mechanically equated with the proffer of inanimate evidentiary objects illegally seized. . . . [The] living witness is an individual human personality whose attributes of will, perception, memory and volition interact to determine what testimony he will give.'"

Because Miranda warnings may inhibit persons from giving information, this Court has determined that they need be administered only after the person is taken into "custody" or his freedom has otherwise been significantly restrained. Unfortunately, the task of defining "custody" is a slippery one, and "policemen investigating serious crimes [cannot realistically be expected to] make no errors whatsoever." If errors are made by law enforcement officers in administering the prophylactic Miranda procedures, they should not breed the same irremediable consequences as police infringement of the Fifth Amendment itself. It is an unwarranted extension of Miranda to hold that a simple failure to administer the warnings, unaccompanied by any actual coercion or other circumstances calculated to undermine the suspect's ability to exercise his free will, so taints the investigatory process that a subsequent voluntary and informed waiver is ineffective for some indeterminate period. Though Miranda requires that the unwarned admission must be suppressed, the admissibility of any subsequent statement should turn in these circumstances solely on whether it is knowingly and voluntarily made.

B.

The Oregon court, however, believed that the unwarned remark compromised the voluntariness of respondent's later confession. It was the court's view that the prior answer and not the unwarned questioning impaired respondent's ability to give a valid waiver and that only lapse of time and change of place could dissipate what it termed the "coercive impact" of the inadmissible statement. When a prior statement is actually coerced, the time that passes between confessions, the change in place of interrogations, and the change in identity of the interrogators all bear on whether that coercion has carried over into the second confession. The failure of police to administer Miranda warnings does not mean that the statements received have actually been coerced, but only that courts will presume the privilege against compulsory self-incrimination has not been intelligently exercised. ... In these circumstances, a careful and thorough administration of Miranda warnings serves to cure the condition that rendered the unwarned statement inadmissible. The warning conveys the relevant information and thereafter the suspect's choice whether to exercise his privilege to remain silent should ordinarily be viewed as an "act of free will."

The Oregon court nevertheless identified a subtle form of lingering compulsion, the psychological impact of the suspect's conviction that he has let the cat out of the bag and, in so doing, has sealed his own fate. But endowing the psychological effects of voluntary unwarned admissions with constitutional implications would, practically speaking, disable the police from obtaining the suspect's informed cooperation even when the official coercion proscribed by the Fifth Amendment played no part in either his warned or unwarned confessions. ...

This Court has never held that the psychological impact of voluntary disclosure of a guilty secret qualifies as state compulsion or compromises the voluntariness of a subsequent informed waiver. The Oregon court, by adopting this expansive view of Fifth Amendment compulsion, effectively immunizes a suspect who responds to pre-Miranda warning questions from the consequences of his subsequent informed waiver of the privilege of remaining silent. This immunity comes at a high cost to legitimate law enforcement activity, while adding little desirable protection to the individual's interest in not being compelled to testify against himself. When neither the initial nor the subsequent admission is coerced, little justification exists for permitting the highly probative evidence of a voluntary confession to be irretrievably lost to the factfinder.

There is a vast difference between the direct consequences flowing from coercion of a confession by physical violence or other deliberate means calculated to break the suspect's will and the uncertain consequences of disclosure of a "guilty secret" freely given in response to an unwarned but noncoercive question, as in this case. ... We must conclude that, absent deliberately coercive or improper tactics in obtaining the initial statement, the mere fact that a suspect has made an unwarned admission does not warrant a presumption of compulsion. A subsequent administration of Miranda warnings to a suspect who has given a voluntary but unwarned statement ordinarily should suffice to remove the conditions that precluded admission of the earlier statement. In such circumstances, the finder of fact may reasonably conclude that the suspect made a rational and intelligent choice whether to waive or invoke his rights.

III.

Though belated, the reading of respondent's rights was undeniably complete. ...It is also beyond dispute that respondent's earlier remark was voluntary, within the meaning of the Fifth Amendment. Neither the environment nor the manner of either "interrogation" was coercive. The initial conversation took place at midday, in the living room area of respondent's own home, with his mother in the kitchen area, a few steps away. Although in retrospect the officers testified that respondent was then in custody, at the time he made his statement he had not been informed that he was under arrest. The arresting officers' testimony indicates that the brief stop in the living room before proceeding to the station house was not to interrogate the suspect but to notify his mother of the reason for his arrest.

The State has conceded the issue of custody and thus we must assume that Burke breached Miranda procedures in failing to administer Miranda warnings before initiating the discussion in the living room. This breach may have been the result of confusion as to whether the brief exchange qualified as "custodial interrogation" or it may simply have reflected Burke's reluctance to initiate an alarming police procedure before McAllister had spoken with respondent's mother. Whatever the reason for Burke's oversight, the incident had none of the earmarks of coercion. Nor did the officers exploit the unwarned admission to pressure respondent into waiving his right to remain silent.

This Court has never embraced the theory that a defendant's ignorance of the full consequences of his decisions vitiates their voluntariness. ...Thus we have not held that the sine qua non for a knowing and voluntary waiver of the right to remain silent is a full and complete appreciation of all of the consequences flowing from the nature and the quality of the evidence in the case.

IV.

When police ask questions of a suspect in custody without administering the required warnings, Miranda dictates that the answers received be presumed compelled and that they be excluded from evidence at trial in the State's case in chief. ... there is no warrant for presuming coercive effect where the suspect's initial inculpatory statement, though technically in violation of Miranda, was voluntary. The relevant inquiry is whether, in fact, the second statement was also voluntarily made. As in any such inquiry, the finder of fact must examine the surrounding circumstances and the entire course of police conduct with respect to the suspect in evaluating the voluntariness of his statements. The fact that a suspect chooses to speak after being informed of his rights is, of course, highly probative. We find that the dictates of Miranda and the goals of the Fifth Amendment proscription against use of compelled testimony are fully satisfied in the circumstances of this case by barring use of the unwarned statement in the case in chief. No further purpose is served by imputing "taint" to subsequent statements obtained pursuant to a voluntary and knowing waiver. We hold today that a suspect who has once responded to unwarned yet uncoercive questioning is not thereby disabled from waiving his rights and confessing after he has been given the requisite Miranda warnings.

The judgment of the Court of Appeals of Oregon is reversed, and the case is remanded for further proceedings not inconsistent with this opinion.

It is so ordered.

JUSTICE BRENNAN, with whom JUSTICE MARSHALL joins, dissenting.

...Today's decision ... delivers a potentially crippling blow to Miranda and the ability of courts to safeguard the rights of persons accused of crime. For at least with respect to successive confessions, the Court today appears to strip remedies for Miranda violations of the "fruit of the poisonous tree" doctrine prohibiting the use of evidence presumptively derived from official illegality.

Two major premises undergird the Court's decision. The Court rejects as nothing more than "speculative" the long-recognized presumption that an illegally extracted confession causes the accused to confess again out of the mistaken belief that he already has sealed his fate, and it condemns as "'extravagant'" the requirement that the prosecution affirmatively rebut the presumption before the subsequent confession may be admitted. The Court instead adopts a new rule that, so long as the accused is given the usual Miranda warnings before further interrogation, the taint of a previous confession obtained in violation of Miranda "ordinarily" must be viewed as automatically dissipated.

In the alternative, the Court asserts that neither the Fifth Amendment itself nor the judicial policy of deterring illegal police conduct requires the suppression of the "fruits" of a confession obtained in violation of Miranda, reasoning that to do otherwise would interfere with "legitimate law enforcement activity." As the Court surely understands, however, ... If violations of constitutional rights may not be remedied through the well-established rules respecting derivative evidence, as the Court has held today, there is a critical danger that the rights will be rendered nothing more than a mere "form of words."

I.

If this Court's reversal of the judgment below reflected mere disagreement with the Oregon court's application of the "cat out of the bag" presumption to the particular facts of this case, the outcome, while clearly erroneous, would be of little lasting consequence. But the Court rejects the "cat out of the bag" presumption entirely and instead adopts a new rule presuming that "ordinarily" there is no causal connection between a confession extracted in violation of Miranda and a subsequent confession preceded by the usual Miranda warnings...

The Court today sweeps aside this common-sense approach as "speculative" reasoning, adopting instead a rule that "the psychological impact of voluntary disclosure of a guilty secret" neither "qualifies as state compulsion" nor "compromises the voluntariness" of subsequent confessions. So long as a suspect receives the usual Miranda warnings before further interrogation, the Court reasons, the fact that he "is free to exercise his own volition in deciding whether or not to make" further confessions "ordinarily" is a sufficient "cure" and serves to break any causal connection between the illegal confession and subsequent statements.

The Court's marble-palace psychoanalysis is tidy, but it flies in the face of our own precedents, demonstrates a startling unawareness of the realities of police interrogation...

A.

(1).

This Court has had long experience with the problem of confessions obtained after an earlier confession has been illegally secured. Subsequent confessions in these circumstances are not per se inadmissible, but the prosecution must demonstrate facts "sufficient to insulate the [subsequent] statement from the effect of all that went before."...

One of the factors that can vitiate the voluntariness of a subsequent confession is the hopeless feeling of an accused that he has nothing to lose by repeating his confession, even where the circumstances that rendered his first confession illegal have been removed. ...

...Although we have thus rejected a per se rule forbidding the introduction of subsequent statements in these circumstances, we have emphasized that the psychological impact of admissions and confessions of criminal guilt nevertheless can have a decisive impact in undermining the voluntariness of a suspect's responses to continued police interrogation and must be accounted for in determining their admissibility. ...

Our precedents did not develop in a vacuum. They reflect an understanding of the realities of police interrogation and the everyday experience of lower courts. Expert interrogators, far from dismissing a first admission or confession as creating merely a "speculative and attenuated" disadvantage for a suspect, understand that such revelations frequently lead directly to a full confession. Standard interrogation manuals advise that "[the] securing of the first admission is the biggest stumbling block. . . ." If this first admission can be obtained, "there is every reason to expect that the first admission will lead to others, and eventually to the full confession."

Interrogators describe the point of the first admission as the "breakthrough" and the "beachhead"...

One police practice that courts have frequently encountered involves the withholding of Miranda warnings until the end of an interrogation session. ... In such situations, where "it was all over except for reading aloud and explaining the written waiver of the Miranda safeguards," courts have time and again concluded that "[the] giving of the Miranda warnings before reducing the product of the day's work to written form could not undo what had been done or make legal what was illegal."

I would have thought that the Court, instead of dismissing the "cat out of the bag" presumption out of hand, would have accounted for these practical realities. ...

Instead, we have instructed courts to consider carefully such factors as the strength of the causal connection between the illegal action and the challenged evidence, their proximity in time and place, the presence of intervening factors, and the "purpose and flagrancy of the official misconduct."

The Court today shatters this sensitive inquiry and decides instead that, since individuals possess "'will, perception, memory and volition,'" a suspect's "exercise [of] his own volition in deciding whether or not to make a [subsequent] statement to the authorities" must "ordinarily" be viewed as sufficient to dissipate the coercive influence of a prior confession obtained in violation of Miranda. But "[will], perception, memory and volition are only relevant as they provide meaningful alternatives in the causal chain, not as mystical qualities which in themselves invoke the doctrine of attenuation." Thus we have always rejected, until today, the notion that "individual will" alone presumptively serves to insulate a person's actions from the taint of earlier official illegality. ...

Nor have we ever allowed Miranda warnings alone to serve talismanically to purge the taint of prior illegalities. ..."

This logic applies with even greater force to the Fifth Amendment problem of successive confessions. Where an accused believes that it is futile to resist because the authorities already have elicited an admission of guilt, the mere rendition of Miranda warnings does not convey the information most critical at that point to ensuring his informed and voluntary decision to speak again: that the earlier confession may not be admissible and thus that he need not speak out of any feeling that he already has sealed his fate. The Court therefore is flatly wrong in arguing, as it does repeatedly, that the mere provision of Miranda warnings prior to subsequent interrogation supplies the accused with "the relevant information" and ensures that a subsequent confession "ordinarily" will be the product of "a rational and intelligent choice" and "'an act of free will.'"

The Court simply has not confronted the basic premise of the derivative-evidence rule: that "[to] forbid the direct use of methods . . . but to put no curb on their full indirect use would only invite the very methods deemed 'inconsistent with ethical standards and destructive of personal liberty.'"

...merely to exclude the statement itself while putting no curbs on the admission of derivative evidence "would destroy the whole basis for the rule in the first instance." Yet that is precisely the result that today's disastrous opinion threatens to encourage. How can the Court possibly expect the authorities to obey Miranda when they have every incentive now to interrogate suspects without warnings or an effective waiver, knowing that the fruits of such interrogations "ordinarily" will be admitted, that an admissible subsequent confession "ordinarily" can be obtained simply by reciting the Miranda warnings shortly after the first has been procured and asking the accused to repeat himself, and that unless the accused can demonstrate otherwise his confession will be viewed as an "act of free will" in response to "legitimate law enforcement activity"? By condoning such a result, the Court today encourages practices that threaten to reduce Miranda to a mere "form of words," and it is shocking that the Court nevertheless disingenuously purports that it "in no way retreats" from the Miranda safeguards.

I dissent.

JUSTICE STEVENS, dissenting.

For me, the most disturbing aspect of the Court's opinion is its somewhat opaque characterization of the police misconduct in this case. The Court appears ambivalent on the question whether there was any constitutional violation. This ambivalence is either disingenuous or completely law-less. This Court's power to require state courts to exclude probative self-incriminatory statements rests entirely on the premise that the use of such evidence violates the Federal Constitution. The same constitutional analysis applies whether the custodial interrogation is actually coercive or irrebuttably presumed to be coercive. If the Court does not accept that premise, it must regard the holding in the Miranda case itself, as well as all of the federal jurisprudence that has evolved from that decision, as nothing more than an illegitimate exercise of raw judicial power. If the Court accepts the proposition that respondent's self-incriminatory statement was inadmissible, it must also acknowledge that the Federal Constitution protected him from custodial police interrogation without first being advised of his right to remain silent.

The source of respondent's constitutional protection is the Fifth Amendment's privilege against compelled self-incrimination that is secured against state invasion by the Due Process Clause of the Fourteenth Amendment. Like many other provisions of the Bill of Rights, that provision is merely a procedural safeguard. It is, however, the specific provision that protects all citizens from the kind of custodial interrogation that was once employed by the Star Chamber, by "the Germans of the 1930's and early 1940's," and by some of our own police departments only a few decades ago. Custodial interrogation that violates that provision of the Bill of Rights is a classic example of a violation of a constitutional right.

I respectfully dissent.

NOTES AND QUERIES

What do you make of the Court's analysis of voluntariness of a confession that occurs when a suspect has let the "cat out of the bag"? What does this rule allow law enforcement to do? What do you make of the subtle form of compulsion, the psychological impact of a suspect's conviction that they had just about confessed, that would have a suspect confess to officers even when the words they had said were unwarned admissions? What do you make of the dissent's claim that initial admissions do matter?

Note that the court conducts a due process analysis by using a totality of the circumstances standard. It finds that the initial admission is proper if the individual is warned after and if the person has waived their rights. Fair?

Note that the officers had a warrant for Elstad's arrest. Should that matter? After reading the introductory paragraphs to this case, do you find that the officers were, in fact, interrogating Elstad when he made his admission? Was this a custodial interrogation or simply an "interview" where Elstad was free to leave and not answer questions? Even if he were not free to leave, should the interaction still be characterized as an interview?

REVIEW NOTE ON EDWARDS V. ARIZONA

An individual arrested in Arizona on charges of robbery, burglary, and first-degree murder was informed at the police station of his rights as required by *Miranda v. Arizona*. After initial questioning, the defendant made a request for counsel and the interrogation ceased. The next morning, police officers came to the jail and asked to see the defendant who thereupon informed the detention officer that he did not want to speak to anyone. The guard told him that "he had" to talk and took him to meet the officers. They again informed him of his *Miranda* rights, and the defendant thereupon implicated himself in the crime. Prior to trial, the defendant moved to suppress his confession on the ground that his *Miranda* rights had been violated when the officers returned to question him after he had invoked his right to counsel. The trial court denied the motion, stating that the defendant's statement was voluntary, and he was subsequently convicted. On appeal, the Supreme Court of Arizona held that the defendant had invoked both his right to remain silent and his right to counsel during the first interrogation, but that he had waived both rights during the second meeting when he voluntarily gave his statements to the officers after again being informed that he need not answer questions and that he need not answer without the advice of counsel. Proper waiver?

On certiorari, the United States Supreme Court reversed. The Court held that the admission at the defendant's trial of the confession obtained from him in the second custodial interrogation after he had been advised of his *Miranda* rights and invoked his right to consult counsel before further interrogation violated his Fifth and Fourteenth Amendment right to have counsel present during custodial interrogation, the defendant not having validly waived that right at the second interrogation, where (1) the police officers conducting the first interrogation ceased interrogation when the defendant requested counsel, (2) the police returned to him the next day without making counsel available to him and without the defendant having suggested or requested the meeting, (3) the defendant informed the detention officer that he did not want to talk to anyone, but the guard told him "that he had to talk," and (4) at the meeting, after the officers told the defendant that they wanted to talk to him and again advised him of his *Miranda* rights, he stated that he would talk and made the incriminating statement used against him at trial. *Edwards v. Arizona*, 451 U.S. 477 (1981).

REVIEW NOTE ON ILLINOIS V. PERKINS

In November 1984, Richard Stephenson was murdered in a suburb of East St. Louis, Illinois. The murder remained unsolved until March 1986, when one Donald Charlton told police that he had learned about a homicide from a fellow inmate at the Graham Correctional Facility, where Charlton had been serving a sentence for burglary. The fellow inmate was Lloyd Perkins, who is the respondent here. Charlton told police that, while at Graham, he had befriended respondent, who told him in detail about a murder that respondent had committed in East St. Louis. On hearing Charlton's account, the police recognized details of the Stephenson murder that were not well known, and so they treated Charlton's story as a credible one.

By the time the police heard Charlton's account, respondent had been released from Graham, but police traced him to a jail in Montgomery County, Illinois, where he was being held pending trial on a charge of aggravated battery, unrelated to the Stephenson murder. The police wanted to investigate further respondent's connection to the Stephenson murder, but feared that the use of an eavesdropping device would prove impracticable and unsafe. They decided instead to place an undercover agent in the cellblock with respondent and Charlton. The plan was for Charlton and undercover agent John Parisi to pose as escapees from a work release program who had been arrested in the course of a burglary. Parisi and Charlton were instructed to engage respondent in casual conversation and report anything he said about the Stephenson murder.

Parisi, using the alias "Vito Bianco," and Charlton, both clothed in jail garb, were placed in the cellblock with respondent at the Montgomery County jail. The cellblock consisted of 12 separate cells that opened onto a common room. Respondent greeted Charlton who, after a brief conversation with respondent, introduced Parisi by his alias. Parisi told respondent that he "wasn't going to do any more time," and suggested that the three of them escape. Respondent replied that the Montgomery County jail was "rinky-dink" and that they could "break out." The trio met in respondent's cell later that evening, after the other inmates were asleep, to refine their plan. Respondent said that his girlfriend could smuggle in a pistol. Charlton said "Hey, I'm not a murderer, I'm a burglar. That's your guys' profession." After telling Charlton that he would be responsible for any murder that occurred, Parisi asked respondent if he had ever "done" anybody. Respondent said that he had, and proceeded to describe at length the events of the Stephenson murder. Parisi and respondent then engaged in some casual conversation before respondent went to sleep. Parisi did not give respondent *Miranda* warnings before the conversations.

Respondent was charged with the Stephenson murder. Before trial, he moved to suppress the statements made to Parisi in the jail. The trial court granted the motion to suppress, and the state appealed. The Appellate Court of Illinois affirmed, holding that *Miranda v. Arizona*, prohibits all undercover contacts with incarcerated suspects which are reasonably likely to elicit an incriminating response.

The United States Supreme Court reversed. *Miranda* forbids coercion, but mere strategic deception by taking advantage of a suspect's misplaced trust in one he supposes to be a fellow prisoner. *Miranda* was not meant to protect suspects from boasting about their criminal activities in front of persons whom they believe to be their cellmates.

In an opinion by Justice Kennedy, the majority held that (1) under the Federal Constitution's Fifth Amendment privilege against self-incrimination, *Miranda* warnings are not required when a suspect is unaware that the suspect is speaking to a law enforcement officer and gives a voluntary statement; (2) an undercover law enforcement officer posing as a fellow inmate is not required to give *Miranda* warnings to an incarcerated suspect before the officer asks questions that may elicit an incriminating response, because the interests protected by *Miranda* are not implicated in such circumstances, in which there is no interaction between custody and official interrogation; and (3) thus, there was no federal obstacle to the admissibility of the statements in the instant case, in which (a) the suspect had been motivated solely by his desire to impress his fellow inmates, (b) the suspect had had no reason to feel that the undercover agent had any legal authority to force the suspect to answer questions or that the agent could affect the suspect's future treatment, (c) the suspect had viewed the cellmate-agent as an equal and had showed no hint of being intimidated by the atmosphere of the jail, and (d) precedents as to restrictions, under the Constitution's Sixth Amendment right to counsel, on the use of undercover agents were not applicable, since, at the time the statements had been made, no charges had been filed on the subject of the interrogation.

Justice Brennan concurred and expressed the view that (1) although he did not subscribe to the court's characterization of *Miranda v. Arizona* in its entirety, he agreed that, when a suspect does not know that his questioner is a police agent, such questioning does not amount to interrogation in an inherently coercive environment so as to require the application of *Miranda*; but (2) if the suspect in the case at hand had previously invoked his *Miranda* rights with respect to the unrelated charge, the suspect might be able to challenge the admissibility of the statements; (3) if the suspect had been formally charged on the unrelated charge and had invoked his right to counsel, the suspect might have a challenge to the admissibility of the statements under the Sixth Amendment; and (4) the deception and manipulation practiced on the suspect raised a substantial claim, which it was open to the lower court on remand to determine, as to whether the confession had been obtained in violation of the due process clause of the Constitution's Fourteenth Amendment.

Justice Marshall dissented and argued that (1) the suspect's confession was inadmissible, because the suspect had received no *Miranda* warnings before the suspect had been subjected to custodial interrogation, since (a) the compulsion proscribed by *Miranda* includes deception by the police, for the pressures unique to custody allow the police to use deceptive interrogation tactics to compel a suspect to make an incriminating statement, and (b) such compulsion is not eliminated by the suspect's ignorance of the interrogator's true identity; and (2) the court's adoption of an "undercover agent" exception to the *Miranda* doctrine (a) was incompatible with the principle that the *Miranda* doctrine should remain simple and clear, and (b) established a substantial loophole in the jurisprudence protecting suspects' Fifth Amendment rights. *Illinois v. Perkins*, 496 U.S. 292 (1990).

FINAL NOTE ON MIRANDA'S PROMISE

Fifth Amendment law is still evolving. Many of the cases we have reviewed revealed that the Supreme Court decisions continue to chip away at *Miranda*'s protections. There are many other examples. Police need not give the warnings when doing so would pose a threat to public safety because, for example, a suspect's silence might prevent police from discovering a dangerous weapon. *New York v. Quarles*, 467

U.S. 649 (1984). Likewise, although questioning must cease when the suspect asserts the right to counsel, if the defendant who has invoked that right reinitiates conversation – a concept the Court has defined broadly – the police may continue questioning him. *Edwards v. Arizona*, 451 U.S. 477 (1981). Moreover, if the suspect merely asserts his right to remain silent (as opposed to his right to counsel), police probably need not wait for the defendant to reinitiate conversation, so long as there is a reasonable interval between interrogations and they rewarn him. *Michigan v. Mosley*, 423 U.S. 96 (1975). The Court also has sanctioned several forms of trickery after the warnings are given. For instance, on two occasions the Court held valid a confession given by a suspect who apparently thought that so long as his statements were not reduced to writing they could not be used against him, a misimpression the police failed to correct. *North Carolina v. Butler*, 441 U.S. 369 (1979); *Connecticut v. Barrett*, 479 U.S. 523 (1987). In another case, the Court upheld the confession of a suspect who was misinformed about the subject matter of the investigation. *Colorado v. Spring*, 479 U.S. 564 (1987). The Court has also refused to exclude confessions obtained after police lied about finding fingerprints at the scene of the crime, *Oregon v. Mathiason*, 429 U.S. 492 (1977), after they falsely told the suspect that his colleague had already confessed to the crime, *Frazier v. Cupp*, 394 U.S. 731 (1969), and after they deceived the defendant's attorney about when interrogation would take place. *Moran v. Burbine*, 475 U.S. 412 (1986). In addition, a confession obtained by an undercover agent, even one posing as a cellmate, does not violate *Miranda*. *Illinois v. Perkins*, 496 U.S. 292 (1990). In each case, the Supreme Court reasoned that the police action was insufficiently coercive to violate the Fifth Amendment prohibition against compelled testimony. Finally, the Court has narrowed the scope of exclusion after a *Miranda* violation. Although a statement obtained by an unwarned suspect must be excluded from the prosecution's case-in-chief, the Court has not required exclusion of evidence obtained as a result of such a statement (e.g., a witness identified in the statement, or another confession given under the impression that the unwarned statement "let the cat out of the bag"). *Oregon v. Elstad*, 470 U.S. 298 (1985). Furthermore, even a statement obtained in violation of *Miranda* is admissible for impeachment purposes. *Harris v. New York*, 401 U.S. 222, 226 (1971). Likewise, officers may also question "outside of *Miranda*" (continue questioning after the individual has invoked his right to remain silent or to have an attorney). As long as officers avoid overbearing tactics that offend Fourteenth Amendment due process (but still outside of *Miranda*), the statements may be used: (a) to impeach a defendant; (b) as a basis for obtaining physical evidence; and (c) for other investigative purposes, such as locating contraband, locating the crime scene, identifying co-suspects, locating witnesses, clearing cases in order to re-prioritize investigative time, and putting to rest community fears. Charles D. Weisselberg, Saving *Miranda*, 84 Cornell L. Rev. 109 (1998). What do you make of these developments?

PART II:
DETERMINING DEFENDANTS' GUILT OR INNOCENCE

Chapter 6

BARGAINING WITH DEFENDANTS

INTRODUCTION

Negotiated pleas now replace convictions obtained through trials by juries and judges. In the federal system, the proportion of convictions obtained through pleas has reached 95%, and has been climbing steadily for over 30 years.[1] In state systems, guilty pleas now account for 94% of felony convictions since the late 1990s.[2] These are rather remarkable findings. For our purposes, these findings are important for three reasons.

The significance of negotiated pleas relates to their impact on defendants' rights. Under the process of plea bargaining, defendants agree to waive their constitutional right to trial and plead guilty in exchange for discretionary consideration on the part of the government.[3] The bargaining process involves negotiations between defense counsel and the prosecution regarding the conditions under which the defendant will enter a plea of guilty or *nolo contendere*.[4] As with the other areas we have studied, conferring discretion to attorneys and judicial officials raises many important issues. Most notably, the conferral of discretion could involve investigating which cases attorneys decide to plea, determining which factors are permissible in making those decisions, and monitoring those decision-making processes. As we will see, this area of law virtually ignores those issues and instead focuses on their outcomes, which involves obtaining judicial approval for the contents of the plea agreement as well as ensuring that at least basic rights were followed in the process that lead to the plea.[5]

The importance of negotiated pleas also relates to the manner by which the system bestows such discretion to bargain on attorneys and state officials. This issue differs from the first in that the first focuses on the discretion itself while this issue centers on the process by which the legal system confers that discretion in the first place. The concern that arises from this process involves the manner and extent to

---

[1] Ronald Wright and Marc Miller, The screening/bargaining tradeoff, 55 Stan. L. Rev. 29 (2002).

[2] Bureau of Justice Statistics, U.S. Dep't of Justice, Felony Sentences in State Courts, 1998 (2001).

[3] By waiving those rights, of course, they also essentially forfeit the right to assert legal claims pertaining to events that occurred prior to the plea. Defendants are not barred from challenging the plea itself, but the general rule is that they cannot claim violations that occurred prior to the guilty plea even if the violation would have barred conviction had the defendant chosen to go to trial. See *McMann v. Richardson*, 397 U.S. 759 (1970). When a defendant pleads guilty, he does so under the law then existing and takes the risk of ordinary errors in his attorney's assessment of laws and facts. As we will see, that general rule raises a few exceptions, such as those relating to incompetent attorneys.

[4] A *nolo* plea is a plea of no contest. Although it is not an admission of guilt, it essentially has the same legal result as a guilty plea. Note too that a defendant may also plea a conditional plea, which permits the defendant to appeal a specific issue that otherwise would be lost by a plea of guilty. A successful appeal would then allow the defendant to withdraw the guilty plea.

[5] The basic constitutional safeguards include effective representation by counsel, or waiver of that right, and the requirement that the waiver of trial rights be competent, knowing (intelligent) and voluntary. See *Parke v. Raley*, 506 U.S. 20, 28-29 (1992) and *Godinez v. Moran*, 509 U.S. 389 (1993). Likewise, there must be a factual basis for the plea. *North Carolina v. Alford*, 400 U.S. 25 (1970).

which offenders can waive fundamental trial rights in a context potentially fraught with inappropriate coercion. We already have seen in previous chapters the immense literature on social coercion, especially subtle coercion that the legal system fails to consider as much as it could. One of the general themes that we have seen relates to the problem criminal justice processes have in considering subtle (and sometimes even overt) coercion. Negotiated pleas similarly attempt to address these concerns, and part of our task centers on determining how effectively the law does address those concerns and to evaluate the reasonableness of those efforts.

Negotiated bargains also are important for us to consider because of the pervasive failure of psychological sciences to examine them. That the legal system settles the vast majority of criminal cases in this fashion makes it peculiar that psychological sciences virtually have ignored this decision point in criminal justice processes. That failure of psychological sciences, with a few notable exceptions, to focus on this area of law makes us center on the justifications for bargaining. An examination of justifications will help us understand why psychological sciences have tended to focus on other areas of criminal adjudication. In addition, a focus on those justifications will help us to consider how this area of law potentially offers meaningful but largely neglected roles for psychological sciences.

JUSTIFYING BARGAINS

The critical factor to understand about bargaining involves the power and limits of proving guilt. Whether defendants actually have committed the crimes charged does not necessarily impact the strength of the government's case against defendants. The strength of prosecution rests on the government's evidence to prove that defendants did commit the crimes. As a result, trials carry significant risks for both the prosecution and the defendant, but they also provide potential benefits for them as well as the court system. These factors involving risks associated with costs and benefits serve to justify the use of bargains.[6]

Both prosecutors and defendants potentially have an enormous stake in plea bargaining. Bargaining fundamentally responds to the significant public and private expense of trials. Both prosecutors and public defenders, for example, generally operate on set budgets, which can be significantly strained by the preparation for and presentation of cases at trial. Given these practical restraints, key players have an interest in resolving disputes, under appropriate circumstances, as early in the process as possible. In addition to producing similar motives, bargaining may serve different interests for prosecutors and defendants. A prosecutor may be faced with issues affecting the substance or admissibility of evidence. This may occur, for example, when evidence is obtained by illegal or constitutionally impermissible means, such as through a coerced or otherwise infirm confession or an improper search or seizure. In addition, trials always carry the risk of acquittals, which in turn may result in a loss of the prosecutor's credibility and hold political consequences, particularly when prosecutors are elected or work for elected officials. For most defendants, the principal benefit of plea bargaining takes the form of a lighter sentence for a less severe charge than might result from taking the case to trial and losing. For some it may mean that they obtain immediate release from jail following the judge's acceptance of a plea. It may also mean that some will have fewer or less serious offenses on their record. Bargaining may also appeal to those who do not want to have socially stigmatizing offenses on their records or who want to avoid publicity or keep others out of the case.[7] In addition, trials may result in convictions on one or more charges arising out of the same

---

[6] For a more in-depth account and analysis of this and the next section of this introduction, see Stephen J. Schulhofer, Plea bargaining as disaster, 101 Yale L.J. 1979 (1992); Robert E. Scott and William J. Stuntz, Plea bargaining as contract, 101 Yale L.J. 1909 (1992); Douglas D. Guidorizzi, Should we really "ban" plea bargaining?: The core concerns of plea bargaining critics, 47 Emory L.J. 753 (1998); Stephanos Bibas, Judicial fact-finding and sentence enhancements in a world of guilty-pleas, 110 Yale L.J. 1097 (2001); Fred C. Zacharias, Justice in plea bargaining, 39 Wm. and Mary L. Rev. 1121 (1998); and George Fisher, Plea bargaining's triumph, 109 Yale L.J. 857 (2000).

[7] Note, in this regard, that going to trial and winning (being acquitted) simply means that the prosecution failed to prove the defendant's guilt beyond a reasonable doubt by following constitutional mandates. It does not necessarily mean that they

transaction and may also result in the presentation of evidence of aggravating factors that may affect sentencing. Negotiated plea bargaining, then, obviates the need for trial and concomitant expenses, relieves uncertainty, and gives the parties greater control over the resulting disposition.

Although often ignored, courts also have an interest in aggressive plea negotiations. Courts typically are not party to the actual negotiations themselves. However, courts encourage the early and expeditious resolution of the criminal process as they accept plea bargains and take seriously stipulated sentencing negotiations. The argument is that early resolution helps ease the strain on over-scheduled dockets and preserves public funds that would otherwise be expended in jury trials. In addition, plea bargaining permits a prompt resolution of criminal proceedings with all the benefits that result from final dispositions, such as avoiding delays and the uncertainties of trial and appeal. These arguments all support the view that pleas promote judicial efficiency.

Plea bargaining also has been justified on the grounds that it promotes the greater public good as it permits the system to act more equitably. It may do so in many ways. Bargaining may be more equitable, for example, insofar as rigid sentencing guidelines may fail to account for a defendant's particular circumstances. Bargaining also may protect the public from those accused persons who are prone to continue criminal conduct even while on pretrial release. Bargaining also potentially serves the greater good by allowing the government to prosecute higher-level criminals where such prosecution would not be possible without the information or testimony of the cooperating defendant. Lastly, bargaining may avoid much of the corrosive impact of enforced idleness during pretrial confinement for those denied pretrial release. These reasons help justify plea bargaining systems and complement justifications based on the practical necessity of conserving judicial, prosecutorial, and law enforcement resources.

Challenging Justifications Supporting Bargains

Although bargains may be viewed as win-win procedures for all participants, they are not without controversy. Arguably the most important challenge to the justifications for plea bargaining deals with the manner the system presupposes fairness in securing the agreement. That concern centers on promises made to defendants that lead to guilty pleas and on the general voluntariness of bargains. The extent to which these issues are properly addressed retains considerable significance to the extent that guilty pleas constitute a waiver of defendants' important Fifth Amendment right not to incriminate themselves and Sixth Amendment right to a trial in which the government must prove guilt beyond a reasonable doubt. In addition to bargaining the specifics of their cases, then, all defendants who accept bargains waive fundamental trial rights. The challenges to bargaining focus on that waiver, especially in terms of its importance to particular defendants, the criminal justice system, and society.

The Relative Coerciveness of Bargains

The accepted view that bargains present good options for defendants makes it difficult to recognize the potential coerciveness of bargains. Important justifications for some level of coercion certainly exist, as we have seen above and throughout the previous chapters. Despite justifications for some type of coercion, coercion may still exist enough to be problematic in practice. For our purposes, understanding that concern involves three different analyses. The first involves whether the legal system does in fact allow coercion, whether subtle or blatant. The second involves the fear that innocent individuals may plead guilty due to the inherent coerciveness of plea agreements. The third concerns whether those who actually are guilty also inappropriately may be coerced by fear that they will be punished more severely if they proceed with trial.

---

were found actually innocent. See Andrew D. Leipold, The problem of the innocent, acquitted defendant, 94 Nw. U.L. Rev. 1297 (2000).

To understand how the legal system approaches issues of voluntariness, compare the features of plea bargaining in criminal law to those of contracts in civil law transactions. Both require that offers are made and accepted, that entitlements are given up and obtained, and that both parties receive a fair exchange. Both also require voluntary acceptance of offers. Contract law views negotiations under duress as clearly unfair and, for that reason, typically as void. Plea bargains have a higher standard for determining voluntariness to plead. Viewed from a contractual perspective, plea bargains could be seen as inappropriately made under duress. That line of argument suggests that those bargains are void because too much coercion removes free choice and voluntariness. The difference in standards for determining involuntariness is seen as especially problematic because plea bargaining involves the criminal justice system, which typically uses greater care to scrutinize the role of the state in infringing someone's rights.

To understand the analogy between criminal and civil bargains and the fundamental difference between them, consider the paradigmatic example of unfair agreements made at gunpoint. Such scenarios typically involve thieves who threaten to shoot someone unless they give them their money. Although a reasonable person may readily agree to hand over their money, the rules of duress would void the effects of such agreements. Although the analogy is not perfect, it reveals the possible upper-hand prosecutors may have and similarly apply duress to the defendant. The duress may not always come in the form of a threat of death, via the death penalty, but at least in the form of a more harsh sentence than a plea bargain would receive. Both the gunman and the prosecutor require persons to make hard and unfair choices between a very certain smaller imposition and an uncertain greater imposition. Some commentators argue that, since duress makes the gunman transaction unfair, it should follow that the plea bargain also is unfair.[8] Given that we retain the constitutional right to a jury trial, unless we waive it, it often is counter-argued that duress is absent in plea bargains since individuals retain the option to go to trial. The argument further supposes that prosecutorial threats, such as to seek the death penalty, are valid and justified when juries could find defendants guilty as charged. Those two counter-arguments, in turn, are rebutted by the extent to which a judge would not allow such potentially unbalanced negotiating in contract law, which makes it peculiar that they would take an active part in approving it in criminal law. Whether or not one concludes that the criminal justice system acts appropriately, it seems difficult to escape the reality that defendants can face enormous pressure to negotiate a bargain.

The concern that bargaining tips the balance of power in favor of prosecutors raises the issue of whether the pressures of law enforcement can overbear the will of innocent defendants who see no alternative but to plead guilty. We do know that the possibility exists. Some defendants plead guilty even though they have committed no crime, or have committed some crime less serious or substantially different from the one charged.[9] We already have seen in previous chapters the distinct possibility that some individuals are indeed innocent.[10] One might explain such bargains on grounds that the defense attorney cannot perfectly represent the interest of the defendant. However, a lawyer may be representing her client perfectly when she advises him to plead guilty even in the face of assertions of innocence. The evidence simply may be overwhelming in the face of the inability to refute it. Courts openly recognize such a dilemma to the extent that they allow defendants to plead guilty without admitting guilt, a procedure known as *Alford* pleas.[11] Importantly, as with any other plea, the legal system does not take such pleas lightly: The leading opinion on this matter revealed the Court's own struggle with the concept as it required courts to scrutinize the evidence closely to find a "strong factual basis" to support the defendant's plea.[12] Despite

---

[8] See Kenneth Kipnis, Criminal justice and the negotiated plea, in Controversies in Criminal Law 245 (Michael J. Gorr and Sterling Harwood, eds., 1992).

[9] Michael O. Finkelstein, A statistical analysis of guilty plea practices in federal courts, 89 Harv. L. Rev. 293, 309-10 (1975).

[10] See also Richard A. Leo and Richard J. Ofshe, The truth about false confessions and advocacy scholarship, 37 Crim. L. Bull. 293 (2001).

[11] North Carolina v. Alford, 400 U.S. 25 (1970).

[12] North Carolina v. Alford, 400 U.S. 25, 37-38 (1970). What this means is that, even if all other constitutional standards are met, a defendant does not necessarily have a federal constitutional right to forego a criminal trial by pleading guilty. The Court in Alford noted that "a criminal defendant does not have an absolute right under the Constitution to have his guilty plea accepted by the court, ... although the States may by statute or otherwise confer such a right." Id. at 38, n.1. The

these protections, however, the reality remains that the legal system sanctions guilty pleas by innocent defendants.[13]

Related to concerns of coercion is the issue regarding whether defendants actually are punished if they choose trials because sentences would likely be longer if they did not plead. The logic of the plea bargain opens itself to the following question and criticism: Is a defendant who elects to stand trial, rather than plead guilty in expectation of a more lenient sentence, being punished more severely, if found to be guilty, for having exercised his constitutional right to trial by jury? Trial convictions of crimes generally receive much longer sentences than their plea bargained counterparts.[14] Studies frequently find shorter sentences for convictions based on plea bargains.[15] And those differences can be far from trivial. In a comprehensive analysis of imprisonment for rape, for example, the method of conviction affected both the probability of receiving a prison sentence and the term of imprisonment for rape. Defendants convicted by a jury were substantially more likely to receive a prison term than those convicted by bench trials or by plea, and the term was substantially longer.[16] The average prison term for rape following a jury conviction is nearly 13 years longer than the average sentence received by those pleading guilty to rape: 292 months for jury trials; 173 months for bench trials; and 139 months for guilty pleas. The chances of getting a prison term also increased with the method of convictions: 89% of jury trials; 71% of bench trials; and 63% of guilty pleas resulted in sentences. Although it may be difficult to evaluate results from pleas and those from trials, the evidence has been interpreted as suggesting that defendants do get considerable discounts for waiving their rights.

The most robust support for the claim that people may be punished for exercising their rights comes from the federal system. The U.S. Sentencing Commission assessed plea discounts in the federal system to be about one third of the sentence before the implementation of new sentencing guidelines in the 1980s; as a result, it actually instituted a similar discount for pleading guilty in the sentencing guideline system.[17] Research, however, remains complicated and sometimes inconsistent. While it is true that in most cases defendants receive stronger sentences when convicted by jury trials than those that are plea bargained, it may not follow that they are being punished more severely for going to trial. A National Institute of Justice report on plea bargaining found that several studies suggest that tried defendants are punished more severely than pleaders but most of these studies have not controlled for variables which might account for both the fact that the case went to trial and the fact that it was sentenced more severely. Equally importantly, the evaluation reported a few studies which had controlled such confounding variables and had found that the mere fact of going to trial did not account for the sentence difference.[18] Many factors may explain the failure to find differences. It is true that judges may not overstep what penalty ranges are for the charges supporting conviction, but the reality increasingly seems to be that plea bargaining deals with the nature of charges and also may involve pleading to certain facts of cases, such as pleading to cocaine rather than crack cocaine which would bring a longer sentence.[19] Bargains that include bargaining

---

Court did not address in that case, nor any one since then, whether a trial judge's discretion to reject a plea is subject to constitutional restrictions.

[13] As we will see, for example, the legal system sets up procedures to ensure that defendants understand the significance of their actions and requests defendants to assert that they were not coerced, which leaves the conclusion that the decision was made under their own free will. That assumption and conclusion is viewed as problematic by those who view such pleas as inherently coercive.

[14] Surveys of judges support those findings. A highly cited study, for example, reported that "87 per cent of the judges who acknowledged that the plea was [a relevant factor in sentencing] indicated that a defendant pleading guilty to a crime was given a more lenient punishment than a defendant who pleaded not guilty." Comment, The influence of the defendant's plea on judicial determination of sentence, 66 Yale L.J. 204, 206-07 (1956).

[15] J. Fred Springer, Burglary and robbery plea bargaining in California: An organizational perspective, 8 Jus. Sys. J. 157, 168-71 (1983).

[16] Lawrence A. Greenfeld, Sex Offenses and Offenders: An Analysis of Data on Rape and Sexual Assault, Bureau of Justice Statistics, Office of Justice Programs, U.S. Department of Justice, NCJ-163392(revised 2/7/97) (1997).

[17] U.S. Sentencing Comm'n, Supplementary Report on the Initial Sentencing Guidelines and Policy Statements (1987).

[18] William F. McDonald, Plea Bargaining: Critical Issues and Common Practices. National Institute of Justice (1982).

[19] Ilene H. Nagel and Stephen J. Schulhofer, A tale of three cities: An empirical study of charging and bargaining practices under the federal sentencing guidelines, 66 S. Cal. L. Rev. 501 (1992).

facts make the process difficult to evaluate for the simple reason that we may not know the actual crime that can serve as a comparison point.

Systemic Concerns

Beyond issues of coercion, one of the most important sets of concerns about plea bargaining involves the extent to which the system may be perpetuating systemic injustice. The system may do so by punishing those who do not deserve to be punished or, in the alternative, by not punishing those who do deserve punishment to the extent fitting their crime. Relatedly, systemic concerns involve the potential differential impact of bargaining on vulnerable groups, including victims who may have preferred trials and more aggressive punishments in particular cases.

A fundamental concern involves the extent to which plea bargaining forces economically disadvantaged defendants to plead guilty to a charge that they otherwise would not have. Impoverished defendants who cannot finance a lengthy criminal trial may be forced to agree to plead guilty to a lesser charge because they cannot afford the process of forcing the state to prove guilt. Important counter-arguments often are made to this charge. For example, we know that everyone is entitled to counsel, even if at public expense. Although public defenders may be viewed as less effective than privately-hired counsel, evidence actually does not support that ill reputation. For example, a National Center for State Courts study found that public defenders actually were as good as paid counsel at meeting the standards of timeliness and performance without sacrificing their clients' interests. The conviction rates of defendants represented by public defenders, assigned counsel, contract attorneys, and privately retained counsel revealed "no statistically significant differences". The research also revealed little difference in the guilty plea rate between publicly appointed counsel, at 76 percent, and privately retained counsel, at 69 percent.[20] Interestingly, federal public defenders have been found to be more knowledgeable, and by implication more effective, than private defense attorneys.[21] Given adequate resources, public appointed attorneys do as well as retained attorneys when representing clients in felony cases. Importantly, however, the research does not address how the use of private or public counsel impacts the nature of punishments or other legal sanctions. And, again, it is difficult to compare cases without knowing more about the relevant crimes themselves

The system also may be unjust to the extent that the offense of conviction does not match either the charges the state filed or the reality of the offender's behavior.[22] The argument is that the public in general, and victims in particular, lose faith in a system with a primary goal of processing and a secondary goal of justice. The argument is that the public doubts that justice has been done when the sanction in a negotiated plea case does not match the actual behavior. Another concern is that defense attorneys in systems driven by bargains believe that they must convince most of their clients – even innocent defendants – to accept lesser punishments to avoid a substantial risk of much greater punishment. Although these concerns could be taken as powerful arguments for the unjustness of the outcomes of plea bargains, it is important to note that the trial process itself is not without its problems and it too often ends up finding guilt for charges lower than the highest charged; and no research has comprehensively compared both ways of determining legal guilt.

A third claim about the effects of plea bargaining considers the impact of improper prosecutorial motives for discounting charges. A potentially suspect practice involves overcharging by prosecutors – the filing of charges with the expectation that defendants will trade excess charges for a guilty plea. The line

---

[20] Roger Hanson and Brian Ostrom, Litigation and the courts: Myths and misconceptions, 29 Trial 40 (April 1993).

[21] Ilene H. Nagel and Stephen J. Schulhofer, A tale of three cities: An empirical study of charging and bargaining practices under the federal sentencing guidelines, 66 S. Cal. L. Rev. 501 (1992).

prosecutor might charge or settle cases selectively, giving unduly generous treatment to some defendants but not to other similar defendants. Problems may arise, for example, when this selective treatment could be based on factors such as conscious or unconscious race or gender bias.[23] Available evidence does suggest biases, or at least significant differences in results. Black offenders are less likely to resolve their cases through plea bargaining than whites.[24] And estimates reveal a higher plea bargaining rate for women (97 percent) than men (92 percent).[25] Numerous studies have focused on the effects of extralegal defendant characteristics on sentence outcomes and have produced important findings establishing a relationship between a defendant's gender, ethnicity, and sentence outcomes. A series of studies of federal sentencing guidelines found important sex differences: only male defendants receive a significant reduction in sentence length due to pleading guilty; female defendants who pled guilty, rather than pursuing a trial, do not experience a significant sentence reduction.[26] A highly cited study of determinant sentencing in California found that the effects on sentence severity of type of offense, mode of disposition, and the defendant's prior record were conditioned by a defendant's ethnicity. The study further found that the effect of prior record of convictions and mode of disposition resulted in significantly more severe punishment for Chicano defendants compared with white defendants. Furthermore, it found that pleading guilty produced a significantly shorter sentence for black defendants than for Chicano defendants.[27] It is unclear whether these findings transfer to other jurisdictions, but they at least do support the claim that bargaining may involve suspect factors that may evade detection.

Another issue is that plea bargaining systems create resentment among the public, police, and crime victims. Many note that, for each of these groups, plea bargains create disappointment and a sense of helplessness.[28] The problem can arise when the prosecutor sets expectations through the initial charges. After reducing and dropping charges during negotiations, the prosecutor actually need not explain why the public, along with the investigators and the victims of the alleged crime, should accept something less than originally announced.[29] The prosecutor also may agree to punishments that the public has not authorized by law, given that pleas may involve stipulating to certain facts and ignoring others. The public also may lose confidence in the system of criminal justice when it appears that some innocent defendants are pleading guilty.[30] Furthermore, the public might mistrust a criminal justice process that allows a defendant to waive procedures that are considered the bare minimum for a civilized system of justice.[31]

A final concern deals with the manner the process remains largely inaccessible. The bargaining process essentially remains closed to review or evaluation. Only the final product of each negotiation is reported on paper and in the courtroom. Negotiations may turn on a range of factors going well beyond the

---

[22] Albert W. Alschuler, The prosecutor's role in plea bargaining, 36 U. Chi. L. Rev. 50, 85-105 (1968).

[23] Developments in the law – Race and the criminal process, 101 Harv. L. Rev. 1473, 1520-57 (1988); Angela J. Davis, The American prosecutor: Independence, power, and the threat of tyranny, 86 Iowa L. Rev. 393 (2001); Dwight L. Greene, Abusive prosecutors: Gender, race and class discretion and the prosecution of drug-addicted mothers, 39 Buff. L. Rev. 737 (1991); and Richard H. McAdams, Race and selective prosecution: Discovering the pitfalls of *Armstrong*, 73 Chi.-Kent L. Rev. 605 (1998).

[24] Marjorie S. Zats, The changing forms of racial/ethnic biases in sentencing, 24 J. of Res. in Crime and Delinq. 69 (1987).

[25] Kathleen Daly, Gender, Crime, and Punishment (1994).

[26] See Celesta A. Albonetti, The joint conditioning effect of defendant's gender and ethnicity on length of imprisonment under the federal sentencing guidelines for drug trafficking/manufacturing offenders, 6 J. Gender Race and Just 39 (2002).

[27] Marjorie S. Zatz, Race, ethnicity, and determinate sentencing: A new dimension to an old controversy, 22 Criminology 147 (1984).

[28] Alan F. Arcuri, Police perceptions of plea bargaining: A preliminary inquiry, 1 J. Police Sci. and Admin. 93, 100-01 (1973); and Markus Dirk Dubber, American plea bargains, German lay judges, and the crisis of criminal procedure, 49 Stan. L. Rev. 547, 591-97 (1997).

[29] But the better practice would be to explain. See John Kaplan, American merchandising and the guilty plea: Replacing the bazaar with the department store, 5 Am. J. Crim. L. 215, 218 (1977).

[30] Abraham S. Goldstein, The Passive Judiciary: Prosecutorial Discretion and the Guilty Plea 44-45 (1981); and Abraham S. Goldstein, Converging criminal justice systems: Guilty pleas and the public interest, 49 S.M.U. L. Rev. 567, 573-75 (1996).

[31] The reality, of course, is that the last two factors may not weigh heavily on the public's mind; but we will see how the legal system necessarily considers these possibilities to ensure greater compliance with legal mandates; see Chapter 11 which deals with treatment and crime prevention.

elements of the offense and the strength of the government's evidence. Some of these factors may be appropriate, others inappropriate, but only the parties themselves ever know the actual factors that determined the outcome of the public proceeding. This has lead commentators to argue that the clearest effect of plea bargains on trial judges is to marginalize them.[32] Judges have little voice in traditional plea bargains. In fact, for example, the federal rules of criminal procedure prohibit judicial participation in plea agreement discussions.[33] Even after negotiations, as we will see, the judge's role remains quite limited.

PSYCHOLOGICAL SCIENCE'S ROLE

The psychological sciences have not examined bargaining between defendants and the state as much as we would have expected given the high use of plea bargaining to dispose of cases. That is not to say that psychological findings are irrelevant. Much of the literature we have reviewed dealing with coercion, for example, would seem applicable to this context. In addition, the literature on decision making we have reviewed and will explore more deeply in the chapters that follow would seem appropriate. Likewise, the literature on evaluating competency to waive the right to trial will be an area we will explore in chapters that follow. For now, it is important to address two areas of research that have received attention.

The first area of research derives from field studies and experiments that attempt to understand the psychological rules people use when making decisions in situations analogous to bargaining. To be sure, it is difficult to simulate protracted negotiations with real life concerns. Psychologists nevertheless seek to identify decision making tendencies. Existing studies actually reveal that individuals readily accept a plea bargain if the conditions are right and in order to cut their losses.[34] This research suggests that individuals simply acquiesce, that defendants typically try to weigh how much time they will need to spend in prison.[35] Contrary to popular beliefs for bargaining, those who bargain do not seem to do so in order to avoid responsibility or repenting for wrong-doing.[36]

The above findings may seem intuitive and not very insightful. But, there would be other possible decision making rules.[37] Defendants could use an optimizing strategy when deciding whether to accept a plea. Optimizing would involve considering several choices of information and choosing the alternatives that lead to the most reward while minimizing costs. In plea bargaining situations, this would mean that the defendant would consider several choices, such as reject or accept, that lead to the most reward and the least punishment. As it turns out, we may be incapable of optimizing. There simply are too many variables that enter into such complex decisions to make a rational decision based on optimizing strategies. In the alternative, individuals may take a "satisficing" strategy. Defendants who adopt this strategy simply take what seems "good enough" when the course of action meets their minimal standard of acceptability.[38] In such cases, defendants tend to adopt a simple rule, such as anything to not go to prison. Simulation studies

---

[32] Ronald Wright and Marc Miller, The screening/bargaining tradeoff, 55 Stan. L. Rev. 29 (2002).

[33] Fed. R. Crim. P. 11(e)(1). Importantly, though, it does seem that judicial participation does still remain extensive in some jurisdictions. See Allen F. Anderson, Judicial participation in the plea negotiation process: Some frequencies and disposing factors, 10 Hampline J. Pub. L. and Pol'y 29 (1990).

[34] Kenneth S. Bordens, The effects of likelihood of conviction, threatened punishment, and assumed role on mock plea bargaining decisions, 5 Basic and Appl. Soc. Psych. 59 (1984).

[35] See Arthur Rosett and Donald R. Cressey, Justice by Consent: Plea Bargains in the American Courthouse (1976).

[36] See Arthur Rosett and Donald R. Cressey, Justice by Consent: Plea Bargains in the American Courthouse (1976).

[37] See Irivin Lester Janis and Leon Mann, Decisionmaking: A Psychological Analysis of Conflict, Choice, and Commitment (1977).

[38] The term actually derives from economics. Herbert Simon identified it as the decision making process whereby one chooses an option that is, while perhaps not the best, good enough. Herbert A. Simon, Administrative Behavior (3rd ed., 1976). Simon himself seemed to have viewed satisficing as the best we can do in the direction of optimizing: "If computational powers were unlimited, a person would simply consult his or her preferences (utility functions) and choose the course of action that would yield the maximum utility under the given circumstances.... But real human beings, of bounded rationality, cannot follow this procedure. Faced with complexity and uncertainty, lacking the wits to optimize, they must be content to satisfice." Herbert A. Simon, Models of Thought 3 (1979).

and research asking actual defendants reveal that defendants, whether guilty or innocent, are likely to plead guilty when there are many charges filed and if the threatened punishment upon conviction was severe.[39] Those findings reveal the use of satisficing strategies.

The second area of research relates to the ability of individuals to understand what they are doing. This involves matters of competency. We will devote an entire chapter to assessing how psychological sciences can contribute to efforts to evaluate competency. For now, the issue is whether those acting in the process actually do recognize that their clients' competencies may be in doubt and what they do with that information. That issue goes to the heart of the concern that the system may be unjustly usurping a defendant's free will and may be increasing the system's capacity to arrogate discretion to itself which could then be misused. One leading study examined attorney-client decision making in order to determine client's participation in over 400 cases, half of which were resolved by trial and the other half of which were resolved by any other legal means. Attorneys doubted the competence of 8-25% of clients charged with felonies and 3-8% of clients charged with misdemeanors. Attorneys viewed clients of doubtful competence as less helpful and as less actively involved in their cases, but as actively involved in making key decisions. Defendants' perceptions accorded with those of the attorneys. Importantly, only 20% of doubtful competence cases were referred for evaluation.[40] These findings reveal important points, the most important of which perhaps is the extent to which the legal system may be setting a high standard, either in law or in practice, for showing incompetence.

NOTES AND QUERIES

Given the arguments justifying plea bargaining and the factors challenging those justifications, what do you make of this approach to adjudicating crime?

What do you make of the findings regarding race and gender differences in plea outcomes? What about evidence questioning the competency of defendants?

If the legal system does recognize that coercion exists, how does the legal system justify it? Is it because it is not coercive enough? What does the psychological evidence reveal on this matter?

In the cases that follow, consider closely the role of judges. Should you find their role limited, how would you increase it? Would increasing judicial scrutiny make a difference? And what would that difference be? Would it do more harm? And what would that harm be? One account suggests that judicial involvement would be too coercive, as in when judges would "suggest" that particular offers are good ones or when the defendant would want to reject suggestions of the judge who will be the one trying the case (e.g., how fair would a judge be if a defendant refused to take his suggestions?). Another account suggests that including judges makes the negotiations more fruitful since judges must accept the pleas' terms or that the inclusion of the judge makes the process more fair since the defendant would know more clearly the judge's view on sentencing options. Which position would you take?

What do you make of the pervasive failure of psychological sciences to explore directly this area of legal processes? Do you attribute it to the fact that the legal justifications make empirical investigations futile and that practicalities necessitate pleas anyway?

Explain the two dominant decision making rules (optimizing and "satisficing") individuals can take when they decide to plea bargain. What do you make of these different approaches. Which approach do you suppose most people adopt when they are making potentially major life-altering decisions, such as choosing a college or career, choosing a spouse, or choose to have children. How "voluntary" do you deem those choices? Suppose the evidence regarding the strategies people adopt when bargaining actually does

[39] Kenneth S. Bordens, The effects of likelihood of conviction, threatened punishment, and assumed role on mock plea bargaining decisions, 5 Basic and Appl. Soc. Psych. 59 (1984); and Kenneth S. Bordens and John Bassett, The plea bargaining process from the defendant's perspective: A field investigation, 6 Basic and Appl. Soc. Psych. 93 (1985).

reflect reality. What implications would follow from such evidence? How much voluntariness could we realistically expect? How much involuntariness should we tolerate?

Admittedly, when evaluating the effectiveness and legitimacy of plea bargaining, the concern becomes what society is willing to tolerate and determine as fair in exchanges between defendants and the state. The hope is that psychological sciences and research could highlight key factors in that exchange and could help us make informed decisions about its fairness. When reading the cases that follow, consider how research could help evaluate justifications for plea bargaining.

PRACTICE NOTES

After a plea agreement has been finalized, the parties present the agreement to the court. The trial judge must decide whether to accept the defendant's guilty plea. Although there are many versions of court colloquies, the Federal Rules of Criminal Procedure's Rule 11 illustrates well the procedures by which courts determine the acceptability of the plea agreement. The rules require that a defendant's guilty plea be made knowingly, intelligently, and voluntarily. In order for a court to perform adequately its required review of the circumstances of a guilty plea, the court asks a number of questions of the defendant during what is commonly referred to as the "plea colloquy." This colloquy occurs in open court in the presence of all parties. When a defendant pleads guilty pursuant to a plea agreement, the court must be informed of the essence of any promises made to the defendant. The court must satisfy itself that no improper or illegal promises have been made to the defendant in order to induce the decision to plead guilty. During the plea colloquy, the court typically attempts to satisfy itself that, *inter alia*, the defendant: (1) is fully aware of, and understands, the nature of the charges against him or her; (2) is aware of the maximum and possible mandatory minimum penalties for the charge or charges to which the defendant is pleading guilty; (3) understands and concurs with all important terms of any plea agreement; (4) understands that the court is not bound by any government sentencing recommendations promised in the plea agreement, and the defendant has no right to withdraw the guilty plea if the court does not accept the sentencing recommendation unless the plea agreement is a special and rare type of agreement valid only if its terms are approved and followed by the court; (5) fully understands and waives his constitutional rights, including the right to be represented by an attorney, the right to persist in a plea of not guilty, and the right to trial by jury, at which the defendant would have the right to assistance of counsel, the right to confront and cross-examine witnesses, and the right against compelled self-incrimination; makes a guilty plea free of force, threats, or any promises apart from any plea agreement; (6) and admits to a factual basis for the guilty plea, that is, the defendant admits to facts that satisfy the elements of the crime or crimes to which the defendant is pleading guilty. The defendant is then typically required to give a factual basis for the plea, or, in the case of a *nolo plea*, the state or the defense attorney may give a factual basis. The court, if it finds the factual basis insufficient to support a finding of guilt, may choose to reject the plea and require the case to be tried. While there is no specific requirement that the court do so, the court may conduct further inquiry into the factual basis with both the prosecutor and the defense attorney in the defendant's presence. The court may ask the defense attorney whether the defense attorney is aware of any defenses that may have been asserted or of any reason why the defendant's guilty plea is not appropriate. The judge may also inform the defendant that, if the sentence imposed is greater than the recommendation, the defendant can withdraw the plea. The option to withdraw is only available when the original plea agreement was tendered on the condition that the judge would accept the sentence recommendation. In most cases, a guilty plea may not be withdrawn.

Given that plea bargains often touch on issues of sentencing, it is important to understand how such sentencing works. The federal guidelines are again illustrative. According to the federal sentencing

---

[40] Norman G. Poythress, Richard J Bonnie, Steven K Hoge, John Monahan, and Lois Oberlander, Client abilities to assist counsel and make decisions in criminal cases: Findings from three studies, 18 L. and Hum. Beh. 437 (1994).

guidelines, judicial discretion is limited by requiring the sentencing judge to follow a "path" to sentencing that begins with the convicted offense from the statutory index. From this determination, the judge is to identify the base offense level, consider (1) any increases to the base offense level due to the defendant's relevant conduct (i.e., the defendant acts as a pilot), (2) any specific offense characteristics (i.e., use of a weapon, the amount of drugs, type of drugs), (3) any applicable adjustments for acceptance of responsibility or substantial assistance to the government, and (4) any special provisions (i.e., defendant's career criminal status). Having determined the final offense level (the base offense level plus enhancements due to defendant's relevant conduct and specific offense characteristics and departure adjustments) and the total number of criminal history points, the judge then locates on the sentencing grid the cell defined by the intersection of these two variables. Importantly, the guidelines ordinarily find irrelevant a defendant's education, age, family ties, employment record, and physical and mental condition (see U.S. Sentencing Commission 1989: Part H). Likewise, the sentencing guidelines explicitly state that defendant characteristics such as gender and ethnicity are legally irrelevant to sentencing outcomes (see U.S. Sentencing Commission 1989: Section 5H1.10).

Given high levels of dissatisfaction with some pleas (such as for drunk-driving, sex offending, etc), important attempts have been made simply to ban plea bargaining, either for targeted crimes or for the entire criminal docket. Although research investigating these experiments report mixed reviews, all agree that the efforts never produced the expected large increases in the trial rate. See Douglas D. Guidorizzi, Should we really "ban" plea bargaining?: The core concerns of plea bargaining critics, 47 Emory L.J. 753 (1998). The experiments demonstrate how negotiations between defense lawyers and prosecutors will persist in some form despite a nominal "ban" on negotiations. The most famous American plea bargaining bans occurred in Alaska during the 1970s and 1980s. In that effort, the attorney general declared that prosecutors would no longer engage in charge bargaining or sentence bargaining in order to restore public confidence in the system. The new policy would also further increase the number of trials, improve the litigation skills of prosecutors, and return prosecutors to their traditional roles of evaluating evidence and trying cases instead of negotiating. Major studies in 1978 and 1991 evaluated the impact of the Alaska plea ban. By all accounts, both charge bargaining and sentence bargaining became rare events during the first ten years of the policy. During the late 1980s, charge bargains reappeared, but prosecutors continued to avoid sentence bargains. For a few years, the trial rate increased modestly. Seven percent of charged cases went to trial before the ban, and the rate moved to 10% before returning to 7% by the end of the 1980s. The ban on negotiated pleas coupled with no major impact on trial rates meant that cases were more aggressively screened and disposed through open guilty pleas (pleas without bargaining). See Teresa White Carns and John Kruse, A re-evaluation of Alaska's plea bargaining ban, 8 Alaska L. Rev. 27, 33-65 (1991); Michael L. Rubinstein and Teresa J. White, Alaska's ban on plea bargaining, 13 L. and Soc'y Rev. 367, 369-78 (1979); Michael L. Rubinstein and Teresa J. White, Plea bargaining: Can Alaska live without it?, 62 Judicature 266, 268-69 (1979); and Teresa White Carns and John A. Kruse, Alaska's ban on plea bargaining reevaluated, 75 Judicature 310, 310-11 (1992).

THE PROSECUTOR'S BARGAINS

BRADY v. U.S.
397 U.S. 742 (1970)

MR. JUSTICE WHITE delivered the opinion of the Court.

In 1959, petitioner was charged with kidnapping in violation of 18 U. S. C. § 1201 (a). Since the indictment charged that the victim of the kidnapping was not liberated unharmed, petitioner faced a maximum penalty of death if the verdict of the jury should so recommend. Petitioner, represented by competent counsel throughout, first elected to plead not guilty. Apparently because the trial judge was unwilling to try the case without a jury, petitioner made no serious attempt to reduce the possibility of a death penalty by waiving a jury trial. Upon learning that his codefendant, who had confessed to the authorities, would plead guilty and be available to testify against him, petitioner changed his plea to guilty. His plea was accepted after the trial judge twice questioned him as to the voluntariness of his plea. Petitioner was sentenced to 50 years' imprisonment, later reduced to 30.

In 1967, petitioner sought relief ... claiming that his plea of guilty was not voluntarily given because § 1201 (a) operated to coerce his plea, because his counsel exerted impermissible pressure upon him, and because his plea was induced by representations with respect to reduction of sentence and clemency. It was also alleged that the trial judge had not fully complied with Rule 11 of the Federal Rules of Criminal Procedure.

After a hearing, the District Court for the District of New Mexico denied relief. According to the District Court's findings, petitioner's counsel did not put impermissible pressure on petitioner to plead guilty and no representations were made with respect to a reduced sentence or clemency. The court held that § 1201 (a) was constitutional and found that petitioner decided to plead guilty when he learned that his codefendant was going to plead guilty: petitioner pleaded guilty "by reason of other matters and not by reason of the statute" or because of any acts of the trial judge. The court concluded that "the plea was voluntarily and knowingly made."

The Court of Appeals for the Tenth Circuit affirmed, determining that the District Court's findings were supported by substantial evidence and specifically approving the finding that petitioner's plea of guilty was voluntary. We granted certiorari ...We affirm.

I.

In United States v. Jackson, the defendants were indicted under § 1201 (a). The District Court dismissed the § 1201 (a) count of the indictment, holding the statute unconstitutional because it permitted imposition of the death sentence only upon a jury's recommendation and thereby made the risk of death the price of a jury trial. This Court held the statute valid, except for the death penalty provision; with respect to the latter, the Court agreed with the trial court "that the death penalty provision . . . imposes an impermissible burden upon the exercise of a constitutional right . . . ." The problem was to determine "whether the Constitution permits the establishment of such a death penalty, applicable only to those defendants who assert the right to contest their guilt before a jury." The inevitable effect of the provision was said to be to discourage assertion of the Fifth Amendment right not to plead guilty and to deter exercise of the Sixth Amendment right to demand a jury trial. Because the legitimate goal of limiting the death penalty to cases in which a jury recommends it could be achieved without penalizing those defendants who plead not guilty and elect a jury trial, the death penalty provision "needlessly penalize[d] the assertion of a constitutional right," and was therefore unconstitutional.

Since the "inevitable effect" of the death penalty provision of § 1201 (a) was said by the Court to be the needless encouragement of pleas of guilty and waivers of jury trial, Brady contends that Jackson requires the invalidation of every plea of guilty entered under that section, at least when the fear of death is shown to have been a factor in the plea. Petitioner, however, has read far too much into the Jackson opinion.

Plainly, it seems to us, Jackson ruled neither that all pleas of guilty encouraged by the fear of a possible death sentence are involuntary pleas nor that such encouraged pleas are invalid whether involuntary or not. Jackson prohibits the imposition of the death penalty under § 1201 (a), but that decision neither fashioned a new standard for judging the validity of guilty pleas nor mandated a new application of the test theretofore fashioned by courts and since reiterated that guilty pleas are valid if both "voluntary" and "intelligent."

That a guilty plea is a grave and solemn act to be accepted only with care and discernment has long been recognized. Central to the plea and the foundation for entering judgment against the defendant is the defendant's admission in open court that he committed the acts charged in the indictment. He thus stands as a witness against himself and he is shielded by the Fifth Amendment from being compelled to do so – hence the minimum requirement that his plea be the voluntary expression of his own choice. But the plea is more than an admission of past conduct; it is the defendant's consent that judgment of conviction may be entered without a trial – a waiver of his right to trial before a jury or a judge. Waivers of constitutional rights not only must be voluntary but must be knowing, intelligent acts done with sufficient awareness of the relevant circumstances and likely consequences. On neither score was Brady's plea of guilty invalid.

II.

The trial judge in 1959 found the plea voluntary before accepting it; the District Court in 1968, after an evidentiary hearing, found that the plea was voluntarily made; the Court of Appeals specifically approved the finding of voluntariness. We see no reason on this record to disturb the judgment of those courts. Petitioner, advised by competent counsel, tendered his plea after his codefendant, who had already given a confession, determined to plead guilty and became available to testify against petitioner. It was this development that the District Court found to have triggered Brady's guilty plea.

The voluntariness of Brady's plea can be determined only by considering all of the relevant circumstances surrounding it. One of these circumstances was the possibility of a heavier sentence following a guilty verdict after a trial. It may be that Brady, faced with a strong case against him and recognizing that his chances for acquittal were slight, preferred to plead guilty and thus limit the penalty to life imprisonment rather than to elect a jury trial which could result in a death penalty. But even if we assume that Brady would not have pleaded guilty except for the death penalty provision of § 1201 (a), this assumption merely identifies the penalty provision as a "but for" cause of his plea. That the statute caused the plea in this sense does not necessarily prove that the plea was coerced and invalid as an involuntary act.

The State to some degree encourages pleas of guilty at every important step in the criminal process. For some people, their breach of a State's law is alone sufficient reason for surrendering themselves and accepting punishment. For others, apprehension and charge, both threatening acts by the Government, jar them into admitting their guilt. In still other cases, the post-indictment accumulation of evidence may convince the defendant and his counsel that a trial is not worth the agony and expense to the defendant and his family. All these pleas of guilty are valid in spite of the State's responsibility for some of the factors motivating the pleas; the pleas are no more improperly compelled than is the decision by a defendant at the close of the State's evidence at trial that he must take the stand or face certain conviction.

Of course, the agents of the State may not produce a plea by actual or threatened physical harm or by mental coercion overbearing the will of the defendant. But nothing of the sort is claimed in this case; nor is there evidence that Brady was so gripped by fear of the death penalty or hope of leniency that he did not or could not, with the help of counsel, rationally weigh the advantages of going to trial against the advantages of pleading guilty. Brady's claim is of a different sort: that it violates the Fifth Amendment to influence or encourage a guilty plea by opportunity or promise of leniency and that a guilty plea is coerced and invalid if influenced by the fear of a possibly higher penalty for the crime charged if a conviction is obtained after the State is put to its proof.

Insofar as the voluntariness of his plea is concerned, there is little to differentiate Brady from (1) the defendant, in a jurisdiction where the judge and jury have the same range of sentencing power, who pleads guilty because his lawyer advises him that the judge will very probably be more lenient than the jury; (2) the defendant, in a jurisdiction where the judge alone has sentencing power, who is advised by counsel that the judge is normally more lenient with defendants who plead guilty than with those who go to trial; (3) the defendant who is permitted by prosecutor and judge to plead guilty to a lesser offense included in the offense charged; and (4) the defendant who pleads guilty to certain counts with the understanding that other charges will be dropped. In each of these situations, as in Brady's case, the defendant might never plead guilty absent the possibility or certainty that the plea will result in a lesser penalty than the sentence that could be imposed after a trial and a verdict of guilty. We decline to hold, however, that a guilty plea is compelled and invalid under the Fifth Amendment whenever motivated by the defendant's desire to accept the certainty or probability of a lesser penalty rather than face a wider range of possibilities extending from acquittal to conviction and a higher penalty authorized by law for the crime charged.

The issue we deal with is inherent in the criminal law and its administration because guilty pleas are not constitutionally forbidden, because the criminal law characteristically extends to judge or jury a range of choice in setting the sentence in individual cases, and because both the State and the defendant often find it advantageous to preclude the possibility of the maximum penalty authorized by law. For a defendant who sees slight possibility of acquittal, the advantages of pleading guilty and limiting the probable penalty are obvious – his exposure is reduced, the correctional processes can begin immediately, and the practical burdens of a trial are eliminated. For the State there are also advantages – the more promptly imposed punishment after an admission of guilt may more effectively attain the objectives of punishment; and with the avoidance of trial, scarce judicial and prosecutorial resources are conserved for those cases in which there is a substantial issue of the defendant's guilt or in which there is substantial doubt that the State can sustain its burden of proof. It is this mutuality of advantage that perhaps explains the fact that at present well over three-fourths of the criminal convictions in this country rest on pleas of guilty, a great many of them no doubt motivated at least in part by the hope or assurance of a lesser penalty than might be imposed if there were a guilty verdict after a trial to judge or jury.

Of course, that the prevalence of guilty pleas is explainable does not necessarily validate those pleas or the system which produces them. But we cannot hold that it is unconstitutional for the State to extend a benefit to a defendant who in turn extends a substantial benefit to the State and who demonstrates by his plea that he is ready and willing to admit his crime and to enter the correctional system in a frame of mind that affords hope for success in rehabilitation over a shorter period of time than might otherwise be necessary.

A contrary holding would require the States and Federal Government to forbid guilty pleas altogether, to provide a single invariable penalty for each crime defined by the statutes, or to place the sentencing function in a separate authority having no knowledge of the manner in which the conviction in each case was obtained. In any event, it would be necessary to forbid prosecutors and judges to accept guilty pleas to selected counts, to lesser included offenses, or to reduced charges. The Fifth Amendment does not reach so far.

The standard as to the voluntariness of guilty pleas must be essentially that defined by Judge Tuttle of the Court of Appeals for the Fifth Circuit:

> [A] plea of guilty entered by one fully aware of the direct consequences, including the actual value of any commitments made to him by the court, prosecutor, or his own counsel, must stand unless induced by threats (or promises to discontinue improper harassment), misrepresentation (including unfulfilled or unfulfillable promises), or perhaps by promises that are by their nature improper as having no proper relationship to the prosecutor's business (e. g. bribes).'

Under this standard, a plea of guilty is not invalid merely because entered to avoid the possibility of a death penalty.

III.

The record before us also supports the conclusion that Brady's plea was intelligently made. He was advised by competent counsel, he was made aware of the nature of the charge against him, and there was nothing to indicate that he was incompetent or otherwise not in control of his mental faculties; once his confederate had pleaded guilty and became available to testify, he chose to plead guilty, perhaps to ensure that he would face no more than life imprisonment or a term of years. Brady was aware of precisely what he was doing when he admitted that he had kidnaped the victim and had not released her unharmed.

Often the decision to plead guilty is heavily influenced by the defendant's appraisal of the prosecution's case against him and by the apparent likelihood of securing leniency should a guilty plea be offered and accepted. Considerations like these frequently present imponderable questions for which there are no certain answers; judgments may be made that in the light of later events seem improvident, although they were perfectly sensible at the time. The rule that a plea must be intelligently made to be valid does not require that a plea be vulnerable to later attack if the defendant did not correctly assess every relevant factor entering into his decision. A defendant is not entitled to withdraw his plea merely because he discovers long after the plea has been accepted that his calculus misapprehended the quality of the State's case or the likely penalties attached to alternative courses of action. More particularly, absent misrepresentation or other impermissible conduct by state agents, a voluntary plea of guilty intelligently made in the light of the then applicable law does not become vulnerable because later judicial decisions indicate that the plea rested on a faulty premise. A plea of guilty triggered by the expectations of a competently counseled defendant that the State will have a strong case against him is not subject to later attack because the defendant's lawyer correctly advised him with respect to the then existing law as to possible penalties but later pronouncements of the courts, as in this case, hold that the maximum penalty for the crime in question was less than was reasonably assumed at the time the plea was entered.

...We find no requirement in the Constitution that a defendant must be permitted to disown his solemn admissions in open court that he committed the act with which he is charged simply because it later develops that the State would have had a weaker case than the defendant had thought or that the maximum penalty then assumed applicable has been held inapplicable in subsequent judicial decisions.

This is not to say that guilty plea convictions hold no hazards for the innocent or that the methods of taking guilty pleas presently employed in this country are necessarily valid in all respects. This mode of conviction is no more foolproof than full trials to the court or to the jury. Accordingly, we take great precautions against unsound results, and we should continue to do so, whether conviction is by plea or by trial. We would have serious doubts about this case if the encouragement of guilty pleas by offers of leniency substantially increased the likelihood that defendants, advised by competent counsel, would falsely condemn themselves. But our view is to the contrary and is based on our expectations that courts will satisfy themselves that pleas of guilty are voluntarily and intelligently made by competent defendants with adequate advice of counsel and that there is nothing to question the accuracy and reliability of the defendants' admissions that they committed the crimes with which they are charged. In the case before us, nothing in the record impeaches Brady's plea or suggests that his admissions in open court were anything but the truth.

Although Brady's plea of guilty may well have been motivated in part by a desire to avoid a possible death penalty, we are convinced that his plea was voluntarily and intelligently made and we have no reason to doubt that his solemn admission of guilt was truthful.

Affirmed.

MR. JUSTICE BLACK, concurring. [omitted]

MR. JUSTICE BRENNAN, concurring. [omitted]

NOTES AND QUERIES

The Court makes clear that waivers of constitutional rights not only must be voluntary but must be knowing, intelligent acts done with sufficient awareness of the relevant circumstances and likely consequences. The Court determines voluntariness by considering the totality of circumstances. The Court also notes that the state cannot produce a plea by actual or threatened physical harm or by mental coercion overbearing the will of the defendant. Why does the potential use of the death penalty not qualify as sufficient mental coercion to overbear the defendant's will? The Court notes that Brady was not so overwhelmed that he could not or did not interact with his attorney and make a rational decision weighing the advantages of a guilty plea. Persuasive argument?

Do you find it fair that a justification for the plea is that the state saves resources when there is substantial doubt that the state can prove guilt? If they cannot prove guilt, why seek a plea bargain instead of simply not proceeding with the prosecution.

Do you think Brady made a reasoned, rational choice to plead guilty? Do you agree with the Court's reasoning that a plea is not compelled if the defendant pleads guilty to obtain the probability of a lesser sentence?

Note that once a court accepts a bargain, prosecutors must follow through with the bargain. That was the ruling in *Santobello v. New York*, 404 U.S. 257 (1971). In that case, a court had accepted a guilty plea but a new prosecutor appeared at the sentencing hearing and, apparently unaware of the agreement that the prosecutor would not make a sentencing recommendation, requested the maximum sentence. The defense objected, but the judge still imposed the maximum sentence stating that he was not influenced by the prosecutor's recommendation. The Supreme Court voided the plea as a matter of due process on the grounds that plea negotiations presuppose fairness in securing agreements between an accused and a prosecutor. As the Court noted, when a plea rests in any significant degree on a promise or agreement of the prosecutor, so that it can be said to be part of the inducement or consideration, such promise must be fulfilled. This is quite significant in that the promise is to be followed even if a judge clearly can ignore the prosecution's position and, as in this case, the court actually states that it had.

THE DEFENDANT'S PLEA: UNDERSTANDING CHARGES

HENDERSON v. MORGAN
426 U.S. 637 (1976)

MR. JUSTICE STEVENS delivered the opinion of the Court.

I.

On April 6, 1965, respondent killed Mrs. Ada Francisco in her home.

When he was in seventh grade, respondent was committed to the Rome State School for Mental Defectives where he was classified as "retarded." He was released to become a farm laborer and ultimately went to work on Mrs. Francisco's farm. Following an argument, she threatened to return him to state custody. He then decided to abscond. During the night he entered Mrs. Francisco's bedroom with a knife, intending to collect his earned wages before leaving; she awoke, began to scream, and he stabbed her. He took a small amount of money, fled in her car, and became involved in an accident about 80 miles away.

The knife was found in the glove compartment of her car. He was promptly arrested and made a statement to the police. He was then 19 years old and substantially below average intelligence.

Respondent was indicted for first-degree murder and arraigned on April 15, 1965. Two concededly competent attorneys were appointed to represent him. The indictment, which charged that he "willfully" stabbed his victim, was read in open court. His lawyers requested, and were granted, access to his written statement and to earlier psychiatric reports. A new psychiatric examination was requested and ordered.

Respondent was found competent to stand trial. Defense counsel held a series of conferences with the prosecutors, with the respondent, and with members of his family. The lawyers "thought manslaughter first would satisfy the needs of justice." They therefore endeavored to have the charge reduced to manslaughter, but the prosecution would agree to nothing less than second-degree murder and a minimum sentence of 25 years. The lawyers gave respondent advice about the different sentences which could be imposed for the different offenses, but, as the District Court found, did not explain the required element of intent.

On June 8, 1965, respondent appeared in court with his attorneys and entered a plea of guilty to murder in the second degree in full satisfaction of the first-degree murder charge made in the indictment. In direct colloquy with the trial judge respondent stated that his plea was based on the advice of his attorneys, that he understood he was accused of killing Mrs. Francisco in Fulton County, that he was waiving his right to a jury trial, and that he would be sent to prison. There was no discussion of the elements of the offense of second-degree murder, no indication that the nature of the offense had ever been discussed with respondent, and no reference of any kind to the requirement of intent to cause the death of the victim.

At the sentencing hearing a week later his lawyers made a statement explaining his version of the offense, particularly noting that respondent "meant no harm to that lady" when he entered her room with the knife. The prosecutor disputed defense counsel's version of the matter, but did not discuss it in detail. After studying the probation officer's report, the trial judge pronounced sentence.

At the evidentiary hearing in the Federal District Court, respondent testified that he would not have pleaded guilty if he had known that an intent to cause the death of his victim was an element of the offense of second-degree murder. The District Judge did not indicate whether or not he credited this testimony.

II.

Petitioner contends that the District Court applied an unrealistically rigid rule of law. Instead of testing the voluntariness of a plea by determining whether a ritualistic litany of the formal legal elements of an offense was read to the defendant, petitioner argues that the court should examine the totality of the circumstances and determine whether the substance of the charge, as opposed to its technical elements, was conveyed to the accused. We do not disagree with the thrust of petitioner's argument, but we are persuaded that even under the test which he espouses, this judgment finding respondent guilty of second-degree murder was defective.

We assume, as petitioner argues, that the prosecutor had overwhelming evidence of guilt available. We also accept petitioner's characterization of the competence of respondent's counsel and of the wisdom of their advice to plead guilty to a charge of second-degree murder. Nevertheless, such a plea cannot support a judgment of guilt unless it was voluntary in a constitutional sense. And clearly the plea could not be voluntary in the sense that it constituted an intelligent admission that he committed the offense unless the defendant received "real notice of the true nature of the charge against him, the first and most universally recognized requirement of due process."

The charge of second-degree murder was never formally made. Had it been made, it necessarily would have included a charge that respondent's assault was "committed with a design to effect the death of the person killed." That element of the offense might have been proved by the objective evidence even if respondent's actual state of mind was consistent with innocence or manslaughter. But even if such a design to effect death would almost inevitably have been inferred from evidence that respondent repeatedly stabbed Mrs. Francisco, it is nevertheless also true that a jury would not have been required to draw that inference. The jury would have been entitled to accept defense counsel's appraisal of the incident as involving only manslaughter in the first degree. Therefore, an admission by respondent that he killed Mrs. Francisco does not necessarily also admit that he was guilty of second-degree murder

There is nothing in this record that can serve as a substitute for either a finding after trial, or a voluntary admission, that respondent had the requisite intent. Defense counsel did not purport to stipulate to that fact; they did not explain to him that his plea would be an admission of that fact; and he made no factual statement or admission necessarily implying that he had such intent. In these circumstances it is impossible to conclude that his plea to the unexplained charge of second-degree murder was voluntary.

Petitioner argues that affirmance of the Court of Appeals will invite countless collateral attacks on judgments entered on pleas of guilty, since frequently the record will not contain a complete enumeration of the elements of the offense to which an accused person pleads guilty. We think petitioner's fears are exaggerated.

Normally the record contains either an explanation of the charge by the trial judge, or at least a representation by defense counsel that the nature of the offense has been explained to the accused. Moreover, even without such an express representation, it may be appropriate to presume that in most cases defense counsel routinely explain the nature of the offense in sufficient detail to give the accused notice of what he is being asked to admit. This case is unique because the trial judge found as a fact that the element of intent was not explained to respondent. Moreover, respondent's unusually low mental capacity provides a reasonable explanation for counsel's oversight; it also forecloses the conclusion that the error was harmless beyond a reasonable doubt, for it lends at least a modicum of credibility to defense counsel's appraisal of the homicide as a manslaughter rather than a murder.

Since respondent did not receive adequate notice of the offense to which he pleaded guilty, his plea was involuntary and the judgment of conviction was entered without due process of law.

Affirmed.

MR. JUSTICE WHITE, with whom MR. JUSTICE STEWART, MR. JUSTICE BLACKMUN, and MR. JUSTICE POWELL join, concurring.

The problem in this case is that the defendant's guilt has been established neither by a finding of guilt beyond a reasonable doubt after trial nor by the defendant's own admission that he is in fact guilty. The defendant did not expressly admit that he intended the victim's death (such intent being an element of the crime for which he stands convicted); and his plea of guilty cannot be construed as an implied admission that he intended her death because the District Court has found that he was not told and did not know that intent to kill was an element of the offense with which he was charged.

Accordingly, the best that can be said for the judgment of conviction entered against the defendant is that it rests on strong evidence - never presented to a trier of fact - or that it rests on the judgment of his lawyer that he would probably be convicted of second-degree murder if he went to trial. It should hardly need saying that a judgment of conviction cannot be entered against a defendant no matter how strong the evidence is against him, unless that evidence has been presented to a jury (or a judge, if a jury is waived) and unless the jury (or judge) finds from that evidence that the defendant's guilt has been proved beyond a reasonable doubt. It cannot be "harmless error" wholly to deny a defendant a jury trial on one or all elements of the offense with which he is charged. Similarly, it is too late in the day to permit a guilty plea to be entered against a defendant solely on the consent of the defendant's agent - his lawyer. Our cases make absolutely clear that the choice to plead guilty must be the defendant's: it is he who must be informed of the consequences of his plea and what it is that he waives when he pleads; and it is on his admission that he is in fact guilty that his conviction will rest.

In this case the defendant's factual guilt of second-degree murder has never been established in any fashion permitted by the Due Process Clause of the Fourteenth Amendment.

MR. JUSTICE REHNQUIST, with whom THE CHIEF JUSTICE joins, dissenting.

The Court's opinion affirms a judgment which directs the release on federal habeas of a state prisoner who, on advice of counsel, pleaded guilty in the New York State courts 11 years ago to a charge of second-degree murder. The Court declares its agreement with petitioner's contention that the test for reviewing the constitutional validity of a counseled plea of guilty should be "the totality of the circumstances." But the Court's holding can be justified only if the Constitution requires that "a ritualistic litany of the formal legal elements of an offense [be] read to the defendant," a requirement which it purports to eschew. The Court accomplishes this result by imposing on state courts, as a constitutional requirement, a definition of "voluntariness" announced by this Court in, in which the Court interpreted a provision of the Federal Rules of Criminal Procedure. Yet that case has been held to have only prospective application even as to the federal courts.

These cases thus set forth a three-pronged test: The plea of guilty must be made voluntarily, it must be made after proper advice, and it must be made with full understanding of the consequences. There can be no doubt that respondent entered his plea "with full understanding of the consequences" because the District Court expressly so found. ...

There was no contention in the federal habeas court that respondent's guilty plea was not "voluntary" in the normal sense of that word. There was no hint of physical or psychological coercion, and respondent was represented by not one but two admittedly capable defense attorneys. ...

Respondent was originally indicted for the crime of first-degree murder, and that indictment charged that in April 1965, he had "willfully, feloniously and of malice aforethought, stabbed and cut Ada Francisco with a dangerous knife... and that thereafter... the said Ada Francisco died of said wounds and injuries, said killing being inexcusable and unjustifiable." Respondent's attorney at the habeas hearing testified that respondent had stabbed his victim "many times," which suggests that experienced counsel would not consider the "design to effect death" issue to be in serious dispute. The habeas judge, in deciding that there was a factual basis for the entry of the plea, took much the same approach...

I do not see how this Court, or any court, could conclude on this state of the record that respondent was not "properly advised" at the time he entered his plea of guilty to the charge of second-degree murder.

His attorneys were motivated by the eminently reasonable tactical judgment on their part that he should plead guilty to second-degree murder in order to avoid the possibility of conviction for first-degree murder with its more serious attendant penalties. Since the Court concedes both the competence of respondent's counsel and the wisdom of their advice, that should be the end of the matter.

There are intimations in the Court's opinion that the vice which it finds in the guilty plea is not that respondent was not informed of all the elements of the offense, but that instead he did not admit to all of those elements. But it is quite clear under our decision in North Carolina v. Alford,, that the latter fact, standing alone, is not sufficient to invalidate a guilty plea. In Alford the defendant not only was not asked to admit to a certain element of the offense, as here, but affirmatively denied having committed the crime at all. Yet we upheld the guilty plea because, as here, it was a tactically sound decision for the defendant to plead to second-degree murder in order to escape the greater penalties which might result from a first-degree murder conviction. In Alford we placed great weight on the fact that, as in this case, "the defendant was represented by competent counsel whose advice was that the plea would be to the defendant's advantage."

The "totality of the circumstances" in this case shows that respondent pleaded guilty to second-degree murder upon the advice of competent counsel. His plea was in no way the result of physical or psychological coercion or overreaching by the State, and he was fully advised as to the consequences of that plea. True, he was not expressly advised that the "design to effect death" was an element of the offense to which he was pleading, although the original first-degree-murder indictment charging "malice aforethought" had been read to him. Given the finding of the habeas judge that there was more than ample evidence from which the jury could have found that respondent had the requisite intent, I cannot subscribe to the Court's invalidation of his...guilty plea for such an extremely technical defect.

In adopting the rule it does, the Court opens the door to countless similarly situated prisoners to withdraw their guilty pleas many years after they were entered. Since it is unlikely that prosecutors will be able to reassemble witnesses and evidence at this late date to try these prisoners, the practical effect of the Court's ruling will be to release these prisoners who at one time freely admitted their guilt.

Notes and Queries

As the dissent makes clear, a plea of guilty must be made voluntarily, it must be made after proper advice, and it must be made with full understanding of the consequences. Based on these factors, did the defendant properly waive his rights? The majority focuses on the need for the defendant to plead formally to each element of offenses, the need to plead to each charge. Does that seem fair to the state in this case? Do you find that he in fact did not receive adequate notice of the charges?

The dissent makes the important point that the defendant actually need not admit to all elements of the offenses, that defendants could actually plead guilty and deny having committed the crime at all. Persuasive? The counter-argument, of course, is that even if they deny the charge, they at least must know what the charge was. Correct?

The dissent conducts a totality of circumstances analysis. Persuasive? What do you make of the majority's own analysis made under the totality of circumstances standard? Do you find this to be a technical defect that inappropriately lets an offender go free? What do you make of the argument that there actually was sufficient evidence to find him guilty anyway?

The Defendant's Plea: Understanding Bargains

BLACKLEDGE v. ALLISON
431 U.S. 63 (1977)

MR. JUSTICE STEWART delivered the opinion of the Court

I.

Allison was indicted by a North Carolina grand jury for breaking and entering, attempted safe robbery, and possession of burglary tools. At his arraignment, where he was represented by court-appointed counsel, he initially pleaded not guilty. But after learning that his codefendant planned to plead guilty, he entered a guilty plea to a single count of attempted safe robbery, for which the minimum prison sentence was 10 years and the maximum was life.

In accord with the procedure for taking guilty pleas then in effect in North Carolina, the judge in open court read from a printed form 13 questions, generally concerning the defendant's understanding of the charge, its consequences, and the voluntariness of his plea. Allison answered "yes" or "no" to each question, and the court clerk transcribed those responses on a copy of the form, which Allison signed. So far as the record shows, there was no questioning beyond this routine; no inquiry was made of either defense counsel or prosecutor. Two questions from the form are of particular relevance to the issues before us: Question No. 8 - "Do you understand that upon your plea of guilty you could be imprisoned for as much as minimum [sic] of 10 years to life?" to which Allison answered "Yes"; and Question No. 11 - "Has the Solicitor, or your lawyer, or any policeman, law officer or anyone else made any promises or threat to you to influence you to plead guilty in this case?" to which Allison answered "No."

The trial judge then accepted the plea by signing his name at the bottom of the form under a text entitled "Adjudication," which recited the three charges for which Allison had been indicted, that he had been fully advised of his rights, was in fact guilty, and pleaded guilty to attempted safe robbery "freely, understandingly and voluntarily," with full awareness of the consequences, and "without undue... compulsion... duress, [or] promise of leniency." Three days later, at a sentencing hearing, of which there is no record whatsoever, Allison was sentenced to 17-21 years in prison.

After unsuccessfully exhausting a state collateral remedy, Allison filed a pro se petition in a Federal District Court seeking a writ of habeas corpus. The petition alleged:

> [h]is guilty plea was induced by an unkept promise, and therefore was not the free and willing choice of the petitioner, and should be set aside by this Court. An unkept bargain which has induced a guilty plea is grounds for relief.

The petition went on to explain and support this allegation as follows:

> The petitioner was led to believe and did believe, by Mr. Pickard [Allison's attorney], that he Mr. N. Glenn Pickard had talked the case over with the Solicitor and the Judge, and that if the petitioner would plead guilty, that he would only get a 10 year sentence of penal servitude. This conversation, where the petitioner was assured that if he plea[ded] guilty, he would only get ten years was witnessed by another party other than the petitioner and counsel.
>
> ...
>
> The petitioner believing that he was only going to get a ten year active sentence, allowed himself to be pled guilty to the charge of attempted safe robbery, and was shocked by the Court with a 17-21 year sentence.
>
> ...
>
> The petitioner was promised by his Attorney, who had consulted presumably with the Judge and Solicitor, that he was only going to get a ten year sentence, and therefore because of this unkept bargain, he is entitled to relief in this Court.
>
> ...
>
> The petitioner is aware of the fact that he was questioned by the trial Judge prior to sentencing, but as he thought he was only going to get ten years, and had been instructed to answer the questions, so that the Court would accept the guilty plea, this fact does not preclude him from raising this matter especially since he was not given the promised sentence by the Court.
>
> ...
>
> The fact that the Judge, said that he could get more, did not affect, the belief of the petitioner, that he was only going to get a ten year sentence.

The Court of Appeals for the Fourth Circuit ... held that Allison's allegation of a broken promise, as amplified by the explanation that his lawyer instructed him to deny the existence of any promises, was not foreclosed by his responses to the form questions at the state guilty-plea proceeding. ... The case was therefore remanded for an evidentiary hearing.

The petitioner warden sought review in this Court, and we granted certiorari...

II.

Whatever might be the situation in an ideal world, the fact is that the guilty plea and the often concomitant plea bargain are important components of this country's criminal justice system. Properly administered, they can benefit all concerned. The defendant avoids extended pretrial incarceration and the anxieties and uncertainties of a trial; he gains a speedy disposition of his case, the chance to acknowledge his guilt, and a prompt start in realizing whatever potential there may be for rehabilitation. Judges and prosecutors conserve vital and scarce resources. The public is protected from the risks posed by those charged with criminal offenses who are at large on bail while awaiting completion of criminal proceedings.

These advantages can be secured, however, only if dispositions by guilty plea are accorded a great measure of finality. To allow indiscriminate hearings in federal postconviction proceedings ... would eliminate the chief virtues of the plea system - speed, economy, and finality. And there is reason for concern about that prospect. More often than not a prisoner has everything to gain and nothing to lose from filing a collateral attack upon his guilty plea. If he succeeds in vacating the judgment of conviction, retrial may be difficult. If he convinces a court that his plea was induced by an advantageous plea agreement that was violated, he may obtain the benefit of its terms. A collateral attack may also be inspired by "a mere desire to be freed temporarily from the confines of the prison."

Yet arrayed against the interest in finality is the very purpose of the writ of habeas corpus - to safeguard a person's freedom from detention in violation of constitutional guarantees. "The writ of habeas corpus has played a great role in the history of human freedom. It has been the judicial method of lifting undue restraints upon personal liberty." And a prisoner in custody after pleading guilty, no less than one tried and convicted by a jury, is entitled to avail himself of the writ in challenging the constitutionality of his custody.

[In] the later case of Fontaine v. United States. ... The defendant there, having waived counsel, had also pleaded guilty to federal bank robbery charges. Before accepting the plea, the District Judge addressed the defendant personally, and the defendant stated in substance "that his plea was given voluntarily and knowingly, that he understood the nature of the charge and the consequences of the plea, and that he was in fact guilty." The defendant later filed a ... motion to vacate his sentence on the ground that his plea had been coerced "by a combination of fear, coercive police tactics, and illness, including mental illness." The motion included supporting factual allegations, as well as hospital records documenting some of the contentions.

Although noting that in collaterally attacking a plea of guilty a prisoner "may not ordinarily repudiate" statements made to the sentencing judge when the plea was entered, the Court observed that no procedural device for the taking of guilty pleas is so perfect in design and exercise as to warrant a per se rule rendering it "uniformly invulnerable to subsequent challenge." Because the record of the plea hearing did not, in view of the allegations made, "'conclusively show that the prisoner [was] entitled to no relief,'" the Court ruled that the prisoner should be given an evidentiary hearing.

These cases do not in the least reduce the force of the original plea hearing. For the representations of the defendant, his lawyer, and the prosecutor at such a hearing, as well as any findings made by the judge accepting the plea, constitute a formidable barrier in any subsequent collateral proceedings. Solemn declarations in open court carry a strong presumption of verity. The subsequent presentation of conclusory allegations unsupported by specifics is subject to summary dismissal, as are contentions that in the face of the record are wholly incredible.

...the barrier of the plea or sentencing proceeding record, although imposing, is not invariably insurmountable. ... the federal courts cannot fairly adopt a per se rule excluding all possibility that a defendant's representations at the time his guilty plea was accepted were so much the product of such factors as misunderstanding, duress, or misrepresentation by others as to make the guilty plea a constitutionally inadequate basis for imprisonment.

III.

The allegations in this case were not in themselves so "vague [or] conclusory," as to warrant dismissal for that reason alone. Allison alleged as a ground for relief that his plea was induced by an unkept promise. But he did not stop there. He proceeded to elaborate upon this claim with specific factual allegations. The petition indicated exactly what the terms of the promise were; when, where, and by whom the promise had been made; and the identity of one witness to its communication. The critical question is whether these allegations, when viewed against the record of the plea hearing, were so "palpably incredible," ibid., so "patently frivolous or false," as to warrant summary dismissal. In the light of the nature of the record of the proceeding at which the guilty plea was accepted, and of the ambiguous status of the process of plea bargaining at the time the guilty plea was made, we conclude that Allison's petition should not have been summarily dismissed.

Only recently has plea bargaining become a visible practice accepted as a legitimate component in the administration of criminal justice. For decades it was a sub rosa process shrouded in secrecy and deliberately concealed by participating defendants, defense lawyers, prosecutors, and even judges...

...No transcript of the proceeding was made. The only record was a standard printed form. There is no way of knowing whether the trial judge in any way deviated from or supplemented the text of the form. The record is silent as to what statements Allison, his lawyer, or the prosecutor might have made regarding promised sentencing concessions. And there is no record at all of the sentencing hearing three days later, at which one of the participants might well have made a statement shedding light upon the veracity of the allegations Allison later advanced.

The litany of form questions followed by the trial judge at arraignment nowhere indicated to Allison (or indeed to the lawyers involved) that plea bargaining was a legitimate practice that could be freely disclosed in open court. Neither lawyer was asked to disclose any agreement that had been reached, or sentencing recommendation that had been promised. The process thus did nothing to dispel a defendant's belief that any bargain struck must remain concealed - a belief here allegedly reinforced by the admonition of Allison's lawyer himself that disclosure could jeopardize the agreement. Rather than challenging respondent's counsel's contention at oral argument in this Court that "at that time in North Carolina plea bargains were never disclosed in response to such a question on such a form," counsel for the petitioners conceded at oral argument that "[that] form was a minimum inquiry."

Although "[l]ogically the general inquiry should elicit information about plea bargaining,... it seldom has in the past." Particularly if, as Allison alleged, he was advised by counsel to conceal any plea bargain, his denial that any promises had been made might have been a courtroom ritual more sham than real. We thus cannot conclude that the allegations in Allison's habeas corpus petition, when measured against the "record" of the arraignment, were so "patently false or frivolous" as to warrant summary dismissal.

North Carolina has recently undertaken major revisions of its plea-bargaining procedures, in part to prevent the very kind of problem now before us. Plea bargaining is expressly legitimated. The judge is directed to advise the defendant that courts have approved plea bargaining and he may thus admit to any promises without fear of jeopardizing an advantageous agreement or prejudicing himself in the judge's eyes. Specific inquiry about whether a plea bargain has been struck is then made not only of the defendant, but also of his counsel and the prosecutor. Finally, the entire proceeding is to be transcribed verbatim.

Had these commendable procedures been followed in the present case, Allison's petition would have been cast in a very different light. The careful explication of the legitimacy of plea bargaining, the questioning of both lawyers, and the verbatim record of their answers at the guilty-plea proceedings would almost surely have shown whether any bargain did exist and, if so, insured that it was not ignored. But the salutary reforms recently implemented by North Carolina highlight even more sharply the deficiencies in the record before the District Court in the present case.

In short, it may turn out upon remand that a full evidentiary hearing is not required. But Allison is "entitled to careful consideration and plenary processing of [his claim,] including full opportunity for presentation of the relevant facts." Upon that understanding, the judgment of the Court of Appeals is affirmed.

It is so ordered.

THE CHIEF JUSTICE concurs in the judgment.

MR. JUSTICE REHNQUIST took no part in the consideration or decision of this case.

MR. JUSTICE POWELL, concurring. [omitted]

NOTES AND QUERIES

Allison pleaded in open court and signed a statement indicating that he knew the sentence and that no one had made promises or threats. How does the Court justify the need to not summarily dismiss the claim? Why would we want to have such claims heard? Why is the interest in finality insufficient to uphold a *per se* rule that would exclude challenges to reasons for guilty pleas?

The Court notes that North Carolina has changed its procedures so that it now asks all parties to advise all defendants to admit promises without fear of jeopardizing agreements. How protective do you find that rule? Do you think that having that rule could actually work to the disadvantage of defendants like Allison? How so? Does this mean that the Court misunderstands the power of coercion and the nature of involuntariness?

THE DEFENDANT'S PLEA: PLEADING FACTUALLY

NORTH CAROLINA v. ALFORD
400 U.S. 25 (1970)

MR. JUSTICE WHITE delivered the opinion of the Court

On December 2, 1963, Alford was indicted for first-degree murder, a capital offense under North Carolina law. The court appointed an attorney to represent him, and this attorney questioned all but one of the various witnesses who appellee said would substantiate his claim of innocence. The witnesses, however, did not support Alford's story but gave statements that strongly indicated his guilt. Faced with strong evidence of guilt and no substantial evidentiary support for the claim of innocence, Alford's attorney recommended that he plead guilty, but left the ultimate decision to Alford himself. The prosecutor agreed to accept a plea of guilty to a charge of second-degree murder, and on December 10, 1963, Alford pleaded guilty to the reduced charge.

Before the plea was finally accepted by the trial court, the court heard the sworn testimony of a police officer who summarized the State's case. Two other witnesses besides Alford were also heard. Although there was no eyewitness to the crime, the testimony indicated that shortly before the killing Alford took his gun from his house, stated his intention to kill the victim, and returned home with the declaration that he had carried out the killing. After the summary presentation of the State's case, Alford took the stand and testified that he had not committed the murder but that he was pleading guilty because he faced the threat of the death penalty if he did not do so. In response to the questions of his counsel, he acknowledged that his counsel had informed him of the difference between second- and first-degree murder and of his rights in case he chose to go to trial. The trial court then asked appellee if, in light of his denial of guilt, he still desired to plead guilty to second-degree murder and appellee answered, "Yes, sir. I plead guilty on – from the circumstances that he [Alford's attorney] told me." After eliciting information about Alford's prior criminal record, which was a long one, the trial court sentenced him to 30 years' imprisonment, the maximum penalty for second-degree murder.

Alford sought post-conviction relief ... Among the claims raised was the claim that his plea of guilty was invalid because it was the product of fear and coercion. After a hearing, the state court in 1965 found that the plea was "willingly, knowingly, and understandingly" made on the advice of competent counsel and in the face of a strong prosecution case. ... On appeal, a divided panel of the Court of Appeals for the Fourth Circuit reversed on the ground that Alford's guilty plea was made involuntarily. ... the Court of Appeals ruled that Alford's guilty plea was involuntary because its principal motivation was fear of the death penalty. By this standard, even if both the judge and the jury had possessed the power to impose the death penalty for first-degree murder or if guilty pleas to capital charges had not been permitted, Alford's plea of guilty to second-degree murder should still have been rejected because impermissibly induced by his desire to eliminate the possibility of a death sentence. ... We vacate the judgment of the Court of Appeals and remand the case for further proceedings.

We held in Brady v. United States, that a plea of guilty which would not have been entered except for the defendant's desire to avoid a possible death penalty and to limit the maximum penalty to life imprisonment or a term of years was not for that reason compelled within the meaning of the Fifth Amendment. ... The standard was and remains whether the plea represents a voluntary and intelligent choice among the alternative courses of action open to the defendant. That he would not have pleaded except for the opportunity to limit the possible penalty does not necessarily demonstrate that the plea of guilty was not the product of a free and rational choice, especially where the defendant was represented by competent counsel whose advice was that the plea would be to the defendant's advantage. The standard fashioned and applied by the Court of Appeals was therefore erroneous and we would, without more, vacate and remand the case for further proceedings with respect to any other claims of Alford which are properly before that court, if it were not for other circumstances appearing in the record which might seem to warrant an affirmance of the Court of Appeals.

As previously recounted, after Alford's plea of guilty was offered and the State's case was placed before the judge, Alford denied that he had committed the murder but reaffirmed his desire to plead guilty to avoid a possible death sentence and to limit the penalty to the 30-year maximum provided for second-degree murder. Ordinarily, a judgment of conviction resting on a plea of guilty is justified by the defendant's admission that he committed the crime charged against him and his consent that judgment be entered without a trial of any kind. The plea usually subsumes both elements, and justifiably so, even though there is no separate, express admission by the defendant that he committed the particular acts claimed to constitute the crime charged in the indictment. Here Alford entered his plea but accompanied it with the statement that he had not shot the victim.

If Alford's statements were to be credited as sincere assertions of his innocence, there obviously existed a factual and legal dispute between him and the State. Without more, it might be argued that the conviction entered on his guilty plea was invalid, since his assertion of innocence negatived any admission of guilt, which, as we observed last Term in Brady, is normally "central to the plea and the foundation for entering judgment against the defendant. ...

In addition to Alford's statement, however, the court had heard an account of the events on the night of the murder, including information from Alford's acquaintances that he had departed from his home with his gun stating his intention to kill and that he had later declared that he had carried out his intention. Nor had Alford wavered in his desire to have the trial court determine his guilt without a jury trial. Although denying the charge against him, he nevertheless preferred the dispute between him and the State to be settled by the judge in the context of a guilty plea proceeding rather than by a formal trial. Thereupon, with the State's telling evidence and Alford's denial before it, the trial court proceeded to convict and sentence Alford for second-degree murder.

State and lower federal courts are divided upon whether a guilty plea can be accepted when it is accompanied by protestations of innocence and hence contains only a waiver of trial but no admission of guilt. Some courts, giving expression to the principle that "our law only authorizes a conviction where guilt is shown," require that trial judges reject such pleas. But others have concluded that they should not "force any defense on a defendant in a criminal case," particularly when advancement of the defense might "end in disaster . . . ." They have argued that, since "guilt, or the degree of guilt, is at times uncertain and elusive," "an accused, though believing in or entertaining doubts respecting his innocence, might reasonably conclude a jury would be convinced of his guilt and that he would fare better in the sentence by pleading guilty. ...As one state court observed nearly a century ago, "reasons other than the fact that he is guilty may induce a defendant to so plead. ...[and] he must be permitted to judge for himself in this respect."

These cases would be directly in point if Alford had simply insisted on his plea but refused to admit the crime. The fact that his plea was denominated a plea of guilty rather than a plea of nolo contendere is of no constitutional significance with respect to the issue now before us, for the Constitution is concerned with the practical consequences, not the formal categorizations, of state law. Thus, while most pleas of guilty consist of both a waiver of trial and an express admission of guilt, the latter element is not a constitutional requisite to the imposition of criminal penalty. An individual accused of crime may voluntarily, knowingly, and understandingly consent to the imposition of a prison sentence even if he is unwilling or unable to admit his participation in the acts constituting the crime.

Nor can we perceive any material difference between a plea that refuses to admit commission of the criminal act and a plea containing a protestation of innocence when, as in the instant case, a defendant intelligently concludes that his interests require entry of a guilty plea and the record before the judge contains strong evidence of actual guilt. Here the State had a strong case of first-degree murder against Alford. Whether he realized or disbelieved his guilt, he insisted on his plea because in his view he had absolutely nothing to gain by a trial and much to gain by pleading. Because of the overwhelming evidence against him, a trial was precisely what neither Alford nor his attorney desired. Confronted with the choice between a trial for first-degree murder, on the one hand, and a plea of guilty to second-degree murder, on the other, Alford quite reasonably chose the latter and thereby limited the maximum penalty to a 30-year term. When his plea is viewed in light of the evidence against him, which substantially negated his claim of innocence and which further provided a means by which the judge could test whether the plea was being intelligently entered, its validity cannot be seriously questioned. In view of the strong factual basis for the plea demonstrated by the State and Alford's clearly expressed desire to enter it despite his professed belief in his innocence, we hold that the trial judge did not commit constitutional error in accepting it.

...Alford now argues in effect that the State should not have allowed him this choice but should have insisted on proving him guilty of murder in the first degree. The States in their wisdom may take this course by statute or otherwise and may prohibit the practice of accepting pleas to lesser included offenses under any circumstances. But this is not the mandate of the Fourteenth Amendment and the Bill of Rights. The prohibitions against involuntary or unintelligent pleas should not be relaxed, but neither should an exercise in arid logic render those constitutional guarantees counterproductive and put in jeopardy the very human values they were meant to preserve.

...the case is remanded to the Court of Appeals for further proceedings consistent with this opinion.

It is so ordered.

MR. JUSTICE BLACK, concurring. [omitted]

MR. JUSTICE BRENNAN, with whom MR. JUSTICE DOUGLAS and MR. JUSTICE MARSHALL join, dissenting.

Last Term, this Court held, over my dissent, that a plea of guilty may validly be induced by an unconstitutional threat to subject the defendant to the risk of death, so long as the plea is entered in open court and the defendant is represented by competent counsel who is aware of the threat, albeit not of its unconstitutionality. Today the Court makes clear that its previous holding was intended to apply even when the record demonstrates that the actual effect of the unconstitutional threat was to induce a guilty plea from a defendant who was unwilling to admit his guilt.

I adhere to the view that, in any given case, the influence of such an unconstitutional threat "must necessarily be given weight in determining the voluntariness of a plea." And, without reaching the question whether due process permits the entry of judgment upon a plea of guilty accompanied by a contemporaneous denial of acts constituting the crime, I believe that at the very least such a denial of guilt is also a relevant factor in determining whether the plea was voluntarily and intelligently made. With these factors in mind, it is sufficient in my view to state that the facts set out in the majority opinion demonstrate that Alford was "so gripped by fear of the death penalty" that his decision to plead guilty was not voluntary but was "the product of duress as much so as choice reflecting physical constraint." Accordingly, I would affirm the judgment of the Court of Appeals.

NOTES AND QUERIES

After giving his version of the events of the night of the murder, Alford stated:

> I pleaded guilty on second degree murder because they said there is too much evidence, but I ain't shot no man, but I take the fault for the other man. We never had an argument in our life and I just pleaded guilty because they said if I didn't they would gas me for it, and that is all."
>
> In response to questions from his attorney, Alford affirmed that he had consulted several times with his attorney and with members of his family and had been informed of his rights if he chose to plead not guilty. Alford then reaffirmed his decision to plead guilty to second-degree murder:
>
> "Q [by Alford's attorney]. And you authorized me to tender a plea of guilty to second degree murder before the court?
>
> "A. Yes, sir.
>
> "Q. And in doing that, that you have again affirmed your decision on that point?
>
> "A. Well, I'm still pleading that you all got me to plead guilty. I plead the other way, circumstantial evidence; that the jury will prosecute me on – on the second. You told me to plead guilty, right. I don't – I'm not guilty but I plead guilty.

Do Alford's statements sway you in any direction?

By what burden of proof do you think a judge must find that the defendant did in fact commit the alleged acts? The Court has not spoken to the issue. It seems that the standard may well not be a "beyond a reasonable doubt" standard. What do you make of that reduced standard? It does seem that all that is required is a factual basis for the plea, not that the judge believes the defendant's guilt.

Do you find Alford's plea to be voluntary and intelligent? Are you concerned that the fear of the death penalty may have induced his plea and thus making it involuntary?

Alford makes clear that a judge accepting a guilty plea must establish the existence of a strong factual basis for the plea. The case left open, however, the scope of the factual basis requirement. Although the judge must determine that there is a factual basis for the charge, it remained unsettled whether a judge must determine the factual assumptions underlying the dispositional (sentencing/punishment) aspects of the plea. The Supreme Court addressed the issue at least in terms of what federal jurisdictions must follow; and it held that a judge need only determine the facts underlying the criminal offense, not those related to punishment. The Court did so in *Libretti v. U.S.*, 516 U.S. 29 (1995), which involved a defendant's forfeiture of virtually all of his property to the government in exchange for a recommendation of a reduced sentence for violations of drug, firearms, and money-laundering laws. Although he apparently had made a good bargain given the potential penalties, he eventually challenged the plea on the grounds that the judge had failed to inquire sufficiently into the nexus between the forfeited property and his crimes. The Supreme Court held, however, that determinations of forfeiture actually deal with punishments which do not relate to the actual plea. Do you agree with the Court's assessment? Does the punishment actually factor into factual bases for the plea? Do you suppose that, in real life, the punishment does indeed factor into the plea? Recall that most who plead guilty seem to do so in expectation of a reduced penalty. Indeed, that expectation helps justify the plea bargain system. What does the distinction between punishment and plea reveal about the standard for addressing guilty pleas? Do you agree that it highlights how pleas actually need not be that rational or reasoned after all? In *Libretti*, the plea agreement actually did allow the sentencing judge to impose the sentence he saw fit. What do you make of that point? Would the system be more fair if the judge were required to make a factual basis for the forfeitures? If so, then why not require such factual findings?

THE DEFENDANT'S PLEA: PLEADING COMPETENTLY

GODINEZ v. MORAN
509 U.S. 389 (1993)

JUSTICE THOMAS delivered the opinion of the Court.

This case presents the question whether the competency standard for pleading guilty or waiving the right to counsel is higher than the competency standard for standing trial. We hold that it is not.

I.

On August 2, 1984, in the early hours of the morning, respondent entered the Red Pearl Saloon in Las Vegas, Nevada, and shot the bartender and a patron four times each with an automatic pistol. He then walked behind the bar and removed the cash register. Nine days later, respondent arrived at the apartment of his former wife and opened fire on her; five of his seven shots hit their target. Respondent then shot himself in the abdomen and attempted, without success, to slit his wrists. Of the four victims of respondent's gunshots, only respondent himself survived. On August 13, respondent summoned police to his hospital bed and confessed to the killings.

After respondent pleaded not guilty to three counts of first-degree murder, the trial court ordered that he be examined by a pair of psychiatrists, both of whom concluded that he was competent to stand trial. The State thereafter announced its intention to seek the death penalty. On November 28, 1984, 2 1/2 months after the psychiatric evaluations, respondent again appeared before the trial court. At this time respondent informed the court that he wished to discharge his attorneys and change his pleas to guilty. The reason for the request, according to respondent, was to prevent the presentation of mitigating evidence at his sentencing.

On the basis of the psychiatric reports, the trial court found that respondent

> is competent in that he knew the nature and quality of his acts, had the capacity to determine right from wrong; that he understands the nature of the criminal charges against him and is able to assist in his defense of such charges, or against the pronouncement of the judgment thereafter; that he knows the consequences of entering a plea of guilty to the charges; and that he can intelligently and knowingly waive his constitutional right to assistance of an attorney.

The court advised respondent that he had a right both to the assistance of counsel and to self-representation, warned him of the "dangers and disadvantages" of self-representation, inquired into his understanding of the proceedings and his awareness of his rights, and asked why he had chosen to represent himself. It then accepted respondent's waiver of counsel. The court also accepted respondent's guilty pleas, but not before it had determined that respondent was not pleading guilty in response to threats or promises, that he understood the nature of the charges against him and the consequences of pleading guilty, that he was aware of the rights he was giving up, and that there was a factual basis for the pleas. The trial court explicitly found that respondent was "knowingly and intelligently" waiving his right to the assistance of counsel, and that his guilty pleas were "freely and voluntarily" given.

On January 21, 1985, a three-judge court sentenced respondent to death for each of the murders. The Supreme Court of Nevada affirmed respondent's sentences for the Red Pearl Saloon murders, but reversed his sentence for the murder of his ex-wife and remanded for imposition of a life sentence without the possibility of parole.

On July 30, 1987, respondent filed a petition for post-conviction relief in state court. Following an evidentiary hearing, the trial court rejected respondent's claim that he was "mentally incompetent to represent himself," concluding that "the record clearly shows that he was examined by two psychiatrists both of whom declared [him] competent." The Supreme Court of Nevada dismissed respondent's appeal, and we denied certiorari.

Respondent then filed a habeas petition in the United States District Court for the District of Nevada. The District Court denied the petition, but the Ninth Circuit reversed. The Court of Appeals concluded that the "record in this case" should have led the trial court to "entertain a good faith doubt about [respondent's] competency to make a voluntary, knowing, and intelligent waiver of constitutional rights," and that the Due Process Clause therefore "required the court to hold a hearing to evaluate and determine [respondent's] competency . . . before it accepted his decision to discharge counsel and change his pleas." Rejecting petitioner's argument that the trial court's error was "cured by the postconviction hearing," and that the competency determination that followed the hearing was entitled to deference under 28 U.S.C. § 2254(d), the Court of Appeals held that "the state court's postconviction ruling was premised on the wrong legal standard of competency." "Competency to waive constitutional rights," according to the Court of Appeals, "requires a higher level of mental functioning than that required to stand trial"; while a defendant is competent to stand trial if he has "a rational and factual understanding of the proceedings and is capable of assisting his counsel," a defendant is competent to waive counsel or plead guilty only if he has "the capacity for 'reasoned choice' among the alternatives available to him." The Court of Appeals determined that the trial court had "erroneously applied the standard for evaluating competency to stand trial, instead of the correct 'reasoned choice' standard," and further concluded that when examined "in light of the correct legal standard," the record did not support a finding that respondent was "mentally capable of the reasoned choice required for a valid waiver of constitutional rights." The Court of Appeals accordingly instructed the District Court to issue the writ of habeas corpus within 60 days, "unless the state court allows [respondent] to withdraw his guilty pleas, enter new pleas, and proceed to trial with the assistance of counsel."

Whether the competency standard for pleading guilty or waiving the right to counsel is higher than the competency standard for standing trial is a question that has divided the Federal Courts of Appeals and state courts of last resort. We granted certiorari to resolve the conflict.

II.

A criminal defendant may not be tried unless he is competent, and he may not waive his right to counsel or plead guilty unless he does so "competently and intelligently." In Dusky v. United States, we held that the standard for competence to stand trial is whether the defendant has "sufficient present ability to consult with his lawyer with a reasonable degree of rational understanding" and has "a rational as well as factual understanding of the proceedings against him." While we have described the standard for competence to stand trial, however, we have never expressly articulated a standard for competence to plead guilty or to waive the right to the assistance of counsel.

Relying in large part upon our decision in Westbrook v. Arizona, the Ninth Circuit adheres to the view that the competency standard for pleading guilty or waiving the right to counsel is higher than the competency standard for standing trial. In Westbrook, a two-paragraph per curiam opinion, we vacated the lower court's judgment affirming the petitioner's conviction, because there had been "a hearing on the issue of [the petitioner's] competence to stand trial," but "no hearing or inquiry into the issue of his competence to waive his constitutional right to the assistance of counsel." The Ninth Circuit has reasoned that the "clear implication" of Westbrook is that the Dusky formulation is not "a high enough standard" for determining whether a defendant is competent to waive a constitutional right. We think the Ninth Circuit has read too much into Westbrook, and we think it errs in applying two different competency standards.

A.

The standard adopted by the Ninth Circuit is whether a defendant who seeks to plead guilty or waive counsel has the capacity for "reasoned choice" among the alternatives available to him. How this standard is different from (much less higher than) the Dusky standard – whether the defendant has a "rational understanding" of the proceedings – is not readily apparent to us. In fact, respondent himself opposed certiorari on the ground that the difference between the two standards is merely one of "terminology," and he devotes little space in his brief on the merits to a defense of the Ninth Circuit's standard. But even assuming that there is some meaningful distinction between the capacity for "reasoned choice" and a "rational understanding" of the proceedings, we reject the notion that competence to plead guilty or to waive the right to counsel must be measured by a standard that is higher than (or even different from) the Dusky standard.

We begin with the guilty plea. A defendant who stands trial is likely to be presented with choices that entail relinquishment of the same rights that are relinquished by a defendant who pleads guilty: He will ordinarily have to decide whether to waive his "privilege against compulsory self-incrimination," by taking the witness stand; if the option is available, he may have to decide whether to waive his "right to trial by jury," ibid.; and, in consultation with counsel, he may have to decide whether to waive his "right to confront [his] accusers," by declining to cross-examine witnesses for the prosecution. A defendant who pleads not guilty, moreover, faces still other strategic choices: In consultation with his attorney, he may be called upon to decide, among other things, whether (and how) to put on a defense and whether to raise one or more affirmative defenses. In sum, all criminal defendants – not merely those who plead guilty – may be required to make important decisions once criminal proceedings have been initiated. And while the decision to plead guilty is undeniably a profound one, it is no more complicated than the sum total of decisions that a defendant may be called upon to make during the course of a trial. (The decision to plead guilty is also made over a shorter period of time, without the distraction and burden of a trial.) This being so, we can conceive of no basis for demanding a higher level of competence for those defendants who choose to plead guilty. If the Dusky standard is adequate for defendants who plead not guilty, it is necessarily adequate for those who plead guilty.

Nor do we think that a defendant who waives his right to the assistance of counsel must be more competent than a defendant who does not, since there is no reason to believe that the decision to waive counsel requires an appreciably higher level of mental functioning than the decision to waive other constitutional rights. Respondent suggests that a higher competency standard is necessary because a defendant who represents himself "'must have greater powers of comprehension, judgment, and reason than would be necessary to stand trial with the aid of an attorney.'" But this argument has a flawed premise; the competence that is required of a defendant seeking to waive his right to counsel is the competence to waive the right, not the competence to represent himself. In Faretta v. California, we held that a defendant choosing self-representation must do so "competently and intelligently," but we made it clear that the defendant's "technical legal knowledge" is "not relevant" to the determination whether he is competent to waive his right to counsel, and we emphasized that although the defendant "may conduct his own defense ultimately to his own detriment, his choice must be honored." Thus, while "[i]t is undeniable that in most criminal prosecutions defendants could better defend with counsel's guidance than by their own unskilled efforts," a criminal defendant's ability to represent himself has no bearing upon his competence to choose self-representation.

B.

A finding that a defendant is competent to stand trial, however, is not all that is necessary before he may be permitted to plead guilty or waive his right to counsel. In addition to determining that a defendant who seeks to plead guilty or waive counsel is competent, a trial court must satisfy itself that the waiver of his constitutional rights is knowing and voluntary. In this sense there is a "heightened" standard for pleading guilty and for waiving the right to counsel, but it is not a heightened standard of competence.

This two-part inquiry is what we had in mind in Westbrook. When we distinguished between "competence to stand trial" and "competence to waive [the] constitutional right to the assistance of counsel," we were using "competence to waive" as a shorthand for the "intelligent and competent waiver" requirement of Johnson v. Zerbst. This much is clear from the fact that we quoted that very language from Zerbst immediately after noting that the trial court had not determined whether the petitioner was competent to waive his right to counsel. Thus, Westbrook stands only for the unremarkable proposition that when a defendant seeks to waive his right to counsel, a determination that he is competent to stand trial is not enough; the waiver must also be intelligent and voluntary before it can be accepted.

III.

Requiring that a criminal defendant be competent has a modest aim: It seeks to ensure that he has the capacity to understand the proceedings and to assist counsel. While psychiatrists and scholars may find it useful to classify the various kinds and degrees of competence, and while States are free to adopt competency standards that are more elaborate than the Dusky formulation, the Due Process Clause does not impose these additional requirements. The judgment of the Court of Appeals is reversed, and the case is remanded for further proceedings consistent with this opinion.

So ordered.

JUSTICE KENNEDY, with whom JUSTICE SCALIA joins, concurring in part and concurring in the judgment.

The Due Process Clause does not mandate different standards of competency at various stages of or for different decisions made during the criminal proceedings. That was never the rule at common law, and it would take some extraordinary showing of the inadequacy of a single standard of competency for us to require States to employ heightened standards. Indeed, we should only overturn Nevada's use of a single standard if it "'offends some principle of justice so rooted in the traditions and conscience of our people as to be ranked as fundamental.'"

A single standard of competency to be applied throughout criminal proceedings does not offend any "'principle of justice so rooted in the traditions and conscience of our people as to be ranked as fundamental.'" Nothing in our case law compels a contrary conclusion, and adoption of a rule setting out varying competency standards for each decision and stage of a criminal proceeding would disrupt the orderly course of trial and, from the standpoint of all parties, prove unworkable both at trial and on appellate review.

With these observations, I concur in the judgment and in Parts I, II-B, and III of the Court's opinion.

JUSTICE BLACKMUN, with whom JUSTICE STEVENS joins, dissenting.

Today, the majority holds that a standard of competence designed to measure a defendant's ability to consult with counsel and to assist in preparing his defense is constitutionally adequate to assess a defendant's competence to waive the right to counsel and represent himself. In so doing, the majority upholds the death sentence for a person whose decision to discharge counsel, plead guilty, and present no defense well may have been the product of medication or mental illness. I believe the majority's analysis is contrary to both common sense and longstanding case law. Therefore, I dissent.

I.

As a preliminary matter, the circumstances under which respondent Richard Allan Moran waived his right to an attorney and pleaded guilty to capital murder bear elaboration. For, although the majority's exposition of the events is accurate, the most significant facts are omitted or relegated to footnotes.

In August 1984, after killing three people and wounding himself in an attempt to commit suicide, Moran was charged in a Nevada state court with three counts of capital murder. He pleaded not guilty to all charges, and the trial court ordered a psychiatric evaluation. At this stage, Moran's competence to represent himself was not at issue.

The two psychiatrists who examined him therefore focused solely upon his capacity to stand trial with the assistance of counsel. Dr. Jack A. Jurasky found Moran to be "in full control of his faculties insofar as his ability to aid counsel, assist in his own defense, recall evidence and to give testimony if called upon to do so." Dr. Jurasky, however, did express some reservations, observing: "Psychologically, and perhaps legally speaking, this man, because he is expressing and feeling considerable remorse and guilt, may be inclined to exert less effort towards his own defense." Nevertheless, under the circumstances, Dr. Jurasky felt that Moran's depressed state of mind was not "necessarily a major consideration." Dr. William D. O'Gorman also characterized Moran as "very depressed," remarking that he "showed much tearing in talking about the episodes that led up to his present incarceration, particularly in talking about his ex-wife."

But Dr. O'Gorman ultimately concluded that Moran "is knowledgeable of the charges being made against him" and "can assist his attorney, in his own defense, if he so desires."

In November 1984, just three months after his suicide attempt, Moran appeared in court seeking to discharge his public defender, waive his right to counsel, and plead guilty to all three charges of capital murder. When asked to explain the dramatic change in his chosen course of action, Moran responded that he wished to represent himself because he opposed all efforts to mount a defense. His purpose, specifically, was to prevent the presentation of any mitigating evidence on his behalf at the sentencing phase of the proceeding. The trial judge inquired whether Moran was "presently under the influence of any drug or alcohol," and Moran replied: "Just what they give me in, you know, medications." Despite Moran's affirmative answer, the trial judge failed to question him further regarding the type, dosage, or effect of the "medications" to which he referred. Had the trial judge done so, he would have discovered that Moran was being administered simultaneously four different prescription drugs – phenobarbital, dilantin, inderal, and vistaril. Moran later testified to the numbing effect of these drugs, stating: "I guess I really didn't care about anything. ... I wasn't very concerned about anything that was going on...as far as the proceedings and everything were going."

Disregarding the mounting evidence of Moran's disturbed mental state, the trial judge accepted Moran's waiver of counsel and guilty pleas after posing a series of routine questions regarding his understanding of his legal rights and the offenses, to which Moran gave largely monosyllabic answers. In a string of affirmative responses, Moran purported to acknowledge that he knew the import of waiving his constitutional rights, that he understood the charges against him, and that he was, in fact, guilty of those charges. One part of this exchange, however, highlights the mechanical character of Moran's answers to the questions. When the trial judge asked him whether he killed his ex-wife "deliberately, with premeditation and malice aforethought," Moran unexpectedly responded: "No. I didn't do it – I mean, I wasn't looking to kill her, but she ended up dead." Instead of probing further, the trial judge simply repeated the question, inquiring again whether Moran had acted deliberately. Once again, Moran replied: "I don't know. I mean, I don't know what you mean by deliberately. I mean, I pulled the trigger on purpose, but I didn't plan on doing it; you know what I mean?" Ignoring the ambiguity of Moran's responses, the trial judge reframed the question to elicit an affirmative answer, stating: "Well, I've previously explained to you what is meant by deliberation and premeditation. Deliberate means that you arrived at or determined as a result of careful thought and weighing the consideration for and against the proposed action. Did you do that?" This time, Moran responded: "Yes."

It was only after prodding Moran through the plea colloquy in this manner that the trial judge concluded that he was competent to stand trial and that he voluntarily and intelligently had waived his right to counsel. Accordingly, Moran was allowed to plead guilty and appear without counsel at his sentencing hearing. Moran presented no defense, called no witness, and offered no mitigating evidence on his own behalf. Not surprisingly, he was sentenced to death.

II.

It is axiomatic by now that criminal prosecution of an incompetent defendant offends the Due Process Clause of the Fourteenth Amendment. The majority does not deny this principle, nor does it dispute the standard that has been set for competence to stand trial with the assistance of counsel: whether the accused possesses "the capacity to understand the nature and object of the proceedings against him, to consult with counsel, and to assist in preparing his defense." My disagreement with the majority turns, then, upon another standard – the one for assessing a defendant's competence to waive counsel and represent himself.

The majority "reject[s] the notion that competence to plead guilty or to waive the right to counsel must be measured by a standard that is higher than (or even different from)" the standard for competence to stand trial articulated in Dusky and Drope. But the standard for competence to stand trial is specifically designed to measure a defendant's ability to "consult with counsel" and to "assist in preparing his defense." A finding that a defendant is competent to stand trial establishes only that he is capable of aiding his attorney in making the critical decisions required at trial or in plea negotiations. The reliability or even relevance of such a finding vanishes when its basic premise – that counsel will be present – ceases to exist. The question is no longer whether the defendant can proceed with an attorney, but whether he can proceed alone and uncounseled. I do not believe we place an excessive burden upon a trial court by requiring it to conduct a specific inquiry into that question at the juncture when a defendant whose competency already has been questioned seeks to waive counsel and represent himself.

The majority concludes that there is no need for such a hearing because a defendant who is found competent to stand trial with the assistance of counsel is, ipso facto, competent to discharge counsel and represent himself. But the majority cannot isolate the term "competent" and apply it in a vacuum, divorced from its specific context. A person who is "competent" to play basketball is not thereby "competent" to play the violin. The majority's monolithic approach to competency is true to neither life nor the law. Competency for one purpose does not necessarily translate to competency for another purpose. Consistent with this commonsense notion, our cases always have recognized that "a defendant's mental condition may be relevant to more than one legal issue, each governed by distinct rules reflecting quite different policies." To this end, this Court has required competency evaluations to be specifically tailored to the context and purpose of a proceeding.

The record in this case gives rise to grave doubts regarding respondent Moran's ability to discharge counsel and represent himself. Just a few months after he attempted to commit suicide, Moran essentially volunteered himself for execution: He sought to waive the right to counsel, to plead guilty to capital murder, and to prevent the presentation of any mitigating evidence on his behalf. The psychiatrists' reports supplied one explanation for Moran's self-destructive behavior: his deep depression. And Moran's own testimony suggested another: the fact that he was being administered simultaneously four different prescription medications. It has been recognized that such drugs often possess side effects that may "compromise the right of a medicated criminal defendant to receive a fair trial . . . by rendering him unable or unwilling to assist counsel."Moran's plea colloquy only augments the manifold causes for concern by suggesting that his waivers and his assent to the charges against him were not rendered in a truly voluntary and intelligent fashion. Upon this evidence, there can be no doubt that the trial judge should have conducted another competency evaluation to determine Moran's capacity to waive the right to counsel and represent himself, instead of relying upon the psychiatrists' reports that he was able to stand trial with the assistance of counsel.

To try, convict, and punish one so helpless to defend himself contravenes fundamental principles of fairness and impugns the integrity of our criminal justice system. I cannot condone the decision to accept, without further inquiry, the self-destructive "choice" of a person who was so deeply medicated and who might well have been severely mentally ill. I dissent.

Notes and Queries

The Court addresses whether it should extend the use of the *Dusky* standard to evaluate the competency of defendants to make guilty pleas and waive their right to counsel. The *Dusky* standard asks whether the defendant has "sufficient present ability to consult with his lawyer with a reasonable degree of rational understanding" and has "a rational as well as factual understanding of the proceedings against him." The Court notes that it is difficult to distinguish that standard – a rational understanding of the proceedings – from the one offered by the circuit court. The circuit court had ruled that a higher standard was warranted, that there should be a focus on a reasoned choice among available alternatives. How similar do you find those standards? Would adopting either one lead to the same result in this case?

The Court holds that there may well be different levels of competency, but the Due Process clause doe not ask for more than the capacity to understand the proceedings and assist counsel. Fair? Do you find persuasive the concurring opinion's claim that a single standard of competency should operate throughout criminal proceedings?

The dissent asserts that the waivers resulted from medication and mental illness. Persuasive point? What do you think about considering the role of depression in determining levels of voluntariness or competency in the waiver of important trial rights? Do you agree with the claim that our legal system should not allow people to essentially volunteer themselves for death because of a mental illness? If you do agree, which mental illness would you count as a factor in determining the competency to waive rights?

Chapter 7

JUDGING JURIES

INTRODUCTION

The petit jury, the jury that hears cases to decide culpability and determine punishments, remains an integral fixture in law enforcement. The thought of being tried by a jury of one's peers dominates even though, as we already have learned, the vast majority of adjudications results from guilty pleas without ever having facts heard by juries. The popular image of juries often ignores a host of reasons that account for the infrequent use of jury trials, with those reasons ranging from the belief that juries are too costly, inappropriately biased, and incompetent to simply ineffective and inefficient.[1] Such criticisms may have contributed to the reduced use of juries, but the jury system itself remains remarkably resilient. Over 150,000 jury trials take place each year in the U.S. and, as a result, hundreds of thousands of citizens serve on juries within any given year.[2] And efforts to change and adapt to criticisms have not progressed much beyond their identification.[3] The right's constitutional status, of course, accounts for the pervasive hesitancy (and sometimes inability) to embark on systematic reforms. The Sixth Amendment ensures the right to a fair trial by jury, guaranteeing that "in all criminal prosecutions, the accused shall enjoy the right to a speedy and public trial, by an impartial jury."

As with the other constitutional mandates we have examined, turning the Amendment's protections into workable rules, and even deciphering the constitutional language, makes for a difficult task. Generally, however, the Sixth Amendment concerns itself with the identity of those who serve as jurors. For criminal trials, the Amendment's concerns result in two premises that guide the identity of juries. The first holds that the decision making process should involve communities. This premise derives from the Sixth Amendment's concern with a government-dominated justice, a concern which translates into a belief in participatory democracy. As a result, an underlying theme in many legal decisions about juries concerns who has been excluded from jury service as well as who should have an opportunity to serve. The second belief is that decision makers must be neutral. This premise derives form the Sixth Amendment guarantee that "all criminal prosecutions" will be tried by "an impartial jury" and from the 5th Amendment's Due Process Clause that requires an impartial judge. Importantly, the Supreme Court has limited the phrase "all criminal prosecutions" to include only crimes for which there are a possible penalty of imprisonment of at least six months;[4] and those crimes must be adjudicated in adult court, for the Supreme Court has exempted

---

[1] For a review, see Steven Penrod and Larry Heuer, Improving group performance: The case of the jury, in Theory and Research on Small Groups 127 (R. Scott Tindale, Linda Heath, Linda, John Edwards, Emil J. Posavac, Fred B. Bryant, Yolanda Suarez-Balcazar, Eaaron Henderson-King, and Judith Myers, eds., 1998).

[2] Michael J. Saks and Mollie Weighner Marti, A meta-analysis of the effects of jury size, 21 L. and Human Beh. 451 (1997).

[3] Phoebe C. Ellsworth and Alan Reifman, Juror comprehension and public policy: Perceived problems and proposed solutions, 6 Psych. Pub. Pol'y and L. 788 (2000).

[4] *Baldwin v. New York*, 399 U.S. 66 (1970).

the juvenile system from any jury trials.[5] These last two cases present settled law regarding who holds rights to jury trials, but the many aspects regarding the identity of juries and jurors raise many issues both in theory and in practice.

In addition to issues of identity and when juries may be required, the legal system adopts views of the roles juries are to play. The legal system most commonly treats juries as passive participants in trials until the formal beginning of deliberations. Two examples highlight the image of passive jurors. The first involves the admonition by the judge that jurors must simply listen and observe. Following jury selection, the court instructs jurors to listen carefully to the testimony, but not to form impressions or make judgments about the verdict until the presentation of all of the testimony and instructions on the law. Jurors then listen to testimony, arguments, and instructions. Courts typically do not invite jurors to clarify points by raising questions of their own; nor do they allow jurors to discuss amongst themselves the evidence or possible verdicts until the court provides them with final instructions. Common sense may suggest that few jurors can actually achieve the passivity envisioned by these norms, but the legal system proceeds as though such restrictions constitute attainable goals. The second example of the law's image of passive jurors involves the manner courts address matters of pretrial publicity or legally irrelevant testimony. In both instances, courts instruct jurors to set aside information already available to them and to reach their verdicts based simply on the legally permissible evidence the trial presents them. The legal system does offer changes of venue or grants mistrials as remedies in extreme cases where jurors could not be expected to erase powerful outside influences. Despite those mechanisms, the legal system pervasively relies on simple admonitions to disregard inadmissible information, an assumption that reflects a perception of the jury as a blank slate on which the trial writes or erases the admission of evidence.[6]

The blank slate image of juries and the view that juries represent community sentiments may be fundamental components of law enforcement trials, but they are potentially problematic even in cases that may not seem to constitute extreme violations of those assumptions. Empirical research has sought to investigate the law's basic premises. Although this area of research remains highly nuanced and sometimes even presents contradictory findings, research has developed to the point that important themes and key findings have emerged to provide us with an opportunity to think through many of the legal issues and cases dealing with Sixth Amendment law. As we will see, that vast majority of findings challenges the law's fundamental assumptions.

Information Processing Models

We already have seen that the legal system endorses a model of decision making that assumes jurors pay complete attention, withhold judgment until all of the facts are in, discard any information that the judge so instructs, and carefully weigh a host of intangible factors. Given the significance of this vision, research has sought to understand how and whether juries can live up to it. This research repeatedly finds that jurors often do not make decisions in the manner courts intend. As we will see, if research on human cognition reveals anything, it is that this model rarely holds true in practice. Having identified that failure, research has sought to understand whether the legal system's procedural rules appropriately channel and structure jurors' thinking and eventual decisions. Research again reveals that, despite those efforts, the general findings remain. Regardless of how courts instruct jurors, juries have difficulty following legal mandates.

A key example of jury failure to abide by implicit and explicit legal rules deals with the extent to which jurors can put aside their biases. As much as we may want to hold on to the view that jurors can place their biases and other sources of knowledge aside when hearing and deciding cases, reality continues

---

[5] *McKeiver v. Pennsylvania*, 403 U.S. 528 (1971).

[6] Judge Nancy Gertner and Judith H. Mizner, The Law of Juries 7-7 to 7-32 (1997).

to suggest otherwise. Studies of both jurors[7] and other human decision makers[8] reveal that people base decisions on past experience in the form of scripts, schemas, stereotypes,[9] and other cognitive mechanisms as well as personal beliefs and values about what is right, wrong, and fair. To help make sense of a complex and confusing chain of events, jurors almost invariably will use information perceived as relevant and useful. Jurors bring expectations and preconceptions with them to the jury box, actively search for causal explanations to make sense of the events described, and consciously or unconsciously process information so as to fill in missing blanks or interpret ambiguities in evidence in ways that may strongly influence their decisions. Jurors' expectations, beliefs, and values affect the way they see and react to evidence.[10]

The above view of jurors reveals that they are, in many respects, like other decision makers. As we already have seen in Chapter 1, people ordinarily scrutinize more carefully and are more likely to reject information presented as inconsistent with their beliefs and expectations.[11] People also find it easier to remember theory-consistent information than theory-inconsistent information.[12] People likewise tend to interpret ambiguous information as consistent with their previously held theories.[13] Although it may have been presumed that the legal system's strictures ensure a processing of information that effectively produces intended results, jurors may not necessarily act as model decision makers.

To complicate matters even more, we already have seen in the previous chapter the challenge faced by efforts to optimize decision making. It simply may not be humanly possible when decisions involve so many complex factors and contingencies. Cognitive science research, for example, has long revealed that human information processing usually is not "rational" in the sense of maximizing the use of relevant information. Instead, human judgment relies heavily on the use of prototypes, schemas, scripts, and other mental structures and representations to simplify and speed decision making. Few doubt that these mechanisms are at work; the main concern involves determining how they work and influence jury decisions.

Early models of jury decision making relied on cognitive science research that challenges the belief that we act rationally. That field of study led researchers to produce two important models. The first group of models are known as averaging models. These models view jurors as assessing and weighing pieces of

---

[7] W. Lance Bennett and Martha S. Feldman, Reconstructing Reality in the Courtroom: Justice and Judgment in American Culture (1981); Shari Seidman Diamond and Jonathan D. Casper, Blindfolding the jury to verdict consequences: Damages, experts, and the civil jury, 26 L. and Soc'y Rev. 513, 557 (1992); Shari Seidman Diamond, Michael J. Saks, and Stephan Landsman, Juror judgments about liability and damages: Sources of variability and ways to increase consistency, 48 DePaul L. Rev. 301, 315 (1998); Shari Seidman Diamond, Jonathan D Casper, Cami L Heiert, and Anna-Maria Marshall, Juror reactions to attorneys at trial, 87 J. Crim. L. and Criminology 17, 43 (1996); Nancy Pennington and Reid Hastie, A cognitive theory of juror decision making: The story model, 13 Cardozo L. Rev. 519, 519 (1991); and Nancy Pennington and Reid Hastie, Explaining the evidence: Tests of the story model for juror decision making, 62 J. Personality and Soc. Psych. 189, 189 (1992).

[8] Paul T.P. Wong and Bernard Weiner, When people ask "why" questions, and the heuristics of attributional search, 40 J. Personality and Soc. Psych. 650, 661-62 (1981).

[9] For our purposes, note that scripts simply are a series of expected events. Scripts govern a body of inferences, which, when activated, organize the comprehension of situations. They are significant in that scripts seem to help "fill the gaps" in comprehension. Schemas simply are the theories and meaning we bring to specific perceptions; when we perceive something, we incorporate it into our cognitive schemas. Stereotypes are a kind of schema about members of a social category.

[10] Vicki L. Smith and Christina Studebaker, What do you expect?: The influence of people's prior knowledge of crime categories on fact-finding, 20 L. and Hum. Behav. 517, 528-29 (1996).

[11] Charles G. Lord, Lee Ross, and Mark R. Lepper, Biased assimilation and attitude polarization: The effects of prior theories on subsequently considered evidence, 37 J. Personality and Soc. Psych. 2098, 2099 (1979); and Geoffrey D. Munro and Peter H. Ditto, Biased assimilation, attitude polarization, and affect in reactions to stereotype-relevant scientific information, 23 Personality and Soc. Psych. Bull. 636 (1997).

[12] Anne Locksley, Charles Stangor, Christine Hepburn, Ellen Grosovsky, and Mariann Hochstraser, The ambiguity of recognition memory tests of schema theories, 16 Cognitive Psych. 421, 422 (1984).

[13] Robert P. Vallone, Lee Ross, and Mark R. Lepper, The hostile media phenomenon: Biased perception and perceptions of media bias in coverage of the Beirut massacre, 49 J. Personality and Soc. Psych. 577, 584-85 (1985).

evidence and combining the results to reach a verdict.[14] The second group of models follow Bayesian approaches. These Bayesian models view jurors as considering and evaluating each new piece of information, revising their prior position on the appropriate verdict in light of their earlier position and the additional evidence.[15] Both of these models gained considerable significance. But the reason for the significance was unintended: the models are important for their pervasive failure to explain juries' decision making processes. The formal models may exemplify well the processes of some decision making, but they had limited success as descriptors of how jurors actually decide cases.

The failure of decision making models to help explain juror behaviors led to the construction of models that considered more closely the information jurors bring to the cases and jury room. The belief is that jurors draw on their prior understandings about the world as they evaluate and make sense of information presented at trial. They impose a narrative structure to describe and explain various possible events that led to the outcomes presented at trial. Not surprisingly, then, the most empirically supported model views jury decision making from the perspective of story-making.[16] The story model views jurors as more than simply recording and storing evidence for later use as they receive it. Rather, jurors actively select and organize the trial evidence to construct a story about the presented evidence. They construct a story based on both the evidence and gaps in evidence with inferences based on their understandings about how the world works. Jurors arrange evidence in the form of a sequence of actions that include important events, the circumstances of the case, inferences about character, and the parties' motivations and states of mind. Jurors interpret ambiguous testimony and fill in "blanks"– issues about which there is no testimony at all.[17] In short, the story model asserts that jurors do not approach the trial with a blank slate. Rather, they use their past experiences to filter and understand the various pieces of evidence. This means that, to the extent that jurors do process incoming information as diligently as they can, jurors still are not the passive rational recipients assumed by law. Indeed, the manner juries are formed and what they are required to do seems to ensure that they do not even abide by models developed by the best available cognitive science research.

How juries approach jury instructions illustrates well the power of stories and the significance of the story-making model. As we already have seen, a fundamental assumption underlying the jury system is the belief that juries are willing and able to follow the instructions of the presiding judge. Yet, limiting instructions – those that seek to control how jurors consider specific evidence – generally have proven to be ineffective and even have been associated with a paradoxical increase in the targeted behavior. Specifically, juries have been found to confuse evidence during deliberation, display "spillover" bias against defendants in joined trials, consider pretrial publicity, follow their initial impressions of guilt or innocence, and take into account the defendant's past criminal record.[18] The theme that emerges from these findings is that jurors are unwilling (or unable) to set aside information that appears relevant to determining what happened — regardless of what the judge (and thus the law) has to say about it.

---

[14] Norman H. Anderson, Foundations of Information Integration Theory (1981); and Martin F. Kaplan and Gwen DeArment Kemmerick, Juror judgment as information integration: Combining evidential and nonevidential information, 30 J. Personality and Soc. Psych. 493 (1974).

[15] David A. Schum and Anne W. Martin, Formal and empirical research on cascaded inference in jurisprudence, 17 L. and Soc'y Rev. 105 (1982).

[16] Nancy Pennington and Reid Hastie, A cognitive theory of juror decision making: The story model, 13 Cardozo L. Rev. 519 (1991); and Nancy Pennington and Reid Hastie, Explanation-based decision making: Effects of memory structure on judgment, 14 J. Experimental Psych.: Learning, Mem. and Cognition 521 (1988).

[17] Baruch Fischhoff, Hindsight [not =] foresight: The effect of outcome knowledge on judgment under uncertainty, 1 J. Experimental Psych.: Hum. Perception and Performance 288 (1975); and Jonathan D. Casper, Kennette Benedict, Jo L. Perry, Juror decision making, attitudes, and the hindsight bias, 13 L. and Hum. Beh. 291 (1989).

[18] Sarah Tanford and Steven Penrod, Social inference processes in juror judgments of multiple-offense trials, 47 J. of Personality and Soc. Psych. 749 (1984); Geoffrey P. Kramer, Norbet L. Kerr, and John S. Carroll, Pretrial publicity, judicial remedies, and jury bias, 14 L. and Hum. Beh. 409 (1990); Jerry I. Shaw and Paul Skolnick (1995). Effects of prohibitive and informative judicial instructions on jury decision making, 23 Soc. Beh. and Personality 319 (1995); and Kurt A. Carlson and J. Edward Russo, Biased interpretation of evidence by mock jurors, 7 J. of Exper'l Psych.: Appl. 91 (2001).

Given the overall pattern of findings and their consistency with the growing body of research on social cognition, strong evidence supports the notions that juries will make inferences based on extralegal information they are exposed to and that judicial instructions to the contrary will have little effect. To make matters even more problematic, research examining the degree to which jurors comprehend their instructions, typically assessed in both absolute terms (e.g., percent accuracy) and relative terms (i.e., by contrasting instructed conditions with uninstructed or nondeliberating conditions), invariably reveals that instructed jurors do not perform well in an absolute sense.[19] Importantly, however, instructed jurors tend to display better comprehension than uninstructed jurors[20] and instructed jurors who deliberate do tend to display somewhat better comprehension than nondeliberating jurors.[21] Despite these more encouraging findings, the long-standing rule is that absolute performance universally remains disappointing and that instructions may not be so helpful as we may have hoped.[22]

Importantly, the finding is not that jurors intend to disregard their instructions. The finding is that they may disregard them even when they want to follow them. A study of mock juror's reactions to graphic autopsy photographs at a simulated homicide trial illustrates how juror's inadvertently may be influenced by evidence that should not affect verdicts.[23] The research demonstrated that despite the mock jurors' beliefs that the photographs should not and did not influence their verdicts, those subjects who reported higher levels of outrage or vengefulness as a result of seeing the photos were more likely to render a guilty verdict. The authors concluded that although the graphic photographs clearly influenced verdicts, participants felt that they should not and did not. It is difficult to underestimate the significance of juror's failure to recognize their limitations. Jurors' inability even to recognize the extent to which such evidence affects them makes it rather unlikely for them to reduce or control the impact of the evidence when instructed to do so by a judge.

These findings have obvious practical significance. As with individual jurors, juries appear to have problems processing information in a prescriptively optimal fashion. The problem seems to stem from the manner attitudes are holistic entities that form quickly and influence subsequent information processing; and they are quite robust once formed and can sustain concerted efforts to correct them. Limiting instructions, the primary means of correcting these flaws in jurors' thinking, may do little to counter the inability of jurors to control their fundamental, "hardwired" cognitive processes. These findings lead us to focus on another group of studies, those that examine the impact of juror or jury characteristics and the relative predictive value of individual and group characteristics.

THE SIGNIFICANCE OF JUROR AND JURY CHARACTERISTICS

One of the clearest images people may have of trials most likely involves jury selection, especially the taxing effort made by opposing parties to select jurors they view as more partial to their case and to reject those who would be biased against them. The significance attached to juror selection and rejection has not escaped psychologists. In fact, research to determine the best predictors of verdicts has long been a staple

---

[19] Reid Hastie, David A, Schkade and John W. Payne, A study of juror and jury judgments in civil cases: Deciding liability for punitive damages, 22 L. and Hum. Beh. 287 (1998); and Reid Hastie, Steve Penrod and Nancy Pennington, Inside the Jury 140-41 (1983).

[20] Bradley Saxton, How well do jurors understand jury instructions? A field test using real juries and real trials in Wyoming, 33 Land and Water L. Rev. 59 (1998).

[21] Shari Seidman Diamond and Judith N. Levi, Improving decisions on death by revising and testing jury instructions, 79 Judicature 224 (1996). Accumulating evidence does support the notion that jury deliberations may somehow moderate the effect of biasing factors, such as the jurors' propensity to disregard inadmissible evidence. Kamala London and Narina Nunez, The effect of jury deliberations on jurors' propensity to disregard inadmissible evidence, 85 J. Applied Psych. 932, 937 (2000).

[22] Phoebe C. Ellsworth and Alan Reifman, Juror comprehension and public policy: Perceived problems and proposed solutions, 6 Psych. Pub. Pol. and L. 788 (2000).

of jury research. Although that research ranges widely, investigations tend to take two forms: one focuses on individual juror characteristics and another focuses on how the jury functions as a whole of its members. As we will see, the emerging general rule is that jury characteristics may predict jury outcomes better than individual juror verdict preferences.[24] This may not seem surprising given that it is the jury itself that eventually decides, but it does appear to be a rather striking finding given the focus the law places on the ability of attorneys and judges to exercise their discretion to accept or exclude jurors.

Juror Characteristics

Much of the work on participant characteristics has sought to identify relationships between juror characteristics and predeliberation verdict preferences. However, accumulating research reveals that few juror characteristics strongly predict verdict preferences.[25] In addition, those characteristics found to be related to juror verdict preferences have tended to have weak and inconsistent effects.[26] This is not to conclude that no juror characteristics may impact eventual verdicts. Some juror personality traits at least modestly relate to juror verdict preferences. In addition, juror personality traits, values and attitudes may seem somewhat influential. Although research has examined numerous characteristics, we focus on those factors that have received the most empirical attention.

The most illustrative and examined trait, authoritarianism, relates to the extent to which individuals tend to be rigid, conventional, conservative, power-oriented, and deferential to authority.[27] This trait may be one of the most reliable predictors of juror decision-making.[28] This area of research tends to examine verdict preferences and their relationships to two forms of authoritarianism: traditional and legal.

---

[23] Kevin S. Douglas, David R. Lyon and James R.P. Ogloff, The impact of graphic photographic evidence on mock jurors' decisions in a murder trial: Probative or prejudicial?, 21 L. and Hum. Beh. 485, 494 (1997).

[24] That individual jurors' tendencies are impacted by the others with them on a decision making body may be something intuitive, but it has been ignored by researchers. One particularly interesting study examined the appointment of three-judge panels on courts of appeals to determine evidence of the effect of judicial ideology on judges' votes. The study used the political party of the appointing president as a rough proxy for ideology. It tested three possible hypotheses. The first was whether a judge's votes, in ideologically contested areas, can be predicted by the party of the appointing president. The second was whether a judge's ideological tendency, in such areas, will be amplified if the panel has two other judges appointed by an appointing president of the same political party. The last was whether a judge's ideological tendency, in such areas, will be dampened if the panel has no other judge appointed by an appointing president of the same political party. The study confirmed all hypotheses in many areas, including affirmative action, campaign finance, sex discrimination, sexual harassment, piercing the corporate veil, disability discrimination, race discrimination, and review of environmental regulations. Notably, all three hypotheses were rejected in the areas of federalism, criminal appeals, and takings of private property, because Republican and Democratic appointees vote essentially alike. In the areas of abortion and capital punishment, the first hypothesis was confirmed, but the second and third were rejected; the argument for this finding was that judges voted their convictions in these areas and were unaffected by the composition of the panel. As a whole, the evidence suggests that judges are subject to group polarization, by which groups of like-minded people go to extremes, which supports the important implication that panel composition has a strong effect on likely outcomes. Cass R. Sunstein, David Schkade, and Lia Michelle Ellman, Ideological Voting on Federal Courts of Appeals: A Preliminary Investigation. U Chicago Law and Economics, Olin Working Paper No. 198 (2003).

[25] M. Juliet Bonazzoli, Jury selection and bias: Debunking invidious stereotypes through science, 18 Quinnipiac L. Rev. 247 (1998); and Michael J. Saks, What do jury experiments tell us about how juries (should) make decisions?, 6 S. C. Inter'y L. J. 1 (1997).

[26] Jeffrey R. Boyl, Psychological, cognitive, personality and interpersonal factors in jury verdicts, 15 L. and Psych. Rev 163 (1991); Solomon M. Fulero and Steve D. Penrod (1990). Attorney jury selection folklore: What do they think and how can psychologists help?, 3 Forensic Rep. 233 (1990); Reid Hastie, Steve Penrod and Nancy Pennington, Inside the Jury (1983); and Christy A. Visher, Juror decision making: The importance of evidence, 11 L. and Hum. Beh. 1 (1987).

[27] Theodor W. Adorno, Else Frankel-Brunswick, Daniel J. Levinson, and R. Nevitt Sanford, The Authoritarian Personality (abridged) (1950/1982).

[28] See Kathleen Stirrett Berg and Neil Vidmar, Authoritarianism and recall of evidence about criminal behavior, 9 J. Res. Personality 147 (1975); Robert M. Bray and Audrey M. Noble, Authoritarianism and decision in mock juries: Evidence of jury bias and group polarization, 36 Soc. Psych. 1424 (1978); and Douglas J. Narby, Brian L. Cutler, and Gary Moran, A meta-analysis of the association between authoritarianism and jurors' perceptions of defendant culpability, 78 J. Appl. Psych. 34 (1993).

Traditional authoritarianism refers to an individual's tendency to be politically conservative, hold conventional values, prefer powerful leadership, and manifest overly punitive and rigid thinking. Legal authoritarianism refers to an individual's tendency to engage in anti-libertarian thinking and specifically focuses on beliefs related to the legal system and an inclination to slight a defendant's civil liberties. Both forms help predict juror's responses to evidence and their eventual verdicts. Most notably, for example, a meta-analysis found that both forms of authoritarianism reliably but modestly associate with juror verdict preferences across 20 studies, with legal authoritarianism being a somewhat superior predictor than traditional authoritarianism.[29] In addition to those findings, important research suggests that authoritarians are particularly punitive toward low-status defendants[30] and defendants perceived as dissimilar from themselves.[31] Findings also indicate that authoritarianism associates with attitudes toward capital punishment: High authoritarians tend to favor the death penalty, while low authoritarians tend to oppose it.[32] This latter finding gains considerable significance in light of other research indicating that persons favoring the death penalty are more likely to convict criminal defendants.[33] Aside from being ostensibly predictive of verdicts, authoritarianism may influence other dimensions of juror decision-making critical to verdict determination. Authoritarianism associates with cognitive differences related to the processing and retrieval of information.[34] Memory of defendant's characteristics links with an authoritarian orientation, while memory of situational information, such as crime-related facts, links with a non-authoritarian orientation. Thus, the presence or absence of an authoritarian approach may affect how jurors assimilate, retain, and recall information, and ultimately how they decide cases.[35] The general conclusion that authoritarians tend to be more pro-conviction than non-authoritarians, however, is not without contextual exceptions; the effects of authoritarianism on criminal verdicts may depend on case-specific facts. But researchers have yet to explore the roles of these factors.

Juror values also have been the subject of important inquiry. A "belief in a just world," a personality construct premised on principles of perceived equity and fairness, repeatedly has been found to influence significantly juror decision making.[36] Believers in a just world adhere to the aphorism that people get what they deserve in life. Chance happenings challenge their sense of equity and are perceived as intolerably

---

[29] Douglas J. Narby, Brian L. Cutler, and Gary Moran, A meta-analysis of the association between authoritarianism and jurors' perceptions of defendant culpability, 78 J. Applied Psych. 34 (1993). See also Gary Moran, Brian L. Cutler, and Anthony De Lisa, Attitudes toward tort reform, scientific jury selection, and juror bias: Verdict inclination in criminal and civil trials, 18 L. and Psych. Rev. 309 (1994).

[30] See Kathleen Stirrett Berg and Neil Vidmar, Authoritarianism and recall of evidence about criminal behavior, 9 J. Res. Personality 147 (1975).

[31] Herman E. Mitchell and Donn Byrne, The defendant's dilemma: Effects of jurors' attitudes and authoritarianism on judicial decisions, 25 J. Personality and Soc. Psych. 123 (1973).

[32] Robert M. Bray and Audrey M. Noble, Authoritarianism and decision in mock juries: Evidence of jury bias and group polarization, 36 Soc. Psych. 1424 (1978).

[33] Researchers repeatedly identify one's attitude toward the death penalty as a reliable predictor of death penalty verdicts. William C. Thompson, Claudia L. Cowan, Phoebe C. Ellsworth, and Joan C. Harrington, Death penalty attitudes and conviction proneness: The translation of attitudes into verdicts, 8 L. and Hum. Beh. 95, 96 (1984); and John H. Blume, Sheri Lynn Johnson, and A. Brian Threlkeld, Probing "Death Qualification" through expanded voir dire, 29 Hofstra L. Rev. 1209 (2001). Note, however, that the evidence is not always conclusive. See Rogers Elliot and Robert J.Robinson, Death penalty attitudes and the tendency to convict or acquit, 15 L. and Hum. Beh. 389 (1991). Those researchers discuss three studies that found no significant relationship between one's attitude toward the death penalty and the issue of guilt/innocence. Importantly, and as we will see in the next section, death- qualified juries are more likely both to convict and to sentence a defendant to death than are mixed juries [death-qualified + excludables (those that would automatically vote against the death penalty no matter what the facts of the case)]. Faye Goldberg, Toward expansion of Witherspoon: Capital scruples, jury bias, and use of psychological data to raise presumptions in the law, 5 Harv. C.R. C.L. L. Rev. 53 (1970); George L. Jurow, New data on the effect of a "death qualified" jury on the guilt determination process, 84 Harv. L. Rev. 567 (1971); Samuel R. Gross, Determining the neutrality of death-qualified juries: Judicial appraisal of empirical data, 8 L. and Hum. Beh. 7 (1984); and Edward J. Bronson, On the conviction proneness and representativeness of the death-qualified jury: An empirical study of Colorado veniremen, 42 U. Colo. L. Rev. 1 (1970).

[34] See Kathleen Stirrett Berg and Neil Vidmar, Authoritarianism and recall of evidence about criminal behavior, 9 J. Res. Personality 147 (1975).

[35] See Luis Garcia and William Griffitt, Evaluation and recall of evidence: Authoritarianism and the Patty Hearst case, 12 J. Res. Personality 57 (1978).

threatening to their sense of justice, necessitating resort to justifications. As a result, when confronted with imbalance, believers in a just world, perhaps driven by a sense of cognitive dissonance, search for justifications to explain their result, regardless of the reasonableness of such explanations. Individuals who score high on just world scales tend to sentence defendants more harshly or, alternatively, to cast blame on the victim more than persons with low just world scale scores.[37] Importantly and again, the predictive value of just world scale scores may be gender specific, with beliefs predicting guilty verdicts for female jurors, but not for male jurors.[38] Importantly, the mitigating effect of a just world orientation on verdicts may be a function of crime type and case-specific variables. Certain crimes, in which the victim is readily discernible and perceptions of impropriety are more conceivable, will be particularly conducive to blaming the victim. Jurors attributing responsibility to rape victims, for example, tend to regard them as having acquiesced in the act and equate acquiescence with consent.[39] Again, however and depending on the crime, attitudes are likely to interact with other juror characteristics.[40]

Another factor that has received a considerable amount of empirical attention involves individuals' attitudes toward the death penalty. Results indicate that no cluster of attitudes has reached the level of firm conclusion than individuals' attitudes toward capital punishment. As we will see, in most jury trials involving a capital offense, jurors are screened for an unwillingness to impose the death penalty (i.e., "death-qualified"). Numerous studies have shown that death-qualified jurors are more likely than "excludable" jurors to favor conviction at the close of a trial.[41] Unlike other findings, however, experimental laboratory work on death penalty attitudes has been complemented by a growing body of field research. Most notably, one research report, drawing on data from 916 jurors who served on 257 sentencing-phase capital juries in 11 states, concluded that death-penalty attitudes play a critical role in juror information processing and deliberation conduct in capital trials.[42] Many jurors made premature decisions regarding the defendant's guilt, some as early as the prosecution's presentation of evidence in the guilt trial. Importantly jurors who adopted an early stance in favor of the death penalty tended to hold a cluster of pro-death attitudes in viewing death as the only acceptable punishment for various kinds of murder (including intentional murder), in believing capital punishment to have substantial value in deterring crime, and in lacking moral doubts about death as punishment. Of those taking an early stand on the defendant's guilt, 60% favored imposing the death penalty. These pro-death penalty individuals tended to be more convinced of the correctness of their view than those favoring life sentences and also more likely to inappropriately advocate for imposing the death penalty as the appropriate punishment during the guilt deliberations. The study provides numerous important findings, but for our purposes, one of the important lessons to take from the death penalty research was that the impact of the attitude was felt at the close of trials. Some juror preferences, then, actually do impact eventual verdicts.

---

36 Melvin J. Lerner, The Belief in a Just World (1980).

37 Kathleen C. Gerbasi, Miron Zuckerman, and Harry T. Reis, Justice needs a new blindfold: A review of mock jury research, 84 Psych. Bull. 323 (1977).

38 The finding is that females who convict have higher just world scale scores than females who acquit. See Gary Moran and John Craig Comfort, Scientific jury selection: Sex as a moderator of demographic and personality predictors of impaneled felony juror behavior, 43 J. Personality and Soc. Psych. 1052, 1054 (1982).

39 Hubert S. Feild and Leigh B. Bienen, Jurors and Rape: A Study in Psychology and Law (1980); Nona J. Barnett and Hubert S. Feild, Sex differences in attitudes toward rape, 18 J.C. Student Personnel 93 (1977); Hubert S. Feild, Attitudes toward rape: A comparative analysis of police, rapists, crisis counselors, and citizens, 36 J. Personality and Soc. Psych. 156 (1978); and Hubert S. Feild, Rape trials and jurors' decisions: A psychological analysis of the effects of victim, defendant, and case characteristics, 3 L. and Hum. Beh. 261 (1979).

40 Examining the impact of juror empathy on verdict in rape cases, Deitz reported that female jurors displayed more empathy for the victim of rape, and consequently believed more strongly that the defendant was guilty. See Sheila R. Deitz, Measurement of empathy toward victims and rapists, 43 J. Personality and Soc. Psych. 372 (1982).

41 Phoebe C. Ellsworth and Robert Mauro, Psychology and law, in 2 The Handbook of Social Psychology 684 (Daniel T. Gilbert, Susan T. Fiske, and Gardner Lindzey, eds., 1998); Jospeh W. Filkins, Christine M. Smith, and R.Scott Tindale (1998). An evaluation of the biasing effects of death qualification, in Theory and Research on Small Groups 153 (R. Scott Tindale, Linda Heath, Linda, John Edwards, Emil J. Posavac, Fred B. Bryant, Yolanda Suarez-Balcazar, Eaaron Henderson-King, and Judith Myers, eds., 1998).

Jury Characteristics

The field of jury research arguably has made its most significant contributions when it has examined the impact of jurors' characteristics when they act with other jurors. That research reveals the important point that individual characteristics that do not or only modestly impact individual juror verdict preferences do seem more predictive when the jury as a whole adopts certain characteristics. Having an impact requires reaching a critical threshold.

Bias related to jury composition has tended to occur in studies that manipulated the composition of juries to create juries that were homogeneous with regard to some focal variable. Parallel with the effect on juror verdict preference we have just reviewed, for example, jury-level authoritarianism/dogmatism links consistently to jury outcomes. Specifically, juries containing a high proportion of authoritarian/dogmatic jurors tend to convict more often and impose longer sentences than juries with a low proportion of such individuals.[43] This suggests that composition bias may be limited to situations in which most members of a jury are similar in some regard, such as, for example, when the juries are more female, death-qualified, authoritarian, or highly cynical toward accused persons. This suggestion actually appears to be supported by existing evidence revealing that jury-level effects do exist despite weak juror-level relationships.

Other important examples reveal stronger jury effects for circumstances that are only weakly predictable at the juror level. A particularly interesting example involves the finding that the weak findings associating sex and race with verdict preferences appear stronger when examined in relationship to jury verdicts. Although the research inevitably remains complex and full of nuances, a few general findings are worthy of note. In terms of gender, some studies have examined the multivariate influences of juror, defendant, and victim's gender. Findings suggest that an interactive effect may exist between juror and defendant's gender such that jurors may be less likely to convict a defendant of their own sex.[44] Research also suggests that an interactive effect exists between defendant and victim gender. A meta-analysis that integrated mock juror research examining the influence of defendant and victim gender on judgments of guilt and punishment indicated that the defendant's gender did not affect judgments of guilt.[45] But the study did find that jurors were slightly more punitive in sentencing male defendants and that, when the victim was female, jurors were more likely to find the defendant guilty and to punish the defendant more severely.[46]

---

[42] William J. Bowers, Marla Sandys and Benjamin D. Steiner, Foreclosed impartiality in capital sentencing: Jurors' predispositions, guilt-trial experience, and premature decision making, 83 Cornell L. Rev. 1476 (1998).

[43] Ramsey McGowen and Glen D. King, Effects of authoritarian, anti-authoritarian, and egalitarian legal attitudes on mock juror and jury decisions, 51 Psych. Rep. 1067 (1982); David R. Shaffer and Thomas Case, On the decision to testify in one's own behalf: Effects of withheld evidence, defendant's sexual preferences, and juror dogmatism on juridic decisions, 42 J. of Personality and Soc. Psych. 335 (1982); Robert M. Bray and Audrey M. Noble, Authoritarianism and decision in mock juries: Evidence of jury bias and group Polarization, 36 Soc. Psych. 1424 (1978); David R. Shaffer, Diane Plummer and Georgina Hammock, Hath he suffered enough? Effects of jury dogmatism, defendant similarity, and defendant's pretrial suffering on juridic decisions, 50 J. of Personality and Soc. Psych. 1059 (1986).

[44] See Aarnold M. Rose and Arthur E. Prell, Does the punishment fit the crime? A study in social valuation, 61 Am. J. Soc. 247 (1995); Cookie Stephan and Judy Corder Tully, The influence of physical attractiveness of a plaintiff on the decisions of simulated jurors, 101 J. Soc. Psych. 149 (1977); Cookie Stephan, Sex prejudice in jury simulation, 88 J. Psych. 305 (1974); and Stuart S. Nagel and Lenore J. Weitzman, Women as litigants, 23 Hastings L.J. 171 (1971). This same-sex bias also may be a function of juror empathy. Jurors may find it easier to identify with and take the perspective of same-sex defendants.

[45] See Ronald Mazzella and Alan Feingold, The effects of physical attractiveness, race, socioeconomic status, and gender of defendants and victims on judgments of mock jurors: A meta-analysis, 24 J. Applied Soc. Psych. 1315, 1316-17 (1994).

[46] See Ronald Mazzella and Alan Feingold, The effects of physical attractiveness, race, socioeconomic status, and gender of defendants and victims on judgments of mock jurors: A meta-analysis, 24 J. Applied Soc. Psych. 1315, 1316-17 (1994).

With regard to race, little evidence suggests simple effects.[47] Again, several studies yield interactions between jury race composition and defendant race, consistent with the similarity bias noted previously.[48] A substantial body of research has focused on the interactive effects of the juror, defendant, and victim's race, and the main effects of defendant and victim's race. An insightful group of studies used the same methodology but varied, for example, the racial composition of the subject pool.[49] Those studies indicated that both white and black mock jurors perceived racially dissimilar defendants as more culpable, particularly when the crime involved interracial rape. Specifically, white mock jurors rated black defendants as more culpable than white defendants, and offenses against white victims as more culpable than offenses against black victims. White mock jurors ascribed greater culpability to black defendants who committed interracial rape than white defendants who committed interracial rape. Similarly, black mock jurors rated white defendants as more culpable than black defendants, and offenses against black victims as more culpable than offenses against white victims. Black mock jurors ascribed greater culpability to white defendants who committed interracial rape than black defendants who committed interracial rape. The defendant's race also interacted with the strength of the evidence. When the evidence was arguably too weak to meet the required burden of proof, white mock jurors gave only white defendants the benefit of doubt. Interestingly, black mock jurors rated white defendants as being significantly more culpable than black defendants in both the marginal and strong evidence categories. Thus, black mock jurors gave black defendants the benefit of doubt when the evidence was arguably too weak for conviction and when the evidence strongly favored conviction. Importantly, support for a jury-defendant similarity bias also comes from field studies. One study observed that white-majority juries were much more likely to convict Hispanic defendants than white defendants, whereas Hispanic-majority juries tended to show the opposite pattern.[50] Another study found that sentence length for white defendants was positively correlated with the number of Hispanic jurors on the jury.[51] In summary, both groups of jurors exhibit preferential treatment for same-race defendants and victims: mock jurors were more punitive toward defendants when the victim was of the same race as the mock juror and the defendant was of a different race; and field studies reveal a similar trend.

Despite revealing important trends, it increasingly seems clear that this area of research becomes complicated by the strength of the evidence. What has been labeled the similarity-leniency theory has been challenged when examined in light of the strength of evidence. The issue has been whether individuals would still abide by the similarity-leniency theory or express the "black sheep effect," which proposes that when the evidence strongly favors conviction, individual jurors, in an effort to preserve the positive image of the juror's own race, will treat racially similar defendants more harshly than racially dissimilar defendants.[52] Thus, the similarity-leniency theory and the black sheep effect predict opposite results for cases in which the evidence strongly attests to the defendant's guilt. Research results have confirmed the similarity-leniency effect for weak evidence of guilt and the black sheep effect for strong evidence of guilt in the racial minority condition. Thus, when jurors anticipated being a member of the jury's racial minority, findings revealed a significant three-way interactive effect for juror race, defendant race, and strength of

---

[47] Jerry L. Shaw and Paul Skolnick (1995). Effects of prohibitive and informative judicial instructions on jury decision making, 23 Soc. Beh. and Personality 319 (1995).

[48] Howard C. Daudistel, Harmon M. Hosch, Malcolm D. Holmes and Jospeh B. Graves, Effects of defendant ethnicity on juries' dispositions of felony cases, 29 J. of Applied Soc. Psych. 317 (1999); Ramsey McGowen and Glen D. King, Effects of authoritarian, anti-authoritarian, and egalitarian legal attitudes on mock juror and jury decisions, 51 Psych. Rep. 1067 (1982); and DoloresA. Perez, Harom M. Hosch, Bruce Ponder and Gloria C. Trejo, Ethnicity of defendants and jurors as influences on jury decisions, 23 J. of Applied Soc. Psych. 1249 (1993).

[49] Denis Chimaeze E. Ugwuegbu, Racial and evidential factors in juror attribution of legal responsibility, 15 J. Exper'l Soc. Psych. 133 (1979).

[50] DoloresA. Perez, Harom M. Hosch, Bruce Ponder and Gloria C. Trejo, Ethnicity of defendants and jurors as influences on jury decisions, 23 J. of Applied Soc. Psych. 1249 (1993).

[51] Howard C. Daudistel, Harmon M. Hosch, Malcolm D. Holmes and Jospeh B. Graves, Effects of defendant ethnicity on juries' dispositions of felony cases, 29 J. of App. Soc. Psych. 317 (1999).

[52] Norbert L. Kerr, Robert W. Hymes, Alonzo B. Anderson, and James E. Weathers, Defendant-juror similarity and mock juror judgments, 19 L. and Hum. Beh. 545, 550-51, 556-57 (1995).

evidence. Jurors were less likely to convict same-race than different-race defendants when confronted with weak evidence. Conversely, jurors were more likely to convict same-race than different-race defendants when confronted with strong evidence. Victim race had no impact on the similarity-leniency or the black sheep effects. Importantly, the black sheep effect was not observed when jurors anticipated being in the jury's racial majority, suggesting that the jury's racial composition acts as a moderator for the black sheep effect. The study's findings support the conclusion that jurors, fueled by a psychological need to maintain a positive self-perception, may engage in ethnocentrism when rendering verdicts. Jury-defendant similarity bias has been observed across a number of studies and contexts and appears to be a robust phenomenon.[53] When the evidence against the defendant is weak or ambiguous, juries comprised of jurors who are demographically similar to the defendant tend to be lenient; however, when the defendant's culpability is clear, those juries tend to be harsher.

As may be the case with many areas of research investigating complex matters, some factors other than those investigated may be explaining trends. In this area, the study of race has been complicated by yet other factors. And those factors probably may transfer to other characteristics deemed important in predicting jury outcomes. Most notably, it may not be the defendant's race, but instead the defendant's "positive appeal" that influences verdicts.[54] Research which varies the defendant's overall attractiveness (as determined by participants' own judgments), including social and physical attractiveness, reveals that those factors are better predictors of verdicts than race of the defendant. Researchers, for example, manipulated defendant and victim race in a videotaped simulated rape trial. Findings revealed that a defendant perceived by jurors as having positive appeal was more likely to be judged not guilty, regardless of the defendant's race. Participants also rated the victim's positive appeal, but this variable had no effect on verdicts. These provocative findings call into doubt all research that failed to control for the extraneous variable of defendant attractiveness. Importantly, the study is not alone. Many studies examining the effect of defendant attractiveness on verdicts have reported attractiveness to be associated with leniency in criminal cases,[55] and studies report similar findings to hold even after deliberation.[56] In failing to address race and

---

[53] Other convincing support stems from a mock jury study which revealed an interaction between jury-defendant similarity and strength of evidence. Derek Chadee, Race, trial evidence and jury decision making, 1 Caribbean J. of Criminology and Soc. Psych. 59 (1996). Jurors in white-majority juries were more likely to vote to convict a black defendant and were more severe in their preferred verdict than jurors in black-majority juries when the prosecution's evidence was weak. In contrast, jurors in black-majority juries tended to be harsher on a black defendant when the evidence strongly pointed to the defendant's guilt, consistent with the "black sheep" effect observed in several studies with mock jurors. M. Juliet Bonazzoli, Jury selection and bias: Debunking invidious stereotypes through science, 18 Quinnipiac L. Rev. 247 (1998); and Nancy J. King, Postconviction review of jury discrimination: Measuring the effects of juror race on jury decisions, 92 Mich. L. Rev. 63 (1993).

[54] R. Michael Bagby, James D.A. Parker, Neil A. Rector, and Valery Kalemba, Racial prejudice in the Canadian legal system, 18 L. and Hum. Beh. 339 (1994).

[55] See Martin F. Kaplan and Gwen D. Kemmerick, Juror judgment as information integration: Combining evidential and non-evidential information, 30 J. Personality and Soc. Psych. 493 (1974); John E. Stewart, II, Defendant's attractiveness as a factor in the outcome of criminal trials: An observational study, 10 J. Applied Soc. Psych. 348 (1980); and Wayne Weiten, The attraction-leniency effect in jury research: An examination of external validity, 10 J. Applied Soc. Psych. 340 (1980). Research also suggests that the effect of attractiveness may be moderated by crime type and case-specific facts. For example, researchers have found that attractive defendants were treated more leniently for crimes of rape, robbery, and cheating, but more punitively for negligent homicide. Ronald Mazzella and Alan Feingold, The effects of physical attractiveness, race, socioeconomic status, and gender of defendants and victims on judgments of mock jurors: A meta-analysis, 24 J. Applied Soc. Psych. 1315, 1316-17 (1994). Note too that attractiveness may operate to the defendant's detriment when attractiveness is believed to have facilitated commission of the offense. Harold Sigall and Nancy Ostrove, Beautiful but dangerous: Effects of offender attractiveness and nature of crime on juridic judgments, 31 J. Personality and Soc. Psych. 410 (1975).

[56] One study, for example, provided mock jurors with a picture of an attractive or unattractive defendant and found postdeliberation verdict preferences to be more lenient for the attractive defendant and more severe with regard to the unattractive defendant after deliberation. Richard R. Izzett and Walter Leginski, Group discussion and the influence of defendant characteristics in a simulated jury setting, 93 J. of Soc. Psych. 271 (1974). Another study manipulated defendant attractiveness by presenting pictures of attractive and unattractive defendants and found that the attractive defendant was almost twice as likely to be acquitted than the unattractive defendant. Robert J. MacCoun, The emergence of extralegal bias during jury deliberations, 17 Crim. Jus. and Beh. 303 (1990). Consistent with Izzett and Leginski's

attractiveness as covariables, research designed to measure the effect of race may have inadvertently measured the effect of attractiveness.[57]

Notes and Queries

Describe the three models that address how jurors receive and evaluate information. What significance do you attach to the "story-making" model? Do you take seriously the finding that jurors have difficulty following judicial instructions? Note that, even if they do, the concern becomes to what extent is such an inability problematic. What issues does that raise? Suppose we do realize that some biases are problematic, what are we to do about it? As you read the cases that follow, consider the forces (legal rationales) against change as well as those that would allow for change.

Consider the research exploring the impact of juror characteristics on verdict opinions. How believable and useful is that research? Do you think, despite those findings, that experienced lawyers could still have the types of jury selection skills to actually end up with a jury favorable to her side? Despite the wide variety of participants to choose from, research has focused on characteristics of the jury and the defendant, with some attention directed toward victims and/or plaintiffs and very little toward attorneys or judges. How useful would that research be? What do you make of the jury deliberation research that moves beyond merely examining the impact of individual juror characteristics? Although deliberation findings are more empirically significant than research findings from individual juror characteristics, what do you make of their practical significance? Consider, for example, the similarity-leniency theory and the black sheep effect. Do you think attorneys would actually find that evidence useful when selecting juries? You may well end up thinking that this type of research is not very useful. When you read the cases that follow, consider the legal rationales that would allow us to take that research seriously, assuming that it is useful in the first place.

Law Note on the Process of Jury Selection

Understanding issues relating to juries first requires understanding the process of jury selection. That process proceeds in the following manner. The process first requires the creation of a list of names typically aimed to reach as many random adults as possible by, for example, taking voter registration rolls (sometimes complimented by other lists like welfare rolls) to create what is known as jury pools, jury lists, or jury wheels. In some states, judges appoint a commissioner or "key man" to select and maintain jury lists. A smaller venire or panel is then selected from the large list of potential jurors. This process uses simple questionnaires that provide information regarding those who are exempted. Typically, some individuals are routinely exempted (such as aliens, those under 18, felons, those suffering from mental defects) or some may request an exemption (if they have a critical occupation, doctor, nurse, mortician or if they can show that serving would pose un undue hardship or inconvenience). Some of the venirepersons who remain are then excluded through voir dire ("to see what is said"), the final phase of the screening

---

study, deliberation produced a sizeable leniency shift in favor of the attractive defendants but not for unattractive defendants.

[57]It is also possible that a relationship may exist between perceptions of attractiveness and racial bias. Familiarity and repeated exposure to stimuli, including people of different races, have been found to increase liking. This phenomenon, labeled the "mere exposure effect," may be an element in the development of racial bias. See generally David G. Myers, Exploring Psychology 511-13 (3d ed. 1996). Because people generally interact within their own racial groups, perceptions of attractiveness and racial bias may be codependent. As one is repeatedly exposed to members of one's own race, the race to which one is habituated is perceived as more attractive, and this perception may simultaneously evoke in-group bias. As one commentator put it, the syllogism is simply that familiarity breeds liking which in turn breeds in-group bias. See Douglas O. Linder, Juror empathy and race, 63 Tenn. L. Rev. 887 (1996).

process to produce a jury and a handful of alternate jurors that are acceptable to the parties and the court. This process permits parties to receive information about the potential jurors so that they may be excluded through challenges. Although the theoretical goal of the process is a fair and impartial jury, the parties aim to eliminate venire members they consider to be biased against them and a threat to their prospects of success. Jury selection is driven by challenges for cause (objections based on the qualifications or fitness of the juror) and peremptory challenges (discretionary challenges granted to parties by statute or rule). Challenges for cause are based on narrowly specified, provable, legally cognizable and explicitly stated grounds that directly implicate the venire member's impartiality. There is no limit to the number of challenges for cause that the parties may present, but the general rule is that a strike for cause will not be granted unless the evidence suggests a "fixed" opinion on the part of the venire member that would prevent an impartial verdict. Peremptory challenges, in contrast, are limited in number, but are presented as a matter of right – with no justification or explanation required; thus the name "peremptory." Moreover, until recently, peremptories were not subject to meaningful challenge by opposing counsel on any ground. Because an articulated foundation for such a challenge is normally not required, they generally reflect the moving party's "real or imagined" fear that the venire member threatens their interests. Voir dire procedures typically vary on three important dimensions, in terms of the: (1) questioning of venire members – what questions are asked, by whom (judge, counsel, or a combination), in what form (verbally or in a written questionnaire), with what level of specificity, with what types of answers expected, and with what follow up expected from the court or counsel; (2) forum in which venire members are questioned, such as whether the questioning is of the venire as a group, with venire member answers heard by all present, or whether the questioning is of individual candidates outside the hearing of the other venire members; and (3) the number of peremptories allowed each side, and whether the numbers for each are the same or different.

ETHICS NOTE ON THE USE OF JURY SCIENCE

Given that researchers have observed statistically significant effects for some demographic, attitudinal and group variables, these effects can be used to influence particular cases. Not surprisingly, there has been a rising interest in scientific jury selection to assist in detecting bias. Rather than relying on conventional jury selection, a technique in which attorneys rely on personal skills, intuition, and experience to select jurors, some now move toward a more scientific jury selection, a technique in which attorneys collaborate with social scientists in applying research findings to select jurors. Jury selection is a fast-growing application of the psycho-social sciences. Its practitioners use public opinion surveys, in-depth interviews, computer analysis correlating jurors' backgrounds and attitudes and laboratory simulations of impending trials to help lawyers select jurors likely to favor their side, exclude those likely to be hostile to it, and present their cases in ways psychologically designed to benefit from the unconscious needs and motives of the jurors. Both techniques obviously embrace the same goal: impaneling jurors who will be favorably disposed to the client's side of the case. In the aggregate, research suggests that scientific jury selection may be slightly more accurate in detecting bias than traditional jury selection methods relying on attorneys' intuitions and experiences.

The potential advantage of scientific jury selection raises several concerns: whether the advantage is fair, whether only a select few can afford the advantage, and whether their use perpetuates stereotypes. These ethical considerations have continued to plague the role of social science in the jury selection process. Those opposing the use of scientific jury selection argue that it undermines principles of justice embodied in the Sixth Amendment by allowing attorneys to select jurors partial to their side, and may be unconstitutional because it takes juror race into account in a way prohibited by *Batson v. Kentucky*, 476 U.S. 79 (1986). As one leading law review analysis put it, scientific jury selection "... violates the fundamental principle that juries should be impartial. Although some consultants claim that they merely equalize their clients' chances for a fair trial, lawyers and consultants concede that their ultimate goal is to win cases, even if that entails selecting prejudiced jurors." Note, The civil jury, 110 Harv. L. Rev. 1408, 1464 (1997). There is much to be said about this criticism. Obviously, accepting that demographic and attitudinal variables may predict jurors' verdicts, the risk of perpetuating stereotypes in the jury selection process becomes a legitimate concern. For further discussion, see Jose Felipe Anderson, Catch me if you can! Resolving the ethical tragedies in the brave new world of jury selection, 32 New Eng. L. Rev. 343 (1998).

Advocates of the scientific technique argue that both scientific jury selection and conventional jury selection seek the same outcome, but from different perspectives. Both selection techniques endeavor to eliminate jurors biased against their clients, while impaneling impartial jurors or jurors more favorable to their clients' position. Both techniques are rooted in an ability to detect biases and employ such determinations to their clients' advantage. Jury consultants applying scientific jury selection base their predictions of suspected bias on experiments using community members to assess bias. Attorneys applying conventional jury selection base their judgments of bias on experience, intuition, and perhaps even knowledge of general psychological research. The essential distinction between scientific jury selection and conventional jury selection is the former's use of scientific methodology and statistical analysis. In principle, there is no ethical distinction between the two techniques with regard to constitutional concerns. One is grounded in science, the other in experience and personal beliefs. Neither technique is flawless. Both an attorney's intuitions and a scientist's predictions may prove fallible. Given that attorneys, whether using the scientific or the conventional technique, will seek to impanel jurors most favorable to their client's position, the ethical concern may involve the selection process itself rather than particular techniques used in that process.

The costliness of scientific jury selection, which frequently enables the more wealthy to benefit from the technique, also creates a distinct ethical concern. Jeremy W. Barber, The jury is still out: The role of jury science in the modern American courtroom, 31 Am. Crim. L. Rev. 1225 (1994). Debate on the subject will no doubt continue given the essentially adversarial nature of our system. Given this foundation, the use of scientific jury selection would seem consistent with an adversarial approach in representing clients, particularly for attorneys who recognize their own weaknesses in the area of jury selection and endeavor to represent their clients zealously. In addition, it may well be that psychological research on juror biases and cognitive capacities may be justifiable in that identifying existing barriers to rational decision making and devising strategies to reduce their impact may improve the chances that juries will understand and consider each litigant's case without bias. For an important exchange on this issue, compare Victor Gold, Covert advocacy: Reflections on the use of psychological persuasion techniques in the courtroom, 65 N.C. L. Rev. 481 (1987) with J. Alexander Tanford and Sarah Tanford, Better trials through science: A defense of psychologist-lawyer collaboration, 66 N.C. L. Rev. 741 (1988).

Research Note on the Nature and Limits of Jury Research

The study of juries produces an enormous wealth of research findings. Unlike other areas of behavioral sciences examining legal processes, the study started with a massive multiyear project, initiated in 1953 by a team of researchers at the University of Chicago. The Chicago Jury Project generated a great deal of data and numerous publications in the late 1950s and early 1960s. The most well-known and influential report stemming from the project is Harry Kalven, Jr. and Hans Zeisel, The American Jury (1966), which reported the results of a massive field study comparing actual jury verdicts with the verdicts favored by trial judges in 3,500 civil and criminal jury trials. They found that judges and juries agreed on the appropriate verdict in 78% of the jury trials examined, with juries being more lenient than judges in 19% of the trials and more severe than judges in just 3% of the cases. However, to identify the source of these discrepancies, Kalven and Zeisel also conducted extensive postdeliberation interviews with jurors from 225 trials to reconstruct the distribution of verdict preferences on the first ballot during deliberation. When the distribution of verdict preferences was compared with final verdicts, Kalven and Zeisel discovered one of the most robust and widely replicated findings in jury research: The verdict preferred by the majority of jurors on the first ballot was the jury's final verdict over 90% of the time. Since the 1970s and 1980s, jury research has mushroomed.

Researchers primarily adopt four methodologies to study jury decision making: (1) mock jury experiments involving simulated trials, (2) post-deliberation interviews with, or surveys of, ex-jurors, (3) analyses of jury verdicts obtained from archival sources, and (4) field studies or experiments involving real juries. The mock jury paradigm has been used most frequently, and each approach clearly has its strengths and weaknesses. Mock jury studies allow a small number of focal variables to be examined with a high level of control over extraneous influences, and they also allow direct access to the deliberation process. However, these advantages come at a cost in terms of structural verisimilitude, which sometimes calls into question the relevance of their findings to actual juries. Field studies involving actual juries are obviously more realistic and their results more generalizable, but they require extensive cooperation from one or more courts, tend to involve small samples as a result, and confounding variables plague the interpretation of their findings. Surveys or interviews of ex-jurors also can serve as a source of data on real deliberations, but these methods are limited by the cognitive biases and limitations of respondents, which can make it difficult to reconstruct an accurate picture of what happened during deliberation. Finally, archival analyses also have the benefit of using real juries and often attain reasonable sample sizes, but relying on court records limits the variables that can be examined and confounding case differences can complicate the interpretation of findings. Ideally, then, any given topic would use multiple approaches and produce consistent findings across methodologies.

Importantly and as we have seen in our examination of research examining the abilities of juries, there has been a notable rise in the use of behavioral sciences, especially cognitive sciences. That research too is not without its limitations. One of the leading critics of the current rise in behavioral science research has reported an impressive analysis of three sets of limitations on behavioral decision theory research that legal behavioralists are often accused of failing to appreciate in their conclusions about human rationality: (1) features of this research that mask individual and situational differences in rational behavior and artificially heighten the apparent frequency of irrational behavior; (2) features unique to the experimental research setting that intentionally and unintentionally increase the likelihood of finding irrational behavior and distort perceptions of the frequency of irrational behavior outside of the laboratory; and (3) features of this research that diminish its real-world importance and its ability to provide prescriptive guidance in the law. See Gregory Mitchell, Taking behavioralism too seriously? The unwarranted pessimism of the new behavioral analysis of law, 43 Wm. and Mary L. Rev. 1907 (2002).

Admittedly, the use of behavioral sciences often runs the risk of ignoring important nuances, and the failure to do so may in turn run the risk of ignoring significant ways the sciences may assist the law. For example, dual-process models of information-processing hold immediate importance for specific areas of legal decision theory. Legal scholars interested in how the law may encourage or discourage the use and existence of social stereotypes and in how social stereotypes are or should be taken into account in the law recently have drawn on psychological research on social stereotyping to inform their work. Some of these scholars treat social stereotypes as automatic and uncontrollable, occurring through a heuristic mode of thought. See, e.g., Joseph W. Rand, The demeanor gap: Race, lie detection, and the jury, 33 Conn. L. Rev. 1, 41 (2000); Amy L. Wax, Discrimination as accident, 74 Ind. L.J. 1129, 1158 (1999). Yet, dual-process models of social cognition suggest that, while social stereotypes may serve as a default heuristic in much person perception, individuating information may also be taken into account via a less-automatic processing mode, and this mode may override the social stereotype arising from the heuristic mode under certain conditions. See Galen V. Bodenhausen, C. Neil Macrae, and Jeffrey S. Sherman, On the dialectics of discrimination: Dual processes in social stereotyping, in Dual-Process Theories in Social Psychology, 271-90 (Shelly Chaiken and Yaacov Trope, eds., 1999). The body of research on person perception is quite complex, and questions remain over the degree of control that individuals may exert over the stereotyping process, if any. See Susan T. Fiske, Stereotyping, prejudice, and discrimination, in 2 Handbook of Social Psychology, 364-75, 385-91 (Daniel T. Gilbert, Susan T. Fiske, and Gardner Lindzey, eds., 4th ed. 1998). The dual-process theories of person perception should, at a minimum, be taken into account when working in this area in order to ensure proper qualifications to one's conclusions. At any rate, it would be important to recognize the debate within psychology about the controllability of social stereotypes and biases. See Clark Freshman, Whatever happened to anti-Semitism? How social science theories of identify discrimination and promote coalitions between "different" minorities, 85 Cornell L. Rev. 313 (2000).

DETERMINING THE STRUCTURE OF JURIES: JURY SIZES

BALLEW v. GEORGIA
435 U.S. 223 (1977)

MR. JUSTICE BLACKMUN announced the judgment of the Court and delivered an opinion in which MR. JUSTICE STEVENS joined.

I.

In November 1973 petitioner Claude Davis Ballew was the manager of the Paris Adult Theatre at 320 Peachtree Street, Atlanta, Ga. On November 9 two investigators from the Fulton County Solicitor General's office viewed at the theater a motion picture film entitled "Behind the Green Door." After they had seen the film, they obtained a warrant for its seizure, returned to the theater, viewed the film once again, and seized it. Petitioner and a cashier were arrested. Investigators returned to the theater on November 26, viewed the film in its entirety, secured still another warrant, and on November 27 once again viewed the motion picture and seized a second copy of the film.

On September 14, 1974, petitioner was charged in a two-count misdemeanor accusation with

> distributing obscene materials ... in that the said accused did, knowing the obscene nature thereof, exhibit a motion picture film entitled 'Behind the Green Door' that contained obscene and indecent scenes. ...

...After a jury of 5 persons had been selected and sworn, petitioner moved that the court impanel a jury of 12 persons. That court, however, tried its misdemeanor cases before juries of five persons ... Petitioner contended that for an obscenity trial, a jury of only five was constitutionally inadequate to assess the contemporary standards of the community. He also argued that the Sixth and Fourteenth Amendments required a jury of at least six members in criminal cases.

The motion for a 12-person jury was overruled, and the trial went on to its conclusion before the 5-person jury that had been impaneled. At the conclusion of the trial, the jury deliberated for 38 minutes and returned a verdict of guilty on both counts of the accusation. ... After a subsequent hearing, the court denied an amended motion for a new trial.

Petitioner took an appeal to the Court of Appeals of the State of Georgia. There he argued: ... the use of the five-member jury deprived him of his Sixth and Fourteenth Amendment right to a trial by jury.

The Court of Appeals rejected petitioner's contentions. ... In its consideration of the five-person-jury issue, the court noted that Williams v. Florida had not established a constitutional minimum number of jurors...

In his petition for certiorari here, petitioner raised ... the unconstitutionality of the five-person jury We granted certiorari...

II.

III

When the Court in Williams permitted the reduction in jury size - or, to put it another way, when it held that a jury of six was not unconstitutional - it expressly reserved ruling on the issue whether a number smaller than six passed constitutional scrutiny. The Court refused to speculate when this so-called "slippery slope" would become too steep. We face now, however, the two-fold question whether a further reduction in the size of the state criminal trial jury does make the grade too dangerous, that is, whether it inhibits the functioning of the jury as an institution to a significant degree, and, if so, whether any state interest counterbalances and justifies the disruption so as to preserve its constitutionality.

Williams v. Florida ... generated a quantity of scholarly work on jury size. These writings do not draw or identify a bright line below which the number of jurors would not be able to function as required by the standards enunciated in Williams. On the other hand, they raise significant questions about the wisdom and constitutionality of a reduction below six. We examine these concerns:

First, recent empirical data suggest that progressively smaller juries are less likely to foster effective group deliberation. At some point, this decline leads to inaccurate factfinding and incorrect application of the common sense of the community to the facts. Generally, a positive correlation exists between group size and the quality of both group performance and group productivity. A variety of explanations have been offered for this conclusion. Several are particularly applicable in the jury setting. The smaller the group, the less likely are members to make critical contributions necessary for the solution of a given problem. Because most juries are not permitted to take notes, memory is important for accurate jury deliberations. As juries decrease in size, then, they are less likely to have members who remember each of the important pieces of evidence or argument. Furthermore, the smaller the group, the less likely it is to overcome the biases of its members to obtain an accurate result. When individual and group decisionmaking were compared, it was seen that groups performed better because prejudices of individuals were frequently counterbalanced, and objectivity resulted. Groups also exhibited increased motivation and self-criticism. All these advantages, except, perhaps, self-motivation, tend to diminish as the size of the group diminishes. Because juries frequently face complex problems laden with value choices, the benefits are important and should be retained. In particular, the counterbalancing of various biases is critical to the accurate application of the common sense of the community to the facts of any given case.

Second, the data now raise doubts about the accuracy of the results achieved by smaller and smaller panels. Statistical studies suggest that the risk of convicting an innocent person (Type I error) rises as the size of the jury diminishes. Because the risk of not convicting a guilty person (Type II error) increases with the size of the panel, an optimal jury size can be selected as a function of the interaction between the two risks. Nagel and Neef concluded that the optimal size, for the purpose of minimizing errors, should vary with the importance attached to the two types of mistakes. After weighting Type I error as 10 times more significant than Type II, perhaps not an unreasonable assumption, they concluded that the optimal jury size was between six and eight. As the size diminished to five and below, the weighted sum of errors increased because of the enlarging risk of the conviction of innocent defendants.

Another doubt about progressively smaller juries arises from the increasing inconsistency that results from the decreases. Saks argued that the "more a jury type fosters consistency, the greater will be the proportion of juries which select the correct (i.e., the same) verdict and the fewer 'errors' will be made." From his mock trials held before undergraduates and former jurors, he computed the percentage of "correct" decisions rendered by 12-person and 6-person panels. In the student experiment, 12-person groups reached correct verdicts 83% of the time; 6-person panels reached correct verdicts 69% of the time. The results for the former-juror study were 71% for the 12-person groups and 57% for the 6-person groups. ... Nagel and Neef tested the average conviction propensity of juries, that is, the likelihood that any given jury of a set would convict the defendant. They found that half of all 12-person juries would have average conviction propensities that varied by no more than 20 points. Half of all six-person juries, on the other hand, had average conviction propensities varying by 30 points, a difference they found significant in both real and percentage terms. Lempert reached similar results when he considered the likelihood of juries to compromise over the various views of their members, an important phenomenon for the fulfillment of the commonsense function. In civil trials averaging occurs with respect to damages amounts. In criminal trials it relates to numbers of counts and lesser included offenses. And he predicted that compromises would be more consistent when larger juries were employed. For example, 12-person juries could be expected to reach extreme compromises in 4% of the cases, while 6-person panels would reach extreme results in 16%. All three of these post -Williams studies, therefore, raise significant doubts about the consistency and reliability of the decisions of smaller juries.

Third, the data suggest that the verdicts of jury deliberation in criminal cases will vary as juries become smaller, and that the variance amounts to an imbalance to the detriment of one side, the defense. Both Lempert and Zeisel found that the number of hung juries would diminish as the panels decreased in size. Zeisel said that the number would be cut in half - from 5% to 2.4% with a decrease from 12 to 6 members. Both studies emphasized that juries in criminal cases generally hang with only one, or more likely two, jurors remaining unconvinced of guilt. Also, group theory suggests that a person in the minority will adhere to his position more frequently when he has at least one other person supporting his argument. In the jury setting the significance of this tendency is demonstrated by the following figures: If a minority viewpoint is shared by 10% of the community, 28.2% of 12-member juries may be expected to have no minority representation, but 53.1% of 6-member juries would have none. Thirty-four percent of 12-member panels could be expected to have two minority members, while only 11% of six-member panels would have two. As the numbers diminish below six, even fewer panels would have one member with the minority viewpoint and still fewer would have two. The chance for hung juries would decline accordingly.

Fourth, what has just been said about the presence of minority viewpoint as juries decrease in size foretells problems not only for jury decisionmaking, but also for the representation of minority groups in the community. The Court repeatedly has held that meaningful community participation cannot be attained with the exclusion of minorities or other identifiable groups from jury service. "It is part of the established tradition in the use of juries as instruments of public justice that the jury be a body truly representative of the community." The exclusion of elements of the community from participation "contravenes the very idea of a jury... composed of 'the peers or equals of the person whose rights it is selected or summoned to determine.'" Although the Court in Williams concluded that the six-person jury did not fail to represent adequately a cross-section of the community, the opportunity for meaningful and appropriate representation does decrease with the size of the panels. Thus, if a minority group constitutes 10% of the community, 53.1% of randomly selected six-member juries could be expected to have no minority representative among their members, and 89% not to have two. Further reduction in size will erect additional barriers to representation.

Fifth, several authors have identified in jury research methodological problems tending to mask differences in the operation of smaller and larger juries. For example, because the judicial system handles so many clear cases, decisionmakers will reach similar results through similar analyses most of the time. One study concluded that smaller and larger juries could disagree in their verdicts in no more than 14% of the cases. Disparities, therefore, appear in only small percentages. Nationwide, however, these small percentages will represent a large number of cases. And it is with respect to those cases that the jury trial right has its greatest value. When the case is close, and the guilt or innocence of the defendant is not readily apparent, a properly functioning jury system will insure evaluation by the sense of the community and will also tend to insure accurate factfinding.

Studies that aggregate data also risk masking case-by-case differences in jury deliberations. ... They found that judges held for plaintiffs 57% of the time and that juries held for plaintiffs 59%, an insignificant difference. Yet case-by-case comparison revealed judge-jury disagreement in 22% of the cases. ... Again, the averages masked significant case-by-case differences that must be considered when evaluating jury function and performance.

IV.

While we adhere to, and reaffirm our holding in Williams v. Florida, these studies, most of which have been made since Williams was decided in 1970, lead us to conclude that the purpose and functioning of the jury in a criminal trial is seriously impaired, and to a constitutional degree, by a reduction in size to below six members. We readily admit that we do not pretend to discern a clear line between six members and five. But the assembled data raise substantial doubt about the reliability and appropriate representation of panels smaller than six. Because of the fundamental importance of the jury trial to the American system of criminal justice, any further reduction that promotes inaccurate and possibly biased decisionmaking, that causes untoward differences in verdicts, and that prevents juries from truly representing their communities, attains constitutional significance.

Georgia here presents no persuasive argument that a reduction to five does not offend important Sixth Amendment interests...

Second, Georgia argues that its use of five-member juries does not violate the Sixth and Fourteenth Amendments because they are used only in misdemeanor cases. If six persons may constitutionally assess the felony charge in Williams, the State reasons, five persons should be a constitutionally adequate number for a misdemeanor trial. The problem with this argument is that the purpose and functions of the jury do not vary significantly with the importance of the crime...

Third, the retention by Georgia of the unanimity requirement does not solve the Sixth and Fourteenth Amendment problem. Our concern has to do with the ability of the smaller group to perform the functions mandated by the Amendments. That a five-person jury may return a unanimous decision does not speak to the questions whether the group engaged in meaningful deliberation, could remember all the important facts and arguments, and truly represented the sense of the entire community. Despite the presence of the unanimity requirement, then, we cannot conclude that "the interest of the defendant in having the judgment of his peers interposed between himself and the officers of the State who prosecute and judge him is equally well served" by the five-person panel.

Fourth, Georgia submits that the five-person jury adequately represents the community because there is no arbitrary exclusion of any particular class. We agree that it has not been demonstrated that the Georgia system violates the Equal Protection Clause by discriminating on the basis of race or some other improper classification. But the data outlined above raise substantial doubt about the ability of juries truly to represent the community as membership decreases below six. If the smaller and smaller juries will lack consistency, as the cited studies suggest, then the sense of the community will not be applied equally in like cases. Not only is the representation of racial minorities threatened in such circumstances, but also majority attitude or various minority positions may be misconstrued or misapplied by the smaller groups. Even though the facts of this case would not establish a jury discrimination claim under the Equal Protection Clause, the question of representation does constitute one factor of several that, when combined, create a problem of constitutional significance under the Sixth and Fourteenth Amendments.

V.

With the reduction in the number of jurors below six creating a substantial threat to Sixth and Fourteenth Amendment guarantees, we must consider whether any interest of the State justifies the reduction. We find no significant state advantage in reducing the number of jurors from six to five.

The States utilize juries of less than 12 primarily for administrative reasons. Savings in court time and in financial costs are claimed to justify the reductions. The financial benefits of the reduction from 12 to 6 are substantial; this is mainly because fewer jurors draw daily allowances as they hear cases. On the other hand, the asserted saving in judicial time is not so clear. Pabst in his study found little reduction in the time for voir dire with the six-person jury because many questions were directed at the veniremen as a group. Total trial time did not diminish, and court delays and backlogs improved very little. The point that is to be made, of course, is that a reduction in size from six to five or four or even three would save the States little. They could reduce slightly the daily allowances, but with a reduction from six to five the saving would be minimal. If little time is gained by the reduction from 12 to 6, less will be gained with a reduction from 6 to 5...

Petitioner, therefore, has established that his trial on criminal charges before a five-member jury deprived him of the right to trial by jury guaranteed by the Sixth and Fourteenth Amendments.

VI.

The judgment of the Court of Appeals is reversed, and the case is remanded for further proceedings not inconsistent with this opinion.

It is so ordered.

MR. JUSTICE STEVENS, concurring. [opinion omitted]

MR. JUSTICE WHITE, concurring in the judgment. [opinion omitted]

MR. JUSTICE POWELL, with whom THE CHIEF JUSTICE and MR. JUSTICE REHNQUIST join, concurring in the judgment. [opinion omitted]

MR. JUSTICE BRENNAN, with whom MR. JUSTICE STEWART and MR. JUSTICE MARSHALL join. [opinion omitted]

Notes and Queries

Ballew refers to *Williams v. Florida*, 399 U.S. 78 (1970). *Williams* had held that the Constitution does not require a 12-person jury. In making its decision, the Court noted that there was "no discernible evidence" for functional differences between juries of 6 and 12 members. That statement sparked criticism and a flurry of empirical research by social scientists in the mid-1970s. *Ballew* marked the end of the legal debate. *Ballew* makes an impressive use of research to examine the functioning of juries. Those findings are clearly identified and reviewed by the Court. What is your sense of those findings? How persuasive do you find that research? How much of a role do you suppose the psychological research played in the Court's ruling?

After taking a close look at the research findings, how relevant do you find them to the legal issue presented in this case? What exactly was the contested legal issue? Can you discern how the reviewed literature actually addressed that issue?

The Court also examines the state's interest in reducing the number of jurors below the number established in *Williams*. How thorough do you find that analysis? Can you think of other justifications? In this regard, consider the Supreme Court's reasoning offered in *Williams*. In that case, the Court had reasoned that the jury's purpose is to reach a commonsense judgment by a group of laymen and to ensure community participation and shared responsibility for determinations of guilt or innocence. The Court found no reason to believe that that purpose could not be served with a six person jury. In addition, the Court also noted that there was no concern with reaching a cross-section of the community as long as some groups were not arbitrarily excluded. These factors will figure prominently in the cases that follow. Note that this suggests that these factors precisely are the ones that research must address if it seeks to influence the Court's views of the number of jurors needed to hear cases. Based on this case, how responsive do you suppose the Court would be to empirical evidence examining the rationales for juries?

The research on jury size still suggests several small but reliable differences in the functioning of 6- and 12-person juries. A recent meta-analysis quantitatively assessed the effects of jury size on deliberation outcomes, using 17 studies that compared 6-person and 12-person juries. The researchers found that larger juries took significantly longer to deliberate (although the mean difference was only 20 minutes across all studies and 44 minutes in three studies based on actual juries), but participation tended to be greater and less variable in smaller juries. Larger juries were also much more likely to include an individual from a racial or ethnic minority. Finally, 12-person juries hung less often but were no more likely to arrive at the "correct" verdict as defined by preference of the majority of individuals in the population. Michael J. Saks and Mollie Weighner Marti, A meta-analysis of the effects of jury size, 21 L. and Hum. Beh. 451 (1997).

DETERMINING THE STRUCTURE OF JURIES: JURY VOTES

JOHNSON v. LOUISIANA
406 U.S. 356 (1972)

MR. JUSTICE WHITE delivered the opinion of the Court.

I.

Appellant Johnson was arrested at his home on January 20, 1968. There was no arrest warrant, but the victim of an armed robbery had identified Johnson from photographs as having committed the crime. He was then identified at a lineup, at which he had counsel, by the victim of still another robbery. The latter crime is involved in this case. Johnson pleaded not guilty, was tried on May 14, 1968, by a 12-man jury and was convicted by a nine-to-three verdict. His due process and equal protection challenges to the Louisiana constitutional and statutory provisions were rejected by the Louisiana courts, and he appealed here. We noted probable jurisdiction...

II.

Appellant argues that in order to give substance to the reasonable-doubt standard, which the State, by virtue of the Due Process Clause of the Fourteenth Amendment, must satisfy in criminal cases, that clause must be construed to require a unanimous-jury verdict in all criminal cases. In so contending, appellant does not challenge the instructions in this case. Concededly, the jurors were told to convict only if convinced of guilt beyond a reasonable doubt. Nor is there any claim that, if the verdict in this case had been unanimous, the evidence would have been insufficient to support it. Appellant focuses instead on the fact that less than all jurors voted to convict and argues that, because three voted to acquit, the reasonable-doubt standard has not been satisfied and his conviction is therefore infirm.

We note at the outset that this Court has never held jury unanimity to be a requisite of due process of law...

Entirely apart from these cases, however, it is our view that the fact of three dissenting votes to acquit raises no question of constitutional substance about either the integrity or the accuracy of the majority verdict of guilt. Appellant's contrary argument breaks down into two parts, each of which we shall consider separately: first, that nine individual jurors will be unable to vote conscientiously in favor of guilt beyond a reasonable doubt when three of their colleagues are arguing for acquittal, and second, that guilt cannot be said to have been proved beyond a reasonable doubt when one or more of a jury's members at the conclusion of deliberation still possess such a doubt. Neither argument is persuasive.

Numerous cases have defined a reasonable doubt as one "'based on reason which arises from the evidence or lack of evidence.'". ... the Court [has] recognized this evidentiary standard as "'impress[ing] on the trier of fact the necessity of reaching a subjective state of certitude of the facts in issue.'" In considering the first branch of appellant's argument, we can find no basis for holding that the nine jurors who voted for his conviction failed to follow their instructions concerning the need for proof beyond such a doubt or that the vote of any one of the nine failed to reflect an honest belief that guilt had been so proved. Appellant, in effect, asks us to assume that, when minority jurors express sincere doubts about guilt, their fellow jurors will nevertheless ignore them and vote to convict even if deliberation has not been exhausted and minority jurors have grounds for acquittal which, if pursued, might persuade members of the majority to acquit. But the mere fact that three jurors voted to acquit does not in itself demonstrate that, had the nine jurors of the majority attended further to reason and the evidence, all or one of them would have developed a reasonable doubt about guilt. We have no grounds for believing that majority jurors, aware of their responsibility and power over the liberty of the defendant, would simply refuse to listen to arguments presented to them in favor of acquittal, terminate discussion, and render a verdict. On the contrary it is far more likely that a juror presenting reasoned argument in favor of acquittal would either have his arguments answered or would carry enough other jurors with him to prevent conviction. A majority will cease discussion and outvote a minority only after reasoned discussion has ceased to have persuasive effect or to serve any other purpose – when a minority, that is, continues to insist upon acquittal without having persuasive reasons in support of its position. At that juncture there is no basis for denigrating the vote of so large a majority of the jury or for refusing to accept their decision as being, at least in their minds, beyond a reasonable doubt. Indeed, at this point, a "dissenting juror should consider whether his doubt was a reasonable one . . . [when it made] no impression upon the minds of so many men, equally honest, equally intelligent with himself." Appellant offers no evidence that majority jurors simply ignore the reasonable doubts of their colleagues or otherwise act irresponsibly in casting their votes in favor of conviction, and before we alter our own longstanding perceptions about jury behavior and overturn a considered legislative judgment that unanimity is not essential to reasoned jury verdicts, we must have some basis for doing so other than unsupported assumptions.

We conclude, therefore, that, as to the nine jurors who voted to convict, the State satisfied its burden of proving guilt beyond any reasonable doubt. The remaining question under the Due Process Clause is whether the vote of three jurors for acquittal can be said to impeach the verdict of the other nine and to demonstrate that guilt was not in fact proved beyond such doubt. We hold that it cannot.

Of course, the State's proof could perhaps be regarded as more certain if it had convinced all 12 jurors instead of only nine; it would have been even more compelling if it had been required to convince and had, in fact, convinced 24 or 36 jurors. But the fact remains that nine jurors – a substantial majority of the jury – were convinced by the evidence. In our view disagreement of three jurors does not alone establish reasonable doubt, particularly when such a heavy majority of the jury, after having considered the dissenters' views, remains convinced of guilt. That rational men disagree is not in itself equivalent to a failure of proof by the State, nor does it indicate infidelity to the reasonable-doubt standard. Jury verdicts finding guilt beyond a reasonable doubt are regularly sustained even though the evidence was such that the jury would have been justified in having a reasonable doubt; even though the trial judge might not have reached the same conclusion as the jury; and even though appellate judges are closely divided on the issue whether there was sufficient evidence to support a conviction. That want of jury unanimity is not to be equated with the existence of a reasonable doubt emerges even more clearly from the fact that when a jury in a federal court, which operates under the unanimity rule and is instructed to acquit a defendant if it has a reasonable doubt about his guilt, cannot agree unanimously upon a verdict, the defendant is not acquitted, but is merely given a new trial. If the doubt of a minority of jurors indicates the existence of a reasonable doubt, it would appear that a defendant should receive a directed verdict of acquittal rather than a retrial. We conclude, therefore, that verdicts rendered by nine out of 12 jurors are not automatically invalidated by the disagreement of the dissenting three. Appellant was not deprived of due process of law.

III.

In order to "facilitate, expedite, and reduce expense in the administration of criminal justice," Louisiana has permitted less serious crimes to be tried by five jurors with unanimous verdicts, more serious crimes have required the assent of nine of 12 jurors, and for the most serious crimes a unanimous verdict of 12 jurors is stipulated. In appellant's case, nine jurors rather than five or 12 were required for a verdict. We discern nothing invidious in this classification. We have held that the States are free under the Federal Constitution to try defendants with juries of less than 12 men. Three jurors here voted to acquit, but from what we have earlier said, this does not demonstrate that appellant was convicted on a lower standard of proof. To obtain a conviction in any of the categories under Louisiana law, the State must prove guilt beyond reasonable doubt, but the number of jurors who must be so convinced increases with the seriousness of the crime and the severity of the punishment that may be imposed. We perceive nothing unconstitutional or invidiously discriminatory, however, in a State's insisting that its burden of proof be carried with more jurors where more serious crimes or more severe punishments are at issue.

The judgment of the Supreme Court of Louisiana is therefore

Affirmed.

MR. JUSTICE BLACKMUN, concurring. [omitted]

MR. JUSTICE POWELL, concurring in No. 69-5035 and concurring in the judgment in No. 69-5046. [omitted]

DISSENT: MR. JUSTICE DOUGLAS, with whom MR. JUSTICE BRENNAN and MR. JUSTICE MARSHALL concur, dissenting.

The result of today's decisions is anomalous: though unanimous jury decisions are not required in state trials, they are constitutionally required in federal prosecutions. How can that be possible when both decisions stem from the Sixth Amendment?

It is said ... that the Sixth Amendment, as applied to the States by reason of the Fourteenth, does not mean what it does in federal proceedings, that it has a "due process" gloss on it, and that that gloss gives the States power to experiment with the explicit or implied guarantees in the Bill of Rights.

Do today's decisions mean that States may apply a "watered down" version of ...[constitutional protections]? Or are today's decisions limited to a paring down of civil rights protected by the Bill of Rights and up until now as fully applicable to the States as to the Federal Government?

These civil rights – whether they concern speech, searches and seizures, self-incrimination, criminal prosecutions, bail, or cruel and unusual punishments extend, of course, to everyone, but in cold reality touch mostly the lower castes in our society. I refer, of course, to the blacks, the Chicanos, the one-mule farmers, the agricultural workers, the offbeat students, the victims of the ghetto. Are we giving the States the power to experiment in diluting their civil rights? It has long been thought that the "thou shalt nots" in the Constitution and Bill of Rights protect everyone against governmental intrusion or overreaching. The idea has been obnoxious that there are some who can be relegated to second-class citizenship. But if we construe the Bill of Rights and the Fourteenth Amendment to permit States to "experiment" with the basic rights of people, we open a veritable Pandora's box. For hate and prejudice are versatile forces that can degrade the constitutional scheme.

I would construe the Sixth Amendment, when applicable to the States, precisely as I would when applied to the Federal Government.

II.

The plurality approves a procedure which diminishes the reliability of a jury. First, it eliminates the circumstances in which a minority of jurors (a) could have rationally persuaded the entire jury to acquit, or (b) while unable to persuade the majority to acquit, nonetheless could have convinced them to convict only on a lesser-included offense. Second, it permits prosecutors in Oregon and Louisiana to enjoy a conviction-acquittal ratio substantially greater than that ordinarily returned by unanimous juries.

The diminution of verdict reliability flows from the fact that nonunanimous juries need not debate and deliberate as fully as must unanimous juries. As soon as the requisite majority is attained, further consideration is not required ... even though the dissident jurors might, if given the chance, be able to convince the majority. Such persuasion does in fact occasionally occur in States where the unanimous requirement applies: "In roughly one case in ten, the minority eventually succeeds in reversing an initial majority, and these may be cases of special importance." One explanation for this phenomenon is that because jurors are often not permitted to take notes and because they have imperfect memories, the forensic process of forcing jurors to defend their conflicting recollections and conclusions flushes out many nuances which otherwise would go overlooked. This collective effort to piece together the puzzle of historical truth, however, is cut short ... Indeed, if a necessary majority is immediately obtained, then no deliberation at all is required in these States. To be sure, ... initial majorities normally prevail in the end, but about a tenth of the time the rough-and-tumble of the jury room operates to reverse completely their preliminary perception of guilt or innocence. The Court now extracts from the jury room this automatic check against hasty factfinding by relieving jurors of the duty to hear out fully the dissenters.

It is said that there is no evidence that majority jurors will refuse to listen to dissenters whose votes are unneeded for conviction. Yet human experience teaches that polite and academic conversation is no substitute for the earnest and robust argument necessary to reach unanimity...

Moreover, even where an initial majority wins the dissent over to its side, the ultimate result in unanimous-jury States may nonetheless reflect the reservations of uncertain jurors. I refer to many compromise verdicts on lesser-included offenses and lesser sentences. Thus, even though a minority may not be forceful enough to carry the day, their doubts may nonetheless cause a majority to exercise caution.

The new rule also has an impact on cases in which a unanimous jury would have neither voted to acquit nor to convict, but would have deadlocked. In unanimous-jury States, this occurs about 5.6% of the time. Of these deadlocked juries, Kalven and Zeisel say that 56% contain either one, two, or three dissenters. In these latter cases, the majorities favor the prosecution 44% (of the 56%) but the defendant only 12% (of the 56%). n5 Thus, by eliminating these deadlocks, Louisiana wins 44 cases for every 12 that it loses, obtaining in this band of outcomes a substantially more favorable conviction ratio (3.67 to 1) than the unanimous-jury ratio of slightly less than two guilty verdicts for every acquittal. By eliminating the one-and-two-dissenting-juror cases, Oregon does even better, gaining 4.25 convictions for every acquittal. While the statutes on their face deceptively appear to be neutral, the use of the nonunanimous jury stacks the truth-determining process against the accused. Thus, we take one step more away from the accusatorial system that has been our proud boast.

It is my belief that a unanimous jury is necessary if the great barricade known as proof beyond a reasonable doubt is to be maintained. This is not to equate proof beyond a reasonable doubt with the requirement of a unanimous jury. That would be analytically fallacious since a deadlocked jury does not bar, as double jeopardy, retrial for the same offense. Nevertheless, one is necessary for a proper effectuation of the other.

We therefore have always held that in criminal cases we would err on the side of letting the guilty go free rather than sending the innocent to jail. We have required proof beyond a reasonable doubt as "concrete substance for the presumption of innocence."

That procedure has required a degree of patience on the part of the jurors, forcing them to deliberate in order to reach a unanimous verdict. Up until today the price has never seemed too high. Now a "law and order" judicial mood causes these barricades to be lowered.

Proof beyond a reasonable doubt and unanimity of criminal verdicts and the presumption of innocence are basic features of the accusatorial system. What we do today is not in that tradition but more in the tradition of the inquisition. Until amendments are adopted setting new standards, I would let no man be fined or imprisoned in derogation of what up to today was indisputably the law of the land.

MR. JUSTICE BRENNAN, with whom MR. JUSTICE MARSHALL joins, dissenting. [omitted]

MR. JUSTICE STEWART, with whom MR. JUSTICE BRENNAN and MR. JUSTICE MARSHALL join, dissenting. [omitted]

MR. JUSTICE MARSHALL, with whom MR. JUSTICE BRENNAN joins, dissenting. [omitted]

NOTES AND QUERIES

What do you make of the argument that having so many dissenters creates a reasonable doubt? Do you find that the state's interest justifies the reduced number of juror members needed for finding guilt?

The case was decided along with *Apodaca v. Oregon*, 406 U.S. 404 (1972). In that case, pursuant to Oregon constitutional provisions authorizing a verdict by 10 of 12 jurors in criminal cases, except for first degree murder verdicts, three defendants were convicted of criminal offenses other than first degree murder in separate state prosecutions, two by 11 to 1 verdicts and one by a 10 to 2 verdict. The majority ruled that the Sixth Amendment's right to a jury trial did not require a unanimous verdict, thus creating no constitutional requirement under the Fourteenth Amendment that state law require a unanimous verdict. The majority also held that a unanimous verdict was not necessary for effective application of the Fourteenth Amendment's requirement that jury panels reflect a cross section of the community, without systematic exclusion of identifiable segments of the community.

Not surprisingly, one of the issues left open after *Johnson* was whether a conviction could be based on a non-unanimous six-member jury verdict without violating the 6th Amendment right to a jury trial. The Court directly addressed the issue in *Birch v. Louisiana*, 441 U.S. 130 (1979). In that case, the Court returned to *Ballew* to support the conclusion that a conviction by five-members of a six-person jury posed a threat to the preservation of the substance of the jury trial guarantee. Again, the Court rejected the state interest in saving the time and expense of trying cases in this manner due to reduced deliberation time and the reduced number of hung juries.

Several studies have examined the impact of allowing juries to reach a verdict without consensus; and several consistent findings have emerged. Specifically, juries not required to be unanimous tend to take less time to reach a verdict and take fewer poles. James H. Davis, Lorne Hulbert, Wing Tung Au, Xiao-Ping Chen, and Paul Zarnoth, Effects of group size and procedural influence on consensual judgments of quantity: The example of damage awards and mock civil juries, 73 J. Pers. and Soc. Psych. 703 (1997). Likewise, they hang (unable to reach a verdict) less often and also tend to cease deliberating when a quorum is reached, and jurors serving on juries required to reach unanimous verdicts have tended to report being more satisfied and confident that the jury reached the correct verdict. Michael J. Saks, Jury verdicts: The role of group size and social decision rule (1977). Importantly, the reality is that decision rule effects appear to be small but real and also likely to be contingent on other factors, such as the strength of the evidence. In other words, there may be only a small range of evidence in which decision rule effects consistently appear (i.e., when the prosecution/plaintiff's case is not particularly weak or strong).

Claiming Improper Jury Selection: Deriving Standards

DUREN v. MISSOURI
439 U.S. 357 (1979)

MR. JUSTICE WHITE delivered the opinion of the Court.

I.

Petitioner Duren was indicted in 1975 in the Circuit Court of Jackson County, Mo., for first-degree murder and first-degree robbery. In a pretrial motion to quash his petit jury panel, and again in a post-conviction motion for a new trial, he contended that his right to trial by a jury chosen from a fair cross section of his community was denied by provisions of Missouri law granting women who so request an automatic exemption from jury service. Both motions were denied.

At hearings on these motions, petitioner established that the jury-selection process in Jackson County begins with the annual mailing of a questionnaire to persons randomly selected from the Jackson County voter registration list. Approximately 70,000 questionnaires were mailed in 1975. The questionnaire contains a list of occupations and other categories which are the basis under Missouri law for either disqualification or exemption from jury service. Included on the questionnaire is a paragraph prominently addressed "TO WOMEN" that states in part:

> "Any woman who elects not to serve will fill out this paragraph and mail this questionnaire to the jury commission at once."

A similar paragraph is addressed "TO MEN OVER 65 YEARS OF AGE," who are also statutorily exempt upon request.

The names of those sent questionnaires are placed in the master jury wheel for Jackson County, except for those returning the questionnaire who indicate disqualification or claim an applicable exemption. Summonses are mailed on a weekly basis to prospective jurors randomly drawn from the jury wheel. The summons, like the questionnaire, contains special directions to men over 65 and to women, this time advising them to return the summons by mail if they desire not to serve. The practice also is that even those women who do not return the summons are treated as having claimed exemption if they fail to appear for jury service on the appointed day. Other persons seeking to claim an exemption at this stage must make written or personal application to the court.

Petitioner established that according to the 1970 census, 54% of the adult inhabitants of Jackson County were women. He also showed that for the periods June-October 1975 and January-March 1976, n15 11,197 persons were summoned and that 2,992 of these, or 26.7%, were women. Of those summoned, 741 women and 4,378 men appeared for service. Thus, 14.5% (741 of 5,119) of the persons on the postsummons weekly venires during the period in which petitioner's jury was chosen were female. In March 1976, when petitioner's trial began, 15.5% of those on the weekly venires were women (110 of 707). Petitioner's jury was selected from a 53-person panel on which there were 5 women; all 12 jurors chosen were men. None of the foregoing statistical evidence was disputed.

In affirming petitioner's conviction, the Missouri Supreme Court questioned two aspects of his statistical presentation. First, it considered the census figures inadequate because they were six years old and might not precisely mirror the percentage of women registered to vote. Second, petitioner had not unequivocally demonstrated the extent to which the low percentage of women appearing for jury service was due to the automatic exemption for women, rather than to sex-neutral exemptions such as that for persons over age 65.

The court went on to hold, however, that even accepting petitioner's statistical proof, "the number of female names in the wheel, those summoned and those appearing were well above acceptable constitutional standards." We granted certiorari ...

II.

> ... "petit juries must be drawn from a source fairly representative of the community,"

> jury wheels, pools of names, panels, or venires from which juries are drawn must not systematically exclude distinctive groups in the community and thereby fail to be reasonably representative thereof.

In order to establish a prima facie violation of the fair-cross-section requirement, the defendant must show (1) that the group alleged to be excluded is a "distinctive" group in the community; (2) that the representation of this group in venires from which juries are selected is not fair and reasonable in relation to the number of such persons in the community; and (3) that this underrepresentation is due to systematic exclusion of the group in the jury-selection process.

A.

With respect to the first part of the prima facie test ... women "are sufficiently numerous and distinct from men" so that "if they are systematically eliminated from jury panels, the Sixth Amendment's fair-cross-section requirement cannot be satisfied."

B.

The second prong of the prima facie case was established by petitioner's statistical presentation. Initially, the defendant must demonstrate the percentage of the community made up of the group alleged to be underrepresented, for this is the conceptual benchmark for the Sixth Amendment fair-cross-section requirement. ... Duren has relied upon a census measurement of the actual percentage of women in the community (54%). In the trial court, the State of Missouri never challenged these data. Although the

Missouri Supreme Court speculated that changing population patterns between 1970 and 1976 and unequal voter registration by men and women rendered the census figures a questionable frame of reference, there is no evidence whatsoever in the record to suggest that the 1970 census data significantly distorted the percentage of women in Jackson County at the time of trial. Petitioner's presentation was clearly adequate prima facie evidence of population characteristics for the purpose of making a fair-cross-section violation.

Given petitioner's proof that in the relevant community slightly over half of the adults are women, we must disagree with the conclusion of the court below that jury venires containing approximately 15% women are "reasonably representative"of this community. If the percentage of women appearing on jury pools in Jackson County had precisely mirrored the percentage of women in the population, more than one of every two prospective jurors would have been female. In fact, less than one of every six prospective jurors was female; 85% of the average jury was male. Such a gross discrepancy between the percentage of women in jury venires and the percentage of women in the community requires the conclusion that women were not fairly represented in the source from which petit juries were drawn in Jackson County.

C.

Finally, in order to establish a prima facie case, it was necessary for petitioner to show that the underrepresentation of women, generally and on his venire, was due to their systematic exclusion in the jury-selection process. Petitioner's proof met this requirement. His undisputed demonstration that a large discrepancy occurred not just occasionally, but in every weekly venire for a period of nearly a year manifestly indicates that the cause of the underrepresentation was systematic – that is, inherent in the particular jury-selection process utilized.

Petitioner Duren's statistics and other evidence also established when in the selection process the systematic exclusion took place. There was no indication that underrepresentation of women occurred at the first stage of the selection process – the questionnaire canvass of persons randomly selected from the relevant voter registration list. The first sign of a systematic discrepancy is at the next stage – the construction of the jury wheel from which persons are randomly summoned for service. Less than 30% of those summoned were female, demonstrating that a substantially larger number of women answering the questionnaire claimed either ineligibility or exemption from jury service. Moreover, at the summons stage women were not only given another opportunity to claim exemption, but also were presumed to have claimed exemption when they did not respond to the summons. Thus, the percentage of women at the final, venire, stage (14.5%) was much lower than the percentage of women who were summoned for service (26.7%).

The resulting disproportionate and consistent exclusion of women from the jury wheel and at the venire stage was quite obviously due to the system by which juries were selected. Petitioner demonstrated that the underrepresentation of women in the final pool of prospective jurors was due to the operation of Missouri's exemption criteria – whether the automatic exemption for women or other statutory exemptions – as implemented in Jackson County. Women were therefore systematically underrepresented. ...

III.

The demonstration of a prima facie fair-cross-section violation by the defendant is not the end of the inquiry into whether a constitutional violation has occurred. We have explained that "States remain free to prescribe relevant qualifications for their jurors and to provide reasonable exemptions so long as it may be fairly said that the jury lists or panels are representative of the community." However, we cautioned that "[the] right to a proper jury cannot be overcome on merely rational grounds." Rather, it requires that a significant state interest be manifestly and primarily advanced by those aspects of the jury-selection process, such as exemption criteria, that result in the disproportionate exclusion of a distinctive group.

The Supreme Court of Missouri suggested that the low percentage of women on jury venires in Jackson County may have been due to a greater number of women than of men qualifying for or claiming permissible exemptions, such as those for persons over 65, teachers, and government workers. Respondent further argues that petitioner has not proved that the exemption for women had "any effect" on or was responsible for the underrepresentation of women on venires.

However, once the defendant has made a prima facie showing of an infringement of his constitutional right to a jury drawn from a fair cross section of the community, it is the State that bears the burden of justifying this infringement by showing attainment of a fair cross section to be incompatible with a significant state interest. Assuming, arguendo, that the exemptions mentioned by the court below would justify failure to achieve a fair community cross section on jury venires, the State must demonstrate that these exemptions caused the underrepresentation complained of. The record contains no such proof, and mere suggestions or assertions to that effect are insufficient.

The other possible cause of the disproportionate exclusion of women on Jackson County jury venires is, of course, the automatic exemption for women. Neither the Missouri Supreme Court nor respondent in its brief has offered any substantial justification for this exemption. In response to questioning at oral argument, counsel for respondent ventured that the only state interest advanced by the exemption is safeguarding the important role played by women in home and family life. But exempting all women because of the preclusive domestic responsibilities of some women is insufficient justification for their disproportionate exclusion on jury venires...

> It is untenable to suggest these days that it would be a special hardship for each and every woman to perform jury service or that society cannot spare any women from their present duties. This may be the case with many, and it may be burdensome to sort out those who should be exempted from those who should serve. But that task is performed in the case of men, and the administrative convenience in dealing with women as a class is insufficient justification for diluting the quality of community judgment represented by the jury in criminal trials.
>
> If it was ever the case that women were unqualified to sit on juries or were so situated that none of them should be required to perform jury service, that time has long since passed.

We recognize that a State may have an important interest in assuring that those members of the family responsible for the care of children are available to do so. An exemption appropriately tailored to this interest would, we think, survive a fair-cross-section challenge. We stress, however, that the constitutional guarantee to a jury drawn from a fair cross section of the community requires that States exercise proper caution in exempting broad categories of persons from jury service. Although most occupational and other reasonable exemptions may inevitably involve some degree of overinclusiveness or underinclusiveness, any category expressly limited to a group in the community of sufficient magnitude and distinctiveness so as to be within the fair-cross-section requirement – such as women – runs the danger of resulting in underrepresentation sufficient to constitute a prima facie violation of that constitutional requirement. We also repeat the observation ... that it is unlikely that reasonable exemptions, such as those based on special hardship, incapacity, or community needs, "would pose substantial threats that the remaining pool of jurors would not be representative of the community."

The judgment of the Missouri Supreme Court is reversed, and the case is remanded for further proceedings not inconsistent with this opinion.

So ordered.

MR. JUSTICE REHNQUIST, dissenting.

The lot of a legislator or judge attempting to conform a State's jury selection process to the dictates of today's opinion, and yet recognize what may be very valid state interests in excusing some individuals or classes of individuals from jury service, is surely not a happy one. ...

The probability, then, is that today's decision will cause States to abandon not only gender-based but also occupation-based classifications for purposes of jury service. Doctors and nurses, though virtually irreplaceable in smaller communities, may ultimately be held by the Court to bring their own "flavor" or "indefinable something" to a jury venire. If so, they could then be exempted from jury service only on a case-by-case basis, and would join others with skills much less in demand whiling away their time in jury rooms of countless courthouses.

No one but a lawyer could think that this was a managerially sound solution to an important problem of judicial administration, and no one but a lawyer thoroughly steeped in the teachings of cases ... could think that such a solution was mandated by the United States Constitution. ...

The short of it is that the only winners in today's decision are those in the category of petitioner, now freed of his conviction of first-degree murder. They are freed not because of any demonstrable unfairness at any stage of their trials, but because of the Court's obsession that criminal venires represent a "fair cross section" of the community, whatever that may be. The losers are the remaining members of that community – men and women seeking to do their duty as jurors and yet minimize the inconvenience that such service entails, judicial administrators striving to make the criminal justice system function, and the citizenry in general seeking the incarceration of those convicted of serious crimes after a fair trial. I do not believe that the Fourteenth Amendment was intended or should be interpreted to produce such a quixotic result.

NOTES AND QUERIES

This case establishes the standard for determining violations of the "fair cross-section" requirement that petit juries must be drawn from a source fairly representative of the community. We can conceive the standard as follows. First, it must be determined whether the jury pool systematically excluded a distinctive group from the community which fails to make the pool reasonably representative of the community. Second, if a fair cross-section violation is shown, simply by making a *prima facie* (at first sight) case, then the state acquires the burden to demonstrate that it has a significant interest in having the violation. The first part of the standard requires three determinations: (1) whether the excluded group is "distinctive," (2) whether the representation of the excluded group is not fair and reasonable in relation to the number of individuals from that group in the community, and (3) whether the under-representation is due to systematic exclusion by the jury-selection process. The second part of the standard simply addresses whether the process furthers an appropriate state interest. As is clear, the analysis involves making numerous arguments, such as: What qualifies as a distinctive group? What is reasonable under-representation? and What appropriate state interest can justify the challenged selection process? What do you make of the Court's analysis of the challenge to the fair-cross section requirement in this case?

Given what we have learned about group decisions, is the outcome of this case sound? What psychological evidence would you use in support of the Court's ruling? How relevant is that research to the manner the Court approaches challenges to constitutional deficiencies in the jury pool?

How would you analyze this case? Suppose a deaf woman has been murdered and the defendant is deaf. The crime occurred in a small college town with the leading college for deaf students. The defendant is found guilty by a jury comprised of no deaf jurors. What would the defendant need to show if he wanted to challenge the deficiency of the jury pool on grounds that no deaf jurors were called to serve? What are his chances of winning? What state interests could the state marshal to support its case? Are deaf individuals a distinctive group? Should they count as a distinctive group? Do you suppose that the process of making the jury pool would systematically exclude them because of their disability? Does conceiving deafness as a disability make it easier or harder to make your case that the defendant' rights were violated?

Claiming Improper Jury Selection: Applying Standards

SWAIN v. ALABAMA
380 U.S. 202 (1965)

MR. JUSTICE WHITE delivered the opinion of the Court.

The petitioner, Robert Swain, a Negro, was indicted and convicted of rape in the Circuit Court of Talladega County, Alabama, and sentenced to death. His motions to quash the indictment, to strike the trial jury venire and to declare void the petit jury chosen in the case, all based on alleged invidious discrimination in the selection of jurors, were denied. The Alabama Supreme Court affirmed the conviction and we granted certiorari.

In support of his claims, petitioner invokes the constitutional principle announced in 1880 in Strauder v. West Virginia, where the Court struck down a state statute qualifying only white people for jury duty. Such a statute was held to contravene the central purposes of the Fourteenth Amendment: "exemption from unfriendly legislation against [Negroes] distinctively as colored, – exemption from legal discriminations, implying inferiority in civil society, lessening the security of their enjoyment of the rights which others enjoy . . . ." Although a Negro defendant is not entitled to a jury containing members of his race, a State's purposeful or deliberate denial to Negroes on account of race of participation as jurors in the administration of justice violates the Equal Protection Clause. This principle ... has been consistently and repeatedly applied in many cases coming before this Court. The principle of these cases is broadly based.

> For racial discrimination to result in the exclusion from jury service of otherwise qualified groups not only violates our Constitution and the laws enacted under it but is at war with our basic concepts of a democratic society and a representative government.

Further, "jurymen should be selected as individuals, on the basis of individual qualifications, and not as members of a race." Nor is the constitutional command forbidding intentional exclusion limited to Negroes. It applies to any identifiable group in the community which may be the subject of prejudice.

But purposeful discrimination may not be assumed or merely asserted. It must be proven, the quantum of proof necessary being a matter of federal law. It is not the soundness of these principles, which is unquestioned, but their scope and application to the issues in this case that concern us here.

I.

We consider first petitioner's claims concerning the selection of grand jurors and the petit jury venire. The evidence was that while Negro males over 21 constitute 26% of all males in the county in this age group, only 10 to 15% of the grand and petit jury panels drawn from the jury box since 1953 have been Negroes, there having been only one case in which the percentage was as high as 23%. In this period of time, Negroes served on 80% of the grand juries selected, the number ranging from one to three. There were four or five Negroes on the grand jury panel of about 33 in this case, out of which two served on the grand jury which indicted petitioner. Although there has been an average of six to seven Negroes on petit jury venires in criminal cases, no Negro has actually served on a petit jury since about 1950. In this case there were eight Negroes on the petit jury venire but none actually served, two being exempt and six being struck by the prosecutor in the process of selecting the jury.

It is wholly obvious that Alabama has not totally excluded a racial group from either grand or petit jury panels. Moreover, we do not consider an average of six to eight Negroes on these panels as constituting forbidden token inclusion within the meaning of the cases in this Court. Nor do we consider the evidence in this case to make out a prima facie case of invidious discrimination under the Fourteenth Amendment.

Alabama law requires that the three jury commissioners in Talladega County place on the jury roll all male citizens in the community over 21 who are reputed to be honest, intelligent men and are esteemed for their integrity, good character and sound judgment. In practice, however, the commissioners do not place on the roll all such citizens, either white or colored. A typical jury roll at best contains about 2,500 names, out of a total male population over 21, according to the latest census, of 16,406 persons. Each commissioner, with the clerk's assistance, produces for the jury list names of persons who in his judgment are qualified. The sources are city directories, registration lists, club and church lists, conversations with other persons in the community, both white and colored, and personal and business acquaintances.

Venires drawn from the jury box made up in this manner unquestionably contained a smaller proportion of the Negro community than of the white community. But a defendant in a criminal case is not constitutionally entitled to demand a proportionate number of his race on the jury which tries him nor on the venire or jury roll from which petit jurors are drawn. Neither the jury roll nor the venire need be a perfect mirror of the community or accurately reflect the proportionate strength of every identifiable group. "Obviously the number of races and nationalities appearing in the ancestry of our citizens would make it impossible to meet a requirement of proportional representation. Similarly, since there can be no exclusion of Negroes as a race and no discrimination because of color, proportional limitation is not permissible." We cannot say that purposeful discrimination based on race alone is satisfactorily proved by showing that an identifiable group in a community is underrepresented by as much as 10%. Here the commissioners denied that racial considerations entered into their selections of either their contacts in the community or the names of prospective jurors. There is no evidence that the commissioners applied different standards of qualifications to the Negro community than they did to the white community. Nor was there any meaningful attempt to demonstrate that the same proportion of Negroes qualified under the standards being administered by the commissioners. It is not clear from the record that the commissioners even knew how many Negroes were in their respective areas, or on the jury roll or on the venires drawn from the jury box. The overall percentage disparity has been small, and reflects no studied attempt to include or exclude a specified number of Negroes. Undoubtedly the selection of prospective jurors was somewhat haphazard and little effort was made to ensure that all groups in the community were fully represented. But an imperfect system is not equivalent to purposeful discrimination based on race. We do not think that the burden of proof was carried by petitioner in this case.

II.

Petitioner makes a further claim relating to the exercise of peremptory challenges to exclude Negroes from serving on petit juries.

In Talladega County the petit jury venire drawn in a criminal case numbers about 35 unless a capital offense is involved, in which case it numbers about 100. After excuses and removals for cause, the venire in a capital case is reduced to about 75. The jury is then "struck" – the defense striking two veniremen and the prosecution one in alternating turns, until only 12 jurors remain. This essentially is the Alabama struck-jury system, applicable in all criminal cases and available in civil cases. In this case, the six Negroes available for jury service were struck by the prosecutor in the process of selecting the jury which was to try petitioner.

In the trial court after the jury was selected, petitioner moved to have the jury declared void on Fourteenth Amendment grounds. Among other things the motion alleged:

> (4) That because of the systematic and arbitrary method of selecting the names of qualified male citizens, negro male citizens, by the Jury Commission of Talladega County, Alabama, the State can, and did in this case, readily strike members of the negro race and that there were only six negroes remaining on the final venire in this cause, in violation of the Fourteenth Amendment of the Constitution of the United States and also the Constitution of the State of Alabama . . . .

The main thrust of the motion according to its terms was the striking of the six Negroes from the petit jury venire. No evidence was taken, petitioner apparently being content to rely on the record which had been made in connection with the motion to quash the indictment. We think the motion, seeking as it did to invalidate the alleged purposeful striking of Negroes from the jury which was to try petitioner, was properly denied.

In providing for jury trial in criminal cases, Alabama adheres to the common-law system of trial by an impartial jury of 12 men who must unanimously agree on a verdict, the system followed in the federal courts by virtue of the Sixth Amendment. As part of this system it provides for challenges for cause and substitutes a system of strikes for the common-law method of peremptory challenge. Alabama contends that its system of peremptory strikes – challenges without cause, without explanation and without judicial scrutiny – affords a suitable and necessary method of securing juries which in fact and in the opinion of the parties are fair and impartial. This system, it is said, in and of itself, provides justification for striking any group of otherwise qualified jurors in any given case, whether they be Negroes, Catholics, accountants or those with blue eyes. Based on the history of this system and its actual use and operation in this country, we think there is merit in this position.

In contrast to the course in England, where both peremptory challenge and challenge for cause have fallen into disuse, peremptories were and are freely used and relied upon in this country, perhaps because juries here are drawn from a greater cross-section of a heterogeneous society. The voir dire in American trials tends to be extensive and probing, operating as a predicate for the exercise of peremptories, and the process of selecting a jury protracted. The persistence of peremptories and their extensive use demonstrate the long and widely held belief that peremptory challenge is a necessary part of trial by jury. Although " there is nothing in the Constitution of the United States which requires the Congress [or the States] to grant peremptory challenges," nonetheless the challenge is "one of the most important of the rights secured to the accused." The denial or impairment of the right is reversible error without a showing of prejudice...

The function of the challenge is not only to eliminate extremes of partiality on both sides, but to assure the parties that the jurors before whom they try the case will decide on the basis of the evidence placed before them, and not otherwise. In this way the peremptory satisfies the rule that "to perform its high function in the best way 'justice must satisfy the appearance of justice.'" Indeed the very availability of peremptories allows counsel to ascertain the possibility of bias through probing questions on the voir dire and facilitates the exercise of challenges for cause by removing the fear of incurring a juror's hostility through examination and challenge for cause. Although historically the incidence of the prosecutor's challenge has differed from that of the accused, the view in this country has been that the system should guarantee "not only freedom from any bias against the accused, but also from any prejudice against his prosecution. Between him and the state the scales are to be evenly held."

The essential nature of the peremptory challenge is that it is one exercised without a reason stated, without inquiry and without being subject to the court's control. While challenges for cause permit rejection of jurors on a narrowly specified, provable and legally cognizable basis of partiality, the peremptory permits rejection for a real or imagined partiality that is less easily designated or demonstrable.

It is often exercised upon the "sudden impressions and unaccountable prejudices we are apt to conceive upon the bare looks and gestures of another," upon a juror's "habits and associations," or upon the feeling that "the bare questioning [a juror's] indifference may sometimes provoke a resentment." It is no less frequently exercised on grounds normally thought irrelevant to legal proceedings or official action, namely, the race, religion, nationality, occupation or affiliations of people summoned for jury duty. For the question a prosecutor or defense counsel must decide is not whether a juror of a particular race or nationality is in fact partial, but whether one from a different group is less likely to be. It is well known that these factors are widely explored during the voir dire, by both prosecutor and accused. This Court has held that the fairness of trial by jury requires no less. Hence veniremen are not always judged solely as individuals for the purpose of exercising peremptory challenges. Rather they are challenged in light of the limited knowledge counsel has of them, which may include their group affiliations, in the context of the case to be tried.

With these considerations in mind, we cannot hold that the striking of Negroes in a particular case is a denial of equal protection of the laws. In the quest for an impartial and qualified jury, Negro and white, Protestant and Catholic, are alike subject to being challenged without cause. To subject the prosecutor's challenge in any particular case to the demands and traditional standards of the Equal Protection Clause would entail a radical change in the nature and operation of the challenge. The challenge, pro tanto, would no longer be peremptory, each and every challenge being open to examination, either at the time of the challenge or at a hearing afterwards. The prosecutor's judgment underlying each challenge would be subject to scrutiny for reasonableness and sincerity. And a great many uses of the challenge would be banned.

In the light of the purpose of the peremptory system and the function it serves in a pluralistic society in connection with the institution of jury trial, we cannot hold that the Constitution requires an examination of the prosecutor's reasons for the exercise of his challenges in any given case. The presumption in any particular case must be that the prosecutor is using the State's challenges to obtain a fair and impartial jury to try the case before the court. The presumption is not overcome and the prosecutor therefore subjected to examination by allegations that in the case at hand all Negroes were removed from the jury or that they were removed because they were Negroes. Any other result, we think, would establish a rule wholly at odds with the peremptory challenge system as we know it. Hence the motion to strike the trial jury was properly denied in this case.

III.

Petitioner, however, presses a broader claim in this Court. His argument is that not only were the Negroes removed by the prosecutor in this case but that there never has been a Negro on a petit jury in either a civil or criminal case in Talladega County and that in criminal cases prosecutors have consistently and systematically exercised their strikes to prevent any and all Negroes on petit jury venires from serving on the petit jury itself. This systematic practice, it is claimed, is invidious discrimination for which the peremptory system is insufficient justification.

We agree that this claim raises a different issue and it may well require a different answer. We have decided that it is permissible to insulate from inquiry the removal of Negroes from a particular jury on the assumption that the prosecutor is acting on acceptable considerations related to the case he is trying, the particular defendant involved and the particular crime charged. But when the prosecutor in a county, in case after case, whatever the circumstances, whatever the crime and whoever the defendant or the victim may be, is responsible for the removal of Negroes who have been selected as qualified jurors by the jury commissioners and who have survived challenges for cause, with the result that no Negroes ever serve on petit juries, the Fourteenth Amendment claim takes on added significance. In these circumstances, giving even the widest leeway to the operation of irrational but trial-related suspicions and antagonisms, it would appear that the purposes of the peremptory challenge are being perverted. If the State has not seen fit to leave a single Negro on any jury in a criminal case, the presumption protecting the prosecutor may well be overcome. Such proof might support a reasonable inference that Negroes are excluded from juries for reasons wholly unrelated to the outcome of the particular case on trial and that the peremptory system is being used to deny the Negro the same right and opportunity to participate in the administration of justice enjoyed by the white population. These ends the peremptory challenge is not designed to facilitate or justify.

We need pursue this matter no further, however, for even if a State's systematic striking of Negroes in the selection of petit juries raises a prima facie case under the Fourteenth Amendment, we think it is readily apparent that the record in this case is not sufficient to demonstrate that the rule has been violated by the peremptory system as it operates in Talladega County.

The difficulty with the record before us, perhaps flowing from the fact that it was made in connection with the motion to quash the indictment, is that it does not with any acceptable degree of clarity, show when, how often, and under what circumstances the prosecutor alone has been responsible for striking those Negroes who have appeared on petit jury panels in Talladega County. The record is absolutely silent as to those instances in which the prosecution participated in striking Negroes, except for the indication that the prosecutor struck the Negroes in this case and except for those occasions when the defendant himself indicated that he did not want Negroes on the jury. Apparently in some cases, the prosecution agreed with the defense to remove Negroes. There is no evidence, however, of what the prosecution did or did not do on its own account in any cases other than the one at bar. In one instance the prosecution offered the defendant an all-Negro jury but the defendant in that case did not want a jury with any Negro members. There was other testimony that in many cases the Negro defendant preferred an all-white to a mixed jury. One lawyer, who had represented both white and Negro defendants in criminal cases, could recall no Negro client who wanted Negroes on the jury which was to try him. The prosecutor himself, who had served since 1953, said that if the Negro defendant wanted Negroes on the jury it would depend "upon the circumstances and the conditions and the case and what I thought justice demanded and what [it] was in that particular case," and that striking is done differently depending on the race of the defendant and the victim of the crime. These statements do not support an inference that the prosecutor was bent on striking Negroes, regardless of trial-related considerations. The fact remains, of course, that there has not been a Negro on a jury in Talladega County since about 1950. But the responsibility of the prosecutor is not illuminated in this record. There is no allegation or explanation, and hence no opportunity for the State to rebut, as to when, why and under what circumstances in cases previous to this one the prosecutor used his strikes to remove Negroes. In short, petitioner has not laid the proper predicate for attacking the peremptory strikes as they were used in this case. Petitioner has the burden of proof and he has failed to carry it.

...This is not to say that a defendant attacking the prosecutor's use of peremptory challenges over a period of time need elicit an admission from the prosecutor that discrimination accounted for his rejection of Negroes, any more than a defendant attacking jury selection need obtain such an admission from the jury commissioners. But the defendant must, to pose the issue, show the prosecutor's systematic use of peremptory challenges against Negroes over a period of time. ... We see no reason, except for blind application of a proof standard developed in a context where there is no question of state responsibility for the alleged exclusion, why the defendant attacking the prosecutor's systematic use of challenges against Negroes should not be required to establish on the record the prosecutor's conduct in this regard, especially where the same prosecutor for many years is said to be responsible for this practice and is quite available for questioning on this matter. Accordingly the judgment is

Affirmed.

MR. JUSTICE HARLAN, concurring. [omitted]

MR. JUSTICE GOLDBERG, with whom THE CHIEF JUSTICE and MR. JUSTICE DOUGLAS join, dissenting.

Regrettably, however, the Court today while referring with approval to Strauder and the cases which have followed, seriously impairs their authority and creates additional barriers to the elimination of jury discrimination practices which have operated in many communities to nullify the command of the Equal Protection Clause. This is evident from an analysis of the Court's holding as applied to the facts which are virtually undisputed.

Petitioner, a 19-year-old Negro, was indicted in Talladega County for the rape of a 17-year-old white girl, found guilty, and sentenced to death by an all-white jury. The petitioner established by competent evidence and without contradiction that not only was there no Negro on the jury that convicted and sentenced him, but also that no Negro within the memory of persons now living has ever served on any petit jury in any civil or criminal case tried in Talladega County, Alabama. Yet, of the group designated by Alabama as generally eligible for jury service in that county, 74% (12,125) were white and 26% (4,281) were Negro.

Under well-established principles this evidence clearly makes out "a prima facie case of the denial of the equal protection which the Constitution guarantees."

It is clear that, unless the State here can "justify such an exclusion as having been brought about for some reason other than racial discrimination," this conviction "cannot stand." "Long continued omission of Negroes from jury service establishes a prima facie case of systematic discrimination. The burden of proof is then upon the State to refute it."

Alabama here does not deny that Negroes as a race are excluded from serving on juries in Talladega County. The State seeks to justify this admitted exclusion of Negroes from jury service by contending that the fact that no Negro has ever served on a petit jury in Talladega County has resulted from use of the jury-striking system, which is a form of peremptory challenge. While recognizing that no Negro has ever served on any petit jury in Talladega County, that the method of venire selection was inadequate, that the prosecutor in this case used the peremptory challenge system to exclude all Negroes as a class, and that the systematic misuse by the State of a peremptory challenge system to exclude all Negroes from all juries is prohibited by the Fourteenth Amendment, the Court affirms petitioner's conviction on the ground that petitioner has "failed to carry" his burden of proof. The Court holds this because it believes the record is silent as to whether the State participated in this total exclusion of all Negroes in previous cases; it would require petitioner specifically to negative the possibility that total exclusion of Negroes from jury service in all other cases was produced solely by the action of defense attorneys.

I cannot agree that the record is silent as to the State's involvement in the total exclusion of Negroes from jury service in Talladega County. The Alabama Supreme Court found that "Negroes are commonly on trial venires but are always struck by attorneys in selecting the trial jury." In response to a question concerning the operation of the jury-striking system, the Circuit Solicitor, the state prosecuting attorney, stated:

> Sometimes, it depends on who is involved in a case. We have been very fortunate in this county, we have not had any white against black or black against white. If we have – where we have a situation arising in a case such as that, in the cases that we have had – we have had no capital felonies, but, we strike a jury different from what if it was two white men involved or two colored men.

This statement, it seems to me, plainly indicates that, at the very least, the State – "we" – participates, in Talladega County, in employing the striking or peremptory challenge system to exclude Negroes from jury service in cases where white men are involved.

Also, the state prosecuting attorney testified as follows:

> Many times I have asked, Mr. Love for instance, I would say there are so many colored men on this jury venire, do you want to use any of them, and he would say, my client doesn't want them, or we don't see fit to use them. And then if I didn't see fit to use them, then we would take them off. We would strike them first, or take them off.
>
> If I am trying a case for the State, I will ask them what is their wish, do they want them [Negro jurors], and they will as a rule discuss it with their client, and then they will say, we don't want them. If we are not going to want them, if he doesn't want them, and if I don't want them, what we do then is just take them off. Strike them first.

These quotations show either that the State "many times" abandons even the facade of the jury-striking system and agrees with the defense to remove all Negroes as a class from the jury lists even before the striking begins, or that pursuant to an agreement the State directly participates in the striking system to remove Negroes from the venire. Indeed the Court recognizes that "apparently in some cases, the prosecution agreed with the defense to remove Negroes." The Court, however, goes on to state that "the record makes clear that this was not a general practice . . . ." With all deference, it seems clear to me that the record statement quoted by the Court to support this conclusion, cuts against rather than in favor of the Court's statement and inference that the general practice was not to exclude Negroes by agreement between the prosecution and defense or by the State acting alone. The prosecutor, in the statement quoted by the court, denied that he had stated that Negro defendants "generally do not want" Negroes to serve on juries and stated that there had only "been occasion here where that has happened." Since it is undisputed that no Negro has ever served on a jury in the history of the county, and a great number of cases have involved Negroes, the only logical conclusion from the record statement that only on occasion have Negro defendants desired to exclude Negroes from jury service, is that in a good many cases Negroes have been excluded by the state prosecutor, either acting alone or as a participant in arranging agreements with the defense.

Moreover, the record shows that in one case, the only one apparently in the history of the county where the State offered Negroes an opportunity to sit on a petit jury, the state prosecutor offered a Negro accused an all-Negro jury where the case involved an alleged crime against another Negro. The offer was refused but it tends to confirm the conclusion that the State joins in systematically excluding Negroes from jury service because it objects to any mixing of Negro and white jurors and to a Negro sitting in a case in which a white man is in any way involved.

Furthermore, the State concededly is responsible for the selection of the jury venire. As the Court recognizes, the evidence showed that while Negroes represent 26% of the population generally available to be called for jury service in Talladega County, Negroes constituted a lesser proportion, generally estimated from 10% to 15%, of the average venire. The Alabama Supreme Court noted that under state law "the jury commission is required to keep a roll containing the names of all male citizens living in the county who possess the qualifications prescribed by law and who are not exempted by law from serving on juries," and, in fact, this had not been done in Talladega County. The Alabama Supreme Court concluded that the method of jury selection in Talladega County was "not exhaustive enough to insure the inclusion of all qualified persons," ibid., and this Court admits it is "imperfect," and that "venires drawn from the jury box made up in this manner unquestionably contained a smaller proportion of the Negro community than of the white community." It may be, for the reasons stated by the Court, that this "haphazard" method of jury selection standing alone as an alleged constitutional violation does not show unlawful jury discrimination. However, this method of venire selection cannot be viewed in isolation and must be considered in connection with the peremptory challenge system with which it is inextricably bound. When this is done it is evident that the maintenance by the State of the disproportionately low number of Negroes on jury panels enables the prosecutor, alone or in agreement with defense attorneys, to strike all Negroes from panels without materially impairing the number of peremptory challenges available for trial strategy purposes.

Finally, it is clear that Negroes were removed from the venire and excluded from service by the prosecutor's use of the peremptory challenge system in this case and that they have never served on the jury in any case in the history of the county. On these facts, and the inferences reasonably drawn from them, it seems clear that petitioner has affirmatively proved a pattern of racial discrimination in which the State is significantly involved, or for which the State is responsible. As this Court held in Strauder, systematic exclusion of Negroes from jury service constitutes a brand of inferiority affixed upon them and state involvement in affixing such a brand is forbidden by the Fourteenth Amendment.

There is, however, a more fundamental defect in the Court's holding. Even if the Court were correct that the record is silent as to state involvement in previous cases in which Negroes have been systematically excluded from jury service, nevertheless, it is undisputed that no Negro has ever served on any petit jury in the history of Talladega County. Under ... the other cases discussed above, it is clear that petitioner by proving this made out a prima facie case of unlawful jury exclusion. The burden of proof then shifted to the State to prove, if it could, that this exclusion was brought about for some reason other than racial discrimination in which the State participated.

Finally, the Court's reasoning on this point completely overlooks the fact that the total exclusion of Negroes from juries in Talladega County results from the interlocking of an inadequate venire selection system, for which the State concededly is responsible, and the use of peremptory challenges. All of these factors confirm my view that no good reason exists to fashion a new rule of burden of proof, which will make it more difficult to put an end to discriminatory selection of juries on racial grounds and will thereby impair the constitutional promise of "Equal Protection of the Laws" ...

... I believe, however, that the preference granted by the Court to the State's use of the peremptory challenge is both unwarranted and unnecessary.

To begin with, the peremptory challenge has long been recognized primarily as a device to protect defendants. ...

While peremptory challenges are commonly used in this country both by the prosecution and by the defense, we have long recognized that the right to challenge peremptorily is not a fundamental right, constitutionally guaranteed, even as applied to a defendant, much less to the State. This Court has sanctioned numerous incursions upon the right to challenge peremptorily. Defendants may be tried together even though the exercise by one of his right to challenge peremptorily may deprive his codefendant of a juror he desires or may require that codefendant to use his challenges in a way other than he wishes. A defendant may be required to exercise his challenges prior to the State, so that some may be wasted on jurors whom the State would have challenged. Congress may regulate the number of peremptory challenges available to defendants by statute and may require codefendants to be treated as a single defendant so that each has only a small portion of the number of peremptories he would have if tried separately. ... "There is nothing in the Constitution of the United States which requires the Congress to grant peremptory challenges to defendants in criminal cases; trial by an impartial jury is all that is secured." ...

Were it necessary to make an absolute choice between the right of a defendant to have a jury chosen in conformity with the requirements of the Fourteenth Amendment and the right to challenge peremptorily, the Constitution compels a choice of the former. ...

NOTES AND QUERIES

Obviously, this case was heard and decided a long time before the Court offered a more systematic approach to challenging the selection of jury pools. The case, however, still is instructive for two reasons. The case is instructive for the lesson it provides us in determining what constitutes a *prima facie* case for the purpose of challenging systematic exclusion. What do you make of the majority's analysis? Reasonable? Recall that blacks were 26% of all male in the county over 21, and that only 10 to 15% have been asked to serve on grand and petit juries. Do you agree with the majority that this difference is enough to render the exclusion constitutionally deficient? Most students tend to agree that the exclusion is not dramatic enough. Yet, after *Swain*, a statistical study used the binomial distribution to analyze the venire data rejected as a *prima facie* case in *Swain*. The analysis determined that the chances of five or fewer African-Americans appearing in any given grand jury venire in Talladega County was approximately 20%. However, five or less African-American members of the venire occurred thirty consecutive times. Therefore, using the product rule, the analysis determined that "on the average, only one in more than one hundred million trillion groups each containing thirty venires would consist solely of venires which were not more than 15% African-American." Apparently, the Court in Swain may have been too quick to conclude that the absolute disparity of 10% was not statistically significant. Michael O. Finkelstein, The application of statistical decision theory to the jury discrimination cases, 80 Harvard L. Rev. 338, 356-58 (1976). What does this tell you about the burden needed to make a *prima facie* case?

Importantly, the Court has not always deferred to the state. For example, in the first case to expand the equal protection formula to a group other than blacks, *Castaneda v. Partida*, 430 U.S. 482 (1972), the Court invalidated a "key man" system which had resulted, over an 11-year period, in a 40% disparity (79% to 39%) between the proportion of those with Spanish surnames in the community and the proportion summoned for grand jury service. Importantly, however, the state had produced no evidence to explain its method of selection. The Court reasoned that the Spanish surnames were easily identifiable and subject to discrimination. Ultimately, the case suggested that procedures susceptible to abuse may mean that disparities necessary to show purposeful discrimination need not be as large as otherwise required, which also suggested that large disparities may support a *prima facie* case regardless of whether the procedure appears racially neutral. Note, again, that simply making a *prima facie* case does not mean that the defendant wins; it means that the burden then shifts to the state to provide adequate reasons to justify or explain the suspected discrimination.

Swain also is important for the manner it introduces and addresses the claim about peremptory challenges. Note that *Swain* also challenges the finding that there have been, on average, five to six black potential jurors who served on petit jury venires, but those jurors were excluded, with the result being that no black jurors serving on petit juries in the history of the county. Do you find that problematic? To address the claim, the Court examines the use of peremptory challenges. The majority and dissent both come to different conclusions on this matter. What are their rationales? How does the majority approach what would need to be proven in order to challenge peremptory challenges? Do you find it appropriate for the Court to assume that prosecutors are acting with pure motives? What do you make of the argument that there is no discrimination since any group could be excluded by peremptory challenges? What do you make of the finding that the prosecutors and defense at least some times collude to exclude black jurors? Given the psychological evidence we reviewed at the beginning of this chapter, what do you make of the use of peremptories? Good or bad idea?

Research Note on Race and Sentencing

A great deal of research has examined the role of race in criminal sentencing, particularly for capital crimes. Initial studies in the 1950s and 1960s revealed that the chances of an African American being sentenced to death were much higher than for a White individual. In 1972, the U.S. Supreme Court declared Georgia's death penalty law to be unconstitutional in *Furman v. Georgia*, 408 U.S. 238 (1972), as a result of the arbitrary and discriminatory manner in which it had been implemented. In response, many states passed new legislation featuring additional constraints on the capital sentencing process in an effort to make it more systematic. In particular, many state death penalty laws explicitly identified one or more "aggravating" factors that must be present to warrant a death sentence as well as a number of "mitigating" factors that, if one or more were present, could justify a life sentence. In 1976, Georgia's new death penalty law was upheld by the U.S. Supreme Court, in *Gregg v. Georgia*, 428 U.S. 153 (1976), and by implication the laws of other states as well. This initiated the modern era of the death penalty in the United States, with 37 states currently sanctioning capital punishment.

After *Gregg*, social scientists began working in earnest to determine if the new state laws were indeed less arbitrary and less discriminatory. Since 1976, numerous studies have examined relationships between the victim's race, defendant's race, and the imposition of the death penalty, using data gleaned from court records and/or interviews with ex-jurors. Most of these studies supported the notion that the race of the victim is an important factor in the determination of who received the death penalty, with the killers of White victims generally found to have higher odds than the killers of Black victims. Furthermore, a number of studies also found disparities suggesting that a victim's race interacted with a defendant's race such that a Black convicted of killing a White stood a much greater chance of receiving the death penalty than a White who killed another White. The most famous research in this area became known as the "Baldus study." David C. Baldus, Charles Pulaski, and George Woodworth, Comparative review of death sentences: An empirical dtudy of the Georgia experience, 74 J. Crim. L. and Criminology 661 (1983). In the early 1980s, researchers became increasingly concerned with accounting for the impact of case characteristics associated with the crime on racial disparities in capital sentencing. Using various methodologies, several studies conducted in the 1980s suggested that disparities in death sentencing rates were smaller (and sometimes eliminated) when characteristics of the crime were included. One study reanalyzed the post-Furman cases from the Baldus study after grouping cases into homogeneous clusters on the basis of seriousness of the crime (i.e., deliberateness of the killing, the victim – defendant relationship, and the heinousness of the killing). In contrast to the Baldus findings, Barnett observed that Whites were more likely to be the victims of more serious killings and noted that sentencing disparities as a function of victim race were concentrated in the middle range of the seriousness index. Arnold Barnett, Some distribution patterns for the Georgia death sentence, 18 U. C.Davis L.Rev. 1327 (1985). Other studies have found similar effects, such as one conducted in California noting that White defendants and killers with White victims were more likely to be sentenced to death but that these disparities vanished when case characteristics were taken into account. Stephen P. Klein and John E. Rolph, Relationship of offender and victim race to death sentences in California, 32 Jurimetrics 33 (1991).

Arguably, the best overview of the early research assessing post-Furman evidence about race discrimination and the death penalty appeared in 1990. The General Accounting Office ("GAO"), at the request of the United States Senate, published the results of a systematic review of the empirical studies conducted by a variety of investigators in the 1970s and 1980s. See U.S. Gen. Acct. Off., Death Penalty Sentencing: Research Indicates Pattern of Racial Disparities (1990). The agency evaluated twenty-eight empirical studies. It sought to assess the extent to which the existing literature supported claims of (1) race-of-defendant discrimination and (2) race-of-victim discrimination. On the issue of race-of-victim discrimination, the agency reported that:

> In 82 percent of the studies, race of victim was found to influence the likelihood of being charged with capital murder or receiving the death penalty, i.e., those who murdered whites were found to be more likely to be sentenced to death than those who murdered blacks. This finding was remarkably

> consistent across data sets, states, data collection methods, and analytic techniques. The finding held for high, medium, and low quality studies.
>
> The race of victim influence was found at all stages of the criminal justice system process, although there were variations among studies as to whether there was a race of victim influence at specific stages. The evidence for the race of victim influence was stronger for the earlier stages of the judicial process (e.g., prosecutorial decision to charge defendant with a capital offense, decision to proceed to trial rather than plea bargain) than in later stages. This was because the earlier stages were comprised of larger samples allowing for more rigorous analyses. However, decisions made at every stage of the process necessarily affect an individual's likelihood of being sentenced to death. Id. at 5-6

The largest of the studies the GAO reviewed was based on a stratified sample of 1066 cases drawn from a universe of 2484 cases processed in the Georgia charging and sentencing system in the period 1973-80 ("the Baldus study"). These results, which were the basis of the petitioner's claim of racial discrimination in *McCleskey v. Kemp*, 481 U.S. 279 (1987) indicated that, after controlling for the presence or absence of hundreds of legitimate case characteristics, defendants with white victims faced, on average, odds of receiving a death sentence that were 4.3 times higher than the odds of similarly situated defendants whose victims were black. This study also demonstrated that in Fulton County, where the jury sentenced McCleskey to death, significant race-of-victim disparities existed.

With regard to an effect for race of defendant, the data were more equivocal. More than half of the studies showed an effect for defendant race, but simple effects differed considerably in magnitude across studies and sometimes race of defendant interacted with other factors. The study concluded:

> Although more than half of the studies found that race of defendant influenced the likelihood of being charged with a capital crime or receiving the death penalty, the relationship between race of defendant and outcome varied across studies. For example, sometimes the race of defendant interacted with another factor. In one study researchers found that in rural areas black defendants were more likely to receive death sentences, and in urban areas white defendants were more likely to receive death sentences. In a few studies, analyses revealed that the black defendant/white victim combination was the most likely to receive the death penalty. However, the extent to which the finding was influenced by race of victim rather than race of defendant was unclear. Id. at 6.

Baldus and his colleagues recently extended the earlier GAO review by reexamining the extent of racial discrimination in all of the studies included in the GAO's review as well as subsequent studies on the topic. They were able to obtain some sentencing data from 29 of the 37 states with death penalty statutes; they found that race-of-victim disparities existed in 90% of those states, whereas race-of-defendant effects were observed in 55% of the states. David C. Baldus, Racial discrimination and the death penalty in the post-*Furman* era: An empirical and legal overview, with recent findings from Philadelphia, 83 Cornell L. Rev. 1638 (1998). They then presented the results of an exceptional archival study of capital sentencing in Pennsylvania. Beginning with a sophisticated sampling plan that included the entire population of death-eligible cases, they examined race-of-defendant and race-of-victim effects at several decision points in the Philadelphia criminal justice system between 1983 and 1993. One noteworthy feature of their study was the use of four independent measures of defendant culpability, including the number of aggravating and mitigating factors found to be present by the jury. Strong effects for race of defendant and race of victim were observed with all four measures, and these effects were generally stronger for jury decisions as opposed to prosecutorial decisions. Moreover, sentencing disparities were greatest when defendant culpability (as measured by the four different approaches) was moderate. In their effort to isolate the source of the jury's bias, the study found that the race-of-victim effect was linked to juries' being less likely to find mitigation when the victim was not Black; the race-of-defendant effect resulted from the jury's being more likely to find aggravating circumstances, as well as placing less weight on mitigating factors, when the defendant was Black.

To summarize, the pattern appears overwhelmingly clear: Defendant race and victim race are related to the decisions of juries in the sentencing phase of capital trials. In addition to main effects, the two racial variables also appear to interact such that Black defendants who kill White victims are especially likely to receive the death penalty relative to White defendants and Black defendants convicted of killing Black victims. High-quality studies show convincingly that race of victim and race of defendant effects do influence jury decisions, probably in an interactive fashion.

QUESTIONING POTENTIAL JURORS

HAM v. SOUTH CAROLINA
409 U.S. 524 (1973)

MR. JUSTICE REHNQUIST delivered the opinion of the Court.

Petitioner was convicted in the South Carolina trial court of the possession of marihuana in violation of state law. He was sentenced to 18 months' confinement, and on appeal his conviction was affirmed by a divided South Carolina Supreme Court. We granted certiorari limited to the question of whether the trial judge's refusal to examine jurors on voir dire as to possible prejudice against petitioner violated the latter's federal constitutional rights.

Petitioner is a young, bearded Negro who has lived most of his life in Florence County, South Carolina. He appears to have been well known locally for his work in such civil rights activities as the Southern Christian Leadership Conference and the Bi-Racial Committee of the City of Florence. He has never previously been convicted of a crime. His basic defense at the trial was that law enforcement officers were "out to get him" because of his civil rights activities, and that he had been framed on the drug charge.

Prior to the trial judge's voir dire examination of prospective jurors, petitioner's counsel requested the judge to ask jurors four questions relating to possible prejudice against petitioner. The first two questions sought to elicit any possible racial prejudice against Negroes; the third question related to possible prejudice against beards; and the fourth dealt with pretrial publicity relating to the drug problem. The trial judge, while putting to the prospective jurors three general questions as to bias, prejudice, or partiality that are specified in the South Carolina statutes, declined to ask any of the four questions posed by petitioner.

The dissenting justices in the Supreme Court of South Carolina thought that this Court's decision in Aldridge v. United States, was binding on the State. There a Negro who was being tried for the murder of a white policeman requested that prospective jurors be asked whether they entertained any racial prejudice. This Court reversed the judgment of conviction because of the trial judge's refusal to make such an inquiry. Mr. Chief Justice Hughes, writing for the Court, stated that the "essential demands of fairness" required the trial judge under the circumstances of that case to interrogate the veniremen with respect to racial prejudice upon the request of counsel for a Negro criminal defendant.

... Since one of the purposes of the Due Process Clause of the Fourteenth Amendment is to insure these "essential demands of fairness," and since a principal purpose of the adoption of the Fourteenth Amendment was to prohibit the States from invidiously discriminating on the basis of race, we think that the Fourteenth Amendment required the judge in this case to interrogate the jurors upon the subject of racial prejudice. South Carolina law permits challenges for cause, and authorizes the trial judge to conduct voir dire examination of potential jurors. The State having created this statutory framework for the selection of juries, the essential fairness required by the Due Process Clause of the Fourteenth Amendment requires that under the facts shown by this record the petitioner be permitted to have the jurors interrogated on the issue of racial bias.

We agree with the dissenting justices of the Supreme Court of South Carolina that the trial judge was not required to put the question in any particular form, or to ask any particular number of questions on the subject, simply because requested to do so by petitioner. ... In this context, either of the brief, general questions urged by the petitioner would appear sufficient to focus the attention of prospective jurors on any racial prejudice they might entertain.

The third of petitioner's proposed questions was addressed to the fact that he wore a beard. While we cannot say that prejudice against people with beards might not have been harbored by one or more of the potential jurors in this case, this is the beginning and not the end of the inquiry as to whether the Fourteenth Amendment required the trial judge to interrogate the prospective jurors about such possible prejudice. Given the traditionally broad discretion accorded to the trial judge in conducting voir dire, and our inability to constitutionally distinguish possible prejudice against beards from a host of other possible similar prejudices, we do not believe the petitioner's constitutional rights were violated when the trial judge refused to put this question. The inquiry as to racial prejudice derives its constitutional stature from the firmly established precedent of Aldridge and the numerous state cases upon which it relied, and from a principal purpose as well as from the language of those who adopted the Fourteenth Amendment. The trial judge's refusal to inquire as to particular bias against beards, after his inquiries as to bias in general, does not reach the level of a constitutional violation.

Because of the trial court's refusal to make any inquiry as to racial bias of the prospective jurors after petitioner's timely request therefore, the judgment of the Supreme Court of South Carolina is

Reversed.

MR. JUSTICE DOUGLAS, concurring in part and dissenting in part.

I concur in that portion of the majority's opinion that holds that the trial judge was constitutionally compelled to inquire into the possibility of racial prejudice on voir dire. I think, however, that it was an abuse of discretion for the trial judge to preclude the defendant from an inquiry by which prospective jurors' prejudice to hair growth could have been explored.

It is unquestioned that a defendant has the constitutional right to a trial by a neutral and impartial jury. Criminal convictions have been reversed when the limitations on voir dire have unreasonably infringed the exercise of this right...

Prejudices involving hair growth are unquestionably of a "serious character." Nothing is more indicative of the importance currently being attached to hair growth by the general populace than the barrage of cases reaching the courts evidencing the attempt by one segment of society officially to control the plumage of another. On the issue of a student's right to wear long hair alone there are well over 50 reported cases. In addition, the issue of plumage has surfaced in the employment-discrimination context, as well as the military area.

The prejudices invoked by the mere sight of nonconventional hair growth are deeply felt. Hair growth is symbolic to many of rebellion against traditional society and disapproval of the way the current power structure handles social problems. Taken as an affirmative declaration of an individual's commitment to a change in social values, nonconventional hair growth may become a very real personal threat to those who support the status quo. For those people, nonconventional hair growth symbolizes an undesirable lifestyle characterized by unreliability, dishonesty, lack of moral values, communal ("communist") tendencies, and the assumption of drug use. If the defendant, especially one being prosecuted for the illegal use of drugs, is not allowed even to make the most minimal inquiry to expose such prejudices, can it be expected that he will receive a fair trial?

Since hair growth is an outward manifestation by which many people determine whether to apply deep-rooted prejudices to an individual, to deny a defendant the right to examine this aspect of a prospective juror's personality is to deny him his most effective means of voir dire examination.

MR. JUSTICE MARSHALL, concurring in part and dissenting in part.

We have never suggested that this right to impartiality and fairness protects against only certain classes of prejudice or extends to only certain groups in the population. It makes little difference to a criminal defendant whether the jury has prejudged him because of the color of his skin or because of the length of his hair. In either event, he has been deprived of the right to present his case to neutral and detached observers capable of rendering a fair and impartial verdict. It is unsurprising, then, that this Court has invalidated decisions reached by juries with a wide variety of different prejudices.

Moreover, the Court has also held that the right to an impartial jury carries with it the concomitant right to take reasonable steps designed to insure that the jury is impartial. A variety of techniques is available to serve this end, but perhaps the most important of these is the jury challenge. Indeed, the first Mr. Justice Harlan, speaking for a unanimous Court, thought that the right to challenge was "one of the most important of the rights secured to the accused" and that "any system for the empanelling of a jury that [prevents] or embarrasses the full, unrestricted exercise by the accused of that right, must be condemned."

Of course, the right to challenge has little meaning if it is unaccompanied by the right to ask relevant questions on voir dire upon which the challenge for cause can be predicated. ...

I do not mean to suggest that a defendant must be permitted to propound any question or that limitless time must be devoted to preliminary voir dire. Although the defendant's interest in a jury free of prejudice is strong, there are countervailing state interests in the expeditious conduct of criminal trials and the avoidance of jury intimidation. These interests bulk larger as the possibility of uncovering prejudice becomes more attenuated. The trial judge has broad discretion to refuse to ask questions that are irrelevant or vexatious. Thus, where the claimed prejudice is of a novel character, the judge might require a preliminary showing of relevance or of possible prejudice before allowing the questions.

But broad as the judge's discretion is in these matters, I think it clear that it was abused in this case. The defense attorney wished to ask no more than four questions, which would have required a scant 15 additional minutes of the court's time. The inquiries, directed inter alia to possible prejudice against people with beards, were obviously relevant, since the defendant was in fact bearded. Moreover, the judge afforded petitioner no opportunity to show that there were a significant number of potential jurors who might be prejudiced against people with beards. At minimum, I think such an opportunity should have been provided. I cannot believe that in these circumstances an absolute ban on questions designed to uncover such prejudice represents a proper balance between the competing demands of fairness and expedition.

I would therefore hold that the defendant in this case, and subject to the limitations set out above, had a constitutionally protected interest in having the judge propound the additional question, in some form, to the jury.

NOTES AND QUERIES

Do you suppose that the questions sought to be asked actually would have made a difference? Note that these were the four questions sought to be asked:

"1. Would you fairly try this case on the basis of the evidence and disregarding the defendant's race?

"2. You have no prejudice against negroes? Against black people? You would not be influenced by the use of the term 'black'?

"3. Would you disregard the fact that this defendant wears a beard in deciding this case?

"4. Did you watch the television show about the local drug problem a few days ago when a local policeman appeared for a long time? Have you heard about that show? Have you read or heard about recent newspaper articles to the effect that the local drug problem is bad? Would you try this case solely on the basis of the evidence presented in this courtroom? Would you be influenced by the circumstances that the prosecution's witness, a police officer, has publicly spoken on TV about drugs?"

The three questions asked of all prospective jurors in this case were, in substance, the following:

"1. Have you formed or expressed any opinion as to the guilt or innocence of the defendant, Gene Ham?

"2. Are you conscious of any bias or prejudice for or against him?

"3. Can you give the State and the defendant a fair and impartial trial?"

Note that this case moves us from issues regarding jury pools to issues regarding jury selection of those who come to serve. In this context, as we have seen, the major concern involves the removal of jurors for cause or through peremptory challenges. Doing so requires, of course, being able to ask questions to jurors in order to desipher grounds for their exclusion. What do you learn in this case about that process? Do you agree that trial judges should be granted broad discretion? What limits does this case place on judicial discretion?

Should a judge ask about racial prejudice when three black defendants are tried for armed robbery, assault and battery by means of a dangerous weapon, and assault and battery with intent to murder a white man employed as a uniformed security guard? What would you like to know before answering that question? In this case, it turns out that the *voir dire* of prospective jurors was to be conducted by the court, which was required by statute to inquire generally into prejudice. Although the judge asked a general question about prejudice and about affiliations with law enforcement agencies, he refused to ask about racial prejudice. Defense counsel did not claim a particular reason for the request except to note the racial difference between the defendants and the victim. The voire dire led to the excusing of 18 veniremen for cause on grounds of prejudice, including one panelist who admitted a racial bias. The eventually impaneled jury convicted each defendant of all counts. On direct appeal the dfendant contended that his federal constitutional rights were violated by the denial of his request that prospective jurors be questioned specifically about racial prejudice. How should the Court rule if it follows *Ham v. South Carolina*? The Court noted that the Constitution does not always entitle a defendant to have questions posed during *voir dire* specifically directed to matters that conceivably might prejudice veniremen against him. It then emphasized that *voir dire* is conducted under the supervision of the court, and a great deal must be left to its sound discretion because the determination of impartiality, in which demeanor plays such an important part, is particularly within the province of the trial judge. The Court distinguished *Ham* on the grounds that its circumstances strongly suggested the need for voir dire to include specific questioning about racial prejudice. *Ristaino v. Ross*, 424 U.S. 589 (1975). Given the psychological evidence we have discussed, is this an appropriate result? How could you argue, legally, for a result that would be more consistent with psychological science findings?

MU'MIN v. VIRGINIA
500 U.S. 415 (1991)

CHIEF JUSTICE REHNQUIST delivered the opinion of the Court.

Petitioner Dawud Majid Mu'Min was convicted of murdering a woman in Prince William County, Virginia, while out of prison on work detail, and was sentenced to death. The case engendered substantial publicity, and 8 of the 12 venirepersons eventually sworn as jurors answered on voir dire that they had read or heard something about the case. None of those who had read or heard something indicated that they had formed an opinion based on the outside information, or that it would affect their ability to determine petitioner's guilt or innocence based solely on the evidence presented at trial. Petitioner contends, however, that his Sixth Amendment right to an impartial jury and his right to due process under the Fourteenth Amendment were violated because the trial judge refused to question further prospective jurors about the specific contents of the news reports to which they had been exposed. We reject petitioner's submission.

Mu'Min was an inmate at the Virginia Department of Corrections' Haymarket Correctional Unit serving a 48-year sentence for a 1973 first-degree murder conviction. On September 22, 1988, he was transferred to the Virginia Department of Transportation (VDOT) Headquarters in Prince William County and assigned to a work detail supervised by a VDOT employee. During his lunch break, he escaped over a perimeter fence at the VDOT facility and made his way to a nearby shopping center. Using a sharp instrument that he had fashioned at the VDOT shop, Mu'Min murdered and robbed Gladys Nopwasky, the owner of a retail carpet and flooring store. Mu'Min then returned to his prison work crew at the VDOT, discarding his bloodied shirt and the murder weapon near the highway.

About three months before trial, petitioner submitted to the trial court, in support of a motion for a change of venue, 47 newspaper articles relating to the murder. One or more of the articles discussed details of the murder and investigation, and included information about petitioner's prior criminal record, the fact that he had been rejected for parole six times, accounts of alleged prison infractions, details about the prior murder for which Mu'Min was serving his sentence at the time of this murder, a comment that the death penalty had not been available when Mu'Min was convicted for this earlier murder, and indications that Mu'Min had confessed to killing Gladys Nopwasky. Several articles focused on the alleged laxity in the supervision of work gangs and argued for reform of the prison work-crew system. The trial judge deferred ruling on the venue motion until after making an attempt to seat a jury.

Shortly before the date set for trial, petitioner submitted to the trial judge 64 proposed voir dire questions and filed a motion for individual voir dire. The trial court denied the motion for individual voir dire; it ruled that voir dire would begin with collective questioning of the venire, but the venire would be broken down into panels of four, if necessary, to deal with issues of publicity. The trial court also refused to ask any of petitioner's proposed questions relating to the content of news items that potential jurors might have read or seen.

Twenty-six prospective jurors were summoned into the courtroom and questioned as a group. When asked by the judge whether anyone had acquired any information about the alleged offense or the accused from the news media or from any other source, 16 of the potential jurors replied that they had. The prospective jurors were not asked about the source or content of prior knowledge, but the court then asked the following questions:

> Would the information that you heard, received, or read from whatever source, would that information affect your impartiality in this case?
>
> Is there anyone that would say what you've read, seen, heard, or whatever information you may have acquired from whatever the source would affect your impartiality so that you could not be impartial?

> Considering what the ladies and gentlemen who have answered in the affirmative have heard or read about this case, do you believe that you can enter the Jury box with an open mind and await until the entire case is presented before reaching a fixed opinion or conclusion as to the guilt or innocence of the accused?
>
> ...In view of everything that you've seen, heard, or read, or any information from whatever source that you've acquired about this case, is there anyone who believes that you could not become a Juror, enter the Jury box with an open mind and wait until the entire case is presented before reaching a fixed opinion or a conclusion as to the guilt or innocence of the accused?

One of the 16 panel members who admitted to having prior knowledge of the case answered in response to these questions that he could not be impartial, and was dismissed for cause. Petitioner moved that all potential jurors who indicated that they had been exposed to pretrial publicity be excused for cause. This motion was denied, as was petitioner's renewed motion for a change of venue based on the pretrial publicity.

The trial court then conducted further voir dire of the prospective jurors in panels of four. Whenever a potential juror indicated that he had read or heard something about the case, the juror was then asked whether he had formed an opinion and whether he could nonetheless be impartial. None of those eventually seated stated that he had formed an opinion or gave any indication that he was biased or prejudiced against the defendant. All swore that they could enter the jury box with an open mind and wait until the entire case was presented before reaching a conclusion as to guilt or innocence.

If any juror indicated that he had discussed the case with anyone, the court asked follow-up questions to determine with whom the discussion took place and whether the juror could have an open mind despite the discussion. One juror who equivocated as to whether she could enter the jury box with an open mind was removed sua sponte by the trial judge. One juror was dismissed for cause because she was not "as frank as she could [be]" concerning the effect of her feelings toward members of the Islamic Faith and toward defense counsel. One juror was dismissed because of her inability to impose the death penalty, while another was removed based upon his statement that upon a finding of capital murder, he could not consider a penalty less than death. The prosecution and the defense each peremptorily challenged 6 potential jurors, and the remaining 14 were seated and sworn as jurors (two as alternates). Petitioner did not renew his motion for change of venue or make any other objection to the composition of the jury. Of the 12 jurors who decided petitioner's case, 8 had at one time or another read or heard something about the case. None had indicated that he had formed an opinion about the case or would be biased in any way. → 2—automatically form biases

The jury found petitioner guilty of capital murder and recommended that he be sentenced to death. After taking the matter under advisement and reviewing a presentence report, the trial judge accepted the jury's recommendation and sentenced Mu'Min to death. Mu'Min appealed, contending that he was entitled to a new trial as a result of the judge's failure to permit the proposed voir dire questions. By a divided vote, the Supreme Court of Virginia affirmed his conviction and sentence, finding that, while a criminal defendant may properly ask on voir dire whether a juror has previously acquired any information about the case, the defendant does not have a constitutional right to explore the content of the acquired information. Rather, an accused is only entitled to know whether the juror can remain impartial in light of the previously obtained information. We granted certiorari. ...

Our cases dealing with the requirements of voir dire are of two kinds: those that were tried in federal courts, and are therefore subject to this Court's supervisory power; and those that were tried in state courts, with respect to which our authority is limited to enforcing the commands of the United States Constitution.

We enjoy more latitude in setting standards for voir dire in federal courts under our supervisory power than we have in interpreting the provisions of the Fourteenth Amendment with respect to voir dire in state courts. But two parallel themes emerge from both sets of cases: First, the possibility of racial prejudice against a black defendant charged with a violent crime against a white person is sufficiently real that the Fourteenth Amendment requires that inquiry be made into racial prejudice; second, the trial court retains great latitude in deciding what questions should be asked on voir dire. ...

Petitioner asserts that the Fourteenth Amendment requires more in the way of voir dire with respect to pretrial publicity than our cases have held that it does with respect to racial or ethnic prejudice. Not only must the court "cover the subject," but it must make precise inquiries about the contents of any news reports that potential jurors have read. Petitioner argues that these "content" questions would materially assist in obtaining a jury less likely to be tainted by pretrial publicity than one selected without such questions. There is a certain commonsense appeal to this argument.

Undoubtedly, if counsel were allowed to see individual jurors answer questions about exactly what they had read, a better sense of the juror's general outlook on life might be revealed, and such a revelation would be of some use in exercising peremptory challenges. But, since peremptory challenges are not required by the Constitution, this benefit cannot be a basis for making "content" questions about pretrial publicity a constitutional requirement. Such questions might also have some effect in causing jurors to reevaluate their own answers as to whether they had formed any opinion about the case, but this is necessarily speculative.

Acceptance of petitioner's claim would require that each potential juror be interrogated individually; even were the interrogation conducted in panels of four jurors, as the trial court did here, descriptions of one juror about pretrial publicity would obviously be communicated to the three other members of the panel being interrogated, with the prospect that more harm than good would be done by the interrogation. Petitioner says that the questioning can be accomplished by juror questionnaires submitted in advance at trial, but such written answers would not give counsel or the court any exposure to the demeanor of the juror in the course of answering the content questions. The trial court in this case expressed reservations about interrogating jurors individually because it might make the jurors feel that they themselves were on trial. While concern for the feelings and sensibilities of potential jurors cannot be allowed to defeat inquiry necessary to protect a constitutional right, we do not believe that "content" questions are constitutionally required.

Whether a trial court decides to put questions about the content of publicity to a potential juror or not, it must make the same decision at the end of the questioning: is this juror to be believed when he says he has not formed an opinion about the case? Questions about the content of the publicity to which jurors have been exposed might be helpful in assessing whether a juror is impartial. To be constitutionally compelled, however, it is not enough that such questions might be helpful. Rather, the trial court's failure to ask these questions must render the defendant's trial fundamentally unfair.

As noted above, our own cases have stressed the wide discretion granted to the trial court in conducting voir dire in the area of pretrial publicity and in other areas of inquiry that might tend to show juror bias. Particularly with respect to pretrial publicity, we think this primary reliance on the judgment of the trial court makes good sense. The judge of that court sits in the locale where the publicity is said to have had its effect and brings to his evaluation of any such claim his own perception of the depth and extent of news stories that might influence a juror. The trial court, of course, does not impute his own perceptions to the jurors who are being examined, but these perceptions should be of assistance to it in deciding how detailed an inquiry to make of the members of the jury venire.

Petitioner relies heavily on our opinion in Irvin v. Dowd to support his position. In that case, we held that pretrial publicity in connection with a capital trial had so tainted the jury pool in Gibson County,

Indiana, that the defendant was entitled as a matter of federal constitutional law to a change of venue to another county. Our opinion in that case details at great length the extraordinary publicity that attended the defendant's prosecution and conviction for murder.

> [A] barrage of newspaper headlines, articles, cartoons and pictures was unleashed against [the defendant] during the six or seven months preceding his trial. . . . The newspapers in which the stories appeared were delivered regularly to approximately 95% of the dwellings in Gibson County and . . . the Evansville radio and TV stations, which likewise blanketed that county, also carried extensive newscasts covering the same incidents."

Two-thirds of the jurors actually seated had formed an opinion that the defendant was guilty, and acknowledged familiarity with material facts and circumstances of the case. Although each of these jurors said that he could be impartial, we concluded:

> With his life at stake, it is not requiring too much that petitioner be tried in an atmosphere undisturbed by so huge a wave of public passion and by a jury other than one in which two-thirds of the members admit, before hearing any testimony, to possessing a belief in his guilt.

We believe that this case is instructive, but not in the way petitioner employs it. It did not deal with any constitutional requirement of voir dire inquiry, and it is not clear from our opinion how extensive an inquiry the trial court made. But the contrast between that case and the present one is marked. In Irvin, the trial court excused over half of a panel of 430 persons because their opinions of the defendant's guilt were so fixed that they could not be impartial, and 8 of the 12 jurors who sat had formed an opinion as to guilt. In the present case, 8 of the 12 jurors who sat answered that they had read or heard something about the case, but none of those 8 indicated that he had formed an opinion as to guilt, or that the information would affect his ability to judge petitioner solely on the basis of the evidence presented at trial.

A trial court's findings of juror impartiality may "be overturned only for 'manifest error.'" ... Had the trial court in this case been confronted with the "wave of public passion" engendered by pretrial publicity that occurred in connection with Irvin's trial, the Due Process Clause of the Fourteenth Amendment might well have required more extensive examination of potential jurors than it undertook here. But the showings are not comparable; the cases differ both in the kind of community in which the coverage took place and in extent of media coverage...

The voir dire examination conducted by the trial court in this case was by no means perfunctory. The court asked the entire venire of jurors four separate questions about the effect on them of pretrial publicity or information about the case obtained by other means. One juror admitted to having formed a belief as to petitioner's guilt and was excused for cause. The trial court then conducted further voir dire in panels of four, and each time an individual juror indicated that he had acquired knowledge about the case from outside sources, he was asked whether he had formed an opinion; none of the jurors seated indicated that he had formed an opinion. One juror who equivocated as to her impartiality was excused by the trial court on its own motion. Several other jurors were excused for other reasons. It is quite possible that if voir dire interrogation had revealed one or more jurors who had formed an opinion about the case, the trial court might have decided to question succeeding jurors more extensively.

Voir dire examination serves the dual purposes of enabling the court to select an impartial jury and assisting counsel in exercising peremptory challenges. In ... Ham we held that the subject of possible racial bias must be "covered" by the questioning of the trial court in the course of its examination of potential jurors, but we were careful not to specify the particulars by which this could be done. We did not, for instance, require questioning of individual jurors about facts or experiences that might have led to racial bias. Petitioner in this case insists, as a matter of constitutional right, not only that the subject of possible bias from pretrial publicity be covered – which it was – but that questions specifically dealing with the content of what each juror has read be asked. For the reasons previously stated, we hold that the Due Process Clause of the Fourteenth Amendment does not reach this far, and that the voir dire examination conducted by the trial court in this case was consistent with that provision. The judgment of the Supreme Court of Virginia is accordingly

Affirmed.

JUSTICE O'CONNOR, concurring.

No one doubts that Dawud Majid Mu'Min's brutal murder of Gladys Nopwasky attracted extensive media coverage. For days on end, the case made headlines because it involved a macabre act of senseless violence and because it added fuel to an already heated political controversy about the wisdom of inmate work-release programs. But the question we decide today is not whether the jurors who ultimately convicted Mu'Min had previously read or heard anything about the case; everyone agrees that eight of them had. Nor is the question whether jurors who read that Mu'Min had confessed to the murder should have been disqualified as a matter of law. ... The only question before us is whether the trial court erred by crediting the assurances of eight jurors that they could put aside what they had read or heard and render a fair verdict based on the evidence. *can't put natural judgements/biases aside

JUSTICE MARSHALL insists that the trial judge could not have assessed realistically the jurors' credibility without first identifying the information to which each individual juror had been exposed. I disagree. It is true that the trial judge did not know precisely what each individual juror had read about the case. He was undeniably aware, however, of the full range of information that had been reported.

With this information in mind, the trial judge had to determine whether or not to believe the jurors' assurances that they would be able to enter the jury box with an open mind. To this end, he questioned prospective jurors repeatedly about whether exposure to pretrial publicity had impaired their ability to be impartial. One juror who equivocated was excused by the trial court on its own motion. As to the jurors ultimately selected, the trial judge determined that their assurances of impartiality were credible. ... credibility determinations of this kind are entitled to '"special deference,'" and will be reversed only for '"manifest error.'".

The dissent is correct to point out that the trial judge could have done more. He could have decided, in his discretion, to ask each juror to recount what he or she remembered reading about the case. The fact remains, however, that the trial judge himself was familiar with the potentially prejudicial publicity to which the jurors might have been exposed. Hearing individual jurors repeat what the judge already knew might still have been helpful: A particular juror's tone of voice or demeanor might have suggested to the trial judge that the juror had formed an opinion about the case and should therefore be excused. I cannot conclude, however, that "content" questions are so indispensable that it violates the Sixth Amendment for a trial court to evaluate a juror's credibility instead by reference to the full range of potentially prejudicial information that has been reported. Accordingly, I join the Court's opinion.

JUSTICE MARSHALL, with whom JUSTICE BLACKMUN and JUSTICE STEVENS join as to all but Part IV, dissenting.

The majority's reasoning is unacceptable. When a prospective juror has been exposed to prejudicial pretrial publicity, a trial court cannot realistically assess the juror's impartiality without first establishing what the juror already has learned about the case. The procedures employed in this case were wholly insufficient to eliminate the risk that two-thirds of Mu'Min's jury entered the jury box predisposed against him. I dissent.

I.

II.

In my view, once a prospective juror admits exposure to pretrial publicity, content questioning must be part of the voir dire for at least three reasons. First, content questioning is necessary to determine whether the type and extent of the publicity to which a prospective juror has been exposed would disqualify the juror as a matter of law. Our cases recognize that, under certain circumstances, exposure to particularly inflammatory publicity creates so strong a presumption of prejudice that "the jurors' claims that they can be impartial should not be believed."...

Second, even when pretrial publicity is not so extreme as to make a juror's exposure to it per se disqualifying, content questioning still is essential to give legal depth to the trial court's finding of impartiality. One of the reasons that a "juror may be unaware of" his own bias, is that the issue of impartiality is a mixed question of law and fact, the resolution of which necessarily draws upon the trial court's legal expertise. Where, as in this case, a trial court asks a prospective juror merely whether he can be "impartial," the court may well get an answer that is the product of the juror's own confusion as to what impartiality is. By asking the prospective juror in addition to identify what he has read or heard about the case and what corresponding impressions he has formed, the trial court is able to confirm that the impartiality that the juror professes is the same impartiality that the Sixth Amendment demands.

Third, content questioning facilitates accurate trial court factfinding. As this Court has recognized, the impartiality "determination is essentially one of credibility." Where a prospective juror acknowledges exposure to pretrial publicity, the precise content of that publicity constitutes contextual information essential to an accurate assessment of whether the prospective juror's profession of impartiality is believable. If the trial court declines to develop this background, its finding of impartiality simply does not merit appellate deference.

In my view, the circumstances of this case presented a clear need for content questioning. Exactly two-thirds of the persons on Mu'Min's jury admitted having been exposed to information about the case before trial. As I have shown, the stories printed prior to trial were extraordinarily prejudicial, and were made no less so by the inflammatory headlines typically used to introduce them. Much of the pretrial publicity was of the type long thought to be uniquely destructive of a juror's ability to maintain an open mind about a case – in particular, reports of Mu'Min's confession; statements by prominent public officials attesting to Mu'Min's guilt; and reports of Mu'Min's unsavory past. Because of the profoundly prejudicial nature of what was published in the newspapers prior to trial, any juror exposed to the bulk of it certainly would have been disqualified as a matter of law ... Indeed, the single story headlined "Murderer confesses to killing woman," alternatively the story headlined "Accused killer says he stabbed Dale City woman after argument, " in my opinion would have had just as destructive an effect upon the impartiality of anyone who read it ... At minimum, without inquiry into what stories had been read by the eight members of the jury who acknowledged exposure to pretrial publicity, the trial court was in no position to credit their individual professions of impartiality.

IV.

Even if I were to believe that the procedures employed at Mu'Min's jury selection satisfied the requirements of the Sixth Amendment, I still would vacate his death sentence. I adhere to my view that the death penalty is in all circumstances cruel and unusual punishment prohibited by the Eighth and Fourteenth Amendments.

JUSTICE KENNEDY, dissenting.

...I find the voir dire in this case was inadequate for an informed ruling that the jurors were qualified to sit. In my view, a juror's acknowledgment of exposure to pretrial publicity initiates a duty to assess that individual juror's ability to be impartial. ... Our willingness to accord substantial deference to a trial court's finding of juror impartiality rests on our expectation that the trial court will conduct a sufficient voir dire to determine the credibility of a juror professing to be impartial.

My difficulty with the voir dire in this case was expressed by the dissenting justices of the Virginia Supreme Court:

> The questions in this case were deficient in that the prospective jurors could simply remain silent as an implied indication of a lack of bias or prejudice. This gave the trial court no effective opportunity to assess the demeanor of each prospective juror in disclaiming bias.

I fail to see how the trial court could evaluate the credibility of the individuals seated on this jury. The questions were asked of groups, and individual jurors attested to their own impartiality by saying nothing. I would hold, as a consequence, that when a juror admits exposure to pretrial publicity about a case, the court must conduct a sufficient colloquy with the individual juror to make an assessment of the juror's ability to be impartial. The trial judge should have substantial discretion in conducting the voir dire, but, in my judgment, findings of impartiality must be based on something more than the mere silence of the individual in response to questions asked en masse.

I submit my respectful dissent.

Notes and Queries

The Court reasons that questions about the content of pretrial publicity are not constitutionally required because peremptories are not constitutionally required unless not asking the questions would make the trial fundamentally unfair. How are we to know if not asking the questions were unfair if we do not know what the jurors knew in the first instance? How does this case deal with that concern? Do you find that the ultimate process used in this case was fair?

The case notes that a court's findings on juror impartiality are overturned only for manifest error. How could that error be determined if the court does not ask jurors questions that would be needed to indicate manifested error? How does the Court deal with this issue?

Given your understanding of the psychology of biases of decision making, do you find that the Court properly addresses issues of pretrial publicity? Do you think that asking general questions about bias and prejudice cures the concern? What about asking very specific questions, would that help?

Note on the Psychology of Pretrial Publicity and its Cures

Social science research clearly has demonstrated the biasing effects of exposure to pre-trial publicity. Most of this research has focused on the potential effects on jurors, primarily with regard to criminal trials. Prejudicial pretrial publicity influences evaluations of the defendant's likability, sympathy for the defendant, perceptions of the defendant as a typical criminal, pretrial judgments of the defendant's guilt, and final verdicts. Indeed, it has been demonstrated that the more people know about a case, the more likely they are to presume the defendant guilty even when they claim to be impartial. It seems that simply knowing more about a case increases a juror's chance that they will vote for conviction. Gary Moran and Brian L. Cutler, The prejudicial impact of pretrial publicity, 21 J. Appl. Soc. Psych. 345 (1991); Norbert L. Kerr, Geoffrey P. Kramer, John S. Carroll and James J. Alfini, On the effectiveness of voir dire in criminal cases with prejudicial pretrial publicity: An empirical study, 40 Am. U. L. Rev. 665 (1991); and Christina

A. Studebaker and Steven D. Penrod, Pretrial publicity: The media, the law, and common sense, 3 Psych. Pub. Pol'y and L. 428 (1997).

Many psychological mechanisms help explain the identified effects of pretrial publicity. In earlier chapters, we already examined research recognizing the potential for innocent but familiar persons to be misidentified as the perpetrator of a crime. Several such studies found that innocent individuals are more likely to be identified as perpetrators if they were present at the scene of the crime than if they were not. Thus, the presence of an innocent but familiar person increases the rate of false identification. Mark R. Phillips, Edward R. Geiselman, David Haghighi and Cynthia M. Lin, Some boundary conditions for bystander misidentification, 24 Crim. Jus. and Beh. 370 (1997); Davis R. Ross, Stephen J. Ceci, David Dunning, Michael P. Toglia, Unconscious transference and mistaken identity: When a witness misidentifies a familiar with an innocent person, 79 J. Appl. Psych. 918 (1994); and Edward R. Geiselman, David Haghighi and Ronna Stown, Unconscious transference and characteristics of accurate and inaccurate eyewitnesses, 2 Psych. Crime and L. 197 (1996).

The process works similarly in the context of pretrial information. The transference may involve not only one's behavior but also a mistaken attribution of one person's statements to another. The information or person becomes "familiar" because the witness/juror did see or hear the information, as through media reports. The danger is that feelings of familiarity later may become confused with actual memory of personally observing the information or evidence in question. Importantly, this effect may be exacerbated by the media's potential to persuade a possible juror or witness that the evidence reported is true or that the suspect presented is the actual perpetrator. Presentations of unreliable reports may become persuasive even though they initially were deemed not credible. It may be true that we are typically sensitive to the expertise, knowledgeability, and trustworthiness of the source of information when we first hear it. We are more likely to believe those that are more credible and trustworthy than those who are not. But, the ability to evaluate information may be compromised by the failure to actually monitor sources, a process known as source dissociation. The dissociation involves remembering information heard but forgetting where it came from. Source dissociation tends to occur with the passage of time so that we later become more persuaded by information coming from a low-credibility source. We tend to forget that the source lacked credibility and consequently forget to discount the information. Anthony R. Pratkanis, Anthony G. Greenwald, Michael R. Leippe, Michael H. Baumgardner, In search of reliable persuasion effects: III. The sleeper effect is dead: Long live the sleeper effect, 54 J. Pers. and Soc. Psych. 203 (1988). In addition, when people are initially exposed to pretrial publicity, there is usually no reason for them to tag the information as unreliable or inadmissible. Yaacov Schul, When warning succeeds: The effect of warning on success in ignoring invalid information, 29 J. of Exper'l Soc. Psych. 42 (1993). Without these cues at the time of encoding, individuals may see no reason to discount or disregard the pretrial publicity. Regrettably, we are biased to believe in the truth of what we hear. This may be the case because it takes much more cognitive effort to disbelieve than to believe. Daniel T. Gilbert, How mental systems believe, 46 Am. Psych. 107 (1991). Thus, particularly when we fail to remember source cues that would cast doubt on the truth of particular information, we will tend to accept it as truth. Ian M. Begg, Ann Anas and Suzanne Farinacci, Dissociation of processes in belief: Source recollection, statement familiarity, and the illusion of truth, 21 J. Exp. Psych. Gen. 446 (1992). Source dissociation leads to a general failure in witness ability to accurately report where information has come from and in their ability to remain unaffected by unreliable information.

Pretrial publicity's effects can be exacerbated by the integrative aspect of information processing. We integrate information as we receive it and we use that integration to construct future information. In addition to integration, once we form the belief, it is highly resistant to change. This constitutes the "belief perseverance" phenomenon. This phenomenon explains why it is difficult to remove the influence of pretrial publicity; people process information in an integrative manner which resists change once it has integrated. People make connections between various pieces of information and base judgments on overall impressions rather than on specific pieces of information, and it is difficult to determine the impact of early, unreliable information. Nancy Pennington and Reid Hastie, Evidence evaluation in complex decision making, 51 J. of Personality and Soc. Psych. 242 (1986). If anything, this makes it quite difficult to be aware of all the ways in which pretrial publicity may impact memory and judgment processes.

These basic psychological processes raise concerns about the effectiveness of efforts to cure pretrial publicity. The safeguards that have been implemented include extended *voir dire* (questioning of potential jurors), judicial admonitions (instructions to jurors), trial evidence, jury deliberation, change of venue (moving the trial to another jurisdiction) or change of venire (changing the group from which jurors are selected). The effectiveness of these safeguards is debatable. For example, extended *voir dire* and judicial admonitions appear to be the most commonly used remedies for prejudicial pretrial publicity. In cases that have received substantial pretrial publicity, the judge may instruct the jurors before deliberation that they should not discuss or consider any of the pretrial publicity during the verdict decision-making process. This judicial admonition is based on the assumptions that jurors are aware of how pretrial publicity has influenced their opinions about the case and that they can intentionally disregard that influence when instructed to do so. The use of extended *voir dire* consists of thorough questioning of potential jurors by attorneys, the judge, or both during the jury selection process. It is based on the assumption that jurors will report bias or provide responses that are indicative of bias resulting from exposure to pretrial publicity and the assumption that attorneys and judges can detect bias in jurors when it is present. Available research challenges all of the assumptions that support attempts to cure the prejudicial effects of pretrial publicity. See Christina A. Studebaker and Steven D. Penrod, Pretrial publicity: The media, the law, and common sense, 3 Psych. Pub. Pol'y and L. 428 (1997);

Research questioning the effects of available safeguards presents may problems. Most jurors are likely to claim that they can ignore biased information, when the reality is that they over-rate their abilities to do so when, in fact, they already developed prejudicial opinions against defendants. Gary Moran and Brian L. Cutler, The prejudicial impact of pretrial publicity, 21 J. Appl. Soc. Psych. 345 (1991). Likewise, simply raising concern about problematic evidence runs the risk of making it more salient in the minds of jurors and, hence, more influential. Christina A. Studebaker and Steven D. Penrod, Pretrial publicity: The media, the law, and common sense, 3 Psych. Pub. Pol'y and L. 428 (1997). Moreover, reactance theory predicts that if jurors perceive limiting instructions as restricting their freedom to make decisions, jurors may be motivated to assert that freedom and attend more strongly to the evidence that is ruled inadmissible. (Reactance theory holds that when individuals perceive a threat to their ability to perform "free behaviors," they become psychologically aroused. Note that a free behavior simply is any behavior in which individuals feel that they have either the requisite physical or psychological ability to engage. Reactive theory suggests that the stronger the threat to the freedom, and the more important the perceived freedom, the higher the level of psychological arousal. And, the higher the arousal, the more attractive the threatened behavior becomes.) Joel D. Lieberman and Jamie Arndt, Social psychological explanations for the failures of instructions to disregard pretrial publicity and other inadmissible evidence, 6 Psych. Pub. Pol'y and L. 677 (2000).

What does psychology suggest we do? Researchers have suggested that judges explain the reasons for asking jurors to ignore certain evidence, which would reduce reactance. Another approach places strong emphasis on the presumption of innocence at the beginning of the trial to help control the effects of pretrial publicity, a process that may serve to inoculate against later damaging inadmissible information. This may work because persuasion studies demonstrate that forewarning effectively allows subjects to resist the effects of persuasive messages. Likewise, social psychological research demonstrates that when individuals are forced to make a public commitment to behave in a specific way, they are ultimately more likely to behave in that manner. This raises the possibility that requiring jurors to make a public pledge to follow admonitions may increase their effectiveness. See J. Alexander Tanford, Law and psychology of jury instructions, 69 Neb. L. Rev. 71 (1990); and Joel D. Lieberman and Jamie Arndt, Social psychological explanations for the failures of instructions to disregard pretrial publicity and other inadmissible evidence, 6 Psych. Pub. Pol. and L. 677 (2000).

REJECTING JURORS: PEREMPTORY CHALLENGES

BATSON v. KENTUCKY
476 U.S. 79 (1986)

JUSTICE POWELL delivered the opinion of the Court.

This case requires us to reexamine that portion of Swain v. Alabama, concerning the evidentiary burden placed on a criminal defendant who claims that he has been denied equal protection through the State's use of peremptory challenges to exclude members of his race from the petit jury.

I.

Petitioner, a black man, was indicted in Kentucky on charges of second-degree burglary and receipt of stolen goods. On the first day of trial in Jefferson Circuit Court, the judge conducted voir dire examination of the venire, excused certain jurors for cause, and permitted the parties to exercise peremptory challenges. The prosecutor used his peremptory challenges to strike all four black persons on the venire, and a jury composed only of white persons was selected. Defense counsel moved to discharge the jury before it was sworn on the ground that the prosecutor's removal of the black veniremen violated petitioner's rights under the Sixth and Fourteenth Amendments to a jury drawn from a cross section of the community, and under the Fourteenth Amendment to equal protection of the laws. Counsel requested a hearing on his motion. Without expressly ruling on the request for a hearing, the trial judge observed that the parties were entitled to use their peremptory challenges to "strike anybody they want to." The judge then denied petitioner's motion, reasoning that the cross-section requirement applies only to selection of the venire and not to selection of the petit jury itself.

The jury convicted petitioner on both counts. On appeal to the Supreme Court of Kentucky, petitioner pressed, among other claims, the argument concerning the prosecutor's use of peremptory challenges. Conceding that Swain v. Alabama apparently foreclosed an equal protection claim based solely on the prosecutor's conduct in this case, petitioner urged the court to follow decisions of other States and to hold that such conduct violated his rights under the Sixth Amendment ... to a jury drawn from a cross section of the community. Petitioner also contended that the facts showed that the prosecutor had engaged in a "pattern" of discriminatory challenges in this case and established an equal protection violation under Swain.

The Supreme Court of Kentucky affirmed. ... The court observed that it recently had reaffirmed its reliance on Swain, and had held that a defendant alleging lack of a fair cross section must demonstrate systematic exclusion of a group of jurors from the venire. ...We granted certiorari ...

II.

In Swain v. Alabama, this Court recognized that a "State's purposeful or deliberate denial to Negroes on account of race of participation as jurors in the administration of justice violates the Equal Protection Clause." This principle has been "consistently and repeatedly" reaffirmed, in numerous decisions of this Court both preceding and following Swain. We reaffirm the principle today.

A.

In holding that racial discrimination in jury selection offends the Equal Protection Clause, the Court in Strauder recognized, however, that a defendant has no right to a "petit jury composed in whole or in part of persons of his own race." "The number of our races and nationalities stands in the way of evolution of such a conception" of the demand of equal protection. But the defendant does have the right to be tried by a jury whose members are selected pursuant to non-discriminatory criteria. The Equal Protection Clause guarantees the defendant that the State will not exclude members of his race from the jury venire on account of race, or on the false assumption that members of his race as a group are not qualified to serve as jurors.

Purposeful racial discrimination in selection of the venire violates a defendant's right to equal protection because it denies him the protection that a trial by jury is intended to secure. "The very idea of a jury is a body . . . composed of the peers or equals of the person whose rights it is selected or summoned to determine; that is, of his neighbors, fellows, associates, persons having the same legal status in society as that which he holds." The petit jury has occupied a central position in our system of justice by safeguarding a person accused of crime against the arbitrary exercise of power by prosecutor or judge. Those on the venire must be "indifferently chosen," to secure the defendant's right under the Fourteenth Amendment to "protection of life and liberty against race or color prejudice."

Racial discrimination in selection of jurors harms not only the accused whose life or liberty they are summoned to try. Competence to serve as a juror ultimately depends on an assessment of individual qualifications and ability impartially to consider evidence presented at a trial. A person's race simply "is unrelated to his fitness as a juror." As long ago as Strauder, therefore, the Court recognized that by denying a person participation in jury service on account of his race, the State unconstitutionally discriminated against the excluded juror.

The harm from discriminatory jury selection extends beyond that inflicted on the defendant and the excluded juror to touch the entire community. Selection procedures that purposefully exclude black persons from juries undermine public confidence in the fairness of our system of justice. Discrimination within the judicial system is most pernicious because it is "a stimulant to that race prejudice which is an impediment to securing to [black citizens] that equal justice which the law aims to secure to all others."

B.

In Strauder, the Court invalidated a state statute that provided that only white men could serve as jurors. We can be confident that no State now has such a law. The Constitution requires, however, that we look beyond the face of the statute defining juror qualifications and also consider challenged selection practices to afford "protection against action of the State through its administrative officers in effecting the prohibited discrimination." Thus, the Court has found a denial of equal protection where the procedures implementing a neutral statute operated to exclude persons from the venire on racial grounds, and has made clear that the Constitution prohibits all forms of purposeful racial discrimination in selection of jurors. While decisions of this Court have been concerned largely with discrimination during selection of the venire, the principles announced there also forbid discrimination on account of race in selection of the petit jury. Since the Fourteenth Amendment protects an accused throughout the proceedings bringing him to justice, the State may not draw up its jury lists pursuant to neutral procedures but then resort to discrimination at "other stages in the selection process."

III.

B.

Since the decision in Swain, we have explained that our cases concerning selection of the venire reflect the general equal protection principle that the "invidious quality" of governmental action claimed to be racially discriminatory "must ultimately be traced to a racially discriminatory purpose." As in any equal protection case, the "burden is, of course," on the defendant who alleges discriminatory selection of the venire "to prove the existence of purposeful discrimination." In deciding if the defendant has carried his burden of persuasion, a court must undertake "a sensitive inquiry into such circumstantial and direct evidence of intent as may be available." Circumstantial evidence of invidious intent may include proof of disproportionate impact. We have observed that under some circumstances proof of discriminatory impact "may for all practical purposes demonstrate unconstitutionality because in various circumstances the discrimination is very difficult to explain on nonracial grounds." For example, "total or seriously disproportionate exclusion of Negroes from jury venires," "is itself such an 'unequal application of the law ...as to show intentional discrimination.'"

Moreover, since Swain, we have recognized that a black defendant alleging that members of his race have been impermissibly excluded from the venire may make out a prima facie case of purposeful discrimination by showing that the totality of the relevant facts gives rise to an inference of discriminatory purpose. Once the defendant makes the requisite showing, the burden shifts to the State to explain adequately the racial exclusion. The State cannot meet this burden on mere general assertions that its officials did not discriminate or that they properly performed their official duties. Rather, the State must demonstrate that "permissible racially neutral selection criteria and procedures have produced the monochromatic result."

The showing necessary to establish a prima facie case of purposeful discrimination in selection of the venire may be discerned in this Court's decisions. The defendant initially must show that he is a member of a racial group capable of being singled out for differential treatment. In combination with that evidence, a defendant may then make a prima facie case by proving that in the particular jurisdiction members of his race have not been summoned for jury service over an extended period of time. Proof of systematic exclusion from the venire raises an inference of purposeful discrimination because the "result bespeaks discrimination."

Since the ultimate issue is whether the State has discriminated in selecting the defendant's venire, however, the defendant may establish a prima facie case "in other ways than by evidence of long-continued unexplained absence" of members of his race "from many panels." In cases involving the venire, this Court has found a prima facie case on proof that members of the defendant's race were substantially underrepresented on the venire from which his jury was drawn, and that the venire was selected under a practice providing "the opportunity for discrimination."This combination of factors raises the necessary inference of purposeful discrimination because the Court has declined to attribute to chance the absence of black citizens on a particular jury array where the selection mechanism is subject to abuse. When circumstances suggest the need, the trial court must undertake a "factual inquiry" that "takes into account all possible explanatory factors" in the particular case.

Thus, since the decision in Swain, this Court has recognized that a defendant may make a prima facie showing of purposeful racial discrimination in selection of the venire by relying solely on the facts concerning its selection in his case. These decisions are in accordance with the proposition that "a consistent pattern of official racial discrimination" is not "a necessary predicate to a violation of the Equal Protection Clause. A single invidiously discriminatory governmental act" is not "immunized by the absence of such discrimination in the making of other comparable decisions." For evidentiary requirements to dictate that "several must suffer discrimination" before one could object would be inconsistent with the promise of equal protection to all.

C.

The standards for assessing a prima facie case in the context of discriminatory selection of the venire have been fully articulated since Swain. These principles support our conclusion that a defendant may establish a prima facie case of purposeful discrimination in selection of the petit jury solely on evidence concerning the prosecutor's exercise of peremptory challenges at the defendant's trial. To establish such a case, the defendant first must show that he is a member of a cognizable racial group and that the prosecutor has exercised peremptory challenges to remove from the venire members of the defendant's race. Second, the defendant is entitled to rely on the fact, as to which there can be no dispute, that peremptory challenges constitute a jury selection practice that permits "those to discriminate who are of a mind to discriminate." Finally, the defendant must show that these facts and any other relevant circumstances raise an inference that the prosecutor used that practice to exclude the veniremen from the petit jury on account of their race. This combination of factors in the empaneling of the petit jury, as in the selection of the venire, raises the necessary inference of purposeful discrimination.

In deciding whether the defendant has made the requisite showing, the trial court should consider all relevant circumstances. For example, a "pattern" of strikes against black jurors included in the particular venire might give rise to an inference of discrimination. Similarly, the prosecutor's questions and statements during voir dire examination and in exercising his challenges may support or refute an inference of discriminatory purpose. These examples are merely illustrative. We have confidence that trial judges, experienced in supervising voir dire, will be able to decide if the circumstances concerning the prosecutor's use of peremptory challenges creates a prima facie case of discrimination against black jurors.

Once the defendant makes a prima facie showing, the burden shifts to the State to come forward with a neutral explanation for challenging black jurors. Though this requirement imposes a limitation in some cases on the full peremptory character of the historic challenge, we emphasize that the prosecutor's explanation need not rise to the level justifying exercise of a challenge for cause. But the prosecutor may not rebut the defendant's prima facie case of discrimination by stating merely that he challenged jurors of the defendant's race on the assumption – or his intuitive judgment – that they would be partial to the defendant because of their shared race. Just as the Equal Protection Clause forbids the States to exclude black persons from the venire on the assumption that blacks as a group are unqualified to serve as jurors, so it forbids the States to strike black veniremen on the assumption that they will be biased in a particular case simply because the defendant is black. The core guarantee of equal protection, ensuring citizens that their State will not discriminate on account of race, would be meaningless were we to approve the exclusion of jurors on the basis of such assumptions, which arise solely from the jurors' race. Nor may the prosecutor rebut the defendant's case merely by denying that he had a discriminatory motive or "[affirming] [his] good faith in making individual selections." If these general assertions were accepted as rebutting a defendant's prima facie case, the Equal Protection Clause "would be but a vain and illusory requirement." The prosecutor therefore must articulate a neutral explanation related to the particular case to be tried. The trial court then will have the duty to determine if the defendant has established purposeful discrimination.

IV.

The State contends that our holding will eviscerate the fair trial values served by the peremptory challenge. Conceding that the Constitution does not guarantee a right to peremptory challenges and that Swain did state that their use ultimately is subject to the strictures of equal protection, the State argues that the privilege of unfettered exercise of the challenge is of vital importance to the criminal justice system.

While we recognize, of course, that the peremptory challenge occupies an important position in our trial procedures, we do not agree that our decision today will undermine the contribution the challenge generally makes to the administration of justice. The reality of practice, amply reflected in many state- and federal-court opinions, shows that the challenge may be, and unfortunately at times has been, used to discriminate against black jurors. By requiring trial courts to be sensitive to the racially discriminatory use of peremptory challenges, our decision enforces the mandate of equal protection and furthers the ends of justice. In view of the heterogeneous population of our Nation, public respect for our criminal justice system and the rule of law will be strengthened if we ensure that no citizen is disqualified from jury service because of his race.

Nor are we persuaded by the State's suggestion that our holding will create serious administrative difficulties. In those States applying a version of the evidentiary standard we recognize today, courts have not experienced serious administrative burdens, and the peremptory challenge system has survived. We decline, however, to formulate particular procedures to be followed upon a defendant's timely objection to a prosecutor's challenges.

V.

In this case, petitioner made a timely objection to the prosecutor's removal of all black persons on the venire. Because the trial court flatly rejected the objection without requiring the prosecutor to give an explanation for his action, we remand this case for further proceedings. If the trial court decides that the facts establish, prima facie, purposeful discrimination and the prosecutor does not come forward with a neutral explanation for his action, our precedents require that petitioner's conviction be reversed.

It is so ordered.

JUSTICE WHITE, concurring.

The Court overturns the principal holding in Swain v. Alabama that the Constitution does not require in any given case an inquiry into the prosecutor's reasons for using his peremptory challenges to strike blacks from the petit jury panel in the criminal trial of a black defendant and that in such a case it will be presumed that the prosecutor is acting for legitimate trial-related reasons. The Court now rules that such use of peremptory challenges in a given case may, but does not necessarily, raise an inference, which the prosecutor carries the burden of refuting, that his strikes were based on the belief that no black citizen could be a satisfactory juror or fairly try a black defendant.

The Court emphasizes that using peremptory challenges to strike blacks does not end the inquiry; it is not unconstitutional, without more, to strike one or more blacks from the jury. The judge may not require the prosecutor to respond at all. If he does, the prosecutor, who in most cases has had a chance to voir dire the prospective jurors, will have an opportunity to give trial-related reasons for his strikes – some satisfactory ground other than the belief that black jurors should not be allowed to judge a black defendant.

JUSTICE MARSHALL, concurring.

...The decision today will not end the racial discrimination that peremptories inject into the jury-selection process. That goal can be accomplished only by eliminating peremptory challenges entirely.

JUSTICE STEVENS, with whom JUSTICE BRENNAN joins, concurring. [omitted]
JUSTICE O'CONNOR, concurring. [omitted]

CHIEF JUSTICE BURGER, joined by JUSTICE REHNQUIST, dissenting.

I.

Today the Court sets aside the peremptory challenge, a procedure which has been part of the common law for many centuries and part of our jury system for nearly 200 years. It does so on the basis of a constitutional argument that was rejected, without a single dissent, in Swain v. Alabama.

In short, it is quite probable that every peremptory challenge could be objected to on the basis that, because it excluded a venireman who had some characteristic not shared by the remaining members of the venire, it constituted a "classification" subject to equal protection scrutiny. Compounding the difficulties, under conventional equal protection principles some uses of peremptories would be reviewed under "strict scrutiny and . . . sustained only if . . . suitably tailored to serve a compelling state interest;" others would be reviewed to determine if they were "substantially related to a sufficiently important government interest," and still others would be reviewed to determine whether they were "a rational means to serve a legitimate end."

The Court never applies this conventional equal protection framework to the claims at hand, perhaps to avoid acknowledging that the state interest involved here has historically been regarded by this Court as substantial, if not compelling. Peremptory challenges have long been viewed as a means to achieve an impartial jury that will be sympathetic toward neither an accused nor witnesses for the State on the basis of some shared factor of race, religion, occupation, or other characteristic. ... Under conventional equal protection principles, a state interest of this magnitude and ancient lineage might well overcome an equal protection objection to the application of peremptory challenges. However, the Court is silent on the strength of the State's interest, apparently leaving this issue, among many others, to the further "litigation [that] will be required to spell out the contours of the Court's equal protection holding today . . . ."

...Our system permits two types of challenges: challenges for cause and peremptory challenges. Challenges for cause obviously have to be explained; by definition, peremptory challenges do not. "It is called a peremptory challenge, because the prisoner may challenge peremptorily, on his own dislike, without showing of any cause." Analytically, there is no middle ground: A challenge either has to be explained or it does not. It is readily apparent, then, that to permit inquiry into the basis for a peremptory challenge would force "the peremptory challenge [to] collapse into the challenge for cause." Indeed, the Court recognized without dissent in Swain that, if scrutiny were permitted, "[the] challenge, pro tanto, would no longer be peremptory, each and every challenge being open to examination, either at the time of the challenge or at a hearing afterwards."

Confronted with the dilemma it created, the Court today attempts to decree a middle ground. To rebut a prima facie case, the Court requires a "neutral explanation" for the challenge, but is at pains to "emphasize" that the "explanation need not rise to the level justifying exercise of a challenge for cause." I am at a loss to discern the governing principles here. A "clear and reasonably specific" explanation of "legitimate reasons" for exercising the challenge will be difficult to distinguish from a challenge for cause. Anything short of a challenge for cause may well be seen as an "arbitrary and capricious" challenge, to use Blackstone's characterization of the peremptory. Apparently the Court envisions permissible challenges short of a challenge for cause that are just a little bit arbitrary – but not too much. While our trial judges are "experienced in supervising voir dire," they have no experience in administering rules like this.

A further painful paradox of the Court's holding is that it is likely to interject racial matters back into the jury selection process, contrary to the general thrust of a long line of Court decisions and the notion of our country as a "melting pot." ...

Today we mark the return of racial differentiation as the Court accepts a positive evil for a perceived one. Prosecutors and defense attorneys alike will build records in support of their claims that peremptory challenges have been exercised in a racially discriminatory fashion by asking jurors to state their racial background and national origin for the record, despite the fact that "such questions may be offensive to some jurors and thus are not ordinarily asked on voir dire." This process is sure to tax even the most capable counsel and judges since determining whether a prima facie case has been established will "require a continued monitoring and recording of the 'group' composition of the panel present and prospective . . .."

The Court does not tarry long over any of these difficult, sensitive problems, preferring instead to gloss over them as swiftly as it slides over centuries of history: "[We] make no attempt to instruct [trial] courts how best to implement our holding today." That leaves roughly 7,000 general jurisdiction state trial judges and approximately 500 federal trial judges at large to find their way through the morass the Court creates today. The Court essentially wishes these judges well as they begin the difficult enterprise of sorting out the implications of the Court's newly created "right." I join my colleagues in wishing the Nation's judges well as they struggle to grasp how to implement today's holding...

JUSTICE REHNQUIST, with whom THE CHIEF JUSTICE joins, dissenting.

I cannot subscribe to the Court's unprecedented use of the Equal Protection Clause to restrict the historic scope of the peremptory challenge, which has been described as "a necessary part of trial by jury." In my view, there is simply nothing "unequal" about the State's using its peremptory challenges to strike blacks from the jury in cases involving black defendants, so long as such challenges are also used to exclude whites in cases involving white defendants, Hispanics in cases involving Hispanic defendants, Asians in cases involving Asian defendants, and so on. This case-specific use of peremptory challenges by the State does not single out blacks, or members of any other race for that matter, for discriminatory treatment. Such use of peremptories is at best based upon seat-of-the-pants instincts, which are undoubtedly crudely stereotypical and may in many cases be hopelessly mistaken. But as long as they are applied across-the-board to jurors of all races and nationalities, I do not see – and the Court most certainly has not explained – how their use violates the Equal Protection Clause.

Nor does such use of peremptory challenges by the State infringe upon any other constitutional interests. The Court does not suggest that exclusion of blacks from the jury through the State's use of peremptory challenges results in a violation of either the fair-cross-section or impartiality component of the Sixth Amendment. And because the case-specific use of peremptory challenges by the State does not deny blacks the right to serve as jurors in cases involving nonblack defendants, it harms neither the excluded jurors nor the remainder of the community.

The use of group affiliations, such as age, race, or occupation, as a "proxy" for potential juror partiality, based on the assumption or belief that members of one group are more likely to favor defendants who belong to the same group, has long been accepted as a legitimate basis for the State's exercise of peremptory challenges. Indeed, given the need for reasonable limitations on the time devoted to voir dire, the use of such "proxies" by both the State and the defendant may be extremely useful in eliminating from the jury persons who might be biased in one way or another. The Court today holds that the State may not use its peremptory challenges to strike black prospective jurors on this basis without violating the Constitution. But I do not believe there is anything in the Equal Protection Clause, or any other constitutional provision, that justifies such a departure from the substantive holding contained in ... Swain. Petitioner in the instant case failed to make a sufficient showing to overcome the presumption announced in Swain that the State's use of peremptory challenges was related to the context of the case. I would therefore affirm the judgment of the court below.

NOTES AND QUERIES

The Court notes that "[there] are any number of bases" on which a prosecutor reasonably may believe that it is desirable to strike a juror who is not excusable for cause. As we explained in another context, however, the prosecutor must give a "clear and reasonably specific" explanation of his "legitimate reasons" for exercising the challenges. The Court finds that race simply is not a legitimate reason. What practical effect emerges from the Court's approach to dealing with the invidiously discriminatory use of peremptory challenges?

The Court highlights that a defendant can challenge based on many panels or one's own panel. How much protection does either of those approaches grant defendants? The Court again returns to the need to find that, when arguing violation in one's own case, that the challenger is a member of a cognizable group, that peremptory challenges allow for discrimination, and that the prosecutor used peremptory challenges in a discriminatory manner. Does that seem to be an appropriate standard?

Recall that *Swain* had upheld the use of even discriminatory peremptories. That leaves us with three options: allow discriminatory peremptories, prohibit those that are discriminatory, or simply ban the use of all peremptories. Which approach do you find most appropriate? Recall that peremptories are not constitutionally required. What problems arise from efforts to prohibit discriminatory practices? In that regard, how persuasive do you find Justice Burger and Justice Rhenquist's dissent?

Without doubt, most litigation about venire selection focuses on the Sixth Amendment's "fair cross-section" requirement. Before that approach was developed, the Equal Protection Clause served as the only constitutional means to challenge a state's venire selection procedure. Initially, this meant that intentional exclusion of a suspect class (e.g., racial minorities) meant that two rights were violated: those of the defendant and those of potential jurors excluded from the venire. This line of cases has developed so that only the second violation can sustain an Equal protection challenge. The leading case, *Holland v. Illinois*, 493 U.S. 474 (1990), held that a defendant may make an equal protection challenge not to vindicate any personal right but can set in motion and vindicate the rights of excluded jurors who would have little incentive to vindicate their own rights. This may seem a bit strange, but the practical significance is that, as was the case in *Holland*, a member of a non-minority, non-suspect group may raise a claim. In light of what we have seen, the standing to raise a claim turns out to be a minor issue given the challenge of proving discrimination.

NOTE ON PEREMPTORY CHALLENGES

A substantial body of literature addresses the effectiveness of *Batson* and its progeny in reducing the level of race and gender discrimination in the use of peremptories. All evidence points in the direction of only a limited, if any, impact. On a national level, in both state and federal courts, claims of discrimination are not frequently raised. When they are used, a *prima facie* case is often recognized. However, following the respondent's rebuttal, an ultimate finding of race or gender discrimination and a grant of relief is quite infrequent. The explanations offered in the literature for *Batson*'s ineffectiveness closely track Justice Marshall's concurring critique. First, the Supreme Court has failed to provide clear standards to guide the judicial review of *Batson* claims. This has been largely left to the discretion of state and lower federal courts that have set standards which sometimes make proof of a *prima facie* case difficult, set a very low standard for the rebuttal of a *prima facie* case, and provide only minimal scrutiny on appellate review. In addition, the *Batson* line of decisions failed to appreciate the interest litigants have in continuing to discriminate by race and gender if they can get away with it; the profession does not consider it irrational for attorneys seeking to protect the best interests of their clients to discriminate on the basis of race and gender. There also is empirical evidence in the form of interviews with, and questionnaires from, both the prosecution and defense counsel supporting the continued use of peremptories, in spite of the apparent ineffectiveness of the *Batson* line of cases. See David C. Baldus, George Woodworth, David Zuckerman, Neil Alan Weiner, and Barbara Broffitt, The use of peremptory challenges in capital murder trials: A legal and empirical analysis, 3 U. Pa. J. Const. L. 3 (2001).

REJECTING JURORS: CHALLENGES FOR CAUSE

WITHERSPOON v. ILLINOIS
391 U.S. 510 (1968)

MR. JUSTICE STEWART delivered the opinion of the Court.

The petitioner was brought to trial in 1960 in Cook County, Illinois, upon a charge of murder. The jury found him guilty and fixed his penalty at death. At the time of his trial an Illinois statute provided:

> In trials for murder it shall be a cause for challenge of any juror who shall, on being examined, state that he has conscientious scruples against capital punishment, or that he is opposed to the same.

Through this provision the State of Illinois armed the prosecution with unlimited challenges for cause in order to exclude those jurors who, in the words of the State's highest court, "might hesitate to return a verdict inflicting [death]." At the petitioner's trial, the prosecution eliminated nearly half the venire of prospective jurors by challenging, under the authority of this statute, any venireman who expressed qualms about capital punishment. From those who remained were chosen the jurors who ultimately found the petitioner guilty and sentenced him to death. The Supreme Court of Illinois denied post-conviction relief, and we granted certiorari to decide whether the Constitution permits a State to execute a man pursuant to the verdict of a jury so composed.

I.

The issue before us is a narrow one. It does not involve the right of the prosecution to challenge for cause those prospective jurors who state that their reservations about capital punishment would prevent them from making an impartial decision as to the defendant's guilt. Nor does it involve the State's assertion of a right to exclude from the jury in a capital case those who say that they could never vote to impose the death penalty or that they would refuse even to consider its imposition in the case before them. For the State of Illinois did not stop there, but authorized the prosecution to exclude as well all who said that they were opposed to capital punishment and all who indicated that they had conscientious scruples against inflicting it.

In the present case the tone was set when the trial judge said early in the voir dire, "Let's get these conscientious objectors out of the way, without wasting any time on them." In rapid succession, 47 veniremen were successfully challenged for cause on the basis of their attitudes toward the death penalty. Only five of the 47 explicitly stated that under no circumstances would they vote to impose capital punishment. Six said that they did not "believe in the death penalty" and were excused without any attempt to determine whether they could nonetheless return a verdict of death. Thirty-nine veniremen, including four of the six who indicated that they did not believe in capital punishment, acknowledged having "conscientious or religious scruples against the infliction of the death penalty" or against its infliction "in a proper case" and were excluded without any effort to find out whether their scruples would invariably compel them to vote against capital punishment.

Only one venireman who admitted to "a religious or conscientious scruple against the infliction of the death penalty in a proper case" was examined at any length. She was asked: "You don't believe in the death penalty?" She replied: "No. It's just I wouldn't want to be responsible." The judge admonished her not to forget her "duty as a citizen" and again asked her whether she had "a religious or conscientious scruple" against capital punishment. This time, she replied in the negative. Moments later, however, she repeated that she would not "like to be responsible for . . . deciding somebody should be put to death." Evidently satisfied that this elaboration of the prospective juror's views disqualified her under the Illinois statute, the judge told her to "step aside."

II.

The petitioner contends that a State cannot confer upon a jury selected in this manner the power to determine guilt. He maintains that such a jury, unlike one chosen at random from a cross-section of the community, must necessarily be biased in favor of conviction, for the kind of juror who would be unperturbed by the prospect of sending a man to his death, he contends, is the kind of juror who would too readily ignore the presumption of the defendant's innocence, accept the prosecution's version of the facts, and return a verdict of guilt. To support this view, the petitioner refers to what he describes as "competent scientific evidence that death-qualified jurors are partial to the prosecution on the issue of guilt or innocence."

The data adduced by the petitioner, however, are too tentative and fragmentary to establish that jurors not opposed to the death penalty tend to favor the prosecution in the determination of guilt. We simply cannot conclude, either on the basis of the record now before us or as a matter of judicial notice, that the exclusion of jurors opposed to capital punishment results in an unrepresentative jury on the issue of guilt or substantially increases the risk of conviction. In light of the presently available information, we are not prepared to announce a per se constitutional rule requiring the reversal of every conviction returned by a jury selected as this one was.

III.

It does not follow, however, that the petitioner is entitled to no relief. For in this case the jury was entrusted with two distinct responsibilities: first, to determine whether the petitioner was innocent or guilty; and second, if guilty, to determine whether his sentence should be imprisonment or death. It has not been shown that this jury was biased with respect to the petitioner's guilt. But it is self-evident that, in its role as arbiter of the punishment to be imposed, this jury fell woefully short of that impartiality to which the petitioner was entitled under the Sixth and Fourteenth Amendments.

The only justification the State has offered for the jury-selection technique it employed here is that individuals who express serious reservations about capital punishment cannot be relied upon to vote for it even when the laws of the State and the instructions of the trial judge would make death the proper penalty. But in Illinois, as in other States, the jury is given broad discretion to decide whether or not death is "the proper penalty" in a given case, and a juror's general views about capital punishment play an inevitable role in any such decision.

A man who opposes the death penalty, no less than one who favors it, can make the discretionary judgment entrusted to him by the State and can thus obey the oath he takes as a juror. But a jury from which all such men have been excluded cannot perform the task demanded of it. Guided by neither rule nor standard, "free to select or reject as it [sees] fit," a jury that must choose between life imprisonment and capital punishment can do little more – and must do nothing less – than express the conscience of the community on the ultimate question of life or death. Yet, in a nation less than half of whose people believe in the death penalty, a jury composed exclusively of such people cannot speak for the community. Culled of all who harbor doubts about the wisdom of capital punishment – of all who would be reluctant to pronounce the extreme penalty – such a jury can speak only for a distinct and dwindling minority.

If the State had excluded only those prospective jurors who stated in advance of trial that they would not even consider returning a verdict of death, it could argue that the resulting jury was simply "neutral" with respect to penalty. But when it swept from the jury all who expressed conscientious or religious scruples against capital punishment and all who opposed it in principle, the State crossed the line of neutrality. In its quest for a jury capable of imposing the death penalty, the State produced a jury uncommonly willing to condemn a man to die.

It is, of course, settled that a State may not entrust the determination of whether a man is innocent or guilty to a tribunal "organized to convict." It requires but a short step from that principle to hold, as we do today, that a State may not entrust the determination of whether a man should live or die to a tribunal organized to return a verdict of death. Specifically, we hold that a sentence of death cannot be carried out if the jury that imposed or recommended it was chosen by excluding veniremen for cause simply because they voiced general objections to the death penalty or expressed conscientious or religious scruples against its infliction. No defendant can constitutionally be put to death at the hands of a tribunal so selected.

Whatever else might be said of capital punishment, it is at least clear that its imposition by a hanging jury cannot be squared with the Constitution. The State of Illinois has stacked the deck against the petitioner. To execute this death sentence would deprive him of his life without due process of law.

Reversed.

*proper findings of guilty conviction but such a jury should not be entrusted to decide life or death sentence

MR. JUSTICE DOUGLAS.

The constitutional question is whether the jury must be "impartially drawn from a cross-section of the community," or whether it can be drawn with systematic and intentional exclusion of some qualified groups. ...

The idea that a jury should be "impartially drawn from a cross-section of the community" certainly should not mean a selection of only those with a predisposition to impose the severest sentence or with a predisposition to impose the least one that is possible.

A fair cross-section of the community may produce a jury almost certain to impose the death penalty if guilt were found; or it may produce a jury almost certain not to impose it. The conscience of the community is subject to many variables, one of which is the attitude toward the death sentence. If a particular community were overwhelmingly opposed to capital punishment, it would not be able to exercise a discretion to impose or not impose the death sentence. A jury representing the conscience of that community would do one of several things depending on the type of state law governing it: it would avoid the death penalty by recommending mercy or it would avoid it by finding guilt of a lesser offense.

In such instance, why should not an accused have the benefit of that controlling principle of mercy in the community? Why should his fate be entrusted exclusively to a jury that was either enthusiastic about capital punishment or so undecided that it could exercise a discretion to impose it or not, depending on how it felt about the particular case?

I see no constitutional basis for excluding those who are so opposed to capital punishment that they would never inflict it on a defendant. Exclusion of them means the selection of jurors who are either protagonists of the death penalty or neutral concerning it. That results in a systematic exclusion of qualified groups, and the deprivation to the accused of a cross-section of the community for decision on both his guilt and his punishment.

Although the Court reverses as to penalty, it declines to reverse the verdict of guilt rendered by the same jury. It does so on the ground that petitioner has not demonstrated on this record that the jury which convicted him was "less than neutral with respect to guilt," because of the exclusion of all those opposed in some degree to capital punishment. The Court fails to find on this record "an unrepresentative jury on the issue of guilt." But we do not require a showing of specific prejudice when a defendant has been deprived of his right to a jury representing a cross-section of the community. We can as easily assume that the absence of those opposed to capital punishment would rob the jury of certain peculiar qualities of human nature as would the exclusion of women from juries. I would not require a specific showing of a likelihood of prejudice, for I feel that we must proceed on the assumption that in many, if not most, cases of class exclusion on the basis of beliefs or attitudes some prejudice does result and many times will not be subject to precise measurement. Indeed, that prejudice "is so subtle, so intangible, that it escapes the ordinary methods of proof." In my view, that is the essence of the requirement that a jury be drawn from a cross-section of the community.

MR. JUSTICE BLACK, with whom MR. JUSTICE HARLAN and MR. JUSTICE WHITE join, dissenting.

...With all due deference it seems to me that one might much more appropriately charge that this Court has today written the law in such a way that the States are being forced to try their murder cases with biased juries. If this Court is to hold capital punishment unconstitutional, I think it should do so forthrightly, not by making it impossible for States to get juries that will enforce the death penalty.

...I would agree with the following statement of the Court of Appeals for the District of Columbia Circuit:

> No proof is available, so far as we know, and we can imagine none, to indicate that, generally speaking, persons not opposed to capital punishment are so bent in their hostility to criminals as to be incapable of rendering impartial verdicts on the law and the evidence in a capital case. Being not opposed to capital punishment is not synonymous with favoring it. Individuals may indeed be so prejudiced in respect to serious crimes that they cannot be impartial arbiters, but that extreme is not indicated by mere lack of opposition to capital punishment. The two antipathies can readily coexist; contrariwise either can exist without the other; and, indeed, neither may exist in a person. It seems clear enough to us that a person or a group of persons may not be opposed to capital punishment and at the same time may have no particular bias against any one criminal or, indeed, against criminals as a class; people, it seems to us, may be completely without a controlling conviction one way or the other on either subject. . . .

It seems to me that the Court's opinion today must be read as holding just the opposite from what has been stated above. For no matter how the Court might try to hide it, the implication is inevitably in its opinion that people who do not have conscientious scruples against the death penalty are somehow callous to suffering and are, as some of the commentators cited by the Court called them, "prosecution prone." This conclusion represents a psychological foray into the human mind that I have considerable doubt about my ability to make, and I must confess that the two or three so-called "studies" cited by the Court on this subject are not persuasive to me.

Finally, I want to point out that the real holding in this case is, at least to me, very ambiguous. If we are to take the opinion literally, then I submit the Court today has decided nothing of substance, but has merely indulged itself in a semantic exercise. For as I read the opinion, the new requirement placed upon the States is that they cease asking prospective jurors whether they have "conscientious or religious scruples against the infliction of the death penalty," but instead ask whether "they would automatically vote against the imposition of capital punishment without regard to any evidence that might be developed at the trial of the case before them." I believe that this fine line the Court attempts to draw is based on a semantic illusion and that the practical effect of the Court's new formulation of the question to be asked state juries will not produce a significantly different kind of jury from the one chosen in this case. And I might add that the States will have been put to a great deal of trouble for nothing. ...

I believe that the Court's decision today goes a long way to destroying the concept of an impartial jury as we have known it. ...

...I shall not contribute in any way to the destruction of our ancient judicial and constitutional concept of trial by an impartial jury by forcing the States through "constitutional doctrine" laid down by this Court to accept jurors who are bound to be biased. For this reason I dissent.

MR. JUSTICE WHITE, dissenting.

...The Court does not deny that the legislature can impose a particular penalty, including death, on all persons convicted of certain crimes. Why, then, should it be disabled from delegating the penalty decision to a group who will impose the death penalty more often than would a group differently chosen?

All Illinois citizens, including those who oppose the death penalty, are assured by the Constitution a fair opportunity to influence the legislature's determinations about criminal sentences. Those opposing the death penalty have not prevailed in that forum, however. The representatives of the people of Illinois have determined that the death penalty decision should be made in individual cases by a group of those citizens without conscientious scruples about one of the sentencing alternatives provided by the legislature. ... The legislature undoubtedly felt that if all citizens could serve on the jury, and if one citizen with especially pronounced "scruples" could prevent a decision to impose death, the penalty would almost never be imposed. We need not decide today whether any possible delegation of the sentencing decision, for example a delegation to the surviving relatives of the victim, would be constitutionally impermissible because it would offend the conscience of civilized men. The delegation by Illinois, which merely excludes those with doubts in policy about one of the punishments among which the legislature sought to have them choose, seems an entirely reasonable and sensible legislative act.

NOTES AND QUERIES

The petitioner argues that the jury did not represent a fair-cross section of the community in that it was biased for convicting and presuming guilt. The Court did not even examine research relating to the penalty phase; it found the bias self-evident. In his brief, the petitioner cited two surveys, one involving 187 college students, W. C. Wilson, Belief in Capital Punishment and Jury Performance (Unpublished Manuscript, University of Texas, 1964), and the other involving 200 college students, F. J. Goldberg, Attitude Toward Capital Punishment and Behavior as a Juror in Simulated Capital Cases (Unpublished Manuscript, Morehouse College, undated). In his petition for certiorari, he cited a study based upon interviews with 1,248 jurors in New York and Chicago. A preliminary, unpublished summary of the results of that study stated that "a jury consisting only of jurors who have no scruples against the death penalty is likely to be more prosecution prone than a jury on which objectors to the death penalty sit," and that "the defendant's chances of acquittal are somewhat reduced if the objectors are excluded from the jury." H. Zeisel, Some Insights Into the Operation of Criminal Juries 42 (Confidential First Draft, University of Chicago, November 1957). What do you make of this evidence?

The case deals only with jurors who had conscientious scruples against the death penalty. Those who would refuse to consider the death penalty were automatically excluded, as were those who were not impartial. The Court notes the need to distinguish between the guilt and penalty phase. As for the guilt phase, the Court refuses to create a rule for not allowing the automatic exclusion of those who have conscientious scruples against the death penalty. (The judge essentially had automatically excused those who had conscientious objections to the death penalty.) The next issue became whether the practice of excluding conscientious objectors biased the jury during the penalty phase. The Court found the bias obvious, that it is impermissible to have a jury predisposed to imposing the death penalty. Do you find the dissents' claims persuasive when they note nothing wrong with having a jury that is ready to apply the law of the state which has a legislature that favors the death penalty?

The case is obviously complex. Recall the major holding that the Constitution does not prohibit the removal of conscientious objectors at the guilt phase, but it does prohibit the removal, for cause, at the penalty phase. Those removed are known as "*Witherspoon*-excludables." *

LOCKHART v. McCREE
476 U.S. 162 (1986)

*Constitution states: juror removal based on biases is allowable in guilt phase but prohibited in penalty phase.

JUSTICE REHNQUIST delivered the opinion of the Court.

In this case we address the question left open by our decision nearly 18 years ago in Witherspoon v. Illinois: Does the Constitution prohibit the removal for cause, prior to the guilt phase of a bifurcated capital trial, of prospective jurors whose opposition to the death penalty is so strong that it would prevent or substantially impair the performance of their duties as jurors at the sentencing phase of the trial? We hold that it does not.

On the morning of February 14, 1978, a combination gift shop and service station in Camden, Arkansas, was robbed, and Evelyn Boughton, the owner, was shot and killed. That afternoon, Ardia McCree was arrested in Hot Springs, Arkansas, after a police officer saw him driving a maroon and white Lincoln Continental matching an eyewitness' description of the getaway car used by Boughton's killer. The next evening, McCree admitted to police that he had been at Boughton's shop at the time of the murder. He claimed, however, that a tall black stranger wearing an overcoat first asked him for a ride, then took McCree's rifle out of the back of the car and used it to kill Boughton. McCree also claimed that, after the murder, the stranger rode with McCree to a nearby dirt road, got out of the car, and walked away with the rifle. McCree's story was contradicted by two eyewitnesses who saw McCree's car between the time of the murder and the time when McCree said the stranger got out and walked away, and who stated that they saw only one person in the car. The police found McCree's rifle and a bank bag from Boughton's shop alongside the dirt road. Based on ballistics tests, a Federal Bureau of Investigation officer testified that the bullet that killed Boughton had been fired from McCree's rifle.

McCree was charged with capital felony murder... In accordance with Arkansas law, the trial judge at voir dire removed for cause, over McCree's objections, those prospective jurors who stated that they could not under any circumstances vote for the imposition of the death penalty. Eight prospective jurors were excluded for this reason. The jury convicted McCree of capital felony murder, but rejected the State's request for the death penalty, instead setting McCree's punishment at life imprisonment without parole. McCree's conviction was affirmed on direct appeal and his petition for state post-conviction relief was denied.

McCree then filed a federal habeas corpus petition raising, inter alia, the claim that "death qualification," or the removal for cause of the so-called "Witherspoon-excludable" prospective jurors, violated his right under the Sixth and Fourteenth Amendments to have his guilt or innocence determined by an impartial jury selected from a representative cross section of the community. By stipulation of the parties, this claim was consolidated with another pending habeas case involving the same claim ... The District Court denied the remainder of McCree's petition, and the Eighth Circuit affirmed.

The District Court held a hearing on the "death qualification" issue in July 1981, receiving in evidence numerous social science studies concerning the attitudes and beliefs of "Witherspoon-excludables," along with the potential effects of excluding them from the jury prior to the guilt phase of a bifurcated capital trial. In August 1983, the court concluded, based on the social science evidence, that "death qualification" produced juries that "were more prone to convict" capital defendants than "non-death-qualified" juries. The court ruled that "death qualification" thus violated both the fair-cross-section and impartiality requirements of the Sixth and Fourteenth Amendments, and granted McCree habeas relief.

The Eighth Circuit found "substantial evidentiary support" for the District Court's conclusion that the removal for cause of "Witherspoon-excludables" resulted in "conviction-prone" juries, and affirmed the grant of habeas relief on the ground that such removal for cause violated McCree's constitutional right to a jury selected from a fair cross section of the community. The Eighth Circuit did not address McCree's impartiality claim. The Eighth Circuit left it up to the discretion of the State "to construct a fair process" for future capital trials that would comply with the Sixth Amendment. ...

Before turning to the legal issues in the case, we are constrained to point out what we believe to be several serious flaws in the evidence upon which the courts below reached the conclusion that "death qualification" produces "conviction-prone" juries. McCree introduced into evidence some 15 social science studies in support of his constitutional claims, but only 6 of the studies even purported to measure the potential effects on the guilt-innocence determination of the removal from the jury of "Witherspoon-excludables." Eight of the remaining nine studies dealt solely with generalized attitudes and beliefs about the death penalty and other aspects of the criminal justice system, and were thus, at best, only marginally relevant to the constitutionality of McCree's conviction. The 15th and final study dealt with the effects on prospective jurors of voir dire questioning about their attitudes toward the death penalty, an issue McCree raised in his brief to this Court but that counsel for McCree admitted at oral argument would not, standing alone, give rise to a constitutional violation.

Of the six studies introduced by McCree that at least purported to deal with the central issue in this case, namely, the potential effects on the determination of guilt or innocence of excluding "Witherspoon-excludables" from the jury, three were also before this Court when it decided Witherspoon. ...

It goes almost without saying that if these studies were "too tentative and fragmentary" to make out a claim of constitutional error in 1968, the same studies, unchanged but for having aged some 18 years, are still insufficient to make out such a claim in this case.

Nor do the three post-Witherspoon studies introduced by McCree on the "death qualification" issue provide substantial support for the "per se constitutional rule" McCree asks this Court to adopt. All three of the "new" studies were based on the responses of individuals randomly selected from some segment of the population, but who were not actual jurors sworn under oath to apply the law to the facts of an actual case involving the fate of an actual capital defendant. We have serious doubts about the value of these studies in predicting the behavior of actual jurors. In addition, two of the three "new" studies did not even attempt to simulate the process of jury deliberation, and none of the "new" studies was able to predict to what extent, if any, the presence of one or more "Witherspoon-excludables" on a guilt-phase jury would have altered the outcome of the guilt determination.

Finally, and most importantly, only one of the six "death qualification" studies introduced by McCree even attempted to identify and account for the presence of so-called "nullifiers," or individuals who, because of their deep-seated opposition to the death penalty, would be unable to decide a capital defendant's guilt or innocence fairly and impartially. McCree concedes, as he must, that "nullifiers" may properly be excluded from the guilt-phase jury, and studies that fail to take into account the presence of such "nullifiers" thus are fatally flawed. Surely a "per se constitutional rule" as far reaching as the one McCree proposes should not be based on the results of the lone study that avoids this fundamental flaw.

Having identified some of the more serious problems with McCree's studies, however, we will assume for purposes of this opinion that the studies are both methodologically valid and adequate to establish that "death qualification" in fact produces juries somewhat more "conviction-prone" than "non-death-qualified" juries. We hold, nonetheless, that the Constitution does not prohibit the States from "death qualifying" juries in capital cases.

The Eighth Circuit ruled that "death qualification" violated McCree's right under the Sixth Amendment, as applied to the States via incorporation through the Fourteenth Amendment, to a jury selected from a representative cross section of the community. But we do not believe that the fair-cross-section requirement can, or should, be applied as broadly as that court attempted to apply it. We have never invoked the fair-cross-section principle to invalidate the use of either for-cause or peremptory challenges to prospective jurors, or to require petit juries, as opposed to jury panels or venires, to reflect the composition of the community at large. The limited scope of the fair-cross-section requirement is a direct and inevitable consequence of the practical impossibility of providing each criminal defendant with a truly "representative" petit jury, a basic truth that the Court of Appeals itself acknowledged for many years prior to its decision in the instant case. We remain convinced that an extension of the fair-cross-section requirement to petit juries would be unworkable and unsound, and we decline McCree's invitation to adopt such an extension.

But even if we were willing to extend the fair-cross-section requirement to petit juries, we would still reject the Eighth Circuit's conclusion that "death qualification" violates that requirement. The essence of a "fair-cross-section" claim is the systematic exclusion of "a 'distinctive' group in the community." In our view, groups defined solely in terms of shared attitudes that would prevent or substantially impair members of the group from performing one of their duties as jurors, such as the "Witherspoon-excludables" at issue here, are not "distinctive groups" for fair-cross-section purposes.

We have never attempted to precisely define the term "distinctive group," and we do not undertake to do so today. But we think it obvious that the concept of "distinctiveness" must be linked to the purposes of the fair-cross-section requirement. In Taylor, we identified those purposes as (1) "[guarding] against the exercise of arbitrary power" and ensuring that the "commonsense judgment of the community" will act as "a hedge against the overzealous or mistaken prosecutor," (2) preserving "public confidence in the fairness of the criminal justice system," and (3) implementing our belief that "sharing in the administration of justice is a phase of civic responsibility."

Our prior jury-representativeness cases, whether based on the fair-cross-section component of the Sixth Amendment or the Equal Protection Clause of the Fourteenth Amendment, have involved such groups as blacks, women, and Mexican-Americans. The wholesale exclusion of these large groups from jury service clearly contravened all three of the aforementioned purposes of the fair-cross-section requirement. Because these groups were excluded for reasons completely unrelated to the ability of members of the group to serve as jurors in a particular case, the exclusion raised at least the possibility that the composition of juries would be arbitrarily skewed in such a way as to deny criminal defendants the benefit of the common-sense judgment of the community. In addition, the exclusion from jury service of large groups of individuals not on the basis of their inability to serve as jurors, but on the basis of some immutable characteristic such as race, gender, or ethnic background, undeniably gave rise to an "appearance of unfairness." Finally, such exclusion improperly deprived members of these often historically disadvantaged groups of their right as citizens to serve on juries in criminal cases.

The group of "Witherspoon-excludables" involved in the case at bar differs significantly from the groups we have previously recognized as "distinctive." "Death qualification," unlike the wholesale exclusion of blacks, women, or Mexican-Americans from jury service, is carefully designed to serve the State's concededly legitimate interest in obtaining a single jury that can properly and impartially apply the law to the facts of the case at both the guilt and sentencing phases of a capital trial. There is very little danger, therefore, and McCree does not even argue, that "death qualification" was instituted as a means for the State to arbitrarily skew the composition of capital-case juries.

Furthermore, unlike blacks, women, and Mexican-Americans, "Witherspoon-excludables" are singled out for exclusion in capital cases on the basis of an attribute that is within the individual's control. It is important to remember that not all who oppose the death penalty are subject to removal for cause in capital cases; those who firmly believe that the death penalty is unjust may nevertheless serve as jurors in capital cases so long as they state clearly that they are willing to temporarily set aside their own beliefs in deference to the rule of law. Because the group of "Witherspoon-excludables" includes only those who cannot and will not conscientiously obey the law with respect to one of the issues in a capital case, "death qualification" hardly can be said to create an "appearance of unfairness."

Finally, the removal for cause of "Witherspoon-excludables" in capital cases does not prevent them from serving as jurors in other criminal cases, and thus leads to no substantial deprivation of their basic rights of citizenship. They are treated no differently than any juror who expresses the view that he would be unable to follow the law in a particular case.

In sum, "Witherspoon-excludables," or for that matter any other group defined solely in terms of shared attitudes that render members of the group unable to serve as jurors in a particular case, may be excluded from jury service without contravening any of the basic objectives of the fair-cross-section requirement. It is for this reason that we conclude that "Witherspoon-excludables" do not constitute a "distinctive group" for fair-cross-section purposes, and hold that "death qualification" does not violate the fair-cross-section requirement.

McCree argues that, even if we reject the Eighth Circuit's fair-cross-section holding, we should affirm the judgment below on the alternative ground, adopted by the District Court, that "death qualification" violated his constitutional right to an impartial jury. McCree concedes that the individual jurors who served at his trial were impartial, as that term was defined by this Court in cases such as Irvin v. Dowd ["It is sufficient if the juror can lay aside his impression or opinion and render a verdict based on the evidence presented in court"]. He does not claim that pretrial publicity, ex parte communications, or other undue influence affected the jury's deliberations. In short, McCree does not claim that his conviction was tainted by any of the kinds of jury bias or partiality that we have previously recognized as violative of the Constitution. Instead, McCree argues that his jury lacked impartiality because the absence of "Witherspoon-excludables" "slanted" the jury in favor of conviction.

We do not agree. McCree's "impartiality" argument apparently is based on the theory that, because all individual jurors are to some extent predisposed towards one result or another, a constitutionally impartial jury can be constructed only by "balancing" the various predispositions of the individual jurors. Thus, according to McCree, when the State "tips the scales" by excluding prospective jurors with a particular viewpoint, an impermissibly partial jury results. We have consistently rejected this view of jury impartiality, including as recently as last Term when we squarely held that an impartial jury consists of nothing more than "jurors who will conscientiously apply the law and find the facts."

The view of jury impartiality urged upon us by McCree is both illogical and hopelessly impractical. McCree characterizes the jury that convicted him as "slanted" by the process of "death qualification." But McCree admits that exactly the same 12 individuals could have ended up on his jury through the "luck of the draw," without in any way violating the constitutional guarantee of impartiality. Even accepting McCree's position that we should focus on the jury rather than the individual jurors, it is hard for us to understand the logic of the argument that a given jury is unconstitutionally partial when it results from a state-ordained process, yet impartial when exactly the same jury results from mere chance. On a more practical level, if it were true that the Constitution required a certain mix of individual viewpoints on the jury, then trial judges would be required to undertake the Sisyphean task of "balancing" juries, making sure that each contains the proper number of Democrats and Republicans, young persons and old persons, white-collar executives and blue-collar laborers, and so on. Adopting McCree's concept of jury impartiality would also likely require the elimination of peremptory challenges, which are commonly used by both the State and the defendant to attempt to produce a jury favorable to the challenger.

McCree argues, however, that this Court's decisions ... stand for the proposition that a State violates the Constitution whenever it "slants" the jury by excluding a group of individuals more likely than the population at large to favor the criminal defendant. We think McCree overlooks two fundamental differences between [those decisions]... and the instant case, and therefore misconceives the[ir] import and scope...

...the removal for cause of "Witherspoon-excludables" serves the State's entirely proper interest in obtaining a single jury that could impartially decide all of the issues in McCree's case. Arkansas by legislative enactment and judicial decision provides for the use of a unitary jury in capital cases. We have upheld against constitutional attack the Georgia capital sentencing plan which provided that the same jury must sit in both phases of a bifurcated capital murder trial, and since then have observed that we are "unwilling to say that there is any one right way for a State to set up its capital sentencing scheme."

The Arkansas Supreme Court recently explained the State's legislative choice to require unitary juries in capital cases:

> It has always been the law in Arkansas, except when the punishment is mandatory, that the same jurors who have the responsibility for determining guilt or innocence must also shoulder the burden of fixing the punishment. That is as it should be, for the two questions are necessarily interwoven.

Another interest identified by the State in support of its system of unitary juries is the possibility that, in at least some capital cases, the defendant might benefit at the sentencing phase of the trial from the jury's "residual doubts" about the evidence presented at the guilt phase. ...

JUSTICE MARSHALL's dissent points out that some States which adhere to the unitary jury system do not allow the defendant to argue "residual doubts" to the jury at sentencing. But while this may justify skepticism as to the extent to which such States are willing to go to allow defendants to capitalize on "residual doubts," it does not wholly vitiate the claimed interest. Finally, it seems obvious to us that in most, if not all, capital cases much of the evidence adduced at the guilt phase of the trial will also have a bearing on the penalty phase; if two different juries were to be required, such testimony would have to be presented twice, once to each jury. As the Arkansas Supreme Court has noted, "[such] repetitive trials could not be consistently fair to the State and perhaps not even to the accused."

...the Arkansas system excludes from the jury only those who may properly be excluded from the penalty phase of the deliberations... That State's reasons for adhering to its preference for a single jury to decide both the guilt and penalty phases of a capital trial are sufficient to negate the inference which the Court drew in Witherspoon concerning the lack of any neutral justification for the Illinois rule on jury challenges.

Second, and more importantly, both [prior cases]... dealt with the special context of capital sentencing, where the range of jury discretion necessarily gave rise to far greater concern over the possible effects of an "imbalanced" jury. ...

In the case at bar, by contrast, we deal not with capital sentencing, but with the jury's more traditional role of finding the facts and determining the guilt or innocence of a criminal defendant, where jury discretion is more channeled. ...

In our view, it is simply not possible to define jury impartiality, for constitutional purposes, by reference to some hypothetical mix of individual viewpoints. Prospective jurors come from many different backgrounds, and have many different attitudes and predispositions. But the Constitution presupposes that a jury selected from a fair cross section of the community is impartial, regardless of the mix of individual viewpoints actually represented on the jury, so long as the jurors can conscientiously and properly carry out their sworn duty to apply the law to the facts of the particular case. We hold that McCree's jury satisfied both aspects of this constitutional standard. The judgment of the Court of Appeals is therefore

Reversed.

JUSTICE BLACKMUN concurs in the result

JUSTICE MARSHALL, with whom JUSTICE BRENNAN and JUSTICE STEVENS join, dissenting.

Respondent contends here that the "death-qualified" jury that convicted him, from which the State, as authorized by Witherspoon, had excluded all venirepersons unwilling to consider imposing the death penalty, was in effect "organized to return a verdict" of guilty. In support of this claim, he has presented overwhelming evidence that death-qualified juries are substantially more likely to convict or to convict on more serious charges than juries on which unalterable opponents of capital punishment are permitted to serve. Respondent does not challenge the application of Witherspoon to the jury in the sentencing stage of bifurcated capital cases. Neither does he demand that individuals unable to assess culpability impartially ("nullifiers") be permitted to sit on capital juries. All he asks is the chance to have his guilt or innocence determined by a jury like those that sit in noncapital cases – one whose composition has not been tilted in favor of the prosecution by the exclusion of a group of prospective jurors uncommonly aware of an accused's constitutional rights but quite capable of determining his culpability without favor or bias.

With a glib nonchalance ill suited to the gravity of the issue presented and the power of respondent's claims, the Court upholds a practice that allows the State a special advantage in those prosecutions where the charges are the most serious and the possible punishments, the most severe. The State's mere announcement that it intends to seek the death penalty if the defendant is found guilty of a capital offense will, under today's decision, give the prosecution license to empanel a jury especially likely to return that very verdict. Because I believe that such a blatant disregard for the rights of a capital defendant offends logic, fairness, and the Constitution, I dissent.

I.

In the wake of Witherspoon, a number of researchers set out to supplement the data that the Court had found inadequate in that case. ... The data strongly suggest that death qualification excludes a significantly large subset – at least 11% to 17% – of potential jurors who could be impartial during the guilt phase of trial. Among the members of this excludable class are a disproportionate number of blacks and women.

The perspectives on the criminal justice system of jurors who survive death qualification are systematically different from those of the excluded jurors. Death-qualified jurors are, for example, more likely to believe that a defendant's failure to testify is indicative of his guilt, more hostile to the insanity defense, more mistrustful of defense attorneys, and less concerned about the danger of erroneous convictions. This pro-prosecution bias is reflected in the greater readiness of death-qualified jurors to convict or to convict on more serious charges. And, finally, the very process of death qualification – which focuses attention on the death penalty before the trial has even begun – has been found to predispose the jurors that survive it to believe that the defendant is guilty.

The evidence thus confirms, and is itself corroborated by, the more intuitive judgments of scholars and of so many of the participants in capital trials – judges, defense attorneys, and prosecutors.

II.

A.

Respondent's case would of course be even stronger were he able to produce data showing the prejudical effects of death qualification upon actual trials. Yet, until a State permits two separate juries to deliberate on the same capital case and return simultaneous verdicts, defendants claiming prejudice from death qualification should not be denied recourse to the only available means of proving their case, recreations of the voir dire and trial processes. ...

The chief strength of respondent's evidence lies in the essential unanimity of the results obtained by researchers using diverse subjects and varied methodologies. Even the Court's haphazard jabs cannot obscure the power of the array. Where studies have identified and corrected apparent flaws in prior investigations, the results of the subsequent work have only corroborated the conclusions drawn in the earlier efforts. Thus, for example, some studies might be faulted for failing to distinguish within the class of Witherspoon-excludables, between nullifiers (whom respondent concedes may be excluded from the guilt phase) and those who could assess guilt impartially. Yet their results are entirely consistent with those obtained after nullifiers had indeed been excluded. And despite the failure of certain studies to "allow for group deliberations," the value of their results is underscored by the discovery that initial verdict preferences, made prior to group deliberations, are a fair predictor of how a juror will vote when faced with opposition in the jury room.

The evidence adduced by respondent is quite different from the "tentative and fragmentary" presentation that failed to move this Court in Witherspoon. Moreover, in contrast to Witherspoon, the record in this case shows respondent's case to have been "subjected to the traditional testing mechanisms of the adversary process." At trial, respondent presented three expert witnesses and one lay witness in his case in chief, and two additional lay witnesses in his rebuttal. Testimony by these witnesses permitted the District Court, and allows this Court, better to understand the methodologies used here and their limitations. Further testing of respondent's empirical case came at the hands of the State's own expert witnesses. Yet even after considering the evidence adduced by the State, the Court of Appeals properly noted: "there are no studies which contradict the studies submitted [by respondent]; in other words, all of the documented studies support the district court's findings."

B.

The true impact of death qualification on the fairness of a trial is likely even more devastating than the studies show. Witherspoon placed limits on the State's ability to strike scrupled jurors for cause, unless they state "unambiguously that [they] would automatically vote against the imposition of capital punishment no matter what the trial might reveal." It said nothing, however, about the prosecution's use of peremptory challenges to eliminate jurors who do not meet that standard and would otherwise survive death qualification. There is no question that peremptories have indeed been used to this end, thereby expanding the class of scrupled jurors excluded as a result of the death-qualifying voir dire challenged here. The only study of this practice has concluded: "For the five-year period studied a prima facie case has been demonstrated that prosecutors in Florida's Fourth Judicial Circuit systematically used their peremptory challenges to eliminate from capital juries venirepersons expressing opposition to the death penalty."

C.

Faced with the near unanimity of authority supporting respondent's claim that death qualification gives the prosecution a particular advantage in the guilt phase of capital trials, the majority here makes but a weak effort to contest that proposition. Instead, it merely assumes for the purposes of this opinion "that 'death qualification' in fact produces juries somewhat more 'conviction-prone' than 'non-death-qualified' juries," and then holds that this result does not offend the Constitution. This disregard for the clear import of the evidence tragically misconstrues the settled constitutional principles that guarantee a defendant the right to a fair trial and an impartial jury whose composition is not biased toward the prosecution.

III.

In Witherspoon the Court observed that a defendant convicted by a jury from which those unalterably opposed to the death penalty had been excluded "might still attempt to establish that the jury was less than neutral with respect to guilt." Respondent has done just that. And I believe he has succeeded in proving that his trial by a jury so constituted violated his right to an impartial jury, guaranteed by both the Sixth Amendment and principles of due process. We therefore need not rely on respondent's alternative argument that death qualification deprived him of a jury representing a fair cross section of the community.

A.

Respondent does not claim that any individual on the jury that convicted him fell short of the constitutional standard for impartiality. Rather, he contends that, by systematically excluding a class of potential jurors less prone than the population at large to vote for conviction, the State gave itself an unconstitutional advantage at his trial. Thus, according to respondent, even though a nonbiased selection procedure might have left him with a jury composed of the very same individuals that actually sat on his panel, the process by which those 12 individuals were chosen violated the Constitution.

I am puzzled by the difficulty that the majority has in understanding the "logic of the argument." For the logic is precisely that which carried the day in Witherspoon, and which has never been repudiated by this Court – not even today, if the majority is to be taken at its word. There was no question in Witherspoon that if the defendant's jury had been chosen by the "luck of the draw," the same 12 jurors who actually sat on his case might have been selected. Nonetheless, because the State had removed from the pool of possible jurors all those expressing general opposition to the death penalty, the Court overturned the defendant's conviction, declaring "that a State may not entrust the determination of whether a man should live or die to a tribunal organized to return a verdict of death." Witherspoon had been denied a fair sentencing determination, the Court reasoned, not because any member of his jury lacked the requisite constitutional impartiality, but because the manner in which that jury had been selected "stacked the deck" against him. Here, respondent adopts the approach of the Witherspoon Court and argues simply that the State entrusted the determination of his guilt and the level of his culpability to a tribunal organized to convict.

IV.

A.

One need not rely on the analysis and assumptions of ... Witherspoon to demonstrate that the exclusion of opponents of capital punishment capable of impartially determining culpability infringes a capital defendant's constitutional right to a fair and impartial jury. For the same conclusion is compelled by the analysis that in Ballew v. Georgia led a majority of this Court to hold that a criminal conviction rendered by a five-person jury violates the Sixth and Fourteenth Amendments.

Faced with an effort by Georgia to reduce the size of the jury in a criminal case beyond the six-member jury approved by this Court in Williams v. Florida, this Court articulated several facets of the inquiry whether the reduction impermissibly "[inhibited] the functioning of the jury as an institution to a significant degree." First, the Court noted that "recent empirical data" had suggested that a five-member jury was "less likely to foster effective group deliberation" and that such a decline in effectiveness would likely lead "to inaccurate factfinding and incorrect application of the common sense of the community to the facts." The Court advanced several explanations for this phenomenon:

> As juries decrease in size..., they are less likely to have members who remember each of the important pieces of evidence or argument. Furthermore, the smaller the group, the less likely it is to overcome the biases of its members to obtain an accurate result. When individual and group decisionmaking were compared, it was seen that groups performed better because prejudices of individuals were frequently counterbalanced, and objectivity resulted.

The Court also cited empirical evidence suggesting "that the verdicts of jury deliberation in criminal cases will vary as juries become smaller, and that the variance amounts to an imbalance to the detriment of one side, the defense." Lastly, the Court observed that further reductions in jury size would also foretell problems "for the representation of minority groups in the community."

B.

Each of the concerns that led this Court in Ballew to find that a misdemeanor defendant had been deprived of his constitutional right to a fair trial by jury is implicated by the process of death qualification, which threatens a defendant's interests to an even greater extent in cases where the stakes are substantially higher. When compared to the juries that sit in all other criminal trials, the death-qualified juries of capital cases are likely to be deficient in the quality of their deliberations, the accuracy of their results, the degree to which they are prone to favor the prosecution, and the extent to which they adequately represent minority groups in the community.

The data considered here, as well as plain common sense, leave little doubt that death qualification upsets the "counter-balancing of various biases" among jurors that Ballew identified as being so critical to the effective functioning of juries. The evidence demonstrates that "a person's attitude toward capital punishment is an important indicator of a whole cluster of attitudes about crime control and due process." Members of the excluded group have been shown to be significantly more concerned with the constitutional rights of criminal defendants and more likely to doubt the strength of the prosecution's case. No doubt because diversity promotes controversy, which in turn leads to a closer scrutiny of the evidence, one study found that "the members of mixed juries [composed of Witherspoon-excludables as well as death-qualified jurors] remember the evidence better than the members of death-qualified juries." This study found that not only is the recall of evidence by a death-qualified jury likely to be below the standard of ordinary juries, but its testing of that evidence will be less rigorous. It thus appears that in the most serious criminal cases – those in which the State has expressed an intention to seek the death penalty – the ability of the jury to find historical truth may well be impaired.

The role of a jury in criminal cases, however, is not limited to the determination of historical facts. The task of ascertaining the level of a defendant's culpability requires a jury to decide not only whether the accused committed the acts alleged in the indictment, but also the extent to which he is morally blameworthy. Thus, especially in capital cases, where a defendant invariably will be charged with lesser included offenses having factual predicates similar to those of the capital murder charges, it may be difficult to classify a particular verdict as "accurate" or "inaccurate." However, the Ballew Court went beyond a concern for simple historical accuracy and questioned any jury procedure that systematically operated to the "detriment of . . . the defense."

With even more clarity than the data considered in Ballew, the studies adduced by respondent show a broad pattern of "biased decisionmaking." It is not merely that the jurors who survive death qualification are more likely to accept the word of the prosecution and be satisfied with a lower standard of proof than those who are excluded. The death-qualified jurors are actually more likely to convict than their peers. Whether the verdict against a particular capital defendant will actually be different depends on the strength of the evidence against him, the likelihood that, absent death qualification, one or more Witherspoon-excludables would have sat on his jury, and a host of other factors. However, Ballew points to the importance of considering the effects of a particular jury procedure over a range of cases, and not focusing on the fairness of any single trial. Because it takes only one juror unwilling to find that the prosecution has met its burden for a trial to end in either a mistrial or a compromise verdict, "it can be confidently asserted that, over time, some persons accused of capital crimes will be convicted of offenses – and to a higher degree – who would not be so convicted" had all persons able to assess their guilt impartially been permitted to sit on their juries.

Death qualification also implicates the Ballew Court's concern for adequate representation of minority groups. Because opposition to capital punishment is significantly more prevalent among blacks than among whites, the evidence suggests that death qualification will disproportionately affect the representation of blacks on capital juries. Though perhaps this effect may not be sufficient to constitute a violation of the Sixth Amendment's fair-cross-section principle, it is similar in magnitude to the reduction in minority representation that the Ballew Court found to be of "constitutional significance" to a defendant's right to a fair jury trial.

The principle of "impartiality" invoked in Witherspoon is thus not the only basis for assessing whether the exclusion of jurors unwilling to consider the death penalty but able impartially to determine guilt infringes a capital defendant's constitutional interest in a fair trial. By identifying the critical concerns that are subsumed in that interest, the Ballew Court pointed to an alternative approach to the issue, drawing on the very sort of empirical data that respondent has presented here. And viewed in light of the concerns articulated in Ballew, the evidence is sufficient to establish that death qualification constitutes a substantial threat to a defendant's Sixth and Fourteenth Amendment right to a fair jury trial – a threat constitutionally acceptable only if justified by a sufficient state interest.

C.

Respondent's challenge ... appears to limit his constitutional claim to only those cases in which jurors have actually been struck for cause because of their opposition to the death penalty. However, this limitation should not blind the Court to prejudice that occurs even in cases in which no juror has in fact been excluded for refusing to consider the death penalty.

There is considerable evidence that the very process of determining whether any potential jurors are excludable for cause under Witherspoon predisposes jurors to convict. One study found that exposure to the voir dire needed for death qualification "increased subjects' belief in the guilt of the defendant and their estimate that he would be convicted." Even if this prejudice to the accused does not constitute an independent due process violation, it surely should be taken into account in any inquiry into the effects of death qualification. ...

The majority contends that any prejudice attributed to the process of death-qualifying jurors is justified by the State's interest in identifying and excluding nullifiers before the guilt stage of trial. It overlooks, however, the ease with which nullifiers could be identified before trial without any extended focus on how jurors would conduct themselves at a capital sentencing proceeding. Potential jurors could be asked, for example, "if there be any reason why any of them could not fairly and impartially try the issue of defendant's guilt in accordance with the evidence presented at the trial and the court's instructions as to the law." The prejudice attributable to the current pretrial focus on the death penalty should therefore be considered here and provides but another reason for concluding that death qualification infringes a capital defendant's "interest in a completely fair determination of guilt or innocence."

V.

The only two reasons that the Court invokes to justify the State's use of a single jury are efficient trial management and concern that a defendant at his sentencing proceedings may be able to profit from "residual doubts" troubling jurors who have sat through the guilt phase of his trial. The first of these purported justifications is merely unconvincing. The second is offensive.

In Ballew, the Court found that the State's interest in saving "court time and . . . financial costs" was insufficient to justify further reductions in jury size. The same is true here. The additional costs that would be imposed by a system of separate juries are not particularly high. ...

In a system using separate juries for guilt and penalty phases, time and resources would be saved every time a capital case did not require a penalty phase. The voir dire needed to identify nullifiers before the guilt phase is less extensive than the questioning that under the current scheme is conducted before every capital trial. The State could, of course, choose to empanel a death-qualified jury at the start of every trial, to be used only if a penalty stage is required. However, if it opted for the cheaper alternative of empaneling a death-qualified jury only in the event that a defendant were convicted of capital charges, the State frequently would be able to avoid retrying the entire guilt phase for the benefit of the penalty jury. Stipulated summaries of prior evidence might, for example, save considerable time. Thus, it cannot fairly be said that the costs of accommodating a defendant's constitutional rights under these circumstances are prohibitive, or even significant.

Even less convincing is the Court's concern that a defendant be able to appeal at sentencing to the "residual doubts" of the jurors who found him guilty. Any suggestion that the current system of death qualification "may be in the defendant's best interests, seems specious unless the state is willing to grant the defendant the option to waive this paternalistic protection in exchange for better odds against conviction." Furthermore, this case will stand as one of the few times in which any legitimacy has been given to the power of a convicted capital defendant facing the possibility of a death sentence to argue as a mitigating factor the chance that he might be innocent. Where a defendant's sentence but not his conviction has been set aside on appeal, States have routinely empaneled juries whose only duty is to assess punishment, thereby depriving defendants of the chance to profit from the "residual doubts" that jurors who had already sat through a guilt phase might bring to the sentencing proceeding. In its statute authorizing resentencing without any reassessment of culpability, Arkansas has noted: "it is a waste of judicial resources to require the retrying of an error-free trial if the State wishes to seek to reimpose the death penalty."

But most importantly, it ill-behooves the majority to allude to a defendant's power to appeal to "residual doubts" at his sentencing when this Court has consistently refused to grant certiorari in state cases holding that these doubts cannot properly be considered during capital sentencing proceedings. Any suggestion that capital defendants will benefit from a single jury thus is more than disingenuous. It is cruel.

VI.

...I dissent.

NOTES AND QUERIES

In note 1, the Court notes: In *Wainwright v. Witt*, 469 U.S. 412 (1985), this Court emphasized that the Constitution does not require "ritualistic adherence" to the "talismanic" standard for juror exclusion set forth in the *Witherspoon* opinion. Rather, the proper constitutional standard is simply whether a prospective juror's views would "'prevent or substantially impair the performance of his duties as a juror in accordance with his instructions and his oath.'" Id., at 433, quoting *Adams v. Texas*, 448 U.S. 38, 45 (1980). Thus, the term "*Witherspoon*-excludable" is something of a misnomer. Nevertheless, because the parties and the courts below have used the term "*Witherspoon*-excludables" to identify the group of prospective jurors at issue in this case, we will use the same term in this opinion.

Recall that *Witherspoon*-excludables were those who were excused because they had conscientious objections to the death penalty and that the vast majority of those who had been excused had not been asked if those scruples would invariably compel them to vote against capital punishment.

This case deals with those who would not, under any circumstances, vote for the imposition of the death penalty. Is that a notable difference to *Witherspoon*-excludables.

The case also deals with research that examines the impact of removing *Witherspoon*-excludables on jury decisions of guilt and penalty. Justice Rhenquist very precisely attacks the evidence that has accumulated to address the controversies raised in *Witherspoon*. Do you find his analysis on target? Is his legal analysis on target when he notes that, even if the psychological science were persuasive, the result would be the same since the constitutional attack based on fair cross-section requirements apply to the venire, not petit juries. We deal with peremptory challenges through the 14th Amendments equal protection clause, not the 6th Amendment. The argument also is that *Witherspoon*-excludables are not a distinctive group. Is it appropriate to exclude jurors who would not obey the law? The case is famous for the analysis that, even though the jury is not impartial in some ways, all that is needed to meet the partiality requirement is to have a jury constituted of those who will conscientiously apply the law and find the facts. Fair enough standard? What implications arise from such a standard?

Justice Marshall's dissent enumerates the research findings in this area. What are the key findings? Why would that not be persuasive enough? The dissenting opinion further notes that the very process of determining whether any potential jurors are excludable for cause under *Witherspoon* predisposes jurors to convict. How are we to deal with that concern?

Witherspoon constrained the challenges for cause made by the state. One of the issues that arises is whether a capital defendant is entitled to specific voir dire questions designed to determine whether potential jurors would automatically impose the death penalty upon conviction. Importantly, the case that first addressed the issue, *Morgan v. Illinois,* 504 U.S. 719 (1992), arose out of a jurisdiction that only required that a juror "may" reject the death penalty if mitigating circumstances were present; there was no obligation not to impose the death penalty once the jury had found guilt and aggravating circumstances. Yet, the Court still held that the defendant was entitled to specific question about the automatic imposition of the death penalty. Importantly, the Court based its decision on the Due Process Clause, because the Sixth Amendment applies to "criminal prosecutions." The argument was that the defendant had the right to remove jurors who automatically would vote for death because they could fail to consider the evidence of mitigating circumstances. What do you make of the argument that the finding of aggravating factors is mandatory and that finding mitigators are optional? Should the legislature be free to bias juries in favor of the death penalty? What about the argument that we elect judges partially on their beliefs and attitudes? Is it a matter that some attitudes are too extreme? How could we know if they in fact are or not? What does psychological science tell us on this matter?

Research Note on Bifurcated Trials

Two studies have examined the impact of bifurcation in cases involving capital punishment. Recall that bifurcation means splitting the determination of guilt and sentence between separate juries. Both of the studies are consistent with the conclusion that juries empaneled for both the guilt and the sentencing phases of trial are somewhat more likely to convict in the guilt phase. The first study manipulated the belief that mock juries would be responsible for sentencing if they convicted. Juries told that they would reconvene to determine a sentence if the defendant was found guilty subsequently convicted 10% more often than juries told only to determine guilt. James H. Davis, Robert W. Holt, Craig E. Spitzer, and Garold Stasser, The effects of consensus requirements and multiple decisions on mock juror verdict preferences, 17 J. of Exper'l Soc. Psych. 1 (1981). The second study found that juries responsible for determining guilt as well as a sentence were 23% more likely to convict than juries responsible only for determining guilt in a capital murder case. The limited available research suggests that juries responsible for determining both guilt and sentence are more likely to convict than juries responsible for determining only guilt. Iriwn A. Horowitz and David G. Seguin, The effects of bifurcation and death qualification on assignment of penalty in capital crimes, 16 J. of Appl. Soc. Psych. 165 (1986). Relatedly, another study pointed to the manner joined trials, rather than separate trials, result in increasing the odds of a particular defendant being found guilty. Research reveals the existence of an assimilation effect wherein juries perceive less distinction among defendants in joined trials than in separate trials. For example, one study found that conviction for a focal defendant was twice as likely in a joined trial compared with separate trials, and intrusion errors evident in the recall of testimony in the unitary trial were worse to the extent that the charges were similar. Sarah Tanford and Steve Penrod, Social inference processes in juror judgments of multiple-offense trials, 47 J. of Personality and Soc. Psych. 749 (1984).

Chapter 8

EVALUATING EXPERTS

INTRODUCTION

Testimony, documents, and records vary in their relevance, reliability and potential for prejudicial affects. As a result, unless opposing parties stipulate to the truth of evidence, courts must apply a complex set of rules to decide whether evidence will be presented to assist in deciding a dispute. The court assumes this gatekeeper role in order to insure, as much as practicable, a fair, impartial, and just result. This chapter examines this court's role as it examines the place of expert testimony and the use of psychological sciences. Importantly, this means examining both psychological science as proffered testimony as well as psychology's role in understanding the influence of expert testimony. To do so, we will examine leading cases in evidence law that actually do not appear related to our inquiry, but a close look reveals their impact on the use of psychological science in criminal justice processes as well as a place for psychology to help us understand the proper use of expert testimony.

A BRIEF OVERVIEW OF THE USE OF EXPERTS

What experts may testify to and the scope of their testimony is one of the most fundamental issues to consider in understanding the place of psychological sciences in criminal law enforcement. We will return to these issues in the cases that follow. For now, it is important to familiarize ourselves with the use of experts, a necessary foundation for considering the impact of experts on triers of fact (judges or juries).

The courts rarely permit experts to testify directly about two points. Experts must not testify whether they believe a witness is telling the truth about the alleged crime or render an opinion about witness credibility. Those determinations are within the exclusive province of the jury or judge's power. Likewise, most states still prohibit expert testimony as to the ultimate issue (e.g., whether a woman was, in fact, battered), since this too is considered within the role of the judge or jury alone. As we will see, however, these rules often become difficult to apply in practice. The opinion of experts can be highly persuasive and their findings on certain matters may run the risk of becoming tantamount to determining the veracity of another witness's claim and, by implication, to determining guilt or liability.

Generally, once a witness has been qualified as an expert, the witness may render an opinion based on that expertise. Typically, the admissibility of expert testimony depends on four factors: whether the subject matter of the testimony is outside the average judge's or jury's knowledge or experience, whether the state of the art of that field permits an expert opinion, whether the witness qualifies as an expert on that subject matter, and whether the basis of the expert's opinion is reasonably reliable. In addition, however, courts necessarily must consider the relevance of the testimony to the disputed claim and the precedential nature and long-term impact of the rule that would be set if the court admitted the testimony. Importantly, psychological science experts may testify to issues based on their clinical knowledge or based on their specific expert knowledge about a phenomenon. These two possibilities raise important concerns, the most critical of which involves the extent to which experts must rely on scientific evidence, an issue that becomes rather controversial when experts proffer evidence based on novel scientific principles. As will become obvious, we want to protect against the admission of what has become known as "junk science" and "junk testimony." The fear is that such evidence runs the risk of contributing to unjust outcomes to the extent that they inappropriately can sway triers of fact.

Once it has been determined that an expert may testify, the central issue then becomes determining the scope of the testimony. For example, an expert witness may (depending on the state) be permitted to corroborate a claim of child maltreatment by testifying that the alleged victim presents psychological and behavioral patterns similar to those of other children known to have been maltreated. Again, depending on the state, the court may allow expert testimony regarding syndromes. Such testimony involves the expert's description of a cluster of factors that have been identified with child maltreatment and have become known, collectively, as a syndrome. The witness (or another witness) will then explain consistencies between these factors and the child's condition.

Psychological Models of Experts' Influence on Juries

Decisions to admit testimony and evidence necessarily must consider their impact on triers of fact. We have just seen that a central concern involves whether junk science and testimony may inappropriately sway triers of fact. In addition to guarding against such evidence, the system also seeks to guard against experts and their testimony which may well be based on legitimate science but nevertheless inappropriately influence the outcomes of cases, such as through the usurpation of a jury's role in determining facts of cases. These concerns have led researchers to address the manner and extent to which experts and their testimony impact juries. Two theoretical perspectives continue to influence empirical research investigating expert testimony and juror decision making: heuristic models of persuasion and the story model of juror decision making.[1] Although the models are not mutually exclusive, each contributes concepts important to furthering the understanding of jurors' perception of and use of expert testimony in reaching verdicts.

The heuristic model of persuasion posits that the quality of an argument determines the persuasiveness of the message. However, when the message is too difficult to comprehend, individuals rely on cognitive shortcuts or heuristics to evaluate the value of the communication. As a result, rather than focusing on the message's quality, decision makers may use heuristic shortcuts that focus on such peripheral issues as the perceived expertise, trustworthiness, and appearance of the communicator. The theory implies that juror decision making may be unduly influenced by the credentials of an expert rather than by the quality of the proffered testimony.[2] During trials, jurors may use the heuristic method of evaluation to interpret expert testimony or scientific evidence because of the testimony's complexity and jurors' preexisting willingness to rely on the opinion of experts.[3] Unlike the heuristic model, the story model envisions a more global view

---

[1] Reid Hastie, Steve Penrod and Nancy Pennington, Inside the Jury (1983).

[2] Nancy Brekke and Eugene Borgida, Expert psychological testimony in rape trials: A social-cognitive analysis, 55 J. Personality and Soc. Psych. 372 (1988); Joel Cooper, Elizabeth A. Bennett, and Holly L. Sukel, Complex scientific testimony: How do jurors make decisions?, 20 L. and Hum. Beh. 379 (1996); and Regina A. Schuller and Neil Vidmar, Battered wife syndrome evidence in the courtroom: A review of the literature, 16 L. and Hum. Beh. 273 (1992).

[3] This is an admittedly complex area of research that reveals the use of two basic types of cognitive processes to integrate information: central processing and peripheral processing. See generally Alice Eagly and Shelly Chaiken, Attitude structure and function, in 1 The Handbook of Social Psycholology 269 (Daniel T. Gilbert, Susan T. Fiske, and Gardner Lindzey, eds., 1998); Richard Petty and Duane Wegener, Attitude change: Multiple roles for persuasion variables, in 1 The Handbook of Soc. Psych. 323 (Daniel T. Gilbert, Susan T. Fiske, and Gardner Lindzey, eds., 1998); Shelly Chaiken, Heuristic versus systematic information processing and the use of source versus message cues in persuasion, 39 J. Personality and Soc. Psych. 752 (1980); and Shelly Chaiken and Duriaraj Maheswaran, Heuristic processing can bias systematic processing: Effects of source credibility, argument ambiguity, and task importance on attitude judgment, 66 J. Personality and Soc. Psych. 460 (1994). When people engage in central or systematic processing, they carefully scrutinize the message and examine the quality of the arguments that are being made. When they engage in peripheral or

of expert testimony. Expert testimony influences decision making processes through its relationship with the stories the juror constructs about other evidence and testimony presented during the trial. The fit between the expert testimony, the juror's preexisting views concerning the issues, and the juror's final story determines the weight placed on the proffered expert testimony in decision making. As a consequence, effective experts specifically link their testimony to other trial evidence.[4]

In terms of evaluating the impact of expert testimony, empirical research actually supports both the story model and the heuristic model of juror decision making. Research reveals, for example, that psychological expert testimony strongly affects (real and mock) trial outcomes when it is presented on: the fallibility of eyewitness identifications,[5] clinical syndromes (i.e., battered woman syndrome, rape trauma syndrome, child sexual abuse syndrome, and repressed memory syndrome),[6] insanity,[7] and a defendants' future dangerousness.[8] The social psychology literature also demonstrates that a number of physical factors (i.e., attractiveness, age, demeanor, etc.) also affect an expert's persuasiveness.[9]

Although expert testimony can affect juror thinking and models have been developed to understand how jurors approach evidence, much remains to be understood in terms of the substantive factors that actually determine decisional outcomes. It remains a challenge to identify key factors, and how they influence one another, to determine legal decisions. Yet, empirical research on expert testimony successfully highlights a number of substantive factors that are important in influencing juror decision making.[10] The complexity of the testimony presented by the expert and the expert's credentials have been found to affect mock juror decisions.[11] As the heuristic model predicts, the complexity of the expert

---

heuristic processing of persuasive messages, they take mental short cuts. Rather than attending to the quality of arguments, they may, for example, make their decision based on the length of the message, the relative number of arguments for one side or another, or the prestige or purported expertise of the source. The claim that juries defer to the credentials of the expert, rather than scrutinizing the quality of the testimony, is, in psychological terms, a claim that jurors engage in peripheral rather than central processing. Research on persuasion indicates that central processing takes place when people are strongly motivated to understand the message and have the intellectual ability to grasp the arguments. When they are unmotivated or unable to process the message, they take cognitive shortcuts and rely on peripheral cues. Thus, this body of research would suggest that if two experts provide testimony of equal quality, but one expert is perceived to be of higher prestige than the other, the higher prestige person would tend to prevail in persuasiveness. Similarly, this research would suggest that the more difficult the testimony, the greater the likelihood that jurors would revert to peripheral cues.

[4] Scott Sundby, The jury as critic: An empirical look at how capital juries perceive expert and law testimony, 83 Va L. Rev. 1109 (1997).

[5] Brian L. Cutler, Steven D. Penrod and Hedy R. Dexter, The eyewitness, the expert psychologist, and the jury, 13 L. and Hum. Beh. 311 (1989); and Steven G. Fox and H.A. Walters, The impact of general versus specific expert testimony and eyewitness confidence upon mock juror judgment, 10 L. and Hum. Beh. 215 (1986).

[6] Nancy Brekke and Eugene Borgida, Expert psychological testimony in rape trials: A social-cognitive analysis, 55 J. Personality and Soc. Psych. 372 (1988); Nancy J. Brekke, Peter J. Enko, Gail Clavet, and Eric Seelau, Of juries and court appointed experts: The impact of nonadversarial versus adversarial expert testimony, 15 L. and Hum. Beh. 451 (1991); Natalie J. Gabora, Nicholas P. Spanos, and Amanda Joab, The effects of complaint age and expert psychological testimony in a simulated child sexual abuse trial, 17 L. and Hum. Beh. 103 (1993); Margaret Bull Kovera, April W. Gresham, Eugene Borgida, Ellen Gray, Does expert psychological testimony inform or influence juror decision making? A social cognitive analysis, 82 J. of Appl. Psych.178 (1997); and Regina A. Schuller and Neil Vidmar, Battered wife syndrome evidence in the courtroom: A review of the literature, 16 L. and Hum. Beh. 273 (1992).

[7] Richard Roger, Michael R. Baby, Mei-mei K. Chow, Psychiatrists and the parameter of expert testimony, 15 Int'l J. of L. and Psychiatry 387 (1992); Richard Rogers, R. Michael Baby, Mamie Crouch, and Brian Cutler, Effects of ultimate opinions on juror perceptions of insanity, 13 Int'l J. of L. and Psychiatry 225 (1990); and Jeff Greenberg and April Wursten, The psychologist and the psychiatrist as expert witnesses: Perceived credibility and influence, 19 Professional Psych.: Res. and Practice 373 (1988).

[8] Daniel A. Krauss and Bruce D. Sales, The effects of clinical and scientific expert testimony on juror decision making in capital sentencing, 7 Psych. Pub. Pol'y and L. 267 (2001).

[9] See Ronald Mazzella and Alan Feingold, The effects of physical attractiveness, race, socioeconomic status, and gender of defendants and victims on judgments of mock jurors: A meta analysis, 24 J. Appl. Soc. Psych. 1315 (1994).

[10] M. Juliet Bonazzoli, Jury selection and bias: Debunking invidious stereotypes through science, 18 Quinnipiac L. Rev. 247 (1998).

[11] Joel Cooper, Elizabeth A. Bennett, and Holly L. Sukel, Complex scientific testimony: How do jurors make decisions?, 20 L. and Hum. Beh. 379 (1996); and Jeff Greenberg and April Wursten, The psychologist and the psychiatrist as expert witnesses: Perceived credibility and influence, Professional Psych.: Res. and Practice, 19, 373-378 (1988).

testimony relates directly to the juror's reliance on an expert's credentials in reaching a decision, and jurors' decisions are not related to the content of the expert's testimony.[12] This effect may occur even when the expert testimony is neither particularly complex nor difficult to understand.[13]

The type of information presented by the expert also may influence the persuasiveness of the testimony. Mock studies as well as studies of actual jurors reveal that expert testimony specifically linked to the facts of a case is more influential in mock juror decisions than more general expert testimony.[14] A growing line of research indicates that mock jurors,[15]as well as judges and attorneys,[16] prefer clinical-opinion expert testimony to research-based on actuarial testimony. Moreover, recent research also has shown that mock jurors are sometimes leery of highly paid academic experts.[17] A number of persuasion experiments reveals that information originating from one case or one event is more influential in decision making than more statistically based information (i.e., information that is presented as a statistical summary of a large number of events).[18] It may be that individuals may have a special affinity for case information, a distrust of statistics, or bias against complex information, but this effect occurs even though case-specific information is often more inaccurate than statistical information.

The failure of decision makers to use statistical information in expected ways deserves emphasis. Much research supports how jurors make bad decisions in their interpretations when presented with statistical information. A relatively small but important body of research has shown that mock jurors are not very competent in utilizing probability estimates when they are presented in the form of abstract evidence bearing on guilt or liability.[19] The jurors either gave the evidence more weight than it deserved or not enough weight. In a series of insightful experiments, Gary Wells presented college students with different forms of information bearing on the likelihood that a bus belonging to a particular company was responsible for killing a dog.[20] The participants in the experiments were able to draw appropriate probability inferences, but they did not exhibit very good reasoning skills in translating those probabilities into verdicts. Wells concluded that rather than reasoning from the evidence to consider whether the dog was killed by a bus belonging to the particular bus company, many persons focused on the possibility of reaching an incorrect decision in holding the bus company liable and how they could justify their decision if it turned out to be wrong. Wells gave the same tasks to a sample of judges and found that they performed no better than the other participants in his experiments.

---

[12] Joel Cooper, Elizabeth A. Bennett, and Holly L. Sukel, Complex scientific testimony: How do jurors make decisions?, 20 L. and Hum. Beh. 379 (1996).

[13] In a simulated insanity trial, Greenberg and Wursten found that jurors were influenced more by medical expert testimony than by psychological expert testimony even when the testimony presented by each expert was identical in form and complexity. Jeff Greenberg and April Wursten, The psychologist and the psychiatrist as expert witnesses: Perceived credibility and influence,19 Professional Psych.: Res. and Practice 373 (1988).

[14] Scott Sundby, The jury as critic: An empirical look at how capital juries perceive expert and law testimony, 83 Virginia L. Rev. 1109 (1997); Steven G. Fox and H.A. Walters,The impact of general versus specific expert testimony and eyewitness confidence upon mock juror judgment, 10 L. and Hum. Beh. 215 (1986); and Margaret Bull Kovera, April W. Gresham, Eugene Borgida, Ellen Gray, Does expert psychological testimony inform or influence juror decision making? A social cognitive analysis, 82 J. of Appl. Psych. 178 (1997).

[15] Daniel A. Krauss and Bruce D. Sales, The effects of clinical and scientific expert testimony on juror decision making in capital sentencing, 7 Psych. Pub. Pol'y and L. 267 (2001).

[16] Richard E. Redding, What judges and lawyers think about the testimony of mental health experts: A survey of the courts and bar, 19 Beh. Sci. and the L. 583 (2001).

[17] Joel Cooper and Isaac M. Neuhaus, The "hired gun" effect: Assessing the effect of pay, frequency of testifying, and credentials on the perception of expert testimony, 24 L. and Hum. Beh. 149 (2000).

[18] Daniel J. O'Keefe, Persuasion Theory and Research (1990).

[19] David L. Faigman and A.J. Baglioni, Jr., Bayes' Theorem in the trial process: Instructing jurors on the value of statistical evidence, 12 Law and Hum. Beh. 1, 15-16 (1988); Jane Goodman, Jurors' comprehension and assessment of probabilistic evidence, 16 Am. J. Trial Advoc. 361 (1992); Brian C. Smith, Steven D. Penrod, Amy L. Otto, and Roger C. Park, Jurors' use of probabilistic evidence, 20 L. and Hum. Beh. 49, 79 (1996); and William C. Thompson, Are juries competent to evaluate statistical evidence?, 52 L. and Contemp. Probs. 9 (1989).

[20] Gary Wells, Naked statistical evidence of liability: Is subjective probability enough?, 62 J. Personality and Soc. Psych. 739 (1992).

The above generalities, however, are complex. Studies increasingly examine whether jurors attempt to understand the content of expert testimony, and the testimony's link to facts of the case (juror sensitivity), or simply favor the side that has the expert or the more credentialed expert regardless of the content of the expert's testimony (juror skepticism). Studies examining the effect of expert testimony on the fallibility of eyewitness identification in mock juror decision making have demonstrated that mock jurors do not simply base final decisions on the credentials and side of the expert (i.e., juror skepticism). On a variety of variables, mock jurors exhibit sensitivity to expert testimony by basing their verdicts on the fit between the expert testimony and the facts of the case.[21] Yet, juror sensitivity may not exist for all aspects of expert testimony. The spurious relationship between witness confidence and accuracy has not always produced a sensitivity effect, even when expert testimony is presented explicitly on this issue.[22] Jurors strongly believe that witness confidence in identification relates to accuracy of identification,[23] even though they correlate only weakly.[24] Numerous studies reveal that mock jurors tend to discount or ignore expert testimony on this issue because it does not fit with the jurors' strongly held preconceived notions.[25] Similar results have emerged with expert testimony on insanity, which apparently does little to change mock jurors' attitudes and final decisions when the mock jurors hold strong beliefs concerning the insanity defense prior to the trial. Mock jurors who held these strong prior-beliefs were also found to be less likely to engage in heuristic biases (i.e., expert credentials had less effect on their decisions).[26] Likewise, studies of actual death penalty cases reveal that jurors' prior beliefs influence the interpretation of expert testimony: Jurors expressly stated that they ignored the testimony of experts when it differed significantly from their preconceived notions of a phenomenon.[27]

In yet another important area, research consistently demonstrates that mock jurors do hold strong beliefs concerning the ability of clinicians to accurately predict future dangerousness.[28] Yet, research also consistently reveals the pervasive inability of clinicians to predict inaccurately. A large body of literature suggests that, as clinicians, mental health practitioners exhibit an unimpressive ability to make accurate future predictions of dangerousness, although it does seem that their abilities actually are better than previously thought, which was ranging from 65 to 85% inaccuracy to now at being inaccurate in the mid forty percent range.[29] Despite that, individuals believe clinicians can predict future dangerousness, a belief which causes jurors to be unfairly biased by the expert clinical opinion testimony and even to discount expert testimony and cross-examination that disagrees with their beliefs.[30] Yet another related example relates to situations when experts report their own levels of confidence. Survey data suggests that judges, jurors, and lawyers place confidence in an expert's own confidence. Judges and lawyers rated experts'

---

[21] Brian L. Cutler, The eyewitness, the expert psychologist, and the jury, 13 L. and Hum. Beh. 311 (1989).

[22] Brian L. Cutler, Steven D. Penrod, and Thomas E. Stuve, Juror decision making in eyewitness identification cases, 12 L. and Hum. Beh. 41 (1988).

[23] Brian L. Cutler, Steven D. Penrod, and Thomas E. Stuve, Juror decision making in eyewitness identification cases, 12 L. and Hum. Beh. 41 (1988); and Steven G. Fox and H.A. Walters, The impact of general versus specific expert testimony and eyewitness confidence upon mock juror judgment, 10 L. and Hum. Beh. 215 (1986).

[24] Robert K. Bothwell, Kenneth A. Deffenbacher, and John C. Brigham, Correlations of eyewitness accuracy and confidence: Optimality hypothesis revised, 72 J. of Appl. Psych. 691 (1987); and Thomas A. Busey, Jennifer Tunnicliff, Geoffrey R. Loftus, and Elizabeth F. Loftus, Accounts of the confidence-accuracy relation in recognition memory, 7 Psychonomic Bull. and Rev. 26 (2000).

[25] Brian L. Cutler, The eyewitness, the expert psychologist, and the jury, 13 L. and Hum. Beh. 311 (1989).

[26] Solomon M. Fulero and Norman J. Finkel, Barring ultimate issue testimony: An "insane" rule?, 15 L. and Hum. Beh. 495 (1991). Finkel's program of research offers the most complete in this area. His findings over many experiments show that evidence about a defendant's insanity is interpreted in the light of jurors' own social-cognitive schemata of what constitutes insane behavior. See generally Norman Finkel, Commonsense Justice: Juror's Notions of the Law (1995).

[27] Scott Sundby, The jury as critic: An empirical look at how capital juries perceive expert and law testimony, 83 Va L. Rev. 1109 (1997).

[28] Daniel A. Krauss and Bruce D. Sales, The effects of clinical and scientific expert testimony on juror decision making in capital sentencing, 7 Psych. Pub. Pol'y and L. 267 (2001).

[29] Randy Borum, Improving the clinical practice of violence risk assessment, 51 Am. Psych. 945 (1996); and Randy K. Otto, Predictions of dangerous behavior: A review and analysis of 'second generation' research, 5 Forensic Rep. 103 (1992).

[30] Daniel A. Krauss and Bruce D. Sales, The effects of clinical and scientific expert testimony on juror decision making in capital sentencing, 7 Psych. Pub. Pol'y and L. 267 (2001).

failure to state definitive conclusions as the most troubling aspect of their relationship with experts, whereas jurors rated experts who conveyed low confidence as a signal for strong concern.[31] These results are consistent with the story model of juror decision making and its emphasis on relating expert testimony to other evidentiary facts; it also highlights the importance of measuring jurors' pretrial beliefs.

Deliberation conditions also may affect the impact of expert testimony on juror decision making. Although the effects of deliberation conditions on jury verdicts remain in dispute in the jury research literature,[32] one important study reveals the differential effects for expert testimony pre- and post-deliberation.[33] Pre-deliberation, jurors view one-sided (clearly advocating one party's position) expert testimony more favorably than balanced testimony, but this effect disappears post-deliberation. Deliberation thus may influence juries to avoid heuristic evaluations of the expert as it allows them to explore more closely the content of an expert's testimony. In addition, deliberation studies reveal that time pressures and testimony complexity contribute to heuristic processing.[34] Having more time to explore the content of expert testimony through multiple viewpoints reduces the complexity of expert testimony. The failure to consider the role of deliberation, then, may mistakenly overvalue the importance of heuristic processing in juror decisions.

Research examining judge's abilities also reveals important points. Despite the important role that judges play in the courtroom, psychologists have focused their research efforts almost exclusively on juries. Importantly, in the operation of the legal system, judges are much more important than juries. They decide roughly as many cases at trial as juries do, they determine the outcome of roughly seven times as many cases as juries by ruling on dispositive motions, and they often play an active role in settling cases.[35] Even in those cases that juries decide, judges preside. They determine what evidence juries will be allowed to hear and interpret and instruct juries on the law they are to apply. Therefore, understanding judicial decision making is the key to understanding the outcome of particular cases and the development of law.

PSYCHOLOGICAL UNDERSTANDINGS OF EXPERTS' INFLUENCE ON JUDGES

Despite the importance of judicial thinking and reasoning in the admission and use of evidence, few systematic studies of judicial decision making exist. Most of the empirical work on judicial decision making has been motivated by concerns that judges make decisions that are self-serving or politically driven.[36] Few have dealt with the sources of judicial error. Psychologists suspect that even though judges are experienced, well-trained, and highly motivated decision makers, they remain vulnerable to cognitive illusions. Research on human judgment and choice indirectly supports this suspicion. Empirical studies demonstrate that cognitive illusions plague assessments that many professionals make. Several studies have found that experts display either roughly the same biases as college students or the same biases at

---

[31] Anthony Champagne, Daniel W. Shuman, and Elizabeth Whitaker, Expert witnesses in the courts: An empirical examination, 75 Judicature 5 (1992); and Daniel W. Shuman, Elizabeth Whitaker, and Anthony Champagne, An empirical examination of the use of expert witnesses in the courts – Part II: A three part study, 343 Jurimetrics 193 (1994).

[32] Shari Seidman Diamond, Illumination and shadow from jury simulations, 21 L. and Hum. Beh. 561 (1997).

[33] Nancy J. Brekke, Peter J. Enko, Gail Clavet, and Eric Seelau, Of juries and court appointed experts: The impact of nonadversarial versus adversarial expert testimony, 15 L. and Hum. Beh. 451 (1991).

[34] Richard E. Petty and John C. Caccioppo, Communication and Persuasion: Central and Peripheral Routes in Attitude Change (1986).

[35] Kevin M. Clermont and Theodore Eisenberg, Trial by jury or judge: Transcending empiricism, 77 Cornell L. Rev. 1124, 1127 n.7 (1992); see also Leonidas Ralph Mecham, Judicial Business of the United States Courts: 1999 Annual Report of the Director 172-74 tbl.C-7 (1999); and Chris Guthrie, Jeffrey J. Rachlinski, and Andrew J. Wistrich, Inside the judicial mind, 86 Cornell L. Rev. 777 (2001).

[36] See generally Lawrence Baum, The Puzzle of Judicial Behavior (1997); and Gregory C. Sisk, Michael Heise, and Andrew P. Morris, Charting the influences on the judicial mind: An empirical study of judicial reasoning, 73 N.Y.U. L. Rev. 1377 (1998).

somewhat reduced levels.[37] Even lawyers fall prey to cognitive illusions.[38] Inasmuch as "judging is choice," the conclusions drawn from psychological research on human judgment and choice likely apply to judges as well. Furthermore, judges make decisions under uncertain, time-pressured conditions that encourage reliance on cognitive shortcuts that sometimes cause illusions of judgment.

Decades of research on juries indicates that cognitive illusions adversely affect the quality of adjudication. We already have seen how juries allow irrelevant or inadmissible information to influence liability determinations.[39] We have viewed these influences as mental shortcuts, which psychologists often refer to as "heuristics," to make complex decisions.[40] We have seen how reliance on these heuristics facilitates good judgment most of the time, but it can also produce systematic errors in judgment. Judges do not seem immune to heuristic errors. One of the most recent studies of judicial decision-making examined a sample of 167 federal magistrate judges to explore the influence of cognitive illusions on judicial decision making.[41] The study tested for the influence of: anchoring (making estimates based on irrelevant starting points); framing (treating economically equivalent gains and losses differently); hindsight bias (perceiving past events to have been more predictable than they actually were); the representativeness heuristic (ignoring important background statistical information in favor of individuating information); and egocentric biases (overestimating one's own abilities). The study found that each of these cognitive illusions influenced the decision-making processes of the judges. Although the judges did display less vulnerability on some illusions than lawpeople, the study revealed that, under certain circumstances, judges rely on heuristics that can lead to systematically erroneous judgments.

The manner law enforcement makes use of experts in trials reveals several important assumptions about the abilities of judges. Although the vast majority of these assumptions go unnoticed, many have been the subject of empirical inquiry. The legal system assumes that judges can identify flawed expert evidence. Given that most judges probably have scientific reasoning abilities similar to the abilities of other lay people, the social psychological literature on the scientific reasoning abilities of lay people provides us with important insights on judges' abilities. Research conducted with lay persons on methodological and statistical reasoning skills suggests that they cannot differentiate between valid and flawed research.[42] Moreover, research suggests that law school education does not improve methodological and statistical reasoning skills.[43] It is possible, though, that judges' extensive experience in evaluating the admissibility of expert evidence will have provided them with knowledge about scientific methodology that lay people do not possess. However, judges report relying on experts' credentials and experience rather than the content of their testimony when judging the credibility of expert testimony.[44] Thus, in addition to admitting flawed testimony, judges may routinely exclude valid evidence. Other research suggests that judges' sociopolitical attitudes influence whether they would admit expert evidence in court; that is, social science findings that support a judge's political orientation toward a particular issue may be more likely to find their way into

---

[37] Scott Plous, The Psychology of Judgment and Decision Making (1993).

[38] Linda Babcock, Henry S. Farber, Cynthia Fobian, and Eldar Shafir, Forming beliefs about adjudicated outcomes: Perceptions of risk and reservation values, 15 Int'l Rev. L. and Econ. 289 (1995); and Darrin R. Lehman, Richard O. Lempert, and Richard E. Nisbett, The effects of graduate training on reasoning, 43 Am. Psych. 431 (1988).

[39] Stanley Sue, Ronald E. Smith, and Cathy Caldwell, Effects of inadmissible evidence on the decisions of simulated jurors: A moral dilemma, 3 J. Appl. Soc. Psych. 345, 350-51 (1973); William C. Thompson, Geoffrey T. Fong, and D. L. Rosenhan, Inadmissible evidence and juror verdicts, 40 J. Personality and Soc. Psych. 453, 457-62 (1981); and Sharon Wolf and David A. Montgomery, Effects of inadmissible evidence and level of judicial admonishment to disregard on the judgments of mock jurors, 7 J. Appl. Soc. Psych. 205, 212-16 (1977).

[40] Amos Tversky and Daniel Kahneman, Judgment under uncertainty: Heuristics and biases, 185 Science 1124, 1124 (1974). For a detailed description of this work, see Judgment Under Uncertainty: Heuristics and Biases (Daniel Kahneman, Paul Slovic, and Amos Tversky, eds., 1982); see also Scott Plous, The Psychology of Judgment and Decision Making 109-30, 145-52 (1993).

[41] Chris Guthrie, Jeffrey J. Rachlinski, and Andrew J. Wistrich, Inside the judicial mind, 86 Cornell L. Rev. 777 (2001).

[42] See generally Rules for Reasoning (Richard E. Nisbett, ed., 1993).

[43] Darrin R. Lehman, Richard O. Lempert, and Richard E. Nisbett, The effects of graduate training on reasoning: Formal discipline and thinking about everyday-life events, 43 Am. Psych. 431, 432 (1988).

[44] Daniel W. Shuman and Anthony Champagne, Removing the people from the legal process: The rhetoric and research on judicial selection and juries, 3 Psych., Pub. Pol'y, and L. 242 (1997).

court.[45] Importantly and not surprisingly, attorneys are not more methodologically sophisticated either; attorneys are just as likely to object to expert testimony whether it is valid or flawed, and given their inadequacy in differentiating good from less good science, are even likely to lead the judge astray.[46]

Taken as a whole, research on the influence of expert testimony on judge and juror decision making suggests the importance of controlling for or evaluating the effects of the physical appearance of the expert, the expert's credentials, the complexity of the expert's testimony, the jurors' prior beliefs concerning the facts at issue, the specific link between the expert testimony and the facts of the case, the confidence of the expert in his or her opinion, the deliberation of jurors, and the extent to which judges and attorneys are able to understand the nature of empirical research.

Notes and Queries

What is an expert generally not allowed to testify about?

What useful knowledge may be gained from the theoretical perspectives used to examine the influence of empirical research: the heuristic and the story telling model? Generally, how persuasive is psychological expert testimony? What kind of expert psychological testimony is most effective? What is so wrong with having jurors or judges base their opinions on, for example, an expert's credentials?

What are the effects of deliberation? How effective are judges in evaluating expert psychological evidence? What types of cognitive illusions do judges use in their decision making?

Law Note on The Federal Rules of Evidence

Consider the following key rules of evidence. The cases that follow will apply them. Note that the rules may appear straightforward but their application is a bit of a challenge. For example, Rule 102 below creates many goals that may often conflict. In addition, the goals in Rule 102 may often conflict within themselves: the focus on truth may refer to accuracy of the testimony presented in court, to the result of how evidence is used in the adversarial process, and/or to how trials in general, rather than specific cases, reveal truth. The goal is to consider how to weigh all of the relevant rules when making decisions about whether particular forms of evidence can be admitted to help decide a case.

Rule 102. Purpose and Construction

These rules shall be construed to secure fairness in administration, elimination of unjustifiable expense and delay, and promotion of growth and development of the law of evidence to the end that the truth may be ascertained and proceedings justly determined.

Rule 401. Definition of "Relevant Evidence"

"Relevant evidence" means evidence having any tendency to make the existence of any fact that is of consequence to the determination of the action more probable or less probable than it would be without the evidence.

Rule 402. Relevant Evidence Generally Admissible; Irrelevant Evidence Inadmissible

---

45 Richard E. Redding and N.Dickon Reppucci, Effects of lawyers' socio-political attitudes on their judgments of social science in legal decision making, 23 L. and Hum. Beh. 31 (1999).

46 Margaret Bull Kovera, Melissa B. Russano, and Bradley D. McAuliff, Assessment of the commonsense psychology underlying *Daubert:* Legal decision makers' abilities to evaluate expert evidence in hostile work environment cases, 8 Psych., Pub. Pol'y and L. 180 (2002).

All relevant evidence is admissible, except as otherwise provided by the Constitution of the United States, by Act of Congress, by these rules, or by other rules prescribed by the Supreme Court pursuant to statutory authority. Evidence which is not relevant is not admissible.

Rule 403. Exclusion of Relevant Evidence on Grounds of Prejudice, Confusion, or Waste of Time

Although relevant, evidence may be excluded if its probative value is substantially outweighed by the danger of unfair prejudice, confusion of the issues, or misleading the jury, or by considerations of undue delay, waste of time, or needless presentation of cumulative evidence.

Rule 701. Opinion Testimony by Lay Witnesses

If the witness is not testifying as an expert, the witness' testimony in the form of opinions or inferences is limited to those opinions or inferences which are (a) rationally based on the perception of the witness, and (b) helpful to a clear understanding of the witness' testimony or the determination of a fact in issue, and (c) not based on scientific, technical, or other specialized knowledge within the scope of Rule 702.

Rule 702. Testimony by Experts

If scientific, technical, or other specialized knowledge will assist the trier of fact to understand the evidence or to determine a fact in issue, a witness qualified as an expert by knowledge, skill, experience, training, or education, may testify thereto in the form of an opinion or otherwise, if (1) the testimony is based upon sufficient facts or data, (2) the testimony is the product of reliable principles and methods, and (3) the witness has applied the principles and methods reliably to the facts of the case.

Rule 703. Bases of Opinion Testimony by Experts

The facts or data in the particular case upon which an expert bases an opinion or inference may be those perceived by or made known to the expert at or before the hearing. If of a type reasonably relied upon by experts in the particular field in forming opinions or inferences upon the subject, the facts or data need not be admissible in evidence in order for the opinion or inference to be admitted. Facts or data that are otherwise inadmissible shall not be disclosed to the jury by the proponent of the opinion or inference unless the court determines that their probative value in assisting the jury to evaluate the expert's opinion substantially outweighs their prejudicial effect.

Rule 704. Opinion on Ultimate Issue

(a) Except as provided in subdivision (b), testimony in the form of an opinion or inference otherwise admissible is not objectionable because it embraces an ultimate issue to be decided by the trier of fact.

(b) No expert witness testifying with respect to the mental state or condition of a defendant in a criminal case may state an opinion or inference as to whether the defendant did or did not have the mental state or condition constituting an element of the crime charged or of a defense thereto. Such ultimate issues are matters for the trier of fact alone.

CONSIDERING SCIENTIFIC EVIDENCE

DAUBERT v. MERRELL DOW
509 U.S. 579 (1993)

Justice Blackman delivered the opinion of the Court.

In this case we are called upon to determine the standard for admitting expert scientific testimony in a federal trial.

I.

Petitioners Jason Daubert and Eric Schuller are minor children born with serious birth defects. They and their parents sued respondent in California state court, alleging that the birth defects had been caused by the mothers' ingestion of Bendectin, a prescription antinausea drug marketed by respondent. Respondent removed the suits to federal court on diversity grounds.

After extensive discovery, respondent moved for summary judgment, contending that Bendectin does not cause birth defects in humans and that petitioners would be unable to come forward with any admissible evidence that it does. In support of its motion, respondent submitted an affidavit of Steven H. Lamm, physician and epidemiologist, who is a well-credentialed expert on the risks from exposure to various chemical substances. Doctor Lamm stated that he had reviewed all the literature on Bendectin and human birth defects • more than 30 published studies involving over 130,000 patients. No study had found Bendectin to be a human teratogen (i.e., a substance capable of causing malformations in fetuses). On the basis of this review, Doctor Lamm concluded that maternal use of Bendectin during the first trimester of pregnancy has not been shown to be a risk factor for human birth defects.

Petitioners did not (and do not) contest this characterization of the published record regarding Bendectin. Instead, they responded to respondent's motion with the testimony of eight experts of their own, each of whom also possessed impressive credentials. These experts had concluded that Bendectin can cause birth defects. Their conclusions were based upon "in vitro" (test tube) and "in vivo" (live) animal studies that found a link between Bendectin and malformations; pharmacological studies of the chemical structure of Bendectin that purported to show similarities between the structure of the drug and that of other substances known to cause birth defects; and the "reanalysis" of previously published epidemiological (human statistical) studies.

The District Court granted respondent's motion for summary judgment. The court stated that scientific evidence is admissible only if the principle upon which it is based is "'sufficiently established to have general acceptance in the field to which it belongs.'" The court concluded that petitioners' evidence did not meet this standard. Given the vast body of epidemiological data concerning Bendectin, the court held, expert opinion which is not based on epidemiological evidence is not admissible to establish causation. Thus, the animal-cell studies, live-animal studies, and chemical-structure analyses on which petitioners had relied could not raise by themselves a reasonably disputable jury issue regarding causation. Petitioners' epidemiological analyses, based as they were on recalculations of data in previously published studies that had found no causal link between the drug and birth defects, were ruled to be inadmissible because they had not been published or subjected to peer review.

The United States Court of Appeals for the Ninth Circuit affirmed. Citing Frye v. United States (1923), the court stated that expert opinion based on a scientific technique is inadmissible unless the technique is "generally accepted" as reliable in the relevant scientific community. The court declared that expert opinion based on a methodology that diverges "significantly from the procedures accepted by recognized authorities in the field ... cannot be shown to be 'generally accepted as a reliable technique.'"

The court emphasized that other Courts of Appeals considering the risks of Bendectin had refused to admit reanalyses of epidemiological studies that had been neither published nor subjected to peer review. Those courts had found unpublished reanalyses "particularly problematic in light of the massive weight of the original published studies supporting [respondent's] position, all of which had undergone full scrutiny from the scientific community." Contending that reanalysis is generally accepted by the scientific community only when it is subjected to verification and scrutiny by others in the field, the Court of Appeals rejected petitioners' reanalyses as "unpublished, not subjected to the normal peer review process and generated solely for use in litigation." The court concluded that petitioners' evidence provided an insufficient foundation to allow admission of expert testimony that Bendectin caused their injuries and, accordingly, that petitioners could not satisfy their burden of proving causation at trial.

We granted certiorari in light of sharp divisions among the courts regarding the proper standard for the admission of expert testimony.

II.

A.

In the 70 years since its formulation in the Frye case, the "general acceptance" test has been the dominant standard for determining the admissibility of novel scientific evidence at trial. Although under increasing attack of late, the rule continues to be followed by a majority of courts, including the Ninth Circuit.

The Frye test has its origin in a short and citation-free 1923 decision concerning the admissibility of evidence derived from a systolic blood pressure deception test, a crude precursor to the polygraph machine. In what has become a famous (perhaps infamous) passage, the then Court of Appeals for the District of Columbia described the device and its operation and declared:

> Just when a scientific principle or discovery crosses the line between the experimental and demonstrable stages is difficult to define. Somewhere in this twilight zone the evidential force of the principle must be recognized, and while courts will go a long way in admitting expert testimony deduced from a well-recognized scientific principle or discovery, the thing from which the deduction is made must be sufficiently established to have gained general acceptance in the particular field in which it belongs.

Because the deception test had "not yet gained such standing and scientific recognition among physiological and psychological authorities as would justify the courts in admitting expert testimony deduced from the discovery, development, and experiments thus far made," evidence of its results was ruled inadmissible.

The merits of the Frye test have been much debated, and scholarship on its proper scope and application is legion. Petitioners' primary attack, however, is not on the content but on the continuing authority of the rule. They contend that the Frye test was superseded by the adoption of the Federal Rules of Evidence. We agree.

We interpret the legislatively enacted Federal Rules of Evidence as we would any statute. Rule 402 provides the baseline:

> All relevant evidence is admissible, except as otherwise provided by the Constitution of the United States, by Act of Congress, by these rules, or by other rules prescribed by the Supreme Court pursuant to statutory authority. Evidence which is not relevant is not admissible.

"Relevant evidence" is defined as that which has "any tendency to make the existence of any fact that is of consequence to the determination of the action more probable or less probable than it would be without the evidence." Rule 401. The Rules' basic standard of relevance thus is a liberal one.

Frye, of course, predated the Rules by half a century. In United States v. Abel we considered the pertinence of background common law in interpreting the Rules of Evidence. We noted that the Rules occupy the field, ... explained that the common law nevertheless could serve as an aid to their application:

> In principle, under the Federal Rules no common law of evidence remains. "All relevant evidence is admissible, except as otherwise provided . ..." In reality, of course, the body of common law knowledge continues to exist, though in the somewhat altered form of a source of guidance in the exercise of delegated powers.

We found the common-law precept at issue in the Abel case entirely consistent with Rule 402's general requirement of admissibility, and considered it unlikely that the drafters had intended to change the rule. In Bourjaily v. United States, (1987), on the other hand, the Court was unable to find a particular common-law doctrine in the Rules, and so held it superseded.

Here there is a specific Rule that speaks to the contested issue. Rule 702, governing expert testimony, provides:

> If scientific, technical, or other specialized knowledge will assist the trier of fact to understand the evidence or to determine a fact in issue, a witness qualified as an expert by knowledge, skill, experience, training, or education, may testify thereto in the form of an opinion or otherwise.

Nothing in the text of this Rule establishes "general acceptance" as an absolute prerequisite to admissibility. Nor does respondent present any clear indication that Rule 702 or the Rules as a whole were intended to incorporate a "general acceptance" standard. The drafting history makes no mention of Frye, and a rigid "general acceptance" requirement would be at odds with the "liberal thrust" of the Federal Rules and their "general approach of relaxing the traditional barriers to 'opinion' testimony." Given the Rules' permissive backdrop and their inclusion of a specific rule on expert testimony that does not mention "general acceptance," the assertion that the Rules somehow assimilated Frye is unconvincing. Frye made "general acceptance" the exclusive test for admitting expert scientific testimony. That austere standard, absent from, and incompatible with, the Federal Rules of Evidence, should not be applied in federal trials.

B.

That the Frye test was displaced by the Rules of Evidence does not mean, however, that the Rules themselves place no limits on the admissibility of purportedly scientific evidence. Nor is the trial judge disabled from screening such evidence. To the contrary, under the Rules the trial judge must ensure that any and all scientific testimony or evidence admitted is not only relevant, but reliable.

The primary locus of this obligation is Rule 702, which clearly contemplates some degree of regulation of the subjects and theories about which an expert may testify. "If scientific, technical, or other specialized knowledge will assist the trier of fact to understand the evidence or to determine a fact in issue" an expert "may testify thereto." The subject of an expert's testimony must be "scientific ... knowledge." The adjective "scientific" implies a grounding in the methods and procedures of science. Similarly, the word "knowledge" connotes more than subjective belief or unsupported speculation. The term "applies to any body of known facts or to any body of ideas inferred from such facts or accepted as truths on good grounds." Of course, it would be unreasonable to conclude that the subject of scientific testimony must be "known" to a certainty; arguably, there are no certainties in science. sing and refining theoretical explanations about the world that are subject to further testing and refinement". But, in order to qualify as "scientific knowledge," an inference or assertion must be derived by the scientific method. Proposed testimony must be supported by appropriate validation • i.e., "good grounds," based on what is known. In short, the requirement that an expert's testimony pertain to "scientific knowledge" establishes a standard of evidentiary reliability.

Rule 702 further requires that the evidence or testimony "assist the trier of fact to understand the evidence or to determine a fact in issue." This condition goes primarily to relevance. "Expert testimony which does not relate to any issue in the case is not relevant and, ergo, non-helpful." The consideration has been aptly described by Judge Becker as one of "fit." "Fit" is not always obvious, and scientific validity for one purpose is not necessarily scientific validity for other, unrelated purposes. The study of the phases of the moon, for example, may provide valid scientific "knowledge" about whether a certain night was dark, and if darkness is a fact in issue, the knowledge will assist the trier of fact. However (absent creditable grounds supporting such a link), evidence that the moon was full on a certain night will not assist the trier of fact in determining whether an individual was unusually likely to have behaved irrationally on that night. Rule 702's "helpfulness" standard requires a valid scientific connection to the pertinent inquiry as a precondition to admissibility.

That these requirements are embodied in Rule 702 is not surprising. Unlike an ordinary witness, see Rule 701, an expert is permitted wide latitude to offer opinions, including those that are not based on knowledge or observation. Presumably, this relaxation of the usual requirement of firsthand knowledge • a rule which represents "a 'most pervasive manifestation' of the common law insistence upon 'the most reliable sources of information,'" is premised on an assumption that the expert's opinion will have a reliable basis in the knowledge and experience of his discipline.

C.

Faced with a proffer of expert scientific testimony, then, the trial judge must determine at the outset, pursuant to Rule 104(a), whether the expert is proposing to testify to (1) scientific knowledge that (2) will assist the trier of fact to understand or determine a fact in issue. This entails a preliminary assessment of whether the reasoning or methodology underlying the testimony is scientifically valid and of whether that reasoning or methodology properly can be applied to the facts in issue. We are confident that federal judges possess the capacity to undertake this review. Many factors will bear on the inquiry, and we do not presume to set out a definitive checklist or test. But some general observations are appropriate.

Ordinarily, a key question to be answered in determining whether a theory or technique is scientific knowledge that will assist the trier of fact will be whether it can be (and has been) tested. "Scientific methodology today is based on generating hypotheses and testing them to see if they can be falsified; indeed, this methodology is what distinguishes science from other fields of human inquiry."

Another pertinent consideration is whether the theory or technique has been subjected to peer review and publication. Publication (which is but one element of peer review) is not a sine qua non of admissibility; it does not necessarily correlate with reliability and in some instances well-grounded but innovative theories will not have been published. Some propositions, moreover, are too particular, too new, or of too limited interest to be published. But submission to the scrutiny of the scientific community is a component of "good science," in part because it increases the likelihood that substantive flaws in methodology will be detected. The fact of publication (or lack thereof) in a peer reviewed journal thus will be a relevant, though not dispositive, consideration in assessing the scientific validity of a particular technique or methodology on which an opinion is premised.

Additionally, in the case of a particular scientific technique, the court ordinarily should consider the known or potential rate of error and the existence and maintenance of standards controlling the technique's operation.

Finally, "general acceptance" can yet have a bearing on the inquiry. A "reliability assessment does not require, although it does permit, explicit identification of arelevant scientific community and an express determination of a particular degree of acceptance within that community." Widespread acceptance can be an important factor in ruling particular evidence admissible, and "a known technique which has been able to attract only minimal support within the community" may properly be viewed with skepticism.

The inquiry envisioned by Rule 702 is, we emphasize, a flexible one. Its overarching subject is the scientific validity • and thus the evidentiary relevance and reliability • of the principles that underlie a proposed submission. The focus, of course, must be solely on principles and methodology, not on the conclusions that they generate.

Throughout, a judge assessing a proffer of expert scientific testimony under Rule 702 should also be mindful of other applicable rules. Rule 703 provides that expert opinions based on otherwise inadmissible hearsay are to be admitted only if the facts or data are "of a type reasonably relied upon by experts in the particular field in forming opinions or inferences upon the subject." Rule 706 allows the court at its discretion to procure the assistance of an expert of its own choosing. Finally, Rule 403 permits the exclusion of relevant evidence "if its probative value is substantially outweighed by the danger of unfair prejudice, confusion of the issues, or misleading the jury . ..." Judge Weinstein has explained: "Expert evidence can be both powerful and quite misleading because of the difficulty in evaluating it. Because of this risk, the judge in weighing possible prejudice against probative force under Rule 403 of the present rules exercises more control over experts than over lay witnesses."

III.

We conclude by briefly addressing what appear to be two underlying concerns of the parties and amici in this case. Respondent expresses apprehension that abandonment of "general acceptance" as the exclusive requirement for admission will result in a "free-for-all" in which befuddled juries are confounded by absurd and irrational pseudoscientific assertions. In this regard respondent seems to us to be overly pessimistic about the capabilities of the jury and of the adversary system generally. Vigorous cross-examination, presentation of contrary evidence, and careful instruction on the burden of proof are the traditional and appropriate means of attacking shaky but admissible evidence. Additionally, in the event the trial court concludes that the scintilla of evidence presented supporting a position is insufficient to allow a reasonable juror to conclude that the position more likely than not is true, the court remains free to direct a judgment and likewise to grant summary judgment. These conventional devices, rather than wholesale exclusion under an uncompromising "general acceptance" test, are the appropriate safeguards where the basis of scientific testimony meets the standards of Rule 702.

Petitioners and, to a greater extent, their amici exhibit a different concern. They suggest that recognition of a screening role for the judge that allows for the exclusion of "invalid" evidence will sanction a stifling and repressive scientific orthodoxy and will be inimical to the search for truth.It is true that open debate is an essential part of both legal and scientific analyses. Yet there are important differences between the quest for truth in the courtroom and the quest for truth in the laboratory. Scientific conclusions are subject to perpetual revision. Law, on the other hand, must resolve disputes finally and quickly. The scientific project is advanced by broad and wide-ranging consideration of a multitude of hypotheses, for those that are incorrect will eventually be shown to be so, and that in itself is an advance. Conjectures that are probably wrong are of little use, however, in the project of reaching a quick, final, and binding legal judgment • often of great consequence • about a particular set of events in the past. We recognize that, in practice, a gatekeeping role for the judge, no matter how flexible, inevitably on occasion will prevent the jury from learning of authentic insights and innovations. That, nevertheless, is the balance that is struck by Rules of Evidence designed not for the exhaustive search for cosmic understanding but for the particularized resolution of legal disputes.

V.

To summarize: "General acceptance" is not a necessary precondition to the admissibility of scientific evidence under the Federal Rules of Evidence, but the Rules of Evidence • especially Rule 702 • do assign to the trial judge the task of ensuring that an expert's testimony both rests on a reliable foundation and is relevant to the task at hand. Pertinent evidence based on scientifically valid principles will satisfy those demands.

The inquiries of the District Court and the Court of Appeals focused almost exclusively on "general acceptance," as gauged by publication and the decisions of other courts. Accordingly, the judgment of the Court of Appeals is vacated, and the case is remanded for further proceedings consistent with this opinion.

It is so ordered.

Chief Justice Rehnquist, with whom Justice Stevens joins, concurring in part and dissenting in part.

The petition for certiorari in this case presents two questions: first, whether the rule of Frye v. United States (1923), remains good law after the enactment of the Federal Rules of Evidence; and second, if Frye remains valid, whether it requires expert scientific testimony to have been subjected to a peer review process in order to be admissible. The Court concludes, correctly in my view, that the Frye rule did not survive the enactment of the Federal Rules of Evidence, and I therefore join Parts I and II-A of its opinion. The second question presented in the petition for certiorari necessarily is mooted by this holding, but the Court nonetheless proceeds to construe Rules 702 and 703 very much in the abstract, and then offers some "general observations."

"General observations" by this Court customarily carry great weight with lower federal courts, but the ones offered here suffer from the flaw common to most such observations • they are not applied to deciding whether particular testimony was or was not admissible, and therefore they tend to be not only general, but vague and abstract. This is particularly unfortunate in a case such as this, where the ultimate legal question depends on an appreciation of one or more bodies of knowledge not judicially noticeable, and subject to different interpretations in the briefs of the parties and their amici. Twenty-two amicus briefs have been filed in the case, and indeed the Court's opinion contains no fewer than 37 citations to amicus briefs and other secondary sources.

The various briefs filed in this case are markedly different from typical briefs, in that large parts of them do not deal with decided cases or statutory language • the sort of material we customarily interpret. Instead, they deal with definitions of scientific knowledge, scientific method, scientific validity, and peer review • in short, matters far afield from the expertise of judges. This is not to say that such materials are not useful or even necessary in deciding how Rule 702 should be applied; but it is to say that the unusual subject matter should cause us to proceed with great caution in deciding more than we have to, because our reach can so easily exceed our grasp.

But even if it were desirable to make "general observations" not necessary to decide the questions presented, I cannot subscribe to some of the observations made by the Court. In Part II-B, the Court concludes that reliability and relevancy are the touchstones of the admissibility of expert testimony. Federal Rule of Evidence 402 provides, as the Court points out, that "evidence which is not relevant is not admissible." But there is no similar reference in the Rule to "reliability." The Court constructs its argument by parsing the language "if scientific, technical, or other specialized knowledge will assist the trier of fact to understand the evidence or to determine a fact in issue, ... an expert ... may testify thereto . ..." It stresses that the subject of the expert's testimony must be "scientific ... knowledge," and points out that "scientific" "implies a grounding in the methods and procedures of science" and that the word "knowledge" "connotes more than subjective belief or unsupported speculation." From this it concludes that "scientific knowledge" must be "derived by the scientific method." Proposed testimony, we are told, must be supported by "appropriate validation." Indeed, the Court decides that "in a case involving scientific evidence, evidentiary reliability will be based upon scientific validity."

Questions arise simply from reading this part of the Court's opinion, and countless more questions will surely arise when hundreds of district judges try to apply its teaching to particular offers of expert testimony. Does all of this dicta apply to an expert seeking to testify on the basis of "technical or other specialized knowledge" • the other types of expert knowledge to which Rule 702 applies • or are the "general observations" limited only to "scientific knowledge"? What is the difference between scientific knowledge and technical knowledge; does Rule 702 actually contemplate that the phrase "scientific, technical, or other specialized knowledge" be broken down into numerous subspecies of expertise, or did its authors simply pick general descriptive language covering the sort of expert testimony which courts have customarily received? The Court speaks of its confidence that federal judges can make a "preliminary assessment of whether the reasoning or methodology underlying the testimony is scientifically valid and of whether that reasoning or methodology properly can be applied to the facts in issue." The Court then states that a "key question" to be answered in deciding whether something is "scientific knowledge" "will be whether it can be (and has been) tested." Following this sentence are three quotations from treatises, which not only speak of empirical testing, but one of which states that the "'criterion of the scientific status of a theory is its falsifiability, or refutability, or testability.'"

I defer to no one in my confidence in federal judges; but I am at a loss to know what is meant when it is said that the scientific status of a theory depends on its "falsifiability," and I suspect some of them will be, too.

I do not doubt that Rule 702 confides to the judge some gatekeeping responsibility in deciding questions of the admissibility of proffered expert testimony. But I do not think it imposes on them either the obligation or the authority to become amateur scientists in order to perform that role. I think the Court would be far better advised in this case to decide only the questions presented, and to leave the further development of this important area of the law to future cases.

NOTES AND QUERIES

Did the *Frye* rule survive the Federal Rules of Evidence?

Are we to interpret the Court's approach as a liberal rule (one which would admit more evidence)?

The dissent complains about the Court's focus on reliability. Do you prefer a focus on relevance to one on reliability? How does the Court guide reliability analyses?

Should we have greater faith in juries to parcel out junk science from good science? Was the rejected evidence here junk science?

Chief Justice Rehnquist demonstrated remarkable candor when he wrote about the difficulties judges may face when assessing the scientific status of theories, such as their falsifiability. A recent survey of 400 judges, from all 50 states, demonstrates that the vast majority do not understand even the most basic scientific concepts described by the *Daubert* Court. The first criterion listed by the *Daubert* court was falsifiability, that is, the ability of the expert's theory to be empirically tested against plausible alternative explanations. Although 89 percent of the judges asserted that falsifiability was a useful decision-making tool, only 4 percent of them could provide an explanation that involved a clear understanding of falsifiability and 35 percent of the judges gave answers that were unequivocally wrong. The second *Daubert* criterion was error rate, and ninety-one percent indicated that error rate was a useful criterion but only 4 percent demonstrated a clear understanding of the concept, while 86 percent gave answers that can be classified at best as equivocal and 10 percent gave an answer that was inaccurate. With respect to the peer review processes, 71 percent of judges clearly understood that concept, but 10 percent clearly did not.

Lastly, 82 percent demonstrated a clear understanding of the general acceptance criterion. Sophia I. Gatowski, Shirley A. Dobbin, James T. Richardson, Gerald P. Ginsburg, Mara L. Merlino, and Veronica Dahir, Asking the gatekeepers: A national survey of judges on judging expert evidence in a post-*Daubert* world, 25 L.and Hum. Beh. 433 (2001).

The above study is actually quite important given the role of trial judges. Trial judges are to examine the methodology and application of the evidence to the facts, not to examine the facts themselves. If they have difficulty understanding methodology, then it is unclear how well they can see how the evidence applies to the facts. Yet, and this too is quite important, the study fails to address the important question of the extent to which problems judges may have as a group in providing definitions translate into poor admissibility decisions. Even if a survey of federal judges demonstrated that they could provide a clear definition of the *Daubert* criteria, this does not mean that they then employ the criteria wisely. Knowledge is not equivalent to good judgment. Unfortunately, at the federal level there does not exist any individual level data on the merits of judicial decisions to admit or exclude. It would be important to address the question of how well judges are performing the gatekeeping function.

One researcher interviewed jurors who had heard cases involving Bendictin. He noted that the great majority of knowledgeable scientists agree that the research on the question of whether the drug caused birth defects in the offspring of the mothers who took it to control morning sickness clearly pointed in the direction of no causal relationship. Yet, the jurors generally concluded that scientists were divided equally on the issue, or that most scientists thought Bendectin was a teratogen. In addition and contrary to what scientists would believe, the jurors tended to discount the epidemiological evidence and rate epidemiology in general as less probative than animal studies, and in vitro research. This misunderstanding was seen as not surprising. The jurors heard approximately an equal number of experts on each side of the issue, lending to an impression that the scientific community was closely divided on the causal question. Likewise, plaintiff's experts stressed the importance of other types of evidence and frequently denigrated epidemiology. Joseph Sanders, Bendectin On Trial, 126-130 (1998). Although the finding may not surprise experts, what do you make of them?

Note that intensive litigation involving Bendectin ultimately caused Merrell Dow to withdraw it from the American market in the early 1980s. By the mid 1980s, however, a substantial body of evidence that the drug was non-teratogenic (did not cause birth defects) quickly formed with the major peer-reviewed epidemiological studies concluding that Bendectin does not cause birth defects. The courts took note of this consensus, and increasingly granted judgments in favor of Merrell Dow. Bendectin has since been re-introduced. Edward K. Cheng, Changing scientific evidence, 88 Minn. L. Rev. 315 (2003).

RESEARCH NOTE ON RESPONDING TO PROBLEMATIC EXPERT TESTIMONY

Because jurors appear to lack the necessary skills to identify flawed research, it is important to evaluate the effectiveness of the procedural safeguards that the justices in *Daubert* presumed would help jurors evaluate the reliability of expert evidence. Instruction on the standard of proof provides one of the clearest efforts to enhance juror decisions. In the *Daubert* decision, the majority stated that careful instruction on the standard of proof could help jurors give proper weight to unreliable expert testimony. Although no studies directly assess the accuracy of this assumption, existing research questions the very logic underlying the belief that instructions on the standard of proof help jurors make better decisions. The goal of an effective safeguard against unreliable evidence should be to sensitize jurors to the methodological quality of the evidence and help jurors differentiate between valid and flawed evidence. Research has shown that certain factors can increase or decrease reliance on the standards of proof that jurors use when evaluating evidence. For a review, see Irwin A. Horowitz, Reasonable doubt instructions: Commonsense justice and standard of proof, 3 Psych., Pub. Pol'y, and L. 285 (1997). These findings suggest that judicial instructions on the standard of proof will alter the stringency of the standards jurors use to evaluate expert evidence (e.g., make them more skeptical) but will not help them distinguish between high quality research and poor quality research. In addition, for instructions on the standard of proof to be effective, it is important that jurors understand the instructions. Unfortunately, most jurors appear not to understand judicial instructions on the standard of proof. Alan Reifman, Spencer M. Gusick and Phoebe C. Ellsworth, Real jurors' understanding of the law in real cases, 16 L. and Hum. Beh. 539 (1992). In sum, judicial instructions on the standard of proof, if understood, tend to cause jurors to become more skeptical of expert evidence.

Cross examination provides another procedural safeguard against problematic expert testimony and scientific claims. If attorneys have any hope of illuminating the methodological flaws present in expert evidence during cross-examination, they need to recognize flaws when they exist. Studies of attorneys' cross-examinations, however, reveal cause for concern. Attorneys' ratings of the reliability of expert evidence do not relate to the presence or absence of methodological flaws, such as a control group or a confound. Even so, attorneys may still ask questions that highlight the inadequacies of an expert's methodology during cross-examination. However, attorneys mention such key issues as internal validity relatively infrequently in their reported cross-examination strategies. Moreover, attorneys who read valid studies devote as much attention to issues of internal validity in their proposed cross-examination as do attorneys who read flawed studies. Rather than focusing their cross-examinations on the methodological quality of an expert's research, attorneys tend to address the expert's qualifications or potential sources of bias (e.g., payment for testimony, disproportionate appearances on behalf of plaintiffs). Margaret Bull Kovera, Melissa B. Russano, and Bradley D. McAuliff, Assessment of the commonsense psychology underlying Daubert: Legal decision makers' abilities to evaluate expert evidence in hostile work environment cases, 8 Psych. Pub. Pol'y and L. 180 (2002).

Providing opposing experts offers yet another key way to address inadequacies in expert testimony. Even if we assume that attorneys will consult experts to assist them with their evaluations of expert evidence, the concern is whether even experts will recognize and report research flaws. Although it would appear that experts would in fact be experts, many factors militate against their recognition and reporting of flaws. One study demonstrated that peer reviewers' theoretical orientations influence their evaluations of the methodological quality of research, such that they find studies to be of higher quality when the findings agree with their orientation. Michael J. Mahoney, Publication prejudices: An experimental study of confirmatory bias in the peer review system, 1 Cognitive Therapy and Res. 161 (1997). Even meta-analyses examining the same group of studies reached conclusions that were consistent with the theoretical orientation of the meta-analysts. Norman Miller and Vicki E. Pollock, Meta-analysis and some science-compromising problems of social psychology, in The Social Psychology of Science 230 (William R. Shadish and Steve Fuller, eds., 1994). Moreover, scientists appear to be willing to ignore fundamental methodological flaws, such as missing control groups or nonrandom assignment, if they find the research question important. Timothy D. Wilson, Bella M. DePaulo, Douglas G. Mook, Kristen J. Klaaren, Scientists evaluations of research: The biasing effects of the importance of the topic, 4 Psych. Sci. 322 (1993). Experts participating in the legal system face additional challenges that may hinder their ability to distinguish flawed and valid research. Because of the adversarial nature of the legal system, experts run the risk of becoming advocates for the side that hired them, rather than impartial educators or evaluators. Anthony Champagne, Daniel W. Shuman and Elizabeth Whitaker, An empirical examination of the use of expert witnesses in American courts, 31 Jurimetrics 375 (1991). At least one question regarding the effectiveness of the opposing expert safeguard remains: Can opposing experts sensitize jurors to the quality of expert evidence? Grave concerns exist about the damage that the battles of the experts may pose to the quality of juror decision making. See, e.g., Michael McCloskey and Howard E. Egeth, Eyewitness identification: What can a psychologist tell a jury?, 38 Am. Psych. 550 (1983). Yet, surprisingly few researchers have subjected these concerns to empirical scrutiny. Although no studies examine whether opposing experts do sensitize jurors to the methodological quality of research presented by an expert, research does suggest that cross-examination and the presentation of opposing expert testimony may not sensitize jurors to flawed research. Brian L. Cutler and Steven D. Penrod, Mistaken Identification: The Eyewitness, Psychology, and the Law (1995); and Margaret Bull Kovera, Bradley D. McAuliff, and Kellye

S. Hebert, Reasoning about scientific evidence: The effects of juror gender and evidence quality on juror decisions in a hostile work environment case, 84 J. of Appl. Psych. 362 (1999).

JUDGING SCIENTIFIC EVIDENCE

G.E. v. JOINER
522 U.S. 136 (1997)

Chief Justice Rehnquist delivered the opinion of the Court.

We granted certiorari in this case to determine what standard an appellate court should apply in reviewing a trial court's decision to admit or exclude expert testimony under Daubert v. Merrell Dow Pharmaceuticals, Inc., (1993). We hold that abuse of discretion is the appropriate standard. We apply this standard and conclude that the District Court in this case did not abuse its discretion when it excluded certain proffered expert testimony.

I.

Respondent Robert Joiner began work as an electrician in the Water and Light Department of Thomasville, Georgia (City) in 1973. This job required him to work with and around the City's electrical transformers, which used a mineral-based dielectric fluid as a coolant. Joiner often had to stick his hands and arms into the fluid to make repairs. The fluid would sometimes splash onto him, occasionally getting into his eyes and mouth. In 1983 the City discovered that the fluid in some of the transformers was contaminated with polychlorinated biphenyls (PCBs). PCBs are widely considered to be hazardous to human health. Congress, with limited exceptions, banned the production and sale of PCBs in 1978.

Joiner was diagnosed with small cell lung cancer in 1991. He sued petitioners in Georgia state court the following year. Petitioner Monsanto manufactured PCBs from 1935 to 1977; petitioners General Electric and Westinghouse Electric manufactured transformers and dielectric fluid. In his complaint Joiner linked his development of cancer to his exposure to PCBs and their derivatives, polychlorinated dibenzofurans (furans) and polychlorinated dibenzodioxins (dioxins). Joiner had been a smoker for approximately eight years, his parents had both been smokers, and there was a history of lung cancer in his family. He was thus perhaps already at a heightened risk of developing lung cancer eventually. The suit alleged that his exposure to PCBs "promoted" his cancer; had it not been for his exposure to these substances, his cancer would not have developed for many years, if at all.

Petitioners removed the case to federal court. Once there, they moved for summary judgment. They contended that (1) there was no evidence that Joiner suffered significant exposure to PCBs, furans, or dioxins, and (2) there was no admissible scientific evidence that PCBs promoted Joiner's cancer. Joiner responded that there were numerous disputed factual issues that required resolution by a jury. He relied largely on the testimony of expert witnesses. In depositions, his experts had testified that PCBs alone can promote cancer and that furans and dioxins can also promote cancer. They opined that since Joiner had been exposed to PCBs, furans, and dioxins, such exposure was likely responsible for Joiner's cancer.

The District Court ruled that there was a genuine issue of material fact as to whether Joiner had been exposed to PCBs. But it nevertheless granted summary judgment for petitioners because (1) there was no genuine issue as to whether Joiner had been exposed to furans and dioxins, and (2) the testimony of Joiner's experts had failed to show that there was a link between exposure to PCBs and small cell lung cancer. The court believed that the testimony of respondent's experts to the contrary did not rise above "subjective belief or unsupported speculation." Their testimony was therefore inadmissible.

The Court of Appeals for the Eleventh Circuit reversed. It held that "because the Federal Rules of Evidence governing expert testimony display a preference for admissibility, we apply a particularly stringent standard of review to the trial judge's exclusion of expert testimony." Applying that standard, the Court of Appeals held that the District Court had erred in excluding the testimony of Joiner's expert witnesses. The District Court had made two fundamental errors. First, it excluded the experts' testimony because it "drew different conclusions from the research than did each of the experts." The Court of Appeals opined that a district court should limit its role to determining the "legal reliability of proffered expert testimony, leaving the jury to decide the correctness of competing expert opinions." Second, the District Court had held that there was no genuine issue of material fact as to whether Joiner had been exposed to furans and dioxins. This was also incorrect, said the Court of Appeals, because testimony in the record supported the proposition that there had been such exposure.

We granted petitioners' petition for a writ of certiorari and we now reverse.

II.

Petitioners challenge the standard applied by the Court of Appeals in reviewing the District Court's decision to exclude respondent's experts' proffered testimony. They argue that that court should have applied traditional "abuse of discretion" review. Respondent agrees that abuse of discretion is the correct standard of review. He contends, however, that the Court of Appeals applied an abuse of discretion standard in this case. As he reads it, the phrase "particularly stringent" announced no new standard of review. It was simply an acknowledgment that an appellate court can and will devote more resources to analyzing district court decisions that are dispositive of the entire litigation. All evidentiary decisions are reviewed under an abuse of discretion standard. He argues, however, that it is perfectly reasonable for appellate courts to give particular attention to those decisions that are outcome-determinative.

We have held that abuse of discretion is the proper standard of review of a district court's evidentiary rulings. ... The Court of Appeals suggested that Daubert somehow altered this general rule in the context of a district court's decision to exclude scientific evidence. But Daubert did not address the standard of appellate review for evidentiary rulings at all. It did hold that the "austere" Frye standard of "general acceptance" had not been carried over into the Federal Rules of Evidence. But the opinion also said:

> That the Frye test was displaced by the Rules of Evidence does not mean, however, that the Rules themselves place no limits on the admissibility of purportedlyscientific evidence. Nor is the trial judge disabled from screening such evidence. To the contrary, under the Rules the trial judge must ensure that any and all scientific testimony or evidence admitted is not only relevant, but reliable.

Thus, while the Federal Rules of Evidence allow district courts to admit a somewhat broader range of scientific testimony than would have been admissible under Frye, they leave in place the "gatekeeper" role of the trial judge in screening such evidence. A court of appeals applying "abuse of discretion" review to such rulings may not categorically distinguish between rulings allowing expert testimony and rulings which disallow it.

We hold that the Court of Appeals erred in its review of the exclusion of Joiner's experts' testimony. In applying an overly "stringent" review to that ruling, it failed to give the trial court the deference that is the hallmark of abuse of discretion review.

III.

We believe that a proper application of the correct standard of review here indicates that the District Court did not abuse its discretion. Joiner's theory of liability was that his exposure to PCBs and their derivatives "promoted" his development of small cell lung cancer. In support of that theory he proffered the deposition testimony of expert witnesses. Dr. Arnold Schecter testified that he believed it "more likely than not that Mr. Joiner's lung cancer was causally linked to cigarette smoking and PCB exposure." Dr. Daniel Teitelbaum testified that Joiner's "lung cancer was caused by or contributed to in a significant degree by the materials with which he worked."

Petitioners contended that the statements of Joiner's experts regarding causation were nothing more than speculation. Petitioners criticized the testimony of the experts in that it was "not supported by epidemiological studies ... [and was] based exclusively on isolated studies of laboratory animals." Joiner responded by claiming that his experts had identified "relevant animal studies which support their opinions." He also directed the court's attention to four epidemiological studies on which his experts had relied.

The District Court agreed with petitioners that the animal studies on which respondent's experts relied did not support his contention that exposure to PCBs had contributed to his cancer. The studies involved infant mice that had developed cancer after being exposed to PCBs. The infant mice in the studies had had massive doses of PCBs injected directly into their peritoneums or stomachs. Joiner was an adult human being whose alleged exposure to PCBs was far less than the exposure in the animal studies. The PCBs were injected into the mice in a highly concentrated form. The fluid with which Joiner had come into contact generally had a much smaller PCB concentration of between 0-500 parts per million. The cancer that these mice developed was alveologenic adenomas; Joiner had developed small-cell carcinomas. No study demonstrated that adult mice developed cancer after being exposed to PCBs. One of the experts admitted that no study had demonstrated that PCBs lead to cancer in any other species.

Respondent failed to reply to this criticism. Rather than explaining how and why the experts could have extrapolated their opinions from these seemingly far-removed animal studies, respondent chose "to proceed as if the only issue [was] whether animal studies can ever be a proper foundation for an expert's opinion." Of course, whether animal studies can ever be a proper foundation for an expert's opinion was not the issue. The issue was whether these experts' opinions were sufficiently supported by the animal studies on which they purported to rely. The studies were so dissimilar to the facts presented in this litigation that it was not an abuse of discretion for the District Court to have rejected the experts' reliance on them.

The District Court also concluded that the four epidemiological studies on which respondent relied were not a sufficient basis for the experts' opinions. The first such study involved workers at an Italian capacitor plant who had been exposed to PCBs. The authors noted that lung cancer deaths among ex-employees at the plant were higher than might have been expected, but concluded that "there were apparently no grounds for associating lung cancer deaths (although increased above expectations) and exposure in the plant." Given that [the authors] were unwilling to say that PCB exposure had caused cancer among the workers they examined, their study did not support the experts' conclusion that Joiner's exposure to PCBs caused his cancer.

The second study followed employees who had worked at Monsanto's PCB production plant. The authors of this study found that the incidence of lung cancer deaths among these workers was somewhat higher than would ordinarily be expected. The increase, however, was not statistically significant and the authors of the study did not suggest a link between the increase in lung cancer deaths and the exposure to PCBs.

The third and fourth studies were likewise of no help. The third involved workers at a Norwegian cable manufacturing company who had been exposed to mineral oil. A statistically significant increase in lung cancer deaths had been observed in these workers. The study, however, (1) made no mention of PCBs and (2) was expressly limited to the type of mineral oil involved in that study, and thus did not support these experts' opinions. The fourth and final study involved a PCB-exposed group in Japan that had seen a statistically significant increase in lung cancer deaths. The subjects of this study, however, had been exposed to numerous potential carcinogens, including toxic rice oil that they had ingested.

Respondent points to Daubert's language that the "focus, of course, must be solely on principles and methodology, not on the conclusions that they generate." He claims that because the District Court's disagreement was with the conclusion that the experts drew from the studies, the District Court committed legal error and was properly reversed by the Court of Appeals. But conclusions and methodology are not entirely distinct from one another. Trained experts commonly extrapolate from existing data. But nothing in either Daubert or the Federal Rules of Evidence requires a district court to admit opinion evidence which is connected to existing data only by the ipse dixit of the expert. A court may conclude that there is simply too great an analytical gap between the data and the opinion proffered. That is what the District Court did here, and we hold that it did not abuse its discretion in so doing.

We hold, therefore, that abuse of discretion is the proper standard by which to review a district court's decision to admit or exclude scientific evidence. We further hold that ... the District Court did not abuse its discretion in excluding their testimony. ...

It is so ordered.

Justice Breyer, concurring.

The Court's opinion, which I join, emphasizes Daubert's statement that a trial judge, acting as "gatekeeper," must "'ensure that any and all scientific testimony or evidence admitted is not only relevant, but reliable.'" This requirement will sometimes ask judges to make subtle and sophisticated determinations about scientific methodology and its relation to the conclusions an expert witness seeks to offer • particularly when a case arises in an area where the science itself is tentative or uncertain, or where testimony about general risk levels in human beings or animals is offered to prove individual causation. Yet, as amici have pointed out, judges are not scientists and do not have the scientific training that can facilitate the making of such decisions.

Of course, neither the difficulty of the task nor any comparative lack of expertise can excuse the judge from exercising the "gatekeeper" duties that the Federal Rules impose. ... ... To the contrary, when law and science intersect, those duties often must be exercised with special care.

...It is, thus, essential in this science-related area that the courts administer the Federal Rules of Evidence in order to achieve the "ends" that the Rules themselves set forth, not only so that proceedings may be "justly determined," but also so "that the truth may be ascertained."

I therefore want specially to note that, as cases presenting significant science-related issues have increased in number, judges have increasingly found in the Rules of Evidence and Civil Procedure ways to help them overcome the inherent difficulty of making determinations about complicated scientific or otherwise technical evidence. Among these techniques are an increased use of Rule 16's pretrial conference authority to narrow the scientific issues in dispute, pretrial hearings where potential experts are subject to examination by the court, and the appointment of special masters and specially trained law clerks.

In the present case, the New England Journal of Medicine has filed an amici brief "in support of neither petitioners nor respondents" in which the Journal writes:

> [A] judge could better fulfill this gatekeeper function if he or she had help from scientists. Judges should be strongly encouraged to make greater use of their inherent authority ... to appoint experts . ...

Reputable experts could be recommended to courts by established scientific organizations, such as the National Academy of Sciences or the American Association for the Advancement of Science.

Given this kind of offer of cooperative effort, from the scientific to the legal community, and given the various Rules-authorized methods for facilitating the courts' task, it seems to me that Daubert's gatekeeping requirement will not prove inordinately difficult to implement; and that it will help secure the basic objectives of the Federal Rules of Evidence; which are, to repeat, the ascertainment of truth and the just determination of proceedings.

Justice Stevens, concurring in part and dissenting in part.

The Court of Appeals' discussion of admissibility is faithful to the dictum in Daubert that the reliability inquiry must focus on methodology, not conclusions. Thus, even though I fully agree with both the District Court's and this Court's explanation of why each of the studies on which the experts relied was by itself unpersuasive, a critical question remains unanswered: When qualified experts have reached relevant conclusions on the basis of an acceptable methodology, why are their opinions inadmissible?

In any event, it bears emphasis that the Court has not held that it would have been an abuse of discretion to admit the expert testimony. The very point of today's holding is that the abuse of discretion standard of review applies whether the district judge has excluded or admitted evidence. And nothing in either Daubert or the Federal Rules of Evidence requires a district judge to reject an expert's conclusions and keep them from the jury when they fit the facts of the case and are based on reliable scientific methodology.

Accordingly, while I join Parts I and II of the Court's opinion, I do not concur in the judgment or in Part III of its opinion.

NOTES AND QUERIES

Justice Breyer emphasizes that a court should not hesitate to go beyond the expertise proffered by the parties and utilize its powers to appoint independent experts, as Rule 706 of the Federal Rules of Evidence authorizes. Helpful suggestion?

If the experts would be qualified as experts, why is it that a court can reject their evidence derived from their expertise?

What is meant by "abuse of discretion"? How wrong must a judge be to abuse her discretion? Were animal studies good and relevant enough at least to be presented to a jury?

ESTABLISHING SCIENTIFIC EXPERTISE

KUMHO TIRE v. CARMICHAEL
526 U.S. 137 (1999)

Justice Breyer delivered the opinion of the Court.

In Daubert v. Merrell Dow Pharmaceuticals, Inc. (1993), this Court focused upon the admissibility of scientific expert testimony. It pointed out that such testimony is admissible only if it is both relevant and reliable. And it held that the Federal Rules of Evidence "assign to the trial judge the task of ensuring that an expert's testimony both rests on a reliable foundation and is relevant to the task at hand." The Court also discussed certain more specific factors, such as testing, peer review, error rates, and "acceptability" in the relevant scientific community, some or all of which might prove helpful in determining the reliability of a particular scientific "theory or technique."

This case requires us to decide how Daubert applies to the testimony of engineers and other experts who are not scientists. We conclude that Daubert's general holding setting forth the trial judge's general "gatekeeping" obligation applies not only to testimony based on "scientific" knowledge, but also to testimony based on "technical" and "other specialized" knowledge.. We also conclude that a trial court may consider one or more of the more specific factors that Daubert mentioned when doing so will help determine that testimony's reliability. But, as the Court stated in Daubert, the test of reliability is "flexible," and Daubert's list of specific factors neither necessarily nor exclusively applies to all experts or in every case. Rather, the law grants a district court the same broad latitude when it decides how to determine reliability as it enjoys in respect to its ultimate reliability determination. Applying these standards, we determine that the District Court's decision in this case not to admit certain expert testimony was within its discretion and therefore lawful.

I.

On July 6, 1993, the right rear tire of a minivan driven by Patrick Carmichael blew out. In the accident that followed, one of the passengers died, and others were severely injured. In October 1993, the Carmichaels brought this diversity suit against the tire's maker and its distributor, whom we refer to collectively as Kumho Tire, claiming that the tire was defective. The plaintiffs rested their case in significant part upon deposition testimony provided by an expert in tire failure analysis, Dennis Carlson, Jr., who intended to testify in support of their conclusion.

Carlson's depositions relied upon certain features of tire technology that are not in dispute. A steel-belted radial tire like the Carmichaels' is made up of a "carcass" containing many layers of flexible cords, called "plies," along which (between the cords and the outer tread) are laid steel strips called "belts." Steel wire loops, called "beads," hold the cords together at the plies' bottom edges. An outer layer, called the "tread," encases the carcass, and the entire tire is bound together in rubber, through the application of heat and various chemicals. The bead of the tire sits upon a "bead seat," which is part of the wheel assembly. That assembly contains a "rim flange," which extends over the bead and rests against the side of the tire.

Carlson's testimony also accepted certain background facts about the tire in question. He assumed that before the blowout the tire had traveled far. ... He conceded that the tire tread had at least two punctures which had been inadequately repaired.

Despite the tire's age and history, Carlson concluded that a defect in its manufacture or design caused the blow-out. He rested this conclusion in part upon three premises which for present purposes, we must assume are not in dispute: First, a tire's carcass should stay bound to the inner side of the tread for a significant period of time after its tread depth has worn away. Second, the tread of the tire at issue had separated from its inner steel-belted carcass prior to the accident. Third, this "separation" caused the blowout.

Carlson added that he had inspected the tire in question. He conceded that the tire to a limited degree showed greater wear on the shoulder than in the center, some signs of "bead groove," some discoloration, a few marks on the rim flange, and inadequately filled puncture holes (which can also cause heat that might lead to separation). But, in each instance, he testified that the symptoms were not significant, and he explained why he believed that they did not reveal overdeflection. For example, the extra shoulder wear, he said, appeared primarily on one shoulder, whereas an overdeflected tire would reveal equally abnormal wear on both shoulders. Carlson concluded that the tire did not bear at least two of the four overdeflection symptoms, nor was there any less obvious cause of separation; and since neither overdeflection nor the punctures caused the blowout, a defect must have done so.

Kumho Tire moved the District Court to exclude Carlson's testimony on the ground that his methodology failed Rule 702's reliability requirement. The court agreed with Kumho that it should act as a Daubert-type reliability "gatekeeper," even though one might consider Carlson's testimony as "technical," rather than "scientific." The court then examined Carlson's methodology in light of the reliability-related factors that Daubert mentioned, such as a theory's testability, whether it "has been a subject of peer review or publication," the "known or potential rate of error," and the "degree of acceptance ... within the relevant scientific community." The District Court found that all those factors argued against the reliability of Carlson's methods, and it granted the motion to exclude the testimony (as well as the defendants' accompanying motion for summary judgment).

The plaintiffs, arguing that the court's application of the Daubert factors was too "inflexible," asked for reconsideration. And the Court granted that motion. After reconsidering the matter, the court agreed with the plaintiffs that Daubert should be applied flexibly, that its four factors were simply illustrative, and that other factors could argue in favor of admissibility. It conceded that there may be widespread acceptance of a "visual-inspection method" for some relevant purposes. But the court found insufficient indications of the reliability of

> the component of Carlson's tire failure analysis which most concerned the Court, namely, the methodology employed by the expert in analyzing the data obtained in the visual inspection, and the scientific basis, if any, for such an analysis.

It consequently affirmed its earlier order declaring Carlson's testimony inadmissable and granting the defendants' motion for summary judgment.

The Eleventh Circuit reversed. ... It noted that "the Supreme Court in Daubert explicitly limited its holding to cover only the 'scientific context,'" adding that "a Daubert analysis" applies only where an expert relies "on the application of scientific principles," rather than "on skill- or experience-based observation." It concluded that Carlson's testimony, which it viewed as relying on experience, "falls outside the scope of Daubert," that "the district court erred as a matter of law by applying Daubert in this case," and that the case must be remanded for further (non-Daubert-type) consideration under Rule 702.

Kumho Tire petitioned for certiorari, asking us to determine whether a trial court "may" consider Daubert's specific "factors" when determining the "admissibility of an engineering expert's testimony.". We granted certiorari in light of uncertainty among the lower courts about whether, or how, Daubert applies to expert testimony that might be characterized as based not upon "scientific" knowledge, but rather upon "technical" or "other specialized" knowledge.

II.

A.

In Daubert, this Court held that Federal Rule of Evidence 702 imposes a special obligation upon a trial judge to "ensure that any and all scientific testimony ... is not only relevant, but reliable." The initial question before us is whether this basic gatekeeping obligation applies only to "scientific" testimony or to all expert testimony. We, like the parties, believe that it applies to all expert testimony.

For one thing, Rule 702 itself says:

> If scientific, technical, or other specialized knowledge will assist the trier of fact to understand the evidence or to determine a fact in issue, a witness qualified as an expert by knowledge, skill, experience, training, or ducation, may testify thereto in the form of an opinion or otherwise.

This language makes no relevant distinction between "scientific" knowledge and "technical" or "other specialized" knowledge. It makes clear that any such knowledge might become the subject of expert testimony. In Daubert, the Court specified that it is the Rule's word "knowledge," not the words (like "scientific") that modify that word, that "establishes a standard of evidentiary reliability." Hence, as a matter of language, the Rule applies its reliability standard to all "scientific," "technical," or "other specialized" matters within its scope. We concede that the Court in Daubert referred only to "scientific" knowledge. But as the Court there said, it referred to "scientific" testimony "because that was the nature of the expertise" at issue.

Neither is the evidentiary rationale that underlay the Court's basic Daubert "gatekeeping" determination limited to "scientific" knowledge. ... The Rules grant that latitude to all experts, not just to "scientific" ones.

Finally, it would prove difficult, if not impossible, for judges to administer evidentiary rules under which a gatekeeping obligation depended upon a distinction between "scientific" knowledge and "technical" or "other specialized" knowledge. There is no clear line that divides the one from the others. Disciplines such as engineering rest upon scientific knowledge. Pure scientific theory itself may depend for its development upon observation and properly engineered machinery. And conceptual efforts to distinguish the two are unlikely to produce clear legal lines capable of application in particular cases.

Neither is there a convincing need to make such distinctions. Experts of all kinds tie observations to conclusions ... And whether the specific expert testimony focuses upon specialized observations, the specialized translation of those observations into theory, a specialized theory itself, or the application of such a theory in a particular case, the expert's testimony often will rest "upon an experience confessedly foreign in kind to [the jury's] own." The trial judge's effort to assure that the specialized testimony is reliable and relevant can help the jury evaluate that foreign experience, whether the testimony reflects scientific, technical, or other specialized knowledge.

We conclude that Daubert's general principles apply to the expert matters described in Rule 702. The Rule, in respect to all such matters, "establishes a standard of evidentiary reliability." It "requires a valid ... connection to the pertinent inquiry as a precondition to admissibility." And where such testimony's factual basis, data, principles, methods, or their application are called sufficiently into question, see Part III, infra, the trial judge must determine whether the testimony has "a reliable basis in the knowledge and experience of [the relevant] discipline."

B.

The petitioners ask more specifically whether a trial judge determining the "admissibility of an engineering expert's testimony" may consider several more specific factors that Daubert said might "bear on" a judge's gate-keeping determination. These factors include:

Whether a "theory or technique ... can be (and has been) tested";
Whether it "has been subjected to peer review and publication";
Whether, in respect to a particular technique, there is a high "known or potential rate of error" and whether there are "standards controlling the technique's operation"; and
Whether the theory or technique enjoys "general acceptance" within a "relevant scientific community."

Emphasizing the word "may" in the question, we answer that question yes.

Engineering testimony rests upon scientific foundations, the reliability of which will be at issue in some cases. In other cases, the relevant reliability concerns may focus upon personal knowledge or experience. ... Our emphasis on the word "may" thus reflects Daubert's description of the Rule 702 inquiry as "a flexible one." Daubert makes clear that the factors it mentions do not constitute a "definitive checklist or test." And Daubert adds that the gatekeeping inquiry must be "'tied to the facts'" of a particular "case. ... Too much depends upon the particular circumstances of the particular case at issue.

We must therefore disagree with the Eleventh Circuit's holding that a trial judge may ask questions of the sort Daubert mentioned only where an expert "relies on the application of scientific principles," but not where an expert relies "on skill- or experience-based observation." We do not believe that Rule 702 creates a schematism that segregates expertise by type while mapping certain kinds of questions to certain kinds of experts. Life and the legal cases that it generates are too complex to warrant so definitive a match.

To say this is not to deny the importance of Daubert's gatekeeping requirement. The objective of that requirement is to ensure the reliability and relevancy of expert testimony. It is to make certain that an expert, whether basing testimony upon professional studies or personal experience, employs in the courtroom the same level of intellectual rigor that characterizes the practice of an expert in the relevant field. Nor do we deny that, as stated in Daubert, the particular questions that it mentioned will often be appropriate for use in determining the reliability of challenged expert testimony. Rather, we conclude that the trial judge must have considerable leeway in deciding in a particular case how to go about determining whether particular expert testimony is reliable. That is to say, a trial court should consider the specific factors identified in Daubert where they are reasonable measures of the reliability of expert testimony.

C.

The trial court must have the same kind of latitude in deciding how to test an expert's reliability, and to decide whether or when special briefing or other proceedings are needed to investigate reliability, as it enjoys when it decides whether that expert's relevant testimony is reliable. Our opinion in Joiner makes clear that a court of appeals is to apply an abuse-of-discretion standard when it "reviews a trial court's decision to admit or exclude expert testimony. ... Thus, whether Daubert's specific factors are, or are not, reasonable measures of reliability in a particular case is a matter that the law grants the trial judge broad latitude to determine. And the Eleventh Circuit erred insofar as it held to the contrary.

III.

In sum, Rule 702 grants the district judge the discretionary authority, reviewable for its abuse, to determine reliability in light of the particular facts and circumstance of the particular case. The District Court did not abuse its discretionary authority in this case. Hence, the judgment of the Court of Appeals is

Reversed.

Justice Scalia, with whom Justice O'Connor and Justice Thomas join, concurring.

I join the opinion of the Court, which makes clear that the discretion it endorses- trial-court discretion in choosing the manner of testing expert reliability- is not discretion to abandon the gatekeeping function. I think it worth adding that it is not discretion to perform the function inadequately. Rather, it is discretion to choose among reasonable means of excluding expertise that is fausse and science that is junky. Though, as the Court makes clear today, the Daubert factors are not holy writ, in a particular case the failure to apply one or another of them may be unreasonable, and hence an abuse of discretion.

Justice Stevens, concurring in part and dissenting in part. [omitted].

NOTES AND QUERIES

Note that all Justices agree that the Court's reliability factors may be used by lower courts to exclude expert testimony.

Kumho Tires arguably is more important than *Daubert*. The case is known for making clear the Rule 702 gatekeeping obligation in regard to non-science "experience-based" expertise. The case, however, also is important for what it says about the general construction and proper approach to the requirements of Rule 702 even in regard to the products of science. *Kumho Tires'* approach, whether dealing with scientific expertise or not, involves three considerations. A court must first review the reliability of the proffered expertise specifically as it applies to the task for which it is offered, not a more global reliability. Because the court retains discretion and flexibility, it then must consider and select the most appropriate criteria of reliability for the kind of expertise being proffered, given the circumstances of the particular case. Lastly, while a court may use the "*Daubert* factors," the presence or absence of one or more is not necessarily dispositive of sufficient reliability to gain admission. What emerges is a focus on the processing of information and an effort to ensure that the evidence has a level of reliability appropriate for the case at hand. The issue that remains involves the extent to which the courts take the process seriously. Relatedly, *Kumho* teaches that judges can ignore all of *Daubert's* "court factors" as long as the other considerations they choose are reasonable indicators of reliability.

The focus on experience is quite significant, but it may matter whose side of a criminal case the expert happens to sit. For example, police often provide expert testimony, such as structure and membership in drug organizations, the modus operandi of drug dealers, and the habits of drug users. Often, the police officer testifying as an expert was also the detective who investigated the case. This experience and testimony seems somewhat similar to those of clinicians. The extent to which they are similar would lead us to expect at least some parity in the admission of both clinical and police expert testimony. Yet, a study of several hundred appellate court cases revealed that police officers are admitted as experts at the appellate court level at a very high rate, more frequently than any other type of expert. For example, psychologists were only admitted 49.7% of the time overall, as compared to the 85.7% admissibility rate for police officers, a statistically significant difference. The courts, however, differentially treated clinical psychologists and experimental psychologists. Experimental psychologists' testimony is the type of testimony in a criminal case that is least likely to be admitted, with only 22.1% of these experts admitted at the appellate level. Clinical psychologists were admitted significantly more often than experimental psychologists, with 55.8% of the clinical psychologists admitted. Jennifer L. Groscup and Steven D. Penrod, Battle of the standards for experts in criminal cases: Police vs. psychologists, 33 Seton Hall L. Rev. 1141 (2003).

To understand the broad range of testimony police officers may offer, consider what you would make of an officer's expertise in horizontal gaze nystagmus (HGN) cases? HGN is a means of assessing impairment due to intoxication based on an investigator's observations of eyeball tremors when the eyes of a subject shift from straight ahead to the side. Although the technique may be used frequently to assess suspects of drunk driving, HGN testimony actually is of questionable dependability. The science behind the phenomenon makes it a proper subject of serious reliability concern. See Charles R. Honts and Susan L. Amato-Henderson, Horizontal gaze nystagmus test: The state of the science in 1995, 71 N.D. L. Rev. 671, 693-94 (1995). Likewise, the subjectivity of the evaluation of the nystagmus also raises issues about reliability. Although some defendants have mounted successful attacks, there have been well over a thousand reported state opinions indicating the presence on the record of HGN evidence since the *Daubert* decision and the vast bulk of them have accepted the testimony without much question. See D. Michael Risinger, Navigating expert reliability: Are criminal standards of certainty being left on the dock?, 64 Alb. L. Rev. 99 (2000).

Note that forensic experts testifying for the prosecution also seem to have an advantage in some areas of scientific evidence. For example, what do you make of bite mark evidence? Much controversy surrounds the extent to which a forensic odontologist can attribute the origin of a human bite mark to a particular person. Under certain conditions, the skill may be obvious. Few would question an identification that resulted when the dentition was shaped and aligned in a clearly unusual manner (such as with significant defects), and the bite mark involved all or most of the dentition left in a medium that was both plastic enough to receive an impression and sufficiently implastic to retain a high quality outline of the reciprocal of the dentition pattern. Yet, none of these ideal conditions are commonly present in criminal actions. A bite mark often reflects only a few teeth without clearly unusual alignment, and the most common medium in litigated cases, human flesh, does not receive and retain impressions very well. This reality means that the wound often ends up being controversial as to whether it even represents a bite mark. These circumstances raise important concerns about the reliability of identifications. What do you think courts would make of this type of evidence? A review of bite mark cases since the 1970s and after *Daubert* found forty-eight cases, all but one of which were criminal cases. In only four or five of those cases is there any indication that the foundational reliability of such evidence was challenged. All of the challenges were generally ignored by the courts, even though some of the testimony involved in these cases went beyond mere identification to the timing of the bites, and even to the intent with which they were inflicted. Only one opinion dealing with bite mark evidence actually cited to *Daubert*. D. Michael Risinger, Navigating expert reliability: Are criminal standards of certainty being left on the dock?, 64 Alb. L. Rev. 99 (2000). Note that similar concern has been raised about the routine admission of fingerprint testimony. In addition to the lack of basic reliability studies, no testing has been conducted to determine the probability of two different people having a number of fingerprint ridge characteristics in common. The concern lead the Department of Justice, in 2000, to recognize that basic validation studies in the fingerprint field have never been conducted and to solicit calls for basic research to (1) determine the scientific validity on the measurement of features, quantification, and statistical analysis of fingerprint expertise and (2) develop standardized procedures for comparing fingerprints and that these procedures must achieve acceptable error rates. Robert Epstein, Fingerprints meet *Daubert*: The myth of fingerprint "science" is revealed, 75 S. Cal. L. Rev. 605 (2002). What do you make of this frequent use of potentially unreliable evidence?

How would you assess the reliability of dogs trained to sniff and identify drugs? Could we simply assess the dog's past tracking record or his current ability to identify drugs? Would that suffice under *Kumho*? See *United States v. Elgin*, 2003 U.S. App. Lexis 1872 (6th Cir. 2003).

The *Daubert* trilogy involved civil cases. Criminal and civil cases use the same federal rules of evidence. Do you suppose that they may be administered differently in criminal than civil cases? Obviously, the criminal cases involve more basic constitutional issues and may be more restrictive. It would seem that that restriction would be on the part of restricting the prosecution and being more generous to defendants' proffers of expert/scientific evidence. The opposite seems to be the case. There is reason to believe that district courts have held criminal defendants' proffers to a higher standard of threshold reliability than prosecution proffers. See D. Michael Risinger, Navigating expert reliability: Are criminal standards of certainty being left on the dock, 64 Alb. L. Rev. 99 (2000). There may be many reasons for this. One suggestion is that exclusion of prosecution proffers by the trial court is unreviewable, whereas exclusion of defense proffers, in the mind of the trial judge, can be corrected on appeal if erroneous. This can incline the trial judge toward admission. See R. Erik Lilquist, A comment on the admissibility of forensic evidence, 33 Seton Hall L. Rev. 1189, 1191-92 (2003). Another commentator notes that the low "abuse of discretion" standard results in virtual automatic affirmance by the courts of appeal and creates a situation where nobody takes responsibility for seriously evaluating the actual reliability of prosecution-proffered expertise. See Mark P. Denbeaux and D. Michael Risinger, *Kumho Tire* and expert reliability: How the question you ask gives the answer you get, 34 Seton Hall L. Rev. 15 (2003).

NOTE ON THE BIASES OF EXPERT WITNESSES

A substantial body of psychological literature suggests that adopting a role affects attention to details, memory retrieval, and decision thresholds. This effect was noted over two decades ago in two psychological experiments. The first experiment had undergraduates view a slide show and heard an audio tape depicting a fight. The "witnesses" then were interviewed by an adversary or non-adversary lawyer and a week later testified about what they saw. Witnesses interviewed by the adversary lawyer biased their testimony in favor of the lawyer's client and this affected the impressions of the factual evidence and the responsibility judgments of "naive" adjudicators who did not know who had interviewed the witness. Blair H. Sheppard and Neil Vidmar, Adversary Pretrial procedures and testimonial evidence: Effects of lawyer's role and Machiavellianism, 39 J. Pers. and Soc. Psych. 320 (1980). The second study had students witness the same fight stimulus. This time the experimenters manipulated the students' role simply by telling the students they would appear either as a witness of the court or as a witness for either the plaintiff or the defendant. Student "judges" who were blind to this manipulation were asked to rate whether the evidence provided by the witness favored the plaintiff or the defendant. Separately, a set of raters heard the testimony of the witnesses and rated it as more or less pro-plaintiff. For both "judges" and raters, when compared to witnesses who testified from a neutral role, witnesses who testified for an adversary party produced testimony favorable to that party. Interestingly, when the witnesses themselves were asked to rate the evidence as pro-plaintiff or pro-defendant, their assigned role did not influence their judgment, i.e. the ratings of "plaintiff," "defendant," and neutral witnesses did not significantly differ from one another. Neil Vidmar and Nancy MacDonald Laird, Adversary social roles: Their effects on witnesses' communications of evidence and the assessments of adjudicators, 44 J. Pers. and Soc. Psych. 888 (1983). Although critics may note that the study exhibits rather weak ecological validity, the study does suggest that even very weak role manipulations can produce biasing effects even among witnesses who themselves have no psychological or economic interest in a given outcome.

CONSIDERING SYNDROME EVIDENCE

ESTELLE v. McGUIRE
502 U.S. 62 (1991)

Chief Justice Rehnquist delivered the opinion of the Court.

Respondent Mark Owen McGuire was found guilty in a California state court of second-degree murder for the killing of his infant daughter. After unsuccessfully challenging his conviction on appeal in the state courts, McGuire sought federal habeas relief, and the United States Court of Appeals for the Ninth Circuit set aside his conviction. We hold that in so doing the Court of Appeals exceeded the limited scope of federal habeas review of state convictions.

McGuire and his wife brought their 6-month-old daughter, Tori, to a hospital in Hayward, California. The baby was bluish in color and was not breathing. The attending physician noticed a large and relatively recent bruise on Tori's chest with multiple bruises around it, as well as black and blue marks around her ears. Efforts to revive the child were unsuccessful; Tori died 45 minutes after being brought to the hospital. An autopsy revealed 17 contusions on the baby's chest, 29 contusions in her abdominal area, a split liver, a split pancreas, a lacerated large intestine, and damage to her heart and one of her lungs. The autopsy also uncovered evidence of rectal tearing, which was at least six weeks old, and evidence of partially healed rib fractures, which were approximately seven weeks old.

The police questioned McGuire and his wife. McGuire stated his belief that Tori's injuries must have resulted from a fall off the family couch. He told the police that when his wife went out to make a telephone call, he went upstairs, leaving Tori lying on the couch; when he heard the baby cry, he came back downstairs to find her lying on the floor. After a police officer expressed skepticism at this explanation, McGuire replied that "maybe some Mexicans came in" while he was upstairs. During separate questioning, McGuire's wife stated that she had not hit Tori, and that she was unsure whether her husband had done so.

McGuire was charged with second-degree murder. At trial, the prosecution introduced both the statements made by McGuire to police and the medical evidence, including the evidence of prior rectal tearing and fractured ribs. Two physicians testified that Tori was a battered child, relying in part on the prior rib and rectal injuries, as well as on the more recent injuries. McGuire's neighbor testified that she had seen McGuire carry Tori by one of her arms to the car and roughly pinch her cheeks together when she cried. The neighbor added that McGuire's wife had expressed fear in leaving Tori alone with McGuire, because he had been rough with the baby and "did bad things" to her.

In addition, the prosecution called a witness who had overheard a conversation between McGuire and his wife in the hospital emergency room the night of Tori's death. According to the witness, McGuire's wife several times insistently asked, "What really happened?" McGuire replied that he "didn't know," and that he "guessed" the baby fell off the couch. His wife continued to press for an answer, stating, "I am very patient. I can wait a long time. I want to know what really happened." Finally, she told McGuire that "the baby was alright when I left. You are responsible." McGuire's wife was called by the prosecution to testify at trial, after having been granted transactional immunity from future prosecution. In contrast to her prior statement to the police and her declarations at the hospital, she stated that she had beaten Tori on the day of her death before her husband arrived home. The jury convicted McGuire of second-degree murder.

The California Court of Appeal affirmed McGuire's conviction. The court observed that the evidence of prior rib and rectal injuries was introduced to prove "battered child syndrome." That syndrome exists when a child has sustained repeated and/or serious injuries by nonaccidental means. After reviewing California authority on the subject, the court concluded that "proof of Tori's 'prior injuries' tending to establish the 'battered child syndrome' was patently proper." The California Supreme Court denied review.

McGuire then filed a petition for habeas corpus relief in the United States District Court for the Northern District of California. That court denied relief. The Court of Appeals for the Ninth Circuit reversed and granted McGuire's habeas petition. The court ruled that the prior injury evidence was erroneously admitted to establish battered child syndrome, because no evidence linked McGuire to the prior injuries and no claim had been made at trial that the baby died accidentally. In addition, the court believed that the trial court's instruction on the use of prior act evidence allowed a finding of guilt based simply on a judgment that McGuire committed the prior bad acts. The court concluded that the admission of the evidence, in conjunction with the prejudicial instruction, "rendered [McGuire's] trial arbitrary and fundamentally unfair" in violation of due process. We hold that none of the alleged errors rise to the level of a due process violation, and so reverse.

[Note: The court instructed the jury as follows:

> Evidence has been introduced for the purpose of showing that the Defendant committed acts similar to those constituting a crime other than that for which he is on trial. Such evidence, if believed, was not received, and may not be considered by you[,] to prove that he is a person of bad character or that he has a disposition to commit crimes. Such evidence was received and may be considered by you only for the limited purpose of determining if it tends to show three things:
>
> 1. The impeachment of Daisy McGuire's testimony that she had no cause to be afraid of the Defendant; 2. To establish the battered child syndrome; and 3. Also a clear connection between the

other two offense[s] and the one of which the Defendant is accused, so that it may be logically concluded that if the Defendant committed other offenses, he also committed the crime charged in this case. For the limited purpose for which you may consider such evidence, you must weigh it in the same manner as you do all other evidence in the case. You are not permitted to consider evidence for any other purpose.]

I.

We first consider whether the admission of the prior injury evidence justified habeas relief. In ruling that McGuire's due process rights were violated by the admission of the evidence, the Court of Appeals relied in part on its conclusion that the evidence was "incorrectly admitted ... pursuant to California law." Such an inquiry, however, is no part of a federal court's habeas review of a state conviction. We have stated many times that "federal habeas corpus relief does not lie for errors of state law."...

We thus turn to the question whether the admission of the evidence violated McGuire's federal constitutional rights. California law allows the prosecution to introduce expert testimony and evidence related to prior injuries in order to prove "battered child syndrome." The demonstration of battered child syndrome "simply indicates that a child found with [serious, repeated injuries] has not suffered those injuries by accidental means." Thus, evidence demonstrating battered child syndrome helps to prove that the child died at the hands of another and not by falling off a couch, for example; it also tends to establish that the "other," whoever it may be, inflicted the injuries intentionally. When offered to show that certain injuries are a product of child abuse, rather than accident, evidence of prior injuries is relevant even though it does not purport to prove the identity of the person who might have inflicted those injuries. Because the prosecution had charged McGuire with second-degree murder, it was required to prove that Tori's death was caused by the defendant's intentional act. Proof of Tori's battered child status helped to do just that; although not linked by any direct evidence to McGuire, the evidence demonstrated that Tori's death was the result of an intentional act by someone, and not an accident. The Court of Appeals, however, ignored the principle of battered child syndrome evidence in holding that this evidence was incorrectly admitted. For example, the court stated that "evidence cannot have probative value unless a party connects it to the defendant in some meaningful way." We conclude that the evidence of prior injuries presented at McGuire's trial, whether it was directly linked to McGuire or not, was probative on the question of the intent with which the person who caused the injuries acted.

In holding the prior injury evidence inadmissible, the Court of Appeals also relied on the theory that, because no claim was made at trial that Tori died accidentally, the battered child syndrome evidence was irrelevant and violative of due process. This ruling ignores the fact that the prosecution must prove all the elements of a criminal offense beyond a reasonable doubt. In this second-degree murder case, for example, the prosecution was required to demonstrate that the killing was intentional. By eliminating the possibility of accident, the evidence regarding battered child syndrome was clearly probative of that essential element, especially in light of the fact that McGuire had claimed prior to trial that Tori had injured herself by falling from the couch. The Court of Appeals, however, ruled that the evidence should have been excluded because McGuire did not raise the defense of accidental death at trial. But the prosecution's burden to prove every element of the crime is not relieved by a defendant's tactical decision not to contest an essential element of the offense. In the federal courts, "[a] simple plea of not guilty ... puts the prosecution to its proof as to all elements of the crime charged." Neither the Court of Appeals nor the parties have given us any reason to think that the rule is different in California. The evidence of battered child syndrome was relevant to show intent, and nothing in the Due Process Clause of the Fourteenth Amendment requires the State to refrain from introducing relevant evidence simply because the defense chooses not to contest the point.

II.

The Court of Appeals, however, did not rely solely on a finding that the admission of the evidence was unconstitutional. It based its decision in part on a belief that the instruction given by the trial court, allowed the jury to consider the prior injury evidence for more than simply proof of the battered child syndrome, and thereby violated McGuire's due process rights. McGuire focuses on the portion of the instruction explaining to the jury that the prior injury evidence

> was received and may be considered by you only for the limited purpose of determining if it tends to show ... a clear connection between the other two offense[s] and the one of which the Defendant is accused, so that it may be logically concluded that if the Defendant committed other offenses, he also committed the crime charged in this case.

McGuire argues that, despite the absence of any direct evidence showing that he caused the rib and rectal injuries, the instruction told the jury to find that he had committed those prior offenses. Furthermore, he argues, the instruction left the jury with the mistaken impression that it could base its finding of guilt on the simple fact that he had previously harmed Tori. Under McGuire's reading, the instruction is transformed into a propensity instruction, allowing the jury to consider as evidence of his guilt the fact that his prior acts show a disposition to commit this type of crime. This, he contends, violates the Due Process Clause.

In arguing his point, McGuire makes much of the fact that, in giving its instruction, the trial court deviated in part from standard jury instruction. As we have stated above, however, the fact that the instruction was allegedly incorrect under state law is not a basis for habeas relief...

McGuire first claims that the instruction directed the jury to find that he had caused the prior injuries, thereby effectively taking that question from the jury. One might argue that the "two offense[s]" referred to in the instruction were McGuire's pinching of the child's cheeks and the lifting of the child by her arm. When read in context, however, we conclude that the most likely interpretation is that the reference was to the rectal tearing and fractured ribs. McGuire argues that, despite the lack of any direct evidence linking him to those injuries, the instruction directed the jury to find that he had committed them. This claim is clearly foreclosed, however, by the language of the instruction. The challenged portion of the instruction included the words "if the Defendant committed other offenses." By including this phrase, the trial court unquestionably left it to the jury to determine whether McGuire committed the prior acts; only if the jury believed he was the perpetrator could it use the evidence in deciding whether McGuire was guilty of the crime charged. Therefore, if the jury did not believe McGuire caused the prior injuries, he was not harmed by the challenged portion of the instruction. To the extent that the jury may have believed McGuire committed the prior acts and used that as a factor in its deliberation, we observe that there was sufficient evidence to sustain such a jury finding by a preponderance of the evidence. The proof of battered child syndrome itself narrowed the group of possible perpetrators to McGuire and his wife, because they were the only two people regularly caring for Tori during her short life. A neighbor testified that she had seen McGuire treat Tori roughly on two occasions, and that McGuire's wife was scared to leave Tori alone with McGuire because he "did bad things" to her; the neighbor further testified that she had never seen McGuire's wife abuse the child in any way. Futhermore, when being questioned by the police after Tori died, McGuire's wife stated that she observed bruises on the baby's body when bathing her. When asked by the police for an explanation, she replied, "I don't really know, you know, I am not the only one who is taking care of her." The evidence described, along with other evidence in the record, convinces us that there was sufficient proof for the jury to conclude, if it so desired, that McGuire caused the prior rib and rectal injuries.

We therefore hold that neither the introduction of the challenged evidence, nor the jury instruction as to its use, "so infused the trial with unfairness as to deny due process of law." The judgment of the Court of Appeals is therefore

Reversed.

Justice O'Connor, with whom Justice Stevens joins, concurring in part and dissenting in part.

I agree with the Court that the evidence of battered child syndrome was relevant. The State had to prove that Mark McGuire intended to kill his daughter, and the evidence that Tori was a battered child was probative of causation and intent. I therefore join Part I of the Court's opinion.

I do not join Part II of the opinion because I think there is a reasonable likelihood that the jury misapplied the prior acts instruction. The trial court instructed the jury that evidence of Tori's prior injuries had been admitted to show that McGuire had committed offenses similar to that for which he was on trial, and that, if the jury found a "clear connection" between the prior offenses and the charged offense, "it may be logically concluded that if the Defendant committed other offenses, he also committed the crime charged in this case." In my view, the instruction encouraged the jury to assume that McGuire had inflicted the prior injuries and then directed the jury to conclude that the prior abuser was the murderer. Because the instruction may have relieved the State of its burden of proving the identity of Tori's murderer beyond a reasonable doubt, I would hold that the instruction was error and remand to the Court of Appeals for a determination of whether that error was harmless.

The fact that a 6-month-old child was repeatedly beaten in the course of her short life is so horrifying that a trial court should take special care to inform the jury as to the significance of that evidence. As the Court notes, the demonstration of battered child syndrome is relevant because it "'indicates that a child found with [serious, repeated injuries] has not suffered those injuries by accidental means.'" I therefore agree that proof of Tori's battered child status, although "not linked by any direct evidence to McGuire," was properly admitted because "the evidence demonstrated that Tori's death was the result of an intentional act by someone, and not an accident." Precisely because the relevance of battered child syndrome is not tied to the identity of the abuser, however, I believe that a jury instruction clarifying the limited probative value of that evidence was required.

Instead of an instruction limiting the use of evidence of Tori's prior injuries, the trial judge gave an instruction limiting the use of evidence of McGuire's prior bad acts. In so doing, the trial judge himself appears to have assumed that the prior injuries could be attributed to McGuire. The judge told the jury that "evidence has been introduced for the purpose of showing that the Defendant committed acts similar to those constituting a crime other than that for which he is on trial." The State concedes that this category of evidence encompasses both the acts for which McGuire was positively identified as the actor (carrying the child by one arm and roughly pinching her cheeks) and the far more brutal acts for which no actor was identified (the fractured ribs and the rectal tearing). The grouping of these two distinct classes of evidence created a reasonable likelihood that the jury would believe that McGuire had been identified • at least in the eyes of the trial judge • as the prior abuser.

The trial court's error in implying that McGuire had been identified as the prior abuser was compounded by its further instruction that, if the jury found a "clear connection" between the prior offenses and the charged offense, "it may be logically concluded that if the Defendant committed other offenses, he also committed the crime charged in this case." The Court finds it "likely" that the jury understood the instruction to mean that "if it found a 'clear connection' between the prior injuries and the instant injuries, and if it found that McGuire had committed the prior injuries, then it could use that fact in determining that

McGuire committed the crime charged." In my view, there is a reasonable likelihood that the jury did not understand this single sentence to establish a two-step process.

The jury was instructed to "consider" the evidence that McGuire had "committed acts similar" to the crime charged and to "determine" whether there was a "clear connection" between these prior acts and the ones that resulted in Tori's death. The trial court did not instruct the jury that it must first "determine" whether McGuire had in fact inflicted the prior injuries. The part of the instruction relied upon by the Court • "it may be logically concluded that if the defendant committed other offenses, he also committed the crime charged in this case" • does not make clear that it is the jury's role to ascertain whether McGuire was the perpetrator of the prior abuse. Rather, coming as it does in the middle of what appears to be a conclusion of law, it is reasonably likely that the jury understood that such a determination had already been made and that its role was merely to determine if there was a "clear connection" between Tori's prior injuries and the injuries that killed her.

...it is well established that the fundamental fairness guarantee of the Due Process Clause requires the prosecution to prove beyond a reasonable doubt every element of the offense. This constitutional principle "prohibits the State from using evidentiary presumptions in a jury charge that have the effect of relieving the State of its burden of persuasion beyond a reasonable doubt of every essential element of a crime."...

In this case, the instruction perhaps was intended to posit a permissive inference that whoever had inflicted Tori's prior injuries was likely to have inflicted the injuries that caused her death. But the trial court did not make clear that the State first had to prove the predicate facts from which the inference was to be drawn. Furthermore, the wording of the instruction is such that the jury may well have assumed that it had no choice but to "logically conclude" that McGuire was the murderer once it found a "clear connection" between the prior injuries and the fatal ones. Because I cannot say with any confidence that the instruction allowed a mere permissive inference drawing from proven facts, I think the instruction should be treated as a mandatory presumption that may have relieved the State of its burden of proving the identity of Tori's killer beyond a reasonable doubt.

Had the instruction been clearly worded, I would agree with the Court that there is sufficient circumstantial evidence in the record to support a finding that McGuire was the perpetrator of the prior injuries. After all, as the Court points out, "the proof of battered child syndrome itself narrowed the group of possible perpetrators to McGuire and his wife, because they were the only two people regularly caring for Tori." In this case, however, it is important to remember that the other person regularly caring for Tori • Daisy McGuire • took the stand and testified, under a grant of immunity, that she was the one who inflicted the fatal injuries on the night of July 7, 1981.

McGuire's jury deliberated for three days before returning a verdict of guilty. Any evaluation of the jury instruction must be conducted against the background of Daisy McGuire's surprise testimony and the dilemma it so clearly posed for the jury. In my view, the jury instruction on similar acts was so "ambiguous," that there was a reasonable likelihood that the jury was encouraged to make assumptions and conclusions about the identity of Tori's murderer that relieved the State of having to prove that element of the offense beyond a reasonable doubt. In cases where the Court has found that jury instructions included mandatory presumptions inconsistent with the guarantees of the Due Process Clause, the Court has remanded to determine whether the erroneous instruction was harmless, which is the course that should be followed here.

NOTES AND QUERIES

Do the facts of this case leave you comfortable with the decision that the father was guilty of battering his child? What do you do with the mother's in-court testimony that she beat her child?

Does the evidence that Tori was a battered child seem strong?

Does it seems fair to find someone guilty of a crime because of actions that are not proven in court? Do you think that the testimony of acts constituting the battered child mean that the facts are proven?

Evidence of the battered child syndrome was admitted to help prove intent, a necessary element of the charges against the defendant. Should the state simply forgo charging such crimes?

Assuming that the case was tried in federal court, do the Federal Rules of Evidence require more from the expert witnesses? Would their evidence be excluded?

RESEARCH NOTES ON SYNDROMES

A syndrome is a group of signs and symptoms that are based on their frequent mutual occurrence that may suggest a common underlying course, pattern, or treatment selection, but do not necessarily imply a specific cause. In thinking of syndromes, it is important to consider the extent to which they are diagnostic. The classic example of a diagnostic syndrome is the battered child syndrome because a group of findings convincingly indicate abuse. The battered child syndrome has a very high degree of diagnostic certainty; physicians look for injuries to the child that are inconsistent with the description of how the injuries came about and they also look for previous unreported injuries. Other syndromes fall outside the traditional meaning of syndrome as they do not point to a particular cause. The Child Sexual Abuse Accommodation Syndrome (CSAAS) is an excellent example of a non-diagnostic syndrome. The Child Sexual Abuse Accommodation Syndrome (CSAAS) was first identified by Dr. Roland Summit in a 1983 article in which he described five experiences typically occurring in sexually abused children: (1) secrecy about the sexual abuse, often ensured by threats of negative consequences of disclosure; (2) emotional helplessness to resist or complain; (3) entrapment and accommodation, where the child sees no way to escape ongoing abuse and thus learns to adapt; (4) delayed, conflicted, and unconvincing disclosure of the abuse; and (5) retraction of the child's allegations in an attempt to restore order to the family structure when the disclosure threatens to destroy it. Roland C. Summit, The child sexual abuse accommodation syndrome, 7 Child Abuse and Neglect 177 (1983). Rather than detecting abuse, the CSAAS makes the assumption that sex abuse already has occurred and it explains the possible reactions that an abused child may experience. Accommodation is not evidence of abuse. Moreover, a child need not show a cluster of accommodation symptoms in order to be accommodating abuse. For example, a child may delay reporting, yet never recant. The syndrome was developed not to prove that abuse occurred but to explain children's reactions to sexual abuse.

If a syndrome is not diagnostic, it would seem that it should not be admissible to establish the cause of a patient's symptom. This seems to make sense given that there is no single behavioral symptom, or syndrome, that is characteristic or indicative of child sexual maltreatment. In an authoritative meta-analysis of the effects of sexual maltreatment, a review of 45 studies found that no one symptom characterized a majority of the sexually abused children. Most importantly, they found that approximately one-third of the victims had no identifiable symptoms whatsoever. Kathleen A. Kendall-Tackett, Linda Meyer Williams and David Finkelhor, Impact of sexual abuse on children: A review and synthesis of recent empirical studies, 113 Psych. Bull. 164 (1993). When a child exhibits one or more symptoms of child sexual abuse accommodation (e.g. delayed disclosure), this does not increase the likelihood that the child was abused. There is no reason to believe that true allegations are more likely than false allegations to be delayed. Therefore, it is inappropriate to use accommodation symptoms as "substantive evidence" of abuse. The purpose of proposed accommodation symptoms, however, is to challenge the assumption that children who exhibit accommodation symptoms must not have been abused. From this perspective, it seems appropriate to tell the jury that accommodation frequently occurs among abused children in order to disabuse the jury of misconceptions regarding how abused children ought to behave. In legal terms, describing the symptoms of accommodation is an appropriate means by which one may "rebut" attacks on or "rehabilitate" a child's credibility. For example, if the defense argues that abuse did not occur since the child did not report abuse until long after exposure to the defendant, the prosecution could offer expert testimony that victims of abuse often delay reporting due to guilt and fear. The proper foundation for relevance of CSAAS testimony is the inference raised by the defense that an inconsistent pattern of disclosures by the child indicates deceit. It is generally believed that an abstract presentation of the CSAAS by an expert who has never seen the child and knows virtually nothing about the case would provide the jury with a demonstrably objective refection. What do you make of this approach to using evidence that otherwise would not be admissible? Does admitting this type of testimony invade the province of the jury?

Base rates are one of the most critical points to understand when evaluating indicators, signs, symptoms, or syndromes of maltreatment. Witnesses may testify, for example, that, if a given child displays a number of signs, symptoms, or behaviors (such as "sexualized behavior" or "recantation" or "delayed recall"), then the child has most likely experienced sexual abuse. The problem with such statements is that some behaviors that have been put forth, including sexualized behavior, as indicators of sexual abuse are also found in non-abused children. To understand the reliability of a syndrome, we must know the prevalence of the syndrome in abused versus non-abused children. The current understanding of sexualized behavior is illustrative. Freud asserted that children are polymorphous perverse and are capable of generating sexual fantasies without sexual experience. As Freud was psychoanalyzing young women with hysteria, he found that they related childhood histories of sexual victimization. He concluded that the etiology of hysteria was a childhood experience of sexual abuse. He apparently was severely criticized by his colleagues and eventually altered his theory. He decided it was not actual incest but incestuous fantasies or wishes that were being reported by his female patients. See Jeffrey Moussaieff Masson, Assault on the Truth (1998). The controversy continues. An opinion that advanced sexual knowledge and explicit sexual behavior can be self-generated is not supported by research findings. Yet, not all sexually abused children exhibit sexualized behavior nor manifest advanced sexual knowledge. In addition, children may learn about sex from sources other than sexual victimization. Nevertheless, sexualized behavior is the marker most often asserted as most likely to distinguish sexually abused from nonabused children. See William Friedrich, Sexual victimization and sexual behavior in children: A review of recent literature, 17 Child Abuse and Neglect 59 (1993).

LAW NOTES ON THE BREADTH OF EXPERT TESTIMONY

Consideration of evidence means much more than determining whether evidence could be admitted. When evidence is deemed admissible, the next concern involves determining what can be said about the evidence. Evidence and testimony involving post-traumatic stress disorder (PTSD) is illustrative. PTSD is quite relevant to child maltreatment because it is a common diagnosis for individuals who have been sexually maltreated. For PTSD to be diagnosed, the individual must have experienced events involving injury (including threats) and the response to those events involve intense fear, helplessness, or horror. In addition, the individual must re-experience the symptoms, avoid certain stimuli (e.g., avoid cars), experience increased arousal symptoms (e..g, unable to sleep), have symptoms that reach clinical levels (e.g., really serious), and those symptoms must last at least one month. Several issues are raised by efforts to link PTSD with sexual maltreatment: (1) PTSD does not mean maltreatment occurred; (2) PTSD may be present with other disorders and comorbidity means that the other disorder may have caused the problem and that PTSD is not a distinct disorder; (3) individuals may be malingering to make a stronger case; and (4) from 80 to 90 percent of cases are correctly identified, which means that 20% are potentially inaccurate. In addition to issues involving PTSD diagnoses, several issues arise when it becomes sought as evidence in trials. The issues involve the breadth of the testimony. Typically, five forms of testimony may be offered and each varies in terms of its admissibility. Evidence may be proffered to understand typical victim's behavior during or after maltreatment, which generally is allowed. Testimony also may seek to provide a general education for jurors about PTSD, which generally is allowed. Testimony also may seek to apply PTSD testimony to the particular case by demonstrating consistency between the victim's behavior and PTSD, all offered without the expert's examination of the victim or commenting about the victim's credibility. That testimony is more controversial, even though research reveals that the testimony does tend to counteract myths and does not seem to prejudice defendants. Testimony stating that the victim does have PTSD is also quite controversial; and research is less clear about the impact of that evidence. Lastly, testimony may move beyond the diagnosis and state that the victim has been maltreated or that the victim is telling the truth, which tends to be viewed as inappropriate. What breadth of testimony do you see as appropriate? What rationales do you use to support your position: Is it because of the nature of the science, the role of the jury, the abilities of experts, or another factor? For an analysis dealing with these issues in the context of PTSD diagnosis for rape trauma testimony. See Laura E. Boeschen, Bruce D. Sales, and Mary P. Koss, Rape trauma experts in the courtroom, 4 Psych., Pub. Pol'y, and L. 414 (1998).

Consider a similar analysis involving offenders, such as a case dealing with a defendant's insanity defense to an assault charge. During the interview, the defendant engages in a conversation with people who in fact are not there, makes irrelevant and incomprehensible statements to himself, and insists that the person he assaulted was the devil trying to kill him and his family. The facts of the case support some of the defendant's statements: the victim does not know the defendant and cannot explain why he was the target. Again psychological testimony may be conceptualized in terms of multiple levels of inference, with each succeeding level incorporating a greater degree of generalization. Based on this evidence, the evaluator might offer these inferences: (1) a particular symptomology (the defendant was delusional at the time of the offense), (2) a diagnosis (the defendant was suffering from paranoid schizophrenia at the time of the offense), (3) the presence of legally relevant impairments (the defendant thought killing the victim was justified); and (4) an ultimate legal conclusion (the defendant was insane at the time of the offense). Rather than providing inferences, the testimony may simply report the facts. Do you suppose that a jury would need the evaluator's inferences? Would the facts about the defendants' behavior during the interview suffice? If so (i.e., if there will be no inferences presented to the jury), is there even a need for an expert evaluation?

LAW NOTE ON PRIOR BAD ACTS

Generally, a person is tried for his specific acts, not for his bad character or his alleged propensity to commit bad acts. The Supreme Court identified the underlying concerns that motivated the character bar in *Michelson v. United States*, 335 U.S. 469 (1948). Explaining why common law had disallowed the admission of evidence of a defendant's evil character to demonstrate that he did the alleged act, Justice Jackson stated: "The inquiry is not rejected because character is irrelevant; on the contrary, it is said to weigh too much with the jury and to so overpersuade them as to prejudge one with a bad general record and deny him a fair opportunity to defend against a particular charge." Id. at 475-76.

The battered child syndrome explicitly concerns prior bad acts. The syndrome is defined as the collection of injuries sustained by a child as a result of repeated mistreatment or beating. Battered child syndrome is suspected if a child's injuries indicate intentional trauma or appear to be more severe than could reasonably be expected to result from an accident. Some of the most suspicious signs include: (1) appearance at an emergency room with an injured child and an improbable explanation; (2) delayed appearance at an emergency room with an injured child; (3) bruise marks shaped like hands, fingers, or objects (belt); (4) specific patterns of scalding seen when a conscious child is immersed in hot water; (5) burns from an electric stove, radiator, heater or other hot objects on the child's hands or buttocks; (6) cigarette burns on exposed areas or the genitals; (7) black eyes in an infant; (8) human bite marks; (9) lash marks; (10) choke marks around neck; (11) circular marks around wrists or ankles (twisting); (12) sutures-separated; (13) bulging soft spot (fontanel) on the infants head; and (14) unexplained unconsciousness in infant. National attention to this syndrome emerged in 1962, with the publication of a now-famous article that conceptualized the "battered child syndrome," reframed society's concept of child physical abuse, and lead to the massive reforms in child protection laws. C. Henry Kempe, N. Freederick Silverman, Brandt F. Steele, William Droegemueller and Henry K. Silver, The battered child syndrome, 181 J. Am. Med. Assoc. 17 (1962).

Prior bad acts also have become an important and controversial issue in sexual maltreatment cases. Today, the majority of states govern the admission of prior sexual misconduct evidence either with the "lustful disposition" doctrine or the *Molineux* rule. The *Molineux* rule was set forth in the case of *People v. Molineux*, 61 N.E. 286 (N.Y. 1901), where the New York court stated that evidence of other offenses of misconduct by the defendant that are not part of the charged offense should not be received into evidence. However, the *Molineux* approach provided a list of exceptions that allow for admitting prior acts for non-propensity purposes such as motive, intent, absence of mistake, common scheme or plan, and identity. Many states broadly interpret the enumerated Molineux exceptions when for sex offense cases. In these states, evidence of past conduct is admitted as evidence of "intent" or "plan," even though under the normal understanding of those exceptions such evidence arguably would not be allowed. The majority of states adopt the "lustful disposition" exception for prior acts evidence in sex offense cases. Under this rule, evidence of past misconduct is admitted to show that the defendant has a propensity to engage in aberrant sexual behavior. Thomas J. Reed, Reading gaol revisited: Admission of uncharged misconduct evidence in sex offender cases, 21 Am. J. of Crim. L.127 (1993).

In September of 1994, the United States Congress turned two centuries of evidentiary common law upside down. The Federal Rules generally follow the character bar, which is contained in Federal Rule 404(b). That Rule states, in part, that " Evidence of other crimes, wrongs, or acts is not admissible to prove the character of a person in order to show action in conformity therewith. It may, however, be admissible for other purposes, such as proof of motive, opportunity, intent, preparation, plan, knowledge, identity, or absence of mistake or accident. ..." But how the rule applies to sex offenders was radically transformed by the *Violent Crime Control and Law Enforcement Act of 1994*, Pub. L. No. 103-322, §§ 3209-35, 108 Stat. 1796, §§ 2135-37 (1994) (codified as amended at 28 U.S.C. app. Fed. R. Evid. 413-415 (1994), which contained three new Federal Rules of Evidence (Rules 412, 413, 414, and 415). These new rules, now being referred to as the "sexual character evidence rules," were designed to bolster prosecution of sexual assault and child molestation offenders, as well as to assist plaintiffs in civil cases predicated on sexual assault or child molestation. The rules allow the admission of evidence of charged or uncharged prior sexual misconduct to be used against a defendant in a sexual offense case and apparently changes the well-established rule against the use of propensity evidence to show that the defendant was acting in conformity with the defendant's character. Rules 413 through 415 address this admissibility in both criminal and civil cases. Rule 413 applies to criminal prosecutions for "sexual assault." The Rule states, "In a criminal case in which the defendant is accused of an offense of sexual assault, evidence of the defendant's commission of another offense or offenses of sexual assault is admissible, and may be considered for its bearing on any matter to which it is relevant." Rule 414 substitutes "child molestation" for "sexual assault." The Rule states, "In a criminal case in which the defendant is accused of an offense of child molestation, evidence of the defendant's commission of another offense or offenses of child molestation is admissible, and may be considered for its bearing on any matter to which it is relevant." Rule 415 is the civil analog to Rules 413 and 414. Rule 415 states: "In a civil case in which a claim for damages or other relief is predicated on a party's alleged commission of conduct constituting an offense of sexual assault or child molestation, evidence of that party's commission of another offense or offenses of sexual assault or child molestation is admissible and may be considered as provided in Rule 413 and Rule 414. ..." The new rules also set forth time frames for the disclosure to the other party that the other acts evidence is expected to be used. In criminal and civil cases, disclosure must occur at least fifteen days prior to trial, except for good cause, and disclosure must include any "statements of witnesses or a summary of the substance of any testimony that is expected to be offered." See Rules 413(b), 414(b), 415(b).

In deciding if prior acts evidence should be admitted under the new federal rules, the Tenth Circuit provided a useful four-prong test to use in determining if the evidence is substantially similar. In *United*

States v. Guardia, 135 F.3d 1326, 1332 (10th Cir. 1998), the court reasoned that: (1) the case must be a trial for a sexual offense; (2) the prior bad acts evidence must be another sexual- type offense; (3) the evidence must be relevant, showing both that the defendant had a certain propensity and the propensity has bearing on the crime charged; and (4) the court must perform a Rule 403 balancing test to determine if the probative value of the evidence outweighs the prejudice to the defendant.

REVIEW PROBLEMS

1. LeCompte was charged under 18 U.S.C. sections 2244(a)(1) and 2246(3) for the alleged sexual abuse of C.D., his wife's eleven-year-old niece. On at least one occasion, LeCompte allegedly exposed himself to C.D. while they played games together at her aunt's trailer. On another occasion, LeCompte allegedly joined C.D. on the couch, forced her to touch his penis, and touched her breasts while C.D.'s siblings were sleeping on the floor next to her. Before trial, the government provided LeCompte with notice that it intended to offer evidence under Rule 414 of prior uncharged sex offenses against T.T., another of his nieces. The incidents involving T.T. allegedly had occurred eight to ten years prior to the current incidents on which he was being tried. According to the prosecutors, T.T. was prepared to testify at trial that LeCompte had played games with her at her aunt's house, had exposed himself to her, had forced her to touch his penis, and had touched her private parts. LeCompte moved to exclude the evidence. After applying the Rule 403 balancing test, the district court ruled that the evidence was inadmissible because the potential for unfair prejudice outweighed the limited probative value of the evidence. The district court found significant the eight year period separating the incidents. The court also found that the testimony obviously would be highly prejudicial evidence against the defendant given that child sexual abuse carries a unique stigma in our society. Given that the evidence was highly prejudicial, the court reasoned that the evidence should carry a very high degree of probative value for it is to be admitted. How should the circuit court reviewing this case rule? The Eighth Circuit rejected the district court's analysis. The court stated that although Rule 414 is subject to the requirements of Rule 403, it must be applied to allow Rule 414 its intended effect, namely to supersede the restrictive aspects of Rule 404(b). The court ruled, "In light of the strong legislative judgment that evidence of prior sexual offenses should ordinarily be admissible, we think the District Court erred in its assessment that the probative value of T.T.'s testimony was substantially outweighed by the danger of unfair prejudice." *United States v. LeCompte*, 131 F.3d 767, 769 (8th Cir. 1997). The court found that the offenses committed against the two girls were substantially similar. The court also noted that even the district court acknowledged that the eight year period between the offenses may not be as significant as it appears at first glance; in fact, the defendant was imprisoned for a portion of the time between [the offenses] which deprived defendant of the opportunity to abuse any children. Arguably even more significantly, the court flatly rejected the district court's emphasis on the "unique stigma" of child sexual abuse • the danger that the jury might convict based on LeCompte's propensity to commit child sexual abuse, rather than on the facts directly supporting the offense against C.D. The court concluded that "it is for this reason that the evidence was previously excluded, and it is precisely such holdings that Congress intended to overrule." Id. at 770.

2. Fumiko Kimura lives in a fairly isolated Japanese immigrant enclave in Los Angeles. Upon learning of her husband's adulterous conduct, she attempts to drown herself and her two children in Santa Monica bay. Both children die but she is rescued by good samaritans. Kimura contends that she was attempting a traditional Japanese ritual, *oyako-shinju*, parent-child suicide. According to this ancient custom, when women have been wronged by their husbands, they may choose to remove themselves from this world rather than bring shame to their families and communities. Taking their children with them into the afterlife is encouraged; leaving children behind with no one to attend to them would be a sign of poor motherhood. *Oyako-shinju*, although not officially condoned, is rarely prosecuted in Japan. How should a court go about determining whether to consider the appropriateness of expert evidence on *oyako-shinju*? See Roger J.R. Levesque, Cultural evidence, child maltreatment, and the law, 5 Child Maltreatment 146 (2000).

3. Kim Logerquist alleges that her pediatrician sexually abused her on several occasions between 1971 and 1973, when she was eight- to ten-years-old. She further alleges that she had amnesia about those events until 1991, when her memory was triggered by watching a television commercial featuring a pediatrician. She sought to introduce evidence, through expert testimony, that severe childhood trauma, including sexual abuse, can cause a repression of memory, and that in later years this memory can be recalled with accuracy. The trial judge granted Defendant's motion that a Frye hearing be held to assess the admissibility of expert testimony regarding repressed memory. [Note that the jurisdiction in which she sought relief, Arizona, follows the Frye standard.] Two experts testified at the Frye hearing. Plaintiff called Dr. Bessell van der Kolk, a clinical psychiatrist who specializes in dissociative amnesia. He testified regarding the large number of patients who alleged such phenomenon and about his diagnoses of dissociative amnesia or post-traumatic stress disorder in such patients. He would testify among other things, that his experience and observations over many years, together with the extensive literature on the subject, have led him to conclude the phenomenon exists in some patients. Defendant's expert, Dr. Richard Kihlstrom, a research psychologist, testified there were serious flaws in the many studies supporting repressed memory and cited other studies finding trauma usually enhances memory rather than causes amnesia. Doctor Kihlstrom did not, however, have any personal experience treating or dealing with people claiming to suffer from repressed memory; nor had he participated in any studies on trauma's effect on memory. After a lengthy hearing, the trial judge determined the theories advanced by Plaintiff's experts were not generally accepted in the relevant scientific community of trauma memory researchers. The judge therefore ordered excluding expert testimony of Plaintiff's alleged repressed memory and Plaintiff's theory that such evidence can be recalled with accuracy. How should the reviewing court rule? The reviewing court ruled Frye inapplicable. The court noted that it was apparent that they were not dealing with an alchemist attempting to change lead into gold or an astrologer predicting events from the movements of the stars but one of the leading researchers and authorities in psychological science. The court found it strange that a witness so well qualified and experienced would not be permitted to testify on an issue beyond the experience of the average juror. The court then noted that Frye applies to the use of novel scientific theories or processes to produce results and that the issues at hand were not scientific. Neither parties had claimed that some scientific process, theory, or formula may be applied to test whether her memories of having been molested are true and accurate or whether the memories were imagined, suggested, implanted, or even invented. As a result, the court concluded that the truth of Plaintiff's testimony that she actually and accurately recalled or remembered the events, as distinguished from inventing them or having had them suggested or implanted, is for a jury to decide. The court also examined the issue, assuming Frye applied, of whether the trial judge abused his discretion by concluding the theory of repressed memory, post-traumatic stress disorder, or dissociative amnesia did not meet the general acceptance test. The court noted that court rulings have split on that question but that, from the record, one might conclude that in finding a lack of general acceptance, the judge gave undue weight to the views of research psychologists and too little to those of clinicians – psychiatrists and psychologists – who work in the field. *Logerquist v. McVey*, 1 P.3d 113 (Ariz. 2000) (en banc). Note that the psychiatric and psychological community remains divided over whether reliable scientific support exists to validate repressed memories. See Recovered Memories of Child Sexual Abuse: Psychological, Social, and Legal Perspectives on a Contemporary Mental Health Controversy (Sheila Taub, ed., 1999). These concerns would seem important to the legal decision to admit such testimony at trial as courts address whether to admit expert testimony on repressed memories. Courts differ, however, as to what evidentiary standard applies to such testimony. Some jurisdictions apply a heightened evidentiary standard by requiring the trial court to assess the reliability of the expert testimony; others merely require that the testimony pass on general relevance grounds, a rather low-level evidentiary standard. Which admissibility standard seems appropriate?

4. Consider the following case. Velarde appeals his conviction by a jury on one count of aggravated sexual abuse of a child on grounds that expert testimony was unreliable and erroneously admitted. Dr. Ornelas began her testimony by recounting her usual procedures in examining a child where sexual abuse has been alleged and then testified that L. had a "normal" physical exam, which was, she opined, "consistent with what [L.] said happened." Dr. Ornelas testified that a normal exam is "the most common

physical findings for a child who has been sexually abused." This is so, Dr. Ornelas opined, because "the type of contact that most commonly occurs between adults and children that's sexual is oral kinds of contact, touching, and what's called labial coitus." Dr. Ornelas also testified that L.'s behavior of withdrawing from her family, staying inside of her room, not being communicative, not being her regular bubbly, running-around kind of self, and ... waking up at night and touching her mother to make sure that her mother was there in bed with her, ... having sleep disturbances and some behavioral changes," was "consistent with child sexual abuse." Finally, she testified as follows: "Q. Doctor, if you had those symptoms or some of those symptoms and a report by a child of sexual abuse, are you comfortable forming a diagnosis of child sexual abuse in such a case? A. I would base that diagnosis on the child's statements about what had happened to them." When the defendant challenged the expert's reliability on the grounds that she exceeded her expertise in testifying about psychology, the trial judge refused a separate hearing, stating that he had "heard this testimony before in trials." The Tenth Circuit reversed because of a lack of any reliability determination by the court. The court also noted that the trial court improperly assumed that Dr. Ornelas' proffered testimony fell within the category of testimony in "ordinary" cases where courts may "avoid unnecessary 'reliability' proceedings ... where the reliability of an expert's methods is properly taken for granted" and gave no indication why this case could be viewed as such an "ordinary" case, or why Dr. Ornelas' methods could be "properly taken for granted," except for the court's remark that "I've had this testimony before in trials, and it's not new and novel." The court further found the testimony problematic because she had testified that the victims had normal physical exams but exhibited behaviors consistent with sexual abuse; and she had testified that she believed sexual abuse had in fact occurred because the victim alleged that such abuse had occurred. *United States v. Velarde*, 214 F.3d 1204 (10th Cir. 2000).

5. What do you make of testimony offered in *United States v. Romero*, 189 F.3d 576 (7th Cir. 1999)? Thirty-six year-old Romero "met" a 12-year-old Erich in a "chat room" on the Internet devoted to UFOs and extraterrestrials. After developing a relationship through e-mail, he enticed the boy to run away from home in Illinois. The two boarded a bus in Chicago bound for St. Petersburg. Some quick investigative work by the local police and the FBI foiled the trip, as Romero and Erich were intercepted at the Greyhound bus station in Louisville, Kentucky. Among other charges, Romero was eventually charged with kidnaping and transporting a minor with intent to engage in criminal sexual activity for inveigling Erich to leave his home and travel to Kentucky; and charged with traveling in interstate commerce for the purpose of engaging in a sexual act with a juvenile. At closing argument in his second trial, the defense argued that Erich consented to travel with Romero, which negated, if believed, the kidnaping charge. Romero did not dispute his keen interest in child pornography or his sexual fantasies about Erich, but he argued that he did not intend to follow through on his fantasies. The second jury rejected these defenses and convicted Romero of the kidnaping and transportation charges. Judge Kocoras then sentenced him to 327 months in prison.

At issue on appeal was whether Judge Kocoras abused his discretion when he admitted the testimony of the prosecution's FBI expert on child molesters. Before trial, the government filed a notice of its intent to use the testimony of Agent Kenneth V. Lanning, who had spent many years studying the sexual exploitation of children and produced over 20 publications, to inform the jury about child molestation. The prosecution proposed to have Agent Lanning testify regarding (1) characteristics of "preferential" child molesters and the methods they used to attract and abuse children and (2) his opinion that Romero is a child molester with an interest in adolescent boys and that Romero had a sexual interest in Erich. Romero had filed a motion *in limine* to exclude Agent Lanning's testimony, arguing that the expert could not offer his opinion about Romero's intent with respect to Erich under Federal Rule of Evidence 704(b) because it would involve the ultimate issue the jury was impaneled to decide. Romero also had argued that Lanning's testimony would be unduly prejudicial under Rule 403 because it amounted to impermissible "profiling."

In response to the defense arguments, the government had offered that it would limit Lanning's testimony to the methods and techniques employed by preferential child molesters. The prosecution would not ask Lanning to give his opinion about Romero or to comment about his intent or culpability. Subject to these limitations, Judge Kocoras allowed Agent Lanning to testify, noting that the testimony would be highly probative:

> Here is a man who studied the field extensively, an acknowledged expert in the field. And I do not think there is any question whatever that his testimony meets all the criteria of the 700 series, and is particularly helpful to the jury because he has had an abundance of training and experience far beyond any lay person, certainly, and far beyond, I think, most experts in the field.

Judge Kocoras thus denied the motion to exclude Lanning's "testimony in general." Kocoras, however, agreed with the defense's concern that Lanning's testimony could possibly invade the province of the jury and usurp their function in determining whether Romero had the requisite criminal intent. For that reason, Judge Kocoras encouraged the defense to object to Lanning's testimony on a question-by-question basis if it seemed that he was going too far.

At trial Lanning testified that his observations arose from his expertise about child molesters in general, not from the specific facts of the case. He then explained his role:

> As I understand it, what I am going to do is provide or share the information that I have concerning the nature of certain types of offenders and provide this information to people who would not otherwise be aware and have this kind of knowledge because of their experiences and work.

Lanning then opined that child sex offenders fall on a spectrum from "situational sex offenders," whose activities are based on an accident of circumstance, to "preferential sex offenders," who have a definite preference for sexual contact with children and methodically pursue such contact. He identified four general traits usually exhibited by preferential sex offenders, all of which he had described in published materials long before the Romero case. He noted that the conduct of a preferential child molester occurs over a long period of time, extremely persistent, and can involve enormous amounts of time on the Internet trying to meet children and develop seemingly innocent relationships with them; that preferential sex offenders have very specific interests and that they focus on certain kinds of children; that preferential sex offenders typically identify a need in a child and then move forward to temporarily fill that need in the child as part of this process; and that preferential offenders engage in fantasy and need-driven behavior. Not surprisingly, the hypotheticals described actions taken by Romero that had already been produced in evidence: Establishing a 9-month relationship with a young (age 12 at the time it started) boy on the Internet; traveling hundreds of miles to meet a 13-year-old; meeting a young boy in a hotel room; spending long hours communicating with multiple young boys; and discussing a sexual interest in children with another adult. Lanning testified that each of these actions would indicate that the offender in question would act upon his fantasies.

The appellate court rejected the defense's claim that Judge Kocoras erred in finding that Lanning's testimony generally would be reliable and helpful to the jury. The court viewed the testimony as critical in dispelling from the jurors' minds the widely held stereotype of a child molester and the court recognized the value of expert testimony in explaining a complicated criminal methodology that may look innocent on the surface but is not as innocent as it appears. Would you have admitted Lanning's testimony about the spectrum of sex offenders? Would it matter whether his research writings are peer-reviewed?

PART III. FORMULATING CRIMINAL DISPOSITIONS

Chapter 9

DETERMINING THE DEFENDANT'S MENTAL STATE AND CAPACITY

INTRODUCTION

A variety of contexts reveals the law's interest in a criminal defendant's subjective mental state. The most obvious examples that often readily come to mind are the insanity defense and the diminished capacity defense (or lack of required *mens rea*[1]). Once established, these defenses lead to finding defendants less blameworthy and thus less legally responsible for their actions. Concern about mental states, however, spreads to other contexts that previously did not make relevant the particular defendant's desires and beliefs at the time of the crime. In many jurisdictions, for example, the self-defense, duress, and provocation doctrines no longer rest on comparing the defendant's position and actions to those of a hypothetical reasonable person. They now focus on issues more closely associated with determining particular individuals' mental states. For example, many states now recognize that the test for self-defense in a case in which a woman kills a man who has repeatedly battered her focuses on what a "battered woman," rather than on what a "reasonable person," would have done in her situation.[2] Although the expansion of these defenses is not as great as popular beliefs and commentaries about "abuse excuse" suggest,[3] the developments foster intense debates.[4] Nevertheless, criminal law requires trials to address subjective and quasi-subjective mental states relevant to inquiries of blameworthiness.

---

[1] *Mens rea* essentially means a guilty mind and refers to the state of mind of the accused at the time the actus reas (act of the crime) is committed. Note that all crimes, except strict liability crimes, necessitate both an act (*actus reus*) and criminal intent (*mens rea*). This area of the law is complex and differs from state to state. Generally, though, there are four levels of relevant *mens rea*. The highest level is specific intent, which exists when a person intended to commit a crime. For example, if you do not intend to kill someone, you cannot be convicted of murder as you do not have the neccesary *mens rea*. (You would be convicted of manslaughter instead.) The second level is recklessness, which is a conscious disregard for the welfare of others and creation of a significant and unjustifiable risk. The next level is negligence, which occurs when one is under a duty to take care and their behavior is below the standard of care required of a reasonable person. The last level, strict liability, requires no proof of intention, negligence or recklessness. If the accused committed the *actus reus*, no *mens rea* need be proved. (Statutory rape tends to be viewed as an example of a strict liability offense.)

[2] See Robert P. Mosteller, Syndromes and politics in criminal trials and evidence law, 46 Duke L.J. 461, 484 and n.77 (1996).

[3] Inspired by psychology-dependent defenses invoked by the Menendez brothers, Lorena Bobbitt, Colin Ferguson, and others, Alan Dershowitz coined the now familiar phrase "abuse excuse" to describe a "legal tactic by which criminal defendants claim a history of abuse as an excuse for violent retaliation." Alan. M. Dershowitz, The Abuse Excuse and Other Cop-Outs, Sob Stories, and Evasions of Responsibility 3, 45 (1994). The extent to which the excuses are used, however, remains debatable. See Peter Arenella, Demystifying the abuse excuse: Is there one?, 19 Harv. J.L. and Pub. Pol'y 703, 703-05 (1996) (noting that successful "abuse excuses" are very rare and that typically only those claiming insanity are eligible to be excused under abuse excuse theories).

[4] The most long-standing debate involves whether criminal liability requires subjective culpability. Holmes, for example, argued that criminal law should "take no account of incapacities, unless the weakness is so marked as to fall into well-known exceptions, such as infancy or madness," while others argued for more flexibility. Oliver Wendell Holmes, The Common Law 43 (1881); see also Jerome Hall, Negligent behavior should be excluded from penal liability, 63

The relevance of mental states derives from the manner the criminal justice system generally treats individuals as having a sense of moral agency (the ability to understand and determine ones actions). The law ascribes individuals with moral qualities and treats them accordingly. For example, the imposition of punishment rests on a model of behavior in which actors exercise a choice whether to violate the law; and that choice must derive from a certain level of maturity, rationality, and sensitivity. When an offender lacks a sense of moral agency, the system offers opportunities for exoneration. Most notably, for example, the insanity defense exempts from public condemnation and punishment those individuals who commit wrongful acts due to an irrational mental state. Offenders who are not of sound mind are deemed less blameworthy due to deficiencies in their sense of moral agency.

Although issues of mental state typically focus on offenders' capacities at the time of the offense, offenders' mental capacities may play other important roles in the state's effort to determine culpability and blameworthiness. For example, a defendant must have the capacity or "competency" to understand and respond to the state's effort to determine their culpability. Thus, unlike the focus on someone's capacities at the time of the offense, issues of competency involve a person's capacities as it relates to adjudicative processes. Although competency may be involved in the early phases of law enforcement (such as competency to waive *Miranda* rights or waive rights against searches), the general belief is that issues of competency most frequently arise during trial processes. In the study of law and psychology, issues of competency arising in trial contexts often are termed "adjudicative competencies" or "adjudicative capacities." That competency involves trial processes is not surprising; issues of competency tend to be challenged when the state commences formal procedures against defendants. Given this reality, concern about a defendant's competency may be raised at any point. If a court doubts a defendant's competency, it must consider this issue formally, and usually after a forensic evaluation.[5]

Concepts of adjudicative capacity and mental states at the time of offenses obviously differ fundamentally. Yet, we consider them together in this chapter in order to understand how the legal system approaches a defendant's psychological inabilities. For our purposes, the goal is to examine how the legal system makes use of this type of psychological evidence and the extent to which the law reflects what psychology can in fact deliver.

ADDRESSING ISSUES OF ADJUDICATIVE COMPETENCY

Provisions allowing for trial delays because a defendant was incompetent to proceed have long been a part of criminal justice processes. English common law allowed for the arraignment, trial, judgment, or execution of an alleged capital offender to be stayed if he or she became "absolutely mad."[6] Over time, states created statutes that have further defined and extended the common-law practice. These statutes generally look to *Dusky v. United States,*[7] which established the modern standard. In *Dusky*, the Supreme Court ruled that constitutional law required a minimum level of rational understanding of the proceedings and ability to assist one's attorney. We will read this remarkably short opinion; for now, it is important to

Colum. L. Rev. 632 (1963). Another debate concerns the extent to which policy reasons require us to ignore some relevant subjective mental states that are logically relevant to culpability, such as the negative impact evidence explaining the mental state might have on views about particular groups in society (e.g., evidence that fear of blacks or gays explains defendant's actions). See Peter Marguilies, Identity on trial: Subordination, social science evidence, and criminal defense, 51 Rutgers L. Rev. 45 (1998). Yet another debate involves how far to carry subjective liability (e.g., should self-defense in battered woman situations be defined in terms of the reasonable battered woman or the honest beliefs and feelings of the woman in question?). See Naomi R. Cahn, The looseness of legal language: The reasonable woman standard in theory and in practice, 77 Cornell L. Rev. 1398 (1992).

[5] Note, however, that, in practice, issues relating to competency may go ignored unless lack of competency highly disrupts the criminal justice process. Norman G. Poythress, Richard J Bonnie, Steven K Hoge, John Monahan, and Lois Oberlander, Client abilities to assist counsel and make decisions in criminal cases: Findings from three studies, 18 L. and Hum. Beh. 437 (1994).

[6] Peter R. Silten and Richard Tullis, Mental competency in criminal proceedings, 28 Hastings L.J. 1053, 1053 (1977).

note that it found that it is not enough for the court to find that "the defendant [is] oriented to time and place and [has] some recollection of events," but that the "test must be whether he has sufficient present ability to consult with his lawyer with a reasonable degree of rational understanding – and whether he has a rational as well as factual understanding of the proceedings against him."[8]

Although all states now use a variant of the *Dusky* standard to define competency, the standard leaves much to be desired. *Dusky* left ambiguous the concept of competency. The case left undetermined what was meant by "sufficient present ability." Equally ambiguous was the phrase requiring a determination of whether a defendant "has a rational as well as factual understanding." These ambiguities continue and leave the typical forensic evaluation largely unguided except by a common principle that evaluators cannot reach a finding of incompetency independent of the facts of the case at hand. The need to focus on specific cases creates considerable challenges for efforts to evaluate a defendant's competencies. Despite the law's preference for individualized proceedings to ensure fundamental rights, the need for individualized, case by case determinations in psychology runs the risk of creating unreliable and potentially unjust determinations. This is particularly true in the context of competency assessments.

Forensic assessment instruments to assess competency typically lack the characteristics of many traditional psychological tests. They tend to use, for example, semi-structured elicitation procedures. Given that specific cases require determinations of different competencies, the use of sem-structured approaches remains necessary. The procedures may help make assessments more systematic as they help evaluators collect important and relevant information and follow the decision-making process that the law requires. But problems still may attach to the collection and evaluation of responses. The central concern involves the extent to which researchers and evaluators can sufficiently generalize competency determinations to reach more consistent findings.

Although efforts historically have not sought to divine broad competencies, the most ambitious research project in this area has sought just that. The MacArthur Network on Mental Health and the Law developed The MacArthur Competence Assessment Tool – Criminal Adjudication (MacCAT-CA),[9] from a number of research instruments to assess three main abilities: understanding, reasoning, and appreciation. The MacCAT-CA consists of 22 items that ask a defendant to respond to a short story about two men who get into a fight and which ends with one being charged with a criminal offense. The first eight items assess the individual's understanding of the legal system. Most of these items consist of two parts. The defendant's ability to understand is first assessed and, if it is unsatisfactory or appears to be questionable, the information is then disclosed to the defendant and his or her understanding is again assessed.[10] This allows the evaluator to determine whether or not the individual can learn disclosed information. The next eight items assess the individual's reasoning skills by asking which of two disclosed facts would be most relevant to the case.[11] Finally, the last six items assess the individual's appreciation of his or her own circumstances.[12] This assessment tool is unusual in that evaluators may consult published national norms.[13]

---

[7] 362 U.S. 402 (1960).

[8] 362 U.S. 402, 402 (1960).

[9] Steven K. Hoge, Richard J. Bonnie, Norman Poythress, John Monahan, Marlene Eisenberg, and Thomas Faucht-Haviar, The MacArthur adjudicative competence study: Development and validation of a research instrument, 21 L. and Hum. Beh. 141 (1997).

[10] The legal content of the Understanding Measure includes: • Understanding the roles of defense attorney and prosecutor. • Understanding both the act and mental elements of a serious offense. • Understanding the elements of a less serious offense. • Understanding the role of a jury. • Understanding the responsibilities of a judge at a jury trial. • Understanding sentencing as a function of the severity of the offense. • Understanding the process of a guilty plea. • Understanding the rights waived in pleading guilty. Randy K. Otto, Norman G. Poythress, Robert A. Nicholson, John F. Edens, John Monahan, Richard J. Bonnie, Steven K. Hoge, and Marlene Eisenberg, Psychometric properties of the MacArthur Competence Assessment Tool-Criminal Adjudication, 10 Psych. Assessment 435 (1998).

[11] The legal content of the Reasoning Measure includes: • Reasoning about evidence suggesting self-defense. • Reasoning about evidence related to criminal intent. • Reasoning about evidence of provocation. • Reasoning about motivation for one's behavior. • Reasoning about the potential impact of alcohol on one's behavior. • Capacity to identify information that might inform the decision to plead guilty versus plead not guilty. • Capacity to identify both potential costs and potential benefits of a legal decision (e. g. , pleading guilty). • Capacity to compare one legal option (e. g. , accepting a plea bargain) with another legal option (e. g. , going to trial) in terms of advantages and disadvantages. Randy K. Otto,

In addition to the MacCAT-CA, a number of measures have been specifically designed to assess defendants' capacities to participate in legal proceedings. These assessment instruments include, for example, the Competence Screening Test [CST], Georgia Court Competency Test [GCCT], CADCOMP, Competency Assessment Instrument [CAI], Interdisciplinary Fitness Interview [IFI], and the Fitness to Stand Trial Interview.[14] In addition, researchers have sought to develop competence assessment instruments for specialized populations of defendants, such as an instrument designed to assess competence with mentally retarded defendants called the Competence Assessment for Standing Trial for Defendants with Mental Retardation (CAST-MR).[15] Although these measures may be used frequently, their limitations are well known and accepted. Some measures were designed to serve primarily as screening instruments and appear mainly to be collections of items having various legal content but little or no underlying conceptual structure. Others lack standardized administration and criterion-based scoring, relying instead on the judgment of the clinician to determine, on a case-by-case basis, which questions to pose to the defendant and how to rate the received responses. None provide quantitative indexes of discrete competence-related abilities, and none of these measures provide interpretative norms based on large, national samples. These are important considerations, especially in light of the manner evaluators and offenders may hold different views of the legal system and of the legal actors.[16]

Although there are numerous ways by which to conduct competency evaluations, researchers increasingly suggest that the most reasonable approach to the assessment of competency does not seek to determine a generalizable standard but instead does what the law requires: it seeks to provide a functional evaluation of a defendant's ability matched to the contextualized demands of the case. As leading researchers note, the famous amnesia case of *Wilson v. United States*[17] illustrates well the functional view. In that decision, the U.S. Court of Appeals for the District of Columbia held that six factors should be considered in determining whether a defendant's amnesia impaired the ability to stand trial: (1) The extent to which the amnesia affected the defendant's ability to consult with and assist his lawyer. (2)The extent to

Norman G. Poythress, Robert A. Nicholson, John F. Edens, John Monahan, Richard J. Bonnie, Steven K. Hoge, and Marlene Eisenberg, Psychometric properties of the MacArthur Competence Assessment Tool-Criminal Adjudication, 10 Psych. Assessment 435 (1998).

[12] The legal content of the Appreciation Measure includes: • Plausibility of defendant's beliefs about the likelihood of being treated fairly by the legal system. • Plausibility of defendant's beliefs about likelihood of being helped by his/her lawyer. • Plausibility of defendant's beliefs about whether to disclose case information to his/her attorney. • Plausibility of defendant's beliefs about likelihood of being found guilty. • Plausibility of defendant's beliefs about likelihood of being punished if found guilty. • Plausibility of defendant's beliefs about whether to accept a plea bargain. Randy K. Otto, Norman G. Poythress, Robert A. Nicholson, John F. Edens, John Monahan, Richard J. Bonnie, Steven K. Hoge, and Marlene Eisenberg, Psychometric properties of the MacArthur Competence Assessment Tool-Criminal Adjudication, 10 Psych. Assessment 435 (1998).

[13] Steven K. Hoge, Richard J. Bonnie, Norman Poythress, and John Monahan, The MaCarthur Competence Assessment Tool – Criminal Adjudication (MacCAT-CA) (1999). Thomas Grisso, Paul S. Appelbaum, Edward P. Mulvey and Kenneth Fletcher, The MacArthur treatment competence study II: Measures of abilities related to competence to consent to treatment, 19 L. and Hum. Beh . 127 (1995); Karen E. Whittemore, James R. P. Ogloff, and Ronald Roesch, An investigation of competency to participate in legal proceedings in Canada, 42 Canadian J. Psych. 1 (1997). One of the most recent studies reported, for example, that the MacCAT-CA measures of Understanding, Reasoning, and Appreciation have good interrater reliability (intraclass Rs ranging from . 75 to . 90) and strong internal consistency (as > . 80, mean interitem rs ranging from . 36 to . 54), as well as evidence of construct validity (expected patterns of correlation with measures of cognitive ability, psychopathology, and clinical judgments of degree of impaired competence). Randy K. Otto, Norman G. Poythress, Robert A. Nicholson, John F. Edens, John Monahan, Richard J. Bonnie, Steven K. Hoge, and Marlene Eisenberg, Psychometric properties of the MacArthur Competence Assessment Tool-Criminal Adjudication, 10 Psych. Assessment 435 (1998).

[14] Gary B. Melton, John Petrila, Norman G. Poythress, and Christopher Slobogin, Psychological Evaluations for the Courts: A Handbook for Mental Health Professionals and Lawyers (1997, 2nd ed.).

[15] Carol T. Everington, The competence assessment for standing trial for defendants with mental retardation (CAST-MR): A validation study, 17 Crim. J. and Beh. 147 (1990).

[16] For example, the CST asks a subject's view of a judge. Only a positive view counts for competency. ("The judge would ...be fair to Jack" gets a 1, while "The judge would ... screw him over" gets a 0.). See Ronald Roesch and Stephen L. Golding, Defining and assessing competence to stand trial, in The Handbook of Forensic Psychology 378 (Irving Weiner and Allen Hess, eds., 1987).

[17] 391 F. 2d. 460 (D.C. 1968).

which the amnesia affected the defendant's ability to testify in his own behalf. (3) The extent to which the evidence in suit could be extrinsically reconstructed in view of the defendant's amnesia. Such evidence would include evidence relating to the crime itself as well as any reasonable possible alibi. (4) The extent to which the government assisted the defendant and his counsel in that reconstruction. (5) The strength of the prosecution's case. Most important here will be whether the government's case is such as to negate all reasonable hypotheses of innocence. If there is any substantial possibility that the accused could, but for his amnesia, establish an alibi or other defense, it should be presumed that he would have been able to do so. (6) Any other facts and circumstances that would indicate whether or not the defendant had a fair trial.[18] Some argue that simply substituting any symptom for amnesia would create the most appropriate standard to determine competency needed for specific legal proceedings.[19] Rather than attempting to reach a broad definition and general approach to determining competency, then, this approach focuses on the relevant legal rule and the needed psychological competencies the rule requires.

The apparent need to focus on case specifics has lead to misunderstandings about the use of the MacCAT-CA. The research group that developed the instrument emphasizes that it is useful in evaluating criminal defendants whose competence has been questioned, but that it is not offered as a measure of legal competence in and of itself. That is, the MacCarthur group does not anticipate the derivation of a single optimal cutoff score for the empirical classification of a defendant as competent or incompetent. The group notes that other psycholegal abilities are relevant to the ultimate determination of competence (e. g., memory for specific events related to one's own case; coherency of speech) and a court may consider other nonpsychological factors (e. g., legal complexity of the case) in making the dichotomous judgment about "competence. " As a result, no single measure, no matter how nuanced, can encompass all of the potentially relevant factors. Additionally, the MacCAT-CA includes no scales designed to assess the examinee's test-taking set. As with any forensic evaluation, the examiner must consider the possibility of exaggerated and fabricated deficits or psychopathology. When suspected, such deception may require other measures designed to assess the defendant's test-taking set. Thus, used as part of a comprehensive evaluation that includes a relevant history (e. g. , psychiatric history), current mental-status evaluation, and inquiry about case-specific memories, the MacCAT-CA should enhance the thoroughness and quality of clinical evaluations of adjudicative competence. But no current index of competency can be used by itself.

As a tool to assist in determining an individual's competency, the promise of the MacCAT-CA cannot be underestimated. But even that promise must be evaluated quite carefully. Despite confusion over the definition of competency *per se* and the need to operate case-by-case, there nevertheless appears to be strong agreement between evaluators' conclusions about a defendant's competency. Even early studies of reliability reported that pairs of evaluators agreed in 80% or more of the cases.[20] Researchers even have reported higher agreement rates when evaluators are highly trained and use semi-structured competence assessment instruments.[21] Such high reliability, however, may be deceptive. When base rates of findings of competency are considered, these high levels of agreement become less impressive. A look at base rates suggests that evaluators are necessarily in agreement about the criteria for a determination of competency. A psychologist, without even directly assessing a group of defendants, could reach high levels of agreement with an examining clinician, simply by calling all defendants competent (the base-rate decision). Since approximately 80% of all referred defendants are deemed competent,[22] the psychologist and the examiner necessarily would have modest agreement, even without making any decisions at all. The misleading nature of the 80% becomes obvious when examining specific psycholegal deficits (as opposed

---

[18] 391 F. 2d. 460, 463-464 (D.C. 1968).

[19] Patricia A. Zapf and Ronald Roesch, Mental competency evaluations: Guidelines for judges and attorneys, 37 Court Rev. 28 (2000).

[20] Norman G. Poythress and Harley V. Stock, Competency to stand trial: A historical review and some new data, 8 J. Psychiarty and L.131 (1980).

[21] Robert A. Nicholson, and Karen E. Kugler, Competent and incompetent criminal defendants: A quantitative review of comparative research, 109 Psych. Bull. 355 (1991).

[22] Ronald Roesch, Patricia A. Zapf, Stephen L. Golding, and Jennifer L. Skeem, Defining and assessing competency to stand trial, in The Handbook of Forensic Psychology 327, 332 (Allen K. Hess and Irving B. Weiner, 1999, 2nd ed.).

to overall competency). For example, specific competency domains set out in each state's competency statutes might include the ability to understand the nature of the proceedings, a factual understanding of the proceedings, and rational understanding of the proceedings. By focusing on agreement on deficits, some researchers have demonstrated that examiners agree only 25% of the time across a series of competency domains.[23] Even this low level may be misleading when competency is truly a serious question; and no study has accumulated enough difficult cases to determine forensic reliability. Importantly, even high levels of reliability do not, of course, ensure that evaluators make valid decisions. Two evaluators could agree that the presence of psychosis automatically leads to a finding of incompetency. As long as the evaluators agree about their criteria for determining psychosis, the reliability of their final judgments about competency will be high. It is quite possible that the criteria used by too many evaluators inappropriately rely on traditional mental status issues without considering the functional aspects of a particular defendant's case.

In addition to issues of reliability, the state of research reveals something problematic when we consider the manner courts evaluate competency evaluations. Most important are the very high levels of examiner-judge agreement. Although that may seem as a good indicator of assessment effectiveness, that agreement does not make the finding valid: courts often accept evaluators' definitions of competency and their conclusions without review.[24] Once a competency evaluation has been completed and the written report submitted, the court may schedule a hearing. If, however, both the defense and the prosecution accept the findings and recommendations in the report, a hearing need not occur. Indeed, most cases do not call for formal hearings. If a hearing is held, the evaluators may be asked to testify, but most hearings are quite brief and usually only use the written report of an evaluator. In fact, the majority of hearings last only a few minutes and are held simply to confirm the findings of evaluators.[25] Even if a hearing is held and although the court's ultimate decisions about competency are not bound by the evaluators' recommendations, courts still tend to accept evaluators' recommendations.[26]

Although it may well be that competency issues raise concerns, it is important to realize the extent to which the concerns infiltrate the legal system. It has been estimated that between 25,000 and 39,000 competency evaluations are conducted in the United States annually.[27] That is, between 2% and 8% of all felony defendants are referred for competency evaluations.[28] As we have seen, however, approximately 80%, the vast majority, are found competent. Although most may be found competent, it is important to note that incompetency determinations vary widely across jurisdictions and evaluation settings, ranging from 7 to 60 percent.[29] Researchers attribute the wide variation to differences in examiner training and use of forensic assessment tools, inadequate treatment of the mentally ill and the need to use the criminal justice system, the availability of mental health services, and variation in judicial scrutiny of evaluator's conclusions.[30] The wide variety may seem problematic, but perhaps more problematic is whether defendants are even referred for evaluation. Three recent studies directly addressed that concern as they examined the place of competency in relationships between clients and attorneys.[31] In that study, attorneys

---

23 Jennifer L. Skeem, Stephen L. Golding, Nancy B. Cohn and Gerald Berge, The logic and reliability of evaluations of competence to stand trial, 22 L.and Hum. Beh. 519 (1998).

24 Jennifer L. Skeem, Stephen L. Golding, Nancy B. Cohn and Gerald Berge, The logic and reliability of evaluations of competence to stand trial, 22 L. and Hum. Beh. 519 (1998).

25 Henry J. Steadman, Beating a Rap?: Defendants Found Incompetent to Stand Trial (1979).

26 Henry J. Steadman, Beating a Rap?: Defendants Found Incompetent to Stand Trial (1979).

27 Steven K. Hoge, Richard J. Bonnie, Norman Poythress, John Monahan, Marlene Eisenberg, and Thomas Faucht-Haviar, The MacArthur adjudicative competence study: Development and validation of a research instrument, 21 L. and Hum. Beh. 141 (1997).

28 Richard J. Bonnie, The competence of criminal defendants: A theoretical reformulation, 10 Beh. Sci. and L. 291 (1992).

29 Robert A. Nicholson and Karen E. Kulger, Competent and incompetent criminal defendants: A qualitative review of comparative research, 109 Psych. Bull. 355 (1991).

30 Stephen L. Golding, Studies of incompetent defendants: Research and social policy implications, 5 Forensic Reports 77 (1992).

31 Norman G. Poythress, Richard J Bonnie, Steven K Hoge, John Monahan, and Lois Oberlander, Client abilities to assist counsel and make decisions in criminal cases: Findings from three studies, 18 L. and Hum. Beh. 437 (1994).

doubted the competence of 8-25% of clients charged with felonies and 3-8% of clients charged with misdemeanors. As compared with clients whose competence was presumed, attorneys viewed clients of doubtful competence as less helpful and as less actively involved in their cases, but as actively involved in making key decisions. Defendants' perceptions accorded with those of the attorneys. Importantly, only 20% of doubtful competence cases were referred for evaluation.

ADDRESSING ISSUES OF INSANITY

The tradition behind the American criminal justice system's formulation of the insanity defense began in earnest in nineteenth-century Great Britain, when a jury found Daniel M'Naghten not guilty by reason of insanity.[32] M'Naghten attempted to kill the prime minister of England but mistakenly killed the prime minister's secretary. His motivation for this attempted assassination was his belief that the prime minister was involved in a conspiracy to kill him. The *M'Naghten* case held:

> Every man is to be presumed to be sane, and ...that to establish a defense on the ground of insanity, it must be clearly proved that, at the time of the committing of the act, the party accused was laboring under such a defect of reason, from disease of mind, as not to know the nature and quality of the act he was doing; or if he did know it, that he did not know he was doing what was wrong.[33]

This approach to assessing insanity hinges on a version of rationality that emphasizes instrumental reasoning skills. At its core stands an offender's understanding of the difference between good and evil conduct. From this perspective, the *M'Naghten* test primarily relies upon the notion of cognitive ability to distinguish right from wrong. A literal reading of the *M'Naghten* court's rendition of the insanity test, however, also includes a reference to an additional requirement that the offender know the nature and quality of the wrongful act. This additional prong suggests that the knowledge requirement might be augmented by a different capacity other than instrumental reasoning, perhaps a richer account of understanding why the act is wrongful. However, commentators and courts rarely present this additional phrase as a separate requirement under the *M'Naghten* test. Instead, courts interpret the phrase to support the central requirement of the *M'Naghten* formula – that is, knowledge of right from wrong.[34]

The *M'Naghten* rule has been the subject of important criticisms. First, the *M'Naghten* formula requires that an offender suffer from a "disease of mind," but the rule never fully clarifies exactly what that constitutes. Second, the most common criticism of the *M'Naghten* rule is that it distills the ability to know down to a purely cognitive function.[35] Critics find that focus on intellectual awareness too restrictive. Most of the individuals who seem seriously mentally ill know intellectually the wrongfulness of their conduct. Third, it is extremely difficult to separate intellectual abilities from other, noncognitive capacities.[36] The *M'Naghten* rule may offer a much broader notion of knowledge that encompasses a rich capacity of understanding and affect, but the standard grants emotions far less consideration than cognition. In any event, a majority of the courts do not define what they mean by the term "to know," leaving the matter to juries and their common sense.[37]

Despite its criticisms, the *M'Naghten* rule still would serve as the basis for other standards to determine insanity. Three other notable standards would emerge: the irresistible impulse test, the American

---

[32] See *M'Naghten's Case*, 8 Eng. Rep. 718 (1843). See Wayne R. LaFave and Austin W. Scott, Jr., Substantive Criminal Law 4.2 (1986). See also Abraham S. Goldstein, The Insanity Defense 45-66 (1967); Abraham L. Halpern, The insanity verdict, the psychopath, and post-acquittal confinement, 24 Pac. L.J. 1125 (1993); and Lloyd I. Weinreb, Criminal Law: Cases, Comment, Questions 529-561 (7th ed. 2003).

[33] *M'Naghten's Case*, 8 Eng. Rep. 718, 722 (1843).

[34] John Kaplan, Robert Weisberg, Guyora Binder, Criminal Law: Cases and Materials 702 (4d ed. 2000).

[35] See Herbert Fingarette, The Meaning of Criminal Insanity (1972).

[36] See Wayne R. LaFave and Austin W. Scott, Jr., Substantive Criminal Law 313-314 (1986).

[37] See Wayne R. LaFave and Austin W. Scott, Jr., Substantive Criminal Law 313-314 (1986).

Law Institute's Model Penal Code, and the Durham rule. In addition to those tests, the federal government would enact its own statute which combines components of prior standards.[38] Each of these rules highlights important aspects of legal issues relating to insanity and build on one another.

In contrast to *M'Naghten*, the irresistible impulse test asks if the mental disease impaired the offender's ability to control his actions.[39] This is known as a volitional test which looks to an individual's ability for self-control to determine the nature of involuntariness in the person's actions. This approach examines whether the defendant had a mental disease that kept him from controlling his conduct, even if he knew what he was doing something wrong. The irresistible impulse differs from the *M'Naghten* rule's focus on the ability to distinguish right from wrong. Thus, the volitional test makes it possible for an offender to be able to distinguish between right and wrong yet still be found legally insane because of lack of control.[40]

Critics were not kind to the irresistible impulse test.[41] Some commentators argue that this test does not add anything to *M'Naghten*; that is, once the *M'Naghten* rule is properly defined, the two tests merge. These commentators believe that a failure of control also implicates a failure of knowledge. A competing group of theorists makes a much more fundamental complaint. These critics argue that the irresistible impulse component overexpands the insanity test, that it makes it available to psychopaths, to neurotics, perhaps to all who commit crime. This is said to follow from the impossibility of determining which acts were uncontrollable, rather than merely uncontrolled, and the attendant suspicion that the former category may not really exist.

More recent tests used to identify whether an offender can qualify for the insanity defense identify as central criteria both the ability to know right from wrong and the ability to control impulses. The American Law Institute's Model Penal Code (ALI), for example, combines the attributes of both the *M'Naghten* test and the irresistible impulse test. It reads: "A person is not responsible for criminal conduct if at the time of such conduct as a result of mental disease or defect he lacks substantial capacity either to appreciate the criminality of his conduct or to conform his conduct to the requirements of the law."[42] The ALI furthers defines mental disease or defect as exempting "an abnormality manifested only by repeated criminal or otherwise antisocial conduct."[43] In addition, the ALI test alters the *M'Naghten* test first by asking whether the offender could "appreciate the criminality of his conduct." This expanded construction of *M'Naghten's* cognitive component allows for the possibility of an increased emotional component to the test for insanity. Instead of relying solely on instrumental reasoning, the ALI model asks how deeply offenders understood the wrongfulness of their conduct. As such, this version of the insanity test crystallizes the more expansive reading of the *M'Naghten* rule. The ALI model further changes the traditional *M'Naghten* test by incorporating a variant of the irresistible impulse test by inquiring into individuals' abilities to "conform" their behavior. The final noteworthy change to the insanity test includes a revision of both the *M'Naghten* rule and the irresistible impulse test. Whereas the *M'Naghten* rule and the irresistible impulse test were criticized for requiring complete incapacitation, the ALI model only requires the absence of "substantial capacity" for either prong of its test. While the notion of appreciation of criminal conduct is distinguishable from the more narrow conception of knowing right from wrong, the ALI model still emphasizes offenders' cognition of the criminality of their acts. In practice, the ALI model continues to rely on instrumental reasoning capacities without fully incorporating the critical role that emotions play in the context of decision making and judgments.

---

[38] See Rita J. Simon and David E. Aaronson, The Insanity Defense: A Critical Assessment of Law and Policy in the Post-Hinckley Era 45-56 (1988).

[39] John Kaplan, Robert Weisberg, Guyora Binder, Criminal Law: Cases and Materials 708 (4d ed. 2000).

[40] Abraham S. Goldstein, The Insanity Defense 67 (1967). Importantly, some argue that there actually were not two distinct, well-defined tests but rather a collection of closely related phrases that borrowed from both approaches and, equally importantly, it was not clear that making a choice among the various approaches impacted case outcomes. Lloyd I. Weinreb, Criminal Law: Cases, Comment, Questions 556 (7th ed. 2003).

[41] Abraham S. Goldstein, The Insanity Defense 67 (1967).

[42] Model Penal Code 4.01 (1962).

[43] Model Penal Code 4.01 (1962).

Another important rule worth discussing is the *Durham* rule.[44] This rule perceived the basis for the insanity defense as applying to actions that stem from a disease of the mind.[45] This approach is known as the "product rule" which finds an offender not responsible if the offense was the product of a diseased mind. More specifically, the *Durham* rule states: "An accused is not criminally responsible if his unlawful act was the product of mental disease or mental defect."[46] This approach may seem unduly deferential to mental illness. However, courts turned to a definition of the insanity test in which the notion of mental disease or defect played a central role when science began to reveal that the human mind could not be divided into discrete subsections and instead operated as an integrated unit.[47] As a result, the test was more concerned with mental illness than with *mens rea*. *Durham* implied that mental illness itself, not the state of mind arising from mental illness, was the excusing factor. This approach allowed the conclusion, as one commentator observed, that "if the defendant had a mental disease, his mind could not be expected to respond properly to threats of sanction."[48]

Critics claimed that the *Durham* rule provided no standard and instead left the jury without adequate guidance. In addition, this absence of guidance was seen as granting too much authority to mental health experts. Without further definition of the mental disease or defect, the jury had no choice but to defer to one expert or choose between the more persuasive of the dueling experts. Because the rule stressed the existence of a mental disease without further demanding proof of actual incapacitation, the jury was left entirely dependent on the expert's classification of conduct as the product of mental disease. While other tests such as *M'Naghten* focus on an incapacitating condition resulting from mental illness or defect, *Durham* ignored causes of incapacitation apart from mental illness.[49] These criticisms were effective enough to lead to the dismantling of *Durham* in *United States v. Brawner,*[50] which discarded the "product" test, but which added a volitional question to *M'Naghten's* cognitive inquiry.

The last significant standard, known as the federal approach, resulted form the public uproar that occurred in the wake of a jury's finding John Hinckley Not Guilty by Reason of Insanity (NGRI) for attempting to assassinate President Reagan. The verdict led to the enactment of the Insanity Defense Reform Act of 1984 (IDRA). The IDRA provides that:

> It is an affirmative defense to a prosecution under any Federal statute that, at the time of the commission of the acts constituting the offense, the defendant, as a result of a severe mental disease or defect, was unable to appreciate the nature and quality or the wrongfulness of his acts.

The statute fundamentally changed the law in numerous material ways: (1) it shifted the burden of proof to defendants, by a quantum of clear and convincing evidence; (2) it eliminated the volitional prong, and thus brought us back to the *M'Naughten* rule; (3) it established strict procedures for the hospitalization and release of defendants found not responsible and incompetent to stand trial; (4) it severely limited the scope of expert testimony in insanity cases (especially in terms of prohibiting testimony to the ultimate issue); and (5) it rendered mental illness other than "severe mental disease or defect" insufficient to prevent the attribution of guilt.

Although the federal government formally rejected the ALI rule when it passed the IDRA, approximately 20 states still retain the ALI test, while the rest of the states permit an insanity defense only

---

[44] See *Durham v. United States*, 214 F.2d 862, 874-75 (D.C. Cir. 1954), overruled by *United States v. Brawner*, 471 F.2d 969, 971 (D.C. Cir. 1972).

[45] Abraham S. Goldstein, The Insanity Defense 82 (1967).

[46] *Durham v. United States*, 214 F.2d 862, 862 (D.C. Cir. 1954). Although the *Durham* rule sparked great debates among legal and moral theorists, even at the height of its popularity it was applied only in the District of Columbia, Maine and the Virgin Islands. See John Kaplan, Robert Weisberg, Guyora Binder, Criminal Law: Cases and Materials 709 (4d ed. 2000); Lloyd I. Weinreb, Criminal Law: Cases, Comment, Questions 568 (7th ed. 2003).

[47] Abraham S. Goldstein, The Insanity Defense 82 (1967).

[48] Abraham S. Goldstein, The Insanity Defense 82 (1967).

[49] Rudolph Joseph Gerber, The Insanity Defense 47 (1984).

[50] 471 F.2d 969 (D.C. Cir. 1972).

when the mental disease or defect causes a "substantial incapacity to appreciate the wrongfulness of the conduct" or words to that effect.[51] Under the current tests for insanity, the threshold requirements for moral agency are fixed quite low. Fewer than 1% of defendants in criminal cases try to use the insanity defense and even fewer, one-quarter of these defendants, use it successfully.[52] The insanity defense is unavailable as long as offenders can distinguish right from wrong and, in some jurisdictions, are not overwhelmed by irresistible impulses.

Note that many states have enacted statutes that offer juries the option of rendering a verdict of guilty but mentally ill in cases that raise insanity defenses.[53] The goal has been to limit the scope of the insanity defense and to ensure that defendants are not set free without being punished or not set free simply because they were mentally ill at the time of the offense. The approach allows for treatment, but the offender typically is to be incarcerated if he is found no longer mentally ill and if he has not been detained for a period longer than he would have been incarcerated had he not been mentally ill.

Given the strict limits in terms of who qualifies for using the insanity defense, it is important to understand the role of forensic assessment. The most frequently used forensic instrument in insanity evaluations provides a good example of the best instrument of this type developed to date: the R-CRAS (for Rogers Criminal Responsibility Assessment Scales).[54]

The instrument calls for examination of thirty different domains, such as reliability of the patient's self- report; level of intoxication at the time of the offense; observable bizarre behavior at the time of the alleged offense; delusions, hallucinations and thought disorders at the time of the alleged crime; general level of anxiety, depression and verbal coherence at the time of the alleged crime; focus of the alleged crime; and behavior during the week prior to the crime.[55] Although the instrument does not (and cannot) produce a quantified assessment of sanity, it does structure an evaluation of mental state at the time of the offense around relevant variables.[56] Importantly, inter-rater reliability on the issue of whether a person is "insane" can be relatively high, from 70 to 90%.[57] The reason reliability increases is attributable to structured interview formats which are designed to ensure that evaluators focus on the variables that legal tests make relevant. Importantly, these high rates of reliability are rather important in that inter-rater reliability from field research using the relatively refined criteria found in recent editions of the official Diagnostic and Statistical Manual (DSM IV), published by the American Psychiatric Association[58] indicates that mental health professionals involved in everyday practice may disagree more than half the time even on major diagnostic categories such as schizophrenia and organic brain syndrome.[59] Diagnostic

---

[51] Gary B. Melton, John Petrila, Norman G. Poythress, and Christopher Slobogin, Psychological Evaluations for the Courts: A Handbook for Mental Health Professionals and Lawyers 193 (2d ed. 1997).

[52] See Rita D. Buitendorp, Note, A statutory lesson from "Big Sky Country" on abolishing the insanity defense, 30 Val. U. L. Rev. 965, 971 n.35 (1996).

[53] John Kaplan, Robert Weisberg, Guyora Binder, Criminal Law: Cases and Materials 724-728 (4d ed. 2000); Lloyd I. Weinreb, Criminal Law: Cases, Comment, Questions 576 (7th ed. 2003).

[54] Randy Borum and Thomas Grisso, Psychological tests use in criminal forensic evaluations, 26 Professional Psych.: Res. and Practice 465 (1995).

[55] Richard Rogers and Daniel W. Shuman, Conducting Insanity Evaluations (2nd ed., 2000). See also Christopher Slobogin, Doubts about Daubert: Psychiatric anecdata as a case study, 57 Wash. and Lee. L. Rev. 919 (2000)

[56] See generally Richard Rogers and Kenneth W. Sewell, The R-CRAS and insanity evaluations: A re-examination of construct validity, 17 Beh. Sci. and L. 181 (1999).

[57] Richard Rogers and Kenneth W. Sewell, The R-CRAS and insanity evaluations: A re-examination of construct validity, 17 Beh. Sci. and L. 181 (1999). Earlier research had noted very high reliability, with one study finding 92% reliability. Kenneth K. Fukunaga, Richard A. Pasewark, Michael Hawkins, and Howard Gudeman, Insanity plea: Interexaminer agreement and concordance of psychiatric opinion and court verdict, 5 L.and Hum. Beh. 325 (1981). Another group had found 76% reliability. Michael R. Phillips, Aron S. Wolf, and David J. Coons, Psychiatry and the criminal justice system: Testing the myths, 145 Am. J. Psychiatry 605 (1988).

[58] American Psychiatric Association, Diagnostic and Statistical Manual (4th ed. 1994).

[59] One group of researchers found 57.1% agreement on schizophrenia. Samuel Fennig, Thomas J Craig, Marsha Tanenberg-Karant, and Evelyn H. Bromet, Comparison of facility and research diagnoses in first-admission psychotic patients, 151 Am. J. Psychiatry 1423, 1426 (1994). Another found 41% agreement on schizophrenia, 50% agreement on mood disorders, and 37% agreement on organic brain syndromes. Paul B. Lieberman and Frances M. Baker, The reliability of psychiatric diagnosis in the emergency room, 36 Hosp. and Community Psychiatry 291, 292 (1985).

opinions concerning people who are not psychotic are even less reliable in the scientific sense.[60] The reliability of determinations about symptoms, such as whether a person is engaging in bizarre thought processes, may be low as well.[61] These are important findings. As we will see, assessments of insanity often involve a diagnosis.

NOTES AND QUERIES

Why is it that researchers have been unable to create an index for competency that can be sued across all cases? Why has there been so much confusion in defining competency? What is the significance of adopting a case-by-case approach to competency? Why is there so much focus on evaluator reliability and why is it so difficult to reach high levels of reliability for specific domains of competency? What significance do you attach to the high levels of examiner-judge agreement on competency evaluations?

The four general models relating to the insanity defense are understandable as follow. The *M'Naghten* Rule (disease of the mind rule) finds the accused not responsible if he did not know what he was doing or did not know what he was doing was wrong. The *Durham* Rule (the "product rule"), finds the accused not responsible if the act was the product of a "mental disease or defect." The ALI Rule finds the accused not responsible if: at the time of the conduct and as a result of mental disease or defect accused lacks substantial capacity either to appreciate the criminality of the conduct or to conform conduct to the requirements of the law. Note that the rule also excludes abnormality manifested only by repeated criminal or antisocial conduct. Lastly, the Insanity Reform Act shifts shift burden of proof to the defense, eliminates requirement of volition, changes the verdict to not guilty ONLY by reason of insanity, and prohibits experts from testifying to the ultimate issue. Importantly, note that some states provide for "guilty but mentally ill" verdicts in addition to the insanity defense. Do you find that the tests to determine insanity determine the decision of whether or not the perpetrator is to be held responsible? How are evaluators not determining the ultimate issue of particular cases, which they theoretically are not supposed to do? What do you make of the guilty but mentally ill verdict? Does it provide a true alternative given that all jurisdictions already provide for mental health treatment (but do not necessarily provide it)? What impact do you suppose requesting that verdict has on juries as opposed to the more traditional not guilty by reason of insanity approach?

What do you make of this scenario? Joseph was 22 months old when he was adopted. His adoptive parents were psychologically abusive, such as threatening to cut off his penis and locking him in a closet when he misbehaved. Joseph grew to have a fear of knives, so much so that he hallucinated about them. By 15, Joseph started to show bizarre behavior, such as laughing uncontrollably and having uncontrollable head movements. The foster parents took to locking him in his room simply because they were afraid of him. By 16, Joseph had left his parents and had gotten married. He had two children and appeared to be a conscientious father. A few years later, his wife left him. Joseph then remarried and fathered five more children. During his marriage, he hid his hallucinations from his wife, for fear that she would leave him. He became very possessive and protective, even to the point that he would beat his children when they did not follow his simple rules. He eventually spent eight months in prison for child abuse. Upon release, he became even more delusional. He heard voices from God that told him to kill everyone. He enlisted the

---

[60] Paul B. Lieberman and Frances M. Baker, The reliability of psychiatric diagnosis in the emergency room, 36 Hosp. and Community Psychiatry 291, 292 (1985). One group of researchers found, for example, that reliability of personality disorder diagnoses in everyday clinical settings ranged from 49% for antisocial personality to 1% for schizoid personality. Graham Mellsop, Frank Varghese, Stephen Joshua, and Anthony Hicks, The reliability of Axis II of DSM-III, 139 Am. J. Psychiatry 1360, 1361 (1982). Other reviews note, for example, that a number of studies showed that rate of disagreement of specific diagnostic categories often equals or exceeds rate of agreement. David Faust and Jay Ziskin, The expert witness in psychology and psychiatry, 241 Science 31 (1988).

[61] See Michael Flaum, Stephan Arndt, and Nancy J. Andreasen, The reliability of "bizarre" delusions, 32 Comprehensive Psychiatry 59 (1991).

help of his oldest son and went from house to house in search of people to kill. At the end of his rampage, they had mutilated and killed two children, one of whom was one of Joseph's own children. Do you think that Joseph is legally insane? What result do you get from using different approaches to determining insanity?

What about this scenario? Texas uses the *Mc'Naughten* test, under which a defendant can be found not guilty by reason of insanity if it is determined that, because of a mental disease or defect, she did not know the difference between right and wrong at the time the crime was committed. Here are a few facts.

A 37-year-old wife and former nurse decided to quit work and stay at home in order to raise her children. One morning, she took each of her children from the breakfast table where they were eating cereal – seven-year-old Noah, five-year-old John, three-year-old Paul, two-year-old Luke, and six-month-old Mary – and drowned them one by one in the bathtub. For four out of the five children, after each one had died, she laid them face up on the bed in the master bedroom and covered their bodies with a sheet. Her eldest child, Noah, the last to be killed, was left in the bathtub. She called 911 right after the murder and told the police in a straightforward manner that she had killed her children.

At trial, she pled not guilty by reason of insanity to two capital murder charges. Both the prosecution and the defense called psychiatric and psychological experts to testify about her mental state at the time of the offense. The prosecution relied solely on the testimony of Dr. Park Dietz, Dietz presented a picture of the defendant as a manipulative woman who deliberately used the murders as a way to gain her life back. He noted how her previous suicide attempts resulted in improved life changes, such as a move from a trailer to a house. The prosecution emphasized the deliberate and premeditated nature of the murders, as well as her seeming sense of orientation, to demonstrate that she knew right from wrong. The prosecution focused on the fact that she had been thinking about killing her children for two years, and that she deliberately planned the murders the night before. It noted several motives, such as revenge against her husband for leaving all the child-rearing up to her, pure frustration, or perhaps just personal gain. It noted that her call to 911 did not say that she was Satan, or that she was trying to save the children, or that she needed to be punished. Her deceptiveness was further shown by the manner she lay each dead child in her bed and covering them with a sheet so that the other children would not understand what was happening. The state argued that these facts proved not only that she was aware of what she was doing and how she was doing it when she killed her children, but also that she knew her conduct was illegal and immoral.

The defense noted a long history of mental illness, included two suicide attempts and hearing Satan's command to kill her child with a knife. After the first suicide attempt, she had been hospitalized and diagnosed with major depressive disorder with psychotic features occurring postpartum. After the second attempt, she had been hospitalized again and began taking Haldol, an anti-psychotic drug often prescribed to people suffering from schizophrenia. Upon her discharge, she and her husband saw a psychiatrist who warned them that having another child could trigger another psychotic episode. She was hospitalized two more times before the murders, including a time soon after her father's death. The defense argued that her state of mind immediately before and after the murder of her children parallels the severe mental impairments that were evident in her past. Not long after the murders, she told some of her doctors that she had done a poor job of raising her children and that killing them was the only way to save them from Satan. She stated during her confession to the police that by drowning her children, she could be punished for having harmed them through her inadequate parenting. When admitted to jail on the day of the murders, she had fresh cuts on her scalp where she had scratched her head to the point of baldness in a spot where she believed Satan had etched the numbers "666."

The defense presented numerous experts who testified to her severe mental disturbances and her inability to distinguish right from wrong at the time of the offense. The defense emphasized the diagnoses of experts who believed her to be schizophrenic, which would have made her more likely to develop full-blown psychosis and depression after the birth of a child. More importantly, the defense argued that while she had a "general concept that the world perceives drowning people is wrong," she believed it was the right thing to do. One expert testified that she was trying to send her children to God, and that she would kill the Satan within her by being executed by the criminal justice system for what she had done; she viewed the murder as "altruistic," as killing her children out of love for them, and to save them from what she perceived as a danger. The defense argued that she saw her children as headed for hell if she did not act.

Based on Texas law, how should a jury rule? Note that the jury found her guilty after only three and a half hours of deliberation and sentenced her to life in prison, with no eligibility for parole for at least forty years. See Christine Michalopoulos, Filling the holes of the insanity defense: The Andrea Yates case and the need for a new prong, 10 Va. J. Soc. Pol'y and L. 383 (2003); Deborah W. Denno, Who is Andrea Yates? A short story about insanity, 10 Duke J. Gender L. and Pol'y 1 (2003).

NOTE ON THE SELF-AWARENESS OF MENTAL ILLNESS

The prosecution's expert witness in the Yates case highlighted that her most consistent story was that she did not think that she was psychotic, that she did not want to be thought of that way and resented someone calling her that. Deborah W. Denno, Who is Andrea Yates? A short story about insanity, 10 Duke J. Gender L. and Pol'y 1 (2003). What do you make of that statement?

Many psychotic people are wrong about their mental status. The argument is that the nature of mental illness alters and controls the afflicted individual's perception and will. Recent research reveals that denial or inability to accept that one is mentally ill is actually a symptom of the disease. See Sonia Johnson and Martin Orrell, Insight and psychosis: A social perspective, 25 Psychol. Med. 515, 515-20 (1995). For example, research suggests that a severe deficit in self-awareness may constitute a distinguishing psychopathological characteristic of patients with bipolar II disorder. Stephano Pallanti, Leonardo Quercioli, Adolfo Pazzagli, Akessadri Rossi, Liliana Dell'Osso, Stefano Pini, and Giovanni Battista Cassano, Awareness of illness and subjective experience of cognitive complaints in patients with bipolar I and bipolar II disorders, 156 Am. J. of Psychiatry, 1094 (1999). Research reveals that from one quarter to over half of schizophrenics do not believe they are mentally ill. See, e.g., Jeffrey M Pyne, Donna Bean, and Greer Sullivan, Characteristics of patients with schizophrenia who do not believe they are mentally ill, 189 J. of Nervous and Mental Disease 146 (2001). In addition, comparisons of the reports of mental health patients with those of psychiatrists reveals that patients often fail to report, with failures ranging form 27-89% for 20 symptoms, J.P. Selten, D. Wiersma, and R.J. van den Bosch, Discrepancy between subjective and object ratings for negative symptoms, 34 J. of Psychiatric Res. 11 (2000). Research also reveals that first-episode patients with a schizophrenia spectrum disorder are less aware of having a mental illness than multiple-episode patients. Katherine N. Thompson, Patrick D. McGorry, Susan M. Harrigan, Reduced awareness of illness in first-episode psychosis, 42 Comprehensive Psychiatry 498 (2001). Importantly, research has shown that the more individuals realize that they are mentally ill, the more they exhibit depressive symptoms. Researchers have found, for example, that a linear insight- demoralization-depression- suicidality syndrome develops in many schizophrenic patients. Robert C. Schwartz, Self-awareness in schizophrenia: Its relationship to depressive symptomatology and broad psychiatric impairments, 189 J. of Nervous and Mental Disease 401 (2001). What implications arise from these findings?

DETERMINING COMPETENCY

DUSKY v. U.S.
362 U.S. 402 (1960)

Per Curiam (Warren, Black, Frankfurter, Douglas, Clark, Harlan, Brennan, Whittaker, Stewart)

The motion for leave to proceed in forma pauperis and the petition for a writ of certiorari are granted. Upon consideration of the entire record we agree with the Solicitor General that "the record in this case does not sufficiently support the findings of competency to stand trial," for to support those findings under 18 U. S. C. § 4244 the district judge "would need more information than this record presents." We also agree with the suggestion of the Solicitor General that it is not enough for the district judge to find that "the defendant [is] oriented to time and place and [has] some recollection of events," but that the "test must be whether he has sufficient present ability to consult with his lawyer with a reasonable degree of rational understanding – and whether he has a rational as well as factual understanding of the proceedings against him."

In view of the doubts and ambiguities regarding the legal significance of the psychiatric testimony in this case and the resulting difficulties of retrospectively determining the petitioner's competency as of more than a year ago, we reverse the judgment of the Court of Appeals affirming the judgment of conviction, and remand the case to the District Court for a new hearing to ascertain petitioner's present competency to stand trial, and for a new trial if petitioner is found competent.

It is so ordered.

NOTES AND QUERIES

1.The Court explained the now widely accepted criteria for evaluating defendants' competency: a trial court must determine whether the defendant "has sufficient present ability to consult with his lawyer with a reasonable degree of rational understanding – and whether he has a rational as well as factual understanding of the proceedings against him." Note that the Court left the trial judge to decide whether the defendant fit the standard. Appropriate? *Dusky* contains substantial ambiguity. How effectively must the defendant participate in the trial or interact with his attorney? What does reasonable degree of rational understanding mean? As you examine the cases that follow, determine whether the *Dusky* standard provides adequate guidance in assessing competency.

Incompetence is not synonymous with mental illness; a person can be mentally ill, for example, yet still competent to stand trial. One may be suffering from a mental disease yet also simultaneously have a rational and factual understanding of court proceedings and be able to consult with a lawyer on a reasonably rational basis. What does this tell you about the competency standard?

As *Dusky* tells us and the following cases we review confirm, the Supreme Court concerns itself with the procedural aspects of inquiries into competency and what should be done with incompetent defendants. It tends to ignore the ultimate question of incompetency. Appropriate? Necessary?

Note that *Dusky* is a *per curiam* decision. A "*per curiam*" decision is a decision delivered via an opinion issued in the name of the Court rather than specific justices. It literally means "by the court." As we have seen, most decisions on the merits by the Supreme Court take the form of one or more opinions signed by individual justices and often joined in by others. Even when such signed opinions are unanimous, they are not termed "*per curiam*." "*Per curiam*" decisions are given that label by the Court itself, tend to be short without in-depth legal analysis, and tend to deal with issues the Court views as relatively non-controversial. No justices take individualized responsibility for the opinion.

DROPE v. MISSOURI
420 U.S. 162 (1975)

MR. CHIEF JUSTICE BURGER delivered the opinion of the Court.

We granted certiorari in this case to consider petitioner's claims that he was deprived of due process of law by the failure of the trial court to order a psychiatric examination with respect to his competence to stand trial ...

I.

In February 1969 an indictment was returned in the Circuit Court of St. Louis, Mo., charging petitioner and two others with the forcible rape of petitioner's wife. Following severance of petitioner's case from those of the other defendants and a continuance, on May 27 his counsel filed a motion for a continuance until September, in order that petitioner might be examined and receive psychiatric treatment. Treatment had been suggested by a psychiatrist who had examined petitioner at his counsel's request and whose report was attached to the motion. On the same date respondent, through the Assistant Circuit Attorney, filed a document stating that the State did not oppose the motion for a psychiatric examination. Apparently no action was taken on the motion, and petitioner's case was continued until June 23, at which time his counsel objected to proceeding with the trial on the ground that he had understood the case would be continued until September and consequently was not prepared. He objected further "for the reason that the defendant is not a person of sound mind and should have a further psychiatric examination before the case should be forced to trial." The trial judge noted that the motion for a continuance was not in proper form and that, although petitioner's counsel had agreed to file another, he had failed to do so, and he overruled his objections and directed that the case proceed to trial.

On June 24 a jury was empaneled, and the prosecution called petitioner's wife as its first witness. She testified that petitioner participated with four of his acquaintances in forcibly raping her and subjecting her to other bizarre abuse and indignities, but that she had resumed living with him after the incident on the advice of petitioner's psychiatrist and so that their children would be taken care of. On cross-examination, she testified that she had told petitioner's attorney of her belief that her husband was sick and needed psychiatric care and that for these reasons she had signed a statement disavowing a desire to prosecute. She related that on several occasions when petitioner did not "get his way or [was] worried about something," he would roll down the stairs. She could explain such behavior only by relating "what they told him many times at City Hospital, that is something he does upon himself [sic]." However, she also stated that she was not convinced petitioner was sick after talking to his psychiatrist, and that she had changed her mind about not wanting to prosecute petitioner because, as she testified, he had "tried to choke me, tried to kill me" on the Sunday evening prior to trial.

The prosecution called three more witnesses, but did not conclude its case, before adjournment on June 24. The following morning, petitioner did not appear. When the trial judge directed counsel to proceed, petitioner's attorney moved for a mistrial "in view of the fact that the defendant, I am informed, shot himself this morning." The trial judge denied the motion, stating that he had already decided the matter would proceed for trial, and when petitioner's counsel complained of the difficulty of proceeding without a client, the trial judge replied that the difficulty was brought about by petitioner, who was on bond and had a responsibility to be present. The prosecution then called four more witnesses and, after producing proof of a prior conviction, rested its case. Petitioner's "Motion for Verdict of Acquittal," including in effect a renewal of the motion for a mistrial, was denied, and his counsel stated that he had "no evidence to produce at this time under the circumstances." The jury returned a verdict of guilty, and on July 21, 1969, petitioner, who had been in the hospital for three weeks recovering from a bullet wound in the abdomen, appeared, and the trial court fixed the penalty at life imprisonment.

Petitioner filed a motion for a new trial, the burden of which was that the trial court had erred in proceeding with the trial when no evidence had been produced that his absence from the trial was voluntary. A hearing was held before the judge who had presided at trial. Petitioner testified that on June 25 he had gone to his brother's house and that he remembered nothing concerning the shooting except that he felt a burning pain in his stomach and later woke up in the hospital. He testified he did not remember talking to anyone at the hospital. The State presented evidence that upon admission to the hospital petitioner stated that he had shot himself because of "'some problem with the law,'" and that he had told a policeman he had shot himself because "he was supposed to go to court for rape, and he didn't do it; he rather be [sic] dead than to go to trial for something he didn't do." The trial judge denied the motion. Stating that on the morning of petitioner's failure to appear he had received information on the telephone which was checked with the hospital, the judge concluded that petitioner had the burden of showing that his absence was not voluntary and found on the basis of the evidence that his absence "'was due to his own voluntary act in shooting himself; done for the very purpose of avoiding trial.'"

In April 1971 petitioner filed a motion to vacate the judgment of conviction and sentence ... He alleged that ... his constitutional rights had been violated by the failure to order a psychiatric examination prior to trial and by conducting the trial to conclusion in his absence. ...

In July 1971 a hearing was held on the motion; petitioner called two psychiatrists as witnesses. The psychiatrist who had examined petitioner prior to his trial testified that in his opinion there was reasonable cause to believe that a person who attempted to commit suicide in the midst of a trial might not be mentally competent to understand the proceedings against him. Another psychiatrist ... testified that in his opinion a man who was charged with raping his wife and attempted suicide during his trial was in need of a psychiatric evaluation to find out his mental condition, and that there should be an evaluation to determine whether the person was competent to assist in his own defense and whether he was "malingering or did it intentionally or if it was due to a true psychiatric disorder." The same psychiatrist stated that he had examined petitioner at City Hospital in 1965 and had found that he had psychiatric problems and was in need of care. Petitioner took the stand, repeating his previous testimony with respect to the shooting.

In June 1972 the sentencing judge denied petitioner's ... motion, and the Missouri Court of Appeals affirmed...

As to the situation before trial, the court held that the psychiatric report attached to petitioner's motion for a continuance did not raise a reasonable doubt of his fitness to proceed. Turning to the second time period, "during the trial after the suicide attempt," the court held that Pate v. Robinson, which involved a competence hearing rather than a competence examination followed by a hearing, did not require that the examination and hearing be held during the trial rather than immediately thereafter. With regard to the period after trial, and accepting petitioner's contention that his was a "bona fide attempt at suicide," the court was of the view that the ... petitioner's suicide attempt did not create a reasonable doubt of his competence as a matter of law, that petitioner had failed to demonstrate the inadequacy of the procedures employed for protecting his rights, and that the finding of the trial court was not clearly erroneous.

...We granted certiorari, and we now reverse.

II.

It has long been accepted that a person whose mental condition is such that he lacks the capacity to understand the nature and object of the proceedings against him, to consult with counsel, and to assist in preparing his defense may not be subjected to a trial. ... Accordingly, as to federal cases, we have approved a test of incompetence which seeks to ascertain whether a criminal defendant "'has sufficient present ability to consult with his lawyer with a reasonable degree of rational understanding – and whether he has a rational as well as factual understanding of the proceedings against him.'"

... Missouri's statutory scheme "jealously guards" a defendant's right to a fair trial. Missouri Rev. Stat. § 552.020 (1) provides: "No person who as a result of mental disease or defect lacks capacity to understand the proceedings against him or to assist in his own defense shall be tried, convicted or sentenced for the commission of an offense so long as the incapacity endures." Section 552.020 (2), provides that a judge or magistrate shall, "upon his own motion or upon motion filed by the state or by or on behalf of the accused," order a psychiatric examination whenever he "has reasonable cause to believe that the accused has a mental disease or defect excluding fitness to proceed." Section 552.020 (3) prescribes the contents of a report of the psychiatric examination, and § 552.030 (6) requires the court to hold a hearing if the opinion relative to fitness to proceed which is required to be included in the report is contested. In addition, the trial court may conduct a hearing on its own motion. Such a procedure is, on its face, constitutionally adequate to protect a defendant's right not to be tried while legally incompetent. Our task is to determine whether the proceedings in this case were consistent with petitioner's right to a fair trial.

III.

The sentencing judge and the Missouri Court of Appeals concluded that the psychiatric evaluation of petitioner attached to his pretrial motion for a continuance did not contain sufficient indicia of incompetence to stand trial to require further inquiry. Both courts mentioned aspects of the report suggesting competence, such as the impressions that petitioner did not have "any delusions, illusions, hallucinations . . . ," was "well oriented in all spheres," and "was able, without trouble, to answer questions testing judgement," but neither court mentioned the contrary data. The report also showed that petitioner, although cooperative in the examination, "had difficulty in participating well," "had a difficult time relating," and that he "was markedly circumstantial and irrelevant in his speech." In addition, neither court felt that petitioner's episodic irrational acts described in the report or the psychiatrist's diagnoses of "[borderline] mental deficiency" and "[chronic] [anxiety] reaction with depression" created a sufficient doubt of competence to require further inquiry.

It does not appear that the examining psychiatrist was asked to address himself to medical facts bearing specifically on the issue of petitioner's competence to stand trial, as distinguished from his mental and emotional condition generally. Thus, it is not surprising that before this Court the dispute centers on the inferences that could or should properly have been drawn from the report. Even where the issue is in focus we have recognized "the uncertainty of diagnosis in this field and the tentativeness of professional judgment." Here the inquiry is rendered more difficult by the fact that a defendant's mental condition may be relevant to more than one legal issue, each governed by distinct rules reflecting quite different policies.

Like the report itself, the motion for a continuance did not clearly suggest that petitioner's competence to stand trial was the question sought to be resolved. ... we are constrained to disagree with the sentencing judge that counsel's pretrial contention that "the defendant is not a person of sound mind and should have a further psychiatric examination before the case should be forced to trial," did not raise the issue of petitioner's competence to stand trial. This statement also may have tended to blur the aspect of petitioner's mental condition which would bear on his criminal responsibility and that which would bear on his competence to stand trial. However, at that stage, and with the obvious advantages of hindsight, it seems to us that it would have been, at the very least, the better practice to order an immediate examination. It is unnecessary for us to decide whether such examination was constitutionally required on the basis of what was then known to the trial court since in our view the question was settled by later events.

IV.

Turning to the situation at petitioner's trial, the state courts viewed the evidence as failing to show that during trial petitioner had acted in a manner that would cause the trial court to doubt his competence. The testimony of petitioner's wife, some of which repeated and confirmed information contained in the psychiatric evaluation attached to petitioner's motion for a continuance, was given little weight. Finally, the sentencing judge, relying on his finding on petitioner's motion for a new trial and although stating "that it does not take a psychiatrist to know that such a man has a problem and indicates poor judgment," concluded that the "fact that Mr. Drope shot himself to avoid trial suggests very strongly an awareness of what was going on." The Missouri Court of Appeals, accepting arguendo petitioner's contention that his was "a bona fide attempt at suicide," refused to conclude "that as a matter of law an attempt at suicide creates a reasonable doubt as to the movant's competency to stand trial."

Notwithstanding the difficulty of making evaluations of the kind required in these circumstances, we conclude that the record reveals a failure to give proper weight to the information suggesting incompetence which came to light during trial. This is particularly so when viewed in the context of the events surrounding petitioner's suicide attempt and against the background of the pretrial showing. Although a defendant's demeanor during trial may be such as to obviate "the need for extensive reliance on psychiatric prediction concerning his capabilities," ... "this reasoning offers no justification for ignoring the uncontradicted testimony of . . . [a] history of pronounced irrational behavior." ... we believe the Missouri courts failed to consider and give proper weight to the record evidence. Too little weight was given to the testimony of petitioner's wife that on the Sunday prior to trial he tried to choke her to death. For a man whose fate depended in large measure on the indulgence of his wife, who had hesitated about pressing the prosecution, this hardly could be regarded as rational conduct. Moreover, in considering the indicia of petitioner's incompetence separately, the state courts gave insufficient attention to the aggregate of those indicia in applying the objective standard of Mo. Rev. Stat. § 552.020 (2). We need not address the Court of Appeals' conclusion that an attempt to commit suicide does not create a reasonable doubt of competence to stand trial as a matter of law. As was true of the psychiatric evaluation, petitioner's attempt to commit suicide "did not stand alone." We conclude that when considered together with the information available prior to trial and the testimony of petitioner's wife at trial, the information concerning petitioner's suicide attempt created a sufficient doubt of his competence to stand trial to require further inquiry on the question.

...evidence of a defendant's irrational behavior, his demeanor at trial, and any prior medical opinion on competence to stand trial are all relevant in determining whether further inquiry is required, but that even one of these factors standing alone may, in some circumstances, be sufficient. There are, of course, no fixed or immutable signs which invariably indicate the need for further inquiry to determine fitness to proceed; the question is often a difficult one in which a wide range of manifestations and subtle nuances are implicated. That they are difficult to evaluate is suggested by the varying opinions trained psychiatrists can entertain on the same facts.

...Petitioner's absence bears on the analysis in two ways: first, it was due to an act which suggests a rather substantial degree of mental instability contemporaneous with the trial; second, as a result of petitioner's absence the trial judge and defense counsel were no longer able to observe him in the context of the trial and to gauge from his demeanor whether he was able to cooperate with his attorney and to understand the nature and object of the proceedings against him.

Even when a defendant is competent at the commencement of his trial, a trial court must always be alert to circumstances suggesting a change that would render the accused unable to meet the standards of competence to stand trial. Whatever the relationship between mental illness and incompetence to stand trial, in this case the bearing of the former on the latter was sufficiently likely that, in light of the evidence of petitioner's behavior including his suicide attempt, and there being no opportunity without his presence to evaluate that bearing in fact, the correct course was to suspend the trial until such an evaluation could be made. That this might have aborted the trial is a hard reality, but we cannot fail to note that such a result might have been avoided by prompt psychiatric examination before trial, when it was sought by petitioner.

V.

Our resolution of the first issue raised by petitioner makes it unnecessary to decide whether, as he contends, it was constitutionally impermissible to conduct the remainder of his trial on a capital offense in his enforced absence from a self-inflicted wound. However, even assuming the right to be present was one that could be waived, what we have already said makes it clear that there was an insufficient inquiry to afford a basis for deciding the issue of waiver.

The question remains whether petitioner's due process rights would be adequately protected by remanding the case now for a psychiatric examination aimed at establishing whether petitioner was in fact competent to stand trial in 1969. Given the inherent difficulties of such a nunc pro tunc determination under the most favorable circumstances, we cannot conclude that such a procedure would be adequate here. The State is free to retry petitioner, assuming, of course, that at the time of such trial he is competent to be tried.

The judgment is reversed, and the cause is remanded for proceedings not inconsistent with this opinion.

Reversed and remanded.

NOTES AND QUERIES

This was the initial report in support of seeking a continuance:

> The motion recites: "Comes now the Defendant, JAMES E. DROPE, and states to the court that he has had a psychiatric examination made by Dr. Joseph F. Shuman, M.D., a copy of which report is attached hereto.
>
> "Defendant moves the court to continue his case until September, 1969 in order that he might receive an Examination, Evaluation and psychiatric treatment, as suggested by Dr. Shuman, at the Malcomb Bliss Hospital in the City of St. Louis, Missouri."
>
> The report, in the form of a letter to petitioner's attorney, states that the psychiatrist examined petitioner on February 20, 1969. In a section entitled "Past Medical History" it describes petitioner as "markedly agitated and upset," noting that he "appeared to be cooperative in this examination, but he had difficulty in participating well." The report continues: "The patient had a difficult time relating. He was markedly circumstantial and irrelevant in his speech. . . . There was no sign as to the presence of any delusions, illusions, hallucinations, obsessions, ideas of reference, compulsions or phobias at this time.
>
> "In a simple IQ exam Mr. Drope was able to achieve a score in the low normal range . . . . Mr. Drope was well oriented in all spheres. With much difficulty he was able to explain a few abstractions. . . . He was able, without trouble, to answer questions testing judgment. He had much difficulty even doing the simple counting and calculation problems." The report then recounts the details of a conversation between the psychiatrist and petitioner's wife. The latter admitted that she had left petitioner on a number of occasions because of his sexual perversions and described the "strange behavior" of petitioner, including falling down flights of stairs, as an attempt to gain sympathy from her. In a section entitled "Impression," the report states that petitioner had "always led a marginal existence," that he had a "history of anti-social conduct," but that there were no "strong signs of psychosis at this time." It concludes that petitioner "certainly needs the aid of a psychiatrist," and that he "is a very neurotic individual who is also depressed and perhaps he is depressed for most of the time," and it offers as diagnoses: "(1) Sociopathic personality disorder, sexual perversion. (2) Borderline mental deficiency. (3) Chronic Anxiety reaction with depression."

What is your response to the facts of this case? Do you think that the defendant's competency was suspect enough that the judge should have ordered him examined? How useful is the initial report seeking a continuance so that the defendant could have his level of competency determined? Is the diagnosis helpful? On what grounds does the Supreme Court rule that there was insufficient inquiry about the defendant's competency?

What is meant by a *nunc pro tunc* determination?

Note that a trial judge may have a duty to inquire without request into a defendant's competency under certain circumstances. Those circumstances were articulated in *Pate v. Robinson*, 383 U.S. 375 (1966). In that case, Robinson conceded at trial that he shot and killed his common-law wife, Flossie May. Robinson claimed, however, that he was insane at the time of the shooting and raised the issue of his incompetence to stand trial. The lower courts rejected his claim but noted that no hearing on mental capacity to stand trial had been requested, that the evidence had failed to raise sufficient doubt as to his competence to require the trial court to conduct a hearing on its own motion, and that the evidence did not raise a reasonable doubt as to his sanity at the time of the offense. The Supreme Court concluded that Robinson was entitled to a hearing on the issue of his competency to stand trial. Robinson had a history of violence and mental illness stemming from being hit, as a child, in the head by a brick dropped from a third floor. At trial, even the prosecutor had suggested that testimony should be heard about Robinson's current sanity. The Court approved of the state standard that requires a judge on his own motion to impanel a jury and conduct a sanity hearing when evidence raises a *bona fide* doubt as to a defendant's competence to stand trial.

We will examine later in this chapter, in *Ake v. Oklahoma*, 470 U.S. 68 (1985), whether the Constitution can require an examination by psychiatrists or other mental health professionals. We also will examine, in *Medina v. California*, 505 U.S. 437 (1992), the constitutional limits on the allocation and the burden of proof regarding competency to stand trial.

Note on the Limits of Confining Incompetent Defendants

Defendants deemed incompetent to participate in adjudications against them typically are hospitalized in an effort to restore their competency. The practice may result in indefinitely confining defendants well beyond the sentence expected from the charges. The Supreme Court has held, in *Jackson v. Indiana*, 406 U.S. 715 (1972), that some limits may apply. In that case, a 27 year-old mentally defective deaf mute with a mental level of a pre-school child was charged with separate robberies of two women, one involving four dollars and another involving five dollars. At a competency hearing, he was deemed incompetent and committed to a state hospital until he would be deemed sane by the staff. In reality, this disposition amounted to a commitment for life. The Supreme Court ruled that, under due process grounds, the commitment must bear some reasonable relation to the purpose for which the individual is committed. It clearly did not in this case. Although the Court did not place any outer time limit on the duration of hospitalization for Jackson, it did find that Jackson himself should be released or civilly committed on the same standard that would be used to commit indefinitely any other citizen. The Court further held that, even if it is determined that the defendant probably soon will be able to stand trial, his continued commitment must be justified by progress toward that goal. The Court ended with noting that it would be inappropriate to attempt to prescribe arbitrary time limits, given the differing state facilities and procedures.

Although *Jackson* was decided more than thirty years ago, a review of legislation in the fifty states and the District of Columbia, conducted twenty years after *Jackson v. Indiana* was decided, revealed that the majority of jurisdictions still had ignored or circumvented the Supreme Court's decision. See Grant H. Morris and J. Reid Meloy, Out of mind? Out of sight: The uncivil commitment of permanently incompetent criminal defendants, 27 U.C. Davis L. Rev. 1, 4 (1993). Some states ignore *Jackson* by continuing to allow incompetent defendants to be detained until their competence has been restored. Others evade *Jackson* by imposing a lengthy period of treatment before acknowledging that the defendant is permanently incompetent, that is, that there is no substantial probability that the defendant will become competent to stand trial in the foreseeable future. Some states mandate a specific treatment period, e.g., Florida mandates five years for any incompetent felony defendant. Several states tie the maximum length of the treatment period to the maximum sentence that could have been imposed if the defendant were convicted of the crime charged. These laws do not conform to the Supreme Court's requirement that conditions an incompetent defendant's treatment on progress toward the goal of restoration to competence. A defendant charged with a serious crime is not by that fact alone more difficult to treat or less responsive to treatment than a defendant charged with a less serious crime. Treatment progress simply cannot be measured by the seriousness of the criminal charge or the possible sentence that could be imposed if the defendant were found guilty in a trial that has yet to be held. And yet, these laws allow continued confinement of permanently incompetent criminal defendants even though further treatment will not result in restoration of their competency. "At the least," stated the Court in *Jackson*, "due process requires that the nature and duration of commitment bear some reasonable relation to the purpose for which the individual is committed." That purpose is restoration to competence, not incapacitation for the length of a maximum sentence that can only be imposed if the defendant is tried and found guilty. Do you agree that that is the purpose?

REFUSING COMPETENCY

RIGGINS v. NEVADA
504 U.S. 127 (1992)

JUSTICE O'CONNOR delivered the opinion of the Court.

Petitioner David Riggins challenges his murder and robbery convictions on the ground that the State of Nevada unconstitutionally forced an antipsychotic drug upon him during trial. Because the Nevada courts failed to make findings sufficient to support forced administration of the drug, we reverse.

I.

During the early hours of November 20, 1987, Paul Wade was found dead in his Las Vegas apartment. An autopsy revealed that Wade died from multiple stab wounds, including wounds to the head, chest, and back. David Riggins was arrested for the killing 45 hours later.

A few days after being taken into custody, Riggins told Dr. R. Edward Quass, a private psychiatrist who treated patients at the Clark County Jail, about hearing voices in his head and having trouble sleeping. Riggins informed Dr. Quass that he had been successfully treated with Mellaril in the past. Mellaril is the trade name for thioridazine, an antipsychotic drug. After this consultation, Dr. Quass prescribed Mellaril at a level of 100 milligrams per day. Because Riggins continued to complain of voices and sleep problems in the following months, Dr. Quass gradually increased the Mellaril prescription to 800 milligrams per day. Riggins also received a prescription for Dilantin, an antiepileptic drug.

In January 1988, Riggins successfully moved for a determination of his competence to stand trial. Three court-appointed psychiatrists performed examinations during February and March, while Riggins was taking 450 milligrams of Mellaril daily. Dr. William O'Gorman, a psychiatrist who had treated Riggins for anxiety in 1982, and Dr. Franklin Master concluded that Riggins was competent to stand trial. The third psychiatrist, Dr. Jack Jurasky, found that Riggins was incompetent. The Clark County District Court determined that Riggins was legally sane and competent to stand trial, so preparations for trial went forward.

In early June, the defense moved the District Court for an order suspending administration of Mellaril and Dilantin until the end of Riggins' trial. Relying on both the Fourteenth Amendment and the Nevada Constitution, Riggins argued that continued administration of these drugs infringed upon his freedom and that the drugs' effect on his demeanor and mental state during trial would deny him due process. Riggins also asserted that, because he would offer an insanity defense at trial, he had a right to show jurors his "true mental state." In response, the State noted that Nevada law prohibits the trial of incompetent persons and argued that the court therefore had authority to compel Riggins to take medication necessary to ensure his competence.

On July 14, 1988, the District Court held an evidentiary hearing on Riggins' motion. At the hearing, Dr. Master "guessed" that taking Riggins off medication would not noticeably alter his behavior or render him incompetent to stand trial. Dr. Quass testified that, in his opinion, Riggins would be competent to stand trial even without the administration of Mellaril, but that the effects of Mellaril would not be noticeable to jurors if medication continued. Finally, Dr. O'Gorman told the court that Mellaril made the defendant calmer and more relaxed but that an excessive dose would cause drowsiness. Dr. O'Gorman was unable to predict how Riggins might behave if taken off antipsychotic medication, yet he questioned the need to give Riggins the high dose he was receiving. The court also had before it a written report in which Dr. Jurasky held to his earlier view that Riggins was incompetent to stand trial and predicted that if taken off Mellaril the defendant "would most likely regress to a manifest psychosis and become extremely difficult to manage."

The District Court denied Riggins' motion to terminate medication with a one-page order that gave no indication of the court's rationale. Riggins continued to receive 800 milligrams of Mellaril each day through the completion of his trial the following November.

At trial, Riggins presented an insanity defense and testified on his own behalf. He indicated that on the night of Wade's death he used cocaine before going to Wade's apartment. Riggins admitted fighting with Wade, but claimed that Wade was trying to kill him and that voices in his head said that killing Wade would be justifiable homicide. A jury found Riggins guilty of murder with use of a deadly weapon and robbery with use of a deadly weapon. After a penalty hearing, the same jury set the murder sentence at death.

Riggins presented several claims to the Nevada Supreme Court, among them that forced administration of Mellaril denied him the ability to assist in his own defense and prejudicially affected his attitude, appearance, and demeanor at trial. This prejudice was not justified, Riggins said in his opening brief, because the State neither demonstrated a need to administer Mellaril nor explored alternatives to giving him 800 milligrams of the drug each day. Riggins amplified this claim in his reply brief, objecting that the State intruded upon his constitutionally protected liberty interest in freedom from antipsychotic drugs without considering less intrusive options. ...

The Nevada Supreme Court affirmed Riggins' convictions and death sentence. With respect to administration of Mellaril, the court held that expert testimony presented at trial "was sufficient to inform the jury of the effect of the Mellaril on Riggins' demeanor and testimony." Thus, although Riggins' demeanor was relevant to his insanity defense, the court held that denial of the defense's motion to terminate medication was neither an abuse of discretion nor a violation of Riggins' trial rights. ...

We granted certiorari, to decide whether forced administration of antipsychotic medication during trial violated rights guaranteed by the Sixth and Fourteenth Amendments.

II.

The record in this case narrowly defines the issues before us. The parties have indicated that once the District Court denied Riggins' motion to terminate use of Mellaril, subsequent administration of the drug was involuntary. Given the parties' positions on this point and the absence of any record evidence to the contrary, we adhere to the understanding of the State Supreme Court.

We also presume that administration of Mellaril was medically appropriate. Although defense counsel stressed that Riggins received a very high dose of the drug, at no point did he suggest to the Nevada courts that administration of Mellaril was medically improper treatment for his client.

Finally, the record is dispositive with respect to Riggins' Eighth Amendment claim that administration of Mellaril denied him an opportunity to show jurors his true mental condition at the sentencing hearing. Because this argument was presented neither to the Nevada Supreme Court nor in Riggins' petition for certiorari, we do not address it here.

With these considerations in mind, we turn to Riggins' core contention that involuntary administration of Mellaril denied him "a full and fair trial." ... "The forcible injection of medication into a nonconsenting person's body," ... "represents a substantial interference with that person's liberty." In the case of antipsychotic drugs like Mellaril, that interference is particularly severe:

> The purpose of the drugs is to alter the chemical balance in a patient's brain, leading to changes, intended to be beneficial, in his or her cognitive processes. While the therapeutic benefits of antipsychotic drugs are well documented, it is also true that the drugs can have serious, even fatal, side effects. One such side effect identified by the trial court is acute dystonia, a severe involuntary spasm of the upper body, tongue, throat, or eyes. The trial court found that it may be treated and reversed within a few minutes through use of the medication Cogentin. Other side effects include akathesia (motor restlessness, often characterized by an inability to sit still); neuroleptic malignant syndrome (a relatively rare condition which can lead to death from cardiac dysfunction); and tardive dyskinesia, perhaps the most discussed side effect of antipsychotic drugs. Tardive dyskinesia is a neurological disorder, irreversible in some cases, that is characterized by involuntary, uncontrollable movements of various muscles, especially around the face. . . . The proportion of patients treated with antipsychotic drugs who exhibit the symptoms of tardive dyskinesia ranges from 10% to 25%. According to the American Psychiatric Association, studies of the condition indicate that 60% of tardive dyskinesia is mild or minimal in effect, and about 10% may be characterized as severe.

Taking account of the unique circumstances of penal confinement ... due process allows a mentally ill inmate to be treated involuntarily with antipsychotic drugs where there is a determination that "the inmate is dangerous to himself or others and the treatment is in the inmate's medical interest."

...Thus, once Riggins moved to terminate administration of antipsychotic medication, the State became obligated to establish the need for Mellaril and the medical appropriateness of the drug.

Although we have not had occasion to develop substantive standards for judging forced administration of such drugs in the trial or pretrial settings, Nevada certainly would have satisfied due process if the prosecution had demonstrated, and the District Court had found, that treatment with antipsychotic medication was medically appropriate and, considering less intrusive alternatives, essential for the sake of Riggins' own safety or the safety of others. Similarly, the State might have been able to justify medically appropriate, involuntary treatment with the drug by establishing that it could not obtain an adjudication of Riggins' guilt or innocence by using less intrusive means. We note that during the July 14 hearing Riggins did not contend that he had the right to be tried without Mellaril if its discontinuation rendered him incompetent. The question whether a competent criminal defendant may refuse antipsychotic medication if cessation of medication would render him incompetent at trial is not before us.

Contrary to the dissent's understanding, we do not "adopt a standard of strict scrutiny." We have no occasion to finally prescribe such substantive standards as mentioned above, since the District Court allowed administration of Mellaril to continue without making any determination of the need for this course or any findings about reasonable alternatives. The court's laconic order denying Riggins' motion did not adopt the State's view, which was that continued administration of Mellaril was required to ensure that the defendant could be tried; in fact, the hearing testimony casts considerable doubt on that argument. Nor did the order indicate a finding that safety considerations or other compelling concerns outweighed Riggins' interest in freedom from unwanted antipsychotic drugs.

Efforts to prove or disprove actual prejudice from the record before us would be futile, and guesses whether the outcome of the trial might have been different if Riggins' motion had been granted would be purely speculative. We accordingly reject the dissent's suggestion that Riggins should be required to demonstrate how the trial would have proceeded differently if he had not been given Mellaril. Like the consequences of compelling a defendant to wear prison clothing, or of binding and gagging an accused during trial, the precise consequences of forcing antipsychotic medication upon Riggins cannot be shown from a trial transcript. What the testimony of doctors who examined Riggins establishes, and what we will not ignore, is a strong possibility that Riggins' defense was impaired due to the administration of Mellaril.

We also are persuaded that allowing Riggins to present expert testimony about the effect of Mellaril on his demeanor did nothing to cure the possibility that the substance of his own testimony, his interaction with counsel, or his comprehension at trial were compromised by forced administration of Mellaril. Even if the Nevada Supreme Court was right that expert testimony allowed jurors to assess Riggins' demeanor fairly, an unacceptable risk of prejudice remained.

To be sure, trial prejudice can sometimes be justified by an essential state interest. Because the record contains no finding that might support a conclusion that administration of antipsychotic medication was necessary to accomplish an essential state policy, however, we have no basis for saying that the substantial probability of trial prejudice in this case was justified.

The judgment of the Nevada Supreme Court is reversed, and the case is remanded for further proceedings not inconsistent with this opinion.

It is so ordered.

JUSTICE KENNEDY, concurring in the judgment.

The medical and pharmacological data in the amicus briefs and other sources indicate that involuntary medication with antipsychotic drugs poses a serious threat to a defendant's right to a fair trial. In the case before us, there was no hearing or well-developed record on the point, and the whole subject of treating incompetence to stand trial by drug medication is somewhat new to the law, if not to medicine. On the sparse record before us, we cannot give full consideration to the issue. I file this separate opinion, however, to express my view that absent an extraordinary showing by the State, the Due Process Clause prohibits prosecuting officials from administering involuntary doses of antipsychotic medicines for purposes of rendering the accused competent for trial, and to express doubt that the showing can be made in most cases, given our present understanding of the properties of these drugs.

At the outset, I express full agreement with the Court's conclusion that one who was medicated against his will in order to stand trial may challenge his conviction. When the State commands medication during the pretrial and trial phases of the case for the avowed purpose of changing the defendant's behavior, the concerns are much the same as if it were alleged that the prosecution had manipulated material evidence. ...

...The avowed purpose of the medication is not functional competence, but competence to stand trial. In my view elementary protections against state intrusion require the State in every case to make a showing that there is no significant risk that the medication will impair or alter in any material way the defendant's capacity or willingness to react to the testimony at trial or to assist his counsel. Based on my understanding of the medical literature, I have substantial reservations that the State can make that showing. Indeed, the inquiry itself is elusive, for it assumes some baseline of normality that experts may have some difficulty in establishing for a particular defendant, if they can establish it at all. These uncertainties serve to underscore the difficult terrain the State must traverse when it enters this domain.

...the effects of antipsychotic drugs must be addressed. First introduced in the 1950's, antipsychotic drugs such as Mellaril have wide acceptance in the psychiatric community as an effective treatment for psychotic thought disorders. The medications restore normal thought processes by clearing hallucinations and delusions.

Although these drugs have changed the lives of psychiatric patients, they can have unwanted side effects. ... More relevant to this case are side effects that, it appears, can compromise the right of a medicated criminal defendant to receive a fair trial. The drugs can prejudice the accused in two principal ways: (1) by altering his demeanor in a manner that will prejudice his reactions and presentation in the courtroom, and (2) by rendering him unable or unwilling to assist counsel.

It is a fundamental assumption of the adversary system that the trier of fact observes the accused throughout the trial, while the accused is either on the stand or sitting at the defense table. This assumption derives from the right to be present at trial, which in turn derives from the right to testify and rights under the Confrontation Clause. At all stages of the proceedings, the defendant's behavior, manner, facial expressions, and emotional responses, or their absence, combine to make an overall impression on the trier of fact, an impression that can have a powerful influence on the outcome of the trial. If the defendant takes the stand, as Riggins did, his demeanor can have a great bearing on his credibility and persuasiveness, and on the degree to which he evokes sympathy. The defendant's demeanor may also be relevant to his confrontation rights.

The side effects of antipsychotic drugs may alter demeanor in a way that will prejudice all facets of the defense. Serious due process concerns are implicated when the State manipulates the evidence in this way. ...

If the State cannot render the defendant competent without involuntary medication, then it must resort to civil commitment, if appropriate, unless the defendant becomes competent through other means. If the defendant cannot be tried without his behavior and demeanor being affected in this substantial way by involuntary treatment, in my view the Constitution requires that society bear this cost in order to preserve the integrity of the trial process. The state of our knowledge of antipsychotic drugs and their side effects is evolving and may one day produce effective drugs that have only minimal side effects. Until that day comes, we can permit their use only when the State can show that involuntary treatment does not cause alterations raising the concerns enumerated in this separate opinion.

With these observations, I concur in the judgment reversing the conviction.

JUSTICE THOMAS, with whom JUSTICE SCALIA joins except as to Part II-A, dissenting.

Petitioner David Edward Riggins killed Paul William Wade by stabbing him 32 times with a knife. He then took cash, drugs, and other items from Wade's home. A Nevada jury convicted Riggins of first-degree murder and robbery with a deadly weapon and sentenced him to death. The Nevada Supreme Court affirmed. This Court reverses the conviction, holding that Nevada unconstitutionally deprived Riggins of his liberty interest in avoiding unwanted medication by compelling him to take an antipsychotic drug. I respectfully dissent.

I.

A.

Riggins first argued that the trial court improperly prevented him from presenting relevant evidence of his demeanor. As the Court notes, Riggins suffers from a mental illness and raised insanity as a defense at trial. When Riggins killed Wade, he was not using any antipsychotic medication. During his trial, however, Riggins was taking large doses of the antipsychotic drug Mellaril. Riggins believed that this drug would make his appearance at trial different from his appearance when he attacked Wade and that this difference might cause the jury to misjudge his sanity. To show his mental condition as it existed at the time of the crime, Riggins requested permission to appear before the jury in an unmedicated state. The trial court denied the request, and the Nevada Supreme Court affirmed.

This Court has no power to decide questions concerning the admissibility of evidence under Nevada law. We therefore may conduct only a limited review of a Nevada court's decision to exclude a particular form of demeanor evidence. Except in cases involving a violation of a specific constitutional provision such as the Confrontation Clause, this Court may not reverse a state "trial judge's action in the admission of evidence" unless the evidentiary ruling "so infuse[s] the trial with unfairness as to deny due process of law." In this case, I see no basis for concluding that Riggins had less than a full and fair trial.

The Court declines to decide whether Mellaril actually affected Riggins' appearance. On the basis of some pretrial psychiatric testimony it speculates only that Riggins might have looked less uptight, drowsy, or confused if he had not taken the drug. Other evidence casts doubt on this possibility. At least one psychiatrist believed that a jury would not "be able to notice whether or not [Riggins] was on Mellaril as compared to the period of the time when he was not medicated by that drug."Yet, even if Mellaril noticeably affected Riggins' demeanor, the Court fails to explain why the medication's effects rendered Riggins' trial fundamentally unfair.

The trial court offered Riggins the opportunity to prove his mental condition as it existed at the time of the crime through testimony instead of his appearance in court in an unmedicated condition. Riggins took advantage of this offer by explaining to the jury the history of his mental health, his usage of Mellaril, and the possible effects of Mellaril on his demeanor. Riggins also called Dr. Jack A. Jurasky, a psychiatrist, who testified about Riggins' condition after his arrest and his likely mental state at the time of the crime. Dr. Jurasky also explained Riggins' use of Mellaril and how it might be affecting him.

The Nevada Supreme Court concluded that this "testimony was sufficient to inform the jury of the effect of the Mellaril on Riggins' demeanor and testimony." Its analysis comports with that of other state courts that also have held that expert testimony may suffice to clarify the effects of an antipsychotic drug on a defendant's apparent demeanor. Having reviewed the record as a whole, I see no reason to disturb the conclusion of the Nevada Supreme Court. On the facts of this case, Riggins' inability to introduce evidence of his mental condition as he desired did not render his trial fundamentally unfair.

B.

Riggins also argued in the Nevada Supreme Court, although not in his briefs to this Court, that he did not have a "'full and fair' trial" because Mellaril had side effects that interfered with his ability to participate in his defense. He alleged, in particular, that the drug tended to limit his powers of perception. The Court accepts this contention, stating: "It is clearly possible that such side effects had an impact upon .

. . the content of his testimony on direct or cross examination, his ability to follow the proceedings, or the substance of his communication with counsel." I disagree. We cannot conclude that Riggins had less than a full and fair trial merely because of the possibility that Mellaril had side effects.

Riggins has no claim of legal incompetence in this case. The trial court specifically found him competent while he was taking Mellaril under a statute requiring him to have "sufficient mentality to be able to understand the nature of the criminal charges against him, and . . . to aid and assist his counsel in the defense interposed upon the trial." Riggins does not assert that due process imposes a higher standard.

The record does not reveal any other form of unfairness relating to the purported side effects of Mellaril. Riggins has failed to allege specific facts to support his claim that he could not participate effectively in his defense. He has not stated how he would have directed his counsel to examine or cross-examine witnesses differently. He has not identified any testimony or instructions that he did not understand. The record, moreover, does not even support his assertion that Mellaril made him worse off. As Justice Rose noted in his concurring opinion below: "Two psychiatrists who had prescribed Mellaril for Riggins, Dr. Quass and Dr. O'Gorman, testified that they believed it was helpful to him. Additional psychiatric testimony established that Mellaril may have increased Riggins' cognitive ability . . . ." Riggins' competence, moreover, tends to confirm that he had a fair trial. I thus see no basis for reversing the Nevada Supreme Court.

II.

Riggins also argues for reversal on the basis ... that the Due Process Clause protects a substantive "liberty interest" in avoiding unwanted medication. Riggins asserts that Nevada unconstitutionally deprived him of this liberty interest by forcing him to take Mellaril. The Court agrees, ruling that "the Nevada courts failed to make findings sufficient to support forced administration of the drug" in this case. I consider reversal on this basis improper.

A.

...Shortly after his arrest, as the Court notes, Riggins told a psychiatrist at his jail that he was hearing voices and could not sleep. The psychiatrist prescribed Mellaril. When the prescription did not eliminate the problem, Riggins sought further treatment and the psychiatrist increased the dosage. Riggins thus began taking the drug voluntarily.

The Court concludes that the medication became involuntary when the trial court denied Riggins' motion for permission not to take the drug during the trial. I disagree. Although the court denied Riggins' motion, it did not order him to take any medication. Moreover, even though Riggins alleges that the state physicians forced him to take the medication after the court's order, the record contains no finding of fact with respect to this allegation. The Court admits that it merely assumes that the physicians drugged him, and attempts to justify its assumption by observing that the Nevada Supreme Court also assumed that involuntary medication occurred. The Nevada Supreme Court, however, may have made its assumption for the purpose of argument; the assumption, in its view, did not change the result of the case. The Court cannot make the same assumption if it requires reversal of Riggins' conviction.

Finally, we did not grant certiorari to determine whether the Nevada courts had made the findings…to support forced administration of a drug. ...

B.

We have held that plaintiffs may receive civil remedies for all manner of constitutional violations under § 1983. This Court, however, has reversed criminal convictions only on the basis of two kinds of constitutional deprivations: those "which occur during the presentation of the case" to the trier of fact, and those which cause a "structural defect affecting the framework" of the trial. The Court does not reveal why it considers a deprivation of a liberty interest in avoiding unwanted medication to fall into either category of reversible error. Even if Nevada failed to make the findings necessary to support forced administration of Mellaril, this failure, without more, would not constitute a trial error or a flaw in the trial mechanism. Although Riggins might be entitled to other remedies, he has no right to have his conviction reversed.

...Because Riggins had a full and fair trial in this case, I would affirm the Nevada Supreme Court.

NOTES AND QUERIES

The Court actually did not decide "whether" the administration of involuntary medication during trial violates rights guaranteed by the Sixth and Fourteenth Amendments, but rather that such medication "may well" violate these rights. The narrow holding seems to be that administering involuntary medications violates constitutional rights if not justified by an appropriate government interest. The Court stopped short of clearly articulating either the circumstances under or standard by which the Court could medicate a defendant solely to render him competent for legal proceedings, such as, in this case, standing trial. If this view of the case is correct, what guidance does the case provide lower courts? Can medications be used to help defendants gain competency?

The Court fails to distinguish government actions involving the administration of involuntary psychotropic medications to a detainee who has been convicted of a crime and the administration of involuntary psychotropic medications to a defendant who is on trial. The Court does note that involuntary medications generally infringe on a detainee's interest in refusing medical treatment, which the government's interests in preventing harm to the detainee and others can justify. During a trial, however, involuntary medications infringe on the detainee's right to a fair trial, which government interests may not justify. Justice Kennedy's concurrence provides ample reason to suspect that forced medication may interfere with a defendant's trial rights. Although the record in this case was not developed enough to explore these issues in depth, commentators have offered three reasons for concerns which admittedly raise complex matters and elusive answers.

The first notable concern involves the impact of medication on the ability of the defendant to exercise his trial rights. It does seem that medications can interfere with a defendant's ability to exercise trial rights by producing feelings of restlessness and anxiety, inducing sedation, diminishing awareness of and interest in the trial and its consequences, and disrupting memory. As a result, involuntary medication may interfere with the defendant's general right to be present, as well as with his more specific rights to receive effective assistance of counsel, to confront witnesses, to present evidence, and to testify on his own behalf. On the other hand, it may well be that involuntary psychotropic medications actually enhance rather than diminish a defendant's ability to exercise procedural rights. As *Riggins* reveals, a trial must be fair, but it need not be perfect. As we already have seen, courts generally can cure trial defects, even those undeniably prejudicial to the defense, by allowing such measures as instructions to the jury or the admission of additional evidence, including the testimony of expert and lay witnesses. As we also have seen, however, some defects do create prejudice that so undermines the fairness of the trial that it renders curative measures insufficient. A key question, then, is whether jury instructions, witness testimony, or any other additional measures may cure the prejudicial effects of administering involuntary psychotropic drugs to a defendant during trial. What do you make of this concern?

A second important concern involves the impact of a defendant's medication on the jury. Involuntary medication could prejudice fact finders' views of the defendant's credibility and impact their views of the defendant's demeanor. The influence of antipsychotic medications may make the defendant appear emotionally unresponsive, bored, nervous, or restless. Arguably, this may mean that the government is manipulating the jury's impression of the defendant in a way that may inappropriately influence the verdict. On the other hand, the effect of involuntary psychotropic drugs on a defendant's demeanor is amenable to cure. One cure for the government's manipulation of the evidence involves providing juries with relevant instructions about the medication's effects. Another cure would allow the defendant to present additional evidence about the effects of involuntary psychotropic drugs. Do you find these cures sufficiently effective to warrant involuntary treatment? Are these cures even necessary?

A last concern involves the manner medication impacts a defendant's mental state. A defendant's mental state at the time of the offense almost always is relevant in a criminal trial, given the prosecution's usual burden of proving that the defendant had the requisite *mens rea* to be convicted of the charged offense. It also, of course, is an issue when an accused may be excused from legal responsibility for behaviors that would otherwise constitute criminal offenses, such as the insanity defense and other defenses that reduce culpability based on a defendant's abnormal mental state at the time he committed the offense. Medications alter the evidence of a defendant's mental state in two ways. First, medications affect the way that a defendant, if he chooses to testify, describes his mental state at the time of the offense. Antipsychotic medications alleviate those symptoms, such as delusions and hallucinations, that would be most likely to convince a jury that the defendant was insane at the time of the offense. Second, medications can alter the defendant's demeanor during the trial; a defendant may appear completely well. This appearance at the time of the trial also will make a jury less likely to believe the defendant's claim that a serious mental illness actually is relevant to his defense. Again, however, the impact of involuntary psychotropic medications on a defendant's ability to present evidence in support of a claim about his mental state at the time of the offense is also an evidentiary problem that might potentially be cured by jury instructions or additional evidence. Some have suggested that the defendant be allowed to present to the jury some type of record, such as a videotape, of the defendant made prior to initiating medication. In the alternative, the defendant might be allowed to discontinue the medications for a brief period during trial. What do you make of these suggestions? See Henry A. Dlugacz, *Riggins v. Nevada*: Towards a unified standard for a prisoner's right to refuse medication?, 17 L. and Psych. Rev. 41 (1993); David M. Siegel, Albert J. Grudzinskas, Jr., and Debra A. Pinals, Old law meets new medicine: Revisiting involuntary psychotropic medication of the criminal defendant, 2001 Wis. L. Rev. 307; and Dora W. Klein, Trial rights and psychotropic drugs: The case against administering involuntary medications to a defendant during trial, 55 Vand. L. Rev. 165 (2002).

It may be argued that any prejudice caused by psychotropic medications can be addressed properly as a competency to stand trial issue. Do you find that proposition persuasive? This is what Justice Thomas noted in his dissenting opinion. Recall that courts interpret the competency to stand trial standard very narrowly, as essentially requiring only a basic cognitive ability to understand and assist in the proceedings. This narrow interpretation may mean that drug-induced impairments in a defendant's emotional, motivational, attentional, or behavioral ability to participate are unlikely even to trigger a review of the defendant's competency to stand trial, much less support a finding of incompetence. Should that matter? Do you agree with the view that the defendant was competent, therefore he had a fair trial? What do you make of the claim that the defendant had started to use the drugs voluntarily? Do you think he had a fair trial?

THE COURT REVISITS RIGGINS IN *SELL V. UNITED STATES*

Recall that the *Riggins* Court indicated that the constitutionality of forcibly medicating a nondangerous defendant to preserve other law enforcement interests remained unsettled. In *Sell v. United States*, 123 S. Ct. 2174 (2003), the Court held that the government may, in certain circumstances, forcibly administer antipsychotic medications to a mentally ill criminal defendant to render him competent to stand trial for serious crimes. In that case, dentist Charles Sell, following at least fourteen years of mental illness, was charged with defrauding health care insurance providers. After release on bond, a grand jury indicted Sell and his wife on fifty-six counts of mail fraud, six counts of Medicaid fraud, and one count of money laundering. At a bond revocation hearing six months later, Sell lashed out erratically at the magistrate. His bond was revoked, and a grand jury indicted Sell in April 1998 on charges of conspiring and attempting to kill a witness and an FBI agent. Early the following year, Sell requested a new hearing to determine his competence. The magistrate found that Sell was incompetent to stand trial and ordered that he be hospitalized at a medical center for federal prisoners to determine whether he would be able to regain competence.

At a hearing, a reviewing psychiatrist granted the center staff's request to administer antipsychotic medications to Sell against his will, finding that medication was necessary to treat Sell's "dangerous" delusional disorder and would restore his trial competence. A Bureau of Prisons official affirmed the psychiatrist's determination on substantially the same grounds. The magistrate held another hearing to consider further evidence, including a "boundary-breaching incident" between Sell and a nurse. The magistrate then authorized the medication. On appeal, the district court reversed the magistrate's finding regarding Sell's dangerousness, but affirmed the order authorizing administration of the medication. The court held that the medication was medically appropriate, was necessary to restore Sell's trial competence, and served the compelling state interest in adjudicating the serious charges against Sell. Both sides appealed; the Circuit court affirmed.

The Supreme Court vacated and remanded. The majority, inferring from *Harper* and *Riggins* a four-part framework, held that the Fifth Amendment, on "rare" occasions, permits forced administration of antipsychotic drugs to render a defendant competent to stand trial. Id. at 2184-86. The Court provided a four-pronged standard. First, though the government interest in trying a defendant for a serious crime generally is "important," that interest is subject to a fact-specific inquiry. The Court observed that "special circumstances," such as civil commitment rather than release of an intransigent defendant, could diminish the government's interest. Second, forced medication must be "substantially likely to render the defendant competent to stand trial" and "substantially unlikely to have side effects" that would compromise "the defendant's ability to assist counsel." Third, forced medication must be "necessary to further [the government's] interests," such that "less intrusive treatments are unlikely to achieve substantially the same results." Finally, the administration must be "medically appropriate, [that is], in the patient's best medical interest in light of his medical condition." The Court further concluded that courts analyzing forced medication should "ordinarily" begin not with trial competence, but with "other Harper-type grounds" – namely, the more "objective and manageable" consideration of a defendant's dangerousness. Begrudgingly accepting the determination below that Sell was not dangerous, the Court vacated the circuit court's holding that Sell was properly medicated. Specifically, the Court noted that the magistrate had not approved forced medication on "trial competence grounds alone," expert witnesses had failed "to focus upon trial competence," and the lower courts had not considered either that Sell had already been confined "for a long period of time" or that "his refusal [of drugs] might result in further lengthy confinement." Id. at 2187. Do you find that *Sell* cures the many inadequacies left by *Riggins*?

THE CASE OF RUSSELL EUGENE WESTON, JR.

In 1996, Weston, diagnosed with paranoid schizophrenia years earlier, arrived at the Central Intelligence Agency headquarters just outside of Washington, D.C. and introduced himself as an operative named "the Moon." In suit-and-tie, he calmly explained the Ruby Surveillance System that he had created while working at NASA. Constructed of a ruby, a watch, and a small wheel, this covert satellite system could reverse the march of time. Fifty minutes later, after explaining his cloning at birth, but never threatening the life of the President, Weston was sent on his way. Two years later, on July 24, 1998, Weston returned to the national capital area – this time armed and ready to stop the work of the Ruby Surveillance System. Cannibals had overused the system, he believed, and had spawned the development and spread of "Black Heva," a plague-like disease that could kill over one-third of America's population.

Weston was determined to reach the override switch located in the "great safe of the U.S. Senate" and halt the spread of "Black Heva."

Running through the security magnetometers positioned in the entrance of the U.S. Capitol Building, Weston opened fire with a .38-caliber revolver, fatally shooting two police officers. He was charged with two counts of capital murder, attempted murder, and firearms offenses. Once incarcerated immediately after his deadly rampage and quickly called the "Capital Killer," Weston refused to take antipsychotic medication to tame the symptoms of his schizophrenia, and a D.C. District Court Judge declared Weston incompetent for trial. For more than three years, the federal courts in the District of Columbia struggled with the question of whether Weston could be compelled to take psychotropic medications involuntarily. The government argued that the medications were necessary both to prevent Weston from harming himself and others and also to render Weston competent to stand trial. Weston's attorneys argued that compelling Weston to take psychotropic medications would violate Weston's liberty interest in refusing medical treatment and his right to a fair trial. At what was thought of as the end of the legal drama, the D.C. Circuit Court of Appeals eventually decided that government interests justified administering involuntary psychotropic medications to render Weston competent to stand trial.

Finding for the government, however, did not resolve the problem. The case reveals the risk of using the antipsychotic medication to pull an insane defendant out his insane condition. A new competency hearing was held for Weston in November of 2002, ten months after he began receiving forcible medication for his psychosis. Weston was rolled into court in a wheelchair because he had gained so much weight, as a side effect of the medications, that he could not walk under his own power. Weston's prison psychiatrist stated that she expected even more weight gain. At the hearing, Weston's lawyers related their client's considered projection for the ultimate resolution of his case. Weston thinks that the judge is an escaped alien prisoner from Mozambique and that "the case will be over soon because his honor will be arrested." Nevertheless, the prosecutor requested that Weston be medicated for paranoid schizophrenia for at least another year. See *United States v. Weston*, 255 F.3d 873 (D.C. Cir. 2001), petition for cert. filed, Sept. 5, 2001 (No. 01-6161). Do you find, as some now argue, that Weston's case exemplifies how involuntary medication constitutes unjustifiable medical experimentation on unwilling subjects? See Aimee Feinberg, Forcible medication of mentally ill criminal defendants: The case of Russell Eugene Weston, Jr., 54 Stan. L. Rev. 769 (2002); and Aaron M. Nance, Balking at buying what the Eighth Circuit is *Sell*-ing: *United States v. Sell* and the involuntary medication of incompetent, non-dangerous, pretrial detainees cloaked with the presumption of innocence, 71 UMKC L. Rev. 685 (2003).

EXCUSES AND DIMINISHED CAPACITIES: SANITY

SHANNON v. UNITED STATES
512 U.S. 573 (1994)

JUSTICE THOMAS delivered the opinion of the Court.

In this case, we consider whether a federal district court is required to instruct the jury regarding the consequences to the defendant of a verdict of "not guilty by reason of insanity," either under the Insanity Defense Reform Act of 1984 or as a matter of general federal practice. We conclude that such an instruction is not required, and therefore affirm.

I.

A.

Prior to the enactment of the Insanity Defense Reform Act of 1984 (IDRA or Act), federal courts generally did not recognize a verdict of "not guilty by reason of insanity" (NGI). Defendants who mounted a successful insanity defense – that is, those who raised a reasonable doubt as to their sanity at the time of the offense – were simply found "not guilty." In addition, there was no general federal civil commitment procedure available to ensure that an insanity acquittee would receive proper care and treatment. Only in the District of Columbia was a defendant who successfully presented an insanity defense to a federal criminal charge subject to a federal commitment process – a process governed by a 1955 congressional enactment. Elsewhere, federal authorities were forced to rely on the willingness of state authorities to institute civil commitment proceedings. Reliance on state cooperation was "at best a partial solution to a serious problem," however, and federal courts "time and again . . . decried this gaping statutory hole."

Before the IDRA was enacted, the Federal Courts of Appeals generally disapproved of instructing the jury concerning the post-trial consequences of an insanity acquittal. Thus, jurors typically were given no information with regard to what would happen to a defendant acquitted by reason of insanity. The courts in general gave two reasons for disapproving such instructions. First, they pointed out that, given the absence of a federal commitment procedure, the consequences of an insanity acquittal were far from certain. Second, they concluded that such instructions would run afoul of the well-established principle that a jury is to base its verdict on the evidence before it, without regard to the possible consequences of the verdict.

The acquittal of John Hinckley on all charges stemming from his attempt on President Reagan's life, coupled with the ensuing public focus on the insanity defense, prompted Congress to undertake a comprehensive overhaul of the insanity defense as it operated in the federal courts. The result of this effort was the IDRA. In the IDRA, Congress made insanity an affirmative defense to be proved by the defendant by clear and convincing evidence, and created a special verdict of "not guilty only by reason of insanity." In addition, Congress filled the "statutory hole" that had been identified by federal courts, by creating a comprehensive civil commitment procedure. Under that procedure, a defendant found NGI is held in custody pending a court hearing, which must occur within 40 days of the verdict. At the conclusion of the hearing, the court determines whether the defendant should be hospitalized or released.

B.

At about 4 a.m. on August 25, 1990, a police officer stopped petitioner Terry Lee Shannon, a convicted felon, on a street in Tupelo, Mississippi. For reasons not explained in the record before us, the officer asked Shannon to accompany him to the station house to speak with a detective. After telling the officer that he did not want to live anymore, Shannon walked across the street, pulled a pistol from his coat, and shot himself in the chest.

Shannon survived his suicide attempt and was indicted for unlawful possession of a firearm by a felon...At trial, he raised the insanity defense, and asked the District Court to instruct the jury that he would be involuntarily committed if the jury returned an NGI verdict. The District Court refused to give Shannon's proposed charge. Instead, it instructed the jury "to apply the law as [instructed] regardless of the consequence," and that "punishment . . . should not enter your consideration or discussion." The jury returned a guilty verdict.

The Court of Appeals for the Fifth Circuit affirmed Shannon's conviction. The court noted that under its pre-IDRA precedent, juries were not to be instructed concerning the consequences of an insanity acquittal. Turning to the text of the IDRA, the court observed that Congress had "said nothing about informing juries of the consequences" of an NGI verdict. Because there was no "statutory requirement" to the contrary, the court "adhered to the established axiom that it is inappropriate for a jury to consider or be informed about the consequences of its verdict."

We granted certiorari in order to consider whether federal district courts are required to instruct juries with regard to the consequences of an NGI verdict.

II.

It is well established that when a jury has no sentencing function, it should be admonished to "reach its verdict without regard to what sentence might be imposed." The principle that juries are not to consider the consequences of their verdicts is a reflection of the basic division of labor in our legal system between judge and jury. The jury's function is to find the facts and to decide whether, on those facts, the defendant is guilty of the crime charged. The judge, by contrast, imposes sentence on the defendant after the jury has arrived at a guilty verdict. Information regarding the consequences of a verdict is therefore irrelevant to the jury's task. Moreover, providing jurors sentencing information invites them to ponder matters that are not within their province, distracts them from their factfinding responsibilities, and creates a strong possibility of confusion.

Despite these familiar precepts, Shannon contends that an instruction informing the jury of the consequences of an NGI verdict is required under the IDRA whenever requested by the defendant. He also argues that such an instruction is required as a matter of general federal criminal practice. We address each argument in turn.

A.

To determine whether Congress intended courts to depart from the principle that jurors are not to be informed of the consequences of their verdicts, we turn first, as always, to the text of the statute. The IDRA refers to the subject of jury instructions only once, and that reference occurs in its description of the possible verdicts a jury may return. Under the Act, "the jury shall be instructed to find . . . the defendant – (1) guilty; (2) not guilty; or (3) not guilty only by reason of insanity." The text of the Act gives no indication that jurors are to be instructed regarding the consequences of an NGI verdict. As the court below observed, the Act "leaves the jury solely with its customary determination of guilt or innocence." The Act's text thus gives no support to Shannon's contention that an instruction informing the jury of the consequences of an NGI verdict is required.

Shannon asserts, however, that an express statutory directive is not necessary because, by modeling the IDRA on D. C. Code Ann. Congress impliedly adopted the ... practice ... of instructing the jury as to the consequences of an NGI verdict...

Members of this Court have expressed differing views regarding the role that legislative history should play in statutory interpretation. ... We agree with the District of Columbia Circuit that "courts have no authority to enforce [a] principle gleaned solely from legislative history that has no statutory reference point." We thus conclude that there is no support in the Act for the instruction Shannon seeks.

B.

Setting the Act aside, Shannon argues that the instruction he proposes is required as a matter of general federal criminal practice. Presumably, Shannon asks us to invoke our supervisory power over the federal courts. According to Shannon, the instruction is necessary because jurors are generally unfamiliar with the consequences of an NGI verdict, and may erroneously believe that a defendant who is found NGI will be immediately released into society. Jurors who are under this mistaken impression, Shannon continues, may also fear that the defendant, if released, would pose a danger to the community. Shannon concludes that such jurors, in order to ensure that the defendant will not be released, may be tempted to return a guilty verdict in a case in which an NGI verdict would be appropriate.

Even assuming Shannon is correct that some jurors will harbor the mistaken belief that defendants found NGI will be released into society immediately – an assumption that is open to debate – the jury in his case was instructed "to apply the law as [instructed] regardless of the consequence," and that "punishment … should not enter your consideration or discussion." That an NGI verdict was an option here gives us no reason to depart from "the almost invariable assumption of the law that jurors follow their instructions."...

We also are not persuaded that the instruction Shannon proposes would allay the fears of the misinformed juror about whom Shannon is concerned. "If the members of a jury are so fearful of a particular defendant's release that they would violate their oaths by convicting [the defendant] solely in order to ensure that he is not set free, it is questionable whether they would be reassured by anything short of an instruction strongly suggesting that the defendant, if found NGI, would very likely be civilly committed for a lengthy period." An accurate instruction about the consequences of an NGI verdict, however, would give no such assurance. Under the IDRA, a postverdict hearing must be held within 40 days to determine whether the defendant should be released immediately into society or hospitalized. Thus, the only mandatory period of confinement for an insanity acquittee is the period between the verdict and the hearing. Instead of encouraging a juror to return an NGI verdict, as Shannon predicts, such information might have the opposite effect – that is, a juror might vote to convict in order to eliminate the possibility that a dangerous defendant could be released after 40 days or less. Whether the instruction works to the advantage or disadvantage of a defendant is, of course, somewhat beside the point. Our central concern here is that the inevitable result of such an instruction would be to draw the jury's attention toward the very thing – the possible consequences of its verdict – it should ignore.

Moreover, Shannon offers us no principled way to limit the availability of instructions detailing the consequences of a verdict to cases in which an NGI defense is raised. Jurors may be as unfamiliar with other aspects of the criminal sentencing process as they are with NGI verdicts. But, as a general matter, jurors are not informed of mandatory minimum or maximum sentences, nor are they instructed regarding probation, parole, or the sentencing range accompanying a lesser included offense. Because it is conceivable that some jurors might harbor misunderstandings with regard to these sentencing options, a district court, under Shannon's reasoning, might be obligated to give juries information regarding these possibilities as well. In short, if we pursue the logic of Shannon's position, the rule against informing jurors of the consequences of their verdicts would soon be swallowed by the exceptions.

Finally, Congress' recent action in this area counsels hesitation in invoking our supervisory powers. As noted above, the IDRA was the product of a thorough and exhaustive review of the insanity defense as used in the federal courts. Given the comprehensive nature of the task before it, Congress certainly could have included a provision requiring the instruction Shannon seeks. For whatever reason, Congress chose not to do so. Under these circumstances, we are reluctant to depart from well-established principles of criminal practice without more explicit guidance from Congress.

Because the District Court properly refused to give the instruction Shannon requested, we affirm.

So ordered.

JUSTICE STEVENS, with whom JUSTICE BLACKMUN joins, dissenting.

A rule that has minimized the risk of injustice for almost 40 years should not be abandoned without good reason. In 1957, shortly after Congress enacted the statute providing for civil commitment of persons found not guilty by reason of insanity in trials conducted in the District of Columbia, the Court of Appeals, sitting in banc, considered whether juries should be instructed about the significance of that provision. Recognizing that an uninformed jury might erroneously find an insane defendant guilty to avoid the risk that a dangerous individual would otherwise go free, the court held that such an instruction should be given. In an opinion jointly authored by Judge Prettyman and then-Judge Warren Burger, the court explained that the doctrine that the jury has no concern with the consequences of a verdict "does not apply in the problem before us"...

When Congress enacted the Insanity Defense Reform Act of 1984 (Act), it established a civil commitment process for the entire federal system, thus making the basis for the District of Columbia Circuit's holding in Lyles applicable to all federal courts. The Act's legislative history unmistakably demonstrates that the Act's sponsors assumed that the Lyles precedent would thereafter be followed nationwide. That assumption does not have the force of a statutory mandate, but it verifies that thoughtful legislators familiar with the issue believed that precedent to be entirely sound. That this Court should now decide to change an established rule that Congress accepted and that protects defendants meaningfully against an obvious risk of injustice is startling – particularly when that change is for no reason other than a perceived inconsistency with another rule that is generally protective of defendants' rights. A far wiser disposition would allow the defendant to choose between the two rules, rather than tilt the scales to favor the prosecutor in every case.

...When there is a realistic danger that jurors' deliberations may be distorted by an incorrect assumption about those consequences, elementary notions of fairness demand that a clarifying instruction be given.

The Court suggests that the instruction might actually prejudice the defendant. That argument lacks merit, as there is no need to give the instruction unless the defendant requests it. ...

The Court also contends that jurors today are more familiar with the consequences of a verdict of not guilty by reason of insanity ... No one has suggested, however, that the level of understanding even approximates that of the conventional choice between "guilty" and "not guilty." Indeed, one recent study concluded that "the public overestimates the extent to which insanity acquittees are released upon acquittal and underestimates the extent to which they are hospitalized as well as the length of confinement of insanity acquittees who are sent to mental hospitals." As long as significant numbers of potential jurors believe that an insanity acquittee will be released at once, the instruction serves a critical purpose. Yet even if, as the Court seems prepared to assume, all jurors are already knowledgeable about the issue, surely telling them what they already know can do no harm.

An increasing number of States that have considered the question endorses use of the instruction, as has the American Bar Association. Judge Newman's succinct assessment of the pros and cons is exactly right: "There is no reason to keep this information from the jurors and every reason to make them aware of it."

I respectfully dissent.

Notes and Queries

The case provides an overview of the federalization of the insanity defense. The key concern here, however, involves whether a jury should be informed that the not guilty verdict would result in civil commitment. The Court reasoned that there was no reason to provide an exception to the general rule that jurors are not to advert to the punishment consequences of their verdicts. The Court also noted that it simply could not provide any assurance to jurors given that it was not clear how long the defendant would be civilly detained.

What do you suppose uninstructed jurors assume to be the consequences of not guilty by reason of insanity verdicts? The Court reasons that jurors may hold mistaken beliefs and that such beliefs do not justify instructions. Fair? Does the dissent have the better argument?

RESEARCH NOTE ON VERDICT OPTIONS

Although the Court tends to distinguish the penalty phase from the guilt phase of trials, the charge does seem to impact verdict/sentencing options. Collectively, studies suggest that allowing juries the opportunity to convict the defendant on a lesser charge substantially impacts their verdicts. The first study to examine this issue compared a condition with the verdict options "not guilty" (NG) and "guilty of premeditated murder" (G) to another condition with the choice of "not guilty," "guilty of unpremeditated murder," or "guilty of premeditated murder." The resulting conviction rate was lower when only two verdict options were available, but sentence length was unaffected. V. Lee Hamilton, Obedience and responsibility: A jury simulation, 36 J. of Personality and Soc. Psych. 126 (1978). Another study examined the "not guilty by reason of insanity" (NGRI) and "guilty but mentally ill" (GBMI) verdict options using three verdict option sets: G/NG, G/NG/NGRI, and G/NG/GBMI/NGRI. Verdict options interacted with the strength of evidence against the defendant such that, when evidence was strong, all juries convicted with two traditional options, most convicted with the addition of NGRI in the three-option set, and all chose GBMI in the four-option set. Conversely, when evidence was weak, all juries acquitted in the two-option set, all chose NGRI in the three-option set, and most chose GBMI when four verdict options were available. Jeffrey C. Savitsky and William D. Lindblom, The impact of the Guilty But Mentally Ill verdict on juror decisions: An empirical analysis, 16 J. of Appl. Soc. Psych. 686 (1986). Finally, the most recent study found that the option of convicting on a lesser included charge resulted in a higher conviction rate when "reasonable doubt" was not defined but not when reasonable doubt was defined as being "firmly convinced." Chantal Mees Koch and Dennis J. Devine, Effects of reasonable doubt and inclusion of a lesser charge on jury verdicts, 23 L. and Hum. Beh. 653 (1999). With respect to sentencing options, two studies failed to find an effect associated with the severity of a mandatory sentence attached to conviction. One study found that mandatory sentence length (0-2 years vs. 15 or more years) did not affect verdicts, but juries deliberated longer when the mandatory sentence was not commensurate with the victim's suffering. James H. Davis, Norbet L. Kerr, Garold S. Strasser, David Meek, and Robert W. Holt, Victim consequences, sentence severity, and decision processes in mock juries, 18 Organiz'l Beh. and Hum. Performance 346 (1977). Similarly, a more recent study found a negligible difference in conviction rates as a function of sentence severity ($ 500 fine vs. 25 years in prison). Keith E. Niedermeier, Irwin A. Horowitz and Norbert L. Kerr, Informing jurors of their nullification power: A route to a just verdict or judicial chaos?, 23 L. and Hum. Beh. 331, 333-48 (1999). Juries thus appear fairly responsive to verdict options, but the impact of verdict options likely interacts with the strength of evidence against the defendant.

A related group of studies examined the impact of varying the standard of proof the prosecution/plaintiff must meet for a jury to convict or assign liability to the defendant. Most notably, Horowitz and Kirkpatrick examined five different supplementary definitions of reasonable doubt and found that one (involving the phrase "firmly convinced") associated with more discussion of the evidence and instructions and fewer convictions when the prosecution's case was weak, but these differences disappeared when the case was strong. Irwin A. Horowitz and Laird C. Kirkpatrick, A concept in search of a definition: The effects of reasonable doubt instructions on certainty of guilt standards and jury verdicts, 20 L. and Hum. Beh. 655 (1996). Building on Horowitz and Kirkpatrick's work, Koch and Devine found that wording associated with reasonable doubt interacted with the availability of a lesser verdict option to affect jury verdicts. When reasonable doubt was defined in terms of being "firmly convinced," there was no impact of lesser included charge on conviction rates; however, when reasonable doubt was not explicitly defined and the lesser included charge was available, more convictions occurred compared with when it was not available. Chantal Mees Koch and Dennis J. Devine, Effects of reasonable doubt and inclusion of a lesser charge on jury verdicts, 23 L. and Hum. Beh. 653 (1999). In sum, despite meaningful differences in content, the wording associated with the standard of proof appears to substantially impact jury verdicts.

NOTE ON THE INSANITY DEFENSE

One of the most intriguing aspects of the insanity defense is the extent to which the public has adopted numerous myths about the insanity plea. One leading commentator identified the following myths, examined relevant empirical research and concluded that all were false: The insanity defense is overused, use of the insanity defense is limited to murder cases, there is no risk to the defendant who pleads insanity, Not Guilty by Reason of Insanity (NGRI) acquittees are quickly released from custody, NGRI acquittees spend much less time in custody than do defendants convicted of the same offenses, criminal defendants who plead insanity are usually faking, most insanity defense trials feature "battles of the experts," criminal defense attorneys-perhaps inappropriately-employ the insanity defense solely to "beat the rap." See Michael L. Perlin, Unpacking the myths: The symbolism mythology of insanity defense jurisprudence, 40 Case W. Res. L. Rev. 599 (1990). Other misconceptions, aside from empirical myths, include: that being insane necessarily means that one's appearance is distinguishable from sane individuals and that insanity should not be sufficient to escape the punishment of an otherwise guilty individual. See Michael L. Perlin, The Jurisprudence of the Insanity Defense 232-33 (1994).

The insanity defense is raised in only about 1% of felony cases in the U.S. and, although success rates vary widely across jurisdiction, it is successful only in 26% of cases where it is raised. Lisa A. Callahan, Henry J. Steadman, Maragaret A. McGreevy, and Pamela C. Robbins, The volume and characteristics of insanity defense pleas: An eight-state study, 19 Bull. of the Am. Academy of Psychiatry and L. 331 (1991). One might expect, then, that cases resulting in successful insanity acquittals would represent clear-cut cases of mentally disordered offenders. Yet, overlap exists between those found guilty and those found insane in both diagnosis and psychiatric history.

One leading study compared male insanity acquittees with two groups: (1) a random sample of convicted offenders who had been sent for pretrial psychiatric assessments and (2) a sample of convicted offenders matched for committed offenses. Compared with the randomly selected convicted offenders, the insanity acquittees were much more likely to have committed murder or attempted murder (74% vs. 7%), more likely to be diagnosed as psychotic (75% vs. 41%), and less likely to be diagnosed as personality disordered (13% vs. 46%) than other offenders. Compared with convicted offenders matched for severity of offense, the insanity acquittees were even more likely to be diagnosed as psychotic (75% vs. 13%) and even less likely to be diagnosed as personality disordered (13% vs. 65%). Lastly, the insanity acquittees had, on average, fewer prior psychiatric admissions than the random control group. Marnie E. Rice and Grant T. Harris, The predictors of insanity acquittal, 13 Int'l J. of L. and Psychiatry 217 (1990).

Some may believe that, once an offender has been found guilty or not guilty by reason of insanity, the verdict impacts placement, length of stay, and treatment. Yet, verdicts have little impact on those factors. Although most insanity acquittees are sent to a hospital (usually to secure hospitals) and most convicted persons are sent to prison, little difference may exist between secure hospitals and prisons. Although insanity acquittees may require treatment for their mental disorder, there may be no effective treatments available. And even if available, patients may refuse the treatment. Likewise, even when effective treatments are known and patients are willing to participate, the programs may be unavailable in institutions. Offenders also actually could get better treatment in prison; for treatment programs are often available inside prison. See Eric Cullen, The Grendon reconviction study: Part 1, 90 Prison Service J. 35 (1993). Similarly, for both insanity acquittees and convicted offenders, length of stay strongly relates to seriousness of the offense and offense history. Grant T. Harris, Marnie E. Rice, and Catherine A. Cormier, Length of detention in matched groups of insanity acquittees and convicted offenders, 14 Int'l J. of L. and Psychiatry 223 (1991). These studies also show that, especially for serious offenses, the two groups do not differ on average lengths of stay. Why do you suppose there is such a large investment made in determining to which system the patient should be attached when the consequences vary so little?

Review Problem on Applying Legal Standards

Serravo was charged in a multi-count information with crimes of attempt to commit first degree murder after deliberation, assault in the first degree, and the commission of crimes of violence. The charges arose out of the stabbing of his wife, Joyce Serravo. After the charges were filed, Serravo entered a plea of not guilty by reason of insanity and was thereafter examined by several psychiatrists.

The evidence at the insanity trial established that the stabbing occurred under the following circumstances. Serravo arrived home at approximately 12:30 a.m. on May 10. After sitting in the kitchen and reading the Bible, he went upstairs to the bedroom where his wife was sleeping, stood over her for a few minutes, and then stabbed her in the back just below the shoulder blade. When his wife awoke, Serravo told her that she had been stabbed by an intruder and that she should stay in bed while he went downstairs to call for medical help. Police officers were later dispatched to the home. Serravo told the officers that he had gone to the King Soopers store and had left the garage door open, that the door leading to the house from the garage was unlocked, that when he returned home and was reading the Bible he heard his front door slam, and that he went upstairs to check on his wife and children and saw that his wife was bleeding from a wound in her back. Serravo signed a consent to search his home and gave the police clothes that he was wearing at the time of his discovery of his wife's injury.

Several weeks after the stabbing, Serravo's wife found letters written by Serravo. In these letters Serravo admitted the stabbing, stating that "our marriage was severed on Mother's Day when I put the knife in your back," that "I have gone to be with Jehovah in heaven for three and one-half days," and that "I must return for there is still a great deal of work to be done." After reading the letters, Serravo's wife telephoned him in order to confront him about the letters. Serravo told his wife that God had told him to stab her in order to sever their marriage bond. Mrs. Serravo informed the police of these facts and Serravo was thereafter arrested and charged.

The prosecution presented expert psychiatric testimony on Serravo's sanity at the time of the stabbing. A resident psychiatrist in training examined Serravo pursuant to a court ordered evaluation of his mental state. Serravo gave the doctor a history of having worked on a plan, inspired by his relationship to God, to establish a multi-million dollar sports complex called Purely Professionals. This facility, according to Serravo, would enable him to achieve his goal of teaching people the path to perfection. On the night of the stabbing, Serravo, according to the history given to the psychiatrist, was excited because he finally believed that he had received some positive encouragement in his endeavor from fellow union members, but he was discouraged by some inner "evil spirits" who kept raising troublesome questions about how he would deal with his wife's lack of encouragement and support. The psychiatrist diagnosed Serravo as suffering either from an organic delusional disorder related to left temporal lobe damage as a result of an automobile accident some years ago or paranoid schizophrenia. Either diagnosis would adequately account for Serravo's delusional belief that he had a privileged relationship with God as the result of which he was in direct communication with God. The expert testified that Serravo was operating under this delusional system when he stabbed his wife and these delusions caused him to believe that his act was morally justified. The expert, however, was of the view that Serravo, because he was aware that the act of stabbing was contrary to law, was sane at the time of the stabbing.

Serravo presented four psychiatrists and a clinical psychologist on the issue of his legal insanity. The first psychiatrist was of the opinion that on the night of the stabbing Serravo was under the psychotic delusion that it was his divine mission to kill his wife and that he was morally justified in stabbing her because God had told him to do so. The psychiatrist was not quite certain whether Serravo's psychotic disorder was paranoid schizophrenia, a paranoid delusional disorder, or an organic delusional disorder. Although uncertain of the exact diagnostic label applicable to Serravo, the expert was of the opinion that

Serravo's mental illness made it impossible for him to distinguish right from wrong even though Serravo was probably aware that such conduct was legally wrong.

Another psychiatrist also testified. This psychiatrist actually was the supervisor of the prosecution witness who also had supervised the examination and made an independent evaluation of Serravo's mental condition. It was his opinion that Serravo was suffering from paranoid schizophrenia at the time of the stabbing and was laboring under the paranoid delusion that his wife stood in the way of his divine mission of completing the large sports complex, that Serravo believed that the stabbing was the right thing to do, and that Serravo, as a result of his mental illness, was unable to distinguish right from wrong with respect to the stabbing. Two other psychiatrists, offered the opinion that Serravo, at the time of the stabbing, was suffering from paranoid schizophrenia and a paranoid delusion about God which so affected his cognitive ability as to render him incapable of distinguishing right from wrong as normal people would be able to do in accordance with societal standards of morality.

A clinical psychologist also testified about Serravo's mental condition at the time of the stabbing. Having conducted extensive psychological testing of Serravo, she was able to offer an opinion on Serravo's reality testing, his emotional reactivity, and his volition, all of which were relevant to the functioning of his conscience. The doctor was of the opinion that Serravo's conscience was based on a false belief or delusion about his magical powers as a result of his direct communication with God. Serravo, in the doctor's view, was suffering from a psychotic disorder that rendered him incapable of distinguishing right from wrong at the time of the stabbing. Although she acknowledged that Serravo appeared to cover up his conduct when the police arrived at his home, the doctor explained that conduct as the product of a small part of his still intact reality testing. In her opinion, Serravo did so because police would not understand his complex reasoning. Explore how a jury would rule based on the following standard: a person "is not accountable who is so diseased or defective in mind at the time of the commission of the act as to be incapable of distinguishing right from wrong, with respect to the act." Note that this is the *Mc'Naughten* test. See *People v. Serravo*, 823 P.2d 128 (Col.1992), where the jury found the defendant not guilty by reason of insanity.

EXCUSES AND DIMINISHED CAPACITIES: SUBSTANCE ABUSE

MONTANA v. EGELHOFF
518 U.S. 37 (1996)

JUSTICE SCALIA announced the judgment of the Court and delivered an opinion, in which THE CHIEF JUSTICE, JUSTICE KENNEDY, and JUSTICE THOMAS join.

We consider in this case whether the Due Process Clause is violated by Montana Code Annotated § 45-2-203, which provides, in relevant part, that voluntary intoxication "may not be taken into consideration in determining the existence of a mental state which is an element of [a criminal] offense."

I.

In July 1992, while camping out in the Yaak region of northwestern Montana to pick mushrooms, respondent made friends with Roberta Pavola and John Christenson, who were doing the same. On Sunday, July 12, the three sold the mushrooms they had collected and spent the rest of the day and evening drinking, in bars and at a private party in Troy, Montana. Some time after 9 p.m., they left the party in Christenson's 1974 Ford Galaxy station wagon. The drinking binge apparently continued, as respondent was seen buying beer at 9:20 p.m. and recalled "sitting on a hill or a bank passing a bottle of Black Velvet back and forth" with Christenson.

At about midnight that night, officers of the Lincoln County, Montana, sheriff's department, responding to reports of a possible drunk driver, discovered Christenson's station wagon stuck in a ditch along U.S. Highway 2. In the front seat were Pavola and Christenson, each dead from a single gunshot to the head. In the rear of the car lay respondent, alive and yelling obscenities. His blood-alcohol content measured .36 percent over one hour later. On the floor of the car, near the brake pedal, lay respondent's .38 caliber handgun, with four loaded rounds and two empty casings; respondent had gunshot residue on his hands.

Respondent was charged with two counts of deliberate homicide, a crime defined by Montana law as "purposely" or "knowingly" causing the death of another human being. A portion of the jury charge, uncontested here, instructed that "[a] person acts purposely when it is his conscious object to engage in conduct of that nature or to cause such a result," and that "[a] person acts knowingly when he is aware of his conduct or when he is aware under the circumstances his conduct constitutes a crime; or, when he is aware there exists the high probability that his conduct will cause a specific result." Respondent's defense at trial was that an unidentified fourth person must have committed the murders; his own extreme intoxication, he claimed, had rendered him physically incapable of committing the murders, and accounted for his inability to recall the events of the night of July 12. Although respondent was allowed to make this use of the evidence that he was intoxicated, the jury was instructed, pursuant to Mont. Code Ann. § 45-2-203, that it could not consider respondent's "intoxicated condition . . . in determining the existence of a mental state which is an element of the offense." The jury found respondent guilty on both counts, and the court sentenced him to 84 years' imprisonment.

The Supreme Court of Montana reversed. It reasoned (1) that respondent "had a due process right to present and have considered by the jury all relevant evidence to rebut the State's evidence on all elements of the offense charged,"and (2) that evidence of respondent's voluntary intoxication was "clearly . . . relevant to the issue of whether [respondent] acted knowingly and purposely." Because § 45-2-203 prevented the jury from considering that evidence with regard to that issue, the court concluded that the State had been "relieved of part of its burden to prove beyond a reasonable doubt every fact necessary to constitute the crime charged," and that respondent had therefore been denied due process. We granted certiorari.

II.

The cornerstone of the Montana Supreme Court's judgment was the proposition that the Due Process Clause guarantees a defendant the right to present and have considered by the jury "all relevant evidence to rebut the State's evidence on all elements of the offense charged." Respondent does not defend this categorical rule; he acknowledges that the right to present relevant evidence "has not been viewed as absolute." That is a wise concession, since the proposition that the Due Process Clause guarantees the right to introduce all relevant evidence is simply indefensible. ... Of course, to say that the right to introduce relevant evidence is not absolute is not to say that the Due Process Clause places no limits upon restriction of that right. But it is to say that the defendant asserting such a limit must sustain the usual heavy burden that a due process claim entails:

> Preventing and dealing with crime is much more the business of the States than it is of the Federal Government, and . . . we should not lightly construe the Constitution so as to intrude upon the administration of justice by the individual States. Among other things, it is normally 'within the power of the State to regulate procedures under which its laws are carried out,' . . . and its decision in this regard is not subject to proscription under the Due Process Clause unless 'it offends some principle of justice so rooted in the traditions and conscience of our people as to be ranked as fundamental.'

Respondent's task, then, is to establish that a defendant's right to have a jury consider evidence of his voluntary intoxication in determining whether he possesses the requisite mental state is a "fundamental principle of justice."

Our primary guide in determining whether the principle in question is fundamental is, of course, historical practice. Here that gives respondent little support. ...

The historical record does not leave room for the view that the common law's rejection of intoxication as an "excuse" or "justification" for crime would nonetheless permit the defendant to show that intoxication prevented the requisite mens rea. Hale, Coke, and Blackstone were familiar, to say the least, with the concept of mens rea, and acknowledged that drunkenness "deprive[s] men of the use of reason." It is inconceivable that they did not realize that an offender's drunkenness might impair his ability to form the requisite intent; and inconceivable that their failure to note this massive exception from the general rule of disregard of intoxication was an oversight. ...

...Instead of the uniform and continuing acceptance we would expect for a rule that enjoys "fundamental principle" status, we find that fully one-fifth of the States either never adopted the "new common-law" rule at issue here or have recently abandoned it.

It is not surprising that many States have held fast to or resurrected the common-law rule prohibiting consideration of voluntary intoxication in the determination of mens rea, because that rule has considerable justification – which alone casts doubt upon the proposition that the opposite rule is a "fundamental principle." A large number of crimes, especially violent crimes, are committed by intoxicated offenders; modern studies put the numbers as high as half of all homicides, for example. Disallowing consideration of voluntary intoxication has the effect of increasing the punishment for all unlawful acts committed in that state, and thereby deters drunkenness or irresponsible behavior while drunk. The rule also serves as a specific deterrent, ensuring that those who prove incapable of controlling violent impulses while voluntarily intoxicated go to prison. And finally, the rule comports with and implements society's moral perception that one who has voluntarily impaired his own faculties should be responsible for the consequences.

In sum, not every widespread experiment with a procedural rule favorable to criminal defendants establishes a fundamental principle of justice. Although the rule allowing a jury to consider evidence of a defendant's voluntary intoxication where relevant to mens rea has gained considerable acceptance, it is of too recent vintage, and has not received sufficiently uniform and permanent allegiance, to qualify as fundamental, especially since it displaces a lengthy commonlaw tradition which remains supported by valid justifications today. n6

III.

The Supreme Court of Montana's conclusion that Mont. Code Ann. § 45-2-203 (1995) violates the Due Process Clause purported to rest on two lines of our jurisprudence. First, it derived its view that the Due Process Clause requires the admission of all relevant evidence from the statement in Chambers v. Mississippi, that "the right of an accused in a criminal trial to due process is, in essence, the right to a fair opportunity to defend against the State's accusations." Respondent relies heavily on this statement, which he terms "the Chambers principle."

We held in Chambers that "the exclusion of [certain] critical evidence, coupled with the State's refusal to permit [petitioner] to cross-examine McDonald, denied him a trial in accord with traditional and fundamental standards of due process." We continued, however:

> In reaching this judgment, we establish no new principles of constitutional law. Nor does our holding signal any diminution in the respect traditionally accorded to the States in the establishment and implementation of their own criminal trial rules and procedures. Rather, we hold quite simply that under the facts and circumstances of this case the rulings of the trial court deprived Chambers of a fair trial.

In other words, Chambers was an exercise in highly case-specific error correction. At issue were two rulings by the state trial court at Chambers' murder trial: denial of Chambers' motion to treat as an adverse witness one McDonald, who had confessed to the murder for which Chambers was on trial, but later retracted the confession; and exclusion, on hearsay grounds, of testimony of three witnesses who would testify that McDonald had confessed to them. We held that both of these rulings were erroneous, the former because McDonald's testimony simply was adverse, and the second because the statements "were originally made and subsequently offered at trial under circumstances that provided considerable assurance of their reliability," and were "well within the basic rationale of the exception for declarations against interest." Thus, the holding of Chambers – if one can be discerned from such a fact-intensive case – is certainly not that a defendant is denied "a fair opportunity to defend against the State's accusations" whenever "critical evidence" favorable to him is excluded, but rather that erroneous evidentiary rulings can, in combination, rise to the level of a due process violation.

The second line of our cases invoked by the Montana Supreme Court's opinion requires even less discussion. In re Winship announced the proposition that the Due Process Clause requires proof beyond a reasonable doubt of every fact necessary to constitute the charged crime, and Sandstrom v. Montana established a corollary, that a jury instruction which shifts to the defendant the burden of proof on a requisite element of mental state violates due process. These decisions simply are not implicated here because, as the Montana court itself recognized, "the burden is not shifted" under § 45-2-203. The trial judge instructed the jury that "the State of Montana has the burden of proving the guilt of the Defendant beyond a reasonable doubt," and that "[a] person commits the offense of deliberate homicide if he purposely or knowingly causes the death of another human being." Thus, failure by the State to produce evidence of respondent's mental state would have resulted in an acquittal. That acquittal did not occur was presumably attributable to the fact, noted by the Supreme Court of Montana, that the State introduced considerable evidence from which the jury might have concluded that respondent acted "purposely" or "knowingly." For example, respondent himself testified that, several hours before the murders, he had given his handgun to Pavola and asked her to put it in the glove compartment of Christenson's car. That he had to retrieve the gun from the glove compartment before he used it was strong evidence that it was his "conscious object" to commit the charged crimes; as was the execution-style manner in which a single shot was fired into the head of each victim.

Finally, we may comment upon the Montana Supreme Court's citation of the following passage in Martin v. Ohio, a case upholding a state law that placed on the defendant the burden of proving self-defense by a preponderance of the evidence:

> It would be quite different if the jury had been instructed that self-defense evidence could not be considered in determining whether there was a reasonable doubt about the State's case, i. e., that self-defense evidence must be put aside for all purposes unless it satisfied the preponderance standard. Such an instruction would relieve the State of its burden and plainly run afoul of [In re] Winship's mandate. The instructions in this case . . . are adequate to convey to the jury that all of the evidence, including the evidence going to self-defense, must be considered in deciding whether there was a reasonable doubt about the sufficiency of the State's proof of the elements of the crime.

This passage can be explained in various ways – e. g., as an assertion that the right to have a jury consider self-defense evidence (unlike the right to have a jury consider evidence of voluntary intoxication) is fundamental, a proposition that the historical record may support. But the only explanation needed for present purposes is the one given in Kokkonen v. Guardian Life Ins. Co.: "It is to the holdings of our cases, rather than their dicta, that we must attend." If the Martin dictum means that the Due Process Clause requires all relevant evidence bearing on the elements of a crime to be admissible, the decisions we have discussed show it to be incorrect.

* * *

"The doctrines of actus reus, mens rea, insanity, mistake, justification, and duress have historically provided the tools for a constantly shifting adjustment of the tension between the evolving aims of the criminal law and changing religious, moral, philosophical, and medical views of the nature of man. This process of adjustment has always been thought to be the province of the States." The people of Montana have decided to resurrect the rule of an earlier era, disallowing consideration of voluntary intoxication when a defendant's state of mind is at issue. Nothing in the Due Process Clause prevents them from doing so, and the judgment of the Supreme Court of Montana to the contrary must be reversed.

It is so ordered.

JUSTICE GINSBURG, concurring in the judgment.

Comprehended as a measure redefining mens rea, § 45-2-203 encounters no constitutional shoal. States enjoy wide latitude in defining the elements of criminal offenses, particularly when determining "the extent to which moral culpability should be a prerequisite to conviction of a crime." When a State's power to define criminal conduct is challenged under the Due Process Clause, we inquire only whether the law "offends some principle of justice so rooted in the traditions and conscience of our people as to be ranked as fundamental." Defining mens rea to eliminate the exculpatory value of voluntary intoxication does not offend a "fundamental principle of justice," given the lengthy common-law tradition, and the adherence of a significant minority of the States to that position today.

Other state courts have upheld statutes similar to § 45-2-203, not simply as evidentiary rules, but as legislative redefinitions of the mental-state element. Legislation of this order, if constitutional in Arizona, Hawaii, and Pennsylvania, ought not be declared unconstitutional by this Court when enacted in Montana.

The Montana Supreme Court's judgment, in sum, strikes down a statute whose text displays no constitutional infirmity. If the Montana court considered its analysis forced by this Court's precedent, it is proper for this Court to say what prescriptions federal law leaves to the States, and thereby dispel confusion to which we may have contributed, and attendant state-court misperception.

JUSTICE O'CONNOR, with whom JUSTICE STEVENS, JUSTICE SOUTER, and JUSTICE BREYER join, dissenting.

The Montana Supreme Court unanimously held that Mont. Code Ann. § 45-2-203 violates due process. I agree. Our cases establish that due process sets an outer limit on the restrictions that may be placed on a defendant's ability to raise an effective defense to the State's accusations. Here, to impede the defendant's ability to throw doubt on the State's case, Montana has removed from the jury's consideration a category of evidence relevant to determination of mental state where that mental state is an essential element of the offense that must be proved beyond a reasonable doubt. Because this disallowance eliminates evidence with which the defense might negate an essential element, the State's burden to prove its case is made correspondingly easier. The justification for this disallowance is the State's desire to increase the likelihood of conviction of a certain class of defendants who might otherwise be able to prove that they did not satisfy a requisite element of the offense. In my view, the statute's effect on the criminal proceeding violates due process.

I.

This Court's cases establish that limitations placed on the accused's ability to present a fair and complete defense can, in some circumstances, be severe enough to violate due process. "The right of an accused in a criminal trial to due process is, in essence, the right to a fair opportunity to defend against the State's accusations." Applying our precedent, the Montana Supreme Court held that keeping intoxication evidence away from the jury, where such evidence was relevant to establishment of the requisite mental state, violated the due process right to present a defense, and that the instruction pursuant to § 45-2-203 was not harmless error. In rejecting the Montana Supreme Court's conclusion, the Court emphasizes that "any number of familiar and unquestionably constitutional evidentiary rules" permit exclusion of relevant evidence. It is true that a defendant does not enjoy an absolute right to present evidence relevant to his defense. But none of the "familiar" evidentiary rules operates as Montana's does. The Montana statute places a blanket exclusion on a category of evidence that would allow the accused to negate the offense's mental-state element. In so doing, it frees the prosecution, in the face of such evidence, from having to prove beyond a reasonable doubt that the defendant nevertheless possessed the required mental state. In my view, this combination of effects violates due process.

... Due process demands that a criminal defendant be afforded a fair opportunity to defend against the State's accusations. Meaningful adversarial testing of the State's case requires that the defendant not be prevented from raising an effective defense, which must include the right to present relevant, probative evidence. To be sure, the right to present evidence is not limitless ... Nevertheless, "an essential component of procedural fairness is an opportunity to be heard. That opportunity would be an empty one if the State were permitted to exclude competent, reliable evidence" that is essential to the accused's defense. Section 45-2-203 forestalls the defendant's ability to raise an effective defense by placing a blanket exclusion on the presentation of a type of evidence that directly negates an element of the crime, and by doing so, it lightens the prosecution's burden to prove that mental-state element beyond a reasonable doubt.

Where the defendant may introduce evidence to negate a subjective mental-state element, the prosecution must work to overcome whatever doubts the defense has raised about the existence of the required mental state. On the other hand, if the defendant may not introduce evidence that might create doubt in the factfinder's mind as to whether that element was met, the prosecution will find its job so much the easier. A subjective mental state is generally proved only circumstantially. If a jury may not consider the defendant's evidence of his mental state, the jury may impute to the defendant the culpability of a mental state he did not possess.

... It seems to me that a State may not first determine the elements of the crime it wishes to punish, and then thwart the accused's defense by categorically disallowing the very evidence that would prove him innocent.

JUSTICE SOUTER, dissenting. [omitted].

JUSTICE BREYER, with whom JUSTICE STEVENS joins, dissenting. [omitted]

Notes and Queries

Egelhoff was charged with purposefully and knowing causing the death of another human being. Is it fair that he is not allowed to present his defense that he was drunk? Does the dissent have the better argument as it emphasized a violation of due process? How does the majority support its finding? How persuasive do you find the argument that a state should have the power to limit testimony based on the principle that the state has the power to determine elements of offenses?

Studies estimate that approximately sixty percent of people arrested in major cities in the United States used drugs at the time of arrest. In 1999, from a sample of 556 male arrestees in New York City, forty-six percent tested positive for cocaine (and "crack" cocaine), forty percent for marijuana, and twenty-two percent for opiates. Overall, in this New York City sample, seventy-nine percent tested positive for any of the measured drugs, forty-one percent were at risk for drug dependence, and twenty-three percent were at risk for alcohol dependence based on heavy usages (including binge drinking). Nahama Broner, Stacy S. Lamon, Damon W. Mayrl, and Martin G. Karopkin, Arrested adults awaiting arraignment: Mental health, substance abuse, and criminal justice characteristics and needs, 30 Fordham Urban L. J. 663 (2003). What implications arise from these and similar findings that reveal a link between substance abuse and crime?

Proving Mental States: Assistance from Experts

AKE v. OKLAHOMA
470 U.S. 68 (1985)

JUSTICE MARSHALL delivered the opinion of the Court.

The issue in this case is whether the Constitution requires that an indigent defendant have access to the psychiatric examination and assistance necessary to prepare an effective defense based on his mental condition, when his sanity at the time of the offense is seriously in question.

I.

Late in 1979, Glen Burton Ake was arrested and charged with murdering a couple and wounding their two children. He was arraigned in the District Court for Canadian County, Okla., in February 1980. His behavior at arraignment, and in other prearraignment incidents at the jail, was so bizarre that the trial judge, sua sponte, ordered him to be examined by a psychiatrist "for the purpose of advising with the Court as to his impressions of whether the Defendant may need an extended period of mental observation." The examining psychiatrist reported: "At times [Ake] appears to be frankly delusional. . . . He claims to be the 'sword of vengeance' of the Lord and that he will sit at the left hand of God in heaven." He diagnosed Ake as a probable paranoid schizophrenic and recommended a prolonged psychiatric evaluation to determine whether Ake was competent to stand trial.

In March, Ake was committed to a state hospital to be examined with respect to his "present sanity," i. e., his competency to stand trial. On April 10, less than six months after the incidents for which Ake was indicted, the chief forensic psychiatrist at the state hospital informed the court that Ake was not competent to stand trial. The court then held a competency hearing, at which a psychiatrist testified:

> [Ake] is a psychotic . . . his psychiatric diagnosis was that of paranoid schizophrenia – chronic, with exacerbation, that is with current upset, and that in addition . . . he is dangerous. . . . [Because] of the severity of his mental illness and because of the intensities of his rage, his poor control, his delusions, he requires a maximum security facility within – I believe – the State Psychiatric Hospital system.

The court found Ake to be a "mentally ill person in need of care and treatment" and incompetent to stand trial, and ordered him committed to the state mental hospital.

Six weeks later, the chief forensic psychiatrist informed the court that Ake had become competent to stand trial. At the time, Ake was receiving 200 milligrams of Thorazine, an antipsychotic drug, three times daily, and the psychiatrist indicated that, if Ake continued to receive that dosage, his condition would remain stable. The State then resumed proceedings against Ake.

At a pretrial conference in June, Ake's attorney informed the court that his client would raise an insanity defense. To enable him to prepare and present such a defense adequately, the attorney stated, a psychiatrist would have to examine Ake with respect to his mental condition at the time of the offense. During Ake's 3-month stay at the state hospital, no inquiry had been made into his sanity at the time of the offense, and, as an indigent, Ake could not afford to pay for a psychiatrist. Counsel asked the court either to arrange to have a psychiatrist perform the examination, or to provide funds to allow the defense to arrange one. The trial judge rejected counsel's argument that the Federal Constitution requires that an indigent defendant receive the assistance of a psychiatrist when that assistance is necessary to the defense, and he denied the motion for a psychiatric evaluation at state expense ...

Ake was tried for two counts of murder in the first degree, a crime punishable by death in Oklahoma, and for two counts of shooting with intent to kill. At the guilt phase of trial, his sole defense was insanity. Although defense counsel called to the stand and questioned each of the psychiatrists who had examined Ake at the state hospital, none testified about his mental state at the time of the offense because none had examined him on that point. The prosecution, in turn, asked each of these psychiatrists whether he had performed or seen the results of any examination diagnosing Ake's mental state at the time of the offense, and each doctor replied that he had not. As a result, there was no expert testimony for either side on Ake's sanity at the time of the offense. The jurors were then instructed that Ake could be found not guilty by reason of insanity if he did not have the ability to distinguish right from wrong at the time of the alleged offense. They were further told that Ake was to be presumed sane at the time of the crime unless he presented evidence sufficient to raise a reasonable doubt about his sanity at that time. If he raised such a doubt in their minds, the jurors were informed, the burden of proof shifted to the State to prove sanity beyond a reasonable doubt. The jury rejected Ake's insanity defense and returned a verdict of guilty on all counts.

At the sentencing proceeding, the State asked for the death penalty. No new evidence was presented. The prosecutor relied significantly on the testimony of the state psychiatrists who had examined Ake, and who had testified at the guilt phase that Ake was dangerous to society, to establish the likelihood of his future dangerous behavior. Ake had no expert witness to rebut this testimony or to introduce on his behalf evidence in mitigation of his punishment. The jury sentenced Ake to death on each of the two murder counts, and to 500 years' imprisonment on each of the two counts of shooting with intent to kill.

On appeal to the Oklahoma Court of Criminal Appeals, Ake argued that, as an indigent defendant, he should have been provided the services of a court-appointed psychiatrist. The court rejected this argument, observing: "We have held numerous times that, the unique nature of capital cases notwithstanding, the State does not have the responsibility of providing such services to indigents charged with capital crimes." Finding no error in Ake's other claims, the court affirmed the convictions and sentences. We granted certiorari.

We hold that when a defendant has made a preliminary showing that his sanity at the time of the offense is likely to be a significant factor at trial, the Constitution requires that a State provide access to a psychiatrist's assistance on this issue if the defendant cannot otherwise afford one. Accordingly, we reverse.

II.

III.

This Court has long recognized that when a State brings its judicial power to bear on an indigent defendant in a criminal proceeding, it must take steps to assure that the defendant has a fair opportunity to present his defense. This elementary principle, grounded in significant part on the Fourteenth Amendment's due process guarantee of fundamental fairness, derives from the belief that justice cannot be equal where, simply as a result of his poverty, a defendant is denied the opportunity to participate meaningfully in a judicial proceeding in which his liberty is at stake. ...

Meaningful access to justice has been the consistent theme of these cases. We recognized long ago that mere access to the courthouse doors does not by itself assure a proper functioning of the adversary process, and that a criminal trial is fundamentally unfair if the State proceeds against an indigent defendant without making certain that he has access to the raw materials integral to the building of an effective defense. Thus, while the Court has not held that a State must purchase for the indigent defendant all the assistance that his wealthier counterpart might buy, it has often reaffirmed that fundamental fairness entitles indigent defendants to "an adequate opportunity to present their claims fairly within the adversary system." To implement this principle, we have focused on identifying the "basic tools of an adequate defense or appeal," and we have required that such tools be provided to those defendants who cannot afford to pay for them.

To say that these basic tools must be provided is, of course, merely to begin our inquiry. In this case we must decide whether, and under what conditions, the participation of a psychiatrist is important enough to preparation of a defense to require the State to provide an indigent defendant with access to competent psychiatric assistance in preparing the defense. Three factors are relevant to this determination. The first is the private interest that will be affected by the action of the State. The second is the governmental interest that will be affected if the safeguard is to be provided. The third is the probable value of the additional or substitute procedural safeguards that are sought, and the risk of an erroneous deprivation of the affected interest if those safeguards are not provided. We turn, then, to apply this standard to the issue before us.

A.

The private interest in the accuracy of a criminal proceeding that places an individual's life or liberty at risk is almost uniquely compelling. Indeed, the host of safeguards fashioned by this Court over the years to diminish the risk of erroneous conviction stands as a testament to that concern. The interest of the individual in the outcome of the State's effort to overcome the presumption of innocence is obvious and weighs heavily in our analysis.

We consider, next, the interest of the State. Oklahoma asserts that to provide Ake with psychiatric assistance on the record before us would result in a staggering burden to the State. We are unpersuaded by this assertion. Many States, as well as the Federal Government, currently make psychiatric assistance available to indigent defendants, and they have not found the financial burden so great as to preclude this assistance. This is especially so when the obligation of the State is limited to provision of one competent psychiatrist, as it is in many States, and as we limit the right we recognize today. At the same time, it is difficult to identify any interest of the States, other than that in its economy, that weighs against recognition of this right. The State's interest in prevailing at trial – unlike that of a private litigant – is necessarily tempered by its interest in the fair and accurate adjudication of criminal cases. Thus, also unlike a private litigant, a State may not legitimately assert an interest in maintenance of a strategic advantage over the defense, if the result of that advantage is to cast a pall on the accuracy of the verdict obtained. We therefore conclude that the governmental interest in denying Ake the assistance of a psychiatrist is not substantial, in light of the compelling interest of both the State and the individual in accurate dispositions.

Last, we inquire into the probable value of the psychiatric assistance sought, and the risk of error in the proceeding if such assistance is not offered. We begin by considering the pivotal role that psychiatry has come to play in criminal proceedings. More than 40 States, as well as the Federal Government, have decided either through legislation or judicial decision that indigent defendants are entitled, under certain circumstances, to the assistance of a psychiatrist's expertise. ... And in many States that have not assured access to psychiatrists through the legislative process, state courts have interpreted the State or Federal Constitution to require that psychiatric assistance be provided to indigent defendants when necessary for an adequate defense, or when insanity is at issue.

These statutes and court decisions reflect a reality that we recognize today, namely, that when the State has made the defendant's mental condition relevant to his criminal culpability and to the punishment he might suffer, the assistance of a psychiatrist may well be crucial to the defendant's ability to marshal his defense. In this role, psychiatrists gather facts, through professional examination, interviews, and elsewhere, that they will share with the judge or jury; they analyze the information gathered and from it draw plausible conclusions about the defendant's mental condition, and about the effects of any disorder on behavior; and they offer opinions about how the defendant's mental condition might have affected his behavior at the time in question. They know the probative questions to ask of the opposing party's psychiatrists and how to interpret their answers. Unlike lay witnesses, who can merely describe symptoms they believe might be relevant to the defendant's mental state, psychiatrists can identify the "elusive and often deceptive" symptoms of insanity, and tell the jury why their observations are relevant. Further, where permitted by evidentiary rules, psychiatrists can translate a medical diagnosis into language that will assist the trier of fact, and therefore offer evidence in a form that has meaning for the task at hand. Through this process of investigation, interpretation, and testimony, psychiatrists ideally assist lay jurors, who generally have no training in psychiatric matters, to make a sensible and educated determination about the mental condition of the defendant at the time of the offense.

Psychiatry is not, however, an exact science, and psychiatrists disagree widely and frequently on what constitutes mental illness, on the appropriate diagnosis to be attached to given behavior and symptoms, on cure and treatment, and on likelihood of future dangerousness. Perhaps because there often is no single, accurate psychiatric conclusion on legal insanity in a given case, juries remain the primary factfinders on this issue, and they must resolve differences in opinion within the psychiatric profession on the basis of the evidence offered by each party. When jurors make this determination about issues that inevitably are complex and foreign, the testimony of psychiatrists can be crucial and "a virtual necessity if an insanity plea is to have any chance of success." By organizing a defendant's mental history, examination results and behavior, and other information, interpreting it in light of their expertise, and then laying out their investigative and analytic process to the jury, the psychiatrists for each party enable the jury to make its most accurate determination of the truth on the issue before them. It is for this reason that States rely on psychiatrists as examiners, consultants, and witnesses, and that private individuals do as well, when they can afford to do so. In so saying, we neither approve nor disapprove the widespread reliance on psychiatrists but instead recognize the unfairness of a contrary holding in light of the evolving practice.

The foregoing leads inexorably to the conclusion that, without the assistance of a psychiatrist to conduct a professional examination on issues relevant to the defense, to help determine whether the insanity defense is viable, to present testimony, and to assist in preparing the cross-examination of a State's psychiatric witnesses, the risk of an inaccurate resolution of sanity issues is extremely high. With such assistance, the defendant is fairly able to present at least enough information to the jury, in a meaningful manner, as to permit it to make a sensible determination.

A defendant's mental condition is not necessarily at issue in every criminal proceeding, however, and it is unlikely that psychiatric assistance of the kind we have described would be of probable value in cases where it is not. The risk of error from denial of such assistance, as well as its probable value, is most predictably at its height when the defendant's mental condition is seriously in question. When the defendant is able to make an ex parte threshold showing to the trial court that his sanity is likely to be a significant factor in his defense, the need for the assistance of a psychiatrist is readily apparent. It is in such cases that a defense may be devastated by the absence of a psychiatric examination and testimony; with such assistance, the defendant might have a reasonable chance of success. In such a circumstance, where the potential accuracy of the jury's determination is so dramatically enhanced, and where the interests of the individual and the State in an accurate proceeding are substantial, the State's interest in its fisc must yield.

We therefore hold that when a defendant demonstrates to the trial judge that his sanity at the time of the offense is to be a significant factor at trial, the State must, at a minimum, assure the defendant access to a competent psychiatrist who will conduct an appropriate examination and assist in evaluation, preparation, and presentation of the defense. This is not to say, of course, that the indigent defendant has a constitutional right to choose a psychiatrist of his personal liking or to receive funds to hire his own. Our concern is that the indigent defendant have access to a competent psychiatrist for the purpose we have discussed, and as in the case of the provision of counsel we leave to the States the decision on how to implement this right.

B.

C.

IV.

We turn now to apply these standards to the facts of this case. On the record before us, it is clear that Ake's mental state at the time of the offense was a substantial factor in his defense, and that the trial court was on notice of that fact when the request for a court-appointed psychiatrist was made. For one, Ake's sole defense was that of insanity. Second, Ake's behavior at arraignment, just four months after the offense, was so bizarre as to prompt the trial judge, sua sponte, to have him examined for competency. Third, a state psychiatrist shortly thereafter found Ake to be incompetent to stand trial, and suggested that he be committed. Fourth, when he was found to be competent six weeks later, it was only on the condition that he be sedated with large doses of Thorazine three times a day, during trial. Fifth, the psychiatrists who examined Ake for competency described to the trial court the severity of Ake's mental illness less than six months after the offense in question, and suggested that this mental illness might have begun many years earlier. Finally, Oklahoma recognizes a defense of insanity, under which the initial burden of producing evidence falls on the defendant. Taken together, these factors make clear that the question of Ake's sanity was likely to be a significant factor in his defense.

Accordingly, we reverse and remand for a new trial.

It is so ordered.

CHIEF JUSTICE BURGER, concurring in the judgment.

The facts of the case and the question presented confine the actual holding of the Court. In capital cases the finality of the sentence imposed warrants protections that may or may not be required in other cases. Nothing in the Court's opinion reaches noncapital cases.

JUSTICE REHNQUIST, dissenting.

The Court holds that "when a defendant has made a preliminary showing that his sanity at the time of the offense is likely to be a significant factor at trial, the Constitution requires that a State provide access to a psychiatrist's assistance on this issue if the defendant cannot otherwise afford one." I do not think that the facts of this case warrant the establishment of such a principle; and I think that even if the factual predicate of the Court's statement were established, the constitutional rule announced by the Court is far too broad. I would limit the rule to capital cases, and make clear that the entitlement is to an independent psychiatric evaluation, not to a defense consultant.

Petitioner Ake and his codefendant Hatch quit their jobs on an oil field rig in October 1979, borrowed a car, and went looking for a location to burglarize. They drove to the rural home of Reverend and Mrs. Richard Douglass, and gained entrance to the home by a ruse. Holding Reverend and Mrs. Douglass and their children, Brooks and Leslie, at gunpoint, they ransacked the home; they then bound and gagged the mother, father, and son, and forced them to lie on the living room floor. Ake and Hatch then took turns attempting to rape 12-year-old Leslie Douglass in a nearby bedroom. Having failed in these efforts, they forced her to lie on the living room floor with the other members of her family.

Ake then shot Reverend Douglass and Leslie each twice, and Mrs. Douglass and Brooks once, with a .357 magnum pistol, and fled. Mrs. Douglass died almost immediately as a result of the gunshot wound; Reverend Douglass' death was caused by a combination of the gunshots he received, and strangulation from the manner in which he was bound. Leslie and Brooks managed to untie themselves and to drive to the home of a nearby doctor. Ake and his accomplice were apprehended in Colorado following a month-long crime spree that took them through Arkansas, Louisiana, Texas, and other States in the western half of the United States.

Ake was extradited from Colorado to Oklahoma on November 20, 1979, and placed in the city jail in El Reno, Oklahoma. Three days after his arrest, he asked to speak to the Sheriff. Ake gave the Sheriff a detailed statement concerning the above crimes, which was first taped, then reduced to 44 written pages, corrected, and signed by Ake.

Ake was arraigned on November 23, 1979, and again appeared in court with his codefendant Hatch on December 11th. Hatch's attorney requested and obtained an order transferring Hatch to the state mental hospital for a 60-day observation period to determine his competency to stand trial; although Ake was present in court with his attorney during this proceeding, no such request was made on behalf of Ake.

On January 21, 1980, both Ake and Hatch were bound over for trial at the conclusion of a preliminary hearing. No suggestion of insanity at the time of the commission of the offense was made at this time. On February 14, 1980, Ake appeared for formal arraignment, and at this time became disruptive. The court ordered that Ake be examined by Dr. William Allen, a psychiatrist in private practice, in order to determine his competency to stand trial. On April 10, 1980, a competency hearing was held at the conclusion of which the trial court found that Ake was a mentally ill person in need of care and treatment, and he was transferred to a state institution. Six weeks later, the chief psychiatrist for the institution advised the court that Ake was now competent to stand trial, and the murder trial began on June 23, 1980. At this time Ake's attorney withdrew a pending motion for jury trial on present sanity. Outside the presence of the jury the State produced testimony of a cellmate of Ake, who testified that Ake had told him that he was going to try to "play crazy."

The State at trial produced evidence as to guilt, and the only evidence offered by Ake was the testimony of the doctors who had observed and treated him during his confinement pursuant to the previous order of the court. Each of these doctors testified as to Ake's mental condition at the time of his confinement in the institution, but none could express a view as to his mental condition at the time of the offense. Significantly, although all three testified that Ake suffered from some form of mental illness six months after he committed the murders, on cross-examination two of the psychiatrists specifically stated that they had "no opinion" concerning Ake's capacity to tell right from wrong at the time of the offense, and the third would only speculate that a psychosis might have been "apparent" at that time. The Court makes a point of the fact that "there was no expert testimony for either side on Ake's sanity at the time of the offense." In addition, Ake called no lay witnesses, although some apparently existed who could have testified concerning Ake's actions that might have had a bearing on his sanity at the time of the offense; and although two "friends" of Ake's who had been with him at times proximate to the murders testified at trial at the behest of the prosecution, defense counsel did not question them concerning any of Ake's actions that might have a bearing on his sanity.

The Court's opinion states that before an indigent defendant is entitled to a state-appointed psychiatrist the defendant must make "a preliminary showing that his sanity at the time of the offense is likely to be a significant factor at trial." But nowhere in the opinion does the Court elucidate how that requirement is satisfied in this particular case. Under Oklahoma law, the burden is initially on the defendant to raise a reasonable doubt as to his sanity at the time of the offense. Once that burden is satisfied, the burden shifts to the State to prove sanity beyond a reasonable doubt. Since the State introduced no evidence concerning Ake's sanity at the time of the offense, it seems clear that as a matter of state law Ake failed to carry the initial burden. Indeed, that was the holding of the Oklahoma Court of Criminal Appeals.

Nor is this a surprising conclusion on the facts here. The evidence of the brutal murders perpetrated on the victims, and of the month-long crime spree following the murders, would not seem to raise any question of sanity unless one were to adopt the dubious doctrine that no one in his right mind would commit a murder. The defendant's 44-page confession, given more than a month after the crimes, does not suggest insanity; nor does the failure of Ake's attorney to move for a competency hearing at the time the codefendant moved for one. The first instance in this record is the disruptive behavior at the time of formal arraignment, to which the trial judge alertly and immediately responded by committing Ake for examination. The trial commenced some two months later, at which time Ake's attorney withdrew a pending motion for jury trial on present sanity, and the State offered the testimony of a cellmate of Ake who said that the latter had told him that he was going to try to "play crazy." The Court apparently would infer from the fact that Ake was diagnosed as mentally ill some six months after the offense that there was a reasonable doubt as to his ability to know right from wrong when he committed it. But even the experts were unwilling to draw this inference.

Before holding that the State is obligated to furnish the services of a psychiatric witness to an indigent defendant who reasonably contests his sanity at the time of the offense, I would require a considerably greater showing than this. And even then I do not think due process is violated merely because an indigent lacks sufficient funds to pursue a state-law defense as thoroughly as he would like. ...

Finally, even if I were to agree with the Court that some right to a state-appointed psychiatrist should be recognized here, I would not grant the broad right to "access to a competent psychiatrist who will conduct an appropriate examination and assist in evaluation, preparation, and presentation of the defense." A psychiatrist is not an attorney, whose job it is to advocate. His opinion is sought on a question that the State of Oklahoma treats as a question of fact. Since any "unfairness" in these cases would arise from the fact that the only competent witnesses on the question are being hired by the State, all the defendant should be entitled to is one competent opinion – whatever the witness' conclusion – from a psychiatrist who acts independently of the prosecutor's office. Although the independent psychiatrist should be available to answer defense counsel's questions prior to trial, and to testify if called, I see no reason why the defendant should be entitled to an opposing view, or to a "defense" advocate.

For the foregoing reasons, I would affirm the judgment of the Court of Criminal Appeals of Oklahoma.

NOTES AND QUERIES

Oklahoma Stat., Tit. 21, § 152 (1981), provides that "[all] persons are capable of committing crimes, except those belonging to the following classes . . . (4) Lunatics, insane persons and all persons of unsound mind, including persons temporarily or partially deprived of reason, upon proof that at the time of committing the act charged against them they were incapable of knowing its wrongfulness."

The Oklahoma Court of Criminal Appeals also dismissed Ake's claim that the Thorazine he was given during trial rendered him unable to understand the proceedings against him or to assist counsel with his defense. The court acknowledged that Ake "stared vacantly ahead throughout the trial" but rejected Ake's challenge in reliance on a state psychiatrist's word that Ake was competent to stand trial while under the influence of the drug. Ake petitioned for a writ of certiorari on this issue as well. The Court did not address this claim.

The central concern is whether the judge inappropriately denied the motion for a psychiatric evaluation at the state's expense to address the insanity defense claim. The Court holds that he had a right to psychiatric assistance because the defendant needed a fair opportunity to present his defense and that fair opportunity involved meaningful access to justice. To determine the "basic tools" that the state must provide a defendant to defend himself against a state's claims, the court used a three-pronged test, which balances the private interest at stake, the government interest affected if the tool is provided, and the value of the safeguard and risk of error if it is not provided.

The dissent presents an account of the brutal acts. Why do you suppose we do not get a sense of that brutality from reading the majority opinion? Do you find the dissent's claim fair when it notes that the expert should be an independent expert, not a defense advocate? Are you convinced by the dissent's argument that the defendant clearly was not insane at the time of the offense?

PROVING MENTAL STATES: BURDEN OF PROOF

MEDINA v. CALIFORNIA
505 U.S. 437 (1992)

JUSTICE KENNEDY delivered the opinion of the Court.

It is well established that the Due Process Clause of the Fourteenth Amendment prohibits the criminal prosecution of a defendant who is not competent to stand trial. The issue in this case is whether the Due Process Clause permits a State to require a defendant who alleges incompetence to stand trial to bear the burden of proving so by a preponderance of the evidence.

I.

In 1984, petitioner Teofilo Medina, Jr., stole a gun from a pawnshop in Santa Ana, California. In the weeks that followed, he held up two gas stations, a drive-in dairy, and a market, murdered three employees of those establishments, attempted to rob a fourth employee, and shot at two passers-by who attempted to follow his getaway car. Petitioner was apprehended less than one month after his crime spree began and was charged with a number of criminal offenses, including three counts of first-degree murder. Before trial, petitioner's counsel moved for a competency hearing, on the ground that he was unsure whether petitioner had the ability to participate in the criminal proceedings against him.

Under California law, "[a] person cannot be tried or adjudged to punishment while such person is mentally incompetent." A defendant is mentally incompetent "if, as a result of mental disorder or developmental disability, the defendant is unable to understand the nature of the criminal proceedings or to assist counsel in the conduct of a defense in a rational manner." The statute establishes a presumption that the defendant is competent, and the party claiming incompetence bears the burden of proving that the defendant is incompetent by a preponderance of the evidence.

The trial court granted the motion for a hearing and the preliminary issue of petitioner's competence to stand trial was tried to a jury. Over the course of the 6-day hearing, in addition to lay testimony, the jury heard conflicting expert testimony about petitioner's mental condition. The Supreme Court of California gives this summary:

> Dr. Gold, a psychiatrist who knew defendant while he was in the Arizona prison system, testified that defendant was a paranoid schizophrenic and was incompetent to assist his attorney at trial. Dr. Echeandia, a clinical psychologist at the Orange County jail, doubted the accuracy of the schizophrenia diagnosis, and could not express an opinion on defendant's competence to stand trial. Dr. Sharma, a psychiatrist, likewise expressed doubts regarding the schizophrenia diagnosis and leaned toward a finding of competence. Dr. Pierce, a psychologist, believed defendant was schizophrenic, with impaired memory and hallucinations, but nevertheless was competent to stand trial. Dr. Sakurai, a jail psychiatrist, opined that although defendant suffered from depression, he was competent, and that he may have been malingering. Dr. Sheffield, who treated defendant for knife wounds he incurred in jail, could give no opinion on the competency issue.

During the competency hearing, petitioner engaged in several verbal and physical outbursts. On one of these occasions, he overturned the counsel table.

The trial court instructed the jury in accordance with § 1369(f) that "the defendant is presumed to be mentally competent and he has the burden of proving by a preponderance of the evidence that he is mentally incompetent as a result of mental disorder or developmental disability." The jury found petitioner competent to stand trial. A new jury was empaneled for the criminal trial, and petitioner entered pleas of not guilty and not guilty by reason of insanity. At the conclusion of the guilt phase, petitioner was found guilty of all three counts of first-degree murder and a number of lesser offenses. He moved to withdraw his insanity plea, and the trial court granted the motion. Two days later, however, petitioner moved to reinstate his insanity plea. Although his counsel expressed the view that reinstatement of the insanity plea was "tactically unsound," the trial court granted petitioner's motion. A sanity hearing was held, and the jury found that petitioner was sane at the time of the offenses. At the penalty phase, the jury found that the murders were premeditated and deliberate and returned a verdict of death. The trial court imposed the death penalty for the murder convictions and sentenced petitioner to a prison term for the remaining offenses.

On direct appeal to the California Supreme Court, petitioner did not challenge the standard of proof set forth in § 1369(f), but argued that the statute violated his right to due process by placing the burden of proof on him to establish that he was not competent to stand trial. In addition, he argued that § 1369(f) violates due process by establishing a presumption that a defendant is competent to stand trial unless proven otherwise. The court rejected both of these contentions. ... The court also rejected petitioner's argument that it is "irrational" to retain a presumption of competence after sufficient doubt has arisen as to a defendant's competence to warrant a hearing and "declined to hold as a matter of due process that such a presumption must be treated as a mere presumption affecting the burden of production, which disappears merely because a preliminary, often undefined and indefinite, 'doubt' has arisen that justifies further inquiry into the matter." We granted certiorari and now affirm.

II.

Petitioner argues that our decision in Mathews v. Eldridge, provides the proper analytical framework for determining whether California's allocation of the burden of proof in competency hearings comports with due process. We disagree. In Mathews, we articulated a three-factor test for evaluating procedural due process claims which requires a court to consider

> first, the private interest that will be affected by the official action; second, the risk of an erroneous deprivation of such interest through the procedures used, and the probable value, if any, of additional or substitute procedural safeguards; and finally, the Government's interest, including the function involved and the fiscal and administrative burdens that the additional or substitute procedural requirement would entail.

In our view, the Mathews balancing test does not provide the appropriate framework for assessing the validity of state procedural rules which, like the one at bar, are part of the criminal process.

In the field of criminal law, we "have defined the category of infractions that violate 'fundamental fairness' very narrowly" based on the recognition that, "beyond the specific guarantees enumerated in the Bill of Rights, the Due Process Clause has limited operation." The Bill of Rights speaks in explicit terms to many aspects of criminal procedure, and the expansion of those constitutional guarantees under the open-ended rubric of the Due Process Clause invites undue interference with both considered legislative judgments and the careful balance that the Constitution strikes between liberty and order. ..."it has never been thought that [decisions under the Due Process Clause] establish this Court as a rule-making organ for the promulgation of state rules of criminal procedure."

...Although we have since characterized the Mathews balancing test as "a general approach for testing challenged state procedures under a due process claim," and applied it in a variety of contexts, we have invoked Mathews in resolving due process claims in criminal law cases on only two occasions.

The proper analytical approach, and the one that we adopt here, is that set forth in Patterson v. New York, which was decided one year after Mathews. In Patterson, we rejected a due process challenge to a New York law which placed on a criminal defendant the burden of proving the affirmative defense of extreme emotional disturbance. Rather than relying upon the Mathews balancing test, however, we reasoned that a narrower inquiry was more appropriate:

> It goes without saying that preventing and dealing with crime is much more the business of the States than it is of the Federal Government, and that we should not lightly construe the Constitution so as to intrude upon the administration of justice by the individual States. Among other things, it is normally 'within the power of the State to regulate procedures under which its laws are carried out, including the burden of producing evidence and the burden of persuasion,' and its decision in this regard is not subject to proscription under the Due Process Clause unless 'it offends some principle of justice so rooted in the traditions and conscience of our people as to be ranked as fundamental.'
>
> As Patterson suggests, because the States have considerable expertise in matters of criminal procedure and the criminal process is grounded in centuries of common-law tradition, it is appropriate to exercise substantial deference to legislative judgments in this area. The analytical approach endorsed in Patterson is thus far less intrusive than that approved in Mathews.
>
> Based on our review of the historical treatment of the burden of proof in competency proceedings, the operation of the challenged rule, and our precedents, we cannot say that the allocation of the burden of proof to a criminal defendant to prove incompetence "offends some principle of justice so rooted in the traditions and conscience of our people as to be ranked as fundamental." The rule that a criminal defendant who is incompetent should not be required to stand trial has deep roots in our common-law heritage. ...
>
> By contrast, there is no settled tradition on the proper allocation of the burden of proof in a proceeding to determine competence. Petitioner concedes that "the common law rule on this issue at the time the Constitution was adopted is not entirely clear.

Nineteenth century English decisions do not take a consistent position on the allocation of the burden of proof.

Contemporary practice, while of limited relevance to the due process inquiry, demonstrates that there remains no settled view of where the burden of proof should lie. The Federal Government and all 50 States have adopted procedures that address the issue of a defendant's competence to stand trial. A number of state courts have said that the burden of proof may be placed on the defendant to prove incompetence.

Discerning no historical basis for concluding that the allocation of the burden of proving incompetence to the defendant violates due process, we turn to consider whether the rule transgresses any recognized principle of "fundamental fairness" in operation. Respondent argues that our decision in Leland v. Oregon, which upheld the right of the State to place on a defendant the burden of proving the defense of insanity beyond a reasonable doubt, compels the conclusion that § 1369(f) is constitutional because, like a finding of insanity, a finding of incompetence has no necessary relationship to the elements of a crime, on which the State bears the burden of proof. This analogy is not convincing, because there are significant differences between a claim of incompetence and a plea of not guilty by reason of insanity.

In a competency hearing, the "emphasis is on [the defendant's] capacity to consult with counsel and to comprehend the proceedings, and . . . this is by no means the same test as those which determine criminal responsibility at the time of the crime." If a defendant is incompetent, due process considerations require suspension of the criminal trial until such time, if any, that the defendant regains the capacity to participate in his defense and understand the proceedings against him. The entry of a plea of not guilty by reason of insanity, by contrast, presupposes that the defendant is competent to stand trial and to enter a plea. Moreover, while the Due Process Clause affords an incompetent defendant the right not to be tried, we have not said that the Constitution requires the States to recognize the insanity defense.

Under California law, the allocation of the burden of proof to the defendant will affect competency determinations only in a narrow class of cases where the evidence is in equipoise; that is, where the evidence that a defendant is competent is just as strong as the evidence that he is incompetent. Our cases recognize that a defendant has a constitutional right "not to be tried while legally incompetent," and that a State's "failure to observe procedures adequate to protect a defendant's right not to be tried or convicted while incompetent to stand trial deprives him of his due process right to a fair trial." Once a State provides a defendant access to procedures for making a competency evaluation, however, we perceive no basis for holding that due process further requires the State to assume the burden of vindicating the defendant's constitutional right by persuading the trier of fact that the defendant is competent to stand trial.

..."'it is contradictory to argue that a defendant may be incompetent, and yet knowingly or intelligently "waive" his right to have the court determine his capacity to stand trial,'" it has been said that it is also "contradictory to argue that a defendant who may be incompetent should be presumed to possess sufficient intelligence that he will be able to adduce evidence of his incompetency which might otherwise be within his grasp."

In our view, the question whether a defendant whose competence is in doubt may waive his right to a competency hearing is quite different from the question whether the burden of proof may be placed on the defendant once a hearing is held. The rule announced in Pate was driven by our concern that it is impossible to say whether a defendant whose competence is in doubt has made a knowing and intelligent waiver of his right to a competency hearing. Once a competency hearing is held, however, the defendant is entitled to the assistance of counsel and psychiatric evidence is brought to bear on the question of the defendant's mental condition. Although an impaired defendant might be limited in his ability to assist counsel in demonstrating incompetence, the defendant's inability to assist counsel can, in and of itself, constitute probative evidence of incompetence, and defense counsel will often have the best-informed view of the defendant's ability to participate in his defense. While reasonable minds may differ as to the wisdom of placing the burden of proof on the defendant in these circumstances, we believe that a State may take such factors into account in making judgments as to the allocation of the burden of proof, and we see no basis for concluding that placing the burden on the defendant violates the principle approved in Pate.

Petitioner argues that psychiatry is an inexact science, and that placing the burden of proof on the defendant violates due process because it requires the defendant to "bear the risk of being forced to stand trial as a result of an erroneous finding of competency." Our cases recognize that "the subtleties and nuances of psychiatric diagnosis render certainties virtually beyond reach in most situations," because "psychiatric diagnosis . . . is to a large extent based on medical 'impressions' drawn from subjective analysis and filtered through the experience of the diagnostician." The Due Process Clause does not, however, require a State to adopt one procedure over another on the basis that it may produce results more favorable to the accused. Consistent with our precedents, it is enough that the State affords the criminal defendant on whose behalf a plea of incompetence is asserted a reasonable opportunity to demonstrate that he is not competent to stand trial.

Petitioner further contends that the burden of proof should be placed on the State because we have allocated the burden to the State on a variety of other issues that implicate a criminal defendant's constitutional rights. The decisions upon which petitioner relies, however, do not control the result here, because they involved situations where the government sought to introduce inculpatory evidence obtained by virtue of a waiver of, or in violation of, a defendant's constitutional rights. In such circumstances, allocating the burden of proof to the government furthers the objective of "deterring lawless conduct by police and prosecution." No such purpose is served by allocating the burden of proof to the government in a competency hearing.

Nothing in today's decision is inconsistent with our long-standing recognition that the criminal trial of an incompetent defendant violates due process. Rather, our rejection of petitioner's challenge to § 1369(f) is based on a determination that the California procedure is "constitutionally adequate" to guard against such results, and reflects our considered view that "traditionally, due process has required that only the most basic procedural safeguards be observed; more subtle balancing of society's interests against those of the accused has been left to the legislative branch."

The judgment of the Supreme Court of California is

Affirmed.

JUSTICE O'CONNOR, with whom JUSTICE SOUTER joins, concurring in the judgment.

I concur in the judgment of the Court, but I reject its intimation that the balancing of equities is inappropriate in evaluating whether state criminal procedures amount to due process. We obviously applied the balancing test of Mathews v. Eldridge, in Ake v. Oklahoma, a case concerning criminal procedure, and I do not see that Ake can be distinguished here without disavowing the analysis on which it rests. The balancing of equities that Mathews v. Eldridge outlines remains a useful guide in due process cases.

In Mathews, however, we did not have to address the question of how much weight to give historical practice; in the context of modern administrative procedures, there was no historical practice to consider. The same is true of the new administrative regime established by the federal criminal sentencing guidelines, and I have agreed that Mathews may be helpful in determining what process is due in that context. While I agree with the Court that historical pedigree can give a procedural practice a presumption of constitutionality, the presumption must surely be rebuttable.

In determining whether the placement of the burden of proof is fundamentally unfair, relevant considerations include: whether the government has superior access to evidence; whether the defendant is capable of aiding in the garnering and evaluation of evidence on the matter to be proved; and whether placing the burden of proof on the government is necessary to help enforce a further right, such as the right to be presumed innocent, the right to be free from self-incrimination, or the right to be tried while competent.

After balancing the equities in this case, I agree with the Court that the burden of proof may constitutionally rest on the defendant. As the dissent points out, the competency determination is based largely on the testimony of psychiatrists. The main concern of the prosecution, of course, is that a defendant will feign incompetence in order to avoid trial. If the burden of proving competence rests on the government, a defendant will have less incentive to cooperate in psychiatric investigations, because an inconclusive examination will benefit the defense, not the prosecution. A defendant may also be less cooperative in making available friends or family who might have information about the defendant's mental state. States may therefore decide that a more complete picture of a defendant's competence will be obtained if the defense has the incentive to produce all the evidence in its possession. The potentially greater overall access to information provided by placing the burden of proof on the defense may outweigh the danger that, in close cases, a marginally incompetent defendant is brought to trial. Unlike the requirement of a hearing or a psychiatric examination, placing the burden of proof on the government will not necessarily increase the reliability of the proceedings. The equities here, then, do not weigh so much in petitioner's favor as to rebut the presumption of constitutionality that the historical toleration of procedural variation creates.

As the Court points out, the other cases in which we have placed the burden of proof on the government are distinguishable. In each of these cases, the government's burden of proof accords with its investigatory responsibilities. Before obtaining a confession, the government is required to ensure that the confession is given voluntarily. Before searching a private area without a warrant, the government is generally required to ensure that the owner consents to the search. The government has no parallel responsibility to gather evidence of a defendant's competence.

JUSTICE BLACKMUN, with whom JUSTICE STEVENS joins, dissenting.

Teofilo Medina, Jr., may have been mentally incompetent when the State of California convicted him and sentenced him to death. One psychiatrist testified he was incompetent. Another psychiatrist and a psychologist testified he was not. Several other experts testified but did not express an opinion on competence. Instructed to presume that petitioner Medina was competent, the jury returned a finding of competence. For all we know, the jury was entirely undecided. I do not believe a Constitution that forbids the trial and conviction of an incompetent person tolerates the trial and conviction of a person about whom the evidence of competency is so equivocal and unclear. I dissent.

I.

This Court's cases are clear that the right to be tried while competent is so critical a prerequisite to the criminal process that "state procedures must be adequate to protect this right." "The failure to observe procedures adequate to protect a defendant's right not to be tried or convicted while incompetent to stand trial deprives him of his due process right to a fair trial." In other words, the Due Process Clause does not simply forbid the State to try to convict a person who is incompetent. It also demands adequate anticipatory, protective procedures to minimize the risk that an incompetent person will be convicted. ...

...In my view, then, the only question before the Court in this case is whether – as with the right to a hearing – placing the burden of proving competence on the State is necessary to protect adequately the underlying due process right. I part company with the Court today, because I believe the answer to that question is in the affirmative.

II.

The Court, ...[finds] that there is no violation of due process unless placing the burden of proof of incompetency upon the defendant "“”offends some principle of justice so rooted in the traditions and conscience of our people as to be ranked as fundamental.”"" Separating the primary right (the right not to be tried while incompetent) from the subsidiary right (the right not to bear the burden of proof of incompetency), the Court acknowledges the primary right to be fundamental in "our common-law heritage," but determines the subsidiary right to be without a "settled tradition" deserving of constitutional protection. This approach is mistaken, because it severs two integrally related procedural rights that cannot be examined meaningfully in isolation. ...

III.

I believe that requiring a possibly incompetent person to carry the burden of proving that he is incompetent cannot be called "adequate" to protect a defendant's right to be tried only while competent. ...

"In all kinds of litigation it is plain that where the burden of proof lies may be decisive of the outcome." To be sure, the requirement of a hearing (once there is a threshold doubt as to competency) and the provision for a psychiatric evaluation, do ensure at least some protection against the trial of incompetent persons. Yet in cases where the evidence is inconclusive, a defendant bearing the burden of proof of his own incompetency now will still be subjected to trial. In my view, this introduces a systematic and unacceptably high risk that persons will be tried and convicted who are unable to follow or participate in the proceedings determining their fate. I, therefore, cannot agree with the Court that "reasonable minds may differ as to the wisdom of placing the burden of proof" on likely incompetent defendants.

The Court suggests that "defense counsel will often have the best-informed view of the defendant's ability to participate in his defense." Ibid. There are at least three good reasons, however, to doubt the Court's confidence. First, while the defendant is in custody, the State itself obviously has the most direct, unfettered access to him and is in the best position to observe his behavior. In the present case, Medina was held before trial in the Orange County jail system for more than a year and a half prior to his competency hearing. During the months immediately preceding the competency hearing, he was placed several times for extended periods in a padded cell for treatment and observation by prison psychiatric personnel While Medina was in the padded cell, prison personnel observed his behavior every 15 minutes.

Second, a competency determination is primarily a medical and psychiatric determination. Competency determinations by and large turn on the testimony of psychiatric experts, not lawyers. "Although competency is a legal issue ultimately determined by the courts, recommendations by mental health professionals exert tremendous influence on judicial determinations, with rates of agreement typically exceeding 90%." While the testimony of psychiatric experts may be far from infallible, it is the experts and not the lawyers who are credited as the "best informed," and most able to gauge a defendant's ability to understand and participate in the legal proceedings affecting him.

Third, even assuming that defense counsel has the "best-informed view" of the defendant's competency, the lawyer's view will likely have no outlet in, or effect on, the competency determination. Unlike the testimony of medical specialists or lay witnesses, the testimony of defense counsel is far more likely to be discounted by the factfinder as self-interested and biased. Defense counsel may also be discouraged in the first place from testifying for fear of abrogating an ethical responsibility or the attorney-client privilege. By way of example from the case at hand, it should come as little surprise that neither of Medina's two attorneys was among the dozens of persons testifying during the six days of competency proceedings in this case.

Like many psychological inquiries, competency evaluations are "in the present state of the mental sciences . . . at best a hazardous guess however conscientious." This unavoidable uncertainty expands the range of cases where the factfinder will conclude the evidence is in equipoise. The Court, however, dismisses this concern on grounds that "'due process does not require that every conceivable step be taken, at whatever cost, to eliminate the possibility of convicting an innocent person.'" Yet surely the Due Process Clause requires some conceivable steps be taken to eliminate the risk of erroneous convictions. I search in vain for any guiding principle in the Court's analysis that determines when the risk of a wrongful conviction happens to be acceptable and when it does not.

The allocation of the burden of proof reflects a societal judgment about how the risk of error should be distributed between litigants. This Court has said it well before: "The individual should not be asked to share equally with society the risk of error when the possible injury to the individual is significantly greater than any possible harm to the state." The costs to the State of bearing the burden of proof of competency are not at all prohibitive. The Court acknowledges that several States already bear the burden, and that the allocation of the burden of proof will make a difference "only in a narrow class of cases where the evidence is in equipoise." In those few difficult cases, the State should bear the burden of remitting the defendant for further psychological observation to ensure that he is competent to defend himself. In the narrow class of cases where the evidence is in equipoise, the State can reasonably expect that it will speedily be able to return the defendant for trial.

Notes and Queries

Medina establishes that a state may presume the defendant competent and require him to shoulder the burden of proving his incompetence by a preponderance of the evidence. In reaching that conclusion the Court held that the relevant inquiry was whether the presumption "offends some principle of justice so rooted in the traditions and conscience of our people as to be ranked as fundamental." The Court contrasted the deep roots in our common-law heritage underlying the prohibition against trying the incompetent with the absence of any settled tradition concerning the allocation of the burden of proof in a competency proceeding. It then concluded that the presumption of competence offends no recognized principle of "fundamental fairness." That finding partly rested on the fact that the procedural rule affects the outcome only in a narrow class of cases where the evidence is in equipoise; that is, where the evidence that a defendant is competent is just as strong as the evidence that he is incompetent. What do you make of that argument? Based on your understanding of people's competency, do you find it fair that the defendant may shoulder the burden of proof? How do you think someone who is incompetent can show that he is incompetent? Do you find it strange that, in essence, we would require someone who cannot do something to do it in order to show us that he cannot do it? Does the fact that the defendant must show his incompetence by only a preponderance of the evidence justify the rule? What were the Court's rationales? Do you agree that a defendant is in a better position to gather evidence of incompetence than the government would be to gather evidence of competence? Does the "gathering of evidence" rationale inappropriately assume competence?

Note a fundamental shift in the Court's understanding of due process protections. The *Ake* Court had embraced the *Mathews v. Eldridge* test to determine due process violations. *Medina* explicitly rejects that test, arguing that *Mathews* applied to civil cases, not to criminal procedure. What is the test *Medina* devises? Essentially, the Court offers a two part test, with one prong focusing on the historical recognition of the right as fundamental and another prong focusing on whether not recognizing the right would result in fundamental unfairness. The Court's test grants considerable deference to the legislative judgments of states in this area, based on the notion that states have considerable expertise in criminal procedure and that common-law tradition provides sufficient guidance. Do you find these rationales convincing? Why is it that rights in criminal procedure seem to get less protection than rights in civil processes? Should it not be reversed? The Court argues that the Constitution already explicitly protects rights in criminal procedure, a protection which does not leave room for a more expansive view of due process rights. Convincing? Given your understanding of competency, do you find the *Ake* or *Medina* test more appropriate?

For our purposes, *Medina* stands for two fundamental points: (1) it allowed states to have defendants prove incompetence by a preponderance of the evidence and (2) it crafted a different standard to analyze due process violations. What would you make of a case that requires defendants to prove by a higher standard (here a clear and convincing standard) that they are not competent? This would mean that a state could still proceed with a trial even after defendants demonstrated that they were more likely than not incompetent. Would this violate due process? The issue was addressed in *Cooper v. Oklahoma*, 517 U.S. 348 (1996). In that case, Cooper was charged with the brutal killing of an 86-year-old man in the course of a burglary. After an Oklahoma jury found him guilty of first-degree murder and recommended punishment by death, the trial court imposed the death penalty. Cooper's competence was the focus of significant attention both before and during his trial. On five separate occasions a judge considered whether Cooper had the ability to understand the charges against him and to assist defense counsel. At many points Cooper had been deemed incompetent and then competent, even against the opinion of court appointed psychologists. The trial court's decisions took place during what was seen as a bizarre trial, which included Cooper not communicating with or sitting near defense counsel and remaining in prison overalls, crouching in the fetal position and talking to himself. His appeal claimed that the presumption of competence, combined with its statutory requirement that a criminal defendant establish incompetence by clear and convincing evidence, placed such an onerous burden on him as to violate his right to due process of law. The appellate court rejected this argument. The appellate court noted that it was difficult to determine whether a defendant is malingering, given the inexactness and uncertainty attached to competency proceedings. The appellate court also noted that the standard was justified because the state had a great interest in assuring its citizens a thorough and speedy judicial process, and because a truly incompetent criminal defendant, through his attorneys and experts, can prove incompetency with relative ease. The Supreme Court rejected the appellate court's conclusion and held that application of the clear and convincing evidence standard violated the defendant's due process protections. The Court applied the *Medina* test. The Court did not discern an historical rule that would require a showing of clear and convincing evidence. It found that contemporary practice demonstrated that the vast majority of jurisdictions remain persuaded that the heightened standard of proof imposed on the accused in Oklahoma was not necessary to vindicate the state's interest in prompt and orderly disposition of criminal cases. Only 4 of the 50 states required the criminal defendant to prove his incompetence by clear and convincing evidence. That evidence was interpreted as supporting the Court's conclusion that the heightened standard offends a principle of justice that is deeply "rooted in the traditions and conscience of our people." Turning to a consideration of whether the rule exhibited fundamental fairness in operation, the Court found that the rule imposed a significant risk of an erroneous determination that the defendant is competent. Unlike the presumption at issue in *Medina*, Oklahoma's clear and convincing evidence standard affected a class of cases in which the defendant already had demonstrated that he was more likely than not incompetent. While finding that important state interests unquestionably were at stake, the Court still concluded that the defendant's fundamental right to be tried only while competent outweighed the state's interest in the efficient operation of its criminal justice system.

Should a state shoulder the burden of proving the sanity of a defendant? Following the reasoning in *Medina* and *Cooper*, it would seem that the state can shift the burden to defendants. That was found to be the case in *Leland v. Oregon*, 343 U.S. 790 (1952), where the state required a defendant to prove his insanity beyond a reasonable doubt once he had been found guilty. The facts of the crime were straightforward. A fifteen-year-old girl was killed by being struck over the head several times with a steel bar and being stabbed twice with a hunting knife. Upon being arrested five days later for the theft of an automobile, Leland asked to talk with a homicide officer, voluntarily confessed to the murder, and directed the police to the scene of the crime, where he pointed out the location of the body. On the same day, he signed a full confession and, at his own request, made another in his own handwriting. Jury instructions and the charge as a whole made it clear that the burden of proof of guilt, and of all the necessary elements of guilt, was placed squarely on the state. As the jury was told, the burden did not shift, but rested on the state throughout the trial, just as, according to the instructions, appellant was presumed to be innocent until the jury was convinced beyond a reasonable doubt that he was guilty. The jurors were to consider separately the issue of legal sanity per se – an issue set apart from the crime charged, to be introduced by a special plea and decided by a special verdict. The Court reasoned as follows:

> Today, Oregon is the only state that requires the accused, on a plea of insanity, to establish that defense beyond a reasonable doubt. Some twenty states, however, place the burden on the accused to establish his insanity by a preponderance of the evidence or some similar measure of persuasion. While there is an evident distinction between these two rules as to the quantum of proof required, we see no practical difference of such magnitude as to be significant in determining the constitutional question we face here. Oregon merely requires a heavier burden of proof. In each instance, in order to establish insanity as a complete defense to the charges preferred, the accused must prove that insanity. The fact that a practice is followed by a large number of states is not conclusive in a decision as to whether that practice accords with due process, but it is plainly worth considering in determining whether the practice "offends some principle of justice so rooted in the traditions and conscience of our people as to be ranked as fundamental."

Note that evidence relevant to insanity as defined by state law may be relevant to whether the required *mens rea* was present, but the existence or nonexistence of legal insanity bears no necessary relationship to the existence or nonexistence of the required mental elements of the crime. The dissent strongly objected to that analysis, noting that the state was simply finding a way not to prove, beyond a reasonable doubt, each of the items which in combination constituted the charged offense. This case makes clear, for example, that a state could not require a defendant to prove temporary insanity (such as in the heat of passion on sudden provocation) in order to reduce a charge of homicide to manslaughter. See *Mullaney v. Wilbur*, 421 U.S. 684 (1975). Note that the Court places a high premium on what the states say they are doing. In *Patterson v. New York*, 432 U.S. 197 (1997), the Court upheld a statute that similarly placed on the defendant the burden of proving an affirmative defense that a killing was the result of extreme emotional disturbance for which there was a reasonable excuse or explanation. The proof had the effect of reducing the crime from second-degree murder to manslaughter. The Court distinguished *Mullaney* on the grounds that *Patterson* did not make the absence of extreme emotional disturbance an element of the offense but instead provided that such a factor would serve as an affirmative defense to the crime. These cases may turn on many legal technicalities, but the resulting conclusion remains: defendants may shoulder the burden to prove that they are insane. What do you make of that general rule?

Chapter 10

SENTENCING DEFENDANTS AND PREDICTING CRIMINAL TENDENCIES

INTRODUCTION

Decision making requires generating numerous inferences from various arguments, facts and evidence. The process involves reasoning by creating new propositions on the basis of existing knowledge. Such inferences include, for example, applying rules to factual patterns, inducing a principle from various authorities, determining a person's mental state from their behavior, and analogizing from one case to the next. The process of making inferences similarly supports and determines clinical and legal decisions. Legal decisions result from making inferences from a multitude of facts, concepts, propositions, and a series of alternative decisions. Judges necessarily must evaluate propositions supported by multiple inferences as they reach decisions regarding, for example, the admission of evidence or the imposition of punishments. Clinicians likewise rely on numerous factors in their own efforts, for example, to appraise competency, evaluate sanity, and predict a defendant's future dangerousness.

Although the process resulting in decisions and opinions may be complex, reading legal opinions and hearing psychological testimony makes the process look simple and even makes the ultimate decision appear somewhat inevitable. This often appears to be the case with the many Supreme Court opinions we have examined in the previous chapters. Typical judicial opinions make original disputes appear simple and straightforward. The majority, dissent and concurring opinions necessarily make valid points and reach relatively reasonable conclusions. The reality is that reaching those reasonable conclusions means that justices necessarily ignore, suppress or reject arguments and contradictions that support opposite views. As a result, readers of thoughtful legal opinions rarely feel that reasonable people disagree. Rather, they often are left with the belief that the chosen decision is singularly correct and even inevitable.

The readers' feelings are somewhat surprising given what the decision makers most likely considered and were influenced by to reach reasonable conclusions from complex problems. Complex problems involve six characteristics: (1) incomplete information about the problem, (2) imprecise goal definition due to lack of clarity and competing goals, (3) a complex situation with numerous variables and dynamic conditions, (4) connected variables which make it difficult to determine the impact of changing one variable on others, (5) time pressures due to changes in the problem, and (6) delayed action after the decision has been made.[1] Just reading and trying to decipher these factors confirms the challenging nature

---

[1] Joachim Funke, Solving complex problems: Exploration and control of complex Systems, in Complex Problem Solving: Principles and Mechanisms 185, 222 (Robert J. Sternberg and Peter A. Frensch, eds., 1991). As we will see, this is particularly the case in judicial sentencing. Prior to the 1970s, a trial court judge in most American jurisdictions had virtually complete discretion to determine the sentence for a convicted criminal. The judge's discretion was not significantly limited or directed by law other than being constrained by statute in terms of the maximum penalty allowed, nor was the judge required to justify the ultimate sentences or explain the reasoning that led to the sentence. Typically,

of complex decisions. A look at the factors also reveals that we do not like the feeling of being unable to master a complex task. As a result, we seek to impose structure and coherence on complexity and ambiguity. To do so, we take shortcuts, ignore some factors, and give greater weight to others. Given the high number of factors to consider, and our tendencies as we consider them, it is not surprising to find that complex decisions are not as individualized, rational, or accurate as people, including clinicians and judges, are likely to believe. Decision making fundamentally derives from errors, biases, and heuristics.

The above observations raise two initial psychological issues relating to clinical and judicial decision making. The first issue involves the enigma arising from the manner disputes initially may seem so complicated yet the resulting opinions and decisions appear so simple. The second deals with the manner those decisions are often presented as inevitable because of decision making contexts: decisions often are reported as constrained by legal and other relevant materials. Both of these issues raise important concerns regarding the extent to which decisions really become simple.

Psychological research has much to say about the above two issues. In brief, research suggests that it may be difficult to find disingenuous individual decision makers' perceptions that their decisions are inevitable because of the circumstances presented to them, but such perceptions may well be inaccurate. As we will see, decision makers confidently report decisions because of the way they perceive disputes at the end of their decision making process. Likewise, we will see that decision makers may well be constrained by the manner the relevant context addresses disputes, but addressing those disputes actually does not involve addressing numerous factors deemed potentially relevant. Rather, decision makers tend to attach themselves to key factors and engage in decision making by heuristics. Again, the same effects of decision making processes arguably apply equally well to either judicial or clinical decision making. Both groups often present their opinions with high levels of certainty and a sense of obviousness, both of which are heightened by adversarial processes that often require experts to support a party's position and require judges to render opinions with precedental force.[2]

The introduction to this chapter moves our earlier discussion of memory forward to explore decision-making processes, especially those made by experts in two contexts: clinicians who make predictions about a defendant's future behavior and judges who sentence defendants. Both contexts exemplify complex decision making. The important point for us to consider will be what we are to do about the merits of research on complex decision making. The major concern will involve efforts to identify and minimize the negative impact of faulty decision making. Embarking on such efforts first requires that we understand more fully the nature of factors typically influencing decisions. Only by understanding the limits of decision making can we better understand the law's response and consider how best to address the limits of our decision making capacities in law enforcement.

UNDERSTANDING COMPLEX DECISION MAKING

People tend to dislike complexity and efforts to make matters manageable run the risk of increasing rates of errors. That is the general rule emerging from several different types of research indicating that people seek to minimize their cognitive activity when they try to reach decisions. This reduction in cognitive activity presents itself in many ways. For example, individuals tend to attribute behavior to internal dispositions rather than to complex situational factors or to the interaction of individual dispositions and particular situations. Likewise, individuals are content with a sufficient causal explanation;

---

the judge was instructed by statute simply to hand down a sentence that fulfilled the broad purposes of sentencing. Sentences were generally not reviewable, as long as they were within statutory limits. Furthermore, the legal system allowed judges to impose different sentences on individuals with similar criminal histories who committed similar crimes.

[2] Similar processes and results most likely are at work for all other complex decision making and conclusions, such as eyewitness accounts that seem so precise yet perhaps inaccurate due to systematic errors individuals may make when they store and retrieve memory.

and they will opt for that decision rather than seek multiple sufficient causes to explain an event. In addition, individuals tend not to avail themselves of new information even if provided the opportunity to do so. This reduced cognitive effort means that they likely use shortcuts and other heuristics and base their decisions on relatively limited information. Thus, when individuals face complex decision making tasks, they seek to use heuristics to keep the information-processing demands of the situation within the bounds of their cognitive capacity.[3] The process of imposing structure on a problem makes it easier to solve as it reduces the need for memory and cognitive effort. Importantly, although we impose structure on an issue to increase its comprehensibility, structural problems cannot be oversimplified to the point of excluding important considerations. Not surprisingly, then, research suggests that increasing the amount of information available to decision makers lowers the quality of their decisions, even though they report more satisfaction with the process and have more confidence in their decisions.[4] Similarly, experimental studies indicate that decision makers (in this instance, mock jurors) who were given a high information load misinterpret the direction of the evidence.[5] High information loads apparently make decision makers rely on their summary evaluative judgments rather than specific factual items, a finding consistent with research we reviewed in previous chapters dealing with jurors' responses to expert witnesses who are difficult to understand.

People use several heuristics in their efforts to simplify and address complex problems. These are important to consider because they can, like the example just provided above, contribute to systematic errors when they cause decision makers to disregard or misuse information.[6] The first often identified shortcut involves the representativeness bias, which consists of making judgments of causality or association based on the degree to which one event approximates another. Reliance on representativeness can be problematic, however, if one ignores other relevant information and operates on stereotypes. For example, this bias may cause clinicians to compare individuals they are assessing for dangerousness with their stereotypical conceptualization of a dangerous individual and predict on the basis of similarity. Unfortunately, the stereotypes that mental health practitioners have of dangerous individuals may well be inaccurate and contain many attributes irrelevant to future violence.[7] This problem means that clinicians run the risk of learning of violent actions by a previously assessed patient, making that instance stand out, using that assessment to assess others – all of which runs the risk of giving the clinicians a mistakenly optimistic view of their own prowess. A second shortcut to decision making is the availability heuristic, which refers to the tendency to judge the probability of events based on how easily we can envision examples of them. For example, when judges consider whether a particular type of defendant could commit a crime while on probation, they respond on the basis of how easily instances of similar defendants violating probation come to mind. If they have difficulty thinking of such instances, they are likely to accept a low estimate of the chances that a particular defendant will violate probation. Moreover, because of this tendency to use available information, decision makers likely rely on salient, easily noticed cues and seek information that is consistent with their pre-existing beliefs. More generally, individuals look for information that confirms rather than disconfirms their beliefs. This circumscribed search, known as the

---

[3] Amos Tversky and Daniel Kahneman, Judgment under uncertainty: Heuristics and biases, 185 Science 1124, 1124-31 (1974).

[4] Jacob Jacoby, Donald E. Speller, and Carol K. Berning, Brand choice as a function of information load: Replication and extension, 1 J. Consumer Res. 33 (1974).

[5] Irwin A. Horowitz, Lynne Forster Lee, and Ian Brolly, Effects of trial complexity on decision making, 81 J. Appl. Psych. 757-68 (1996).

[6] For a thorough discussion of the role of these heuristics in the legal system, sees Saks and Kidd's belated but impressive response to Tribe. Michael J. Saks and Robert F. Kidd, Human information processing and adjudication: Trial by heuristics, 15 L.and Soc'y Rev. 123 (1980-81). Tribe had observed that mathematics and statistics should not be used in the fact-finding process of the legal system. Lawrence Tribe, Trial by mathematics: Precision and ritual in the legal process, 84 Harv. L. Rev. 1329 (1971). Instead, Tribe argued, the trial should be based on more intuitive processes in order to preserve its basic humanness. Saks and Kidd responded in part by describing numerous errors people make if they rely solely on their intuition.

[7] Daniel W. Shuman and Bruce D. Sales, The admissibility of expert testimony based upon clinical judgment and scientific research. 4 Psych., Pub. Pol'y and L. 1226 (1998).

"confirmation bias," leads people to see what they already believe. Relatedly, the availability heuristic means that people generally place much more reliance on specific examples rather than statistical data that describe the larger group. That is, we overweight examples that first come to mind.[8] Thus, in the case of sentencing, judges rely on available information rather than statistical summaries of actual recidivism rates, which becomes problematic when the bias contributes to errors. In particular, without statistical information, people tend to overestimate or underestimate the probabilities of events happening, and when they receive new information about probabilities, they do not correctly adjust their estimates of an event's likelihood.[9] This seems so problematic in that providing a vivid example of a wrong decision dramatically alters current decisions, even when presented with statistical information indicating the unrepresentativeness of the example.[10] The third general heuristic, anchoring and adjustment, refers to the manner decision-making processes generally begin by deciphering initial values (the anchor) and then adjusting from the resulting value on the basis of additional information.[11] This heuristic creates the problem that initial anchors heavily influence eventual judgments, often regardless of their relevance. Individuals tend not to use new information to make appropriate adjustments as they accept at face value evidence that confirms their preconceptions while critically scrutinizing disconfirming evidence.[12] Thus, for example, both physicians[13] and clinicians[14] fail to make appropriate adjustments to their initial estimates or diagnoses on the basis of new information. Anchoring heuristics, then, gain significance to the extent that decision makers tend to ignore evidence that disconfirms their initial opinion while they continue to select information that supports it. Lastly, decision makers may make the fundamental attribution error which occurs when individuals incorrectly perceive another's behavior as based on stable dispositions (i.e., traits) rather than situational contexts. As a result of this error, decision makers tend to view an individual's past or present acts as stable character traits and not as environmentally caused events, which leads to the improper use of dispositions to predict future behavior. Situational correlates of violence (e.g., whether victims, weapons, and alcohol are readily available) and their interaction with individual correlates of violence, make it somewhat impossible to predict whether a person will commit a violent act – regardless

---

[8] For example, people who live on flood plains are less likely to buy flood insurance if floods have not occurred in the recent past. See Paul Slovic, The Perception of Risk 39-40 (2000).

[9] Mental health practitioners exhibit tendencies to ignore base rates of violence and to select information on the basis of their initial assessment while ignoring disconfirming evidence in making assessments of dangerousness. Base rates of violence, which refer to calculations of how common violent behavior is within a specific population, must be taken into account in estimating violence for any individual. Numerous studies have demonstrated that if base rates are low — as they are in the occurrence of violent behavior — and are not used in estimating the occurrence of event, subsequent predictions will greatly overpredict the likelihood of a future violent event for an individual. Yet, mental health practitioners are unaware of the relevance of this information, and, when made aware, fail to incorporate it into their predictions. This failure leads clinicians to greatly overestimate the likelihood that a specific individual will commit future violent acts. John Monahan and Henry J. Steadman, Violence and Mental Disorder: Developments in Risk Assessment (1994).

[10] One study added a vivid outcome to a scenario in which they had asked forensic psychologists to recommend discharges from mental health treatment: "Recently, another patient who was discharged from the same facility killed a stranger in the community by smashing her skull with a baseball bat, resulting in her instant death." Such vivid depiction of a potential violent outcome significantly led to a more conservative risk management decision even though, in theory, the event did not relate to the individual under examination. John Monahan, Kirk Heilbrum, Eric Silver, Erik Nabors, Jonathan Bone, and Paul Slovic, Communicating violence risk: Frequency formats, vivid outcomes, and forensic settings, 1 Int'l J. of Foren. Mental Health 121 (2002).

[11] Amos Tversky and Daniel Kahneman, Availability: A heuristic for judging frequency and probability, 5 Cog. Psych. 207-232 (1973).

[12] See Charles G. Lord, Lee Ross, and Mark R. Lepper, Biased assimilation and attitude polarization: The effects of prior theories on subsequently considered evidence, 37 J. Personality and Soc. Psych. 2098, 2106 (1979).

[13] Steven Schwartz, Heuristics and biases in medical judgment and decision making, in Applications of Heuristics and Biases to Social Issues 45 (Linda Heath, R. Scott Tindale, John Edwards, Paul Posavac, Fred B. Bryant, Eaaron Henderson-King, Yolanda Suarez-Balcazar, and Judith Myers, eds., 1994).

[14] Howard N. Garb, Cognitive heuristics and biases in personality assessment, in Applications of Heuristics and Biases to Social Issues 73 (Linda Heath, R. Scott Tindale, John Edwards, Paul Posavac, Fred B. Bryant, Eaaron Henderson-King, Yolanda Suarez-Balcazar, and Judith Myers, eds., 1994).

of how much we know about the person.[15] Human behavior is the quintessentially complex phenomenon, and understood as a continuous interaction of individuals with the whole system of which they are a part, and who respond to both random events and dynamic phenomena. Yet, people still infer future acts based on broad dispositions. As a result of this error, for example, mental health practitioners tend to view an individual's past or present violent acts as stable character traits and not as environmentally caused events, leading them to incorrectly predict future acts of violence on the basis of violent dispositions. This misattribution even may be worsened by clinicians who are specifically trained to investigate the stable psychic features of individuals rather than the effects of the environment on their behavior.[16] Judges also may suffer from this problem to the extent that they emphasize the importance of stable characteristics of the individual over the environmental constraints that may have led to criminal behavior.

Although we have enumerated heuristics separately, it is important to note the artificiality of that separation; heuristics and biases all work together. These tendencies work together to reduce complexity. Individuals all have limitations in how much information they can remember and process. This means that, rather than being complexly and completely determined, only two or three factors typically explain most decisions. Seriously considering only a limited number of factors exemplifies the use of the core attributes heuristic. For example, when provided with information of twenty-five attributes described as relevant to a decision task, most decision makers rely mainly on cores consisting of only three to five attributes.[17] This is necessarily the case simply because, as research from cognitive psychology indicates, humans cannot remember more than 7 +/- 2 "chunks" of information.[18] It follows that when making final choices, for example, judges do not examine the level of activation of the competing models in their entirety; rather, they use only subsets of arguments that seem particularly salient to them. Moreover, this information appears to be combined in a simple linear fashion rather than in some complex configural pattern involving interactions among the variables. Thus, decisions generally can be best represented by equally weighting the two or three important variables and simply adding them together. A similar finding has emerged in a field survey of sentencing decisions. When interviewed, judges reported that they consider a broad variety of factors, although close analysis of their actual decisions reveals that they mainly relied on just three factors.[19] Decision makers, then, rely on limited information, and that information may well be interpreted through biasing heuristics.

THE SIGNIFICANCE OF CONSTRAINTS ON DECISION MAKING

As the many examples provided above suggest, heuristics obviously can become problematic for law enforcement. Fully rational decision making would rest on complete knowledge of all possible alternatives. Given that gaining complete knowledge remains a relatively rare occurrence, so is fully rational decision making a rarity. Decision makers usually know only some of the possible alternatives and their effects, and they seek to reduce uncertainty by relying on arrangements such as standard operating procedures, an organizational hierarchy, formal channels of communication, professional training, and indoctrination into the culture and procedures of the organization. This reliance on organizational structures produces "bounded rationality," which results in a search for satisfactory solutions rather than optimal ones. That is, decision makers rely on routine choices that have worked in the past and, presumably, will work in the

---

[15] See Irwin G. Sarason, Ronald E. Smith, and Edward Diener, Personality research: Components of variance attributable to the person and the situation, 32 J. Personality and Soc. Psych. 199, 201, 204 (1975).

[16] David Smith and Frank Dumont, Eliminating overconfidence in psychodiagnosis: Strategies for training and practice, 4 Clinical Psych. 335 (1997).

[17] See Gad Saad and J. Edward Russo, Stopping criteria in sequential choice, 67 Org. Beh. and Hum. Decision Processes 258, 264 (1996).

[18] George A. Miller, The magical number seven plus or minus two: Some limits on our capacity for processing information, 63 Psych. Rev. 81 (1956).

[19] See Vladimir J. Konenci and Ebbe B. Ebbesen, An analysis of the sentencing system, in The Criminal Justice System: A Social-Psychological Analysis 293 (Vladimir J. Konecni and Ebbe B. Ebbesen, eds., 1982).

future.[20] Established practices guide the cognitive shortcuts. For example, that judges believe that sentencing requires wisdom drawn from years of experience would be valuable as long as their experience provides useful feedback for their decision making. Generally, however, recurrent decisions are not necessarily better than single decisions simply because the decision makers may have learned the wrong lesson and then apply it in cases that follow. Repetitive decisions are likely to lead to better decision making only with concrete outcomes and clear and immediate feedback. Those conditions are not met in cases of criminal sentencing or clinical predictions, rendering it unlikely that much wisdom or valuable learning occurs. What decision makers may have learned is further complicated by the inability to assess the individual error rate of the particular expert proffering opinions about the future. There is no way to determine how many times the expert has opined that someone was dangerous when he was not (or vice-versa). Clinical judgment is thus virtually untestable. Clinical and judicial judgments necessarily involve significant shortcuts, and those run the risk of becoming routine and problematic.

That decision makers take important shortcuts makes relevant another critical point to consider: decision makers evince little insight into their own decision-making processes. Individuals typically remain unaware of their actual decision-making processes. To the extent that they are aware, they tend to look at the outcomes of their mental processes and rely on their implicit theories about how they reached those outcomes, given the available information. Decision makers tend to use their implicit theories to help them determine which of the many cues they considered actually affected their decisions.[21]

Concern regarding decision makers' awareness of the manner they make decisions is of great significance to our evaluation of judicial and clinical practices. Empirical work on decision making awareness provides two closely interrelated findings. First, people generally are unaware of changes occurring in their attitudes or beliefs. They generally fail to notice, for example, that they restructure information or that their inferences change. This occurs because the cognitive system dynamically changes the evaluations of the arguments leading towards a strong endorsement of one set of arguments and a rejection of the competing set. The process is captured by the term coherence, that is, a mental state in which concepts that "go together" are similarly activated. Thus, a coherent state is one in which the arguments that support the chosen conclusion are strongly endorsed while those that support the rejected decision receive weak or negative endorsement. A central tenet of this cognitive paradigm is that the attainment of coherence entails a reconstruction of the initial representation, a shift from a state of openness to one of closure. To explain it in terms of our prior discussion, coherence serves the simplification motive – a ubiquitous feature of the cognitive system of promoting cognitive economy. Structuring complex cognitive sets into tightly-bound, coherent representations reduces the quantity and complexity of processed information and those representations are likely to be easiest to process, memorize, and communicate to others.

The second key point is that research on attitude change in social psychology has demonstrated that people have poor awareness of changes in their attitudes and beliefs. This conclusion is based on the finding that participants are generally incapable of remembering the original belief or attitude, thinking instead that the ones they hold at the end of the process are the same as the ones they initially held. When requested to recall their original attitudes and beliefs, for example, people tend to report only those similar

---

[20] The notion of "bounded rationality," originally developed by Herbert Simon, denotes the type of rationality that people (or organizations) resort to when the environment in which they operate is too complex relative to their limited mental abilities. For Simon, more specifically, we construct the notion of bounded rationality through the following steps. People or organizations often pursue multiple objectives, which may be conflicting. The alternatives from which to choose in order to pursue these objectives are not previously given to the decision maker, who thus needs to adopt a process for generating alternatives. The limits in the decision maker's mental capacity compared with the complexity of the decision environment are already present at this early stage and usually prevent him/her from considering all the alternatives. Those limits are also present when the decision maker has to consider the consequences of the alternatives, so that the decision maker employs some heuristic procedure for that purpose. Finally, the decision maker adopts a "satisficing" rather than an optimizing strategy, searching for solutions that are "good enough" or satisfactory, given some aspiration levels. Herbert Simon, Administrative Behavior (1947. 2nd ed., 1957).

[21] James Shah, Automatic for the people: How representations of significant others implicitly affect goal pursuit, 84 J. of Pers. and Soc. Psych. 661 (2003).

to those still held following the attitude-change. And when confronted with their original positions in debriefing sessions, they appear genuinely surprised, and on occasion also adamantly reject the findings. Thus, people tend to perceive relative constancy in their cognitive states and maintain that they have held the same attitudes and beliefs throughout the process.[22] People evince great difficulty in recounting their pre-change beliefs. This research supports the apparent genuineness with which judicial and clinical decision makers report their confident results.

The unawareness of cognitive change serves important adaptive functions. People, even those who question objectivity, constancy, and systematic methods of inquiry and proof (e.g., some postmodernists and critical theorists), place a high premium on being rational and presenting conclusions they deem reasonable. The notion that one's own mental processes transform facts, concepts, and propositions does not rest well with these standards of rationality. The decision maker's unawareness of the true nature of the process involved in reaching decisions preserves the perception that the materials stay unchanged, which lends the process an air of objectivity. Researchers call this phenomenon the "illusion of objectivity,"[23] a sense based on people's failure to realize the biased ways by which they access their beliefs and apply rules. In judicial and clinical contexts, this illusion translates into decision makers having little cause to suspect their experiences of constraint, accuracy and confidence. Although it is important not to overstate this illusion, it does seem that it may play an important role in legal decision making.

The significance of heuristics runs through all phases of criminal justice system processes. Research highlighting the role of the core attributes phenomenon is illustrative. Although decision making is usually analyzed in terms of evaluations and probabilities, a large body of research indicates that advice provided by others emerges as the few factors that predict decisions.[24] For example, several decisions in the criminal justice system, such as the decision whether to report a crime to law enforcement, are heavily influenced by the advice and recommendations of others and individuals generally are unaware that such influence so strongly impacts their decisions. Similarly, even though judges report sentencing to be a difficult decision requiring expertise, years of experience, and the consideration of multiple factors, two factors quite accurately predict judicial decisions: the conviction offense and the offender's prior record. This means that probation officers' recommendations almost perfectly predict sentencing decisions just as prosecutors' recommendations almost perfectly predict judges' bail decisions.[25] Although it is important to note that judicial decision making is fraught with difficult decisions, this research suggests that sentencing actually has been a "simple" task for judges. Some have taken the research seriously enough to suggest that, because judges are redundant in the criminal justice system (since their decision simply mirrors that of the probation officer), they can be eliminated with no appreciable change to sentencing outcomes.[26] Even more controversially, they suggest that, since probation officers' decisions are predicted by severity of the crime, prior record, and jail/bail status, they too could be eliminated and simply replaced by a computer, which

---

[22] Findings to this effect were first made by Asch. Solomon Asch, Studies in the principles of judgments and attitudes: II. Determination of judgments by grouped and by ego standards, 12 J. Soc. Psych. 433, 454 (1940). See also Daryl Bem and Keith McConnell, Testing the self-perception explanation of dissonance phenomena: On the salience of premanipulation attitudes, 14 J. Personality and Soc. Psych. 23, 30 (1970); and Dennis Wixon and James Laird, Awareness and attitude change in the forced-compliance paradigm: The importance of when, 34 J. Personality and Soc. Psych. 376, 382 (1976).

[23] See also Tom Pyszczynski and Jeff Greenberg, Toward an integration of cognitive and motivational perspectives on social inference: A biased hypothesis-testing model, 20 Advances Exper'l Soc. Psych. 297, 333 (1987).

[24] A substantial number of victims, of different types of crime, consult with others immediately after the crime, and the advice received from these others provides the best predictor of whether or not victims notify police. Martin S. Greenberg and Scott R. Beach, The role of social influence in crime victim's decision to notify the police, in Psychology in the Courts: International Advances in Knowledge 305 (Ronald Roesch, Raymond R. Corrado, and Rebecca Demptster, eds. 2002). Schachter and Singer demonstrated that people will sometimes use information from others to help them determine what their own emotions are. Stanley Schachter and Jerome E. Singer, Cognitive, social, and physiological determinants of emotional states, 69 Psych . Rev. 379 (1962).

[25] Vladimir J. Konenci and Ebbe B. Ebbesen, An analysis of the sentencing system, in The Criminal Justice System: A Social-Psychological Analysis 293 (Vladimir J. Konecni and Ebbe B. Ebbesen, eds., 1982).

[26] Vladimir J. Konenci and Ebbe B. Ebbesen, An analysis of the sentencing system, in The Criminal Justice System: A Social-Psychological Analysis 293 (Vladimir J. Konecni and Ebbe B. Ebbesen, eds., 1982).

would produce consistent, fair, speedy, and more efficient decisions. These findings do more than reveal the importance of heuristics, they raise concerns about effectiveness and the need to consider who or what should make key decisions and the extent to which they should be guided.

THE EFFECTIVENESS OF CLINICAL AND JUDICIAL DECISIONS

Although the legal system places great weight on the decisions of experts, especially judges and clinicians, their actual competency to reach correct decisions may well be debatable. That conclusion would surely be the implication from the above areas of research. Experts, like lay people, tend to use a number of flawed heuristics to simplify decision making. These flawed heuristics contribute to high error rates. Although it is important to not take the research findings to extremes and blanketly find suspect all legal decisions, the findings do suggest a need to weigh carefully the abilities of decision makers who make key decisions. It also means considering how to respond to the limits of decision making.

Although individuals assume that they can make correct decisions if given correct information, regardless of the amount of information involved, we have seen that the lesson that emerges from existing research points to inherent constraints on human decision-making ability. The limitations that arise in virtually all complex decision making render statistical prediction pervasively superior to individualized, case-by-case judgments, regardless of what people believe.[27] Efforts to predict parole violations are illustrative.[28] A statistical model of parole success that includes the offender's age at first arrest, number of convictions, and number of prison violations poorly predicts which parolees are likely to violate parole. The model's correlation coefficient is about .30. Given the significance of this decision, such results may appear strikingly low. However, experienced parole officers do much worse when they use an interview to predict parole success, with a correlation coefficient of only .06. That is, the decision makers would be better off ignoring all information gleaned from the interview, and simply combining the three aforementioned factors using a statistical model. Likewise, decisions that take into account interviews appear systematically worse than decisions that use a simple model comprised of a few factors that reliably predict success.[29] Generally, then, a gatekeeper who makes a decision partly based on an interview less reliably predicts than a gatekeeper who uses a simple statistical prediction model and no interview.[30] We seem disposed to assume that more is better and to think that we will be able to distinguish good information from non-diagnostic or non-informative factors. We are inclined to think that once we have all the information available, we will use our reason to consider all of the pieces of information. Given what we know about heuristics and biases, it is clear that the addition of certain types of information contributes to a less reliable, lower-quality decision. More is not better.

Clinical decisions regarding predictions of future offending and dangerousness have been viewed as highly unreliable. The leading review of the literature on predicting dangerousness, which was noted in the

---

[27] Meehl argued that statistical procedures establishing relations between data and some condition or event are, on average, more accurate than clinical prediction based solely on the decision maker's own judgment. Pa ul E. Meehl, Clinical Versus Statistical Prediction: A Theoretical Analysis and A Review of the Evidence (1954). More recent reviews of about 100 studies have also concluded that statistical prediction is better than clinical prediction. Robyn M. Dawes, David Faust, and Paul E. Meehl, Clinical versus actuarial judgment, 243 Science 1668 (1989); and William M. Grove and Paul E. Meehl, Comparative efficiency of informal (subjective, impressionistic) and formal (mechanical, algorithmic) prediction procedures: The clinical-statistical controversy, 2 Psych., Pub. Pol'y, L. 293 (1996).

[28] John S. Carroll, Richard L. Wiener, Dan Coates, Jolene Galegher, and James J. Alibrio, Evaluation, diagnosis, and prediction in parole decision making, 17 L. and Soc'y Rev. 199, 215-17 (1982).

[29] Robyn M. Dawes, House of Cards: Psychology and Psychotherapy Built on Myth 86-89 (1994).

[30] For example, people incorrectly assume that they can glean a much deeper understanding of a graduate school candidate in a forty-five minute interview than they can from a few simple predictive factors such as test scores. Robyn M. Dawes, A case study of graduate admissions: Application of three principles of human decision making, 26 Am. Psych. 180 (1971).

controlling Supreme Court case on this issue,[31] estimated clinical prediction error rates between 65% and 85%.[32] This translates into clinicians' being wrong essentially two out of three times they make predictions. Researchers have since perceived these striking estimates of inaccuracy as artificially inflated, as artifacts of the low base rates of violence (2-5%) found in the early clinical dangerousness prediction studies.[33] Later studies of dangerousness assessment, with base rates for violence between 25% and 50%,[34] report error rates closer to 44%.[35] The most recent estimates of the ability of mental health practitioners to predict dangerousness using more sophisticated statistical techniques suggest that mental health practitioners at least fair somewhat equally with chance in predicting future dangerousness.[36] This research does not, however, support the idea that clinicians accurately predict the long-term dangerousness of criminal defendants.[37] Importantly, statistical models that capture a person's decision making (referred to as a "bootstrapping model") generally do better than the person by themselves, simply because bias, boredom, or fatigue affect them, whereas statistical models consistently rely only on the limited number of factors that the person actually uses to make decisions. Such bootstraping, however, reduces the predictive power of the statistical model; human judgment about fitting an individual into the model apparently worsens predictions. Individuals tend to be unaware of the research showing the superiority of actuarial prediction, including clinicians who make diagnoses and predictions.[38] Even those aware of the research still are likely to rely on their own judgment because of overconfidence in their own ability. The phenomenon by which many individuals oppose the use of statistical prediction is known as the "broken leg" problem.[39] That problem is understood as knowing that a statistical formula might be very useful at predicting a person's weekly trips to a grocery store, but also thinking (most often wrongly) that the individual has a broken leg and is unable to go to the store leads to a better prediction in this instance than will the formula. Unfortunately, clinicians tend to see more "broken legs" (i.e., exceptions to the rule) than there actually are, which sabotages their attempt to improve on statistical methods. In fact, clinicians generally would benefit from ignoring all broken legs and always relying on actuarial predictions.[40] Yet, even clinicians who view research on risk factors as relevant ignore that research as they rely on perceived variables not subjected to empirical scrutiny.[41]

---

[31] That case is *Barefoot v. Estelle*, 463 U.S. 880 (1983), which we will read.

[32] John Monahan, The Prediction of Violent Behavior (1981).

[33] Randy Borum, Improving the clinical practice of violence risk assessment: Technology, guidelines, and training, 51 Am. Psych. 945 (1996). Of course, other variables are important, such as the length of time the prediction covers. A recent study has demonstrated that clinicians may be fairly accurate in predicting dangerousness when they are confident of their dangerousness assessment and when their prediction concerns an inpatient psychiatric population over a relatively short period of time. Dale E. McNeil, David A. Sandberg, and Renee L.Binder, The relationship between confidence and accuracy in clinical predictions of psychiatric patients' potential for violence, 25 L. and Hum. Beh. 655 (1998).

[34] Randy Borum, Improving the clinical practice of violence risk assessment: Technology, guidelines, and training, 51 Am. Psych. 945 (1996); and Randy K. Otto, Prediction of dangerous behavior: A review and analysis of "second generation" research, 5 Forensic Rep. 103 (1992).

[35] Randy K. Otto, Prediction of dangerous behavior: A review and analysis of "second generation" research, 5 Forensic Rep. 103 (1992).

[36] William Gardner, Charles W. Lidz, Edaward P. Mulvey and Esther C. Shaw, Clinical versus actuarial predictions of violence in patients with mental illness, 64 J. of Consulting and Clinical Psych. 602 (1996); and Douglas Mossman, Assessing predictions of violence: Being accurate about accuracy, 62 J. of Consulting and Clinical Psych. 783 (1994).

[37] The best studies reveal that clinicians have an overall high hit rate when predicting short term assaultive behavior. James M. Wood, Howard N. Garb, Scott O. Lilienfeld, and M. Teressa Nezworski (2002). Clinical assessment, 53 Ann. Rev. Pscyh. 519, 533.

[38] See, e.g., Reid Hastie and Robyn M. Dawes, Rational Choice in an Uncertain World: The Psychology of Judgment and Decision Making 56 (2001).

[39] Paul E. Meehl, Clinical Versus Statistical Prediction: A Theoretical Analysis and A Review of the Evidence (1954).

[40] Robyn M. Dawes, David Faust, and Paul E. Meehl, Clinical versus actuarial judgment, 243 Science 1668 (1989); and William M. Grove and Paul E. Meehl, Comparative efficiency of informal (subjective, impressionistic) and formal (mechanical, algorithmic) prediction procedures: The clinical-statistical controversy, 2 Psych., Pub. Pol'y, and L. 293 (1996).

[41] Eric B. Elbogen, Cynthia Calkins Mercado, Mario J. Scalora, and Alan J. Tomkins, Perceived relevance of factors for violence risk-assessment: A survey of clinicians, 1 Int'l J. of Forensic Mental Health 37 (2002).

As with clinical decisions, those involving sentencing decisions present complex problems. Because judges typically have many decisions to make with limited investigative resources, they generally make decisions under time pressure and with incomplete and sometimes inaccurate information.[42] In many ways, judicial decisions are actually even more complicated in that, historically, judges have not been given clear and consistent goals for their decisions. Given these difficulties and complexities, and consistent research on decision making, judges likely use heuristics to keep decisions within the limits of their cognitive capacities.

Research does indeed indicate that judges do not make decisions the way they think they do or the way they report they do. To make sense of the information they are given and help them understand events in a case, judges construct stories and impose causal schemas. This should not be surprising in light of research indicating that sentencing hearings historically have lasted only five minutes[43] and of the research we discussed in previous chapters about how juries construct evidence. Research on judicial decision making, however, is quite specific. Judges, like clinicians, tend to find "broken legs." As we will explore more fully below, wide sentencing disparities partly accounted for the rise in efforts to impose sentencing guidelines limiting judicial discretion. Yet, even despite the guidelines, judges tend to believe that a particular defendant with an especially mitigating or aggravating circumstance (the "broken leg") not covered by the guidelines presents a worthy exception. These broken legs are important in that judges must justify their sentencing decisions when they do not fall within guideline sentencing ranges. Most federal sentences (approximately 64.5% in 2000) do fall within the sentencing guidelines, however many actually do not (about 35% fall below and about .5% fall above the guidelines).[44] Judges, then, frequently assume that many cases are more severe than the defendant before them, that they must depart from structured guidelines to fit their individual assessments.

IMPROVING DECISIONS AND IDENTIFYING CONTROVERSIES

The limitations of decision makers obviously has not gone unnoticed. Both those involved in research dealing with prediction and sentencing recognize the need for improving decision making. In the clinical context, for example, recognition came early and, as we will see, even reached the legal system. Recognition of judicial limitations actually has been part of the history of law enforcement, but systematic efforts to reform have been less than two decades old. The result of the recognitions contributes to a move toward actuarial methods to guide both clinical and judicial decisions. These efforts, all of which are relatively new, now reveal their own limitations as they produce challenging issues and results.

In response to the pervasive limitations of pure clinical assessments, a small number of actuarial instruments developed during the 1970s, 1980s, and 1990s to predict future violence. The development of these actuarial instruments specifically designed to forecast risk of future dangerousness has significantly improved the accuracy of predictions of future violence.[45] Actuarial instruments make use of empirically

---

[42] Arthur J.Lurigio, John S. Carroll, and Loretta Stalans, Understanding judges' sentencing decisions: Attributions of responsibility and story construction, in Applications of Heuristics and Biases to Social Issues 91 (Linda Heath, R. Scott Tindale, John Edwards, Paul Posavac, Fred B. Bryant, Eaaron Henderson-King, Yolanda Suarez-Balcazar, and Judith Myers, eds., 1994).

[43] Konecni and Ebbesen found that no information from sentencing hearings (e.g., the amount and content of what was said and by whom) significantly predicted the final sentence once all prehearing information (e.g., the probation officer's recommendation, the defendant's jail/bail status) were taken into account. As a result, they characterized hearings as staged rituals that have symbolic value for the defendant and the public at large but which serve no actual function. They went even one step further and characterized individualized justice as a myth, since few of the factors that would separate one individual case from another (e.g., employment history, social background) related to the final decision. Vladimir J. Konenci and Ebbe B. Ebbesen, An analysis of the sentencing system, in The Criminal Justice System: A Social-Psychological Analysis 293 (Vladimir J. Konecni and Ebbe B. Ebbesen, eds., 1982).

[44] U.S. Sentencing Commission, 2000 Sourcebook of Federal Sentencing Statistics (2001), Figure G.

[45] William Gardner, Charles W. Lidz, Edaward P. Mulvey and Esther C. Shaw, Clinical versus actuarial predictions of violence in patients with mental illness, 64 J. of Consulting and Clinical Psych. 602 (1996); and Randy Borum,

established risk factors (i.e., past history of violence, psychopathic tendencies, prior arrest, etc., for dangerousness prediction), which successfully have been demonstrated to predict the appropriate outcome (i.e., violence) across groups within the selected population.[46] The instruments then weigh these risk factors statistically in a way that maximizes the power to predict a specified outcome. These efforts have been deemed positive developments.

One of the most popular instruments, the Psychopathy Checklist (Revised) (PCL-R),[47] measures the psychological construct known as "psychopathy."[48] Although no one seems quite sure what psychopathy means, researchers generally assert that we can best understand psychopathy as what historically has been referred to as sociopathic or antisocial personality disorder, a common characteristic found among the group of offenders who are responsible for a disproportionate amount of crime. The most often mentioned features of this disorder include aggression beginning in early childhood, impulsivity, resistance to punishment, general lack of emotional attachment or concern for others, dishonesty and selfishness in social interactions, and high levels of promiscuous and uncommitted sexual behavior.[49] Although controversy still surrounds the construct itself, researchers seem to agree that the PCL-R can be used to predict recurring violence.[50] The instrument seeks to predict violence in offenders and psychiatric patients by assessing a constellation of affective, interpersonal and behavioral characteristics. The instrument consists of twenty risk factors, scored on a three-point scale, with a score of greater than 30 (on a 40-point scale) indicating a strong propensity for violence.[51] The factors are of two types: one that describes interpersonal dimensions (such as shallowness, callousness, dishonesty), and one that describes behavior (such as juvenile delinquency, criminal versatility, impulsivity), and the factors overlap somewhat with the American Psychiatric Association's concept of antisocial personality disorder.[52] Despite important criticisms relating to the instrument's constructs and use, many researchers consider the instrument to have at least some predictive value for community violence and it is frequently used in prisons to determine eligibility for parole.[53]

Several researchers have sought to enhance the effectiveness of actuarial instruments. The most recent effort, from the MacArthur Risk Assessment group, seeks to validate an actuarial instrument comprising over 30 assessment measures at five sites across the United States.[54] This theory-driven instrument contains variables representing demographic, personality, personal history, contextual, and clinical domains.[55] Although the MacArthur group's effort shows promise, the best researched and validated actuarial tool for assessing dangerousness to date has been the Violence Risk Assessment Guide (VRAG), which has

---

Improving the clinical practice of violence risk assessment: Technology, guidelines, and training, 51 Am. Psych. 945 (1996).

46 John Monahan and Henry J. Steadman, Violence and Mental Disorder: Developments in Risk Assessment (1994).

47 Robert D. Hare, Manual for the Hare Psychopathy Checklist-Revised (1991).

48 Grant T. Harris, Tracey A. Skilling, and Marnie E. Rice, The construct of psychopathy, 28 Crime and Jus. 197, 197 (2001).

49 Grant T. Harris, Tracey A. Skilling, and Marnie E. Rice, The construct of psychopathy, 28 Crime and Jus. 197, 197 (2001).

50 See Darryl G. Kroner and Jeremy F. Mills, The accuracy of five risk appraisal instruments in Predicting Institutional Misconduct and New Convictions, 28 Crim. Jus. and Beh. 471, 473 (2001).

51 The twenty factors are: Glibness/ superficial charm, grandiose sense of self-worth, need for stimulation/ proneness to boredom, pathological lying, conning/ manipulative, lack of remorse or guilt, shallow affect, callous/ lack of sympathy, parasitic lifestyle, poor behavioral controls, promiscuous sexual behavior, early behavioral problems, lack of realistic long-term goals, impulsivity, irresponsibility, failure to accept responsibility, many short-term marital relationships, juvenile delinquency, revocation of conditional release, and criminal versatility. Robert D. Hare, The Hare PCL-R: Some issues concerning its use and misuse, 3 Legal and Crim. Psych. 99, 100 (1998).

52 Grant T. Harris, Tracey A. Skilling, and Marnie E. Rice, The construct of psychopathy, 28 Crime and Jus. 197, 204 (2001).

53 See Robert T. Salekin, Richard Rogers, and Kenneth W. Sewell, A review and meta-analysis of the Psychopathy Checklist and the Psychopathy Checklist-Revised: Predictive validity of dangerousness, 3 Clin. Psych. 203, 208 (1996); and John Monahan, Henry J. Steadman, Paul S. Appelbaum, Pamela C. Robbins, Edward P. Mulvey, Eric Silver, Loren H. Roth, and Thomas Grisso, Developing a clinically useful actuarial tool for assessing violence risk, 176 Brit. J. Psych. 312, 320 (2000).

54 John Monahan and Henry J. Steadman, Violence and Mental Disorder: Developments in Risk Assessment (1994).

55 See Kirk Heilbrun and Gretchen Witte, The MacArthur Risk Assessment Study: Implications for practice, research, and policy, 82 Marq. L. Rev. 733 (1999).

demonstrated a classification accuracy of nearly 75%.[56] The VRAG consists of twelve variables: the Hare Psychopathy Checklist (PCL-R), elementary school maladjustment, age of present offense, diagnosis of personality disorder (DSM-III), separation from parents before the age of 16, failure in prior conditional release, criminal history for property offenses, marital status, diagnosis of schizophrenia (DSM-III), victim injury in present offense, history of alcohol abuse, and female victim in present offense. Although the authors of the VRAG now argue explicitly and strongly for the "complete replacement" of clinical assessments of dangerousness with actuarial methods,[57] their efforts are not immune from criticism.[58] As a group, however, it does appear that actuarial dangerousness prediction instruments significantly outperform pure clinical predictions.[59]

Decisional trees also have been developed to formulate more successful violence predictions. This approach seeks to guide clinician's decision making by structuring the decision making process in a logical sequence of critical questions. One important study has reported how several screening instruments significantly outperform the accuracy of pure clinical opinion predictions of dangerousness, with very high effect sizes increasing from .618 for clinical predictions to .736 for full screenings.[60] The findings are somewhat striking; a screening instrument based on historical behavior alone (prior incident of violence and seriousness of violence) performed no differently than an instrument that contained those variables plus a variety of other measures (age, hostility measured on the Brief Symptom Inventory, drug use, and a thought disorder measure). Other leading commentators also have advocated the use of a dangerousness assessment decision tree, which has demonstrated moderate success in predicting violence.[61] One highly touted approach focuses on hostility ratings, age of first offense, the number of prior violent offenses, and drug use.[62] Given these successes, it is surprising that clinicians rarely use at least some of the actuarial or decisional instruments in their everyday practice to predict future violence.[63]

---

[56] Marnie E. Rice and Grant T. Harris, Violent recidivism: Assessing predictive validity, 63 J. of Consulting and Clinical Psych. 737 (1995).

[57] Vernon L. Quinsey, Grant T. Harris, Marnie E. Rice, and Catherine A. Cormier, Violent Offenders: Appraising and Managing Risk 171 (1999).

[58] Although it has been the most successful effort, some authors have challenged the approach to note that (1) actuarial predictions have been demonstrated to be superior to clinical predictions for a fairly wide range of prediction tasks, but that is not the case for assessments of dangerousness; (2) assessments of dangerousness are inherently different from many other predictive tasks, and they are different in ways that make it very difficult to meaningfully compare clinical and actuarial assessments; and (3) if actuarial instruments, or structured assessment guides, are to be used in the fairest and most effective manner, they must be validated in a far more precise manner than has occurred to date. See Thomas R. Litwack, Actuarial versus clinical assessments of dangerousness, 7 Psych. Pub. Pol'y and L. 409 (2001).

[59] This is actually true of comparisons of human judges to mechanical algorithms, as revealed in a meta-analysis that found mechanical algorithms 10% more accurate across studies in medicine, mental health, personality, and education and training settings. William M. Gorve, DavidH. Zald, Boyd S. Lebow, Beth E. Snitz, and Chad Nelson, Clinical versus mechanical prediction: A meta-analysis, 12 Psych. Assessment 19 (2000). Importantly, the authors also reported consistent superiority for mechanical-prediction techniques, regardless of the judgment task, type of judges, judges' amounts of experience, or the types of data being combined. Clinical predictions performed relatively less well when predictors included clinical interview data.

[60] These are the likelihood that a randomly selected violent patient would have been predicted to be more violent than a randomly selected nonviolent person. William Gardner, Charles W. Lidz, Edaward P. Mulvey and Esther C. Shaw, Clinical versus actuarial predictions of violence in patients with mental illness, 64 J. of Consulting and Clinical Psych. 602 (1996).

[61] William Gardner, Charles W. Lidz, Edaward P. Mulvey and Esther C. Shaw, Clinical versus actuarial predictions of violence in patients with mental illness, 64 J. of Consulting and Clinical Psych. 602 (1996); and Randy Borum, Improving the clinical practice of violence risk assessment: Technology, guidelines, and training, 51 Am. Psych. 945 (1996).

[62] Gary Melton, John Petrila, Norman G. Poythress, and Christopher Slobogin, Psychological Evaluations for the Courts: A Handbook for Mental Health Professionals and Lawyers (1997). See also John Monahan, Henry J. Steadman, Paul S. Appelbaum, Pamela C. Robbins, Edward P. Mulvey, Eric Silver, Loren H. Roth, and Thomas Grisso, Developing a clinically useful actuarial tool for assessing violence risk, 176 Brit. J. Psychiatry 312 (2000). The MacArthur group has developed an "Iterative Classification Tree," or ICT. They sought to increase the utility of this actuarial method for real-world clinical decision making by applying the method to a set of violence risk factors commonly available in clinical records or capable of being routinely assessed in clinical practice. Results showed that the ICT partitioned three-quarters of a sample of psychiatric patients into one of two categories with regard to their risk of violence to others during the first twenty weeks after discharge (a period during which 18.7% of all patients committed at least one violent

Despite powerful arguments favoring reliance on actuarial assessments, their use is not without limitations. Even if some clinicians can do better than the best available actuarial assessment instruments, for example, the range of clinicians' skills would mean that fewer errors will be made if we eschewed clinical assessment in favor of actuarial assessment. On the other hand, some criticize these instruments for ignoring case-specific information and suggest that actuarial evidence might be difficult for jurors to weigh appropriately in their decision making.[64] Alternatively, others fear that jurors might rely too heavily on actuarial testimony in their decision making; presenting risk in numerical form may lead the trappings of precision and objectivity to suppress appropriate doubts about validity and certainty of prediction.[65] Empirical evidence leaves at least the latter criticism unsubstantiated. If anything, the weight of evidence suggests that jurors place less weight on statistical measures than on other testimony, especially clinical evidence.[66] As we already have seen in previous chapters, jurors clearly have difficulty evaluating and interpreting complex statistical information and may process it in a biased fashion (i.e., on the basis of the expert's credentials and final opinion rather than on the content). Indeed, even clinicians have difficulty interpreting statistical information, as exemplified by the surprising finding that clinicians are more likely to hospitalize patients if the risk of violence is communicated in a frequency format ("20 out of 100 patients") rather than a probability format ("20% likely").[67]

Despite important criticisms against using actuarial methods to predict offender behavior, these methods have become part of sentencing instruments. The limitations in unstructured decision making for multivariable decisions led some to conclude that sentencing guidelines would increase the accuracy, consistency and fairness of sentencing decisions. The research strongly suggested that sentencing disparity existed because judges differed both in their judgments of the relative seriousness of the case facts and in the particular sentencing policy objectives they sought to achieve through the sentence. For example, one important study found that judges' subjective perceptions were more predictive of sentencing decisions than were more objective views of the data, as coded by the researchers.[68] The fact that sentencing decisions could be explained in part by judges' personality, beliefs, and background and by the race and gender of the defendant suggested the necessity for reform.[69] However, this disparity among judges may have been overstated,[70] and the reality is that many forces, such as issues relating to civil rights, discrimination, and attacks on the notion of rehabilitation had undermined the rationales for indeterminate sentencing. These forces became increasingly important in light of the general concern that all legal processes should be made fairer by clarifying rules and instituting review of decisions.

Evidence of disparity in sentencing surfaced in the 1970s and 1980s from analyses of both actual decisions and simulations. These analyses were among the forces that drove policymakers toward

---

act). One category consisted of groups whose rates of violence were no more than half the base rate of the total patient sample (i.e., equal to or less than 9% violent). The other category consisted of groups whose rates of violence were at least twice the base rate of the total patient sample (i.e., equal to or greater than 37% violent). The prevalence of violence within individual risk groups varied from 3% to 53%, which was deemed considerably more accurate than clinical prediction. Henry J. Steadman, Eric Silver, John Monahan, Paul S. Appelbaum, Pamela Clark Robbins, Edward P. Mulvey, Thomas Grisso, Loren H. Roth, and Steven Banks, A classification tree approach to the development of actuarial violence risk assessment tools, 24 L. and Hum. Beh. 83 (2000).

63 Daniel A. Krauss and Bruce D. Sales, The effects of clinical and scientific expert testimony on juror decision making in capital sentencing, 7 Psych. Pub. Pol'y and L. 267 (2001).

64 Gary Melton, John Petrila, Norman G. Poythress, and Christopher Slobogin, Psychological Evaluations for the Courts: A Handbook for Mental Health Professionals and Lawyers (1997).

65 Lawrence Tribe, Trial by mathematics: Precision and ritual in the legal process, 84 Harv. L. Rev. 1329 (1971).

66 Gary Melton, John Petrila, Norman G. Poythress, and Christopher Slobogin, Psychological Evaluations for the Courts: A Handbook for Mental Health Professionals and Lawyers (1997); and Brian C. Smith, Steven D. Penrod, Amy L. Otto, and Roger C. Park, Jurors' use of probabilistic evidence, 20 L. and Hum. Beh. 49 (1996).

67 John Monahan, Kirk Heilbrum, Eric Silver, Erik Nabors, Jonathan Bone, and Paul Slovic, Communicating violence risk: Frequency formats, vivid outcomes, and forensic settings, 1 Intern'l J. of Forensic Mental Health 121 (2002).

68 John S. Carroll and Richard L. Wiener, Cognitive social psychology and beyond, in Cognitive Social Psychology 213, 232 (Albert H. Hastorf and Alice M. Isen, eds., 1982).

69 Michael Tonry, Sentencing Matters 7 (1996).

70 John Hagan, Extra-legal attributes and criminal sentencing: An assessment of a sociological viewpoint, 8 L. and Soc'y Rev. 357 (1974).

structuring judicial discretion through guidelines. Legislatively, this has been accomplished in a variety of ways. Most prominently, though, efforts to structure sentencing decisions took the form of mandatory minimum statutes and sentencing guidelines. Under mandatory minimum statutes, once charged and convicted of a particular offense, a defendant must receive a specific minimum punishment. Sentencing guidelines make use of a formula created by sentencing commissions, which are administrative agencies assumed to have greater expertise than legislatures. Although there may be variations among states and between states and the federal government, all sentencing formulas include variables relating to offense seriousness, criminal history, and offender characteristics.

Although guidelines and other structured decision making remain fraught with controversy, the general sense is that such models are more accurate, more consistent, and thus fairer than nonstatistical and unstructured decision making. But that may be more debatable than generally believed. Actuarial methods may be superior, but much depends on the factors under consideration. In the context of the U.S. sentencing guidelines, for example, reliability is best determined by comparing the final guidelines' recommendations of different individuals given the same cases; and this standard reveals important signs of weakness. One study seeking to determine the reliability of the guidelines randomly selected 47 federal districts and one probation officer within each of those districts. Participants read a case involving conspiracy to distribute cocaine and were asked to assign a base offense level for each of the three people charged in the conspiracy. For the three defendants, the base offense levels (and sentences in months for offenders with no prior record) ranged from 24 to 32 (57 to 136 months), 20 to 32 (37 to 136 months), and 16 to 32 (24 to 136 months).[71] Given that judges' final sentencing decisions are very likely to follow probation officers' recommendations, the low reliability of these decisions raises concerns. Importantly, judges do not fare that well by themselves either. One study, for example, presented 50 federal judges with 20 identical files based on actual cases and asked them to sentence the hypothetical offenders.[72] The judges gave a wide variation in sentencing decisions. For instance, one case involved a male offender over 40 with a prior record consisting of six other arrests, three convictions, and two incarcerations, who was found guilty of nine counts of extortionate credit transactions and related income tax violations. The recommended sentences ranged from 3 years in prison with no fine to 20 years in prison with a $65,000 fine.

If anything, these findings reveal the important point that much remains to be done in efforts to systematize the way decision makers decide and what they use in their decisions.[73] Although much remains to be done, however, existing research supports well the contention that many critical decisions are both unreliable and unfair. This contention makes urgent the need to examine how law enforcement can benefit from current psychological sciences revealing that human decision makers tend to make systematic errors in the manner they combine pieces of information. Also critical is an effort to understand what aspects of the legal system allow for taking advantage of the best empirical evidence and which aspects ensure that even the best evidence will remain ignored.

NOTES AND QUERIES

Consider the following heuristics: representative bias, availability heuristic, confirmation bias, and anchoring. To the extent that they help us understand complex decisions, what do you make of their significance?

Describe the significance of the illusion of objectivity and of bounded rationality.

---

[71] Pamela B. Lawrence and Paul J. Hofer, An empirical study of the application of relevant conduct guidelines, 4 Fed. Sentencing Rep. 330 (1992).

[72] Anthony Partridge and William B. Eldridge, Federal Jud. Center, The Second Circuit Sentencing Study: A Report on the Judges of the Second Circuit (1974).

[73] R. Barry Ruback and Jonathan Wroblewski, The federal sentencing guidelines: Psychological and policy reasons for simplification, 7 Psych. Pub. Pol'y and L. 739 (2001).

What significance are we to attach to the tendencies of bootstrapping and "broken legs" in clinical decision making?

Discuss the relative effectiveness of clinical versus actuarial models for making complex decisions. Note that one may be tempted to opt for actuarial methods because they seem to increase effectiveness. But greater effectiveness may not mean that such methods should still be used. Statistical analysis may provide an important tool, but one cannot expect statistics to provide an answer about any particular individual. That is, the most that can be said is that someone falls within a group that has a certain statistical propensity for a relevant characteristic under observation, such as violence. What other factors caution against the use of actuarial methods?

When reading the cases that follow, consider thinking of them in light of how the law addresses the complexity of sentencing and/or prediction. Also consider how the law addresses issues of bias and potential decision maker inadequacies.

PREDICTIONS OF FUTURE DANGEROUSNESS

BAREFOOT v. ESTELLE
463 U.S. 880 (1983)

JUSTICE WHITE delivered the opinion of the Court.

We have two questions before us in this case: whether the District Court erred on the merits in rejecting the petition for habeas corpus filed by petitioner, and whether the Court of Appeals for the Fifth Circuit correctly denied a stay of execution of the death penalty pending appeal of the District Court's judgment.

I.

On November 14, 1978, petitioner was convicted of the capital murder of a police officer in Bell County, Tex. A separate sentencing hearing before the same jury was then held to determine whether the death penalty should be imposed. Under Tex. Code Crim. Proc. Ann., two special questions were to be submitted to the jury: whether the conduct causing death was "committed deliberately and with reasonable expectation that the death of the deceased or another would result"; and whether "there is a probability that the defendant would commit criminal acts of violence that would constitute a continuing threat to society." The State introduced into evidence petitioner's prior convictions and his reputation for lawlessness. The State also called two psychiatrists, John Holbrook and James Grigson, who, in response to hypothetical questions, testified that petitioner would probably commit further acts of violence and represent a continuing threat to society. The jury answered both of the questions put to them in the affirmative, a result which required the imposition of the death penalty.

On appeal to the Texas Court of Criminal Appeals, petitioner urged, among other submissions, that the use of psychiatrists at the punishment hearing to make predictions about petitioner's future conduct was unconstitutional because psychiatrists, individually and as a class, are not competent to predict future dangerousness. Hence, their predictions are so likely to produce erroneous sentences that their use violated the Eighth and Fourteenth Amendments. It was also urged, in any event, that permitting answers to hypothetical questions by psychiatrists who had not personally examined petitioner was constitutional error. The court rejected all of these contentions and affirmed the conviction and sentence on March 12, 1980; rehearing was denied on April 30, 1980.

III.

Petitioner's merits submission is that his death sentence must be set aside because the Constitution of the United States barred the testimony of the two psychiatrists who testified against him at the punishment hearing. There are several aspects to this claim. First, it is urged that psychiatrists, individually and as a group, are incompetent to predict with an acceptable degree of reliability that a particular criminal will commit other crimes in the future and so represent a danger to the community. Second, it is said that in any event, psychiatrists should not be permitted to testify about future dangerousness in response to hypothetical questions and without having examined the defendant personally. Third, it is argued that in the particular circumstances of this case, the testimony of the psychiatrists was so unreliable that the sentence should be set aside. As indicated below, we reject each of these arguments.

A.

The suggestion that no psychiatrist's testimony may be presented with respect to a defendant's future dangerousness is somewhat like asking us to disinvent the wheel. In the first place, it is contrary to our cases. If the likelihood of a defendant's committing further crimes is a constitutionally acceptable criterion for imposing the death penalty, which it is and if it is not impossible for even a lay person sensibly to arrive at that conclusion, it makes little sense, if any, to submit that psychiatrists, out of the entire universe of persons who might have an opinion on the issue, would know so little about the subject that they should not be permitted to testify. In Jurek, seven Justices rejected the claim that it was impossible to predict future behavior and that dangerousness was therefore an invalid consideration in imposing the death penalty. JUSTICES Stewart, POWELL, and STEVENS responded directly to the argument:

> It is, of course, not easy to predict future behavior. The fact that such a determination is difficult, however, does not mean that it cannot be made. Indeed, prediction of future criminal conduct is an essential element in many of the decisions rendered throughout our criminal justice system. The decision whether to admit a defendant to bail, for instance, must often turn on a judge's prediction of the defendant's future conduct. Any sentencing authority must predict a convicted person's probable future conduct when it engages in the process of determining what punishment to impose. For those sentenced to prison, these same predictions must be made by parole authorities. The task that a Texas jury must perform in answering the statutory question in issue is thus basically no different from the task performed countless times each day throughout the American system of criminal justice. What is essential is that the jury have before it all possible relevant information about the individual defendant whose fate it must determine. Texas law clearly assures that all such evidence will be adduced.

...Furthermore, in Estelle v. Smith, in the face of a submission very similar to that presented in this case with respect to psychiatric testimony, we approvingly repeated the above quotation from Jurek and went on to say that we were in "no sense disapproving the use of psychiatric testimony bearing on future dangerousness."

Acceptance of petitioner's position that expert testimony about future dangerousness is far too unreliable to be admissible would immediately call into question those other contexts in which predictions of future behavior are constantly made. ...

In the second place, the rules of evidence generally extant at the federal and state levels anticipate that relevant, unprivileged evidence should be admitted and its weight left to the factfinder, who would have the benefit of cross-examination and contrary evidence by the opposing party. Psychiatric testimony predicting dangerousness may be countered not only as erroneous in a particular case but also as generally so unreliable that it should be ignored. If the jury may make up its mind about future dangerousness unaided by psychiatric testimony, jurors should not be barred from hearing the views of the State's psychiatrists along with opposing views of the defendant's doctors.

Third, petitioner's view mirrors the position expressed in the amicus brief of the American Psychiatric Association (APA). As indicated above, however, the same view was presented and rejected in Estelle v. Smith. We are no more convinced now that the view of the APA should be converted into a constitutional rule barring an entire category of expert testimony. We are not persuaded that such testimony is almost entirely unreliable and that the factfinder and the adversary system will not be competent to uncover, recognize, and take due account of its shortcomings.

The amicus does not suggest that there are not other views held by members of the Association or of the profession generally. Indeed, as this case and others indicate, there are those doctors who are quite willing to testify at the sentencing hearing, who think, and will say, that they know what they are talking about, and who expressly disagree with the Association's point of view. Furthermore, their qualifications as experts are regularly accepted by the courts. If they are so obviously wrong and should be discredited, there should be no insuperable problem in doing so by calling members of the Association who are of that view and who confidently assert that opinion in their amicus brief. Neither petitioner nor the Association suggests that psychiatrists are always wrong with respect to future dangerousness, only most of the time. Yet the submission is that this category of testimony should be excised entirely from all trials. We are unconvinced, however, at least as of now, that the adversary process cannot be trusted to sort out the reliable from the unreliable evidence and opinion about future dangerousness, particularly when the convicted felon has the opportunity to present his own side of the case.

We are unaware of and have not been cited to any case, federal or state, that has adopted the categorical views of the Association. Certainly it was presented and rejected at every stage of the present proceeding. After listening to the two schools of thought testify not only generally but also about the petitioner and his criminal record, the District Court found:

> The majority of psychiatric experts agree that where there is a pattern of repetitive assaultive and violent conduct, the accuracy of psychiatric predictions of future dangerousness dramatically rises. The accuracy of this conclusion is reaffirmed by the expert medical testimony in this case at the evidentiary hearing. . . . It would appear that Petitioner's complaint is not the diagnosis and prediction made by Drs. Holbrook and Grigson at the punishment phase of his trial, but that Dr. Grigson expressed extreme certainty in his diagnosis and prediction. . . . In any event, the differences among the experts were quantitative, not qualitative. The differences in opinion go to the weight [of the evidence] and not the admissibility of such testimony. . . . Such disputes are within the province of the jury to resolve. Indeed, it is a fundamental premise of our entire system of criminal jurisprudence that the purpose of the jury is to sort out the true testimony from the false, the important matters from the unimportant matters, and, when called upon to do so, to give greater credence to one party's expert witnesses than another's. Such matters occur routinely in the American judicial system, both civil and criminal.

We agree with the District Court, as well as with the Court of Appeals' judges who dealt with the merits of the issue and agreed with the District Court in this respect.

B.

Whatever the decision may be about the use of psychiatric testimony, in general, on the issue of future dangerousness, petitioner urges that such testimony must be based on personal examination of the defendant and may not be given in response to hypothetical questions. We disagree. Expert testimony, whether in the form of an opinion based on hypothetical questions or otherwise, is commonly admitted as evidence where it might help the factfinder do its assigned job. ...

Today, in the federal system, Federal Rules of Evidence 702-706 provide for the testimony of experts. The Advisory Committee Notes touch on the particular objections to hypothetical questions, but none of these caveats lends any support to petitioner's constitutional arguments. Furthermore, the Texas Court of Criminal Appeals could find no fault with the mode of examining the two psychiatrists under Texas law...

Like the Court of Criminal Appeals, the District Court, and the Court of Appeals, we reject petitioner's constitutional arguments against the use of hypothetical questions. Although cases such as this involve the death penalty, we perceive no constitutional barrier to applying the ordinary rules of evidence governing the use of expert testimony.

C.

IV.

In sum, we affirm the judgment of the District Court. There is no doubt that the psychiatric testimony increased the likelihood that petitioner would be sentenced to death, but this fact does not make that evidence inadmissible, any more than it would with respect to other relevant evidence against any defendant in a criminal case...

The judgment of the District Court is

Affirmed.

JUSTICE STEVENS, concurring in the judgment. [omitted]

JUSTICE MARSHALL, with whom JUSTICE BRENNAN joins, dissenting. [omitted]

JUSTICE BLACKMUN, with whom JUSTICE BRENNAN and JUSTICE MARSHALL join as to Parts I-IV, dissenting.

...I, too, dissent, but I base my conclusion also on evidentiary factors that the Court rejects with some emphasis. The Court holds that psychiatric testimony about a defendant's future dangerousness is admissible, despite the fact that such testimony is wrong two times out of three. The Court reaches this result – even in a capital case – because, it is said, the testimony is subject to cross-examination and impeachment. In the present state of psychiatric knowledge, this is too much for me. One may accept this in a routine lawsuit for money damages, but when a person's life is at stake – no matter how heinous his offense – a requirement of greater reliability should prevail. In a capital case, the specious testimony of a psychiatrist, colored in the eyes of an impressionable jury by the inevitable untouchability of a medical specialist's words, equates with death itself.

I.

To obtain a death sentence in Texas, the State is required to prove beyond a reasonable doubt that "there is a probability that the defendant would commit criminal acts of violence that would constitute a continuing threat to society." As a practical matter, this prediction of future dangerousness was the only issue to be decided by Barefoot's sentencing jury.

At the sentencing hearing, the State established that Barefoot had two prior convictions for drug offenses and two prior convictions for unlawful possession of firearms. None of these convictions involved acts of violence. At the guilt stage of the trial, for the limited purpose of establishing that the crime was committed in order to evade police custody, the State had presented evidence that Barefoot had escaped from jail in New Mexico where he was being held on charges of statutory rape and unlawful restraint of a minor child with intent to commit sexual penetration against the child's will. The prosecution also called several character witnesses at the sentencing hearing, from towns in five States. Without mentioning particular examples of Barefoot's conduct, these witnesses testified that Barefoot's reputation for being a peaceable and law-abiding citizen was bad in their respective communities.

Last, the prosecution called Doctors Holbrook and Grigson, whose testimony extended over more than half the hearing. Neither had examined Barefoot or requested the opportunity to examine him. In the presence of the jury, and over defense counsel's objection, each was qualified as an expert psychiatrist witness. Doctor Holbrook detailed at length his training and experience as a psychiatrist, which included a position as chief of psychiatric services at the Texas Department of Corrections. He explained that he had previously performed many "criminal evaluations," and that he subsequently took the post at the Department of Corrections to observe the subjects of these evaluations so that he could "be certain those opinions that [he] had were accurate at the time of trial and pretrial." He then informed the jury that it was "within [his] capacity as a doctor of psychiatry to predict the future dangerousness of an individual within a reasonable medical certainty," and that he could give "an expert medical opinion that would be within reasonable psychiatric certainty as to whether or not that individual would be dangerous to the degree that there would be a probability that that person would commit criminal acts of violence in the future that would constitute a continuing threat to society."

Doctor Grigson also detailed his training and medical experience, which, he said, included examination of "between thirty and forty thousand individuals," including 8,000 charged with felonies, and at least 300 charged with murder. He testified that with enough information he would be able to "give a medical opinion within reasonable psychiatric certainty as to the psychological or psychiatric makeup of an individual," and that this skill was "particular to the field of psychiatry and not to the average layman."

Each psychiatrist then was given an extended hypothetical question asking him to assume as true about Barefoot the four prior convictions for nonviolent offenses, the bad reputation for being law-abiding in various communities, the New Mexico escape, the events surrounding the murder for which he was on trial and, in Doctor Grigson's case, the New Mexico arrest. On the basis of the hypothetical question, Doctor Holbrook diagnosed Barefoot "within a reasonable [psychiatric] certainty," as a "criminal sociopath." He testified that he knew of no treatment that could change this condition, and that the condition would not change for the better but "may become accelerated" in the next few years. Finally, Doctor Holbrook testified that, "within reasonable psychiatric certainty, " there was "a probability that the Thomas A. Barefoot in that hypothetical will commit criminal acts of violence in the future that would constitute a continuing threat to society," and that his opinion would not change if the "society" at issue was that within Texas prisons rather than society outside prison.

Doctor Grigson then testified that, on the basis of the hypothetical question, he could diagnose Barefoot "within reasonable psychiatric certainty" as an individual with "a fairly classical, typical, sociopathic personality disorder." He placed Barefoot in the "most severe category" of sociopaths (on a scale of one to ten, Barefoot was "above ten"), and stated that there was no known cure for the condition. Finally, Doctor Grigson testified that whether Barefoot was in society at large or in a prison society there was a "one hundred percent and absolute" chance that Barefoot would commit future acts of criminal violence that would constitute a continuing threat to society.

On cross-examination, defense counsel questioned the psychiatrists about studies demonstrating that psychiatrists' predictions of future dangerousness are inherently unreliable. Doctor Holbrook indicated his familiarity with many of these studies but stated that he disagreed with their conclusions. Doctor Grigson stated that he was not familiar with most of these studies, and that their conclusions were accepted by only a "small minority group" of psychiatrists – "[it's] not the American Psychiatric Association that believes that."

After an hour of deliberation, the jury answered "yes" to the two statutory questions, and Thomas Barefoot was sentenced to death.

II.

A.

The American Psychiatric Association (APA), participating in this case as amicus curiae, informs us that "[the] unreliability of psychiatric predictions of long-term future dangerousness is by now an established fact within the profession." The APA's best estimate is that two out of three predictions of long-term future violence made by psychiatrists are wrong. The Court does not dispute this proposition, and indeed it could not do so; the evidence is overwhelming. For example, the APA's Draft Report of the Task Force on the Role of Psychiatry in the Sentencing Process (Draft Report) states that "[considerable] evidence has been accumulated by now to demonstrate that long-term prediction by psychiatrists of future violence is an extremely inaccurate process." John Monahan, recognized as " the leading thinker on this issue" even by the State's expert witness at Barefoot's federal habeas corpus hearing, concludes that "the 'best' clinical research currently in existence indicates that psychiatrists and psychologists are accurate in no more than one out of three predictions of violent behavior," even among populations of individuals who are mentally ill and have committed violence in the past. Another study has found it impossible to identify any subclass of offenders "whose members have a greater-than-even chance of engaging again in an assaultive act." Yet another commentator observes: "In general, mental health professionals . . . are more likely to be wrong than right when they predict legally relevant behavior. When predicting violence, dangerousness, and suicide, they are far more likely to be wrong than right." Neither the Court nor the State of Texas has cited a single reputable scientific source contradicting the unanimous conclusion of professionals in this field that psychiatric predictions of long-term future violence are wrong more often than they are right.

The APA also concludes, as do researchers that have studied the issue, that psychiatrists simply have no expertise in predicting long-term future dangerousness. A layman with access to relevant statistics can do at least as well and possibly better; psychiatric training is not relevant to the factors that validly can be employed to make such predictions, and psychiatrists consistently err on the side of overpredicting violence. Thus, while Doctors Grigson and Holbrook were presented by the State and by self-proclamation as experts at predicting future dangerousness, the scientific literature makes crystal clear that they had no expertise whatever. Despite their claims that they were able to predict Barefoot's future behavior "within reasonable psychiatric certainty," or to a "one hundred percent and absolute" certainty, there was in fact no more than a one in three chance that they were correct.

Like the District Court and the Court of Appeals, the Court seeks to justify the admission of psychiatric testimony on the ground that "'[the] majority of psychiatric experts agree that where there is a pattern of repetitive assaultive and violent conduct, the accuracy of psychiatric predictions of future dangerousness dramatically rises.'" The District Court correctly found that there is empirical evidence supporting the common-sense correlation between repetitive past violence and future violence; the APA states that "[the] most that can be said about any individual is that a history of past violence increases the probability that future violence will occur."

The lower courts and this Court have sought solace in this statistical correlation without acknowledging its obvious irrelevance to the facts of this case. The District Court did not find that the State demonstrated any pattern of repetitive assault and violent conduct by Barefoot. Recognizing the importance of giving some credibility to its experts' specious prognostications, the State now claims that the "reputation" testimony adduced at the sentencing hearing "can only evince repeated, widespread acts of criminal violence." This is simply absurd. There was no testimony worthy of credence that Barefoot had committed acts of violence apart from the crime for which he was being tried; there was testimony only of a bad reputation for peaceable and law-abiding conduct. In light of the fact that each of Barefoot's prior convictions was for a non-violent offense, such testimony obviously could have been based on antisocial but nonviolent behavior. Neither psychiatrist informed the jury that he considered this reputation testimony to show a history of repeated acts of violence. Moreover, if the psychiatrists or the jury were to rely on such vague hearsay testimony in order to show a "pattern of repetitive assault and violent conduct," Barefoot's death sentence would rest on information that might "bear no closer relation to fact than the average rumor or item of gossip," and should be invalid for that reason alone. A death sentence cannot rest on highly dubious predictions secretly based on a factual foundation of hearsay and pure conjecture.

Although I believe that the misleading nature of any psychiatric prediction of future violence violates due process when introduced in a capital sentencing hearing, admitting the predictions in this case – which were made without even examining the defendant – was particularly indefensible. In the APA's words, if prediction following even an in-depth examination is inherently unreliable,

> there is all the more reason to shun the practice of testifying without having examined the defendant at all. . . . Needless to say, responding to hypotheticals is just as fraught with the possibility of error as testifying in any other way about an individual whom one has not personally examined. Although the courts have not yet rejected the practice, psychiatrists should.

Such testimony is offensive not only to legal standards; the APA has declared that "[it] is unethical for a psychiatrist to offer a professional opinion unless he/she has conducted an examination." The Court today sanctions admission in a capital sentencing hearing of "expert" medical testimony so unreliable and unprofessional that it violates the canons of medical ethics.

The danger of an unreliable death sentence created by this testimony cannot be brushed aside on the ground that the "'jury [must] have before it all possible relevant information about the individual defendant whose fate it must determine.'" Although committed to allowing a "wide scope of evidence" at presentence hearings, the Court has recognized that "consideration must be given to the quality, as well as the quantity, of the information on which the sentencing [authority] may rely." Thus, very recently, this Court reaffirmed a crucial limitation on the permissible scope of evidence: "'[so] long as the evidence introduced . . . [does] not prejudice a defendant, it is preferable not to impose restrictions.'" The Court all but admits the obviously prejudicial impact of the testimony of Doctors Grigson and Holbrook; granting that their absolute claims were more likely to be wrong than right, the Court states that "[there] is no doubt that the psychiatric testimony increased the likelihood that petitioner would be sentenced to death."

Indeed, unreliable scientific evidence is widely acknowledged to be prejudicial. The reasons for this are manifest. "The major danger of scientific evidence is its potential to mislead the jury; an aura of scientific infallibility may shroud the evidence and thus lead the jury to accept it without critical scrutiny." Where the public holds an exaggerated opinion of the accuracy of scientific testimony, the prejudice is likely to be indelible. There is little question that psychiatrists are perceived by the public as having a special expertise to predict dangerousness, a perception based on psychiatrists' study of mental disease. It is this perception that the State in Barefoot's case sought to exploit. Yet mental disease is not correlated with violence, and the stark fact is that no such expertise exists. Moreover, psychiatrists, it is said, sometimes attempt to perpetuate this illusion of expertise, and Doctors Grigson and Holbrook – who purported to be able to predict future dangerousness "within reasonable psychiatric certainty," or absolutely – present extremely disturbing examples of this tendency. The problem is not uncommon.

...Surely, this Court's commitment to ensuring that death sentences are imposed reliably and reasonably requires that nonprobative and highly prejudicial testimony on the ultimate question of life or death be excluded from a capital sentencing hearing.

III.

A.

Despite its recognition that the testimony at issue was probably wrong and certainly prejudicial, the Court holds this testimony admissible because the Court is "unconvinced . . . that the adversary process cannot be trusted to sort out the reliable from the unreliable evidence and opinion about future dangerousness." One can only wonder how juries are to separate valid from invalid expert opinions when the "experts" themselves are so obviously unable to do so. Indeed, the evidence suggests that juries are not effective at assessing the validity of scientific evidence.

There can be no question that psychiatric predictions of future violence will have an undue effect on the ultimate verdict. Even judges tend to accept psychiatrists' recommendations about a defendant's dangerousness with little regard for cross-examination or other testimony. There is every reason to believe that inexperienced jurors will be still less capable of "[separating] the wheat from the chaff," despite the Court's blithe assumption to the contrary. The American Bar Association has warned repeatedly that sentencing juries are particularly incapable of dealing with information relating to "the likelihood that the defendant will commit other crimes," and similar predictive judgments. ... "[since] the members of a jury will have had little, if any, previous experience in sentencing, they are unlikely to be skilled in dealing with the information they are given." But the Court in this case, in its haste to praise the jury's ability to find the truth, apparently forgets this well-known and worrisome shortcoming.

...In no area is purportedly "expert" testimony admitted for the jury's consideration where it cannot be demonstrated that it is correct more often than not. "It is inconceivable that a judgment could be considered an 'expert' judgment when it is less accurate than the flip of a coin." The risk that a jury will be incapable of separating "scientific" myth from reality is deemed unacceptably high.

B.

The Constitution's mandate of reliability, with the stakes at life or death, precludes reliance on cross-examination and the opportunity to present rebuttal witnesses as an antidote for this distortion of the truth-finding process. Cross-examination is unlikely to reveal the fatuousness of psychiatric predictions because such predictions often rest, as was the case here, on psychiatric categories and intuitive clinical judgments not susceptible to cross-examination and rebuttal. Psychiatric categories have little or no demonstrated relationship to violence, and their use often obscures the unimpressive statistical or intuitive bases for prediction. The APA particularly condemns the use of the diagnosis employed by Doctors Grigson and Holbrook in this case, that of sociopathy:

> In this area confusion reigns. The psychiatrist who is not careful can mislead the judge or jury into believing that a person has a major mental disease simply on the basis of a description of prior criminal behavior. Or a psychiatrist can mislead the court into believing that an individual is devoid of conscience on the basis of a description of criminal acts alone. . . . The profession of psychiatry has a responsibility to avoid inflicting this confusion upon the courts and to spare the defendant the harm that may result. . . . Given our uncertainty about the implications of the finding, the diagnosis of sociopathy . . . should not be used to justify or to support predictions of future conduct. There is no certainty in this area.

It is extremely unlikely that the adversary process will cut through the facade of superior knowledge. ...

Nor is the presentation of psychiatric witnesses on behalf of the defense likely to remove the prejudicial taint of misleading testimony by prosecution psychiatrists. No reputable expert would be able to predict with confidence that the defendant will not be violent; at best, the witness will be able to give his opinion that all predictions of dangerousness are unreliable. Consequently, the jury will not be presented with the traditional battle of experts with opposing views on the ultimate question. Given a choice between an expert who says that he can predict with certainty that the defendant, whether confined in prison or free in society, will kill again, and an expert who says merely that no such prediction can be made, members of the jury charged by law with making the prediction surely will be tempted to opt for the expert who claims he can help them in performing their duty, and who predicts dire consequences if the defendant is not put to death.

Ultimately, when the Court knows full well that psychiatrists' predictions of dangerousness are specious, there can be no excuse for imposing on the defendant, on pain of his life, the heavy burden of convincing a jury of laymen of the fraud.

IV.

The Court is simply wrong in claiming that psychiatric testimony respecting future dangerousness is necessarily admissible in light of ... Estelle v. Smith. ...

In Smith, the psychiatric testimony at issue was given by the same Doctor Grigson who confronts us in this case, and his conclusions were disturbingly similar to those he rendered here. The APA, appearing as amicus curiae, argued that all psychiatric predictions of future dangerousness should be excluded from capital sentencing proceedings. The Court did not reach this issue, because it found Smith's death sentence invalid on narrower grounds: Doctor Grigson's testimony had violated Smith's Fifth and Sixth Amendment rights. Contrary to the Court's inexplicable assertion in this case Smith certainly did not reject the APA's position. Rather, the Court made clear that "the holding in Jurek was guided by recognition that the inquiry [into dangerousness] mandated by Texas law does not require resort to medical experts." If Jurek and Smith held that psychiatric predictions of future dangerousness are admissible in a capital sentencing proceeding as the Court claims, this guiding recognition would have been irrelevant.

The Court also errs in suggesting that the exclusion of psychiatrists' predictions of future dangerousness would be contrary to the logic of Jurek. Jurek merely upheld Texas' substantive decision to condition the death sentence upon proof of a probability that the defendant will commit criminal acts of violence in the future. Whether the evidence offered by the prosecution to prove that probability is so unreliable as to violate a capital defendant's rights to due process is an entirely different matter, one raising only questions of fair procedure. Jurek's conclusion that Texas may impose the death penalty on capital defendants who probably will commit criminal acts of violence in no way establishes that the prosecution may convince a jury that this is so by misleading or patently unreliable evidence.

Moreover, Jurek's holding that the Texas death statute is not impermissibly vague does not lead ineluctably to the conclusion that psychiatric testimony is admissible. It makes sense to exclude psychiatric predictions of future violence while admitting lay testimony because psychiatric predictions appear to come from trained mental health professionals, who purport to have special expertise. In view of the total scientific groundlessness of these predictions, psychiatric testimony is fatally misleading. Lay testimony, frankly based on statistical factors with demonstrated correlations to violent behavior, would not raise this substantial threat of unreliable and capricious sentencing decisions, inimical to the constitutional standards established in our cases; and such predictions are as accurate as any a psychiatrist could make. Indeed, the very basis of Jurek, as I understood it, was that such judgments can be made by laymen on the basis of lay testimony.

Texas' choice of substantive factors does not justify loading the factfinding process against the defendant through the presentation of what is, at bottom, false testimony.

V.

I would vacate petitioner's death sentence, and remand for further proceedings consistent with these views.

Notes and Queries

The decision reported many studies reaching a similar conclusion to that of the APA Task Force Report, Clinical Aspects of the Violent Individual 28 (1974), noting that "90% error rate '[unfortunately] . . . is the state of the art.'"

The majority directly addresses concerns regarding expert testimony about a defendant's future dangerousness. Identify the three major inadequacies of the expert testimony challenged in this case. What do you make of the majority's response to those challenges?

The Court takes very seriously the emerging empirical research supporting the use of heuristics we identified at the beginning of this chapter. The Court notes that psychiatrists actually may be less accurate predictors of future violence than laymen because of personal biases in favor of predicting violence arising from the fear of being responsible for the erroneous release of a violent individual. It also notes that inaccuracy may be due to a tendency to generalize from experiences with past offenders on bases that have no empirical relationship to future violence, a tendency that may be present in Grigson's and Holbrook's testimony. How important do you think these concerns are to this case?

Do you find persuasive the dissent's point that predictions are not only unreliable but also unethical without directly examining defendants?

What do you make of the APA's position that all psychiatric predictions of future dangerousness should be excluded from capital sentencing proceedings?

The case reveals numerous rights the legal system accords defendants at sentencing. For a thorough analysis of individuals' rights at sentencing, see Alan C. Michaels, Trial rights at sentencing, 81 N.C.L. Rev. 1771 (2003). Michaels examines, for example, the right to counsel, notice of conduct, trial by jury, discovery, double jeopardy protection, public trial, Confrontation Clause protections, present evidence, remain silent, and proof beyond a reasonable doubt. He concludes that more rights apply at sentencing than may have been supposed but nevertheless identifies the principle of no mandated presumption of "sentencing innocence," that there is no requirement that the defendant be given the benefit of the doubt. As a result, rights designed to give the defendant extra protections – particularly by insuring that errors will tend to be resolved in the defendant's favor, but also rights that provide extra protection against state oppression or otherwise champion the defendant's autonomy – generally do not apply. By virtue of convictions, defendants generally lose the constitutional entitlement to have errors resolved in their favor that protected them at trial. When reading the cases that follow, seek to determine the helpfulness of this proposition.

NOTE ON DR. GRIGSON

Dr. James P. Grigson is repeatedly mentioned in Supreme Court cases and capital cases in Texas. Commentators describe well why he has earned the reputation as "Dr. Death." As of 1994, Dr. Grigson had appeared in at least 150 capital trials on behalf of the state, and his predictions of future dangerousness had been used to help convict at least one-third of all Texas death row inmates. Despite clear concern on the part of the psychiatric community regarding the inability of psychiatric professionals to accurately predict future dangerousness, Dr. Grigson has testified repeatedly that he was one hundred percent certain that the defendant would be dangerous in the future; that he could testify to this fact "within reasonable psychiatric certainty;" and, in some cases, that there was "a one thousand percent chance" that the defendant would be a future danger. In 1995, Dr. Grigson was expelled from the American Psychiatric Association (APA) and from the Texas Society of Psychiatric Phsyicians (TSPP). The APA and the TSPP determined that Dr. Grigson's testimony in several cases that he could be one hundred percent certain that the defendant would be dangerous in the future was a violation of ethics which could not be tolerated. Yet, he continues to be appointed by Texas courts to make psychiatric evaluations of defendants and continues to predict future dangerousness of defendants for the State of Texas. Importantly, Dr. Grigson was proven wrong in several cases. The most notable case was that of Randall Dale Adams, whom Dr. Grigson described as an incurable and extreme sociopath with no regard for the life or property of others and who would continue to present a danger to society. He concluded that Adams would kill again. Due mainly to Errol Morris's documentary *The Thin Blue Line*, Adams was exonerated of all charges after twelve years of imprisonment and released from the Texas death row. Importantly, during his twelve years of imprisonment nor in the years since his release, Adams did not commit a known act of violence. Eugenia T. Lafontaine, A dangerous preoccupation with future danger: Why expert predictions of future dangerousness in capital cases are unconstitutional, 44 B. C. L. Rev. 207 (2002). Clearly, Dr. Grigson is not a popular figure in some circles. For our purposes, consider what critics' claims tell us about heuristics in decision making, the role of bounded rationality, and what the legal system can perhaps do differently to address critics' concerns.

NOTE ON SQUARING BAREFOOT WITH DAUBERT

To date, few courts have evaluated the admissibility of expert testimony regarding future violence under the Court's recent *Daubert* decision and its progeny. Given that, the Supreme Court is not likely to address the issue any time soon. Despite the lack of case law, there has been much post-*Daubert* commentary on the issue in legal and scientific literatures. This commentary overwhelmingly suggests that testimony by a qualified expert regarding a properly conducted clinical violence risk assessment will remain admissible evidence. For example, even critics of the use of dangerousness assessments arrive at the following conclusion regarding the admissibility of psychological and psychiatric expertise on violence risk assessments:

> [I]t could be argued that mental health professionals should not be allowed to testify as experts [on violence prediction] under the Daubert standard. However, (a) historically, the Supreme Court has been receptive to professional assessments of dangerousness; (b) in almost any case in which such assessments are made they will be based, at least in part, on validated risk factors (e.g., a history of

violence); (c) mental health professionals could well make the point that they cannot validate their expertise in many circumstances without releasing dangerous individuals; (d) throughout our society, mental health professionals are expected by the law to make professional assessments of dangerousness when patients pose a serious risk of harm to others; (e) the Supreme Court also stated in Daubert that, still, "[w]idespread acceptance can be an important factor in ruling particular evidence admissible," and clinical assessments of dangerousness are widely accepted by the clinical community and increasingly by the academic community; and (f) if nothing else, it is likely that mental health professionals will be better able than laypersons to articulate, highlight, and analyze the factors that go into a dangerousness risk assessment. Given all this, it is highly unlike that the Daubert decision will affect the admissibility of professional assessments of dangerousness in federal courts or in states that follow the Daubert decision. Thomas R. Litwack and Louise B. Schlesinger, Dangerousness risk assessments: Research, legal, and clinical considerations, in The Handbook of Forensic Psychology 192-93 (Allen K. Hess and Irving B. Weiner, eds., 2d ed., 1999).

Note on Actuarial Predictions and Juries

Despite problems with the accuracy of violence predictions, some argue that because actuarial predictions provide the best information available, they should be admitted to help guide decision makers in their determinations. Importantly, the most hotly debated topic in juror sentencing deliberations – next to the crime itself – is the issue of the defendant's dangerousness upon return to society. In death penalty cases, for example, future dangerousness takes precedence in jury deliberations over any mitigating evidence, such as remorse, mental illness, intelligence, or drug/alcohol addiction, and any concern about the defendant's behavior in prison. But whether or not future dangerousness is permitted or required by statute, and whether or not it is even mentioned by prosecutors or presented as evidence in the penalty phase of the case, it remains the major focus of the factfinders. This is true regardless of the presence or absence of expert testimony about future dangerousness in the hearing. John H. Blume, Stephen P. Garvey, and Sheri Lynn Johnson, Future dangerousness in capital cases: Always "at issue", 86 Cornell L. Rev. 397, 398 (2001). Fact-finders focus on dangerousness because they often incorrectly believe that the law requires a death sentence upon a showing of the defendant's future dangerousness. Most people do not believe that defendants sentenced to life will actually be required to spend the rest of their lives in prison. They fear that a dangerous person will be released into the community, a fear that is a highly motivating factor in choosing between death and a life sentence. James Liginbuhl and Julie Howe, Discretion in capital sentencing instructions: Guided or misguided?, 70 Ind. L.J. 1161, 1174 (1995). Jury deliberations exacerbate that fear to the extent that they lack objective information about such predictions and overestimate the threat of future violence. Jurors seldom are informed of the true rate of violent recidivism among murderers released from prison. Jonathan R. Sorensen and Rocky L. Pilgrim, An actuarial risk assessment of violence posed by capital murder defendants, 90 J. Crim. L. and Criminol. 1251(2000). Interviews with capital jurors have revealed that jurors who sentenced the defendant to death had median estimates of future violence of eighty-five percent, with a fifty percent median estimate that the defendant would commit another murder. Yet, empirical studies demonstrate a counter-intuitive decreased base rate for violence among capital commutees in prison. In studies of capital commutees paroled into the community, twenty percent returned to prison, but only eight to ten percent committed new felonies. Unless jurors are informed about population base rates and how they should use them in making their decision, risk estimates amount to little more than speculation. In addition, jurors consistently underestimate the number of years that must be served for a term of "life in prison," which means that the prisoner will be much older and have less opportunity in terms of potential risk period than jurors believe. The decrease in violence and criminal activity with age is a well-established principle of criminology. Base rates of violence are far lower after the age of sixty (when most life prisoners would be eligible for parole) than when individuals are in their twenties. Base rate errors plague human decision making in general, and there is no reason to assume that capital jurors are any different. Mark. D. Cunningham and Thomas J.

Reidy, Don't confuse me with the facts: Common errors in violence risk assessment at capital sentencing, 26 Crim. Jus. and Beh. 20, 23 (1999). Does the evidence constitute sufficient reason to believe that probabilistic estimates, with actuarial estimates being the most accurate, would be helpful to the jury? The empirical evidence may seem quite persuasive, but should it matter? Why not simply allow a jury to use fear as its basis for making sentencing decisions?

RESEARCH NOTE ON THE POWER OF ADVERSARIAL PROCESSES

The majority opinion in *Barefoot* rejected the defense contention that admission of unreliable prediction testimony was unconstitutional. The majority did not seriously dispute the APA's assertion that such predictions were typically wrong and therefore that Dr. Grigson's claim of absolute certainty contradicted well-established evidence in the scientific literature. Rather, the majority opinion placed great faith in the adversarial process. Our legal system obviously relies on the effectiveness of this process; but whether it effectively can counter unreliable evidence seems questionable. Do you suppose that the traditional tools of attorney argument – opposing experts and vigorous cross-examination – sufficiently guard against decisions based on evidence presented by experts like Dr. Grigson? A group of leading researchers examined this proposition by modeling an expert after Dr. Grigson. In the experiment, the jury, drawn from the Cook County, Illinois jury pool, watched a seventy-five minute videotape of a death penalty hearing involving an armed robbery and murder of a stranger who the defendant robbed in order to buy beer.

The researchers developed several conditions to assess the influence of expert testimony. Three conditions began with a similar foundation in which the jurors heard the prosecution's expert state that he had diagnosed the defendant as a sociopath, as a person with no motivation to follow rules, who lies regularly, is manipulative, and lacks empathy, guilt, or remorse. The expert based his diagnosis on examination of records from prior court proceedings, pre-sentence reports, and prison records. These records revealed that the defendant had a long criminal history beginning when he was a juvenile and that he had seven arrests as an adult, including two for armed robbery which involved harm to the victim. The records also showed that he was dependent on alcohol and had a long history of dishonesty. The expert testified that, in his opinion, the defendant was "certain to kill again" if he was not executed. The expert also testified that he had extensive prior experience in making such predictions and that his judgments were generally very accurate.

The above three conditions were varied in terms of the defendant's attorney's response. The first condition involved a "weak cross-examination;" the defense only brought out the fact that the witness usually testified for the state, but did not challenge the future dangerousness prediction. The second condition involved a "strong cross-examination," the defense added to the cross in the weak condition by pointing out at length that the expert's prediction of future killing was inconsistent with prior research and that the expert has not employed the standard methods for diagnosing future dangerousness. The witness admitted on the stand that the best scientific literature indicates that two-thirds of dangerousness predictions prove to be incorrect. The cross-examination also revealed that the expert had never published his findings in peer-reviewed journals. The expert responded that he was focused on clinical diagnosis, not publication, and that he was confident he was correct. The third condition used a "strong cross-examination plus defense expert." In that condition, the defense lawyer conducted the same cross-examination as in the strong-cross condition. In addition, a psychiatrist was presented as a defense expert who testified that the defendant coped reasonably well but on rare occasions excessive drinking interacted with a personality disorder to produce violence. The defense expert also testified that predictions about future violence could not be made with any certainty, but that in his view, the likelihood of future similar violence was not great and the defendant was a good candidate for an alcohol abuse program.

The study also developed a fourth, control condition. In this condition, the expert simply made a realistic prediction without extreme views. The expert essentially agreed with the defense expert that predictions of future dangerousness are accurate only about one-third of the time. However, he also warned about the defendant's potential for future violence. The cross-examination was identical to the cross in the first condition, that the expert usually testified for the state.

The study examined the impact of these conditions on the persuasiveness of the state's expert, the jury verdict preference (death or life), and confidence in the verdict. Taking the Supreme Court's view of the significance of the adversarial processes, it would seem that the first condition (strong prediction of future dangerousness, no opposing expert, and a weak cross) should produce the highest percentage of death penalty verdicts. If cross-examination is an effective prophylactic against unreliable testimony, the second condition should produce lower persuasiveness scores and a lower percentage of death penalty verdicts. And the combination of a powerful cross and an opposing expert should produce still lower persuasiveness scores and even fewer death penalty verdicts. Ideally, this version would produce jury judgments indistinguishable from the fourth version in which the expert reported the limitations in his own testimony.

The study revealed that the efforts to address the strong predictions of dangerousness do not seem to have an appreciable impact. For example, in the weak cross condition forty-seven percent of the juries gave a death verdict, in the strong cross condition fifty-one percent recommended death, and in the strong cross plus opposing expert fifty percent recommended death. The only condition with a different result was in the fourth condition where the plaintiff's expert testified that predictions were wrong two-thirds of the time. In this condition, thirty-nine percent of the juries recommended the death penalty. The study supports, as the researchers concluded, the claim that this type of testimony seems impervious to cross-examination and even opposing experts. Shari Seidman Diamond, Jonathan D Casper, Cami L Heiert, and Anna-Maria Marshall, Juror reactions to attorneys at trial, 87 J. Crim. L. and Criminology 17 (1996). Importantly, the weakest cross-examination appears to be the most typical form of cross examination. The vast majority of cross is devoted to expert qualifications and potential sources of bias. Margaret Kovora, Melissa B. Russano, and Bradley D. McAuliff, Assessment of the commonsense psychology underlying *Daubert*, 8 Psych. Pub. Pol'y and L. 180, 192 (2002).

CONTROLLING JUDICIAL DISCRETION

UNITED STATES v. GRAYSON
438 U.S. 41 (1978)

MR. CHIEF JUSTICE BURGER delivered the opinion of the Court.

We granted certiorari to review a holding of the Court of Appeals that it was improper for a sentencing judge, in fixing the sentence within the statutory limits, to give consideration to the defendant's false testimony observed by the judge during the trial.

I.

In August 1975, respondent Grayson was confined in a federal prison camp under a conviction for distributing a controlled substance. In October, he escaped but was apprehended two days later by FBI agents in New York City. He was indicted for prison escape.

During its case in chief, the United States proved the essential elements of the crime, including his lawful confinement and the unlawful escape. In addition, it presented the testimony of the arresting FBI agents that Grayson, upon being apprehended, denied his true identity.

Grayson testified in his own defense. He admitted leaving the camp but asserted that he did so out of fear: "I had just been threatened with a large stick with a nail protruding through it by an inmate that was serving time at Allenwood, and I was scared, and I just ran." He testified that the threat was made in the presence of many inmates by prisoner Barnes who sought to enforce collection of a gambling debt and followed other threats and physical assaults made for the same purpose. Grayson called one inmate, who testified: "I heard talk to Grayson in a loud voice one day, but that's all. I never seen no harm, no hands or no shuffling whatsoever."

Grayson's version of the facts was contradicted by the Government's rebuttal evidence and by cross-examination on crucial aspects of his story. For example, Grayson stated that after crossing the prison fence he left his prison jacket by the side of the road. On recross, he stated that he also left his prison shirt but not his trousers. Government testimony showed that on the morning after the escape, a shirt marked with Grayson's number, a jacket, and a pair of prison trousers were found outside a hole in the prison fence. Grayson also testified on cross-examination: "I do believe that I phrased the rhetorical question to Captain Kurd, who was in charge of [the prison], and I think I said something if an inmate was being threatened by somebody, what would . . . he do? First of all he said he would want to know who it was." On further cross-examination, however, Grayson modified his description of the conversation. Captain Kurd testified that Grayson had never mentioned in any fashion threats from other inmates. Finally, the alleged assailant, Barnes, by then no longer an inmate, testified that Grayson had never owed him any money and that he had never threatened or physically assaulted Grayson.

The jury returned a guilty verdict, whereupon the District Judge ordered the United States Probation Office to prepare a presentence report. At the sentencing hearing, the judge stated:

> I'm going to give my reasons for sentencing in this case with clarity, because one of the reasons may well be considered by a Court of Appeals to be impermissible; and although I could come into this Court Room and sentence this Defendant to a five-year prison term without any explanation at all, I think it is fair that I give the reasons so that if the Court of Appeals feels that one of the reasons which I am about to enunciate is an improper consideration for a trial judge, then the Court will be in a position to reverse this Court and send the case back for re-sentencing.
>
> In my view a prison sentence is indicated, and the sentence that the Court is going to impose is to deter you, Mr. Grayson, and others who are similarly situated. Secondly, it is my view that your defense was a complete fabrication without the slightest merit whatsoever. I feel it is proper for me to consider that fact in the sentencing, and I will do so.

He then sentenced Grayson to a term of two years' imprisonment, consecutive to his unexpired sentence.

On appeal, a divided panel of the Court of Appeals for the Third Circuit directed that Grayson's sentence be vacated and that he be resentenced by the District Court without consideration of false testimony...

We granted certiorari to resolve conflicts between holdings of the Courts of Appeals. We reverse.

II.

In Williams v. New York, Mr. Justice Black observed that the "prevalent modern philosophy of penology [is] that the punishment should fit the offender and not merely the crime," and that, accordingly, sentences should be determined with an eye toward the "[reformation] and rehabilitation of offenders." But it has not always been so. In the early days of the Republic, when imprisonment had only recently emerged as an alternative to the death penalty, confinement in public stocks, or whipping in the town square, the period of incarceration was generally prescribed with specificity by the legislature. Each crime had its defined punishment. The "excessive rigidity of the [mandatory or fixed sentence] system" soon gave way in some jurisdictions, however, to a scheme permitting the sentencing judge – or jury – to consider aggravating and mitigating circumstances surrounding an offense, and, on that basis, to select a sentence within a range defined by the legislature. Nevertheless, the focus remained on the crime: Each particular offense was to be punished in proportion to the social harm caused by it and according to the offender's culpability. The purpose of incarceration remained, primarily, retribution and punishment.

Approximately a century ago, a reform movement asserting that the purpose of incarceration, and therefore the guiding consideration in sentencing, should be rehabilitation of the offender, dramatically altered the approach to sentencing. A fundamental proposal of this movement was a flexible sentencing system permitting judges and correctional personnel, particularly the latter, to set the release date of prisoners according to informed judgments concerning their potential for, or actual, rehabilitation and their likely recidivism. Indeed, the most extreme formulations of the emerging rehabilitation model, with its "reformatory sentence," posited that "convicts [regardless of the nature of their crime] can never be rightfully imprisoned except upon proof that it is unsafe for themselves and for society to leave them free, and when confined can never be rightfully released until they show themselves fit for membership in a free community."

This extreme formulation, although influential, was not adopted unmodified by any jurisdiction. "The influences of legalism and realism were powerful enough . . . to prevent the enactment of this form of indeterminate sentencing. Concern for personal liberty, skepticism concerning administrative decisions about prisoner reformation and readiness for release, insistence upon the preservation of some measure of deterrent emphasis, and other such factors, undoubtedly, led, instead, to a system – indeed, a complex of systems – in which maximum terms were generally employed." Thus it is that today the extent of a federal prisoner's confinement is initially determined by the sentencing judge, who selects a term within an often broad, congressionally prescribed range; release on parole is then available on review by the United States Parole Commission, which, as a general rule, may conditionally release a prisoner any time after he serves one-third of the judicially fixed term. To an unspecified degree, the sentencing judge is obligated to make his decision on the basis, among others, of predictions regarding the convicted defendant's potential, or lack of potential, for rehabilitation.

Indeterminate sentencing under the rehabilitation model presented sentencing judges with a serious practical problem: how rationally to make the required predictions so as to avoid capricious and arbitrary sentences, which the newly conferred and broad discretion placed within the realm of possibility. An obvious, although only partial, solution was to provide the judge with as much information as reasonably practical concerning the defendant's "character and propensities[,] . . . his present purposes and tendencies," and, indeed, "every aspect of [his] life." Thus, most jurisdictions provided trained probation officers to conduct presentence investigations of the defendant's life and, on that basis, prepare a presentence report for the sentencing judge.

Constitutional challenges were leveled at judicial reliance on such information, however. In Williams v. New York, a jury convicted the defendant of murder but recommended a life sentence. The sentencing judge, partly on the basis of information not known to the jury but contained in a presentence report, imposed the death penalty. The defendant argued that this procedure deprived him of his federal constitutional right to confront and cross-examine those supplying information to the probation officer and, through him, to the sentencing judge. The Court rejected this argument. It noted that traditionally "a sentencing judge could exercise a wide discretion in the sources and types of evidence used to assist him in determining the kind and extent of punishment to be imposed within limits fixed by law." "And modern concepts individualizing punishment have made it all the more necessary that a sentencing judge not be denied an opportunity to obtain pertinent information;" indeed, "[to] deprive sentencing judges of this kind of information would undermine modern penological procedural policies that have been cautiously adopted throughout the nation after careful consideration and experimentation." Accordingly, the sentencing judge was held not to have acted unconstitutionally in considering either the defendant's participation in criminal conduct for which he had not been convicted or information secured by the probation investigator that the defendant was a "menace to society."

Of course, a sentencing judge is not limited to the often far-ranging material compiled in a presentence report. "[Before] making [the sentencing] determination, a judge may appropriately conduct an inquiry broad in scope, largely unlimited either as to the kind of information he may consider, or the source from which it may come." Congress recently reaffirmed this fundamental sentencing principle by enacting 18 U. S. C. § 3577:

> No limitation shall be placed on the information concerning the background, character, and conduct of a person convicted of an offense which a court of the United States may receive and consider for the purpose of imposing an appropriate sentence.

Thus, we have acknowledged that a sentencing authority may legitimately consider the evidence heard during trial, as well as the demeanor of the accused. More to the point presented in this case, one serious study has concluded that the trial judge's "opportunity to observe the defendant, particularly if he chose to take the stand in his defense, can often provide useful insights into an appropriate disposition."

A defendant's truthfulness or mendacity while testifying on his own behalf, almost without exception, has been deemed probative of his attitudes toward society and prospects for rehabilitation and hence relevant to sentencing. Soon after Williams was decided, the Tenth Circuit concluded that "the attitude of a convicted defendant with respect to his willingness to commit a serious crime [perjury] . . . is a proper matter to consider in determining what sentence shall be imposed within the limitations fixed by statute."..

> ...The theory has its critics. While it lasts, however, a fact like the defendant's readiness to lie under oath before the judge who will sentence him would seem to be among the more precise and concrete of the available indicia.

Only one Circuit has directly rejected the probative value of the defendant's false testimony in his own defense. In Scott v. United States, the court argued that

> the peculiar pressures placed upon a defendant threatened with jail and the stigma of conviction make his willingness to deny the crime an unpromising test of his prospects for rehabilitation if guilty. It is indeed unlikely that many men who commit serious offenses would balk on principle from lying in their own defense. The guilty man may quite sincerely repent his crime but yet, driven by the urge to remain free, may protest his innocence in a court of law.

The Scott rationale rests not only on the realism of the psychological pressures on a defendant in the dock – which we can grant – but also on a deterministic view of human conduct that is inconsistent with the underlying precepts of our criminal justice system. A "universal and persistent" foundation stone in our system of law, and particularly in our approach to punishment, sentencing, and incarceration, is the "belief in freedom of the human will and a consequent ability and duty of the normal individual to choose between good and evil." Given that long-accepted view of the "ability and duty of the normal individual to choose," we must conclude that the defendant's readiness to lie under oath – especially when, as here, the trial court finds the lie to be flagrant – may be deemed probative of his prospects for rehabilitation.

III.

Against this background we evaluate Grayson's constitutional argument that the District Court's sentence constitutes punishment for the crime of perjury for which he has not been indicted, tried, or convicted by due process. A second argument is that permitting consideration of perjury will "chill" defendants from exercising their right to testify on their own behalf.

A.

In his due process argument, Grayson does not contend directly that the District Court had an impermissible purpose in considering his perjury and selecting the sentence. Rather, he argues that this Court, in order to preserve due process rights, not only must prohibit the impermissible sentencing practice of incarcerating for the purpose of saving the Government the burden of bringing a separate and subsequent perjury prosecution but also must prohibit the otherwise permissible practice of considering a defendant's untruthfulness for the purpose of illuminating his need for rehabilitation and society's need for protection. He presents two interrelated reasons. The effect of both permissible and impermissible sentencing practices may be the same: additional time in prison. Further, it is virtually impossible, he contends, to identify and establish the impermissible practice. We find these reasons insufficient justification for prohibiting what the Court and the Congress have declared appropriate judicial conduct.

First, the evolutionary history of sentencing demonstrates that it is proper – indeed, even necessary for the rational exercise of discretion – to consider the defendant's whole person and personality, as manifested by his conduct at trial and his testimony under oath, for whatever light those may shed on the sentencing decision. The "parlous" effort to appraise "character" degenerates into a game of chance to the extent that a sentencing judge is deprived of relevant information concerning "every aspect of a defendant's life." The Government's interest, as well as the offender's, in avoiding irrationality is of the highest order. That interest more than justifies the risk that Grayson asserts is present when a sentencing judge considers a defendant's untruthfulness under oath.

Second, in our view, Williams fully supports consideration of such conduct in sentencing. There the Court permitted the sentencing judge to consider the offender's history of prior antisocial conduct, including burglaries for which he had not been duly convicted. This it did despite the risk that the judge might use his knowledge of the offender's prior crimes for an improper purpose.

Third, the efficacy of Grayson's suggested "exclusionary rule" is open to serious doubt. No rule of law, even one garbed in constitutional terms, can prevent improper use of firsthand observations of perjury. The integrity of the judges, and their fidelity to their oaths of office, necessarily provide the only, and in our view adequate, assurance against that.

B.

Grayson's argument that judicial consideration of his conduct at trial impermissibly "chills" a defendant's statutory right and perhaps a constitutional right to testify on his own behalf is without basis. The right guaranteed by law to a defendant is narrowly the right to testify truthfully in accordance with the oath – unless we are to say that the oath is mere ritual without meaning. This view of the right involved is confirmed by the unquestioned constitutionality of perjury statutes, which punish those who willfully give false testimony. Further support for this is found in an important limitation on a defendant's right to the assistance of counsel: Counsel ethically cannot assist his client in presenting what the attorney has reason to believe is false testimony. Assuming, arguendo, that the sentencing judge's consideration of defendants' untruthfulness in testifying has any chilling effect on a defendants' decision to testify falsely, that effect is entirely permissible. There is no protected right to commit perjury.

Accordingly, we reverse the judgment of the Court of Appeals and remand for reinstatement of the sentence of the District Court.

Reversed and remanded.

JUSTICE STEWART, with whom MR. JUSTICE BRENNAN and MR. JUSTICE MARSHALL join, dissenting.

The Court begins its consideration of this case with the assumption that the respondent gave false testimony at his trial. But there has been no determination that his testimony was false. This respondent was given a greater sentence than he would otherwise have received – how much greater we have no way of knowing – solely because a single judge thought that he had not testified truthfully. In essence, the Court holds today that whenever a defendant testifies in his own behalf and is found guilty, he opens himself to the possibility of an enhanced sentence. Such a sentence is nothing more or less than a penalty imposed on the defendant's exercise of his constitutional and statutory rights to plead not guilty and to testify in his own behalf.

Accordingly, I would affirm the judgment of the Court of Appeals.

NOTES AND QUERIES

What do you make of the apparently immense power judges retain in sentencing offenders by using unproven charges and allegations? Does it seem fair to punish offenders for offenses that have not been proven beyond a reasonable doubt?

Do you find persuasive the view that considering uncharged allegations are permissible because (1) the trial judge must consider the defendant's entire history and (2) we simply need to rely on the integrity of judges?

Do you think that considering a defendant's conduct at trial should be relevant to determining his punishment? Do you think that this case does chill defendants' abilities to testify in their own defenses?

The Court relies on *Williams v. New York*, 337 U.S. 241 (1949), which is often seen as the seminal case addressing whether constitutional rights apply at sentencing. In *Williams*, the Supreme Court affirmed a death sentence that a state trial judge had imposed based in part on assertions in a probation report that Williams had committed some thirty burglaries (for which he had not been charged) and on "certain activities of [Williams] as shown by the probation report that indicated [Williams] possessed a "morbid sexuality' and classified him as a "menace to society.'" Id. at 244. The Court concluded that Williams's sentence of death did not violate the Due Process Clause of the Fourteenth Amendment. The Court found no violation even though the probation report was not even disclosed to Williams prior to his sentence and it was conceded to be based on hearsay allegations that he was not given the opportunity to challenge prior to sentencing. The Court justified its conclusion on the ground that looser evidentiary rules were necessary at sentencing to achieve the progressive goals of achieving rehabilitation and reformation through a process of individualized sentencing. What do you make of the Court's rationale?

Grayson clearly opts for providing judges with immense discretion. What do you make of that discretion in light of current research on decision making effectiveness? What positive role does discretion play in judicial decision making?

MISTRETTA v. U.S.
488 U.S. 361 (1989).

JUSTICE BLACKMUN delivered the opinion of the Court.

In this litigation, we granted certiorari before judgment in the United States Court of Appeals for the Eighth Circuit in order to consider the constitutionality of the Sentencing Guidelines promulgated by the United States Sentencing Commission. The Commission is a body created under the Sentencing Reform

Act of 1984 (Act). The United States District Court for the Western District of Missouri ruled that the Guidelines were constitutional.

I.

A.

Background

For almost a century, the Federal Government employed in criminal cases a system of indeterminate sentencing. Statutes specified the penalties for crimes but nearly always gave the sentencing judge wide discretion to decide whether the offender should be incarcerated and for how long, whether restraint, such as probation, should be imposed instead of imprisonment or fine. This indeterminate-sentencing system was supplemented by the utilization of parole, by which an offender was returned to society under the "guidance and control" of a parole officer.

Both indeterminate sentencing and parole were based on concepts of the offender's possible, indeed probable, rehabilitation, a view that it was realistic to attempt to rehabilitate the inmate and thereby to minimize the risk that he would resume criminal activity upon his return to society. It obviously required the judge and the parole officer to make their respective sentencing and release decisions upon their own assessments of the offender's amenability to rehabilitation. As a result, the court and the officer were in positions to exercise, and usually did exercise, very broad discretion. This led almost inevitably to the conclusion on the part of a reviewing court that the sentencing judge "sees more and senses more" than the appellate court; thus, the judge enjoyed the "superiority of his nether position," for that court's determination as to what sentence was appropriate met with virtually unconditional deference on appeal. The decision whether to parole was also "predictive and discretionary." The correction official possessed almost absolute discretion over the parole decision.

Historically, federal sentencing – the function of determining the scope and extent of punishment – never has been thought to be assigned by the Constitution to the exclusive jurisdiction of any one of the three Branches of Government. Congress, of course, has the power to fix the sentence for a federal crime and the scope of judicial discretion with respect to a sentence is subject to congressional control. Congress early abandoned fixed-sentence rigidity, however, and put in place a system of ranges within which the sentencer could choose the precise punishment. Congress delegated almost unfettered discretion to the sentencing judge to determine what the sentence should be within the customarily wide range so selected. This broad discretion was further enhanced by the power later granted the judge to suspend the sentence and by the resulting growth of an elaborate probation system. Also, with the advent of parole, Congress moved toward a "three-way sharing" of sentencing responsibility by granting corrections personnel in the Executive Branch the discretion to release a prisoner before the expiration of the sentence imposed by the judge. Thus, under the indeterminate-sentence system, Congress defined the maximum, the judge imposed a sentence within the statutory range (which he usually could replace with probation), and the Executive Branch's parole official eventually determined the actual duration of imprisonment.

Serious disparities in sentences, however, were common. Rehabilitation as a sound penological theory came to be questioned and, in any event, was regarded by some as an unattainable goal for most cases. In 1958, Congress authorized the creation of judicial sentencing institutes and joint councils to formulate standards and criteria for sentencing. In 1973, the United States Parole Board adopted guidelines that established a "customary range" of confinement. Congress in 1976 endorsed this initiative through the Parole Commission and Reorganization Act, an attempt to envision for the Parole Commission a role, at least in part, "to moderate the disparities in the sentencing practices of individual judges." That Act, however, did not disturb the division of sentencing responsibility among the three Branches. The judge continued to exercise discretion and to set the sentence within the statutory range fixed by Congress, while the prisoner's actual release date generally was set by the Parole Commission.

This proved to be no more than a way station. Fundamental and widespread dissatisfaction with the uncertainties and the disparities continued to be expressed. Congress had wrestled with the problem for more than a decade when, in 1984, it enacted the sweeping reforms that are at issue here.

B.

The Act

The Act, as adopted, revises the old sentencing process in several ways:

It rejects imprisonment as a means of promoting rehabilitation and it states that punishment should serve retributive, educational, deterrent, and incapacitative goals.

It consolidates the power that had been exercised by the sentencing judge and the Parole Commission to decide what punishment an offender should suffer. This is done by creating the United States Sentencing Commission, directing that Commission to devise guidelines to be used for sentencing, and prospectively abolishing the Parole Commission.

It makes all sentences basically determinate. A prisoner is to be released at the completion of his sentence reduced only by any credit earned by good behavior while in custody.

It makes the Sentencing Commission's guidelines binding on the courts, although it preserves for the judge the discretion to depart from the guideline applicable to a particular case if the judge finds an aggravating or mitigating factor present that the Commission did not adequately consider when formulating guidelines. The Act also requires the court to state its reasons for the sentence imposed and to give "the specific reason" for imposing a sentence different from that described in the guideline.

It authorizes limited appellate review of the sentence. It permits a defendant to appeal a sentence that is above the defined range, and it permits the Government to appeal a sentence that is below that range. It also permits either side to appeal an incorrect application of the guideline.

Thus, guidelines were meant to establish a range of determinate sentences for categories of offenses and defendants according to various specified factors, "among others." The maximum of the range ordinarily may not exceed the minimum by more than the greater of 25% or six months, and each sentence is to be within the limit provided by existing law.

C.

The Sentencing Commission

The Commission is established "as an independent commission in the judicial branch of the United States." It has seven voting members (one of whom is the Chairman) appointed by the President "by and with the advice and consent of the Senate." "At least three of the members shall be Federal judges selected after considering a list of six judges recommended to the President by the Judicial Conference of the United States." No more than four members of the Commission shall be members of the same political party. The Attorney General, or his designee, is an ex officio nonvoting member. The Chairman and other members of the Commission are subject to removal by the President "only for neglect of duty or malfeasance in office or for other good cause shown." Except for initial staggering of terms, a voting member serves for six years and may not serve more than two full terms.

D.

The Responsibilities of the Commission

In addition to the duty the Commission has to promulgate determinative-sentence guidelines, it is under an obligation periodically to "review and revise" the guidelines. It is to "consult with authorities on, and individual and institutional representatives of, various aspects of the Federal criminal justice system." It must report to Congress "any amendments of the guidelines." It is to make recommendations to Congress whether the grades or maximum penalties should be modified. It must submit to Congress at least annually an analysis of the operation of the guidelines. It is to issue "general policy statements" regarding their application. And it has the power to "establish general policies . . . as are necessary to carry out the purposes" of the legislation; to "monitor the performance of probation officers" with respect to the guidelines; to "devise and conduct periodic training programs of instruction in sentencing techniques for judicial and probation personnel" and others; and to "perform such other functions as are required to permit Federal courts to meet their responsibilities" as to sentencing.

We note, in passing, that the monitoring function is not without its burden. Every year, with respect to each of more than 40,000 sentences, the federal courts must forward, and the Commission must review, the presentence report, the guideline worksheets, the tribunal's sentencing statement, and any written plea agreement.

II.

This Litigation

On December 10, 1987, John M. Mistretta (petitioner) and another were indicted in the United States District Court for the Western District of Missouri on three counts centering in a cocaine sale. Mistretta moved to have the promulgated Guidelines ruled unconstitutional on the grounds that the Sentencing Commission was constituted in violation of the established doctrine of separation of powers, and that Congress delegated excessive authority to the Commission to structure the Guidelines. As has been noted, the District Court was not persuaded by these contentions.

The District Court rejected petitioner's delegation argument on the ground that, despite the language of the statute, the Sentencing Commission "should be judicially characterized as having Executive Branch status" and that the Guidelines are similar to substantive rules promulgated by other agencies. The court also rejected petitioner's claim that the Act is unconstitutional because it requires Article III federal judges to serve on the Commission. The court stated, however, that its opinion "does not imply that I have no serious doubts about some parts of the Sentencing Guidelines and the legality of their anticipated operation."

Petitioner had pleaded guilty to the first count of his indictment (conspiracy and agreement to distribute cocaine). The Government thereupon moved to dismiss the remaining counts. That motion was granted. Petitioner was sentenced under the Guidelines to 18 months' imprisonment, to be followed by a 3-year term of supervised release. The court also imposed a $ 1,000 fine and a $ 50 special assessment.

Petitioner filed a notice of appeal to the Eighth Circuit, but both petitioner and the United States petitioned for certiorari before judgment. ... we granted those petitions.

III.

Delegation of Power

Petitioner argues that in delegating the power to promulgate sentencing guidelines for every federal criminal offense to an independent Sentencing Commission, Congress has granted the Commission excessive legislative discretion in violation of the constitutionally based nondelegation doctrine. We do not agree.

The nondelegation doctrine is rooted in the principle of separation of powers that underlies our tripartite system of Government. The Constitution provides that "[a]ll legislative Powers herein granted shall be vested in a Congress of the United States," and we long have insisted that "the integrity and maintenance of the system of government ordained by the Constitution" mandate that Congress generally cannot delegate its legislative power to another Branch.. We also have recognized, however, that the separation-of-powers principle, and the nondelegation doctrine in particular, do not prevent Congress from obtaining the assistance of its coordinate Branches. In a passage now enshrined in our jurisprudence, Chief Justice Taft, writing for the Court, explained our approach to such cooperative ventures: "In determining what [Congress] may do in seeking assistance from another branch, the extent and character of that assistance must be fixed according to common sense and the inherent necessities of the government co-ordination." So long as Congress "shall lay down by legislative act an intelligible principle to which the person or body authorized to [exercise the delegated authority] is directed to conform, such legislative action is not a forbidden delegation of legislative power."

Applying this "intelligible principle" test to congressional delegations, our jurisprudence has been driven by a practical understanding that in our increasingly complex society, replete with ever changing and more technical problems, Congress simply cannot do its job absent an ability to delegate power under broad general directives. ...

In light of our approval of these broad delegations, we harbor no doubt that Congress' delegation of authority to the Sentencing Commission is sufficiently specific and detailed to meet constitutional requirements. Congress charged the Commission with three goals: to "assure the meeting of the purposes of sentencing as set forth" in the Act; to "provide certainty and fairness in meeting the purposes of sentencing, avoiding unwarranted sentencing disparities among defendants with similar records . . . while maintaining sufficient flexibility to permit individualized sentences," where appropriate; and to "reflect, to the extent practicable, advancement in knowledge of human behavior as it relates to the criminal justice process." Congress further specified four "purposes" of sentencing that the Commission must pursue in carrying out its mandate: "to reflect the seriousness of the offense, to promote respect for the law, and to provide just punishment for the offense"; "to afford adequate deterrence to criminal conduct"; "to protect the public from further crimes of the defendant"; and "to provide the defendant with needed . . . correctional treatment.".

In addition, Congress prescribed the specific tool – the guidelines system – for the Commission to use in regulating sentencing. More particularly, Congress directed the Commission to develop a system of "sentencing ranges" applicable "for each category of offense involving each category of defendant." ... Moreover, Congress directed the Commission to use current average sentences "as a starting point" for its structuring of the sentencing ranges.

To guide the Commission in its formulation of offense categories, Congress directed it to consider seven factors: the grade of the offense; the aggravating and mitigating circumstances of the crime; the nature and degree of the harm caused by the crime; the community view of the gravity of the offense; the public concern generated by the crime; the deterrent effect that a particular sentence may have on others; and the current incidence of the offense. Congress set forth 11 factors for the Commission to consider in establishing categories of defendants. These include the offender's age, education, vocational skills, mental and emotional condition, physical condition (including drug dependence), previous employment record, family ties and responsibilities, community ties, role in the offense, criminal history, and degree of dependence upon crime for a livelihood. Congress also prohibited the Commission from considering the "race, sex, national origin, creed, and socioeconomic status of offenders," and instructed that the guidelines should reflect the "general inappropriateness" of considering certain other factors, such as current unemployment, that might serve as proxies for forbidden factors.

In addition to these overarching constraints, Congress provided even more detailed guidance to the Commission about categories of offenses and offender characteristics. Congress directed that guidelines require a term of confinement at or near the statutory maximum for certain crimes of violence and for drug offenses, particularly when committed by recidivists. Congress further directed that the Commission assure a substantial term of imprisonment for an offense constituting a third felony conviction, for a career felon, for one convicted of a managerial role in a racketeering enterprise, for a crime of violence by an offender on release from a prior felony conviction, and for an offense involving a substantial quantity of narcotics. Congress also instructed " that the guidelines reflect . . . the general appropriateness of imposing a term of imprisonment" for a crime of violence that resulted in serious bodily injury. On the other hand, Congress directed that guidelines reflect the general inappropriateness of imposing a sentence of imprisonment "in cases in which the defendant is a first offender who has not been convicted of a crime of violence or an otherwise serious offense." Congress also enumerated various aggravating and mitigating circumstances, such as, respectively, multiple offenses or substantial assistance to the Government, to be reflected in the guidelines. In other words, although Congress granted the Commission substantial discretion in formulating guidelines, in actuality it legislated a full hierarchy of punishment – from near maximum imprisonment, to substantial imprisonment, to some imprisonment, to alternatives – and stipulated the most important offense and offender characteristics to place defendants within these categories.

We cannot dispute petitioner's contention that the Commission enjoys significant discretion in formulating guidelines. The Commission does have discretionary authority to determine the relative severity of federal crimes and to assess the relative weight of the offender characteristics that Congress listed for the Commission to consider. The Commission also has significant discretion to determine which crimes have been punished too leniently, and which too severely. Congress has called upon the Commission to exercise its judgment about which types of crimes and which types of criminals are to be considered similar for the purposes of sentencing.

Developing proportionate penalties for hundreds of different crimes by a virtually limitless array of offenders is precisely the sort of intricate, labor-intensive task for which delegation to an expert body is especially appropriate. Although Congress has delegated significant discretion to the Commission to draw judgments from its analysis of existing sentencing practice and alternative sentencing models, "Congress is not confined to that method of executing its policy which involves the least possible delegation of discretion to administrative officers." We have no doubt that in the hands of the Commission "the criteria which Congress has supplied are wholly adequate for carrying out the general policy and purpose" of the Act.

IV.

Separation of Powers

Having determined that Congress has set forth sufficient standards for the exercise of the Commission's delegated authority, we turn to Mistretta's claim that the Act violates the constitutional principle of separation of powers.

This Court consistently has given voice to, and has reaffirmed, the central judgment of the Framers of the Constitution that, within our political scheme, the separation of governmental powers into three coordinate Branches is essential to the preservation of liberty. ...

In applying the principle of separated powers in our jurisprudence ... the Framers did not require – and indeed rejected – the notion that the three Branches must be entirely separate and distinct. ...

In adopting this flexible understanding of separation of powers, we simply have recognized Madison's teaching that the greatest security against tyranny – the accumulation of excessive authority in a single Branch – lies not in a hermetic division among the Branches, but in a carefully crafted system of checked and balanced power within each Branch. "[T]he greatest security," wrote Madison, "against a gradual concentration of the several powers in the same department, consists in giving to those who administer each department, the necessary constitutional means, and personal motives, to resist encroachments of the others."..

It is this concern of encroachment and aggrandizement that has animated our separation-of-powers jurisprudence and aroused our vigilance against the "hydraulic pressure inherent within each of the separate Branches to exceed the outer limits of its power." Accordingly, we have not hesitated to strike down provisions of law that either accrete to a single Branch powers more appropriately diffused among separate Branches or that undermine the authority and independence of one or another coordinate Branch. ...

...In cases specifically involving the Judicial Branch, we have expressed our vigilance against two dangers: first, that the Judicial Branch neither be assigned nor allowed "tasks that are more properly accomplished by [other] branches," and, second, that no provision of law "impermissibly threatens the institutional integrity of the Judicial Branch."

Mistretta argues that the Act suffers from each of these constitutional infirmities. He argues that Congress, in constituting the Commission as it did, effected an unconstitutional accumulation of power within the Judicial Branch while at the same time undermining the Judiciary's independence and integrity. Specifically, petitioner claims that in delegating to an independent agency within the Judicial Branch the power to promulgate sentencing guidelines, Congress unconstitutionally has required the Branch, and individual Article III judges, to exercise not only their judicial authority, but legislative authority – the making of sentencing policy – as well. Such rulemaking authority, petitioner contends, may be exercised by Congress, or delegated by Congress to the Executive, but may not be delegated to or exercised by the Judiciary.

At the same time, petitioner asserts, Congress unconstitutionally eroded the integrity and independence of the Judiciary by requiring Article III judges to sit on the Commission, by requiring that those judges share their rulemaking authority with nonjudges, and by subjecting the Commission's members to appointment and removal by the President. According to petitioner, Congress, consistent with the separation of powers, may not upset the balance among the Branches by co-opting federal judges into the quintessentially political work of establishing sentencing guidelines, by subjecting those judges to the political whims of the Chief Executive, and by forcing judges to share their power with nonjudges.

...Although the unique composition and responsibilities of the Sentencing Commission give rise to serious concerns about a disruption of the appropriate balance of governmental power among the coordinate Branches, we conclude, upon close inspection, that petitioner's fears for the fundamental structural protections of the Constitution prove, at least in this case, to be "more smoke than fire," and do not compel us to invalidate Congress' considered scheme for resolving the seemingly intractable dilemma of excessive disparity in criminal sentencing.

A.

Location of the Commission

The Sentencing Commission unquestionably is a peculiar institution within the framework of our Government. Although placed by the Act in the Judicial Branch, it is not a court and does not exercise judicial power. Rather, the Commission is an "independent" body comprised of seven voting members including at least three federal judges, entrusted by Congress with the primary task of promulgating sentencing guidelines. Our constitutional principles of separated powers are not violated, however, by mere anomaly or innovation. Setting to one side, for the moment, the question whether the composition of the Sentencing Commission violates the separation of powers, we observe that Congress' decision to create an independent rulemaking body to promulgate sentencing guidelines and to locate that body within the Judicial Branch is not unconstitutional unless Congress has vested in the Commission powers that are more appropriately performed by the other Branches or that undermine the integrity of the Judiciary.

Nonetheless ... we have recognized the constitutionality of a "twilight area" in which the activities of the separate Branches merge. ...

What Mistretta's argument comes down to, then, is not that the substantive responsibilities of the Commission aggrandize the Judicial Branch, but that that Branch is inevitably weakened by its participation in policymaking. We do not believe, however, that the placement within the Judicial Branch of an independent agency charged with the promulgation of sentencing guidelines can possibly be construed as preventing the Judicial Branch "from accomplishing its constitutionally assigned functions." Despite the substantive nature of its work, the Commission is not incongruous or inappropriate to the Branch. As already noted, sentencing is a field in which the Judicial Branch long has exercised substantive or political judgment. ... Congress placed the Commission in the Judicial Branch precisely because of the Judiciary's special knowledge and expertise.

B.

C.

Presidential Control

The Act empowers the President to appoint all seven members of the Commission with the advice and consent of the Senate. The Act further provides that the President shall make his choice of judicial appointees to the Commission after considering a list of six judges recommended by the Judicial Conference of the United States. The Act also grants the President authority to remove members of the Commission, although "only for neglect of duty or malfeasance in office or for other good cause shown."

Mistretta argues that this power of Presidential appointment and removal prevents the Judicial Branch from performing its constitutionally assigned functions. ... ...we do not believe that the President's appointment and removal powers over the Commission afford him influence over the functions of the Judicial Branch or undue sway over its members.

The notion that the President's power to appoint federal judges to the Commission somehow gives him influence over the Judicial Branch or prevents, even potentially, the Judicial Branch from performing its constitutionally assigned functions is fanciful. We have never considered it incompatible with the functioning of the Judicial Branch that the President has the power to elevate federal judges from one level to another or to tempt judges away from the bench with Executive Branch positions. The mere fact that the President within his appointment portfolio has positions that may be attractive to federal judges does not, of itself, corrupt the integrity of the Judiciary. Were the impartiality of the Judicial Branch so easily subverted, our constitutional system of tripartite Government would have failed long ago. We simply cannot imagine that federal judges will comport their actions to the wishes of the President for the purpose of receiving an appointment to the Sentencing Commission.

The President's removal power over Commission members poses a similarly negligible threat to judicial independence. ...

V.

We conclude that in creating the Sentencing Commission – an unusual hybrid in structure and authority – Congress neither delegated excessive legislative power nor upset the constitutionally mandated balance of powers among the coordinate Branches. The Constitution's structural protections do not prohibit Congress from delegating to an expert body located within the Judicial Branch the intricate task of formulating sentencing guidelines consistent with such significant statutory direction as is present here. Nor does our system of checked and balanced authority prohibit Congress from calling upon the accumulated wisdom and experience of the Judicial Branch in creating policy on a matter uniquely within the ken of judges. Accordingly, we hold that the Act is constitutional

The judgment of United States District Court for the Western District of Missouri is affirmed.

It is so ordered.

JUSTICE SCALIA, dissenting.

While the products of the Sentencing Commission's labors have been given the modest name "Guidelines," they have the force and effect of laws, prescribing the sentences criminal defendants are to receive. A judge who disregards them will be reversed. I dissent from today's decision because I can find no place within our constitutional system for an agency created by Congress to exercise no governmental power other than the making of laws.

I.

It should be apparent from the above that the decisions made by the Commission are far from technical, but are heavily laden (or ought to be) with value judgments and policy assessments. ...

Petitioner's most fundamental and far-reaching challenge to the Commission is that Congress' commitment of such broad policy responsibility to any institution is an unconstitutional delegation of legislative power. It is difficult to imagine a principle more essential to democratic government than that upon which the doctrine of unconstitutional delegation is founded: Except in a few areas constitutionally committed to the Executive Branch, the basic policy decisions governing society are to be made by the Legislature. Our Members of Congress could not, even if they wished, vote all power to the President and adjourn sine die.

But while the doctrine of unconstitutional delegation is unquestionably a fundamental element of our constitutional system, it is not an element readily enforceable by the courts. Once it is conceded, as it must be, that no statute can be entirely precise, and that some judgments, even some judgments involving policy considerations, must be left to the officers executing the law and to the judges applying it, the debate over unconstitutional delegation becomes a debate not over a point of principle but over a question of degree...

II.

The focus of controversy, in the long line of our so-called excessive delegation cases, has been whether the degree of generality contained in the authorization for exercise of executive or judicial powers in a particular field is so unacceptably high as to amount to a delegation of legislative powers. I say "so-called excessive delegation" because although that convenient terminology is often used, what is really at issue is whether there has been any delegation of legislative power, which occurs (rarely) when Congress authorizes the exercise of executive or judicial power without adequate standards. Strictly speaking, there is no acceptable delegation of legislative power. ... In the present case, however, a pure delegation of legislative power is precisely what we have before us. It is irrelevant whether the standards are adequate, because they are not standards related to the exercise of executive or judicial powers; they are, plainly and simply, standards for further legislation.

By reason of today's decision, I anticipate that Congress will find delegation of its lawmaking powers much more attractive in the future. If rulemaking can be entirely unrelated to the exercise of judicial or executive powers, I foresee all manner of "expert" bodies, insulated from the political process, to which Congress will delegate various portions of its lawmaking responsibility. How tempting to create an expert Medical Commission (mostly M.D.'s, with perhaps a few Ph.D.'s in moral philosophy) to dispose of such thorny, "nowin" political issues as the withholding of life-support systems in federally funded hospitals, or the use of fetal tissue for research. This is an undemocratic precedent that we set – not because of the scope of the delegated power, but because its recipient is not one of the three Branches of Government. The only governmental power the Commission possesses is the power to make law; and it is not the Congress.

III.

I think the Court errs, in other words, not so much because it mistakes the degree of commingling, but because it fails to recognize that this case is not about commingling, but about the creation of a new Branch altogether, a sort of juniorvarsity Congress. It may well be that in some circumstances such a Branch would be desirable; perhaps the agency before us here will prove to be so. But there are many desirable dispositions that do not accord with the constitutional structure we live under. And in the long run the improvisation of a constitutional structure on the basis of currently perceived utility will be disastrous.

I respectfully dissent from the Court's decision, and would reverse the judgment of the District Court.

NOTES AND QUERIES

Federal judges have not welcomed guidelines. Indeed, over 200 federal trial judges ruled the Guidelines unconstitutional before the Supreme Court resolved the issue to the contrary in *Mistretta*. Nearly 10 years after *Mistretta*, in 1997, three-fourths of the federal trial judges felt that mandatory guidelines were "unnecessary." Kate Stith and Jose A. Cabranes, Fear of Judging: Sentencing Guidelines in the Federal Courts 5 (1998). What implications arise from hostility to the Guidelines by those who are to be guided by them? For criticism of the Guidelines, see, for example, Kate Stith and Jose A. Cabranes, Fear of Judging: Sentencing Guidelines in the Federal Courts (1998); Jose A. Cabranes, Sentencing Guidelines: A dismal failure, N.Y. L.J., Feb. 11, 1992, at 2; and Daniel J. Freed, Federal sentencing in the wake of guidelines: Unacceptable limits on the discretion of sentencers, 101 Yale L.J. 1681 (1992). For defense of the Guidelines, see, for example, Frank O. Bowman, III, Fear of law: Thoughts on fear of judging and the state of the Federal Sentencing Guidelines, 44 St. Louis U. L.J. 299 (2000); Frank O. Bowman, III, The quality of mercy must be restrained, and other lessons in learning to love the Federal Sentencing Guidelines, 1996 Wis. L. Rev. 679 (1996); and Marvin E. Frankel, Sentencing Guidelines: A need for creative collaboration, 101 Yale L.J. 2043 (1992).

The Guidelines limit consideration of personal characteristics such as age, education, vocational skills, mental condition, physical condition, employment record, and family and community ties. They also contain a directive that wealth be barred from consideration. These factors are deemed not ordinarily relevant, except that socioeconomic status is barred from consideration in sentencing. What do you make of that exclusion? What do you think it does to the traditional goal of rehabilitation which, it would seem, would have judges use these same factors to inform their decision? Do you find eliminating these factors justifiable in light of the goal of reducing judicial bias? In practice, the rule means that counsel seek to define and redefine "ordinary" and "extraordinary" for the purposes of receiving a departure from the mandatory sentence. For example, some argue that a female inmate who has children is not "ordinary," and thus a departure may be appropriate, despite the large proportion of female inmates who have children. See Myrna S. Raeder, Remember the family: Seven myths about single parenting departures, 13 Fed. Sent. Rep. 251, 251-52 (2001). What do you make of such arguments?

The focus on extraordinary and a-typical factors has contributed to important developments in the use and non-use of cultural considerations. What do you make of the following cases? In one, a Korean-American man who spent the first forty years of his life in Korea pled guilty to bribing an Internal Revenue Service agent, but argued that he should be granted a departure from Guidelines because his cultural beliefs made him unlike the typical defendant convicted of this crime. He claimed that because of his Korean cultural upbringing he believed the money he gave to the agent was not only lawful but also socially mandated. *United States v. Yu*, 954 F.2d 951 (3d Cir. 1992). In another case, a Mexican-American man convicted of illegal reentry argued that the district court abused its discretion by not taking into account the degree of his cultural assimilation to United States norms. He argued that it would be "unusual" to punish the defendant to the same extent as others convicted of this crime given that the United States contained his family and the only way of life he had ever known. *United States v. Lipman*, 133 F.3d 726 (9th Cir. 1998). Are their situations extraordinary enough to warrant consideration? In the first case, the district court refused the departure, stating that the sentencing guidelines denied it the authority to consider the defendant's culture. On appeal, the court noted that culture is uncomfortably close to the prohibited sentencing factor of national origin but declined to decide the propriety of culture as a sentencing factor and affirmed the district court's decision on other grounds. *United States v. Yu*, 954 F.2d 951, 954 (3d Cir. 1992). In the second case, the appellate court found the defendant's degree of assimilation to American culture relevant in sentencing. *United States v. Lipman*, 133 F.3d 726, 729 (9th Cir. 1998). What does this tell you about sentencing decisions? One review of numerous cases dealing with cultural arguments found that, despite willingness to consider a defendant's culture when that culture is consistent with American mores, no judicial circuit has stated that a defendant's degree of cultural difference, which might serve to justify or explain a defendant's rationale for committing a particular crime, is an appropriate consideration for district court judges in making sentencing determinations. Kelly M. Neff, Removing the blinders in federal sentencing: Cultural difference as a proper departure ground, 78 Chi.-Kent. L. Rev. 445 (2003).

The need to eliminate bias serves as the leading rationale for eliminating the above factors from sentencing considerations. Yet, the literature indicates that disparities, especially in terms of race and ethnicity, have continued to plague the system even after the advent of the Guidelines. In fact, studies and commentators appear to be unanimous on this point. See generally Celesta A. Albonetti, Sentencing under the Federal Ssentencing Gguidelines: Effects of defendant characteristics, guilty pleas, and departures on sentence outcomes for drug offenses, 1991-1992, 31 L. and Soc'y Rev. 789, 790, 806 (1997).

At least two explanations reveal why bias may continue despite Guidelines. The first explanation deals with the discretion still remaining in the hands of judges. Judges have the ability to influence sentencing through various other means in addition to the imposition of adjustments and departures. Most notably, judges have virtually unlimited discretion to sentence a defendant to any term within a sentencing range calculated under the Guidelines. Further, many cases allow judges the authority to substitute at least part of a defendant's sentence with a variety of non-prison alternatives. These discretionary measures can and do lead to different sentences, or at least different periods of incarceration, for similarly situated defendants. The Supreme Court approves of this discretion. In *Koon v. United States*, 518 U.S. 81 (1996), a case we review below, the Court established the rule that the federal courts of appeals must review a district court's application of the Guidelines to the facts using an "abuse of discretion" standard. Id. at 91, 96-98 This standard of review applies to the decision to invoke both adjustments and departures. As a result of this highly deferential standard, sentencing judges have considerable leeway in applying the Guidelines. The Court in *Koon* noted that "Congress directed courts of appeals to "give due deference to the district court's application of the guidelines to the facts.'" Id. at 98. As a result of this deference, appellate courts affirm most sentencing decisions. As a consequence, although similar cases might involve similar facts, sentencing results may vary considerably between judges and still be upheld at the appellate level. Depending on the particular facts of a case, results may vary within a particular district and still be upheld at the appellate level. This variance results from the appellate courts' application of the clearly erroneous standard of review, and the "fact-specific' orientation of the Guidelines. Timothy P. Tobin, Drug couriers: A call for action by the U.S. sentencing commission, 7 Geo. Mason L. Rev. 1055, 1083 (1999). The second explanation for the continued disparities has been that the federal guidelines may reduce judicial discretion, but do not restrict prosecutorial discretion. Three important areas of prosecutorial discretion that have an effect on sentencing decisions include: which charges to bring, whether to seek a downward departure for substantial assistance to authorities, and whether and to what extent to enter into a plea agreement. See Jon J. Lambiras, White-collar crime: Why the sentencing disparity despite uniform guidelines?, 30 Pepp. L. Rev. 459 (2003). Leading commentators now argue that prosecutorial discretion has become the key force controlling sentencing in cases involving mandatory minimum statutes (especially narcotics cases), and to a lesser degree, the Guidelines cases in general. Ian Weinstein, Fifteen years after the federal sentencing revolution: How mandatory minimums have undermined effective and just narcotics sentencing, 40 Am. Crim. L. Rev. 87(2003). Although the three factors affecting prosecutorial discretion have been deemed significant, plea bargaining, especially the lack of policies regarding them, has been the subject of considerable research which has lead to the conclusion that bargaining contributes significantly to sentencing disparity. Stephen J. Schulhofer and Ilene H. Nagel, Plea negotiations under the Federal Sentencing Guidelines: Guideline circumvention and its dynamics in the post-*Mistretta* period, 91 Nw. U. L. Rev. 1284, 1296 (1997). Note that office policies regarding pleas often do not exist and that even some U.S. Attorney's Offices are reluctant to adopt formal published guidelines regarding plea bargaining simply because formal policies restrict flexibility. William T. Pizzi, Understanding prosecutorial discretion in the United States: The limits of comparative criminal procedure as an instrument of reform, 54 Ohio St. L.J. 1325, 1365 (1993).

In federal cases, the probation officer typically interviews the defendant as part of preparations to write a presentence report for the sentencing judge. The defendant does have a right to counsel, but counsel's presence is not mandatory. Even if counsel were present, however, it is not clear how helpful counsel would be. At the interview, the defendant must divulge all prior convictions and arrests and may be pressed to discuss the facts of the case at issue. The penalties for failing to tell the truth or give complete information can be grave and can include an enhancement for obstruction of justice. What do you make of sentencing offenders based on the defendant's past rather than the current offense? Are those distinguishable? How would a decision maker respond to prior "bad acts." Christopher P. Yates and Louise E. Herrick, Going on record: The perils of discussing criminal history during the presentence interview, 13 Fed. Sent. Rep. 330 (2001).

The Guidelines focus on real offense sentencing, which bases the sentence on the actual conduct in which the defendant engaged regardless of the charges for which he was indicted or convicted. It does so in contrast to charge offense sentencing, which bases the sentence only upon the conduct that constitutes the elements of the offense for which the defendant was charged and of which he was convicted. The Guidelines allow the defendant to be sentenced for all acts and omissions committed, aided, abetted, counseled, commanded, induced, procured, or willfully caused by the defendant, even when the defendant was not charged with that conduct, or when the defendant has been acquitted of such conduct. See Mark Osler, Must have got lost: Traditional sentencing goals, the false trail of uniformity and process, and the way back home, 54 S.C. L. Rev. 649 (2003). Does this seem appropriate in light of *Grayson* which had approved broad consideration of facts at sentencing premised on the need for such information to craft a rehabilitative sentence? Note too that this doctrine creates the perverse incentive for prosecutors to drop charges in order to increase an offender's sentence. Some have critically noted that, by deferring evidence of that act to sentencing, a prosecutor will enjoy a much lower burden of proof, the ability to use hearsay, freedom from the rules of evidence, and, if the probation officer includes dropped charges in her report, the possibility of getting the higher sentence imposed while essentially placing no evidence before the judge at all. See Daniel J. Freed, Federal sentencing in the wake of Guidelines: Unacceptable limits on the discretion of sentencers, 101 Yale L.J. 1681 (1992).

NOTE ON HOW GUIDELINES SPECIFY SENTENCING RANGES

The U.S. Sentencing Guidelines Manual (2000) provides for a range of penalties appropriate to an individual offender's conviction. Section 1B1.1 provides the general instructions for application of the Guidelines.

Upon conviction for or a guilty plea to a single offense, the sentencing court must first determine the appropriate offense guideline section in Chapter 2. The appropriate offense guideline section (determined from the statutory index) yields a base offense level and describes specific offense characteristics that might increase or decrease the level. Specific offense characteristics include criminal results, degree of bodily injury, and extent of financial injury, to name only a few. The offense guideline section also provides cross-references and special instructions. The sentencing court must adjust the base level for circumstances related to the victim, the role of the offender in the commission of the crime, and obstruction of justice. If the defendant has clearly accepted responsibility for the offense, the level is decreased. After following subsections 1B1.1(a) through (e), the sentencing court has established the level of the offense.

The sentencing court must next categorize the offender. First, the court must establish the defendant's criminal history category in section 4A. The court must next adjust that category for any applicable reasons set forth in section 4B, which refers to career offenders and criminal livelihood. The total determined points equals the criminal history category of the offender.

The sentencing court then applies the criminal history category and the offense level to the sentencing table contained in section 5A to determine the applicable probation and imprisonment guideline range. The court has discretion to sentence within the range provided. Further sentencing requirements and options for probation, imprisonment, supervision, fines, and restitution are provided in sections 5B through G. Finally, the court is directed to refer to sections 5H and K for policy statements regarding specific offender characteristics and departures that warrant consideration in sentencing.

REVISITING JUDICIAL DISCRETION

We have noted that the Federal Sentencing Guidelines have been criticized for eliminating sentencing discretion and producing excessively harsh sentences. We also noted that the Guidelines have been criticized for rendering the offense of conviction irrelevant. How do you square those criticisms with *Koon v. United States*, 518 U.S. 81 (1996).

Koon began on the evening of March 2, 1991, when Rodney King and two of his friends sat in King's wife's car in Altadena, California, a city in Los Angeles County, and drank malt liquor for a number of hours. Then, with King driving, they left Altadena via a major freeway. King was intoxicated. California Highway Patrol officers observed King's car traveling at a speed they estimated to be in excess of 100 m.p. h. The officers followed King with red lights and sirens activated and ordered him by loudspeaker to pull over, but he continued to drive. The Highway Patrol officers called on the radio for help. Units of the Los Angeles Police Department joined in the pursuit, one of them manned by petitioner Laurence Powell and his trainee, Timothy Wind.

King left the freeway, and after a chase of about eight miles, stopped at an entrance to a recreation area. The officers ordered King and his two passengers to exit the car and to assume a felony prone position – that is, to lie on their stomachs with legs spread and arms behind their backs. King's two friends complied. King, too, got out of the car but did not lie down. Petitioner Stacey Koon arrived, at once followed by Ted Briseno and Roland Solano. All were officers of the Los Angeles Police Department, and as sergeant, Koon took charge. The officers again ordered King to assume the felony prone position. King got on his hands and knees but did not lie down. Officers Powell, Wind, Briseno and Solano tried to force King down, but King resisted and became combative, so the officers retreated. Koon then fired taser darts (designed to stun a combative suspect) into King.

The events that occurred next were captured on videotape by a bystander. As the videotape begins, it shows that King rose from the ground and charged toward Officer Powell. Powell took a step and used his baton to strike King on the side of his head. King fell to the ground. From the 18th to the 30th second on the videotape, King attempted to rise, but Powell and Wind each struck him with their batons to prevent him from doing so. From the 35th to the 51st second, Powell administered repeated blows to King's lower extremities; one of the blows fractured King's leg. At the 55th second, Powell struck King on the chest, and King rolled over and lay prone. At that point, the officers stepped back and observed King for about 10 seconds. Powell began to reach for his handcuffs. (At the sentencing phase, the District Court found that Powell no longer perceived King to be a threat at this point.)

At one-minute-five-seconds (1:05) on the videotape, Briseno, in the District Court's words, "stomped" on King's upper back or neck. King's body writhed in response. At 1:07, Powell and Wind again began to strike King with a series of baton blows, and wind-kicked him in the upper thoracic or cervical area six times until 1:26. At about 1:29, King put his hands behind his back and was handcuffed. Where the baton blows fell and the intentions of King and the officers at various points were contested at trial, but, as noted, petitioners' guilt had been established.

Powell radioed for an ambulance. He sent two messages over a communications network to the other officers that said "'ooops'" and "'I havent [sic] beaten anyone this bad in a long time.'" Koon sent a message to the police station that said: "'Unit just had a big time use of force. . . . Tased and beat the suspect of CHP pursuit big time.'"

King was taken to a hospital where he was treated for a fractured leg, multiple facial fractures, and numerous bruises and contusions. Learning that King worked at Dodger Stadium, Powell said to King: "'We played a little ball tonight, didn't we Rodney? . . . You know, we played a little ball, we played a little hardball tonight, we hit quite a few home runs. . . . Yes, we played a little ball and you lost and we won.'"

Koon, Powell, Briseno, and Wind were tried in state court on charges of assault with a deadly weapon and excessive use of force by a police officer. The officers were acquitted of all charges, with the exception of one assault charge against Powell that resulted in a hung jury. The verdicts touched off widespread rioting in Los Angeles. More than 40 people were killed in the riots, more than 2,000 were injured, and nearly $1 billion in property was destroyed.

On August 4, 1992, a federal grand jury indicted the four officers under 18 U.S.C. §242, charging them with violating King's constitutional rights under color of law. Powell, Briseno, and Wind were charged with willful use of unreasonable force in arresting King. Koon was charged with willfully permitting the other officers to use unreasonable force during the arrest. After a trial in United States District Court for the Central District of California, the jury convicted Koon and Powell but acquitted Wind and Briseno.

The Supreme Court considered the District Court's sentencing determinations. It noted that, under the Sentencing Guidelines, a district court identifies the base offense level assigned to the crime in question, adjusts the level as the Guidelines instruct, and determines the defendant's criminal history category. Coordinating the adjusted offense level and criminal history category yields the appropriate sentencing range. The sentencing range for the officers was 70 to 87 months of imprisonment. However, the District Court (1) granted the officers a downward departure under the Guidelines of five offense levels on the basis of a finding that the suspect's misconduct – which included driving while intoxicated, fleeing from the police, refusing to obey the officers' commands, and attempting to escape from police custody – had provoked the officers' offensive behavior; and (2) granted an additional three level downward departure on the basis of the combination of the officers' (a) unusual susceptibility to abuse in prison, (b) job loss and preclusion from law enforcement employment, (c) burdens of successive state and federal prosecutions, and (d) low risk of recidivism; and (3) having thus reduced the sentencing range to 30-37 months, sentenced each officer to 30 months in prison. The petitioners appealed their convictions, and the

Government appealed the sentences, arguing that the District Court erred in granting the downward departures and in failing to adjust the offense level upward for serious bodily injury. The Court of Appeals affirmed petitioners' convictions, and affirmed the District Court's refusal to adjust the offense level, but it reversed the District Court's departure determinations.

The Supreme Court granted certiorari to determine the standard of review governing appeals from a district court's decision to depart from the sentencing ranges in the Guidelines. The Court ruled that an appellate court should not review the departure decision de novo, but instead should ask whether the sentencing court abused its discretion. The Court also held that, having invoked the wrong standard, the Court of Appeals had erred further in rejecting certain of the downward departure factors relied upon by the District Judge.

The Court reasoned that the Sentencing Reform Act did not eliminate all of the district court's discretion. The Court found that the Act acknowledges the wisdom, even the necessity, of sentencing procedures that take into account individual circumstances. This led Congress to allow district courts to depart from the applicable Guideline range if the court finds that there exists an aggravating or mitigating circumstance of a kind, or to a degree, not adequately taken into consideration by the Sentencing Commission in formulating the guidelines that should result in a sentence different from that described. To determine whether a circumstance was adequately taken into consideration by the Commission, Congress instructed courts to consider only the sentencing guidelines, policy statements, and official commentary of the Sentencing Commission. The Court noted that the Commission lists certain factors that never can be bases for departure (race, sex, national origin, creed, religion, socioeconomic status, lack of guidance as a youth, drug or alcohol dependence, and economic hardship), but then states that with the exception of those listed factors, it "does not intend to limit the kinds of factors, whether or not mentioned anywhere else in the guidelines, that could constitute grounds for departure in an unusual case." The Court also noted that the Act authorizes district courts to depart in cases that feature aggravating or mitigating circumstances of a kind or degree not adequately taken into consideration by the Commission. The Commission, in turn, formulated each Guideline to apply to a heartland of typical cases. The Commission noted that atypical cases were not "adequately taken into consideration," and factors that may make a case atypical provide potential bases for departure. It also realized that departure factors "cannot, by their very nature, be comprehensively listed and analyzed in advance." Faced with this reality, the Commission chose to prohibit consideration of only a few factors, and not otherwise to limit, as a categorical matter, the considerations that might bear upon the decision to depart. These considerations led the Court to adopt an abuse-of-discretion standard. The Court found that the Court of Appeals had erred in over-ruling the sentencing departures as it found that those departures were well within the sound discretion of the District Court. Given the facts of the case, what do you make of the District Court's use of its discretion?

CONTROLLING MANDATED PUNISHMENTS

HARMELIN v. MICHIGAN
501 U.S. 957 (1990)

JUSTICE SCALIA announced the judgment of the Court and delivered the opinion of the Court with respect to Part IV, and an opinion with respect to Parts I, II, and III, in which THE CHIEF JUSTICE joins.

Petitioner was convicted of possessing 672 grams of cocaine and sentenced to a mandatory term of life in prison without possibility of parole. The Michigan Court of Appeals initially reversed his conviction because evidence supporting it had been obtained in violation of the Michigan Constitution. On petition for rehearing, the Court of Appeals vacated its prior decision and affirmed petitioner's sentence, rejecting his argument that the sentence was "cruel and unusual" within the meaning of the Eighth Amendment. The Michigan Supreme Court denied leave to appeal, and we granted certiorari.

Petitioner claims that his sentence is unconstitutionally "cruel and unusual" for two reasons: first, because it is "significantly disproportionate" to the crime he committed; second, because the sentencing judge was statutorily required to impose it, without taking into account the particularized circumstances of the crime and of the criminal.

I.

A.

The Eighth Amendment, which applies against the States by virtue of the Fourteenth Amendment, provides: "Excessive bail shall not be required, nor excessive fines imposed, nor cruel and unusual punishments inflicted." In Rummel v. Estelle (1980), we held that it did not constitute "cruel and unusual punishment" to impose a life sentence, under a recidivist statute, upon a defendant who had been convicted, successively, of fraudulent use of a credit card to obtain $ 80 worth of goods or services, passing a forged check in the amount of $ 28.36, and obtaining $ 120.75 by false pretenses. We said that "one could argue without fear of contradiction by any decision of this Court that for crimes concededly classified and classifiable as felonies, that is, as punishable by significant terms of imprisonment in a state penitentiary, the length of the sentence actually imposed is purely a matter of legislative prerogative." We specifically rejected the proposition asserted by the dissent, that unconstitutional disproportionality could be established by weighing three factors: (1) gravity of the offense compared to severity of the penalty, (2) penalties imposed within the same jurisdiction for similar crimes, and (3) penalties imposed in other jurisdictions for the same offense. A footnote in the opinion, however, said: "This is not to say that a proportionality principle would not come into play in the extreme example mentioned by the dissent, . . . if a legislature made overtime parking a felony punishable by life imprisonment."

Two years later, in Hutto v. Davis (1982), we similarly rejected an Eighth Amendment challenge to a prison term of 40 years and fine of $ 20,000 for possession and distribution of approximately nine ounces of marijuana. We thought that result so clear in light of Rummel that our per curiam opinion said the Fourth Circuit, in sustaining the constitutional challenge, "could be viewed as having ignored, consciously or unconsciously, the hierarchy of the federal court system," which could not be tolerated "unless we wish anarchy to prevail." And we again explicitly rejected application of the three factors discussed in the Rummel dissent. However, whereas in Rummel we had said that successful proportionality challenges outside the context of capital punishment "have been exceedingly rare," in Davis we misdescribed Rummel as having said that "'successful challenges . . .' should be 'exceedingly rare,'" and at that point inserted a reference to, and description of, the Rummel "overtime parking" footnote. The content of that footnote was imperceptibly (but, in the event, ominously) expanded: Rummel's "not [saying] that a proportionality principle would not come into play" in the fanciful parking example, became "noting . . . that there could be situations in which the proportionality principle would come into play, such as" the fanciful parking example. This combination of expanded text plus expanded footnote permitted the inference that gross disproportionality was an example of the "exceedingly rare" situations in which Eighth Amendment challenges "should be" successful. Indeed, one might say that it positively invited that inference, were that not incompatible with the sharp per curiam reversal of the Fourth Circuit's finding that 40 years for possession and distribution of nine ounces of marijuana was grossly disproportionate and therefore unconstitutional.

A year and a half after Davis we uttered what has been our last word on this subject to date. Solem v. Helm (1983) set aside under the Eighth Amendment, because it was disproportionate, a sentence of life imprisonment without possibility of parole, imposed under a South Dakota recividist statute for successive offenses that included three convictions of third-degree burglary, one of obtaining money by false pretenses, one of grand larceny, one of third-offense driving while intoxicated, and one of writing a "no account" check with intent to defraud. In the Solem account, Weems no longer involved punishment of a "unique nature," but was the "leading case," exemplifying the "general principle of proportionality," which was "deeply rooted and frequently repeated in common-law jurisprudence," had been embodied in the English Bill of Rights "in language that was later adopted in the Eighth Amendment," and had been "recognized explicitly in this Court for almost a century." The most recent of those "recognitions" were the "overtime parking" footnotes in Rummel and Davis. As for the statement in Rummel that "one could argue without fear of contradiction by any decision of this Court that for crimes concededly classified and classifiable as felonies . . . the length of the sentence actually imposed is purely a matter of legislative prerogative": according to Solem, the really important words in that passage were "'one could argue.'" "The Court [in Rummel] . . . merely recognized that the argument was possible. To the extent that the State . . . makes this argument here, we find it meritless." Having decreed that a general principle of disproportionality exists, the Court used as the criterion for its application the three-factor test that had been explicitly rejected in both Rummel and Davis. Those cases, the Court said, merely "indicated [that] no one factor will be dispositive in a given case" – though Davis had expressly, approvingly, and quite correctly described Rummel as having "disapproved each of [the] objective factors."

It should be apparent from the above discussion that our 5-to-4 decision eight years ago in Solem was scarcely the expression of clear and well accepted constitutional law. We have long recognized, of course, that the doctrine of stare decisis is less rigid in its application to constitutional precedents, and we think that to be especially true of a constitutional precedent that is both recent and in apparent tension with other decisions. Accordingly, we have addressed anew, and in greater detail, the question whether the Eighth Amendment contains a proportionality guarantee – with particular attention to the background of the Eighth Amendment and to the understanding of the Eighth Amendment before the end of the 19th century. We conclude from this examination that Solem was simply wrong; the Eighth Amendment contains no proportionality guarantee.

B.

Solem based its conclusion principally upon the proposition that a right to be free from disproportionate punishments was embodied within the "cruell and unusuall Punishments" provision of the English Declaration of Rights of 1689, and was incorporated, with that language, in the Eighth Amendment. There is no doubt that the Declaration of Rights is the antecedent of our constitutional text. ...

As Solem observed, the principle of proportionality was familiar to English law at the time the Declaration of Rights was drafted. The Magna Carta provided that "[a] free man shall not be fined for a small offence, except in proportion to the measure of the offense; and for a great offence he shall be fined in proportion to the magnitude of the offence, saving his freehold. . . ." When imprisonment supplemented fines as a method of punishment, courts apparently applied the proportionality principle while sentencing. Despite this familiarity, the drafters of the Declaration of Rights did not explicitly prohibit "disproportionate" or "excessive" punishments. Instead, they prohibited punishments that were "cruell and unusuall." The Solem Court simply assumed, with no analysis, that the one included the other. As a textual matter, of course, it does not: a disproportionate punishment can perhaps always be considered "cruel," but it will not always be (as the text also requires) "unusual." The error of Solem's assumption is confirmed by the historical context and contemporaneous understanding of the English guarantee.

Most historians agree that the "cruell and unusuall Punishments" provision of the English Declaration of Rights was prompted by the abuses attributed to the infamous Lord Chief Justice Jeffreys of the King's Bench during the Stuart reign of James II. ...

The preamble to the Declaration of Rights, a sort of indictment of James II that calls to mind the preface to our own Declaration of Independence, specifically referred to illegal sentences and King's Bench proceedings. ...

The only recorded contemporaneous interpretation of the "cruell and unusuall Punishments" clause confirms the focus upon Jeffreys' King's Bench activities, and upon the illegality, rather than the disproportionality, of his sentences. ...

In sum, we think it most unlikely that the English Cruell and Unusuall Punishments Clause was meant to forbid "disproportionate" punishments. ...

C.

Unless one accepts the notion of a blind incorporation, however, the ultimate question is not what "cruell and unusuall punishments" meant in the Declaration of Rights, but what its meaning was to the Americans who adopted the Eighth Amendment. Even if one assumes that the Founders knew the precise meaning of that English antecedent, a direct transplant of the English meaning to the soil of American constitutionalism would in any case have been impossible. There were no common-law punishments in the federal system, so that the provision must have been meant as a check not upon judges but upon the Legislature.

Wrenched out of its common-law context, and applied to the actions of a legislature, the word "unusual" could hardly mean "contrary to law." But it continued to mean (as it continues to mean today) "such as [does not] occur in ordinary practice," "such as is [not] in common use." According to its terms, then, by forbidding "cruel and unusual punishments, " the Clause disables the Legislature from authorizing particular forms or "modes" of punishment – specifically, cruel methods of punishment that are not regularly or customarily employed.

The language bears the construction, however – and here we come to the point crucial to resolution of the present case – that "cruelty and unusualness" are to be determined not solely with reference to the punishment at issue ("Is life imprisonment a cruel and unusual punishment?") but with reference to the crime for which it is imposed as well ("Is life imprisonment cruel and unusual punishment for possession of unlawful drugs?"). The latter interpretation would make the provision a form of proportionality guarantee. The arguments against it, however, seem to us conclusive.

First of all, to use the phrase "cruel and unusual punishment" to describe a requirement of proportionality would have been an exceedingly vague and oblique way of saying what Americans were well accustomed to saying more directly. ...

Secondly, it would seem quite peculiar to refer to cruelty and unusualness for the offense in question, in a provision having application only to a new government that had never before defined offenses, and that would be defining new and peculiarly national ones. Finally, and most conclusively, as we proceed to discuss, the fact that what was "cruel and unusual" under the Eighth Amendment was to be determined without reference to the particular offense is confirmed by all available evidence of contemporary understanding.

The early commentary on the Clause contains no reference to disproportionate or excessive sentences, and again indicates that it was designed to outlaw particular modes of punishment. ...

Perhaps the most persuasive evidence of what "cruel and unusual" meant, however, is found in early judicial constructions of the Eighth Amendment and its state counterparts. ...

Throughout the 19th century, state courts interpreting state constitutional provisions with identical or more expansive wording (i. e., "cruel or unusual") concluded that these provisions did not proscribe disproportionality but only certain modes of punishment. For example, in Aldridge v. Commonwealth

(1824), the General Court of Virginia had occasion to interpret the cruel and unusual punishments clause that was the direct ancestor of our federal provision. In rejecting the defendant's claim that a sentence of so many as 39 stripes violated the Virginia Constitution, the court said:

II.

We think it enough that those who framed and approved the Federal Constitution chose, for whatever reason, not to include within it the guarantee against disproportionate sentences that some State Constitutions contained. It is worth noting, however, that there was good reason for that choice – a reason that reinforces the necessity of overruling Solem. While there are relatively clear historical guidelines and accepted practices that enable judges to determine which modes of punishment are "cruel and unusual," proportionality does not lend itself to such analysis. Neither Congress nor any state legislature has ever set out with the objective of crafting a penalty that is "disproportionate"; yet as some of the examples mentioned above indicate, many enacted dispositions seem to be so – because they were made for other times or other places, with different social attitudes, different criminal epidemics, different public fears, and different prevailing theories of penology. This is not to say that there are no absolutes; one can imagine extreme examples that no rational person, in no time or place, could accept. But for the same reason these examples are easy to decide, they are certain never to occur. The real function of a constitutional proportionality principle, if it exists, is to enable judges to evaluate a penalty that some assemblage of men and women has considered proportionate – and to say that it is not. For that real-world enterprise, the standards seem so inadequate that the proportionality principle becomes an invitation to imposition of subjective values.

This becomes clear, we think, from a consideration of the three factors that Solem found relevant to the proportionality determination: (1) the inherent gravity of the offense, (2) the sentences imposed for similarly grave offenses in the same jurisdiction, and (3) sentences imposed for the same crime in other jurisdictions. As to the first factor: Of course some offenses, involving violent harm to human beings, will always and everywhere be regarded as serious, but that is only half the equation. The issue is what else should be regarded to be as serious as these offenses, or even to be more serious than some of them. On that point, judging by the statutes that Americans have enacted, there is enormous variation – even within a given age, not to mention across the many generations ruled by the Bill of Rights. The State of Massachusetts punishes sodomy more severely than assault and battery; whereas in several States, sodomy is not unlawful at all. In Louisiana, one who assaults another with a dangerous weapon faces the same maximum prison term as one who removes a shopping basket "from the parking area or grounds of any store…without authorization." ...

The difficulty of assessing gravity is demonstrated in the very context of the present case: Petitioner acknowledges that a mandatory life sentence might not be "grossly excessive" for possession of cocaine with intent to distribute. But surely whether it is a "grave" offense merely to possess a significant quantity of drugs – thereby facilitating distribution, subjecting the holder to the temptation of distribution, and raising the possibility of theft by others who might distribute – depends entirely upon how odious and socially threatening one believes drug use to be. Would it be "grossly excessive" to provide life imprisonment for "mere possession" of a certain quantity of heavy weaponry? If not, then the only issue is whether the possible dissemination of drugs can be as "grave" as the possible dissemination of heavy weapons. Who are we to say no? The members of the Michigan Legislature, and not we, know the situation on the streets of Detroit.

The second factor suggested in Solem fails for the same reason. One cannot compare the sentences imposed by the jurisdiction for "similarly grave" offenses if there is no objective standard of gravity. Judges will be comparing what they consider comparable. Or, to put the same point differently: When it happens that two offenses judicially determined to be "similarly grave" receive significantly dissimilar penalties, what follows is not that the harsher penalty is unconstitutional, but merely that the legislature does not share the judges' view that the offenses are similarly grave. Moreover, even if "similarly grave" crimes could be identified, the penalties for them would not necessarily be comparable, since there are many other justifications for a difference. For example, since deterrent effect depends not only upon the amount of the penalty but upon its certainty, crimes that are less grave but significantly more difficult to detect may warrant substantially higher penalties. Grave crimes of the sort that will not be deterred by penalty may warrant substantially lower penalties, as may grave crimes of the sort that are normally committed once in a lifetime by otherwise law-abiding citizens who will not profit from rehabilitation. Whether these differences will occur, and to what extent, depends, of course, upon the weight the society accords to deterrence and rehabilitation, rather than retribution, as the objective of criminal punishment (which is an eminently legislative judgment). In fact, it becomes difficult even to speak intelligently of "proportionality," once deterrence and rehabilitation are given significant weight. Proportionality is inherently a retributive concept, and perfect proportionality is the talionic law.

As for the third factor mentioned by Solem – the character of the sentences imposed by other States for the same crime – it must be acknowledged that that can be applied with clarity and ease. The only difficulty is that it has no conceivable relevance to the Eighth Amendment. That a State is entitled to treat with stern disapproval an act that other States punish with the mildest of sanctions follows a fortiori from the undoubted fact that a State may criminalize an act that other States do not criminalize at all. Indeed, a State may criminalize an act that other States choose to reward – punishing, for example, the killing of endangered wild animals for which other States are offering a bounty. What greater disproportion could there be than that? "Absent a constitutionally imposed uniformity inimical to traditional notions of federalism, some State will always bear the distinction of treating particular offenders more severely than any other State." Diversity not only in policy, but in the means of implementing policy, is the very raison d'etre of our federal system. Though the different needs and concerns of other States may induce them to treat simple possession of 672 grams of cocaine as a relatively minor offense, nothing in the Constitution requires Michigan to follow suit. The Eighth Amendment is not a ratchet, whereby a temporary consensus on leniency for a particular crime fixes a permanent constitutional maximum, disabling the States from giving effect to altered beliefs and responding to changed social conditions.

III.

Our 20th-century jurisprudence has not remained entirely in accord with the proposition that there is no proportionality requirement in the Eighth Amendment, but neither has it departed to the extent that Solem suggests. ...

The first holding of this Court unqualifiedly applying a requirement of proportionality to criminal penalties was issued 185 years after the Eighth Amendment was adopted. In Coker v. Georgia, supra, the Court held that, because of the disproportionality, it was a violation of the Cruel and Unusual Punishments Clause to impose capital punishment for rape of an adult woman. Five years later, in Enmund v. Florida, we held that it violates the Eighth Amendment, because of disproportionality, to impose the death penalty upon a participant in a felony that results in murder, without any inquiry into the participant's intent to kill. Rummel treated this line of authority as an aspect of our death penalty jurisprudence, rather than a generalizable aspect of Eighth Amendment law. We think that is an accurate explanation, and we reassert it. Proportionality review is one of several respects in which we have held that "death is different," and have imposed protections that the Constitution nowhere else provides. We would leave it there, but will not extend it further.

IV.

Petitioner claims that his sentence violates the Eighth Amendment for a reason in addition to its alleged disproportionality. He argues that it is "cruel and unusual" to impose a mandatory sentence of such severity, without any consideration of so-called mitigating factors such as, in his case, the fact that he had no prior felony convictions. He apparently contends that the Eighth Amendment requires Michigan to create a sentencing scheme whereby life in prison without possibility of parole is simply the most severe of a range of available penalties that the sentencer may impose after hearing evidence in mitigation and aggravation.

As our earlier discussion should make clear, this claim has no support in the text and history of the Eighth Amendment. Severe, mandatory penalties may be cruel, but they are not unusual in the constitutional sense, having been employed in various forms throughout our Nation's history. ...

Petitioner's "required mitigation" claim, like his proportionality claim, does find support in our death penalty jurisprudence. We have held that a capital sentence is cruel and unusual under the Eighth Amendment if it is imposed without an individualized determination that that punishment is "appropriate" – whether or not the sentence is "grossly disproportionate." Petitioner asks us to extend this so-called "individualized capital sentencing doctrine" to an "individualized mandatory life in prison without parole sentencing doctrine." We refuse to do so.

Our cases creating and clarifying the "individualized capital sentencing doctrine" have repeatedly suggested that there is no comparable requirement outside the capital context, because of the qualitative difference between death and all other penalties. ...

The judgment of the Michigan Court of Appeals is
Affirmed.

JUSTICE KENNEDY, with whom JUSTICE O'CONNOR and JUSTICE SOUTER join, concurring in part and concurring in the judgment.

I concur in Part IV of the Court's opinion and in the judgment. I write this separate opinion because my approach to the Eighth Amendment proportionality analysis differs from JUSTICE SCALIA'S. Regardless of whether JUSTICE SCALIA or JUSTICE WHITE has the best of the historical argument, stare decisis counsels our adherence to the narrow proportionality principle that has existed in our Eighth Amendment jurisprudence for 80 years. Although our proportionality decisions have not been clear or consistent in all respects, they can be reconciled, and they require us to uphold petitioner's sentence.

I.

A.

B.

Though our decisions recognize a proportionality principle, its precise contours are unclear. ... Despite these tensions, close analysis of our decisions yields some common principles that give content to the uses and limits of proportionality review.

The first of these principles is that the fixing of prison terms for specific crimes involves a substantive penological judgment that, as a general matter, is "properly within the province of legislatures, not courts." Determinations about the nature and purposes of punishment for criminal acts implicate difficult and enduring questions respecting the sanctity of the individual, the nature of law, and the relation between law and the social order. " ... Thus, "reviewing courts . . . should grant substantial deference to the broad authority that legislatures necessarily possess in determining the types and limits of punishments for crimes."

The second principle is that the Eighth Amendment does not mandate adoption of any one penological theory. "The principles which have guided criminal sentencing . . . have varied with the times." The federal and state criminal systems have accorded different weights at different times to the penological goals of retribution, deterrence, incapacitation, and rehabilitation. And competing theories of mandatory and discretionary sentencing have been in varying degrees of ascendancy or decline since the beginning of the Republic.

Third, marked divergences both in underlying theories of sentencing and in the length of prescribed prison terms are the inevitable, often beneficial, result of the federal structure.

The fourth principle at work in our cases is that proportionality review by federal courts should be informed by "'objective factors to the maximum possible extent.'" The most prominent objective factor is the type of punishment imposed. In Weems, "the Court could differentiate in an objective fashion between the highly unusual cadena temporal and more traditional forms of imprisonment imposed under the Anglo-Saxon system." In a similar fashion, because "'the penalty of death differs from all other forms of criminal punishment,'" the objective line between capital punishment and imprisonment for a term of years finds frequent mention in our Eighth Amendment jurisprudence. By contrast, our decisions recognize that we lack clear objective standards to distinguish between sentences for different terms of years. Although "no penalty is per se constitutional," the relative lack of objective standards concerning terms of imprisonment has meant that "'outside the context of capital punishment, successful challenges to the proportionality of particular sentences [are] exceedingly rare.'"

All of these principles – the primacy of the legislature, the variety of legitimate penological schemes, the nature of our federal system, and the requirement that proportionality review be guided by objective factors – inform the final one: The Eighth Amendment does not require strict proportionality between crime and sentence. Rather, it forbids only extreme sentences that are "grossly disproportionate" to the crime.

II.

III.

A penalty as severe and unforgiving as the one imposed here would make this a most difficult and troubling case for any judicial officer. Reasonable minds may differ about the efficacy of Michigan's sentencing scheme, and it is far from certain that Michigan's bold experiment will succeed. ... but we cannot say the law before us has no chance of success and is on that account so disproportionate as to be cruel and unusual punishment. The dangers flowing from drug offenses and the circumstances of the crime committed here demonstrate that the Michigan penalty scheme does not surpass constitutional bounds. Michigan may use its criminal law to address the issue of drug possession in wholesale amounts in the manner that it has in this sentencing scheme. For the foregoing reasons, I conclude that petitioner's sentence of life imprisonment without parole for his crime of possession of more than 650 grams of cocaine does not violate the Eighth Amendment.

JUSTICE WHITE, with whom JUSTICE BLACKMUN and JUSTICE STEVENS join, dissenting.

Petitioner, a first-time offender, was convicted of possession of 672 grams of cocaine. The statute under which he was convicted provides that a person who knowingly or intentionally possesses any of various narcotics, including cocaine, "which is in an amount of 650 grams or more of any mixture containing that controlled substance is guilty of a felony and shall be imprisoned for life." No particular degree of drug purity is required for a conviction. Other statutes make clear that an individual convicted of possessing this quantity of drugs is not eligible for parole. A related statute, which was enacted at the same time as the statute under which petitioner was convicted, mandates the same penalty of life imprisonment without possibility of parole for someone who "manufacture[s], deliver[s], or possess[es] with intent to manufacture or deliver" 650 grams or more of a narcotic mixture. There is no room for judicial discretion in the imposition of the life sentence upon conviction. The asserted purpose of the legislative enactment of these statutes was to "'stem drug traffic'" and reach "'drug dealers.'"

The first Solem factor requires a reviewing court to assess the gravity of the offense and the harshness of the penalty. The mandatory sentence of life imprisonment without possibility of parole "is the most severe punishment that the State could have imposed on any criminal for any crime" for Michigan has no death penalty.

Although these factors are "by no means exhaustive" in evaluating the gravity of the offense, it is appropriate to consider "the harm caused or threatened to the victim or society," based on such things as the degree of violence involved in the crime and "the absolute magnitude of the crime," and "the culpability of the offender," including the degree of requisite intent and the offender's motive in committing the crime.

Drugs are without doubt a serious societal problem. To justify such a harsh mandatory penalty as that imposed here, however, the offense should be one which will always warrant that punishment. Mere possession of drugs – even in such a large quantity – is not so serious an offense that it will always warrant, much less mandate, life imprisonment without possibility of parole. Unlike crimes directed against the persons and property of others, possession of drugs affects the criminal who uses the drugs most directly. The ripple effect on society caused by possession of drugs, through related crimes, lost productivity, health problems, and the like is often not the direct consequence of possession, but of the resulting addiction, something which this Court held in Robinson v. California cannot be made a crime.

To be constitutionally proportionate, punishment must be tailored to a defendant's personal responsibility and moral guilt. JUSTICE KENNEDY attempts to justify the harsh mandatory sentence imposed on petitioner by focusing on the subsidiary effects of drug use, and thereby ignores this aspect of our Eighth Amendment jurisprudence. While the collateral consequences of drugs such as cocaine are indisputably severe, they are not unlike those which flow from the misuse of other, legal substances. For example, in considering the effects of alcohol on society, the Court has stressed that "no one can seriously dispute the magnitude of the drunken driving problem or the States' interest in eradicating it," but at the same time has recognized that the severity of the problem "cannot excuse the need for scrupulous adherence to our constitutional principles." Thus, the Court has held that a drunken driver who has been prosecuted for traffic offenses arising from an accident cannot, consistent with the Double Jeopardy Clause, subsequently be prosecuted for the death of the accident victim. Likewise, the Court scrutinized closely a state program of vehicle checkpoints designed to detect drunken drivers before holding that the brief intrusion upon motorists is consistent with the Fourth Amendment. It is one thing to uphold a checkpoint designed to detect drivers then under the influence of a drug that creates a present risk that they will harm others. It is quite something else to uphold petitioner's sentence because of the collateral consequences which might issue, however indirectly, from the drugs he possessed. Indeed, it is inconceivable that a State could rationally choose to penalize one who possesses large quantities of alcohol in a manner similar to that in which Michigan has chosen to punish petitioner for cocaine possession, because of the tangential effects which might ultimately be traced to the alcohol at issue. "Unfortunately, grave evils such as the narcotics traffic can too easily cause threats to our basic liberties by making attractive the adoption of constitutionally forbidden shortcuts that might suppress and blot out more quickly the unpopular and dangerous conduct." That is precisely the course JUSTICE KENNEDY advocates here.

The "absolute magnitude" of petitioner's crime is not exceptionally serious. Because possession is necessarily a lesser included offense of possession with intent to distribute, it is odd to punish the former as severely as the latter. Nor is the requisite intent for the crime sufficient to render it particularly grave. To convict someone under the possession statute, it is only necessary to prove that the defendant knowingly possessed a mixture containing narcotics which weighs at least 650 grams. There is no mens rea requirement of intent to distribute the drugs, as there is in the parallel statute. Indeed, the presence of a separate statute which reaches manufacture, delivery, or possession with intent to do either undermines the State's position that the purpose of the possession statute was to reach drug dealers. Although "intent to deliver can be inferred from the amount of a controlled substance possessed by the accused," the inference is one to be drawn by the jury. In addition, while there is usually a pecuniary motive when someone possesses a drug with intent to deliver it, such a motive need not exist in the case of mere possession. Finally, this statute applies equally to first-time offenders, such as petitioner, and recidivists. Consequently, the particular concerns reflected in recidivist statutes such as those in Rummel and Solem are not at issue here.

The second prong of the Solem analysis is an examination of "the sentences imposed on other criminals in the same jurisdiction." As noted above, there is no death penalty in Michigan; consequently, life without parole, the punishment mandated here, is the harshest penalty available. It is reserved for three crimes: first-degree murder; manufacture, distribution, or possession with intent to manufacture or distribute 650 grams or more of narcotics; and possession of 650 grams or more of narcotics. Crimes directed against the persons and property of others – such as second-degree murder; and armed robbery – do not carry such a harsh mandatory sentence, although they do provide for the possibility of a life sentence in the exercise of judicial discretion. It is clear that petitioner "has been treated in the same manner as, or more severely than, criminals who have committed far more serious crimes."

The third factor set forth in Solem examines "the sentences imposed for commission of the same crime in other jurisdictions." No other jurisdiction imposes a punishment nearly as severe as Michigan's for possession of the amount of drugs at issue here. Of the remaining 49 States, only Alabama provides for a mandatory sentence of life imprisonment without possibility of parole for a first-time drug offender, and then only when a defendant possesses 10 kilograms or more of cocaine. ... Thus, "it appears that [petitioner] was treated more severely than he would have been in any other State." Indeed, the fact that no other jurisdiction provides such a severe, mandatory penalty for possession of this quantity of drugs is enough to establish "the degree of national consensus this Court has previously thought sufficient to label a particular punishment cruel and unusual."

Application of Solem's proportionality analysis leaves no doubt that the Michigan statute at issue fails constitutional muster. The statutorily mandated penalty of life without possibility of parole for possession of narcotics is unconstitutionally disproportionate in that it violates the Eighth Amendment's prohibition against cruel and unusual punishment. Consequently, I would reverse the decision of the Michigan Court of Appeals.

JUSTICE MARSHALL, dissenting. [omitted]

JUSTICE STEVENS, with whom JUSTICE BLACKMUN joins, dissenting.

While I agree wholeheartedly with JUSTICE WHITE's dissenting opinion, I believe an additional comment is appropriate.

The severity of the sentence that Michigan has mandated for the crime of possession of more than 650 grams of cocaine, whether diluted or undiluted, does not place the sentence in the same category as capital punishment. I remain convinced that Justice Stewart correctly characterized the penalty of death as "unique" because of "its absolute renunciation of all that is embodied in our concept of humanity." Nevertheless, a mandatory sentence of life imprisonment without the possibility of parole does share one important characteristic of a death sentence: The offender will never regain his freedom. Because such a sentence does not even purport to serve a rehabilitative function, the sentence must rest on a rational determination that the punished "criminal conduct is so atrocious that society's interest in deterrence and retribution wholly outweighs any considerations of reform or rehabilitation of the perpetrator." Serious as this defendant's crime was, I believe it is irrational to conclude that every similar offender is wholly incorrigible.

The death sentences that were at issue and invalidated in Furman were "cruel and unusual in the same way that being struck by lightning is cruel and unusual." In my opinion the imposition of a life sentence without possibility of parole on this petitioner is equally capricious. As JUSTICE WHITE has pointed out, under the Federal Sentencing Guidelines, with all relevant enhancements, petitioner's sentence would barely exceed 10 years. In most States, the period of incarceration for a first offender like petitioner would be substantially shorter. No jurisdiction except Michigan has concluded that the offense belongs in a category where reform and rehabilitation are considered totally unattainable. Accordingly, the notion that this sentence satisfies any meaningful requirement of proportionality is itself both cruel and unusual.

I respectfully dissent.

NOTES AND QUERIES

Identify the factors, enumerated in *Solem*, that could indicate disproportionality in sentencing. Do you agree with Justice Scalia's approach to those factors or with Justice White's application in the dissent? What do you make of Justice Kennedy's reasons, in Part IB of his opinion, for concurring in this case?

THE SUPREME COURT REVISITS *HARMELIN*

Under California's three strikes law, a defendant who is convicted of a felony and has previously been convicted of two or more serious or violent felonies must receive an indeterminate life imprisonment term. Such a defendant becomes eligible for parole on a date calculated by reference to a minimum term, which, in this case, is 25 years. While on parole, petitioner Ewing was convicted of felony grand theft for stealing three golf clubs, worth $399 apiece. As required by the three strikes law, the prosecutor formally alleged, and the trial court found, that Ewing had been convicted previously of four serious or violent felonies. In sentencing him to 25 years to life, the court refused to exercise its discretion to reduce the conviction to a misdemeanor – under a state law that permits certain offenses, known as "wobblers," to be classified as either misdemeanors or felonies – or to dismiss the allegations of some or all of his prior relevant convictions. Do you find that his sentence was grossly disproportionate under the Eighth Amendment? Justice O'Connor wrote the opinion of the Court and found: (1) the Eighth Amendment has a "narrow proportionality principle" that "applies to noncapital sentences;" (2) the Constitution "does not mandate adoption of any one penological theory," and nothing in the Eighth Amendment prohibits California from choosing to incapacitate criminals who have already been convicted of at least one serious or violent crime; and (3) in examining Ewing's claim that his sentence is grossly disproportionate, that it is a "wobbler" is of no moment, for it remains a felony unless the trial court imposes a misdemeanor sentence. Justice Scalia agreed that petitioner's sentence did not violate the Eighth Amendment's prohibition against cruel and unusual punishments, but on the ground that prohibition was aimed at excluding only certain modes of punishment. He further noted that this case demonstrated why a proportionality principle cannot be intelligently applied. Justice Thomas concluded that petitioner's sentence did not violate the Eighth Amendment's prohibition against cruel and unusual punishments because the Amendment contains no proportionality principle. Justices Stevens, Souter, Ginsburg and Breyer all dissented to find that the sentence, following a proportionality review, violated the Eighth Amendment. *Ewing v. California*, 123 S.Ct. 1179 (2003).

California charged Andrade with two felony counts of petty theft with a prior conviction after he stole approximately $150 worth of videotapes from two different stores. Under California's three strikes law, any felony can constitute the third strike subjecting a defendant to a prison term of 25 years to life. The jury found Andrade guilty and then found that he had three prior convictions that qualified as serious or violent felonies under the three strikes regime. Because each of his petty theft convictions thus triggered a separate application of the three strikes law, the judge sentenced him to two consecutive terms of 25 years to life. Does his sentence violate the proportionality analysis offered in *Harmelin v. Michigan*? The presented legal issue in this case was whether the lower court had correctly interpreted federal law for the purposes of granting an appeal under the Antiterrorism and Effective Death Penalty Act of 1996 (AEDPA). (That is, the AEDPA allowed an appeal if the lower state court had misinterpreted federal law.) The Supreme Court, in an opinion written by Justice O'Connor, held that the sentence was not so grossly disproportionate as to violate the Eighth Amendment, which meant that the lower court had not incorrectly interpreted federal law for the purposes of granting an appeal under the AEDPA. Justices Souter, Stevens, Ginsberg and Breyer dissented by finding that Andrade's sentence could not survive Eighth Amendment review. They noted that Andrade's criminal history was less grave than Ewing's, and yet he received a prison term twice as long for a less serious triggering offense. *Lockyer v. Andrade*, 123 S. Ct. 1166 (2003).

Considering Sentencing Factors

APPRENDI v. NEW JERSEY
530 U.S. 466 (2000)

JUSTICE STEVENS delivered the opinion of the Court.

A New Jersey statute classifies the possession of a firearm for an unlawful purpose as a "second-degree" offense. Such an offense is punishable by imprisonment for "between five years and 10 years."A separate statute, described by that State's Supreme Court as a "hate crime" law, provides for an "extended term" of imprisonment if the trial judge finds, by a preponderance of the evidence, that "the defendant in committing the crime acted with a purpose to intimidate an individual or group of individuals because of race, color, gender, handicap, religion, sexual orientation or ethnicity." The extended term authorized by the hate crime law for second-degree offenses is imprisonment for "between 10 and 20 years."

The question presented is whether the Due Process Clause of the Fourteenth Amendment requires that a factual determination authorizing an increase in the maximum prison sentence for an offense from 10 to 20 years be made by a jury on the basis of proof beyond a reasonable doubt.

I.

At 2:04 a.m. on December 22, 1994, petitioner Charles C. Apprendi, Jr., fired several .22-caliber bullets into the home of an African-American family that had recently moved into a previously all-white neighborhood in Vineland, New Jersey. Apprendi was promptly arrested and, at 3:05 a.m., admitted that he was the shooter. After further questioning, at 6:04 a.m., he made a statement – which he later retracted – that even though he did not know the occupants of the house personally, "because they are black in color he does not want them in the neighborhood."

A New Jersey grand jury returned a 23-count indictment charging Apprendi with four first-degree, eight second-degree, six third-degree, and five fourth-degree offenses. The charges alleged shootings on four different dates, as well as the unlawful possession of various weapons. None of the counts referred to the hate crime statute, and none alleged that Apprendi acted with a racially biased purpose.

The parties entered into a plea agreement, pursuant to which Apprendi pleaded guilty to two counts (3 and 18) of second-degree possession of a firearm for an unlawful purpose, and one count (22) of the third-degree offense of unlawful possession of an antipersonnel bomb; the prosecutor dismissed the other 20 counts. ...

After the trial judge accepted the three guilty pleas, the prosecutor filed a formal motion for an extended term. The trial judge thereafter held an evidentiary hearing on the issue of Apprendi's "purpose" for the shooting on December 22. Apprendi adduced evidence from a psychologist and from seven character witnesses who testified that he did not have a reputation for racial bias. He also took the stand himself, explaining that the incident was an unintended consequence of overindulgence in alcohol, denying that he was in any way biased against African-Americans, and denying that his statement to the police had been accurately described. The judge, however, found the police officer's testimony credible, and concluded that the evidence supported a finding "that the crime was motivated by racial bias." Having found "by a preponderance of the evidence" that Apprendi's actions were taken "with a purpose to intimidate" as provided by the statute, the trial judge held that the hate crime enhancement applied. Rejecting Apprendi's constitutional challenge to the statute, the judge sentenced him to a 12-year term of imprisonment on count 18, and to shorter concurrent sentences on the other two counts.

Apprendi appealed, arguing, inter alia, that the Due Process Clause of the United States Constitution requires that the finding of bias upon which his hate crime sentence was based must be proved to a jury beyond a reasonable doubt. ... the Appellate Division of the Superior Court of New Jersey upheld the enhanced sentence...

A divided New Jersey Supreme Court affirmed. ...

We granted certiorari and now reverse.

II.

...The question whether Apprendi had a constitutional right to have a jury find such bias on the basis of proof beyond a reasonable doubt is starkly presented.

Our answer to that question was foreshadowed by our opinion in Jones v. United States (1999), construing a federal statute. We there noted that "under the Due Process Clause of the Fifth Amendment and the notice and jury trial guarantees of the Sixth Amendment, any fact (other than prior conviction) that increases the maximum penalty for a crime must be charged in an indictment, submitted to a jury, and proven beyond a reasonable doubt." The Fourteenth Amendment commands the same answer in this case involving a state statute.

III.

In his 1881 lecture on the criminal law, Oliver Wendell Holmes, Jr., observed: "The law threatens certain pains if you do certain things, intending thereby to give you a new motive for not doing them. If you persist in doing them, it has to inflict the pains in order that its threats may continue to be believed." New Jersey threatened Apprendi with certain pains if he unlawfully possessed a weapon and with additional pains if he selected his victims with a purpose to intimidate them because of their race. As a matter of simple justice, it seems obvious that the procedural safeguards designed to protect Apprendi from unwarranted pains should apply equally to the two acts that New Jersey has singled out for punishment. Merely using the label "sentence enhancement" to describe the latter surely does not provide a principled basis for treating them differently.

At stake in this case are constitutional protections of surpassing importance: the proscription of any deprivation of liberty without "due process of law"and the guarantee that "in all criminal prosecutions, the accused shall enjoy the right to a speedy and public trial, by an impartial jury." Taken together, these rights indisputably entitle a criminal defendant to "a jury determination that [he] is guilty of every element of the crime with which he is charged, beyond a reasonable doubt."

Any possible distinction between an "element" of a felony offense and a "sentencing factor" was unknown to the practice of criminal indictment, trial by jury, and judgment by court n4 as it existed during the years surrounding our Nation's founding. ...

The historic link between verdict and judgment and the consistent limitation on judges' discretion to operate within the limits of the legal penalties provided highlight the novelty of a legislative scheme that removes the jury from the determination of a fact that, if found, exposes the criminal defendant to a penalty exceeding the maximum he would receive if punished according to the facts reflected in the jury verdict alone.

We do not suggest that trial practices cannot change in the course of centuries and still remain true to the principles that emerged from the Framers' fears "that the jury right could be lost not only by gross denial, but by erosion." But practice must at least adhere to the basic principles undergirding the requirements of trying to a jury all facts necessary to constitute a statutory offense, and proving those facts beyond reasonable doubt. ...

IV.

It was in McMillan v. Pennsylvania (1986) that this Court, for the first time, coined the term "sentencing factor" to refer to a fact that was not found by a jury but that could affect the sentence imposed by the judge. That case involved a challenge to the State's Mandatory Minimum Sentencing Act. According to its provisions, anyone convicted of certain felonies would be subject to a mandatory minimum penalty of five years imprisonment if the judge found, by a preponderance of the evidence, that the person "visibly possessed a firearm" in the course of committing one of the specified felonies. Articulating for the first time, and then applying, a multifactor set of criteria for determining whether the Winship protections applied to bar such a system, we concluded that the Pennsylvania statute did not run afoul of our previous admonitions against relieving the State of its burden of proving guilt, or tailoring the mere form of a criminal statute solely to avoid Winship's strictures.

We did not, however, there budge from the position that (1) constitutional limits exist to States' authority to define away facts necessary to constitute a criminal offense and (2) that a state scheme that keeps from the jury facts that "expose [defendants] to greater or additional punishment" may raise serious constitutional concern. As we explained:

> Section 9712 neither alters the maximum penalty for the crime committed nor creates a separate offense calling for a separate penalty; it operates solely to limit the sentencing court's discretion in selecting a penalty within the range already available to it without the special finding of visible possession of a firearm. . . . The statute gives no impression of having been tailored to permit the visible possession finding to be a tail which wags the dog of the substantive offense. Petitioners' claim that visible possession under the Pennsylvania statute is 'really' an element of the offenses for which they are being punished – that Pennsylvania has in effect defined a new set of upgraded felonies –

would have at least more superficial appeal if a finding of visible possession exposed them to greater or additional punishment but it does not.

V.

The New Jersey statutory scheme that Apprendi asks us to invalidate allows a jury to convict a defendant of a second-degree offense based on its finding beyond a reasonable doubt that he unlawfully possessed a prohibited weapon; after a subsequent and separate proceeding, it then allows a judge to impose punishment identical to that New Jersey provides for crimes of the first degree based upon the judge's finding, by a preponderance of the evidence, that the defendant's "purpose" for unlawfully possessing the weapon was "to intimidate" his victim on the basis of a particular characteristic the victim possessed. In light of the constitutional rule explained above, and all of the cases supporting it, this practice cannot stand.

New Jersey's defense of its hate crime enhancement statute has three primary components: (1) the required finding of biased purpose is not an "element" of a distinct hate crime offense, but rather the traditional "sentencing factor" of motive; (2) McMillan holds that the legislature can authorize a judge to find a traditional sentencing factor on the basis of a preponderance of the evidence; and (3) Almendarez-Torres extended McMillan's holding to encompass factors that authorize a judge to impose a sentence beyond the maximum provided by the substantive statute under which a defendant is charged. None of these persuades us that the constitutional rule that emerges from our history and case law should incorporate an exception for this New Jersey statute.

New Jersey's first point is nothing more than a disagreement with the rule we apply today. Beyond this, we do not see how the argument can succeed on its own terms. ...

... Despite what appears to us the clear "elemental" nature of the factor here, the relevant inquiry is one not of form, but of effect – does the required finding expose the defendant to a greater punishment than that authorized by the jury's guilty verdict?

As the New Jersey Supreme Court itself understood in rejecting the argument that the required "motive" finding was simply a "traditional" sentencing factor, proof of motive did not ordinarily "increase the penal consequences to an actor." ...

The preceding discussion should make clear why the State's reliance on McMillan is likewise misplaced. The differential in sentence between what Apprendi would have received without the finding of biased purpose and what he could receive with it is not, it is true, as extreme as the difference between a small fine and mandatory life imprisonment. But it can hardly be said that the potential doubling of one's sentence – from 10 years to 20 – has no more than a nominal effect. Both in terms of absolute years behind bars, and because of the more severe stigma attached, the differential here is unquestionably of constitutional significance. When a judge's finding based on a mere preponderance of the evidence authorizes an increase in the maximum punishment, it is appropriately characterized as "a tail which wags the dog of the substantive offense."

New Jersey would also point to the fact that the State did not, in placing the required biased purpose finding in a sentencing enhancement provision, create a "separate offense calling for a separate penalty."As for this, we agree wholeheartedly with the New Jersey Supreme Court that merely because the state legislature placed its hate crime sentence "enhancer" "within the sentencing provisions" of the criminal code "does not mean that the finding of a biased purpose to intimidate is not an essential element of the offense."...

The New Jersey procedure challenged in this case is an unacceptable departure from the jury tradition that is an indispensable part of our criminal justice system. Accordingly, the judgment of the Supreme Court of New Jersey is reversed, and the case is remanded for further proceedings not inconsistent with this opinion.

It is so ordered.

JUSTICE SCALIA, concurring. [omitted]

JUSTICE THOMAS, with whom JUSTICE SCALIA joins as to Parts I and II, concurring.

I.

This case turns on the seemingly simple question of what constitutes a "crime." Under the Federal Constitution, "the accused" has the right (1) "to be informed of the nature and cause of the accusation" (that is, the basis on which he is accused of a crime), (2) to be "held to answer for a capital, or otherwise infamous crime" only on an indictment or presentment of a grand jury, and (3) to be tried by "an impartial jury of the State and district wherein the crime shall have been committed." With the exception of the Grand Jury Clause, the Court has held that these protections apply in state prosecutions. Further, the Court has held that due process requires that the jury find beyond a reasonable doubt every fact necessary to constitute the crime.

All of these constitutional protections turn on determining which facts constitute the "crime" – that is, which facts are the "elements" or "ingredients" of a crime. In order for an accusation of a crime (whether by indictment or some other form) to be proper under the common law, and thus proper under the codification of the common-law rights in the Fifth and Sixth Amendments, it must allege all elements of that crime; likewise, in order for a jury trial of a crime to be proper, all elements of the crime must be proved to the jury (and, under Winship, proved beyond a reasonable doubt).

This authority establishes that a "crime" includes every fact that is by law a basis for imposing or increasing punishment (in contrast with a fact that mitigates punishment). ... One need only look to the kind, degree, or range of punishment to which the prosecution is by law entitled for a given set of facts. Each fact necessary for that entitlement is an element.

JUSTICE O'CONNOR, with whom THE CHIEF JUSTICE, JUSTICE KENNEDY, and JUSTICE BREYER join, dissenting.

I.

Our Court has long recognized that not every fact that bears on a defendant's punishment need be charged in an indictment, submitted to a jury, and proved by the government beyond a reasonable doubt. Rather, we have held that the "legislature's definition of the elements of the offense is usually dispositive." Although we have recognized that "there are obviously constitutional limits beyond which the States may not go in this regard," and that "in certain limited circumstances Winship's reasonable-doubt requirement applies to facts not formally identified as elements of the offense charged," we have proceeded with caution before deciding that a certain fact must be treated as an offense element despite the legislature's choice not to characterize it as such. We have therefore declined to establish any bright-line rule for making such judgments and have instead approached each case individually, sifting through the considerations most relevant to determining whether the legislature has acted properly within its broad power to define crimes and their punishments or instead has sought to evade the constitutional requirements associated with the characterization of a fact as an offense element.

In one bold stroke the Court today casts aside our traditional cautious approach and instead embraces a universal and seemingly bright-line rule limiting the power of Congress and state legislatures to define criminal offenses and the sentences that follow from convictions thereunder. ...

II.

Under our precedent, then, a State may leave the determination of a defendant's sentence to a judge's discretionary decision within a prescribed range of penalties. When a judge, pursuant to that sentencing scheme, decides to increase a defendant's sentence on the basis of certain contested facts, those facts need not be proved to a jury beyond a reasonable doubt. The judge's findings, whether by proof beyond a reasonable doubt or less, suffice for purposes of the Constitution. Under the Court's decision today, however, it appears that once a legislature constrains judges' sentencing discretion by prescribing certain sentences that may only be imposed (or must be imposed) in connection with the same determinations of the same contested facts, the Constitution requires that the facts instead be proved to a jury beyond a reasonable doubt. I see no reason to treat the two schemes differently. In this respect, I agree with the Solicitor General that "[a] sentence that is constitutionally permissible when selected by a court on the basis of whatever factors it deems appropriate does not become impermissible simply because the court is permitted to select that sentence only after making a finding prescribed by the legislature." Although the Court acknowledges the legitimacy of discretionary sentencing by judges, it never provides a sound reason for treating judicial factfinding under determinate-sentencing schemes differently under the Constitution.

Prior to the most recent wave of sentencing reform, the Federal Government and the States employed indeterminate-sentencing schemes in which judges and executive branch officials (e.g., parole board officials) had substantial discretion to determine the actual length of a defendant's sentence. Studies of indeterminate-sentencing schemes found that similarly situated defendants often received widely disparate sentences. Although indeterminate sentencing was intended to soften the harsh and uniform sentences formerly imposed under mandatory-sentencing systems, some studies revealed that indeterminate sentencing actually had the opposite effect.

In response, Congress and the state legislatures shifted to determinate-sentencing schemes that aimed to limit judges' sentencing discretion and, thereby, afford similarly situated offenders equivalent treatment. The most well known of these reforms was the federal Sentencing Reform Act of 1984. In the Act, Congress created the United States Sentencing Commission, which in turn promulgated the Sentencing Guidelines that now govern sentencing by federal judges. ...the apparent effect of the Court's opinion today is to halt the current debate on sentencing reform in its tracks and to invalidate with the stroke of a pen three decades' worth of nationwide reform, all in the name of a principle with a questionable constitutional pedigree. Indeed, it is ironic that the Court, in the name of constitutional rights meant to protect criminal defendants from the potentially arbitrary exercise of power by prosecutors and judges, appears to rest its decision on a principle that would render unconstitutional efforts by Congress and the state legislatures to place constraints on that very power in the sentencing context.

Finally, perhaps the most significant impact of the Court's decision will be a practical one – its unsettling effect on sentencing conducted under current federal and state determinate-sentencing schemes. As I have explained, the Court does not say whether these schemes are constitutional, but its reasoning strongly suggests that they are not. Thus, with respect to past sentences handed down by judges under determinate-sentencing schemes, the Court's decision threatens to unleash a flood of petitions by convicted defendants seeking to invalidate their sentences in whole or in part on the authority of the Court's decision today. ... New Jersey, have determinate-sentencing schemes, the number of individual sentences drawn into question by the Court's decision could be colossal.

III.

Because I do not believe that the Court's "increase in the maximum penalty" rule is required by the Constitution, I would evaluate New Jersey's sentence-enhancement statute, by analyzing the factors we have examined in past cases. First, the New Jersey statute does not shift the burden of proof on an essential ingredient of the offense by presuming that ingredient upon proof of other elements of the offense. Second, the magnitude of the New Jersey sentence enhancement, as applied in petitioner's case, is constitutionally permissible. Under New Jersey law, the weapons possession offense to which petitioner pleaded guilty carries a sentence range of 5 to 10 years' imprisonment. The fact that petitioner, in committing that offense, acted with a purpose to intimidate because of race exposed him to a higher sentence range of 10 to 20 years' imprisonment. The 10-year increase in the maximum penalty to which petitioner was exposed falls well within the range we have found permissible. ...

In sum, New Jersey "simply took one factor that has always been considered by sentencing courts to bear on punishment" – a defendant's motive for committing the criminal offense – "and dictated the precise weight to be given that factor" when the motive is to intimidate a person because of race. ...

JUSTICE BREYER, with whom CHIEF JUSTICE REHNQUIST joins, dissenting.

The majority holds that the Constitution contains the following requirement: "any fact [other than recidivism] that increases the penalty for a crime beyond the prescribed statutory maximum must be submitted to a jury, and proved beyond a reasonable doubt." This rule would seem to promote a procedural ideal – that of juries, not judges, determining the existence of those facts upon which increased punishment turns. But the real world of criminal justice cannot hope to meet any such ideal. It can function only with the help of procedural compromises, particularly in respect to sentencing. And those compromises, which are themselves necessary for the fair functioning of the criminal justice system, preclude implementation of the procedural model that today's decision reflects. At the very least, the impractical nature of the requirement that the majority now recognizes supports the proposition that the Constitution was not intended to embody it. ...

Notes and Queries

Given your understanding of jury decision making and those of judges, do you find *Apprendi* a move in the correct direction? What do you make of the legal arguments regarding sentencing factors?

The Court held that any factor that increases a defendant's penalty beyond the statutory maximum, other than a record of a prior conviction, must be determined by a jury and proven beyond a reasonable doubt. Writing for the majority, Justice Stevens indicated an intent to preserve the traditional structure of criminal law. In its analysis, the majority emphasized that judges have always retained the discretion to sentence a defendant within a statutorily prescribed range of sentences. *Apprendi* established the principle that any fact of fault necessitates a jury determination. More specifically, *Apprendi* reversed a state court's sentencing under New Jersey's hate crimes sentencing enhancer on grounds of unconstitutionality. Do you suppose that a broad reading of the *Apprendi* rationale questions the constitutionality of sentencing under the U.S. Sentencing Guidelines? Do you find the following persuasive? *Apprendi* declared unconstitutional a defendant's sentence because the determination of a key fact at sentencing led to a sentence above the statutory range for the offense of conviction. The Court held that any fact, other than a prior conviction, that increases punishment beyond the prescribed statutory maximum must be proven to a jury beyond a reasonable doubt – a standard that establishes both the factfinder's identity and the prosecution's burden of proof. Controversy arose as to whether *Apprendi's* rationale had a much broader sweep – affecting not only the use of factors to extend sentences beyond the statutory maximum but also the use of factors to extend sentences beyond the statutory minimums. Such a rationale could render unconstitutional sentencing under determinate schemes such as the U.S. Sentencing Guidelines. Under the Sentencing Guidelines, federal judges find, at the sentencing stage and by a preponderance of evidence, the factors relevant to punishment greater than that of the statutory minimums for conviction of federal crimes.

There was much debate regarding whether the Court's decision in *Apprendi* should be extended to facts that increased a defendant's mandatory minimum sentence but did not extend the defendant's sentence beyond the statutory maximum. The Court addressed the issue in *Harris v. United States*, 536 U.S. 545, 568 (2002) and made it clear that statutory schemes that allow a judge to decide facts that alter a defendant's sentence within the statutory range prescribed by law do not violate due process.

Some commentators argue that *Apprendi* will still initiate the demise of guidelines sentencing, even though the Court would hold them constitutional. The argument is that *Apprendi* further empowers prosecutors, giving them greater leverage in shaping sentencing outcomes. See Jeffrey Standen, The end of the era of Sentencing Guidelines: *Apprendi v. New Jersey*, 87 Iowa L. Rev. 775, 798-98 (2002). Persuasive?

Chapter 11

Treating and Controlling Offenders

Introduction

Once sentenced, offenders typically enter the system of correction and management. As with other areas of law enforcement, this context involves numerous complexities, ranging from how law enforcement may control prison conditions and the lives of inmates to what society may do to control individuals upon release from incarceration. Often lost in discussions of treatment and correction, however, is the extent to which criminal justice responses impact broader compliance with the law. How the legal system responds to offenders impacts how offenders, victims, and potential offenders respond to law enforcement. Not surprisingly, both of these aspects of law enforcement provide potentially enormous roles for psychology. Our analysis, then, necessarily begins with a discussion of the place of psychology in efforts to rehabilitate and control offenders. We then proceed to discuss psychological research that seeks to understand why people obey the law, a discussion that reveals much about how the legal system can ensure greater compliance from not just past offenders but also from society at large.

The Psychology of Corrections

The most notable place for psychology in corrections comes in efforts to rehabilitate offenders. Psychology and other helping professions play important roles in prisons, both in terms of controlling and rehabilitating inmates. The impact of psychologists, however, has extended quite further. Unlike any other domain of psychology's role in law enforcement, psychologists' work in this area has had an unusually strong influence on policy. Regrettably, their apparent influence stems from their allegedly massive failure. Understanding the nature of that apparent failure and responses to it provides a good starting point for understanding psychology's place in corrections.

Rehabilitative Failures

In the early 1970s, Robert Martinson examined "what works" through a highly methodical meta-analytic[1] study of the efficacy of 231 rehabilitative prison regimes that met minimal methodological

[1] Recall that a meta-analysis simply is the statistical aggregation of the results from a large collection of independent studies for the purposes of integrating the findings. The results from each of these studies are converted into a common metric, termed an effect size, to enable cross-study comparison. An effect size is an estimate of the size of the relationship between two variables and is the primary unit of analysis within a meta-analysis. The ability of meta-analytic techniques

standards. His conclusion was quite simple: "nothing."[2] He noted that, with "...few and isolated exceptions, the rehabilitative efforts that have been reported so far have had no appreciable effect on recidivism."[3] In delivering his sweeping criticisms, he not only highlighted the failure of prior efforts to rehabilitate offenders but also concluded that we could never meet ideals of prisoner reform. The conclusion that rehabilitation would never work led many penologists, legislators, and judges to abandon the goal of rehabilitating those deemed criminal.[4] Importantly, although Martinson's evaluative study helped mobilize critics of rehabilitative ideals, the report did not stand alone. It was preceded and followed by a succession of studies that came to similar conclusions,[5] including a report commissioned by the National Academy of Sciences.[6]

While the general public and policy makers responded forcefully to criticisms of rehabilitative ideals, critics mounted efforts to highlight the complexities inherent in the broad conclusion that nothing worked. Most notably, they highlighted how estimates of the overall average effects of treatment do not recognize that methodological and treatment variables may be contributing to variation around the average effect. That is, some types of studies and some types of treatment most likely resulted in larger effects on recidivism. As some noted, the broad critique of rehabilitation had overlooked numerous apparently successful programs that Martinson and his colleagues either did not include in their review or evaluated in an overly stringent fashion.[7] Some critics charged that the evaluated programs were too limited and compromised versions of their original conception thwarted by the demands of inadequate correctional budgets. The argument was that programs lacked fidelity to design principles, which made it unfair to use them as failed exemplars of rehabilitative goals. Most importantly, however, critics challenged that the prison rehabilitation programs were not designed to impact the nature of the community outside prisons. Even though prison programs could have effected positive changes inside prisons, those benefits may not have transferred to criminogenic situations faced by offenders upon release. Most notably, it was argued that recidivism rates were poor indicators of prison success; they may mask gains that might occur in prison treatment programs but that erode once outside of prison.[8] Many of these criticisms were legitimate and even Martinson realized some of their merit. Martinson even noted similar limitations in his review and he even retracted his earlier, sweeping conclusions and went so far as to reject his original overall condemnation of rehabilitative regimes.[9] Despite retractions, the initial, uncorrected conclusion prevailed; it already had fueled a trend against rehabilitative efforts.

The dramatic fall of the rehabilitative ideal provided room for an equally dramatic shift in correctional policy. Another theory, one of "just deserts," emerged to replace the void left by rehabilitation's failure to justify imprisonment. Proponents of the new policy mandate argued that lawbreakers should be imprisoned simply because they deserved punishment. Although some desert theorists argued that some lawbreakers deserved to be punished to deter others from crime, the more dominant view simply held that offenders must suffer for their transgressions. Thus, Andrew von Hirsch, who led the theoretical charge to rethink modern punishment, defined desert as the idea that "the response to someone's behavior should depend on

---

to aggregate systematically and compare the findings across several studies is one of the primary advantages of this technique. Robert Rosenthal, Meta-Analytic Procedures for Social Research (1991). Importantly, however, these analyses are only as good as the studies that already exist.

[2] See Robert Martinson, What works? Questions and answers about prison reform, 35 Pub. Int. 22 (1974).

[3] See Robert Martinson, What works? Questions and answers about prison reform, 35 Pub. Int. 22, 25 (1974).

[4] Richard L. Nygaard, Crime, pain, and punishment: A skeptic's view, 102 Dick. L. Rev. 355, 362 (1998).

[5] See generally James Robinson and Gerald Smith, The effectiveness of correctional programs, 17 Crime and Delinq. 67 (1971).

[6] See generally The Rehabilitation of Criminal Offenders: Problems and Prospects (Lee Sechrest, Susan O. White, and Elizabeth D. Brown, eds., 1979).

[7] Ted Palmer, Martinson revisited, 12 J. Res. Crime and Delinq. 133 (1975).

[8] For a more complete account of the research, see generally The Effectiveness of Correctional Treatment: A Survey of Treatment Evaluation Studies (Douglas Lipton, Robert Martinson, and Judith Wilks, eds., 1975).

[9] Robert Martinson, New findings, new views: A note of caution regarding sentencing reform, 7 Hofstra L. Rev. 243, 252 (1979).

the good or bad qualities of that behavior."[10] Under this view, judges would become instruments of retribution as desert-based punishment would grade crime according to blame and prisons would serve to inflict the punishment.

Just deserts theory contributed to the dominance of efforts to punish and incapacitate. A host of legal and criminal justice decision makers enthusiastically embraced the approach as the foundation for a variety of sentencing reforms. Determinate or fixed sentencing schemes replaced indeterminate sentences and parole systems.[11] Law enforcement introduced mandatory prison sentences, mandatory minimums, and mandatory enhanced terms. The effort went so far as to seek to reduce judicial sentencing discretion to a focus on the criminal act itself. This was most notable in what has been viewed as the dismantling of the juvenile court through, for example, efforts to transfer juveniles to adult courts based on specific offenses deemed as needing adult punishment.[12] Presumptive sentencing and sentencing guidelines reflected the same view: Justice was to be apportioned when the judge sentenced an offender, but a limited and legislatively fixed set of considerations would constrain that apportioning. Taken to its theoretical extreme, the model would explicitly exclude from sentencing decisions consideration of who offenders were and, by implication, why they committed criminal offenses.

Responding to Apparent Rehabilitative Failures

Despite a few notable exceptions,[13] laws continue to move toward a just desert approach. Yet, an equally important development erodes the empirical basis for rejecting rehabilitation. Most notably, meta-analyses and individual program evaluations in the 1980s and 1990s advanced the unsurprising idea that the effectiveness of rehabilitation programs depends on the nature of the intervention and the

---

[10] Andrew von Hirsch, "Neoclassicism," proportionality, and the rationale for punishment: Thoughts on the Scandinavian debate, 29 Crime and Delinq. 52, 59 (1983).

[11] Francis Allen, The Decline of the Rehabilitative Ideal: Penal Policy and Social Purpose (1981).

[12] This actually led to efforts to abolish the juvenile court by many who aim to dismantle the current juvenile court structure and incorporate children into the adult criminal court system. Barry C. Feld, Abolish the juvenile court: Youthfulness, criminal responsibility, and sentencing policy, 88 J. Crim. L. and Criminology 68 (1997).

[13] The leading exceptions, of course, are the numerous drug courts; but even they have been subjected to numerous criticisms for their failure to take rehabilitation seriously and for failing to carefully consider the limitations of research. Critics of these specialized courts find them too new to provide reliable data as to their success or failure. See, e.g., Steven Belenko, National Center on Addiction and Substance Abuse (CASA) at Columbia University, Research on Drug Courts: A Critical Review 2001 Update 6 (2001) ("Despite their ongoing popularity and rapid spread, historically there has been a relative paucity of empirically sound and comprehensive research on drug court operations and impacts."); Richard S. Gebelen, U.S. Department of Justice, National Institute of Justice, The Rebirth of Rehabilitation: Promise and Perils of Drug Courts 5 (2000) ("As the results of more sophisticated evaluations become available, preliminary success rates will not be sustained. As less tractable groups participate, rates of compliance and graduation will decline and recidivism will rise."). Others dispute reduced-recidivism claims, arguing that the success of drug courts is statistically meaningless. The argument is that, although their methods do seem to reduce drug recidivism slightly, so many of the drug court "clients" fail to respond to treatment that the courts ultimately sentence larger numbers to prison. As a result, the drug court's emphasis on treatment and monitoring as their initial response to drug crime widens the net of penal control and facilitates the felony prosecution of defendants who earlier would have been prosecuted for misdemeanors if prosecuted at all. See, e.g., District Judge Morris B. Hoffman, The drug court scandal, 78 N.C.L. Rev. 1437, 1497-98, 1534 (2000). See also Steven Belenko, The challenges of integrating drug treatment into the criminal justice process, 63 Albany L. Rev. 833 (2000). Recent research actually reveals that drug treatment courts will not necessarily result in cost reductions because cases from such courts and control cases are incarcerated for approximately equal numbers of days. One of the major reasons for failing to outperform other cases is that drug courts fail to implement programs as they should and fail to offer drug treatment. Denise C. Gottfredson, Stacy S. Najaka, Brook Kearley, Effectiveness of drug treatment courts: Evidence from a randomized trial, 2 Criminology and Pub. Pol'y. 171 (2003). That study found, for example, that recidivism rates for drug treatment court cases who did not receive drug treatment were not significantly different from recidivism rates for the control subjects (75% vs. 81%), despite the use of drug testing and sanctions. But for those who did receive treatment, recidivism rates were much lower (57% vs. 81%), which suggests that treatment is a critical element of the drug court model.

cooperation of the target group.[14] Arguably, the most fundamental finding simply confirmed implementation's crucial role. When the rehabilitation program meets the need and obtains the loyalty of the corrections staff, it will be implemented well, and promises to be effective. When it does not, the program will be implemented poorly and inevitably fail.[15]

Given the significance of rehabilitative efforts and the extent to which they have been challenged, consider the findings of two leading meta-analyses of the offender treatment literature. One of the most comprehensive analyses examined 443 studies of offenders 12 to 21 years of age.[16] That study included all English-language published and unpublished studies conducted since 1950 that met the following criteria: (1) some intervention or treatment (broadly defined) aimed at reducing delinquency or antisocial behavior; (2) at least one quantitative measure of delinquency outcome; and (3) a randomly selected group or a control group sufficiently detailed to determine its pretreatment similarity to the treatment group. The high number of studies allowed the researchers to strongly reject the null hypothesis that nothing works. The most influential moderator variables pertaining to treatment indicated that more specific and structured treatments (e.g., behavioral and skills training) and multimodal treatments were more effective than less-structured, less-specific treatments (e.g., counseling). Importantly, treatments were more effective when the researcher had a high level of involvement. Also important to note was the finding that treatment effects were greater when delivered to higher risk offenders. Likewise, treatment in institutions was less effective than treatment in noninstitutional settings. Among treatments provided outside institutions, more intensive treatment (in terms of duration and frequency of treatment contacts) associated with larger effect sizes. Lastly, subject age did not influence the findings.

The second study worth highlighting categorized prior studies according to how well they followed three theoretically motivated principles of effective correctional treatment: risk, need, and responsivity.[17] First, researchers argued that intensive services should be reserved for high-risk cases and that minimal services should be provided to low-risk cases. Second, they argued that effective treatment to reduce recidivism target dynamic risk factors or criminogenic needs.[18] Third, they argued that offenders generally are most responsive to programs that use behavioral and social learning principles delivered by therapists who use a "fair but firm" approach and who model and reward anticriminal styles of thinking, feeling, and acting.[19] Using these three principles, the researchers categorized studies according to whether they used (a) criminal sanctions without a treatment component, (b) inappropriate correctional service;[20] (c) appropriate service; or (d) unspecified (not well reported) service. The researchers found a small overall positive effect of rehabilitative efforts. Despite that, however, the studies classified as appropriate service yielded larger effects than all other categories. They concluded that appropriate treatment dropped recidivism rates by over 50%. When viewed in light of the study reported above, the findings are impressive. The study reported above had concluded that the best treatment represented decreases in recidivism of 20% to 40%;

---

[14] See Effective Correctional Treatment (Robert Ross and Paul Gendreau, eds., 1980). See generally Paul Gendreau, The principles of effective intervention with offenders, in Choosing Correctional Options That Work (Alan Harland, ed., 1996); D.A. Andrews, Ivan Zinger, Robert D. Hoge, Jim Bonta, Paul Gendreau, and Francis T. Cullen, Does correctional treatment work? A clinically relevant and psychologically informed meta-analysis, 28 Criminology 369 (1990); Paul Gendreau and Robert R. Ross, Revivification of rehabilitation: Evidence from the1980's, 4 Jus. Q. 349 (1987); Ted Palmer, The effectiveness of intervention: Recent trends and current issues, 37 Crime and Delinq. 330 (1991).

[15] See Ann Chih Lin, Reform in the Making: The Implementation of Social Policy in Prison (2000).

[16] Mark W. Lipsey, Juvenile delinquency treatment: A meta-analytic inquiry into the variability of effects, in Meta-analysis for Explanation 83 (Thomas D. Cook, Harris Cooper, David S. Cordray, Heidi Hartmann, Larry Hedges, Richard J. Light, Thomas A. Louis, and Frederick Mosteller, eds., 1992).

[17] D.A. Andrews, Ivan Zinger, Robert D. Hoge, Jim Bonta, Paul Gendreau, and Francis T. Cullen, Does correctional treatment work? A clinically relevant and psychologically informed meta-analysis, 28 Criminology 369 (1990).

[18] They argued that the most promising treatment targets included changing antisocial attitudes and peer associations, reducing chemical dependencies, promoting identification with prosocial role models, developing prosocial skills, and increasing self-control and self-management skills.

[19] They did recognize, however, that a few high-functioning (highly verbal, self-reflective) offenders might benefit from nonbehavioral, evocative, less-structured programs.

[20] They viewed these as services targeted to low-risk offenders; nondirective, relationship -dependent, or psychodynamic therapy; milieu therapy and group approaches that emphasized within-group communication; "scared straight" therapy.

the treatments that led to these effects were, by and large, the same as those defined by this study as appropriate correctional service. Importantly, meta-analytic evidence has supported the applicability of these principles for diverse offender populations, including those within community and institutional settings.[21] More specifically in terms of groups of offenders, these meta-analyses have demonstrated that the principles of effective correctional treatment apply to female offenders,[22] young offenders,[23] and violent offenders (especially those deemed high risk).[24]

The meta-analytic studies support the conclusion that treatment for some offenders can reduce criminal recidivism (compared with the mere application of criminal justice sanctions) as well as have other positive effects. The most effective programs are those that provide highly structured and behavioral or cognitive-behavioral environments, based in the community rather than in institutions, managed with integrity and enthusiasm, target higher rather than lower risk offenders, and are intensive in terms of number of hours and overall length of program.[25] Programs based on fear or punishment as well as traditional psychotherapy have been considerably less effective than other programs, and some of these programs may even be harmful for certain offenders.[26]

Although it is important to emphasize that many policy considerations factor into responses to offenders, it also is important to note that treatment is widely accepted as a viable and effective solution to many forms of specific offenses. For example, therapeutic efforts have been shown to be effective against substance abuse,[27] a major factor linking to many criminal events and especially to recidivism.[28] Likewise, research now highlights effective ways to treat and mange disordered offenders, those with learning disabilities, high-risk violent offenders, and sex offenders.[29] Lastly, it is important to note that even the treatment literature that focuses on youth has special significance given that youth constitute a high crime group and that many adult offenders begin their offending careers early.[30]

---

[21] James K. Hill, D.A. Andrews, and Robert D. Hoge, Meta-analysis of treatment programs for young offenders: The effect of clinically relevant treatment on recidivism, with controls introduced for various methodological variables, 6 Canadian J. of Program Eval. 97 (1991).

[22] Craig Dowden and D.A. Andrews, What works for female offenders: A meta-analytic review, 45 Crime and Delinq. 438 (1999).

[23] Craig Dowden and D.A. Andrews, What works in young offender treatment: A meta-analysis, 11 Forum on Corrections Res. 21 (1999).

[24] Craig Dowden and D A Andrews, Effective correctional treatment and violent reoffending: A meta-analysis, 42 Canadian J. of Criminology 449 (2000).

[25] See also Frank S Pearson, Douglas S Lipton, Charles M Cleland, and Dorline S Yee, The effects of behavioral / cognitive-behavioral programs on recidivism, 48 Crime and Deilinq. 476 (2002).

[26] Marnie E. Rice, Grant T. Harris and Catherine A. Cormier, Evaluation of a maximum security therapeutic community for psychopaths and other mentally disordered offenders, 16 L. and Hum. Beh. 399 (1992). Note, however, that the early evidence came almost exclusively from studies of juveniles.

[27] Frank S. Pearson and Douglas S. Lipton, A meta-analytic review of the effectiveness of corrections-based treatments for drug abuse, 79 Prison J. 384 (1999); David B. Wilson, Meta-analyses in alcohol and other drug abuse treatment research, 95 Addiction S419 (2000); and Michael L. Prendergast, Deborah Podus, Eunice Chang, and Darren Urada, The effectiveness of drug abuse treatment: A meta-analysis of comparison group studies, 67 Drug and Alcohol Dependence 53 (2002).

[28] Craig Dowden and S.L. Brown, The role of substance abuse factors in predicting recidivism: A meta-analysis, 8 Psych. Crime and L. 243 (2002).

[29] Treating Adult and Juvenile Offenders with Special Needs (Jose B. Ashford, Burce Dennis Sales, and William H. Reid, eds., 2002).

[30] For a small percentage of adolescents, their antisocial tendencies that begin in childhood continue in a stable pattern of criminal conduct that defines their adult characters; and it is this small group that eventually commits much of adult crime. Terrie Moffitt, Adolescent-limited and life course persistent antisocial behavior: A developmental taxonomy, 100 Psychol. Rev. 674 (1993); Terrie E. Moffitt, Avshalom Caspi, Honalee Harrington, and Barry J. Milne, Males on the life-course-persistent and adolescence-limited antisocial pathways: Follow-up at age 26 years, 14 Development and Psychopathology 179 (2002); and Alex Piquero, Testing Moffitt's neuropsychological variation hypothesis for the prediction of life-course persistent offending, 7 Psych. Crime and L. 193 (2001).

THE PSYCHOLOGY OF FOLLOWING THE LAW

Fully understanding treatment and punishment means evaluating what psychological sciences tell us about why people obey the law and using those evaluations to examine legal cases like those presented in this chapter. Research actually has much to tell us about effective punishment and the types of legal rules that foster law-abiding behavior. Much of the relevant literature that focuses on human motivation derives from sub-disciplines of psychology, sociology, criminology, and economics. Although many theories address motivations to follow social dictates within those key disciplines, all typically examine motivations for social behavior by focusing on the person (the individual's attitudes and social values) and on the environment (the incentives and risks within the social environment). To help us understand the contours of psychological theories and research about law-related behavior, we will focus on two leading models, one which focuses on internal motivations and another on environmental contingencies.[31]

Deterrence Models

Deterrence theory guides much of the existing research on the effectiveness of justice system interventions.[32] This theory rests on the view that self-interest primarily determines compliance with the law. Individuals decide to commit crimes or obey the law, this account predicts, after calculating whether the benefits of compliance outweigh its costs. People will commit crimes when they receive more out of the crime relative to the punishment they would or could receive. This expectation derives from the assumption that individuals behave rationally to maximize their utility. To shape behavior, then, this rational choice model focuses on the ability of expected losses associated with law-breaking to lessen the likelihood that people will break the law.[33] The theory expects that effectiveness in inhibiting future illegal behavior increases as a negative outcome (or sanction) increases in severity or certainty. Given that individuals interacting with legal authorities simply seek to secure favorable outcomes for themselves, society can shape behavior by considering what people would view as gains and losses.[34] Once those factors are determined, communities can promote obedience by adopting the most cost-effective policies for raising the price of crime.[35] As a result, the model would have us seek to identify optimal levels of punishment and devise appropriate conditions to deter criminal behavior. It is this focus on deterrence and society's ability to control that leads many to describe these approaches as "social control models" when applied to criminal justice processes.[36]

Although deterrence models have considerable dominance in law, much effort continues to evaluate their effectiveness. Research examining deterrence compares the degree of social control imposed through different outcomes of legal proceedings. The dominance of the models probably would have led us to expect that research would focus on fine-tuning appropriate punishments. The focus of research, though,

---

[31] Research in this area views contingencies simply as different results that may occur depending on actions taken.

[32] See Tom R. Tyler, Procedural justice, legitimacy, and the effective rule of law, 30 Crime and Jus. 283 (2003); and Craig Haney and Philip Zimbardo, The past and future of U.S. prison policy: Twenty-five years after the Stanford prison experiment, 53 Am. Psychologist 709 (1998).

[33] See Daniel S. Nagin and Raymond Paternoster, The preventive effects of the perceived risk of arrest: Testing an expanded conception of deterrence, 29 Criminology 561, 580-81 (1991); and Raymond Paternoster, Decisions to participate in and desist from four types of common delinquency: Deterrence and the rational choice perspective, 23 L. and Soc'y Rev. 7, 10-12, 37 (1989).

[34] Raymond Paternoster, Decisions to participate in and desist from four types of common delinquency: Deterrence and the rational choice perspective, 23 L. and Soc'y Rev. 7, 10 (1989).

[35] Richard A. Posner, An economic theory of the criminal law, 85 Colum. L. Rev. 1193 (1985); Steven Shavell, Criminal law and the optimal use of nonmonetary sanctions as a deterrent, 85 Colum. L. Rev. 1232 (1985); and Dan M. Kahan, Social influence, social meaning, and deterrence, 83 Va. L. Rev. 349 (1997).

[36] For a review of models, see Stephen E. Brown, Finn-Aage Esbensen, and Gilbert Geis, Criminology: Explaining Crime and Its Contexts (3rd ed. 1998).

continues to be much more basic. Existing research in this area tends to investigate whether deterrence models actually work.

Few doubt that variations in the perceived certainty and severity of punishment do shape people's compliance with the law.[37] People's estimate of the likelihood that they will get caught and punished if they disobey the law does seem to shape their behavior.[38] Research does reveal that the ability to threaten or deliver sanctions is usually effective in shaping people's law-related behavior. In particular, a number of studies on deterrence suggest that people are less likely to engage in illegal behaviors when they think that they might be caught and punished. This core premise of deterrence models finds support in many studies examining the factors that shape people's law-related behavior.[39]

Although research supports the basic premise of deterrence models, research also suggests that estimates of the likelihood of being caught and punished have, at best, a minor influence on people's law-related behavior. For example, some studies suggest that such estimates do not independently influence behavior when analyses consider the influence of other factors.[40] Other studies do find an independent influence of deterrence, but note that it is typically small in magnitude.[41] Other studies reveal that offenders may be aware in general terms of the possibility of being apprehended and punished but that those prospects are not salient in their thinking in the moments prior to committing crime.[42] Research on aggressive behavior also indicates that individuals are influenced by very short-term motivations and lose sight of long-term consequences.[43] The influence of sanctions, then, may not be as great as we may have thought.

Evidence that sanctions may not be so powerful also comes from the psychological literature on the effectiveness of punishment. Numerous authors have reviewed the conditions that make punishment effective. These stipulations include the following: that the punishment be unavoidable or inevitable, that punishment be administered immediately or with maximum speed, that severity should be high, and that society provide alternative behaviors for pursuing desired goals.[44] As it turns out, however, criminal justice processes cannot meet these requirements. Even though it may increasingly become more punitive, the criminal justice system simply does not effectively use punishment.

Criminological research also actually questions the overall effectiveness of deterrence. For example, reviews of the current body of literature on the effect of sentence severity find no effect on the level of crime in society and find little evidence to support the hypothesis that variation in sentence severity will differentially affect crime rates.[45] Similarly, one would think that at least short-term compliance with a police officer's directives would be high if the deterrent model reflected reality. Yet, research investigating police encounters with citizens reveals high rates of disobedience: about 1 out of 4 individuals fail to obey

---

[37] See, e.g., Harold G. Grasmick and Robert J. Bursik, Jr., Conscience, significant others, and rational choice: Extending the deterrence model, 24 L. and Soc'y Rev. 837, 838-40, 857 (1990).

[38] Raymond Paternoster, The deterrent effect of the perceived certainty and severity of punishment: A review of the evidence and issues, 4 Jus. Q. 173, 174, 211 (1987).

[39] Daniel S. Nagin and Raymond Paternoster, The preventive effects of the perceived risk of arrest: Testing an expanded conception of deterrence, 29 Criminology 561, 580-81 (1991); and Daniel S. Nagin, Criminal deterrence research at the outset of the twenty-first century, 23 Crime and Jus. 1 (1998).

[40] Raymond Paternoster and LeeAnn Iovanni, The deterrent effect of perceived severity: A reexamination, 64 Soc. Forces 751, 769-70 (1986).

[41] See, e.g., Robert J. MacCoun, Drugs and the law: A Psychological analysis of drug prohibition, 113 Psych. Bull. 497, 501 (1993). His review of studies of deterrence of drug use found that around 5 percent of the variance in drug use behavior can be explained by variations in the expected likelihood or severity of punishment. This suggests that much variance in law-related behavior flows from factors other than risk estimates.

[42] For a review of studies, see James McGuire, Criminal sanctions versus psychologically-based interventions with offenders: A comparative empirical analysis, 8 Psych. Crime and L. 183, 190 (2002).

[43] Leonard Berkowitz, Aggression: Its Causes, Consequences, and Control (1993).

[44] James McGuire, Criminal sanctions versus psychologically-based interventions with offenders: A comparative empirical analysis, 8 Psych. Crime and L. 183, 188-190 (2002).

[45] This applies at least to crime rates in Western populations. For a review, see Anthony N. Doob and Cheryl Marie Webster, Sentence severity and crime: Accepting the null hypothesis, 30 Crime and Jus. 143 (2003).

police when police are right there telling them to desist certain illegal behaviors.[46] Obeying law enforcement to avoid certain punishment may be normative, but it is not universal.

In sum, then, research findings suggest that people's compliance with the law does link (but sometimes weakly) to the risks associated with law-breaking behavior. Despite the high popularity of models focusing on deterrence and the need to address people's calculations when they decide to commit crimes, research in this area has yet to address effectively key psychological factors about criminal behavior. Most notably, it does not explain well how individuals who commit crime employ elaborate cognitive mechanisms which function to isolate them psychologically from the consequences of their actions and render illegal action acceptable by helping them avoid responsibility and perceive the experience of punishment as unfair.[47]

Process Models

Psychologists generally reveal little interest in social control models. In fact, the limits of those models have lead psychologists to expand investigations to other factors that psychologists view as central to the determination of people's behavior: the set of internal values that shape feelings about what is ethical or appropriate to do. These researchers connect voluntary compliance with the law to the extent to which individuals believe the law is "just" or to which they believe that the authority enforcing the law has the right to do so.[48] Researchers consider this a normative approach. It is normative because individuals respond to the issues of justice and authority differently from the way they respond to rewards and punishments. This approach differs from the deterrence model which views compliance with the law as a response to externally imposed punishments (if individuals did respond that way, they would be said to act instrumentally). Individuals who comply for normative reasons do so because they feel an internal obligation.

Much attention has been placed on internal motivations that make people feel obligated or responsible to act appropriately. The process models place emphasis on the values that become a part of the person and how those values lead them to exercise self-regulation over their behavior so that their behavior is consistent with the internal principles and values that define their sense of who they are. In such a situation, people do not so much merely comply with the law out of fear of punishment as much as they accept and consent to it. People become law-abiding because they feel that obeying the law and legal authority is the right thing to do. This perspective emphasizes the importance of developing and sustaining a climate of appropriate values, one in which people abide by laws because they feel that obeying is right, fair and appropriate. Given suitable climates, people will internalize values that influence proper behavior, and that internalization makes it unnecessary to shape behavior by threatening them with punishment for wrongdoing. People take upon themselves the responsibility to follow social rules and the responsibility for obeying the directives of legal authorities.

As the above description suggests, this perspective identifies two key values as central to encouraging people to follow legal mandates. The first is the belief that it is morally right to follow the law.[49] This

---

[46] One study observed police encounters with the public in Richmond, Virginia. It found an overall noncompliance rate of 22 percent: 19 percent of the time when the police told a person to leave another person alone, 33 percent of the time when the police told a person to cease some form of disorder, and 18 percent of the time when the police told a person to cease illegal behavior. Stephen D. Mastrofski, Jeffrey B. Snipes, and Anne E. Supina, Compliance on demand: The public's responses to specific police requests, 33 J. of Crime and Delinq. 269 (1996). A replication in Indianapolis, Indiana, and St. Petersburg, Florida, found an overall noncompliance rate of 20 percent: 14 percent of the time when the police told people to leave another person alone, 25 percent of the time when the police told a person to cease some form of disorder, and 21 percent of the time when the police told a person to cease illegal behavior. John D. McCluskey, Stephen D. Mastrofski and Roger B. Parks, To acquiesce and rebel: Predicting citizen compliance with police requests, 2 Police Q. 389 (1999).

[47] In the criminological literature, these are known as techniques of neutralization. See George B. Vold, Thomas J. Bernard, and Jeffrey B. Snipes, Theoretical Criminology (5th ed., 2002).

[48] See Tom R. Tyler, Why People Obey the Law 3-4 (1990).

[49] Paul H. Robinson and John M. Darley, Justice, Liability, and Blame: Community Views and the Criminal Law 201 (1995).

judgment links to people's assessment that the behaviors prohibited by law are contrary to their moral values.[50] The second key value is the belief that everyone has a civic duty to accept legal rules and to obey the directives of legal authorities.[51] Although the threat of punishment looms when dealing with legal authorities, most people accept authorities' decisions, not simply because they fear them. Most people obey because they view authorities as legitimate sources of power who ought to be obeyed and because the laws do not contradict their moral values. The model, then, focuses on the legitimacy of authorities and rules.

Psychologists have investigated the extent to which people's social values matter in determining people's compliance with laws, even in terms of the extent to which they matter beyond predictions derived from the deterrence model. That research reveals that both morality and legitimacy influence compliance in a manner that is both separate from the influence of risk assessments and stronger than the impact of risk assessments.[52] For example, an important study designed to test compliance with the law directly analyzed the relative impact of legitimacy, public deterrence, peer disapproval, and personal morality on compliance. The study found that, compared to deterrence, legitimacy was a much stronger predictor of compliance.[53] Importantly, the argument is not that instrumental means (punishment) of producing compliance have no effect. Deterrence or outcome-based judgements still do influence compliance or related behavior in some way. Research reveals, though, that legitimacy is typically more important than, or just as important to compliance as, instrumental reasons.

The process models help reveal and explain two limitations of the deterrence/social control models. As we have seen, the social control model defines legitimacy in terms of maximizing self-interest. This view suggests that people will evaluate authorities as legitimate when authorities make decisions that benefit them in the long run. However, while the self-interest approach exhibits great explanatory power, it appears incomplete. The process models highlight two key limitations.[54] One limitation of deterrence approaches involves the extent to which they fail to make sense of the fact that individuals confer legitimacy on officials even in the face of repeated negative outcomes. A second limitation deals with the inability of the self-interest perspective to account for the fact that people appear to care very deeply about the way they are treated by authorities quite apart from the outcome of particular encounters. These limitations suggest that real world behavior reflects more a theory relying on norms than one relying on outcomes.

Psychologists have developed a theory of procedural justice that does account for the regular conference in legitimacy in the face of repeated negative outcomes and for the fact that people care a great deal about how governmental authorities treat them.[55] The procedural justice model directs the study of legitimacy and obligation to the feelings, needs, and concerns of the people who deal with legal authorities.[56] This area of research suggests that law abiding behavior is not linked to agreement with the

---

[50] For example, if murder were to become suddenly legal, most people would not commit murder because murder contradicts our sense of what is right and wrong. Likewise, if all abortion were to become illegal, some probably would use it under certain circumstances because they would not consider it contrary to their values of what constitutes murder.

[51] If citizens believe that legal authorities are legitimate, they regard them as entitled to be obeyed. In such situations, people obey laws because they regard deference to social authorities as part of the obligations associated with citizenship. The argument is that people follow police directives without thinking about whether they will be punished for failure to comply. Tom R. Tyler, Why People Obey the Law 3-4 (1990).

[52] Tom R. Tyler, Why People Obey the Law 58-60 (1990). Note that several studies support this finding by demonstrating the important role of both moral values and beliefs about the legitimacy of legal authorities on reactions to law and legal authorities. Tom R. Tyler, Procedural justice, legitimacy, and the effective rule of law, 30 Crime and Jus. 283 (2003).

[53] It found that the regression estimate for legitimacy on compliance was about five times greater than the estimate for deterrence. Tom R. Tyler, Why People Obey the Law 58-60 (1990). Other research supports similar findings. Tom R. Tyler and Yuen J. Huo, Trust in the Law: Encouraging Public Cooperation with the Police and Courts (2002).

[54] See E. Allan Lind and Tom R. Tyler, The Social Psychology of Procedural Justice 228-30 (1988).

[55] In thinking about the utility of this research, the argument tends to be that legitimacy does seem to provide greater and more reliable authority to legal officials than does morality. It may be more reliable because legal officials have discretionary authority to decide what is appropriate. Within the scope of their prescribed roles, the police and courts make decisions, and citizens believe that they ought to obey those decisions. Because legitimacy invests authorities with discretionary authority, it is a more flexible form of social value upon which to base the operation of the legal system. With morality, the discretion rests with citizens who decide whether or not the law corresponds to their moral values.

[56] In order to make this assessment, individuals typically focus on three factors: standing, neutrality and trust. Tom R. Tyler and E. Allan Lind, A relational model of authority in groups, in 25 Advances in Experimental Social Psychology 115,

decisions made by legal authorities. [57] If people believe that the legal authorities are exercising authority in fair ways, they are more likely to defer to those authorities. It is true that fair procedures promote fair outcomes and that the favorable outcomes, in turn, increase compliance.[58] The data, however, support an alternative concept: fair treatment affects compliance regardless of whether the ultimate result is viewed as right or wrong. If people feel unfairly treated by a government official or a court proceeding, they will perceive the source as less legitimate and, as a consequence, obey its orders less frequently.[59] Being treated fairly by authorities, even while being sanctioned by them, influences both a person's view of the legitimacy of the authority figures and ultimately that person's obedience. Perhaps most importantly, from the perspective of the legal system, judgments about procedural fairness link to the willingness both to accept particular legal decisions[60] and to generally follow laws and legal rules.[61] The importance of procedural justice to the legal system also comes in the extent to which procedural justice plays an especially important role in securing compliance over time.[62] It is clear that people's behavioral reactions to law and legal authorities are heavily influenced by their assessments of the fairness of legal procedures.

This area of research presents obvious implications for policing. Legitimacy as a means of producing compliance can be acquired simply by changing procedures and practices of current officials in ways that require few additional resources. For example, some research indicates that police who regularly treat arrestees with courtesy are more likely than those who do not to be viewed as legitimate.[63] This means that

---

158-160 (Mark P. Zanna ed., 1992). By standing, researchers refer to indications that the authority recognizes an individual's status and membership in a valued group, such as polite treatment and treatment that accords dignity and respect, such as concern for rights. Tom R. Tyler, What is procedural justice?: Criteria used by citizens to assess the fairness of legal procedures, 22 L. and Soc'y Rev. 103, 129 (1998). Neutrality refers to indications that decisions in which the perceiver is not made to feel as if she is less worthy than others because of bias, discrimination and incompetence. Tom R. Tyler and E. Allan Lind, A relational model of authority in groups, in 25 Advances in Experimental Social Psychology 115, 157 (Mark P. Zanna, ed., 1992). And trust refers to the extent to which a perceiver believes that the authority in question will act fairly and benevolently in the future. Tom R. Tyler, Trust and democratic governance, in Trust and Governance 269, 270 (Valerie Braithwaite and Margaret Levi, eds., 1998). Of course, individuals making assessments do not disaggregate their assessments in terms of these factors; rather, they come to conclusions about authorities by considering information relevant to these factors. Researchers have been able to disaggregate the various factors for purposes of analysis. Note that these factors differ slightly from the original conception of due process concerns. In addition to the three factors listed above, the model focused on consistency, which involved whether authorities treat similarly situated persons in a similar manner and whether an individual can expect to receive similar treatment over time, in different encounters with the justice system. See Tom R. Tyler, Kenneth Rasinski, and Nancy Spodick, Influence of voice on satisfaction with leaders: Exploring the meaning of process control, 48 J. Personality and Soc. Psych. 72, 72 (1985). See also Tom R. Tyler, Procedural justice, legitimacy, and the effective rule of law, 30 Crime and Jus. 283 (2003). Depending on which context, research uses different conceptualizations of the important aspects of processes. Researchers deem this necessary because no single procedure is universally regarded as fair. People's views of the attributes of a fair procedure vary when the procedure is being used to resolve different types of problems. For example, when the police are dealing with a dispute, people rate having opportunities to state their point of view as being key to the fairness of a procedure; but, when the police are trying to solve a problem, people primarily focus on whether they trust the motives of the officers involved. Tom R. Tyler, What is procedural justice? Criteria used by citizens to assess the fairness of legal procedures, 22 L. and Soc'y Rev.103 (1988).

[57] This is important because if people viewed as legitimate only those authorities who make decisions with which they agree, it would be difficult for legal authorities to maintain their legitimacy. This is so because they are required to make unpopular decisions, which may deliver unfavorable outcomes.

[58] John Thibaut and Laurens Walker, Procedural Justice: A Psychological Analysis (1975); and John Thibaut and Laurens Walker, A theory of procedure, 66 Cal. L. Rev. 541 (1978).

[59] Tom R. Tyler and E. Allen Lind, A relational model of authority in groups, 25 Adv. in Exper'l Soc. Psych. 115 (1992).

[60] See E. Allan Lind and Tom R. Tyler, The Social Psychology of Procedural Justice 65-83 (1988).

[61] See Richard Sparks, Anthony Bottoms and Will Hay, Prisons and the Problem of Order 87-89 (1996).

[62] Raymond Paternoster, Robert Brame, Ronet Bachman, and Lawrence W. Sherman, Do fair procedures matter? The effect of procedural justice on spouse assault, 31 L. and Soc'y Rev. 163, 165-66, 192 (1997).

[63] Several studies are illustrative. In one study, researchers examined what transpired when police were called to homes to deal with issues of domestic violence. The concern of the study was with subsequent compliance to the law on the part of the abusive men whose behavior led to the initial call. From a social control perspective, we would expect threats and/or punishments to increase compliance. From a due process perspective, police can best gain compliance by socializing the offending spouse about the law and their obligation to obey it. They can do so by treating that person fairly, since the roots of the perceived obligation to obey the law lie in judgments about the fairness of the legal process. The results of the study supported the value of the due process perspective. If the police treat the abuser fairly during their encounter,

we could achieve greater compliance by changing how police treat people than by using methods that rely on deterrence.[64] Although the focus on instrumental means continues to be the dominant approach,[65] research on legitimacy means that law enforcement gains could be achieved more cheaply than through more instrumental means simply establishing legitimacy, which can support acceptance of decisions as long as authorities are viewed as legitimate.[66] Even victims' satisfaction with police links to the extent to which they view their actions as legitimate.[67] We should, therefore, expect greater compliance in communities where police treat arrestees with greater respect than communities where police do not. This

---

that abuser is subsequently more likely to comply with the law. Fair treatment increases feelings of respect for the law and leads abusers to be more willing to obey it in the future. This influence is greater than the impact of threatened or enacted punishments. In fact, the reason the study was conducted in the first place is because there were many conflicting findings about arrest policies regarding mandatory arrest in domestic violence situations, and it seems that police behavior was the variable that could explain best the variety of findings. Raymond Paternoster, Robert Brame, Ronet Bachman, and Lawrence W. Sherman, Do fair procedures matter? The effect of procedural justice on spouse assault, 31 L. and Soc'y Rev. 163, 176-182 (1997). Yet another study examined the basis of public willingness to accept the decisions of legal authorities during their personal encounters with police officers and judges. They interviewed 1,656 people living in Oakland and Los Angeles, California, each of whom had recently had a personal experience with legal authorities. The study found that two types of factors shape people's deference to legal authorities during personal encounters. The first links to outcomes. People's willingness to accept decisions is based in part on the degree to which they regard the decisions made by legal authorities as being fair or favorable. Not surprisingly, people are more willing to accept decisions that provide them with outcomes that they view as desirable or fair or both. When people feel that they have won, they are more willing to accept the decisions made. The second factor involves the contact people have with authorities when they seek help, and this study found that most police contact, 85%, were of this form. However, irrespective of the type of contact involved or the authority involved, the process-based model best accounted for people's willingness to accept the decisions made. In this model, people are viewed as influenced by non-outcome-based judgments about procedural justice and motive-based trust. First, they defer to the decisions of legal authorities because those authorities are viewed as exercising their authority in fair ways. Second, people are influenced by their judgments about their trust in the motives of the authorities with whom they deal. People are more willing to defer to authorities when they trust their motives. The study reported that procedural justice judgments and judgments about motive-based trust are more important in shaping both decision acceptance and evaluations of legal authority than are evaluations of the fairness or favorableness of the decisions made by those authorities. The research found that those influences occurred beyond any influence of outcome issues or concerns. In fact, 44 percent of the variance in people's willingness to accept decisions was uniquely shaped by procedural justice and motive-based trust, while only 1 percent of the variance was uniquely shaped by outcome judgments. In addition, procedural justice and motive-based trust were the key factors shaping decision acceptance both when the police imposed themselves on members of the public as part of their social regulatory activities and when people called the police for help. The authors concluded that the findings support the suggestion that legal authorities should engage in process-based regulation in which they are attentive to how they treat members of the public. If police officers and judges behaved in ways that are experienced as fair, they would increase their ability to gain immediate voluntary deference. Tom R. Tyler and Yuen J. Huo, Trust in the Law: Encouraging Public Cooperation with the Police and Courts (2002). See also Tom R. Tyler, Trust and law abidingness: A proactive model of social regulation, 81 B.U. L. Rev. 361, 364-65 (2001).

64 A leading review of prevention studies noted the role of police as follows. "One of the most striking recent findings is the extent to which the police themselves create a risk factor for crime simply by using bad manners. Modest but consistent scientific evidence supports the hypothesis that the less respectful police are towards suspects and citizens generally, the less people will comply with the law. Changing police 'style' may thus be as important as focusing police 'substance.' Making both the style and substance of police practices more 'legitimate' in the eyes of the public, particularly high-risk juveniles, may be one of the most effective long-term police strategies for crime prevention." Lawrence W. Sherman, Denise Gottfredson, Doris MacKenzie, John Eck, Peter Reuter, and Shawn Bushway, Preventing Crime: What Works, What Doesn't, What's Promising: A Report to the United States Congress. 8-1. (1997).

65 Most officers see their role as apprehending perpetrators and adducing sufficient evidence against them to support convictions, not creating an environment in which suspects feel heard and understood. David Lester, Officer attitudes toward police use of force, in Police Violence: Understanding and Controlling Police Abuse of Force 180 (William A. Geller and Hans Toch, eds., 1996); Stephen D. Mastrofski, Jeffrey B. Snipes, and Anne E. Supina, Compliance on demand: The public's response to specific police requests, 33 J. Res. Crime and Delinq. 269, 274 (1996).

66 If deterrence is to be produced by maintaining a certain probability of detection of rule-breakers, then authorities must be willing to devote resources to maintain (or increase) the desired level of police to meet the requisite probability of detection. Therefore, instrumental means of producing compliance always depend on resource limits.

67 Women's satisfaction with police response to domestic violence incidents is highest when the officers comply with the woman's preference, whether that is to arrest, or to refrain from arresting, the perpetrator. Edna Erez and Joanne Belknap, In their own words: Battered women's assessment of the criminal processing system's responses, 13 Violence and Victims 251 (1998).

proposition finds support from research indicating that the manner people are treated affects their perceptions of decision makers throughout the criminal justice system.[68]

The research also has important implications for understanding the effectiveness of prisons. The effects come in two forms. The first way legitimacy's positive impact presents itself emerges from research that indicates how inmates behave differently in different prison settings.[69] For example, the incidence of acts of violence in prisons is influenced not only by the characteristics of inmates but also by aspects of the prison environment and by the continual dynamic interaction between prisoners, prison staff, and the physical and social context within which they are placed. This research suggests that enhanced physical restrictions can often reduce levels of violence due to restrictions on opportunity but may also sometimes lead to a loss of legitimacy that can escalate violence.[70] Some studies, for example, have compared prison environments that differed in their legitimacy in the eyes of prisoners.[71] They found less individual and collective disorder when prisoners view prison as more legitimate; and they found that legitimacy to develop out of the use of fair procedures and the provision of respectful treatment.

The second way legitimacy figures prominently in prison settings deals with its impact on correctional staff. One recent study, for example, examined the impact of organizational justice on the job satisfaction and organizational commitment of correctional staff.[72] It examined both distributive justice (the perception of the fairness of rewards given one's inputs) and procedural justice (perceived fairness in the process of determining distributive outcomes). The study found that distributive and procedural justice are distinct concepts among correctional staff, and both have significant positive effects on job satisfaction. Additionally, procedural justice, but not distributive justice, had a significant positive impact on organizational commitment. The extent to which these factors matter has been shown by the extent to which commitment to organizations and job satisfaction shape employees' productive behaviors and effectiveness.

The focus on process and legitimacy also provides lessons for society's general response to problem behavior. We have learned that individuals do not decide to commit crimes in isolation; rather, their decisions interact with and reinforce each other in various ways. In particular, individuals are much more likely to commit crimes when they perceive criminal activity as widespread. Studies reveal a strong correlation between a person's obedience and her perception of others' behavior and attitudes toward the law.[73] As some researchers note, the perception that one's peers will or will not disapprove exerts a much stronger influence than does the threat of a formal sanction on whether a person decides to engage in a range of common offenses - from larceny, to burglary, to drug use.[74] These findings confirm that individuals' decisions to engage in crime are interlinked in various ways. This finding is supported by research that we discussed in earlier chapters, such as Philip Zimbardo's study of people's decisions to pillage an abandoned automobile.[75] The suggestion that the maintenance of internal values in community

---

[68] For example, one group of researchers used a panel design to interview 628 people accused of felonies. Those people were interviewed prior to and following the adjudication of their cases. The question addressed was how the experience of going through the criminal justice system influenced people's views about that system and its authorities. Procedural justice was the key factor shaping people's overall orientations toward legal authorities, government, and law. Neither outcome fairness nor outcome favorableness separately influenced people's views about the legal system. Tom R. Tyler, Jonathan D. Casper, and Bonnie Fisher, Maintaining allegiance toward political authorities, 33 Am. J. of Pol. Sci. 629 (1989).

[69] Kenneth Adams, Adjusting to prison life K. Adams, 16 Crime and Jus. 275, 315 (1992).

[70] Anthony E. Bottoms, Interpersonal violence and social order in prisons, 26 Crime and Jus. 205 (1999).

[71] Richard J. Sparks and Anthony Bottoms, Legitimacy and order in prisons, 46 Brit. J. of Soc. 45 (1995); and Richard J. Sparks, Anthony Bottoms, and Will Hay, Prisons and the Problem of Order (1996).

[72] Eric Lambert, The impact of organizational justice on correctional staff, 31 J. of Criminal Jus. 155 (2003).

[73] Harold G. Grasmick and Donald E. Green, Legal punishment, social disapproval and internalization as inhibitors of illegal behavior, 71 J. Crim. L. and Criminology 325 (1980).

[74] See, e.g., John Braithwaite, Crime, Shame, and Reintegration 69-70 (1989); and Dan M. Kahan, Social influence, social meaning, and deterrence, 83 Va. L. Rev. 349 (1997).

[75] Philip G. Zimbardo, The human choice: Individuation, reason, and order versus deindividuation, impulse, and chaos, in Nebraska Symposium on Motivation, 1969, at 237, 287-93 (William J. Arnold and David Levie, eds., 1969).

residents is important to effective policing is also made by the literature on restorative justice.[76] The core argument of that literature is that the police and courts should behave in ways that "restore" people to law-following behavior. The restorative model seeks to reconnect offenders to an awareness of their own social values and to their stake in maintaining social relationships. This awareness will discourage them from law-breaking behavior in the future because they will recognize that their behavior violates personal values that define appropriate conduct. They will see that rule breaking damages social relationships with friends, family, and the community. It would, of course, be important not to view these implications as without their own limitations (e.g., deterrence still needs to play a role in combating problem behavior). Yet, these findings reveal the remarkable extent to which laws need not necessarily focus on deterrence and punishment to the exclusion of important process factors.

THE LAW'S RESPONSE

The law has not adapted well to the above findings challenging deterrence and punishment models. The legal system originally framed the area of law regulating punishment and the way the criminal justice system treats (in this case, mistreats) offenders in terms of the Eighth Amendment prohibition against inflicting "cruel and unusual punishments." That Amendment historically provided the most direct legal mechanism to limit the conditions of imprisonment and efforts to control. Although the original intent of the Amendment was to preclude only certain barbarous punishments that had been allowed under English law,[77] its scope was progressively broadened and eventually applied to prisoners.

Despite notable expansion, this area of law remained inadequate to support rehabilitative efforts. Modern 8th Amendment jurisprudence centers on the extent to which the punishment offends an "evolving standard of decency" held by members of the public, an approach to jurisprudence we will return to in the next chapter. For now, it is important to note that this standard does not offer much to efforts arguing that individuals should not simply be warehoused and that they at least should be provided with an environment that fosters their rehabilitative needs. Some Justices do not even view prison conditions as issues involving the 8th Amendment. Rather than carve out protections for inmates and those under surveillance, the Court broadens the latitude granted to, for example, prison officials who confront the day-to-day exigencies of institutional life. The cases that follow will explore how the Court continues to transform this area of jurisprudence.

The Court's move to narrow the use of the 8th Amendment has led to a focus on other protections. We will see, most notably, a focus on Ex Post Facto prohibitions (the impermissibility of passing a law after the occurrence of an action which retrospectively changes the legal consequences of the action), Double Jeopardy (being tried twice for the same offense), and the right to privacy. Likewise, there still remains a focus on ensuring basic Due Process protections. Despite these possible protections, the general finding that emerges from the cases that follow is that very few restrictions apply to society's efforts to enact statutes to punish and control those deemed criminals. In addition, and as we already have seen, the Court grants law enforcement officials (starting with police and ending with corrections officers) considerable discretion. It is perhaps that high level of discretion that opens windows to using psychological findings in efforts to effectively address criminal behavior.

---

[76] John Braithwaite, Crime, Shame, and Reintegration (1989). John Braithwaite, Restorative justice: Assessing optimistic and pessimistic accounts, 25 Crime and Jus. 1 (1999); Heather Strang and John Braithwaite, Restorative Justice and Civil Society (2001).

[77] See Anthony F. Granucci, "Nor cruel and unusual punishments inflicted": The original meaning, 57 Cal. L. Rev. 839 (1969).

When reading the cases that follow, try to keep in mind the potential role psychology may play in permissible, discretionary efforts. We will see, for example, that the strongest factors determining the effectiveness of efforts to rehabilitate are found within the broad setting conditions established by criminal sanctions. Counselors, for example, may have little immediate influence over the boundaries of criminal sanctions, but they can play a role in the discretionary aspects of the management of sentences and the services delivered. Likewise, and as the downfall of the rehabilitative ideal revealed, psychologists' work which resonates with community sentiments may effect change. The lesson of that downfall, however, suggests that psychologists must focus on ensuring that laws remain faithful to established psychological principles. When examining the following cases, consider how they reflect different efforts to control individuals' behaviors. In considering how the law controls behavior, try to include not only the manner the law controls those deemed offenders but also those who would be dealing with offenders, such as corrections officers, mental health officials, and even general laws. In addition, consider how the law controls potential offenders. If the law permits discretion, consider how that discretion can be shaped to take advantage of psychological research findings and theories.

NOTES AND QUERIES

Do you accept the now apparently robust proposition that rehabilitative efforts do work as long as they are implemented faithfully? Even if that proposition is true, does that mean that we are realistic in thinking that rehabilitative efforts are effective? What factors do you suppose would impact implementation efforts? How does the law address these factors?

What is meant by normative approaches to punishment? What about instrumental models? How do the models work together? Now that you have a sense of the literature exploring both models, which do you find most appealing? Can you weigh the costs and benefits of both models? Why do you supposed instrumental models tend to be so dominant and popular?

Obviously, it is important to recognize one's chances of being caught for particular crimes if one is to take the deterrence model seriously. Can you guess what your chances are for stealing a car? What about your chances of getting prison for planning the perfect murder? Do you think that criminals would do better or worse than you in terms of evading punishment? Keep in mind that people tend to be overly optimistic in assessing their abilities (all of us tend to think that we are smarter than others; and criminals probably think that more than non-criminals do). What do you make of recent research indicating that, in most situations, the objective risk of being caught and punished is quite low. For example, according to an analysis of crime and arrest rates, the objective risk of being caught, convicted, and imprisoned for rape is about 12 percent; for robbery 4 percent; and for assault, burglary, larceny, and motor vehicle theft 1 percent. For murder, however, the chances actually are close to 50-50, around 45 percent. Paul H. Robinson and John M. Darley, The utility of desert, 91 N. U. L. Rev. 453 (1997). If the chances of being caught and punished for certain crimes actually are low, why are people not committing more crime? Are these actually low risks? How rational do you think people really are when they are making their deterrence calculations? Does that impact your view of the deterrence model? Does the model still make sense even though people may not be acting rationally in their calculations? The key, of course, is to adapt the penalty structure to the decision-making styles of the people whose behavior one is trying to influence. How are we to do that?

COMMITTING THE DANGEROUS

ADDINGTON v. TEXAS
441 U.S. 418 (1979)

MR. CHIEF JUSTICE BURGER delivered the opinion of the Court.

The question in this case is what standard of proof is required by the Fourteenth Amendment to the Constitution in a civil proceeding brought under state law to commit an individual involuntarily for an indefinite period to a state mental hospital.

I.

On seven occasions between 1969 and 1975, appellant was committed temporarily to various Texas state mental hospitals and was committed for indefinite periods to Austin State Hospital on three different occasions. On December 18, 1975, when appellant was arrested on a misdemeanor charge of "assault by threat" against his mother, the county and state mental health authorities therefore were well aware of his history of mental and emotional difficulties.

Appellant's mother filed a petition for his indefinite commitment in accordance with Texas law. The county psychiatric examiner interviewed appellant while in custody and after the interview issued a Certificate of Medical Examination for Mental Illness. In the certificate, the examiner stated his opinion that appellant was "mentally ill and [required] hospitalization in a mental hospital."

Appellant retained counsel and a trial was held before a jury to determine in accord with the statute:

whether the proposed patient is mentally ill, and if so
whether he requires hospitalization in a mental hospital for his own welfare and protection or the protection of others, and if so
whether he is mentally incompetent.

The trial on these issues extended over six days.

The State offered evidence that appellant suffered from serious delusions, that he often had threatened to injure both of his parents and others, that he had been involved in several assaultive episodes while hospitalized and that he had caused substantial property damage both at his own apartment and at his parents' home. From these undisputed facts, two psychiatrists, who qualified as experts, expressed opinions that appellant suffered from psychotic schizophrenia and that he had paranoid tendencies. They also expressed medical opinions that appellant was probably dangerous both to himself and to others. They explained that appellant required hospitalization in a closed area to treat his condition because in the past he had refused to attend outpatient treatment programs and had escaped several times from mental hospitals.

Appellant did not contest the factual assertions made by the State's witnesses; indeed, he conceded that he suffered from a mental illness. What appellant attempted to show was that there was no substantial basis for concluding that he was probably dangerous to himself or others.

The trial judge submitted the case to the jury with the instructions in the form of two questions:

Based on clear, unequivocal and convincing evidence, is Frank O'Neal Addington mentally ill?
Based on clear, unequivocal and convincing evidence, does Frank O'Neal Addington require hospitalization in a mental hospital for his own welfare and protection or the protection of others?

Appellant objected to these instructions on several grounds, including the trial court's refusal to employ the "beyond a reasonable doubt" standard of proof.

The jury found that appellant was mentally ill and that he required hospitalization for his own or others' welfare. The trial court then entered an order committing appellant as a patient to Austin State Hospital for an indefinite period.

Appellant appealed that order to the Texas Court of Civil Appeals, arguing, among other things, that the standards for commitment violated his substantive due process rights and that any standard of proof for commitment less than that required for criminal convictions, i. e., beyond a reasonable doubt, violated his procedural due process rights. The Court of Civil Appeals agreed with appellant on the standard-of-proof issue and reversed the judgment of the trial court. Because of its treatment of the standard of proof, that court did not consider any of the other issues raised in the appeal.

On appeal, the Texas Supreme Court reversed the Court of Civil Appeals' decision..

...the Texas Supreme Court in this case concluded that the trial court's instruction to the jury, although not in conformity with the legal requirements, had benefitted appellant, and hence the error was harmless. Accordingly, the court reinstated the judgment of the trial court.

We noted probable jurisdiction. ... for a writ of certiorari, we now grant the petition.

II.

The function of a standard of proof, as that concept is embodied in the Due Process Clause and in the realm of factfinding, is to "instruct the factfinder concerning the degree of confidence our society thinks he should have in the correctness of factual conclusions for a particular type of adjudication." The standard serves to allocate the risk of error between the litigants and to indicate the relative importance attached to the ultimate decision.

Candor suggests that, to a degree, efforts to analyze what lay jurors understand concerning the differences among these three tests or the nuances of a judge's instructions on the law may well be largely an academic exercise; there are no directly relevant empirical studies. Indeed, the ultimate truth as to how the standards of proof affect decisionmaking may well be unknowable, given that factfinding is a process shared by countless thousands of individuals throughout the country. We probably can assume no more than that the difference between a preponderance of the evidence and proof beyond a reasonable doubt probably is better understood than either of them in relation to the intermediate standard of clear and convincing evidence. Nonetheless, even if the particular standard-of-proof catchwords do not always make a great difference in a particular case, adopting a "standard of proof is more than an empty semantic exercise." In cases involving individual rights, whether criminal or civil, "[the] standard of proof [at a minimum] reflects the value society places on individual liberty."

III.

In considering what standard should govern in a civil commitment proceeding, we must assess both the extent of the individual's interest in not being involuntarily confined indefinitely and the state's interest in committing the emotionally disturbed under a particular standard of proof. Moreover, we must be mindful that the function of legal process is to minimize the risk of erroneous decisions.

A.

This Court repeatedly has recognized that civil commitment for any purpose constitutes a significant deprivation of liberty that requires due process protection. Moreover, it is indisputable that involuntary commitment to a mental hospital after a finding of probable dangerousness to self or others can engender adverse social consequences to the individual. Whether we label this phenomena "stigma" or choose to call it something else is less important than that we recognize that it can occur and that it can have a very significant impact on the individual.

The state has a legitimate interest under its parens patriae powers in providing care to its citizens who are unable because of emotional disorders to care for themselves; the state also has authority under its police power to protect the community from the dangerous tendencies of some who are mentally ill. Under the Texas Mental Health Code, however, the State has no interest in confining individuals involuntarily if they are not mentally ill or if they do not pose some danger to themselves or others. Since the preponderance standard creates the risk of increasing the number of individuals erroneously committed, it is at least unclear to what extent, if any, the state's interests are furthered by using a preponderance standard in such commitment proceedings.

... Loss of liberty calls for a showing that the individual suffers from something more serious than is demonstrated by idiosyncratic behavior. Increasing the burden of proof is one way to impress the factfinder with the importance of the decision and thereby perhaps to reduce the chances that inappropriate commitments will be ordered.

The individual should not be asked to share equally with society the risk of error when the possible injury to the individual is significantly greater than any possible harm to the state. We conclude that the individual's interest in the outcome of a civil commitment proceeding is of such weight and gravity that due process requires the state to justify confinement by proof more substantial than a mere preponderance of the evidence.

B.

Appellant urges the Court to hold that due process requires use of the criminal law's standard of proof – "beyond a reasonable doubt." He argues that the rationale of the Winship holding that the criminal law standard of proof was required in a delinquency proceeding applies with equal force to a civil commitment proceeding.

...Winship recognized that the basic issue – whether the individual in fact committed a criminal act – was the same in both proceedings. There being no meaningful distinctions between the two proceedings, we required the state to prove the juvenile's act and intent beyond a reasonable doubt.

There are significant reasons why different standards of proof are called for in civil commitment proceedings as opposed to criminal prosecutions. In a civil commitment state power is not exercised in a punitive sense. Unlike the delinquency proceeding in Winship, a civil commitment proceeding can in no sense be equated to a criminal prosecution.

In addition, the "beyond a reasonable doubt" standard historically has been reserved for criminal cases. This unique standard of proof, not prescribed or defined in the Constitution, is regarded as a critical part of the "moral force of the criminal law," and we should hesitate to apply it too broadly or casually in noncriminal cases.

The heavy standard applied in criminal cases manifests our concern that the risk of error to the individual must be minimized even at the risk that some who are guilty might go free. The full force of that idea does not apply to a civil commitment. It may be true that an erroneous commitment is sometimes as undesirable as an erroneous conviction. However, even though an erroneous confinement should be avoided in the first instance, the layers of professional review and observation of the patient's condition, and the concern of family and friends generally will provide continuous opportunities for an erroneous commitment to be corrected. ...

Finally, the initial inquiry in a civil commitment proceeding is very different from the central issue in either a delinquency proceeding or a criminal prosecution. In the latter cases the basic issue is a straightforward factual question – did the accused commit the act alleged? There may be factual issues to resolve in a commitment proceeding, but the factual aspects represent only the beginning of the inquiry. Whether the individual is mentally ill and dangerous to either himself or others and is in need of confined therapy turns on the meaning of the facts which must be interpreted by expert psychiatrists and psychologists. Given the lack of certainty and the fallibility of psychiatric diagnosis, there is a serious question as to whether a state could ever prove beyond a reasonable doubt that an individual is both mentally ill and likely to be dangerous.

The subtleties and nuances of psychiatric diagnosis render certainties virtually beyond reach in most situations. The reasonable-doubt standard of criminal law functions in its realm because there the standard is addressed to specific, knowable facts. Psychiatric diagnosis, in contrast, is to a large extent based on medical "impressions" drawn from subjective analysis and filtered through the experience of the diagnostician. This process often makes it very difficult for the expert physician to offer definite conclusions about any particular patient. ...

That practical considerations may limit a constitutionally based burden of proof is demonstrated by the reasonable-doubt standard, which is a compromise between what is possible to prove and what protects the rights of the individual. If the state was required to guarantee error-free convictions, it would be required to prove guilt beyond all doubt. However, "[due] process does not require that every conceivable step be taken, at whatever cost, to eliminate the possibility of convicting an innocent person." Nor should the state be required to employ a standard of proof that may completely undercut its efforts to further the legitimate interests of both the state and the patient that are served by civil commitments.

...We conclude that it is unnecessary to require states to apply the strict, criminal standard.

C.

Having concluded that the preponderance standard falls short of meeting the demands of due process and that the reasonable-doubt standard is not required, we turn to a middle level of burden of proof that strikes a fair balance between the rights of the individual and the legitimate concerns of the state. We note that 20 states, most by statute, employ the standard of "clear and convincing" evidence; states use "clear, cogent, and convincing" evidence; and 2 states require "clear, unequivocal and convincing" evidence.

We have concluded that the reasonable-doubt standard is inappropriate in civil commitment proceedings because, given the uncertainties of psychiatric diagnosis, it may impose a burden the state cannot meet and thereby erect an unreasonable barrier to needed medical treatment. ... To meet due process demands, the standard has to inform the factfinder that the proof must be greater than the preponderance-of-the-evidence standard applicable to other categories of civil cases.

We noted earlier that the trial court employed the standard of "clear, unequivocal and convincing" evidence in appellant's commitment hearing before a jury. That instruction was constitutionally adequate. However, determination of the precise burden equal to or greater than the "clear and convincing" standard which we hold is required to meet due process guarantees is a matter of state law which we leave to the Texas Supreme Court. Accordingly, we remand the case for further proceedings not inconsistent with this opinion.

Vacated and remanded.

MR. JUSTICE POWELL took no part in the consideration or decision of this case.

NOTES AND QUERIES

The case concerns the appropriate level of proof needed to determine whether a person should be held for an indefinite period of time in a state mental hospital. The Court highlights the dual significance of the standard of proof: it relates to the confidence society has in the correction of factual conclusions and the allocation of the risk of error. Given those two factors, which level of proof do you think most addresses those two concerns, a clear and convincing or beyond a reasonable doubt standard? Consider the evidence we reviewed in previous chapters relating to the actual burden of proof these standards require. Why would the preponderance, the lowest level of proof, not suffice?

The Court notes the two main state powers that can be used to protect communities and citizens from themselves: the *parens patriae* power, which deals with those unable to care for themselves and the police power, which allows society to protect itself from dangerous individuals. Which power should govern the law's approach to mentally ill individuals who happen to be dangerous? What do you make of these determinations given the discussion we had in previous chapters regarding the ability to predict future dangerousness?

What do you make of the Court's rationales regarding the need not to require a reasonable doubt standard? For example, commitment admittedly involves questionable expert testimony and uncertainties. Should that mean that we adopt a higher or lower burden of proof? What does adopting a lower burden of proof reveal about the legal system? Do you find it appropriate to assume that concern from friends and acquaintances provides protection from inappropriate detention? Why do we not consider similar concerns in criminal cases? Or, do we actually consider those factors? What about the argument that the civil justice system simply does not seek to punish? What if it in fact does punish. Should that matter? What if there is no known treatment. Should individuals still be detained for their own good?

NOTE ON CRIME AND MENTAL ILLNESS

Commentators often find staggering the prevalence of mental disorders among persons involved with the criminal justice. Those sentiments find ample support from research. For example, the Department of Justice's statistics indicate that sixteen percent of jail and prison inmates have a serious mental illness. Although quite high, researchers deem this figure a likely underestimate of true prevalence rates given that it fails to include those who were not formally diagnosed. When researchers take into account less serious disorders, these estimates rise to 35 percent. Linda A. Teplin, Psychiatric and substance abuse disorders among male urban jail detainees, 84 Am. J. Pub. Health 292, 292-93 (1994). Other estimates are even higher. The largest study to date, sampling 3,332 inmates in New York prisons, found that 80% had severe disorders requiring treatment and another 16% had mental disorders requiring periodic mental health services. Henry J. Steadman, Stanley Fabisiak, Joel Dvoskin, and Edward J. Holohean, A survey of mental disability among state prison inmates, 38 Hosp. and Comm. Psychiatry 1086, 1086 (1987). Some reviews of the literature reveal that 70% of those admitted to correctional facilities have active symptoms of serious mental illness, an impressive statistic that renders jails and prisons the largest mental hospitals in the country. Paul F. Stavis, Why prisons are brim-full of the mentally ill: Is their incarceration a solution or a sign of failure?, 11 Geo. Mason U. Civ. Rts. L. J. 157, 159 (2000).

Serious mental illness is not only prevalent among those who have been convicted. A recent large-scale study of pre-trial arrestees in Brooklyn, New York found that 18.5% had a serious mental disorder (schizophrenia, bipolar disorder, or major depression) and that 3% had a moderately serious mental disorder (post-traumatic stress disorder, depression, or generalized anxiety disorder), for a total of 22.1% having one of the six disorders addressed in the study. Nahama Broner, Stacy S. Lamon, Damon W. Mayrl, and Martin G. Karopkin, Arrested adults awaiting arraignment: Mental health, substance abuse, and criminal justice characteristics and needs, 30 Fordham Urb. L.J. 663, 681-684 (2003). Others offer a different view by estimating that, each year, about 700,000 adults with serious mental illness come into contact with the criminal justice system. Henry J. Steadman, Martha Williams Deane, Joseph P. Morrissey, Mary L. Westcott, Susan Salasin, and Steven Shapiro, A SAMHSA research initiative assessing the effectiveness of jail diversion programs for mentally ill persons, 50 Psychiatric Serv. 1620, 1620 (1999).

The above statistics may seem strikingly high, but they are not surprising to those who study the history of prisons. Historically, jails and prisons always have housed many people with mental illness, but the numbers have increased in the last several decades due to massive deinstitutionalization from mental hospitals, cutbacks in social services, and the unavailability of community and inpatient psychiatric treatment. These factors have been influenced by a renewed increase in what is being deemed as the "criminalization" of the mentally ill. E. Fuller Torrey, Editorial: Jails and prisons-America's new mental hospitals, 85 Am. J. Pub. Health 1611, 1611-12 (1995); H. Richard Lamb and Linda E. Weinberger, Persons with severe mental illness in jails and prisons: A review, 49 Psychiatric Serv. 483, 486 (1998). This process views the mentally ill as becoming criminalized to the extent that some mentally-disordered offenders who should be diverted to the mental health system are instead shunted to the criminal justice system in the hope that they will receive even minimal services unavailable in the community mental health system. The criminalization finds support from research indicating that mentally ill offenders are far more likely to be arrested, detained, and held without bail than others apprehended for the same offense. They also may be more likely to recidivate than non-mentally ill offenders if treatment is not received. See Nahama Broner, Stacy S. Lamon, Damon W. Mayrl, and Martin G. Karopkin, Arrested adults awaiting arraignment: Mental health, substance abuse, and criminal justice characteristics and needs, 30 Fordham Urb. L.J. 663, 663-664, 686 (2003).

The role of substance abuse in mental illness is worth emphasizing when attempting to understand the role of mental illness in crime. Statistics for mental illness typically do not include substance abuse. If that were taken into account, rates of mental illness would be considerably higher. For example, in terms of substance abuse alone, studies estimate that approximately sixty percent of people arrested in major cities in the United States had used drugs at the time of arrest. Arrestee Drug Abuse Monitoring Program, U.S. Dep't of Justice, 1999 Annual Report on Drug Use Among Adult and Juvenile Arrestees 9 (2000), available at http://www.ncjrs.org/pdffiles1/nij/181426.pdf (last visited March. 15, 2004). In 1999, from a sample of 556 male arrestees in New York City, forty-six percent tested positive for cocaine (and "crack" cocaine), forty percent for marijuana, and twenty-two percent for opiates. Overall, the New York City sample revealed that seventy-nine percent tested positive for any of the measured drugs, forty-one percent were at risk for drug dependence, and twenty-three percent were at risk for alcohol dependence based on heavy usages (including binge drinking). When studies include drug charges and/or regular use prior to the alleged offense, nationally, close to seventy percent of inmates are considered substance-dependent. Bruce G. Taylor, Nora Fitzgerald, Dana Hunt, Judy A. Reardon, Henry H. Brownstein, U.S. Dep't of Justice, ADAM Preliminary 2000 Findings on Drug Use and Drug Markets: Adult Male Arrestees 7-18 (2001), available at http://www.ncjrs.org/pdffiles1/nij/189101.pdf (last visited March 15, 2004). Other studies support the need to consider substance abuse along with other mental illnesses. The study of detainees we cited to above, for example, reported that sixty-nine percent of those having a mental disorder also had a substance abuse or dependence problem, substantially higher than the 45% base-rate for substance abuse in the overall sample. Nahama Broner, Stacy S. Lamon, Damon W. Mayrl, and Martin G. Karopkin, Arrested adults awaiting arraignment: Mental health, substance abuse, and criminal justice characteristics and needs, 30 Fordham Urb. L.J. 663, 681-684 (2003).

The role of substance abuse also is important to consider because the risk of violence by the mentally ill is believed to be primarily driven by substance use rather than mental illness; and problems with substance use link to medication non-compliance which, in turn, significantly increases the risk for violence and triples the risk for arrest. Randy Borum, Jeffrey Swanson, Marvin Swartz, and Virginia

Hiday, Substance abuse, violent behavior and police encounters among persons with severe mental disorder, 13 J. Contemp. Crim. Jus. 236, 245 (1997). Just as studies have shown that rates of mental illness and substance abuse are quite high in incarcerated populations, other studies have shown that the two problems frequently co-occur. In contrast to the general U.S. population, where twenty percent of adults with serious mental illness have a co-occurring substance abuse problem, research studies report that almost three quarters of inmates with mental health diagnoses have co-occurring alcohol and drug abuse problems. Karen M. Abram and Linda A. Teplin, Co-occurring disorders among mentally ill jail detainees: Implications for public policy, 46 Am. Psychologist 1036, 1039, 1044 (1991). This holds true among inmates with diagnoses of schizophrenia (fifty-eight percent of whom were drinking and fifty-two percent of whom were using drugs at the time of arrest), those diagnosed with a bipolar disorder (fifty-eight percent using drugs and thirty-three percent using alcohol), and for those diagnosed with a depressive disorder (fifty-four percent using drugs and forty percent using alcohol). Other researchers have found that seventy percent of inmates with serious mental illness were actively abusing substances at the time of incarceration. Mark R. Munetz. Thomas P. Grande, and Margaret R. Chambers, The incarceration of individuals with severe mental disorders, 34 Cmty. Mental Health J. 361, 369 (2001). These rates are significantly higher than rates found among those without a serious mental health diagnosis. For inmates without a serious mental health diagnoses, researchers have found that thirty-two percent were drinking at the time of arrest, and twenty-seven percent were using drugs at the time of arrest. Karen M. Abram and Linda A. Teplin, Co-occurring disorders among mentally ill jail detainees: Implications for public policy, 46 Am. Psychologist 1036, 1039 (1991).

Beyond legal problems, the mentally ill have many additional documented social service needs. These needs tend to be more acute for individuals with co-occurring disorders. Several reviews of the research literature find that the negative consequences of co-occurring disorders in the general population include the following: the inability to manage finances, greater stress and demands on family, increased risk of homelessness, increased vulnerability to infectious diseases such as HIV and hepatitis, increased risk for suicide, and higher rates of hospitalization and other service utilization. Robert E. Drake, Carolyn Mercer-McFadden, Kim T. Mueser, Gregory J. McHugo, and Gary R. Bond, Review of integrated mental health and substance abuse treatment for patients with dual disorders, 24 Schizophrenia Bull. 589, 601-03 (1998); John F. Edens, Roger H. Peters, and Holly H. Hills, Treating prison inmates with co-occurring disorders: An integrative review of existing programs, 15 Beh. Sci. and L. 439, 440 (1997); Jill RachBeisel Jack Scott, and Lisa Dixon, Co-occurring severe mental illness and substance use disorders: A review of recent research, 50 Psychiatric Serv. 1427, 1430-31 (1999). In effect, researchers understand the mentally ill and substance abusing subset of the criminal justice population as exhibiting a host of medical, social, and behavioral pathology that sets them apart from others in the criminal justice system by the highly varied and complex nature of their problems.

SELING v. YOUNG
531 U.S. 250 (2001)

Justice O'Connor delivered the opinion of the Court.

Washington State's Community Protection Act of 1990 (Act) was a response to citizens' concerns about laws and procedures regarding sexually violent offenders. One of the Act's provisions authorizes civil commitment of such offenders. The Act defines a sexually violent predator as someone who has been convicted of, or charged with, a crime of sexual violence and who suffers from a mental abnormality or personality disorder that makes the person likely to engage in predatory acts of sexual violence if not confined in a secure facility. The statute reaches prisoners, juveniles, persons found incompetent to stand trial, persons found not guilty by reason of insanity, and persons at any time convicted of a sexually violent offense who have committed a recent overt act. Generally, when it appears that a person who has committed a sexually violent offense is about to be released from confinement, the prosecuting attorney files a petition alleging that that person is a sexually violent predator. That filing triggers a process for charging and trying the person as a sexually violent predator, during which he is afforded a panoply of protections including counsel and experts (paid for by the State in cases of indigency), a probable cause hearing, and trial by judge or jury at the individual's option. At trial, the State bears the burden to prove beyond a reasonable doubt that the person is a sexually violent predator.

Upon the finding that a person is a sexually violent predator, he is committed for control, care, and treatment to the custody of the department of social and health services. Once confined, the person has a right to adequate care and individualized treatment. The person is also entitled to an annual examination of his mental condition. If that examination indicates that the individual's condition is so changed that he is not likely to engage in predatory acts of sexual violence, state officials must authorize the person to petition the court for conditional release or discharge. The person is entitled to a hearing at which the State again bears the burden of proving beyond a reasonable doubt that he is not safe to be at large.The person may also independently petition the court for release. At a show cause hearing, if the court finds probable cause to believe that the person is no longer dangerous, a full hearing will be held at which the State again bears the burden of proof.

The Act also provides a procedure to petition for conditional release to a less restrictive alternative to confinement. Before ordering conditional release, the court must find that the person will be treated by a state certified sexual offender treatment provider, that there is a specific course of treatment, that housing exists that will be sufficiently secure to protect the community, and that the person is willing to comply with the treatment and supervision requirements. Conditional release is subject to annual review until the person is unconditionally released.

B.

Respondent, Andre Brigham Young, was convicted of six rapes over three decades. Young was scheduled to be released from prison for his most recent conviction in October 1990. One day prior to his scheduled release, the State filed a petition to commit Young as a sexually violent predator.

At the commitment hearing, Young's mental health experts testified that there is no mental disorder that makes a person likely to reoffend and that there is no way to predict accurately who will reoffend. The State called an expert who testified, based upon a review of Young's records, that Young suffered from a severe personality disorder not otherwise specified with primarily paranoid and antisocial features, and a severe paraphilia, which would be classified as either paraphilia sexual sadism or paraphilia not otherwise specified (rape). In the state expert's opinion, severe paraphilia constituted a mental abnormality under the Act. The State's expert concluded that Young's condition, in combination with the personality disorder, the span of time during which Young committed his crimes, his recidivism, his persistent denial, and his lack of empathy or remorse, made it more likely than not that he would commit further sexually violent acts. The victims of Young's rapes also testified. The jury unanimously concluded that Young was a sexually violent predator.

Young and another individual appealed their commitments in state court, arguing that the Act violated the Double Jeopardy, Ex Post Facto, Due Process, and Equal Protection Clauses of the Federal Constitution...

The Washington court reasoned that the claimants' double jeopardy and ex post facto claims hinged on whether the Act is civil or criminal in nature. Following this Court's precedents, the court examined the language of the Act, the legislative history, and the purpose and effect of the statutory scheme. The court found that the legislature clearly intended to create a civil scheme both in the statutory language and legislative history. The court then turned to examine whether the actual impact of the Act is civil or criminal. The Act, the court concluded, is concerned with treating committed persons for a current mental abnormality, and protecting society from the sexually violent acts associated with that abnormality, rather than being concerned with criminal culpability. The court distinguished the goals of incapacitation and treatment from the goal of punishment. The court found that the Washington Act is designed to further legitimate goals of civil confinement and that the claimants had failed to provide proof to the contrary.

As the Washington Supreme Court held and the Ninth Circuit acknowledged, we proceed on the understanding that the Washington Act is civil in nature. The Washington Act is strikingly similar to a commitment scheme we reviewed four Terms ago in Kansas v. Hendricks (1997). In fact, Kansas patterned its Act after Washington's. In Hendricks, we explained that the question whether an Act is civil or punitive in nature is initially one of statutory construction. A court must ascertain whether the legislature intended the statute to establish civil proceedings. A court will reject the legislature's manifest intent only where a party challenging the Act provides the clearest proof that the statutory scheme is so punitive in either purpose or effect as to negate the State's intention. We concluded that the confined individual in that case had failed to satisfy his burden with respect to the Kansas Act. We noted several factors: The Act did not implicate retribution or deterrence; prior criminal convictions were used as evidence in the commitment proceedings, but were not a prerequisite to confinement; the Act required no finding of scienter to commit a person; the Act was not intended to function as a deterrent; and although the procedural safeguards were similar to those in the criminal context, they did not alter the character of the scheme.

We also examined the conditions of confinement provided by the Act. The Court was aware that sexually violent predators in Kansas were to be held in a segregated unit within the prison system. We explained that the Act called for confinement in a secure facility because the persons confined were dangerous to the community. We noted, however, that conditions within the unit were essentially the same as conditions for other involuntarily committed persons in mental hospitals. Moreover, confinement under the Act was not necessarily indefinite in duration. Finally, we observed that in addition to protecting the public, the Act also provided treatment for sexually violent predators. We acknowledged that not all mental conditions were treatable. For those individuals with untreatable conditions, however, we explained that there was no federal constitutional bar to their civil confinement, because the State had an interest in protecting the public from dangerous individuals with treatable as well as untreatable conditions. Our conclusion that the Kansas Act was "nonpunitive thus removed an essential prerequisite for both Hendricks' double jeopardy and ex post facto claims."

With this in mind, we turn to the Court of Appeals' determination that respondent could raise an "as-applied" challenge to the Act on double jeopardy and ex post facto grounds and seek release from confinement. Respondent essentially claims that the conditions of his confinement at the Center are too restrictive, that the conditions are incompatible with treatment, and that the system is designed to result in indefinite confinement. Respondent's claims are in many respects like the claims presented to the Court in Hendricks, where we concluded that the conditions of confinement were largely explained by the State's goal to incapacitate, not to punish. Nevertheless, we do not deny that some of respondent's allegations are serious. Nor do we express any view as to how his allegations would bear on a court determining in the first instance whether Washington's confinement scheme is civil. Here, we evaluate respondent's allegations as presented in a double jeopardy and ex post facto challenge under the assumption that the Act is civil.

We hold that respondent cannot obtain release through an "as-applied" challenge to the Washington Act on double jeopardy and ex post facto grounds. We agree with petitioner that an "as-applied" analysis would prove unworkable. Such an analysis would never conclusively resolve whether a particular scheme is punitive and would thereby prevent a final determination of the scheme's validity under the Double Jeopardy and Ex Post Facto Clauses. Unlike a fine, confinement is not a fixed event. As petitioner notes, it extends over time under conditions that are subject to change. The particular features of confinement may affect how a confinement scheme is evaluated to determine whether it is civil rather than punitive, but it remains no less true that the query must be answered definitively. The civil nature of a confinement scheme cannot be altered based merely on vagaries in the implementation of the authorizing statute.

Our decision today does not mean that respondent and others committed as sexually violent predators have no remedy for the alleged conditions and treatment regime at the Center. The text of the Washington Act states that those confined under its authority have the right to adequate care and individualized treatment. As petitioner acknowledges, if the Center fails to fulfill its statutory duty, those confined may have a state law cause of action. It is for the Washington courts to determine whether the Center is operating in accordance with state law and provide a remedy.

State courts, in addition to federal courts, remain competent to adjudicate and remedy challenges to civil confinement schemes arising under the Federal Constitution. As noted above, the Washington Supreme Court has already held that the Washington Act is civil in nature, designed to incapacitate and to treat. Accordingly, due process requires that the conditions and duration of confinement under the Act bear some reasonable relation to the purpose for which persons are committed.

Whether a confinement scheme is punitive has been the threshold question for some constitutional challenges. Whatever these cases may suggest about the relevance of conditions of confinement, they do not endorse the approach of the dissent, which would render the inquiry into the effects of the statute, completely open ended. In one case, the Court refused to consider alleged confinement conditions because the parties had entered into a consent decree to improve conditions. The Court presumed that conditions were in compliance with the requirements of the consent decree. In another case, the Court found that anecdotal case histories and a statistical study were insufficient to render a regulatory confinement scheme punitive. In such cases, we have decided whether a confinement scheme is punitive notwithstanding the inherent difficulty in ascertaining current conditions and predicting future events.

We have not squarely addressed the relevance of conditions of confinement to a first instance determination, and that question need not be resolved here. An Act, found to be civil, cannot be deemed punitive "as applied" to a single individual in violation of the Double Jeopardy and Ex Post Facto Clauses and provide cause for release.

The judgment of the United States Court of Appeals for the Ninth Circuit is therefore reversed, and the case is remanded for further proceedings consistent with this opinion.

It is so ordered.

Justice Scalia, with whom Justice Souter joins, concurring.

I agree with the Court's holding that a statute, "found to be civil in nature, cannot be deemed punitive" or criminal "as applied" for purposes of the Ex Post Facto and Double Jeopardy Clauses. The Court accurately observes that this holding gives us "no occasion to consider the extent to which a court may look to actual conditions of confinement and implementation of the statute to determine in the first instance whether a confinement scheme is civil in nature." I write separately to dissociate myself from any implication that this reserved point may be an open question. I do not regard it as such since, three years ago, we rejected a similar double jeopardy challenge (based upon the statute's implementation "as applied" to the petitioner), where the statute had not yet been determined to be civil in nature, and where we were making that determination "in the first instance." ...

The short of the matter is that, for Double Jeopardy and Ex Post Facto Clause purposes, the question of criminal penalty vel non depends upon the intent of the legislature; and harsh executive implementation cannot "transform what was clearly intended as a civil remedy into a criminal penalty," any more than compassionate executive implementation can transform a criminal penalty into a civil remedy.

Justice Thomas, concurring in the judgment.

...I write separately to express my view, first, that a statute which is civil on its face cannot be divested of its civil nature simply because of the manner in which it is implemented. ...

The Washington Act does not provide on its face for punitive conditions of confinement, and the actual conditions under which the Act is implemented are of no concern to our inquiry. I therefore concur in the judgment of the Court.

Justice Stevens, dissenting.

...If a detainee comes forward with "'the clearest proof' that 'the statutory scheme [is] so punitive either in purpose or effect as to negate [the State's] intention' that the proceeding be civil, it must be considered criminal." Accordingly, we have consistently looked to the conditions of confinement as evidence of both the legislative purpose behind the statute and its actual effect. ...

The majority in this case, however, incorrectly assumes that the Act at issue is necessarily civil. The issue the majority purports to resolve is whether an Act that is otherwise civil in nature can be deemed criminal in a specific instance based on evidence of its application to a particular prisoner. However, respondent Young's petition did not present that issue. Rather, consistent with our case law, Young sought to introduce evidence of the conditions of confinement as evidence of the punitive purpose and effect of the Washington statute. Properly read, Hudson acknowledges that resolving whether an Act is civil or criminal in nature can take into account whether the statutory scheme has a punitive effect. ....

To be sure, the question whether an Act is civil or punitive in nature "is initially one of statutory construction." However, under the majority's analysis, there is no inquiry beyond that of statutory construction. In essence, the majority argues that because the constitutional query must be answered definitively and because confinement is not a "fixed event," conditions of confinement should not be considered at all, except in the first challenge to a statute, when, as a practical matter, the evidence of such conditions is most likely not to constitute the requisite "clearest proof." This seems to me quite wrong. If conditions of confinement are such that a detainee has been punished twice in violation of the Double Jeopardy Clause, it is irrelevant that the scheme has been previously labeled as civil without full knowledge of the effects of the statute.

In this case, Young has made detailed allegations concerning both the absence of treatment for his alleged mental illness and the starkly punitive character of the conditions of his confinement. If proved, those allegations establish not just that those detained pursuant to the statute are treated like those imprisoned for violations of Washington's criminal laws, but that, in many respects, they receive significantly worse treatment. If those allegations are correct, the statute in question should be characterized as a criminal law for federal constitutional purposes. I therefore agree with the Court of Appeals' conclusion that respondent should be given the opportunity to come forward with the "clearest proof" that his allegations are true.

Accordingly, I respectfully dissent.

NOTES AND QUERIES

Do the alternative remedies, such as the right to treatment under the state statute, sufficiently protect the interests of sex offenders and society? Obviously, Young's criminal record of 6 rapes over the past three decades does not make him a good candidate for release into society. What do you make of the law's approach to keeping him detained? What do you make of the expert testimony that there is no mental disorder that makes a person more likely to offend and that experts are unable to predict dangerousness? Would you feel confident in finding that Young would re-offend if released to society? Is it his criminal record that increases your confidence? Should one be treated differently for past crimes when the debt to society for those crimes already has been paid, such as through incarceration and then release? Why does the Court reject an "as applied" challenge?

Are we to read the Court's opinion as allowing a civil commitment that is in fact punitive? Why would such facts not matter? The Court notes that a § 1983 action against the Center is pending in the Western District of Washington. The Center operates under an injunction that requires it to adopt and implement a plan for training and hiring competent sex offender therapists, to improve relations between residents and treatment providers, to implement a treatment program for residents containing elements required by prevailing professional standards, to develop individual treatment programs, and to provide a psychologist or psychiatrist expert in the diagnosis and treatment of sex offenders to supervise the staff. A Special Master has assisted in bringing the Center into compliance with the injunction. Should the fact that the center currently is not doing what it is suppose to do matter? Note that the Court states that it does not address conditions of confinement and that the fact that the statute is civil decides the case. Reasonable argument? What do you make of the two concurring opinions? Are they really that different from the majority opinion? The dissent would have us focus on the punitive effect of statutes, that lower courts should at least examine that there is no available treatment and the extent to which the confinement is in fact punitive. Are you surprised to find only one lone dissenter on this issue?

The Supreme Court has advanced various justifications for the Double Jeopardy Clause protections and the articulated reasons relevant to the double jeopardy bar on post-decision changes adverse to the defendant, which include: (1) the risk of convicting an innocent by depleting the defendant's resources, *United States v. Scott*, 437 U.S. 82, 91 (1978); (2) the risk that an innocent defendant will be convicted because of "subtle changes" in the government's evidence, *Arizona v. Washington*, 434 U.S. 497, 504 n.14 (1978); (3) the protection of the finality of criminal judgments, Id. at 503; (4) protection against "embarrassment, expense and ordeal" and a "continuing state of anxiety and insecurity," *Green v. United States*, 355 U.S. 184, 187 (1957); (5) protection against "government oppression," *Lockhart v. Nelson*, 488 U.S. 33, 42 (1988); and (6) "protecting a jury's prerogative to acquit against the evidence," *United States v. DiFrancesco*, 449 U.S. 117, 130 n.11 (1980). Given these considerations, was the majority ruling in *Selig* on target?

COMMENT ON CIVIL COMMITMENT

Involuntary civil commitment statutes exist in every state. They allow the state to commit a person against their will if there is proof of a mental disability that poses a substantial threat of serious harm to oneself or others. The threat of harm must be real and present, and the burden of proof to establish dangerousness (to self or others) must be clear and convincing. Proponents of involuntary commitment view this form of treatment as a last resort effort to help the mentally disabled who are imminently dangerous and in desperate need of mental health treatment. Critics of the practice focus on the fact that there is no assurance that such commitment accomplishes the goal of treatment and improvement of mental conditions. See Robert M. Levy and Leonard S. Rubenstein, The Rights of People with Mental Disabilities (1996).

THE SUPREME COURT REVISITS THE COMMITMENT OF SEX OFFENDERS

In *Kansas v. Hendricks*, 117 S. Ct. 2072 (1997), the Court's opinion pointed out that "States have in certain narrow circumstances provided for the forcible civil detainment of people who are unable to control their behavior and who thereby pose a danger to the public health and safety." The Court noted that the Kansas "Act unambiguously requires a finding of dangerousness either to one's self or to others," and then "links that finding to the existence of a 'mental abnormality' or 'personality disorder' that makes it difficult, if not impossible, for the person to control his dangerous behavior." And the Court ultimately determined that the statute's "requirement of a 'mental abnormality' or 'personality disorder' is consistent with the requirements of ... other statutes that we have upheld in that it narrows the class of persons eligible for confinement to those who are unable to control their dangerousness." The *Hendricks* case was made easier in that (1) Hendricks suffered from pedophilia, (2) the psychiatric profession itself classifies that condition "as a serious mental disorder," and (3) he conceded that he cannot "'control the urge'" to molest children. As a result, the Court concluded that this "admitted lack of volitional control, coupled with a prediction of future dangerousness, adequately distinguishes *Hendricks* from other dangerous persons who are perhaps more properly dealt with exclusively through criminal proceedings." The issue that emerged was whether the state needed always to prove that a dangerous individual is completely unable to control his behavior, which the Court addressed in *Kansas v. Crane*, 534 U.S. 407 (2002).

Crane was convicted of lewd and lascivious behavior and pleaded guilty to aggravated sexual battery for two incidents that took place on the same day in 1993. In the first, Crane exposed himself to a tanning salon attendant. In the second, 30 minutes later, Crane entered a video store, waited until he was the only customer present, and then exposed himself to the clerk. Before running out of the store, he grabbed the clerk by the neck, demanded she perform oral sex on him, and threatened to rape her. Following Crane's plea to aggravated sexual battery, the state filed a petition in State District Court to have him evaluated and adjudicated a sexual predator under the SVPA. Several psychologists examined him and determined that he suffered from exhibitionism and antisocial personality disorder. Though exhibitionism alone would not support classification as a sexual predator, a psychologist concluded that the two in combination did place Crane's condition within the range of disorders covered by the SVPA, "citing the increasing frequency of incidents involving [Crane], increasing intensity of the incidents, [respondent's] increasing disregard for the rights of others, and his increasing daring and aggressiveness." Another psychologist testified that Crane's behavior was marked by "impulsivity or failure to plan ahead," indicating his unlawfulness "was a combination of willful and uncontrollable behavior." The State's experts agreed, however, that "respondent's mental disorder does not impair his volitional control to the degree he cannot control his dangerous behavior."

Crane moved for summary judgment, arguing that for his detention to comport with substantive due process the State was required to prove not merely what the statute requires that by reason of his mental disorder he is "likely to engage in repeat acts of sexual violence" but also that he is unable to control his violent behavior. The Supreme Court agreed with Kansas insofar as it argued that *Hendricks* set forth no requirement of total or complete lack of control. *Hendricks* referred to the Kansas Act as requiring a "mental abnormality" or "personality disorder" that makes it "difficult, if not impossible, for the [dangerous] person to control his dangerous behavior." The Court agreed that an absolutist approach was unworkable in that most severely ill people even those commonly termed "psychopaths" retain some ability to control their behavior and insistence upon absolute lack of control would risk barring the civil commitment of highly dangerous persons suffering severe mental abnormalities. But the Court also held that the Constitution does not permit commitment of the type of dangerous sexual offender considered in *Hendricks* without any lack-of-control determination. The Court, however, did not announce a standard, but only noted that it is enough to say that there must be proof of serious difficulty in controlling behavior.

The American Psychiatric Association denies clinical capacity to predict harm and future dangerousness. Importantly, the Court has allowed clinical predictions of dangerous, even if inaccurate, to justify involuntary confinement. *Barefoot v. Estelle*, 463 U.S. 880 (1983). The American Psychiatric Association argues that relevant disorders, such as pedophilia, are not mental illness. Yet, the Court, in *Kansas v. Hendricks*, 117 S. Ct. 2072 (1997) concluded that such controversies allow the states to set the boundaries of civil commitment for disorders. What arguments are to be made against following the advice of those who will be relied on to implement and enforce the law?

Committing the Insane

FOUCHA v. LOUISIANA
504 U.S. 71 (1992)

JUSTICE WHITE delivered the opinion of the Court, except as to Part III.

When a defendant in a criminal case pending in Louisiana is found not guilty by reason of insanity, he is committed to a psychiatric hospital unless he proves that he is not dangerous. This is so whether or not he is then insane. After commitment, if the acquittee or the superintendent begins release proceedings, a review panel at the hospital makes a written report on the patient's mental condition and whether he can be released without danger to himself or others. If release is recommended, the court must hold a hearing to determine dangerousness; the acquittee has the burden of proving that he is not dangerous. If found to be dangerous, the acquittee may be returned to the mental institution whether or not he is then mentally ill. Petitioner contends that this scheme denies him due process and equal protection because it allows a person acquitted by reason of insanity to be committed to a mental institution until he is able to demonstrate that he is not dangerous to himself and others, even though he does not suffer from any mental illness.

I.

Petitioner Terry Foucha was charged by Louisiana authorities with aggravated burglary and illegal discharge of a firearm. Two medical doctors were appointed to conduct a pretrial examination of Foucha. The doctors initially reported, and the trial court initially found, that Foucha lacked mental capacity to proceed, but four months later the trial court found Foucha competent to stand trial. The doctors reported that Foucha was unable to distinguish right from wrong and was insane at the time of the offense. On October 12, 1984, the trial court ruled that Foucha was not guilty by reason of insanity, finding that he "is unable to appreciate the usual, natural and probable consequences of his acts; that he is unable to distinguish right from wrong; that he is a menace to himself and others; and that he was insane at the time of the commission of the above crimes and that he is presently insane." He was committed to the East Feliciana Forensic Facility until such time as doctors recommend that he be released, and until further order of the court. In 1988, the superintendent of Feliciana recommended that Foucha be discharged or released. A three-member panel was convened at the institution to determine Foucha's current condition and whether he could be released or placed on probation without being a danger to others or himself. On March 21, 1988, the panel reported that there had been no evidence of mental illness since admission and recommended that Foucha be conditionally discharged. The trial judge appointed a two-member sanity commission made up of the same two doctors who had conducted the pretrial examination. Their written report stated that Foucha "is presently in remission from mental illness [but] we cannot certify that he would not constitute a menace to himself or others if released." One of the doctors testified at a hearing that upon commitment Foucha probably suffered from a drug induced psychosis but that he had recovered from that temporary condition; that he evidenced no signs of psychosis or neurosis and was in "good shape" mentally; that he had, however, an antisocial personality, a condition that is not a mental disease and that is untreatable. The doctor also testified that Foucha had been involved in several altercations at Feliciana and that he, the doctor, would not "feel comfortable in certifying that [Foucha] would not be a danger to himself or to other people."

After it was stipulated that the other doctor, if he were present, would give essentially the same testimony, the court ruled that Foucha was dangerous to himself and others and ordered him returned to the mental institution. The... State Supreme Court affirmed, holding that Foucha had not carried the burden placed upon him by statute to prove that he was not dangerous, that our decision in Jones v. United States (1983), did not require Foucha's release, and that neither the Due Process Clause nor the Equal Protection Clause was violated by the statutory provision permitting confinement of an insanity acquittee based on dangerousness alone.

Because the case presents an important issue and was decided by the court below in a manner arguably at odds with prior decisions of this Court, we granted certiorari.

II.

Addington v. Texas held that to commit an individual to a mental institution in a civil proceeding, the State is required by the Due Process Clause to prove by clear and convincing evidence the two statutory preconditions to commitment: that the person sought to be committed is mentally ill and that he requires hospitalization for his own welfare and protection of others. Proof beyond a reasonable doubt was not required, but proof by preponderance of the evidence fell short of satisfying due process.

When a person charged with having committed a crime is found not guilty by reason of insanity, however, a State may commit that person without satisfying the Addington burden with respect to mental illness and dangerousness. Such a verdict, we observed in Jones, "establishes two facts: (i) the defendant committed an act that constitutes a criminal offense, and (ii) he committed the act because of mental illness," an illness that the defendant adequately proved in this context by a preponderance of the evidence. From these two facts, it could be properly inferred that at the time of the verdict, the defendant was still mentally ill and dangerous and hence could be committed.

We held, however, that "the committed acquittee is entitled to release when he has recovered his sanity or is no longer dangerous;" i. e., the acquittee may be held as long as he is both mentally ill and dangerous, but no longer. ..In this case, Louisiana does not contend that Foucha was mentally ill at the time of the trial court's hearing. Thus, the basis for holding Foucha in a psychiatric facility as an insanity acquittee has disappeared, and the State is no longer entitled to hold him on that basis.

The State, however, seeks to perpetuate Foucha's confinement at Feliciana on the basis of his antisocial personality which, as evidenced by his conduct at the facility, the court found rendered him a danger to himself or others. There are at least three difficulties with this position. First, even if his continued confinement were constitutionally permissible, keeping Foucha against his will in a mental institution is improper absent a determination in civil commitment proceedings of current mental illness and dangerousness. ... Here, according to the testimony given at the hearing in the trial court, Foucha is not suffering from a mental disease or illness. If he is to be held, he should not be held as a mentally ill person.

Second, if Foucha can no longer be held as an insanity acquittee in a mental hospital, he is entitled to constitutionally adequate procedures to establish the grounds for his confinement. ...

Third, "the Due Process Clause contains a substantive component that bars certain arbitrary, wrongful government actions 'regardless of the fairness of the procedures used to implement them.'" Freedom from bodily restraint has always been at the core of the liberty protected by the Due Process Clause from arbitrary governmental action. "It is clear that commitment for any purpose constitutes a significant deprivation of liberty that requires due process protection." ...

A State, pursuant to its police power, may of course imprison convicted criminals for the purposes of deterrence and retribution. But there are constitutional limitations on the conduct that a State may criminalize. Here, the State has no such punitive interest. As Foucha was not convicted, he may not be punished. Here, Louisiana has by reason of his acquittal exempted Foucha from criminal responsibility.

The State may also confine a mentally ill person if it shows "by clear and convincing evidence that the individual is mentally ill and dangerous." Here, the State has not carried that burden; indeed, the State does not claim that Foucha is now mentally ill.

We have also held that in certain narrow circumstances persons who pose a danger to others or to the community may be subject to limited confinement and it is on these cases, that the State relies in this case.

Furthermore, if Foucha committed criminal acts while at Feliciana, such as assault, the State does not explain why its interest would not be vindicated by the ordinary criminal processes involving charge and conviction, the use of enhanced sentences for recidivists, and other permissible ways of dealing with patterns of criminal conduct. These are the normal means of dealing with persistent criminal conduct. Had they been employed against Foucha when he assaulted other inmates, there is little doubt that if then sane he could have been convicted and incarcerated in the usual way.

III.

It should be apparent from what has been said earlier in this opinion that the Louisiana statute also discriminates against Foucha in violation of the Equal Protection Clause of the Fourteenth Amendment. Jones established that insanity acquittees may be treated differently in some respects from those persons subject to civil commitment, but Foucha, who is not now thought to be insane, can no longer be so classified. The State nonetheless insists on holding him indefinitely because he at one time committed a criminal act and does not now prove he is not dangerous. Louisiana law, however, does not provide for similar confinement for other classes of persons who have committed criminal acts and who cannot later prove they would not be dangerous. Criminals who have completed their prison terms, or are about to do so, are an obvious and large category of such persons. Many of them will likely suffer from the same sort of personality disorder that Foucha exhibits. However, state law does not allow for their continuing confinement based merely on dangerousness. Instead, the State controls the behavior of these similarly situated citizens by relying on other means, such as punishment, deterrence, and supervised release. Freedom from physical restraint being a fundamental right, the State must have a particularly convincing reason, which it has not put forward, for such discrimination against insanity acquittees who are no longer mentally ill.

Furthermore, in civil commitment proceedings the State must establish the grounds of insanity and dangerousness permitting confinement by clear and convincing evidence. Similarly, the State must establish insanity and dangerousness by clear and convincing evidence in order to confine an insane convict beyond his criminal sentence, when the basis for his original confinement no longer exists. However, the State now claims that it may continue to confine Foucha, who is not now considered to be mentally ill, solely because he is deemed dangerous, but without assuming the burden of proving even this ground for confinement by clear and convincing evidence. The court below gave no convincing reason why the procedural safeguards against unwarranted confinement which are guaranteed to insane persons and those who have been convicted may be denied to a sane acquittee, and the State has done no better in this Court.

For the foregoing reasons the judgment of the Louisiana Supreme Court is reversed.

So ordered.

JUSTICE O'CONNOR, concurring in part and concurring in the judgment. [omitted]

JUSTICE KENNEDY, with whom THE CHIEF JUSTICE joins, dissenting.

This is a criminal case. It began one day when petitioner, brandishing a .357 revolver, entered the home of a married couple, intending to steal. He chased them out of their home and fired on police officers who confronted him as he fled. Petitioner was apprehended and charged with aggravated burglary and the illegal use of a weapon. There is no question that petitioner committed the criminal acts charged. Petitioner's response was to deny criminal responsibility based on his mental illness when he committed the acts. He contended his mental illness prevented him from distinguishing between right and wrong with regard to the conduct in question.

The majority's failure to recognize the criminal character of these proceedings and its concomitant standards of proof leads it to conflate the standards for civil and criminal commitment in a manner not permitted by our precedents...

... In Jones we distinguished criminal from civil commitment, holding that the Due Process Clause permits automatic incarceration after a criminal adjudication and without further process. The majority today in effect overrules that holding. It holds that "keeping Foucha against his will in a mental institution is improper absent a determination in civil commitment proceedings of current mental illness and dangerousness." Our holding in Jones was clear and to the contrary. We should not so disregard controlling precedent.

Our respect for the Court's opinion in Jones should be informed by the recognition that its distinction between civil and criminal commitment is both sound and consistent with long-established precedent. First, as described above, the procedural protections afforded in a criminal commitment surpass those in a civil commitment; indeed, these procedural protections are the most stringent known to our law. Second, proof of criminal conduct in accordance with In re Winship eliminates the risk of incarceration "for mere 'idiosyncratic behavior,' [because a] criminal act by definition is not 'within a range of conduct that is generally acceptable.'" The criminal law defines a discrete category of conduct for which society has reserved its greatest opprobrium and strictest sanctions; past or future dangerousness, as ascertained or predicted in civil proceedings, is different in kind. Third, the State presents distinct rationales for these differing forms of commitment: In the civil context, the State acts in large part on the basis of its parens patriae power to protect and provide for an ill individual, while in the criminal context, the State acts to ensure the public safety. ...

The majority's opinion is troubling at a further level, because it fails to recognize or account for profound differences between clinical insanity and state-law definitions of criminal insanity. It is by now well established that insanity as defined by the criminal law has no direct analog in medicine or science. Consistent with the general rule that the definition of both crimes and defenses is a matter of state law, the States are free to recognize and define the insanity defense as they see fit. ...

JUSTICE THOMAS, with whom THE CHIEF JUSTICE and JUSTICE SCALIA join, dissenting.

II.

The Court today concludes that Louisiana has denied Foucha both procedural and substantive due process. In my view, each of these conclusions is wrong. I shall discuss them in turn.

A.

I cannot agree with the Court's conclusion because I believe that there is a real and legitimate distinction between insanity acquittees and civil committees that justifies procedural disparities. Unlike civil committees, who have not been found to have harmed society, insanity acquittees have been found in a judicial proceeding to have committed a criminal act.

In my view, there was no procedural due process violation in this case. Articles of the Louisiana Code of Criminal Procedure, as noted above, afford insanity acquittees the opportunity to obtain release by demonstrating at regular intervals that they no longer pose a threat to society. These provisions also afford judicial review of such determinations. Pursuant to these procedures, and based upon testimony of experts, the Louisiana courts determined not to release Foucha at this time because the evidence did not show that he ceased to be dangerous. Throughout these proceedings, Foucha was represented by state-appointed counsel. I see no plausible argument that these procedures denied Foucha a fair hearing on the issue involved or that Foucha needed additional procedural protections. ...

B.

The Court next concludes that Louisiana's statutory scheme must fall because it violates Foucha's substantive due process rights. I disagree. Until today, I had thought that the analytical framework for evaluating substantive due process claims was relatively straightforward. Certain substantive rights we have recognized as "fundamental"; legislation trenching upon these is subjected to "strict scrutiny," and generally will be invalidated unless the State demonstrates a compelling interest and narrow tailoring. Such searching judicial review of state legislation, however, is the exception, not the rule, in our democratic and federal system; we have consistently emphasized that "the Court has no license to invalidate legislation which it thinks merely arbitrary or unreasonable." Except in the unusual case where a fundamental right is infringed, then, federal judicial scrutiny of the substance of state legislation under the Due Process Clause of the Fourteenth Amendment is not exacting.

In striking down Louisiana's scheme as a violation of substantive rights guaranteed by the Due Process Clause, the Court today ignores this well-established analytical framework. First, the Court never explains whether we are dealing here with a fundamental right, and, if so, what right. Second, the Court never discloses what standard of review applies. Indeed, the Court's opinion is contradictory on both these critical points.

I respectfully dissent.

NOTES AND QUERIES

In this case, Foucha is no longer insane and the state seeks to use an antisocial personality disorder diagnosis to detain him. The Court rules that, since Foucha is no longer insane, the state can no longer justify civil commitment, it must use criminal law to detain him. Note, in this regard, that since he was acquitted, he cannot be punished. The Court ends by noting that the state must prove that the petitioner is insane and dangerous by clear and convincing evidence.

The dissent and majority disagree about the needed standard. The dissent draws on *Jones v. U.S.*, 463 U.S. 354 (1983); and that case is worth considering. In *Jones*, the petitioner was arrested for attempting to steal a jacket from a department store and charged with attempted petit larceny, a misdemeanor punishable by a maximum prison sentence of one year. The court ordered him committed to a public hospital for the mentally ill for a determination of his competency to stand trial. He was found competent to stand trial but found not guilty by reason of insanity and committed to the hospital. He eventually was hospitalized for more than the time he would have spent in prison had he been convicted. He remained in the hospital because the staff found that he suffered from paranoid schizophrenia and, because of that, was still a danger to himself and to others. Although he was acquitted of the crime by reason of insanity, the Supreme Court reasoned that being found not guilty on those grounds indicates that he is dangerous and mentally ill simply because committing a criminal act indicates dangerousness. The Court reasoned that making such a link is not unreasonable and therefore permissible. The Court also rejected his claim that the indefinite commitment was unconstitutional because the proof of his insanity was based only on a preponderance of the evidence, on the grounds that due process is flexible and varies with the demands of particular situations. The Court then concluded that the purpose of commitment following an insanity acquittal, like that of civil commitment, is to treat the individual's mental illness and protect him and society from his potential dangerousness. As a result, the committed acquittee is entitled to release when he has recovered his sanity or is no longer dangerous. And because it is impossible to predict how long it will take for any given individual to recover it was permissible to leave the length of commitment indeterminate, subject to periodic review of the patient's suitability for release. What do you make of the Court's claim that being found to have committed a crime and being committed because of mental illness constitutes an adequate basis for a determination of dangerousness and mental illness, which qualifies an individual for civil commitment?

The dissenting opinions note that states should be allowed to define insanity defenses as they please, and that the case essentially overrules *Jones* by requiring mental illness and dangerousness while *Jones* only required mental illness or dangerousness. Do you suppose, as the dissent does, that the civil commitment process provides enough protection and that there is no need to require protections consistent with criminal procedure requirements? What do you make of the argument that insanity acquittees have in fact committed criminal acts and that reality allows the law to treat them differently from mere civil commitment? The dissent also properly notes that it remains unclear whether we are in fact dealing with fundamental rights and that, if we are not, then the Court should adopt a more deferential review of the state's laws.

Considering Conditions of Confinement

HUDSON v. PALMER
468 U.S. 517 (1984)

CHIEF JUSTICE BURGER delivered the opinion of the Court.

I.

The facts underlying this dispute are relatively simple. Respondent Palmer is an inmate at the Bland Correctional Center in Bland, Va., serving sentences for forgery, uttering, grand larceny, and bank robbery convictions. On September 16, 1981, petitioner Hudson, an officer at the Correctional Center, with a fellow officer, conducted a "shakedown" search of respondent's prison locker and cell for contraband. During the "shakedown," the officers discovered a ripped pillowcase in a trash can near respondent's cell bunk. Charges against Palmer were instituted under the prison disciplinary procedures for destroying state property. After a hearing, Palmer was found guilty on the charge and was ordered to reimburse the State for the cost of the material destroyed; in addition, a reprimand was entered on his prison record.

Palmer subsequently brought this pro se action in United States District Court under 42 U. S. C. § 1983. Respondent claimed that Hudson had conducted the shakedown search of his cell and had brought a false charge against him solely to harass him, and that, in violation of his Fourteenth Amendment right not to be deprived of property without due process of law, Hudson had intentionally destroyed certain of his noncontraband personal property during the September 16 search. Hudson denied each allegation; he moved for and was granted summary judgment. The District Court accepted respondent's allegations as true but held nonetheless, relying on Parratt v. Taylor (1981), that the alleged destruction of respondent's property, even if intentional, did not violate the Fourteenth Amendment because there were state tort remedies available to redress the deprivation, and that the alleged harassment did not "rise to the level of a constitutional deprivation."

The Court of Appeals affirmed ... the District Court's holding that respondent was not deprived of his property without due process. ... It agreed with the District Court ...that the logic of Parratt applies equally to unauthorized intentional deprivations of property by state officials. ... ...

The Court of Appeals reversed the summary judgment on respondent's claim that the shakedown search was unreasonable. ... Because the Court of Appeals concluded that the record reflected a factual dispute over whether the search of respondent's cell was routine or conducted to harass respondent, it held that summary judgment was inappropriate, and that a remand was necessary to determine the purpose of the cell search.

We granted certiorari. We affirm in part and reverse in part.

II.

A.

The first question we address is whether respondent has a right of privacy in his prison cell entitling him to the protection of the Fourth Amendment against unreasonable searches. ... the Court of Appeals held that the District Court's summary judgment in petitioner's favor was premature because respondent had a "limited privacy right" in his cell that might have been breached. The court concluded that, to protect this privacy right, shakedown searches of an individual's cell should be performed only "pursuant to an established program of conducting random searches . . . reasonably designed to deter or discover the possession of contraband" or upon reasonable belief that the prisoner possesses contraband. Petitioner contends that the Court of Appeals erred in holding that respondent had even a limited privacy right in his cell, and urges that we adopt the "bright line" rule that prisoners have no legitimate expectation of privacy in their individual cells that would entitle them to Fourth Amendment protection.

We have repeatedly held that prisons are not beyond the reach of the Constitution. No "iron curtain" separates one from the other. Indeed, we have insisted that prisoners be accorded those rights not fundamentally inconsistent with imprisonment itself or incompatible with the objectives of incarceration. For example, we have held that invidious racial discrimination is as intolerable within a prison as outside, except as may be essential to "prison security and discipline." Like others, prisoners have the constitutional right to petition the Government for redress of their grievances, which includes a reasonable right of access to the courts.

However, while persons imprisoned for crime enjoy many protections of the Constitution, it is also clear that imprisonment carries with it the circumscription or loss of many significant rights. These constraints on inmates, and in some cases the complete withdrawal of certain rights, are "justified by the considerations underlying our penal system." The curtailment of certain rights is necessary, as a practical matter, to accommodate a myriad of "institutional needs and objectives" of prison facilities, chief among which is internal security. Of course, these restrictions or retractions also serve, incidentally, as reminders that, under our system of justice, deterrence and retribution are factors in addition to correction.

We have not before been called upon to decide the specific question whether the Fourth Amendment applies within a prison cell, but the nature of our inquiry is well defined. We must determine here, as in other Fourth Amendment contexts, if a "justifiable" expectation of privacy is at stake. The applicability of the Fourth Amendment turns on whether "the person invoking its protection can claim a 'justifiable,' a 'reasonable,' or a 'legitimate expectation of privacy' that has been invaded by government action."...

Notwithstanding our caution in approaching claims that the Fourth Amendment is inapplicable in a given context, we hold that society is not prepared to recognize as legitimate any subjective expectation of privacy that a prisoner might have in his prison cell and that, accordingly, the Fourth Amendment proscription against unreasonable searches does not apply within the confines of the prison cell. The recognition of privacy rights for prisoners in their individual cells simply cannot be reconciled with the concept of incarceration and the needs and objectives of penal institutions.

Prisons, by definition, are places of involuntary confinement of persons who have a demonstrated proclivity for anti-social criminal, and often violent, conduct. Inmates have necessarily shown a lapse in ability to control and conform their behavior to the legitimate standards of society by the normal impulses of self-restraint; they have shown an inability to regulate their conduct in a way that reflects either a respect for law or an appreciation of the rights of others. Even a partial survey of the statistics on violent crime in our Nation's prisons illustrates the magnitude of the problem. During 1981 and the first half of 1982, there were over 120 prisoners murdered by fellow inmates in state and federal prisons. A number of prison personnel were murdered by prisoners during this period. Over 29 riots or similar disturbances were reported in these facilities for the same time frame. And there were over 125 suicides in these institutions. ...

The administration of a prison, we have said, is "at best an extraordinarily difficult undertaking." But it would be literally impossible to accomplish the prison objectives identified above if inmates retained a right of privacy in their cells. Virtually the only place inmates can conceal weapons, drugs, and other contraband is in their cells. Unfettered access to these cells by prison officials, thus, is imperative if drugs and contraband are to be ferreted out and sanitary surroundings are to be maintained.

Determining whether an expectation of privacy is "legitimate" or "reasonable" necessarily entails a balancing of interests. ... We are satisfied that society would insist that the prisoner's expectation of privacy always yield to what must be considered the paramount interest in institutional security. We believe that it is accepted by our society that "[loss] of freedom of choice and privacy are inherent incidents of confinement."

Respondent acknowledges that routine shakedowns of prison cells are essential to the effective administration of prisons. He contends, however, that he is constitutionally entitled not to be subjected to searches conducted only to harass. The crux of his claim is that "because searches and seizures to harass are unreasonable, a prisoner has a reasonable expectation of privacy not to have his cell, locker, personal effects, person invaded for such a purpose." This argument, which assumes the answer to the predicate question whether a prisoner has a legitimate expectation of privacy in his prison cell at all, is merely a challenge to the reasonableness of the particular search of respondent's cell. Because we conclude that prisoners have no legitimate expectation of privacy and that the Fourth Amendment's prohibition on unreasonable searches does not apply in prison cells, we need not address this issue.

Our holding that respondent does not have a reasonable expectation of privacy enabling him to invoke the protections of the Fourth Amendment does not mean that he is without a remedy for calculated harassment unrelated to prison needs. Nor does it mean that prison attendants can ride roughshod over inmates' property rights with impunity. The Eighth Amendment always stands as a protection against "cruel and unusual punishments." By the same token, there are adequate state tort and common-law remedies available to respondent to redress the alleged destruction of his personal property.

B.

In his complaint in the District Court ... respondent alleged under 42 U. S. C. § 1983 that petitioner intentionally destroyed certain of his personal property during the search. This destruction, respondent contended, deprived him of property without due process, in violation of the Due Process Clause of the Fourteenth Amendment. ...

In Parratt v. Taylor, a state prisoner sued prison officials under 42 U. S. C. § 1983, alleging that their negligent loss of a hobby kit he ordered from a mail-order catalog deprived him of property without due process of law, in violation of the Fourteenth Amendment. The Court of Appeals for the Eighth Circuit had affirmed the District Court's summary judgment in the prisoner's favor. We reversed, holding that the Due Process Clause of the Fourteenth Amendment is not violated when a state employee negligently deprives an individual of property, provided that the state makes available a meaningful postdeprivation remedy.

While Parratt is necessarily limited by its facts to negligent deprivations of property, it is evident, as the Court of Appeals recognized, that its reasoning applies as well to intentional deprivations of property. The underlying rationale of Parratt is that when deprivations of property are effected through random and unauthorized conduct of a state employee, predeprivation procedures are simply "impracticable" since the state cannot know when such deprivations will occur. We can discern no logical distinction between negligent and intentional deprivations of property insofar as the "practicability" of affording predeprivation process is concerned. The state can no more anticipate and control in advance the random and unauthorized intentional conduct of its employees than it can anticipate similar negligent conduct. Arguably, intentional acts are even more difficult to anticipate because one bent on intentionally depriving a person of his property might well take affirmative steps to avoid signalling his intent.

If negligent deprivations of property do not violate the Due Process Clause because predeprivation process is impracticable, it follows that intentional deprivations do not violate that Clause provided, of course, that adequate state postdeprivation remedies are available. Accordingly, we hold that an unauthorized intentional deprivation of property by a state employee does not constitute a violation of the procedural requirements of the Due Process Clause of the Fourteenth Amendment if a meaningful postdeprivation remedy for the loss is available. For intentional, as for negligent deprivations of property by state employees, the state's action is not complete until and unless it provides or refuses to provide a suitable postdeprivation remedy.

Palmer does not seriously dispute the adequacy of the existing state-law remedies themselves. He asserts in this respect only that, because certain of his legal papers allegedly taken "may have contained things irreplacable [sic], and incompensable" or "may also have involved sentimental items which are of equally intangible value," a suit in tort, for example, would not "necessarily" compensate him fully. If the loss is "incompensable," this is as much so under § 1983 as it would be under any other remedy. In any event, that Palmer might not be able to recover under these remedies the full amount which he might receive in a § 1983 action is not, as we have said, determinative of the adequacy of the state remedies.

III.

We hold that the Fourth Amendment has no applicability to a prison cell. We hold also that, even if petitioner intentionally destroyed respondent's personal property during the challenged shakedown search, the destruction did not violate the Fourteenth Amendment since the Commonwealth of Virginia has provided respondent an adequate postdeprivation remedy.

Accordingly, the judgment of the Court of Appeals reversing and remanding the District Court's judgment on respondent's claim under the Fourth and Fourteenth Amendments is reversed. The judgment affirming the District Court's decision that respondent has not been denied due process under the Fourteenth Amendment is affirmed.

It is so ordered.

JUSTICE O'CONNOR, concurring. [omitted]

JUSTICE STEVENS, with whom JUSTICE BRENNAN, JUSTICE MARSHALL, and JUSTICE BLACKMUN join, concurring in part and dissenting in part.

...The Court correctly concludes that the imperatives of prison administration require random searches of prison cells, and also correctly states that in the prison context "[of] course, there is a risk of maliciously motivated searches, and of course, intentional harassment of even the most hardened criminals cannot be tolerated by a civilized society." But the Court then holds that no matter how malicious, destructive, or arbitrary a cell search and seizure may be, it cannot constitute an unreasonable invasion of any privacy or possessory interest that society is prepared to recognize as reasonable.

Measured by the conditions that prevail in a free society, neither the possessions nor the slight residuum of privacy that a prison inmate can retain in his cell, can have more than the most minimal value. From the standpoint of the prisoner, however, that trivial residuum may mark the difference between slavery and humanity...

Personal letters, snapshots of family members, a souvenir, a deck of cards, a hobby kit, perhaps a diary or a training manual for an apprentice in a new trade, or even a Bible – a variety of inexpensive items may enable a prisoner to maintain contact with some part of his past and an eye to the possibility of a better future. Are all of these items subject to unrestrained perusal, confiscation, or mutilation at the hands of a possibly hostile guard? Is the Court correct in its perception that "society" is not prepared to recognize any privacy or possessory interest of the prison inmate – no matter how remote the threat to prison security may be?

I.

Even if it is assumed that Palmer had no reasonable expectation of privacy in most of the property at issue in this case because it could be inspected at any time, that does not mean he was without Fourth Amendment protection. For the Fourth Amendment protects Palmer's possessory interests in this property entirely apart from whatever privacy interest he may have in it...

There can be no doubt that the complaint adequately alleges a "seizure" within the meaning of the Fourth Amendment. Palmer was completely deprived of his possessory interests in his property; by taking and destroying it, Hudson was asserting "dominion and control" over it; hence his conduct "did constitute a seizure."...

The Court suggests that "the interest of society in the security of its penal institutions" precludes prisoners from having any legitimate possessory interests. That contention is fundamentally wrong for at least two reasons.

First, ... Palmer had a legitimate right under both state law and the Due Process Clause to possess the material at issue. That being the case, the Court's own analysis indicates that Palmer had a legitimate possessory interest in the material within the Fourth Amendment's proscription on unreasonable seizures.

Second, the most significant of Palmer's possessory interests are protected as a matter of substantive constitutional law, entirely apart from the legitimacy of those interests under state law or the Due Process Clause. The Eighth Amendment forbids "cruel and unusual punishments." Its proscriptions are measured by society's "evolving standards of decency." The Court's implication that prisoners have no possessory interests that by virtue of the Fourth Amendment are free from state interference cannot, in my view, be squared with the Eighth Amendment. To hold that a prisoner's possession of a letter from his wife, or a picture of his baby, has no protection against arbitrary or malicious perusal, seizure, or destruction would not, in my judgment, comport with any civilized standard of decency.

II.

Once it is concluded that Palmer has adequately alleged a "seizure," the question becomes whether the seizure was "unreasonable." Questions of Fourth Amendment reasonableness can be resolved only by balancing the intrusion on constitutionally protected interests against the law enforcement interests justifying the challenged conduct.

It is well settled that the discretion accorded prison officials is not absolute. ... When, as here, the material at issue is not contraband it simply makes no sense to say that its seizure and destruction serve "legitimate institutional interests."

The Court's holding is based on its belief that society would not recognize as reasonable the possessory interests of prisoners. Its perception of what society is prepared to recognize as reasonable is not based on any empirical data; rather it merely reflects the perception of the four Justices who have joined the opinion that THE CHIEF JUSTICE has authored. On the question of what seizures society is prepared to consider reasonable, surely the consensus on that issue in the lower courts is of some significance. Virtually every federal judge to address the question over the past decade has concluded that the Fourth Amendment does apply to a prison cell. There is similar unanimity among the commentators. The Court itself acknowledges that "intentional harassment of even the most hardened criminals cannot be tolerated by a civilized society." That being the case, I fail to see how a seizure that serves no purpose except harassment does not invade an interest that society considers reasonable, and that is protected by the Fourth Amendment.

The Court rests its view of "reasonableness" almost entirely upon its assessment of the security needs of prisons. Because deference to institutional needs is so critical to the Court's approach, it is worth inquiring as to the view prison administrators take toward conduct of the type at issue here. On that score the Court demonstrates a remarkable lack of awareness as to what penologists and correctional officials consider "legitimate institutional interests." I am unaware that any responsible prison administrator has ever contended that there is a need to take or destroy noncontraband property of prisoners; the Court certainly provides no evidence to support its conclusion that institutions require this sort of power. To the contrary, it appears to be the near-universal view of correctional officials that guards should neither seize nor destroy noncontraband property...

Depriving inmates of any residuum of privacy or possessory rights is in fact plainly contrary to institutional goals. Sociologists recognize that prisoners deprived of any sense of individuality devalue themselves and others and therefore are more prone to violence toward themselves or others. At the same time, such an approach undermines the rehabilitative function of the institution: "Without the privacy and dignity provided by fourth amendment coverage, an inmate's opportunity to reform, as small as it may be, will further be diminished. It is anomalous to provide a prisoner with rehabilitative programs and services in an effort to build self-respect while simultaneously subjecting him to unjustified and degrading searches and seizures."

To justify its conclusion, the Court recites statistics concerning the number of crimes that occur within prisons. ... Thus, the prison homicide rate, it turns out, is significantly lower than that in many of our major cities. I do not suggest this type of analysis provides a standard for measuring the reasonableness of a search or seizure within prisons, but I do suggest that the Court's use of statistics is less than persuasive.

The size of the inmate population also belies the Court's hypothesis that all prisoners fit into a violent, incorrigible stereotype. Many, of course, become recidivists. But literally thousands upon thousands of former prisoners are now leading constructive law-abiding lives. The nihilistic tone of the Court's opinion – seemingly assuming that all prisoners have demonstrated an inability "to control and conform their behavior to the legitimate standards of society by the normal impulses of self-restraint," is consistent with its conception of prisons as sterile warehouses, but not with an enlightened view of the function of a modern prison system.

In the final analysis, however, any deference to institutional needs is totally undermined by the fact that Palmer's property was not contraband. If Palmer were allowed to possess the property, then there can be no contention that any institutional need or policy justified the seizure and destruction of the property. ... To accord prisoners any less protection is to declare that the prisoners are entitled to no measure of human dignity or individuality – not a photo, a letter, nor anything except standard-issue prison clothing would be free from arbitrary seizure and destruction. Yet that is the view the Court takes today. It declares prisoners to be little more than chattels, a view I thought society had outgrown long ago.

III.

The first Clause of the Fourth Amendment provides that "the right of the people to be secure in their persons, houses, papers and effects, against unreasonable searches and seizures, shall not be violated. . . ." Today's holding means that the Fourth Amendment has no application at all to a prisoner's "papers and effects." This rather astonishing repeal of the Constitution is unprecedented . ...

Accordingly, I respectfully dissent..

NOTES AND QUERIES

The Court finds many reasons to affirm that prison cells must be open to searches, which means that there essentially are no rights to privacy in prison cells. This leads the Court to not address searches to harass, simply because searches do not implicate protections based on privacy. What do you make of that line of reasoning? Do you agree with the Court when it finds that society is not ready to recognize expectations of privacy in prison cells? If you do find that there was a privacy interest, the next issue is whether you find the seizure reasonable. Do you think it was? Is harassment in prison reasonable? Given that Palmer actually did have a right to the property, does it make sense that it is not protected by the Constitution? Do you find the dissent's view more convincing when it focuses on the destruction of and right to property?

The Court notes that protection from cruel and unusual punishment could apply to serious cases. It seems to rest, however, on the view that the state does provide post-deprivation hearings and that protection means that intentional and negligent deprivations of property do not violate due process protections. Is this line of reasoning persuasive? What implications arise from this approach?

The dissent turns to psychology and sociology to reveal why the type of prison official misconduct in this case would be counterproductive and, in essence, unreasonable. How persuasive is that argument in light of the legal requirements the case identifies for bringing actions against officials? Given the introductory materials presented at the beginning of this chapter, how effective do you find this approach to dealing with criminal behavior?

CONTROLLING PRISON OFFICIALS

FARMER v. BRENNAN
511 U.S. 825 (1994)

JUSTICE SOUTER delivered the opinion of the Court.

I.

The dispute before us stems from a civil suit brought by petitioner, Dee Farmer, alleging that respondents, federal prison officials, violated the Eighth Amendment by their deliberate indifference to petitioner's safety. Petitioner, who is serving a federal sentence for credit card fraud, has been diagnosed by medical personnel of the Bureau of Prisons as a transsexual, one who has "[a] rare psychiatric disorder in which a person feels persistently uncomfortable about his or her anatomical sex," and who typically seeks medical treatment, including hormonal therapy and surgery, to bring about a permanent sex change. For several years before being convicted and sentenced in 1986 at the age of 18, petitioner, who is biologically male, wore women's clothing (as petitioner did at the 1986 trial), underwent estrogen therapy, received silicone breast implants, and submitted to unsuccessful "black market" testicle-removal surgery. Petitioner's precise appearance in prison is unclear from the record before us, but petitioner claims to have continued hormonal treatment while incarcerated by using drugs smuggled into prison, and apparently wears clothing in a feminine manner, as by displaying a shirt "off one shoulder." The parties agree that petitioner "projects feminine characteristics."

The practice of federal prison authorities is to incarcerate preoperative transsexuals with prisoners of like biological sex, and over time authorities housed petitioner in several federal facilities, sometimes in the general male prison population but more often in segregation. While there is no dispute that petitioner was segregated at least several times because of violations of prison rules, neither is it disputed that in at least one penitentiary petitioner was segregated because of safety concerns.

On March 9, 1989, petitioner was transferred for disciplinary reasons from the Federal Correctional Institute in Oxford, Wisconsin (FCI-Oxford), to the United States Penitentiary in Terre Haute, Indiana (USP-Terre Haute). Though the record before us is unclear about the security designations of the two prisons in 1989, penitentiaries are typically higher security facilities that house more troublesome prisoners than federal correctional institutes. After an initial stay in administrative segregation, petitioner was placed in the USP-Terre Haute general population. Petitioner voiced no objection to any prison official about the transfer to the penitentiary or to placement in its general population. Within two weeks, according to petitioner's allegations, petitioner was beaten and raped by another inmate in petitioner's cell. Several days later, after petitioner claims to have reported the incident, officials returned petitioner to segregation to await, according to respondents, a hearing about petitioner's HIV-positive status.

Acting without counsel, petitioner ...[alleged] a violation of the Eighth Amendment. As defendants, petitioner named respondents: the warden of USP-Terre Haute and the Director of the Bureau of Prisons (sued only in their official capacities); the warden of FCI-Oxford and a case manager there; and the Director of the Bureau of Prisons North Central Region Office and an official in that office (sued in their official and personal capacities). As later amended, the complaint alleged that respondents either transferred petitioner to USP-Terre Haute or placed petitioner in its general population despite knowledge that the penitentiary had a violent environment and a history of inmate assaults, and despite knowledge that petitioner, as a transsexual who "projects feminine characteristics," would be particularly vulnerable to sexual attack by some USP-Terre Haute inmates. This allegedly amounted to a deliberately indifferent failure to protect petitioner's safety, and thus to a violation of petitioner's Eighth Amendment rights. Petitioner sought compensatory and punitive damages, and an injunction barring future confinement in any penitentiary, including USP-Terre Haute.

Without ruling on respondents' request to stay discovery, the District Court ... granted summary judgment to respondents, concluding that there had been no deliberate indifference to petitioner's safety. The failure of prison officials to prevent inmate assaults violates the Eighth Amendment, the court stated, only if prison officials were "reckless in a criminal sense," meaning that they had "actual knowledge" of a potential danger. Respondents, however, lacked the requisite knowledge, the court found. "[Petitioner] never expressed any concern for his safety to any of [respondents]. Since [respondents] had no knowledge of any potential danger to [petitioner], they were not deliberately indifferent to his safety.".

The United States Court of Appeals for the Seventh Circuit summarily affirmed without opinion. We granted certiorari. ...

II.

A.

The Constitution "does not mandate comfortable prisons," but neither does it permit inhumane ones, and it is now settled that "the treatment a prisoner receives in prison and the conditions under which he is confined are subject to scrutiny under the Eighth Amendment." In its prohibition of "cruel and unusual punishments," the Eighth Amendment places restraints on prison officials, who may not, for example, use excessive physical force against prisoners. The Amendment also imposes duties on these officials, who must provide humane conditions of confinement; prison officials must ensure that inmates receive adequate food, clothing, shelter, and medical care, and must "take reasonable measures to guarantee the safety of the inmates."

In particular, as the lower courts have uniformly held, and as we have assumed, "prison officials have a duty . . . to protect prisoners from violence at the hands of other prisoners." Having incarcerated "persons [with] demonstrated proclivit[ies] for antisocial criminal, and often violent, conduct," having stripped them of virtually every means of self-protection and foreclosed their access to outside aid, the government and its officials are not free to let the state of nature take its course. Prison conditions may be "restrictive and even harsh," but gratuitously allowing the beating or rape of one prisoner by another serves no "legitimate penological objective." Being violently assaulted in prison is simply not "part of the penalty that criminal offenders pay for their offenses against society."

It is not, however, every injury suffered by one prisoner at the hands of another that translates into constitutional liability for prison officials responsible for the victim's safety. Our cases have held that a prison official violates the Eighth Amendment only when two requirements are met. First, the deprivation alleged must be, objectively, "sufficiently serious;" a prison official's act or omission must result in the denial of "the minimal civilized measure of life's necessities." For a claim (like the one here) based on a failure to prevent harm, the inmate must show that he is incarcerated under conditions posing a substantial risk of serious harm.

The second requirement follows from the principle that "only the unnecessary and wanton infliction of pain implicates the Eighth Amendment." To violate the Cruel and Unusual Punishments Clause, a prison official must have a "sufficiently culpable state of mind." In prison-conditions cases that state of mind is one of "deliberate indifference" to inmate health or safety, a standard the parties agree governs the claim in this case. The parties disagree, however, on the proper test for deliberate indifference, which we must therefore undertake to define.

B.

1.

Although we have never paused to explain the meaning of the term "deliberate indifference," the case law is instructive. The term first appeared in the United States Reports in Estelle v. Gamble, and its use there shows that deliberate indifference describes a state of mind more blameworthy than negligence. In considering the inmate's claim in Estelle that inadequate prison medical care violated the Cruel and Unusual Punishments Clause, we distinguished "deliberate indifference to serious medical needs of prisoners," from "negligen[ce] in diagnosing or treating a medical condition," holding that only the former violates the Clause. We have since read Estelle for the proposition that Eighth Amendment liability requires "more than ordinary lack of due care for the prisoner's interests or safety."

While Estelle establishes that deliberate indifference entails something more than mere negligence, the cases are also clear that it is satisfied by something less than acts or omissions for the very purpose of causing harm or with knowledge that harm will result. That point underlies the ruling that "application of the deliberate indifference standard is inappropriate" in one class of prison cases: when "officials stand accused of using excessive physical force." ...

With deliberate indifference lying somewhere between the poles of negligence at one end and purpose or knowledge at the other, the Courts of Appeals have routinely equated deliberate indifference with recklessness. ...

That does not, however, fully answer the pending question about the level of culpability deliberate indifference entails, for the term recklessness is not self-defining. ... The criminal law, however, generally permits a finding of recklessness only when a person disregards a risk of harm of which he is aware. The standards proposed by the parties in this case track the two approaches (though the parties do not put it that way): petitioner asks us to define deliberate indifference as what we have called civil-law recklessness, and respondents urge us to adopt an approach consistent with recklessness in the criminal law.

We reject petitioner's invitation to adopt an objective test for deliberate indifference. We hold instead that a prison official cannot be found liable under the Eighth Amendment for denying an inmate humane conditions of confinement unless the official knows of and disregards an excessive risk to inmate health or safety; the official must both be aware of facts from which the inference could be drawn that a substantial risk of serious harm exists, and he must also draw the inference. This approach comports best with the text of the Amendment as our cases have interpreted it. The Eighth Amendment does not outlaw cruel and unusual "conditions"; it outlaws cruel and unusual "punishments." An act or omission unaccompanied by knowledge of a significant risk of harm might well be something society wishes to discourage, and if harm does result society might well wish to assure compensation. The common law reflects such concerns when it imposes tort liability on a purely objective basis. But an official's failure to alleviate a significant risk that he should have perceived but did not, while no cause for commendation, cannot under our cases be condemned as the infliction of punishment.

2.

Our decision that Eighth Amendment liability requires consciousness of a risk is thus based on the Constitution and our cases, not merely on a parsing of the phrase "deliberate indifference." And we do not reject petitioner's arguments for a thoroughly objective approach to deliberate indifference without recognizing that on the crucial point (whether a prison official must know of a risk, or whether it suffices that he should know) the term does not speak with certainty. ...

...Under the test we adopt today, an Eighth Amendment claimant need not show that a prison official acted or failed to act believing that harm actually would befall an inmate; it is enough that the official acted or failed to act despite his knowledge of a substantial risk of serious harm. We doubt that a subjective approach will present prison officials with any serious motivation "to take refuge in the zone between 'ignorance of obvious risks' and 'actual knowledge of risks.'" Whether a prison official had the requisite knowledge of a substantial risk is a question of fact subject to demonstration in the usual ways, including inference from circumstantial evidence, and a factfinder may conclude that a prison official knew of a substantial risk from the very fact that the risk was obvious. For example, if an Eighth Amendment plaintiff presents evidence showing that a substantial risk of inmate attacks was "longstanding, pervasive, well-documented, or expressly noted by prison officials in the past, and the circumstances suggest that the defendant-official being sued had been exposed to information concerning the risk and thus 'must have known' about it, then such evidence could be sufficient to permit a trier of fact to find that the defendant-official had actual knowledge of the risk."

Nor may a prison official escape liability for deliberate indifference by showing that, while he was aware of an obvious, substantial risk to inmate safety, he did not know that the complainant was especially likely to be assaulted by the specific prisoner who eventually committed the assault. The question under the Eighth Amendment is whether prison officials, acting with deliberate indifference, exposed a prisoner to a sufficiently substantial "risk of serious damage to his future health," and it does not matter whether the risk comes from a single source or multiple sources, any more than it matters whether a prisoner faces an excessive risk of attack for reasons personal to him or because all prisoners in his situation face such a risk. If, for example, prison officials were aware that inmate "rape was so common and uncontrolled that some potential victims dared not sleep [but] instead . . . would leave their beds and spend the night clinging to the bars nearest the guards' station," it would obviously be irrelevant to liability that the officials could not guess beforehand precisely who would attack whom.

Because, however, prison officials who lacked knowledge of a risk cannot be said to have inflicted punishment, it remains open to the officials to prove that they were unaware even of an obvious risk to inmate health or safety. That a trier of fact may infer knowledge from the obvious, in other words, does not mean that it must do so. Prison officials charged with deliberate indifference might show, for example, that they did not know of the underlying facts indicating a sufficiently substantial danger and that they were therefore unaware of a danger, or that they knew the underlying facts but believed (albeit unsoundly) that the risk to which the facts gave rise was insubstantial or nonexistent.

In addition, prison officials who actually knew of a substantial risk to inmate health or safety may be found free from liability if they responded reasonably to the risk, even if the harm ultimately was not averted. ...

We address, finally, petitioner's argument that a subjective deliberate indifference test will unjustly require prisoners to suffer physical injury before obtaining court-ordered correction of objectively inhumane prison conditions. "It would," indeed, "be odd to deny an injunction to inmates who plainly proved an unsafe, life-threatening condition in their prison on the ground that nothing yet had happened to them." But nothing in the test we adopt today clashes with that common sense. Petitioner's argument is flawed for the simple reason that "one does not have to await the consummation of threatened injury to obtain preventive relief." Consistently with this principle, a subjective approach to deliberate indifference does not require a prisoner seeking "a remedy for unsafe conditions [to] await a tragic event [such as an] actual assault before obtaining relief."

In a suit such as petitioner's, insofar as it seeks injunctive relief to prevent a substantial risk of serious injury from ripening into actual harm, "the subjective factor, deliberate indifference, should be determined in light of the prison authorities' current attitudes and conduct": their attitudes and conduct at the time suit is brought and persisting thereafter. An inmate seeking an injunction on the ground that there is "a contemporary violation of a nature likely to continue," must adequately plead such a violation; to survive summary judgment, he must come forward with evidence from which it can be inferred that the defendant-officials were at the time suit was filed, and are at the time of summary judgment, knowingly and unreasonably disregarding an objectively intolerable risk of harm, and that they will continue to do so; and finally to establish eligibility for an injunction, the inmate must demonstrate the continuance of that disregard during the remainder of the litigation and into the future. ... If the court finds the Eighth Amendment's subjective and objective requirements satisfied, it may grant appropriate injunctive relief. ...

Accordingly, we reject petitioner's arguments and hold that a prison official may be held liable under the Eighth Amendment for denying humane conditions of confinement only if he knows that inmates face a substantial risk of serious harm and disregards that risk by failing to take reasonable measures to abate it.

III.

IV.

The judgment of the Court of Appeals is vacated, and the case is remanded for further proceedings consistent with this opinion.

So ordered.
JUSTICE BLACKMUN, concurring. [omitted]

JUSTICE STEVENS, concurring. [omitted]

JUSTICE THOMAS, concurring in the judgment.

I adhere to my belief ... that "judges or juries – but not jailers – impose 'punishment.'" "Punishment," from the time of the Founding through the present day, "has always meant a 'fine, penalty, or confinement inflicted upon a person by the authority of the law and the judgment and sentence of a court, for some crime or offense committed by him.'" Conditions of confinement are not punishment in any recognized sense of the term, unless imposed as part of a sentence. As an original matter, therefore, this case would be an easy one for me: Because the unfortunate attack that befell petitioner was not part of his sentence, it did not constitute "punishment" under the Eighth Amendment.

When approaching this case, however, we do not write on a clean slate. Beginning with Estelle v. (1976), the Court's prison condition jurisprudence has been guided, not by the text of the Constitution, but rather by "evolving standards of decency that mark the progress of a maturing society." I continue to doubt the legitimacy of that mode of constitutional decisionmaking, the logical result of which, in this context, is to transform federal judges into superintendents of prison conditions nationwide. Although Estelle loosed the Eighth Amendment from its historical moorings, the Court is now unwilling to accept the full consequences of its decision and therefore resorts to the "subjective" (state of mind) component of post-Estelle Eighth Amendment analysis in an attempt to contain what might otherwise be unbounded liability for prison officials under the Cruel and Unusual Punishments Clause..

Although I disagree with the constitutional predicate of the Court's analysis, I share the Court's view that petitioner's theory of liability – that a prison official can be held liable for risks to prisoner safety of which he was ignorant but should have known – fails under even "a straightforward application of Estelle." In adopting the "deliberate indifference" standard for challenges to prison conditions, Estelle held that mere "inadverten[ce]" or "negligen[ce]" does not violate the Eighth Amendment. "From the outset, thus, we specified that the Eighth Amendment does not apply to every deprivation, or even every unnecessary deprivation, suffered by a prisoner, but only that narrow class of deprivations involving 'serious' injury inflicted by prison officials acting with a culpable state of mind." ...

The question remains, however, what state of mind is sufficient to constitute deliberate indifference under Estelle. Given my serious doubts concerning the correctness of Estelle in extending the Eighth Amendment to cover challenges to conditions of confinement, I believe the scope of the Estelle "right" should be confined as narrowly as possible. ... The Court today adopts the next highest level of subjective intent, actual knowledge of the type sufficient to constitute recklessness in the criminal law, noting that "due regard" is appropriate "for prison officials' 'unenviable task of keeping dangerous men in safe custody under humane conditions.'"

Even though the Court takes a step in the right direction by adopting a restrictive definition of deliberate indifference, I cannot join the Court's opinion. ...I remain unwilling to subscribe to the view, adopted by ipse dixit in Estelle, that the Eighth Amendment regulates prison conditions not imposed as part of a sentence. ...

NOTES AND QUERIES

Recall that *Hudson v. Palmer*, 468 U.S. 517 (1984), had left open a challenge based on 8th Amendment Cruel and Unusual Punishment grounds. The Court identifies the two key prongs of the standard to determine an 8th Amendment violation on such grounds: The deprivation must be serious enough to deprive individuals of "the minimal civilized measures of life's necessities" and the official responsible for the deprivation must do so in actions that are deliberately indifferent to the inmate's health or safety. The Court then defines its view of deliberate indifference, which is a subjective test requiring that the official must both be aware of the facts from which the inference could be drawn that a substantial risk of serious harm exists and that the official actually draw the inference. The Court explicitly rejects an approach that would focus on an objective standard to impose liability. Does that seem like an appropriate approach? What implications arise from the Court's approach?

The majority, and Justice Thomas' concurring opinion, notes that conditions of confinement are not punishment; and the concurring opinion further notes that evolving standards of decency simply are not legitimate factors in this mode of analysis. Does that make sense? Does it seem intuitive that the condition of punishment is the punishment? How does the Court reason otherwise?

Given the introductory materials presented at the beginning of this chapter, how effective do you find this approach to dealing with criminal behavior?

NOTE ON ESTELLE V. GAMBLE

Estelle v. Gamble, 429 U.S. 97 (1976), involved a prisoner who alleged that prison doctors and guards violated his Eighth Amendment right to be free from "cruel and unusual punishment" when they failed to respond to his repeated complaints about a back injury and forced him to continue the labor that was part of his sentence. The record showed that although some of Gamble's (the prisoner's) ailments were addressed, there was evidence that his back injury could have been better diagnosed and treated if an X-ray had been taken. Despite denying Gamble's Eighth Amendment claim, Justice Marshall wrote for the Court that "deliberate indifference to serious medical needs of prisoners constitutes the 'unnecessary and wanton infliction of pain' ... proscribed by the Eighth Amendment." The Court illuminated the meaning of the phrase "deliberate indifference" in two ways. First, it contrasted situations that, while possibly actionable under state tort law, were not actionable under 42 U.S.C. § 1983 because there was no showing of deliberate indifference to a prisoner's medical needs. While §1983 would preclude, in such situations, "intentionally denying or delaying access to medical care" or "intentionally interfering with ... treatment," it would not prohibit mere "negligence in diagnosing or treating a medical condition," or "an inadvertent failure to provide adequate medical care . ..." Similarly, in the case of a prisoner forced to undergo a second attempt at electrocution when a mechanical malfunction interfered with the first attempt, Marshall observed that the Court had rejected a claim of cruel and unusual punishment because the need for the second attempt was "an unforeseeable accident" and an "innocent misadventure." But, the Court noted, had the second electrocution been part of a "single, cruelly willful attempt" or even just "a series of abortive attempts," it would have violated the Eighth Amendment. Second, the Court compared deliberate indifference to professional judgment and strongly implied that the professional judgment standard was to be construed more harshly against the state. The point was made in the Court's summary of a prisoner's rights case: a "doctor's choosing the 'easier and less efficacious treatment' of throwing away the prisoner's ear and stitching the stump may be attributable to 'deliberate indifference' ... rather than professional judgment." Following the decision to its logical conclusion, the Court set a requirement that plaintiffs show the state of mind (the *mens rea*) of the defendant as it attached significance to the subjective motivation of the defendant as a criterion for determining whether the action involves cruel and unusual punishment.

The Supreme Court Revisits the Immunity of Correctional Officers

We have seen that qualified immunity protects public officials from being sued for damages unless they violated clearly established law of which a reasonable official in his position would have known. How would you approach this case? While he was an inmate at the Limestone Prison in Alabama, Hope filed a claim against three guards as a result of an incident that occurred on June 7th, 1995. On that day in June, Hope took a nap during the bus ride to his chain gang's work site. When Hope's work detail arrived, he was slow to get off the bus and onto the job site. After a verbal altercation and a wrestling match with a prison guard, Hope was subdued and taken back to the prison where he was handcuffed and shackled to a hitching post. Hope remained cuffed to the post for seven hours, shirtless, while the sun burned his skin. During those seven hours, he was given no bathroom breaks and only two water breaks. According to his affidavit, one guard even taunted Hope by giving water to some dogs and then kicking over the water cooler, spilling it at Hope's feet. He suffered from dehydration, sunburn, muscle aches, and burns on his wrists where the cuffs became heated from the sun.

Hope filed suit against three prison guards, claiming under 42 U.S.C.A. 1983 that his constitutional rights had been violated through the use of cruel and unusual punishment. The guards moved for summary judgment on the grounds of qualified immunity. The district court entered judgment for the guards on qualified immunity grounds without deciding whether the hitching post constituted cruel and unusual punishment. On appeal, the court found the treatment to violate constitutional norms, but also found that Hope was not entitled to relief because his treatment did not violate clearly established law and, therefore, the defendants were entitled to qualified immunity. In so finding, the Eleventh Circuit reasoned that pre-existing case law must have found a violation on materially similar facts before the law can be clearly established to overcome a qualified immunity defense. The Supreme Court granted certiorari to review the qualified immunity holding.

After determining that the appellate court was correct in ruling the hitching post to be cruel and unusual punishment, the Supreme Court addressed the issue of qualified immunity. The Court reversed the appellate court's ruling and held that the guards were not entitled to an immunity defense. The Court reasoned that prior case law need not be materially similar, and that conduct can violate established law even in novel factual circumstances. The Court held that officials can still be on notice that their conduct violates established law even in novel factual circumstances. The Court phrased the qualified immunity inquiry as follows: Did the state of the law (prior to the conduct at issue) give respondents fair warning that their alleged treatment of Hope was unconstitutional? Given the guard's actions, do you think that they should have known that they were acting inappropriately and violating his rights? The Court determined that the guards should have known, in light of state regulations and a Department of Justice (DOJ) report, that they were violating Hope's clearly established constitutional rights by chaining him to the hitching post and therefore were not entitled to an immunity defense. *Hope v. Pelzer*, 122 S. Ct. 2508 (2002). Do you think that the guards should still be held responsible for their behavior even though there would have been no state regulation and no report from the DOJ?

CONTROLLING MENTAL HEALTH PROFESSIONALS

WASHINGTON v. HARPER
494 U.S. 210 (1990)

JUSTICE KENNEDY delivered the opinion of the Court.

The central question before us is whether a judicial hearing is required before the State may treat a mentally ill prisoner with antipsychotic drugs against his will. Resolution of the case requires us to discuss the protections afforded the prisoner under the Due Process Clause of the Fourteenth Amendment.

I.

Respondent Walter Harper was sentenced to prison in 1976 for robbery. From 1976 to 1980, he was incarcerated at the Washington State Penitentiary. Most of that time, respondent was housed in the prison's mental health unit, where he consented to the administration of antipsychotic drugs. Antipsychotic drugs, sometimes called "neuroleptics" or "psychotropic drugs," are medications commonly used in treating mental disorders such as schizophrenia. As found by the trial court, the effect of these and similar drugs is to alter the chemical balance in the brain, the desired result being that the medication will assist the patient in organizing his or her thought processes and regaining a rational state of mind.

Respondent was paroled in 1980 on the condition that he participate in psychiatric treatment. While on parole, he continued to receive treatment at the psychiatric ward at Harborview Medical Center in Seattle, Washington, and was later sent to Western State Hospital pursuant to a civil commitment order. In December 1981, the State revoked respondent's parole after he assaulted two nurses at a hospital in Seattle.

Upon his return to prison, respondent was sent to the Special Offender Center (SOC or Center), a 144-bed correctional institute established by the Washington Department of Corrections to diagnose and treat convicted felons with serious mental disorders. At the Center, psychiatrists first diagnosed respondent as suffering from a manic-depressive disorder. At first, respondent gave voluntary consent to treatment, including the administration of antipsychotic medications. In November 1982, he refused to continue taking the prescribed medications. The treating physician then sought to medicate respondent over his objections, pursuant to SOC Policy 600.30.

...The Policy has several substantive and procedural components. First, if a psychiatrist determines that an inmate should be treated with antipsychotic drugs but the inmate does not consent, the inmate may be subjected to involuntary treatment with the drugs only if the (1) suffers from a "mental disorder" and (2) is "gravely disabled" or poses a "likelihood of serious harm" to himself, others, or their property. Only a psychiatrist may order or approve the medication. Second, an inmate who refuses to take the medication voluntarily is entitled to a hearing before a special committee consisting of a psychiatrist, a psychologist, and the Associate Superintendent of the Center, none of whom may be, at the time of the hearing, involved in the inmate's treatment or diagnosis. If the committee determines by a majority vote that the inmate suffers from a mental disorder and is gravely disabled or dangerous, the inmate may be medicated against his will, provided the psychiatrist is in the majority.

Third, the inmate has certain procedural rights before, during, and after the hearing. He must be given at least 24 hours' notice of the Center's intent to convene an involuntary medication hearing, during which time he may not be medicated. In addition, he must receive notice of the tentative diagnosis, the factual basis for the diagnosis, and why the staff believes medication is necessary. At the hearing, the inmate has the right to attend; to present evidence, including witnesses; to cross-examine staff witnesses; and to the assistance of a lay adviser who has not been involved in his case and who understands the psychiatric issues involved. Minutes of the hearing must be kept, and a copy provided to the inmate. The inmate has the right to appeal the committee's decision to the Superintendent of the Center within 24 hours, and the Superintendent must decide the appeal within 24 hours after its receipt. The inmate may seek judicial review of a committee decision in state court by means of a personal restraint petition or extraordinary writ.

Fourth, after the initial hearing, involuntary medication can continue only with periodic review. When respondent first refused medication, a committee, again composed of a nontreating psychiatrist, a psychologist, and the Center's Associate Superintendent, was required to review an inmate's case after the first seven days of treatment. If the committee reapproved the treatment, the treating psychiatrist was required to review the case and prepare a report for the Department of Corrections medical director every 14 days while treatment continued.

In this case, respondent was absent when members of the Center staff met with the committee before the hearing. The committee then conducted the hearing in accordance with the Policy, with respondent being present and assisted by a nurse practitioner from another institution. The committee found that respondent was a danger to others as a result of a mental disease or disorder, and approved the involuntary administration of antipsychotic drugs. On appeal, the Superintendent upheld the committee's findings. Beginning on November 23, 1982, respondent was involuntarily medicated for about one year. Periodic review occurred in accordance with the Policy.

In November 1983, respondent was transferred from the Center to the Washington State Reformatory. While there, he took no medication, and as a result, his condition deteriorated. He was retransferred to the Center after only one month. Respondent was the subject of another committee hearing in accordance with Policy 600.30, and the committee again approved medication against his will. Respondent continued to receive antipsychotic drugs, subject to the required periodic reviews, until he was transferred to the Washington State Penitentiary in June 1986.

In February 1985, respondent filed suit in state court under 42 U.S.C. § 1983 against various individual defendants and the State, claiming that the failure to provide a judicial hearing before the involuntary administration of antipsychotic medication violated the Due Process, Equal Protection, and Free Speech Clauses of both the Federal and State Constitutions, as well as state tort law. He sought both damages and declaratory and injunctive relief. After a bench trial in March 1987, the court held that, although respondent had a liberty interest in not being subjected to the involuntary administration of antipsychotic medication, the procedures contained in the Policy met the requirements of due process...

On appeal, the Washington Supreme Court reversed and remanded the case to the trial court. ... that respondent had a liberty interest in refusing antipsychotic medications, the Court concluded that the "highly intrusive nature" of treatment with antipsychotic medications warranted greater procedural protections than those necessary to protect the liberty interests. ... It held that, under the Due Process Clause, the State could administer antipsychotic medication to a competent, nonconsenting inmate only if, in a judicial hearing at which the inmate had the full panoply of adversarial procedural protections, the State proved by "clear, cogent, and convincing" evidence that the administration of antipsychotic medication was both necessary and effective for furthering a compelling state interest.

We granted certiorari and we reverse.

II.

III.

As a matter of state law, the Policy itself undoubtedly confers upon respondent a right to be free from the arbitrary administration of antipsychotic medication. ... By permitting a psychiatrist to treat an inmate with antipsychotic drugs against his wishes only if he is found to be (1) mentally ill and (2) gravely disabled or dangerous, the Policy creates a justifiable expectation on the part of the inmate that the drugs will not be administered unless those conditions exist.

We have no doubt that, in addition to the liberty interest created by the State's Policy, respondent possesses a significant liberty interest in avoiding the unwanted administration of antipsychotic drugs under the Due Process Clause of the Fourteenth Amendment. Upon full consideration of the state administrative scheme, however, we find that the Due Process Clause confers upon respondent no greater right than that recognized under state law.

...The extent of a prisoner's right under the Clause to avoid the unwanted administration of antipsychotic drugs must be defined in the context of the inmate's confinement. The Policy under review requires the State to establish, by a medical finding, that a mental disorder exists which is likely to cause harm if not treated. Moreover, the fact that the medication must first be prescribed by a psychiatrist, and then approved by a reviewing psychiatrist, ensures that the treatment in question will be ordered only if it is in the prisoner's medical interests, given the legitimate needs of his institutional confinement. These standards, which recognize both the prisoner's medical interests and the State's interests, meet the demands of the Due Process Clause.

The legitimacy, and the necessity, of considering the State's interests in prison safety and security are well established by our cases. ...

In Turner [v. Safley (1987)], we considered various factors to determine the reasonableness of a challenged prison regulation. Three are relevant here. "First, there must be a 'valid, rational connection' between the prison regulation and the legitimate governmental interest put forward to justify it." Second, a court must consider "the impact accommodation of the asserted constitutional right will have on guards and other inmates, and on the allocation of prison resources generally." Third, "the absence of ready alternatives is evidence of the reasonableness of a prison regulation," but this does not mean that prison officials "have to set up and then shoot down every conceivable alternative method of accommodating the claimant's constitutional complaint."

Applying these factors to the regulation before us, we conclude that the Policy comports with constitutional requirements. There can be little doubt as to both the legitimacy and the importance of the governmental interest presented here. There are few cases in which the State's interest in combating the danger posed by a person to both himself and others is greater than in a prison environment, which, "by definition," is made up of persons with "a demonstrated proclivity for antisocial criminal, and often violent, conduct." ...

Special Offender Center Policy 600.30 is a rational means of furthering the State's legitimate objectives. Its exclusive application is to inmates who are mentally ill and who, as a result of their illness, are gravely disabled or represent a significant danger to themselves or others. The drugs may be administered for no purpose other than treatment, and only under the direction of a licensed psychiatrist. There is considerable debate over the potential side effects of antipsychotic medications, but there is little dispute in the psychiatric profession that proper use of the drugs is one of the most effective means of treating and controlling a mental illness likely to cause violent behavior.

The alternative means proffered by respondent for accommodating his interest in rejecting the forced administration of antipsychotic drugs do not demonstrate the invalidity of the State's policy. Respondent's main contention is that, as a precondition to antipsychotic drug treatment, the State must find him incompetent, and then obtain court approval of the treatment using a "substituted judgment" standard. The suggested rule takes no account of the legitimate governmental interest in treating him where medically appropriate for the purpose of reducing the danger he poses. A rule that is in no way responsive to the State's legitimate interests is not a proper accommodation, and can be rejected out of hand. Nor are physical restraints or seclusion "alternative[s] that fully accommodate the prisoner's rights at de minimis cost to valid penological interests." Physical restraints are effective only in the short term, and can have serious physical side effects when used on a resisting inmate, as well as leaving the staff at risk of injury while putting the restraints on or tending to the inmate who is in them. Furthermore, respondent has failed to demonstrate that physical restraints or seclusion are acceptable substitutes for antipsychotic drugs, in terms of either their medical effectiveness or their toll on limited prison resources.

We hold that, given the requirements of the prison environment, the Due Process Clause permits the State to treat a prison inmate who has a serious mental illness with antipsychotic drugs against his will, if the inmate is dangerous to himself or others and the treatment is in the inmate's medical interest. Policy 600.30 comports with these requirements; we therefore reject respondent's contention that its substantive standards are deficient under the Constitution.

IV.

Having determined that state law recognizes a liberty interest, also protected by the Due Process Clause, which permits refusal of antipsychotic drugs unless certain preconditions are met, we address next what procedural protections are necessary to ensure that the decision to medicate an inmate against his will is neither arbitrary nor erroneous under the standards we have discussed above. ...

A.

The primary point of disagreement between the parties is whether due process requires a judicial decisionmaker. ...

The procedural protections required by the Due Process Clause must be determined with reference to the rights and interests at stake in the particular case. The factors that guide us are well established. "Under Mathews v. Eldridge (1976) we consider the private interests at stake in a governmental decision, the governmental interests involved, and the value of procedural requirements in determining what process is due under the Fourteenth Amendment."

Respondent's interest in avoiding the unwarranted administration of antipsychotic drugs is not insubstantial. The forcible injection of medication into a nonconsenting person's body represents a substantial interference with that person's liberty. The purpose of the drugs is to alter the chemical balance in a patient's brain, leading to changes, intended to be beneficial, in his or her cognitive processes. While the therapeutic benefits of antipsychotic drugs are well documented, it is also true that the drugs can have serious, even fatal, side effects. ...

Notwithstanding the risks that are involved, we conclude that an inmate's interests are adequately protected, and perhaps better served, by allowing the decision to medicate to be made by medical professionals rather than a judge. The Due Process Clause "has never been thought to require that the neutral and detached trier of fact be law trained or a judicial or administrative officer." Though it cannot be doubted that the decision to medicate has societal and legal implications, the Constitution does not prohibit the State from permitting medical personnel to make the decision under fair procedural mechanisms. Particularly where the patient is mentally disturbed, his own intentions will be difficult to assess and will be changeable in any event. ...

Under Policy 600.30, the decisionmaker is asked to review a medical treatment decision made by a medical professional. That review requires two medical inquiries: first, whether the inmate suffers from a "mental disorder"; and second, whether, as a result of that disorder, he is dangerous to himself, others, or their property. Under the Policy, the hearing committee reviews on a regular basis the staff's choice of both the type and dosage of drug to be administered, and can order appropriate changes. The risks associated with antipsychotic drugs are for the most part medical ones, best assessed by medical professionals. A State may conclude with good reason that a judicial as administrative review using medical decisionmakers. We hold that due process requires no more.

B.

V.

In sum, we hold that the regulation before us is permissible under the Constitution. It is an accommodation between an inmate's liberty interest in avoiding the forced administration of antipsychotic drugs and the State's interests in providing appropriate medical treatment to reduce the danger that an inmate suffering from a serious mental disorder represents to himself or others. The Due Process Clause does require certain essential procedural protections, all of which are Washington Supreme Court is reversed, and the case is remanded for further proceedings not inconsistent with this opinion.

It is so ordered.
CONCUR: JUSTICE BLACKMUN, concurring. [omitted]

JUSTICE STEVENS, with whom JUSTICE BRENNAN and JUSTICE MARSHALL join, concurring in part and dissenting in part.

I.

The Court acknowledges that under the Fourteenth Amendment "respondent possesses a significant liberty interest in avoiding the unwanted administration of antipsychotic drugs," but then virtually ignores the several dimensions of that liberty. They are both physical and intellectual. Every violation of a person's bodily integrity is an invasion of his or her liberty. The invasion is particularly intrusive if it creates a substantial risk of permanent injury and premature death. Moreover, any such action is degrading if it overrides a competent person's choice to reject a specific form of medical treatment. And when the purpose or effect of forced drugging is to alter the will and the mind of the subject, it constitutes a deprivation of liberty in the most literal and fundamental sense. ...

The record of one of Walter Harper's involuntary medication hearings at the Special Offense Center (SOC) notes: "Inmate Harper stated he would rather die than take medication." That Harper would be so opposed to taking psychotropic drugs is not surprising: as the Court acknowledges, these drugs both "alter the chemical balance in a patient's brain" and can cause irreversible and fatal side effects.

The Washington Supreme Court properly equated the intrusiveness of this mind altering drug treatment with electroconvulsive therapy or psychosurgery. ... There is no doubt, as the State Supreme

Court and other courts that have analyzed the issue have concluded, that a competent individual's right to refuse such medication is a fundamental liberty interest deserving the highest order of protection.

II.

Arguably, any of three quite different state interests might be advanced to justify a deprivation of this liberty interest. The State might seek to compel Harper to submit to a mind altering drug treatment program as punishment for the crime he committed in 1976, as a "cure" for his mental illness, or as a mechanism to maintain order in the prison. The Court today recognizes Harper's liberty interest only as against the first justification.

Forced administration of antipsychotic medication may not be used as a form of punishment. ...

The Court does not suggest that psychotropic drugs... may be forced on prisoners as a necessary condition of their incarceration or as a disciplinary measure. Rather, it holds:

> Given the requirements of the prison environment, the Due Process Clause permits the State to treat a prison inmate who has a serious mental illness with anti-psychotic drugs against his will, if the inmate is dangerous to himself or others and the treatment is in the inmate's medical interest. Policy 600.30 comports with these requirements; we therefore reject respondent's contention that its substantive standards are deficient under the Constitution.

Crucial to the Court's exposition of this substantive due process standard is the condition that these drugs "may be administered for no purpose other than treatment," and that "the treatment in question will be ordered only if it is in the prisoner's medical interests, given the legitimate needs of his institutional confinement." Thus, although the Court does not find, as Harper urges, an absolute liberty interest of a competent person to refuse psychotropic drugs, it does recognize that the substantive protections of the Due Process Clause limit the forced administration of psychotropic drugs to all but those inmates whose medical interests would be advanced by such treatment.

... Whether or not the State's alleged interest in providing medically beneficial treatment to those in its custody who are mentally ill may alone override the refusal of psychotropic drugs by a presumptively competent person, a plain reading of Policy 600.30 reveals that it does not meet the substantive standard set forth by the Court. ...

Although any application of Policy 600.30 requires a medical judgment as to a prisoner's mental condition and the cause of his behavior, the Policy does not require a determination that forced medication would advance his medical interest. Use of psychotropic drugs, the State readily admits, serves to ease the institutional and administrative burdens of maintaining prison security and provides a means of managing an unruly prison population and preventing property damage. By focusing on the risk that the inmate's mental condition poses to other people and property, the Policy allows the State to exercise either parens patriae authority or police authority to override a prisoner's liberty interest in refusing psychotropic drugs. Thus, most unfortunately, there is simply no basis for the Court's assertion that medication under the Policy must be to advance the prisoner's medical interest.

Policy 600.30 sweepingly sacrifices the inmate's substantive liberty interest to refuse psychotropic drugs, regardless of his medical interests, to institutional and administrative concerns. ...

The State advances security concerns as a justification for forced medication in two distinct circumstances. A SOC Policy provision not at issue in this case permits 72 hours of involuntary medication on an emergency basis when "an inmate is suffering from a mental disorder and as a result of that disorder presents an imminent likelihood of serious harm to himself or others." In contrast to the imminent danger of injury that triggers the emergency medication provisions, a general risk of illness-induced injury or property damage – evidenced by no more than past behavior – allows long-term, involuntary medication of an inmate with psychotropic drugs under Policy 600.30. This ongoing interest in security and management is a penological concern of a constitutionally distinct magnitude from the necessity of responding to emergencies. It is difficult to imagine what, if any, limits would restrain such a general concern of prison administrators who believe that prison environments are, "'by definition,' . . . made up of persons with 'a demonstrated proclivity for antisocial criminal, and often violent, conduct.'" A rule that allows prison administrators to address potential security risks by forcing psychotropic drugs on mentally ill inmates for prolonged periods is unquestionably an "exaggerated response" to that concern.

...The flaw in Washington's Policy 600.30 – and the basic error in the Court's opinion today – is the failure to divorce from each other the two justifications for forced medication and to consider the extent to which the Policy is reasonably related to either interest. The State, and arguably the Court, allows the SOC to blend the state interests in responding to emergencies and in convenient prison administration with the individual's interest in receiving beneficial medical treatment. The result is a muddled rationale that allows the "exaggerated response" of forced psychotropic medication on the basis of purely institutional concerns. So serving institutional convenience eviscerates the inmate's substantive liberty interest in the integrity of his body and mind.

III.

The procedures of Policy 600.30 are also constitutionally deficient. Whether or not the State ever may order involuntary administration of psychotropic drugs to a mentally ill person who has been committed to its custody but has not been declared incompetent, it is at least clear that any decision approving such drugs must be made by an impartial professional concerned not with institutional interests, but only with the individual's best interests. The critical defect in Policy 600.30 is the failure to have the treatment decision made or reviewed by an impartial person or tribunal.

These decisionmakers have two disqualifying conflicts of interest. First, the panel members must review the work of treating physicians who are their colleagues and who, in turn, regularly review their decisions. Such an in-house system pits the interests of an inmate who objects to forced medication against the judgment not only of his doctor, but often his doctor's colleagues. Furthermore, the Court's conclusion that "none of the hearing committee members may be involved in the inmate's current treatment or diagnosis," overlooks the fact that Policy 600.30 allows a treating psychiatrist to participate in all but the initial 7-day medication approval...

Second, the panel members, as regular staff of the Center, must be concerned not only with the inmate's best medical interests, but also with the most convenient means of controlling the mentally disturbed inmate. The mere fact that a decision is made by a doctor does not make it "certain that professional judgment in fact was exercised." The structure of the SOC committee virtually insures that it will not be. While the initial inquiry into the mental bases for an inmate's behavior is medical, the ultimate medication decision under Policy 600.30 turns on an assessment of the risk that an inmate's condition imposes on the institution. The prescribing physician and each member of the review committee must therefore wear two hats. This hybrid function disables the independent exercise of each decisionmaker's professional judgment. The structure of the review committee further confuses the objective of the inquiry; two of the committee members are not trained or licensed to prescribe psychotropic drugs, and one has no medical expertise at all. The trump by institutional interests is dramatized by the fact that appeals of committee decisions under the Policy are made solely to the SOC Superintendent.

The institutional bias that is inherent in the identity of the decisionmakers is unchecked by other aspects of Policy 600.30. The committee need not consider whether less intrusive procedures would be effective, or even if the prescribed medication would be beneficial to the prisoner, before approving involuntary medication. Findings regarding the severity or the probability of potential side effects of drugs and dosages are not required. And, although the Policy does not prescribe a standard of proof necessary for any factual determination upon which a medication decision rests, the Court gratuitously advises that the "clear, cogent, and convincing" standard adopted by the State Supreme Court would be unnecessary.

Nor is the 600.30 hearing likely to raise these issues fairly and completely. An inmate recommended for involuntary medication is no more capable of "'speaking effectively for himself'" on these "issues which are 'complex or otherwise difficult to develop or present'" than an inmate recommended for transfer to a mental hospital. Although single doses of some psychotropic drugs are designed to be effective for a full month, the inmate may not refuse the very medication he is contesting until 24 hours before his hearing. Policy 600.30 also does not allow the inmate to be represented by counsel at hearings, but only to have present an adviser, who is appointed by the SOC. These advisers, of questionable loyalties and efficacy, cannot provide the "independent assistance" required for an inmate fairly to understand and participate in the hearing process. In addition, although the Policy gives the inmate a "limitable right to present testimony through his own witnesses and to confront and cross-examine witnesses," in the next paragraph it takes that right away for reasons that "include, but are not limited to such things as irrelevance, lack of necessity, redundancy, possible reprisals, or other reasons relating to institutional interests of security, order, and rehabilitation." Finally, because Policy 600.30 provides a hearing only for the 7-day committee, and just a paper record for the long-term committee, the inmate has no opportunity at all to present his objections to the more crucial decision to medicate him on a long-term basis.

I continue to believe that "even the inmate retains an unalienable interest in liberty – at the very minimum the right to be treated with dignity – which the Constitution may never ignore." A competent individual's right to refuse psychotropic medication is an aspect of liberty requiring the highest order of protection under the Fourteenth Amendment. ...

Notes and Queries

The case deals directly with the due process protections needed for treating mentally ill prisoners with anti-psychotic medications. The case gains significance to the extent that it provides the factors used to determine the reasonableness of challenged prison regulations. There must be a valid, rational connection between the prison regulation and the legitimate governmental interest put forward to justify it. A court must consider the impact accommodation of the asserted constitutional right will have on guards and other inmates, and on the allocation of prison resources generally. And the absence of ready alternatives is evidence of the reasonableness of a prison regulation. How deferential do you find this approach to evaluating the legitimacy of prison regulations? What implications arise from this approach? Consider the significance of this approach in light of the cases we have reviewed that provided immunity for officials. Taken together, what do these cases mean?

Harper is competent and he does not want the medication. Why does his competency not factor into the majority's analysis? Are you concerned about possible institutional bias? What limits does the legal standard place on addressing security requirements through medication?

Note on Youngberg v. Romeo

The mentally ill, retarded and disabled have been the subject of many cases involving the right to treatment. The right-to-treatment movement has raised a number of federal claims, and these claims typically have fallen under one of three categories: 1) due process claims; 2) claims under the Developmental Disabilities Bill of Rights and/or Mental Health Rights and Advocacy Bill of Rights; and 3) claims based on the Americans with Disabilities Act and/or the Rehabilitation Act. These claims have not fared as well as was hoped, particularly because of the leading Supreme Court case, *Youngberg v. Romeo*, 457 U.S. 307 (1982).

The plaintiff in this case was a 33 years-old who had the mental capacity of an 18-month-old child, with an I. Q. between 8 and 10. He could not talk and lacked the most basic self-care skills. Until he was 26, he had lived with his parents. Within two weeks of his father's death, his mother sought his temporary admission to a nearby hospital because she was unable to care for him or control his violence. He was then committed to the hospital. At the hospital, he was injured on numerous occasions, both by his own violence and by the reactions of other residents to him. His mother became concerned about these injuries. After objecting to his treatment several times, she filed this complaint alleging that Romeo had suffered injuries on at least sixty-three occasions. After the suit was brought, he was transferred from his ward to the hospital for treatment of a broken arm. While in the infirmary, and by order of a doctor, he was physically restrained during portions of each day to protect Romeo and others in the hospital. Although he normally would have returned to his ward when his arm healed, the staff involved in the litigation agreed that he should remain in the hospital due to the pending lawsuit. His mother then alleged that the hospital failed to provide him with appropriate "treatment or programs for his mental retardation." An appellate court found that the involuntarily committed retain liberty interests in freedom of movement and in personal security. These were "fundamental liberties" that can be limited only by an "overriding, non-punitive" state interest. It further found that the involuntarily committed have a liberty interest in habilitation designed to "treat" their mental retardation. (This was difficult in this case in that all agreed that he would never leave the institution and be able to care for himself.) The court, however, could not agree on the relevant standard to be used in determining whether Romeo's rights had been violated.

The Supreme Court agreed that Romeo had a right to safe conditions and right to freedom from bodily restraints, based on due process grounds. The Court also agreed that he did have a right to treatment. The right, however, was very limited. Finding that involuntarily institutionalized individuals were only entitled to minimally adequate or reasonable training to ensure safety and freedom from undue restraint, the Court effectively limited the applicability of a due process right to treatment to the most egregiously apparent denials of care. Furthermore, the Court held that in determining whether adequate or reasonable treatment had been provided the courts were generally to defer to the judgment of professionals, including the very professionals charged with providing inadequate care. The Court reasoned that decisions made by the appropriate professional are entitled to a presumption of correctness in order to enable institutions for the mentally ill to function. The Court recognized that these institutions are often overcrowded and understaffed and that a single professional may have to make decisions with respect to a number of residents with widely varying needs and problems in the course of a normal day. The administrators, and particularly professional personnel, the Court argued, should not be required to make each decision in the shadow of an action for damages. For a review of statutory standards and state approaches to the right to treatment, see Katie Eyer, Litigating for treatment: The use of state laws and constitutions in obtaining treatment rights for individuals with mental illness, 28 N.Y.U. Rev. L. and Soc. Change 1 (2003).

Controlling After Incarceration or Commitment: Revoking Probation

BLACK v. ROMANO
471 U.S. 606 (1985)

JUSTICE O'CONNOR delivered the opinion of the Court.

I.

On November 15, 1976, respondent Nicholas Romano pleaded guilty in the Circuit Court of Laclede County, State of Missouri, to two counts of transferring and selling a controlled substance. The charges resulted from Romano's attempt to trade 26 pounds of marihuana, which he had harvested, refined, and packaged, for what he thought was opium. After the Missouri Department of Probation and Parole completed a presentence investigation, the trial judge held a sentencing hearing on April 13, 1977. Romano's attorney urged the court to order probation. He argued that the offenses had not involved any victim, that Romano had no previous felony convictions, and that, except for running a stop sign, he had not violated the law after his arrest on the controlled substance charges. Both the Probation Department and the prosecutor opposed probation. The trial judge nonetheless concluded that probation was appropriate because the underlying charges did not involve an offense against the person.

The judge imposed concurrent sentences of 20 years on each count, suspended execution of the sentences, and placed Romano on probation for 5 years. The trial judge observed that Romano appeared to "have an uphill run on this probation," given the presentence report and the fact that his "past track record [was] not too good." The trial judge warned that if any of the conditions of probation were violated, he would revoke probation and order Romano imprisoned under the terms of the suspended sentence. Only two months after being placed on probation, Romano was arrested for leaving the scene of an automobile accident. ... a felony punishable by up to five years' imprisonment. The information alleged that Romano had struck and seriously injured a pedestrian with his automobile and, knowing that such injury had occurred, "unlawfully and feloniously" left the scene without stopping or reporting the accident.

On July 18, 1977, the judge who had sentenced Romano on the controlled substance charges held a probation revocation hearing. Several witnesses gave testimony indicating that Romano had run over a pedestrian in front of a tavern and then had driven away. Romano offered no explanation of his involvement in the accident. Instead, his counsel challenged the credibility of the witnesses, argued that the evidence did not justify a finding that Romano had violated his probation conditions, and requested the court to continue the defendant's probation. Neither Romano nor his two lawyers otherwise proposed or requested alternatives to incarceration. The judge found that Romano had violated his probation conditions by leaving the scene of an accident, revoked probation, and ordered execution of the previously imposed sentence. Although the judge prepared a memorandum of his findings, he did not expressly indicate that he had considered alternatives to revoking probation. On October 12, 1977, the State filed an amended information reducing the charges arising from the automobile accident to the misdemeanor of reckless and careless driving. Romano was convicted on the reduced charges and ordered to pay a $ 100 fine.

Romano was incarcerated in state prison following the revocation of his probation. After unsuccessfully seeking postconviction relief in state court, he filed a petition for a writ of habeas corpus in Federal District Court. The habeas petition, filed in November 1982, alleged that the state judge had violated the requirements of due process by revoking respondent's probation without considering alternatives to incarceration. The District Court agreed, and held that under the circumstances "alternatives to incarceration should have been considered, on the record, and if [the trial judge] decided still to send Romano to jail, he should have given the reasons why the alternatives were inappropriate." Because Romano had been imprisoned for more than five years and had been paroled after he filed his federal habeas petition, the District Court concluded that the proper relief was to order him released from the custody of the Missouri Department of Probation and Parole. The Court of Appeals agreed that due process required the trial judge to consider alternatives to incarceration in the probation revocation proceeding and to indicate on the record that he had done so.

II.

The Due Process Clause of the Fourteenth Amendment imposes procedural and substantive limits on the revocation of the conditional liberty created by probation. ...

A.

In identifying the procedural requirements of due process, we have observed that the decision to revoke probation typically involves two distinct components: (1) a retrospective factual question whether the probationer has violated a condition of probation; and (2) a discretionary determination by the sentencing authority whether violation of a condition warrants revocation of probation. Probationers have an obvious interest in retaining their conditional liberty, and the State also has an interest in assuring that revocation proceedings are based on accurate findings of fact and, where appropriate, the informed exercise of discretion. Our previous cases have sought to accommodate these interests while avoiding the imposition of rigid requirements that would threaten the informal nature of probation revocation proceedings or interfere with exercise of discretion by the sentencing authority.

Gagnon concluded that ... the final revocation of probation must be preceded by a hearing, although the factfinding body need not be composed of judges or lawyers. The probationer is entitled to written notice of the claimed violations of his probation; disclosure of the evidence against him; an opportunity to be heard in person and to present witnesses and documentary evidence; a neutral hearing body; and a written statement by the factfinder as to the evidence relied on and the reasons for revoking probation. The probationer is also entitled to cross-examine adverse witnesses, unless the hearing body specifically finds good cause for not allowing confrontation. Finally, the probationer has a right to the assistance of counsel in some circumstances. One point relevant to the present case is immediately evident from a review of the minimum procedures set forth in some detail in Gagnon and Morrissey: the specified procedures do not include an express statement by the factfinder that alternatives to incarceration were considered and rejected.

We do not question the desirability of considering possible alternatives to imprisonment before probation is revoked. Nonetheless, incarceration for violation of a probation condition is not constitutionally limited to circumstances where that sanction represents the only means of promoting the State's interest in punishment and deterence. ...

B.

III.

The decision to revoke Romano's probation satisfied the requirements of due process. In conformance with Gagnon and Morrissey, the State afforded respondent a final revocation hearing. The courts below concluded, and we agree, that there was sufficient evidence to support the state court's finding that Romano had violated the conditions of his probation. The memorandum prepared by the sentencing court and the transcript of the hearing provided the necessary written statement explaining the evidence relied upon and the reason for the decision to revoke probation. Romano does not dispute that he had a full opportunity to present mitigating factors to the sentencing judge and to propose alternatives to incarceration. The procedures required by the Due Process Clause of the Fourteenth Amendment were afforded in this case, even though the state judge did not explain on the record his consideration and rejection of alternatives to incarceration.

...The judgment of the Court of Appeals is reversed.

It is so ordered.
JUSTICE POWELL took no part in the consideration or decision of this case.

JUSTICE MARSHALL, with whom JUSTICE BRENNAN joins, concurring. [omitted]

Notes and Queries

This case speaks to the issue of the power of the state over those placed on probation. Part III of the opinion notes the reasons this case complies with due process requirements. What standard can you discern? How well does the standard you envision include the factors Romano claims? How legitimate were his claims?

Given the introductory materials presented at the beginning of this chapter, how effective do you find this approach to dealing with criminal behavior? Does the research indicate that the state should foster an approach that addresses Romano's claims?

Controlling After Incarceration or Commitment: Notifying Communities

DOE v. PORITZ
662 A.2d 367 (NJ Sup. Ct., 1995)

Chief Justice Wilentz delivered the opinion of the court.

I.

The Legislative Purpose: Addressing the Problem of Repetitive Sex Offenders

The challenged laws before us in this case have two basic provisions. First, they require registration with law enforcement authorities of certain convicted sex offenders and spell out the offenses that trigger the registration requirement, registration of those convicted prior to their passage limited to offenders found to have repetitive and compulsive characteristics. Second, they provide for notice of the presence of such offenders in the community, the scope of that notice measured by the likelihood that such offenders will commit another sex offense: where the risk of such reoffense is low, only law enforcement authorities are notified; where it is moderate, institutions and organizations having the responsibility to care for and supervise children and women are notified; and where the risk is high, those members of the public likely to encounter the offender are notified.

Based on statistical and other studies the Legislature could have found, and presumably did find, the following facts, essentially reflected in its statement of purpose, and its enactment of the laws:

> Studies describing recidivism by sex offenders indicate the severity of the problem the Legislature addressed in Megan's Law. Studies report that rapists recidivate at a rate of 7 to 35%; offenders who molest young girls, at a rate of 10 to 29%, and offenders who molest young boys, at a rate of 13 to 40%. Further, of those who recidivate, many commit their second crime after a long interval without offense. In cases of sex offenders, as compared to other criminals, the propensity to commit crimes does not decrease over time. ... In one study, 48% of the recidivist sex offenders repeated during the first five years and 52% during the next 17 years. ...
>
> As Doe acknowledges, successful treatment of sex offenders appears to be rare. ...

Further information gleaned from similar studies strongly reinforces the foregoing:

> Sexual crimes are notoriously underreported. Such data as are available, however, demonstrate that their impact is substantial and widespread. ...
>
> Sexual assault takes a heavy toll on its victims, particularly on children. ... Thus, apart from the substantial personal trauma caused to the victims of such crimes, sexual crimes against children exact heavy social costs as well.

On the critical issue of recidivism, the Legislature presumably adopted the view suggested in the following information, supportive of that stated in the studies relied on by the Attorney General:

> Sex offender recidivism compounds the problem. As a group, sex offenders are significantly more likely than other repeat offenders to reoffend with sex crimes or other violent crimes, and that tendency persists over time. ...
>
> These figures comport with other data on sex offender recidivism. A major Justice Department study of state prisoners released in one year showed that 7.7% of released rapists were rearrested for rape within three years. Moreover, 27.5% of released rapists were rearrested during that period for some kind of violent offense (murder, rape, robbery, or assault). ... A recent review of the most frequently cited studies of sex offender recidivism indicates that rapists repeat their offenses at [] rates up to 35%; offenders who molest young girls, at [] rates up to 29%; and offenders who molest young boys, at [] rates up to 40%. ...

Clearly, both the Legislature's and the public's increasing awareness of the dangers posed by sex...

...The remedy selected by our Legislature goes beyond the ability of citizens to request the criminal record of their neighbors when they may have no reason to make such requests. The remedy goes directly to the question of what a community can do to protect itself against the potential of reoffense by a group the Legislature could find had a relatively high risk of recidivism involving those crimes most feared, and those crimes to which the most vulnerable and defenseless were exposed the children of society. The spectacle of offenses committed by neighbors, known in the public records as significantly potential reoffenders, but not known to anyone else, and especially not known to those most likely to be affected, their neighbors, suggested the most obvious and practical degree of protection: a law that would tell neighbors and others who night be affected, of the presence of such offenders, no more and no less.

The concern for the potential unfairness of identification has some justification, but it is wrong to assume the people of this State and the media will not understand that potential. The Attorney General points to information, far from complete because of the injunction against the implementation of these laws, that suggests that harassment and vigilantism have been minimal. This Court has no right to assume that the public will be punitive when the Legislature was not, that the public, instead of protecting itself as the laws intended, will attempt to destroy the lives of those subject to the laws, and this Court has no right to assume that community leaders, public officials, law enforcement authorities, will not seek to educate the public concerning the Legislature's intent, including appropriate responses to notification information, responses that are not at all punitive, but seek merely to protect their children, their families, and others from reoffense. ...

...We do not perceive in this case a society clamoring for blood, demanding the names of previously-convicted sex offenders in order to further punish them, but rather families concerned about their children who want information only in order to protect them. Presumably, some citizens will harass, and presumably they will be prosecuted, but we believe that overwhelmingly our citizens are law-abiding citizens. We do not share the certainty of the dissent in the probability of community reaction that would gut the protective purpose of these laws and convert them into punishment. We decline to decide this case on that assumption.

II.

The Laws and the Attorney General's Guidelines

Despite complexities of detail, the Registration Law is basically simple. It requires registration of sex offenders convicted after its effective date and all prior-convicted offenders whose conduct was found to be repetitive and compulsive. The sex offenses that trigger the laws for those previously convicted are aggravated sexual assault, sexual assault, aggravated criminal sexual contact, kidnapping pursuant to N.J.S.A. 2C:13-1(c)(2), and for those convicted after their effective date, added to the foregoing are various laws concerning endangering the welfare of a child, luring or enticing, criminal sexual contact if the victim is a minor, and kidnapping, criminal restraint, or false imprisonment if the victim is a minor and the offender not the parent; and in all cases an attempt to commit any of the foregoing.

Registration requires, in the case of those no longer in custody generally those who committed the offense before adoption of the laws appearance at a local police station for fingerprinting, photographing, and providing information for a registration form that will include a physical description, the offense involved, home address, employment or school address, vehicle used, and license plate number. For those in custody, the procedure is effected at that location. The forms, information, fingerprints, and photographs (or copies) are centrally collected by the State Police and prosecutors. The registration requirement applies to all convicts, all juveniles, no matter what their age, found delinquent because of the commission of those offenses, and to all found not guilty by reason of insanity. The requirements apply as well to sex offenders convicted elsewhere who relocate to this state. Registrants whose conduct was repetitive and compulsive must verify their addresses with the local law enforcement agency quarterly, other registrants must do so annually. Upon relocation to another municipality, re-registration is required there, and, apparently, any change of address requires notice to the local law enforcement agency.

All of these are lifetime requirements unless the registrant has been offense-free for fifteen years following conviction or release from a correctional facility (whichever is later) and, on application to terminate these obligations, can persuade the court that he or she is not likely to pose a threat to the safety of others. Registration records are open to any law enforcement agency in the state, or any other state, or any federal law enforcement agency. Failure to comply with the Registration Law is a fourth-degree crime.

The Community Notification Law requires the local chief of police to give notification of the registrant's presence in the community, such notification also required if the registrant changes address (presumably whether within or outside of the community although the statutory language refers only to the latter). The law provides for three levels of notification (referred to as Tiers One, Two and Three in the Guidelines) depending on the risk of reoffense.

If risk of reoffense is low, law enforcement agencies likely to encounter the person registered shall be notified;

If risk of reoffense is moderate, organizations in the community including schools, religious and youth organizations shall be notified in accordance with the Attorney General's Guidelines, in addition to the notice required by paragraph (1) of this subsection;

If risk of reoffense is high, the public shall be notified through means in accordance with the Attorney General's Guidelines designed to reach members of the public likely to encounter the person registered, in addition to the notice required by paragraphs (1) and (2) of this subsection.

No suggestion has been made that any registrant could be classified as posing no risk of reoffense: presumably then, all registrants will be subjected at the very least to Tier One Notification (called "Law Enforcement Alert" in the Guidelines). Although the statute provides that the risk of reoffense, and therefore the extent (the level, the Tier) of notification shall be assessed by the prosecutors of the county of conviction and the county of residence together with any law enforcement officials that either deems appropriate, the Guidelines appear to require the final assessment to be made by one prosecutor, apparently the prosecutor of the county of residence.

We are aware of the uncertainties that surround all aspects of the subject of sex offender recidivism and the effectiveness of preventive measures. Legislatures, despite uncertainty, must sometimes act to deal with public needs, basing such action on what they conclude, in a welter of conflicting opinions, to be the probable best course. Our Legislature could reasonably conclude that risk of reoffense can be fairly measured, and that knowledge of the presence of offenders provides increased defense against them. Given those conclusions, the system devised by the Legislature is propriately designed to achieve the laws' purpose of protecting the public.

IV.

Interpretation of Statute: Revision of Attorney General's Guidelines; Judicial Review

...despite its constitutionality, the statute sufficiently impinges on liberty interests to trigger both procedural due process and the fairness doctrine in our state, those subject to the statute are entitled to the protection of procedures designed to assure that the risk of reoffense and the extent of notification are fairly evaluated before Tier Two or Tier Three notification is implemented. Although the provisions of the statute and the implementing Guidelines are obviously designed to assure such evaluation, and although there is no reason to believe that the prosecutors and other law enforcement personnel charged with the decision-making power that controls both the level of notification and the specific steps that will determine the amount of notification will not discharge their duties competently and fairly, we have concluded that judicial review through a summary proceeding should be available prior to notification if sought by any person covered by the law. The Attorney General, therefore, as a condition to the enforcement of this law, shall formulate procedures designed to assure that notice is given in sufficient time prior to Tier Two or Tier Three notification to allow the offender to object. We realize that in some cases it may be impossible as a practical matter to give such notice, or to give it timely, and in those cases it may be dispensed with.

The only issue for the court on the Tier level of notification is the risk of reoffense. In that sense the factors of the Guidelines noting the characteristics of prior offenses or of the offender are relevant only to the risk of reoffense, i.e., the likelihood of its occurrence. That is the clear intent of the statute. All offenders required to register are, by statute, subject to at least Tier One notification, meaning that no matter how low the risk of reoffense, the Legislature has concluded Tier One notification is required.

We note further that quite obviously none of these standards or classes suggests the court must make a finding of likelihood of reoffense, for the Legislature did not impose either Tier Two or Tier Three notification only when it was probable that reoffense would occur, but rather only when the risk however quantified was sufficient to warrant such notification. The quality of the offense a sex offense undoubtedly led to this legislative conclusion that notification was warranted even when reoffense was not probable, and that legislative conclusion is unassailable in any proceedings before the court. Therefore the probability of reoffense on the part of moderate- or high-risk offenders is not the issue before the court, but rather the relatively greater risk of reoffense compared either to the low-risk offender class or the moderate-risk offender class.

As for the manner of notification, the limitations set forth in our opinion are mandatory. For Tier Two notification, only those community organizations that own or operate an establishment where children gather under their care, or where women are cared for, shall qualify, and only those that are "likely to encounter" the offender as discussed in connection with Tier Three. The notice that goes out to such organizations shall specifically direct them not to notify anyone else, that being the acknowledged intent of the statute as interpreted by the Attorney General, an interpretation with which we agree. Organizations concerned with the welfare of children and women, but not having them under their custody or care, do not qualify, and as we understand the Guidelines, the Attorney General does not take a different position. There shall be no automatic inclusion of an organization simply because it is "registered." Tier Two notification can easily amount to the same notification as required for Tier Three if these limitations are not observed.

That dangers exist beyond those organizations "likely to encounter" the offender is obvious, for the offender may travel many miles before he or she offends, suggesting the possibility that greater safety would be assured if every organization in the state were notified. That is not at all the intent of the Legislature, the law having struck the balance between the need for safety and individual rights through the "likely to encounter" standard. The word "likely" shall be taken in its usual sense: to mean not "possibly" but "likely," not in the sense of "probably" but rather in the sense of "having a fair chance to encounter."

As for the manner and extent of notification under Tier Three, "likely to encounter" clearly includes the immediate neighborhood of the offender's residence and not just the people next door. It presumably would include (since Tier Three includes Tier Two notification) all schools within the municipality, depending on its size, and we see no reason why it should not include schools and other institutions in adjacent municipalities depending upon their distance from the offender's residence, place of work, or school. ...

We do not automatically exclude, however, notification to a group carefully selected to include only those "likely to encounter" the offender. ...

We assume that the media will exercise responsibility in this matter in recognition of the critical societal interest involved. In particular, we assume that the media will not knowingly frustrate the explicit legislative goal of confining notification to those likely to encounter the offender. ...

VI.

Privacy

In assessing plaintiff's claim, we must determine whether, and to what extent, plaintiff has a reasonable expectation of privacy in the information disclosed under the Registration and Notification Laws. If there is a reasonable expectation of privacy in the information disclosed, we must decide whether the intrusion on the right of privacy is justified, balancing the governmental interest in disclosure against the private interest in confidentiality.

We first address plaintiff's expectation of privacy in the information disclosed under the Registration Law. Information that is readily available to the public, which an individual cannot expect to remain private, is not within the ambit of constitutional protection. ... Requiring disclosure of plaintiff's prior arrest and conviction, therefore, does not implicate the right to privacy, as those records are publicly available. ...

Likewise, requiring the disclosure of other information, such as plaintiff's age and legal residence or a description of his vehicle, does not infringe on any expectation of privacy. As the trial court noted, that information is readily available through public records. ... Plaintiff therefore cannot have a reasonable expectation of privacy in the information contained therein.

Lastly, an individual cannot expect to have a constitutionally protected privacy interest in matters that are exposed to public view. Because a person's physical appearance is necessarily and constantly exposed to public view, no person can have a reasonable expectation of privacy in his appearance. Similarly, no person can have a reasonable expectation of privacy in her fingerprints. Requiring a description or photograph and fingerprints, therefore, does not implicate any privacy interest.

X.

Conclusion

We sail on truly uncharted waters, for no other state has adopted such a far-reaching statute. All other notification statutes apparently make public notification discretionary on the part of officials; the statute before us, however, mandates it. Despite the unavoidable uncertainty of our conclusion, we remain convinced that the statute is constitutional. To rule otherwise is to find that society is unable to protect itself from sexual predators by adopting the simple remedy of informing the public of their presence. That the remedy has a potentially severe effect arises from no fault of government, or of society, but rather from the nature of the remedy and the problem; it is an unavoidable consequence of the compelling necessity to design a remedy.

There is no point in predicting the extent of potential ostracism, in avoiding the conclusion that some ostracism will result, or in calming concerns by observing that the offenders themselves are responsible for their plight for having committed their crimes in the first place, for that justification would apply to any excessive punishment by government. Here government has done all it can to confine that impact, allowing it only where clearly necessary to effect public safety, and if the Tier level selected and the methods of notification conform to the statute and its intent, as defined and limited herein, Tier Two and Tier Three public notification will be appropriately confined and applied only to those whose apparent future dangerousness requires it, and the statute will not only have survived constitutional attack, but in fact will operate as the Legislature intended. We must not prejudge society with the ogre of vigilantism or harassment, although its potential obviously calls for the vigorous steps suggested by the Attorney General, and we must not assume that those in responsible positions will violate the intent of this law by giving notification far beyond that which is authorized, and we must not assume that the press, for whatever reason, will disregard the notification confinement which this law requires.

Justice Stein, dissenting. [omitted]

NOTES AND QUERIES

Critics have assailed community notification and registration laws, with charges ranging from their ineffectiveness and their tendency to cause vigilantism, their significant stigmatic and liberty-depriving effects, and their inappropriate focus on crazed sex offenders who commit only a minority of sex crimes. How does *Doe v. Poritz* respond to these criticisms? How adequate do you find that response?

Community notification and registration laws are in a state of flux. Recent efforts engage in actuarial justice. This influence is most apparent in jurisdictions that eschew individual risk assessments in favor of legislative imposition of compulsory registration and notification for those offenders convicted of specified sex offenses. Do you find that trend more or less problematic than individualized assessments? Consider your answer in light of our previous discussion that experts are not necessarily adequate evaluators of risk. What other factors are relevant to your decision?

Given the introductory materials presented at the beginning of this chapter, how effective do you find this approach to dealing with criminal behavior? How could it be made more effective?

RESEARCH COMMENT

One of the arguments for using community notification laws is that offenders simply are not incarcerated long enough. Little research has examined this concern. Existing studies reveal that sentences generally tend to be lenient, ranging from 5 to 9 years of prison with very wide deviations that range even farther than the average sentence. It also has found that the criminal justice system does seem to incarcerate and punish more severely (in terms of prison time) those society is most worried about – persistent predators who abuse several children. Interestingly, research also indicates that individual victims' experiences are generally less predictive of sentencing outcomes than perpetrators' characteristics and that intra-family and stranger abuse seem to be taken equally seriously. See Roger J.R. Levesque, Sentencing sex crimes against children: An empirical and policy analysis, 18 Beh. Sci. and L. 331 (2000).

THE SUPREME COURT VISITS "MEGAN'S LAW"

Under the Alaska Sex Offender Registration Act (Act), any sex offender or child kidnaper incarcerated in the State must register with the Department of Corrections within 30 days before his release, providing his name, address, and other specified information. If the individual is at liberty, he must register with local law enforcement authorities within a working day of his conviction or of entering the State. If he was convicted of a single, nonaggravated sex crime, the offender must provide annual verification of the submitted information for 15 years. If he was convicted of an aggravated sex offense or of two or more sex offenses, he must register for life and verify the information quarterly. The offender's information is forwarded to the Department of Public Safety, which maintains a central registry of sex offenders. Some of the data, such as fingerprints, driver's license number, anticipated change of address, and whether the offender has had medical treatment afterwards is kept confidential. The offender's name, aliases, address, photograph, physical description, driver's license number, motor vehicle identification numbers, place of employment, date of birth, crime, date and place of conviction, length and conditions of sentence, and a statement as to whether the offender is in compliance with the Act's update requirements or cannot be located are, however, published on the Internet. Both the Act's registration and notification requirements are retroactive.

Respondents were convicted of aggravated sex offenses. Both were released from prison and completed rehabilitative programs for sex offenders. Although convicted before the Act's passage, respondents are covered by it. After the initial registration, they are required to submit quarterly verifications and notify the authorities of any changes. Both respondents, along with the wife of one of them, brought an action seeking to declare the Act void as to them under the Ex Post Facto Clause. Justice Kennedy, writing for the majority, held that, because the Alaska Sex Offender Registration Act is nonpunitive, its retroactive application does not violate the Ex Post Facto Clause. The Court reasoned that the determinative question is whether the legislature meant to establish civil proceedings. If the intention was to impose punishment, that ends the inquiry. If, however, the intention was to enact a regulatory scheme that is civil and nonpunitive, the Court must further examine whether the statutory scheme is so punitive either in purpose or effect as to negate the State's intention to deem it civil. Because the Court ordinarily defers to the legislature's stated intent, only the clearest proof will suffice to override that intent and transform what has been denominated a civil remedy into a criminal penalty. In terms of the Alaska statute, the Court found that the legislature's intent was to create a civil, nonpunitive regime. The Court further found that the respondents could not show that the Act's effects negate Alaska's intention to establish a civil regulatory scheme. Justice Stevens dissented by noting that the act did impose stigma, that the act was punitive, and that the state may not impose punishment after the fact. Justice Ginsburg and Breyer also dissented because they found the act to have a punitive effect, which was not permissible. *Smith v. Doe*, 123 S. Ct. 1140 (2003).

In yet another case, *Connecticut v. Doe*, 123 S. Ct. 1160 (2003), the Court examined part of Connecticut's "Megan's Law." That law requires persons convicted of sexual offenses to register with the Department of Public Safety (DPS) upon their release into the community, and requires DPS to post a sex offender registry containing registrants' names, addresses, photographs, and descriptions on an Internet Website and to make the registry available to the public in certain state offices. Respondent, a convicted sex offender who was subject to the law, filed an action on behalf of himself and similarly situated sex offenders, claiming that the law violates, the Fourteenth Amendment's Due Process Clause. The Second Circuit Court had concluded that such disclosure both deprived registered sex offenders of a "liberty interest," and violated the Due Process Clause because officials did not afford registrants a predeprivation hearing to determine whether they are likely to be "currently dangerous." The Supreme Court, without dissent, reversed as it found that due process does not require the opportunity to prove a fact that is not material to the State's statutory scheme. The Court noted that mere injury to reputation, even if defamatory, does not constitute the deprivation of a liberty interest. Even assuming that respondent had been deprived of a liberty interest, due process did not entitle him to a hearing to establish a fact – that he is not currently dangerous – that is not material under the statute. As the DPS Website explained, the law's requirements turn on an offender's conviction alone – a fact that a convicted offender has already had a procedurally safeguarded opportunity to contest.

Chapter 12

TERMINATING THE LIFE OF CRIMINALS

INTRODUCTION

The punishment of offenders often serves a wide variety of different goals, ranging from deterring the offender from crime, deterring others from crime, isolating and incapacitating the offender, and rehabilitating the offender, to simply reattributing against them.[1] We already have examined many of these rationales in the context of sentencing, offering treatment, and otherwise controlling offenders. We also have examined how juries use these rationales, particularly in the context of the death penalty, and how the law deals with juror's views of punishment. At this juncture, we move our discussion further to understand better how the legal system permits various forms of punishment. Although we will see that the Court treats the penalty of death differently from other punishments, exploring which crimes and offenders may qualify for the death penalty and examining the mandated procedures to ensure legally fair outcomes present us with the opportunity to consider how the Court evaluates the extent to which laws reflect the sentiments of the people for the purposes of punishment consistent with the 8th Amendment's proscription against "cruel and unusual punishment." Most fundamentally, we will observe how the law reflects the manner different policy rationales motivate individuals' punishment preferences. Equally importantly, we will examine how the law could better consider those preferences and whether it in fact should.

PEOPLE'S INTUITIVE PUNISHMENT JUDGEMENTS

Research exploring the psychology of justice reveals that a harm-based retributive psychology largely guides people's punishment judgments. For example, comparisons of layperson's views of punishment and those of sentencing guidelines[2] and the Model Penal Code[3] reveal that people's punishment judgments generally track the harm caused by the crime. This results, for example, in the belief that a person who steals a few dollars from a church poor box should be punished less severely than another who embezzles several thousand dollars from the same church.[4] People typically believe that offenders should be punished so as to suffer as he has made others suffer.[5] People base their determination of punishment on the

---

[1] Jeffrie G. Murphy and Jean Hampton, Forgiveness and Mercy 125-26 (1988).
[2] Peter H. Rossi and Richard A. Berk, Just Punishments: Federal Guidelines and Public Views Compared (1997).
[3] Paul H. Robinson and John M. Darley, Justice, Liability, and Blame: Community Views and the Criminal Law (1995).
[4] Importantly, even judges are not immune from similar beliefs. Stanton Wheeler, Kenneth Mann, and Austin Sarat, Sitting in Judgment: The Sentencing of White-Collar Criminals 66-68 (1988).
[5] Sandra Graham, Bernard Weiner, and Gail Sahar Zucker, An attributional analysis of punishment goals and public reactions to O.J. Simpson, 23 Personality and Soc. Psych. Bull. 331 (1997); and V. Lee Hamilton and Joseph Sanders, Punishment and the individual in the United States and Japan, 22 L. and Soc'y Rev. 301 (1988).

committed wrong.[6] Punishment decisions, then, mainly reflect a moral reaction to a wrong, a sense of deservingness.[7] Importantly, the focus on the offense's moral nature appears independent of the punishment's potential to meet other sentencing goals, including deterrence, which figures prominently in rationales for governmental responses to crime. The priority placed on this retributive approach appears so common that it has become known as the "default" sentencing strategy. This strategy accounts, for example, for the finding that the sentences people give without explicit strategy instructions resembles those that result when they are instructed to punish based on retribution.[8] Although it may seem that people default to the retributive strategy unconsciously, that does not appear to be the case. When requested to rank the philosophies they believe should guide sentencing, people explicitly choose retribution as the most important principle.[9] Although state imposed punishments often serve a number of possible goals, then, our understanding of punishment reveals that individuals seek to match retribution to harms.

The attention placed on harm and the desire to punish based on harm tends to be so potent that punishment judgments sometimes concentrate on adventitious harm. For example, the more severe an accident victim's injury, the more blame and responsibility individuals attribute to the person who caused the accident.[10] Although many factors can explain this phenomenon, psychological science tells us that the ascription occurs because people make defensive attributions.[11] Severe harm causes fear which in turn threatens people. People's fear that a similarly serious injury could befall them leads them to reassure themselves that such severe outcomes do not occur accidentally or randomly. As a result, people assign greater responsibility for the harm to the relevant actors; the severity of harm influences judgments of responsibility and blame. Moreover, severity affects judgments about adventitiousness itself. For example, serious harm makes people view adventitious consequences as less adventitious; and the converse is also true. The often used hypothetical in which a bank robber's bullet misses its intended target instead strikes a customer illustrates the tendency. Under these circumstances, people are less willing to acknowledge the chance nature of the harm to the customer when actions result in severe injuries (victim paralysis) than in mild harms (grazed by a bullet).[12] We find it threatening to believe that chance could create a severe outcome because that would mean that similar harms also could happen to us. People's conceptions of fair punishments, then, typically rest on their perceptions of harm, regardless of whether the harm is adventitious or unforeseen.

UNDERSTANDING PUNISHMENT JUDGEMENTS THROUGH VICTIM IMPACT STATEMENTS

The above conclusions gain considerable support from research investigating victim impact statements. Victim impact statements which communicate greater harm produce more severe punishment judgments. Two studies have examined victim impact evidence in capital case simulations. Both studies varied the victims' character and found that portraying victims in a more positive light led mock jurors to view the crime as more serious, and the survivors as having suffered more psychological, physical, and

---

[6] John M. Darley, Kevin M Carlsmith, and Paul H. Robinson, Incapacitation and just deserts as motives for punishment, 24 L. and Hum. Beh. 659, 660-71 (2000).

[7] Cass R. Sunstein, David Schkade, and Daniel Kahneman, Do people want optimal deterrence?, 29 J. Legal Stud. 237 (2000).

[8] Robert M. McFatter, Sentencing strategies and justice: Effects of punishment philosophy on sentencing decisions, 36 J. Personality and Soc. Psych. 1490 (1978); and John M. Darley, Kevin M Carlsmith, and Paul H. Robinson, Incapacitation and just deserts as motives for punishment, 24 L. and Hum. Beh. 659 (2000).

[9] Mark Warr and Mark Stafford, Public goals of punishment and support for the death penalty, 21 J. Res. Crime and Delinq. 95 (1984).

[10] Jennifer K. Robbennolt, Outcome severity and judgments of "responsibility": A meta-analytic review, 30 J. Appl. Soc. Psych. 2575 (2000).

[11] Elaine Walster, Assignment of responsibility for an accident, 3 J. Personality and Soc. Psych. 73 (1966).

[12] D. Chimaeze Ugwuegbu and Clyde Hendrick, Personal causality and attribution of responsibility, 2 Soc. Beh. and Personality 76 (1974).

financial harm.[13] Studies using undergraduate students acting as jurors making mock capital punishment decisions reveal that they also are more likely to vote for a death sentence when victim impact evidence was present and the mock jurors were neutral to or supportive of the death penalty; and this was especially true when the crime involved aggravating circumstances and post-deliberation individual verdicts (rather than group verdicts).[14] Available evidence, then, supports the conclusion that a focus on victims impacts sentencing.

Although this area of research derives mainly from mock juries, the findings gain support from several social psychological mechanisms that would predict the influence of victim impact evidence on punishment judgments. Harm serves as a heuristic that helps us interpret events in the absence of better information.[15] We know, for example, that unknown factors about a crime are filled in by a harm heuristic.[16] Given that perceptions of harm fill in blanks, the resulting concern centers on whether harm can properly evidence culpability. Although physical harm may be a reliable measure, emotional harm appears particularly unreliable as a heuristic simply because of wide variations in individuals' emotional responses to a crime. Victims also vary broadly in the manner they effectively express their emotional experiences in court. This variation gains significance to the extent that, unlike physical injury, the severity of emotional injury permits few reliable inferences about the act that led to the injury, simply because victims vary widely in their emotional responses and emotional expression. Thus, although it may be intuitively compelling to punish offenders more harshly for causing more severe emotional harm, this intuition conceivably derives from the inaccurate but general proposition that harm reliably indicates a defendant's culpability. In applying the general principle, we fail to discount for the unreliability of emotional harm.

Considerable evidence also reveals that people are susceptible to outcome bias, which creates problems when punishment focuses on harms. People make more favorable evaluations when the outcome is positive than when it is negative; and they do so to an extent greater than is warranted by the available information.[17] People take into account information about an event's outcome when judging the person who caused it, even when the outcome provides an unreliable basis for judging. This gains significance in this context because emotional harm contained in victim impact statements do not necessarily provide a reliable proxy for judging relevant but unknown circumstances of the crime, such as the defendant's state of mind. Yet, we are drawn to outcome information even when we are aware of its unreliability. People's general susceptibility to using outcome information in judging behavior suggests that victim impact statements risk unduly influencing jurors.

In addition to focusing on heuristics and their biasing effects, it is important to emphasize the powerful role emotions play in decision making. First we know that anger creates a desire to attack, an instinct that translates easily into a desire for punishment.[18] Given that anger is a punitive emotion, it is not surprising that angry responses to crime lead people to seek greater punishment.[19] Thus, to the extent that the sentencer's anger toward the defendant is evoked or exacerbated by victim impact statements, sentencers prefer harsher punishment judgments. Second, the very demonstration of negative emotions can alter

---

13 Edith Greene, The many guises of victim impact evidence and effects on jurors' judgments, 5 Psych. Crime and L. 331 (1999); and Edith Greene, Heather Koehring, and Melinda Quiat, Victim impact evidence in capital cases: Does the victim's character matter?, 28 J. Appl. Soc. Psych. 145 (1998).

14 James Luginbuhl and Michael Burkhead, Victim impact evidence in a capital trial: Encouraging votes for death, 20 Am. J. Crim. Jus. 1 (1995); and Bryan Myers and Jack Arbuthnot, The effects of victim impact evidence on the verdicts and sentencing judgments of mock jurors, 29 J. Offender Rehab. 95 (1999).

15 Stephen J. Morse, The moral metaphysics of causation and results, 88 Cal. L. Rev. 879 (2000).

16 A frequently cited study that tested memory for eyewitness events found that eyewitness memory of the details of a videotaped car accident varied with the severity of the crash (as characterized by lawyers' leading questions). For example, eyewitnesses estimated that the car involved in the accident was traveling at faster speeds, and they were more likely to report having seen broken glass (although there was none) if the car was described as having "smashed" the other car (as opposed to having "contacted" it). Elizabeth F. Loftus and John C. Palmer, Reconstruction of automobile destruction: An example of the interaction between language and memory, 13 J. Verbal Learning and Verbal Beh. 585, 588 (1974).

17 Jonathan Baron and John C. Hershey, Outcome bias in decision evaluation, 54 J. Personality and Soc. Psych. 569 (1988).

18 Richard S. Lazarus, Emotion and Adaptation (1991).

19 Sandra Graham, Bernard Weiner, and Gail Sahar Zucker, An attributional analysis of punishment goals and public reaction to O.J. Simpson, 23 Personality and Soc. Psych. Bull. 331 (1997).

people's explanations for events. For example, when experimenters induce feelings of anger, subjects are more likely to blame individual persons for negative outcomes than they are to blame impersonal forces, such as bad luck.[20] Anger has this effect because the emotion emerges, in the first instance, through the recognition that another person has done something to harm us, or has harmed someone with whom we sympathize.[21] Once this focus on individual accountability emerges, it is more salient and readily available when we assess other situations. One explanation for the anger-punishment relationship is that exposure to intense emotional suffering heightens decision makers' negative affect and consequently activates "blame-validation processing."[22] In this state, jurors or other decision makers seek ways to hold an offender responsible,[23] even for unforeseeable outcomes. In response to these negative feelings, people rationalize greater blame for an event – and presumably, concomitant levels of punishment – by altering their evidentiary standards. According to the blame-validation model, evidence that a victim or a family member of a victim has suffered severe emotional injury produces both a decision maker's desire to blame and a cognitive search to validate that blame. In short, the anger aroused by hearing victim impact statements often induces decision makers to engage in a search for evidence to support more blame and punishment.[24] That anger arises should not be surprising. Over one third of capital jurors report being afraid of defendants;[25]and researchers have long known that anger (along with contempt and disgust) is a key "moral emotion" that guides people's responses to wrongdoing by others.[26]

Punishment Judgements and the Death Penalty

In the context of the death penalty, concerns about the proper use of punishment arise in terms of the 8th Amendment's prohibition against cruel and unusual punishment. The major issue involves the extent to which the punishment fits "evolving standards of decency." Importantly, the legal system approaches this determination in different ways, some of which are deemed more important than others by different members of the Court. The first standard is the objective test, which examines what capital jurors tend to do with the types of cases brought to them and examines how state statutes approach those cases. A major example would be the prohibition against using the death penalty for minors under age ten, which is something capital jurors tend not to do and which statutes tend not to condone. The second test, known as the subjective tests, tends to focus on either of two considerations. The first consideration deals with the deterrent and retributive value of the death penalty; the second consideration involves the proportionality of the sentence compared to the crime, such as whether imposition of the death penalty is proportional to the crime of rape. The last major test examines the extent to which the procedures leading to the capital sentencing were arbitrary and capricious. Under this test, for example, the Court focuses on the adequacy of jury instructions and the extent to which juries have exercised guided discretion and the extent to which statements heard by juries would produce arbitrarily imposed death sentences. Importantly, the Court often uses many of these tests at once to determine whether a statute's provisions violate 8th Amendment protections.

---

[20] Dacher Keltner, Phoebe C. Ellsworth, and Kari Edwards, Beyond simple pessimism: Effects of sadness and anger on social perception, 64 J. Personality and Soc. Psych. 740 (1993).

[21] Craig A. Smith and Phoebe C. Ellsworth, Patterns of cognitive appraisal in emotion, 48 J. Personality and Soc. Psych. 813 (1985).

[22] Mark D. Alicke, Culpable control and the psychology of blame, 126 Psych. Bull. 556 (2000).

[23] The presumption of guilt, for example, sets in motion a process of behavioral confirmation by which expectations influence an interrogator's behavior, the suspect's behavior, and ultimately the judgments of neutral observers. Saul M. Kassin, Behavioral confirmation in the interrogation room: On the dangers of presuming guilt, 27 L. and Hum. Beh. 187 (2003).

[24] This phenomenon has come to be known as "confirmation bias." Joshua Klayman and Young-Won Ha, Confirmation, disconfirmation, and information in hypothesis testing, 94 Psychol. Rev. 211 (1987).

[25] Stephen P. Garvey, The emotional economy of capital sentencing, 75 N.Y.U. L. Review 26 (2000).

[26] Paul Rozin, Laura Lowery, Sumio Imada, and Jonathan Haidt, The CAD triad hypothesis: A mapping between three moral emotions (contempt, anger, disgust) and three moral codes (community, autonomy, divinity), 76 J. Personality and Soc. Psych. 574 (1999).

It is worth emphasizing that a nationwide effort to improve our understanding of how capital jurors decide cases, the Capital Jury Project, increasingly yields an extensive analysis of jurors' experiences.[27] Some of the reports directly relate to our discussion. One of the most intriguing findings thus far reveals that the psychology of the juror and the facts of the case seem to matter more than the law.[28] This is a profoundly important point. Capital jurors often disappoint the law's expectations. For example, an overview of research from hundreds of jurors from several states found that, while no capital juror should think that the death penalty is the only appropriate punishment for convicted murderers, four out of ten capital jurors believe that they are required to impose the death penalty if they find that the crime was heinous, vile, or depraved.[29] Likewise, three out of ten erroneously think that the death penalty is required if they find that the defendant would be dangerous in the future.[30] Similarly problematic findings have been identified in many states. For example, no capital juror should believe that anyone but they alone are responsible for the defendant's sentence. Yet, some capital jurors nonetheless believe they share that responsibility with trial or appeals court judges. Equally troublesome is the finding that many of the jurors do not fully understand mitigation.[31]

Importantly, we may find it inherently problematic that the process by which capital jurors are selected and instructed does miscarry. The major concern, however, is whether any of these miscarriages actually influence the thoughts and feelings capital jurors have toward the defendants they sentence. Surprisingly, the emotional responses of jurors who do not fully understand their role or the court's instructions differ little from those jurors who do. Regardless of whether jurors do or do not measure up to the law's expectations, they still have much of the same thoughts and feelings about particular defendants.[32] There are, however, some notable exceptions, such as the more a juror tends to believe that anyone convicted of capital murder should be sentenced to death, the angrier and less sympathetic they are likely to feel toward the defendant.[33] And, as we have seen, such emotions play an important role in finding death. As you examine the cases that follow, consider this type of research and its relevance to the law's conceptions of adequate capital jurisprudence protections provided to defendants.

NOTES AND QUERIES

The Court has used two principal methods to determine the "evolving standards of decency" relevant to a particular aspect of the 8th Amendment's prohibition against cruel and unusual punishment. What are those two methods? Additionally, the Court concerns itself with an arbitrary and capricious test. Which test allows for the most influence of psychological research?

Capital jurors apparently tend not to understand their mandates, a fact that may be frightening to some but that in fact may not really matter when jurors actually decide cases. What implications arise from that finding?

What significance do you attach to the finding that people are retributive and that, without instructions, focus on harm caused rather than the law they are supposed to apply? How can the law consider this information when, for example, it tries arguably less culpable individuals?

---

[27] William J. Bowers, The Capital Jury Project: Rationale, design, and preview of early findings, 70 Ind. L.J. 1043 (1995).
[28] Stephen P. Garvey, The emotional economy of capital sentencing, 75 N.Y.U. L. Review 26 (2000).
[29] William J. Bowers, The Capital Jury Project: Rationale, design, and preview of early findings, 70 Ind. L.J. 1043 (1995).
[30] William J. Bowers, The Capital Jury Project: Rationale, design, and preview of early findings, 70 Ind. L.J. 1043 (1995).
[31] Stephen P. Garvey, The emotional economy of capital sentencing, 75 N.Y.U. L. Review 26 (2000).
[32] Stephen P. Garvey, The emotional economy of capital sentencing, 75 N.Y.U. L. Review 26 (2000).
[33] Stephen P. Garvey, The emotional economy of capital sentencing, 75 N.Y.U. L. Review 26 (2000).

Determining Who Can Be Executed: The Insane

FORD v. WAINWRIGHT
477 U.S. 399 (1986)

JUSTICE MARSHALL announced the judgment of the Court and delivered the opinion of the Court with respect to Parts I and II and an opinion with respect to Parts III, IV, and V, in which JUSTICE BRENNAN, JUSTICE BLACKMUN, and JUSTICE STEVENS join.

For centuries no jurisdiction has countenanced the execution of the insane, yet this Court has never decided whether the Constitution forbids the practice. Today we keep faith with our common-law heritage in holding that it does.

I.

Alvin Bernard Ford was convicted of murder in 1974 and sentenced to death. There is no suggestion that he was incompetent at the time of his offense, at trial, or at sentencing. In early 1982, however, Ford began to manifest gradual changes in behavior. They began as an occasional peculiar idea or confused perception, but became more serious over time. After reading in the newspaper that the Ku Klux Klan had held a rally in nearby Jacksonville, Florida, Ford developed an obsession focused upon the Klan. His letters to various people reveal endless brooding about his "Klan work," and an increasingly pervasive delusion that he had become the target of a complex conspiracy, involving the Klan and assorted others, designed to force him to commit suicide. He believed that the prison guards, part of the conspiracy, had been killing people and putting the bodies in the concrete enclosures used for beds. Later, he began to believe that his women relatives were being tortured and sexually abused somewhere in the prison. This notion developed into a delusion that the people who were tormenting him at the prison had taken members of Ford's family hostage. The hostage delusion took firm hold and expanded, until Ford was reporting that 135 of his friends and family were being held hostage in the prison, and that only he could help them. By "day 287" of the "hostage crisis," the list of hostages had expanded to include "senators, Senator Kennedy, and many other leaders." In a letter to the Attorney General of Florida, written in 1983, Ford appeared to assume authority for ending the "crisis," claiming to have fired a number of prison officials. He began to refer to himself as "Pope John Paul, III," and reported having appointed nine new justices to the Florida Supreme Court.

Counsel for Ford asked a psychiatrist who had examined Ford earlier, Dr. Jamal Amin, to continue seeing him and to recommend appropriate treatment. On the basis of roughly 14 months of evaluation, taped conversations between Ford and his attorneys, letters written by Ford, interviews with Ford's acquaintances, and various medical records, Dr. Amin concluded in 1983 that Ford suffered from "a severe, uncontrollable, mental disease which closely resembles 'Paranoid Schizophrenia With Suicide Potential'" – a "major mental disorder . . . severe enough to substantially affect Mr. Ford's present ability to assist in the defense of his life."

Ford subsequently refused to see Dr. Amin again, believing him to have joined the conspiracy against him, and Ford's counsel sought assistance from Dr. Harold Kaufman, who interviewed Ford in November 1983. Ford told Dr. Kaufman that "I know there is some sort of death penalty, but I'm free to go whenever I want because it would be illegal and the executioner would be executed." When asked if he would be executed, Ford replied: "I can't be executed because of the landmark case. I won. Ford v. State will prevent executions all over." These statements appeared amidst long streams of seemingly unrelated thoughts in rapid succession. Dr. Kaufman concluded that Ford had no understanding of why he was being executed, made no connection between the homicide of which he had been convicted and the death penalty, and indeed sincerely believed that he would not be executed because he owned the prisons and could control the Governor through mind waves. Dr. Kaufman found that there was "no reasonable possibility that Mr. Ford was dissembling, malingering or otherwise putting on a performance . . . ." The following month, in an interview with his attorneys, Ford regressed further into nearly complete incomprehensibility, speaking only in a code characterized by intermittent use of the word "one," making statements such as "Hands one, face one. Mafia one. God one, father one, Pope one. Pope one. Leader one."

Counsel for Ford invoked the procedures of Florida law governing the determination of competency of a condemned inmate. Following the procedures set forth in the statute, the Governor of Florida appointed a panel of three psychiatrists to evaluate whether, Ford had "the mental capacity to understand the nature of the death penalty and the reasons why it was imposed upon him." At a single meeting, the three psychiatrists together interviewed Ford for approximately 30 minutes. Each doctor then filed a separate two- or three-page report with the Governor, to whom the statute delegates the final decision. One doctor concluded that Ford suffered from "psychosis with paranoia" but had "enough cognitive functioning to understand the nature and the effects of the death penalty, and why it is to be imposed on him." Another found that, although Ford was "psychotic," he did "know fully what can happen to him." The third concluded that Ford had a "severe adaptational disorder," but did "comprehend his total situation including being sentenced to death, and all of the implications of that penalty." He believed that Ford's disorder, "although severe, seem[ed] contrived and recently learned." Thus, the interview produced three different diagnoses, but accord on the question of sanity as defined by state law.

The Governor's decision was announced on April 30, 1984, when, without explanation or statement, he signed a death warrant for Ford's execution. Ford's attorneys unsuccessfully sought a hearing in state court to determine anew Ford's competency to suffer execution. Counsel then filed a petition for habeas corpus in the United States District Court for the Southern District of Florida, seeking an evidentiary hearing on the question of Ford's sanity, proffering the conflicting findings of the Governor-appointed commission and subsequent challenges to their methods by other psychiatrists. The District Court denied the petition without a hearing. The Court of Appeals granted a certificate of probable cause and stayed Ford's execution, and we rejected the State's effort to vacate the stay of execution. The Court of Appeals then addressed the merits of Ford's claim and a divided panel affirmed the District Court's denial of the writ.This Court granted Ford's petition for certiorari in order to resolve the important issue whether the Eighth Amendment prohibits the execution of the insane and, if so, whether the District Court should have held a hearing on petitioner's claim.

II.

There is now little room for doubt that the Eighth Amendment's ban on cruel and unusual punishment embraces, at a minimum, those modes or acts of punishment that had been considered cruel and unusual at the time that the Bill of Rights was adopted. "Although the Framers may have intended the Eighth Amendment to go beyond the scope of its English counterpart, their use of the language of the English Bill of Rights is convincing proof that they intended to provide at least the same protection . . . ."

...Not bound by the sparing humanitarian concessions of our forebears, the Amendment also recognizes the "evolving standards of decency that mark the progress of a maturing society." In addition to considering the barbarous methods generally outlawed in the 18th century, therefore, this Court takes into account objective evidence of contemporary values before determining whether a particular punishment comports with the fundamental human dignity that the Amendment protects.

A.

We begin, then, with the common law. The bar against executing a prisoner who has lost his sanity bears impressive historical credentials; the practice consistently has been branded "savage and inhuman."

B.

This ancestral legacy has not outlived its time. Today, no State in the Union permits the execution of the insane. It is clear that the ancient and humane limitation upon the State's ability to execute its sentences has as firm a hold upon the jurisprudence of today as it had centuries ago in England. The various reasons put forth in support of the common-law restriction have no less logical, moral, and practical force than they did when first voiced. For today, no less than before, we may seriously question the retributive value of executing a person who has no comprehension of why he has been singled out and stripped of his fundamental right to life. Similarly, the natural abhorrence civilized societies feel at killing one who has no capacity to come to grips with his own conscience or deity is still vivid today. And the intuition that such an execution simply offends humanity is evidently shared across this Nation. Faced with such widespread evidence of a restriction upon sovereign power, this Court is compelled to conclude that the Eighth Amendment prohibits a State from carrying out a sentence of death upon a prisoner who is insane. Whether its aim be to protect the condemned from fear and pain without comfort of understanding, or to protect the dignity of society itself from the barbarity of exacting mindless vengeance, the restriction finds enforcement in the Eighth Amendment.

III.

The Eighth Amendment prohibits the State from inflicting the penalty of death upon a prisoner who is insane. Petitioner's allegation of insanity in his habeas corpus petition, if proved, therefore, would bar his execution. The question before us is whether the District Court was under an obligation to hold an evidentiary hearing on the question of Ford's sanity. ...

A.

B.

Although the condemned prisoner does not enjoy the same presumptions accorded a defendant who has yet to be convicted or sentenced, he has not lost the protection of the Constitution altogether; if the Constitution renders the fact or timing of his execution contingent upon establishment of a further fact, then that fact must be determined with the high regard for truth that befits a decision affecting the life or death of a human being. Thus, the ascertainment of a prisoner's sanity as a predicate to lawful execution calls for no less stringent standards than those demanded in any other aspect of a capital proceeding. Indeed, a particularly acute need for guarding against error inheres in a determination that "in the present state of the mental sciences is at best a hazardous guess however conscientious." That need is greater still because the ultimate decision will turn on the finding of a single fact, not on a range of equitable considerations. In light of these concerns, the procedures employed in petitioner's case do not fare well.

C.

Florida law directs the Governor, when informed that a person under sentence of death may be insane, to stay the execution and appoint a commission of three psychiatrists to examine the prisoner. "The examination of the convicted person shall take place with all three psychiatrists present at the same time." After receiving the report of the commission, the Governor must determine whether "the convicted person has the mental capacity to understand the nature of the death penalty and the reasons why it was imposed on him." If the Governor finds that the prisoner has that capacity, then a death warrant is issued; if not, then the prisoner is committed to a mental health facility. The procedure is conducted wholly within the executive branch, ex parte, and provides the exclusive means for determining sanity.

Petitioner received the statutory process. The Governor selected three psychiatrists, who together interviewed Ford for a total of 30 minutes, in the presence of eight other people, including Ford's counsel, the State's attorneys, and correctional officials. The Governor's order specifically directed that the attorneys should not participate in the examination in any adversarial manner. This order was consistent with the present Governor's "publicly announced policy of excluding all advocacy on the part of the condemned from the process of determining whether a person under a sentence of death is insane."

After submission of the reports of the three examining psychiatrists, reaching conflicting diagnoses but agreeing on the ultimate issue of competency, Ford's counsel attempted to submit to the Governor some other written materials, including the reports of the two other psychiatrists who had examined Ford at greater length, one of whom had concluded that the prisoner was not competent to suffer execution. The Governor's office refused to inform counsel whether the submission would be considered. The Governor subsequently issued his decision in the form of a death warrant. That this most cursory form of procedural review fails to achieve even the minimal degree of reliability required for the protection of any constitutional interest ... is self-evident.

IV.

A.

The first deficiency in Florida's procedure lies in its failure to include the prisoner in the truth-seeking process. Notwithstanding this Court's longstanding pronouncement that "[t]he fundamental requisite of due process of law is the opportunity to be heard," state practice does not permit any material relevant to the ultimate decision to be submitted on behalf of the prisoner facing execution. In all other proceedings leading to the execution of an accused, we have said that the factfinder must "have before it all possible relevant information about the individual defendant whose fate it must determine." And we have forbidden States to limit the capital defendant's submission of relevant evidence in mitigation of the sentence. It would be odd were we now to abandon our insistence upon unfettered presentation of relevant information, before the final fact antecedent to execution has been found.

Rather, consistent with the heightened concern for fairness and accuracy that has characterized our review of the process requisite to the taking of a human life, we believe that any procedure that precludes the prisoner or his counsel from presenting material relevant to his sanity or bars consideration of that material by the factfinder is necessarily inadequate. "[T]he minimum assurance that the life-and-death guess will be a truly informed guess requires respect for the basic ingredient of due process, namely, an opportunity to be allowed to substantiate a claim before it is rejected."

...without any adversarial assistance from the prisoner's representative – especially when the psychiatric opinion he proffers is based on much more extensive evaluation than that of the state-appointed commission – the factfinder loses the substantial benefit of potentially probative information. The result is a much greater likelihood of an erroneous decision.

B.

A related flaw in the Florida procedure is the denial of any opportunity to challenge or impeach the state-appointed psychiatrists' opinions. "[C]ross-examination . . . is beyond any doubt the greatest legal engine ever invented for the discovery of truth." Cross-examination of the psychiatrists, or perhaps a less formal equivalent, would contribute markedly to the process of seeking truth in sanity disputes by bringing to light the bases for each expert's beliefs, the precise factors underlying those beliefs, any history of error or caprice of the examiner, any personal bias with respect to the issue of capital punishment, the expert's degree of certainty about his or her own conclusions, and the precise meaning of ambiguous words used in the report. Without some questioning of the experts concerning their technical conclusions, a factfinder simply cannot be expected to evaluate the various opinions, particularly when they are themselves inconsistent. The failure of the Florida procedure to afford the prisoner's representative any opportunity to clarify or challenge the state experts' opinions or methods creates a significant possibility that the ultimate decision made in reliance on those experts will be distorted.

C.

Perhaps the most striking defect in the procedures ... is the State's placement of the decision wholly within the executive branch. Under this procedure, the person who appoints the experts and ultimately decides whether the State will be able to carry out the sentence that it has long sought is the Governor, whose subordinates have been responsible for initiating every stage of the prosecution of the condemned from arrest through sentencing. The commander of the State's corps of prosecutors cannot be said to have the neutrality that is necessary for reliability in the factfinding proceeding.

V.

A.

Having identified various failings of the Florida scheme, we must conclude that the State's procedures for determining sanity are inadequate to preclude federal redetermination of the constitutional issue. We do not here suggest that only a full trial on the issue of sanity will suffice to protect the federal interests; we leave to the State the task of developing appropriate ways to enforce the constitutional restriction upon its execution of sentences. ...

Yet the lodestar of any effort to devise a procedure must be the overriding dual imperative of providing redress for those with substantial claims and of encouraging accuracy in the factfinding determination. The stakes are high, and the "evidence" will always be imprecise. It is all the more important that the adversary presentation of relevant information be as unrestricted as possible. Also essential is that the manner of selecting and using the experts responsible for producing that "evidence" be conducive to the formation of neutral, sound, and professional judgments as to the prisoner's ability to comprehend the nature of the penalty. Fidelity to these principles is the solemn obligation of a civilized society.

B.

Today we have explicitly recognized in our law a principle that has long resided there. It is no less abhorrent today than it has been for centuries to exact in penance the life of one whose mental illness prevents him from comprehending the reasons for the penalty or its implications. In light of the clear need for trustworthiness in any factual finding that will prevent or permit the carrying out of an execution, we hold that [the statute] provides inadequate assurances of accuracy. Having been denied a factfinding procedure "adequate to afford a full and fair hearing" on the critical issue, petitioner is entitled to an evidentiary hearing in the District Court, de novo, on the question of his competence to be executed.

The judgment of the Court of Appeals is reversed, and the case is remanded for further proceedings consistent with this opinion.

It is so ordered.

JUSTICE POWELL, concurring in part and concurring in the judgment. [omitted]

JUSTICE O'CONNOR, with whom JUSTICE WHITE joins, concurring in the result in part and dissenting in part.

I am in full agreement with JUSTICE REHNQUIST's conclusion that the Eighth Amendment does not create a substantive right not to be executed while insane. Accordingly, I do not join the Court's reasoning or opinion. Because, however, the conclusion is for me inescapable that Florida positive law has created a protected liberty interest in avoiding execution while incompetent, and because Florida does not provide even those minimal procedural protections required by due process in this area, I would vacate the judgment and remand to the Court of Appeals with directions that the case be returned to the Florida system so that a hearing can be held in a manner consistent with the requirements of the Due Process Clause. I cannot agree, however, that the federal courts should have any role whatever in the substantive determination of a defendant's competency to be executed.

JUSTICE REHNQUIST, with whom THE CHIEF JUSTICE joins, dissenting.

The Court today holds that the Eighth Amendment prohibits a State from carrying out a lawfully imposed sentence of death upon a person who is currently insane. This holding is based almost entirely on two unremarkable observations. First, the Court states that it "know[s] of virtually no authority condoning the execution of the insane at English common law." Second, it notes that "[t]oday, no State in the Union permits the execution of the insane." Armed with these facts, and shielded by the claim that it is simply "keep[ing] faith with our common-law heritage," the Court proceeds to cast aside settled precedent and to significantly alter both the common-law and current practice of not executing the insane. It manages this feat by carefully ignoring the fact that the Florida scheme it finds unconstitutional, in which the Governor is assigned the ultimate responsibility of deciding whether a condemned prisoner is currently insane, is fully consistent with the "common-law heritage" and current practice on which the Court purports to rely.

Since no State sanctions execution of the insane, the real battle being fought in this case is over what procedures must accompany the inquiry into sanity. The Court reaches the result it does by examining the common law, creating a constitutional right that no State seeks to violate, and then concluding that the common-law procedures are inadequate to protect the newly created but common-law based right. I find it unnecessary to "constitutionalize" the already uniform view that the insane should not be executed, and inappropriate to "selectively incorporate" the common-law practice. I therefore dissent.

NOTES AND QUERIES

The central concerns in this case involve whether the 8th Amendment prohibits the execution of the insane and whether an individual has a right to a hearing to determine their sanity for the purposes of execution. The Court finds it easy to prohibit the execution of insane individuals, arguing that it violates evolving standards of decency in that no state permits the execution of the insane because it has no retributive value. The Court rules that a petitioner has a right to a hearing. *Ford*, however, leaves many questions unanswered: What is the procedure that the State must follow in cases involving a condemned inmate who has allegedly gone insane awaiting execution? What is the legal definition of insanity in relation to a prisoner awaiting execution, i.e., what is the legal definition of "insanity to be executed"? Who has the initial burden to prove a condemned prisoner's insanity? Who has the burden of proof upon an allegation that sanity has been restored? What quantum of proof can be legally required? After a finding of insanity, can the state forcibly medicate an insane inmate to restore his sanity for execution? What clues do you get from the opinion that would help you approach some of these questions? What does the opinion focus on most when it finds the Florida procedures inadequate?

Do you agree with the dissent which argues that the 8th Amendment does not bar the death penalty of the currently insane? What really is gained by a rule that prohibits the execution of the insane? Would it not be more humane if who was to be executed did not know that they were to be killed in cases where they were in fact sane when they were tried, convicted and sentenced?

DETERMINING WHO CAN BE EXECUTED: THE MENTALLY RETARDED

PENRY v. LYNAUGH
492 U.S. 302 (1989)

JUSTICE O'CONNOR delivered the opinion of the Court, except as to Part IV-C.

I.

On the morning of October 25, 1979, Pamela Carpenter was brutally raped, beaten, and stabbed with a pair of scissors in her home in Livingston, Texas. She died a few hours later in the course of emergency treatment. Before she died, she described her assailant. Her description led two local sheriff's deputies to suspect Penry, who had recently been released on parole after conviction on another rape charge. Penry subsequently gave two statements confessing to the crime and was charged with capital murder.

At a competency hearing held before trial, a clinical psychologist, Dr. Jerome Brown, testified that Penry was mentally retarded. As a child, Penry was diagnosed as having organic brain damage, which was probably caused by trauma to the brain at birth. Penry was tested over the years as having an IQ between 50 and 63, which indicates mild to moderate retardation. Dr. Brown's own testing before the trial indicated that Penry had an IQ of 54. Dr. Brown's evaluation also revealed that Penry, who was 22 years old at the time of the crime, had the mental age of a 6 1/2-year-old, which means that "he has the ability to learn and the learning or the knowledge of the average 6 1/2 year old kid." Penry's social maturity, or ability to function in the world, was that of a 9- or 10-year-old. Dr. Brown testified that "there's a point at which anyone with [Penry's] IQ is always incompetent, but, you know, this man is more in the borderline range."

The jury found Penry competent to stand trial. The guilt-innocence phase of the trial began on March 24, 1980. The trial court determined that Penry's confessions were voluntary, and they were introduced into evidence. At trial, Penry raised an insanity defense and presented the testimony of a psychiatrist, Dr. Jose Garcia. Dr. Garcia testified that Penry suffered from organic brain damage and moderate retardation, which resulted in poor impulse control and an inability to learn from experience. Dr. Garcia indicated that Penry's brain damage was probably caused at birth, but may have been caused by beatings and multiple injuries to the brain at an early age. In Dr. Garcia's judgment, Penry was suffering from an organic brain disorder at the time of the offense which made it impossible for him to appreciate the wrongfulness of his conduct or to conform his conduct to the law.

Penry's mother testified at trial that Penry was unable to learn in school and never finished the first grade. Penry's sister testified that their mother had frequently beaten him over the head with a belt when he was a child. Penry was also routinely locked in his room without access to a toilet for long periods of time. As a youngster, Penry was in and out of a number of state schools and hospitals, until his father removed him from state schools altogether when he was 12. Penry's aunt subsequently struggled for over a year to teach Penry how to print his name.

The State introduced the testimony of two psychiatrists to rebut the testimony of Dr. Garcia. Dr. Kenneth Vogtsberger testified that although Penry was a person of limited mental ability, he was not suffering from any mental illness or defect at the time of the crime, and that he knew the difference between right and wrong and had the potential to honor the law. In his view, Penry had characteristics consistent with an antisocial personality, including an inability to learn from experience and a tendency to be impulsive and to violate society's norms. He testified further that Penry's low IQ scores underestimated his alertness and understanding of what went on around him.

Dr. Felix Peebles also testified for the State that Penry was legally sane at the time of the offense and had a "full-blown anti-social personality." In addition, Dr. Peebles testified that he personally diagnosed Penry as being mentally retarded in 1973 and again in 1977, and that Penry "had a very bad life generally, bringing up." In Dr. Peebles' view, Penry "had been socially and emotionally deprived and he had not learned to read and write adequately."Although they disagreed with the defense psychiatrist over the extent and cause of Penry's mental limitations, both psychiatrists for the State acknowledged that Penry was a person of extremely limited mental ability, and that he seemed unable to learn from his mistakes.

The jury rejected Penry's insanity defense and found him guilty of capital murder. The following day, at the close of the penalty hearing, the jury decided the sentence to be imposed on Penry by answering three "special issues":

whether the conduct of the defendant that caused the death of the deceased was committed deliberately and with the reasonable expectation that the death of the deceased or another would result;

whether there is a probability that the defendant would commit criminal acts of violence that would constitute a continuing threat to society; and

if raised by the evidence, whether the conduct of the defendant in killing the deceased was unreasonable in response to the provocation, if any, by the deceased.

If the jury unanimously answers "yes" to each issue submitted, the trial court must sentence the defendant to death. Otherwise, the defendant is sentenced to life imprisonment.

Defense counsel raised a number of objections to the proposed charge to the jury. With respect to the first special issue, he objected that the charge failed to define the term "deliberately." With respect to the second special issue, he objected that the charge failed to define the terms "probability," "criminal acts of violence," and "continuing threat to society." Defense counsel also objected to the charge because it failed to "authorize a discretionary grant of mercy based upon the existence of mitigating circumstances" and because it "fail[ed] to require as a condition to the assessment of the death penalty that the State show beyond a reasonable doubt that any aggravating circumstances found to exist outweigh any mitigating circumstances." In addition, the charge failed to instruct the jury that it may take into consideration all of the evidence whether aggravating or mitigating in nature which was submitted in the full trial of the case. Defense counsel also objected that, in light of Penry's mental retardation, permitting the jury to assess the death penalty in this case amounted to cruel and unusual punishment prohibited by the Eighth Amendment.

These objections were overruled by the trial court. The jury was then instructed that the State bore the burden of proof on the special issues, and that before any issue could be answered "yes," all 12 jurors must be convinced by the evidence beyond a reasonable doubt that the answer to that issue should be "yes." The jurors were further instructed that in answering the three special issues, they could consider all the evidence submitted in both the guilt-innocence phase and the penalty phase of the trial. The jury charge then listed the three questions, with the names of the defendant and the deceased inserted.

...Penry was sentenced to death. The Texas Court of Criminal Appeals affirmed his conviction and sentence on direct appeal. ...

We granted certiorari to resolve two questions. First, was Penry sentenced to death in violation of the Eighth Amendment because the jury was not adequately instructed to take into consideration all of his mitigating evidence and because the terms in the Texas special issues were not defined in such a way that the jury could consider and give effect to his mitigating evidence in answering them? Second, is it cruel and unusual punishment under the Eighth Amendment to execute a mentally retarded person with Penry's reasoning ability?

II.

III.

Underlying Lockett and Eddings is the principle that punishment should be directly related to the personal culpability of the criminal defendant. If the sentencer is to make an individualized assessment of the appropriateness of the death penalty, "evidence about the defendant's background and character is relevant because of the belief, long held by this society, that defendants who commit criminal acts that are attributable to a disadvantaged background, or to emotional and mental problems, may be less culpable than defendants who have no such excuse." Moreover, Eddings makes clear that it is not enough simply to allow the defendant to present mitigating evidence to the sentencer. The sentencer must also be able to consider and give effect to that evidence in imposing sentence. Only then can we be sure that the sentencer has treated the defendant as a "uniquely individual human bein[g]" and has made a reliable determination that death is the appropriate sentence. "Thus, the sentence imposed at the penalty stage should reflect a reasoned moral response to the defendant's background, character, and crime."

Although Penry offered mitigating evidence of his mental retardation and abused childhood as the basis for a sentence of life imprisonment rather than death, the jury that sentenced him was only able to express its views on the appropriate sentence by answering three questions: Did Penry act deliberately when he murdered Pamela Carpenter? Is there a probability that he will be dangerous in the future? Did he act unreasonably in response to provocation? The jury was never instructed that it could consider the evidence offered by Penry as mitigating evidence and that it could give mitigating effect to that evidence in imposing sentence.

Penry argues that his mitigating evidence of mental retardation and childhood abuse has relevance to his moral culpability beyond the scope of the special issues, and that the jury was unable to express its "reasoned moral response" to that evidence in determining whether death was the appropriate punishment. We agree. Thus, we reject the State's contrary argument that the jury was able to consider and give effect to all of Penry's mitigating evidence in answering the special issues without any jury instructions on mitigating evidence.

The first special issue asks whether the defendant acted "deliberately and with the reasonable expectation that the death of the deceased . . . would result." Neither the Texas Legislature nor the Texas Court of Criminal Appeals have defined the term "deliberately," and the jury was not instructed on the term, so we do not know precisely what meaning the jury gave to it. Assuming, however, that the jurors in this case understood "deliberately" to mean something more than that Penry was guilty of "intentionally" committing murder, those jurors may still have been unable to give effect to Penry's mitigating evidence in answering the first special issue.

Penry's mental retardation was relevant to the question whether he was capable of acting "deliberately," but it also "had relevance to [his] moral culpability beyond the scope of the special verdict questio[n]." Personal culpability is not solely a function of a defendant's capacity to act "deliberately." A rational juror at the penalty phase of the trial could have concluded, in light of Penry's confession, that he deliberately killed Pamela Carpenter to escape detection. Because Penry was mentally retarded, however, and thus less able than a normal adult to control his impulses or to evaluate the consequences of his conduct, and because of his history of childhood abuse, that same juror could also conclude that Penry was less morally "culpable than defendants who have no such excuse," but who acted "deliberately" as that term is commonly understood.

In the absence of jury instructions defining "deliberately" in a way that would clearly direct the jury to consider fully Penry's mitigating evidence as it bears on his personal culpability, we cannot be sure that the jury was able to give effect to the mitigating evidence of Penry's mental retardation and history of abuse in answering the first special issue. Without such a special instruction, a juror who believed that Penry's retardation and background diminished his moral culpability and made imposition of the death penalty unwarranted would be unable to give effect to that conclusion if the juror also believed that Penry committed the crime "deliberately." Thus, we cannot be sure that the jury's answer to the first special issue reflected a "reasoned moral response" to Penry's mitigating evidence.

The second special issue asks "whether there is a probability that the defendant would commit criminal acts of violence that would constitute a continuing threat to society." The mitigating evidence concerning Penry's mental retardation indicated that one effect of his retardation is his inability to learn from his mistakes. Although this evidence is relevant to the second issue, it is relevant only as an aggravating factor because it suggests a "yes" answer to the question of future dangerousness. The prosecutor argued at the penalty hearing that there was "a very strong probability, based on the history of this defendant, his previous criminal record, and the psychiatric testimony that we've had in this case, that the defendant will continue to commit acts of this nature." Even in a prison setting, the prosecutor argued, Penry could hurt doctors, nurses, librarians, or teachers who worked in the prison.

Penry's mental retardation and history of abuse is thus a two-edged sword: it may diminish his blameworthiness for his crime even as it indicates that there is a probability that he will be dangerous in the future. ...

The second special issue, therefore, did not provide a vehicle for the jury to give mitigating effect to Penry's evidence of mental retardation and childhood abuse.

The third special issue asks "whether the conduct of the defendant in killing the deceased was unreasonable in response to the provocation, if any, by the deceased." On this issue, the State argued that Penry stabbed Pamela Carpenter with a pair of scissors not in response to provocation, but "for the purpose of avoiding detection." Penry's own confession indicated that he did not stab the victim after she wounded him superficially with a scissors during a struggle, but rather killed her after her struggle had ended and she was lying helpless. Even if a juror concluded that Penry's mental retardation and arrested emotional development rendered him less culpable for his crime than a normal adult, that would not necessarily diminish the "unreasonableness" of his conduct in response to "the provocation, if any, by the deceased." Thus, a juror who believed Penry lacked the moral culpability to be sentenced to death could not express that view in answering the third special issue if she also concluded that Penry's action was not a reasonable response to provocation.

The State contends, notwithstanding the three interrogatories, that Penry was free to introduce and argue the significance of his mitigating circumstances to the jury. In fact, defense counsel did argue that if a juror believed that Penry, because of the mitigating evidence of his mental retardation and abused background, did not deserve to be put to death, the juror should vote "no" on one of the special issues even if she believed the State had proved that the answer should be "yes." Thus, Penry's counsel stressed the evidence of Penry's mental retardation and abused background, and asked the jurors, "can you be proud to be a party to putting a man to death with that affliction?" He urged the jury to answer the first special issue "no" because "it would be the just answer, and I think it would be a proper answer." As for the prediction of the prosecution psychiatrist that Penry was likely to continue to get into trouble, the defense argued: "That may be true. But, a boy with this mentality, with this mental affliction, even though you have found that issue against us as to insanity, I don't think that there is any question in a single one of you juror's [sic] minds that there is something definitely wrong, basically, with this boy. And I think there is not a single one of you that doesn't believe that this boy had brain damage. . . ." In effect, defense counsel urged the jury to "[t]hink about each of those special issues and see if you don't find that we're inquiring into the mental state of the defendant in each and every one of them."

In rebuttal, the prosecution countered by stressing that the jurors had taken an oath to follow the law, and that they must follow the instructions they were given in answering the special issues:

> You've all taken an oath to follow the law and you know what the law is. . . . In answering these questions based on the evidence and following the law, and that's all that I asked you to do, is to go out and look at the evidence. The burden of proof is on the State as it has been from the beginning, and we accept that burden. And I honestly believe that we have more than met that burden, and that's the reason that you didn't hear Mr. Newman [defense attorney] argue. He didn't pick out these issues and point out to you where the State had failed to meet this burden. He didn't point out the weaknesses in the State's case because, ladies and gentlemen, I submit to you we've met our burden. . . . [Y]our job as jurors and your duty as jurors is not to act on your emotions, but to act on the law as the Judge has given it to you, and on the evidence that you have heard in this courtroom, then answer those questions accordingly.

In light of the prosecutor's argument, and in the absence of appropriate jury instructions, a reasonable juror could well have believed that there was no vehicle for expressing the view that Penry did not deserve to be sentenced to death based upon his mitigating evidence.

The State conceded at oral argument in this Court that if a juror concluded that Penry acted deliberately and was likely to be dangerous in the future, but also concluded that because of his mental retardation he was not sufficiently culpable to deserve the death penalty, that juror would be unable to give effect to that mitigating evidence under the instructions given in this case. The State contends, however, that to instruct the jury that it could render a discretionary grant of mercy, or say "no" to the death penalty, based on Penry's mitigating evidence, would be to return to the sort of unbridled discretion that led to Furman v. Georgia (1972). We disagree.

"In contrast to the carefully defined standards that must narrow a sentencer's discretion to impose the death sentence, the Constitution limits a State's ability to narrow a sentencer's discretion to consider relevant evidence that might cause it to decline to impose the death sentence." Indeed, it is precisely because the punishment should be directly related to the personal culpability of the defendant that the jury must be allowed to consider and give effect to mitigating evidence relevant to a defendant's character or record or the circumstances of the offense. Rather than creating the risk of an unguided emotional response, full consideration of evidence that mitigates against the death penalty is essential if the jury is to give a "'reasoned moral response to the defendant's background, character, and crime.'" In order to ensure "reliability in the determination that death is the appropriate punishment in a specific case," the jury must be able to consider and give effect to any mitigating evidence relevant to a defendant's background and character or the circumstances of the crime.

In this case, in the absence of instructions informing the jury that it could consider and give effect to the mitigating evidence of Penry's mental retardation and abused background by declining to impose the death penalty, we conclude that the jury was not provided with a vehicle for expressing its "reasoned moral response" to that evidence in rendering its sentencing decision. Our reasoning in Lockett and Eddings thus compels a remand for resentencing so that we do not "risk that the death penalty will be imposed in spite of factors which may call for a less severe penalty." "When the choice is between life and death, that risk is unacceptable and incompatible with the commands of the Eighth and Fourteenth Amendments."

IV.

Penry's second claim is that it would be cruel and unusual punishment, prohibited by the Eighth Amendment, to execute a mentally retarded person like himself with the reasoning capacity of a 7-year-old. He argues that because of their mental disabilities, mentally retarded people do not possess the level of moral culpability to justify imposing the death sentence. He also argues that there is an emerging national consensus against executing the mentally retarded. The State responds that there is insufficient evidence of a national consensus against executing the retarded, and that existing procedural safeguards adequately protect the interests of mentally retarded persons such as Penry.

A.

B.

The Eighth Amendment categorically prohibits the infliction of cruel and unusual punishments. At a minimum, the Eighth Amendment prohibits punishment considered cruel and unusual at the time the Bill of Rights was adopted. The prohibitions of the Eighth Amendment are not limited, however, to those practices condemned by the common law in 1789. The prohibition against cruel and unusual punishments also recognizes the "evolving standards of decency that mark the progress of a maturing society." In discerning those "evolving standards," we have looked to objective evidence of how our society views a particular punishment today. The clearest and most reliable objective evidence of contemporary values is the legislation enacted by the country's legislatures. We have also looked to data concerning the actions of sentencing juries.

It was well settled at common law that "idiots," together with "lunatics," were not subject to punishment for criminal acts committed under those incapacities. ...

The common law prohibition against punishing "idiots" for their crimes suggests that it may indeed be "cruel and unusual" punishment to execute persons who are profoundly or severely retarded and wholly lacking the capacity to appreciate the wrongfulness of their actions. Because of the protections afforded by the insanity defense today, such a person is not likely to be convicted or face the prospect of punishment. Moreover, under Ford v. Wainwright (1986), someone who is "unaware of the punishment they are about to suffer and why they are to suffer it" cannot be executed.

Such a case is not before us today. Penry was found competent to stand trial. In other words, he was found to have the ability to consult with his lawyer with a reasonable degree of rational understanding, and was found to have a rational as well as factual understanding of the proceedings against him. In addition, the jury rejected his insanity defense, which reflected their conclusion that Penry knew that his conduct was wrong and was capable of conforming his conduct to the requirements of the law.

Penry argues, however, that there is objective evidence today of an emerging national consensus against execution of the mentally retarded, reflecting the "evolving standards of decency that mark the progress of a maturing society." ... Only one State, however, currently bans execution of retarded persons who have been found guilty of a capital offense. ...

In contrast, in Ford v. Wainwright, which held that the Eighth Amendment prohibits execution of the insane, considerably more evidence of a national consensus was available. No State permitted the execution of the insane, and 26 States had statutes explicitly requiring suspension of the execution of a capital defendant who became insane. Other States had adopted the common law prohibition against executing the insane. Moreover, in examining the objective evidence of contemporary standards of decency in Thompson v. Oklahoma, the plurality noted that 18 States expressly established a minimum age in their death penalty statutes, and all of them required that the defendant have attained at least the age of 16 at the time of the offense. In our view, the two state statutes prohibiting execution of the mentally retarded, even when added to the 14 States that have rejected capital punishment completely, do not provide sufficient evidence at present of a national consensus.

Penry does not offer any evidence of the general behavior of juries with respect to sentencing mentally retarded defendants, nor of decisions of prosecutors. He points instead to several public opinion surveys that indicate strong public opposition to execution of the retarded. For example, a poll taken in Texas found that 86% of those polled supported the death penalty, but 73% opposed its application to the mentally retarded. A Florida poll found 71% of those surveyed were opposed to the execution of mentally retarded capital defendants, while only 12% were in favor. A Georgia poll found 66% of those polled opposed to the death penalty for the retarded, 17% in favor, with 16% responding that it depends how retarded the person is. In addition, the AAMR, the country's oldest and largest organization of professionals working with the mentally retarded, opposes the execution of persons who are mentally retarded. The public sentiment expressed in these and other polls and resolutions may ultimately find expression in legislation, which is an objective indicator of contemporary values upon which we can rely. But at present, there is insufficient evidence of a national consensus against executing mentally retarded people convicted of capital offenses for us to conclude that it is categorically prohibited by the Eighth Amendment.

C.

Relying largely on objective evidence such as the judgments of legislatures and juries, we have also considered whether application of the death penalty to particular categories of crimes or classes of offenders violates the Eighth Amendment because it "makes no measurable contribution to acceptable goals of punishment and hence is nothing more than the purposeless and needless imposition of pain and suffering" or because it is "grossly out of proportion to the severity of the crime." ...

Penry argues that execution of a mentally retarded person like himself with a reasoning capacity of approximately a 7-year-old would be cruel and unusual because it is disproportionate to his degree of personal culpability. ...Penry argues that mentally retarded people do not have the judgment, perspective, and self-control of a person of normal intelligence. In essence, Penry argues that because of his diminished ability to control his impulses, to think in long-range terms, and to learn from his mistakes, he "is not capable of acting with the degree of culpability that can justify the ultimate penalty."

The AAMR and other groups working with the mentally retarded agree with Penry. They argue as amici that all mentally retarded people, regardless of their degree of retardation, have substantial cognitive and behavioral disabilities that reduce their level of blameworthiness for a capital offense. Amici do not argue that people with mental retardation cannot be held responsible or punished for criminal acts they commit. Rather, they contend that because of "disability in the areas of cognitive impairment, moral reasoning, control of impulsivity, and the ability to understand basic relationships between cause and effect," mentally retarded people cannot act with the level of moral culpability that would justify imposition of the death sentence. Thus, in their view, execution of mentally retarded people convicted of capital offenses serves no valid retributive purpose.

It is clear that mental retardation has long been regarded as a factor that may diminish an individual's culpability for a criminal act. In its most severe forms, mental retardation may result in complete exculpation from criminal responsibility. Moreover, virtually all of the States with death penalty statutes that list statutory mitigating factors include as a mitigating circumstance evidence that "[t]he capacity of the defendant to appreciate the criminality of his conduct or to conform his conduct to the requirements of law was substantially impaired." A number of States explicitly mention "mental defect" in connection with such a mitigating circumstance. Indeed, as the Court holds in Part III of this opinion, the sentencing body must be allowed to consider mental retardation as a mitigating circumstance in making the individualized determination whether death is the appropriate punishment in a particular case.

On the record before the Court today, however, I cannot conclude that all mentally retarded people of Penry's ability – by virtue of their mental retardation alone, and apart from any individualized consideration of their personal responsibility – inevitably lack the cognitive, volitional, and moral capacity to act with the degree of culpability associated with the death penalty. Mentally retarded persons are individuals whose abilities and experiences can vary greatly. ... In light of the diverse capacities and life experiences of mentally retarded persons, it cannot be said on the record before us today that all mentally retarded people, by definition, can never act with the level of culpability associated with the death penalty.

Penry urges us to rely on the concept of "mental age," and to hold that execution of any person with a mental age of seven or below would constitute cruel and unusual punishment. Mental age is "calculated as the chronological age of nonretarded children whose average IQ test performance is equivalent to that of the individual with mental retardation." Such a rule should not be adopted today. First, there was no finding below by the judge or jury concerning Penry's "mental age." One of Penry's expert witnesses, Dr. Brown, testified that he estimated Penry's "mental age" to be 6 1/2. That same expert estimated that Penry's "social maturity" was that of a 9- or 10-year-old. As a more general matter, the "mental age" concept, irrespective of its intuitive appeal, is problematic in several respects. As the AAMR acknowledges, "[t]he equivalence between nonretarded children and retarded adults is, of course, imprecise." The "mental age" concept may underestimate the life experiences of retarded adults, while it may overestimate the ability of retarded adults to use logic and foresight to solve problems. The mental age concept has other limitations as well. Beyond the chronological age of 15 or 16, the mean scores on most intelligence tests cease to increase significantly with age. As a result, "[t]he average mental age of the average 20 year old is not 20 but 15 years."

Not surprisingly, courts have long been reluctant to rely on the concept of mental age as a basis for exculpating a defendant from criminal responsibility. Moreover, reliance on mental age to measure the capabilities of a retarded person for purposes of the Eighth Amendment could have a disempowering effect if applied in other areas of the law. Thus, on that premise, a mildly mentally retarded person could be denied the opportunity to enter into contracts or to marry by virtue of the fact that he had a "mental age" of a young child. In light of the inherent problems with the mental age concept, and in the absence of better evidence of a national consensus against execution of the retarded, mental age should not be adopted as a line-drawing principle in our Eighth Amendment jurisprudence.

In sum, mental retardation is a factor that may well lessen a defendant's culpability for a capital offense. But we cannot conclude today that the Eighth Amendment precludes the execution of any mentally retarded person of Penry's ability convicted of a capital offense simply by virtue of his or her mental retardation alone. So long as sentencers can consider and give effect to mitigating evidence of mental retardation in imposing sentence, an individualized determination whether "death is the appropriate punishment" can be made in each particular case. While a national consensus against execution of the mentally retarded may someday emerge reflecting the "evolving standards of decency that mark the progress of a maturing society," there is insufficient evidence of such a consensus today.

Accordingly, the judgment below is affirmed in part and reversed in part, and the case is remanded for further proceedings consistent with this opinion.

It is so ordered.

JUSTICE BRENNAN, with whom JUSTICE MARSHALL joins, concurring in part and dissenting in part. [omitted]

JUSTICE STEVENS, with whom JUSTICE BLACKMUN joins, concurring in part and dissenting in part. [omitted]

JUSTICE SCALIA, with whom THE CHIEF JUSTICE, JUSTICE WHITE, and JUSTICE KENNEDY join, concurring in part and dissenting in part.

...As noted at the outset of this discussion, our law regarding capital sentencing has sought to strike a balance between complete discretion, which produces "wholly arbitary and capricious action," and no discretion at all, which prevents the individuating characteristics of the defendant and of the crime to be taken into account. ... In providing for juries to consider all mitigating circumstances insofar as they bear upon (1) deliberateness, (2) future dangerousness, and (3) provocation, it seems to me Texas had adopted a rational scheme that meets the two concerns of our Eighth Amendment jurisprudence. The Court today demands that it be replaced, however, with a scheme that simply dumps before the jury all sympathetic factors bearing upon the defendant's background and character, and the circumstances of the offense, so that the jury may decide without further guidance whether he "lacked the moral culpability to be sentenced to death," "did not deserve to be sentenced to death," or "was not sufficiently culpable to deserve the death penalty." The Court seeks to dignify this by calling it a process that calls for a "reasoned moral response,"– but reason has nothing to do with it, the Court having eliminated the structure that required reason. It is an unguided, emotional "moral response" that the Court demands be allowed – an outpouring of personal reaction to all the circumstances of a defendant's life and personality, an unfocused sympathy. Not only have we never before said the Constitution requires this, but the line of cases following Gregg sought to eliminate precisely the unpredictability it produces.

The Court cannot seriously believe that rationality and predictability can be achieved, and capriciousness avoided, by "'narrow[ing] a sentencer's discretion to impose the death sentence,'" but expanding his discretion "'to decline to impose the death sentence.'" The decision whether to impose the death penalty is a unitary one; unguided discretion not to impose is unguided discretion to impose as well. ...

I respectfully dissent.

NOTES AND QUERIES

Note1of the Court's opinion indicates that persons who are mentally retarded are described as having "significantly subaverage general intellectual functioning existing concurrently with deficits in adaptive behavior and manifested during the developmental period." To be classified as mentally retarded, a person generally must have an IQ of 70 or below. Individuals with IQ scores between 50-55 and 70 have "mild" retardation. Individuals with scores between 35-40 and 50-55 have "moderate" retardation. "Severely" retarded people have IQ scores between 20-25 and 35-40, and "profoundly" retarded people have scores below 20 or 25.

Penry argues that an evolving standard of decency prohibits his execution. How does his argument proceed? How does the Court address his argument? Does it make sense to simply leave the issue to juries and allow mental age to be one factor in the analysis of determining culpability?

Recall that the majority remands the case to determine whether the state had provided the jury with sufficient discretion, a remand based on the argument that a jury must be able to hear mitigating evidence. The dissent correctly notes that Texas had adopted a rational scheme. Such a rational scheme has been what was required by the Supreme Court in earlier cases. The dissent also notes that the decision will not make the scheme more rational by increasing juror discretion. Good argument? Note that the prior case on point was *Furman v. Georgia*, 408 U.S. 238 (1972), in which a sharply divided Court ruled that any capital punishment statute that lacked judicial guidance violated the Eighth Amendment prohibition of cruel and unusual punishment. The Georgia death penalty statute at issue gave the jury complete and uninhibited discretion to determine whether to sentence a defendant to death. The Court noted that application of death penalty statutes resulted in discrimination toward disadvantaged groups nationwide. The Court ultimately concluded that because of the uniqueness and finality of the death penalty, any death penalty statute that allowed for its arbitrary application violated the Eighth Amendment and must be struck down. By invalidating all death penalty statutes that lacked sentencing guidelines, the Court's decision in *Furman* effectively rendered all death penalty statutes in existence at the time inoperable. In response to the invalidation of these statutes, states adopted two main approaches toward remedying the situation. Note, Discretion and the constitutionality of the new death penalty statutes, 87 Harv. L. Rev. 1690, 1699-1712 (1974). The majority of states created statutes that mandated imposition of the death penalty upon conviction for certain crimes, thus eliminating sentencing discretion altogether. By contrast, a few states created statutes that mandated a bifurcated capital trial in which a defendant's guilt and his resultant punishment were separately decided. During the sentencing stage of a bifurcated trial, a jury would determine whether to impose the death penalty based upon the consideration of aggravating and mitigating factors.

Who do you think should decide whether the level of retardation is sufficient to warrant not executing an inmate: a jury or an expert?

In *Penry v. Johnson*, 532 U.S. 782 (2001), the Supreme Court examined Penry's retrial and again reversed the decision for failure to provide effective jury instructions that would allow it to provide a reasoned moral response to the mitigating evidence of Penry's mental retardation and childhood abuse.

NOTE ON *ATKINS V. VIRGINIA*

Consider the Supreme Court's recent pronouncement on whether the Eight Amendment categorically prohibits death sentences for criminal defendants who were mentally retarded, *Atkins v. Virginia*, 536 U.S. 304 (2002). Atkins was convicted in a Virginia trial court on charges of abduction, armed robbery, and capital murder that arose out of a 1996 incident. At the sentencing hearing, the defense presented testimony by a forensic psychologist who said that the defendant was mildly mentally retarded, with an IQ of 59, while a prosecution expert witness expressed the view that the defendant was of at least average intelligence. A jury sentenced the defendant to death. Justice Stevens' majority opinion held that the execution of criminals who were mentally retarded was excessive and, thus, prohibited by the Eighth Amendment as cruel and unusual punishment, because:

(a) Since the decision in *Penry v Lynaugh*, a national consensus – with the consistency of the direction of change being more significant than the number of states – had developed against such executions, as evidenced by (a) the large number of states which had enacted prohibitions against such executions, (b) the absence of states reinstating the power to conduct such executions, and (c) the rarity of such executions even in states that allowed them. (Recall that in *Penry* the Supreme Court had determined that the two states which then prohibited execution of such defendants, even when added to the 14 states which prohibited the death penalty altogether, did not establish a national consensus against such executions.)

(b) Evidence that such executions were opposed by religious and professional organizations and by the world community – and that polling data showed a widespread consensus among

Americans against such executions – was not dispositive, but lent further support to the conclusion that there was a consensus among those who had addressed the issue.

(c) In light of some deficiencies of persons who were mentally retarded with respect to information processing, communication, abstract and logical reasoning, impulse control, and understanding of others – which deficiencies diminished such persons' culpability – (a) it was questionable whether the death penalty's retribution and deterrence justifications were applicable to such offenders, and (b) such offenders faced a special risk of wrongful execution, due to their lesser ability to make a persuasive showing of mitigation.

Chief Justice Rehnquist (joined by Justices Scalia and Thomas) dissented, expressing the view that (1) the work product of legislatures and sentencing jury determinations ought to be the sole indicators by which courts ascertain the contemporary American conceptions of decency for purposes of the Eighth Amendment; (2) the Supreme Court erred in giving weight to foreign laws, the views of professional and religious organizations, and opinion polls; and (3) even if some opinion polls were to be used, the Supreme Court lacked sufficient information to conclude that the polls cited by the court (a) had been conducted in accordance with generally accepted scientific principles, or (b) were capable of supporting valid empirical inferences. In addition, Justice Scalia (joined by Chief Justice Rehnquist and Justice Thomas), dissented, expressing the view that (1) the execution of offenders who were mildly mentally retarded would not have been considered cruel and unusual punishment when the Eighth Amendment was adopted; (2) the factor that 18 states, which were less than half the number that permitted capital punishment, had recently enacted legislation barring the execution of criminals who were mentally retarded was not sufficient to establish a national consensus, especially since only seven of those states had barred all such executions; (3) some other factors referred to by the Supreme Court – such as the short-term trend toward barring such executions, the margins by which legislatures had enacted such bans, the supposed infrequency of such executions in states which still allowed them, the views of professional and religious organizations, public opinion polls, and the practices of other countries – were irrelevant to establishing a national consensus; (4) the Supreme Court's view that the execution of offenders who were mentally retarded failed to serve the death penalty's legitimate purposes (a) overlooked the purpose of incapacitating dangerous criminals and preventing future crimes, (b) improperly took from the sentencer the determination whether particular defendants' retardation sufficiently reduced their culpability to preclude the death penalty for particular murders, and (c) erred in concluding that deterrence was not served on the theory of the supposed inability of some criminals who were mentally retarded to appreciate fully the death penalty; and (5) the unsupported claim that offenders who were mentally retarded faced a special risk of execution, on the theory that they were less able to make a persuasive showing of mitigation, had no bearing on an Eighth Amendment claim of cruel and unusual punishment.

Note on Assessing Mental Retardation

The *Atkins* Court used definitions provided by the American Association of Mental Retardation (AAMR) and the American Psychiatric Association (APA). The AAMR provides the most widely used definition. It defines mental retardation as being "characterized by significantly sub-average intellectual functioning... [with] related limitations in two or more... adaptive skill areas. Mental retardation manifests before age 18." The AAMR classifies mental retardation in four categories: mild, moderate, severe, and profound. Similarly, the APA defines mental retardation as significantly sub-average general intellectual functioning accompanied by significant limitations in adaptive functioning in at least two of the following skill areas: communication, self-care, home living, social/interpersonal skill, use of community resources, self direction, functional academic skills, work, leisure, health, and safety. The APA also maintains that onset must occur before age 18 years.

Although these tests are widely used, several criticisms may arise when they are used to define mental retardation for the purposes of carrying out the death penalty. First, state statutes rely heavily on the academic or "numbers" side of IQ assessment, rather than assessment of "performance IQ." "Performance IQ" refers to a "measure [of] a person's ability to function effectively under real world situations." Because the Supreme Court left it to the states to determine how to enforce the ban, states are not required to use "performance IQ" when defining mental retardation. Second, mental retardation deals with potential abuse of the mental retardation exemption that could occur if the defendant "feigned symptoms" during assessment. The criteria for determination of mental retardation is subjective and somewhat ambiguous, potentially allowing for borderline assessments that lack concrete reasoning. Third, an individual's "adaptive behavior classification" may differ from his "intelligence classification." For example, an individual may receive a mildly retarded adaptive behavior classification, but a normal intelligence classification. When this case arises, psychologists make a judgment call as to whether the person should be assessed as mildly mentally retarded or of average intelligence. Although the problem may be common when assessing a person for mental retardation, it becomes a critical distinction when deciding whether a person should live or die based upon the final determination. Fourth, IQs may not be stable. IQ test results may vary greatly over time, well outside any 10 point variable and both education and experience can increase IQ's over time. Although some argue that IQ is a relatively stable factor throughout one's life, the issue poses considerable concern especially to the extent that some definitions only recognize its onset as occurring before the age of eighteen. Lastly, many have noted racial bias in intelligence test assessment. The reasons for concern stem from arguments that intelligence tests have a cultural bias and the race of the examiner affects the intelligence score. See generally, Jerome M. Sattler, Assessment of Children (Jerome M. Sattler, 3d. ed., 1988).

Which decision do you find most appropriate: *Penry* or *Atkins*? What do you make of the use of IQ tests and the role of experts in determining the imposition of the death penalty? Is this somehow different than experts' predictions of dangerousness? What do you make of Justice O'Connor's conclusion in *Penry* that, given controversies and lack of clear evolving consensus, we simply should leave matters to juries who are best situated to individualize justice?

DETERMINING WHO CAN BE EXECUTED: JUVENILES

STANFORD v. KENTUCKY
492 U.S. 361 (1989)

JUSTICE SCALIA announced the judgment of the Court and delivered the opinion of the Court with respect to Parts I, II, III, and IV-A, and an opinion with respect to Parts IV-B and V, in which THE CHIEF JUSTICE, JUSTICE WHITE, and JUSTICE KENNEDY join.

These two consolidated cases require us to decide whether the imposition of capital punishment on an individual for a crime committed at 16 or 17 years of age constitutes cruel and unusual punishment under the Eighth Amendment.

I.

The first case, involves the shooting death of 20-year-old Barbel Poore in Jefferson County, Kentucky. Petitioner Kevin Stanford committed the murder on January 7, 1981, when he was approximately 17 years and 4 months of age. Stanford and his accomplice repeatedly raped and sodomized Poore during and after their commission of a robbery at a gas station where she worked as an attendant. They then drove her to a secluded area near the station, where Stanford shot her point-blank in the face and then in the back of her head. The proceeds from the robbery were roughly 300 cartons of cigarettes, two gallons of fuel, and a small amount of cash. A corrections officer testified that petitioner explained the murder as follows: "'He said, I had to shoot her, [she] lived next door to me and she would recognize me. . . . I guess we could have tied her up or something or beat [her up] . . . and tell her if she tells, we would kill her. . . . Then after he said that he started laughing.'"

...Stressing the seriousness of petitioner's offenses and the unsuccessful attempts of the juvenile system to treat him for numerous instances of past delinquency, the juvenile court found certification for trial as an adult to be in the best interest of petitioner and the community.

Stanford was convicted of murder, first-degree sodomy, first-degree robbery, and receiving stolen property, and was sentenced to death and 45 years in prison. ...

The second case before us today, No. 87-6026, involves the stabbing death of Nancy Allen, a 26-year-old mother of two who was working behind the sales counter of the convenience store she and David Allen owned and operated in Avondale, Missouri. Petitioner Heath Wilkins committed the murder on July 27, 1985, when he was approximately 16 years and 6 months of age. The record reflects that Wilkins' plan was to rob the store and murder "whoever was behind the counter" because "a dead person can't talk." While Wilkins' accomplice, Patrick Stevens, held Allen, Wilkins stabbed her, causing her to fall to the floor. When Stevens had trouble operating the cash register, Allen spoke up to assist him, leading Wilkins to stab her three more times in her chest. Two of these wounds penetrated the victim's heart. When Allen began to beg for her life, Wilkins stabbed her four more times in the neck, opening her carotid artery. After helping themselves to liquor, cigarettes, rolling papers, and approximately $450 in cash and checks, Wilkins and Stevens left Allen to die on the floor.

...Relying on the "viciousness, force and violence" of the alleged crime, petitioner's maturity, and the failure of the juvenile justice system to rehabilitate him after previous delinquent acts, the juvenile court made the necessary certification [to adult court].

Wilkins was charged with first-degree murder, armed criminal action, and carrying a concealed weapon. After the court found him competent, petitioner entered guilty pleas to all charges. A punishment hearing was held, at which both the State and petitioner himself urged imposition of the death sentence. Evidence at the hearing revealed that petitioner had been in and out of juvenile facilities since the age of eight for various acts of burglary, theft, and arson, had attempted to kill his mother by putting insecticide into Tylenol capsules, and had killed several animals in his neighborhood. Although psychiatric testimony indicated that Wilkins had "personality disorders," the witnesses agreed that Wilkins was aware of his actions and could distinguish right from wrong.

On mandatory review of Wilkins' death sentence, the Supreme Court of Missouri affirmed, rejecting the argument that the punishment violated the Eighth Amendment.

We granted certiorari in these cases to decide whether the Eighth Amendment precludes the death penalty for individuals who commit crimes at 16 or 17 years of age.

II.

The thrust of both Wilkins' and Stanford's arguments is that imposition of the death penalty on those who were juveniles when they committed their crimes falls within the Eighth Amendment's prohibition against "cruel and unusual punishments." Wilkins would have us define juveniles as individuals 16 years of age and under; Stanford would draw the line at 17.

Neither petitioner asserts that his sentence constitutes one of "those modes or acts of punishment that had been considered cruel and unusual at the time that the Bill of Rights was adopted." Nor could they support such a contention. At that time, the common law set the rebuttable presumption of incapacity to commit any felony at the age of 14, and theoretically permitted capital punishment to be imposed on anyone over the age of 7. In accordance with the standards of this common-law tradition, at least 281 offenders under the age of 18 have been executed in this country, and at least 126 under the age of 17.

Thus petitioners are left to argue that their punishment is contrary to the "evolving standards of decency that mark the progress of a maturing society." They are correct in asserting that this Court has "not confined the prohibition embodied in the Eighth Amendment to 'barbarous' methods that were generally outlawed in the 18th century," but instead has interpreted the Amendment "in a flexible and dynamic manner." In determining what standards have "evolved," however, we have looked not to our own conceptions of decency, but to those of modern American society as a whole. As we have said, "Eighth Amendment judgments should not be, or appear to be, merely the subjective views of individual Justices; judgment should be informed by objective factors to the maximum possible extent." This approach is dictated both by the language of the Amendment – which proscribes only those punishments that are both "cruel and unusual" – and by the "deference we owe to the decisions of the state legislatures under our federal system."

III.

"First" among the "'objective indicia that reflect the public attitude toward a given sanction'" are statutes passed by society's elected representatives. Of the 37 States whose laws permit capital punishment, 15 decline to impose it upon 16-year-old offenders and 12 decline to impose it on 17-year-old offenders. This does not establish the degree of national consensus this Court has previously thought sufficient to label a particular punishment cruel and unusual. In invalidating the death penalty for rape of an adult woman, we stressed that Georgia was the sole jurisdiction that authorized such a punishment. In striking down capital punishment for participation in a robbery in which an accomplice takes a life, we emphasized that only eight jurisdictions authorized similar punishment. In finding that the Eighth Amendment precludes execution of the insane and thus requires an adequate hearing on the issue of sanity, we relied upon (in addition to the common-law rule) the fact that "no State in the Union" permitted such punishment. And in striking down a life sentence without parole under a recidivist statute, we stressed that "it appears that [petitioner] was treated more severely than he would have been in any other State."

IV.

A.

Wilkins and Stanford argue, however, that even if the laws themselves do not establish a settled consensus, the application of the laws does. That contemporary society views capital punishment of 16- and 17-year-old offenders as inappropriate is demonstrated, they say, by the reluctance of juries to impose, and prosecutors to seek, such sentences. Petitioners are quite correct that a far smaller number of offenders under 18 than over 18 have been sentenced to death in this country. From 1982 through 1988, for example, out of 2,106 total death sentences, only 15 were imposed on individuals who were 16 or under when they committed their crimes, and only 30 on individuals who were 17 at the time of the crime. And it appears that actual executions for crimes committed under age 18 accounted for only about two percent of the total number of executions that occurred between 1642 and 1986. As Wilkins points out, the last execution of a person who committed a crime under 17 years of age occurred in 1959. These statistics, however, carry little significance. Given the undisputed fact that a far smaller percentage of capital crimes are committed by persons under 18 than over 18, the discrepancy in treatment is much less than might seem. Granted, however, that a substantial discrepancy exists, that does not establish the requisite proposition that the death sentence for offenders under 18 is categorically unacceptable to prosecutors and juries. To the contrary, it is not only possible, but overwhelmingly probable, that the very considerations which induce petitioners and their supporters to believe that death should never be imposed on offenders under 18 cause prosecutors and juries to believe that it should rarely be imposed.

B.

This last point suggests why there is also no relevance to the laws cited by petitioners and their amici which set 18 or more as the legal age for engaging in various activities, ranging from driving to drinking alcoholic beverages to voting. It is, to begin with, absurd to think that one must be mature enough to drive carefully, to drink responsibly, or to vote intelligently, in order to be mature enough to understand that murdering another human being is profoundly wrong, and to conform one's conduct to that most minimal of all civilized standards. But even if the requisite degrees of maturity were comparable, the age statutes in question would still not be relevant. They do not represent a social judgment that all persons under the designated ages are not responsible enough to drive, to drink, or to vote, but at most a judgment that the vast majority are not. These laws set the appropriate ages for the operation of a system that makes its determinations in gross, and that does not conduct individualized maturity tests for each driver, drinker, or voter. The criminal justice system, however, does provide individualized testing. In the realm of capital punishment in particular, "individualized consideration [is] a constitutional requirement," and one of the individualized mitigating factors that sentencers must be permitted to consider is the defendant's age. Twenty-nine States, including both Kentucky and Missouri, have codified this constitutional requirement in laws specifically designating the defendant's age as a mitigating factor in capital cases. Moreover, the determinations required by juvenile transfer statutes to certify a juvenile for trial as an adult ensure individualized consideration of the maturity and moral responsibility of 16- and 17-year-old offenders before they are even held to stand trial as adults. The application of this particularized system to the petitioners can be declared constitutionally inadequate only if there is a consensus, not that 17 or 18 is the age at which most persons, or even almost all persons, achieve sufficient maturity to be held fully responsible for murder; but that 17 or 18 is the age before which no one can reasonably be held fully responsible. What displays society's views on this latter point are not the ages set forth in the generalized system of driving, drinking, and voting laws cited by petitioners and their amici, but the ages at which the States permit their particularized capital punishment systems to be applied.

V.

Having failed to establish a consensus against capital punishment for 16- and 17-year-old offenders through state and federal statutes and the behavior of prosecutors and juries, petitioners seek to demonstrate it through other indicia, including public opinion polls, the views of interest groups, and the positions adopted by various professional associations. We decline the invitation to rest constitutional law upon such uncertain foundations. A revised national consensus so broad, so clear, and so enduring as to justify a permanent prohibition upon all units of democratic government must appear in the operative acts (laws and the application of laws) that the people have approved.

We also reject petitioners' argument that we should invalidate capital punishment of 16- and 17-year-old offenders on the ground that it fails to serve the legitimate goals of penology. According to petitioners, it fails to deter because juveniles, possessing less developed cognitive skills than adults, are less likely to fear death; and it fails to exact just retribution because juveniles, being less mature and responsible, are also less morally blameworthy. In support of these claims, petitioners and their supporting amici marshall an array of socioscientific evidence concerning the psychological and emotional development of 16- and 17-year-olds.

If such evidence could conclusively establish the entire lack of deterrent effect and moral responsibility, resort to the Cruel and Unusual Punishments Clause would be unnecessary; the Equal Protection Clause of the Fourteenth Amendment would invalidate these laws for lack of rational basis. But as the adjective "socioscientific" suggests (and insofar as evaluation of moral responsibility is concerned perhaps the adjective "ethicoscientific" would be more apt), it is not demonstrable that no 16-year-old is "adequately responsible" or significantly deterred. It is rational, even if mistaken, to think the contrary. The battle must be fought, then, on the field of the Eighth Amendment; and in that struggle socioscientific, ethicoscientific, or even purely scientific evidence is not an available weapon. The punishment is either "cruel and unusual" (i. e., society has set its face against it) or it is not. The audience for these arguments, in other words, is not this Court but the citizenry of the United States. It is they, not we, who must be persuaded. For as we stated earlier, our job is to identify the "evolving standards of decency"; to determine, not what they should be, but what they are. We have no power under the Eighth Amendment to substitute our belief in the scientific evidence for the society's apparent skepticism. In short, we emphatically reject petitioner's suggestion that the issues in this case permit us to apply our "own informed judgment," regarding the desirability of permitting the death penalty for crimes by 16- and 17-year-olds.

While the dissent is correct that several of our cases have engaged in so-called "proportionality" analysis, examining whether "there is a disproportion 'between the punishment imposed and the defendant's blameworthiness,'" and whether a punishment makes any "measurable contribution to acceptable goals of punishment," we have never invalidated a punishment on this basis alone. All of our cases condemning a punishment under this mode of analysis also found that the objective indicators of state laws or jury determinations evidenced a societal consensus against that penalty. In fact, the two methodologies blend into one another, since "proportionality" analysis itself can only be conducted on the basis of the standards set by our own society; the only alternative, once again, would be our personal preferences.

* * *

We discern neither a historical nor a modern societal consensus forbidding the imposition of capital punishment on any person who murders at 16 or 17 years of age. Accordingly, we conclude that such punishment does not offend the Eighth Amendment's prohibition against cruel and unusual punishment.

The judgments of the Supreme Court of Kentucky and the Supreme Court of Missouri are therefore

Affirmed.

JUSTICE O'CONNOR, concurring in part and concurring in the judgment. [omitted]

JUSTICE BRENNAN, with whom JUSTICE MARSHALL, JUSTICE BLACKMUN, and JUSTICE STEVENS join, dissenting.

I believe that to take the life of a person as punishment for a crime committed when below the age of 18 is cruel and unusual and hence is prohibited by the Eighth Amendment.

The method by which this Court assesses a claim that a punishment is unconstitutional because it is cruel and unusual is established by our precedents, and it bears little resemblance to the method four Members of the Court apply in this case. To be sure, we begin the task of deciding whether a punishment is unconstitutional by reviewing legislative enactments and the work of sentencing juries relating to the punishment in question to determine whether our Nation has set its face against a punishment to an extent that it can be concluded that the punishment offends our "evolving standards of decency." The Court undertakes such an analysis in this case. But JUSTICE SCALIA, in his plurality opinion on this point would treat the Eighth Amendment inquiry as complete with this investigation. ... a more searching inquiry is mandated by our precedents interpreting the Cruel and Unusual Punishment Clause. In my view, that inquiry must in this case go beyond age-based statutory classifications relating to matters other than capital punishment, and must also encompass what JUSTICE SCALIA calls, with evident but misplaced disdain, "ethicoscientific" evidence. Only then can we be in a position to judge, as our cases require, whether a punishment is unconstitutionally excessive, either because it is disproportionate given the culpability of the offender, or because it serves no legitimate penal goal.

I.

Our judgment about the constitutionality of a punishment under the Eighth Amendment is informed, though not determined, by an examination of contemporary attitudes toward the punishment, as evidenced in the actions of legislatures and of juries. The views of organizations with expertise in relevant fields and the choices of governments elsewhere in the world also merit our attention as indicators whether a punishment is acceptable in a civilized society.

A.

B.

The application of these laws is another indicator the Court agrees to be relevant. The fact that juries have on occasion sentenced a minor to death shows, the Court says, that the death penalty for adolescents is not categorically unacceptable to juries. This, of course, is true; but it is not a conclusion that takes Eighth Amendment analysis very far. Just as we have never insisted that a punishment have been rejected unanimously by the States before we may judge it cruel and unusual, so we have never adopted the extraordinary view that a punishment is beyond Eighth Amendment challenge if it is sometimes handed down by a jury. ...

Both in absolute and in relative terms, imposition of the death penalty on adolescents is distinctly unusual. Adolescent offenders make up only a small proportion of the current death-row population: 30 out of a total of 2,186 inmates, or 1.37 percent. Eleven minors were sentenced to die in 1982; 9 in 1983; 6 in 1984; 5 in 1985; 7 in 1986; and 2 in 1987. Forty-one, or 2.3 percent, of the 1,813 death sentences imposed between January 1, 1982, and June 30, 1988, were for juvenile crimes. And juvenile offenders are significantly less likely to receive the death penalty than adults. During the same period, there were 97,086 arrests of adults for homicide, and 1,772 adult death sentences, or 1.8 percent; and 8,911 arrests of minors for homicide, compared to 41 juvenile death sentences, or 0.5 percent.

...It is certainly true that in the vast majority of cases, juries have not sentenced juveniles to death, and it seems to me perfectly proper to conclude that a sentence so rarely imposed is "unusual."

C.

Further indicators of contemporary standards of decency that should inform our consideration of the Eighth Amendment question are the opinions of respected organizations. Where organizations with expertise is a relevant area have given careful consideration to the question of a punishment's appropriateness, there is no reason why that judgment should not be entitled to attention as an indicator of contemporary standards. There is no dearth of opinion from such groups that the state-sanctioned killing of minors is unjustified. A number, indeed, have filed briefs amicus curiae in these cases, in support of petitioners...

D.

...It is unnecessary, however, to rest a view that the Eighth Amendment prohibits the execution of minors solely upon a judgment as to the meaning to be attached to the evidence of contemporary values outlined above, for the execution of juveniles fails to satisfy two well-established and independent Eighth Amendment requirements – that a punishment not be disproportionate, and that it make a contribution to acceptable goals of punishment.

II.

JUSTICE SCALIA forthrightly states in his plurality opinion that Eighth Amendment analysis is at an end once legislation and jury verdicts relating to the punishment in question are analyzed as indicators of contemporary values. A majority of the Court rejected this revisionist view as recently as last Term and does so again in this case and in Penry v. Lynaugh. We need not and should not treat this narrow range of factors as determinative of our decision whether a punishment violates the Constitution because it is excessive.

The Court has explicitly stated that "the attitude of state legislatures and sentencing juries do not wholly determine" a controversy arising under the Eighth Amendment.

...This Court abandons its proven and proper role in our constitutional system when it hands back to the very majorities the Framers distrusted the power to define the precise scope of protection afforded by the Bill of Rights, rather than bringing its own judgment to bear on that question, after complete analysis.

III.

There can be no doubt at this point in our constitutional history that the Eighth Amendment forbids punishment that is wholly disproportionate to the blameworthiness of the offender. "The constitutional principle of proportionality has been recognized explicitly in this Court for almost a century."..

Proportionality analysis requires that we compare "the gravity of the offense," understood to include not only the injury caused, but also the defendant's culpability, with "the harshness of the penalty." In my view, juveniles so generally lack the degree of responsibility for their crimes that is a predicate for the constitutional imposition of the death penalty that the Eighth Amendment forbids that they receive that punishment.

A.

Legislative determinations distinguishing juveniles from adults abound. These age-based classifications reveal much about how our society regards juveniles as a class, and about societal beliefs regarding adolescent levels of responsibility.

The participation of juveniles in a substantial number of activities open to adults is either barred completely or significantly restricted by legislation. All States but two have a uniform age of majority, and have set that age at 18 or above. No State has lowered its voting age below 18. Nor does any State permit a person under 18 to serve on a jury. Only four States ever permit persons below 18 to marry without parental consent. Thirty-seven States have specific enactments requiring that a patient have attained 18 before she may validly consent to medical treatment. Thirty-four States require parental consent before a person below 18 may drive a motor car. Legislation in 42 States prohibits those under 18 from purchasing pornographic materials. Where gambling is legal, adolescents under 18 are generally not permitted to participate in it, in some or all of its forms. In these and a host of other ways, minors are treated differently from adults in our laws, which reflects the simple truth derived from communal experience that juveniles as a class have not the level of maturation and responsibility that we presume in adults and consider desirable for full participation in the rights and duties of modern life.

> The reasons why juveniles are not trusted with the privileges and responsibilities of an adult also explain why their irresponsible conduct is not as morally reprehensible as that of an adult." Adolescents "are more vulnerable, more impulsive, and less self-disciplined than adults," and are without the same "capacity to control their conduct and to think in long-range terms." They are particularly impressionable and subject to peer pressure and prone to "experiment, risk-taking and bravado." They lack "experience, perspective, and judgment." Moreover, the very paternalism that our society shows toward youths and the dependency it forces upon them mean that society bears a responsibility for the actions of juveniles that it does not for the actions of adults who are at least theoretically free to make their own choices: "youth crime . . . is not exclusively the offender's fault; offenses by the young represent a failure of family, school, and the social system, which share responsibility for the development of America's youth.

To be sure, the development of cognitive and reasoning abilities and of empathy, the acquisition of experience upon which these abilities operate and upon which the capacity to make sound value judgments depends, and in general the process of maturation into a self-directed individual fully responsible for his or her actions, occur by degrees. But the factors discussed above indicate that 18 is the dividing line that society has generally drawn, the point at which it is thought reasonable to assume that persons have an ability to make, and a duty to bear responsibility for their, judgments. Insofar as age 18 is a necessarily arbitrary social choice as a point at which to acknowledge a person's maturity and responsibility, given the different developmental rates of individuals, it is in fact "a conservative estimate of the dividing line between adolescence and adulthood. Many of the psychological and emotional changes that an adolescent experiences in maturing do not actually occur until the early 20s."

B.

There may be exceptional individuals who mature more quickly than their peers, and who might be considered fully responsible for their actions prior to the age of 18, despite their lack of the experience upon which judgment depends. In my view, however, it is not sufficient to accommodate the facts about juveniles that an individual youth's culpability may be taken into account in the decision to transfer him or her from the juvenile to the adult court system for trial, or that a capital sentencing jury is instructed to consider youth and other mitigating factors. I believe that the Eighth Amendment requires that a person who lacks that full degree of responsibility for his or her actions associated with adulthood not be sentenced to death. Hence it is constitutionally inadequate that a juvenile offender's level of responsibility be taken into account only along with a host of other factors that the court or jury may decide outweigh that want of responsibility.

Immaturity that constitutionally should operate as a bar to a disproportionate death sentence does not guarantee that a minor will not be transferred for trial to the adult court system. Rather, the most important considerations in the decision to transfer a juvenile offender are the seriousness of the offense, the extent of prior delinquency, and the response to prior treatment within the juvenile justice system. Psychological, intellectual, and other personal characteristics of juvenile offenders receive little attention at the transfer stage, and cannot account for differences between those transferred and those who remain in the juvenile court system. Nor is an adolescent's lack of full culpability isolated at the sentencing stage as a factor that determinatively bars a death sentence. A jury is free to weigh a juvenile offender's youth and lack of full responsibility against the heinousness of the crime and other aggravating factors – and, finding the aggravating factors weightier, to sentence even the most immature of 16- or 17-year olds to be killed. By no stretch of the imagination, then, are the transfer and sentencing decisions designed to isolate those juvenile offenders who are exceptionally mature and responsible, and who thus stand out from their peers as a class.

It is thus unsurprising that individualized consideration at transfer and sentencing has not in fact ensured that juvenile offenders lacking an adult's culpability are not sentenced to die. Quite the contrary. Adolescents on death row appear typically to have a battery of psychological, emotional, and other problems going to their likely capacity for judgment and level of blameworthiness. A recent diagnostic evaluation of all 14 juveniles on death rows in four States is instructive. Seven of the adolescents sentenced to die were psychotic when evaluated, or had been so diagnosed in earlier childhood; four others had histories consistent with diagnoses of severe mood disorders; and the remaining three experienced periodic paranoid episodes, during which they would assault perceived enemies. Eight had suffered severe head injuries during childhood, and nine suffered from neurological abnormalities. Psychoeducational testing showed that only 2 of these death-row inmates had IQ scores above 90 (that is, in the normal range) – and both individuals suffered from psychiatric disorders – while 10 offenders showed impaired abstract reasoning on at least some tests. All but two of the adolescents had been physically abused, and five sexually abused. Within the families of these children, violence, alcoholism, drug abuse, and psychiatric disorders were commonplace.

The cases under consideration today certainly do not suggest that individualized consideration at transfer and sentencing ensure that only exceptionally mature juveniles, as blameworthy for their crimes as an adult, are sentenced to death. Transferring jurisdiction over Kevin Stanford to Circuit Court, the Juvenile Division of the Jefferson, Kentucky, District Court nevertheless found that Stanford, who was 17 at the time of his crime,

> has a low internalization of the values and morals of society and lacks social skills. That he does possess an institutionalized personality and has, in effect, because of his chaotic family life and lack of treatment, become socialized in delinquent behavior. That he is emotionally immature and could be amenable to treatment if properly done on a long term basis of psychotherapeutic intervention and reality based therapy for socialization and drug therapy in a residential facility.

At the penalty phase of Stanford's trial, witnesses testified that Stanford, who lived with various relatives, had used drugs from the age of about 13, and that his drug use had caused changes in his personality and behavior. Stanford had been placed at times in juvenile treatment facilities, and a witness who had assessed him upon his admission to an employment skills project found that he lacked age-appropriate social interaction skills; had a history of drug abuse; and wanted for family support or supervision.

Heath Wilkins was 16 when he committed the crime for which Missouri intends to kill him. The juvenile court, in ordering him transferred for trial to adult court, focused upon the viciousness of Wilkins' crime, the juvenile system's inability to rehabilitate him in the 17 months of juvenile confinement available, and the need to protect the public, though it also mentioned that Wilkins was, in its view, "an experienced person, and mature in his appearance and habits." The Circuit Court found Wilkins competent to stand trial. Wilkins then waived counsel, with the avowed intention of pleading guilty and seeking the death penalty and the Circuit Court accepted the waiver and later Wilkins' guilty plea. Wilkins was not represented by counsel at sentencing. Presenting no mitigating evidence, he told the court he would prefer the death penalty to life in prison – "one I fear, the other one I don't," – and after hearing evidence from the State, the Court sentenced Wilkins to die. Wilkins took no steps to appeal and objected to an amicus' efforts on his behalf. The Missouri Supreme Court, however, ordered an evaluation to determine whether Wilkins was competent to waive his right to appellate counsel. Concluding that Wilkins was incompetent to waive his rights, the state-appointed forensic psychiatrist found that Wilkins " suffers from a mental disorder" that affects his "reasoning and impairs his behavior." It would be incredible to suppose, given this psychiatrist's conclusion and his summary of Wilkins' past, set out in the margin, that Missouri's transfer and sentencing schemes had operated to identify in Wilkins a 16-year old mature and culpable beyond his years.

C.

Juveniles very generally lack that degree of blameworthiness that is, in my view, a constitutional prerequisite for the imposition of capital punishment under our precedents concerning the Eighth Amendment proportionality principle. The individualized consideration of an offender's youth and culpability at the transfer stage and at sentencing has not operated to ensure that the only offenders under 18 singled out for the ultimate penalty are exceptional individuals whose level of responsibility is more developed than that of their peers. In that circumstance, I believe that the same categorical assumption that juveniles as a class are insufficiently mature to be regarded as fully responsible that we make in so many other areas is appropriately made in determining whether minors may be subjected to the death penalty. ...

IV.

Under a second strand of Eighth Amendment inquiry into whether a particular sentence is excessive and hence unconstitutional, we ask whether the sentence makes a measurable contribution to acceptable goals of punishment. The two "principal social purposes" of capital punishment are said to be "retribution and the deterrence of capital crimes by prospective offenders." Unless the death penalty applied to persons for offenses committed under 18 measurably contributes to one of these goals, the Eighth Amendment prohibits it.

"Retribution as a justification for executing [offenders] very much depends on the degree of [their] culpability." ... These same considerations persuade me that executing juveniles "does not measurably contribute to the retributive end of ensuring that the criminal gets his just deserts." A punishment that fails the Eighth Amendment test of proportionality because disproportionate to the offender's blameworthiness by definition is not justly deserved.

Nor does the execution of juvenile offenders measurably contribute to the goal of deterrence. Excluding juveniles from the class of persons eligible to receive the death penalty will have little effect on any deterrent value capital punishment may have for potential offenders who are over 18: these adult offenders may of course remain eligible for a death sentence. The potential deterrent effect of juvenile executions on adolescent offenders is also insignificant. The deterrent value of capital punishment rests "on the assumption that we are rational beings who always think before we act, and then base our actions on a careful calculation of the gains and losses involved." As the plurality noted in Thompson, "the likelihood that the teenage offender has made the kind of cost-benefit analysis that attaches any weight to the possibility of execution is so remote as to be virtually nonexistent." First, juveniles "have less capacity . . . to think in long-range terms than adults," and their careful weighing of a distant, uncertain, and indeed highly unlikely consequence prior to action is most improbable. In addition, juveniles have little fear of death, because they have "a profound conviction of their own omnipotence and immortality." Because imposition of the death penalty on persons for offenses committed under the age of 18 makes no measurable contribution to the goals of either retribution or deterrence, it is "nothing more than the purposeless and needless imposition of pain and suffering," and is thus excessive and unconstitutional.

V.

There are strong indications that the execution of juvenile offenders violates contemporary standards of decency: a majority of States decline to permit juveniles to be sentenced to death; imposition of the sentence upon minors is very unusual even in those States that permit it; and respected organizations with expertise in relevant areas regard the execution of juveniles as unacceptable, as does international opinion. These indicators serve to confirm in my view my conclusion that the Eighth Amendment prohibits the execution of persons for offenses they committed while below the age of 18, because the death penalty is disproportionate when applied to such young offenders and fails measurably to serve the goals of capital punishment. I dissent.

NOTES AND QUERIES

In the majority's analysis of the evolving standard of decency regarding the death penalty as applied to juveniles, the Court finds irrelevant the different laws regarding the age of majority. Do you find the Court's reasoning persuasive? The Court's analysis of state statutes finds no national consensus. Do you find that analysis correct? How does the Court respond to popular indicia of changing standards of decency? Do you find persuasive the Court's rejection of arguments based on adolescents' lack of cognitive and moral capacity? The majority obviously relies on state statutes and the decision making patterns of capital juries. By using those two standards, what is the minimal that would need to be shown in order to find the death penalty unconstitutional for 18 year-old juveniles?

Do you agree with the dissent that the penalty is disproportionate to the blameworthiness of adolescents and that the application of the death penalty in these instances does not further goals of deterrence and retribution?

NOTE ON THOMPSON V. OKLAHOMA

The year before *Stanford*, the Court announced, in *Thompson v. Oklahoma*, 487 U.S. 815 (1988) (Stevens, J., plurality), that it was unconstitutional to execute anyone who was under the age of sixteen at the time that the underlying offense was committed. Among the considerations that the Court examined were the lesser culpability of a minor because of the obvious factors like inexperience, less education, and less intelligence. The Court indicated that the death penalty serves two basic purposes, retribution and the deterrence of future crimes by prospective offenders. The Court emphasized that punishment should be related directly to the personal culpability of the criminal defendant. The Court then stated that because of the lesser culpability of a juvenile offender, the teenager's capacity for growth, and society's fiduciary obligations to its children, the retributive rationale was inapplicable to the execution of an offender under the age of sixteen. The Court likewise dismissed the deterrence rationale as applied to offenders under the age of sixteen because there will continue to be executions of adults to deter prospective offenders and because the likelihood that the teenage offender has made the kind of cost-benefit analysis that attaches any weight to the possibility of execution is so remote as to be virtually nonexistent. Given these considerations, how would you justify imposing the death penalty on a 16 year-old but not a 15 ½ year-old?

NOTE ON THE PSYCHOLOGICAL DEVELOPMENT OF ADOLESCENTS

In the wake of *Atkins v. Virginia*, 536 U.S. 304 (2002), commentators have extended the Supreme Court's logic about the prohibition against executing mentally retarded individuals to juveniles. Commentators have found that many of the developmental characteristics that establish the diminished culpability of the mentally retarded also characterize adolescents. They also have found that the age at which adolescents attain relevant competencies and their developmental trajectories reveals that they may not measureably depart from the stable and flat developmental trajectories of the mentally retarded. Most notably, research from the biological sciences complements evidence from behavioral science regarding deficits and incompetencies in adolescents that influence judgment, decision making, and emotional regulation. Adolescents exhibit uneven brain development with regard to various functions, and this irregularity results in significant variation among adolescents in the age at which they attain organic brain developmental thresholds that regulate the emotional and cognitive components of decision making and control. This variation suggests that some adolescents, even some in their twenties, may be immature both in their psychosocial functioning and their organic development that underlies it. These findings have been used to support the argument that the failure to account for these findings invites the risk of executing adolescents whose culpabilities do not reach the constitutional thresholds defined in *Atkins* and other death penalty cases that require a high standard for establishing culpability. See Jeffrey Fagan, *Atkins*, adolescence, and the maturity heuristic: Rationales for a categorical exemption for juveniles from capital punishment, 33 N.M.L. Rev. 207 (2003); George J. Annas, Moral progress, mental retardation, and the death penalty, 347 New Eng. J. Med. 1814, 1817 (2002); Robin M. A. Weeks, Comparing children to the mentally retarded: How the decision in *Atkins v. Virginia* will affect the execution of juvenile offenders, 17 BYU J. Pub. L. 451 (2003); and Lawrence Steinberg and Elizabeth S. Scott, Less guilty by reason of adolescence: Developmental immaturity, diminished responsibility, and the juvenile death penalty, 58 Am. Psychologist 1009 (2003). How relevant do you find this research given the Court's analysis in *Stanford v. Kentucky*?

NOTE ON JUVENILE DEATH PENALTY RESEARCH

One study of Virgina registered voters eligible for the jury pool demonstrated that sixty percent of those polled would recommend execution of a ten-year-old for committing murder. Importantly, 73 percent would execute fifteen-year-olds; 90% would execute sixteen-year-olds; and 96 percent would execute eighteen-year-olds. Catherine A. Crosby; Preston A. Britner; Kathleen M. Jodl, and Sharon G. Portwood, The juvenile death penalty and the Eighth Amendment: An empirical investigation of societal consensus and proportionality, 19 L. and Hum. Beh. 245, 245-61 (1995).

The findings from the above study are, in many regards, remarkably consistent with those from other states. A study using a statewide sample of 539 Tennessee residents, revealed that 72.5 of respondents would allow the death penalty of juveniles. Of that group, 23 percent thought that there should be no minimal age, by age 12, nearly a majority (43.8%) supported executions, and by age 16, the majority (85.6%) endorsed the use of the death penalty. Importantly, when provided with alternative sentences like life without the possibility of parole, 64% reported that they would prefer that alternative to execution. Melissa M. Moon, John Paul Wright, Francis T. Cullen, and Jennifer A. Pealer, Putting kids to death: Specifying public support for juvenile capital punishment, 17 Jus. Q. 663 (2000). In a California study of 535 adults (aged 18-91 years-old), it was found that 28.2% strongly opposed the execution of juveniles. Similar to the other study, this one found that, of those who supported the use of the death penalty for juveniles, 42.5% would support life without parole as an alternative to the death penalty. Brenda L. Vogel and Ronald E. Vogel, The age of death: Appraising public opinion of juvenile capital punishment, 31 J. of Crim. Jus. 169 (2003).

NOTE ON THE JUVENILE DEATH PENALTY AFTER ATKINS: ROPER V. SIMMONS

Commentators' suggestions that the Court would eventually revisit *Stanford* – in which the Court had held that imposition of the death penalty on offenders for murders committed at 16 and 17 years of age did not violate the Eighth Amendment – were prescient and very quickly substantiated. Not long after having decided *Atkins* – in which the Court had held that the execution of offenders who were mentally retarded violated the Eighth Amendment, the Court examined its potential impact on juvenile death penalty jurisprudence. The Court did so in *Roper v. Simmons*, 125 S. Ct. 1183 (2005). The facts of the case are particularly gruesome. At the age of 17, when he was still a junior in high school, Christopher Simmons committed murder. About nine months later, after he had turned 18, he was tried and sentenced to death. There is little doubt that Simmons was the instigator of the crime. Before its commission Simmons said he wanted to murder someone. In chilling, callous terms he talked about his plan, discussing it for the most part with two friends, then aged 15 and 16. Simmons proposed to commit burglary and murder by breaking and entering, tying up a victim, and throwing the victim off a bridge. Simmons assured his friends they could "get away with it" because they were minors. The three met at about 2 a.m. on the night of the murder, but one left before the other two set out. Simmons and his friend entered the home of the victim, Shirley Crook, after reaching through an open window and unlocking the back door. Simmons turned on a hallway light. Awakened, Mrs. Crook called out, "Who's there?" In response, Simmons entered Mrs. Crook's bedroom, where he recognized her from a previous car accident involving them both. Simmons later admitted this confirmed his resolve to murder her. Using duct tape to cover her eyes and mouth and bind her hands, the two perpetrators put Mrs. Crook in her minivan and drove to a state park. They reinforced the bindings, covered her head with a towel, and walked her to a railroad trestle spanning the Meramec River. There they tied her hands and feet together with electrical wire, wrapped her whole face in duct tape and threw her from the bridge, drowning her in the waters below. By the afternoon Steven Crook had returned home from an overnight trip, found his bedroom in disarray, and reported his wife missing. On the same afternoon fishermen recovered the victim's body from the river. Simmons, meanwhile, was bragging about the killing, telling friends he had killed a woman. The jury recommended the death penalty and the trial judge imposed it.

The Supreme Court, in an opinion by Kennedy, joined by Stevens, Souter, Ginsburg, and Breyer, held that the Constitution's Eighth Amendment proscription against cruel and unusual punishment prohibited imposition of the death penalty for crimes committed when offenders were under 18 years of age. The Court found that the evidence of national consensus against the death penalty for juveniles was similar, and in some respects parallel, to the evidence held sufficient in *Atkins* to demonstrate a national consensus against the death penalty for the mentally retarded. Similarly to *Atkins*, 30 states prohibited the juvenile death penalty, comprising (i) 12 that had rejected the death penalty altogether, and (ii) 18 that maintained it but, by express provision or by judicial interpretation, excluded juveniles from its reach. Also similarly to *Atkins*, even in the 20 states without a formal prohibition on executing juveniles, the practice was infrequent. Though less dramatic than the change from a prior contrary decision to *Atkins*, the change from *Stanford* to the current case was significant, for the same consistency of direction of change had been demonstrated, where since *Stanford*, no state that previously had prohibited capital punishment for juveniles had reinstated it.

The Court also found that, as in *Atkins*, the objective indicia of consensus in the instant case – (a) the rejection of death penalty for offenders under 18 in the majority of states; (b) the infrequency of its use even where it remained on the books; and (c) the consistency in the trend toward abolition of the practice – provided sufficient evidence that society presently viewed juveniles as categorically less culpable than the average criminal.

In addition, the Court reasoned that the general maturity-related differences between juveniles under 18 and adults demonstrated that juvenile offenders could not with reliability be classified among the worst offenders. It noted that the reasoning applied by a plurality of the court concerning the immaturity of people under the age of 16 in *Thompson v Oklahoma* (1988) – where the court had held that the Eighth Amendment prohibited imposition of the death penalty for offenses committed when the offenders were under 16 – applied to all offenders under 18. According to the majority, there are three differences between juveniles and adults that demonstrate that juvenile offenders cannot with reliability be classified among the worst offenders. First, the lack of maturity and an underdeveloped sense of responsibility are found in youth more often than in adults and are more understandable among the young. These qualities often result in impetuous and ill-considered actions and decisions. Second, juveniles are more vulnerable or susceptible to negative influences and outside pressures, including peer pressure. Finally, the character of a juvenile is not as well formed as that of an adult. These differences, in the eyes of the Court, render suspect any conclusion that a juvenile falls among the worst offenders. The susceptibility of juveniles to immature and irresponsible behavior means their irresponsible conduct is not as morally reprehensible as that of an adult. Once the diminished culpability of juveniles was recognized, it was evident that the penological justifications (restitution and deterrence) for the death penalty applied to juveniles with lesser force than to adults. The differences between juvenile and adult offenders were too marked and too well understood to risk allowing a youthful person to receive the death penalty despite insufficient culpability. Further support for the claim came from evidence that the age of 18 was the point where, for many purposes, society drew the line between childhood and adulthood; and from international law, which indicated that the United States was the only country in the world that continued to give official sanction to the juvenile death penalty. Thus, despite the problems associated with line drawing, the majority concludes that a line must be drawn.

In a powerful dissent, Justice O'Connor expressed the view that (1) the court's decision was not justified by (a) the objective evidence of contemporary societal values, (b) the court's moral proportionality analysis, or (c) the two in tandem; (2) the evidence before the court failed to demonstrate conclusively that any national consensus against capital punishment of 17-year-old offenders had emerged in the brief period since the court had upheld the constitutionality of this practice in *Stanford*; (3) the court had adduced no evidence impeaching the seemingly reasonable conclusion reached by many state legislatures that at least some 17-year-old murderers were sufficiently mature to deserve the death penalty in an appropriate case; and (4) it had not been shown that capital sentencing juries were incapable of accurately assessing a youthful defendant's maturity or of giving due weight to the mitigating characteristics associated with youth.

Justice Scalia, joined by Rehnquist and Thomas, also forcefully dissented and expressed the view that (1) the court had (a) proclaimed itself sole arbiter of the nation's moral standards, and (b) in the course of discharging that responsibility, had purported to take guidance from the views of foreign courts and legislatures; and (2) the meaning of the Eighth Amendment, no more than the meaning of other provisions of the Constitution, ought not to be determined by the subjective views of (a) five members of the Supreme Court, and (b) like-minded foreigners.

DETERMINING WHO DECIDES

RING v. ARIZONA
122 S. Ct. 2428 (2002)

JUSTICE GINSBURG delivered the opinion of the Court.

This case concerns the Sixth Amendment right to a jury trial in capital prosecutions. In Arizona, following a jury adjudication of a defendant's guilt of first-degree murder, the trial judge, sitting alone, determines the presence or absence of the aggravating factors required by Arizona law for imposition of the death penalty.

In Walton v. Arizona (1990), this Court held that Arizona's sentencing scheme was compatible with the Sixth Amendment because the additional facts found by the judge qualified as sentencing considerations, not as "elements of the offense of capital murder." Ten years later, however, we decided Apprendi v. New Jersey (2000), which held that the Sixth Amendment does not permit a defendant to be "exposed . . . to a penalty exceeding the maximum he would receive if punished according to the facts reflected in the jury verdict alone." This prescription governs, Apprendi determined, even if the State characterizes the additional findings made by the judge as "sentencing factors."

Apprendi's reasoning is irreconcilable with Walton's holding in this regard, and today we overrule Walton in relevant part. Capital defendants, no less than non-capital defendants, we conclude, are entitled to a jury determination of any fact on which the legislature conditions an increase in their maximum punishment.

I.

At the trial of petitioner Timothy Ring for murder, armed robbery, and related charges, the prosecutor presented evidence sufficient to permit the jury to find the facts here recounted. On November 28, 1994, a Wells Fargo armored van pulled up to the Dillard's department store at Arrowhead Mall in Glendale, Arizona. Courier Dave Moss left the van to pick up money inside the store When he returned, the van, and its driver, John Magoch, were gone.

Later that day, Maricopa County Sheriff's Deputies found the van – its doors locked and its engine running – in the parking lot of a church in Sun City, Arizona. Inside the vehicle they found Magoch, dead from a single gunshot to the head. According to Wells Fargo records, more than $562,000 in cash and $271,000 in checks were missing from the van.

Prompted by an informant's tip, Glendale police sought to determine whether Ring and his friend James Greenham were involved in the robbery. The police investigation revealed that the two had made several expensive cash purchases in December 1994 and early 1995. Wiretaps were then placed on the telephones of Ring, Greenham, and a third suspect, William Ferguson.

Testifying in his own defense, Ring said the money seized at his house was startup capital for a construction company he and Greenham were planning to form. Ring testified that he made his share of the money as a confidential informant for the Federal Bureau of Investigation and as a bail bondsman and gunsmith. But an FBI agent testified that Ring had been paid only $458, and other evidence showed that Ring had made no more than $8,800 as a bail bondsman.

The trial judge instructed the jury on alternative charges of premeditated murder and felony murder. The jury deadlocked on premeditated murder, with 6 of 12 jurors voting to acquit, but convicted Ring of felony murder occurring in the course of armed robbery.

As later summed up by the Arizona Supreme Court, "the evidence admitted at trial failed to prove, beyond a reasonable doubt, that [Ring] was a major participant in the armed robbery or that he actually murdered Magoch." Although clear evidence connected Ring to the robbery's proceeds, nothing submitted at trial put him at the scene of the robbery. Furthermore, "for all we know from the trial evidence," the Arizona court stated, "[Ring] did not participate in, plan, or even expect the killing. This lack of evidence no doubt explains why the jury found [Ring] guilty of felony, but not premeditated, murder."

Under Arizona law, Ring could not be sentenced to death, the statutory maximum penalty for first-degree murder, unless further findings were made. The State's first-degree murder statute prescribes that the offense "is punishable by death or life imprisonment as provided by §13-703." The cross-referenced section, §13-703, directs the judge who presided at trial to "conduct a separate sentencing hearing to determine the existence or nonexistence of [certain enumerated] circumstances . . . for the purpose of determining the sentence to be imposed." The statute further instructs: "The hearing shall be conducted before the court alone. The court alone shall make all factual determinations required by this section or the constitution of the United States or this state."

At the conclusion of the sentencing hearing, the judge is to determine the presence or absence of the enumerated "aggravating circumstances" and any "mitigating circumstances." The State's law authorizes the judge to sentence the defendant to death only if there is at least one aggravating circumstance and "there are no mitigating circumstances sufficiently substantial to call for leniency."

Between Ring's trial and sentencing hearing, Greenham pleaded guilty to second-degree murder and armed robbery. He stipulated to a 27 1/2 year sentence and agreed to cooperate with the prosecution in the cases against Ring and Ferguson.

Called by the prosecution at Ring's sentencing hearing, Greenham testified that he, Ring, and Ferguson had been planning the robbery for several weeks before it occurred. According to Greenham, Ring "had I guess taken the role as leader because he laid out all the tactics." On the day of the robbery, Greenham said, the three watched the armored van pull up to the mall. When Magoch opened the door to smoke a cigarette, Ring shot him with a rifle equipped with a homemade silencer. Greenham then pushed Magoch's body aside and drove the van away. At Ring's direction, Greenham drove to the church parking lot, where he and Ring transferred the money to Ring's truck. Later, Greenham recalled, as the three robbers were dividing up the money, Ring upbraided him and Ferguson for "forgetting to congratulate [Ring] on [his] shot."

On cross-examination, Greenham acknowledged having previously told Ring's counsel that Ring had nothing to do with the planning or execution of the robbery. Greenham explained that he had made that prior statement only because Ring had threatened his life. Greenham also acknowledged that he was now testifying against Ring as "pay back" for the threats and for Ring's interference in Greenham's relationship with Greenham's ex-wife.

On October 29, 1997, the trial judge entered his "Special Verdict" sentencing Ring to death. Because Ring was convicted of felony murder, not premeditated murder, the judge recognized that Ring was eligible for the death penalty only if he was Magoch's actual killer or if he was "a major participant in the armed robbery that led to the killing and exhibited a reckless disregard or indifference for human life."

Citing Greenham's testimony at the sentencing hearing, the judge concluded that Ring "is the one who shot and killed Mr. Magoch." The judge also found that Ring was a major participant in the robbery and that armed robbery "is unquestionably a crime which carries with it a grave risk of death."

The judge then turned to the determination of aggravating and mitigating circumstances. He found two aggravating factors. First, the judge determined that Ring committed the offense in expectation of receiving something of "pecuniary value;" "taking the cash from the armored car was the motive and reason for Mr. Magoch's murder and not just the result." Second, the judge found that the offense was committed "in an especially heinous, cruel or depraved manner." In support of this finding, he cited Ring's comment, as reported by Greenham at the sentencing hearing, expressing pride in his marksmanship. The judge found one nonstatutory mitigating factor: Ring's "minimal" criminal record. In his judgment, that mitigating circumstance did not "call for leniency"; he therefore sentenced Ring to death.

On appeal, Ring argued that Arizona's capital sentencing scheme violates the Sixth and Fourteenth Amendments to the U.S. Constitution because it entrusts to a judge the finding of a fact raising the defendant's maximum penalty. The State, in response, noted that this Court had upheld Arizona's system in Walton v. Arizona and had stated in Apprendi that Walton remained good law.

We granted Ring's petition for a writ of certiorari to allay uncertainty in the lower courts caused by the manifest tension between Walton and the reasoning of Apprendi. We now reverse ...

II.

Based solely on the jury's verdict finding Ring guilty of first-degree felony murder, the maximum punishment he could have received was life imprisonment. This was so because, in Arizona, a "death sentence may not legally be imposed . . . unless at least one aggravating factor is found to exist beyond a reasonable doubt." The question presented is whether that aggravating factor may be found by the judge, as

Arizona law specifies, or whether the Sixth Amendment's jury trial guarantee, made applicable to the States by the Fourteenth Amendment, requires that the aggravating factor determination be entrusted to the jury.

The dispositive question, we said, "is one not of form, but of effect." If a State makes an increase in a defendant's authorized punishment contingent on the finding of a fact, that fact – no matter how the State labels it – must be found by a jury beyond a reasonable doubt. A defendant may not be "exposed . . . to a penalty exceeding the maximum he would receive if punished according to the facts reflected in the jury verdict alone."

In an effort to reconcile its capital sentencing system with the Sixth Amendment as interpreted by Apprendi, Arizona first restates the Apprendi majority's portrayal of Arizona's system: Ring was convicted of first-degree murder, for which Arizona law specifies "death or life imprisonment" as the only sentencing options; Ring was therefore sentenced within the range of punishment authorized by the jury verdict. This argument overlooks Apprendi's instruction that "the relevant inquiry is one not of form, but of effect." In effect, "the required finding [of an aggravated circumstance] exposed [Ring] to a greater punishment than that authorized by the jury's guilty verdict." The Arizona first-degree murder statute "authorizes a maximum penalty of death only in a formal sense," for it explicitly cross-references the statutory provision requiring the finding of an aggravating circumstance before imposition of the death penalty. If Arizona prevailed on its opening argument, Apprendi would be reduced to a "meaningless and formalistic" rule of statutory drafting.

Arizona also supports the distinction relied upon in Walton between elements of an offense and sentencing factors. As to elevation of the maximum punishment, however, Apprendi renders the argument untenable. Apprendi repeatedly instructs in that context that the characterization of a fact or circumstance as an "element" or a "sentencing factor" is not determinative of the question "who decides," judge or jury...

Even if facts increasing punishment beyond the maximum authorized by a guilty verdict standing alone ordinarily must be found by a jury, Arizona further urges, aggravating circumstances necessary to trigger a death sentence may nonetheless be reserved for judicial determination. As Arizona's counsel maintained at oral argument, there is no doubt that "death is different."...

Apart from the Eighth Amendment provenance of aggravating factors, Arizona presents "no specific reason for excepting capital defendants from the constitutional protections . . . extended to defendants generally, and none is readily apparent." The notion "that the Eighth Amendment's restriction on a state legislature's ability to define capital crimes should be compensated for by permitting States more leeway under the Fifth and Sixth Amendments in proving an aggravating fact necessary to a capital sentence . . . is without precedent in our constitutional jurisprudence."

In various settings, we have interpreted the Constitution to require the addition of an element or elements to the definition of a criminal offense in order to narrow its scope. .. If a legislature responded to one of these decisions by adding the element we held constitutionally required, surely the Sixth Amendment guarantee would apply to that element. We see no reason to differentiate capital crimes from all others in this regard.

Arizona suggests that judicial authority over the finding of aggravating factors "may . . . be a better way to guarantee against the arbitrary imposition of the death penalty." The Sixth Amendment jury trial right, however, does not turn on the relative rationality, fairness, or efficiency of potential factfinders. Entrusting to a judge the finding of facts necessary to support a death sentence might be

> an admirably fair and efficient scheme of criminal justice designed for a society that is prepared to leave criminal justice to the State...The founders of the American Republic were not prepared to leave it to the State, which is why the jury-trial guarantee was one of the least controversial provisions of the Bill of Rights. It has never been efficient; but it has always been free.

In any event, the superiority of judicial factfinding in capital cases is far from evident. Unlike Arizona, the great majority of States responded to this Court's Eighth Amendment decisions requiring the presence of aggravating circumstances in capital cases by entrusting those determinations to the jury.

For the reasons stated, we hold that Walton and Apprendi are irreconcilable; our Sixth Amendment jurisprudence cannot be home to both. Accordingly, we overrule Walton to the extent that it allows a sentencing judge, sitting without a jury, to find an aggravating circumstance necessary for imposition of the death penalty. Because Arizona's enumerated aggravating factors operate as "the functional equivalent of an element of a greater offense," the Sixth Amendment requires that they be found by a jury.

The right to trial by jury guaranteed by the Sixth Amendment would be senselessly diminished if it encompassed the factfinding necessary to increase a defendant's sentence by two years, but not the factfinding necessary to put him to death. We hold that the Sixth Amendment applies to both. The judgment of the Arizona Supreme Court is therefore reversed, and the case is remanded for further proceedings not inconsistent with this opinion.

It is so ordered.

JUSTICE SCALIA, with whom JUSTICE THOMAS joins, concurring.

...my observing over the past 12 years the accelerating propensity of both state and federal legislatures to adopt "sentencing factors" determined by judges that increase punishment beyond what is authorized by the jury's verdict, and my witnessing the belief of a near majority of my colleagues that this novel practice is perfectly OK, cause me to believe that our people's traditional belief in the right of trial by jury is in perilous decline. That decline is bound to be confirmed, and indeed accelerated, by the repeated spectacle of a man's going to his death because a judge found that an aggravating factor existed. We cannot preserve our veneration for the protection of the jury in criminal cases if we render ourselves callous to the need for that protection by regularly imposing the death penalty without it.

Accordingly, whether or not the States have been erroneously coerced into the adoption of "aggravating factors," wherever those factors exist they must be subject to the usual requirements of the common law, and to the requirement enshrined in our Constitution, in criminal cases: they must be found by the jury beyond a reasonable doubt.

JUSTICE KENNEDY, concurring. [omitted]

JUSTICE BREYER, concurring in the judgment.

I.

II.

This Court has held that the Eighth Amendment requires States to apply special procedural safeguards when they seek the death penalty. Otherwise, the constitutional prohibition against "cruel and unusual punishments" would forbid its use. JUSTICE STEVENS has written that those safeguards include a requirement that a jury impose any sentence of death. ... I therefore conclude that the Eighth Amendment requires that a jury, not a judge, make the decision to sentence a defendant to death.

I am convinced by the reasons that JUSTICE STEVENS has given. These include (1) his belief that retribution provides the main justification for capital punishment, and (2) his assessment of the jury's comparative advantage in determining, in a particular case, whether capital punishment will serve that end.

As to the first, I note the continued difficulty of justifying capital punishment in terms of its ability to deter crime, to incapacitate offenders, or to rehabilitate criminals. Studies of deterrence are, at most, inconclusive.

As to incapacitation, few offenders sentenced to life without parole (as an alternative to death) commit further crimes. And rehabilitation, obviously, is beside the point.

In respect to retribution, jurors possess an important comparative advantage over judges. In principle, they are more attuned to "the community's moral sensibility," because they "reflect more accurately the composition and experiences of the community as a whole." Hence they are more likely to "express the conscience of the community on the ultimate question of life or death," and better able to determine in the particular case the need for retribution, namely, "an expression of the community's belief that certain crimes are themselves so grievous an affront to humanity that the only adequate response may be the penalty of death."

Nor is the fact that some judges are democratically elected likely to change the jury's comparative advantage in this respect. Even in jurisdictions where judges are selected directly by the people, the jury remains uniquely capable of determining whether, given the community's views, capital punishment is appropriate in the particular case at hand.

The importance of trying to translate a community's sense of capital punishment's appropriateness in a particular case is underscored by the continued division of opinion as to whether capital punishment is in all circumstances, as currently administered, "cruel and unusual." Those who make this claim point, among other things, to the fact that death is not reversible, and to death sentences imposed upon those whose convictions proved unreliable.

They point to the potentially arbitrary application of the death penalty, adding that the race of the victim and socio-economic factors seem to matter.

They argue that the delays that increasingly accompany sentences of death make those sentences unconstitutional because of "the suffering inherent in a prolonged wait for execution."

They point to the inadequacy of representation in capital cases, a fact that aggravates the other failings.

And they note that other nations have increasingly abandoned capital punishment.

For these reasons, the danger of unwarranted imposition of the penalty cannot be avoided unless "the decision to impose the death penalty is made by a jury rather than by a single governmental official." And I conclude that the Eighth Amendment requires individual jurors to make, and to take responsibility for, a decision to sentence a person to death.

JUSTICE O'CONNOR, with whom the CHIEF JUSTICE joins, dissenting.

I understand why the Court holds that the reasoning of Apprendi v. New Jersey is irreconcilable with Walton v. Arizona. Yet in choosing which to overrule, I would choose Apprendi, ...

...Apprendi's rule that any fact that increases the maximum penalty must be treated as an element of the crime is not required by the Constitution, by history, or by our prior cases. Indeed, the rule directly contradicts several of our prior cases. And it ignores the "significant history in this country of . . . discretionary sentencing by judges." The Court has failed, both in Apprendi and in the decision announced today, to "offer any meaningful justification for deviating from years of cases both suggesting and holding that application of the 'increase in the maximum penalty' rule is not required by the Constitution."

By expanding on Apprendi, the Court today exacerbates the harm done in that case. Consistent with my dissent, I would overrule Apprendi ...

NOTES AND QUERIES

The majority decided that Arizona's death-sentencing scheme violated the Sixth Amendment by authorizing judges to determine the existence of aggravating factors used to sentence first-degree murder defendants to death. The decision, however, left unanswered two questions that could affect future Sixth Amendment jurisprudence. First, the Court failed to decide whether a defendant's waiver of his or her right to a jury trial nevertheless required a jury determination of aggravating factors upon a guilty verdict. Second, the Court neglected to answer fully whether its decision applied to final sentencing determinations, or merely to the finding of aggravating factors. Would you take *Ring* to mean that juries alone must find facts which could lead to a greater period of sentencing, or does the decision hold that judges alone must not find these facts? The facts of the *Ring* case were of a sentencing scheme which allowed a judge, sitting without a jury, to find the facts relevant to the aggravating factors listed in the Arizona first-degree murder statute. So, the holding is that judges alone must not find the relevant factors that may lead to a death-penalty sentence; but is the obvious extension of this holding that these facts must be found by juries alone? The question is important because of the volume of statutes which employ hybrid judge and jury systems for determining these factors. Note that the exact holding of the case is this: "We hold that *Walton* and *Apprendi* are irreconcilable; our Sixth Amendment jurisprudence cannot be home to both. Accordingly, we overrule *Walton* to the extent that it allows a sentencing judge, sitting without a jury, to find an aggravating circumstance necessary for imposition of the death penalty. Because Arizona's enumerated aggravating factors operate as 'the functional equivalent of an element of a greater offense,' the Sixth Amendment requires that they be found by a jury." It does seem that a scheme by which the judge may increase the maximum sentence of a convicted defendant outside of the presence of the jury is unconstitutional both in death-penalty cases, as well as any non-capital case. As stated above, one question that remains open is whether or not a system can survive Sixth Amendment scrutiny if it uses some combination of the judge and the jury to make the decision relevant to aggravating factors, or if a jury alone must decide those issues beyond a reasonable doubt. The crux of the issue will most likely lie in the nature of the involvement of the two parties, the judge and the jury. It does seem that the system would be acceptable if the fact-finding is truly left to the jury, and the judge has little or no discretion once the jury renders its opinion, then this system should be acceptable.

Justice Breyer presents the possibility that judges' capital sentencing decisions may be less reliable than those of juries even in the normative sense of reliability as accuracy of judgment. Again drawing on empirical data that has emerged in recent years, Justice Breyer supports his view of the intrinsic superiority of jury sentencing in capital cases by referring to an empirical finding that "judges who override jury verdicts for life are especially likely to commit serious errors." The data underlying this observation is the high frequency of appellate reversals of Florida judges' overrides of jury life recommendations. This data would appear to suggest that judges who feel driven by political pressures or other factors to return a sentence of death despite a jury recommendation of life are prone to misconstrue facts or law in an effort to produce a predetermined outcome. Assuming that this phenomenon does indeed take place (and the explanation certainly fits the behavior of judges in a significant number of capital cases), judges' sentences can be viewed as "unreliable" and "inaccurate" in the sense that they are premised on erroneous judgments and findings.

To a large extent, *Ring* was not a watershed decision in that it merely extended *Apprendi* to the death penalty. Review that case as presented in Chapter 10. Do you agree that *Ring* is a simple extension?

CONSIDERING VICTIM IMPACT STATEMENTS

PAYNE v. TENNESSEE
501 U.S. 808 (1991)

CHIEF JUSTICE REHNQUIST delivered the opinion of the Court.

Petitioner, Pervis Tyrone Payne, was convicted by a jury on two counts of first-degree murder and one count of assault with intent to commit murder in the first degree. He was sentenced to death for each of the murders and to 30 years in prison for the assault.

The victims of Payne's offenses were 28-year-old Charisse Christopher, her 2-year-old daughter Lacie, and her 3-year-old son Nicholas. The three lived together in an apartment in Millington, Tennessee, across the hall from Payne's girl-friend, Bobbie Thomas. On Saturday, June 27, 1987, Payne visited Thomas' apartment several times in expectation of her return from her mother's house in Arkansas, but found no one at home. On one visit, he left his overnight bag, containing clothes and other items for his weekend stay, in the hallway outside Thomas' apartment. With the bag were three cans of malt liquor.

Payne passed the morning and early afternoon injecting cocaine and drinking beer. Later, he drove around the town with a friend in the friend's car, each of them taking turns reading a pornographic magazine. Sometime around 3 p.m., Payne returned to the apartment complex, entered the Christophers' apartment, and began making sexual advances towards Charisse. Charisse resisted and Payne became violent. A neighbor who resided in the apartment directly beneath the Christophers heard Charisse screaming, "'Get out, get out,' as if she were telling the children to leave." The noise briefly subsided and then began, "'horribly loud.'" The neighbor called the police after she heard a "blood curdling scream" from the Christophers' apartment.

When the first police officer arrived at the scene, he immediately encountered Payne, who was leaving the apartment building, so covered with blood that he appeared to be "'sweating blood.'" The officer confronted Payne, who responded, "'I'm the complainant.'" When the officer asked, "'What's going on up there?'" Payne struck the officer with the overnight bag, dropped his tennis shoes, and fled.

Inside the apartment, the police encountered a horrifying scene. Blood covered the walls and floor throughout the unit. Charisse and her children were lying on the floor in the kitchen. Nicholas, despite several wounds inflicted by a butcher knife that completely penetrated through his body from front to back, was still breathing. Miraculously, he survived, but not until after undergoing seven hours of surgery and a transfusion of 1,700 cc's of blood – 400 to 500 cc's more than his estimated normal blood volume. Charisse and Lacie were dead.

Charisse's body was found on the kitchen floor on her back, her legs fully extended. She had sustained 42 direct knife wounds and 42 defensive wounds on her arms and hands. The wounds were caused by 41 separate thrusts of a butcher knife. None of the 84 wounds inflicted by Payne were individually fatal; rather, the cause of death was most likely bleeding from all of the wounds.

Lacie's body was on the kitchen floor near her mother. She had suffered stab wounds to the chest, abdomen, back, and head. The murder weapon, a butcher knife, was found at her feet. Payne's baseball cap was snapped on her arm near her elbow. Three cans of malt liquor bearing Payne's fingerprints were found on a table near her body, and a fourth empty one was on the landing outside the apartment door.

Payne was apprehended later that day hiding in the attic of the home of a former girlfriend. As he descended the stairs of the attic, he stated to the arresting officers, "'Man, I ain't killed no woman.'" According to one of the officers, Payne had "'a wild look about him. His pupils were contracted. He was foaming at the mouth, saliva. He appeared to be very nervous. He was breathing real rapid.'" He had blood on his body and clothes and several scratches across his chest. It was later determined that the blood stains matched the victims' blood types. A search of his pockets revealed a packet containing cocaine residue, a hypodermic syringe wrapper, and a cap from a hypodermic syringe. His overnight bag, containing a bloody white shirt, was found in a nearby dumpster.

At trial, Payne took the stand and, despite the overwhelming and relatively uncontroverted evidence against him, testified that he had not harmed any of the Christophers. Rather, he asserted that another man had raced by him as he was walking up the stairs to the floor where the Christophers lived. He stated that he had gotten blood on himself when, after hearing moans from the Christophers' apartment, he had tried to help the victims. According to his testimony, he panicked and fled when he heard police sirens and noticed the blood on his clothes. The jury returned guilty verdicts against Payne on all counts.

During the sentencing phase of the trial, Payne presented the testimony of four witnesses: his mother and father, Bobbie Thomas, and Dr. John T. Hutson, a clinical psychologist specializing in criminal court evaluation work. Bobbie Thomas testified that she met Payne at church, during a time when she was being abused by her husband. She stated that Payne was a very caring person, and that he devoted much time and attention to her three children, who were being affected by her marital difficulties. She said that the children had come to love him very much and would miss him, and that he "behaved just like a father that loved his kids." She asserted that he did not drink, nor did he use drugs, and that it was generally inconsistent with Payne's character to have committed these crimes.

Dr. Hutson testified that based on Payne's low score on an IQ test, Payne was "mentally handicapped." Hutson also said that Payne was neither psychotic nor schizophrenic, and that Payne was the most polite prisoner he had ever met. Payne's parents testified that their son had no prior criminal record and had never been arrested. They also stated that Payne had no history of alcohol or drug abuse, he worked with his father as a painter, he was good with children, and he was a good son.

The State presented the testimony of Charisse's mother, Mary Zvolanek. When asked how Nicholas had been affected by the murders of his mother and sister, she responded:

> He cries for his mom. He doesn't seem to understand why she doesn't come home. And he cries for his sister Lacie. He comes to me many times during the week and asks me, Grandmama, do you miss my Lacie. And I tell him yes. He says, I'm worried about my Lacie.

In arguing for the death penalty during closing argument, the prosecutor commented on the continuing effects of Nicholas' experience, stating:

> But we do know that Nicholas was alive. And Nicholas was in the same room. Nicholas was still conscious. His eyes were open. He responded to the paramedics. He was able to follow their directions. He was able to hold his intestines in as he was carried to the ambulance. So he knew what happened to his mother and baby sister.
>
> There is nothing you can do to ease the pain of any of the families involved in this case. There is nothing you can do to ease the pain of Bernice or Carl Payne, and that's a tragedy. There is nothing you can do basically to ease the pain of Mr. and Mrs. Zvolanek, and that's a tragedy. They will have to live with it the rest of their lives. There is obviously nothing you can do for Charisse and Lacie Jo. But there is something that you can do for Nicholas.

> Somewhere down the road Nicholas is going to grow up, hopefully. He's going to want to know what happened. And he is going to know what happened to his baby sister and his mother. He is going to want to know what type of justice was done. He is going to want to know what happened. With your verdict, you will provide the answer.

In the rebuttal to Payne's closing argument, the prosecutor stated:

> You saw the videotape this morning. You saw what Nicholas Christopher will carry in his mind forever. When you talk about cruel, when you talk about atrocious, and when you talk about heinous, that picture will always come into your mind, probably throughout the rest of your lives. ...
>
> ...
>
> ...No one will ever know about Lacie Jo because she never had the chance to grow up. Her life was taken from her at the age of two years old. So, no there won't be a high school principal to talk about Lacie Jo Christopher, and there won't be anybody to take her to her high school prom. And there won't be anybody there – there won't be her mother there or Nicholas' mother there to kiss him at night. His mother will never kiss him good night or pat him as he goes off to bed, or hold him and sing him a lullaby.
>
> ...
>
> [Petitioner's attorney] wants you to think about a good reputation, people who love the defendant and things about him. He doesn't want you to think about the people who love Charisse Christopher, her mother and daddy who loved her. The people who loved little Lacie Jo, the grandparents who are still here. The brother who mourns for her every single day and wants to know where his best little playmate is. He doesn't have anybody to watch cartoons with him, a little one. These are the things that go into why it is especially cruel, heinous, and atrocious, the burden that that child will carry forever.

The jury sentenced Payne to death on each of the murder counts.

The Supreme Court of Tennessee affirmed the conviction and sentence. The court rejected Payne's contention that the admission of the grandmother's testimony and the State's closing argument constituted prejudicial violations of his rights under the Eighth Amendment as applied in Booth v. Maryland (1987), and South Carolina v. Gathers, (1989). The court characterized the grandmother's testimony as "technically irrelevant," but concluded that it "did not create a constitutionally unacceptable risk of an arbitrary imposition of the death penalty and was harmless beyond a reasonable doubt."

The court determined that the prosecutor's comments during closing argument were "relevant to [Payne's] personal responsibility and moral guilt." The court explained that "when a person deliberately picks a butcher knife out of a kitchen drawer and proceeds to stab to death a twenty-eight-year-old mother, her two and one-half year old daughter and her three and one-half year old son, in the same room, the physical and mental condition of the boy he left for dead is surely relevant in determining his 'blameworthiness.'" The court concluded that any violation of Payne's rights under Booth and Gathers "was harmless beyond a reasonable doubt."

We granted certiorari to reconsider our holdings in Booth and Gathers that the Eighth Amendment prohibits a capital sentencing jury from considering "victim impact" evidence relating to the personal characteristics of the victim and the emotional impact of the crimes on the victim's family.

In Booth, the defendant robbed and murdered an elderly couple. As required by a state statute, a victim impact statement was prepared based on interviews with the victims' son, daughter, son-in-law, and granddaughter. The statement, which described the personal characteristics of the victims, the emotional impact of the crimes on the family, and set forth the family members' opinions and characterizations of the crimes and the defendant, was submitted to the jury at sentencing. The jury imposed the death penalty. The conviction and sentence were affirmed on appeal by the State's highest court.

This Court held by a 5-to-4 vote that the Eighth Amendment prohibits a jury from considering a victim impact statement at the sentencing phase of a capital trial. The Court made clear that the admissibility of victim impact evidence was not to be determined on a case-by-case basis, but that such evidence was per se inadmissible in the sentencing phase of a capital case except to the extent that it "related directly to the circumstances of the crime." In Gathers, decided two years later, the Court extended the rule announced in Booth to statements made by a prosecutor to the sentencing jury regarding the personal qualities of the victim.

The Booth Court began its analysis with the observation that the capital defendant must be treated as a "'uniquely individual human being,'" and therefore the Constitution requires the jury to make an individualized determination as to whether the defendant should be executed based on the "'character of the individual and the circumstances of the crime.' The Court concluded that while no prior decision of this Court had mandated that only the defendant's character and immediate characteristics of the crime may constitutionally be considered, other factors are irrelevant to the capital sentencing decision unless they have "some bearing on the defendant's 'personal responsibility and moral guilt.'" To the extent that victim impact evidence presents "factors about which the defendant was unaware, and that were irrelevant to the decision to kill," the Court concluded, it has nothing to do with the "blameworthiness of a particular defendant." Evidence of the victim's character, the Court observed, "could well distract the sentencing jury from its constitutionally required task [of] determining whether the death penalty is appropriate in light of the background and record of the accused and the particular circumstances of the crime." The Court concluded that, except to the extent that victim impact evidence relates "directly to the circumstances of the crime," the prosecution may not introduce such evidence at a capital sentencing hearing because "it creates an impermissible risk that the capital sentencing decision will be made in an arbitrary manner."

Booth and Gathers were based on two premises: that evidence relating to a particular victim or to the harm that a capital defendant causes a victim's family do not in general reflect on the defendant's "blameworthiness," and that only evidence relating to "blameworthiness" is relevant to the capital sentencing decision. However, the assessment of harm caused by the defendant as a result of the crime charged has understandably been an important concern of the criminal law, both in determining the elements of the offense and in determining the appropriate punishment. Thus, two equally blameworthy criminal defendants may be guilty of different offenses solely because their acts cause differing amounts of harm. "If a bank robber aims his gun at a guard, pulls the trigger, and kills his target, he may be put to death. If the gun unexpectedly misfires, he may not. His moral guilt in both cases is identical, but his responsibility in the former is greater." The same is true with respect to two defendants, each of whom participates in a robbery, and each of whom acts with reckless disregard for human life; if the robbery in which the first defendant participated results in the death of a victim, he may be subjected to the death penalty, but if the robbery in which the second defendant participates does not result in the death of a victim, the death penalty may not be imposed.

The principles which have guided criminal sentencing – as opposed to criminal liability – have varied with the times. The book of Exodus prescribes the Lex talionis, "An eye for an eye, a tooth for a tooth." In England and on the continent of Europe, as recently as the 18th century, crimes which would be regarded as quite minor today were capital offenses. Writing in the 18th century, the Italian criminologist Cesare Beccaria advocated the idea that "the punishment should fit the crime." He said that "we have seen that the true measure of crimes is the injury done to society."

Gradually the list of crimes punishable by death diminished, and legislatures began grading the severity of crimes in accordance with the harm done by the criminal. The sentence for a given offense, rather than being precisely fixed by the legislature, was prescribed in terms of a minimum and a maximum, with the actual sentence to be decided by the judge. With the increasing importance of probation, as opposed to imprisonment, as a part of the penological process, some States such as California developed the "indeterminate sentence," where the time of incarceration was left almost entirely to the penological authorities rather than to the courts. But more recently the pendulum has swung back. The Federal Sentencing Guidelines, which went into effect in 1987, provided for very precise calibration of sentences, depending upon a number of factors. These factors relate both to the subjective guilt of the defendant and to the harm caused by his acts.

Wherever judges in recent years have had discretion to impose sentence, the consideration of the harm caused by the crime has been an important factor in the exercise of that discretion:

> The first significance of harm in Anglo-American jurisprudence is, then, as a prerequisite to the criminal sanction. The second significance of harm – one no less important to judges – is as a measure of the seriousness of the offense and therefore as a standard for determining the severity of the sentence that will be meted out.

Whatever the prevailing sentencing philosophy, the sentencing authority has always been free to consider a wide range of relevant material. In the federal system, we observed that "a judge may appropriately conduct an inquiry broad in scope, largely unlimited either as to the kind of information he may consider, or the source from which it may come." ...

We have held that a State cannot preclude the sentencer from considering "any relevant mitigating evidence" that the defendant proffers in support of a sentence less than death. Thus we have, as the Court observed in Booth, required that the capital defendant be treated as a "'uniquely individual human being.'" But it was never held or even suggested in any of our cases preceding Booth that the defendant, entitled as he was to individualized consideration, was to receive that consideration wholly apart from the crime which he had committed. The language quoted from Woodson in the Booth opinion was not intended to describe a class of evidence that could not be received, but a class of evidence which must be received. Any doubt on the matter is dispelled by comparing the language in Woodson with the language from Gregg v. Georgia, quoted above, which was handed down the same day as Woodson. This misreading of precedent in Booth has, we think, unfairly weighted the scales in a capital trial; while virtually no limits are placed on the relevant mitigating evidence a capital defendant may introduce concerning his own circumstances, the State is barred from either offering "a quick glimpse of the life" which a defendant "chose to extinguish," or demonstrating the loss to the victim's family and to society which has resulted from the defendant's homicide.

The Booth Court reasoned that victim impact evidence must be excluded because it would be difficult, if not impossible, for the defendant to rebut such evidence without shifting the focus of the sentencing hearing away from the defendant, thus creating a "'mini-trial' on the victim's character." In many cases the evidence relating to the victim is already before the jury at least in part because of its relevance at the guilt phase of the trial. But even as to additional evidence admitted at the sentencing phase, the mere fact that for tactical reasons it might not be prudent for the defense to rebut victim impact evidence makes the case no different than others in which a party is faced with this sort of a dilemma. As we explained in rejecting the contention that expert testimony on future dangerousness should be excluded from capital trials, "the rules of evidence generally extant at the federal and state levels anticipate that relevant, unprivileged evidence should be admitted and its weight left to the factfinder, who would have the benefit of cross-examination and contrary evidence by the opposing party."

Payne echoes the concern voiced in Booth's case that the admission of victim impact evidence permits a jury to find that defendants whose victims were assets to their community are more deserving of punishment than those whose victims are perceived to be less worthy. As a general matter, however, victim impact evidence is not offered to encourage comparative judgments of this kind – for instance, that the killer of a hardworking, devoted parent deserves the death penalty, but that the murderer of a reprobate does not. It is designed to show instead each victim's "uniqueness as an individual human being," whatever the jury might think the loss to the community resulting from his death might be. The facts of Gathers are an excellent illustration of this: The evidence showed that the victim was an out of work, mentally handicapped individual, perhaps not, in the eyes of most, a significant contributor to society, but nonetheless a murdered human being.

...Where the State imposes the death penalty for a particular crime, we have held that the Eighth Amendment imposes special limitations upon that process.

> First, there is a required threshold below which the death penalty cannot be imposed. In this context, the State must establish rational criteria that narrow the decisionmaker's judgment as to whether the circumstances of a particular defendant's case meet the threshold. Moreover, a societal consensus that the death penalty is disproportionate to a particular offense prevents a State from imposing the death penalty for that offense. Second, States cannot limit the sentencer's consideration of any relevant circumstance that could cause it to decline to impose the penalty. In this respect, the State cannot challenge the sentencer's discretion, but must allow it to consider any relevant information offered by the defendant.

But, "beyond these limitations ... the Court has deferred to the State's choice of substantive factors relevant to the penalty determination."

Within the constitutional limitations defined by our cases, the States enjoy their traditional latitude to prescribe the method by which those who commit murder shall be punished."...

We are now of the view that a State may properly conclude that for the jury to assess meaningfully the defendant's moral culpability and blameworthiness, it should have before it at the sentencing phase evidence of the specific harm caused by the defendant. ... By turning the victim into a "faceless stranger at the penalty phase of a capital trial," Booth deprives the State of the full moral force of its evidence and may prevent the jury from having before it all the information necessary to determine the proper punishment for a first-degree murder.

The present case is an example of the potential for such unfairness. The capital sentencing jury heard testimony from Payne's girlfriend that they met at church; that he was affectionate, caring, and kind to her children; that he was not an abuser of drugs or alcohol; and that it was inconsistent with his character to have committed the murders. Payne's parents testified that he was a good son, and a clinical psychologist testified that Payne was an extremely polite prisoner and suffered from a low IQ. None of this testimony was related to the circumstances of Payne's brutal crimes. In contrast, the only evidence of the impact of Payne's offenses during the sentencing phase was Nicholas' grandmother's description – in response to a single question – that the child misses his mother and baby sister. Payne argues that the Eighth Amendment commands that the jury's death sentence must be set aside because the jury heard this testimony. But the testimony illustrated quite poignantly some of the harm that Payne's killing had caused; there is nothing unfair about allowing the jury to bear in mind that harm at the same time as it considers the mitigating evidence introduced by the defendant. The Supreme Court of Tennessee in this case obviously felt the unfairness of the rule pronounced by Booth when it said: "It is an affront to the civilized members of the human race to say that at sentencing in a capital case, a parade of witnesses may praise the background, character and good deeds of Defendant (as was done in this case), without limitation as to relevancy, but nothing may be said that bears upon the character of, or the harm imposed, upon the victims."

In Gathers, as indicated above, we extended the holding of Booth barring victim impact evidence to the prosecutor's argument to the jury. Human nature being what it is, capable lawyers trying cases to juries try to convey to the jurors that the people involved in the underlying events are, or were, living human beings, with something to be gained or lost from the jury's verdict. Under the aegis of the Eighth

Amendment, we have given the broadest latitude to the defendant to introduce relevant mitigating evidence reflecting on his individual personality, and the defendant's attorney may argue that evidence to the jury. Petitioner's attorney in this case did just that. For the reasons discussed above, we now reject the view – expressed in Gathers – that a State may not permit the prosecutor to similarly argue to the jury the human cost of the crime of which the defendant stands convicted. ...

We thus hold that if the State chooses to permit the admission of victim impact evidence and prosecutorial argument on that subject, the Eighth Amendment erects no per se bar. A State may legitimately conclude that evidence about the victim and about the impact of the murder on the victim's family is relevant to the jury's decision as to whether or not the death penalty should be imposed. There is no reason to treat such evidence differently than other relevant evidence is treated.

...We accordingly affirm the judgment of the Supreme Court of Tennessee.

It is so ordered.

JUSTICE O'CONNOR, with whom JUSTICE WHITE and JUSTICE KENNEDY join, concurring.

In my view, a State may legitimately determine that victim impact evidence is relevant to a capital sentencing proceeding. A State may decide that the jury, before determining whether a convicted murderer should receive the death penalty, should know the full extent of the harm caused by the crime, including its impact on the victim's family and community. A State may decide also that the jury should see "a quick glimpse of the life petitioner chose to extinguish," to remind the jury that the person whose life was taken was a unique human being.

Given that victim impact evidence is potentially relevant, nothing in the Eighth Amendment commands that States treat it differently than other kinds of relevant evidence. "The Eighth Amendment stands as a shield against those practices and punishments which are either inherently cruel or which so offend the moral consensus of this society as to be deemed 'cruel and unusual.'" Certainly there is no strong societal consensus that a jury may not take into account the loss suffered by a victim's family or that a murder victim must remain a faceless stranger at the penalty phase of a capital trial. Just the opposite is true. Most States have enacted legislation enabling judges and juries to consider victim impact evidence. The possibility that this evidence may in some cases be unduly inflammatory does not justify a prophylactic, constitutionally based rule that this evidence may never be admitted. Trial courts routinely exclude evidence that is unduly inflammatory; where inflammatory evidence is improperly admitted, appellate courts carefully review the record to determine whether the error was prejudicial.

We do not hold today that victim impact evidence must be admitted, or even that it should be admitted. We hold merely that if a State decides to permit consideration of this evidence, "the Eighth Amendment erects no per se bar." If, in a particular case, a witness' testimony or a prosecutor's remark so infects the sentencing proceeding as to render it fundamentally unfair, the defendant may seek appropriate relief under the Due Process Clause of the Fourteenth Amendment.

That line was not crossed in this case. The State called as a witness Mary Zvolanek, Nicholas' grandmother. Her testimony was brief. She explained that Nicholas cried for his mother and baby sister and could not understand why they did not come home. I do not doubt that the jurors were moved by this testimony – who would not have been? But surely this brief statement did not inflame their passions more than did the facts of the crime: Charisse Christopher was stabbed 41 times with a butcher knife and bled to death; her 2-year-old daughter Lacie was killed by repeated thrusts of that same knife; and 3-year-old Nicholas, despite stab wounds that penetrated completely through his body from front to back, survived – only to witness the brutal murders of his mother and baby sister. In light of the jury's unavoidable familiarity with the facts of Payne's vicious attack, I cannot conclude that the additional information provided by Mary Zvolanek's testimony deprived petitioner of due process.

I agree with the Court that Booth v. Maryland and Gathers were wrongly decided. The Eighth Amendment does not prohibit a State from choosing to admit evidence concerning a murder victim's personal characteristics or the impact of the crime on the victim's family and community. Booth also addressed another kind of victim impact evidence – opinions of the victim's family about the crime, the defendant, and the appropriate sentence. As the Court notes in today's decision, we do not reach this issue as no evidence of this kind was introduced at petitioner's trial. Nor do we express an opinion as to other aspects of the prosecutor's conduct. As to the victim impact evidence that was introduced, its admission did not violate the Constitution. Accordingly, I join the Court's opinion.

JUSTICE SCALIA, with whom JUSTICE O'CONNOR and JUSTICE KENNEDY join as to Part II, concurring. [omitted]

JUSTICE SOUTER, with whom JUSTICE KENNEDY joins, concurring. [omitted]

JUSTICE MARSHALL, with whom JUSTICE BLACKMUN joins, dissenting. [omitted]

JUSTICE STEVENS, with whom JUSTICE BLACKMUN joins, dissenting.

...Our cases provide no support whatsoever for the majority's conclusion that the prosecutor may introduce evidence that sheds no light on the defendant's guilt or moral culpability, and thus serves no purpose other than to encourage jurors to decide in favor of death rather than life on the basis of their emotions rather than their reason.

Until today our capital punishment jurisprudence has required that any decision to impose the death penalty be based solely on evidence that tends to inform the jury about the character of the offense and the character of the defendant. Evidence that serves no purpose other than to appeal to the sympathies or emotions of the jurors has never been considered admissible. Thus, if a defendant, who had murdered a convenience store clerk in cold blood in the course of an armed robbery, offered evidence unknown to him at the time of the crime about the immoral character of his victim, all would recognize immediately that the evidence was irrelevant and inadmissible. Evenhanded justice requires that the same constraint be imposed on the advocate of the death penalty.

II.

Today's majority has obviously been moved by an argument that has strong political appeal but no proper place in a reasoned judicial opinion. Because our decision in Lockett, recognizes the defendant's right to introduce all mitigating evidence that may inform the jury about his character, the Court suggests that fairness requires that the State be allowed to respond with similar evidence about the victim. This argument is a classic non sequitur: The victim is not on trial; her character, whether good or bad, cannot therefore constitute either an aggravating or a mitigating circumstance.

Even if introduction of evidence about the victim could be equated with introduction of evidence about the defendant, the argument would remain flawed in both its premise and its conclusion. The conclusion that exclusion of victim impact evidence results in a significantly imbalanced sentencing procedure is simply inaccurate. Just as the defendant is entitled to introduce any relevant mitigating evidence, so the State may rebut that evidence and may designate any relevant conduct to be an aggravating factor provided that the factor is sufficiently well defined and consistently applied to cabin the sentencer's discretion.

The premise that a criminal prosecution requires an evenhanded balance between the State and the defendant is also incorrect. The Constitution grants certain rights to the criminal defendant and imposes special limitations on the State designed to protect the individual from overreaching by the disproportionately powerful State. Thus, the State must prove a defendant's guilt beyond a reasonable doubt. Rules of evidence are also weighted in the defendant's favor. For example, the prosecution generally cannot introduce evidence of the defendant's character to prove his propensity to commit a crime, but the defendant can introduce such reputation evidence to show his law-abiding nature. Even if balance were required or desirable, today's decision, by permitting both the defendant and the State to introduce irrelevant evidence for the sentencer's consideration without any guidance, surely does nothing to enhance parity in the sentencing process.

III.

Victim impact evidence, as used in this case, has two flaws, both related to the Eighth Amendment's command that the punishment of death may not be meted out arbitrarily or capriciously. First, aspects of the character of the victim unforeseeable to the defendant at the time of his crime are irrelevant to the defendant's "personal responsibility and moral guilt" and therefore cannot justify a death sentence.

Second, the quantity and quality of victim impact evidence sufficient to turn a verdict of life in prison into a verdict of death is not defined until after the crime has been committed and therefore cannot possibly be applied consistently in different cases. The sentencer's unguided consideration of victim impact evidence thus conflicts with the principle central to our capital punishment jurisprudence that, "where discretion is afforded a sentencing body on a matter so grave as the determination of whether a human life should be taken or spared, that discretion must be suitably directed and limited so as to minimize the risk of wholly arbitrary and capricious action." Open-ended reliance by a capital sentencer on victim impact evidence simply does not provide a "principled way to distinguish [cases], in which the death penalty is imposed, from the many cases in which it is not."

The majority attempts to justify the admission of victim impact evidence by arguing that "consideration of the harm caused by the crime has been an important factor in the exercise of [sentencing] discretion." This statement is misleading and inaccurate. It is misleading because it is not limited to harm that is foreseeable. It is inaccurate because it fails to differentiate between legislative determinations and judicial sentencing. It is true that an evaluation of the harm caused by different kinds of wrongful conduct is a critical aspect in legislative definitions of offenses and determinations concerning sentencing guidelines. There is a rational correlation between moral culpability and the foreseeable harm caused by criminal conduct. Moreover, in the capital sentencing area, legislative identification of the special aggravating factors that may justify the imposition of the death penalty is entirely appropriate. But the majority cites no authority for the suggestion that unforeseeable and indirect harms to a victim's family are properly considered as aggravating evidence on a case-by-case basis.

IV.

The majority thus does far more than validate a State's judgment that "the jury should see 'a quick glimpse of the life petitioner chose to extinguish.'" Instead, it allows a jury to hold a defendant responsible for a whole array of harms that he could not foresee and for which he is therefore not blameworthy. JUSTICE SOUTER argues that these harms are sufficiently foreseeable to hold the defendant accountable because "every defendant knows, if endowed with the mental competence for criminal responsibility, that the life he will take by his homicidal behavior is that of a unique person, like himself, and that the person to be killed probably has close associates, 'survivors,' who will suffer harms and deprivations from the victim's death." But every juror and trial judge knows this much as well. Evidence about who those survivors are and what harms and deprivations they have suffered is therefore not necessary to apprise the sentencer of any information that was actually foreseeable to the defendant. Its only function can be to "divert the jury's attention away from the defendant's background and record, and the circumstances of the crime."

Arguing in the alternative, JUSTICE SOUTER correctly points out that victim impact evidence will sometimes come to the attention of the jury during the guilt phase of the trial. He reasons that the ideal of basing sentencing determinations entirely on the moral culpability of the defendant is therefore unattainable unless a different jury is empaneled for the sentencing hearing. Thus, to justify overruling Booth, he assumes that the decision must otherwise be extended far beyond its actual holding.

JUSTICE SOUTER's assumption is entirely unwarranted. For as long as the contours of relevance at sentencing hearings have been limited to evidence concerning the character of the offense and the character of the offender, the law has also recognized that evidence that is admissible for a proper purpose may not be excluded because it is inadmissible for other purposes and may indirectly prejudice the jury. In the case before us today, much of what might be characterized as victim impact evidence was properly admitted during the guilt phase of the trial and, given the horrible character of this crime, may have been sufficient to justify the Tennessee Supreme Court's conclusion that the error was harmless because the jury would necessarily have imposed the death sentence even absent the error. The fact that a good deal of such evidence is routinely and properly brought to the attention of the jury merely indicates that the rule of Booth may not affect the outcome of many cases.

In reaching our decision today, however, we should not be concerned with the cases in which victim impact evidence will not make a difference. We should be concerned instead with the cases in which it will make a difference. In those cases, defendants will be sentenced arbitrarily to death on the basis of evidence that would not otherwise be admissible because it is irrelevant to the defendants' moral culpability. The Constitution's proscription against the arbitrary imposition of the death penalty must necessarily proscribe the admission of evidence that serves no purpose other than to result in such arbitrary sentences.

V.

The notion that the inability to produce an ideal system of justice in which every punishment is precisely married to the defendant's blameworthiness somehow justifies a rule that completely divorces some capital sentencing determinations from moral culpability is incomprehensible to me. Also incomprehensible is the argument that such a rule is required for the jury to take into account that each murder victim is a "unique" human being. The fact that each of us is unique is a proposition so obvious that it surely requires no evidentiary support. What is not obvious, however, is the way in which the character or reputation in one case may differ from that of other possible victims. Evidence offered to prove such differences can only be intended to identify some victims as more worthy of protection than others. Such proof risks decisions based on the same invidious motives as a prosecutor's decision to seek the death penalty if a victim is white but to accept a plea bargain if the victim is black.

Given the current popularity of capital punishment in a crime-ridden society, the political appeal of arguments that assume that increasing the severity of sentences is the best cure for the cancer of crime, and the political strength of the "victims' rights" movement, I recognize that today's decision will be greeted with enthusiasm by a large number of concerned and thoughtful citizens. The great tragedy of the decision, however, is the danger that the "hydraulic pressure" of public opinion that Justice Holmes once described – and that properly influences the deliberations of democratic legislatures – has played a role not only in the Court's decision to hear this case, and in its decision to reach the constitutional question without pausing to consider affirming on the basis of the Tennessee Supreme Court's rationale, but even in its resolution of the constitutional issue involved. Today is a sad day for a great institution.

NOTES AND QUERIES

In deciding the constitutionality of crime victim impact statements in capital sentencing hearings, the Court has identified three types of victim impact information: (1) evidence of the victim's unique personal characteristics, (2) evidence of the crime's impact on the victim's family and community, and (3) the victim's sentencing opinion. *Payne* notes that, in *Booth v. Maryland*, 482 U.S. 496 (1987), the Court had banned victim impact testimony at capital sentencing proceedings as cruel and unusual under the Eighth Amendment. In *Payne*, however, the Court overruled *Booth* with respect to the first two types of impact statements, leaving unclear the admissibility of victims' sentencing opinions. Given the introductory materials to this chapter, we already can discern the impact of the first two factors. What do you make of the third form of evidence? In light of current research, which of the three forms of evidence do you find most objectionable? Regardless of the current research, do you find the third form legally objectionable? Do you discern 8th Amendment problems with the third form of evidence? Do you discern due process challenges? See Douglas E. Beloof, Constitutional implications of crime victims as participants, 88 Cornell L. Rev. 282 (2003). Beloof notes that, outside of the death penalty context, many states have granted victims the independent right as participants to communicate victim impact information, including sentencing recommendations. Why not extend the right to capital cases? See also Wayne A. Logan, Through the past darkly: A survey of the uses and abuses of victim impact evidence in capital trials, 41 Ariz. L. Rev. 143, 157-69 (1999).

Payne simply lifted the *per se* ban on the admissibility of victim impact evidence. What do you discern it to permit? Do you feel well guided to determine *Payne's* scope by the Court's dual reasons for permitting victim impact evidence: to offset the defendant's mitigating evidence and to permit the jury to assess the specific harm resulting from the offense? Could you discern any substantive restrictions on the types and modes of victim impact evidence that the prosecution may present, such as what evidence a sentencer may hear or who may be allowed to testify? *Payne* also leaves open issues regarding the procedural safeguards necessary to safeguard a capital defendant's right to a reliable sentencing determination? Possible protections could include providing defendants with notice that the evidence would be sought, pre-admission in *in camera* hearings to allow defendants to respond to the evidence before the jury receives it, and limiting instructions to help guide the jury's use of the evidence. Would you find such protections appropriate or necessary? See John H. Blume, Victim impact evidence in capital cases, 88 Cornell L. Rev. 257 (2003). Note that the majority does not offer much guidance to determine where *Payne* actually stands. Some language sanctions only a very limited victim impact presentation in order to prevent the victim from being faceless, as the majority notes that there would be no constitutional problem if a State were to permit the prosecution to present a capital sentencing jury with a quick glimpse of the life the defendant took. Yet, the Court also seems quite permissive in the evidence it would tolerate because of the enforcement mechanism that the Court chose: whether the evidence is so unduly prejudicial that it renders the trial fundamentally unfair.

Following the Supreme Court's decision to permit surviving friends and family of homicide victims to testify about the character of the victim and the emotional and psychological impact of the victim's death, commentators have criticized this type of testimony for its effects on capital sentencing. Some claim that victim impact statements overwhelm the jury and interfere with its ability to empathize with the defendant, Susan Bandes, Empathy, narrative, and victim impact statements, 63 U. Chi. L. Rev. 361, 392-93 (1996). Others view the statements as inappropriately focusing the jury on the victim and leading them to stereotyping and placing insufficient weight to mitigating factors, Angela P. Harris, The jurisprudence of victimhood, 1991 Sup. Ct. Rev. 77, 96-101. Yet others argue that victim impact statements contribute to arbitrariness in capital sentencing and moves us away from Supreme Court cases – *Furman v. Georgia*, 408 U.S. 238 (1972) and *Gregg v. Georgia*, 428 U.S. 153 (1976) – which emphasized the need for consistency and limits on arbitrariness in capital sentencing systems. Wayne A. Logan, Through the past darkly: A survey of the uses and abuses of victim impact evidence in capital trials, 41 Ariz. L. Rev. 143, 191-92 (1999); and Niru Shanker, Getting a grip on *Payne* and restricting the influence of victim impact statements in capital sentencing: The Timothy McVeigh case and various state approaches compared, 26 Hastings Const. L.Q. 711, 740 (1999).

The harms described in victim impact statements raise a variety of concerns about the adventitious nature of the statements and their impact on capital jurors. First, commentators evince concern that victim impact statements highlight the perceived relative worth of the victim, and consequently that the jury's judgment about whether to impose the death sentence will be influenced by this inappropriate factor. Amy K. Phillips, Note, Thou shalt not kill any nice people: The problem of victim impact statements in capital sentencing, 35 Am. Crim. L. Rev. 93, 105-06 (1997). In this sense, whether someone kills a person of high or low standing is adventitious because the death reflects neither the murderer's mental state nor the morality of the act itself. Empirical data supports this claim. Greater victim "respectability" leads to judgments that the crime was more serious; see Edith Greene, Heather Koehring, and Melinda Quiat, Victim impact evidence in capital cases: Does the victim's character matter?, 28 J. Appl. Soc. Psych. 145, 154 (1998). Second, victim impact statements detail the various harms that befall the victim or the victim's family after a crime, which might include financial complications resulting from a crime, stress-induced illnesses, and various other consequences that a defendant might not have been able to foresee at the time of the crime. The argument is that the emotional fallout of a crime to a victim or a victim's family is a paradigmatic example of adventitious harm. The harm described by victim impact statements is adventitious in the sense that in many cases the victim's character and the nature of the reaction of the victim's family are facts that the defendant has no knowledge of at the time of the crime. Given its adventitiousness, the argument is that efforts must be made to limit the use of such evidence that may inappropriately bias juries; Janice Nadler and Mary R. Rose, Inside and outside the courtroom: Victim impact testimony and the psychology of punishment, 88 Cornell L. Rev. 419 (2003).

Researchers propose a blame-validation model which explains that we ascribe culpability (blame) as we evaluate harmful events. The argument is that we scrutinize evidence concerning harmful events for its contribution to personal control and spontaneously evaluate its favorableness or unfavorableness. These spontaneous evaluations encourage a form of information processing which reviews the event in a manner that favors ascribing blame to the person or persons who evoke the most negative affect or whose behavior confirms unfavorable expectations. Mark D. Alicke, Culpable control and the psychology of blame, 126 Psych. Bull. 556 (2000).

Controlling Punishment Decisions

JONES v. U.S.
527 U.S. 373 (1999).

JUSTICE THOMAS delivered the opinion of the Court, except as to Part III-A

I.

Petitioner Louis Jones, Jr., kidnaped Private Tracie Joy McBride at gunpoint from the Goodfellow Air Force Base in San Angelo, Texas. He brought her to his house and sexually assaulted her. Soon thereafter, petitioner drove Private McBride to a bridge just outside of San Angelo, where he repeatedly struck her in the head with a tire iron until she died. Petitioner administered blows of such severe force that, when the victim's body was found, the medical examiners observed that large pieces of her skull had been driven into her cranial cavity or were missing.

The Government charged petitioner with, inter alia, kidnaping with death resulting to the victim, an offense punishable by life imprisonment or death. Exercising its discretion under the Federal Death Penalty Act of 1994, the Government decided to seek the latter sentencing option. Petitioner was tried in the District Court for the Northern District of Texas and found guilty by the jury.

The District Court then conducted a separate sentencing hearing. As an initial matter, the sentencing jury was required to find that petitioner had the requisite intent; it concluded that petitioner intentionally killed his victim and intentionally inflicted serious bodily injury resulting in her death. Even on a finding of intent, however, a defendant is not death-eligible unless the sentencing jury also finds that the Government has proved beyond a reasonable doubt at least one of the statutory aggravating factors set forth at §3592. Because petitioner was charged with committing a homicide, the Government had to prove 1 of the 16 statutory aggravating factors set forth at 18 U.S.C. §3592(c). The jury unanimously found that two such factors had been proved beyond a reasonable doubt – it agreed that petitioner caused the death of his victim during the commission of another crime, and that he committed the offense in an especially heinous, cruel, and depraved manner.

Once petitioner became death-eligible, the jury had to decide whether he should receive a death sentence. In making the selection decision, the Act requires that the sentencing jury consider all of the aggravating and mitigating factors and determine whether the former outweigh the latter (or, if there are no mitigating factors, whether the aggravating factors alone are sufficient to warrant a death sentence). The Act, however, requires more exacting proof of aggravating factors than mitigating ones – although a jury must unanimously agree that the Government established the existence of an aggravating factor beyond a reasonable doubt, the jury may consider a mitigating factor in its weighing process so long as one juror finds that the defendant established its existence by preponderance of the evidence. In addition to the two statutory aggravators that established petitioner's death-eligibility, the jury also unanimously found two aggravators of the nonstatutory variety[34] had been proved: one set forth victim impact evidence and the other victim vulnerability evidence.[35] As for mitigating factors, at least one juror found 10 of the 11 that petitioner proposed and seven jurors wrote in a factor petitioner had not raised on the Special Findings Form.[36]

After weighing the aggravating and mitigating factors, the jury unanimously recommended that petitioner be sentenced to death. ... We granted certiorari and now affirm.

II.

A.

---

[34] The term "nonstatutory aggravating factor" is used to refer to any aggravating factor that is not specifically described in 18 U.S.C. §3592. Section 3592(c) provides that the jury may consider "whether any other aggravating factor for which notice has been given exists." Pursuant to §3593(a), when the Government decides to seek the death penalty, it must provide notice of the aggravating factors that it proposes to prove as justifying a sentence of death.

[35] As phrased on the Special Findings Form, the nonstatutory aggravating factors read:

3(B). Tracie Joy McBride's young age, her slight stature, her background, and her unfamiliarity with San Angelo, Texas.

3(C). Tracie Joy McBride's personal characteristics and the effect of the instant offense on Tracie Joy McBride's family constitute an aggravating factor of the offense.

[36] The mitigating factors that the jury found as set forth on the Special Findings Form (along with the number of jurors that found for each factor in brackets) are as follows: "1. That the defendant Louis Jones did not have a significant prior criminal record." "2. That the defendant Louis Jones' capacity to appreciate the wrongfulness of the defendant's conduct or to conform to the requirements of law was significantly impaired, regardless of whether the capacity was so impaired as to constitute a defense to the charge." "3. That the defendant Louis Jones committed the offense under severe mental or emotional disturbance." "4. That the defendant Louis Jones was subjected to physical, sexual, and emotional abuse as a child (and was deprived of sufficient parental protection that he needed)." "5. That the defendant Louis Jones served his country well in Desert Storm, Grenada, and for 22 years in the United States Army." "6. That the defendant Louis Jones is likely to be a well-behaved inmate." "7. That the defendant Louis Jones is remorseful for the crime he committed." "8. That the defendant Louis Jones' daughter will be harmed by the emotional trauma of her father's execution." "9. That the defendant Louis Jones was under unusual and substantial internally generated duress and stress at the time of the offense." "10. That the defendant Louis Jones suffered from numerous neurological or psychological disorders at the time of the offense." Seven jurors added petitioner's ex-wife as a mitigating factor without further elaboration.

We first decide the question whether petitioner was entitled to an instruction as to the consequences of jury deadlock. Petitioner requested, in relevant part, the following instruction:

> In the event, after due deliberation and reflection, the jury is unable to agree on a unanimous decision as to the sentence to be imposed, you should so advise me and I will impose a sentence of life imprisonment without possibility of release. ...
>
> ...
>
> In the event you are unable to agree on [a sentence of] Life Without Possibility of Release or Death, but you are unanimous that the sentence should not be less than Life Without Possibility of Release, you should report that vote to the Court and the Court will sentence the defendant to Life Without the Possibility of Release.

In petitioner's view, the Eighth Amendment requires that the jury be instructed as to the effect of their inability to agree. He alternatively argues that we should invoke our supervisory power over the federal courts and require that such an instruction be given.

Before we turn to petitioner's Eighth Amendment argument, a question of statutory interpretation calls for our attention. The Fifth Circuit held that the District Court did not err in refusing petitioner's requested instruction because it was not substantively correct. According to the Court of Appeals, §3593(b)(2)(C), which provides that a new jury shall be impaneled for a new sentencing hearing if the guilt phase jury is discharged for "good cause," requires the District Court to impanel a second jury and hold a second sentencing hearing in the event of jury deadlock. The Government interprets the statute the same way (although its reading is more nuanced) and urges that the judgment below be affirmed on this ground.

Petitioner, however, reads the Act differently. In his view, whenever the jury reaches a result other than a unanimous verdict recommending a death sentence or life imprisonment without the possibility of release, the duty of sentencing falls upon the district court pursuant to §3594, which reads:

> Upon a recommendation under section 3593(e) that the defendant should be sentenced to death or life imprisonment without possibility of release, the court shall sentence the defendant accordingly. Otherwise, the court shall impose any lesser sentence that is authorized by law. Notwithstanding any other law, if the maximum term of imprisonment for the offense is life imprisonment, the court may impose a sentence of life imprisonment without possibility of release.

Petitioner's argument is based on his construction of the term "otherwise." He argues that this term means that when the jury, after retiring for deliberations, reports itself as unable to reach unanimous verdict, the sentencing determination passes to the court.

...petitioner's view of the statute is the better one. The phrase "good cause" in §3593(b)(2)(C) plainly encompasses events such as juror disqualification, but cannot be read so expansively as to include the jury's failure to reach a unanimous decision. Nevertheless, the Eighth Amendment does not require that the jury be instructed as to the consequences of their failure to agree.

To be sure, we have said that the Eighth Amendment requires that a sentence of death not be imposed arbitrarily. In order for a capital sentencing scheme to pass constitutional muster, it must perform a narrowing function with respect to the class of persons eligible for the death penalty and must also ensure that capital sentencing decisions rest upon an individualized inquiry. The instruction that petitioner requested has no bearing on what we have called the "eligibility phase" of the capital sentencing process. As for what we have called the "selection phase," our cases have held that in order to satisfy the requirement that capital sentencing decisions rest upon an individualized inquiry, a scheme must allow a "broad inquiry" into all "constitutionally relevant mitigating evidence." Petitioner does not argue, nor could he, that the District Court's failure to give the requested instruction prevented the jury from considering such evidence.

In theory, the District Court's failure to instruct the jury as to the consequences of deadlock could give rise to an Eighth Amendment problem of a different sort: We also have held that a jury cannot be "affirmatively misled regarding its role in the sentencing process." In no way, however, was the jury affirmatively misled by the District Court's refusal to give petitioner's proposed instruction. The truth of the matter is that the proposed instruction has no bearing on the jury's role in the sentencing process. Rather, it speaks to what happens in the event that the jury is unable to fulfill its role – when deliberations break down and the jury is unable to produce a unanimous sentence recommendation. Petitioner's argument, although less than clear, appears to be that a death sentence is arbitrary within the meaning of the Eighth Amendment if the jury is not given any bit of information that might possibly influence an individual juror's voting behavior. That contention has no merit. We have never suggested, for example, that the Eighth Amendment requires a jury be instructed as to the consequences of a breakdown in the deliberative process. On the contrary, we have long been of the view that "the very object of the jury system is to secure unanimity by a comparison of views, and by arguments among the jurors themselves." We further have recognized that in a capital sentencing proceeding, the Government has "a strong interest in having the jury express the conscience of the community on the ultimate question of life or death." We are of the view that a charge to the jury of the sort proposed by petitioner might well have the effect of undermining this strong governmental interest.

B.

Petitioner further argues that the jury was led to believe that if it could not reach a unanimous sentence recommendation he would receive a judge-imposed sentence less severe than life imprisonment, and his proposed instruction as to the consequences of deadlock was necessary to correct the jury's erroneous impression. Moreover, he contends that the alleged confusion independently warrants reversal of his sentence under the Due Process Clause, the Eighth Amendment, and the Act itself. He grounds his due process claim in the assertion that sentences may not be based on materially untrue assumptions, his Eighth Amendment claim in his contention that the jury is entitled to accurate sentencing information, and his statutory claim in an argument that jury confusion over the available sentencing options constitutes an "arbitrary factor" under §3595(c)(2)(A).

...After instructing the jury on the aggravating and mitigating factors and explaining the process of weighing those factors, the District Court gave the following instructions pertaining to the jury's sentencing recommendation:

> ...If you unanimously conclude that the aggravating factors found to exist sufficiently outweigh any mitigating factor or factors found to exist, or in the absence of any mitigating factors, that the aggravating factors are themselves sufficient to justify a sentence of death, you may recommend a sentence of death. Keep in mind, however, that regardless of your findings with respect to aggravating and mitigating factors, you are never required to recommend a death sentence.
>
> If you recommend the imposition of a death sentence, the court is required to impose that sentence. If you recommend a sentence of life without the possibility of release, the court is required to impose that sentence. If you recommend that some other lesser sentence be imposed, the court is required to impose a sentence that is authorized by the law. ...

...There is no reasonable likelihood that the jury applied the instructions incorrectly. The District Court did not expressly inform the jury that it would impose a lesser sentence in case of deadlock. It simply told the jury that, if they recommended a lesser sentence, the court would impose a sentence "authorized by the law."

Even assuming, arguendo, that an error occurred (and that it was plain), petitioner cannot show that it affected his substantial rights. Any confusion among the jurors over the effect of a lesser sentence recommendation was allayed by the District Court's admonition that the jury should not concern itself with the effect of such a recommendation. The jurors are presumed to have followed these instructions. Even if the jurors had some lingering doubts about the effect of deadlock, therefore, the instructions made clear that they should set aside their concerns and either report that they were unable to reach agreement or recommend a lesser sentence if they believed that this was the only option.

Moreover, even assuming that the jurors were confused over the consequences of deadlock, petitioner cannot show the confusion necessarily worked to his detriment. It is just as likely that the jurors, loathe to recommend a lesser sentence, would have compromised on a sentence of life imprisonment as on a death sentence. Where the effect of an alleged error is so uncertain, a defendant cannot meet his burden of showing that the error actually affected his substantial rights. ...

III.

A.

Apart from the claimed instructional error, petitioner argues that the nonstatutory aggravating factors found and considered by the jury were vague, overbroad, and duplicative in violation of the Eighth Amendment, and that the District Court's error in allowing the jury to consider them was not harmless beyond a reasonable doubt.

The Eighth Amendment, as the Court of Appeals correctly recognized, permits capital sentencing juries to consider evidence relating to the victim's personal characteristics and the emotional impact of the murder on the victim's family in deciding whether an eligible defendant should receive a death sentence. Petitioner does not dispute that, as a general matter, such evidence is appropriate for the sentencing jury's consideration. His objection is that the two nonstatutory aggravating factors were duplicative, vague, and overbroad so as to render their use in this case unconstitutional ...

1.

We first address petitioner's contention that the two nonstatutory aggravating factors were impermissibly duplicative. The Fifth Circuit reasoned that "the plain meaning of the term 'personal characteristics,' used in [nonstatutory aggravator] 3(C), necessarily includes 'young age, slight stature, background, and unfamiliarity,' which the jury was asked to consider in 3(B)." The problem, the court thought, was that this duplication led to "double counting" of aggravating factors. Following a Tenth Circuit decision, the Fifth Circuit was of the view that in a weighing scheme, "double counting" has a tendency to skew the process so as to give rise to the risk of an arbitrary, and thus unconstitutional, death sentence. In the Fifth Circuit's words, there may be a thumb on the scale in favor of death "if the jury has been asked to weigh the same aggravating factor twice."

We have never before held that aggravating factors could be duplicative so as to render them constitutionally invalid, nor have we passed on the "double counting" theory that the Tenth Circuit advanced and the Fifth Circuit appears to have followed here. What we have said is that the weighing process may be impermissibly skewed if the sentencing jury considers an invalid factor. Petitioner's argument (and the reasoning of the Fifth and Tenth Circuits) would have us reach a quite different proposition – that if two aggravating factors are "duplicative," then the weighing process necessarily is skewed, and the factors are therefore invalid.

2.

We also are of the view that the Fifth Circuit incorrectly concluded that factors 3(B) and 3(C) were unconstitutionally vague. In that court's view, the nonstatutory aggravating factors challenged here "failed to guide the jury's discretion, or [to] distinguish this murder from any other murder." The Court of Appeals also was of the opinion that "the use of the terms 'background,' 'personal characteristics,' and 'unfamiliarity' without further definition or instruction left the jury with . . . open-ended discretion."

Ensuring that a sentence of death is not so infected with bias or caprice is our "controlling objective when we examine eligibility and selection factors for vagueness." Our vagueness review, however, is "quite deferential."As long as an aggravating factor has a core meaning that criminal juries should be capable of understanding, it will pass constitutional muster. Assessed under this deferential standard, the factors challenged here surely are not vague. The jury should have had no difficulty understanding that factor 3(B) was designed to ask it to consider whether the victim was especially vulnerable to petitioner's attack. Nor should it have had difficulty comprehending that factor 3(C) asked it to consider the victim's personal traits and the effect of the crime on her family. Even if the factors as written were somewhat vague, the Fifth Circuit was wrong to conclude that the factors were not given further definition; as we have explained, the Government's argument made absolutely clear what each nonstatutory factor meant.

3.

Finally, we turn to petitioner's contention that the challenged nonstatutory factors were overbroad. An aggravating factor can be overbroad if the sentencing jury "fairly could conclude that an aggravating circumstance applies to every defendant eligible for the death penalty." We have not, however, specifically considered what it means for a factor to be overbroad when it is important only for selection purposes and especially when it sets forth victim vulnerability or victim impact evidence. Of course, every murder will have an impact on the victim's family and friends and victims are often chosen because of their vulnerability. It might seem, then, that the factors 3(B) and 3(C) apply to every eligible defendant and thus fall within the Eighth Amendment's proscription against overbroad factors. But that cannot be correct; if it were, we would not have decided Payne as we did. Even though the concepts of victim impact and victim vulnerability may well be relevant in every case, evidence of victim vulnerability and victim impact in a particular case is inherently individualized. And such evidence is surely relevant to the selection phase decision, given that the sentencer should consider all of the circumstances of the crime in deciding whether to impose the death penalty.

What is of common importance at the eligibility and selection stages is that "the process is neutral and principled so as to guard against bias or caprice in the sentencing decision." So long as victim vulnerability and victim impact factors are used to direct the jury to the individual circumstances of the case, we do not think that principle will be disturbed. Because factors 3(B) and 3(C) directed the jury to the evidence specific to this case, we do not think that they were overbroad in a way that offended the Constitution.

B.

The error in this case, if any, rests in loose drafting of the nonstatutory aggravating factors; as we have made clear, victim vulnerability and victim impact evidence are appropriate subjects for the capital sentencer's consideration. Assuming that use of these loosely drafted factors was indeed error, we conclude that the error was harmless.

...Had factors 3(B) and 3(C) been precisely defined in writing, the jury surely would have reached the same recommendation as it did. ... We are satisfied that the jury in this case actually understood what each factor was designed to put before it, and therefore have no doubt that the jury would have reached the same conclusion had the aggravators been precisely defined in writing.

* * *

For the foregoing reasons, the judgment of the Court of Appeals is affirmed.

It is so ordered.

JUSTICE GINSBURG, with whom JUSTICE STEVENS and JUSTICE SOUTER join, and with whom JUSTICE BREYER joins as to Parts I, II, III, and V, dissenting.

The Federal Death Penalty Act of 1994 (FDPA) establishes a complex regime applicable when the Government seeks the ultimate penalty for a defendant found guilty of an offense potentially punishable by death. This case is pathmarking, for it is the first application of the FDPA. Two questions, as I comprehend petitioner's core objections, warrant prime attention.

First, when Congress specifies only two sentencing options for an offense, death or life without possibility of release, must the jury be told exactly that? Or, can a death decision stand despite misleading trial court "lesser sentence" instructions, specifically, instructions open to the construction that lack of a unanimous jury vote for either life or death would allow the judge to impose a sentence less severe than life in prison? Second, when the jury is unable to agree on a unanimous recommendation in a case in which death or life without possibility of release are the only sentencing options, must the judge then impose the life sentence? Or, is the judge required or permitted to impanel a second jury to make the life or death decision?

The Court of Appeals for the Fifth Circuit confronted these two questions and resolved both for the prosecution. ... I would reverse and remand so that the life or death decision may be made by an accurately informed trier.

I.

The jury apparently found the case close. It rejected three of the seven aggravators the Government urged.[37] And one or more jurors found each of the specific mitigating factors submitted by Jones. The jury deliberated for a day and a half before returning a verdict recommending death.

Jones moved for a new trial on the ground, supported by postsentence juror statements, that the court's instructions had misled the jurors. Specifically, Jones urged that the charge led jurors to believe that a deadlock would result in a court-imposed lesser sentence; to avoid such an outcome, Jones asserted, jurors who favored life without possibility of release changed their votes to approve the death verdict. The vote change, Jones maintained, was not hypothetical; it was backed up by juror statements. ...

III.

---

[37] The jury rejected the following aggravators: (1) the crime involved substantial planning and premeditation; (2) the crime created a grave risk to a person other than the victim; and (3) Jones posed a future danger to the lives and safety of other persons. It found as aggravators: (1) Jones killed the victim during the commission of kidnaping; (2) the crime was especially heinous, cruel, and depraved; (3) the victim's young age, slight stature, background, and unfamiliarity with San Angelo, Texas; and (4) the victim's personal characteristics and the effect of the offense on her family.

The governing law gave Jones's jury at the sentencing phase a life (without release) or death choice. The District Court, however, introduced, erroneously, a third prospect, "some other lesser sentence." Moreover, the court told the jury "not to be concerned" with what that lesser sentence might be, for "that [was] a matter for the court to decide." The jury's choice was clouded by that misinformation. I set out below my reasons for concluding that the misinformation rendered the jury's death verdict unreliable.

Misinformation, not the District Court's failure to repeat the unanimity requirement each time it mentioned the jury's sentencing options, or to advise on the consequences of a deadlocked jury, is the harmful error at the heart of Jones's case. I therefore see no cause to dispute that "the Eighth Amendment does not require that the jury be instructed as to the consequences of their failure to agree." In my judgment, however, the court was obliged, in this life or death case, to make clear to the jury that Jones's minimum sentence was life without possibility of release.

IV.

Piled on the key instructional error, the trial court presented the jury with duplicative, vague nonstatutory aggravating factors. The court told the jury to consider as aggravators, if established beyond a reasonable doubt, factors 3(B) – the victim's "young age, her slight stature, her background, and her unfamiliarity with San Angelo, Texas" – and 3(C) – the victim's "personal characteristics and the effect of the instant offense on [her] family."

...Double counting of aggravators "creates the risk of an arbitrary death sentence." ...

Appellate courts should hesitate to assert confidence that "elimination of improperly considered aggravating circumstances could not possibly affect the balance." Adding the overlapping aggravators to the more disturbing misinformation conveyed in the charge, I see no basis for concluding "'it would have made no difference if the thumb had been removed from death's side of the scale.'"

NOTES AND QUERIES

The central concern in this case illustrates the challenge of guiding the discretion of decision makers. In your view, was there a doubling of aggravators in this case? Sentencers must determine the persuasiveness of the totality of aggravating circumstances when compared to the totality of the mitigating circumstances. Does this provide a psychologically feasible and realistic alternative to merely counting up the circumstances? Does it provide enough guidance? How do you think the psychology of punishment plays into the manner jurors weigh mitigators and aggravators?

The introduction to this chapter, as well as our previous discussions of psychological research, suggests that decision makers, like most other human beings, tend to overestimate the causal significance of personal choice and to correspondingly underestimate the causal significance of situational factors in the behavior of others. We also have seen that observers also tend to attribute undesirable consequences to behavior rather than to circumstances. Observers resist the conclusion that serious harm might have resulted from chance rather than from wrongdoing. When harm has occurred, this tendency is magnified by the desire to believe that the world is basically just and a person is to blame. That research appears quite relevant to death penalty jurisprudence because death penalty cases call on observers to evaluate the personal responsibility of the accused for harm caused by balancing mitigating and aggravating factors. Research suggest that observers cannot perform this task in a completely rational way. Quite the contrary; observers are predisposed toward attributing conduct and its consequences to a person's personality and free will. Explain the significance of these psychological mechanisms to this case. How can that research help us address whether jurors were instructed properly and wether they were able to weigh factors appropriately? Importantly, it is difficult to move away from these potential biases; there is no reason to doubt that judges are not also influenced by them and no reason to doubt that the entire criminal justice system does not make the same error. See Donald A. Dripps, Fundamental retribution error: Criminal justice and the social psychology of blame, 56 Vand. L. Rev. 1383 (2003).

As seen in Chapter 7, death penalty jurisprudence may exacerbate biases. The process by which we select jurors, and determine those who eventually are deemed qualified to serve, contributes to biases. The relevant issue that arose in our discussion was whether those biases were acceptable in light of alternatives. That research has now been complimented by studies examining how juries respond to aggravating and mitigating factors. Those studies, again, point to biases. For example, death-qualified venirepersons, when compared to excludables, are more likely to endorse aggravating circumstances. Excludable participants, when compared to death-qualified venirepersons, are more likely to endorse nonstatutory mitigators. Brooke M. Butler and Gary Moran, The role of death qualification in venireperson' evaluations of aggravating and mitigating circumstances in capital trials, 26 L. and Hum. Beh. 175 (2002). What implications arise from this research?

Are you surprised by the numerous mitigating factors found by the jury? Defendants have a right to present any mitigating evidence or circumstances, whether formally listed by statute or not. Note too that the only requirement is that a sentencer must consider and give independent weight to any mitigating circumstance; it need not grant mercy on its basis. What do you make of this approach to guiding jury discretion given that the list of mitigators was so long compared to aggravators?

Do you think that a jury would have decided differently if it had known the consequences of a jury deadlock? What do you make of the dissent's point that Jones actually had jurors' statements indicating that they had, in fact, based their decision on a fact that was not true, regardless of what the trial court may have intended? Do you find the bases for such a verdict harmless error?

The jury was given two options at the sentencing phase; they could choose between either life (without release) or death. Jones had wanted to let the jury know of the existence of a third option. If the jury deadlocked, a judge would impose life without the possibility of release. What would be the impact of that instruction? Psychological science may contribute important suggestions. Research indicates that the movement from a structure of a binary choice to a decision among three or more options alters the actual decisions people make, even though those changes are irrational. Giving a decisionmaker additional options of a certain type will tend to push decisionmakers irrationally toward such decisions. A classic study, for example, investigated how the context of a third option can change the choice that a person makes. It found that the addition of a third option to a choice set can have the counterintuitive effect of increasing the absolute share of one of the two pre-existing choices. Subjects were given the choice between two cameras: a Minolta X-370, priced at $169.99, and a Minolta Maxxum 3000i, priced at $239.99. Subjects were split fifty-fifty between either option. The study then then added a third option to the choice set: a top of the line Maxxum 7000i, priced at $469.99. The popularity of the X-370 dropped from 50% to 22%, but the popularity of the Maxxum 3000i increased from 50% to 57%, and the Maxxum 7000i was the choice of 21% of the subjects. These results persisted even when the third option was not available. The researchers concluded that just knowing about the third possibility had the effect of increasing the absolute share of the middle option. The implication is that, even though a third option or a first option is not good, just having the extra option actually increases the percentage of subjects who choose a compromise middle option. Itamar Simonson and Amos Tversky, Choice in context: Tradeoff contrast and extremeness aversion, 29 J. Marketing Res. 281, 281-90 (1992). What implications arise from these findings which have since been replicated and identified as the "decoy" and "compromise" effects? For explorations of these effects, see Itamar Simonson, Choice based on reasons: The case of attraction and compromise effects, 16 J. of Consumer Res. 158 (1989); and Jerel E. Slaughter, Evan F. Sinar, and Scott Highhouse, Decoy effects and attribute-level inferences, 84 J. of App. Psych. 823 (1999).

NOTE ON INTERSECTIONS BETWEEN PSYCHOLOGY AND LAW

Much of our discussions have focused on the extent to which the legal system uses, abuses, or ignores psychological science. As we reach the end of our inquiry, it makes sense to consider what leading commentators have to say about intersections between the law and psychology. A central issue involves understanding why courts often are reluctant to rely on empirical research. There are many reasons that the law may avoid social sciences. An obvious reason is that it may well be that no empirical research has been conducted on the issues being litigated and in some instances the Court may point to the absence of empirical data as one reason not to take a particular approach. Another reason courts may appear reluctant to make full use of psychological science evidence is that it often rivals law. One commentator has provided a series of contrasting characteristics: (1) Psychology is innovative, while law resists innovation; (2) psychology is based on data and observation, while law is based on precedent and hierarchy; (3) psychology seeks an objective answer to problems, while law seeks an adversarial victory; (4) psychology is descriptive, while law is prescriptive; (5) psychology is nomothetic, while law is idiographic; (6) psychological conclusions are probabilistic and tentative, while legal conclusions are irrevocable and must appear certain; (7) psychology is proactive, while law is reactive; and (8) psychology is abstract, while law deals with concrete issues. Craig Haney, Psychology and legal change: On the limits of a factual jurisprudence, 4 L. and Hum. Beh. 147 (1980). Another important commentator has offered another approach to understanding why the legal system often fails to move toward directions suggested by psychology; he suggests that the courts and social sciences are essentially incompatible. This approach suggests that the Supreme Court will perceive a branch of social science to be relevant to the formation of legal policy only if the science reflects the values advanced by the law. The more the two value systems converge, the more completely the Court's jurisprudence will incorporate social-scientific information. The converse is also true. This approach suggests that we examine which areas of law share values with fields of social science and which do not. It also predicts that the less compatible the two systems are, the less likely it is that legal decisionmakers will incorporate social science information into their decisions. See Alexander J. Tanford, The limits of a scientific jurisprudence: The Supreme Court and psychology, 66 Ind. L. J. 137 (1990).

APPENDIX A
KEY FEDERAL CONSTITUTIONAL PROVISIONS

Amendment I. Congress shall make no law respecting an establishment of religion, or prohibiting the free exercise thereof; or abridging the freedom of speech, or of the press; or the right of the people peaceably to assemble, and to petition the Government for a redress of grievances.

Amendment II. A well regulated militia, being necessary to the security of a free state, the right of the people to keep and bear arms, shall not be infringed.

Amendment III. Section 1. The judicial power of the United States, shall be vested in one Supreme Court, and in such inferior courts as the Congress may from time to time ordain and establish. ... Section 2. The judicial power shall extend to all cases, in law and equity, arising under this Constitution, the laws of the United States, and treaties made, or which shall be made, under their authority; ... to controversies to which the United States shall be a party; • to controversies between two or more states;• between a state and citizens of another state;• between citizens of different states; • between citizens of the same state claiming lands under grants of different states, and between a state, or the citizens thereof ...

Amendment IV. The right of the people to be secure in their persons, houses, papers, and effects, against unreasonable searches and seizures, shall not be violated, and no Warrants shall issue, but upon probable cause, supported by Oath or affirmation, and particularly describing the place to be searched, and the persons or things to be seized.

Amendment V. No person shall be held to answer for a capital, or otherwise infamous crime, unless on a presentment or indictment of a Grand Jury, except in cases arising in the land or naval forces, or in the Militia, when in actual service in time of War or public danger; nor shall any person be subject for the same offence to be twice put in jeopardy of life or limb; nor shall be compelled in any criminal case to be a witness against himself, nor be deprived of life, liberty, or property, without due process of law; nor shall private property be taken for public use, without just compensation.

Amendment VI. In all criminal prosecutions, the accused shall enjoy the right to a speedy and public trial, by an impartial jury of the State and district wherein the crime shall have been committed, which district shall have been previously ascertained by law, and to be informed of the nature and cause of the accusation; to be confronted with the witnesses against him; to have compulsory process for obtaining witnesses in his favor, and to have the Assistance of Counsel for his defence.

Amendment VIII. Excessive bail shall not be required, nor excessive fines imposed, nor cruel and unusual punishments inflicted.

Amendment IX. The enumeration in the Constitution, of certain rights, shall not be construed to deny or disparage others retained by the people.

Amendment X. The powers not delegated to the United States by the Constitution, nor prohibited by it to the States, are reserved to the States respectively, or to the people.

Amendment XIII. Section 1. Neither slavery nor involuntary servitude, except as a punishment for crime whereof the party shall have been duly convicted, shall exist within the United States, or any place subject to their jurisdiction. Section 2. Congress shall have power to enforce this article by appropriate legislation.

Amendment XIV. Section 1. All persons born or naturalized in the United States, and subject to the jurisdiction thereof, are citizens of the United States and of the state wherein they reside. No state shall make or enforce any law which shall abridge the privileges or immunities of citizens of the United States; nor shall any state deprive any person of life, liberty, or property, without due process of law; nor deny to any person within its jurisdiction the equal protection of the laws.

Amendment XV. Section 1. The right of citizens of the United States to vote shall not be denied or abridged by the United States or by any state on account of race, color, or previous condition of servitude. Section 2. The Congress shall have power to enforce this article by appropriate legislation.

APPENDIX B
UNDERSTANDING CASE LAW

Nature of Cases: Formal cases typically begin in the trial court, where a trial judge (sometimes with the assistance of a jury) seeks to resolve a dispute. If one of the parties believes the decision-makers erred in that phase, the party may appeal to a "higher" court, typically called a court of appeal. Courts of appeal review briefs. Briefs are the written arguments submitted by the appellant (the appealing party) and the appellee (the responding party). In addition to the briefs, the reviewing court may examine trial transcripts and documents introduced as evidence during the trial. To render decisions, courts often have attorneys appear to orally state their positions and to respond to questions from the justices. However, no trial takes place during the appellate phase; appellate courts take the facts as they were litigated and apply them to the law. Typically, one of the justices expresses the court's ruling in a written opinion.

Cite or Citation: This includes the parties and "citation" reference where the case can be located. The citation is the group of letters and numbers attached to the case, which tell you where the case was heard and when it was decided; e.g., U.S. or S.Ct. are U.S. Supreme Court case law reporters.

Facts: Material facts are the description of the events between the parties that led to the dispute. The facts indicate how the case came before the trial court and what was decided. If it is on appeal, it includes the alleged error.

Issues: Issues are the legal points or questions disputed by the parties. Typically, an issue combines the applicable rule of law with the material facts of the case.

Holdings: These are the court's rulings. Holdings are unlike dicta. Dicta are the arguments the court makes, but they are only binding on future courts if they relate to the question actually before it. The dicta, however, are important to consider in analyzing the court's thinking and possibilities.

Reasoning: This is the analysis the court used to support is decisions.

Opinions: The opinion of the court is the written decision. When more than one judge has heard the case, one of the judges typically writes the decision for the court, and that judge's name appears at the beginning of the opinion. Cases often have separate opinions, which may be concurring or dissenting. Concurring opinions agree with the principal holding but differ in its reasoning. Dissenting opinions dissent on the holding and the reasoning. If the court's opinion is joined in by a majority, it is called the majority opinion, which binds future cases. The common ground on which a majority agree becomes the law. Concurring opinions do not affect whether the reasoning will bind subsequent cases. However, when the opinion of the court is a plurality opinion, when a majority has concurred in the result only but not in the reasoning, then the plurality's reasoning does not bind future cases.

Policy Considerations: The social policies or goals that the decision-maker seeks to further.

Appendix C
General Categories of Criminal Homicide: Murder and Manslaughter

Murder

Murder typically involves two degrees. First-degree murder includes premeditated, deliberate killing; killings that take place while committing dangerous felonies; and particularly brutal, heinous, or cruel murders. Second-degree murder includes intentional killing without premeditation; killings resulting from the intent to do serious bodily injury; killings resulting from the resisting of lawful arrest; and killings taking place during the commission of less serious felonies.

In understanding the legal category of murder, it is important to consider three worthy points. First, some states consider killings committed in specific ways to be first degree murder. Although these vary by state, they can include killing by poison, by lying in wait, and by torture. Second, second-degree murder generally is viewed as a catchall offense including killings that are neither manslaughter nor first-degree murder. Third, premeditation means with planning or deliberation. The amount of time needed for premeditation of a killing depends on the person and the circumstances. It must be long enough, after forming the intent to kill, for the killer to have been fully conscious of the intent and to have considered the killing.

Manslaughter

Manslaughter either is voluntary or involuntary. Voluntary manslaughter involves the intentional killing of another done under provocation that is actual or adequate, occurs in the heat of passion, or occurs before an adequate cooling off period. To qualify for this charge, defendants must have believed that they were acting in self-defense but where it was unreasonable to do so. Involuntary manslaughter involves the unintentional killing of another either with gross criminal recklessness or with gross criminal negligence while committing certain illegal acts. Negligent homicide includes unintentional killings in which actors should have known they were creating substantial and unjustified risks of death by conduct that deviated from ordinary care. It involves causing death by less than gross negligence.

Properly understanding the legal category of manslaughter requires noting a few key points. First, adequate provocation typically includes only situations involving a threat of deadly force or in which a person acts in the heat of passion (e.g., acts immediately after finding spouse with a lover). Second, gross criminal negligence is very great negligence; actions without even slight care but not amounting to intentional or conscious wrongdoing. The defendant is unaware of risk but should have been aware; it involves substantial and unjustifiable risk (not just everyday risk), gross incompetence. Third, criminal recklessness involves awareness that the risk was substantial and unjustifiable; it involves a gross deviation from the reasonable person standard and is more culpable than criminal negligence. Lastly, the negligent homicide offense often is included in, and considered to be a lesser degree than, involuntary manslaughter.

APPENDIX D
MAJOR PSYCHIATRIC DISORDERS

Many of the cases we will examine involve psychiatric diagnoses and psychological disorders. Most of these can be found in the Diagnostic and Statistical Manual of Mental Disorders-IV (1994) (DSM-IV) published by the American Psychiatric Association. While keeping in mind that many disorders exist, we focus on those that appear most frequently in the criminal justice literature.

DISSOCIATIVE DISORDERS

The key disorder which we will most frequently encounter in this area involves the diagnosis of Multiple Personality Disorder. Although that diagnosis continues to be used, DSM-IV actually has changed it to Dissociative Identity Disorder (DID). That change stresses dissociation, which is understood as a mental process that produces a lack of connection in a person's thoughts, memories, feelings, actions, or sense of identity. The experience of dissociation means that a person fails to associate information that typically would be associated with other information. A classic example involves an individual's dissociation of a traumatic memory from their ongoing memory.

Several diagnostic features distinguish DID. Those features include the presence of two or more distinct identities, each with its own particular way of relating to the world and self. A diagnosis of DID requires at least two identities that recurrently control the person's behavior. In addition, a diagnosis requires an inability to recall important personal information to an extent that is more than ordinary forgetfulness (such as finding oneself in a place without knowing how one got there). In addition to those factors, individuals with DID may experience any of the following: depression, mood swings, suicidal tendencies, sleep disorders (insomnia, night terrors, and sleep walking), panic attacks and phobias (flashbacks or reactions to stimuli), alcohol and drug abuse, compulsions and rituals, psychotic-like symptoms (such as auditory and visual hallucinations), time loss, trances, amnesias, out of body experiences and eating disorders.

DSM-IV describes several types of Dissociative Disorders. Three examples frequently appear in the criminal justice literature. The first form is Dissociative Amnesia. This disorder refers to the inability to recall important personal information when that failure is due to information that has become traumatic or stressful. The second form, Dissociative Fugue, refers to a sudden, unexpected travel away from home with the inability to recall one's past. These symptoms lead to confusion about one's identity or even sometimes to the assumption of a new identity. The third form, Depersonalization Disorder, refers to feeling detached or estranged from one's self. That detachment, however, still has reality testing intact to the extent that individuals know what is happening but do not feel like they are experiencing it themselves. Note that all of these disorders typically will not be diagnosed unless they cause a major disruption in an individual's life or they are not due to a general medical condition or to the physiological effects of substances like drugs or alcohol.

PERSONALITY DISORDERS

The DSM-IV defines a personality disorder as a long-standing and maladaptive pattern of perceiving and responding to other people and to stressful circumstances. It involves an enduring pattern of inner experience and behavior that conspicuously differs from the expectations of the individual's culture, is pervasive and inflexible, has an onset in adolescence or early adulthood, is stable over time, and leads to distress or impairment. Personality disorders exist on a continuum so they can be mild to more severe in terms of how pervasive and to what extent a person exhibits the features of a particular personality disorder. DSM-IV defines ten personality disorders, grouped into three clusters. Cluster A focuses on odd or eccentric behavior; it includes Paranoid Personality, Schizoid Personality, and Schizotypal Personality. Cluster B centers on emotional or erratic behavior; it includes Borderline Personality, Narcissistic Personality, Antisocial Personality, Histrionic (hysterical) Personality. Cluster C focuses on anxious, fearful behavior; it includes Dependent Personality, Avoidant Personality, and Obsessive-compulsive Personality.

Paranoid Personality: This disorder refers to a pervasive distrust and suspiciousness of others to the extent that individuals interpret the actions of others as deliberately threatening, hostile, malevolent, unfaithful, disloyal, condescending, deceitful or demeaning. These motives often represent projections of one's own hostilities onto others. Because of the way they perceive others, persons with this personality disorder are generally cold, distant, untrusting, unforgiving, and prone to anger or aggressive outbursts without justification.

Schizoid Personality: This disorder involves a pattern of detachment from social relationships and a restricted range of expression of emotions in social settings. Persons with this personality disorder are introverted, withdrawn, emotionally cold and distant as they fear closeness and intimacy. They are most often absorbed in their own feelings and thoughts (such as daydreaming).

Schizotypal Personality: This disorder, like schizoid personality disorders, involves a general incapacity to develop and maintain close relationships. This disorder also includes, however, cognitive or perceptual distortions and eccentricities of behavior. For example, people with this disorder express such oddities as magical thinking, clairvoyance, ideas of reference, as well as strange, outlandish or paranoid beliefs.

Borderline Personality: Individuals with this disorder experience unstable relationships, moods, behaviors, and self-image. They often experience the world in extremes, moving abruptly and unpredictably from one view to another. For example, they quickly may feel intensely attached to someone only to reject that person because of a perceived slight.

Narcissistic Personality: This personality disorder refers to an exaggerated sense of self-importance marked by a pervasive pattern of grandiosity in fantasy or behavior. These individuals have an exaggerated sense of superiority and success. This exaggeration leads them to believe that others are less important, which helps them rationalize their tendency to exploit interpersonal relationships. They also are characterized by a need for attention and to be admired. They lack empathy and are extremely sensitive to criticism and failure. They also are prone to mood swings when confronted with a failure to fulfill their high opinion of themselves.

Antisocial Personality: Individuals with this disorder, which was previously called psychopathic or sociopathic, pervasively and callously disregard the rights and feelings of others. They characteristically ignore normal rules of social behavior as they impulsively and irresponsibly exploit others for materialistic gain or personal gratification (unlike narcissistic persons, who exploit others because they think their superiority justifies it). They are generally unable to tolerate frustration. They often fail to anticipate the negative consequences of their antisocial behaviors and typically show no respect for other people and feel no remorse about the effects of their behavior on others. Individuals with this disorder are known for their easy ability to use deceit to rationalize their behavior or blame it on others. Importantly, punishment does not seem to improve their judgment and foresight; nor does it change their behavior. Rather, punishment tends to confirm their view of the world.

Histrionic (hysterical) Personality: Persons with this personality disorder excessively seek attention and dependency on others. They are conscious of appearance and dramatic. To get attention or manipulate others, they may engage in self-mutilation or recurrent suicidal gestures. Their expressions and behaviors often evoke sympathetic or erotic attention from others. Because of their over-exaggerated expressions, their relationships often are established easily but tend to remain superficial and transient.

Dependent Personality: This disorder is characterized by a person's pervasive and excessive need to have others take care of them, which leads to submissive and clinging behavior and fears of separation. Persons with this disorder allow others' needs to supersede their own and surrender responsibility for major areas of their lives to others. Individuals with this disorder lack self-confidence and feel insecure about their ability to take care of themselves. They require excessive reassurance and advice, and are hurt easily by criticism or disapproval.

Avoidant Personality: Persons with this personality disorder are hypersensitive to rejection and fear starting relationships or new efforts for fear that they may fail. As a result, this disorder is known for its pervasive pattern of social inhibition, feelings of inadequacy, and hypersensitivity to criticism. Individuals with an avoidant personality disorder are openly distressed about their isolation and respond to rejection with withdrawal.

Obsessive-compulsive Personality: This disorder involves a pervasive pattern of preoccupation with orderliness, perfectionism, and control. As a result, individuals with this disorder tend to be very reliable, dependable, orderly, and methodical, but their inflexibility often renders them incapable of adapting to changed circumstances because they lack flexibility, openness, and efficiency. The inflexibility accounts for the difficulty of making decisions and completing tasks.

OTHER PERSONALITY TYPES

We will read cases that report personality disorders not classified in the DSM-IV. It is worth identifying three of the most commonly diagnosed disorders.

Passive-aggressive Personality: Persons with this personality disorder typically appear inept or passive. But that appearance tends to be designed covertly either to avoid responsibility or to control or punish others. Passive-aggressive behavior is often evident in procrastination, inefficiency, or protests of inability. Those behaviors serve to deny or conceal hostility or disagreements. Persons exhibiting this personality frequently agree to perform tasks they do not want to perform and then subtly undermine their completion.

Cyclothymic Personality: People with this disorder exhibit high buoyancy that alternates with gloom and pessimism. The mood changes are characteristically regular (lasts weeks or longer) and typically occur without justifiable external cause. This disorder is considered a variant of manic-depressive illness.

Depressive Personality: Persons with depressive personality disorder are chronically morose, worried, and self-conscious. They find self-satisfaction undeserved and sinful. They find their suffering needed to earn the love or admiration of others. This personality disorder is considered a temperament that usually does not result in social dysfunction.

SCHIZOPHRENIA

Schizophrenia refers to a psychotic disorder marked by, for example, delusions, hallucinations, incoherent speech, and disorganized thinking. These symptoms vary in type and severity. Symptoms can be categorized as positive (excess or distorted normal functions) or negative (deficit in normal functions). Some investigators believe schizophrenia is a single disorder while others view it as a syndrome comprised of numerous underlying disease entities.

Schizophrenic symptoms: Positive symptoms are categorized as delusions and hallucinations or thought disorder and bizarre behavior. Delusions and hallucinations essentially are the psychotic dimension of schizophrenia. Hallucinations may occur in any sensory form, but auditory hallucinations are the most common and are characteristic of schizophrenia. Delusions are false beliefs about external reality that are maintained despite obvious proof to the contrary. In persecutory delusions, individuals believe that they are being tormented, followed, tricked, or spied on. In delusions of reference, they believe that passages from books, newspapers, songs or television are directed at them. In delusions of thought withdrawal or thought insertion, individuals believe that others can read their mind, that their thoughts are being transmitted to others, or that thoughts and impulses are being imposed on them by outside forces. Thought disorder and bizarre behavior involve what is termed the disorganized symptom cluster of schizophrenia. Thought disorder refers to disorganized thinking as revealed, for example, by rambling and undirected speech. Bizarre behavior may include childlike silliness, agitation, and inappropriate appearance or conduct. For example, catatonic motor behavior is an extreme form of bizarre behavior that can include maintaining a rigid posture or engaging in purposeless and unstimulated motor activity.

Negative symptoms are often associated with a general loss of motivation and diminished sense of purpose and goals. Negative symptoms include blunted affect, poverty of speech, anhedonia, and asociality. Blunted affect means a flattening of emotions, so much so that individuals may appear immobile as they make poor eye contact and lack expression. Poverty of speech refers to a diminished thought reflected in decreased speech and terse replies to questions. Anhedonia means a diminished capacity to experience pleasure which may be reflected by a lack of interest in activities and excessive time spent in purposeless activity. Asociality refers to a lack of interest in relationships.

Schizophrenic types: Classical subtypes used to classify patients into more uniform groups include paranoid, disorganized (hebephrenic), catatonic, and undifferentiated. Paranoid schizophrenia involves a preoccupation with delusions or auditory hallucinations, without prominent disorganized speech or inappropriate affect. Disorganized schizophrenia is characterized by disorganized speech, disorganized behavior, and flat or inappropriate affect. Catatonic schizophrenia consists of physical symptoms such as immobility or excessive motor activity and the assumption of bizarre postures. Undifferentiated schizophrenia involves mixed symptoms. Among individual patients, subtypes may change over time, generally from paranoid to disorganized or undifferentiated or from nondeficit to deficit.

Schizophrenia also can be classified based on the presence and severity of negative symptoms, such as blunted affect, lack of motivation, and diminished sense of purpose. Patients with a deficit subtype have prominent negative symptoms unaccounted for by other factors (eg, depression, anxiety, an understimulating environment, and drug side effects). These patients typically are more disabled, have a poorer prognosis, and are more resistant to treatment than those with nondeficit subtype, who may have delusions, hallucinations, and thought disorders but are relatively free of negative symptoms.

Mood Disorders

The essential feature of these mental disorders, also referred to as affective disorders, is persistent or episodic exaggeration of mood state. Illnesses in this group of disorders are heterogeneous and typically recurrent illnesses including unipolar (depressive) and bipolar (manic-depressive) disorders that are characterized by pervasive mood disturbances, psychomotor dysfunction, and vegetative symptoms.

Depression: Depression, sometimes referred to as Unipolar Disorder, presents a mood that typically is depressed, irritable, and/or anxious. Depressed patients present a morbid look; they appear miserable, make poor eye contact, and engage in monosyllabic or no speech. Clinically depressed individuals may present a preoccupation with guilt, self-denigrating ideas, decreased ability to concentrate, indecisiveness, diminished interest in usual activities, social withdrawal, helplessness, hopelessness, and recurrent thoughts of death and suicide. These patients often experience sleep disorders and often are known as being so depressed that they cannot feel emotions to the extent that they can no longer cry (either out of grief or joy).

Bipolar Disorders: This disorder, popularly named manic-depressive disorder, involves alternations between depression and manic phases. Symptoms of the depressive phase are similar to those of unipolar depression, except that there may be more extreme sings like depressive stupor (no movement). The manic symptoms are characterized by elation, racing thoughts, and sometimes irritability and hostility. Manic patients are inexhaustibly, excessively, and impulsively involved in various activities without recognizing their inherent social dangers. In the extreme, psychomotor activity is so frenzied that any understandable link between mood and behavior is lost; this senseless agitation is known as delirious mania, which is the counterpart of depressive stupor.

Three types of bipolar disorders exist. Bipolar I disorder is characterized by alternating full-fledged manic and major depressive episodes. Bipolar I disorder commonly begins with depression and is characterized by at least one manic or excited period during its course. Bipolar II disorder involves an alternation between depressive episodes and with hypomanias (relatively mild, nonpsychotic, short periods). Bipolar III, an unofficial category, includes patients with major depressive episodes and a family history of bipolar disorders who exhibit subtle hypomanic tendencies. Their temperament is viewed as hyperthymic, which means that they are driven and ambitious.

Anxiety Disorders

Anxiety disorders differ dramatically from normal feelings of nervousness. Unlike nervousness due to an anticipated event, this disorder is characterized by symptoms that often occur without warning and make simple life routines nearly unbearably discomforting.

Posttraumatic Stress Disorder: This disorder involves the repeated re-experience of an overwhelming physical or emotional event, usually through nightmares or flashbacks. This experience causes intense fear, helplessness, horror, and avoidance of stimuli associated with the traumatic event. Additionally, symptoms may include feeling numb or detached, having trouble sleeping, feeling jittery or on guard or being depressed. The traumatic event typically involves serious injury or threatened death to the person or others or actual death of others; and that event is experienced as intense fear, helplessness, or horror.

Acute Stress Disorder: This disorder resembles posttraumatic stress disorder except that it begins within four weeks of the traumatic event and lasts a minimum of two days but no more than four weeks. A person with this disorder has three or more of the following dissociative symptoms: a sense of numbing, detachment, or absence of emotional responsiveness; reduced awareness of surroundings; a feeling that things are not real; a feeling that they are not real; and amnesia for an important part of the trauma.

Phobic Disorders: These disorders involve persistent, unrealistic, and intense fear of a specific object, situation, or activity. Individuals who have a phobia avoid situations or stimuli related to the phobia or painfully endure those situations. Importantly, however, individuals with phobias retain insight and recognize the excessiveness of their anxiety. Numerous types of phobias exist, with the most popular example being agoraphobia – anxiety about or avoidance of being trapped in situations or places with no way to escape easily if panic develops.

Obsessive-Compulsive Disorder: This disorder involves obsessions, which are recurrent, unwanted, intrusive ideas, images, or impulses that seem silly, weird, nasty, or horrible, and compulsions, which are urges to do something that will lessen the discomfort arising from the obsessions. The overarching obsessional theme is harm, risk, or danger, and common obsessions include contamination, doubt, loss, and aggressivity. Typically, persons with obsessive-compulsive disorder feel compelled to perform repetitive, purposeful, intentional behaviors called rituals to balance their obsessions. Most persons with this disorder are aware that their obsessions do not reflect real risks and that the physical and mental behaviors they perform to relieve their concern are unrealistic and excessive to the point of being bizarre. Preservation of insight differentiates obsessive-compulsive disorder from psychotic disorders. Because persons with this disorder fear embarrassment or stigmatization and have not lost contact with reality, they often conceal their obsessions and rituals.

Panic Disorder: This disorder's core symptom is the panic attack, which is an overwhelming fear of being in danger. During an attack, the individual may experience: Pounding heart or chest pain; sweating, trembling, or shaking, shortness of breath or sensation of choking, nausea or abdominal pain; dizziness or lightheadedness; feeling unreal or disconnected; fear of losing control or dying; numbness; and chills or hot flashes. Individuals with this disorder often feel that they are having a heart attack or stroke because the symptoms occur unexpectedly and seemingly without reason.

PSYCHOSEXUAL DISORDERS

Psychosexual disorders include sexual dysfunctions; the most common form of psychosexual disorder encountered in the criminal justice system are paraphilias. These disorders are characterized by long-standing, intense, sexually arousing fantasies, urges, or behaviors that involve inanimate objects, actual or imagined suffering or humiliation of oneself or one's partner, or nonconsenting partners. To qualify as dysfuntional, these characteristics must reveal clinically important distress or disability.

The most common paraphilias include the following: Fetishism, which involves the use of an inanimate object (the fetish) as the preferred method of producing sexual excitement; pedophilia, which is a preference for repetitive sexual activity with prepubertal children; exhibitionism, which involves obtaining sexual excitement by exposing one's genitals to unsuspecting strangers; voyeurism, which involves achieving sexual arousal by observing unsuspecting persons who are naked, disrobing, or engaging in sexual activity; sexual masochism, which involves sexual excitement from intentional participation in an activity in which one is humiliated, beaten, bound, or otherwise abused; and sexual sadism, which involves achieving sexual gratification by inflicting physical or psychological suffering (such as humiliation or terror) on the sexual partner.

For texts on psychopathology or abnormal psychology that review these and other important disorders, see American Psychiatric Association, Diagnostic and Statistical Manual of Mental Disorders-IV(1994); James Butcher, Susan Mineka, & Jill Hooley, Abnormal Psychology (12th ed., 2004); and David H. Barlow & Vincent Mark Durand, Abnormal Psychology: An Introduction (2002).

APPENDIX E
LEGAL GLOSSARY

-A-

Ab initio: "From the beginning."
Action: A lawsuit or legal proceeding.
Acquit: To find not guilty or free from accusation.
Acquittal: Setting the person free from a charge of guilt by a finding of not guilty.
Actus reas: "Guilty act." Part of the crime that is the act.
Adjudication: Pronouncing a judgment or the process of reaching that judgement.
Adversary system: A judicial system involving opposing parties before an independent decisionmaker.
Affidavit: A written statement made under oath.
Affirm: To agree or uphold.
Affirmative defense: A defense which makes the defendant not guilty of the crime even if the prosecution can prove the elements of the crime. Examples include insanity, self-defense, and entrapment.
Allegation: Assertion or statement that a party expects to prove.
Amend: To change or modify.
Amicus curiae: "Friend of the court." A party that provides information, typically a brief, to a court even though the party is not directly involved in the case at hand.
Answer: Defendant's written response in a civil case.
Appeal: A request to overturn the legal ruling of a lower court.
Appeals court: See "appellate court" in this glossary.
Appellant: The party appealing a decision or judgment to a higher court. Opposite of appellee.
Appellate court: A court having jurisdiction to review a lower court's ruling.
Appellee: The party against whom the appellant appeals a legal decision.
Arraignment: Initial appearance before a judge in a criminal case in which the court formally charges a person with an offense.
Arrest: To deprive a person of his liberty by legal authority. In the technical criminal law sense, seizure of an alleged or suspected offender to answer for a crime.
Assault: The immediate threat of attacking someone. Results from an act that makes another reasonably apprehensive of immediate and harmful contact.
Attempt: An overt act, beyond mere preparation, moving directly toward the actual commission of a substantive offence.
Aver: To allege; to assert formally.

-B-

Bad faith: Dishonesty or fraud.

Bail: A monetary or other form of security given to ensure the appearance of defendants at criminal proceedings.

Battery: The illegal touching of another person. When used in "assault and battery," the assault is the threat of attack and the battery the physical attack itself. The contact may be actually harmful or offensive.

Bench trial: A trial held before a judge and without a jury.

Beyond a reasonable doubt: The highest level of proof required to win a legal action.

Bill of Rights: The first 10 amendments to the U.S. Constitution, which describe the rights and protections guaranteed to each citizen.

Booking: The official process of recording the arrest, which may include taking fingerprints and photographs of the accused.

Brief: Written document that outlines a party's legal arguments in a case.

Burden of proof: The duty of a party in a lawsuit to persuade the judge or the jury that enough facts exist to prove the allegations of the case.

Burglary: The illegal entry into any building with the intent to commit a crime, such as theft.

-C-

Capital crime: A crime punishable by death or life imprisonment.

Capital punishment: Punishment by death for certain crimes.

Case law: The law created by judges when deciding individual disputes or cases; also known as common law.

Case of first impression: First discussion or consideration; refers to the first time a question of law is considered for determination by a court.

Certiorari: "To be informed of." The order a court issues to review the decision and proceedings of a lower court. (pronounced ser-shi-o-ra' ri).

Challenge for cause: During jury selection (voire dire), a request to the court that a potential juror be excused because of a specific reason or cause.

Charge: A formal accusation or indictment.

Citation: (1) Order to appear in court at a certain place at a specified time. (2) Reference to legal authorities and precedents (such as constitutions, statutes and reported cases) to substantiate a legal proposition.

Civil case: A lawsuit between individuals or organizations, which normally seeks monetary compensation for damages.

Civil court: A court that handles civil cases.

Civil law: (1) The system of legal principles forming the basis of the law of most European countries and descended from common law as distinguished from the "common law" tradition of Anglo-American jurisdictions. (2) Body of law governing private or "civil" relationships, as distinguished from criminal law.

Circumstantial evidence: Indirect evidence that implies something occurred but does not directly prove it.

Claimant: Party asserting a right, demand or claim.

Clear and convincing evidence: The trier of fact must be persuaded by the evidence that it is highly probable that the claim is true. Level of proof that is more than a preponderance of the evidence but less than beyond a reasonable doubt.

Code: A collection, compendium or revision of laws, rules and regulations enacted by legislative authority.

Common law: The law created by judges when deciding individual disputes or cases. Also known as case law.

Compensatory damages: Money awarded to reimburse actual costs, such as medical bills or pain and suffering.

Competency: Legally fit and qualified, such as to give testimony, waive rights, etc.

Complainant: Plaintiff, party that individual files the suit, same as plaintiff.

Complaint: The document that initiates a legal action.

Concur: To agree or act together.

Consent search: A search made by law enforcement after a person has agreed to the search.

Conspiracy: A combination of two or more persons to commit a criminal or unlawful act.

Conviction: The result of a criminal trial or plea that ends with the defendant being guilty as charged.

Corrections: The part of the criminal justice system that deals with convicted criminals; it includes jails, prisons, parole, and probation.

Count: The separate charges made in an indictment or information.

Criminal procedure: The rules for processing someone through the criminal justice system.

Cross-examination: The questioning of an opponent's witnesses at trial.

Custody: Legal or physical control of a person or object.

Custodial interrogation: A type of questioning designed to induce a confession or disclosure of certain crimes.

-D-

Damnum absque injuria: "A wrong without injury." The doctrine that the courts will not hear a case in which the wrongful act or omission of the potential defendant did not cause any harm to person, property or rights. (pronounced dam'num abs'kwe in-joo'ri-a)

Decision: Judgment rendered by a court after a consideration of the facts and legal issues before it.

Declaratory judgment: Declares the rights of the parties or expresses the opinion of the courts on a question of law, without ordering anything to be done.

Decree: Decision or order of the court.

Defendant: In criminal cases, the person accused of the crime. In civil matters, the person or organization that is being sued.

De minimis: An abbreviation of "de minimis non curat lex" which literally means the law is not concerned with trivial matters. The phrase is generally used as a way to categorize that which is not worth litigating over.

De novo: Anew.

Deposition: The sworn testimony of a witness taken outside of court and transcribed by a reporter.

Derivative evidence: Evidence derived from other evidence, typically refers to illegally obtained evidence being excluded because it was tainted by the original evidence.

Determinate sentencing: Sentence/punishment for a fixed period of time stated in a statute.

Dicta or Dictum: That part of the opinion of a court which is not necessary for the decision of the issue before it and does not act as a binding precedent in later cases.

Direct evidence: Evidence that stands on its own to prove an alleged fact, such as testimony of a witness who says she saw a defendant pointing a gun at a victim during a robbery.

Direct examination: The initial questioning of a witness by the party that called the witness.

Directed verdict: A judge's order to a jury to return a specified verdict, usually in cases where there has been a failure of evidence, an overwhelming weight of the evidence, or where the law, as applied to the facts, is for one of the parties.

Discovery: Part of the pre-trial litigation process during which each party requests relevant information and documents from the other side in an attempt to "discover" pertinent facts.

Discretion: The power to choose.

Dismissal with prejudice: Case dismissed for good reason, which bars plaintiff from bringing an action on the same claim.

Dismissal without prejudice: Case dismissed, but plaintiff may bring a new suit on the same claim.
Disposition: In criminal cases, the settlement of a case.
Dissent: Denotes the disagreement of one or more judges of a court with the decision of the majority.
Double jeopardy: Generally, being tried twice for the same offense.
Due process: The notion that laws and legal proceedings must be fair. The Constitution guarantees that the government cannot take away a person's basic rights to "life, liberty or property, without due process of law." There are two types of due process, substantive and procedural. Both aim to provide the same treatment for all people. Substantive due process relates to the creation of law and that no law should be created with the intent of discriminating against a particular group of people. Procedural due process concerns the need to order the judicial system so that it remains constant for all people. Note that the source of due process derives from the Due Process Clause in the 5th Amendment that applies to the federal government and made applicable to the states through the 14th Amendment.
Duress: An act committed without the free will.
Duty to warn: The legal obligation to warn people of a danger.

-E-

En banc: "By the full court." When all the members of an appellate court hear an argument, they are sitting en banc.
Entrapment: The affirmative defense that the defendant would not have committed the crime if law enforcement had not enticed the defendant.
Equal Protection Clause: Part of the Fourteenth Amendment to the U.S. Constitution that prohibits discrimination by state government institutions.
Equity: The spirit and habit of fairness and just dealing between people.
Error: An incorrect application of the law to some material aspect of a case, furnishing grounds for the review of the proceedings and reversal of judgment by an appellate court.
Et al.: An abbreviation of *et alia*, meaning "and others."
Et seq.: An abbreviation for *et sequentes*, or *et sequentia*, meaning "and the following."
Evidence: Matters presented in court to prove an alleged fact.
Ex parte: "By or for one party." Situation in which only one party (and not the adversary) appears before a judge.
Exclusionary rule: Prohibits the use of illegally obtained evidence during trial.
Exculpatory evidence: Evidence that clears or tends to clear the defendant from guilt.
Exigent circumstances: Emergency circumstances, such as those that permit law enforcement to enter homes without warrants in order to address an immediate danger to persons or evidence.
Expert witness: A witness with a specialized knowledge of a subject.
Ex post facto: Laws that make an act criminal when it was not criminal at the time that it was committed.

-F-

Fact finder: The one responsible for deciding the facts of a particular case and coming to a verdict; either a judge or jury.
False arrest, imprisonment: The unlawful detention of persons, whereby they are deprived of their personal liberty against their will and without lawful authority.
Felony: Typically, a crime punishable by incarceration for a year or more.
Felony murder: The rule that if any person is killed during a felony, the criminal can be charged with murder.
Findings: A conclusion reached upon some matter by a judge or jury in a legal proceedings, e.g., a "finding of fact".

Foreseeability: A key issue in determining a person's liability. If a defendant could not reasonably have foreseen that someone might be hurt by his or her actions, then there may be no liability.

Frisk: A restricted search of a person to locate weapons.

Fruit of the poisonous tree doctrine: Illegally obtained evidence cannot be admitted against defendants because it is tainted; the taint also applies to the evidence discovered by the process initiated by the illegal activity.

-G-

Good faith: Honestly and without deception.

Grand jury: A group of citizens convened in a criminal case to consider the prosecutor's evidence and determine whether probable cause exists to prosecute a suspect for a felony.

Gross negligence: Failure to use even the slightest amount of care in a way that shows recklessness or willful disregard for the safety of others.

Guardian ad litem: "Guardian at law." The person appointed by the court to look out for the best interests of the child or other legally incompetent person during the course of legal proceedings.

-H-

Habeas corpus: "You have the body." A judicial mandate to a prison official ordering them to bring an inmate to the court so it can determine the lawfulness of the imprisonment.

Harmless error: An error committed by a lower court during a trial which is not prejudicial to the rights of the party and for which the appellate court will not reverse the judgment. The court acknowledges that an error occurred but its consequence was so minimal as to make the error irrelevant.

Hearing: A flexible term for a court proceeding.

Hearsay: Secondhand information that a witness only heard about from someone else and did not see or hear himself.

Holding: Part of a judicial opinion related to the material facts of a case, which bind later cases presenting similar issues.

Homicide: Literally, human killing. The crimes of homicide range from different degrees of murder to different kinds of manslaughter.

Hung jury: A jury that is unable to reach a final verdict.

-I-

Immunity: Exemption from a legal duty, penalty or prosecution.

Impanel: To select a jury.

Impeachment of witness: An attack on the credibility of a witness by the testimony of other witnesses or by the inconsistent testimony or statements of the witness made at an earlier time.

In camera: "In chambers." Refers to a hearing or inspection of documents that takes places in private, often in a judge's chambers.

Incapacity: The lack of power or the legal inability to act.

Inchoate crime: Crimes in which the actual crime has not yet been committed but steps to commit the crime have been made. Examples include solicitation, attempt, and conspiracy.

Incompetent: A person lacking the capacity, legal qualification, or fitness to manage affairs or to discharge a required duty.

Indeterminate sentence: A prison sentence of an indefinite period of time. Under this sentence, prisoners are released when the parole board determines they are rehabilitated.

Indictment: A formal accusation of a felony, issued by a grand jury after considering evidence presented by a prosecutor.

Indigent: Lacking in funds.

Information: A formal accusation of a crime, issued by a prosecutor. An alternative to an indictment.

Infractions: Minor offenses, often traffic tickets, which are punishable only by a fine.

Injunction: A discretionary process of preventative and remedial justice which is exercised by the courts that have equity powers.

In loco parentis: "In the place of the parent"; refers to actions of a custodian, guardian or other person acting in the parent's place.

Insanity: A defendant who claims insanity admits to committing the act, but denies criminal responsibility for the act.

Intent, criminal: The exercise of intelligent will, where the mind is fully aware of the nature and consequences of an act done with such knowledge and with full liberty of action.

Inter alia: Among other things.

Irresistible impulse: Under one form of insanity defense, a defendant is not guilty if he knows that the act is wrong but due to an irresistible impulse still commits the act.

Instruction: An explanation that a trial judge gives to juries to inform them of the law applicable to the case before them.

Interrogation: Questioning of a suspect with the intent of eliciting incriminating admissions.

Inventory search: Securing and recording the contents of lawfully impounded objects (typically vehicles).

Investigatory detention: When police stop someone to investigate their potential involvement in a crime w/o actually arresting them. Often time associated with s stop and frisk known as a *Terry stop*.

Involuntary manslaughter: A killing caused by criminal negligence or an unintended killing that takes place during a misdemeanor offense.

-J-

Judgment: A court's official decision on the matters before it.

Judgment non obstante veredicto: A judgment notwithstanding the verdict. A decision by a trial judge to rule in favor of a losing party even though the jury's verdict was in favor of the other side.

Judgment notwithstanding the verdict (j.n.o.v.): Granted when the judge decides that reasonable people could not have reached the verdict.

Judicial notice: Acceptance by the court, without formal proof shown, of facts of common knowledge.

Jurisdiction: The power of a court to hear and determine cases or controversies brought before the court for resolution.

Jurisprudence: The science of the law. Also a collective term denoting the course of judicial decisions or case law as opposed to legislation.

Jury charge: The judge's instructions to the jurors on the law that applies in a case and definitions of the relevant legal concepts.

Jury nullification: Instance in which a jury deliberately rejects the evidence or refuses to apply the law either because the jury wants to send a message about a social issue or because the result dictated by the law is against the jury's sense of justice or morality.

-K-

Knowingly: With knowledge, willfully or intentionally with respect to a material element of an offense.

-L-

Larceny: The illegal taking of property not belonging to ones self.
Lesser included offenses: Charges that contain elements of the most serious charge against a defendant.
Lex loci delicti commissi: The tradition of the law is to apply the law of the place where the crime was committed.
Liability: Legal responsibility, duty or obligation.

-M-

M'Naughten rule: Specifies that a person is not guilty if at the time the crime was committed the individual had a diseased mind and was unable to distinguish right from wrong.
Magistrate: A court officer who issues warrants; normally a lower-court judge who handles pretrial proceedings or presides over misdemeanor trials.
Mala in se: Crimes that are intrinsically bad such as rape, robbery, murder, arson and theft.
Mala prohibita: Acts that are illegal only because the law prohibits them.
Malice aforethought: A state of mind requirement for murder. It is either an intent to kill or an intent to do an extremely dangerous act with a conscious disregard for the consequences.
Malicious prosecution: A civil suit for the tort of malicious prosecution can result from either a civil or criminal suit if the proceeding was instituted maliciously without probable cause, and with a decision favorable to the defendant.
Malpractice: Failure of a professional to follow the accepted standards of practice of his or her profession.
Mandamus: A writ by which a court commands the performance of a particular act.
Mandatory sentence: A criminal sentence set by a legislature that establishes the minimum length of prison time for specified crimes.
Manslaughter: The unlawful killing of a human being without premeditation. Can be voluntary, like when someone is killed unlawfully under circumstances that do not include a premeditated intent to kill. Or involuntary, like when someone is killed unintentionally as a result of someone else performing another unlawful act or negligently performing a lawful act.
Mayhem: The crime of mutilating or cutting off a part of someone's body.
Mens rea: "Guilty mind". Certain crimes require that a person intended to carry out the crime, and thus the prosecution would have to prove that there was *mens rea* at the time the offense was committed.
Minor: A person who does not have the legal rights of an adult.
Misdemeanor: Crime that is punishable by less than one year in jail.
Mitigating factors: Information about a defendant or the circumstances of a crime that might tend to lessen the severity of a sentence or the crime with which the person is charged.
Moral turpitude: Conduct contrary to honesty, modesty or good morals.
Motion: A formal request asking a judge to issue a ruling or order on a legal matter.
Motion for directed verdict: In civil cases, a request asserting that the plaintiff has raised no genuine issue to be tried and asks the judge to rule in favor of the defense. Typically made after the plaintiff is done presenting his or her case.
Motion for summary judgment: In civil cases, a request asserting that the plaintiff has raised no genuine issue to be tried and asks the judge to rule in favor of the defense. If the parties agree about the facts of the case but disagree about the law the judge can dispose of the case via summary judgment. Typically made before the trial.
Motion in limine: A written motion for a protective order against prejudicial questions and statements.
Motion to dismiss: In a civil case, a defendant's request asserting that even if all the allegations are true, the plaintiff is not entitled to any legal relief and thus the case should be dismissed.
Motion to suppress evidence: A request to keep out evidence at a trial or hearing.

-N-

Named plaintiffs: The originators of a class action suit.

Negligence: Failure to use the degree of care that a reasonable person would use under the same circumstances.

Nisi prius: Courts for the initial trial of issues of fact, as distinguished from appellate courts.

Nolo contendere: The same as a guilty plea, except it cannot be used later against the accused as an admission of guilt.

-O-

Oath: A solemn and formal declaration by a person that what they are about to say or write is the truth.

-P-

Parens patriae: "Parent of his country." Used when the government acts on behalf of a child or incompetent individuals.

Parole: A type of release from prison usually with some conditions. Different from probation in that parole occurs after a person has been sent to prison.

Parties: Plaintiffs and defendants (petitioners and respondents) to lawsuits, also known as appellants and appellees in appeals, and their lawyers.

Per curiam: "By the court." An opinion which expresses the decision in the case but which does not identify the judge who wrote it.

Peremptory challenge: During jury selection, an attorney's rejection of a prospective juror that requires no reason be given to the court. Each side has a limited number of these challenges.

Perjury: A crime in which a person knowingly makes a false statement while under oath in court.

Petition: A written application to the court asking for specific action to be taken.

Petty offenses: Minor crimes, such as traffic violations, which are generally punishable by a fine or short jail term.

Plain view doctrine: Objects in plain view of officers who have the right to be in a particular place are subject to seizure without a warrant and may be admitted as evidence.

Plaintiff: The person who initiates a lawsuit.

Plea: Defendants' formal answer in court to charges contained in a complaint, information, or indictment, regarding their guilt.

Pleadings: In a civil case, the allegations by each party of their claims and defenses.

Police power: The power that resides in every sovereignty to pass laws for its internal regulation and government.

Precedent: Previously decided case considered binding in the court where it was issued and in all lower courts in the same jurisdiction.

Preliminary hearing: Legal proceeding used in some states in which a prosecutor presents evidence to a judge in an attempt to show that there is probable cause that a person committed a crime.

Pretrial conference: Meeting with the judge and attorneys to define the issues, prepare for trial, and discuss the possibility of settlement.

Preventive detention: Laws that enable people who are thought to be dangerous or accused of serious crimes to be denied bail or otherwise detained.

Preponderance of the evidence: The level of proof required to prevail in most civil cases. The judge or jury must be persuaded that the facts are more probably one way (the plaintiff's way) than another (the defendant's).

Prima facie: "At first view." Refers to the minimum amount of evidence a plaintiff/prosecutor must have to avoid having a case dismissed.

Privileged communication: Conversation that takes place within the context of a protected relationship, such as that between an attorney and client, a husband and wife, a priest and penitent, and a doctor and patient.

Pro se: "For himself." A person who represents himself, sometimes with the assistance of a lawyer. (pronounced pro say)

Probable cause: A reasonable belief that a person has committed a crime.

Probation: An alternative to prison. This sentence requires the offender to follow certain conditions, usually under the supervision of a probation officer.

Probative value: That which furnishes, establishes or contributes toward proof.

Procedural Due Process: A right promised by the 5th and 14th amendments to the constitution. Provides that all men are to be granted a certain "due-process" before being deprived of their life, liberty, or property. Typically, these are basic rights that protect individuals from government actions.

Prosecutor: The government lawyer who investigates and tries criminal cases. Generally known as a district attorney, state's attorney, or United States attorney.

Protective order: In litigation, an order that prevents the disclosure of sensitive information except to certain individuals under certain conditions. In a domestic dispute, an order that prevents one party from approaching another, often within a specified distance.

Proximate cause: In tort law, the negligent act which causes a plaintiff's injury or, when combined with other acts or omissions, most directly causes the plaintiff's injury or loss.

Public defender: A lawyer who works for a state or local agency representing clients accused of a crime who cannot afford to pay.

Public policy: That which is best for society as a whole; a subjective determination by an individual such as a judge or a governor, or a group such as a state legislature of what is for the general good of all the people. Also the principle of law which holds that no person can do that which has a tendency to be injurious to the public, or against the public good.

Punitive damages: Money awarded to a victim that is intended to punish a defendant and stop the person or business from repeating the type of conduct that caused an injury.

Purposely: A conscious desire to produce a prohibited result or harm.

-Q-

Query or Queries: A question or questions.

Quash: To nullify, void, or vacate by judicial decision

Quid pro quo: Something for something. Exchanging something of value.

-R-

Reasonable care: The level of care a typical person would use if faced with the same circumstances.

Reasonable doubt: The level of certainty a juror must have to find a defendant guilty of a crime.

Reasonable grounds: Having probable cause to arrest without warrant.

Recidivist: Repeat offender.

Redirect examination: An attorney's requestioning of his or her own witness after cross-examination.

Remand: An appellate court's decision to send a case back to a lower court for further proceedings.

Res ipsa loquitur: "The thing speaks for itself." Refers to situations when it is assumed that a person's injury was caused by the negligent action of another party because the accident was the sort that would not occur unless someone was negligent.

Res judicata: The matter has already been decided. This means that once a suit is brought the same facts cannot be used again in another suit with the same parties.

Respondent: The party against whom an appeal is taken. See "appellee" in this glossary,

Retroactive effect: In relation to precedent, the decision controls the legal consequences of causes of action arising before the announcement of the decision.

Reverse: As used in opinions, judgments, and mandates, the setting aside, annulling, vacating, or changing to the contrary the decision of a lower court or other body.

Right against self-incrimination: The Fifth Amendment right that allows a person to refuse to answer questions that would subject him or her to accusation of a criminal act.

-S-

Search: Any governmental intrusion into something in which a person has a reasonable expectation of privacy.

Seizure: Any taking into possession, custody, or control.

Settlement: The resolution or compromise by the parties in a civil lawsuit.

Sovereign immunity: Principle that no sovereign can be sued without its express consent.

Sovereignty: The supreme authority of an independent nation or state.

Specific intent: The intent to do a prohibited act on purpose.

Standard of care: The standard to which a defendant is held.

Standing: The legal right to initiate a lawsuit. Typically, a person must be sufficiently affected by the matter at hand, and there must be a case or controversy that can be resolved by legal action.

Stare decisis: "To stand by that which is decided." Refers to the principle of adhering to precedent when deciding a case.

Status crime: A type of crime that makes it illegal to be a certain way. The Supreme Court has ruled that such laws are invalid.

Statute: The law as enacted by the legislative body, as opposed to case law developed by the courts.

Statutes of limitations: Laws setting deadlines for filing lawsuits within a certain time after events occur that are the source of a claim.

Strict liability: Liability even when there is no proof of negligence.

Subpoena: An order compelling a person to appear to testify or produce documents.

Substantive Due Process: The principle that laws should be created objectively.

Substantive law: That part of the law dealing with rights, duties and liabilities, as distinguished from procedural law, which is the law regulating procedure.

Summary judgment: Judgment entered when there is no genuine issue of material fact and party is entitled to prevail as a matter of law.

Summation: The closing argument in a trial.

Summons: A legal document that notifies a party that a lawsuit has been initiated and states when and where the party must appear to answer the charges.

Suspect classification: A classification that is used to analyze a law, typically to determine if it is constitutional. If a law is deemed to affect a suspect classification, it will be held up to strict scrutiny and be deemed justifiable only by a "compelling" state interest that is being addressed in a very narrow fashion so as not to infringe excessively on the affected rights.

-T-

Trial de novo: A new trial in which the case begins as though no previous trial existed.

Tort: A civil wrong that results in an injury to a person or property.

-U-

-V-

Valid claim: A grievance that can be resolved by legal action.
Venire: The list of jurors summoned to serve for a particular time.
Venue: The jurisdiction in which a particular lawsuit should be tried; the county from which the jury is pooled.
Verdict: A jury or judge's formal decision on the issues presented at trial.
Vicarious liability: When one person is liable for the negligent actions of another person, even though the first person was not directly responsible for the injury. For instance, a parent sometimes can be vicariously liable for the harmful acts of a child and an employer sometimes can be vicariously liable for the acts of a worker.
Voir dire: Jury selection; the questioning of prospective jurors.
Voluntary manslaughter: The intentional killing of another person done under extreme provocation and in the heat of anger.

-W-

Wanton: An act that is useless for any rightful purpose, is without any adequate legal provocation, and manifests a reckless indifference to the rights and interests of others.
Warrant: An official order authorizing a specific act, such as an arrest or the search of someone's home. Issued if the magistrate decides that (1) the evidence supports the belief that (2) probable cause exists to believe that (3) a crime has been committed and that (4) the suspect is the probable culprit.
Willfully: Intentionally.
Without prejudice: A dismissal "without prejudice" allows a new suit to be brought on the same cause of action.
Writ: A judicial order.
Writ of certiorari: A Supreme Court's order directing a lower court to transmit records for a case for which it will hear on appeal.

-X-

-Y-

-Z-

INDEX

A

B

C

D

E

F

G

H

I

J

K

L

M

N

O

Q

R

S

T

U

V

W

Y